THE GREAT BOOK OF

GUNS

THE GREAT BOOK OF GUNS

An Illustrated History of Military, Sporting, and Antique Firearms

Edited by Chris McNab

THUNDER BAY
P·R·E·S·S
San Diego, California

Thunder Bay Press
An imprint of the Advantage Publishers Group
5880 Oberlin Drive, San Diego, CA 92121-4794
www.thunderbaybooks.com

An imprint of Chrysalis Books Group

All notations of errors or omissions should be addressed to Thunder Bay Press, Editorial Department, at the above address. All other correspondence (author inquiries, permissions) concerning the content of this book should be addressed to Salamander Books Ltd., The Chrysalis Building, Bramley Road, London W10 6SP, United Kingdom.

ISBN 1-59223-304-X

Library of Congress Cataloging-in-Publication Data
available upon request.

Printed in China
1 2 3 4 5 08 07 06 05 04

Credits
Project Editor: Shaun Barrington
Designer: John Heritage
Picture researcher: Rebecca Sodergren
Production: Don Campaniello
Reproduction: ClassicScan Pte. Ltd.

Additional Captions

Page 1: Vickers heavy machine gun 0.303 in., 1912.

Page 2: George Maddox, a noted guerilla fighter of the American Civil War, sports a pair of Remington's 1863 New Model Army pistols. The chambers of the left-hand pistol are clearly seen to be loaded and ready for action. Despite his dandified appearance, Maddox was a cold-blooded killer.

Page 3: The French Châtellerault Service Pistol, 1841.

Page 5: The American Vandenburgh Volley Gun, 1860 (top); the Spanish Bernedo 6.35 mm Pocket Pistol, 1915 (bottom).

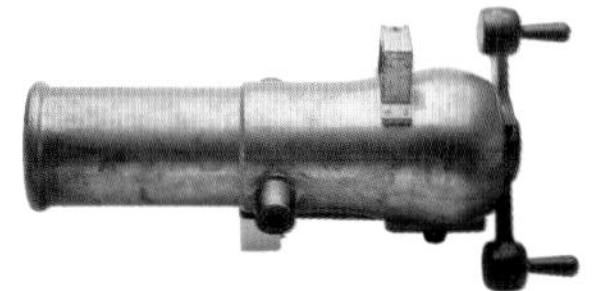

Contents

Introduction

> *"To preserve liberty, it is essential that the whole body of people always possess arms, and be taught alike especially when young, how to use them."*
>
> Richard Henry Lee, 1788, initiator of the Declaration of Independence, and member of the first Senate, which passed the Bill of Rights.

Whatever one's perspective on firearms, there is no denying that they rank among the most influential inventions in the history of mankind. Prior to firearms, personnel weaponry was centrally dependent upon the personal power of the operator, who needed the physical strength and acquired motor skills to wield a sword, ax, or mace as an effective combat tool. Even with projectile weapons such as longbows and crossbows, although the mechanics of the tensed wood or steel were responsible for the range/force of the bolt or arrow, considerable strength in the arms, shoulders, and back was required to pull back the cord (often well over 150 lb. for a yew bow).

Firearms changed the situation profoundly, though slowly. Although the earliest matchlock weapons of the fifteenth century did not have the combat performance of a good bow, the only physical input required was to point the weapon at the target and ignite the powder. With only minimal training and good eyesight, a talented harquebusier could achieve a kill out to 50 m (164 ft.), whereas the skills of an English archer took years to develop and required a lengthy apprenticeship beginning in the late teens. Firearms became the great leveller on the battlefield, reducing the primacy of human body as the winner of battles.

Above: *A Union Army powder flask from the Civil War. These flasks became obsolete when the copper percussion cap was adopted. The cap fit over a nipple fixed to the weapon's breech. The hammer striking the cap sent a spark into the barrel.*

Killing at distance

Firearms provided the ability to kill at ranges and with power not achievable with physical force, and the ranges crept up inexorably. In the fifteenth century, a matchlock rifle would have had an effective range, "effective" meaning the flight of the round is within the intentional

Left: *In the United States Civil War, marksmen began to come into their own, one of the most famous units being the 1st Regiment of United States Sharpshooters, which was also known as "Berdan's Sharpshooters" after its commanding officer, Colonel Hiram Berdan. The majority of men were armed with the Sharps 0.52 in. caliber rifle, as is the man seen here, Private Truman Head, whose nickname was "California Joe." They wore green hats and coats, and although their trousers were originally sky blue (as in the rest of the Union Army), these were later changed to green.*

targeting of the operator) of about 50 m (164 ft.). By the end of the eighteenth century a smoothbore flintlock musket took the range up to around 150 m (492 ft.), and a century later bullets from rifled Confederate firearms in the Civil War were hitting Union soldiers (and vice versa) at up to 500 m (1,640 ft.) in gifted hands. By the opening of World War I in 1914, with the world's armies now equipped with breech-loading bolt-action rifles firing powerful unitary cartridges, killing ranges were in excess of 1.6 km (1 mile), up to 3.2 km (2 miles) when those cartridges were fired from machine guns fitted to elevated mounts in sustained-fire roles. In the present day, a US Marine sniper in the Gulf War in 1990–91, armed with a .50 caliber Barrett

Above: *Target rifle by Samuel Staudenmayer of London. This is the type of target rifle that would have been used by the Regency Duke of Cumberland's Sharpshooters.*

Left: *A group of Coldstream Guards from the Crimean War carrying Minié Rifles. This rifle gave the British superiority in firepower over the Russian smooth-bored muskets.*

Below: *From the early 1700s onwards, many weapons designers sought to perfect an automatic weapon which would bring a new dimension of firepower to the battlefield. The break-through eventually came with Hiram Maxim's machine gun, and an early example is seen here in the hands of a Boer soldier in about 1900.*

M82A1, shot and killed an Iraqi officer from a distance of 1,800 m (5,905 ft.), a phenomenal act of precision fire.

The ability to kill accurately at long range with direct fire—as opposed to the indirect fire of a long-range bow shot—revolutionized infantry warfare. Steadily, exposed frontal assault tactics became suicidal operations when faced by ranks of emplaced riflemen or machine gunners. Although the traditions of the open charge died hard, and were repeated well into the twentieth century, by World War II fire-and-maneuver was the standard infantry tactic, the intelligent use of cover from first contact essential to surviving accurate small-arms fire. Also, along with the development of artillery, the improvement of small arms led armies to appreciate the need for rapid improvised defensive works to enhance survivability.

The ability to shoot targets at a distance not only mutated the battlefield, but also transformed the acquisition of food through hunting. With every increase in the range of weaponry came a decrease in the distance which the hunter needed to track his prey, consequently reducing the chances of startling the target before the shot was taken. Kills increased to such an extent that certain species were taken to the brink of extinction. In the early 1800s about sixty-five million American Plains Buffalo roamed North America. By 1890, hunters had shot all but 1,000 creatures. The shotgun weapon had a similar impact on the hunting of fast-moving or flying targets. In the great estate shoots of nineteenth-century Britain, it was not unusual for over 2,000 driven game birds to be killed in a single day's shooting.

Heavy firepower

While range is to some extent a preoccupation in the design of all types of firearms, it is far from the overriding concern. Indeed, since World War II many military weapons have had their effective ranges reduced to reflect honest assessments of practical combat ranges, particularly in the field of assault rifles that use either shortened rounds such as the 7.62 x 39 mm Soviet round, or small-caliber, high-velocity rounds like the 5.56 x 45 mm NATO, both of which have a practical range of around 500 m (1,640 ft.). Submachine guns and handguns were both developed specifically to serve the needs of close-range warfare. SMGs emerged during World War I for applications in trench combat, long-range rifle cartridges being unnecessary and dangerous to your own side, in

Below: *A United States Marine Corps member undergoing parachute training in 1961. His weapon is the 0.45 in. M3A1 submachine gun, popularly known as the "Grease Gun." Like the British Sten, the M3A1 was designed in a rush at the start of World War II.*

combat ranges of 50 m (164 ft.) and below. Modern handguns rarely have aspirations to range, instead concentrating on takedown power within about 25 m (82 ft.).

The submachine gun reminds us of a concern parallel to range in the development of firearms—volume of fire. Increased volumes of fire serve two main purposes. First, and most obvious, the greater the volume of fire directed against the enemy—as long as it is controlled properly—the greater the likelihood of higher numbers of casualties or a hit upon a single moving target. The second purpose is that a soldier is in a vulnerable position while reloading, so the corollary of increasing the volume of fire is less time spent with weapon downtime.

The seminal leaps in volume of fire occurred with the invention first of the unitary cartridge, then the breech-loading weapon, next magazine feed and finally automatic operating systems such as blowback, gas operation, and recoil operation. Each step permitted the evolution from the 3–4 rpm fired by an eighteenth-century

Left: *An elaborate seventeenth-century flintlock pistol. In these weapons, a piece of flint was held in the jaws of the cock. On pulling the trigger the cock was pushed around by the spring until it hit the steel pan, generating sparks that were able to reach the priming and ignite the charge, which then drove the bullet up the barrel. The beautiful and skillful ornamentation transforms this weapon of death into a work of art.*

Below: *A United States infantryman using his 7.62 mm M60 in the light machine gun role, firing from behind a fallen tree somewhere in Vietnam. The array of ammunition belts is testimony to the weapon's high rate of fire.*

rifleman from his smoothbore muzzle-loading musket, to the 6000 rpm sprayed from a M134 rotary-barrel Gatling weapon fitted aboard a US helicopter gunship.

The huge differences, even amongst modern weapons, in rates of fire reminds us that firearms come in a prodigious variety of purposes and formats, from .22 target pistols to 20 mm antitank rifles. As divergent as such weapons are, however, the development of firearms and firearms ammunition seems to have reached a certain stasis. Almost every firearm today will be firing the unitary metallic cartridge, and this fact dictates the limits of design and performance. Caseless ammunition such as fired by the Heckler & Koch G11 show one possible future direction, while the electronic ignition system of the Australian Metal Storm system shows another. Such futuristic directions will no doubt have to fit in with the other major criteria for a successful weapon: economies of production. World War II demonstrated that it is not necessarily the most sophisticated weapons which have greatest impact, but those which can be put into the hands of as many people as possible through economical and rapid production methods. The AK-47, for instance, is a far less sophisticated weapon system than the US M16, but its simplicity of manufacture means that over eighty million AK-type weapons now litter the globe, fueling entire conflicts in some regions. With millions of new small arms emerging into the world each year, there seems little reason to believe that in a futuristic age the conventional firepower of small arms will become any less influential than it was 100 or 200 years ago.

Above: *Firearms took to the skies within a decade of the first successful aircraft flights. Here a Luftwaffe gunner in World War II mans a 13mm MG-131 in a Rheinmetall Dorsig dorsal turret mounting.*

Left: *U.S. soldiers man the frontline in the Meuse valley, north of Verdun, on October 3, 1918. The standard firearms of U.S. infantry during World War I were the .30in caliber Springfield M1903 and the M1917, both sturdy and reliable bolt-action weapons working from five-round internal magazines.*

A note on arrangement and data

This book is organized by type of weapon—handguns, rifles and shotguns, submachine guns, light machine guns, and heavy machine guns. Within these sections the gun entries are arranged chronologically in order of their initial year of production or, if this date cannot be precisely ascertained, a judged approximation. The features throughout this book bring out important technological or historical aspects of firearms, and will provide some context and discussion surrounding the individual entries.

The reader can refer to the glossary for explanations of specific terms. Measurements for weapons manufactured before about 1870, particularly caliber, are approximate, and even after that date minor variations in dimensions may be found in the various reference books, depending upon who took the measurements and the method used. In specifications "n.k." means not known. In gun descriptions "qv"—"quod vide"—indicates a separate gun entry.

Above: *US Rangers in action around Salines airport during the Grenada operation, 1983. They carry the standard 5.56mm M16A1 rifle, which was replaced by the improved M16A2 from the early 1990s.*

Left: *The Steyr AUG, despite its awkward appearance, is a superb assault rifle. It uses a "bullpup" operating system to reduce its length and relies heavily on plastics in its construction, even in the firing mechanism. The rifle shown here is actually the Australian Army's version, known as the F88.*

Left: *The very latest in submachine gun design, the Parker-Hale Personal Defense Weapon (PDW) fires 9 mm ammunition and was introduced in 1999. A traditional problem with submachine guns has been "weapon climb" when firing on automatic, but the PDW is claimed to have completely eliminated this, using a new, patented technique. In the configuration seen here it weighs 2.4 kg (5.25 lb.) and the magazine holds thirty-two rounds.*

- Length is overall and, in the case of weapons with folding butts, is the length with butt extended.

- Barrel length is measured from the forward end of the chamber to the muzzle.

- Weight is the total weight of the weapon, plus (where applicable) one empty magazine, but less bayonet (if fitted), and without ammunition. In the case of heavy machine guns, the weight with tripod is given separately.

- Caliber is as given by the makers. It should be noted that calibers originally given in inches are not always converted to metric measurement.

Below: *A British soldier fires his 5.56 mm L85A1 rifle, using the bipod for sustained, semi-automatic fire. This was one of a number of rifles introduced in the 1980s and 1990s to use the new NATO standard 5.56 x 45 mm round.*

Left: *Two members of the "A" team 743, 7th Special Forces Group, take stock of the terrain on exercise, Fort Bragg, 1980. Sometimes, but not always, special forces employ special weaponry.*

- Rifling, if known or appropriate, is given in the specifications list of many entries.

- Operation is also given in the specifications list of many entries, or described in the text of the entry in other instances.

- Cyclic rate of fire is the rate at which an automatic weapon would fire if it had a continuous supply of ammunition in unlimited quantities, expressed in rounds per minute (rpm). This is essentially a theoretical figure, since weapons are very rarely required to fire continuously, and, in any case, there are inevitable pauses for reloading, clearing stoppages, and over-heating.

- Muzzle velocity (abbreviated to "Muz vel") is as given by makers and, except with the most modern weapons, is an approximate figure.

- Range is given only for heavy machine guns which could be fired from a fixed mount—e.g., a tripod. In all other weapons, the range is not given since it depends to such a large extent on the firer's skill and expertise, all the circumstances in which he/she is firing (i.e., in the calm on a range or in the face of imminent attack from an approaching enemy, in clear daylight or adverse weather). It should also be noted that in the case of weapons being fired on "automatic" the accuracy decreases rapidly with the length of the burst.

Below: *Quite apart from their role in war, rifles and pistols are also widely used for sport, both for target shooting and, as in this example, for trap shooting. All firearms are inherently dangerous, particularly so in the wrong hands, but when properly used and under careful control they can be safe and can give considerable pleasure.*

Pistols & Revolvers

> *"I cannot impress upon an individual too strongly the propriety of remaining perfectly calm and collected when hit...if he dies, go off with as good a grace as possible."*
>
> Anonymous author writing in *The Art of Duelling*, published in 1836.

Handguns have several distinct disadvantages. For a start, handguns are notoriously difficult to shoot accurately. Whereas a shooting novice is quite capable of putting a bullseye in a target with a rifle (with proper tuition and a bench support, of course), the same cannot be said if he or she were using a handgun. Even a trained handgun user will struggle to accurately engage targets over 50–66 ft. (15–20 m) away, exploding many of the myths of handgun use represented in movies. Handgun recoil can be troublesome, particularly with large-caliber magnum loads, and so handguns require extended training time to master.

So what is the redeeming quality of handguns, which makes them so desirable to own in both military and civilian markets? In a word, portability. A modern handgun is the ultimate transportable firepower, and (very) generally speaking, the history of handguns has seen a steady evolutionary increase in firepower with an accompanying decrease in size.

Above: *The Annely flintlock revolver dates from around 1705 and allied the flintlock mechanism with an eight-chamber cylinder, each cylinder having its own pan and touch-hole. Only with the invention of the percussion cap, however, did revolvers become practical guns.*

Ancient and Modern

To make the point, we can compare two different firearms from opposite ends of firearm history: an extant Italian wheel-lock pistol from the early years of the sixteenth century and a modern Beretta 92 handgun. The wheel-lock was certainly a challenge to fire. To load it a charge of powder with ball and wadding was first compacted into the barrel, and the pan primed. A spring-loaded arm holding a piece of pyrites was cocked, and the wheel-lock's metal wheel was cranked against the spring tension using a key. The weapon could now be fired, but this unsighted handgun weighed 2.25 lb. (1.02 kg) and was 15.5 in. (394 mm) long, statistics which would have compromised accuracy from the start. Although the weapon had a long barrel (11.5 in./292 mm), the barrel was not rifled and upon firing the bullet would have achieved a muzzle velocity of only 400 ft./sec (122 m/sec). The .437 in. (10.9 mm) ball fired by the wheel-lock would certainly have killed somebody at close ranges, but at ranges of over 50 ft. (15.2 m) the shooter would have been unlikely to hit his target.

While there is no denying the revolutionary status of the wheel-lock in its own time, the modern handgun of course employs different materials and technology. A comparison nevertheless can provide a useful perspective on the direction of handgun development over the centuries. What is better, how much better, and why? The Beretta Model 92 is the handgun selected to replace the US Army's Colt M1911 in 1985. It is an automatic weapon, recoil-operated, feeding from a 15-round magazine filled with 9mm Parabellum ammunition. The gun is 8.54 in. (217 mm) in length and although the barrel is far shorter than the wheel-lock, being only 4.9 in. (125 mm), it is rifled (six grooves, right-hand) for accuracy. The muzzle velocity of the Model 92 is 1,280 ft./sec (390 m/sec), the lethality of its rounds extending well beyond 330 ft. (100 m). Accurate shooting range is probably about 70 ft. (21 m), the range a trained user will be confident of an accurate hit on a human-sized target. The comparison is most significant when looking at the improvement in

Above: *US Army servicemen train in handling the powerful Colt M1911 pistol. The .45 in. caliber M1911 served in the US Army from 1911 to 1990, such was the reliability of its design. However, it was replaced by the Beretta 92 during the 1980s, the Beretta offering a higher magazine capacity and easier handling.*

firing procedure. To unleash fifteen rounds of high-velocity pistol ammunition the operator will have to do no more than insert a magazine into the grip, pull back the slide, release the safety, then pull the trigger fifteen times.

So the key differences between an ancient and a modern handgun are dimensions, weight, operating system, ammunition capacity, and lethality; but not, in any dramatic sense, practical combat range. An army officer of the early nineteenth century firing a flintlock pistol would probably have been able, if he was well-trained, to hit a human target over similar practical ranges to the Beretta user. The comparison reveals the fundamental limitation inherent in handguns, that is, they are held and fired single-handed. The point is highlighted more if ancient and modern rifle technologies are compared. A smoothbore musket of the seventeenth century could fire two or three rounds a minute with an accurate range of around 164 ft. (50 m). A modern assault rifle, such as an M16A2 or Israeli Galil, can unleash thirty rounds in about fifteen seconds (less if full-auto mode is used) with killing ranges of more than 1,640 ft. (500 m). The accurate range of modern sniper weapons is up to and even exceeding 6,000 ft. (1,830 m).

Whereas rifles have an inherently stable hold using shoulder support and two hands, the pistol will forever be limited by the grip. That said, within those limitations the last 500 years have turned the pistol into a lethal weapon.

From wheel-lock to revolver

The wheel-lock was the first effective form of firearm ignition, and had a major significance to the development of handguns. Prior to the advent of the wheel-lock in the early sixteenth century, the matchlock had provided a basic firing mechanism but it was ill-suited for a handgun—the smoldering slowmatch meant that matchlock weapons could not be concealed. The wheel-lock, however, meant that a pre-loaded pistol could be transported on the body ready for instant application. For the military, the wheel-lock gave the cavalry its first usable firearm, able to be fired with one hand while the other controlled the horse. Wheel-locks were expensive, and that restricted their distribution, but not enough to stop governments and royalty across Europe being alarmed at the rise in gun crime and attempting to levy various restrictions upon gun ownership.

It was the arrival of the snaphance lock, then the flintlock in the late sixteenth and seventeenth centuries, that truly galvanized the market for handguns, especially the flintlock. Flintlocks dramatically reduced the cost of a gun, and by the eighteenth century, handguns were widely distributed throughout the military and civilian populations. Wealthier citizens took to traveling with a pistol or keeping one by the side of their beds for personal protection; just as criminals took advantage of the new, cheaper weaponry.

During this period handguns also became more diverse in type. There were tiny "traveler's pistols," which would fit in a waistcoat pocket; there were high-quality dueling pistols with refined lock mechanisms; the Royal Navy equipped boarding parties with bell-mouthed handguns to create a scatter-shot effect for deck combat. Whatever the role, however, all flintlock weapons were limited by their single-shot configuration, with reloading almost impossible in combat (after the first shot the pistol was often turned around and held by the muzzle as a club).

The problem was overcome by a true revolution in firearm design—the introduction of percussion pistols and the unitary cartridge in the nineteenth century. Alexander Forsythe's application of fulminates led to the creation of the percussion cap around 1820, and this made firearms more reliable, as well as dramatically speeding up the whole cycle of ignition from hammer fall to the bullet leaving the muzzle, hence making handguns more accurate. Handguns became more streamlined and compact, and more lethal, with the introduction of the revolver.

The first revolvers of the early 1800s worked by rotating the barrels (they were generally known as "pepperbox" revolvers), but the famous Samuel Colt rejected this principle to make a rotating cylinder instead. Combined with the percussion cap, Colt's early revolvers gave soldiers and civilians a powerful six-shot firearm, and the revolver principle soon spread across North America and into Europe.

When loaded, the nineteenth-century percussion revolvers had a performance almost indistinguishable from their modern counterparts, and in the military the heavy caliber handguns (often approaching 0.5 in.) ensured lethality at close ranges, as was proved most terribly in the American Civil War.

By the end of the century the problem of slow reloading of revolvers was overcome by the spreading use of the unitary cartridge, first developed back in 1812 by the Swiss inventor Samuel Johannes Pauly.

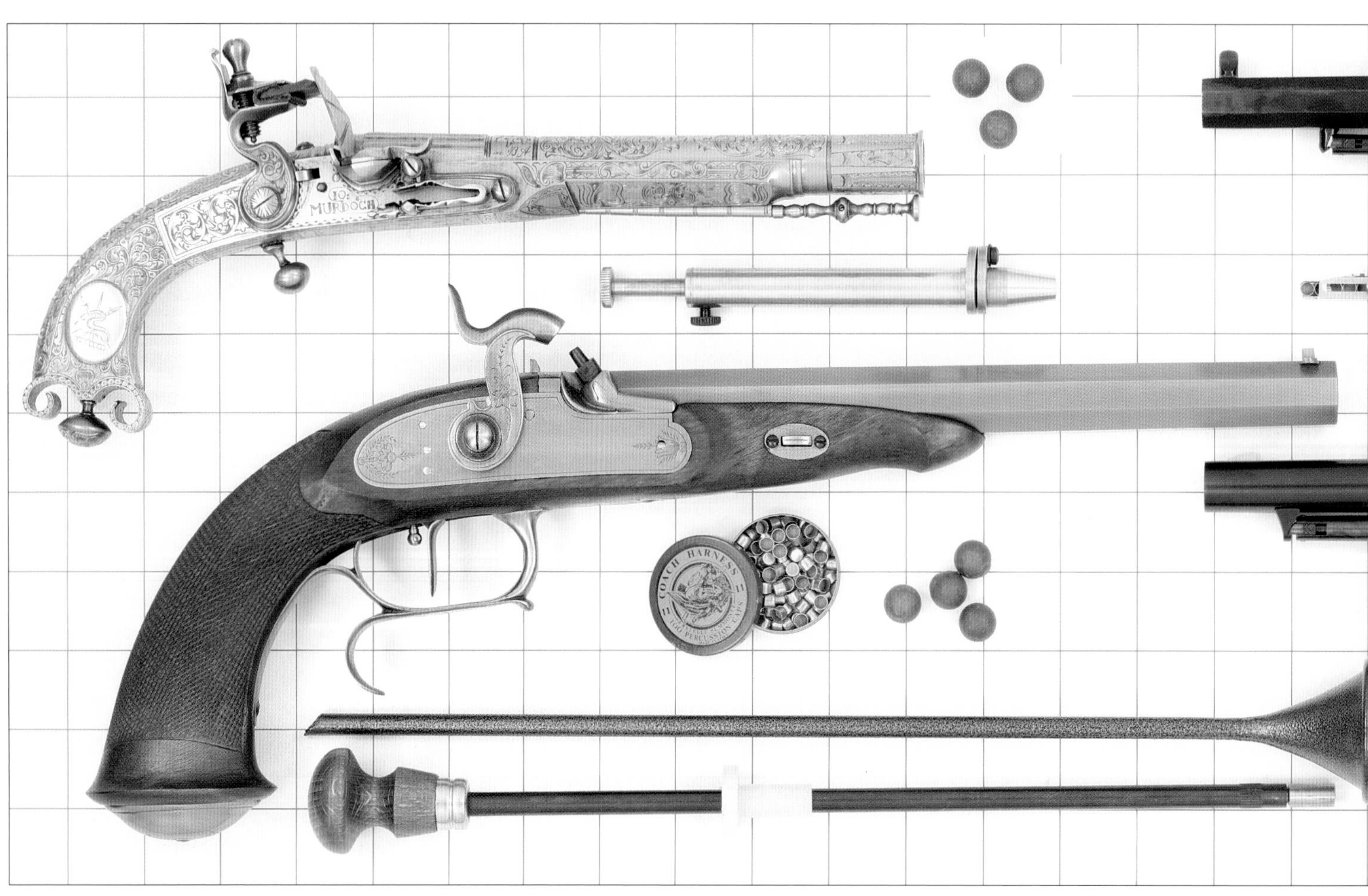

Below: *A selection of replica firearms, all from Italy, showing the evolution from flintlock to percussion weapons. The replica handgun market has experienced considerable growth in recent years, focused particularly on weapons of the Wild West and the US Civil War. Below: Scottish flintlock pistol by Uberti, with powder charge measure. Bottom: Le Page target pistol by Pedersoli, with ramrod and rod guide. Below right: Uberti's Remington New Model Army percussion revolver. Bottom right: Armi San Marco's Colt model 1860 army percussion revolver.*

Smith & Wesson produced the first cartridge revolvers in the 1850s and Colt soon joined them, when S&W's initial patents expired. Pinfire, rimfire, and then centerfire revolvers evolved, and by the end of the nineteenth century the development of the modern revolver was essentially complete.

Since that period, revolvers have been improved in terms of manufacturing quality, sighting, and in mechanism changes, but the fundamentals remain the same.

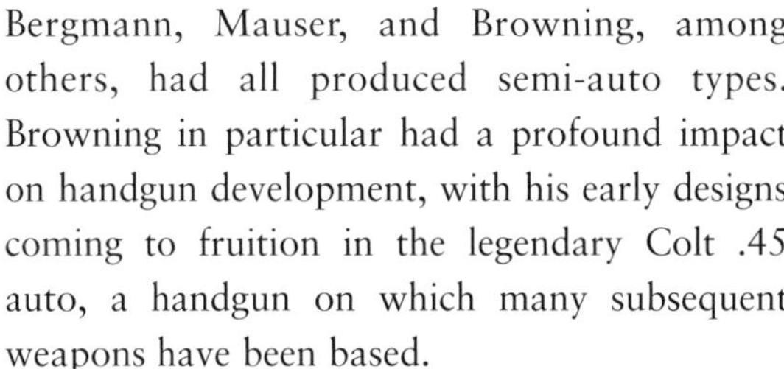

Above: *Pistol target shooting is an exacting sport, requiring strength in the arms and shoulders, acute concentration and a first-rate weapon. Here the shooter fires a customized target gun from a seated rest.*

The automatic pistol

The end of the nineteenth century also introduced a new handgun type that would rival the revolver and ultimately dominate the handgun market—the automatic pistol. Building on the self-loading mechanism pioneered in machine guns by Hiram Maxim, the German Hugo Borchardt invented the first commercially successful self-loading handgun in 1893, which was recoil-operated with a toggle-joint, allowing separation of barrel and breech to enable cycling. It was fed from an eight-round magazine and was, admittedly, of such bulk that it was difficult to fire with one hand. However, others refined the concept of the self-loading pistol, and soon Bergmann, Mauser, and Browning, among others, had all produced semi-auto types. Browning in particular had a profound impact on handgun development, with his early designs coming to fruition in the legendary Colt .45 auto, a handgun on which many subsequent weapons have been based.

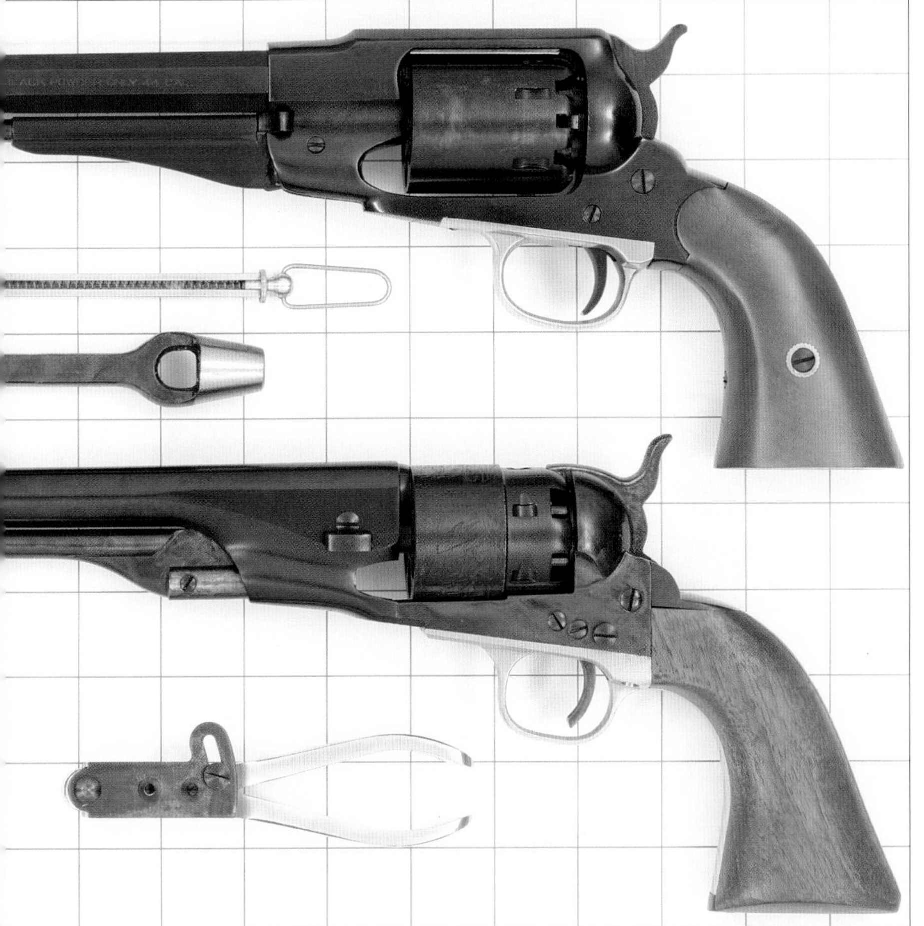

By the outbreak of World War II, automatic handguns had reached their modern configuration, and there has been no major redesign of either automatic or revolver design ever since.

There have of course been numerous minor refinements. Modern handguns use precision castings and lightweight metals. Magazine capacities of auto handguns have crept up to around 15 rounds, even for weapons of larger caliber like the .45. Sight pictures have also been radically improved using technologies such as tritium dots.

Yet while advances in rifle and machine gun technology continue apace, the handgun has settled into conventional forms. The main reason for this is that handguns are militarily unimportant weapons, and so do not attract the big R&D budgets that rifles do. Handguns are back-up weapons, to be used when all else fails. However, the importance of handguns should not be underestimated.

Handguns are the primary form of armament for police forces the world over, and lives do hang upon the quality of a sidearm. As to future developments, perhaps the very conformity of handgun design is a kind of reassurance that handguns that actually make it into production are reliable, serviceable weapons, which can be depended on for either sport or self-protection.

BERETTA MODEL 1984 PISTOL

The Model 84 was chambered to fire the internationally standardized 9mm Short cartridge, and since this round is relatively low-powered, the weapon works on the simple blowback principle, without any requirement for breech-locking. The firer pulls the slide to the rear by hand, which cocks the hammer, and then releases the slide which is driven forward by the spring to chamber the round. To fire a round the trigger is pulled and the hammer strikes the rear of the firing-pin, which then hits the cartridge and fires the round. As the round leaves the barrel the recoil forces thrust the slide to the rear, compressing the recoil spring, ejecting the spent case and chambering the next round. There is a manual safety that can be operated by either the left or right hand. The Model 84 has a double-column magazine, but without the long grooves which characterized the magazine of the Model 81. The weapon has an anodized aluminum frame and is considered to be both safe and reliable.

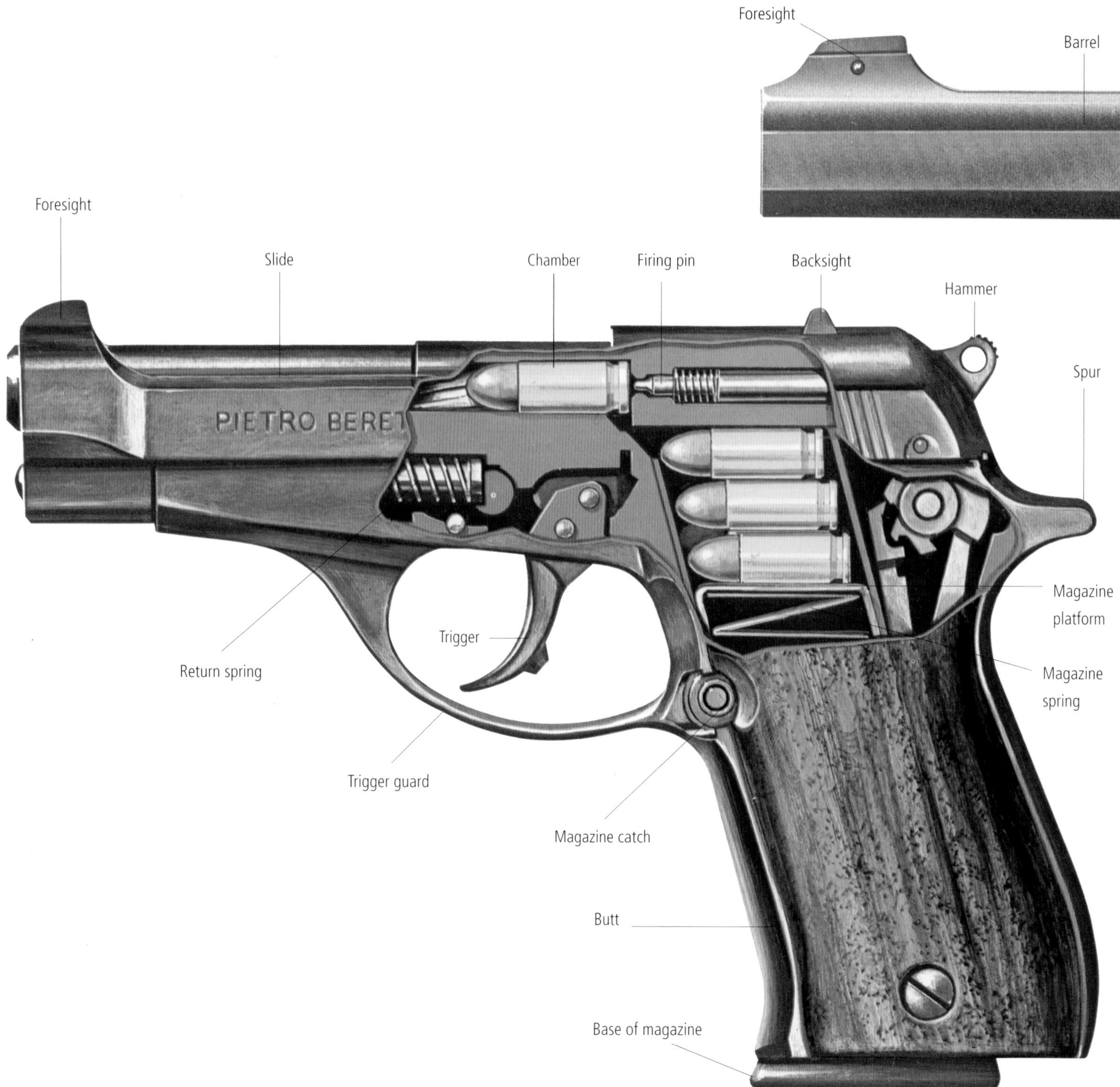

BERETTA MODEL 84 PISTOL

WEBLEY AND SCOTT MARK VI REVOLVER

Almost certainly the most common and best known of the many Webley and Scott revolver designs was the Mark VI, first introduced in 1915 and remaining in service until well into the 1930s. It was issued to the British Army and was also used extensively by various Commonwealth forces and also occasionally by the police.

In operation, pressure on the trigger depressed the cylinder stop and allowed the cylinder to rotate and bring the next chamber in line. Continuing steady pressure on the trigger caused the hammer to fall so that its nose struck the cap of the cartridge. At this stage the cylinder was prevented from rotating by the stop. The hammer could also be first drawn back manually to the cocked position, which decreased the amount of pressure required and so aided accurate shooting. The sequence was repeated either at double or single action until all the rounds were fired. The empty cases were then ejected.

WEBLEY AND SCOTT MARK VI REVOLVER

ITALY

WHEEL-LOCK PISTOL 1530

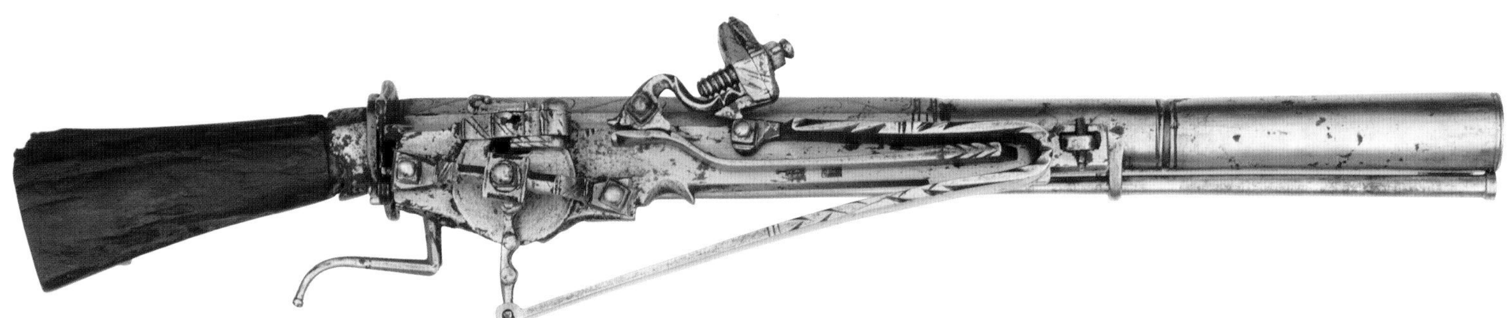

Length (gun): 15.5 in. (394 mm)
Barrel: 11.5 in. (292 mm)
Weight: 36.0 oz. (1.0 kg)
Caliber: 0.437 in. (10.9 mm)
Rifling: none
Capacity: one
Muz vel: 400 ft./sec. (122 m/sec.)

The wheel, which gave the lock its name, was spun by a spring, so that its roughened edge rubbed briskly against a piece of pyrites and caused sparks. The upper part of the wheel protruded through a close-fitting slot in the pan, connected to the barrel by a touch hole. Once the arm was loaded and the pan primed, the wheel was wound (usually about three-quarters of a turn) with a key, the pan opened, and the hinged jaws holding the piece of pyrites pulled down until it was held firmly against the wheel. Pressure on the trigger then allowed the wheel to spin against the pyrites, striking sparks and igniting the priming. This mechanism, when well made, was reasonably reliable in dry weather, although the relatively poor quality temper of the springs made it advisable not to leave it wound (or "spanned," as it was often referred to). The arm illustrated was made in Italy in about 1530, and was a plain but well-made weapon. Note in particular the straight grip, presumably a legacy of the mace. This gave a good hold on the arm but must have made it virtually impossible to direct the ball accurately, except at very close quarters.

GERMANY

SNAPHANCE PISTOL 1575

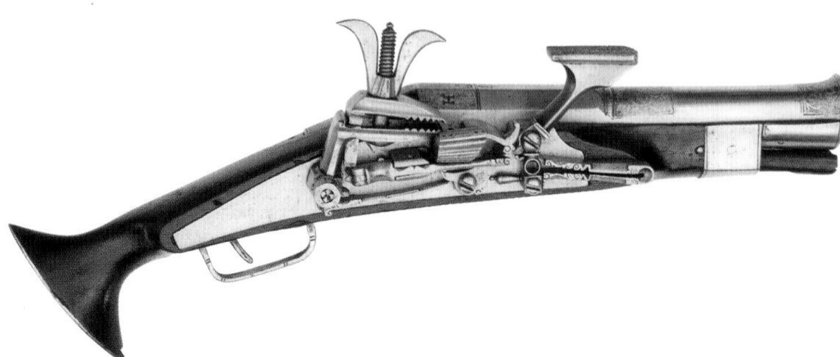

Length (gun): 15.8 in. (400 mm)
Barrel: 8.2 in. (208 mm)
Weight: 59.0 oz. (1.7 kg)
Caliber: 0.675 in. (17.1 mm)
Rifling: none
Capacity: one
Muz vel: 450 ft./sec. (138 m/sec.)

The snaphance (or snaphaunce) was a form of flintlock. Although the name is of Dutch derivation, there is no evidence that the type originated in the Low Countries; the lock on this example appears to be Franco-German. The pistol has some gold damascening on the barrel but is otherwise plain, although well made. The pistol had a "cock" which "pecked" forward when the trigger was pressed. The flint struck a steel plate positioned over the shallow priming pan, from which the touch hole led into the breech. The steel was at the end of a pivoted arm, which could be held safely forward (as in the photograph), or backward, over the pan. The steel was usually linked to a sliding pan cover, which thus opened automatically when the steel was pulled back. The cock had a short throw, so a strong spring was fitted to give it sufficient impetus to strike a shower of good hot sparks.

SPAIN

FLINTLOCK PISTOL 16TH CENTURY (1575)

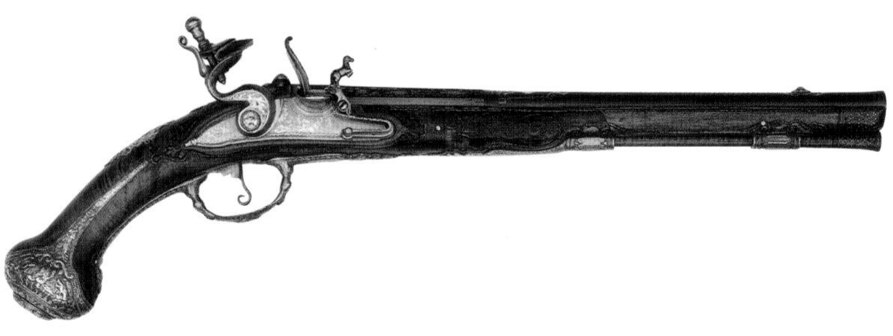

Length (gun): 20.5 in. (521 mm)
Barrel: 13.4 in (340 mm)
Weight: 36.0 oz. (1.0 kg)
Caliber: 0.665 in. (16.9 mm)
Rifling: none
Capacity: one
Muz vel: 400 ft./sec. (122 m/sec.)

This Spanish pistol has a round barrel, except for about 2 in. (51 mm) at the breech which is rounded octagonal, and is slightly swamped at the muzzle. The lock is a miquelet (or miguelet), a type believed to have originated in Catalonia in the early sixteenth century. When the trigger was pressed, the sear was withdrawn and the cock fell, the flint in its jaws striking the vertical steel and knocking it forward, taking with it the integral horizontal pan cover. The mainspring was necessarily very strong, so a ring was fitted to the cock to provide a firm grip. The tip of the trigger is turned back on itself; the butt had a steel cap with long spurs reaching almost the whole way up the butt. The ramrod (missing) was held in a groove on the underside of the stock by a brass loop and tailpipe. It was designed to be carried in a saddle holster, and was a plain, robust arm.

THE HAND-GONNE

The history of firearms begins at some point during the first half of the fourteenth century. The first weapons to fire missiles from an enclosed tube using gunpowder were large vase-shaped, cast-bronze cannon, generally firing either loose stones or a single large stone, although an early artistic representation in Walter de Millemete's "On the Duties of Kings" (1325) also shows one of these bell cannons firing an arrow. Bell casting was an expensive and skilled process and was gradually replaced by the coopering process in which a long, straight barrel was built up from strips of metal, these being heated and welded together and strengthened with reinforcing bands.

The early cannon were the beginnings of the artillery revolution—outside the consideration of this book—but it was not long before man-portable versions of the new weapons were considered. The hand-gonne was effectively the first hand-held firearm in history, appearing around 1350, probably in Germany or Belgium. It was little more than a diminutive bronze or iron cannon fitted onto a cut-down pike haft using metal bands. To fire the weapon, the user would load, with powder and ball, tuck the haft under his armpit, sprinkle powder into the vent hole, then a second man would apply either a hot metal rod or a burning slowmatch (cord impregnated with saltpeter) to the vent hole. The caliber of these weapons tended to be around 0.7 in. (18 mm).

The hand-gonne was of limited military application. It would have been highly inaccurate, heavy to transport, and time-consuming to load. To improve accuracy, some hand-gonnes featured a hook beneath the muzzle which, when engaged with a solid feature such as a wall or tree, would allow the shooter to achieve more stable aiming. However, with a typical muzzle velocity of around 100 mps (320 fps), no rifling, and a poor fit between projectile and bore, the lethality of the hand-gonne at anything less than 20–30 m (66–100 ft.) must have been extremely poor. Evidence of burst weapons also suggests that they could have been more dangerous to the user than the target.

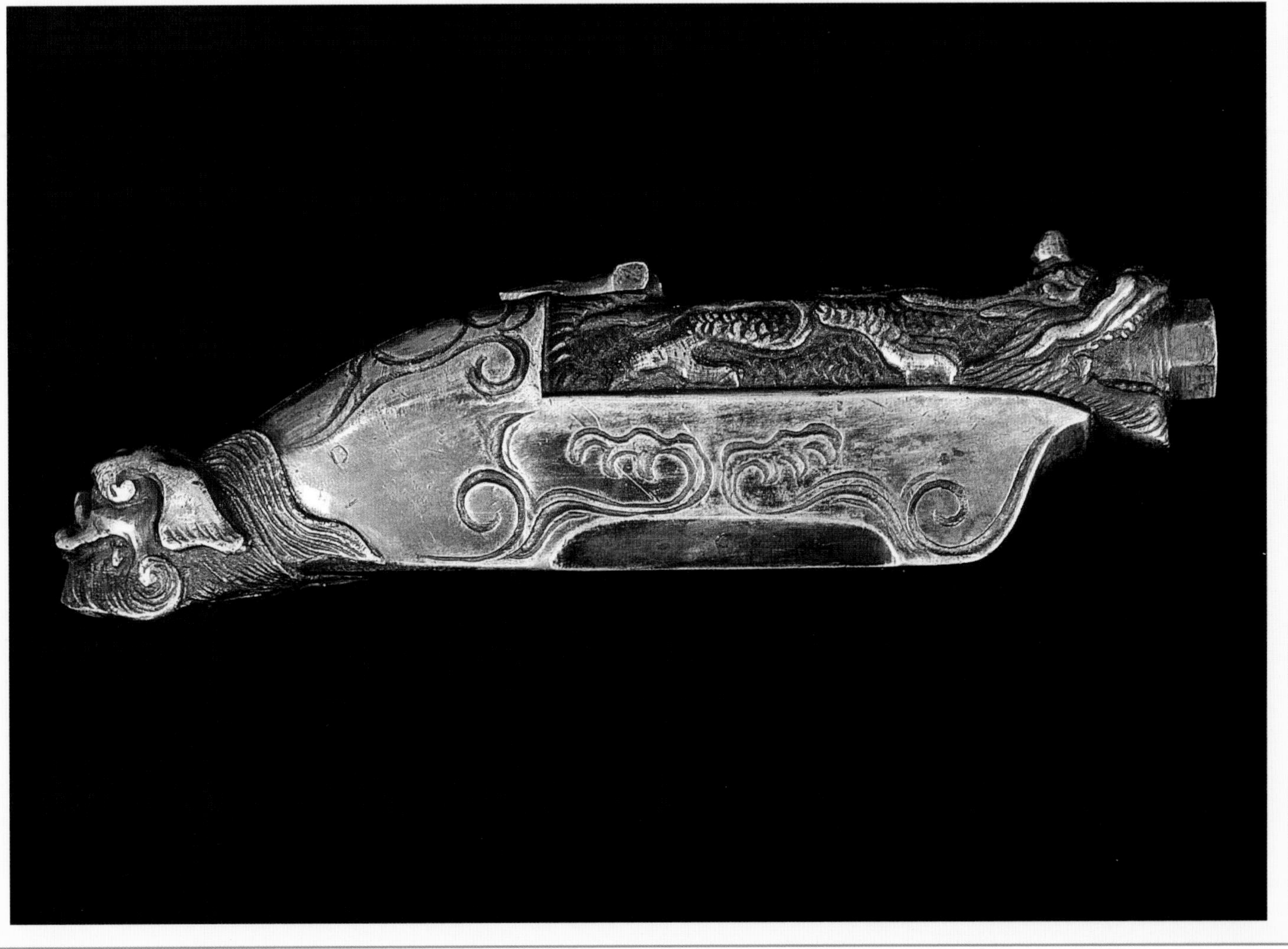

Below: *This fourteenth-century Japanese brass hand cannon was more beautiful than useful. Japan would prove to be one of the most conservative nations in terms of firearms development, persisting with the matchlock even into the nineteenth century.*

EARLY GUNPOWDER COMPOSITIONS

Above: *A sixteenth-century woodcut of the German monk and alchemist Berthold Schwarz at work on the production of gunpowder, supposedly in the early fourteenth century. The first to attribute the "invention" of gunpowder to the friar of Freiburg seems to have been Felix Hemmelin (1389–1464) of Zurich in his "De Nobilitate et Rusticitate Dialogus" (ca. 1450). He writes rather cautiously that the discovery was made within 200 years of the time of his writing. It is now known that the Chinese were there first.*

During the fourteenth century, the composition of English gunpowder was roughly standardized to around six parts saltpeter to two parts charcoal and one part sulphur. Although these proportions in themselves will produce a reasonably powerful powder, with a gas expansion of around x100 of volume, the powder quality itself could be extremely variable. The problem lay mainly in the base ingredients. The sulphur, saltpeter, and charcoal were all manufactured through crude processes that left a powder with a high degree of impurity.

Further deficiencies were imbued in the mixing process. Gunpowder was hand mixed, which allowed the potential for errors in quantity and inconsistent distribution of the constituents throughout the mix.

The result for firearms users was an unpredictable experience. If held loaded in a firearm for some time, the powder would also settle with no air gaps. This produced a slow-burning powder, so slow that the ball could be propelled from the muzzle before the whole charge was burned, with a consequent reduction in performance. In addition, when the powder was carried over a distance, lighter particles would shake to the bottom, resulting in a separation of the constituents and poor burning.

The dramatic leap forward in the quality of gunpowder came in the mid-fourteenth century with the French invention of the process of "corning." Corning involved turning the gunpowder into granular rather than powdered form by mixing the powder with water (or later a water/alcohol mix) and spreading the mix onto metal plates to dry, forming it into "cakes." Once dried, it could then be crumbled up into grains, the size of the grain controlled through a process of sieving.

Corned powder was dramatically more efficient than a simple mixed powder. The corning process ensured a uniform distribution of the elements throughout each grain. Most importantly, the irregular shape of the grains created air gaps between each grain, which produced almost instantaneous ignition of the whole charge and therefore more effective propulsion. Later corned powders were also glazed in graphite to make a moisture-resistant coating over the grains.

RUSSIA

CAUCASIAN FLINTLOCK PISTOL 1650

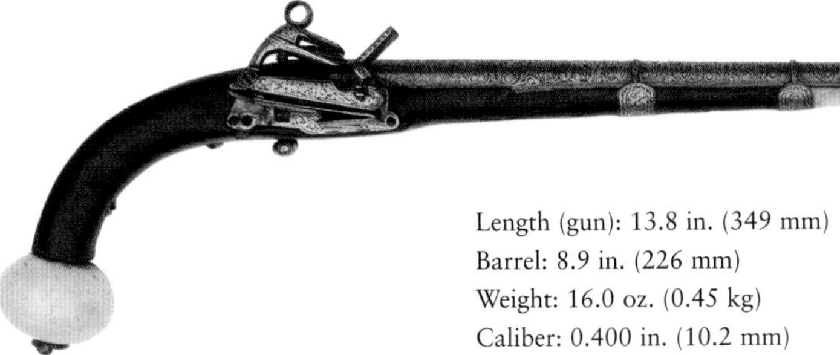

Length (gun): 13.8 in. (349 mm)
Barrel: 8.9 in. (226 mm)
Weight: 16.0 oz. (0.45 kg)
Caliber: 0.400 in. (10.2 mm)
Rifling: none
Capacity: one
Muz vel: 400 ft./sec. (122 m/sec.)

These arms were made in the Caucasus region, and are sometimes known as "Cossack pistols." They were probably assembled by local craftsmen, although the locks and barrels were frequently imported from Spain, Italy, and elsewhere. The barrel is decorated with an elaborate pattern of silver inlaid with black, in the Italianate style known as niello. The lock is characteristically miquelet. The sear projected horizontally from the lockplate and acted directly on the projection at the bottom of the cock. The sear can be seen just above the button trigger, which is practically universal on pistols of this kind. The pan cover and steel are combined; the face of the steel is scored with eight vertical grooves to ensure a good spark. The lock and all metal parts except the barrel and lanyard ring are gold damascened. Ramrods were carried separately, often on a cord or ribbon around the user's neck.

GERMANY

RIFLED CAVALRY PISTOL 1715

Length (gun): 19.5 in. (495 mm)
Barrel: 13.3 in. (337 mm)
Weight: 40.0 oz. (1.13 kg)
Caliber: 0.55 in. (14.0 mm)
Rifling: 7 grooves, r/hand
Capacity: one
Muz vel: 500 ft./sec. (152 m/sec.)

This pistol, although severely plain (apart from a little shallow engraving on the trigger-guard), as befits a service arm, is of excellent quality. The lock is standard, with the slight down-droop at the rear characteristic of the period, and it is stocked in a hardwood. The octagonal barrel is very sturdy, rifled with seven rounded grooves; rifled barrels necessitated tight-fitting bullets, and these, in turn, led to increased pressures at the breech. The pistol's foresight is square in section, while the backsight (which is just visible behind the steel) has a shallow V-notch. The flat metal plate at the back of the butt incorporates a keyhole: it was clearly the attachment point for a stock, which would convert the arm into a carbine. When used in this way, with a carefully measured charge and a well-cast ball wrapped in an oiled patch, it is probable that it would have shot fairly well up to an impressive 150 yards (137 m).

UNITED KINGDOM

CANNON-BARRELED FLINTLOCK PISTOL 1725

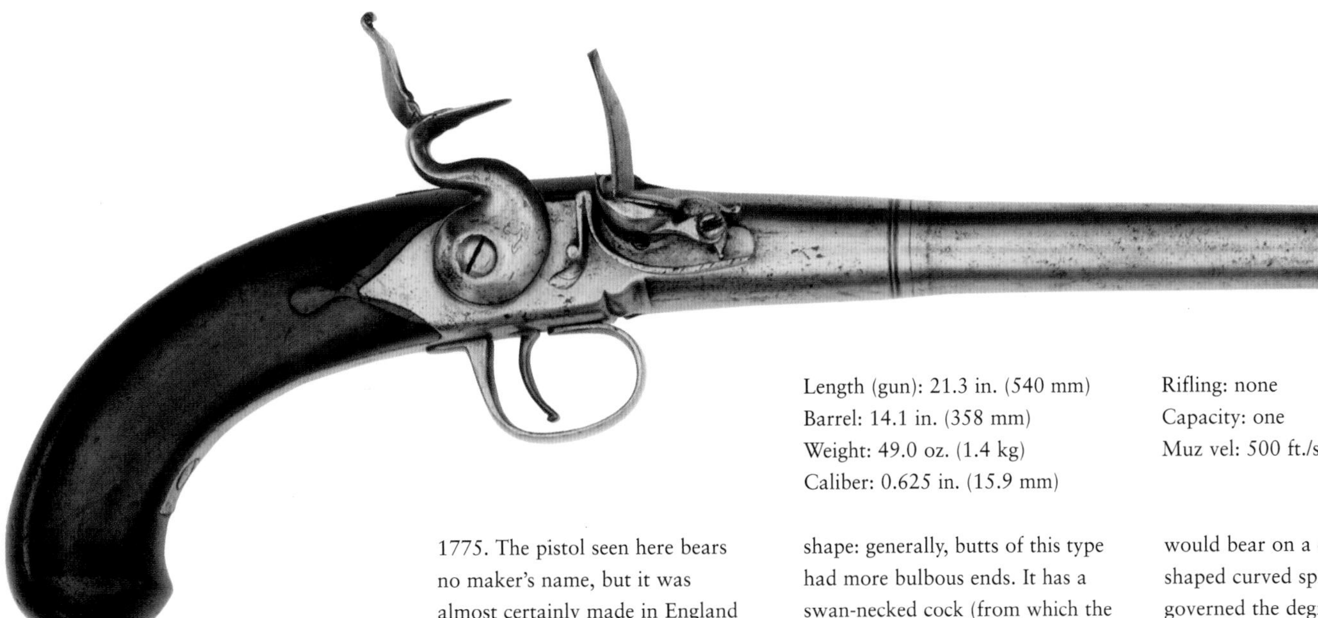

Length (gun): 21.3 in. (540 mm)
Barrel: 14.1 in. (358 mm)
Weight: 49.0 oz. (1.4 kg)
Caliber: 0.625 in. (15.9 mm)
Rifling: none
Capacity: one
Muz vel: 500 ft./sec. (152 m/sec.)

Weapons of this type are frequently known as "Queen Anne pistols," although they only began to appear around the time she died in 1714. They continued to be made until at least 1775. The pistol seen here bears no maker's name, but it was almost certainly made in England in about 1725. It is a holster pistol and probably one of a pair, of medium quality, typically carried by the guard on a coach or by a mounted servant escorting his master. The pistol has no butt cap. The butt is of slightly unusual shape: generally, butts of this type had more bulbous ends. It has a swan-necked cock (from which the top jaw and screw are missing); the slight roughening on the jaw surface was to ensure that the flint, which was often seated in leather, was held firmly. The tail of the combined pan cover and steel (now often known as the frizzen) would bear on a characteristically shaped curved spring, which governed the degree of resistance to the falling flint: it was necessary for the pan to open quickly and smoothly, while still offering enough resistance to ensure good sparks. Some weapons of this type had ramrods held in a pipe or pipes below the barrel.

SPAIN

FLINTLOCK PISTOL 1720

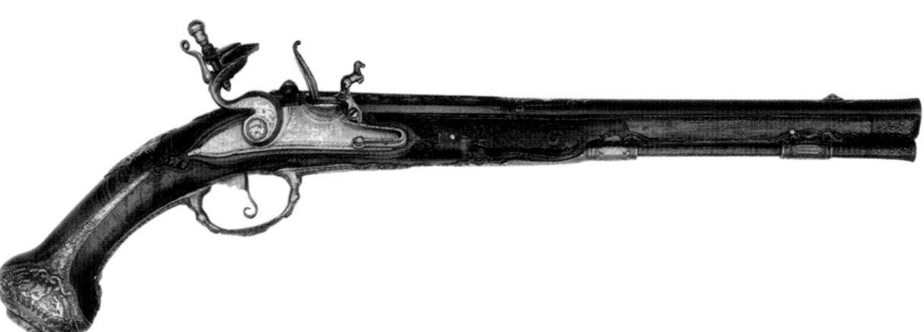

Length (gun): 21.3 in. (540 mm)
Barrel: 14.1 in. (358 mm)
Weight: 49.0 oz. (1.4 kg)
Caliber: 0.625 in. (15.9 mm)
Rifling: none
Capacity: one
Muz vel: 500 ft./sec. (152 m/sec.)

This very fine pistol was made by Juan Fernandez, who worked in Madrid from 1717 until 1739, at the height of French influence. The barrel, well blued and heavily decorated with gold inlay, is round for two-thirds of its length, the breech end being octagonal for strength. The lock is of the usual French type and the lock plate is beautifully ornamented with battle scenes in gold and silver damascene. The cock is of the graceful type known as "swan-necked." The flint is seated in a small patch of leather to hold the flint rigid and cushion it. The combined steel and pan cover (later often known as frizzens) are decorated with rearing horses; mainly ornamental, they also prevented the pans from opening too far by exerting pressure on the frizzen springs.

UNITED KINGDOM

BARBAR POCKET SCREW-OFF PISTOL 1740

Length (gun): 6.6 in. (168 mm)
Barrel: 3.0 in. (76 mm)
Weight: 12.0 oz. (0.34 kg)
Caliber: 0.500 in. (12.7 mm)
Rifling: none
Capacity: one
Muz vel: 350 ft./sec. (107 m/sec.)

The well-known London gunsmith Barbar made this weapon in about 1740. Although most gentlemen then habitually carried swords, many liked to have a pair of pistols handy also. These were usually carried in the capacious flapped pockets of the long waistcoats then worn, where they were available for instant use. The weapon seen here (which was originally one of a pair) is a strictly fundamental piece, without ornamentation of any kind, but its quality is excellent—as is only to be expected from a maker of Barbar's repute. Because it has a screw-off barrel, it could be loaded with a tight ball that would stay in place. A common enough problem with muzzle-loaders was that the ball, unless held in position by an over wad, would move forward if the arm was jolted.

UNITED KINGDOM

BUMFORD SCREW-OFF FLINTLOCK PISTOL 1755

Length (gun): 11.8 in. (298 mm)
Barrel: 5.5 in. (140 mm)
Weight: 27.0 oz. (0.76 kg)
Caliber: 0.62 in. (15.7 mm)
Rifling: none
Capacity: one
Muz vel: 450 ft./sec. (122 m/sec.)

This has a removable cannon-shaped barrel. To remove the barrel, a circular key was slipped over it and locked near the breech by a stud, which fitted a corresponding notch in the inner circumference of the key. This enabled the barrel to make a good, gas-tight fit with the breech. The somewhat abrupt swell at the bottom of the butt is characteristic of the general type, as is the cast-brass butt cap with its simple design of foliage and the brass escutcheon plate just visible above it. Screw-off barrels made possible the use of a carefully measured charge and a tight-fitting ball. In this weapon, the powder chamber is contained within the male screw and has a concave top. The chamber was loaded vertically, the ball was balanced on the top, and the barrel then screwed on again with the key. This system was a slow process, but it eliminated the need for ramming and was particularly useful in rifled barrels.

FRANCE

SAINT-ÉTIENNE MODÈLE 1777

Length (gun): 13.3 in. (337 mm)
Barrel: 7.5 in. (190 mm)
Weight: 46.0 oz. (1.3 kg)
Caliber: 0.700 in. (17.8 mm)
Rifling: none
Capacity: one
Muz vel: 500 ft./sec. (152 m/sec.)

This pistol was made at Saint-Étienne, and is a plain, robust weapon, built on a solid brass frame and fitted with a walnut butt with a heavy brass butt cap, the top strap being of iron. The cock is of the common ring-necked type, which gave much greater strength than the more elegant swan-necked type. The tapered barrel, firing a ball of about 1 oz. (28.35 g), has no sight. The lack of any stock in front of the trigger guard necessitated special arrangements for the ramrod (here at full length below the arm). It was normally housed in a hole in the front of the frame, which is just visible here. This pistol was the pattern for one of the earliest military pistols to be made in the United States. In 1799 and 1800, Simon North, a famous American maker, received contracts to make very similar pistols in partnership with his brother-in-law, Cheny. Such arms are rare.

The Wheel Lock

Above: *The expense of manufacture of the cleverly designed wheel lock almost precluded its use on military small arms altogether.*

While the matchlock system of ignition was in use from the mid-fifteenth century to the early 1700s, it was an impractical system to apply to handguns. A pistol is a close-quarters weapon, which is usually carried about the person for more or less instant use—a burning slow match would preclude this transportation. However, in the first two decades of the sixteenth century emerged a new system of firing a weapon that was directly applicable to pistols—the wheel lock.

The origins of the wheel lock are much debated. Leonardo da Vinci sketched out two wheel lock type systems in his "Codice Atlantico" in 1508, and in 1517 Johann Kiefuss of Nuremberg produced working examples. Other specimens from around this period are sourced to Hungary. Regardless of the point of origin, by the 1520s Europe was given a new system of weapon ignition which, unlike the matchlock, could be fired instantaneously hours after loading, making it ideal for the "snap-shooting" usage of game weapons and handguns.

The wheel lock works in a similar way to a modern flint-type cigarette lighter. The lock featured a metal wheel that was wound up against spring tension using a purpose-designed key. The upper part of the wheel protruded through a close-fitting slot in the pan, which was connected to the barrel by a touch hole. The other part of the mechanism was an arm with jaws gripping a piece of pyrites.

To load and fire the weapon, the barrel was first charged with gunpowder, shot, and wadding, the arm cocked, and the pan primed. The wheel was wound up, usually with a three-quarter turn, and the pyrites brought into contact with the wheel. When the trigger was pulled, the wheel spun in contact with the pyrites (which had dropped onto the wheel), producing sparks and a pan-to-main charge ignition.

Wheel locks were a satisfactory method of firing a weapon, although they were unreliable in damp weather and suffered from spring weakening if the wheel spring was left under tension for prolonged periods. Wheel-lock pistols were highly expensive and soon became something of a status symbol among the aristocracy, often with inlay of gold, silver, ivory, and horn. They also fell into enough criminal hands for the governments and royalty of Europe to issue prohibitions on handgun ownership in the sixteenth and seventeenth centuries.

UNITED KINGDOM

MURDOCH SCOTTISH ALL-STEEL PISTOL 1770

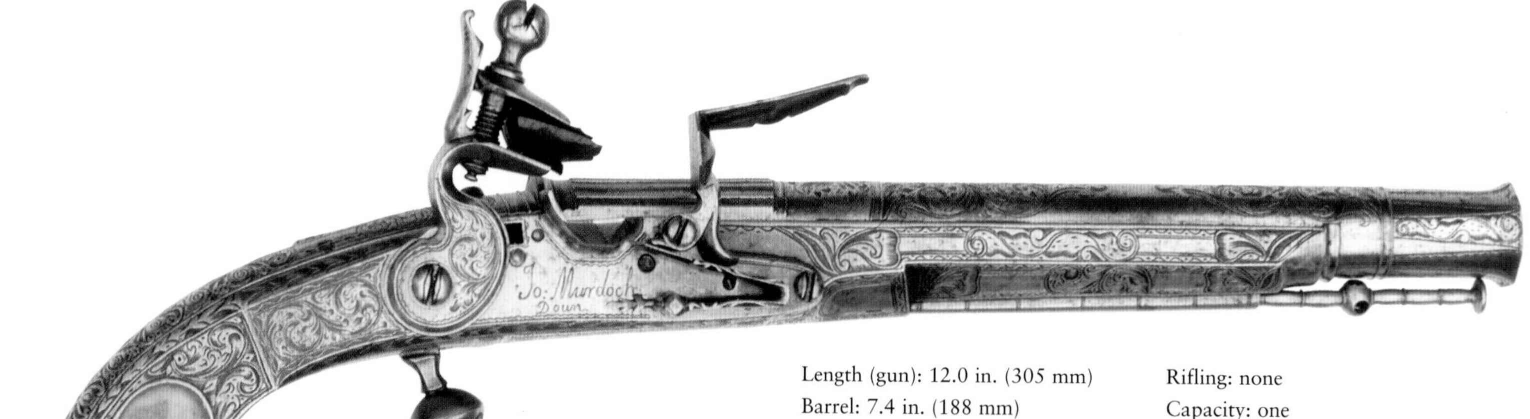

Length (gun): 12.0 in. (305 mm)
Barrel: 7.4 in. (188 mm)
Weight: 22.0 oz. (0.62 kg)
Caliber: 0.556 in. (14.1 mm)
Rifling: none
Capacity: one
Muz vel: 500 ft./sec. (152 m/sec.)

This pistol was made by Murdoch of Doune, a noted center for manufacturing pistols in Scotland. It has a round steel barrel, with slight flares at the muzzle, and an elegant lock. The butt terminates in the incurved horns. The small knob between the horn is the handle of a pricker, which could be unscrewed from the butt and used to remove fouling from the touch hole. The trigger is of the universal button type and there is no trigger guard, a universal characteristic of the type. Almost every part is covered with fine engraving. When the Royal Highland Regiment was first raised in the mid-eighteenth century, its soldiers carried a musket, bayonet, broadsword, and Highland pistol, the latter being worn in an arrangement of straps, not unlike a modern shoulder holster, under the left arm. It was soon found that the pistol had no military value. Frugal colonels then bought cheap Birmingham-made versions, usually from Isaac Bissell, until pistols ceased to be worn by the rank and file in 1776. They experienced a brief resurgence in the first half of the nineteenth century, when Scotland had a period of romantic popularity.

UNITED KINGDOM

MEMORY HOLSTER PISTOL 1780

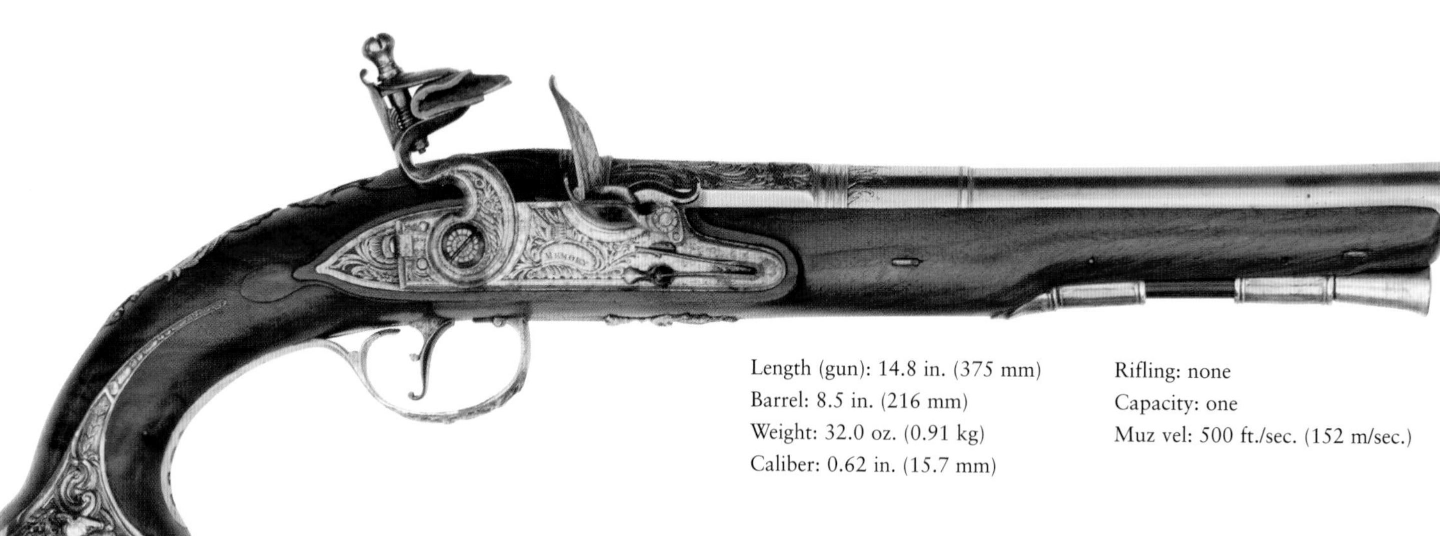

Length (gun): 14.8 in. (375 mm)
Barrel: 8.5 in. (216 mm)
Weight: 32.0 oz. (0.91 kg)
Caliber: 0.62 in. (15.7 mm)
Rifling: none
Capacity: one
Muz vel: 500 ft./sec. (152 m/sec.)

This fine pistol was made in 1780 by Memory of Southwark, London. The barrel is of brass, the front two-thirds being round and the breech end octagonal. The breech is highly ornamented, while the muzzle is slightly swamped. The barrel is held to the stocks by a flat key passing through a loop on its underside. In later years it became customary to inset a small plate around these keys, so that they could be tapped out without bruising the stock. The lock is typically English, the plate being beautifully engraved and bearing the name "MEMORY" within a small ornamental scroll. The cock, also decorated, is swan-necked, the angle of the edge of the flint to the steel ensuring a good shower of sparks with the fastest possible opening time for the pan; rapid ignition was an essential requirement for accurate shooting. The pan speed depended also on the frizzen spring; on this pistol it has a small semicircular projection on its upper surface. When the pan is closed, the tail of the pan cover is forward of the projection and snaps down on the other side, thus shortening the opening time. The stock is of fine walnut and the butt cap is finely chiseled.

UNITED KINGDOM

MORTIMER REPEATING PISTOL 1790

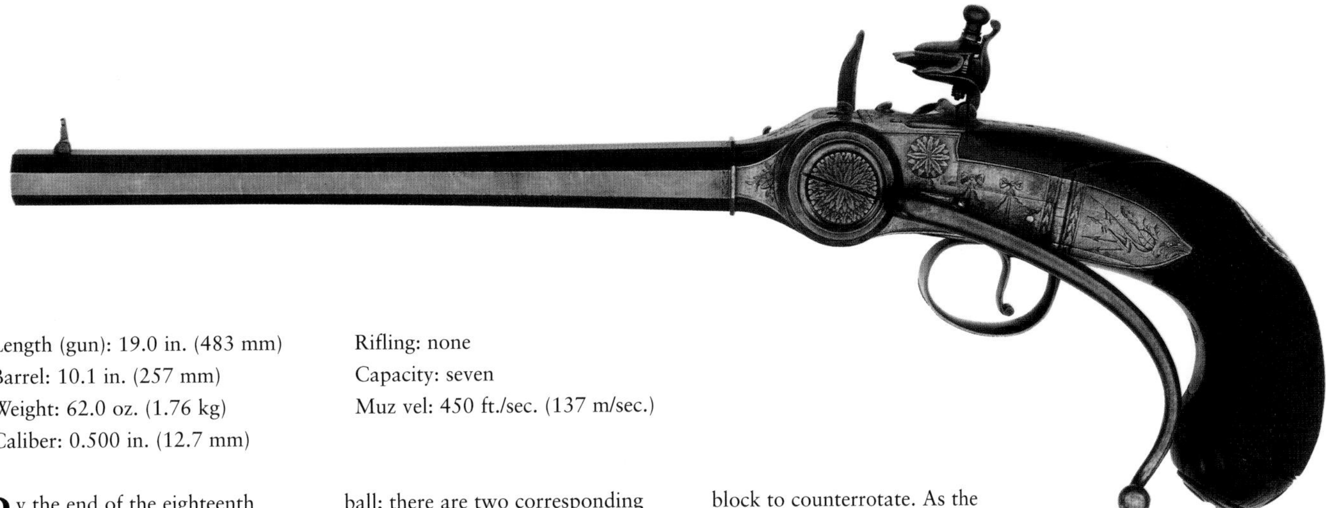

Length (gun): 19.0 in. (483 mm)
Barrel: 10.1 in. (257 mm)
Weight: 62.0 oz. (1.76 kg)
Caliber: 0.500 in. (12.7 mm)
Rifling: none
Capacity: seven
Muz vel: 450 ft./sec. (137 m/sec.)

By the end of the eighteenth century, manufacturing techniques had improved enough to persuade a few London makers to turn their attention to repeating weapons. Among them was H. W. Mortimer. This pistol has at its breech end a horizontally revolving block into which two recesses are cut, one for powder and one for a ball; there are two corresponding tubular magazines in its butt. To load, the weapon was held muzzle downward and the loading lever was pushed forward. This brought the recesses in the block into line with the magazine, and one ball and one charge were fed into them by gravity. The action of pulling the lever backward caused the block to counterrotate. As the recess holding the ball passed the breech, the ball rolled in; the recess holding the charge then moved into position behind it to act as a temporary chamber. This second motion of the lever also cocked and primed the arm. Although ingenious, arms with this kind of repeating system never became popular, mainly because of the problems of obturation—that is, the escape of burning gases. Any minor discrepancy in fitting the various parts could lead to the explosion of the powder in the magazine—with disastrous results to the firer.

UNITED KINGDOM

TOWER SEA SERVICE PISTOL 1790

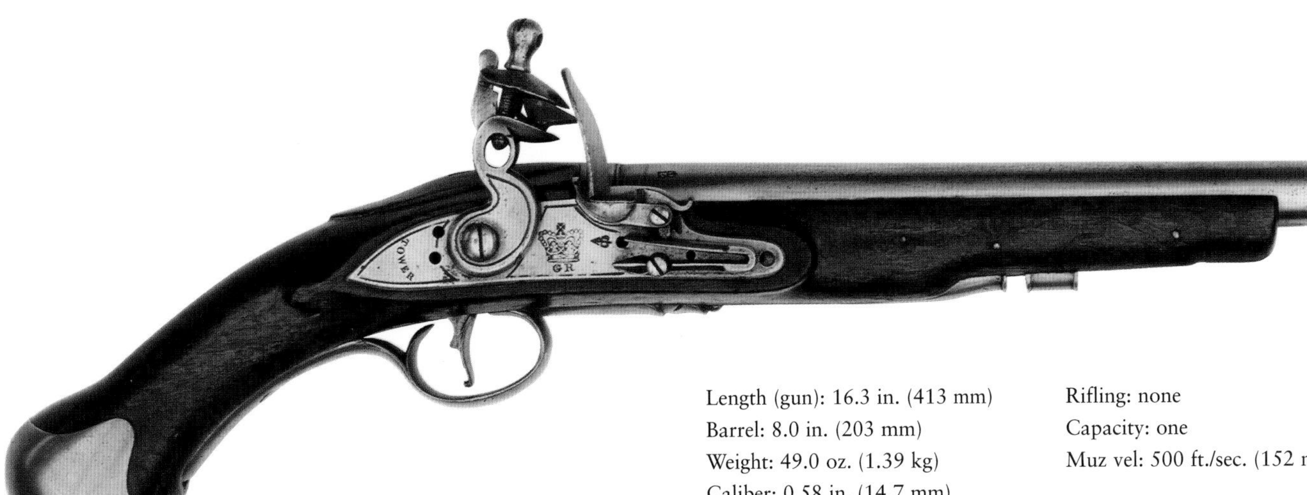

Length (gun): 16.3 in. (413 mm)
Barrel: 8.0 in. (203 mm)
Weight: 49.0 oz. (1.39 kg)
Caliber: 0.58 in. (14.7 mm)
Rifling: none
Capacity: one
Muz vel: 500 ft./sec. (152 m/sec.)

This weapon is broadly representative of British martial pistols of 1740–1840. It was made in about 1790 and differs from earlier models chiefly in having a shorter barrel and lacking the long ears on the butt cap. It is of very plain and robust construction, fully stocked in walnut with a very heavy cast-brass butt cap, capable of cracking a skull. The lock plate bears a crown with "GR" beneath it and the word "TOWER" across the tail; the weapon was assembled in the great armory at the Tower of London, although its parts would almost certainly have been manufactured elsewhere by government contractors. The small crown and arrow below the pan is a lock-viewer's mark. The cock is of the ring-necked type, popular in military weapons because of its strength. The bottom end of the screw holding the top jaw can be seen protruding into the aperture. The smooth-bored barrel is without sights and bears proof and view marks at the breech end. The ramrod (not shown) was of plain steel with the usual slightly domed head. The weapon has a belt hook, basically a flat spring, the rear end of which is screwed firmly through the brass side plate and into the stock, the spring lying along the stock.

THE SNAPHANCE LOCK

The snaphance lock was a major evolutionary leap forward in the history of firearms. The matchlock had been a crude and frequently ineffective method of ignition, and the wheel lock a prohibitively expensive one for mass production. Snaphance ignition relied on the process of striking a flint against steel, one already in use by the sixteenth century for lighting fires, candles, or pipes.

The first snaphances emerged as early as 1550 in northern Europe, and laid the foundations for future flintlock mechanisms. In the earliest weapons, a piece of shaped flint was held in a pair of pivoted jaws, known as the "cock" because of an imagined resemblance to the head of a cockerel. The cock was spring-loaded, and pulling the trigger caused the cock to "peck" forward and downward, driving the flint against a steel striker plate angled (under the tension of a leaf spring) above the "pan"—a shallow, spoon-like container that held fine priming powder. The pan charge was linked to the main barrel charge by a hole; once the priming charge had been ignited by the sparks from the flint striking the steel, the sparks traveled through the hole to ignite the main charge and complete the firing of the weapon. Note that the striker plate (also referred to variously as the battery, frizzen, hammer, or hen) was hinged, allowing it to be pushed forward when the gun was not in use to avoid accidental misfire.

The term "snaphance" is an English derivation from the Dutch words *schnapp hahn* (pecking cock) or *schapphahns* (cock thieves), and the Netherlands was probably, though not certainly, the country from which the snaphance spread throughout Europe. The snaphance offered a seminal advantage over matchlocks and wheel locks. Unlike matchlocks, they did not require the maintenance of a burning slowmatch, and, unlike the wheel lock, their relative cheapness extended the ownership of quality guns downward through the classes. By the beginning of the seventeenth century, Dutch snaphance locks (and native copies/variants) had spread throughout northern Europe and down to the Mediterranean. Examples were even to be found in Africa and the Far East.

Below: *The snaphance was the most common pistol ignition system among the early New England Pilgrims. Although its name derives from the Dutch, this is not certain provenance of its origins. Here the steel is positioned forward on its pivoted arm, away from the pan.*

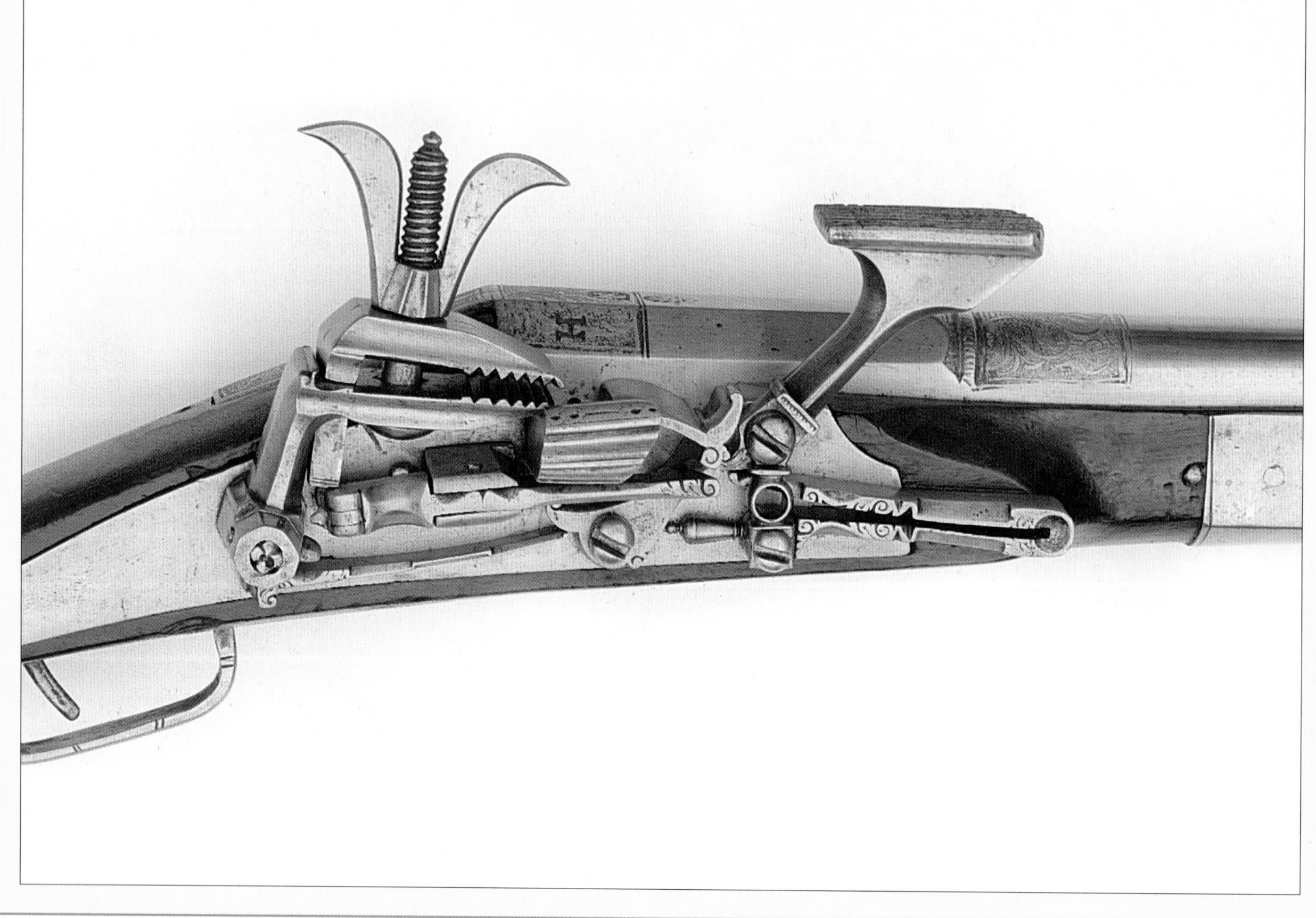

UNITED KINGDOM

MANTON DUELING PISTOL 1795

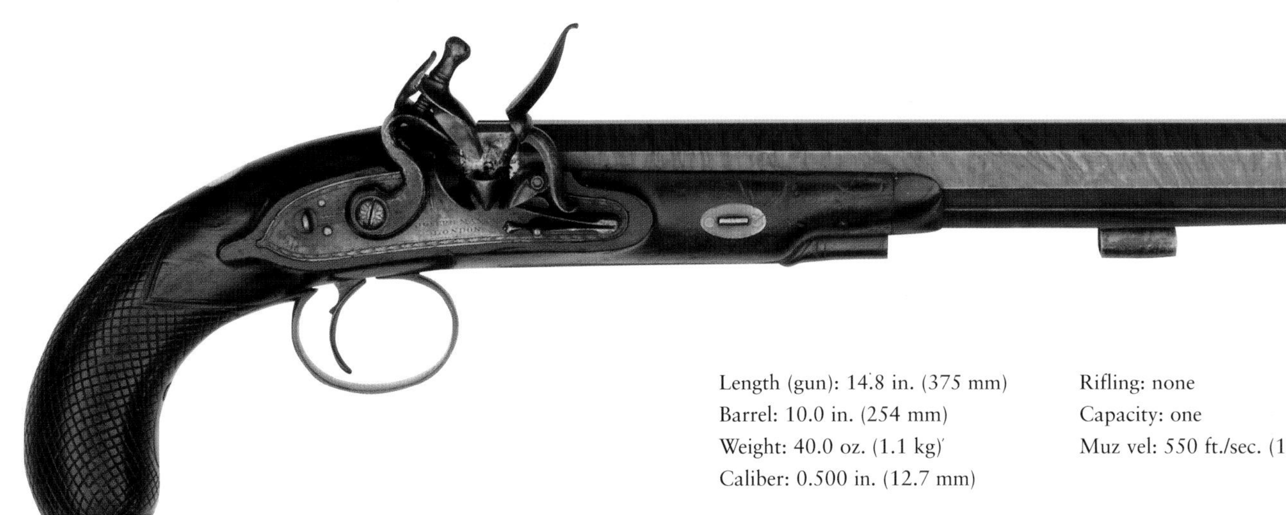

Length (gun): 14.8 in. (375 mm)
Barrel: 10.0 in. (254 mm)
Weight: 40.0 oz. (1.1 kg)
Caliber: 0.500 in. (12.7 mm)
Rifling: none
Capacity: one
Muz vel: 550 ft./sec. (167 m/sec.)

The lock on this pistol is of fine quality, with graceful swan-necked cock and a deep pan with a flash guard to protect the firer from back-blown sparks. The tail of the frizzen is fitted with a small roller, which bears on the small projection visible on top of the frizzen spring. The lock plate, lightly engraved, bears the inscription "JOSEPH MANTON, LONDON." The small stud near the tail of the lock is a sliding safety; the cock could be firmly locked at half-cock. The octagonal barrel is of excellent quality, being 0.2 in. (5.08 mm) thick. Barrels like this, usually known as "twist" or "damascus" barrels, were made by a process in which thin rods of iron and steel were twisted, then welded side by side into long flat ribbons. These were then twisted around iron mandrels and hammer-welded. This process gave the barrel considerable strength, because the long fibers of the metal were twisted around it. Cheap damascus barrels were never very reliable; poor hammer-welding could lead to the barrel opening or partially untwisting under pressure. This pistol is fitted with Manton's patent breech, which ensured good ignition and allowed the pan to be more closely inset, thus reducing bulk.

UNITED KINGDOM

TOWER PERCUSSION PISTOL CONVERSION 1800s

Length (gun): 15.0 in. (381 mm)
Barrel: 9.0 in. (229 mm)
Weight: 36.0 oz. (1.1 kg)
Caliber: 0.700 in. (17.8 mm)
Rifling: none
Capacity: one
Muz vel: 500 ft./sec. (152 m/sec.)

This weapon was made for the Light Dragoons and is a good example of one of the methods used to convert flintlocks to the percussion system. The new system allowed reliable ignition, particularly in bad weather. It also made the arm less bulky by doing away with the cock and pan. A hollow metal tube, closed at one end, was screwed into the touch hole. This tube, known as the drum, was threaded on its upper side to receive a screw-in percussion nipple on which the cap fitted. The old flint cock was replaced by a hooded hammer, and the pan and frizzen were removed. This simple method made conversion quick and cheap and was widely used by civilian gunsmiths. It was not generally employed in military conversions, where the favored method was to weld or braze a nipple lump into the required position and drill it for a nipple.

UNITED KINGDOM

BIRMINGHAM BOX-LOCK PISTOL 1800

Length (gun): 7.4 in. (188 mm)
Barrel: 2.0 in. (51 mm)
Weight: 10.0 oz. (0.28 kg)
Caliber: 0.400 in. (10.2 mm)
Rifling: none
Capacity: one
Muz vel: 400 ft./sec. (122 m/sec.)

The box-lock was more compact for pocket arms than the side lock. The breech consists of two parallel side plates, between which the cock is mounted centrally, with its own separate flat plate cover incorporating a rear tang for fixing the butt. The trigger has a similar plate, incorporating the butt tang. There is no tumbler because the bottom of the cock is notched to hold the sear. The arrangement necessitates the placing of the pan on top of the breech, with a flat frizzen spring inset into the breech in front of it. The butt is slab-sided, cut from a plank and its edges chamfered. The barrel screw-off mechanism is typical, and a key would have been used. The pistol is lightly engraved and bears private Birmingham proof marks, indicating that it was made before the establishment of the official proof house in 1813.

UNITED KINGDOM

MORTIMER DUELING PISTOL 1800

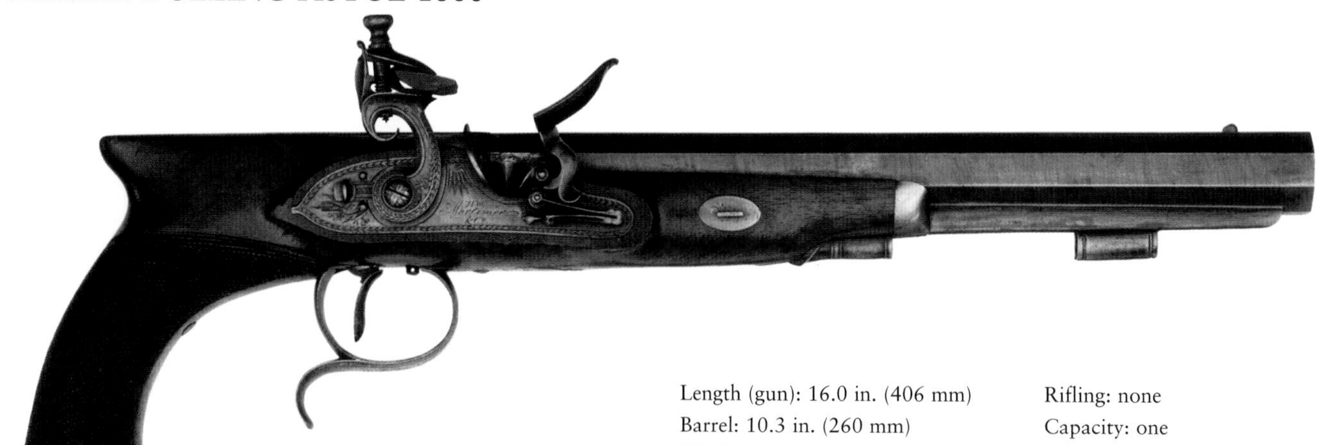

Length (gun): 16.0 in. (406 mm)
Barrel: 10.3 in. (260 mm)
Weight: 37.0 oz. (1.1 kg)
Caliber: 0.62 in. (15.7 mm)

Rifling: none
Capacity: one
Muz vel: 550 ft./sec. (167 m/sec.)

Gunsmiths developed highly specialized arms for dueling, almost invariably in pairs, and usually handsomely cased with a variety of accessories. This pistol, of the highest quality, was one of a pair made soon after 1800 by the well-known London maker H. W. Mortimer. The heavy, octagonal, damascus twist barrel is extremely carefully bored, attractively figured, and discreetly ornamented with gold inlay at the breech-end. The barrel bears the proud inscription: "H. W. MORTIMER AND CO LONDON, GUNMAKERS TO HIS MAJESTY." The fixed sights consist of a front bead and a deep U-backsight, with top ears which curve inward so that the sight becomes almost an aperture. A long groove is cut along the top of the stock to guide the eye quickly to the line of sight. The "saw-handled" stock is of fine walnut. The back spur is designed to fit neatly over the fork of the thumb, to help keep the muzzle down. The spur below the trigger-guard, which was held by the second finger, also helped to achieve this, as did the heavy barrel. As the pistol is half-stocked, the front part of the barrel has lower ribs along which the ramrod lay (not shown), made of wood with horn tips.

UNITED KINGDOM

MULEY BLUNDERBUSS PISTOL 1800

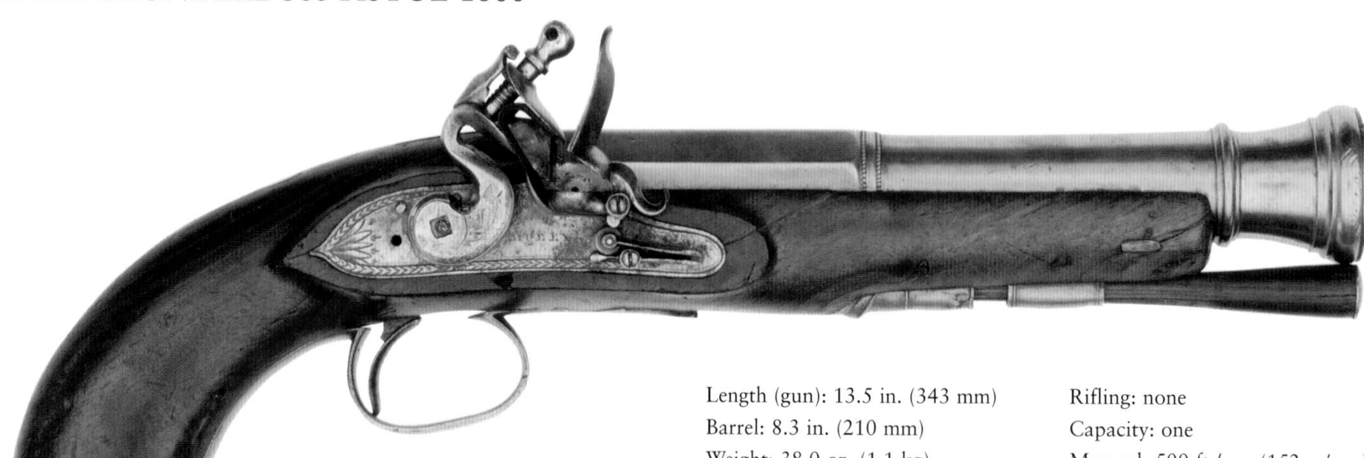

Length (gun): 13.5 in. (343 mm)
Barrel: 8.3 in. (210 mm)
Weight: 38.0 oz. (1.1 kg)
Caliber: 0.62 in. (15.7 mm)

Rifling: none
Capacity: one
Muz vel: 500 ft./sec. (152 m/sec.)

This British musketoon pistol was made by Muley of Dublin, a well-known maker of pistols in the late eighteenth and early nineteenth centuries. It is of good quality, severely plain in the best tradition of British arms, but fabricated of good materials and well finished. The lock is of orthodox type, with a graceful swan-necked cock and some light engraving on the plate, together with the name of the maker. A refinement is the addition of a roller on the frizzen spring, which speeded lock time very considerably by minimizing friction. The brass barrel is part octagonal and part round; by about 1800 the trumpet-type barrel of the earlier arms had given place to a much more restrained variety, incorporating quite a narrow muzzle with molded rings for ornament. On the breech plug there is a hook that fits into a corresponding socket on the steel standing breech; and the front end of the barrel is held in place by a flat key passing through a loop. The top flat is marked "MULEY, DUBLIN." The remaining furniture is of brass, the ramrod pipes being held by pins in the usual way. The ramrod (which may not be original) is of wood with a brass tip.

UNITED KINGDOM

ANNELY FLINTLOCK REVOLVER 1805

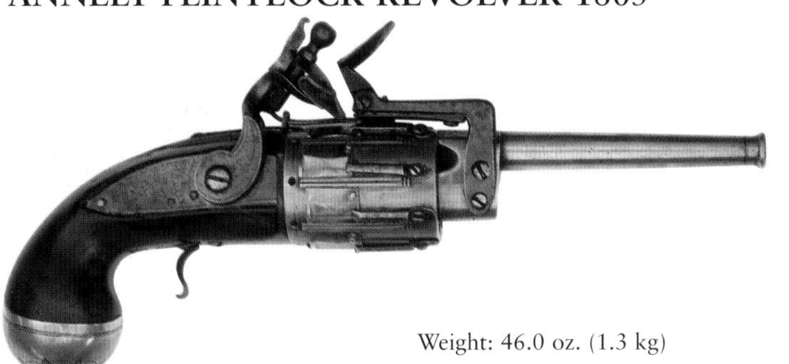

Length (gun): 12 in. (305 mm)
Barrel: 5.37 in. (137 mm)
Weight: 46.0 oz. (1.3 kg)
Caliber: 0.400 in. (10.2 mm)
Rifling: nil
Capacity: eight
Muz vel: 400 ft./sec. (122 m/sec.)

This revolver was made by T. Annely. It has a round, cannon-type brass barrel (most of the metal is brass), fastened to the frame by the cylinder axis pin. The brass cylinder has eight chambers, each with its own pan and touch hole, normally covered by a sliding cover. The hinged steel is mounted on an arm attached to the barrel lump, and the neck of the cock is therefore bent over so that the flint will strike it. The lock is of back-action type, and its plate (which may not be original) is engraved with the maker's name. The action of cocking caused the cylinder to rotate by means of a pawl and ratchet; when the cock fell, a lever attached to it pushed open the cover of the pan aligned with the barrel. The butt has a rounded plate bearing a Tudor rose. There is no trigger guard. Weapons of this type were reasonably efficient, but were very difficult to make; the drilling of the chambers presented a particular problem.

FRANCE

LEPAGE NAPOLEON PISTOL 1810

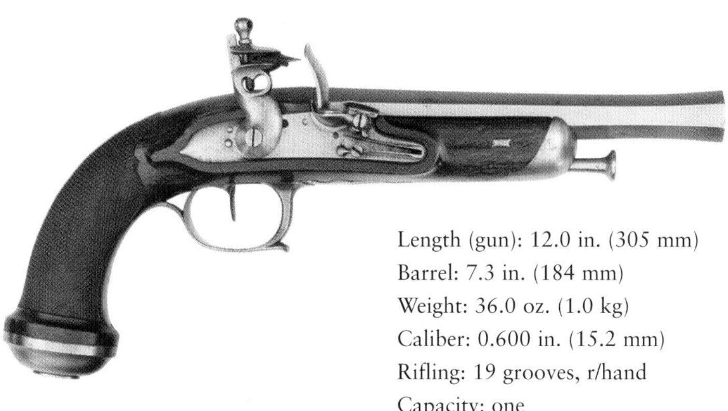

Length (gun): 12.0 in. (305 mm)
Barrel: 7.3 in. (184 mm)
Weight: 36.0 oz. (1.0 kg)
Caliber: 0.600 in. (15.2 mm)
Rifling: 19 grooves, r/hand
Capacity: one
Muz vel: 500 ft./sec. (152 m/sec.)

In June 1815, the allied armies of Great Britain and Prussia fought a brief but bloody campaign against the French army under Napoleon. The campaign ended with the victory at Waterloo. Napoleon was subsequently exiled on the remote island of St. Helena. At some stage toward the end of Napoleon's life, Dr. Arnott, medical officer of the 20th Regiment (later the Lancashire Fusiliers), which then formed part of the garrison, was called in to treat him, effecting at least a temporary cure. Napoleon gave Arnott a number of presents, including a fine pair of holster pistols, one of which is seen here. This is characteristic of its maker, Lepage of Paris, whose name is engraved on the top flat of its octagonal barrel. It is a flintlock and unusual in that it has multi-grooved rifling, which meant it could throw a ball of about 0.8 oz. (23 g) to a considerable distance with great accuracy.

UNITED KINGDOM

RIGBY OVERCOAT POCKET PISTOL 1818

Length (gun): 8.3 in. (210 mm)
Barrel: 3.2 in. (81 mm)
Weight: 19.0 oz. (210 mm)
Caliber: 0.75 in. (19 mm)
Rifling: none
Capacity: one
Muz vel: 500 ft./sec. (152 m/sec.)

Flintlock pocket pistols could be very small waistcoat-pocket arms, or heavier types designed to be carried conveniently by a traveler in his overcoat pocket. The example shown here is by John Rigby of Dublin, Ireland, and was probably made in the first quarter of the nineteenth century. Like most British arms of the period, it is severely plain, with no more than a trifle of engraving on cock and trigger guard—but well-made arms had little need of ornament to point up their quality. It has a horn-tipped, wooden ramrod and is fully stocked, with a neatly checkered butt. The elegant lock is of the type often found on dueling pistols. Perhaps its main characteristic is its stubby, octagonal twist barrel, the yawning muzzle of which might prove a deterrent to would-be robbers. It fired a lead ball of 12-bore—i.e., twelve bullets aggregated 1 lb. (0.45 kg) of lead – and would have been a formidable arm at close quarters. It is fitted with both foresight and backsight; but these would hardly have been necessary at the range at which it was most likely to be used.

UNITED KINGDOM

COLLIER FLINTLOCK REVOLVER 1818

Length: 14.3 in. (362 mm)
Weight: 35 oz. (0.99 kg)
Barrel: 6.25 in. (159 mm)
Caliber: 0.473 in. (12 mm)
Rifling: none
Capacity: Five
Muz Vel: 550 ft./sec. (167 m/sec.)

Elisha Collier, an American living in London, patented this flintlock revolver. It has an octagonal, smooth-bore barrel attached to the frame by a top strap, and an axis pin on which the five-chambered cylinder revolved. Each chamber vent is successively aligned with an opening at the bottom of the pan. The combined pan cover and steel, attached to the top strap, incorporates a small magazine that deposited a measure of priming in the pan as the cover was closed. After each shot, it was necessary to rotate the cylinder manually to bring the next loaded chamber into the firing position. The breech is coned, the mouths of the cylinders being countersunk to fit over it; before rotating the cylinder it had to be drawn back against a spring to disengage it. The forward action of the cock thrust a steel wedge against the rear of the cylinder, holding it in position to ensure barrel/chamber alignment.

BELGIUM

DOUBLE-BARRELED POCKET PISTOL 1820

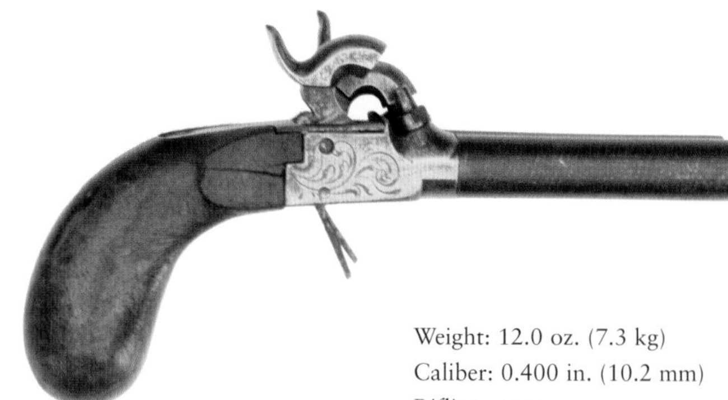

Length (gun): 6.5 in. (165 mm)
Barrel: 2.7 in. (67 mm)
Weight: 12.0 oz. (7.3 kg)
Caliber: 0.400 in. (10.2 mm)
Rifling: none
Capacity: two
Muz vel: 500 ft./sec. (152 m/sec.)

Muzzle-loaded pistols were far too slow to reload in action, so double-barreled arms were popular. This particular specimen, which is of medium quality, is fairly typical of the small pocket pistols turned out by the thousands by Belgian makers in the first half of the nineteenth century. The screw-off barrels fit over male screws of about 0.3 in. (7.6 mm) diameter, containing the chambers. Each muzzle has four deep notches, equally spaced around the circumference, which take a key. The barrels have a very marked damascus-type spiral figure; but this was probably etched with acid as they are solid metal tubes. The two locks have folding triggers that were extruded only when the hammers were placed at half-cock, which made it possible to dispense with the bulky trigger-guard while still avoiding the risk of the triggers catching in the lining of a pocket when the weapon was drawn.

UNITED KINGDOM

MANTON PERCUSSION DUELING PISTOL 1823

Length (gun): 14.8 in. (375 mm)
Barrel: 9.3 in. (235 mm)
Weight: 38.0 oz. (1.1 kg)
Caliber: 0.42 in. (10.7 mm)
Rifling: 30 grooves, r/hand
Capacity: one
Muz vel: 600 ft./sec. (183 m/sec.)

This pistol has an octagonal twist barrel with unusually thick walls. The top flat is engraved: "JOHN MANTON AND SON, DOVER STREET, LONDON." It is unusual in being lightly rifled. The barrel is screwed into a breech plug about 0.7 in. (17.8 mm) long, and is fitted with a hook which locks into a recess in the standing breech. The top flat of the breech plug is inset with rectangular gold plates (each bearing a crown and the words "MANTON, LONDON") and the nipple bolster is fitted with a circular platinum safety plug, intended to blow out if the internal pressure was too high, to prevent the barrel bursting. The half-stock is of fine walnut with horn tip, the butt being finely checkered to give a secure grip. The barrel is held to it with a single flat key. The lower flat of the barrel is fitted with half ribs, equipped with a single pipe to hold the ramrod (not shown), which was of ebony with brass tip and ferrule. The trigger guard has a pineapple finial, and a long rear tang let into the butt. This is a beautiful weapon, plain and austere, and almost certainly extremely accurate at short range.

UNITED KINGDOM

BIRMINGHAM POCKET PERCUSSION PISTOL 1830

Length (gun): 5.8 in. (147 mm)
Barrel: 1.5 in. (38 mm)
Weight: 9.0 oz. (1.25 kg)
Caliber: 0.500 in. (12.7 mm)
Rifling: none
Capacity: one
Muz vel: 400 ft./sec. (122 m/sec.)

This kind of small pocket pistol was turned out by the thousands, small and compact but of man-stopping caliber at close quarters. It is of the common box-lock pattern, with the mechanism retained between two rear projections from the side of the breech and enclosed by top and bottom plates. This weapon has a sliding safety; when the pistol was at half-cock, the safety could be pushed forward until it engaged a notch at the rear of the hammer. The most interesting feature of this specimen is a device to prevent the percussion cap from falling off the nipple while the arm was in the user's pocket. There is a spring-loaded ring around the nipple: once the hammer had been placed at half-cock, this ring was raised by forward pressure on the vertical lever against a small spring, which allowed a cap to be placed in position. The ring was then lowered again, and held the cap firmly in place.

UNITED KINGDOM

BLANCH PERCUSSION PISTOL 1830

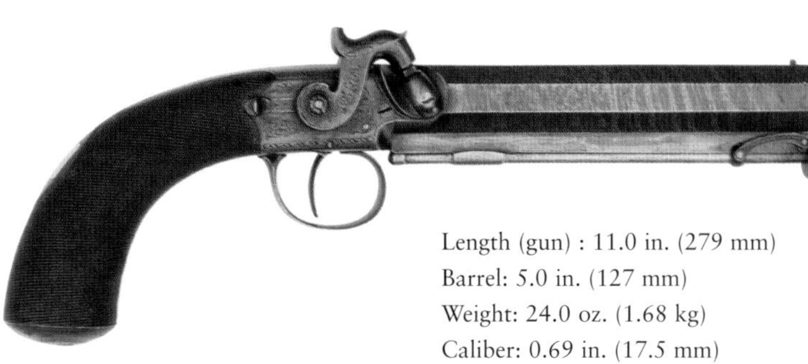

Length (gun) : 11.0 in. (279 mm)
Barrel: 5.0 in. (127 mm)
Weight: 24.0 oz. (1.68 kg)
Caliber: 0.69 in. (17.5 mm)
Rifling: none
Capacity: one
Muz vel: 550 ft./sec. (167 m/sec.)

This streamlined percussion pistol is of excellent quality, made by J. Blanch and Son of London, whose name appears on the top flat of the barrel. The octagonal damascus barrel was treated with acid to bring out the figuring. It is fitted with a Manton patent breech, with a rear fence to protect the firer's eye from flying fragments of the copper cap. The flat hammer has a deep recess in the nose with a slot at its forward end. The hammer comb has been broken off, a common casualty. The butt is finely checkered, except for a diamond-shaped area at the rear with a rectangular escutcheon plate. The butt cap incorporates a small compartment for percussion caps. The swivel ramrod lies against a metal rib on the lower flat of the barrel. Swivel ramrods were especially useful on service pistols, since they could not be dropped. This weapon fired a heavy ball of musket bore, and was probably one of a pair.

UNITED KINGDOM

PINCHES TURN-OVER PISTOL 1830

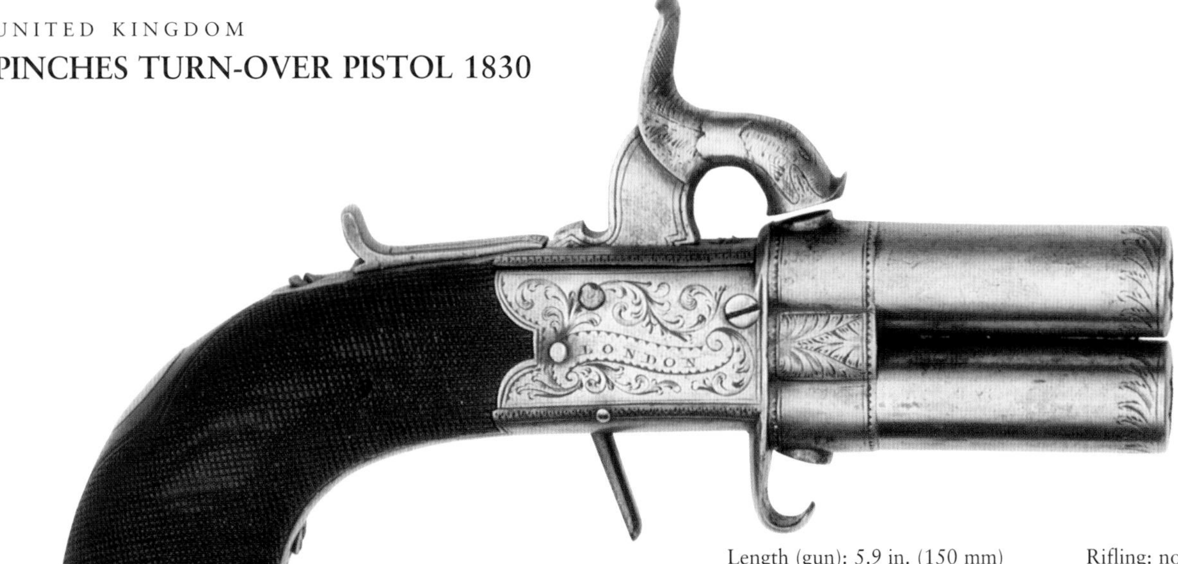

Length (gun): 5.9 in. (150 mm)
Barrel: 1.6 in. (41 mm)
Weight: 11.0 oz. (1.31 kg)
Caliber: 0.31 in. (8 mm)
Rifling: none
Capacity: two
Muz vel: 450 ft./sec. (137 m/sec.)

This is a small, pocket percussion pistol, sometimes known as an "over-and-under" because of the position of its barrels. It is of good quality and was made by Pinches of London. The barrels are of screw-off type: their muzzles have deep, star-shaped indentations to take a key of similar section. The barrels are screwed into a standing breech and rechambered. The pistol has a single hammer with a pop-out trigger and a strongly made sliding safety, the front end of which engaged over a projection on the back of the hammer when the latter was set at half-cock. The top barrel was fired first; the pistol was then placed at half-cock and the barrels rotated manually through 180 degrees to bring the second barrel uppermost. The standing breech has a spring device to prevent accidental rotation. The hook-shaped device in front of the trigger was intended to ensure that the cap did not slip off the lower nipple when the pistol was drawn.

UNITED KINGDOM

WILKINSON DOUBLE-BARREL OVER-AND-UNDER PISTOL 1830

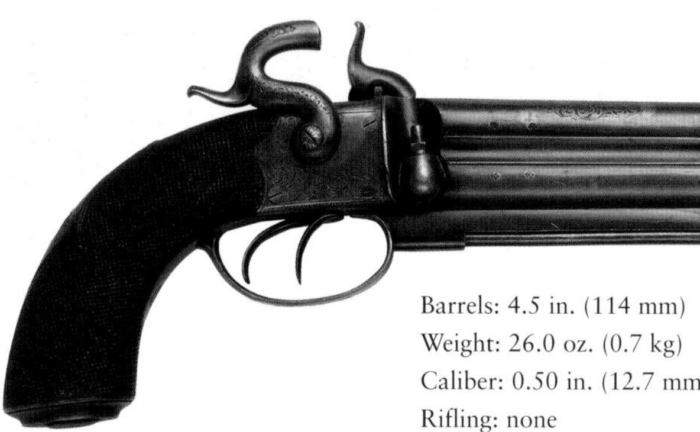

Length (gun): 10.0 in. (254 mm)
Barrels: 4.5 in. (114 mm)
Weight: 26.0 oz. (0.7 kg)
Caliber: 0.50 in. (12.7 mm)
Rifling: none
Capacity: two
Muz vel: 500 ft./sec. (152 m/sec.)

One of the first answers to the requirement for greater firepower was the double-barreled pistol, although the requirement for a flintlock on each side, one for each barrel, made all such weapons heavy and clumsy. Note that in the picture the left-hand barrel has been discharged, while the right-hand side is cocked. The barrels were "over-and-under" with the ramrod being retained by a swiveling stirrup to ensure that it did not fall to the ground or get lost. This weapon, made by Wilkinson of London in about 1830, for example, weighed 26.0 oz. (0.7 kg), a hefty weight for such a relatively small weapon. The problem would, however, soon be solved by the appearance of the revolver.

FRANCE

ST. ÉTIENNE DUELING PISTOL 1835

Length (gun): 16.5 in. (419 mm)
Barrel: 10.3 in. (260 mm)
Weight: 32.0 oz. (0.9 kg)
Caliber: 0.52 in. (13.2 mm)
Rifling: none
Capacity: one
Muz vel: 550 ft./sec. (167 m/sec.)

This is a plain but well-made weapon. The damascus barrel is smooth-bored, but appears to have been made with single twist only. Appreciable swamping at the muzzle end is clearly visible. The pistol has a patent breech, the nipple being inset into a fence, and is fitted with a bead foresight and a simple V backsight, both fixed. The barrel is held onto the stock, which appears to be of walnut, by a very long top tang which reaches almost to the bulbous butt, together with a second, lower, tang incorporating the trigger guard; the two are connected by a screw running through the butt. A single flat key passes through a loop below the barrel; its end has a protective oval plate of German silver. The lock is a back-action, in which the mainspring is behind the hammer. The ramrod is of steel and with a brass end.

UNITED KINGDOM

BLANCH FOUR-BARRELED PISTOL 1835

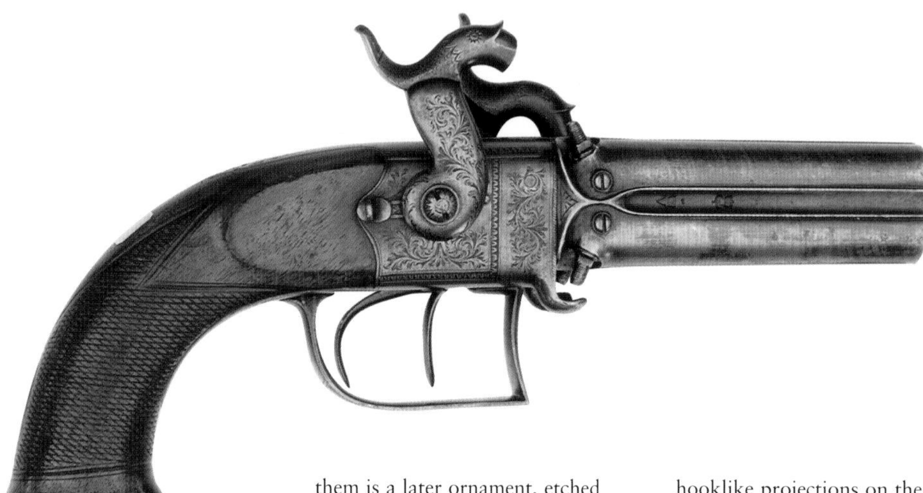

Length (gun): 8.5 in. (216 mm)
Barrel: 4.0 in. (102 mm)
Weight: 37.0 oz. (1.1 kg)
Caliber: 0.500 in. (12.7 mm)
Rifling: none
Capacity: four
Muz vel: 500 ft./sec. (152 m/sec.)

This weapon was made by Blanch of London and bears the maker's name on the left-hand side of the breech, below the hammer. The barrels have been bored out of a solid piece of metal, and the damascus-type figuring on them is a later ornament, etched with acid. Each has its own nipple with a screw plug beneath it to facilitate cleaning. The barrels were held in position by a spring catch; when it was desired to rotate them, it was first necessary to release this catch by pressing back the squared front of the trigger guard—hence its somewhat unusual shape. There are two hooklike projections on the lower part of the frame to hold the lower pair of percussion caps in position. The hammers are gracefully shaped and have deep hoods, which completely enclose the nipples. The latter, rather unusually, are lightly threaded, presumably to help keep the caps in position. The pistol has sliding safety catches that held the hammers securely at half-cock. The checkered walnut butt is of an essentially modern shape, clearly looking forward to the revolver rather than back to the pistol. The ramrod below the weapon was normally screwed upward into the butt. All in all, this is a most elegant pistol, although—hardly surprising, with four barrels—rather bulky.

THE FLINTLOCK

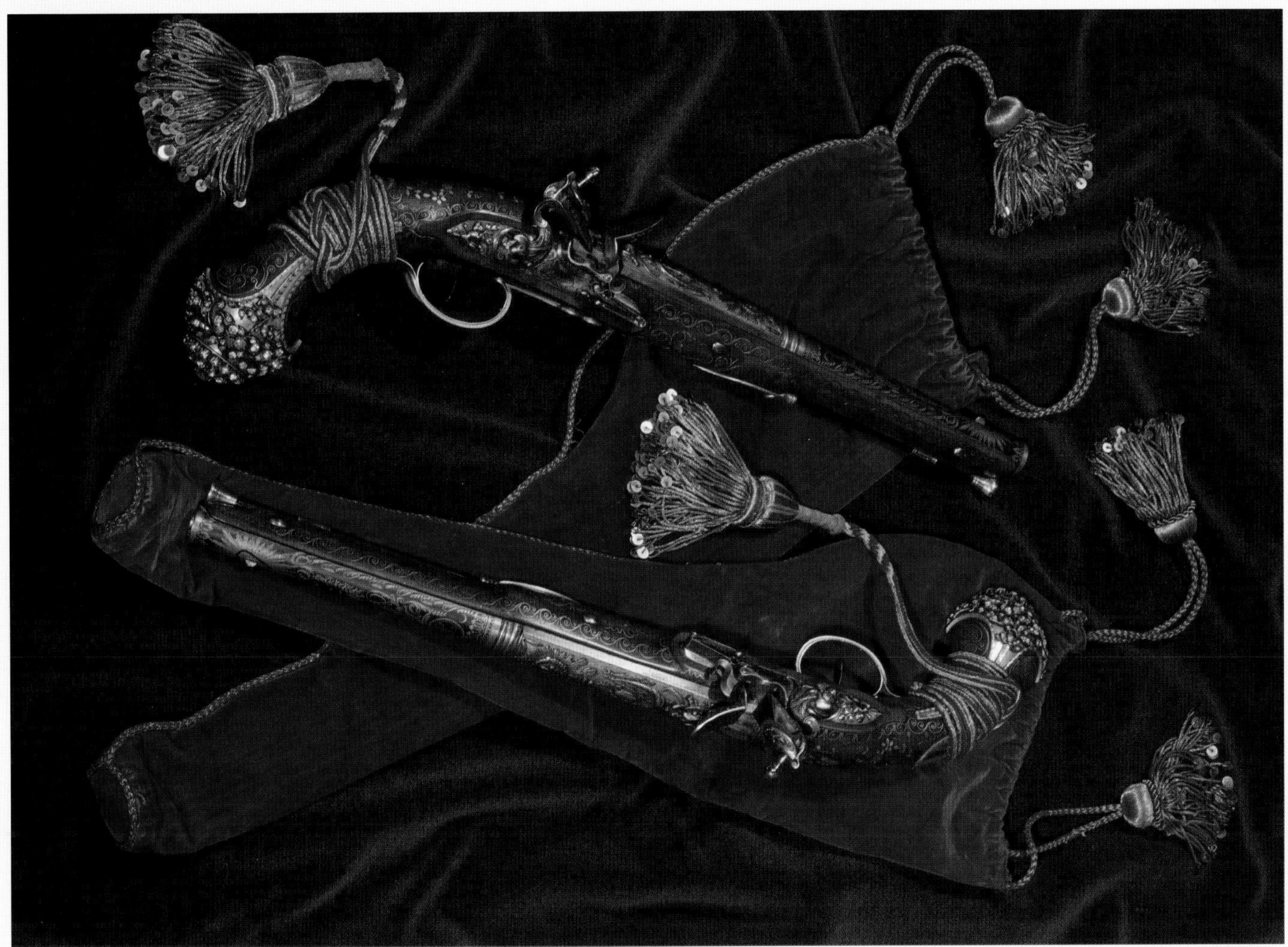

The flintlock developed from the snaphance lock in the early part of the seventeenth century and would become the dominant system of firearms ignition for around 200 years, only supplanted by the percussion system in the nineteenth century. The origins of the flintlock lay in an earlier lock system developed in Spain in the 1580s, known as the miquelet lock. In the standard snaphance, the pan featured a cover, which had to be moved to one side before firing to expose the priming charge. In the miquelet lock, the pan cover and striking steel were unified so that the cover moved automatically with the drop of the cock.

The flintlock improved on this system, fusing the snaphance mechanism with the miquelet steel and pan cover combination to make a weapon with faster ignition and greater reliability. The creator of the flintlock proper is likely to have been the French gunsmith Marin le Bourgeoys of Lisieux, Normandy. Around the beginning of the seventeenth century he revealed his new flintlock system to the French court, and by the mid-century much of Europe was imitating his design.

The basic flintlock mechanism worked as follows. When the cock was drawn back it rotated a tumbler, which compressed a mainspring (of leaf type) by forcing the longer arm of the spring upward. At the same time, the nose of the sear engaged with the half- and full-cock notches. Pulling the trigger released the sear, allowing the cock to spring forward in a vertical motion (snaphance cocks had a more horizontal fall). As the flint struck the steel, the pan cover was simultaneously knocked open to allow the sparks to ignite the priming composition, which in turn fired the main charge.

The flintlock would go through numerous variations over its two-century lifespan, although the relatively minor nature of the changes attests to the basic success of the design. The principal challenge for gunsmiths was to get the springwork and the angle of strike in the correct balance. The variability in skills of different gunsmiths meant widely differing levels of reliability in their products.

Above: *A pair of flintlock pistols dated 1857; the overlap in the development of handguns is sometimes surprising. Colt had been busy suing companies for ignoring its patent for the revolving cylinder some years before. These flintlocks employ a system more than 250 years old: they are almost "gentiques."*

UNITED KINGDOM

BOOTH POCKET PERCUSSION PISTOL 1835

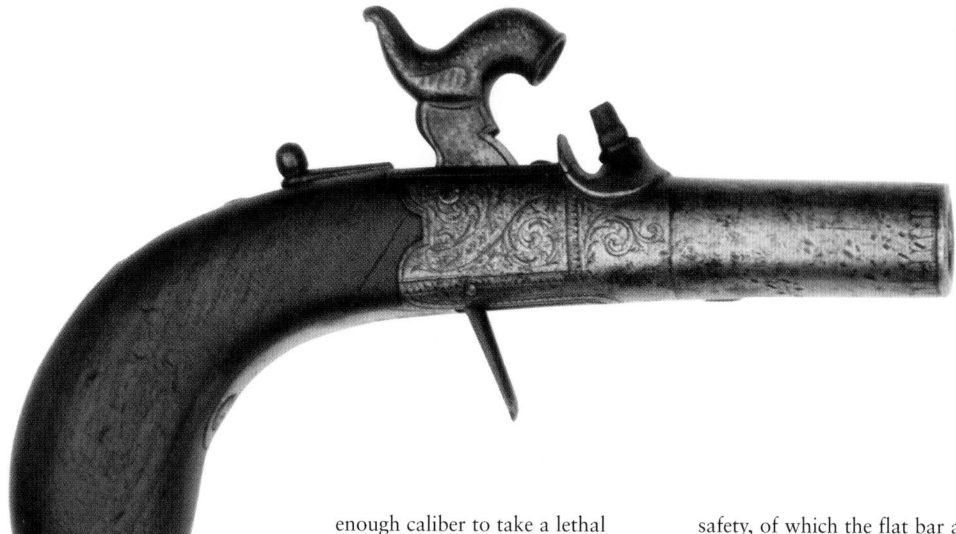

Length: 6.0 in. (152 mm)
Weight: 9.0 oz. (1.25 kg)
Barrel: 1.5 in. (38 mm)
Caliber: 0.500 in. (12.7 mm)
Rifling: none
Capacity: one
Muz vel: 400 ft./sec. (122 m/sec.)

This percussion pocket pistol probably dates from about 1835. It is of the box-lock type. Its short, stubby barrel is of the screw-off variety and is of large enough caliber to take a lethal ball, although the pistol's small charge would make it ineffective at anything above point-blank range. There is a fence behind the nipple to deflect any fragments of copper that might fly from the cap; the nose of the hammer is deeply recessed for the same purpose. The hammer is fitted with a sliding safety, of which the flat bar and knob are visible behind the hammer in the photograph. The mechanism was so designed that when the hammer was down, the trigger folded forward into a recess in the bottom of the breech: cocking the action caused it to pop out in readiness for firing. The characteristic rounded butt, often referred to as "bag-shaped," has a small silver escutcheon plate let into it. The curved scroll visible on the breech bears the word "SUNDERLAND," while a similar scroll on the other side is inscribed "R. D. BOOTH."

BELGIUM

MARIETTE PEPPERBOX PISTOL 1839

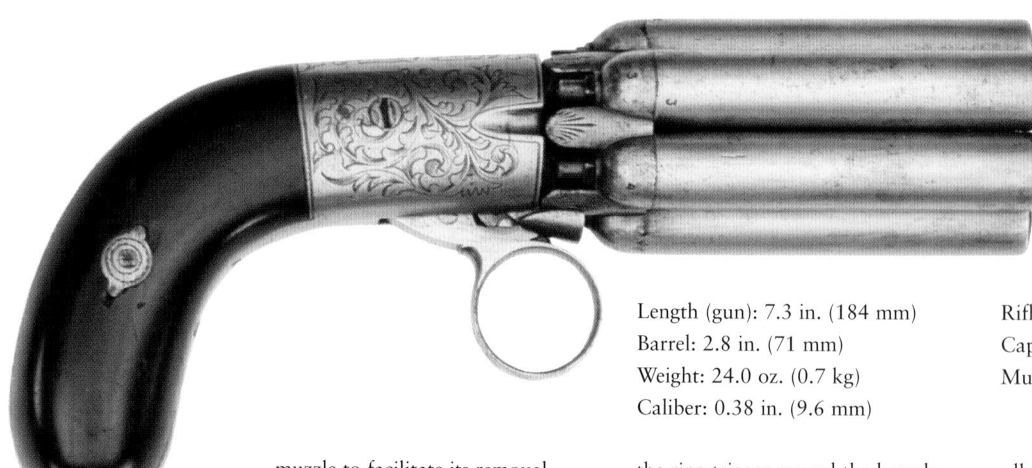

Length (gun): 7.3 in. (184 mm)
Barrel: 2.8 in. (71 mm)
Weight: 24.0 oz. (0.7 kg)
Caliber: 0.38 in. (9.6 mm)
Rifling: none
Capacity: six
Muz vel: 500 ft./sec. (152 m/sec.)

This Mariette-type pistol, made to a design patented in Belgium in 1837, bears Liège proof marks. Its barrels are screwed separately onto six chambers, into which the nipples are fixed. Each barrel has four rectangular slots at ninety-degree intervals around the muzzle to facilitate its removal with a special key; each barrel is numbered, as is each chamber. The cluster of barrels is screwed to a spindle on the standing breech, access to which was via the central space left in the cluster of barrels. The nipples are in the same axis as the barrels; this reduced the chances of a misfire and made the arm neat and compact. Pressure on the ring trigger caused the barrels to rotate, bringing each in turn into line, and drew back and released the internal hammer, which struck the nipple on the lowest barrel. There are partitions between the nipples; another shield rose as the hammer fell to guard completely the nipple being fired. Recapping was achieved by pressing the trigger sufficiently to allow the barrels to be manually rotated: a small slot was exposed in the right-hand side of the frame, allowing the caps to be slid into place. The butt is of ebonized plates, on a strap inscribed "MARIETTE BREVETTE."

UNITED KINGDOM

COOPER PEPPERBOX PISTOL 1837

Length (gun): 7.8 in. (197 mm)
Barrel: 3.0 in. (76 mm)
Weight: 26.0 oz. (0.7 kg)
Caliber: 0.400 in. (10.2 mm)
Rifling: none
Capacity: six
Muz vel: 500 ft./sec. (152 m/sec.)

This pepperbox pistol was made by J. R. Cooper, who was well known for the production of arms of this type; most of his pistols were based on the design of Mariette arms, widely manufactured in Belgium and France. It is typical of most of Cooper's Mariette-type arms: there is little elegance about it and the finish is rough. The left-hand side of the breech bears the inscription "J R COOPER, PATENT," although it is not certain that it was, in fact, patented. The barrels were bored out of a solid cylinder of steel, with shallow grooves between them; each groove bears a Birmingham proof mark. The nipples are in the same axis as the barrels and have flat, rectangular shields between them. A V-shaped groove on the right-hand side of the frame allowed the caps to be placed in position. Pressure on the ring trigger drew back an under-hammer and a spring on the trigger released the hammer.

EASTERN EUROPE

TURKISH BLUNDERBUSS PISTOL 1840

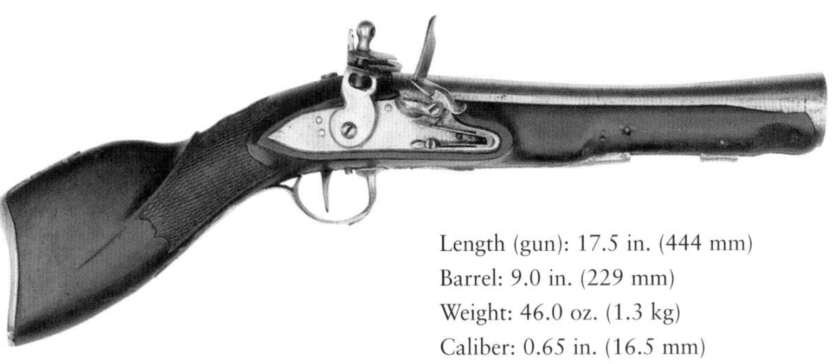

Length (gun): 17.5 in. (444 mm)
Barrel: 9.0 in. (229 mm)
Weight: 46.0 oz. (1.3 kg)
Caliber: 0.65 in. (16.5 mm)
Rifling: none
Capacity: slugs
Muz vel: not available

This pistol is plain and ugly. Parts of it, or perhaps the entire weapon, were probably made in Europe for export to the Middle East. The lock is plain, with a brass pan, and the cock is of the ring-necked type commonly found on European military arms. The furniture is of plain cast brass, while the stock, with its characteristic checkered dwarf butt, is of walnut. A rectangular brass loop attached to the side plate on the left-hand side of the stock allowed the pistol to be carried on a crossbelt. The barrel is narrowest at its midpoint. Its external diameters are: breech 1.2 in. (30.5 mm); center: 0.95 in. (24 mm); and muzzle 1.5 in. (38 mm). There are signs the barrel was originally of octagonal section and that the muzzle has been beaten out. Unusually, it is fitted with a ramrod, suggesting European origins; many indigenous weapons had a separate rod, slung around the neck.

UNITED STATES

ALLEN AND THURBER PEPPERBOX 1837

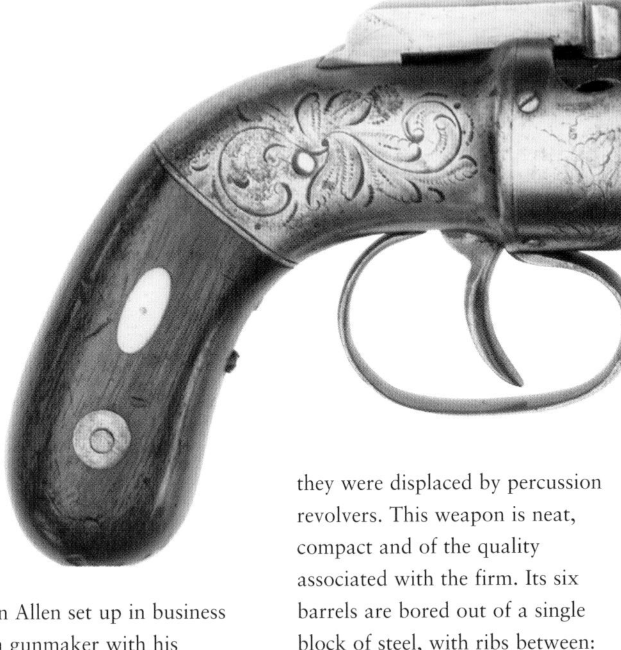

Length: 7.5 in. (190 mm)
Barrel: 3.0 in. (76 mm)
Weight: 23.0 oz. (0.7 kg)
Caliber: 0.31 in. (8 mm)
Rifling: none
Capacity: six
Muz vel: 400 ft./sec. (122 m/sec.)

Ethan Allen set up in business as a gunmaker with his brother-in-law in the late 1830s. Their pepperbox pistols were by far the most popular repeating arms in the United States, until they were displaced by percussion revolvers. This weapon is neat, compact and of the quality associated with the firm. Its six barrels are bored out of a single block of steel, with ribs between: two of the ribs bear the inscriptions "PATENTED 1837, CAST STEEL" and "ALLEN & THURBER WORCESTER." The double-action bar hammer mechanism was the subject of the patent. Steady pressure on the trigger caused the rear-hinged hammer (inscribed "ALLEN PATENT") to rise until the lifter hook disengaged, allowing it to fall and strike the cap. The action of the trigger rotated the barrel cluster by means of a pawl and ratchet. The nipples, which are set at right-angles to the barrels, are covered by a close-fitting shield. Light pressure on the trigger lifted the nose clear of the nipple and allowed the barrels to be rotated clockwise for recapping. The butt is a continuous metal strap integral with the body; its wooden side plates bear oval escutcheon plates.

FRANCE

MARIETTE FOUR-BARRELED PEPPERBOX 1840

Length (gun): 7.0 in. (178 mm)
Barrel: 2.5 in. (63 mm)
Weight: 18.0 oz. (0.5 kg)
Caliber: 0.35 in. (9 mm)
Rifling: none
Capacity: four
Muz vel: 450 ft./sec. (137 m/sec.)

The arm seen here is another of the continental Mariette pepperbox pistols. This particular arm, which has four barrels, is one of the immediate successors to the four-barreled, double-locked, turn-over pistols, but with additional refinements peculiar to pepperbox arms. It has a rotating breech with four chambers: a separate barrel is screwed onto each chamber, and each barrel is numbered to correspond with its own chamber. The rotating breech is screwed onto a spindle in the standing breech, to which access could be gained—with some difficulty—by way of the narrow space between the barrels, which very nearly touch each other. The barrels could be removed individually by means of a squared key, which fitted into four slots equally spaced around the muzzle; these slots may give the quite incorrect impression that the barrels are rifled. The nipples, which are set in shallow depressions, are in prolongation of the axis of the barrels; they could be capped by way of the U-shaped aperture seen on the right-hand side of the frame. The ring trigger rotated the barrels and activated the hammer, and also incorporated the usual hood, which masked completely the nipple that was actually being fired.

UNITED KINGDOM

LANG DOUBLE-BARRELED HOLSTER PISTOL 1840

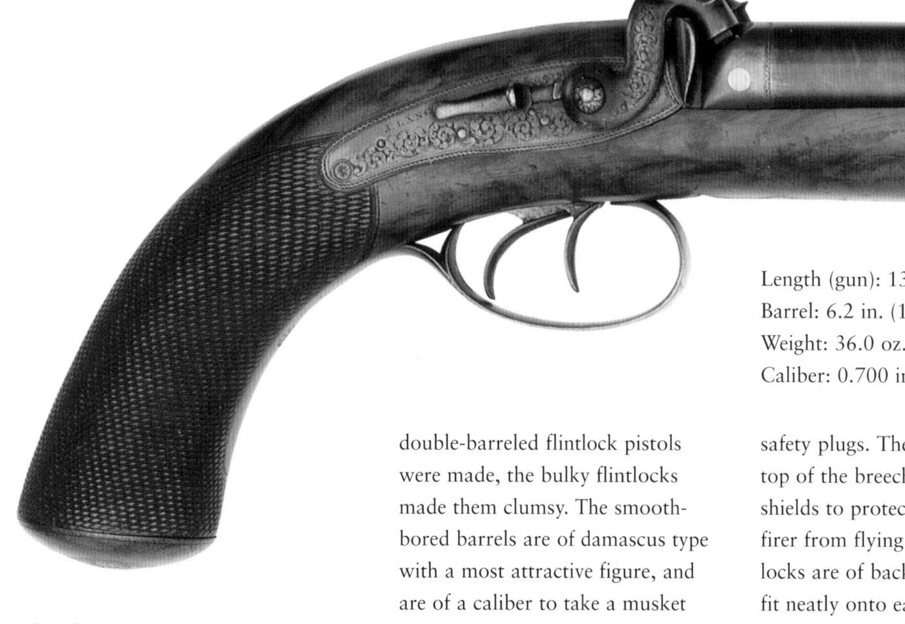

Length (gun): 13.0 in. (330 mm)
Barrel: 6.2 in. (157 mm)
Weight: 36.0 oz. (1.1 kg)
Caliber: 0.700 in. (17.8 mm)
Rifling: none
Capacity: two
Muz vel: 550 ft./sec. (167 m/sec.)

This percussion pistol (one of a pair) was intended for use by generals and staff officers and was made by Joseph Lang, of 7 Haymarket, London. Although double-barreled flintlock pistols were made, the bulky flintlocks made them clumsy. The smooth-bored barrels are of damascus type with a most attractive figure, and are of a caliber to take a musket ball. A bead foresight is mounted on the top rib between the barrels; the backsight consists of a shallow V-groove on the standing breech. The chambers have platinum safety plugs. The nipples are on top of the breeches and have shields to protect the eyes of the firer from flying fragments. The locks are of back-action type and fit neatly onto each side of the carefully tapered stock, so that the hammers do not protrude beyond the outside line of the barrels; this ensures that the pistols are reasonably narrow across the breech. The locks are equipped with sliding safeties, which engaged in slots in the hammers when the latter were in half-cock position. The barrels are held to the stock by a hook at the breech end and by a single flat key. The pistol has an ingenious swivel ramrod.

UNITED KINGDOM

LANG FOUR-BARRELED TURN-OVER PISTOL 1840

Length (gun): 9.0 in. (229 mm)
Barrel: 4.0 in. (102 mm)
Weight: 37.0 oz. (1.1 kg)
Caliber: 0.500 in. (12.7 mm)
Rifling: none
Capacity: four
Muz vel: 550 ft./sec. (167 m/sec.

This very fine weapon by Joseph Lang is intermediate between the double-barreled type and the early pepperbox revolvers. The four barrels of this weapon are bored out of a solid block of steel; the attractive damascus effect has been etched on. Each barrel has its own nipple and shield, and each has a platinum safety plug. The two hooklike projections on the standing breech prevented the caps on the lower nipples from being blown off when the upper barrels were discharged. Each pair of barrels has a small, fixed bead foresight on the rib between them, the ramrod being carried in two pipes in the third rib, while the fourth rib bears the proof marks. The butt is finely checkered and has the usual butt cap, with a compartment for spare caps. The hammers are gracefully shaped; both have deeply hooded heads with front slots, and both are fitted with sliding safeties. Once the top pair of barrels had been discharged and the hammers recocked, the cluster of barrels was turned clockwise (from the firer's point of view) on its central spindle, to bring the second pair into position. The barrels are held by a simple spring catch in order to prevent accidental movement.

UNITED KINGDOM

OVER-AND-UNDER PISTOL 1840

Length (gun): 9.8 in. (248 mm)
Barrel: 4.0 in. (102 mm)
Weight: 30.0 oz. (1.9 kg)
Caliber: 0.500 in. (12.7 mm)
Rifling: none
Capacity: two
Muz vel: 550 ft./sec. (167 m/sec.)

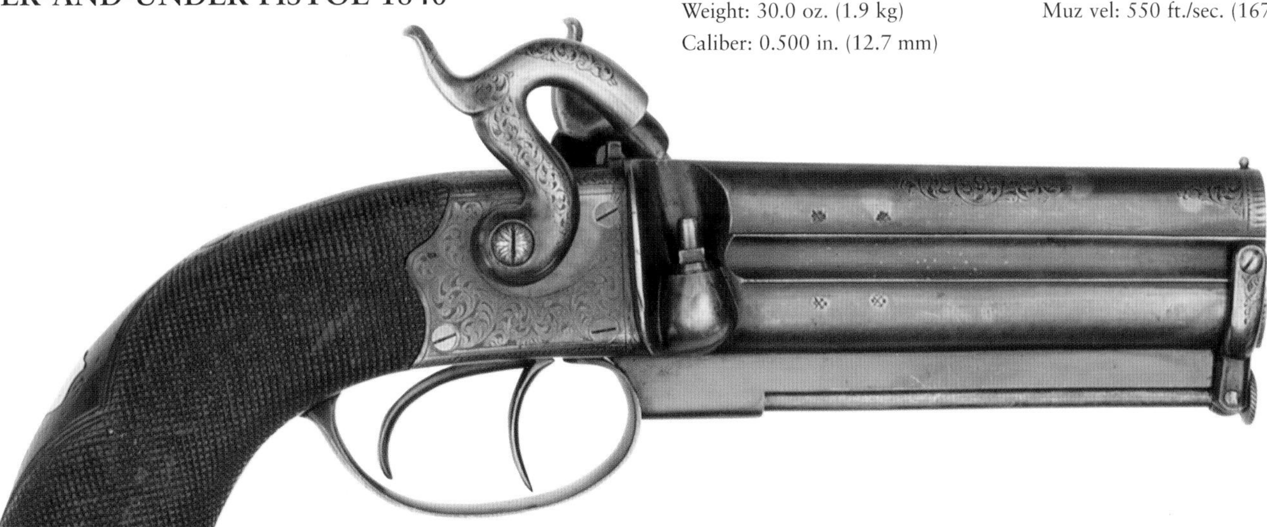

Having one barrel set above the other was a less bulky arrangement than having them side by side, and ensured better weight distribution. The pistol seen here is a good example of the type. Although of good quality, it has no maker's mark: this is rather surprising, but since it bears Birmingham proof marks, it may well be one of the many pirated copies of fine arms, which were turned out in large quantities, and in widely varying quality, by a number of small Birmingham makers. The barrels, with fixed sights, are bored out of a single block of steel, with a flat top rib, complete with fore- and backsight, and concave side ribs. The lower barrel has a separate rib to accommodate the swivel ramrod, which is held securely in place by a small spring catch situated inside the end pipe, in front of the trigger guard. The breeches have flash shields, the right-hand one being longer than the left because of the lowness of the nipple on the under barrel. This also necessitates the long, trunklike (and rather ugly) nose on the right-hand hammer. The checkered butt, which is of modern shape, contains the usual cap compartment, and all the metalwork is lightly engraved.

UNITED KINGDOM

LANG GAS-SEAL REVOLVER 1840

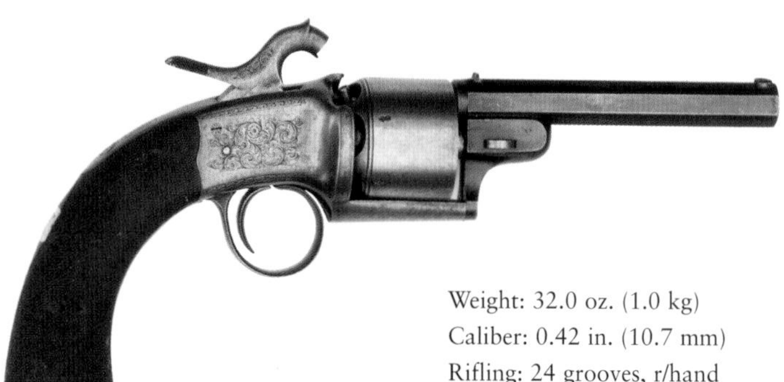

Length (gun): 11.0 in. (279 mm)
Barrel: 4.8 in. (121 mm)
Weight: 32.0 oz. (1.0 kg)
Caliber: 0.42 in. (10.7 mm)
Rifling: 24 grooves, r/hand
Capacity: six
Muz vel: 600 ft./sec. (183 m/sec.)

This revolver is fitted with laterally adjustable sights, the hammer being offset a little to the right. The barrel is keyed to the axis pin, with the usual projection engaging the lower edge of the frame. The cylinder is rebated at the rear, the different diameters being joined by a coned section containing circular depressions for the nipples, which are inclined slightly backward. The frame is of case-hardened iron. Drawing the hammer back to half-cock allowed an internal spring to force the cylinder back so that the top chamber cleared the barrel cone, while drawing the hammer back to full-cock rotated the cylinder. As the trigger fell, a cylindrical metal ram was thrust forward to lock the cylinder to the barrel at the moment of firing. As in many gas-seal weapons, the chambers were larger in caliber than the bore. This ensured that a ball which loaded easily into the chamber made a gas-tight fit in the barrel.

UNITED KINGDOM

TURNER PEPPERBOX PISTOL 1840

Length (gun): 9.3 in. (235 mm)
Barrel: 3.5 in. (89 mm)
Weight: 32.0 oz. (0.9 kg)
Caliber: 0.476 in. (12.1 mm)
Rifling: none
Capacity: six
Muz vel: 500 ft./sec. (152 m/sec.)

This weapon was made by Thomas Turner of Reading, and is of excellent construction. Its six smooth-bored barrels are drilled from a single block of steel; unusually, each is numbered at the breech end, the ribs between them being stamped alternately with a view mark or a proof mark. The nipples are at right angles to the axis, without partitions. A nipple shield prevents the percussion caps from being brushed or shaken off; however, canalizing the flash from the cap must also have contributed to the risk of more than one barrel firing from a single cap. The bar hammer is of standard double-action type; considerable pressure on the trigger was required to operate it. The trigger action activated a pawl and ratchet, rotating the barrels on an axis pin screwed into the standing breech; they are held in place by an engraved brass-headed screw which fits flush with the muzzles.

UNITED KINGDOM

PARKER FIELD GAS-SEAL REVOLVER 1840

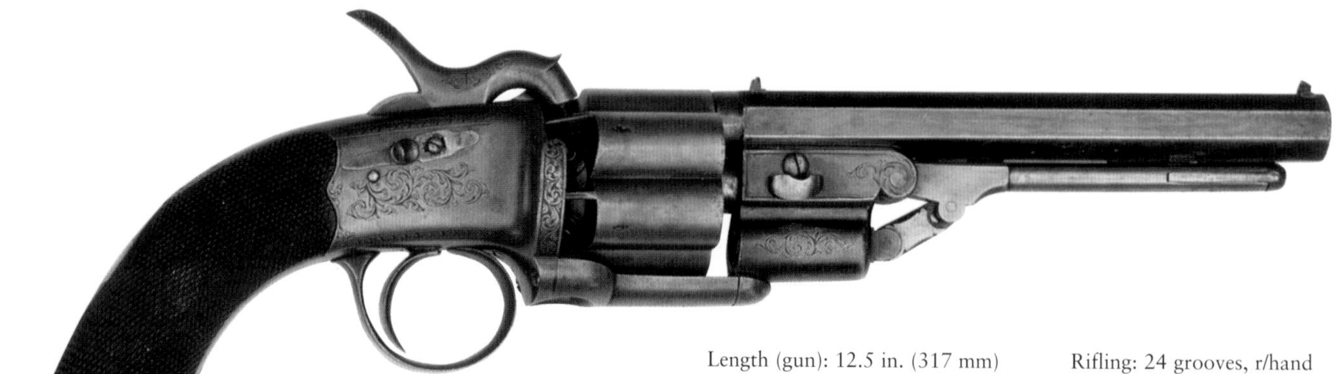

Length (gun): 12.5 in. (317 mm)
Barrel: 6.0 in. (152 mm)
Weight: 38.0 oz. (1.1 kg)
Caliber: 0.42 in. (10.7 mm)
Rifling: 24 grooves, r/hand
Capacity: six
Muz vel: 600 ft./sec. (183 m/sec.)

This gas-seal revolver bears the maker's inscription of "PARKER FIELD AND SONS, 233 HIGH HOLBORN, LONDON," a firm well known for the production of weapons of this type. As might be expected, it is a very well-made and finished arm, the usual multigrooved, blued barrel firmly wedged to the lower edge of the frame and fitted with laterally adjustable sights. The case-hardened cylinder is, however, fluted, giving the weapon a distinctive appearance, and there are flat shields between the nipples to eliminate the risk of multiple discharge. The hammer had the customary three rearward positions, with a safety that locked it securely in the first; the system of rotation and reciprocation was the same as that of the Beattie revolver. The major point of interest in this arm is the existence of a compound rammer below the barrel: when the long arm was pulled down, a horizontal rammer housed in the cylinder below the axis key exerted powerful pressure on the bullet and ensured that it was seated very securely in the chamber. This refinement went some way toward making the application of the gas-seal principle unnecessary.

FRANCE

CHÂTELLERAULT SERVICE PISTOL 1841

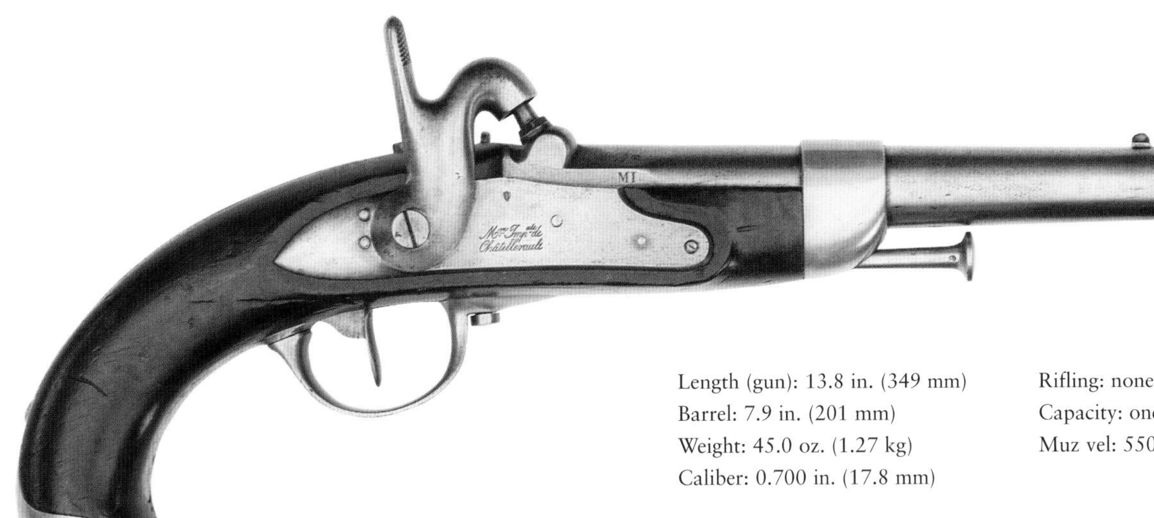

Length (gun): 13.8 in. (349 mm)
Barrel: 7.9 in. (201 mm)
Weight: 45.0 oz. (1.27 kg)
Caliber: 0.700 in. (17.8 mm)
Rifling: none
Capacity: one
Muz vel: 550 ft./sec. (167 m/sec.)

French arms developed certain easily recognizable characteristics. This pistol is plainly made and of robust construction, well suited to service use. The slightly tapered smooth-bored barrel has both fixed foresight and backsight. The tang is marked "Mle (Model) 1842" and bears the date "1855" and the letters "MI" may be seen just in front of the nipple lump. There are further markings on the left-hand side of the breech. The lockplate, which is severely plain, bears the (abbreviated) inscription "Manufacture Imperiale de Châtellerault," one of the great French factories. The hammer, with its near-vertical checkered comb and its massive, turned-in nose is typically French. The solid brass cap holding the barrel to the front of the stock has a rearward projection on the left side with a retaining screw, and connects up to the sideplate on which the heads of the lock screws rest. The steel ramrod is retained in a recess running through the brass cap and into the stock. The stock is of walnut, the top and bottom of the butt being reinforced with steel strips: the top strip just touches the massive brass butt cap with its swivel lanyard ring.

UNITED KINGDOM

TOWER SEA SERVICE PERCUSSION PISTOL 1842

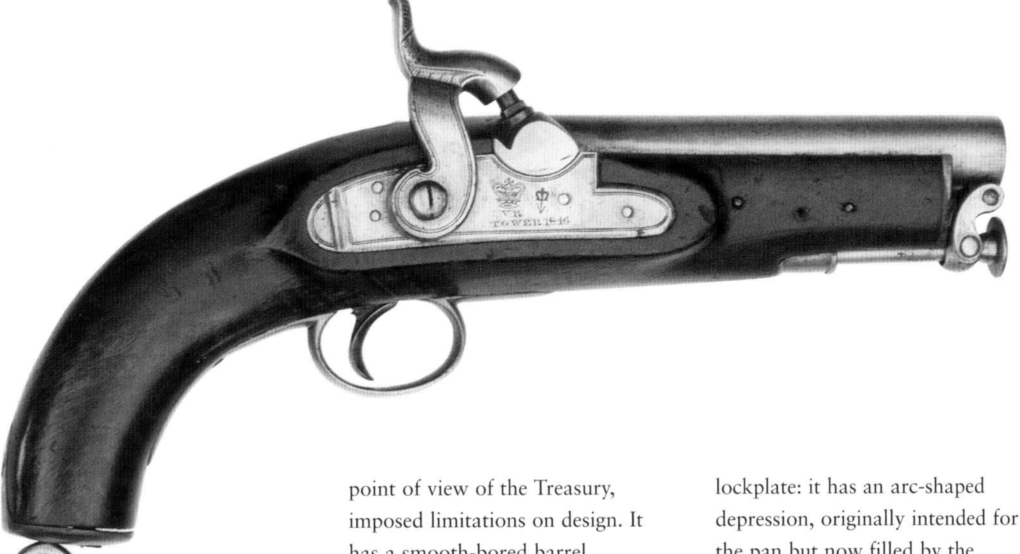

Length (gun): 11.0 in. (279 mm)
Barrel: 5.9 in. (150 mm)
Weight: 36.0 oz. (1.1 kg)
Caliber: 0.56 in. (14.2 mm)
Rifling: none
Capacity: one
Muz vel: 500 ft./sec. (152 m/sec.)

George Lovell produced this percussion pistol in 1842 from the large stocks of flintlock parts in store. This practice, although highly desirable from the point of view of the Treasury, imposed limitations on design. It has a smooth-bored barrel profusely marked with proof and inspection stamps. The barrel is held to the butt by a long screw and a single pin passing through a loop about 3 in. (76 mm) from the muzzle. The fact that this arm is a conversion is obvious from the shape of the upper edge of the lockplate: it has an arc-shaped depression, originally intended for the pan but now filled by the nipple lump, which appears to have been welded onto an original flintlock barrel. The hammer is of basic Lovell type, although the neck is flat rather than rounded. The swivel ramrod is held in a single tail pipe. The butt cap and trigger guard are of cast brass, the former having a steel lanyard ring. As this arm was for naval and coastguard use, it is fitted with a long belt hook, screwed to the left-hand side of the stock. Thus it could be carried on the cutlass belt, leaving both hands free. This was of considerable advantage to men on pitching vessels.

GERMANY

KUFAHL'S NEEDLE-FIRE REVOLVER 1842

Length (gun): 9.6 in. (244 mm)
Barrel: 3.2 in. (81 mm)
Weight: 22.0 oz. (0.6 kg)
Caliber: 0.300 in. (7.62 mm)
Rifling: 5 grooves, l/hand
Capacity: six
Muz vel: 500 ft./sec. (152 m/sec.)

The barrel and frame were made from a single piece of iron, although the top strap was welded on. The rifled octagonal barrel has a swamped muzzle. There is a laterally adjustable foresight; the backsight consists of a V-notch. The single-piece wooden butt is held in place by a screw through the lower tang. The trigger guard is hooked into this tang, its front end held in place by a screw. A small hole at the rear of each chamber allowed the needle to reach the front-loaded consumable cartridge. The cylinder axis pin could be removed by turning it through ninety degrees and drawing it out from the front; a small spring stud on the left side of the frame held it in place. Steady pressure on the trigger forced the bolt forward, rotating and locking the cylinder; then the needle-holder and needle went forward and fired the cartridge. Once the trigger was released, the needle and holder retracted, allowing the cylinder to rotate. The pistol is well made and finished, and bears the inscription, "Fv. V. Dreyse Sommerda" on the top strap. It is numbered "12620" on the left side of the frame; the right side bears the inscription "Cal 0.30," suggesting that it was made for the British or American markets.

UNITED KINGDOM

TOWER CAVALRY PISTOL 1842

Length (gun): 15.5 in. (394 mm)
Barrel: 9.0 in. (229 mm)
Weight: 52.0 oz. (1.5 kg)
Caliber: 0.75 in. (19 mm)
Rifling: none
Capacity: one
Muz vel: 500 ft./sec. (152 m/sec.)

By 1838 the pistol was no longer a general issue to British cavalry regiments, although lancer regiments were allowed to retain one pistol per trooper, and sergeant-majors and trumpeters continued to be armed with them. The weapon illustrated is the Model 1842, designed by George Lovell, who was Inspector of Small Arms and well known for his work on percussion weapons. Lovell was a great believer in the virtues of strength and simplicity in military arms, and he introduced a common caliber to facilitate the supply of ammunition in the field. He dedicated himself to bringing the new percussion system to the British military, and as early as 1830 began experimenting to that end. This is a very solid, robust arm with a rather short butt, which detracts somewhat from its general appearance. It has a smooth-bored barrel of full musket bore, held on the stock by a long screw and one flat key. Its swivel ramrod is retained by a combined nose cap and pipe of cast brass. The lock is unusually large, being the standard Pattern 1842 musket lock, and is held in position by two screws, the heads of which rest on small brass cups. The full stock is walnut; the butt cap and trigger guard are brass. Instead of the usual ring in the butt, a steel sling swivel is screwed into the front of the trigger guard.

FRANCE

CHÂTELLERAULT GENDARMERIE PISTOL 1845

Length (gun): 9.5 in. (241 mm)
Barrel: 5.0 in. (127 mm)
Weight: 23.0 oz. (0.7 kg)
Caliber: 0.600 in. (15.2 mm)
Rifling: none
Capacity: one
Muz vel: 500 ft./sec. (152 m/sec.)

This pistol was made at the Royal Factory at Châtellerault in 1845, three years after this model was introduced. (Among other famous weapons, the Châtellerault arsenal would be first to manufacture the 1891 Mosin Nagant rifle that armed Russia's armies.) The pistol has a short stubby barrel, about 1 in. (25.4 mm) of which is octagonal at the breech end. The nipple stands somewhat higher than on comparable British weapons. It is possible that the barrel is a conversion from a flintlock. There are the usual tang screws, the front end of the barrel being secured to the stock by a steel collar with its long lower tang inset into the woodwork, where its rear end meets the front end of the trigger guard. The hammer is mounted on a back-action lock neatly let into the stock, where it is retained by a screw with its lower end sited in a small plate. The tail of the lock is held in position by a second small screw, the head of which hooks over it. The stock has a steel cap, and the trigger guard is made of the same metal. The ramrod, the front end of which is badly corroded and blackened in this example, passes through the collar and into a hole in the stock. This is a very neat and compact arm.

FRANCE

PINFIRE REVOLVER 1845

Length (gun): 9.0 in. (229 mm)
Barrel: 4.3 in. (109 mm)
Weight: 22.0 oz. (0.6 kg)
Caliber: 0.39 in. (9.9 mm)
Rifling: 9 grooves, l/hand
Capacity: six
Muz vel: 600 ft./sec. (183 m/sec.)

This typical French pinfire revolver has a round barrel, with a lump that appears to have been made separately, held on by the usual means of cylinder axis pin and lower frame, the latter being held by a screw. The general construction is flimsy and much daylight is visible between the face of the cylinder and the breech end of the rifled barrel. The mechanism is of the self-cocking variety, with the hammer head in the form of an animal, possibly a hippopotamus. It has a folding trigger, allowing it to be easily carried in a pocket. The crude engraving on the cylinder may have been cast in it. The frame, loading gate, and butt strap are of a yellow alloy. The better pinfire arms were good enough for all practical purposes. Indeed, they continued to be made well into the twentieth century. They were essentially a continental European product with manufacture centering in Belgium and France, although some were produced in Germany. Pinfire arms appear never to have been made in the United States: a number were used by both sides in the Civil War, but otherwise there was a direct transition from percussion to rim- or centerfire—as in Britain.

DERINGER POCKET GUNS: THE PERCUSSION MODELS, 1845–1860

Henry Deringer was a Philadelphia gunsmith who developed a range of small, very compact, but large-caliber pocket pistols, which were so successful that his name soon became synonymous with all such weapons, whether or not they were made by his company. (Here, all except weapons actually produced by Deringer are referred to as "derringers.")

There were, in effect, two subtypes: the original percussion type, which appeared in the early 1830s and continued in production and use for many years, and its much superior replacement, the cartridge type, which appeared in 1861 and ultimately achieved much greater popularity. One of the most infamous applications for the Deringer was as an assassin's weapon, its most dramatic use in such a role being in the hand of John Wilkes Booth, who assassinated President Abraham Lincoln in 1865. (It is appropriate to note here that it was in a newspaper report on this incident that the name was written "Derringer," resulting in a misspelling that has persisted for many years.) The main characteristics of the Deringer were that it was small—usually less than 6.0 in. (152 mm) long—and of large

caliber, which resulted in a short-range weapon, but one with considerable power. A few had rudimentary sights, but these were of little practical use, since ranges were usually so short that all that was necessary was for the firer to point and shoot. The derringer was much favored as an offensive weapon by gamblers and gunfighters, and as a personal defense weapon by anyone who feared being caught unawares or at a disadvantage.

The weapons shown here include a number of genuine Deringers of varying sizes: (1–13), of which the 0.4 in. caliber (8) is the most significant, being identical to the weapon used by John Wilkes Booth to murder President Lincoln. Another maker of such small pistols was Ethan Allen, most of whose products employed an unusual bar hammer (14, 15, 23), although some used a more conventional center hammer (19). A number of other identifiable products are also shown: Blunt & Symes side hammer pocket pistol (16), Bacon & Co. single-shot ring trigger pocket pistol (22), Lindsay two-shot belt pistol with brass frame (21, 25), and the Massachusetts Arms Co. single-shot pistol fitted with Maynard's tape primer mechanism (24). However, many derringers were not stamped with their makers' names, such anonymous weapons including: 0.28 in. (7 mm) caliber pinfire pistol shown opened for loading (17), screw-on barrel pistol (18, seen here with barrel removed), a type which was more popular in Europe than in the United States, an English pocket pistol converted from flintlock to percussion (20), and a 0.2 in. caliber single-shot, breech-loading, pocket pistol (26).

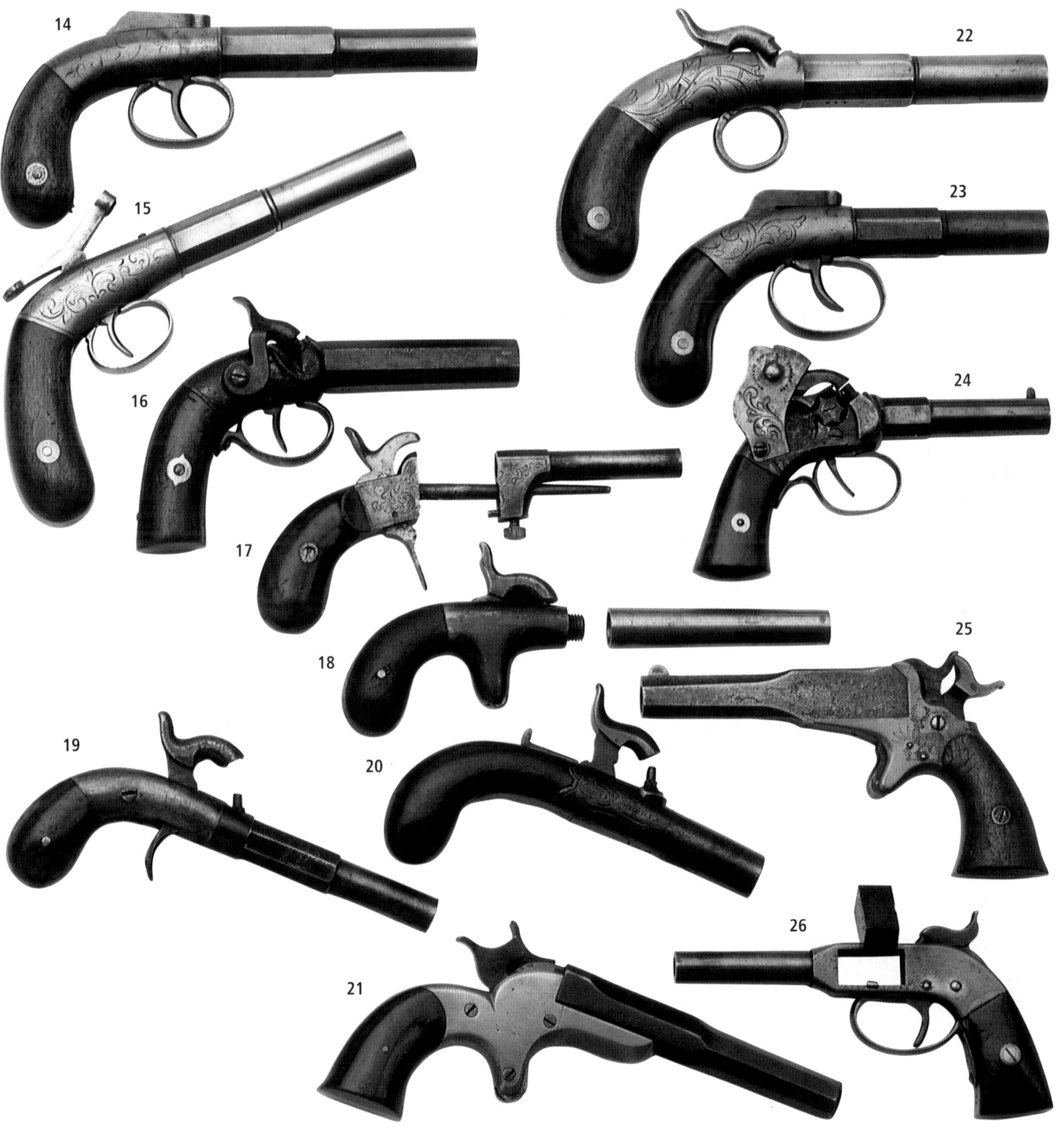

DERRINGER POCKET GUNS: THE RIMFIRE CARTRIDGE AND OTHER MODELS, 1860–1875

Rimfire cartridges started to become widely available in the early 1860s and derringer-type single- or double-barreled pistols using them were soon in great demand. Hiding places for such weapons gave rise to much ingenuity: some men, for example, used their boot tops, sleeve cuffs, or waistbands, while others hid them in their hats. These pistols were also popular with ladies, of whom the well-bred tended to carry them in their handbags, while those of lesser virtue hid them in their stocking tops or even, occasionally, in a form of "crotch pouch." The first shot from a derringer might not always have achieved the desired result, giving rise to the need for a multishot weapon. The double-barreled Remington model is shown in its original packing (7) and opened for loading (8). Next came three-barreled weapons, such as those made by William Marston (4) and (12), and even four-barreled pepper-boxes produced by Sharp & Co. (1, 2, 9, 10, 11), Starr (13), and Remington-Eliot (6).

Another solution to the same problem was to combine the pistol with a stabbing weapon, as in the Wesson two-shot pistol, which had a central tube housing a small bayonet (3), while some of the Marstons not only had three barrels but also a nasty-looking bayonet attachment (5). These

weapons obtained their multishot capability by having multiple barrels, but others sought a different method, such as the Schoop two-shot "harmonica" 0.30 in. rimfire pocket pistol (28), which had only a single barrel, while the American Arms Co Wheeler "roll-over" pistol (24) used two barrels that could be twisted to align the barrels with the hammer one at a time.

The great majority of derringers were, however, single-shot weapons, with Samuel Colt being one of the most prolific producers; starting with the first model (16) and the No. 3 (23), and, as usual, some of these were highly decorated (18). There was also a wide range available from the numerous gunsmiths then at work around the United States, including: Dexter Smith (17), Dickinson (25), Merwin & Bray (22), Remington (14), Rupertus (19, 27), and Union Arms Co. (20). Also among this group was the Hammond Bulldog 0.44 in. pistol (26), which was very reliable and effective, and, as a consequence, was particularly popular during the American Civil War as a "second" weapon.

Some designers sought unusual answers for the users' requirements. David Williamson, for example, modeled his rimfire derringer (15) on Henry Deringer's original, but incorporated a percussion insert, to be used in the event that rimfire ammunition was not available. The inventor of the drilled-through cylinder, Rollin White, also produced a pocket pistol with a swiveling breech (21). The great majority of pistols whose barrels "broke" for loading/unloading had the pivot either under the barrel (as shown in (13)) or above it (as in the "tip-up" models), but the Brown Manufacturing Company's "Southerner" (29) was most unusual in having a barrel which swung out sideways.

UNITED STATES

COLT DRAGOON MODEL 1849 REVOLVER

Length: 13.5 in. (343 mm)
Barrel: 7.5 in. (190 mm)
Weight: 68.0 oz. (1.9 kg)
Caliber: 0.44 in. (11.2 mm)
Rifling: 7 grooves, l/hand
Capacity: six
Muz vel: 850 ft./sec. (259 m/sec.)

The earliest versions of the unusually heavy arm seen here were the Walker or Witneyville-Walker models, which appeared as a result of the increased demand for arms caused by the Mexican War of 1846. These were followed by the Dragoon series, so called because the weapons were primarily used to arm cavalry of that description. This particular specimen is the Colt Dragoon Model 1849 (although it should be noted that it has the square-backed trigger guard not often found at such a late date). It has a round barrel with a fixed foresight; the backsight is incorporated into the top of the hammer. The barrel is keyed to the very robust axis pin and is further supported by a solid lug butted to the lower frame. Below the barrel is the arm's very powerful compound rammer, which forced the bullets into the chambers so tightly that neither damp nor the flash from previous shots could enter.

BELGIUM

CONTINENTAL PINFIRE REVOLVER 1850

Length (gun): 10.0 in. (245 mm)
Barrel: 5.8 in. (147 mm)
Weight: 21.0 oz. (0.6 kg)
Caliber: 0.39 in. (9.9 mm)
Rifling: 6 grooves, l/hand
Capacity: six
Muz vel: 550 ft./sec. (167 m/sec.)

This is a medium-quality pinfire revolver of quite large caliber. Like many of its kind, it is anonymous, bearing no name or markings other than a number and Belgian proofmarks on the cylinder. It has an octagonal barrel with a very high and flimsy foresight; the backsight is a simple notch on the top of the hammer nose. The cylinder has long, machined projections, the higher parts being almost level with the pin apertures. These were engaged by a cylinder stop, which rose from the lower frame when the trigger was pressed, locking the cylinder when a chamber was in line. The lock is of a later type than on most weapons of this kind, and the hammer could be manually cocked. The revolver is fitted with an ejector rod, held by the tension of a small, flat spring, which prevented it being accidentally pushed into a chamber. The arm is blued, except for the hammer, trigger, and ejector rod.

UNITED KINGDOM

COGSWELL PEPPERBOX PISTOL 1850

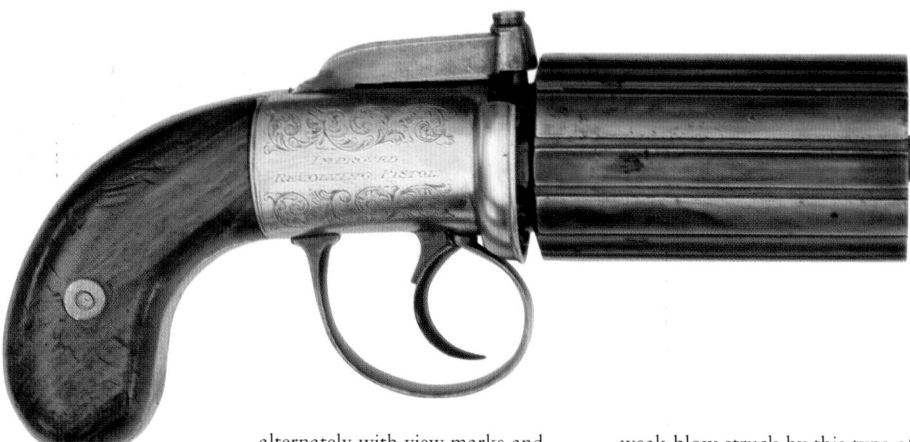

Length (gun): 7.6 in. (193 mm)
Barrel: 3.0 in. (76 mm)
Weight: 28.0 oz. (0.8 kg)
Caliber: 0.476 in. (12.1 mm)
Rifling: none
Capacity: six
Muz vel: 500 ft./sec. (152 m/sec.)

This pistol is a well-finished arm of good quality. Its six smooth-bored barrels have been drilled out of a single steel cylinder, with the intervals between the barrels machined out into plain but elegant grooves. Each barrel is numbered at the breech end, while the grooves are stamped alternately with view marks and proof marks. The chambers are in a cylinder of somewhat smaller diameter than the barrel cluster, and the nipples are screwed into the chambers at right angles to the axis of the barrels. There are no partitions between the nipples, increasing the risk of multiple discharge; such pistols usually employed especially sensitive caps to compensate for the relatively weak blow struck by this type of hammer. The breech mechanism is of German silver and is discreetly engraved in the English style. The left-hand side bears the inscription "B. COGSWELL, 224 STRAND, LONDON," while the right-hand side bears the words "IMPROVED REVOLVING PISTOL." The breech includes a nipple shield: the advantages and disadvantages of such a provision roughly balance out, for the protection afforded to the caps was offset by the increased risk of several barrels firing together. The butt consists of a continuous strap of German silver, with walnut plates held in position by a screw.

UNITED KINGDOM

BAKER TRANSITIONAL REVOLVER 1851

Length (gun): 11.5 in. (292 mm)
Barrel: 5.6 in. (142 mm)
Weight: 35.0 oz. (1.0 kg)
Caliber: 0.44 in. (11.2 mm)
Rifling: 14 grooves, r/hand
Capacity: six
Muz vel: 500 ft./sec. (152 m/sec.)

This revolver was made by T. K. Baker of London. The rifled barrel is octagonal for just over half its length. The cylinder is deeply rebated to give a seating for the nipples, which have no partitions. The cylinder's back is cut into a ratchet, with a further, outer row of six slots for the cylinder stops. The hammer had to be cocked for each shot; hence the long hammer spur. Half-cocking the hammer very slightly rotated the cylinder counterclockwise; pulling the hammer back to full cock brought the next chamber in line and locked the cylinder. The hammer was slightly angled, so when the arm was cocked, the foresight could be aligned with a shallow V backsight on the hammer. The frame is of German silver. The method of holding the barrel in place, screwed to the axis pin without any secondary brace to the frame, was unsatisfactory. There must have been a tendency for the barrel to work loose.

UNITED KINGDOM

ADAMS 0.44 IN. SELF-COCKING REVOLVER 1851

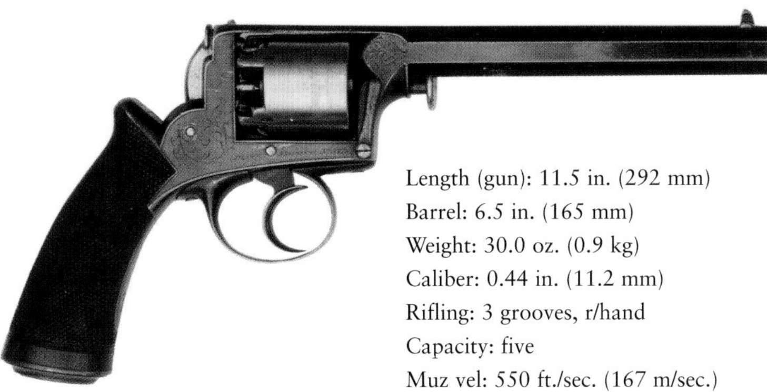

Length (gun): 11.5 in. (292 mm)
Barrel: 6.5 in. (165 mm)
Weight: 30.0 oz. (0.9 kg)
Caliber: 0.44 in. (11.2 mm)
Rifling: 3 grooves, r/hand
Capacity: five
Muz vel: 550 ft./sec. (167 m/sec.)

The original Adams "Dragoon" type, 38-bore revolver was rather too heavy for a man on foot. This revolver is the next size down and was of nominal 54-bore (about 0.44 in./11.2 mm caliber). However, some of the earliest models, like this one, were 56-bore and bear the small number "56" on the front of the frame. It is of the usual strong, one-piece construction. The cylinder, which is bright, has the usual five chambers and horizontal nipples separated by partitions. It is slightly unusual, in that it rotated counterclockwise. The cylinder could be removed by withdrawing the small plug on the upper end of the vertical spring on the front of the frame, then drawing the axis pin forward. The lock is self-cocking and a safety device to hold the hammer clear of the nipples is on the left-hand side of the frame. The bullets, with oversized felt wads attached to their bases, were only thumb-tight in the chambers for fast loading.

UNITED KINGDOM

ADAMS SELF-COCKING REVOLVER 1851

Length (gun): 13.0 in. (330 mm)
Barrel: 7.5 in. (190 mm)
Weight: 45.0 oz. (1.3 kg)
Caliber: 0.49 in. (12.4 mm)
Rifling: 5 grooves, r/hand
Capacity: five
Muz vel: 700 ft./sec. (213 m/sec.)

The Adams revolver was put into large-scale production following interest generated at the 1851 Great Exhibition. This example is number 419. Unlike Colt pistols, the barrels, frames, and butts of Adams pistols were forged as single entities, which gave them great strength and rigidity. The barrel is octagonal; the top flat is engraved "DEANE ADAMS AND DEANE (MAKER TO HRH PRINCE ALBERT) 30 KING WILLIAM ST LONDON BRIDGE." It is rifled and fitted with a foresight capable of lateral adjustment. The plain, five-chambered cylinder, with nipples adequately separated by partitions, rotated on an axis pin and could be removed by drawing the pin forward and clear of the frame. A small, flat spring on the right-hand side of the frame prevented this happening accidentally. The lock was self-cocking; the pistol was fired by steady pressure on the trigger, causing the hammer to rise and fall. The small, flat spring behind the cylinder is a safety device: there is an inward-facing stud at its top end, which, when depressed, held the hammer clear of the nipples; the slightest pressure on the trigger caused the stud to spring clear, leaving the revolver ready for action The arm has a one-piece butt of checkered walnut, with a cap compartment in the base.

UNITED KINGDOM

LANCASTER DOUBLE-BARRELED PISTOL 1851

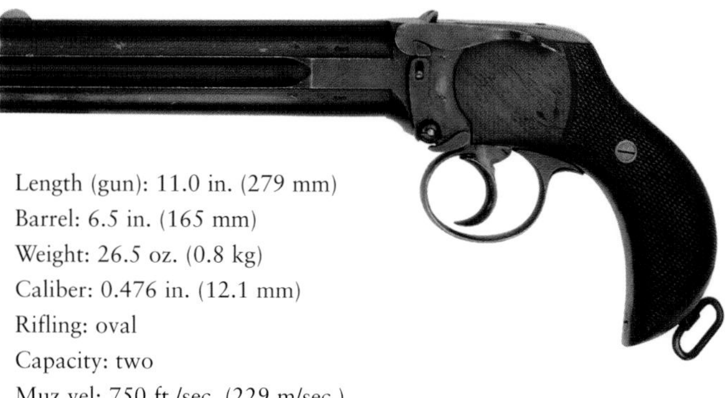

Length (gun): 11.0 in. (279 mm)
Barrel: 6.5 in. (165 mm)
Weight: 26.5 oz. (0.8 kg)
Caliber: 0.476 in. (12.1 mm)
Rifling: oval
Capacity: two
Muz vel: 750 ft./sec. (229 m/sec.)

Although similar in principle to the four-barreled weapons, this Lancaster double-barreled pistol differed in detail. The locking system was identical. The difference lay in the system of extraction. In the double-barreled Lancaster, when the barrels were opened, the vertical lever at their breech end initially moved with them, until its lower end caught the horizontal projection just above the trigger. When this happened, the lever stopped, but as the barrels continued to move, the extractor was drawn out by means of a protruding pin, which engaged in a slot at the upper end of the lever. This extractor was not spring-operated: when the barrels were closed, it was pushed back into place by the face of the standing breech. This pistol was lighter and better balanced than the four-barreled version. The trigger pull was so long and heavy that accuracy would have been difficult—except for close action.

UNITED STATES

WESSON & LEAVITT TAPE-PRIMER REVOLVER 1851

Length: 6.6 in. (168 mm)
Barrel: 3.0 in. (76 mm)
Weight: 10.0 oz. (0.3 kg)
Caliber: 0.28 in. (7.1 mm)
Rifling: 7 grooves, l/hand
Capacity: six
Muz vel: 500 ft./sec. (152 m/sec.)

The Massachusetts Arms Co. was sued by Colt in 1851 for infringement of its patent for a revolving cylinder. The revolver, designed by Wesson and Leavitt, used a system of bevel gears rather than a pawl and ratchet to rotate the cylinder, but the court found against the company. This is one of the pistols modified to avoid the patent. The rear end of the top strap, which is integral with the barrel, is hinged to the standing breech so that it could be turned upward through about forty-five degrees, allowing the cylinder to be removed by pulling it forward off its axis pin. When the cylinder was fully home, about 1 in. (25.4 mm) protruded beyond its front face. A single nipple is screwed into the top of the breech so that it is aligned with the vent into the rear of each chamber. Use of one nipple was made possible by a device called a tape-primer.

UNITED STATES

MASSACHUSETTS TAPE-PRIMER REVOLVER 1852

Length: 10.5 in. (267 mm)
Barrel: 6.0 in. (152 mm)
Weight: 24.0 oz. (0.7 kg)
Caliber: 0.32 in. (8.1 mm)
Rifling: 7 grooves, l/hand
Capacity: six
Muz vel: 550 ft./sec. (167 m/sec.)

The weapon illustrated is another of the modified revolvers, made in the interval between the court case and the expiry of Colt's patent in 1857. The barrel of this weapon, which is rifled, is attached to the top of the standing breech by a hinged strap that permitted it to be raised to an angle of about forty-five degrees in order to remove the cylinder. The latter is mounted on a stout axis pin that protrudes slightly more than 1 in. (25.4 mm) beyond the front face of the cylinder; the object of this extension was to provide a firm locking point for a hook which pivoted around the breech end of the barrel, a fitting clearly visible in the illustration. There is a small retaining spring on the end of the axis pin to prevent it being released accidentally. The lock is fitted with a tape-primer, which made possible the use of a single nipple only: the flash was transmitted to the charge by means of a small hole at the rear of each chamber. When the cylinder stop pin (visible in front of the trigger) was pushed, the cylinder could be rotated manually.

UNITED STATES

COLT NAVY REVOLVER 1851

Length: 12.9 in. (328 mm)
Barrel: 7.5 in. (190 mm)
Weight: 39.0 oz. (1.1 kg)
Caliber: 0.36 in. (9.1 mm)
Rifling: 7 grooves, r/hand
Capacity: six
Muz vel: 700 ft./sec. (213 m/sec.)

The Great Exhibition held in London in 1851 provided Colt with an opportunity for publicity. The revolver was then little known in England. There were one or two excellent British-made arms of similar type on view, notably the Adams revolver; but these were largely handmade prototypes and there was little immediate chance of their being made in numbers, unlike Colt. This revolver is of broadly similar type to the Dragoon, but smaller. It has an octagonal barrel with a bead foresight; the barrel is secured to the frame by means of a wedge through the very stout cylinder axis pin and is firmly braced against the lower frame. The six-chambered cylinder is plain, except for rectangular depressions for the stop. The revolver has a hemispherical standing breech, in which a depression is located on the right for access to the nipples. It was made in Colt's London factory.

UNITED KINGDOM

BAKER GAS-SEAL REVOLVER 1852

Length (gun): 13.3 in. (337 mm)
Barrel: 6.5 in. (165 mm)
Weight: 49.0 oz. (1.4 kg)
Caliber: 0.577 in. (14.6 mm)
Rifling: 16 grooves, r/hand
Capacity: six
Muz vel: 600 ft./sec. (183 m/sec.)

The gas-seal type had a cylinder that reciprocated so that each chamber was locked securely to the barrel at the time of firing. Most British gas-seal revolvers bear a strong resemblance to each other. Many of this type were not developed until after the Great Exhibition. This is a heavy, service-type weapon with an octagonal, blued barrel with multigrooved rifling. The barrel is held rigidly to the weapon by the combination of a key through the axis pin and a lower extension locking onto the bottom of the frame. The short, case-hardened cylinder is rebated at the rear in order to provide a seating for the nipples, which are at right angles to the barrel axis and without partitions. Its hammer is of the bar variety and is single-action, with a long, rearward spur for cocking; it is slightly angled, so that the fixed sights could be aligned when it was cocked, and is fitted with a sliding safety.

UNITED KINGDOM

TRANSITIONAL REVOLVER WITH BAYONET 1852

Length (gun): 12.0 in. (305 mm)
Barrel: 5.8 in. (147 mm)
Weight: 32.0 oz. (0.9 kg)
Caliber: 0.42 in. (10.7 mm)
Rifling: 9 grooves, r/hand
Capacity: six
Muz vel: 500 ft./sec. (152 m/sec.)

This interesting arm shows the lines along which the transitional revolver developed in the mid-nineteenth century. The revolver has a folding bayonet, part of which is just visible above the barrel. It will, however, be seen that there is a strong projection below the cylinder to which a corresponding projection below the barrel is firmly screwed, thus making a very considerable contribution to the strength and rigidity of the weapon. The frame is made of iron and the butt is of a handy size and it is in most respects a robust and serviceable arm. The exact function of arms like this cannot be defined with certainty: it was probably intended to be for self-defense; but the presence of the bayonet (although of little larger size than a penknife) suggests at least some degree of offensive intent. The weapon may possibly have been of the naval type that are often referred to as boarding pistols.

UNITED KINGDOM

TRANTER REVOLVER, FIRST MODEL 1853

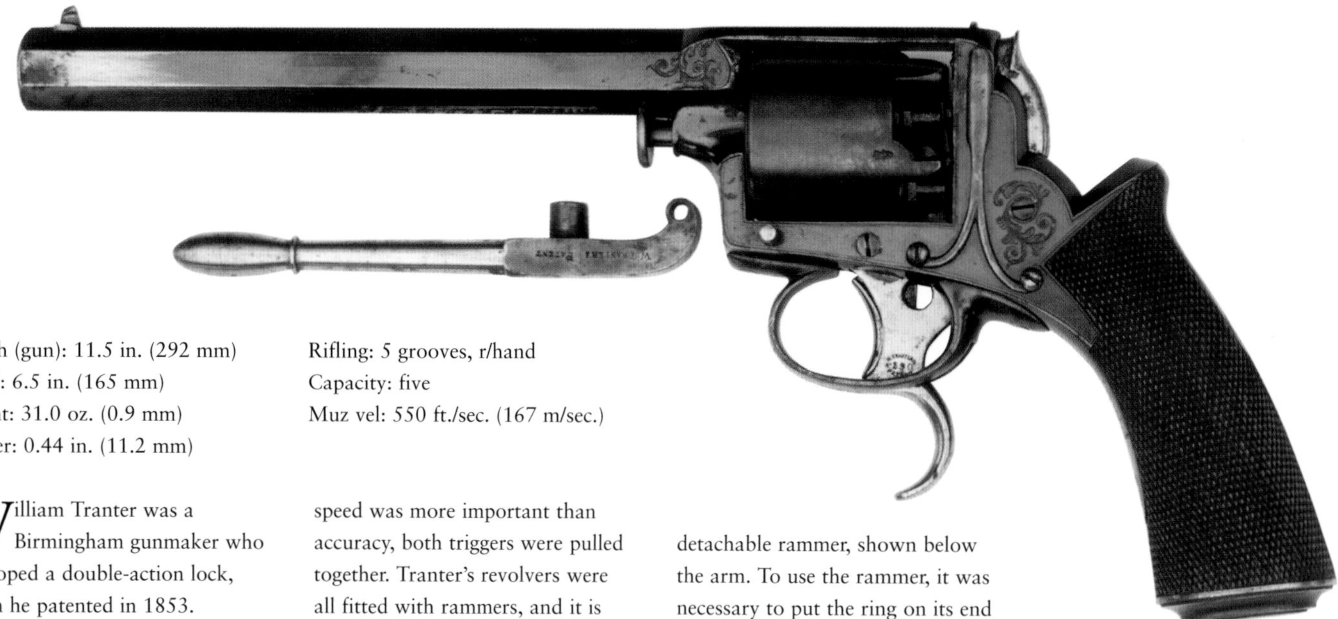

Length (gun): 11.5 in. (292 mm)
Barrel: 6.5 in. (165 mm)
Weight: 31.0 oz. (0.9 mm)
Caliber: 0.44 in. (11.2 mm)
Rifling: 5 grooves, r/hand
Capacity: five
Muz vel: 550 ft./sec. (167 m/sec.)

William Tranter was a Birmingham gunmaker who developed a double-action lock, which he patented in 1853. Pressure on the lower trigger (which is, in effect, a cocking lever) cocked the combless hammer; a very light pressure on the upper trigger was then sufficient to fire the shot. When speed was more important than accuracy, both triggers were pulled together. Tranter's revolvers were all fitted with rammers, and it is by the variations in these that the different models are identified. The numbering of the models does not necessarily relate to their chronological order. This is the first model; it is equipped with a detachable rammer, shown below the arm. To use the rammer, it was necessary to put the ring on its end over a peg (visible) on the bottom of the frame, then raise the lever so that the ram bore on the bullet and forced it into the chamber. Around the base of each bullet was a cannelure, which contained a beeswax mixture: the expansion of the bullet on firing forced beeswax into the bore, helping to reduce hard fouling and facilitating cleaning.

UNITED KINGDOM

WEBLEY LONGSPUR REVOLVER 1853

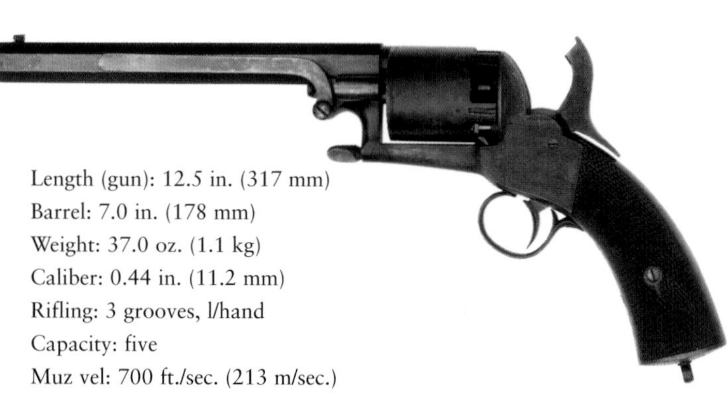

Length (gun): 12.5 in. (317 mm)
Barrel: 7.0 in. (178 mm)
Weight: 37.0 oz. (1.1 kg)
Caliber: 0.44 in. (11.2 mm)
Rifling: 3 grooves, l/hand
Capacity: five
Muz vel: 700 ft./sec. (213 m/sec.)

This revolver was patented in 1853; this is the third model. The frame is of malleable iron. The octagonal barrel is attached to the axis pin by a threaded sleeve in the lump at the rear end of the barrel. The lower part of this lump butts onto the lower projection of the frame and is attached to it by a thumbscrew. The case-hardened cylinder has five chambers with horizontal nipples separated by partitions. The first model had a detachable rammer; the second had a swivel rammer pivoted back horizontally across the frame below the cylinder. It has an integral spring that held the lever flush against a small stud on the left-hand barrel flat when not in use. Raising the lever thrust the hollow-nosed rammer into the chamber with sufficient force to allow the use of tight-fitting bullets. The lock is single-action and has a half-cock to hold the hammer clear of the nipples. The trigger and guard are rather small.

FRANCE

LEFAUCHEUX PINFIRE REVOLVER 1854

Length (gun): 8.4 in. (213 mm)
Barrel: 4.0 in. (102 mm)
Weight: 20.0 oz. (0.56 kg)
Caliber: 0.35 in. (9 mm)
Rifling: 4 grooves, r/hand
Capacity: six
Muz vel: 600 ft./sec. (183 m/sec.)

The pinfire cartridge was invented by Frenchman Casimir Lefaucheux as early as 1828, and was in quite extensive use, mainly in Europe, before 1840. It did not arouse much interest in Britain until its appearance at the Great Exhibition in 1851, when it was shown in conjunction with an arm of the pepperbox type. A more modern type of arm was then developed by Casimir's son Eugène, who patented it in Great Britain in 1854. The weapon is plain and robust: the octagonal barrel is attached to the axis pin (as in Colt arms) and is further braced against the lower part of the frame, making a reasonably rigid joint. The heavy standing breech is fitted with a top-hinged loading gate with a spring catch, and a simple sliding rod is provided for knocking out the empty cases. The small, square studs on the cylinder engaged with the cylinder stop on firing.

UNITED KINGDOM

BEATTIE GAS-SEAL REVOLVER 1855

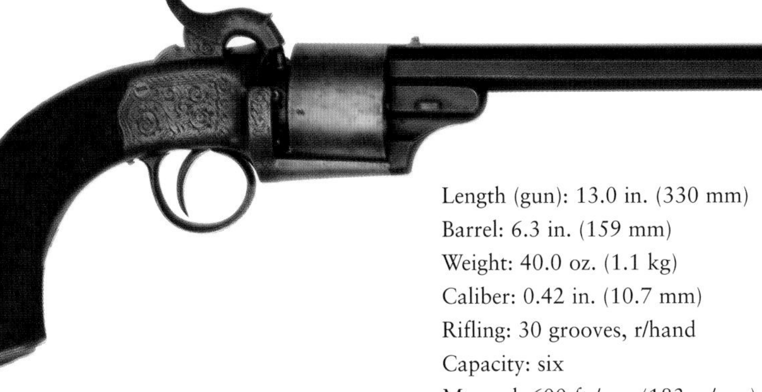

Length (gun): 13.0 in. (330 mm)
Barrel: 6.3 in. (159 mm)
Weight: 40.0 oz. (1.1 kg)
Caliber: 0.42 in. (10.7 mm)
Rifling: 30 grooves, r/hand
Capacity: six
Muz vel: 600 ft./sec. (183 m/sec.)

The browned barrel is octagonal and has multi-grooved rifling. The rear end of the cylinder is rebated to provide a seating for the nipples, which are at right angles to the axis of the chambers. The barrel is securely wedged to the axis pin by means of a flat, sliding key with a retaining screw; it also has an extension that engaged with the lower part of the frame. The hammer is single-action. Early percussion revolvers had no rammer, which meant that the bullets could be no more than finger-tight in the cylinders. That part of the burning gases which was inevitably deflected down into the gap between the face of the cylinder and the end of the barrel, was liable to flash past the bullets in the neighboring chambers and ignite their charges. Gas-seal revolvers overcame this by having slightly coned barrel rear ends and chamber front ends opened out, so that they fitted closely.

UNITED KINGDOM

ADAMS POCKET REVOLVER 1855

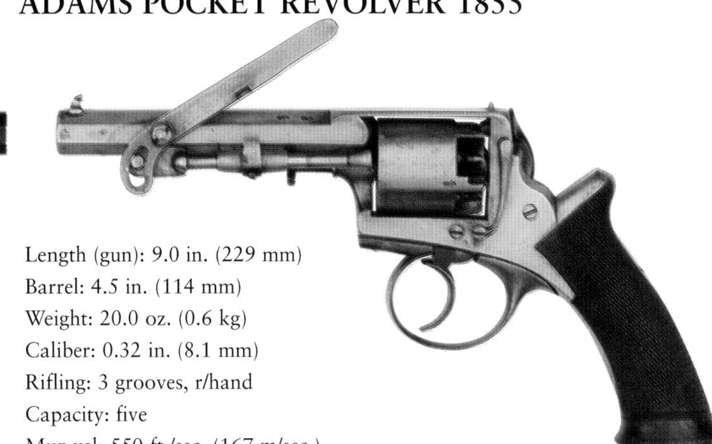

Length (gun): 9.0 in. (229 mm)
Barrel: 4.5 in. (114 mm)
Weight: 20.0 oz. (0.6 kg)
Caliber: 0.32 in. (8.1 mm)
Rifling: 3 grooves, r/hand
Capacity: five
Muz vel: 550 ft./sec. (167 m/sec.)

This pocket pistol has the usual solid frame and octagonal barrel. The system of mounting the cylinder was also the same as other Adams designs; the axis pin was drawn forward to remove it. The lock is self-cocking. The spring safety plunger can be seen on the left-hand side of the frame. This held the hammer nose clear of the nipple and allowed the pistol to be carried loaded. It released itself automatically when the trigger was pulled. The most distinctive feature is probably the patent Brazier rammer attached to the left-hand flat of the barrel. Joseph Brazier, who patented it in 1855, was a well-known Birmingham gunmaker who made Adams revolvers under license. A number of other licensees, in Britain, continental Europe, and the United States, also made revolvers on the Adams pattern: the weapon illustrated may be the product of one of these firms. The revolver has been overcleaned.

UNITED KINGDOM

BEAUMONT-ADAMS 0.44 IN. REVOLVER 1855

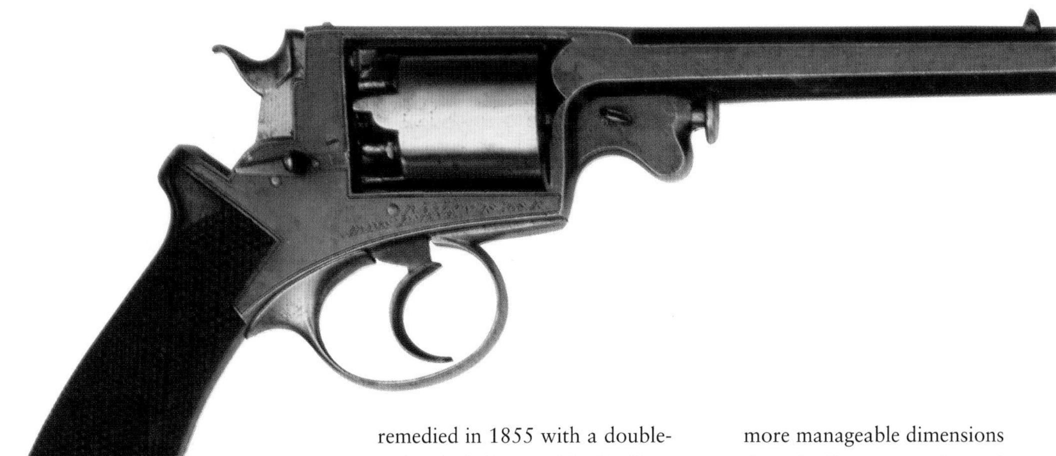

Length (gun): 11.8 in. (298 mm)
Barrel: 5.8 in. (146 mm)
Weight: 38.0 oz. (1.1 kg)
Caliber: 0.44 in. (11.2 mm)
Rifling: 3 grooves, r/hand
Capacity: five
Muz vel: 550 ft./sec. (167 m/sec.)

The Adams revolvers of 1851 were self-cockers and could only be fired by applying quite heavy pressure on the trigger, making them fast but inaccurate, except at close range. This was remedied in 1855 with a double-action lock, invented by Lt. F. Beaumont of the Royal Engineers. This allowed preliminary cocking for deliberate shooting, without affecting the rate of fire. It appears that only two calibers were made: the massive Dragoon arm and the smaller 54-bore (about 0.44 in./11.2 mm caliber) shown here. This weapon, while still having adequate stopping power, was of more manageable dimensions than the Dragoon, and was thus favored by unmounted officers. The revolver is of strong construction. It has the usual one-piece frame with integral octagonal barrel, which is rifled and bears the foresight; the backsight is a simple notch on the frame above the standing breech. The plain cylinder, with its horizontal nipples separated by partitions, is somewhat longer than those of the original Adams, to allow for a heavier charge, and bears London proof marks. There is a Kerr-type rammer on the left-hand side of the barrel. The lower frame is marked "B14886" and "Adams Patent No 30550 R," and carries an "L.A.C." (London Armoury Company) stamp near the axis pin.

A DUEL OF HONOR

One day in 1838, two London society gentlemen, Mr. Francis Lionel Eliot and Mr. Charles Flower Mirfin, were attending the Epsom races. An accident occurred between the two gentlemen's carriages, and Mirfin's gig was overturned. Mirfin suffered fractured ribs, and a violent argument blew up between the two men, during which Eliot struck Mirfin with his stick.

Insults were traded and the two men separated, but for Mirfin, the slight on his honor remained, and he proceeded to spend the next two months attempting to track down Eliot. By accident, on August 21, he heard Eliot's name mentioned in a salon in Piccadilly, and was finally able to extract an address.

Mirfin sent his associate, Edward Delves Broughton, to challenge Eliot over the incident and demand an apology. No diplomatic resolution was achieved, so a duel by pistol was scheduled for the following morning on Wimbledon Common.

The principals in the duel were the duelists themselves, Eliot and Mirfin, plus their seconds—Broughton for Mirfin and John Young and Henry Webber for Eliot. The seconds fulfilled the role of observing that correct dueling etiquette was observed on both sides. A doctor, Dr. Scott, was also in attendance.

Above: *One of the most famous duels in the United States took place in 1804 between the federalist politician Alexander Hamilton and Aaron Burr, who had been appointed vice president in 1800. Moves had been made by Hamilton's associates to turn Burr to their side, but Hamilton had doubts. One New York newspaper reported that Hamilton said he "looked upon Mr. Burr to be a dangerous man, and one who ought not to be trusted with the reins of government." Burr demanded a duel; Hamilton agreed, but decided not to fire. Burr had no such qualms: at Weehawken, New Jersey, Hamilton was hit and died thirty-one hours later.*

The duelists met at first light, and again attempted a verbal resolution. Mirfin, however, turned down an apology. A distance of twelve paces was measured out on the ground. The dueling pistols were loaded, and Eliot and Mirfin separated to dueling distance.

At a signal, both men fired simultaneously. Eliot showed his skill at arms from the beginning, taking Mirfin's hat off with the ball while Mirfin's shot flew wide. Deeming that honor was not satisfied, Mirfin requested another gun. According to a later court report, Mirfin "declared he would face a dozen shots rather than submit." It was not a wise course. On the second firing, Mirfin was shot fatally through the heart, declaring "He's hit me," before dying in the arms of Scott and Broughton.

Although socially accepted, dueling in the mid-nineteenth century remained a criminal act, and in September, Eliot, Young, and Webber were all convicted of murder as either principals or accessories. Broughton received a similar conviction when he stood trial in February 1839. Typically, however, none of the participants was executed. Eliot, Young, and Webber had their death sentences commuted to one year in Guildford prison, with a month in solitude, while Broughton also received twelve months in jail.

UNITED KINGDOM

DAW REVOLVER 1855

Length (gun): 10.5 in. (267 mm)
Barrel: 5.6 in. (142 mm)
Weight: 26.0 oz. (0.7 kg)
Caliber: 0.38 in. (9.6 mm)
Rifling: 5 grooves, r/hand
Capacity: five
Muz vel: 550 ft./sec. (167 m/sec.)

G. H. Daw was in partnership with D. W. Witton until 1860, but thereafter traded alone as George H. Daw. In 1855, the firm of Pryse and Cashmore patented a double-action lock which Daw enthusiastically took up. The barrel is wedged to the axis pin and is further braced against the lower frame, and it is fitted with a compound rammer of Colt type. The barrel is cylindrical with top and bottom flats, the former bearing the inscription "GEORGE H DAW, 57 THREADNEEDLE ST LONDON, PATENT NO 112." It has a double-action "hesitation" lock: by slowly pressing the trigger, the hammer was brought to full-cock, whence a further slight pressure fired it. It could also be cocked manually, and a stronger pressure on the trigger caused the arm to fire double-action. The standing breech has a large, U-shaped cutaway at the top, allowing ample room for recapping, and the hammerhead has a hood which fitted it exactly when lowered, thus preventing the blowback of cap fragments. Each nipple partition has a small stud, which corresponds with a recess in the bottom of the hammer-nose. This allowed the hammer to be left down on a partition when a fully capped and loaded revolver was carried, without any risk of accident.

UNITED KINGDOM

TRANTER REVOLVER, SECOND MODEL 1855

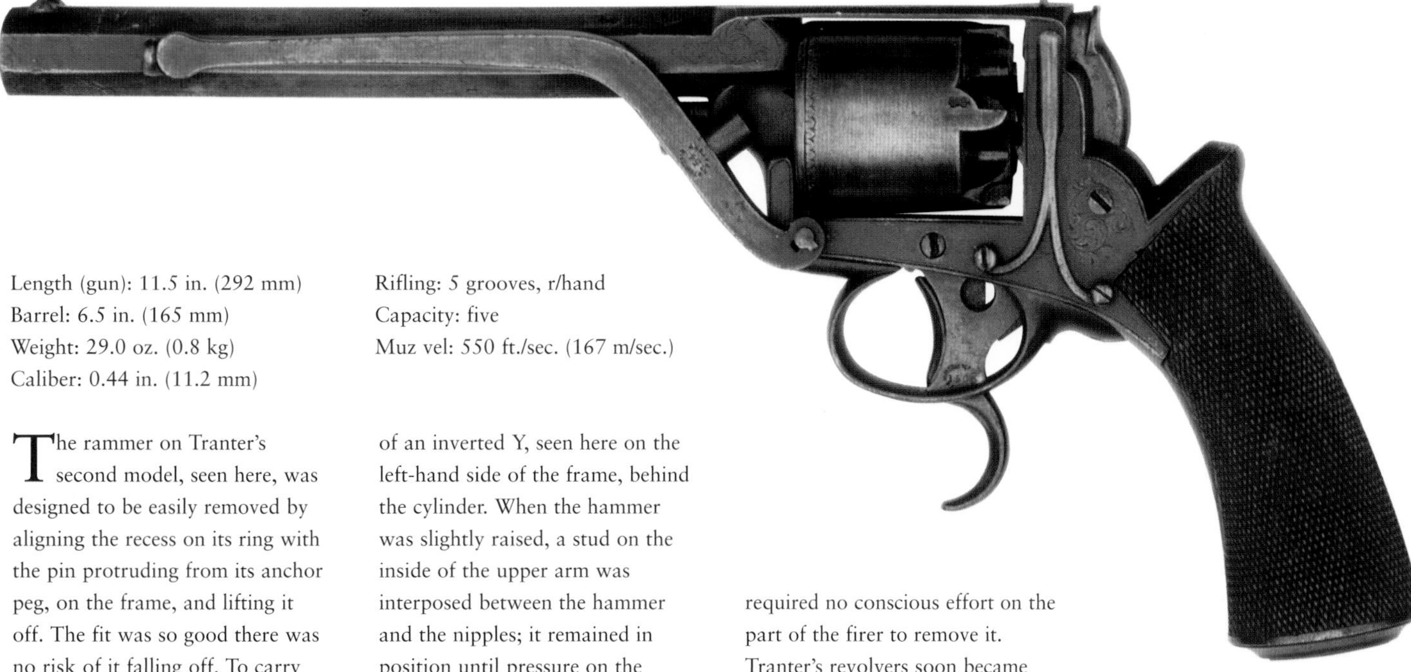

Length (gun): 11.5 in. (292 mm)
Barrel: 6.5 in. (165 mm)
Weight: 29.0 oz. (0.8 kg)
Caliber: 0.44 in. (11.2 mm)
Rifling: 5 grooves, r/hand
Capacity: five
Muz vel: 550 ft./sec. (167 m/sec.)

The rammer on Tranter's second model, seen here, was designed to be easily removed by aligning the recess on its ring with the pin protruding from its anchor peg, on the frame, and lifting it off. The fit was so good there was no risk of it falling off. To carry the loaded revolver safely, it was necessary to keep the nose of the hammer clear of the caps. Tranter's solution was a spring in the shape of an inverted Y, seen here on the left-hand side of the frame, behind the cylinder. When the hammer was slightly raised, a stud on the inside of the upper arm was interposed between the hammer and the nipples; it remained in position until pressure on the lower trigger brought the hammer back to full-cock, when it automatically disengaged. This was a simple and effective device that required no conscious effort on the part of the firer to remove it. Tranter's revolvers soon became popular with service officers, because they were both mechanically sound and well made. There were initially some criticisms of Tranter's system, but it proved fast and simple in operation, remaining in service for a long time.

UNITED KINGDOM

BEAUMONT-ADAMS 0.49 IN. DRAGOON REVOLVER 1855

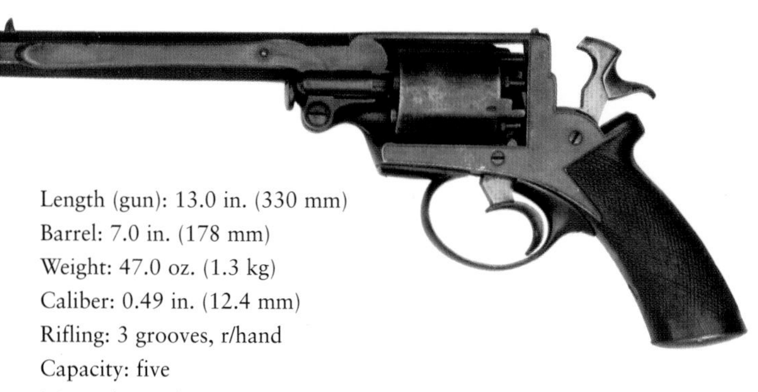

Length (gun): 13.0 in. (330 mm)
Barrel: 7.0 in. (178 mm)
Weight: 47.0 oz. (1.3 kg)
Caliber: 0.49 in. (12.4 mm)
Rifling: 3 grooves, r/hand
Capacity: five
Muz vel: 750 ft./sec. (229 m/sec.)

This revolver has the solid frame and octagonal barrel of the earlier Adams, but the shape of the butt is of more modern appearance and the curve in the trigger is less pronounced. The new mechanism made it possible to place the hammer at half-cock; thus, the spring plug was no longer necessary, but there is a sliding safety on the right-hand side of the frame. This intervened between a nipple and a partition, thus preventing the cylinder from rotating and making it impossible to draw the hammer back to full-cock. Another interesting addition was a rammer. The first Adams was loaded with wadded, finger-tight bullets in slightly oversized chambers; but although this speeded reloading, there was a risk of a bullet slipping forward and jamming the cylinder. A tight bullet also gave better shooting and a good, watertight seal, so Adams followed Colt's example and fitted a rammer.

FRANCE

LEFAUCHEUX PINFIRE NAVAL REVOLVER 1856

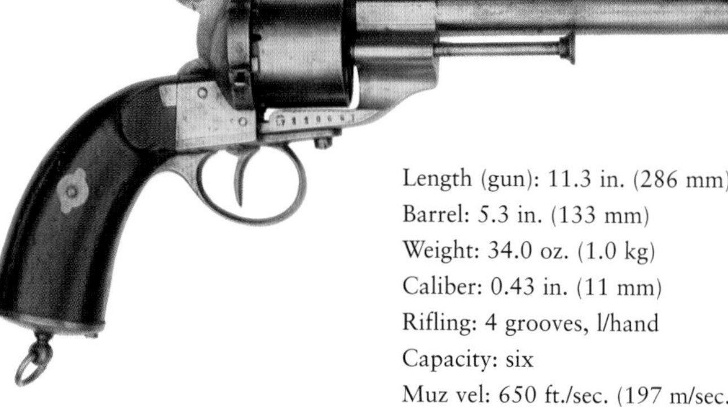

Length (gun): 11.3 in. (286 mm)
Barrel: 5.3 in. (133 mm)
Weight: 34.0 oz. (1.0 kg)
Caliber: 0.43 in. (11 mm)
Rifling: 4 grooves, l/hand
Capacity: six
Muz vel: 650 ft./sec. (197 m/sec.)

The French government carried out extensive trials with pinfire weapons during the Crimean War (the other arms were the American Colt and the British Beaumont-Adams—both, of course, percussion arms), and as a result a Lefaucheux pinfire revolver was selected in 1856 for use by the French Navy. It is in every respect a well-made and reliable weapon: plain, solid, well balanced, and a worthy service arm. It has a round barrel with a lump fitting over the cylinder axis pin and fastened also to the lower frame, to which it is both slotted and screwed to make a rigid joint. It has the usual solid standing breech with a loading gate on the right-hand side. The cylinder revolved freely except at full cock, when a stop protruded from the standing breech lower part to lock the cylinder by acting on the rectangular blocks between the pin apertures. It was also adopted by the Italian Navy in 1858.

UNITED KINGDOM

TRANTER REVOLVER, THIRD MODEL 1855

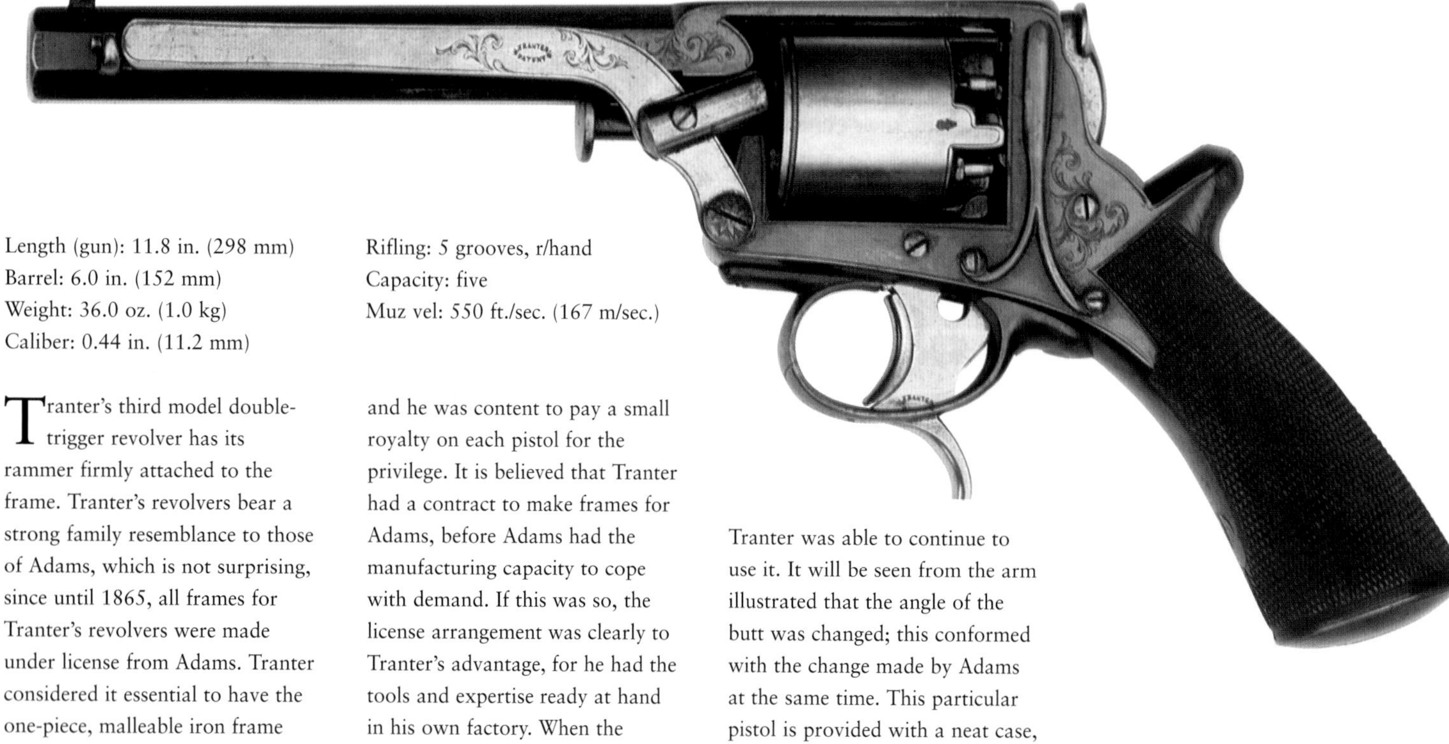

Length (gun): 11.8 in. (298 mm)
Barrel: 6.0 in. (152 mm)
Weight: 36.0 oz. (1.0 kg)
Caliber: 0.44 in. (11.2 mm)
Rifling: 5 grooves, r/hand
Capacity: five
Muz vel: 550 ft./sec. (167 m/sec.)

Tranter's third model double-trigger revolver has its rammer firmly attached to the frame. Tranter's revolvers bear a strong family resemblance to those of Adams, which is not surprising, since until 1865, all frames for Tranter's revolvers were made under license from Adams. Tranter considered it essential to have the one-piece, malleable iron frame incorporating the barrel that was a major feature of Adams's arms—and he was content to pay a small royalty on each pistol for the privilege. It is believed that Tranter had a contract to make frames for Adams, before Adams had the manufacturing capacity to cope with demand. If this was so, the license arrangement was clearly to Tranter's advantage, for he had the tools and expertise ready at hand in his own factory. When the patent expired in 1865, the system became common property and Tranter was able to continue to use it. It will be seen from the arm illustrated that the angle of the butt was changed; this conformed with the change made by Adams at the same time. This particular pistol is provided with a neat case, with bullet mold, lubricating compound, and other accessories.

FORSYTHE'S PERCUSSION SYSTEM

Above: *This lithograph of an Englishman on a pheasant shoot was produced in the same year as the Reverend Forsythe patented his new percussion system, in 1807. And the new system was designed primarily to increase such a sportsman's hunting success, by eliminating the flash of the flintlock priming pan and increasing the rate of fire.*

Although the flintlock gave good service for around 200 years, and certainly revolutionized battlefield combat, it had severe limitations. It was slow to load, susceptible to damp, the flint would need frequent renewal (sometimes as often as every thirty shots), the steel required periodic retempering, and the time lag between pulling the trigger and firing the main charge reduced accuracy. What was needed was a new system of ignition.

Progress toward this new system began in the late 1700s, when the French scientist Count Claude Louis Berthollet began experiments with fulminates—metallic chemical compounds—which would detonate under blow or friction. Attempts were made to use fulminates as gunpowder substitutes, a totally inadvisable application that resulted in some devastating factory explosions and blown-open firearms. However, fulminates would have a vital role in the history of firearms, courtesy of the Scottish minister Dr. Reverend Alexander John Forsythe.

Forsythe began to experiment with fulminate of mercury in the early 1800s. As a keen shot as well as a scientist, Forsythe had observed while hunting that game would be alerted to a flintlock shot by the flash of the priming pan. This led him to apply the fulminate to priming rather than as a main propellant. By mixing the fulminate with other fast-igniting but stable chemicals, a chemical was produced that provided near instantaneous ignition of a powder charge without the "flaring" of loose gunpowder.

Forsythe patented his new invention in 1807, and designed the "scent-bottle" lock to utilize it in weaponry. This lock was a container that held the fulminate. When this was rotated through ninety degrees and back, a small quantity of the percussion powder was deposited under the gun's hammer for firing. The scent-bottle lock worked reasonably well, and caught on in sporting use, but there remained the danger of the entire bottle exploding. Forysthe conducted further experiments to overcome this problem, combining the fulminate with gum arabic to form detonating pellets, and also placing small quantities of fulminate in slim metal tubes to be set on the touch hole and detonated by the hammer. Although Forysthe did not invent the percussion cap, which truly transformed firearms and led to the unitary cartridge, his priming system using fulminates made weaponry more accurate, quicker to fire, and more dependable in combat or hunting.

UNITED KINGDOM

WESTLEY RICHARDS REVOLVER 1856

Length (gun): 12.3 in. (311 mm)
Barrel: 6.0 in. (152 mm)
Weight: 39.0 oz. (1.1 kg)
Caliber: 0.49 in. (12.4 mm)
Rifling: 12 grooves, r/hand
Capacity: five
Muz vel: 550 ft./sec. (167 m/sec.)

The name of Westley Richards has long been well respected in British gunmaking, with a reputation for a wide variety of firearms. Their revolvers are, however, comparatively rare. This arm, which was made in about 1856, is of unusual design and construction. The barrel and top straps are a completely separate component. The barrel is held to the frame by the combination of two parts: a hook at the rear of the strap engaged in the top of the standing breech, where it was locked by means of a rotating pin, the handle of which is on the left-hand side. A sleeve below the barrel fits over the forward extension of the axis pin. This sleeve also has a small catch that engaged a slot in the axis pin to prevent accidental removal. The revolver has a double-action lock with a combless side-hammer. As this is positioned off-center, the nipples are angled so that the chamber aligns with the bore.

UNITED STATES

STARR REVOLVER 1856

Length (gun): 18.1 in. (460 mm)
Barrel: see text
Weight: 61.0 oz. (1.7 kg)
Caliber: 0.30 in.-30
Rifling: not available
Capacity: one
Muz vel: not available

The Starr Arms Company of New York made three types: a Navy double-action model of 0.36 in. (9.1 mm) caliber, a double-action Army model of 0.44 in. (11.2 mm) caliber, and a heavier 0.44 in. (11.2 mm) caliber single-action model (above). The Starr has a top strap and the barrel is hinged at the front of the frame. The removal of the screw visible below the hammer nose enabled the revolver to be broken and stripped. The cylinder was mounted by its rear-projecting ratchet and a forward plug fitting into recesses in the frame. The cylinder is plain, except for twelve oval slots, which allowed the cylinder to be locked with the hammer between nipples, thus eliminating the chance of accidental discharge. The one-piece walnut butt is held between two tangs. All metalwork is steel. It has a blade foresight, adjustable laterally; the backsight is a notch on top of the nose of the hammer.

UNITED STATES

LE MAT REVOLVER 1856

Length (gun): 13.3 in. (337 mm)
Barrel: 7.0 in. (178 mm)
Weight: 58.0 oz. (1.6 kg)
Caliber: 0.300 in./0.65 in. (7.62 mm/16.5 mm)
Rifling: 5 grooves, r/hand
Capacity: nine/one
Muz vel: 600 ft./sec. (183 m/sec.)

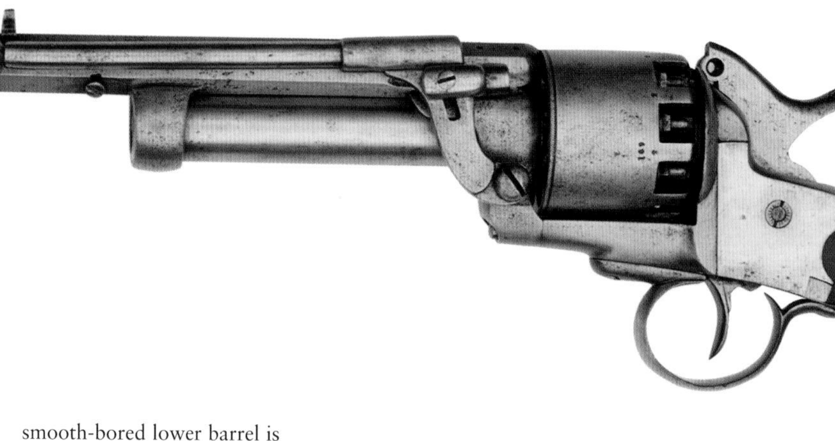

The Le Mat was patented in the United States in 1856. The frame, including the butt, is made in one piece, the lower barrel being an integral part of it. The cylinder is mounted on this lower barrel, which thus doubles as an axis pin. The upper barrel is mounted on the lower one by means of a front and rear ring, the latter having an extension which locks firmly onto the lower part of the frame. The smooth-bored lower barrel is cylindrical; the upper rifled barrel is octagonal and fitted with a foresight. The weapon's rearsight was an integral part of the hammer nose, unfortunately missing in this specimen. The revolver is fitted with a rammer of similar type to that designed by Kerr and used on the Beaumont-Adams. The cylinder, bearing English proof marks, has nine chambers. The nipple for the lower barrel is set in a deep, cylindrical recess on top of the standing breech: the hammer had a rotatable nose, which could be set to fire either barrel. The lock is single-action, access to its mechanism being via an inspection plate on the left-hand side of the frame. The top flat of the barrel is inscribed "LEMAT AND GIRARDS PATENT, LONDON." The weapon was used by the Confederate Army.

UNITED KINGDOM

BENTLEY REVOLVER 1857

UNITED KINGDOM

KERR REVOLVER (NO. 27) 1858

Length (gun): 12.0 in. (305 mm)
Barrel: 7.0 in. (178 mm)
Weight: 33.0 oz. (0.9 kg)
Caliber: 0.44 in. (11.2 mm)
Rifling: 14 grooves, r/hand
Capacity: five
Muz vel: 600 ft./sec. (183 m/sec.)

The earliest Webley-Bentley revolvers appeared in about 1853. The frame and butt were forged from a single piece of iron; the hexagonal barrel is a separate component, fastened to the axis pin by a wedge. The bottom of the lump, which has a small aperture on its inner side, is braced against a peg in the lower part of the frame. This Bentley invention was also used on the Longspur. The cylinder has wide arc-shaped partitions between the nipples and the bullets were forced into its five chambers by a Colt-type rammer. The lock is self-cocking and incorporates a safety device, also a Bentley invention, upon the hammer head: if the trigger was pressed sufficiently to bring the nose of the hammer clear of the frame, the flat stud visible at the back of the hammer could be depressed, causing the hammer's front end to rise so that it fouled the upper edge of the frame and was held clear of the nipples.

Length (gun) : 11.0 in. (279 mm)
Barrel: 5.8 in. (146 mm)
Weight: 42.0 oz. (1.2 kg)
Caliber: 0.44 in. (11.2 mm)
Rifling: 5 grooves, l/hand
Capacity: five
Muz vel: 550 ft./sec. (167 m/sec.)

When the partnership of Deane, Adams, and Deane was dissolved in 1856, it was replaced by the London Armoury Company, which was able to provide capital for the large-scale manufacture of Adams revolvers to meet military contracts. One of the shareholders was the company superintendent, James Kerr, inventor of the rammer used on the Beaumont-Adams revolver. In 1858, Kerr patented a percussion revolver (of which this, No. 27, is an early example). It had a detachable lock, which could be removed by two screws, on the assumption that any blacksmith could replace a spring to which he had easy access. The idea was successful: Kerr's revolvers proved popular in the various British colonies and also as service arms with the Confederate forces in the Civil War. The locks of the early models were of single-action type, but double-action locks were sometimes fitted later.

UNITED STATES

ALLEN AND WHEELOCK REVOLVER 1858

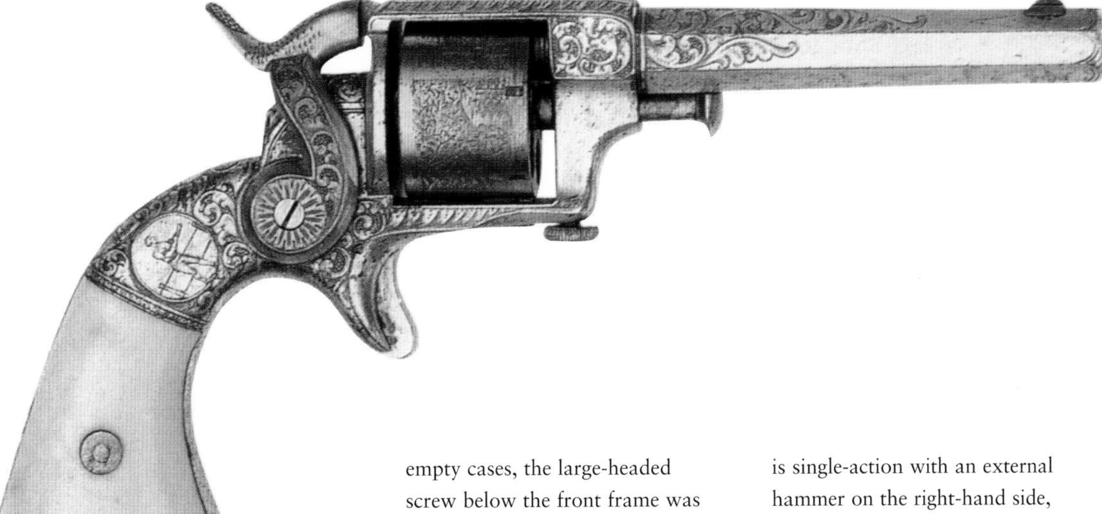

Length: 8.0 in. (203 mm)
Barrel: 4.0 in. (102 mm)
Weight: 15.0 oz. (0.4 kg)
Caliber: 0.32 in. (8.1 mm)
Rifling: 6 grooves, l/hand
Capacity: six
Muz vel: 500 ft./sec. (152 m/sec.)

This revolver, made by Ethan Allen and Thomas P. Wheelock, has a solid frame, including the butt, into which an octagonal barrel is screwed. To load the revolver or eject the empty cases, the large-headed screw below the front frame was removed, allowing the cylinder to be taken out. Empty cases could then be punched out by the axis pin, the chambers reloaded, and the cylinder replaced. This made the revolver very slow to reload, but it also greatly simplified manufacture and thus made it cheap to produce. The weapon is single-action with an external hammer on the right-hand side, access to the mechanism being gained via an oval inspection plate on the left. The trigger is "sheathed"; this reduced its bulk and made it a suitable pocket arm. The barrel and frame are crudely engraved with a standing pugilist on the right side and a kneeling one on the left, with a further motif of boxing gloves on the inspection plate cover. The butt plates are of ivory or, more likely, bone. The arm is garishly cheap in overall appearance. The left-hand flat of the barrel is marked "ALLEN AND WHEELOCK, WORCESTER, MS US" and "ALLENS PAT'S SEP 7 NOV 9 1858," and the weapon is numbered 444.

UNITED KINGDOM

DEANE-HARDING REVOLVER 1858

Length (gun): 12.0 in. (305 mm)
Barrel: 5.3 in. (133 mm)
Weight: 41.0 oz. (1.2 kg)
Caliber: 0.44 in. (11.2 mm)
Rifling: 3 grooves, r/hand
Capacity: five
Muz vel: 550 ft./sec. (167 m/sec.)

Deane was the older of Adams's two original partners. In 1858, Deane began the manufacture of a new revolver patented that year by William Harding. This is the 54-bore service caliber. The barrel, barrel lump, and upper strap constitute a completely separate component from the frame. To strip the weapon, the pin from the hole in front of the hammer nose was removed. The barrel was thus pushed down to an angle of forty-five degrees to disengage a hook at the bottom of the lump from a corresponding socket in the lower frame. The barrel group incorporates a rammer, also patented by Harding. When the lever below the barrel was released and pulled downward, a hook drew the ram into the bottom chamber until the lever was vertically downward.

EUROPE

LONGSPUR-TYPE REVOLVER 1860

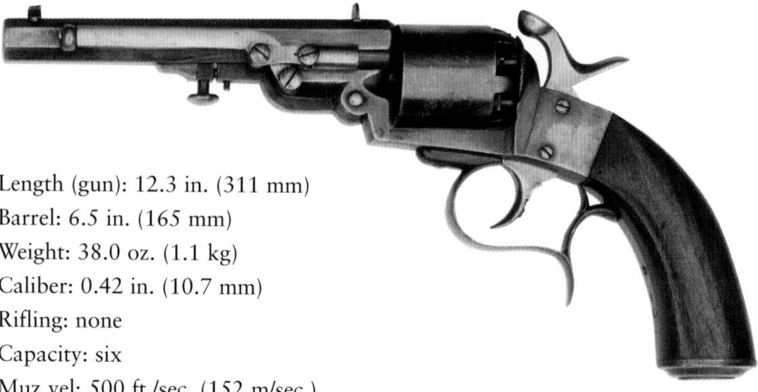

Length (gun): 12.3 in. (311 mm)
Barrel: 6.5 in. (165 mm)
Weight: 38.0 oz. (1.1 kg)
Caliber: 0.42 in. (10.7 mm)
Rifling: none
Capacity: six
Muz vel: 500 ft./sec. (152 m/sec.)

The style of this weapon suggests that it is a Western Europe copy of the Webley Longspur (qv). The octagonal barrel is fitted to the frame in a complex way: a cylindrical hole in the lump below the breech end fits over a very long axis pin; the bottom of the lump is also braced against the lower frame to make a very rigid joint. To remove the barrel it would have been necessary to slide back the mushroom-shaped stud below it, then draw down the lever behind it. This disengaged a half-round locking pin from a corresponding recess on the axis pin, allowing the entire barrel to be drawn forward. The lever of the Kerr rammer locked into a hook on the left-hand side of the barrel. When the lever was raised vertically, the ram was forced into the chamber.

FRANCE

LEFAUCHEUX FIST PISTOL 1860

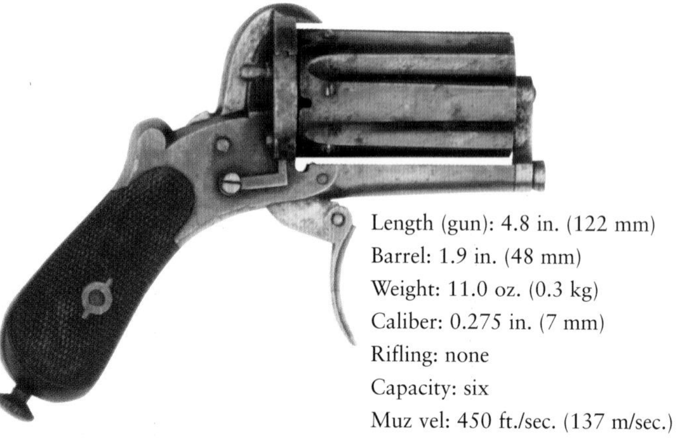

Length (gun): 4.8 in. (122 mm)
Barrel: 1.9 in. (48 mm)
Weight: 11.0 oz. (0.3 kg)
Caliber: 0.275 in. (7 mm)
Rifling: none
Capacity: six
Muz vel: 450 ft./sec. (137 m/sec.)

This type of pistol is called a *coup de poing* (fist pistol) in France. Its fluted, pepperbox cylinder is made from a single piece of metal, and the front end of the cylinder axis pin is supported by a bracket screwed to the front end of the lower frame. The standing breech is a flat, circular plate: a semicircular portion is cut out on the right-hand side for loading. This aperture is filled by a bottom-hinged gate fitted with a small stud to give purchase; its bottom end bore on the L-shaped spring below it. The lock is self-cocking; the trigger hinges forward. The cylinder was free to rotate until the trigger was pressed; a cylinder-stop rose from the lower frame and engaged one of the cylinder studs. After firing, the empty cases were pushed out through the loading gate with an extractor pin. Such arms sometimes incorporated brass knuckles and a dagger, and are known as "Apache pistols," a term for the denizens of the underworld of nineteenth-century Paris.

UNITED KINGDOM

ADAMS REVOLVER CONVERSION 1860

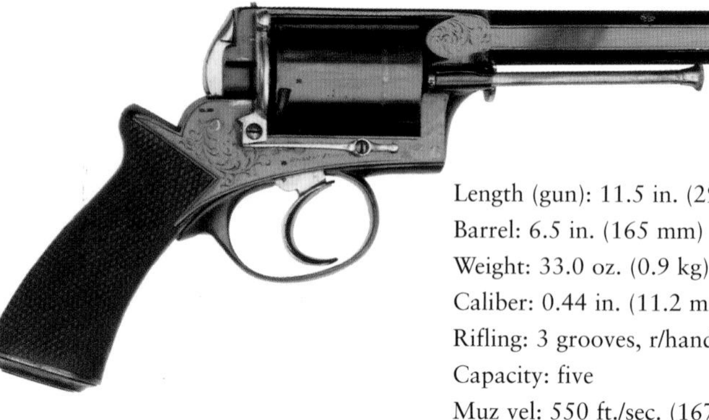

Length (gun): 11.5 in. (292 mm)
Barrel: 6.5 in. (165 mm)
Weight: 33.0 oz. (0.9 kg)
Caliber: 0.44 in. (11.2 mm)
Rifling: 3 grooves, r/hand
Capacity: five
Muz vel: 550 ft./sec. (167 m/sec.)

This revolver is an Adams self-cocking percussion arm, converted to take centerfire cartridges. The weapon has a bored-through, five-chambered cylinder: this necessitated the fitting of a loading gate. The gate is hinged at the bottom and opened backward. Its bottom end was supported on a flat spring screwed to the lower part of the frame; the pressure of the spring held the gate firmly open or closed. A piece of metal of the required shape has been screwed to the left-hand side of the frame to prevent the cartridges slipping out, fitted in front of the spring safety which holds the hammer clear of the rounds. The only other addition is an ejector rod working in a sleeve, which has been brazed onto the frame. The barrel is engraved "P.W. ADAIR COLDSTREAM GUARDS." An upper flat is engraved "CRIMEA, SEBASTOPOL." He was later appointed Colonel-Commandant of the 4th (Militia) Battalion of the Somerset Light Infantry.

UNITED KINGDOM

DUAL-IGNITION REVOLVER 1860

Length (gun): 10.8 in. (274 mm)
Barrel: 5.5 in. (140 mm)
Weight: 33.0 oz. (0.9 kg)
Caliber: 0.44 in. (11.2 mm)
Rifling: 12 grooves, r/hand
Capacity: five
Muz vel: 550 ft./sec. (167 m/sec.)

Dual-ignition revolvers were transitional between the percussion and centerfire systems. All that was necessary to switch from percussion to centerfire was to change the cylinder. The revolver seen here is one such. Its origin is by no means certain. It is of Webley style and is marked "WEBLEYS PATENT," but since this inscription appears on many arms with little or no connection with the firm, it is not a reliable guide. Webley did make a dual-purpose revolver of similar type, but it had a Kerr-type rammer on the left-hand side. In fact, the arm shown is probably a hybrid from some unknown workshop. It is of robust construction and the cylinders were easily changed (the cartridge cylinder is, unfortunately, missing from this example). The rammer, the lever of which acted downward, drove a very tight ram into the chambers and was equally effective for loading bullets or ejecting cases, the latter by bearing on their front edges. It was, however, slow to operate, because of the need for absolute alignment of ram and chamber. It has a hinged loading-gate for use with centerfire cartridges. This type of arm had a short life.

UNITED KINGDOM

TRANTER REVOLVER CONVERSION 1860

Length (gun): 10.3 in. (260 mm)
Barrel: 6.0 in. (152 mm)
Weight: 26.0 oz. (0.7 kg)
Caliber: 0.38 in. (9.6 mm)
Rifling: 5 grooves, r/hand
Capacity: five
Muz vel: 600 ft./sec. (183 m/sec.)

Although he is, perhaps, best known for his double-trigger arms, William Tranter also made a number of single-trigger, double-action revolvers from 1856 until 1863, and this weapon was originally of that type, although it subsequently underwent conversion. The perfection of the metallic rimfire cartridge naturally led to a demand for revolvers to fire it, and many existing arms were converted to meet this demand. In this Tranter conversion, the main change was the provision of a new, bored-through cylinder, with the addition of a loading gate on the right-hand side of the frame and a shield on the left to prevent the cartridges from slipping out. A new hammer, suitable for the firing of rimfire rounds, was added. There is no integral ejector, but the empty cases could be pushed out through the loading gate by means of a rod, which screwed into the butt when it was not in use.

1848–1862
THE HANDGUNS OF THE AMERICAN WEST

Seldom has one particular type of weapon become so associated with a historical era as the handgun and the American West, where a large proportion of the population carried a weapon. Many of these weapons were the products of famous names such as Colt, Remington, and Smith & Wesson. They were sold in vast numbers and, like today's automobiles, the customer was faced with a bewildering variety of models and calibers. Then, having settled on the model, there was a further variety of options, such as barrel length, metal finish, type of butt grip, and, for the wealthier, engravings. Apart from such big-name manufacturers, however, there was also a large number of much smaller gunsmiths whose names are now all but forgotten, but whose products also took part in the stirring events on the frontier. A small selection of what was available is shown here.

Samuel Colt (1814–1862) never claimed to have invented the revolver, but he certainly brought it to an unprecedented state of perfection. Initially lacking his own factory, one of Colt's earliest models was produced by Eli Whitney, an example being the 2nd Model Navy Revolver (9), but then Colt was able to buy Whitney out and set up his factory at Hartford, Connecticut, where he started to produce weapons under his own name. One of the first was the Dragoon revolver of 1848; an example of the 3rd Model Dragoon is shown (3). Then, as now, the placing of an order by the Army or Navy inevitably impressed civilian customers and among the most famous Colt products were the Model 1851 Navy revolver (6, shown here in 0.36 in. caliber) and the long series for the Army. The latter included the Model 1860 Army revolver 0.44 in. (7), and the most famous of all, the single-action, which appeared in a variety of calibers, including 0.38-40 (14), and in various barrel lengths, such as the 0.45 in. caliber, long barrel (15), and the 0.45 in. caliber short barrel (17). Later came the Model 1878 double-action Army revolver (18). Colt also produced special models for law enforcement officers, such as this Model 1862 police revolver in 0.36 in. caliber (8), while weapons intended for the civilian market bore dramatic and eye-catching names, such as Thunderer (16). Smaller firearms produced for self-defense included the Model 1849 pocket revolver 0.31 in. (4) and the Model 1855 side hammer pocket revolver 2nd series (5). Innovations not only resulted in new models, but in modifications for older models, such as this Model 1861 Navy (10), factory-modified in Colt's own works or by outside agencies, such as the Reynolds-modified Model 1860 Army (11).

Other big-name players included Smith & Wesson, among whose products were the No. 2 Army 0.32 in. (23); and the No. 3 Single-Action Army (24) and 1st Model American Single-Action (25), both firing the 0.44 in. S&W round. Another Smith & Wesson weapon was the Double-Action 1st Model (26), while Remington, which was more famous for its rifles, also produced some revolvers, including the New Model Army (12).

The weapons produced by the Volcanic Company, which enjoyed a limited popularity in the 1850s, used a lever action to load from a tubular magazine housing eight or ten rounds, and their products such as the Navy

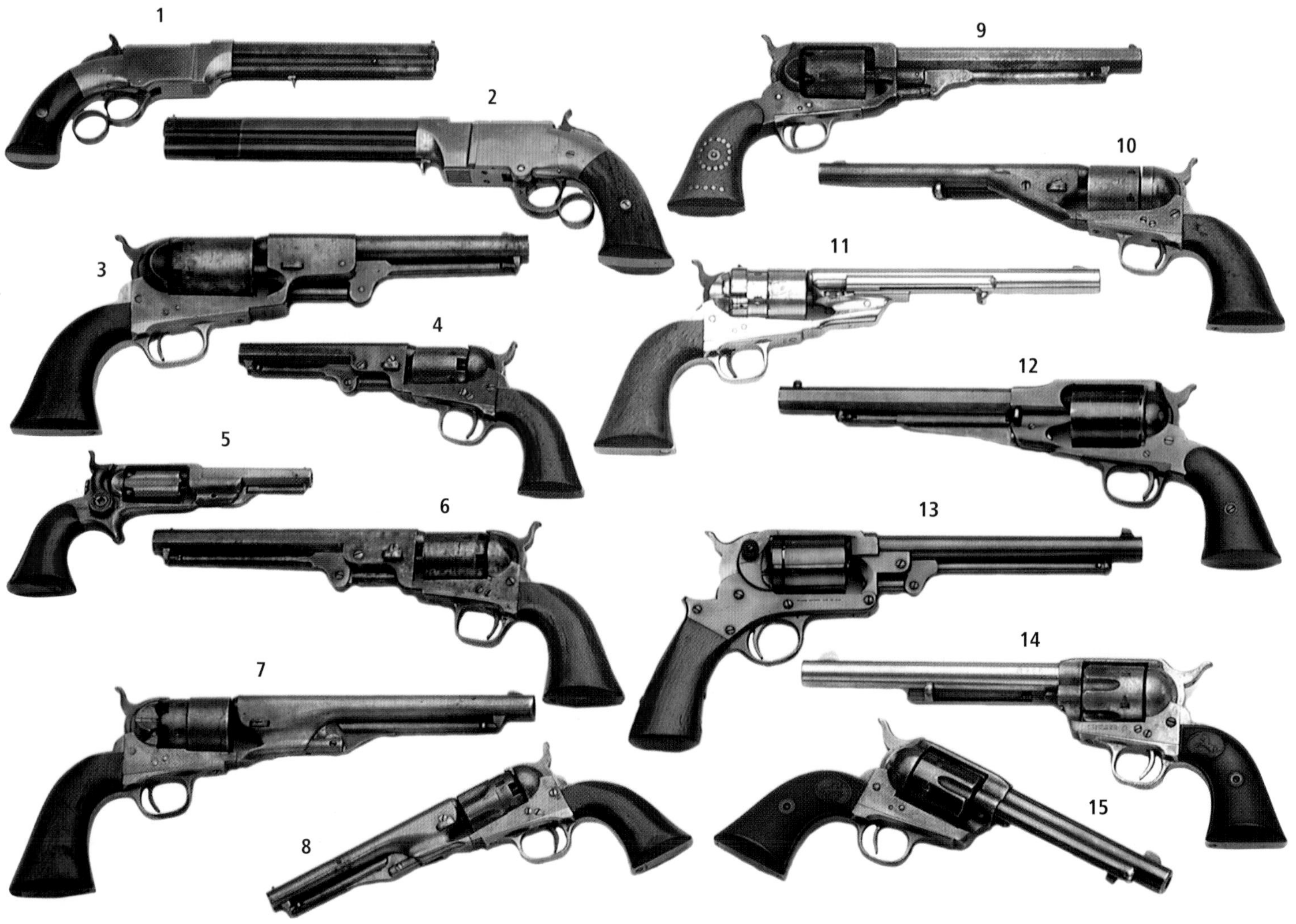

No. 1 (1) and Navy No. 2 pistols (2) were both well made and accurate. Volcanic was subsequently renamed, first as the New Haven Arms Company and then as the Winchester Arms Company, after which time it concentrated on the famous rifles.

Other gunsmiths were less well known, but had their own niches in the market. These included the Starr single-action Model 1863 Army (13); Merwin & Hulbert Army revolver, early type with square butt (19) and bird's-head butt (20); Forehand & Wadsworth New Model Army revolver (22); Manhattan Firearms Company pocket model 0.31 in. caliber (27); and the Hopkins & Allen XL No. 8 Army revolver (21).

That famous men did not always use famous-name guns is borne out by the two revolvers carried by Sheriff Patrick Floyd Garrett at Fort Sumner, who on the night of July 14, 1881, shot Billy the Kid with a 0.45 in. Colt Single-Action. Among his extensive personal armory, however, was this Merwin & Hulbert 0.38 in. caliber with ivory grips (29) and the Hopkins & Allen 0.32 in. (28), both of them inscribed with his name.

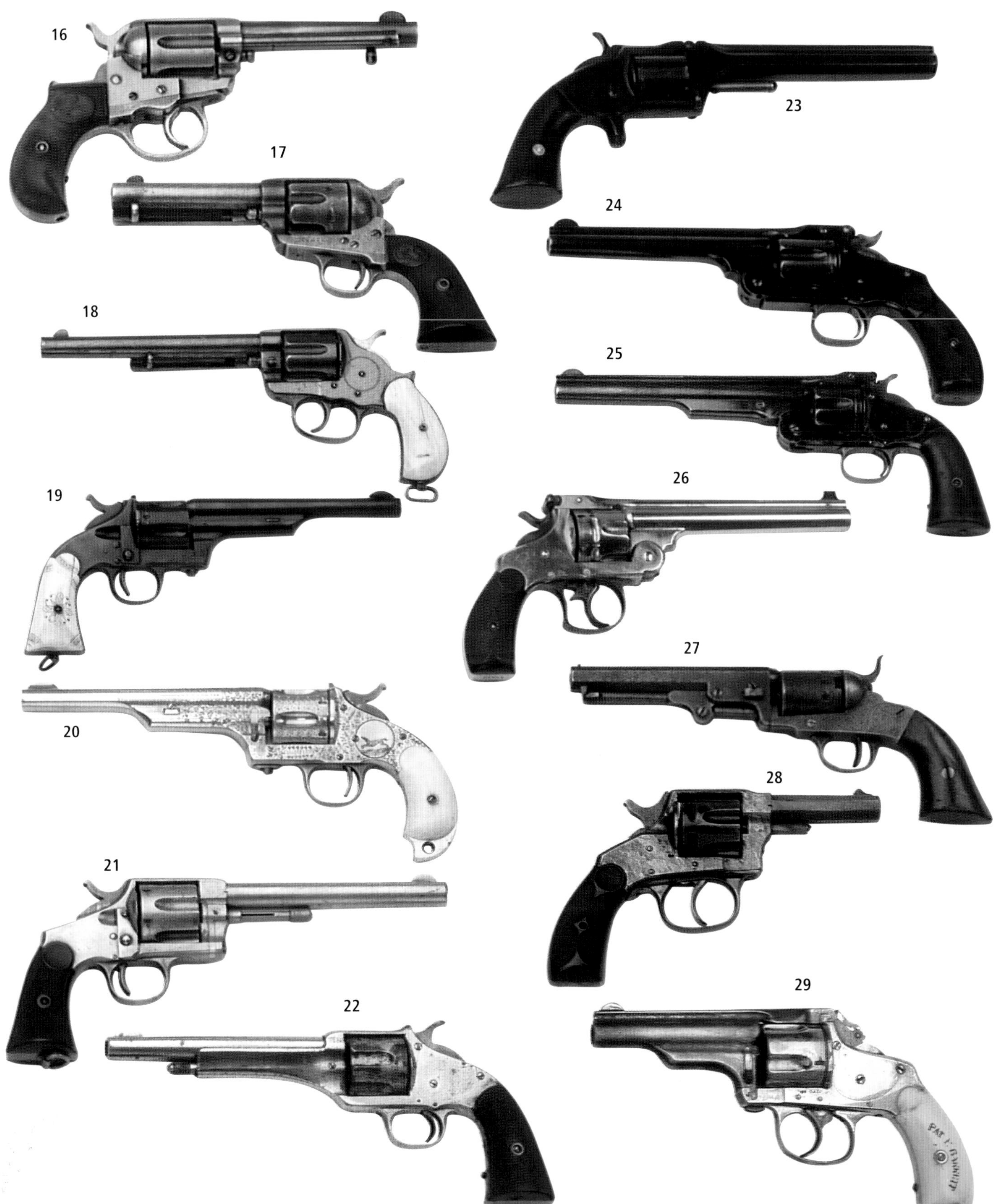

UNITED STATES

SMITH & WESSON TIP-UP POCKET REVOLVER 1860

Length (gun): 7.0 in. (178 mm)
Barrel: 3.2 in. (81 mm)
Weight: 11.5 oz. (0.3 kg)
Caliber: 0.22 in. (5.6 mm)
Rifling: 5 grooves, r/hand
Capacity: seven
Muz vel: 500 ft./sec. (152 m/sec.)

By the mid-1850s, Smith & Wesson had designed a pocket revolver to fire rimfire cartridges and were only awaiting the expiry of Colt's patent for a revolving cylinder to put it onto the market. They also acquired Rollin White's American patent for a bored-through cylinder and agreed to pay him twenty-five cents for every weapon of that type they made. The first, or Model No. 1, appeared in 1857. Because the shape of its brass frame made it difficult to manufacture economically, a second series, of which this is a specimen, was produced. The octagonal barrel is hinged at the top of the frame, just above the front of the cylinder, and opened upward when the small catch just below the front of the cylinder was pushed up. The cylinder stop consisted of a flat spring on top of the frame. To reload, the cylinder was removed and the empty copper rimfire cases were pushed out with the pin below the barrel.

UNITED STATES

SMITH & WESSON 0.32 IN. NO 2 (ARMY) REVOLVER 1861

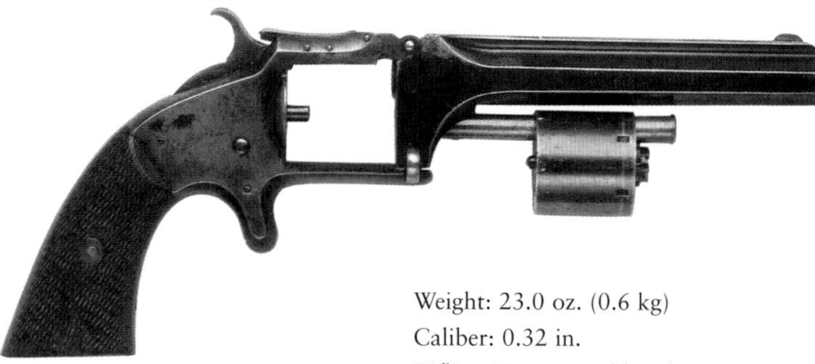

Length (gun): 10.0 in. (254 mm)
Barrel: 5.2 in. (132 mm)
Weight: 23.0 oz. (0.6 kg)
Caliber: 0.32 in.
Rifling: 7 grooves, l/hand
Capacity: six
Muz vel: 550 ft./sec. (167 m/sec.)

Smith & Wesson had acquired the Rollin White patent for revolvers with bored-through cylinders which would take self-contained metallic cartridges. In 1857, the company produced such a cartridge, made of copper with the percussion powder arranged around the internal circumference of the rim, thus known as "rimfire" cartridges. Smith & Wesson's first designs using this principle were all on the lines of the No. 2 revolver seen here. There was a hinge at the top of the front plate of the frame and a catch at the foot, so that when the catch was released, the octagonal barrel could be lifted up, giving rise to the generic name "tip-up revolver." Once the barrel was out of the way, the cylinder was removed, reversed in the shooter's hand, and then each chamber was pressed in turn against the built-in spike. Once all six empty cases had been ejected, the shooter reloaded and replaced the cylinder.

UNITED STATES

COLT 0.44 IN. MODEL 1860 ARMY REVOLVER

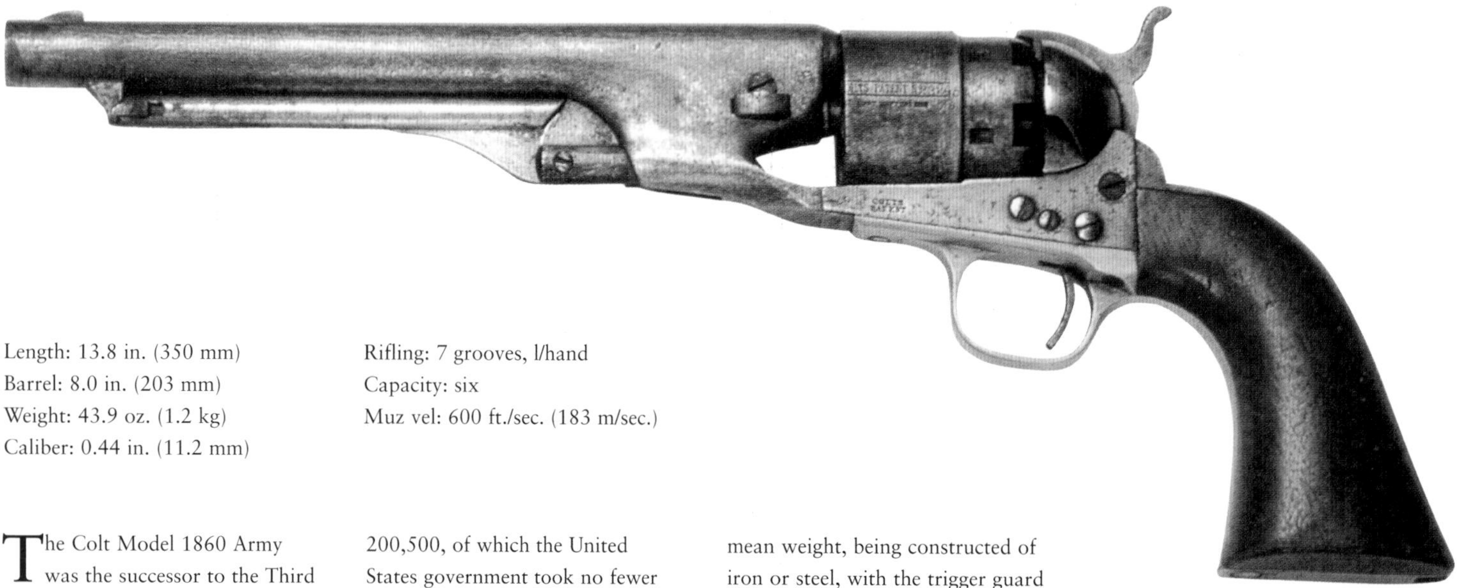

Length: 13.8 in. (350 mm)
Barrel: 8.0 in. (203 mm)
Weight: 43.9 oz. (1.2 kg)
Caliber: 0.44 in. (11.2 mm)
Rifling: 7 grooves, l/hand
Capacity: six
Muz vel: 600 ft./sec. (183 m/sec.)

The Colt Model 1860 Army was the successor to the Third Model Dragoon and became probably the most widely used of all handguns during the American Civil War—by both sides. The production figures speak for themselves, with production over the period 1860 to 1873 totaling 200,500, of which the United States government took no fewer than 127,156. It was a percussion weapon, using rammer loading from the front of the cylinder, with the great majority of shooters taking the precaution of having a stock of ready-prepared paper cartridges. The weapon was no mean weight, being constructed of iron or steel, with the trigger guard and front strap made of brass. Aiming was by means of a brass blade foresight and a notch cut in the hammer's nose serving as the rearsight. There were many minor variations over the long production run, but the caliber remained unchanged at 0.44 in., unlike the Colt Navy Model 1861, which came in either 0.36 or 0.44 in. caliber.

UNITED KINGDOM

BEAUMONT-ADAMS 0.32 IN. REVOLVER 1861

Length (gun): 8.5 in. (216 mm)
Barrel: 4.5 in. (114 mm)
Weight: 24.0 oz. (0.7 kg)
Caliber: 0.32 in.
Rifling: 3 grooves, r/hand
Capacity: five
Muz vel: 450 ft./sec. (137 m/sec.)

This is a very ornate example of a Beaumont-Adams revolver, which was made by the London Armoury Company in about 1861. It is well blued and inlaid with gold, with a crew on the butt. It is of 12-bore (0.32 in.) which was about the smallest caliber considered to have adequate stopping power. These weapons could be fired either by simple pressure on the trigger or by the preliminary manual cocking of the hammer, which, in effect, combined the best locking features of the Colts and the original Adams in a somewhat more orthodox manner than that of Tranter. Deane, one of Adams's original partners, in his *Manual of Firearms* published in 1858, suggested that the addition of the Beaumont lock to Adams' original revolver made it over-complex and liable to derangement.

UNITED KINGDOM

TRANTER RIMFIRE REVOLVER 1863

Length (gun): 12.0 in. (305 mm)
Barrel: 6.5 in. (165 mm)
Weight: 50.0 oz. (1.4 kg)
Caliber: 0.45 in. (11.4 mm)
Rifling: 5 grooves, r/hand
Capacity: six
Muz vel: 650 ft./sec. (197 m/sec.)

Tranter produced a good many double-action percussion revolvers, in a variety of sizes, in order to compete with Beaumont-Adams arms, especially military arms in service calibers. Once the popularity of the new Smith & Wesson breech-loading revolvers was assured, Tranter, a competent and enterprising individual, wasted little time: by 1863, he had placed on the market the rimfire revolver seen here. This was the first of its type to be produced (or, it might be safer to say, acknowledged) by a British maker. Tranter had used the Adams frame, under license, for his revolvers, and the cylinder (which is, of course, bored through) has six chambers instead of the five customary in Tranter's earlier models; the rear ends of the chambers are recessed to accommodate the rims of the cartridges. There is a bottom-hinged loading gate on the right-hand side of the standing breech.

UNITED STATES

REMINGTON ARMY MODEL 1863 REVOLVER

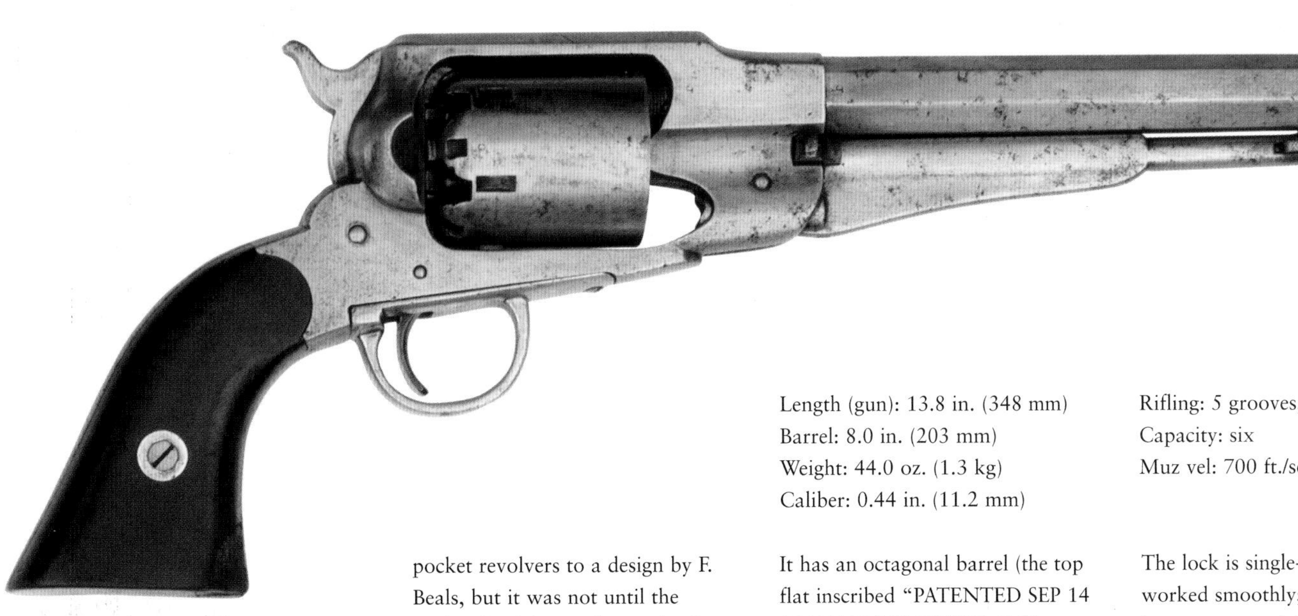

Length (gun): 13.8 in. (348 mm)
Barrel: 8.0 in. (203 mm)
Weight: 44.0 oz. (1.3 kg)
Caliber: 0.44 in. (11.2 mm)
Rifling: 5 grooves, r/hand
Capacity: six
Muz vel: 700 ft./sec. (213 m/sec.)

Eliphalet Remington was a blacksmith who turned to gunmaking fairly early in his career. He initially specialized in military rifles and gained an enviable reputation for quality. By 1857, he had begun to make a few pocket revolvers to a design by F. Beals, but it was not until the outbreak of the Civil War that he began to produce revolvers in quantity. This example is the improved Army Model of 1863; it was a fine arm in its day, perhaps its major feature being its solid frame, which gave it great rigidity. It has an octagonal barrel (the top flat inscribed "PATENTED SEP 14 1850 E REMINGTON AND SONS ILION NEW YORK USA NEW MODEL") that screws into the frame, and a plain, six-shot cylinder with rectangular slots for the stop. The axis pin could be removed by drawing it forward. The lock is single-action and worked smoothly; cocking the hammer rotated the cylinder. The brass trigger guard is rather small; it would not have been easy to operate the trigger wearing gloves. This arm was used extensively by Union troops in the Civil War and remained popular afterwards.

HANDGUNS USED BY THE CONFEDERATE STATES ARMY

The Confederated States Army had control of only a few of its own armaments manufacturing facilities at the start of the Civil War. It developed more during the course of the conflict, but it was always limited by lack of production equipment and skilled manpower, as well as by the scarcity of materials. The Army had to use a mixture of weapons it could find at the start of the war, new manufacture of antiquated designs and of a few new designs of its own, weapons captured from Union forces, and a small number of imports, especially from Great Britain.

At the outbreak of war, the weapons immediately available included antiquated flintlock pistols like the government-pattern Model 1836 (1) and Model 1842 (2), and production of such weapons continued at the Virginia Manufactory, resulting in their 1st Model (3) and 2nd Model (4) pistols. Not all production was of such old designs; modern weapons came from many small gunsmiths, among whom were T. W. Cofer (8), J. H. Dance and Brothers (12), J. F. Garrett & Co. (7), Griswold & Gurnison (9), Leech & Rigdon (10), Le Mat's 1st Model (5) and 2nd Model (11), and Wesson & Leavitt (6). Perhaps the largest single source was weapons captured from the Union Army, which covered the entire range of Northern equipment, in which Colt products were inevitably largely featured. These are just a few representative examples of such captured Colt equipment: Model 1848 Army (19), Model 1849 pocket revolver (13), Whitney Navy (a Colt design) (14), Model 1851 Navy (21), Model 1860 with fluted cylinder (15) and with non-fluted cylinder (20), and the Massachusetts Arms Company Adams-patent Navy revolver (22)—actually, a British design produced under license in the United States.

Another source was direct importation from Europe, particularly Great Britain, some examples being: Beaumont-Adams (16), Kerr (23), Tranter with single trigger (17) and with double-trigger (18), and Webley (24).

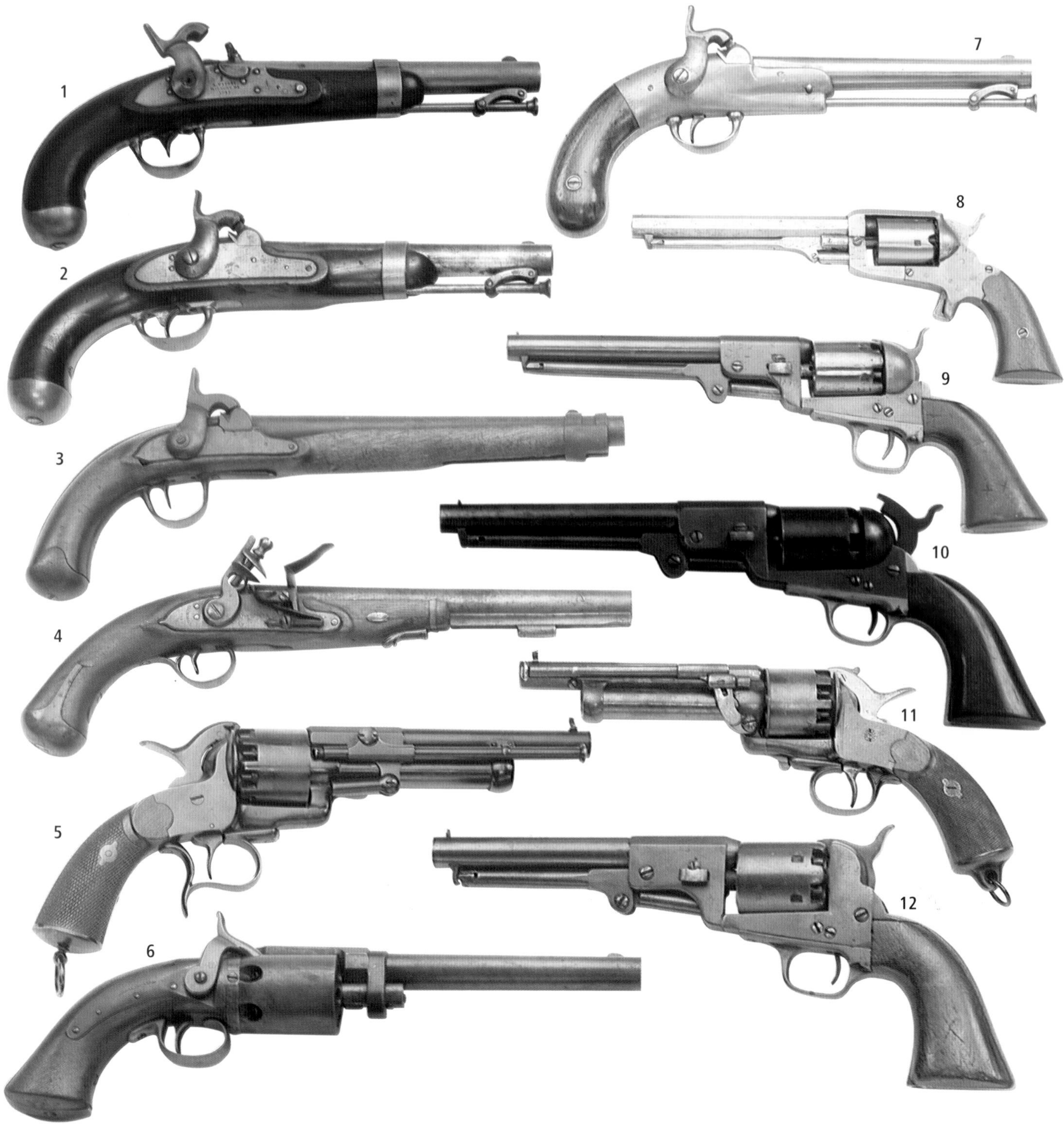

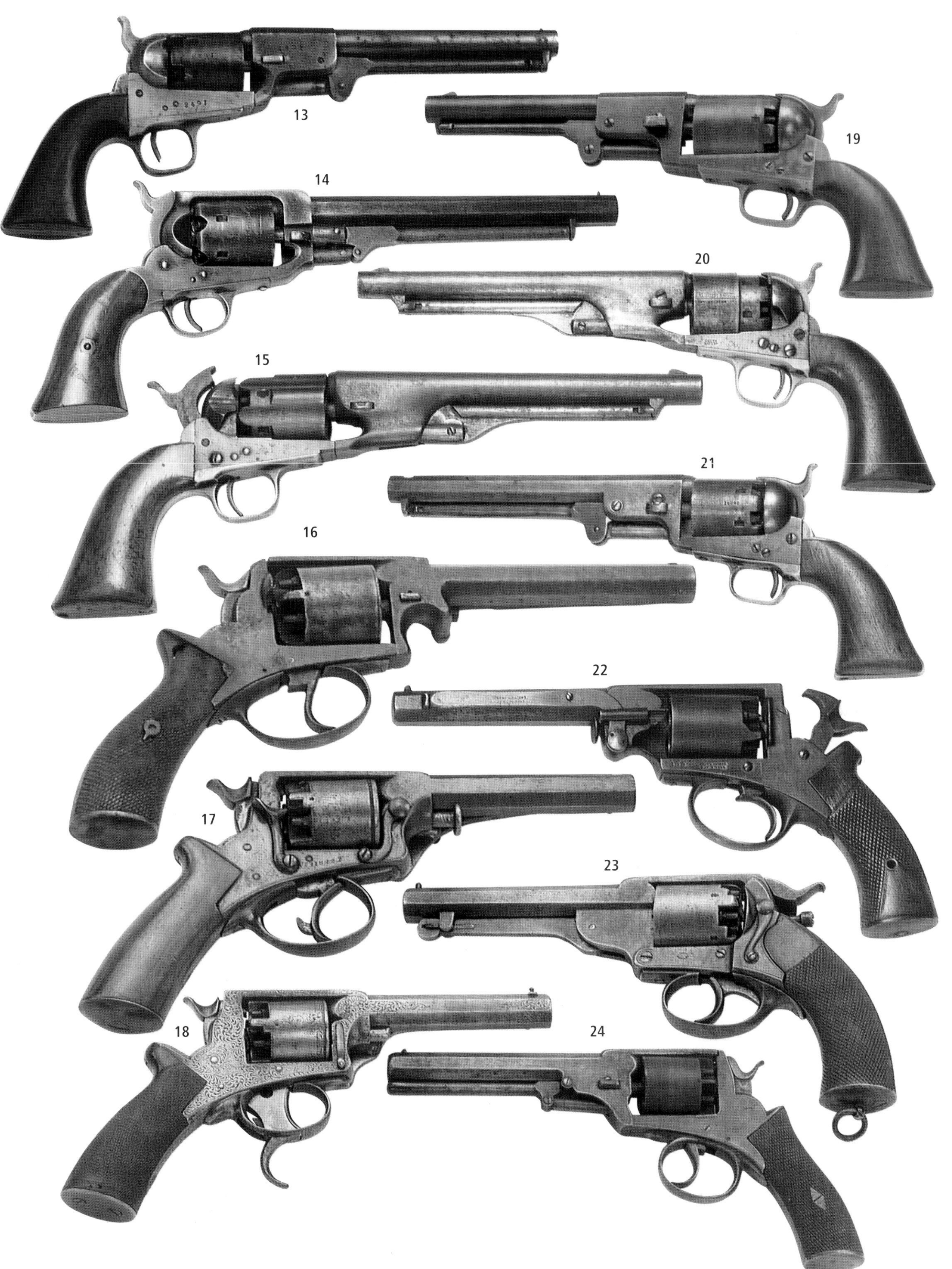
13
19
14
20
15
21
16
22
17
23
18
24

1863-1898
COLT'S CARTRIDGE COMPETITORS

The Rollin White patent for the bored-through cylinder was held by Smith & Wesson and they challenged any infringement with great vigor, but when it expired a host of new revolvers appeared on the market, of which the most successful was the Colt Single-Service Army and its civilian versions, such as the Peacemaker. The US Army Ordnance Department conducted official tests, concluding that what the Colt lacked in manufacturing precision it more than made up for in reliability and its ability to withstand rough handling, making it an ideal weapon for military and frontier use. But Colt by no means had matters all their own way, and there were a number of serious competitors, some of which are shown here.

Smith & Wesson's success in winning an order from Russia meant that it had to devote its entire capacity for five years to meeting the order. The model that won this order was the No. 3 Model Army Russian (20), which used a special 0.44 in. cartridge specified by the Russian Army. This was later succeeded by the New Model No. 3 Russian (23), in the same 0.44 in. caliber, which incorporated some changes; note, for example, the absence of the finger spur in the later gun. In an effort to regain its place in the domestic market, Smith & Wesson produced the No. 3 American model (21) in 0.32 in. caliber, which was later improved by Schofield who installed a better barrel latch (22). Then Smith & Wesson themselves upgraded the design with the 0.44 in. double-action 1881 Frontier revolver (24), but it never supplanted the Colt.

Remington was, of course, one of the major contenders. The original Remington Model 1863 was a percussion weapon, but various conversions

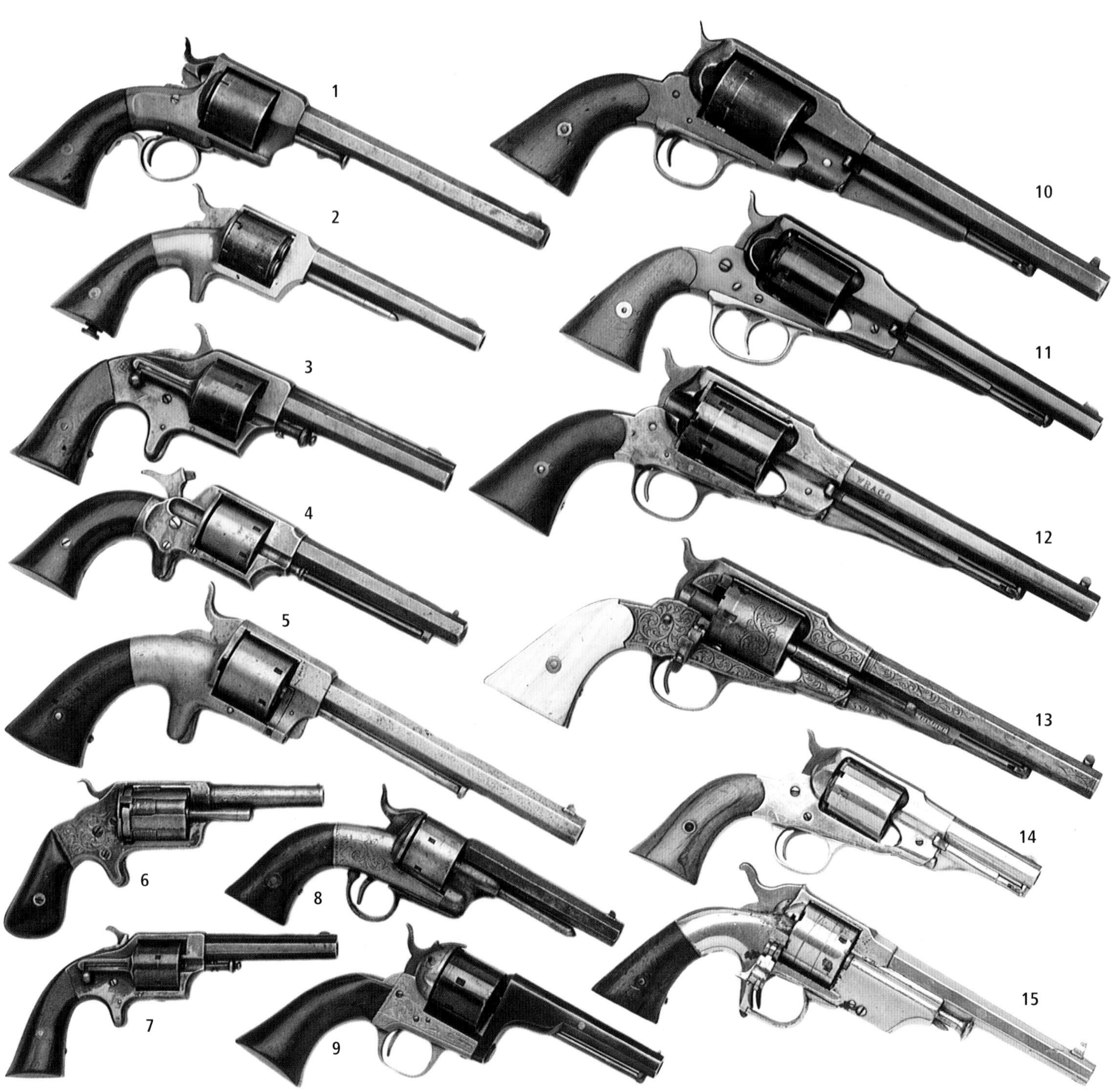

to rimfire cartridges were designed, resulting in the New Model Army of 1875, various versions of which are shown at (10), (12), and, in an elaborately engraved version (13). Other products on the market were the Double-Action New Model belt pistol (11), No. 2 Pocket Revolver (14), and, albeit slightly later, the Model 1890 Single-Action Army revolver (19), of which about 2,000 were made.

A company with a high reputation in the West for well-made products was Merwin & Hulbert, whose guns included the Open-top Army revolver shown here in blued (16) and nickel-plated finishes (17), which was later produced with a top strap (18).

Allen & Wheelock produced a number of revolver designs. Its "center hammer/lipfire" (15) had a notch cut into the rear of the each chamber to enable the hammer face to strike the cartridge "lips." The Bacon Company encountered the wrath of Smith & Wesson when it marketed its 0.32 in. rimfire pocket pistol (8), which incorporated a cylinder with bored-through cylinders; having been found guilty of infringing the copyright, the company was ordered to withdraw it. A later model (5), produced after the copyright had expired, was more successful.

Other models challenging Colt's supremacy included: Brooklyn Firearm Company's "Slocum" pocket pistol in 0.32 in. rimfire (6), Eagle Arms Company's cup-primed pocket revolver (7), Merwin & Bray's pocket pistol (3), Moore's "Seven-Shooter" 0.32 in. rimfire pocket revolver (9), Pond's pocket/belt pistol (2), Prescott's single-action, six-shot Navy revolver in 0.38 in. rimfire (1), and Uhlinger's pocket revolver in 0.32 in. rimfire (4).

UNITED STATES

HAMMOND BULLDOG PISTOL 1864

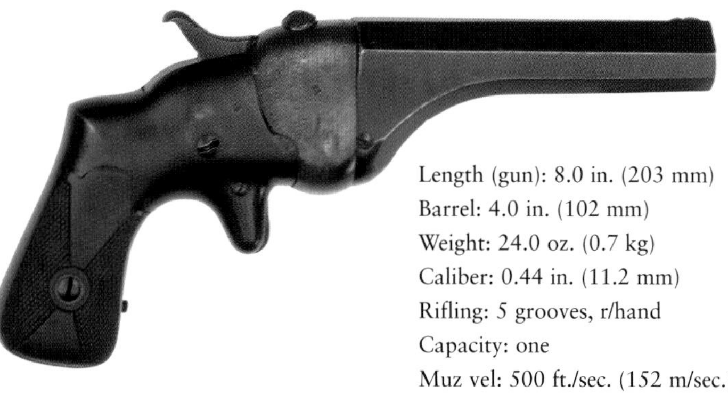

Length (gun): 8.0 in. (203 mm)
Barrel: 4.0 in. (102 mm)
Weight: 24.0 oz. (0.7 kg)
Caliber: 0.44 in. (11.2 mm)
Rifling: 5 grooves, r/hand
Capacity: one
Muz vel: 500 ft./sec. (152 m/sec.)

Single-shot cartridge weapons of the type broadly classed as derringers became popular during the American Civil War, when many soldiers, particularly on the Northern side, liked to carry a small, concealed pistol as a back-up gun for use in emergency. The weapon illustrated here was produced by the Connecticut Arms and Manufacturing Company, Naubuc, Connecticut, under a patent dated October 25, 1864. It was generally known under the trade name of "Hammond Bulldog." It was a solid, robust arm capable of firing a powerful cartridge. Access to the breech was gained by placing the hammer at half-cock, pressing the top stud, and then pushing the breechblock to the left. The pivot of the block was so arranged that, as the block moved, it also retracted about 0.2 in. (5 mm), thus bringing the extractor into play.

SPAIN

ARRIABAN PINFIRE REVOLVER 1865

Length (gun): 11.5 in. (292 mm)
Barrel: 6.4 in. (163 mm)
Weight: 34.0 oz. (1.0 kg)
Caliber: 0.43 in. (11 mm)
Rifling: 4 grooves, l/hand
Capacity: six
Muz vel: 650 ft./sec. (197 m/sec.)

This weapon is very closely based on the Lefaucheux Pinfire Naval revolver (qv). The pinfire was adopted by Norway, Sweden, and Spain as an arm for officers and certain categories of mounted troops. The weapon illustrated here was made by Arriaban of Eibar, probably in the mid-1860s, when Spain first adopted the arm. Spanish gunsmiths were noted for their barrels; they had considerable deposits of high-grade iron ore in the Biscayan area. Although they were never able to compete in the highly industrialized areas of Northern Europe, they maintained a considerable export trade with their colonies in South America, where cheapness was much more important than high quality. The weapon seen here is of solid construction, with a round barrel fastened to the axis pin and the lower frame. A rearward extension to the barrel lump slides over the lower extension of the frame (to which it is screwed) and fits into a slot in the lower part of the standing breech. The lock is single-action and there is a lower spur on the trigger guard to give added grip for the firer's fingers.

UNITED KINGDOM

TRANTER REVOLVER, POCKET MODEL 1866

Length (gun): 9.5 in. (241 mm)
Barrel: 4.3 in. (109 mm)
Weight: 22.0 oz. (0.6 kg)
Caliber: 0.38 in. (9.6 mm)
Rifling: 3 grooves, r/hand
Capacity: five
Muz vel: 500 ft./sec. (152 m/sec.)

Tranter's revolvers were made in a variety of calibers: 38-bore (0.500 in./12.7 mm), 50-bore (0.45 in./11.4 mm), 54-bore (0.44 in./11.2 mm), 80-bore (0.38 in./9.6 mm), 90-bore (0.36 in./9.1 mm), and 120-bore (0.32 in./8.1 mm). This pistol is 80-bore (0.38 in./9.6 mm), and it is the second model, with detachable rammer. Like all Tranter's revolvers in this series, it conformed closely to the standard design and was fitted with the patent safety device and the usual cylinder axis retaining spring on the right-hand side. Like all Tranter's arms, it bears the inscription "W. TRANTER PATENT" on the upper trigger, just above the guard, and on the rammer, opposite the ram itself. The frame is of the later pattern, with raked-back butt; as it does not bear the words "Adams Patent," it must be presumed to have been made after the patent's expiry in 1865. It bears the usual light engraving on the sides of the frame and at the breech end of the barrel, the top flat of which is engraved "GASQUOINE AND DYSON, MARKET PLACE, MANCHESTER," this being the name of the retailer. This is in every respect a neat and compact weapon and, although a pocket pistol, it is of sufficient caliber to give it very reasonable stopping-power.

Highwaymen and Pistols

Although armed robbery has been a feature of society since the invention of weapons, it was the pistol that gave rise to the highwayman. A highwayman required a weapon that was easily concealed, enabled him to control his victims (not necessarily kill them) from a distance, and left him with a free hand to remove or accept valuables. These criteria generally ruled out the sword and the matchlock pistol—a smoldering match could not be concealed (it would either extinguish or cause a fire if hidden under clothing).

The advent of the wheel-lock pistol in the first half of the sixteenth century, however, brought a marked increase in incidents of mounted robbery. The wheel-lock was portable and easily concealed, and it could be loaded in advance and operated with one hand while the other controlled the horse and the flow of valuables. In England, the threat posed by the wheel-lock was soon recognized by the government. In 1537 Henry VIII imposed legal restrictions on ownership of firearms less than 0.75 m (2.5 ft.) long. Queen Elizabeth also attempted similar prohibitions between 1575 and 1600 as concern about pistol crime grew, as evidenced by this extract from a letter from the Privy Council to the Lord Keeper and the Lord Treasurer in 1575:

> Her Majesty having been advertised of numerous highway robberies which have lately been committed in divers parts of the realm, and that it is a common thing for the thieves to carry pistols whereby they either murder out of hand before they rob, or else put her subjects in such fear that they dare not resist, their lordships are requested to take such steps as may be necessary to redress this mischief.

Despite the evident concern, wheel-locks were prohibitively expensive for most criminals. With the advent of the far cheaper flintlock system in the mid-seventeenth century, highway robbery entered its heyday (the word highwayman entered the lexicon in 1617).

Figures such as James Maclaine, Dick Turpin, and Claude Duval entered popular legend as romantic heroes. Yet the life of a highwayman was short, and he often ended his days as a rotting corpse hung up as a public warning. This fact, and the increasingly common distribution of pistols amongst coachmen and victims, led to a decline in mounted robbery in the late eighteenth century. The last officially designated highway robbery in England took place in 1831, just as the new percussion pistols were beginning to replace the flintlocks. High tobymen, or horsed robbers, had yielded the field to low tobymen, or footpads.

Below: *The blunderbuss was developed as a horseman's weapon, though originally it was most commonly used as a naval weapon, becoming popular in Europe in the middle of the seventeenth century and spreading widely thereafter. They were used not only by some highwaymen but also by coach guards. Firing either pistol balls or buckshot, they would have been effective at close range. This relatively modern 1800 example does not have the daunting bell-mouth of earlier types: interestingly, the trumpet-type barrel made no difference to the spread, something not discovered for decades.*

UNITED KINGDOM

TRANTER POCKET REVOLVER 1865

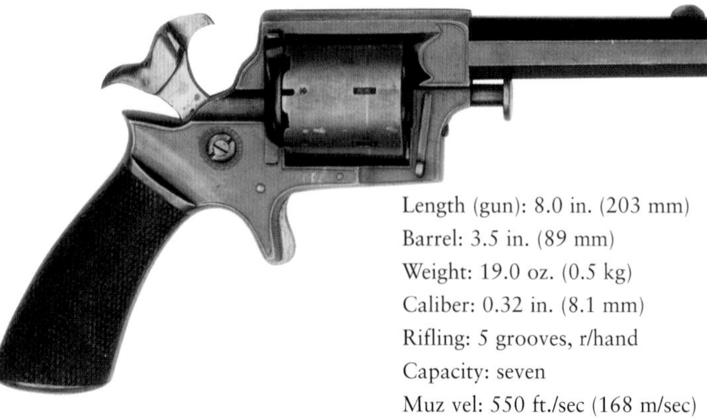

Length (gun): 8.0 in. (203 mm)
Barrel: 3.5 in. (89 mm)
Weight: 19.0 oz. (0.5 kg)
Caliber: 0.32 in. (8.1 mm)
Rifling: 5 grooves, r/hand
Capacity: seven
Muz vel: 550 ft./sec (168 m/sec)

This is a typical Tranter with a solid, robust frame, into which the barrel is screwed, and a plain seven-shot cylinder with recesses for the cartridge rims. The cylinder was rotated by a pawl, worked by the hammer, acting on a ratchet cut out of the cylinder. The cylinder stop rose from the bottom of the frame and engaged rectangular slots toward the front. The cylinder pin was retained by a small, vertical spring: pressure on the bottom of the spring allowed the pin to be withdrawn. The weapon has a bottom-hinged loading gate on the right-hand side of the frame, into which a groove has been machined to allow the copper rimfire cartridges to be inserted. With no ejector, the cylinder pin had to be used, or the cases could be levered out by inserting a knifepoint into the wide slots around the rear cylinder edge. The single-action lock has a half-cock operated by the sheathed trigger common on pocket arms.

FRANCE

LAGRESE REVOLVER 1866

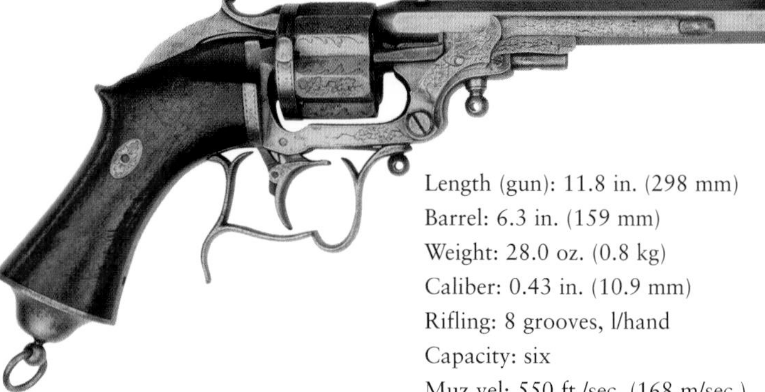

Length (gun): 11.8 in. (298 mm)
Barrel: 6.3 in. (159 mm)
Weight: 28.0 oz. (0.8 kg)
Caliber: 0.43 in. (10.9 mm)
Rifling: 8 grooves, l/hand
Capacity: six
Muz vel: 550 ft./sec. (168 m/sec.)

This revolver, made by Lagrese of Paris, is somewhat ornate and complex. The frame, including the butt, is one piece without any top strap; the octagonal barrel is screwed to the front end of the frame, through which also passes the cylinder axis pin. There is a gap between the barrel and the cylinder of about 0.05 in. (1.3 mm), which must have led to considerable gas loss. The arrangement of the cylinder is strange. It has a separate back plate incorporating a loading gate. Conical apertures through the back plate allowed the nose of the hammer to reach the cartridges. To load, it was necessary to put the nose of the hammer into a safety hole in the plate, holding the plate rigid but allowing the gate to be opened and the cylinder to be rotated clockwise. A groove on the right side of the butt allowed the rounds to be slid in. Ejection was by an upward pull of the lever forcing the ram into the chamber.

UNITED STATES

REMINGTON DOUBLE DERRINGER 1866

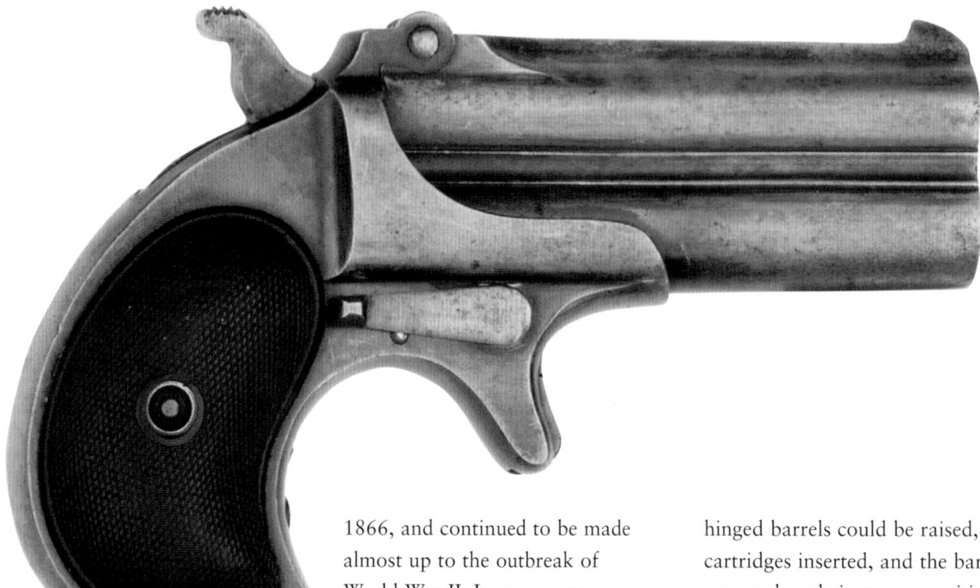

Length (gun): 4.8 in. (121 mm)
Barrel: 3.0 in. (76 mm)
Weight: 12.0 oz. (0.34 kg)
Caliber: 0.410 in. (10.4 mm)
Rifling: 6 grooves, l/hand
Capacity: one
Muz vel: 450 ft./sec. (137 m/sec.)

This is another of the famous derringer-type weapons designed by William H. Elliott of the Remington company. This model first appeared in about 1866, and continued to be made almost up to the outbreak of World War II. It was a neat, compact weapon which, in spite of its small size, handled surprisingly well, even though the butt could be gripped only by the second finger. To load the pistol, it was necessary first to turn the lever (visible above the trigger) until it pointed forward; then the top-hinged barrels could be raised, the cartridges inserted, and the barrels returned to their proper position and locked. The hammer was of single-action type, but was, most ingeniously, equipped with a floating nose which fired the top and bottom barrels in succession. The extractor, situated on the left-hand side of the barrels, was worked by the user's thumb.

BELGIUM

R.I.C. POCKET-TYPE REVOLVER 1867

Length (gun): 8.0 in. (203 mm)
Barrel: 3.0 in. (76 mm)
Weight: 28.0 oz. (0.8 kg)
Caliber: 0.45 in. (11.4mm)
Rifling: 7 grooves, r/hand
Capacity: five
Muz vel: 600 ft./sec. (183 m/sec.)

The Royal Irish Constabulary (R.I.C.) revolver first appeared in 1867, establishing the reputation of its manufacturer, P. Webley and Son of Birmingham. It was widely copied: it is probable that imitation R.I.C. revolvers greatly outnumbered the originals. Civilian purchasers of weapons were not always very selective. Nor was their trust always misplaced, for many of the R.I.C. copies were perfectly adequate. The example illustrated stands at the lower end of the scale: it was hardly worth the little money it sold for. In general appearance it resembles the earliest version of the original Webley, with a plain cylinder and the distinctive hump in the top strap just in front of the trigger. It has the usual round, stubby barrel cast integrally with the frame, and it was so badly made that the right barrel wall is appreciably thicker than the left. Although it bears Birmingham proof marks and the barrel is stamped "TRULOCK & HARRIS, 9 DAWSON ST DUBLIN" its origin is uncertain; it could have been made by one of many back-street Belgian workshops which made copies of several weapons.

UNITED STATES

REMINGTON DERRINGER 1867

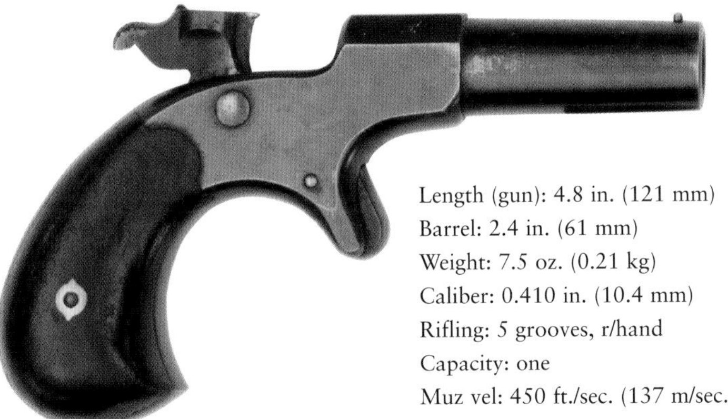

Length (gun): 4.8 in. (121 mm)
Barrel: 2.4 in. (61 mm)
Weight: 7.5 oz. (0.21 kg)
Caliber: 0.410 in. (10.4 mm)
Rifling: 5 grooves, r/hand
Capacity: one
Muz vel: 450 ft./sec. (137 m/sec.)

Many of the small pocket pistols produced by Remington were designed by William H. Elliott, who became well known for such arms. Some were of pepperbox design; others had fixed barrels and rotating firing pins; and yet others were of single- or double-barreled type, in which form they continued to be made until well into the twentieth century. This is the single-barreled Remington version of 1867, a simple but quite powerful arm that sold well. It was of very basic construction, since it had, in effect, no breechblock of any kind: the cartridge was held in position at the moment of firing by the heavy hammer. When the weapon was at full-cock, a short rimfire round of 0.41 in. caliber could be inserted. When the hammer fell, a small projection below it engaged in front of the sear and held the round in position to be fired by an integral striker situated on the top of the hammer face.

FRANCE

DEVISME REVOLVER 1867

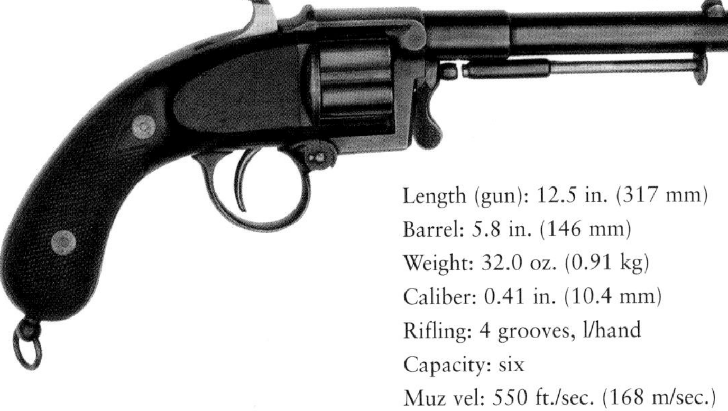

Length (gun): 12.5 in. (317 mm)
Barrel: 5.8 in. (146 mm)
Weight: 32.0 oz. (0.91 kg)
Caliber: 0.41 in. (10.4 mm)
Rifling: 4 grooves, l/hand
Capacity: six
Muz vel: 550 ft./sec. (168 m/sec.)

This revolver, based on an earlier percussion arm, was first shown at the 1867 Paris Exhibition. It has a cylindrical steel barrel screwed into a frame hinged at the bottom of the standing breech. Pressure on the milled lever in front of the frame allowed the barrel to drop, giving access to the cylinder. The locking device is based on the cylinder axis pin. The front end of the pin passes through the frame and is attached to the opening lever. The rear end has a rectangular stud which entered a socket on the standing breech when the arm was closed. The extractor pin sleeve is attached to another sleeve around the barrel: the movement of the lever activated a simple rack-and-pinion, swinging the extractor pin out to the right, to knock out each empty case. The single-action lock has a half-cock. The weapon is of excellent quality and finish, with barrel and cylinder blued and the remainder case-hardened.

BELGIUM

GALAND & SOMMERVILLE REVOLVER 1868

Length (gun): 10.0 in. (254 mm)
Barrel: 5.0 in. (127 mm)
Weight: 35.0 oz. (1.0 kg)
Caliber: 0.45 in. (11.4 mm)
Rifling: 5 grooves, r/hand
Capacity: six
Muz vel: 600 ft./sec. (183 m/sec.)

Charles François Galand of Liège in Belgium and Sommerville, a partner in a Birmingham firm, took out a joint patent in 1868 for a self-extracting cartridge revolver of the general type illustrated. The arm was made in Birmingham and on the continent. It does not appear ever to have become popular in Britain, but a good many revolvers on this principle were made in Europe. This one is well made but is unnamed, although it carries the name "Wm POWELL of BIRMINGHAM," probably the retailer. It bears Birmingham proof marks, and, somewhat unusually, an Enfield Small Arms mark of crossed lances with a "B" beneath them. The revolver was opened by gripping the milled studs at the bottom of the frame and drawing them forward. This activated a plunger below the barrel (very like the ram on a percussion revolver), and forced both barrel and cylinder forward, leaving the empty cases held by their rims on the extractor. The partial return of the cylinder to the extractor allowed fresh rounds to be loaded.

FRANCE

LE MAT REVOLVER 1868

Length (gun): 10.2 in. (259 mm)
Barrel: 4.6 in. (117 mm)
Weight: 49.0 oz. (1.4 kg)
Caliber: 0.44 in./0.65 in. (11.2 mm/16.5 mm)
Rifling: 5 grooves, l/hand
Capacity: nine/one
Muz vel: 600 ft./sec. (183 m/sec.)

This is a cartridge version of the earlier percussion Le Mat, made in France. It is complex and based on its lower barrel, which was firmly seated in the standing breech and acted as an axis pin for the revolver cylinder. The lower frame of the upper barrel has a sleeve which fits over the lower barrel; an extension from this is screwed firmly to the lower frame, making what appears to be a rigid joint. The upper barrel and cylinder (which has nine chambers) allowed the arm to be used as an orthodox single-action cartridge revolver, with a loading gate and a sliding ejector rod of Colt type. To load the lower shot barrel, it was necessary to cock the weapon, then open the side-hinged breechblock by manipulating the catch behind the cylinder. The breechblock has its own firing pin. The action of opening the breech-block activated a semicircular extractor which engaged under the rim of the cartridge case and pushed it clear. This powerful arm was used in French penal colonies.

UNITED KINGDOM

TRANTER CENTERFIRE REVOLVER 1868

Length (gun): 10.5 in. (267 mm)
Barrel: 5.0 in. (127 mm)
Weight: 35.0 oz. (1.0 kg)
Caliber: 0.45 in. (11.4 mm)
Rifling: 5 grooves, r/hand
Capacity: six
Muz vel: 650 ft./sec. (198 m/sec.)

William Tranter was an early entrant in the field of cartridge revolvers: by 1868, he had produced a revolver for use with the new Boxer cartridges. The Tranter revolver illustrated here was still broadly based on the Adams frame that Tranter had used so successfully in his earlier weapons. The frame is still solid, with an integral, octagonal barrel, and the six-chambered cylinder is plain, except for the slots cut for the cylinder stop. The loading gate has a rearward spring catch; light downward pressure was required to operate it. The lock is double-action. An innovation is the provision of a built-in firing pin on the standing breech; the end of the pin was struck by the hammer. The extractor pin is attached to a swivel mount, which allowed it to be swung out into line with the right-hand chamber. A small spring catch held the pin in position but allowed it to be removed for cleaning. An irregularly shaped plate on the left side allowed access to the lock mechanism.

UNITED STATES

SMITH & WESSON TIP-UP REVOLVER 1868

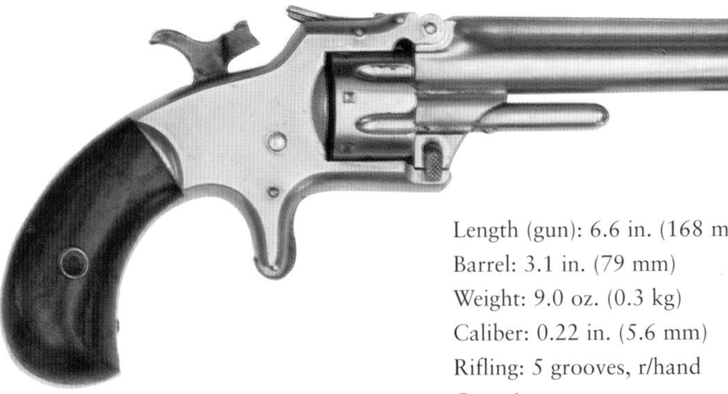

Length (gun): 6.6 in. (168 mm)
Barrel: 3.1 in. (79 mm)
Weight: 9.0 oz. (0.3 kg)
Caliber: 0.22 in. (5.6 mm)
Rifling: 5 grooves, r/hand
Capacity: seven
Muz vel: 500 ft./sec. (152 m/sec.)

When the Civil War ended in 1865, there was a recession in the United States. In particular, the sales of revolvers fell. Smith & Wesson therefore decided to discontinue their second issue and introduce a third issue of more attractive appearance. There was always a demand for pocket pistols in the United States, particularly, perhaps, in the more settled Eastern States where, although fewer people carried a revolver openly, many—both men and women—liked to have one handy in pocket or handbag. The new model did not differ very much mechanically from its predecessor: it had the same tip-up barrel, removable cylinder, and single-action lock. However, instead of having a brass frame, like the earlier model, it was made entirely of iron and the whole weapon was plated. The traditional flat-edged butt gave way to the type known as "bird's-beak," with walnut side-plates held in place by a screw.

AUSTRIA

GASSER REVOLVER 1870

Length (gun): 14.8 in. (375 mm)
Barrel: 9.3 in. (236 mm)
Weight: 52.0 oz. (1.5 kg)
Caliber: 0.43 in. (11 mm)
Rifling: 6 grooves, l/hand
Capacity: six
Muz vel: 900 ft./sec. (274 m/sec.)

The great Austrian firm of Gasser was founded in 1862 by Leopold Gasser, who patented this revolver in 1870. Gasser revolvers were used by the Austro-Hungarian Army and were sold as civilian arms throughout the Balkans. Its open frame is common to all original Gasser revolvers. Its basic construction is similar to the early Colt, except that there is a threaded hole below the barrel that screws onto the front end of the axis pin instead of the wedge. It has a bottom-hinged loading gate and a sliding ejector rod on the right-hand side. The double-action lock has a safety device in the form of the flat bar above the trigger-guard. This massive arm is marked with "GASSER PATENT, GUSS-STAHL," an Austrian eagle, and an emblem showing an arrow transfixing an apple. Chambered to fire the cartridge developed for the Werndl carbine, it was only suitable for use by mounted men.

UNITED KINGDOM

THOMAS REVOLVER 1869

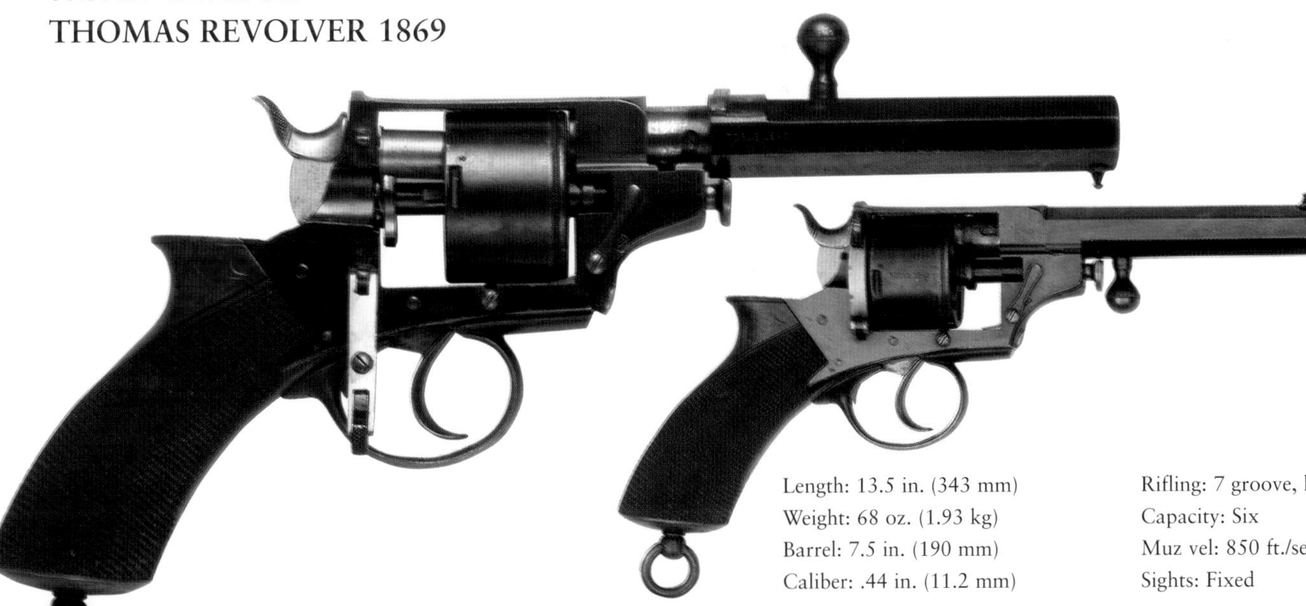

Length: 13.5 in. (343 mm)
Weight: 68 oz. (1.93 kg)
Barrel: 7.5 in. (190 mm)
Caliber: .44 in. (11.2 mm)
Rifling: 7 groove, l/hand
Capacity: Six
Muz vel: 850 ft./sec. (259 m/sec.)
Sights: Fixed

In 1869, Birmingham gunmaker J. Thomas patented this double-action revolver. The weapon is of cast steel with a heavy octagonal barrel, a very long cylinder aperture, and a knob beneath its barrel (bottom photo). To eject the empty cases, pressure on the small spring on the front of the frame released the barrel catch, allowing the barrel to be rotated until the knob was uppermost (top photo). The barrel was then drawn forward, taking the cylinder with it to the front of the aperture. A star-shaped extractor attached to the standing breech held the cases firmly by their rims until they were fully out of the chambers. They were then thrown clear by a flick of the wrist. There is a flange on the barrel which worked in a slot on the frame. This flange was set at a slight angle to the circumference of the barrel: when the latter was turned it exerted a powerful camming action and drew the cylinder very slightly forward, thus loosening the tightest of cases. The system was effective but was soon overtaken by better ones: revolvers on this system were made in small numbers and are now rare.

1869–1890 COLT DERRINGERS AND POCKET PISTOLS

Colt started to design derringers from about 1869 and, as usual with the company, they appeared in a wide variety of models. The line started with the First Model in about 1870, and the example shown here (1) is of 0.41 in. caliber and is engraved. It was shaped so that it could be used as iron knuckles in a fist fight, although whether this was deliberate or accidental on the part of Colt is no longer known. The next to appear was the Second Model derringer, which remained in production from 1870-1890; the model shown here (2) fired a 0.42 in. rimfire cartridge. Also appearing in 1870 (and remaining in production until 1912) was the Third Model derringer (3) which was 4.8 in. (122 mm) long and weighed 8.0 oz. (230 g), firing a 0.41 in. round. The weapon had a brass frame, a 2.5 in. (63 mm) long steel barrel, and a wooden bird's-beak butt. The weapon was opened by swinging the barrel laterally to the right, which automatically ejected the spent cartridge case. Once the Rollin White patent held by Smith & Wesson expired in 1869, Colt was able to start manufacturing revolvers, including a compact range which started with the Open Top Pocket line. There was a basic steel version (7) and a nickel-plated version with pearl grips (8); both were 0.22 in. caliber and held seven rounds. A slightly heavier version, from 1880, was chambered for 0.32 in. rimfire (8). Nor had the increase in caliber ended, for this was followed by even larger calibers, by now restricted to five rounds: 0.38 in. (9)—this is an unfinished factory prototype—and then 0.41 in. (10).

Another line of development resulted in a slightly heavier, if more conventional weapon known as a "House Revolver," which was intended to provide self-defense against burglars and other uninvited intruders. Products included the Cloverleaf House Model revolver of 1874 (5), which was the company's first solid frame weapon made to fire metallic cartridges and carried four 0.41 in. cartridges in a somewhat rudimentary cylinder. This was followed in 1881 by the New House Model (6), which fired five 0.38 in. centerfire rounds.

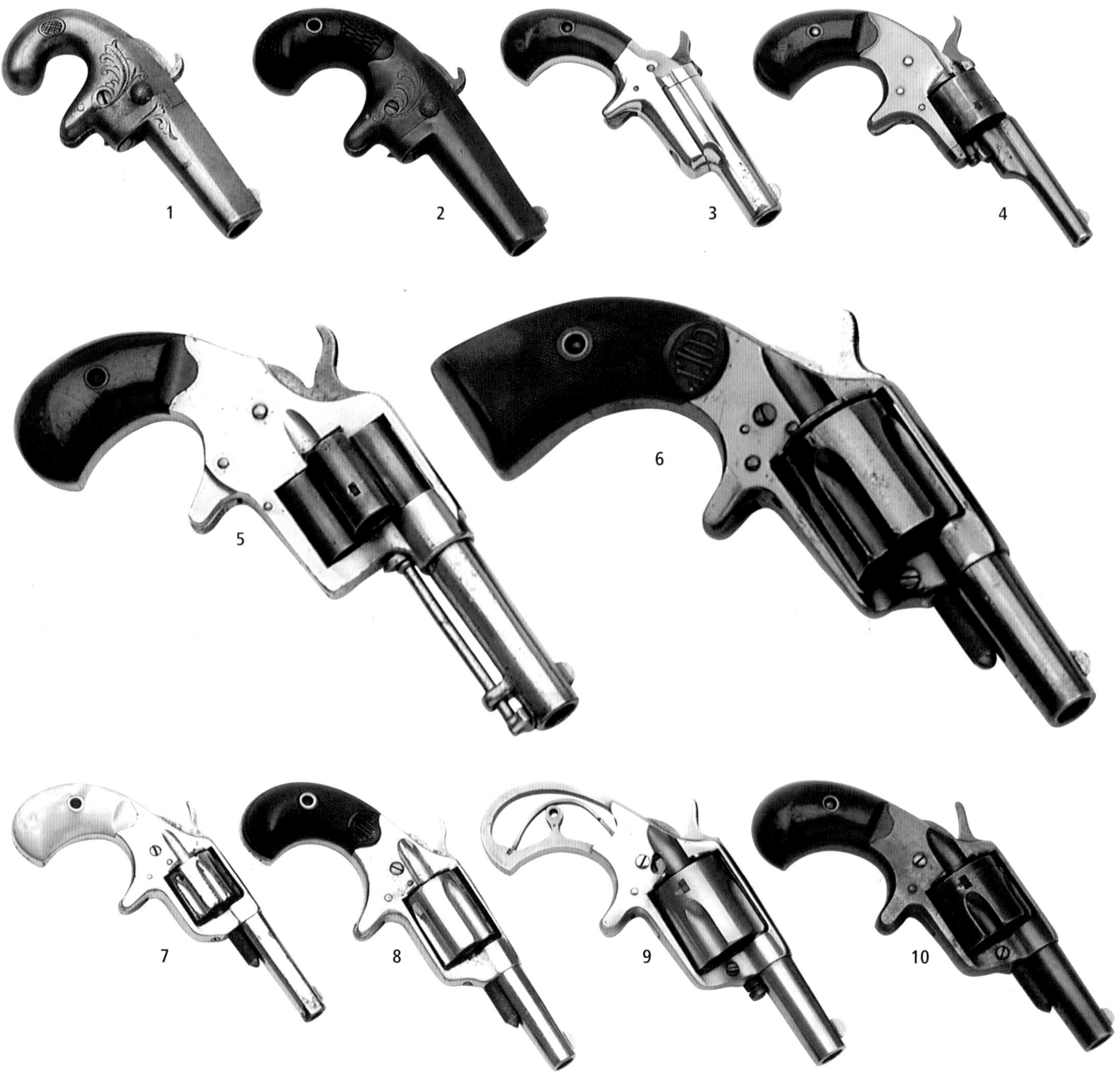

BELGIUM

ADAMS CENTER-FIRE REVOLVER (COPY) 1870

Length (gun): 11.0 in. (279 mm)
Barrel: 6.0 in. (152 mm)
Weight: 35.0 oz. (0.99 kg)
Caliber: 0.42 in. (10.7 mm)
Rifling: 6 grooves, r/hand
Capacity: six
Muz vel: 600 ft./sec. (183 m/sec.)

By 1868, John Adams, brother of Robert and managing director of the Adams Patent Small Arms Company, had patented and produced a centerfire cartridge revolver based on the original percussion revolvers produced by Beaumont-Adams a dozen years earlier. The conversion involved a new bored-through cylinder; a loading gate; and a sliding ejector rod brazed to the right front of the frame, permanently in line with the chamber opposite the loading gate. A deep cartridge groove was cut into the frame behind the gate. The new Adams was quickly copied by Belgian makers. Although this copy appears to have a solid frame, it is in two parts: there are screws at the bottom front of the frame and by the hammer nose—the construction is similar, to that of the Deane-Harding revolver. The plain cylinder with its top-hinged gate and cartridge groove is nearly identical to that of the original Adams. The only real difference is the Webley-type swivel ejector rod, which was normally housed in the hollow axis pin, pulled forward, and swiveled. To remove the cylinder, the ejector rod was withdrawn and the small stud on the front frame was depressed. Then the milled end of the axis pin was drawn forward.

BELGIUM

COPY OF ADAMS REVOLVER 1870

Length (gun): 13.0 in. (330 mm)
Barrel: 6.9 in. (175 mm)
Weight: 33.0 oz. (0.9 kg)
Caliber: 0.38 in. (9.6 mm)
Rifling: 8 grooves, r/hand
Capacity: six
Muz vel: 500 ft./sec. (152 m/sec.)

Although Adams revolvers were made under license in Belgium, the name on this pistol—"DAVID H. BREVETTE"—is not that of a licensee. The arm resembles those made by D. Herman of Liège and is probably a pirated copy. The frame is made separately from the octagonal barrel, which is attached to it Colt-fashion by means of a robust cylinder pin and a lump screwed to the lower part of the frame. A rammer is attached to the left-hand flat of the barrel. The cylinder bears Liège proof marks. The lock is of the Adams self-cocking type; on the left-hand side is fitted a spring safety bolt to hold the hammer clear of the nipples. A flat plate protrudes far enough forward from the top of the frame to cover completely the nipple under the hammer. The trigger is of the ring type found on earlier pepperbox pistols. The one-piece butt is fitted with a cap of German silver and contains a percussion cap compartment, with a lid in the form of a grotesque mask.

BELGIUM

GALAND-TYPE REVOLVER 1870

Length (gun): 13.0 in. (330 mm)
Barrel: 4.8 in. (122 mm)
Weight: 46.0 oz. (1.3 kg)
Caliber: 0.43 in. (11 mm)
Rifling: 10 grooves, r/hand
Capacity: six
Muz vel: 700 ft./sec. (213 m/sec.

Charles François Galand, the well-known Belgian gunmaker, patented a number of improvements to the revolver, including an improved method of extracting cartridges. Although Galand made a number of these arms in conjunction with the British maker Sommerville of Birmingham, the type was more popular on the continent. The spur on the trigger guard formed the rear extremity of a long lever hinged to a very long front extension of the cylinder axis pin. When the milled catch at the rear of the trigger guard was pulled backward, the lever could be drawn down to the vertical position, drawing forward the barrel and cylinder along the axis pin. During the last part of its travel, the rear plate of the cylinder, which is pierced with holes for the cartridges, stopped, while the main cylinder went on for a further 0.5 in. (13 mm), leaving the empty cases behind it on the plate. The flimsy folding skeleton stock was ineffective.

THE PERCUSSION CAP

Above: *The percussion cap was a tremendous boon to Deringer and eventually to every other handgun manufacturer. The tin of Hicks percussion caps—"foil lined, central fire"—was American-made.*

The invention of the percussion cap in the early nineteenth century heralded the true advent of modern small arms, as it ultimately made possible the unitary cartridge and all the firearms dependent upon it. Various individuals have claims to its invention, such as the sportsman Peter Hawker and the gunmakers Joseph Manton and Joseph Egg. The English artist Joshua Shaw, however, is known to have invented a percussion cap in 1814 and managed a successful patent application in the United States in 1822. (His previous patent application had been refused.)

The percussion cap system was simplicity itself. A small brass cup was filled with fulminate of mercury and was placed on a nipple beneath the gun's hammer. When the trigger was pulled, the hammer crushed the brass cap, detonating the percussion powder and sending an instant flame down through a hole in the nipple into the gun's chamber to ignite the main charge.

The percussion system offered major advantages over the flintlock. It was more reliable and more resistant to adverse weather. The lock action was faster, resulting in improved accuracy, and the muzzle velocity of the weapon was increased by the more efficient burning of the main charge under the intense jet of flame from the cap. Percussion lock weapons were also more streamlined than the flintlock, as the new system could do away with the pan, which in turn made possible the use of the back-action lock (the mainspring located behind the trigger).

The reduction of bulk offered by the percussion lock system was particularly advantageous in the development of pistols. Pistols could now be significantly reduced in size, sufficiently so to be carried concealed in a coat pocket as a genuinely effective self-defense weapon. Taking advantage of this development, gun designers began to produce multi-barrel weapons, usually two barrels in an over-and-under configuration, but four to six barrel pepperbox pistols were also popular.

Two-barrel guns generally had their barrels rotated manually to align cap with hammer, but the better pepperbox pistols turned through each barrel in turn using the mechanical action of pulling the trigger. While these guns could be clumsy, unbalanced weapons, their advantage in a close-quarter fight was obvious, and they laid the foundations for the modern revolver.

GERMANY

SCHULER "REFORM" PISTOL 1870

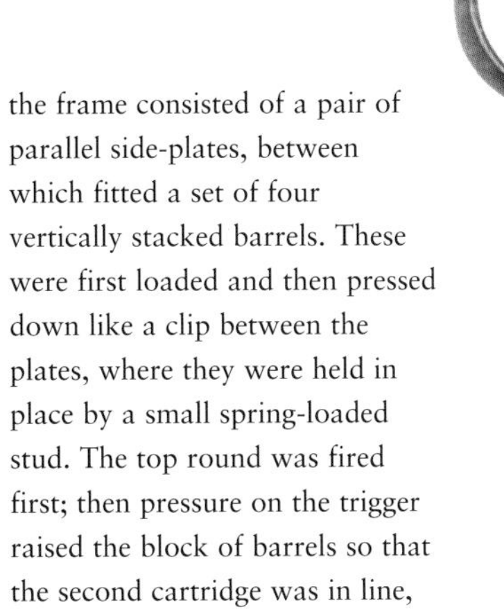

Length (gun): 5.3 in. (133 mm)
Barrel: 3.0 in. (76 mm)
Weight: 12.0 oz. (0.3 kg)
Caliber: 6 mm
Rifling: 7 grooves, r/hand
Capacity: four
Muz vel: 780 ft./sec.

In the early days of cartridge weapons, before the self-loading arm had been invented, many ingenious attempts were made to solve the problem of the physical bulk of revolvers. The weapon illustrated here is a Belgian copy of a design by August Schuler of Suhl, Germany. The basic lock mechanism was that of a normal double-action revolver, in which the hammer acted on a firing pin in the frame. The forward end of the frame consisted of a pair of parallel side-plates, between which fitted a set of four vertically stacked barrels. These were first loaded and then pressed down like a clip between the plates, where they were held in place by a small spring-loaded stud. The top round was fired first; then pressure on the trigger raised the block of barrels so that the second cartridge was in line, ready for the next shot. The three lower barrels had small holes drilled on their upper sides to connect each to the barrel immediately above; thus, when the second and subsequent barrels were fired, enough gas passed upwards to blow out the empty case in the barrel above. The comb of the hammer was shaped in such a way as to deflect these ejected cases away from the direction of the firer's face.

UNITED KINGDOM

PRYSE 0.455 IN. SERVICE REVOLVER (UNKNOWN MAKER) 1870

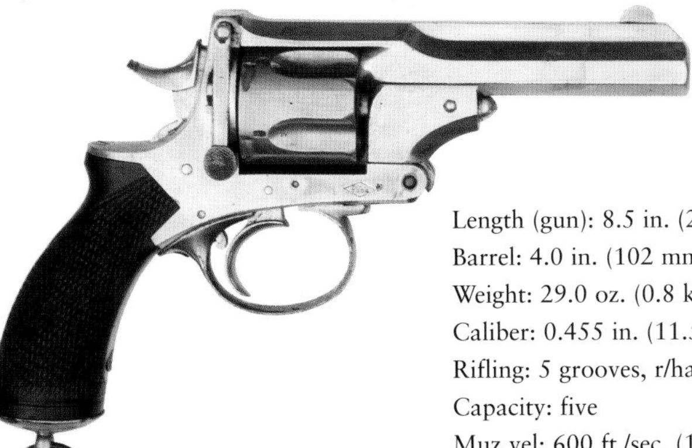

Length (gun): 8.5 in. (216 mm)
Barrel: 4.0 in. (102 mm)
Weight: 29.0 oz. (0.8 kg)
Caliber: 0.455 in. (11.5 mm)
Rifling: 5 grooves, r/hand
Capacity: five
Muz vel: 600 ft./sec. (183 m/sec.)

This British Army revolver has Birmingham proof marks. The right side of the frame is marked "Patent 3096" and the left bears the legend "First Quality." Pryse revolvers were popular for many years in the British Army and one of the greatest generals of the late Victorian era, Field Marshal Lord Roberts of Kandahar, is known to have carried one. One of several good features in the gun was that the end of the top strap fitted into a slot in the top of the standing breech, where it was secured by a cylindrical lug entering from either side. This was a strong and successful feature, although, curiously, it was not mentioned in the patent document. The characteristic feature of Pryse revolvers is that they are of break-open type, with a star-shaped ejector at the rear of the cylinder. Opening the revolver to the full brought this automatically into play, driving backward with force to throw out the empty cases.

UNITED KINGDOM

WEBLEY DOUBLE-ACTION REVOLVER 1870

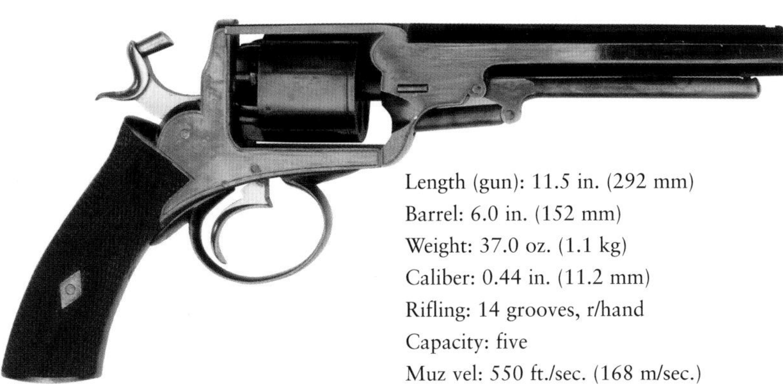

Length (gun): 11.5 in. (292 mm)
Barrel: 6.0 in. (152 mm)
Weight: 37.0 oz. (1.1 kg)
Caliber: 0.44 in. (11.2 mm)
Rifling: 14 grooves, r/hand
Capacity: five
Muz vel: 550 ft./sec. (168 m/sec.)

Webley produced two types of double-action pistol: one with a solid frame, with a barrel screwed in; the other, shown here, of two-piece construction. The octagonal, multigrooved barrel is made with a top strap and a lump. The rear end of the strap fits into a slot cut across the top of the standing breech above the nose of the hammer, a hole in the lump fits over the front end of the axis pin, and a small stud projects from the lower frame to fit a corresponding hole at the bottom of the lump—thus giving a rigid, three-way locking system. The whole is held firmly together by a Colt-type wedge driven in from the left-hand side and retained by a small grub screw. The cylinder is of the usual Webley type, each chamber being numbered serially from one to five counterclockwise. The double-action lock has a half-cock but no safety catch. The revolver is fitted with a Colt-type rammer. The butt has a cap integral with the tang.

UNITED KINGDOM

WEBLEY R.I.C. REVOLVER NO. 1 1870

Length (gun): 9.3 in. (235 mm)
Barrel: 14.5 in. (114 mm)
Weight: 30.0 oz. (0.9 kg)
Caliber: 0.45 in. (11.4 mm)
Rifling: 5 grooves, r/hand
Capacity: six
Muz vel: 650 ft./sec. (198 m/sec.)

The No. 1 Model has a basically round barrel that is, however, slightly raised on its upper side, and on which a flat rib has been machined. The barrel is screwed into a solid frame. The six-chambered cylinder is plain, except for recesses for the cylinder stop at the rear end. Plain cylinders are usually indicative of earlier models: later cylinders are fluted to achieve a small reduction in weight. The extractor is of the usual type, although its knob is acorn-shaped. The loading gate is standard. The revolver has a double-action lock, with a half-cock that held the nose of the hammer well clear of the cartridges in the chambers. The checkered walnut butt is of one-piece type and is held by two vertical screws. These revolvers were made in several calibers, the smallest was 0.41 in. (10.4 mm), and were widely used all over the British Empire, and copied in various European countries.

UNITED KINGDOM

WEBLEY NO. 1 REVOLVER 1870

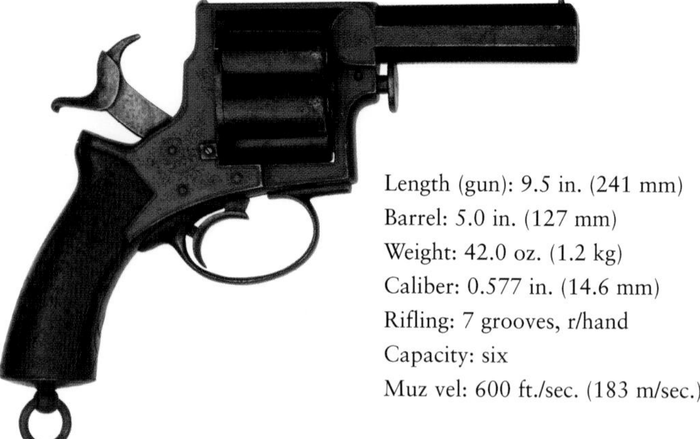

Length (gun): 9.5 in. (241 mm)
Barrel: 5.0 in. (127 mm)
Weight: 42.0 oz. (1.2 kg)
Caliber: 0.577 in. (14.6 mm)
Rifling: 7 grooves, r/hand
Capacity: six
Muz vel: 600 ft./sec. (183 m/sec.)

The Webley No. 1 Revolver was of 0.577 in. (14.6 mm) caliber, exactly the same as that of the service rifle. The revolver is built on a robust, solid frame with integral barrel. The cylinder is fully fluted and the lock is double-action. One of the problems connected with the early Boxer cartridge was a marked tendency for the primer to bulge backward under the force of the explosion. In some breech mechanisms, this was not particularly important; but in a revolver of orthodox type—i.e., one in which the base of the cartridge was forced back against a robust standing breech—there was always the risk that a bulged primer would prevent the cylinder from rotating. The Webley No. 1 was therefore fitted with a detachable backplate that rotated with the cylinder; it was pierced with holes for the hammer nose, into which the primers could expand without fouling the mechanism.

UNITED STATES

COLT HOUSE PISTOL 1871

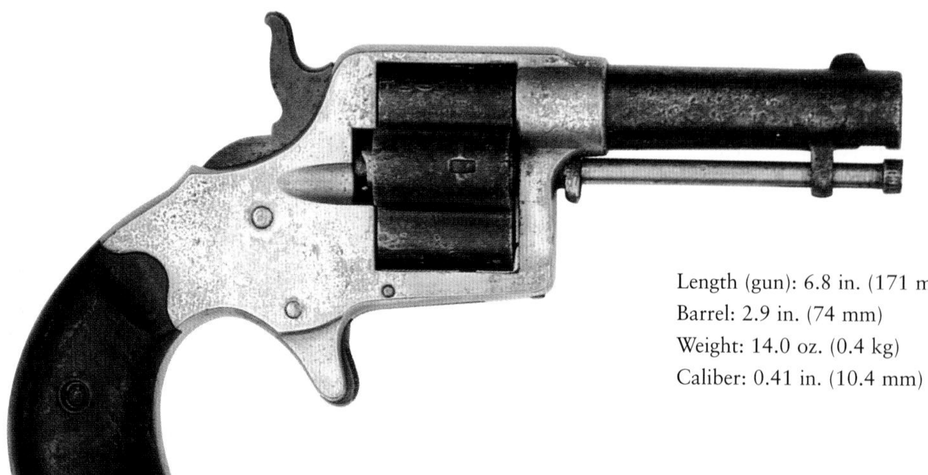

Length (gun): 6.8 in. (171 mm)
Barrel: 2.9 in. (74 mm)
Weight: 14.0 oz. (0.4 kg)
Caliber: 0.41 in. (10.4 mm)
Rifling: 7 grooves, r/hand
Capacity: four
Muz vel: 450 ft./sec. (137 m/sec.)

This revolver is one of the earliest house pistols. It has a solid brass frame into which is screwed a steel barrel, available in a variety of lengths. It has a four-chambered cylinder with a section shaped like a four-leafed clover; hence the nickname of "Cloverleaf Colt." The lock is single-action. The hammer comb on the earlier models was almost vertical; in later models, it was slanted much farther back. The hammer activated the cylinder stop, housed in a long slot below the frame. The trigger is of the sheathed type. There is no loading gate, but the side of the frame is grooved to help loading. A flat fence on the left-hand side of the frame kept the cartridges in their chambers. The rod below the barrel is a forward extension of the cylinder axis pin; it could be drawn forward to remove the cylinder. A retaining ring is fitted below the barrel to ensure that the pin could not be dropped. To make the weapon more compact, the cylinder could be partially rotated so that two chambers were on each side of the frame. The hammer then fitted into one of the small apertures between each chamber to prevent the cylinder rotating. It has a bird's-beak butt.

UNITED STATES

ETHAN ALLEN POCKET REVOLVER 1871

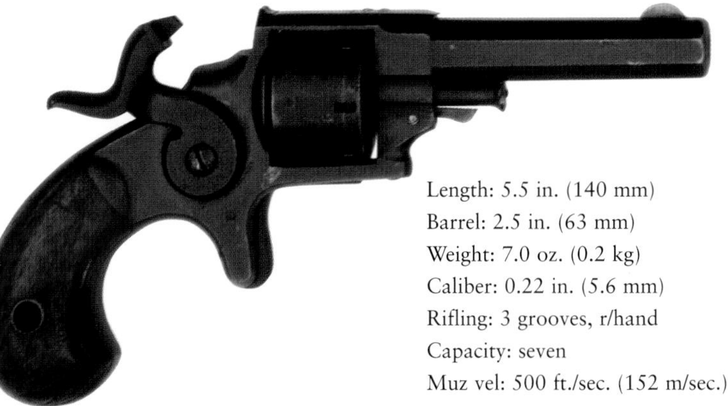

Length: 5.5 in. (140 mm)
Barrel: 2.5 in. (63 mm)
Weight: 7.0 oz. (0.2 kg)
Caliber: 0.22 in. (5.6 mm)
Rifling: 3 grooves, r/hand
Capacity: seven
Muz vel: 500 ft./sec. (152 m/sec.)

The perfection of the rimfire cartridge and the expiry of Smith & Wesson's patent for the bored-through cylinder in 1869 gave rise to a great increase in production of small, cheap pocket pistols—for which there was apparently an almost insatiable demand in the United States. Ethan Allen continued to manufacture pepperbox pistols for some time, but after his death in 1871, his company switched to pistols of the type seen here. It has an octagonal steel barrel screwed into a gunmetal frame, and a seven-chambered steel cylinder to take rimfire cartridges. In order to load the weapon, it was necessary first to press up the catch under the cylinder axis pin, which would then be drawn out and the cylinder removed. The empty cases were knocked out with the axis pin; this made the weapon relatively cheap to manufacture.

UNITED STATES

SMITH & WESSON NEW MODEL NO 3 REVOLVER 1871

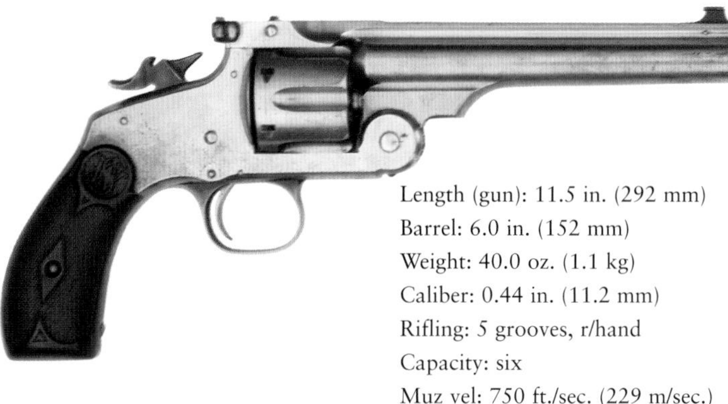

Length (gun): 11.5 in. (292 mm)
Barrel: 6.0 in. (152 mm)
Weight: 40.0 oz. (1.1 kg)
Caliber: 0.44 in. (11.2 mm)
Rifling: 5 grooves, r/hand
Capacity: six
Muz vel: 750 ft./sec. (229 m/sec.)

This arm is chambered to take the 0.44 in. (11.2 mm) Russian cartridge. It has a round, tapered barrel with a full top rib, and is fitted with a target sight instead of the round blade usually found on service models. The revolver was opened by pushing up the milled catch in front of the hammer and pushing down the barrel. This automatically forced out the star-shaped ejector, which was mounted on a hexagonal rod, and activated by a rack and gear. The six-chambered cylinder is 1.44 in. (37 mm) long; a few later models had cylinders of 1.56 in. (40 mm). The lock is single-action with a rebounding hammer and is case-hardened. Although this was a very fine arm and popular with expert target shots, it never really caught on in the United States. Users preferred a more powerful cartridge than was considered safe or practical in a break-open arm.

UNITED STATES

COLT NEW LINE 0.22 IN. POCKET MODEL REVOLVER 1872

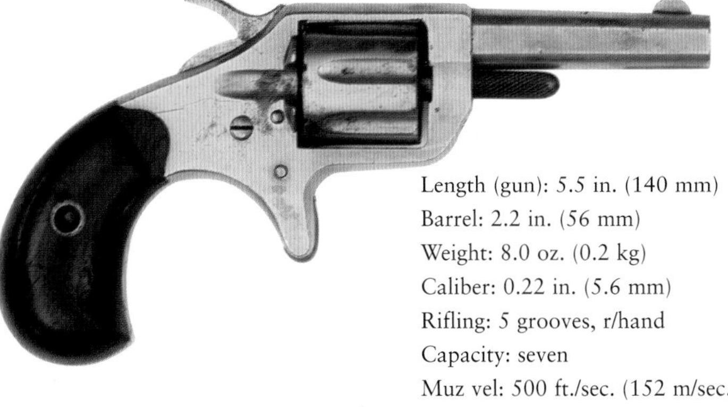

Length (gun): 5.5 in. (140 mm)
Barrel: 2.2 in. (56 mm)
Weight: 8.0 oz. (0.2 kg)
Caliber: 0.22 in. (5.6 mm)
Rifling: 5 grooves, r/hand
Capacity: seven
Muz vel: 500 ft./sec. (152 m/sec.)

It was not until 1872 that the Colt New Line series of pocket revolvers firing metallic cartridges went onto the market (because of Smith & Wesson patents) in a variety of calibers from 0.41 in. (10.4 mm) down to 0.22 in. (5.6 mm). The example shown is of the smallest caliber. It has an octagonal barrel complete with foresight, screwed into a solid frame. The cylinder was rotated by means of the usual pawl and ratchet and held steady by a cylinder stop. This projected from the bottom of the standing breech and engaged slots cut into the rear of the cylinder between the chambers. The cylinder was removed by pressing a retaining spring on the right-hand side of the frame and drawing forward the axis pin. There was no loading gate, but cartridges could be inserted through a small gap in the rear of the frame.

FRANCE

ST. ETIENNE SERVICE REVOLVER MODEL 1873

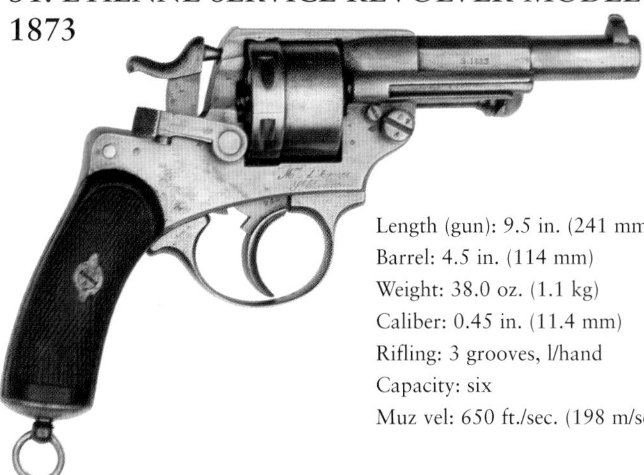

Length (gun): 9.5 in. (241 mm)
Barrel: 4.5 in. (114 mm)
Weight: 38.0 oz. (1.1 kg)
Caliber: 0.45 in. (11.4 mm)
Rifling: 3 grooves, l/hand
Capacity: six
Muz vel: 650 ft./sec. (198 m/sec.)

This was the first centerfire revolver to be adopted by the French Army. It has a solid frame and is very heavy and robust. The barrel is half round and half octagonal. The revolver has a Colt-type extractor rod, working in a sleeve. When it was not in use, the front end of the rod was turned under the barrel, where it was held against the end of the cylinder axis rod by light spring pressure. To remove the cylinder, the rod was turned down, the large-headed screw just beneath it loosened, and the axis pin drawn forward. The loading gate is hinged at the bottom and was opened by being drawn backward. The lock is of orthodox double-action Chamelot-Delvigne type. The hammer is set at half-cock. A large, irregularly shaped inspection plate on the left-hand side of the frame is held by two pins and a screw.

GERMANY

PINFIRE REVOLVER 1873

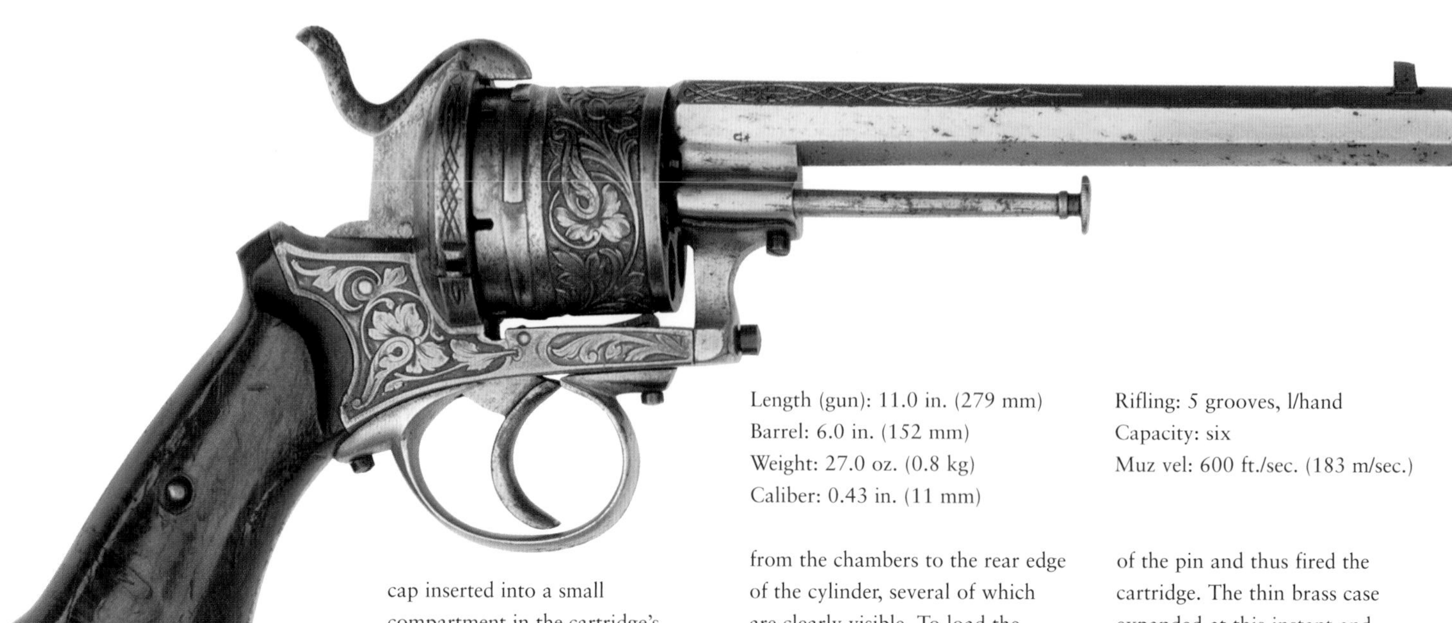

Length (gun): 11.0 in. (279 mm)
Barrel: 6.0 in. (152 mm)
Weight: 27.0 oz. (0.8 kg)
Caliber: 0.43 in. (11 mm)
Rifling: 5 grooves, l/hand
Capacity: six
Muz vel: 600 ft./sec. (183 m/sec.)

The pinfire cartridge consisted of a rimless, cylindrical brass case containing the charge, a bullet, and an internal percussion cap inserted into a small compartment in the cartridge's base. The inner end of the small brass-wire pin, which gave the cartridge its name, rested on this cap. When it was driven inward by the blow of the hammer, it set off the cap and fired the charge. The most interesting aspects of this weapon are the apertures running from the chambers to the rear edge of the cylinder, several of which are clearly visible. To load the revolver, it was necessary to open the top-hinged loading gate, place the hammer at half-cock, and insert the cartridges into the chambers in such a way that the pins protruded from the apertures. The hammer was so shaped that when it fell, it struck the outer end of the pin and thus fired the cartridge. The thin brass case expanded at this instant and prevented any rearward escape of burning gases. Then the metal's natural elasticity caused it to contract, so that it could be easily removed by the sliding rod below the barrel. Copper was also used for cases, although it was somewhat less elastic.

UNITED STATES

COLT NEW LINE 0.41 IN. POCKET REVOLVER 1873

Length (gun): 6.0 in. (152 mm)
Barrel: 2.0 in. (51 mm)
Weight: 11.0 oz. (0.3 kg)
Caliber: 0.41 in. (10.4 mm)
Rifling: 7 grooves, r/hand
Capacity: five
Muz vel: 450 ft./sec. (137 m/sec.)

New Line single-action pocket revolvers, superseding the Colt House Pistol, were made in calibers, from 0.22 in. (5.6 mm) to 0.41 in. (10.4 mm), including some centerfire models, and with barrel lengths from 1.5 in. (38 mm) to 3.5 in. (89 mm). This revolver is the 0.41 in. (10.4 mm) rimfire version with a 2 in. (51 mm) barrel. It is a compact, streamlined weapon. The round barrel, with a noticeable taper from muzzle to breech, is screwed into a solid iron frame that has a half-fluted, five-chambered cylinder without recesses for cartridge rims. The loading gate could be opened when the gun was cocked or half-cocked. Pressure on a small stud at the front of the frame on the right-hand side allowed the cylinder axis pin to be withdrawn and used to push out the empty cases. A circular inspection plate on the left side of the frame gave access to the lock. It has the typical bird-beak butt.

UNITED STATES

COLT SINGLE-ACTION ARMY (ARTILLERY MODEL) REVOLVER 1873

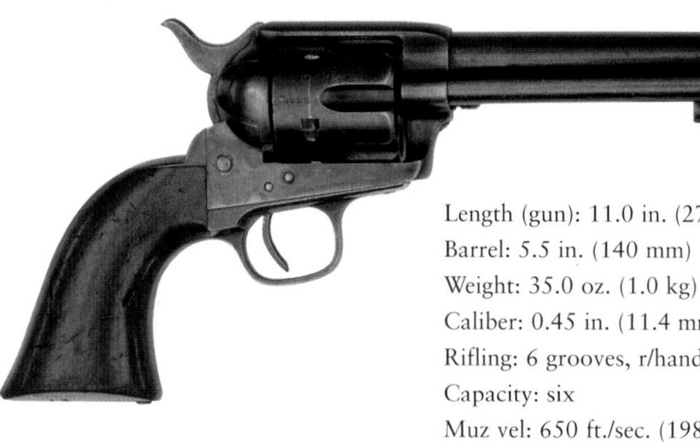

Length (gun): 11.0 in. (279 mm)
Barrel: 5.5 in. (140 mm)
Weight: 35.0 oz. (1.0 kg)
Caliber: 0.45 in. (11.4 mm)
Rifling: 6 grooves, r/hand
Capacity: six
Muz vel: 650 ft./sec. (198 m/sec.)

Colt's first venture into the rimfire field was to develop a slightly tapered cartridge that could be loaded into the front face of the cylinder and firmly seated with the orthodox percussion rammer. But this method, known as the Thuer conversion, was only temporary, and soon after the expiry of the Smith & Wesson patent, Colt had a revolver of its own to offer. It appeared in 1873 and is sometimes referred to as the Model 1873. It fired a brass-cased centerfire cartridge with a copper cap in its base and was an immediate success. It was first known by the awkward title of "New Metallic Cartridge Revolving Pistol" but later became known by the more familiar "Single-Action Army Revolver." The earliest model was of 0.45 in. (11.4 mm) caliber and fired a 235-grain (15 g) lead bullet by means of 617 grains (40 g) of black powder, but it was later made in a wide variety of different calibers.

1877–1878 UNUSUAL COLTS

A company the size of Colt produced a large number of new designs: some never got beyond the drawing board; some resulted in a prototype but stopped there; the others went into production. In addition, production models differed widely, partly as a result of options offered by the company and partly as a result of requests from customers.

The standard production 1878 double-action Frontier revolver (1) has been fitted with the long 7.5 in. barrel, while the Model 1877 double-action Lightning revolver (4) of 0.41 in. caliber is in standard blued finish but has been fitted with the more expensive pearl grips. The Model 1877 double-action Lightning revolver of 0.38 in. caliber (5) has been heavily engraved and is fitted with ivory grips, a longer barrel, and an attached ejector rod. Another type of weapon which is of particular interest to the historian as much as to the modern collector is one which bears its owner's name, such as this Third Model 1877 double-action 0.38 in. caliber Lightning revolver (3), whose backstrap is engraved "Capt Jack Crawford," who was a well-known scout.

Two weapons which reached the prototype stage but did not go into production were a hammerless double-action weapon of 1878 (2) and a gun that was probably the first ever with a swing-out cylinder, a device that Colt patented in 1884 (6). This particular design did not go into production, but five years later, Colt started to sell their first models with this swing-out device, and it soon became the standard.

1873
THE COLT SINGLE-ACTION ARMY REVOLVER

Few firearms are as readily identified with the gunfighter and the combats of the American West as the Colt Single-Action Army revolver, which was first fielded in 1873 and quickly spread from the military to civilian users. Its many names —Peacemaker, Frontier Six-Shooter, Thumb-Buster, Colt '45, and Hog-Leg, among others—convey the ideas of frontiersmen and gunmen but, whatever name they had for it, the gun was widely used and relied upon by both men and women on both sides of the law, and by civilians and the military alike. Indeed, if it seldom earned affection, it was always treated with the greatest respect.

The name "Single-Action" meant that the hammer had to be pulled rearward to the cocked position, using the thumb or free hand, each time the weapon was to be fired, as is shown by this company demonstration plate (1) and the cutaway model (19). The first-ever Single-Action Colt to come off the production line (6) did so in 1873 and was followed by 357,858 more before production ended (temporarily) in 1942.

Various barrel lengths were available, of which the 4.75 in. (121 mm) was the most popular (13) The longest "normal" version was the 7.5 in. (191 mm) (5), although an "extra-long" version with a detachable shoulder-stock became available by special order in 1876 (9). Many different calibers were also available, although the most popular were 0.45 in. (18), followed by 0.44-40 in. (16). Various experimental models were also produced, such as this model with an automatic cartridge extractor (7).

Among the variables were the finish of the gun and the type of grip to be fitted. The latter depended simply on the imagination of the Colt factory and its customers. Some examples of special finishes are this gold-plated gun (10) with pearl steer-head grips and the owner's name inlaid in silver on the backstab, a second model (11) that is nickel-plated and fitted with ivory grips, a third (3) with pearl handgrips, and a fourth (12) that can be identified by the carved Mexican eagles on the ivory grips as being intended for a customer "south of the border."

Several special models were produced, including this competition model (8), the Bisley (named after the premier British target ranges), which had longer curved grips and special target sights, and was popular in both the US and the UK. This, too, came in a variety of models and finishes, including one with fixed sights and a 5.5 in. (140 mm) barrel (4), and another with chrome-plating (2).

The Colt Single-Action was also produced to meet bulk orders by specific groups or companies. Such orders were placed by the Texas Rangers (14), Wells Fargo (15), and the Adams Express Company (17), among many others.

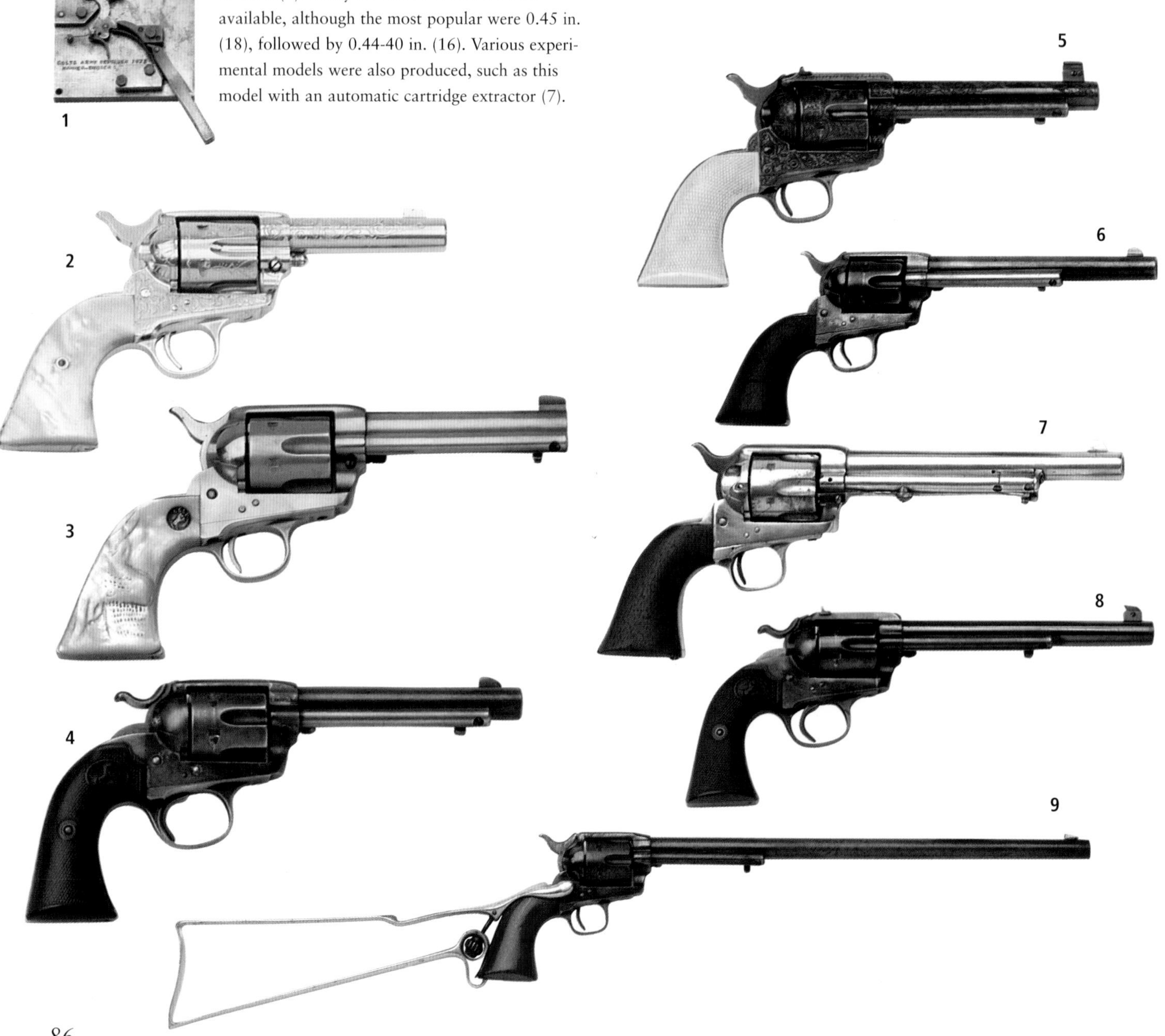

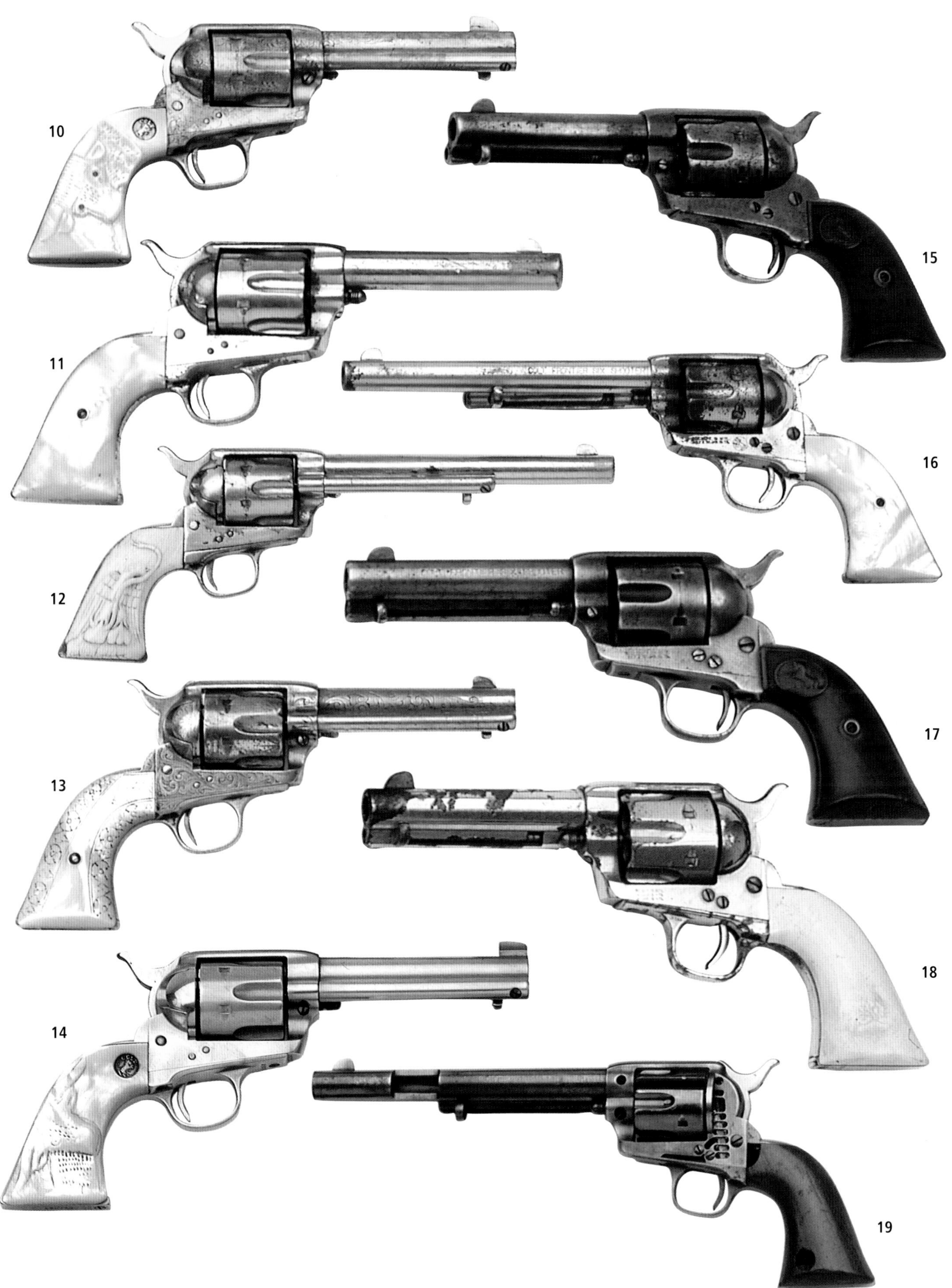
10
11
12
13
14
15
16
17
18
19

UNITED STATES

COLT SINGLE-ACTION ARMY (CAVALRY MODEL) REVOLVER 1873

Length (gun): 13.0 in. (330 mm)
Barrel: 7.5 in. (190 mm)
Weight: 38.0 oz. (1.1 kg)
Caliber: 0.44 in. (11.2 mm)
Rifling: 6 grooves, r/hand
Capacity: six
Muz vel: 650 ft./sec. (198 m/sec.)

This remains the archetypal American handgun and was manufactured in many different versions and under a variety of names. To the company it was known as the Model P, but to the military it was the Single-Action Army model 1873 and was issued in two barrel lengths: Cavalry Model, 7.5 in. (190 mm); and Artillery Model, 5.5 in. (140 mm). Both military versions were characterized by a solid frame with a top strap, a round barrel screwed into the frame, and a bored-through cylinder. There was a robust, hemispherical standing breech, with a contoured loading gate built into its right side, and ejection was by means of a rod sliding in a sleeve below and to the right of the barrel. As its name implies, the lock was of the single-action type. The weapon shown is of 0.44 in. (11.2 mm) caliber, which was popular since the Winchester 1873 Model rifle used the same cartridge.

BELGIUM

CHAMELOT-DELVIGNE SERVICE-TYPE REVOLVER 1874

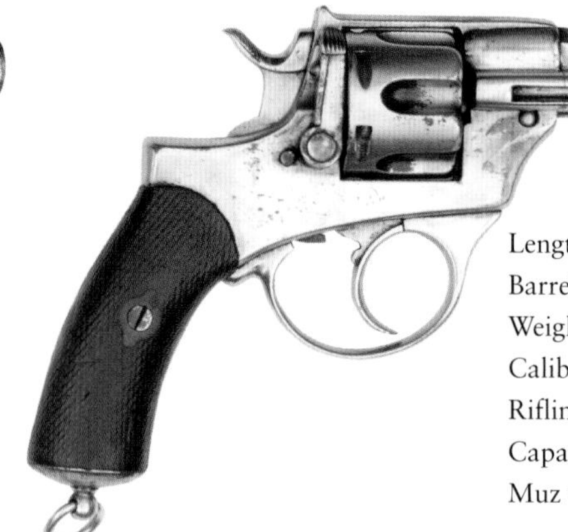

Length (gun): 9.5 in. (241 mm)
Barrel: 4.5 in. (114 mm)
Weight: 38.0 oz. (1.1 kg)
Caliber: 0.45 in. (11.4 mm)
Rifling: 4 grooves, l/hand
Capacity: six
Muz vel: 600 ft./sec. (183 m/sec.)

The first firm to patent and manufacture the Chamelot-Delvigne double-action lock for revolvers was Pirlot Frères of Liège, Belgium. Although little is known of the lock's origins, it proved to be strong, simple, and reliable, which made it highly suitable for use on military arms. It was used by a number of countries—notably Belgium, France, Italy, and Switzerland—in the last thirty years of the nineteenth century. The weapon shown is fairly typical, although its origin is obscure: it has few visible markings but is probably of Belgian make. It has an octagonal barrel, screwed into a solid frame. There is a bottom-hinged loading gate that opened to the rear and a small stop projected from the frame to prevent it from dropping too far. The ejector rod worked in a sleeve, the head of the rod being turned inward when not in use to fit over the long forward extension of the axis pin.

EUROPE

CONTINENTAL TIP-UP REVOLVER 1874

Length (gun): 10.8 in. (273 mm)
Barrel: 5.5 in. (140 mm)
Weight: 32.0 oz. (0.9 kg)
Caliber: 0.44 in. (11.2 mm)
Rifling: 7 grooves, r/hand
Capacity: five
Muz vel: 600 ft./sec. (183 m/sec.)

Smith & Wesson patented a 0.22 in. (5.6 mm) centerfire cartridge in the United States in 1855–56, and subsequently produced it in 0.32 in. (8.1 mm). The company only patented the bored-through cylinder in the United States and had no patent protection elsewhere; as a result, pirated copies soon began to appear. It is generally thought that Webley produced unlicensed copies in the early 1860s, but as these were unmarked, it is impossible to be certain. The weapon illustrated here is something of a mystery: although obviously of Smith & Wesson type, it bears no name or mark other than the date, 1874, on the left-hand side of the barrel frame, and one or two manufacturing numbers on the cylinder. The major differences (apart from size) from the genuine arm are the provision of a backsight on the top frame, the fact that the cylinder stop rose from the bottom, and that the weapon is of centerfire rather than rimfire type and is fitted with a sliding safety behind the hammer. The weapon appears well made, although it lacks the finish of the real thing. Its size, and the lanyard ring, suggest it was intended for military use.

BELGIUM

MINIATURE REVOLVER 1875

Length (gun): 4.3 in. (109 mm)
Barrel: 1.6 in. (41 mm)
Weight: 6.0 oz. (0.2 kg)
Caliber: 0.22 in. (5.6 mm)
Rifling: 5 grooves, r/hand
Capacity: six
Muz vel: 500 ft./sec. (152 m/sec.)

The tiny pistol seen here is a cheap but well-finished and reliable revolver of the type produced in Belgium in the nineteenth century. It has a solid frame with an integral round barrel, complete with foresight. Its cylinder is chambered to take six short, copper-cased rimfire cartridges. It was loaded through a bottom-hinged loading gate, the insertion of the cartridges being facilitated by a groove in the frame, and the chambers are recessed to accommodate the cartridge rims. The ejector rod is housed in the hollow axis pin and could be drawn forward and then swiveled in order to bring it in line with the chamber opposite the loading gate. The double-action lock was activated by a folding trigger. Unusually, there is a safety lever on the left side of the frame; when this was pressed down, it prevented the hammer from rising. Apart from the hammer, trigger, ejector, and safety, the weapon is blued and bears appropriate proof marks and the number "8345." Around 1,900 revolvers like this could be bought in England very cheaply; they were particularly recommended to cyclists!

ITALY

GLISENTI CHAMELOT-DELVIGNE-PATTERN ITALIAN SERVICE REVOLVER 1875

Length (gun): 11.2 in. (284 mm)
Barrel: 6.3 in. (159 mm)
Weight: 40.0 oz. (1.1 kg)
Caliber: 0.41 in. (10.4 mm)
Rifling: 5 grooves, r/hand
Capacity: six
Muz vel: 625 ft./sec. (190 m/sec.)

This revolver is the Italian version of the Chamelot-Delvigne et Schmidt Model 1872 (Schmidt was a Swiss officer who made some design changes). The arm has a solid frame, and the octagonal barrel is screwed into it. The foresight is slotted in and the backsight is a U-notch on the lump. The six-chambered cylinder is grooved and has rear notches for the cylinder stop. The ejector rod worked in a sleeve. To remove the cylinder, it was necessary to turn down the head of the ejector rod and press in a stud on the left front of the frame; this allowed the pin to be drawn forward. The spring loading gate is hinged at the bottom and was opened by drawing it to the rear. The lock is double-action; very slight pressure on the trigger lifted the hammer to the half-cock position, for the cylinder to be rotated for loading. These revolvers were made in various Italian factories until 1930.

UNITED STATES

COLT DERRINGER NO. 3 1875

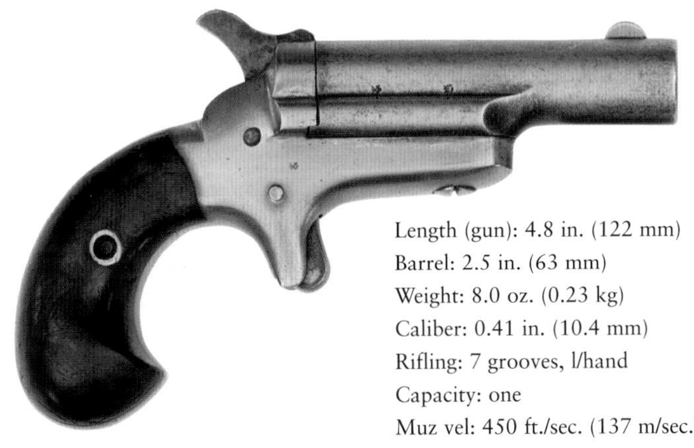

Length (gun): 4.8 in. (122 mm)
Barrel: 2.5 in. (63 mm)
Weight: 8.0 oz. (0.23 kg)
Caliber: 0.41 in. (10.4 mm)
Rifling: 7 grooves, l/hand
Capacity: one
Muz vel: 450 ft./sec. (137 m/sec.)

Weapons of this type take their names from Henry Deringer of Philadelphia, who specialized, from the 1830s onward, in the production of small pocket pistols of quite large caliber. These soon achieved popularity as easily concealed weapons. A pistol of this type was used to assassinate Abraham Lincoln. This brought the arm increased "fame" and led to extensive copying, until eventually the word "derringer" (spelled as it is owing to a mistake in a newspaper headline) came to denote a type rather than a trademark. The specimen shown here was made by Colt and is classed as the company's Model No. 3. To load, it was necessary to put the hammer at half-cock and swing the breech out to the right to insert the cartridge. The barrel was swung back and the pistol was cocked. The empty case was ejected automatically when the breech was opened.

UNITED STATES

REMINGTON MODEL 1875 REVOLVER

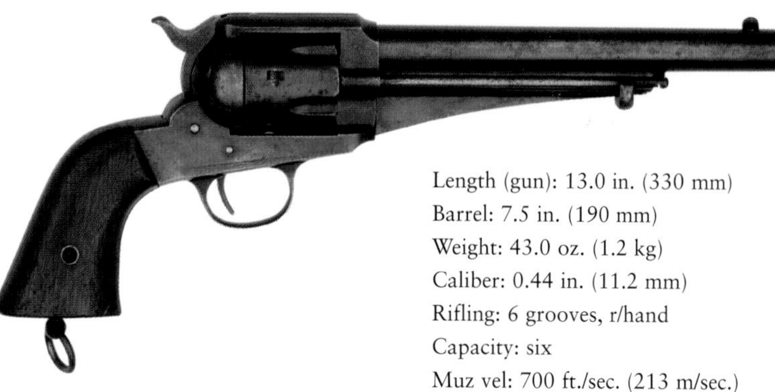

Length (gun): 13.0 in. (330 mm)
Barrel: 7.5 in. (190 mm)
Weight: 43.0 oz. (1.2 kg)
Caliber: 0.44 in. (11.2 mm)
Rifling: 6 grooves, r/hand
Capacity: six
Muz vel: 700 ft./sec. (213 m/sec.)

Once the Civil War was over, the demand for arms, particularly revolvers, remained fairly high. The first Remington cartridge revolver, which appeared in 1875, differed very little in general appearance from the firm's earlier percussion arm. The major mechanical differences were the bored-through cylinder, the loading gate, and the provision of a Colt-type ejector rod working in a sleeve. The distinctively tapered rammer handle of the earlier arm had, of course, become unnecessary; but it was replaced by a rib of similar dimensions, leaving the silhouette unchanged. The top of the barrel is engraved "E REMINGTON & SONS, ILION, NEW YORK, UNITED STATES." Although the Western scene was largely dominated by Colt arms, the new cartridge Remingtons were fine weapons—robust, well-made, and accurate. A new version appeared in 1891, but by then Colt was unassailable.

UNITED KINGDOM

WEBLEY-PRYSE 0.45 IN. REVOLVER 1876

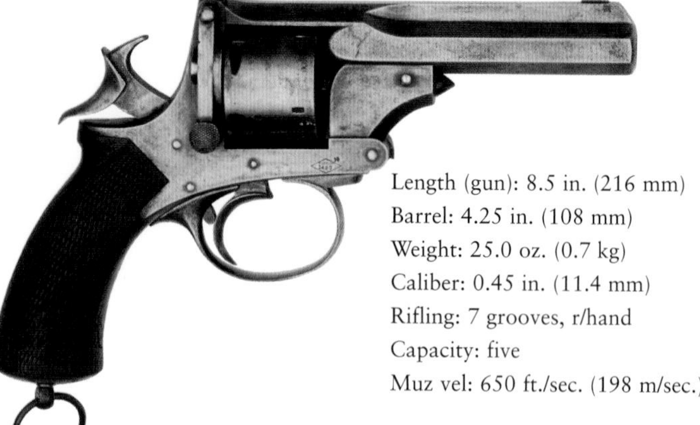

Length (gun): 8.5 in. (216 mm)
Barrel: 4.25 in. (108 mm)
Weight: 25.0 oz. (0.7 kg)
Caliber: 0.45 in. (11.4 mm)
Rifling: 7 grooves, r/hand
Capacity: five
Muz vel: 650 ft./sec. (198 m/sec.)

In 1876, Charles Pryse patented a new type of break-down, self-extracting revolver. The gun was hinged at the lower front of the frame; when the barrel was pushed down to an angle of about ninety degrees, a star-shaped ejector was forced from the cylinder, throwing out the empty cartridge cases. Two long register pins working in holes in the cylinder were attached to the base of the extractor. The barrel hinge was formed by two lugs on the barrel, with the extractor lever between them, and two outer lugs on the frame. It was held by a threaded pin. The cocking system consisted of two vertical arms, one on each side of the frame. A rear extension of the barrel entered a slot in front of the hammer; the bolts on the arms passed through holes in the side of this slot and engaged in recesses on the extension; they were held in place by springs. Pryse revolvers were always produced under license.

UNITED KINGDOM

WEBLEY R.I.C. REVOLVER NO. 2 1876

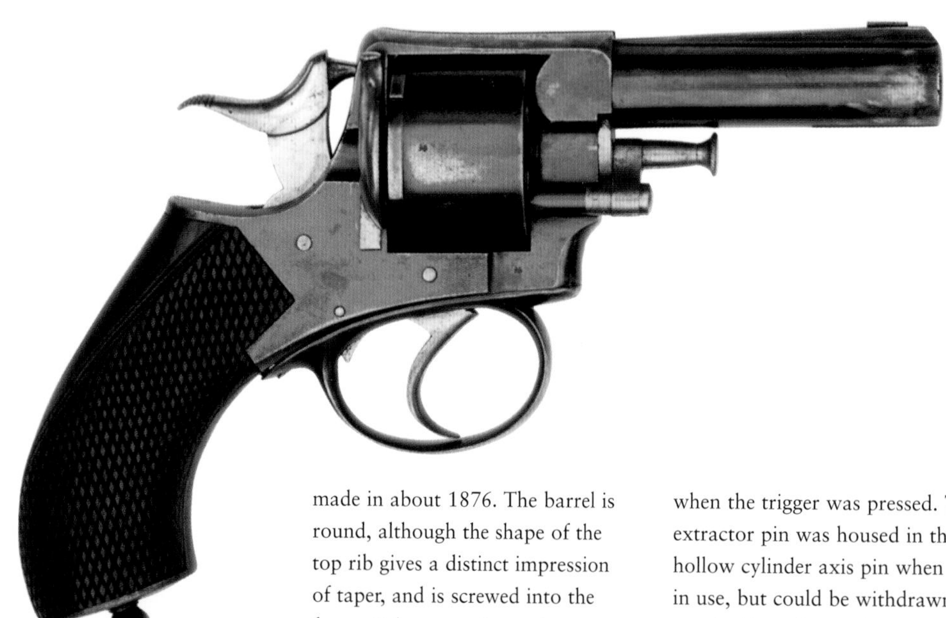

Length (gun): 8.3 in. (210 mm)
Barrel: 3.5 in. (89 mm)
Weight: 27.0 oz. (0.8 kg)
Caliber: 0.45 in. (11.4 mm)
Rifling: 5 grooves, r/hand
Capacity: six
Muz vel: 650 ft./sec. (198 m/sec.)

The first R.I.C. arm adopted was the Webley revolver, which was known thereafter as the Royal Irish Constabulary revolver. This specimen is the No. 2 Model, made in about 1876. The barrel is round, although the shape of the top rib gives a distinct impression of taper, and is screwed into the frame. It has a semi-round foresight, slotted in; the backsight is a long, V-shaped groove along the top strap. The six-chambered cylinder is plain except for raised flanges at the rear; the ends of these are held by the cylinder stop, which rose from the lower frame when the trigger was pressed. The extractor pin was housed in the hollow cylinder axis pin when not in use, but could be withdrawn on a swivel in order to align it with the appropriate chamber. Access to the chamber was via a loading gate hinged at the bottom. The lock is double-action. This revolver was carried by Major Webb of the Bengal Cavalry in the Second Afghan War of 1878–80; it is marked "MANTON & CO, LONDON & CALCUTTA" on the strap. The left side of the frame is stamped "WEBLEYS RIC NO 2 .450 CF," with the flying bullet trademark, and also bears the serial number "10974." Production of the No. 2 models lasted from about 1876 to 1914.

UNITED STATES

COLT DOUBLE-ACTION ARMY REVOLVER 1877

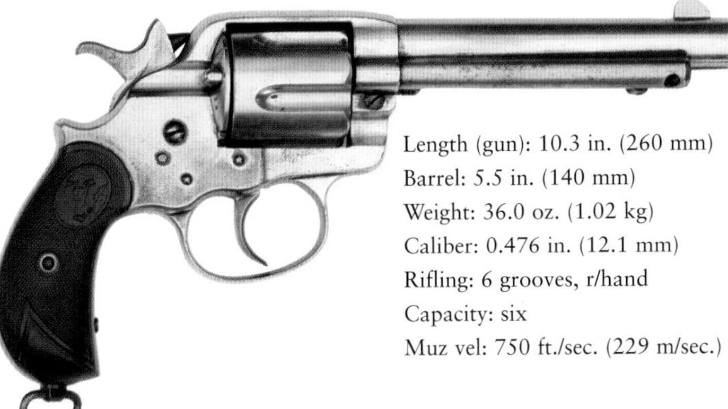

Length (gun): 10.3 in. (260 mm)
Barrel: 5.5 in. (140 mm)
Weight: 36.0 oz. (1.02 kg)
Caliber: 0.476 in. (12.1 mm)
Rifling: 6 grooves, r/hand
Capacity: six
Muz vel: 750 ft./sec. (229 m/sec.)

In 1877, Colt introduced the Double-Action Army model. It has the usual solid frame, with a round barrel screwed into it and an ejector rod sliding in a sleeve. The six-chambered cylinder has a loading gate, and a cartridge groove is provided on the right-hand side of the frame. It is the first Colt revolver to have been fitted with a double-action lock. The revolver was made in three major calibers—0.32 in. (8.1 mm), 0.38 in. (9.6 mm), and 0.45 in. (11.4 mm)—and in three barrel lengths: 4.75 in. (121 mm), 5.5 in. (140 mm), and 7.5 in. (190 mm). The caliber of the revolver shown is, however, 0.476 in. (12.1 mm), which indicates that this particular specimen was probably made for the British market—for this was the standard British service caliber at the time. Made in the US until 1909, it never proved popular: it had the reputation of being both badly balanced and mechanically unreliable—a Colt!

UNITED KINGDOM

PRYSE 0.577 IN. (BLAND-PRYSE) REVOLVER 1877

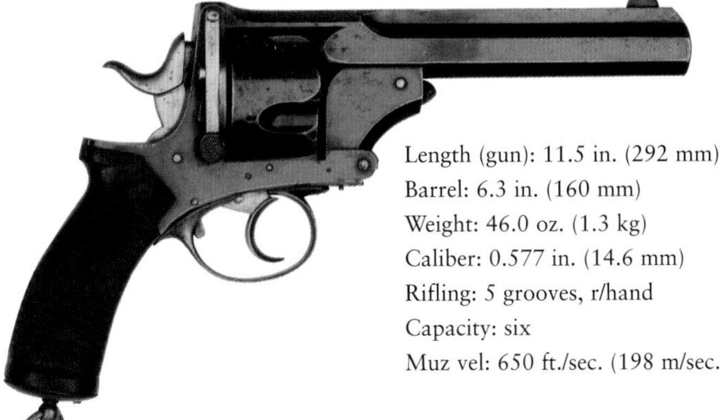

Length (gun): 11.5 in. (292 mm)
Barrel: 6.3 in. (160 mm)
Weight: 46.0 oz. (1.3 kg)
Caliber: 0.577 in. (14.6 mm)
Rifling: 5 grooves, r/hand
Capacity: six
Muz vel: 650 ft./sec. (198 m/sec.)

Webley was one of several patentees manufacturing the Pryse new design of break-open revolver. Although this specimen has no markings, it was probably marketed by a firm called Bland. The major point of interest is its massive 0.577 in. (14.6 mm) caliber, a true "man-stopping" round, which would have halted any assailant in mid-stride. Indeed, the size and weight of the revolver, coupled to the very hefty recoil, must have posed a considerable challenge to the shooter, and it is worth noting that the marginally smaller, modern 0.5 in. (12.7 mm) Browning round is considered a heavyweight when fired from a rifle. The 0.577 in. round was adopted as the British Army's rifle round in the late 1860s, and the War Office then approved a revolver round of the same caliber. Webley produced their No. 1 Revolver, while Bland-Pryse produced this as a competitor.

GERMANY

COSTER PINFIRE REVOLVER 1877

Length (gun): 10.4 in. (264 mm)
Barrel: 5.4 in. (137 mm)
Weight: 26.0 oz. (0.7 kg)
Caliber: 0.35 in. (9 mm)
Rifling: 6 grooves, r/hand
Capacity: six
Muz vel: 550 ft./sec. (168 m/sec.)

This is an attractive arm, strong and well made and of unusually good quality and finish. It has a one-piece frame with a top strap and an octagonal barrel on which the top flat is narrowed to form a distinct rib. It has an unusually high foresight, while the backsight is a V-shaped notch. The cylinder is unfluted and has long and elegantly formed projections: these engaged against the cylinder stop, which rose from the lower frame when the trigger was pressed. It has the usual loading gate, with a thumb piece and a spring catch that held the gate in position yet allowed it to be opened with quite light thumb pressure. The lock is double-action. There is an upward bulge at the end of the top strap which prevented the protruding pins from fouling it when the cylinder rotated, and there is a correspon-ding notch on the bottom of the frame. The pistol is well blued and competently engraved, with the exception of the hammer, trigger, foresight, and ejector rod, which are of bright steel. The one-piece butt—its shape typical of German arms—is held by two tangs. The top strap bears the inscription "J A COSTER IN HANAU," and there is a gold monogram on the top tang.

UNITED KINGDOM

WEBLEY-PRYSE REVOLVER NO. 4 1877

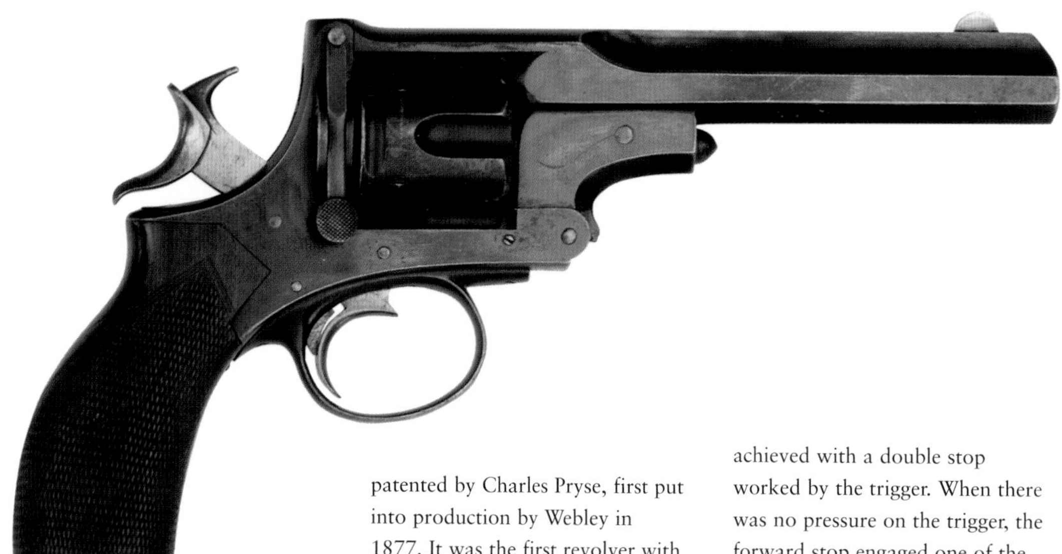

Length (gun): 10.8 in. (273 mm)
Barrel: 5.8 in. (146 mm)
Weight: 36.0 oz. (1.0 kg)
Caliber: 0.476 in. (12.1 mm)
Rifling: 7 grooves, r/hand
Capacity: six
Muz vel: 650 ft./sec. (198 m/sec.)

This is one of the early hinged-frame, self-extracting revolvers incorporating the system patented by Charles Pryse, first put into production by Webley in 1877. It was the first revolver with a rebounding hammer; this automatically lifted about 0.15 in. (4 mm) when the trigger was released after firing, thus holding it clear of the next cartridge. The fluted cylinder was reliably locked at all times, except when the lock was being operated. This was achieved with a double stop worked by the trigger. When there was no pressure on the trigger, the forward stop engaged one of the smaller slots; when the trigger was pressed, the cylinder rotated, and the rear part of the stop engaged in one of the long, bullet-shaped slots at the rear of the cylinder. The cylinder has a star extractor that was forced sharply outward when the revolver was opened by pressing in the milled discs on the lower ends of the locking arms, disengaging two bolts from an extension of the top frame. The extractor was provided with two register pins that fitted into holes in the cylinder. The left side of the frame of this specimen is marked "WEBLEYS NO4 .476CF." Below this is the famous flying-bullet trademark and the serial number "7546."

UNITED KINGDOM

WEBLEY-PRYSE-TYPE 0.45 IN. REVOLVER 1878

Length (gun): 7.5 in. (190 mm)
Weight: 25.0 oz. (0.7 kg)
Barrel: 3.5 in. (89 mm)
Caliber: 0.45 in. (11.4 mm)
Rifling: 3 grooves, r/hand
Capacity: five
Muz vel: 650 ft./sec. (198 m/sec.)

Charles Pryse licensed a number of gunsmiths to manufacture revolvers to his patent design, and even Webley was one of these, despite the fact that it had its own designs on the market, as has already been mentioned. Other makers of Pryse-type revolvers included British makers such as Thomas Horsley and Christopher Bonehill, while copies were inevitably made by Belgian manufacturers in Liège. The arm illustrated here is marked "T.W. WATSON, 4, PALL MALL, LONDON" on the top flat of the barrel, but this is almost certainly the name of the retailer rather than that of the maker. The weapon bears London proof marks and has the number "358" on the frame. Although of the same caliber as the Webley-Pryse shown earlier, this weapon had a much shorter barrel (3.5 in./89 mm, compared to 4.25 in./108 mm), and there were differences in the trigger group and butt.

BELGIUM

BULLDOG PISTOL (COPY) 1878

Length (gun): 5.5 in. (140 mm)
Barrel: 1.9 in. (48 mm)
Weight: 12.0 oz. (0.3 kg)
Caliber: 0.32 in. (8.1 mm)
Rifling: 5 grooves, r/hand
Capacity: six
Muz vel: 550 ft./sec. (168 m/sec.)

In 1878, the British firm of P. Webley and Sons (which had by then begun to establish its excellent reputation for revolvers) introduced a group of weapons under the general title of "British Bulldog." They were solid-frame, five-chambered arms of 0.44 in. (11.2 mm) and 0.45 in. (11.4 mm) caliber, and were intended primarily as civilian arms. Despite the fact that Britain was then a relatively well-settled and generally law-abiding country, many people liked to keep a pistol handy in the house for protection against aggressive vagrants or burglars. There was also a considerable demand from civilians going out to work in the more remote parts of the British Empire. These reliable Bulldog weapons soon became popular; they were quickly copied in France, Belgium, German, Spain—and even in the United States. The weapon illustrated is a Belgian copy of poor quality, with a folding trigger.

RIFLING: A QUANTUM LEAP

Rifling refers to the method of imparting spin to a bullet as it passes down the barrel of a firearm. Although the introduction of rifling cannot be dated with any precision, it is clear that rifled firearms had emerged by the end of the sixteenth century. It was first introduced as a way to reduce the pervasive problem of barrel fouling in early smoothbore weapons. Gasper Zollner of Vienna at first attempted to counter this problem by cutting two straight grooves into the walls of the barrel, these being intended to capture most of the fouling. However, gunsmiths had observed the archer's technique of achieving greater distance and accuracy by angling the flights to spin the arrow. By cutting twisting grooves down the barrel, then hammering the ball down tightly so that it engaged the grooves, the ball was spun upon firing and produced great improvements in performance. The depth and number of grooves steadily increased, rifled weapons of the 1800s generally having between three and twelve grooves. By the end of the nineteenth century, almost all weapons except shotguns were rifled, and even the shortest handgun barrel had rifling.

Above: *It is not so easy to photograph the inside of a pistol barrel, so here is what the inside of a 12-inch gun looks like. The soldier's head is at the muzzle end and the rifling that gives the shell its spin uses exactly the same principles as the grooves inside a handgun. This gun was one of the links in a chain of such guns that encircled the English coast to guard against invasion during World War II.*

Rifling works on a simple principle. In flight, any object will try to present its heaviest face first and is also subject to the interference of wind, temperature, humidity, air pressure, and other factors. A bullet fired from an unrifled barrel, therefore, is prone to twisting erratically in flight, forcing it to deviate from its intended flight path. A rifled barrel, however, spins the bullet around its central axis, cancelling the effect of weight shift and also making it more resistant to environmental interference.

The consequence is a far more accurate round, which will fly further and hold its velocity for longer. Even though the bullet bites hard into the grooves, only about 20 percent of the energy at firing is directed into its rotation.

There are numerous types of rifling, including concentric, polygonal, and ratchet (a series of small arcs rather than grooves). Some weapons have progressive pitching (pitch refers to the speed at which the bullet turns, as in the pitch of a screw), with slow pitch in front of the chamber quickening to a tight, fast pitch in front of the muzzle.

GERMANY

MAUSER ZIG-ZAG REVOLVER 1878

Length (gun): 11.8 in. (298 mm)
Barrel: 6.5 in. (165 mm)
Weight: 42.0 oz. (1.2 kg)
Caliber: 0.43 in. (10.9 mm)
Rifling: 5 grooves, r/hand
Capacity: six
Muz vel: 650 ft./sec. (198 m/sec.)

This proposed German service revolver was designed by Peter Paul Mauser. It is top-hinged. When a lever on the left-hand side of the frame was pushed upward, it allowed the ring in front of the trigger to be pulled downward. This freed the catch and allowed the entire barrel and cylinder to be raised just past the vertical, where it locked. Increased pressure on the ring operated a cam which forced a star ejector out of the rear face of the cylinder, throwing out the empty cases. The weapon had an unusual method of cylinder rotation. When the trigger was pressed, a rod with a stud on its upper surface was forced forward so that its front end protruded through the barrel catch, ensuring that it could not be opened by accident. The stud engaged one of the diagonal slots on the cylinder and thus caused the cylinder to rotate through one-sixth of its circumference. When the trigger was released, the rod was retracted.

UNITED KINGDOM

KERR REVOLVER (LATER MODEL) 1878

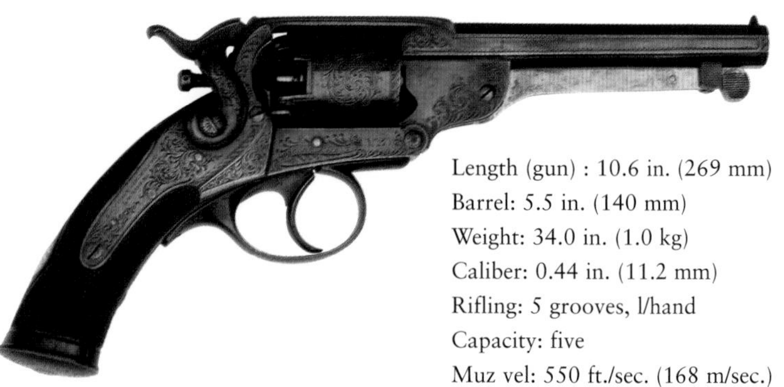

Length (gun) : 10.6 in. (269 mm)
Barrel: 5.5 in. (140 mm)
Weight: 34.0 in. (1.0 kg)
Caliber: 0.44 in. (11.2 mm)
Rifling: 5 grooves, l/hand
Capacity: five
Muz vel: 550 ft./sec. (168 m/sec.)

Kerr's revolvers had the barrel and top strap forged as a separate component, fastened to the frame by two screws: one just below the aperture for the hammer nose, the other at the front lower end of the frame. The fit is so accurate that the revolver could be taken to have a solid frame. This revolver is fitted with a new type of rammer, also the invention of Kerr. It is centrally placed below the barrel: when not in use, the lever was held between two lugs on the lower side of the barrel by means of a spring catch. Drawing the lever downward forced the ram into the lowest chamber. The central position of the rammer meant that the cylinder axis had to be inserted from the the rear. It has a sliding safety on the lockplate; when pushed forward, it engaged a slot at the rear of the hammer and prevented it from being drawn back. Kerr revolvers were used by the Confederates.

UNITED KINGDOM

WEBLEY BULLDOG REVOLVER 1878

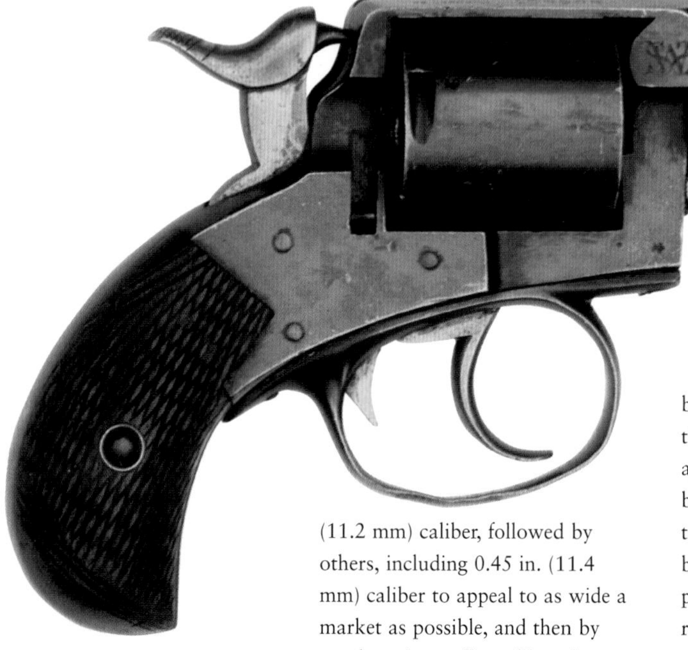

Length (gun): 5.5 in. (140 mm)
Barrel: 2.1 in. (53 mm)
Weight: 11.0 oz. (0.3 kg)
Caliber: 0.32 in. (8.1 mm)
Rifling: 5 grooves, r/hand
Capacity: five
Muz vel: 500 ft./sec. (152 m/sec.)

As previously mentioned (see page 92, Bulldog Copy), Webley produced a whole series of Bulldog weapons. The first was a heavy, centerfire arm in 0.442 in. (11.2 mm) caliber, followed by others, including 0.45 in. (11.4 mm) caliber to appeal to as wide a market as possible, and then by revolvers in smaller calibers better suited for use as pocket arms. The revolver seen here is the smallest of these pocket types and is classed as the second model. It is constructed on a solid frame with an integral barrel. The vertical dimension of the barrel at the muzzle is appreciably greater than it is at the breech end; this gives a markedly tapered effect, even in a very short barrel. As was the universal practice in these early Webley revolvers, the cylinder is plain—except for the slots at its rear end to accommodate the cylinder stop, which rose from the bottom of the frame when the action was cocked. It was originally fitted with a bottom-hinged loading gate. The ejector pin was normally housed in the hollow cylinder axis pin, whence it could be withdrawn and swiveled for use. Once this had been done, the cylinder axis pin could also be withdrawn by means of its flat, milled head; thus, the cylinder could be removed. The mechanism is of double-action type, and the arm was designed to take centerfire cartridges. Rimfire versions were also made, and were so stamped for identification on the frame.

UNITED KINGDOM

WEBLEY-KAUFMANN REVOLVER 1878

Length (gun): 11.0 in. (279 mm)
Barrel: 6.8 in. (173 mm)
Weight: 38.0 oz. (1.1 kg)
Caliber: 0.455/0.476 in. (11.5/12.1 mm)
Rifling: 7 grooves, r/hand
Capacity: six
Muz vel: 650 ft./sec. (198 m/sec.)

Michael Kaufmann was a very talented British inventor of firearms. His association with Webley in the period 1878-81 led to the appearance of the revolver seen here, which bears his name and which provided, in effect, the basic design for Webley's famous range of Government (Webley-Green) models, produced from 1882 onward. The Webley-Kaufmann revolver has an octagonal barrel with its top flat drawn up into a rib. It is of break-open type, and perhaps its main point of interest is the locking system. A rear extension on the top strap fits into a corresponding slot in the standing breech, and running through both is a cylindrical hole, with a diameter of about 0.16 in. (4 mm), in which the locking bolt worked. Pressure on a lever on the left side of the body caused a spring bolt (the milled end of which is visible in the photograph) to be forced outward, thus allowing the revolver to be closed. When the lever was released, the bolt was returned inward, entering the hole in the rear extension. This held a floating bolt, which was pushed over to the left in order to engage with the far hole on the standing breech, thus providing a very strong locking device indeed.

UNITED KINGDOM

WEBLEY NEW MODEL ARMY EXPRESS REVOLVER 1878

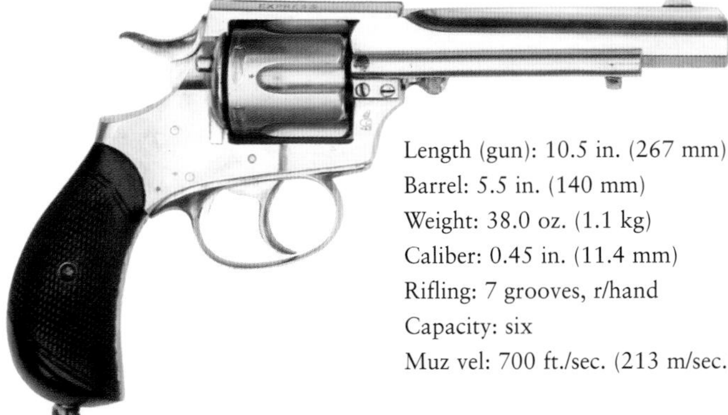

Length (gun): 10.5 in. (267 mm)
Barrel: 5.5 in. (140 mm)
Weight: 38.0 oz. (1.1 kg)
Caliber: 0.45 in. (11.4 mm)
Rifling: 7 grooves, r/hand
Capacity: six
Muz vel: 700 ft./sec. (213 m/sec.)

Like the 1877 Colt double-action revolver (though probably not based on it), the Webley is a solid-frame revolver, with a loading gate and a sliding ejector rod. Its barrel, which is basically octagonal but with a higher and narrower top flat, is screwed into the frame, although the joint is virtually imperceptible. It has an unusually large trigger guard, presumably so that it could be used by a man wearing gloves. Its bird's-beak butt is larger than that of the corresponding Colt, and was a good deal more comfortable to handle as a result. The arm was made in one caliber only, nominally 0.45 in. (11.4 mm), but, like all Webley service arms of the period, it would accept cartridges of both 0.455 in. (11.5 mm) and 0.476 in. (12.1 mm) caliber. There was only one standard length of barrel 5.5 in. (140 mm), as seen here—but a few models were made with 12 in. (305 mm) barrels to special order, and these were supplied with a detachable shoulder stock.

UNITED KINGDOM

TRANTER "ARMY" REVOLVER 1879

Length (gun): 11.8 in. (298 mm)
Barrel: 6.0 in. (152 mm)
Weight: 36.0 oz. (1.0 kg)
Caliber: 0.45 in. (11.4 mm)
Rifling: 7 grooves, r/hand
Capacity: six
Muz vel: 650 ft./sec. (198 m/sec.)

The obvious advantage of the hinged-frame or break-open revolver—particularly as regards speed of ejection or reloading—were quickly seen by Tranter, who, by 1879, had patented and put into production his own revolver of this type. It has an octagonal barrel with a raised top rib and a round foresight (the backsight being a groove on the back end of the top strap), and a six-chambered fluted cylinder with an automatic ejector. The cylinder could be removed by first opening the revolver and then pressing the milled catch visible below the barrel; the cylinder could then be lifted off its axis pin. The lock is of double-action type and has a rebounding hammer. The locking system consists of a rear extension to the top strap, with a rectangular aperture that fits over a shaped projection on top of the standing breech. The long, pivoted hook on the left of the frame is basically similar to that found on the Webley, but fits over a projection on the top frame.

THE BIRTH OF MODERN PROPELLANTS

Black powder was an adequate propellant for over 200 years, producing a respectable gas expansion of about 290 times its own volume. It certainly enabled a ball or bullet to be lethal, but it had many associated problems. Black powder produces intense smoke upon firing, obscuring the ground for subsequent shots. Producing potassium nitrate (saltpeter) required labor-intensive production processes, and the quality of a powder could be variable depending on the type of raw materials used. Furthermore, black powder creates intense, solid fouling in the barrel, increasing cleaning times significantly.

The move away from black powder began in 1838, when the scientist Theophile Pelouze treated cotton with nitric acid, producing an explosive substance that lay the foundations for nitrocellulose propellants. In the mid 1840s, Professor Christian F. Schoenbein of Switzerland and Professor Bottger of Germany both produced nitrocellulose (also known as guncotton) by treating cotton with concentrated nitric and sulphuric acids.

What these scientists produced was a propellant with around 300 percent more gas-to-volume expansion than black powder. However, the new propellant was far too powerful to use in most weapons, so scientists subsequently sought ways to reduce its burn rate to manageable levels. Various methods were applied. The Prussian artillery officer Major E. Schultze nitrated wood instead of cotton to produce a more manageable propellant, but the most important step came in the 1870s, when scientists discovered that nitrocellulose was soluble in an alcohol/ether mix. When the solution was dried, it could be formed into powder granules, and using this method, Frenchman Paul Vielle made the first effective smokeless propellant synthesized from guncotton, known as Poudre B.

The final leap into modern propellants came with Alfred Nobel's work in 1887, in which he gelatinized guncotton in the explosive nitroglycerine (in a 60/40 mix). This discovery formed the basis for all subsequent smokeless powders, as in its final state the mixture gave a controllable burn, high power, and limited fouling.

Right: *Gathering nitrocellulose produced at a Melbourne plant in the 1950s; it is easy to see why it became known as guncotton. Nitrocellulose makes cordite when it is put with nitroglycerine, as discovered by Alfred Nobel, and is still the basis for gun propellants today.*

UNITED STATES

SMITH & WESSON REVOLVING RIFLE 1879

Length (gun): 35.0 in. (889 mm)
Barrel: 18.0 in. (457 mm)
Weight: 80.0 oz. (2.3 kg)
Caliber: 0.32 in. (8.1 mm)
Rifling: 6 grooves, r/hand
Capacity: six
Muz vel: 820 ft./sec. (250 m/sec.)

This rare weapon first appeared in 1879. It is closely modeled on the No. 3 revolver, but with a two-piece barrel which is screwed together about 2 in. (51 mm) in front of the breech, although the joint is barely visible. The rifle was made in three barrel lengths: 16 in. (406 mm), 18 in. (457 mm) as illustrated, and 20 in. (508 mm). It has a blued foresight on the top rib and an L-shaped backsight to give two elevations. The aperture backsight, an optional extra, may be seen on the clamp which holds the rifle butt onto the pistol. The grips and fore end are of hard, mottled rubber. The rifle butt, which is clamped to the revolver by means of the milled screw below the backsight pillar, is of fine-quality Circassian walnut and has a rubber butt plate. This specimen was captured by British troops in Ireland in 1916—the year of the Easter Rising—and would presumably have been useful in guerrilla warfare.

AUSTRIA-HUNGARY

MONTENEGRIN GASSER REVOLVER 1880

Length (gun): 10.4 in. (264 mm)
Barrel: 5.3 in. (135 mm)
Weight: 33.0 oz. (0.94 kg)
Caliber: 0.42 in. (10.7 mm)
Rifling: 6 grooves, l/hand
Capacity: five
Muz vel: 550 ft./sec. (168 m/sec.)

The term Montenegrin Gasser is used to describe a fairly broad category rather than a particular arm. The revolver illustrated here has a solid frame, but is otherwise generally similar in principle to the Gasser arm. In particular, it has the same flat safety bar that acted against the hammer until the trigger was pressed. Some Montenegrin Gassers are of breakdown type, with a circular pierced extractor plate at the rear of the cylinder, others have open frames, and some were made with single-action locks. They are often highly decorated. The story is told that in the late nineteenth-century King Nicholas of Montenegro had a considerable financial interest in the factory and, in order to maintain his income, insisted that every adult male in his kingdom possess one of these revolvers. The story may well be apocryphal—but it has an authentic Ruritanian flavor!

BELGIUM

COPY OF R.I.C. REVOLVER 1880

Length (gun): 8.8 in. (222 mm)
Barrel: 4.0 in. (102 mm)
Weight: 24.0 oz. (0.7 kg)
Caliber: 0.45 in. (11.4 mm)
Rifling: 7 grooves, l/hand
Capacity: six
Muz vel: 650 ft./sec. (198 m/sec.)

The original Royal Irish Constabulary revolver was first put on the market by P. Webley and Son of Birmingham in 1867 and proved an immediate success. The force from which its title was derived adopted it in 1868, as did many other colonial forces, both military and police; it also proved extremely popular as an arm for civilian use. The revolver inevitably went through a number of changes in its long history, but its essential characteristics remained. Inevitably, such a popular arm was very widely copied in the United Kingdom, in continental Europe, and even occasionally in the United States. The quality and reliability of these pirated versions varied considerably. The weapon illustrated here is characteristic of the type: it is a copy of the Webley Model of 1880. It has a solid frame with an octagonal barrel screwed into it; the cylinder is unusual in having elliptical fluting. The lock is of double-action type with a wide hammer comb. The ejector rod is housed in the hollow axis pin. This appears to be one of the better copies, for it is well made and finished, but it bears no marks other than a crown over the letter "R." This is the Belgian mark for black-powder revolver barrels that have been tested with a charge 30 percent above the intended norm.

UNITED KINGDOM

ENFIELD MARK II SERVICE REVOLVER 1880

Length (gun): 11.5 in. (292 mm)
Barrel: 5.8 in. (146 mm)
Weight: 40.0 oz. (1.1 kg)
Caliber: 0.476 in. (12.1 mm)
Rifling: 7 grooves, r/hand
Capacity: six
Muz vel: 700 ft./sec. (213 m/sec.)

Colonial campaigns during the 1870s had shown the British that the 0.45 in. (11.4 mm) would not always stop a charging enemy; thus, a more powerful round of 0.476 in. (12.1 mm) caliber was developed. There were doubts that a top-break revolver could handle such rounds, and so a new arm was developed. The designer was a Philadelphian, Owen Jones; his revolver was approved for service in 1880. This specimen is a Mark II. The barrel is hinged to the front of the frame and fastened with a spring catch just in front of the hammer. When the revolver was opened and the barrel forced downward, the cylinder remained in the same axis and was simply drawn forward along its pin. This left the cases held by their rims in a star-shaped extractor on the standing breech, whence they could be shaken clear. The need for the cylinder to be drawn well forward accounts for the rather ugly bulge below the barrel.

UNITED KINGDOM

HILL'S SELF-EXTRACTING REVOLVER 1880

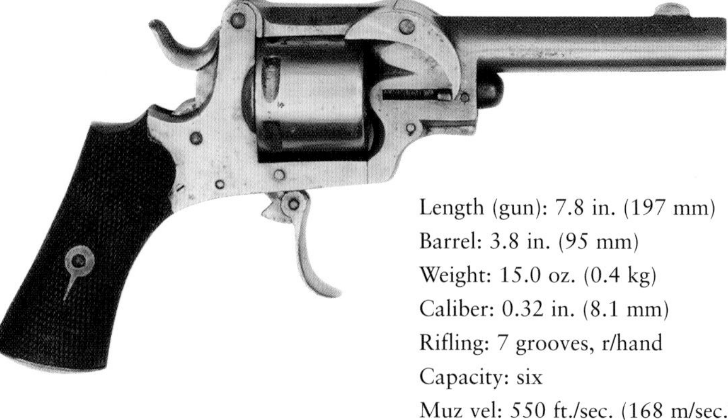

Length (gun): 7.8 in. (197 mm)
Barrel: 3.8 in. (95 mm)
Weight: 15.0 oz. (0.4 kg)
Caliber: 0.32 in. (8.1 mm)
Rifling: 7 grooves, r/hand
Capacity: six
Muz vel: 550 ft./sec. (168 m/sec.)

This revolver is more complex than other tip-ups because no special manual operation was necessary to eject the empty cases. There are two hinges: one where the top frame is attached to the standing breech, and a second where the barrel joins the frame. To open the weapon, it was necessary first to press the flat lever (just visible) on the lower front corner of the frame and raise the barrel. At this stage, the front hinge remained rigid and only the rear one opened. When the barrel was vertical, the limit of the rear hinge was reached and the crescent-shaped lever also locked. Continued pressure on the barrel caused the front hinge to come into play, allowing the barrel to continue backward beyond the vertical. The small stud protruding from the front of the frame, and attached to the extractor rod, bore on the front end of the crescent and was thrust downward, pushing out the star extractor.

UNITED KINGDOM

TIP-UP REVOLVER 1880

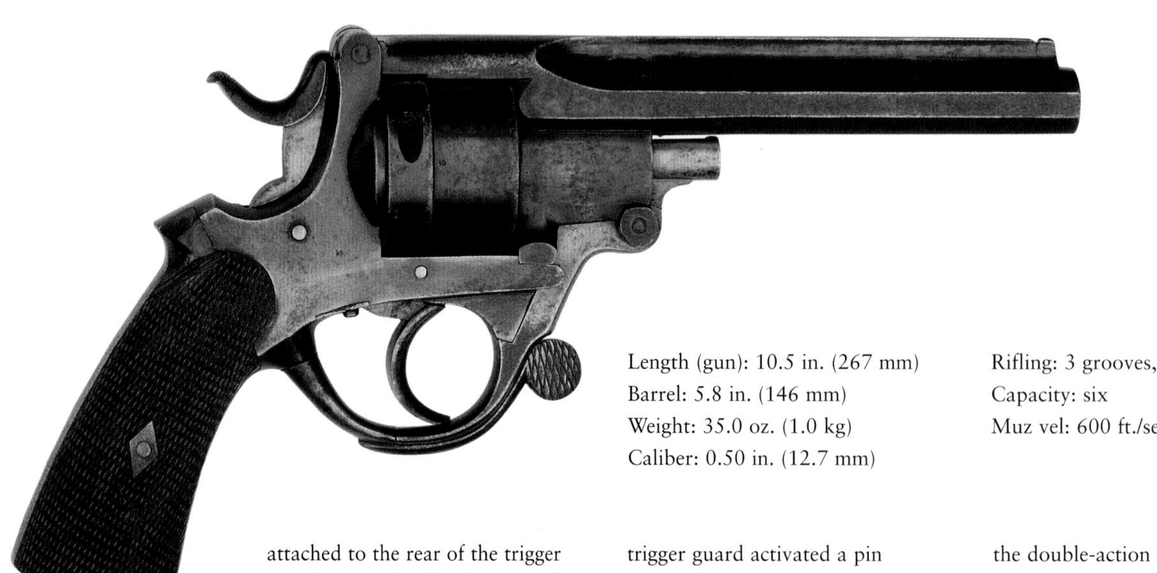

Length (gun): 10.5 in. (267 mm)
Barrel: 5.8 in. (146 mm)
Weight: 35.0 oz. (1.0 kg)
Caliber: 0.50 in. (12.7 mm)
Rifling: 3 grooves, r/hand
Capacity: six
Muz vel: 600 ft./sec. (183 m/sec.)

This large and robust revolver by an unknown maker has Birmingham proof marks and bears the words "CAST STEEL" on the barrel. It is of tip-up type. When the milled head of an arm attached to the rear of the trigger guard was pushed hard over to the left, it locked the hammer at half-cock and unlocked the barrel catch. This allowed the barrel and cylinder to be turned over well beyond the vertical, until the top strap rested on the head of the hammer. Increased pressure on the lever forming the front half of the trigger guard activated a pin attached to a star extractor, forcing it out from the cylinder. When the lever was released, the extractor returned to its original position. The barrel and cylinder were then closed and locked with the lever with the milled head. This action also had the effect of freeing the hammer and allowing the double-action lock mechanism to function in the normal way. It was desirable that the pistol be held on its side during this process; otherwise, there was a considerable risk that the rounds would fall out of the chambers under their own weight. Cylinder rotation in this arm was by the usual method of pawl and ratchet.

UNITED KINGDOM

TIP-UP REVOLVER 1880

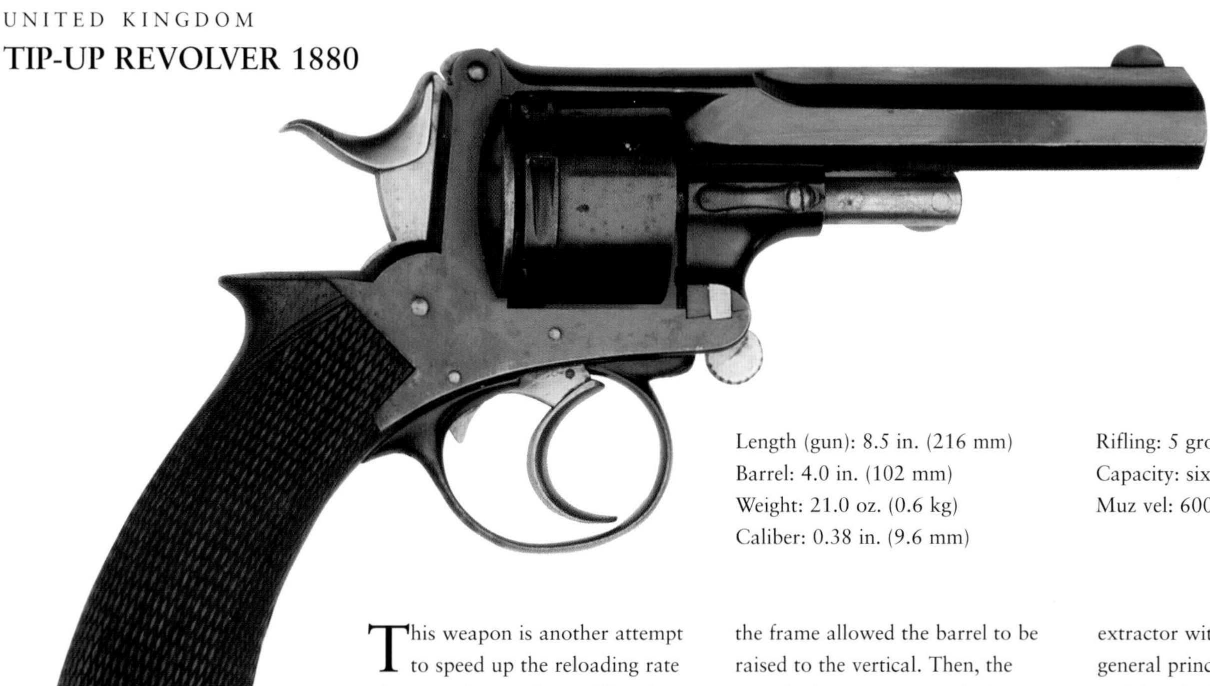

Length (gun): 8.5 in. (216 mm)
Barrel: 4.0 in. (102 mm)
Weight: 21.0 oz. (0.6 kg)
Caliber: 0.38 in. (9.6 mm)
Rifling: 5 grooves, r/hand
Capacity: six
Muz vel: 600 ft./sec. (183 m/sec.)

This weapon is another attempt to speed up the reloading rate of a cartridge revolver. Although of good quality, it bears no maker's name; but its general style and London proof marks indicate that it is of British origin. It is a cartridge revolver of the tip-up type: upward pressure on the circular catch at the lower front of the frame allowed the barrel to be raised to the vertical. Then, the very thick ejector pin—which is, in fact, shaped with a right-angled knob like an ordinary door bolt—was first rotated as far as possible, exerting a powerful camming action on the star-shaped extractor, and then pushed sharply backward, thus thrusting out the extractor with its empty cases. The general principle was a sound one and foreshadowed the introduction of the tip-down revolver with its automatic ejector. Its main weakness appears to lie in the catch, which did not engage deeply with the frame and might have opened accidentally.

UNITED KINGDOM

BULLDOG-TYPE REVOLVER 1880

Length (gun): 9.0 in. (229 mm)
Barrel: 4.0 in. (102 mm)
Weight: 29.0 oz. (0.8 kg)
Caliber: 0.45 in. (11.4 mm)
Rifling: 7 grooves, r/hand
Capacity: five
Muz vel: 600 ft./sec. (183 m/sec.)

This particular specimen has the usual ovate barrel with top rib and is of solid-frame construction. The five-chambered cylinder is plain, except for slots for the cylinder stop, and bears Birmingham proof marks. The ejector is of the usual pin pattern, and it was carried inside the hollow cylinder axis pin. It is fitted with a swivel carrier on the right front of the frame, allowing it to be drawn out and swung over to come into line with the chamber aligned with the loading gate. The gate itself is hinged at the bottom and turned down sideways; the usual groove is cut in the frame beside it to facilitate loading. The lock is double-action, with a fairly wide, milled comb on the hammer. The arm has a one-piece, wrap-over grip of checkered walnut, fastened to the revolver by two vertical screws, one running downward from the rear of the frame behind the hammer, and the other running upward from the butt plate. The revolver's swivel ring is missing.

UNITED STATES

COLT FRONTIER/PEACEMAKER 0.44 IN. REVOLVER 1880

Length (gun): 10.3 in. (262 mm)
Barrel: 4.8 in. (121 mm)
Weight: 34.0 oz. (1.0 kg)
Caliber: 0.44 in. (11.2 mm)
Rifling: 6 grooves, r/hand
Capacity: six
Muz vel: 650 ft./sec. (198 m/sec.)

The civilian version of the Colt Single-Action Army became one of the most widely used handguns in the American West, where it was known either as the Peacemaker or, in this 0.44-40 in. form, as the Frontier. The gun had excellent balance and felt right in anyone's hand. The gun shown here is a presentation version of the Colt Frontier, silver-plated and embellished by an artist named Cuno Helfricht in about 1880. It has engraved, mother-of-pearl butt grips and is a superior example of the gunmaker's art. Most civilian models had a 4.75 in. (121 mm) barrel, but some were much longer and the Buntline Model (named after the author of Westerns who commissioned them) had a 12.0 in. (305 mm) barrel. The Colt Peacemaker/Frontier remained in production until 1941, by which time 357,859 had been produced in around 36 different calibers. After a gap of some fifteen years, Colt was persuaded to put it back in production. This was one of the best revolvers Colt ever produced.

DUELING PISTOLS

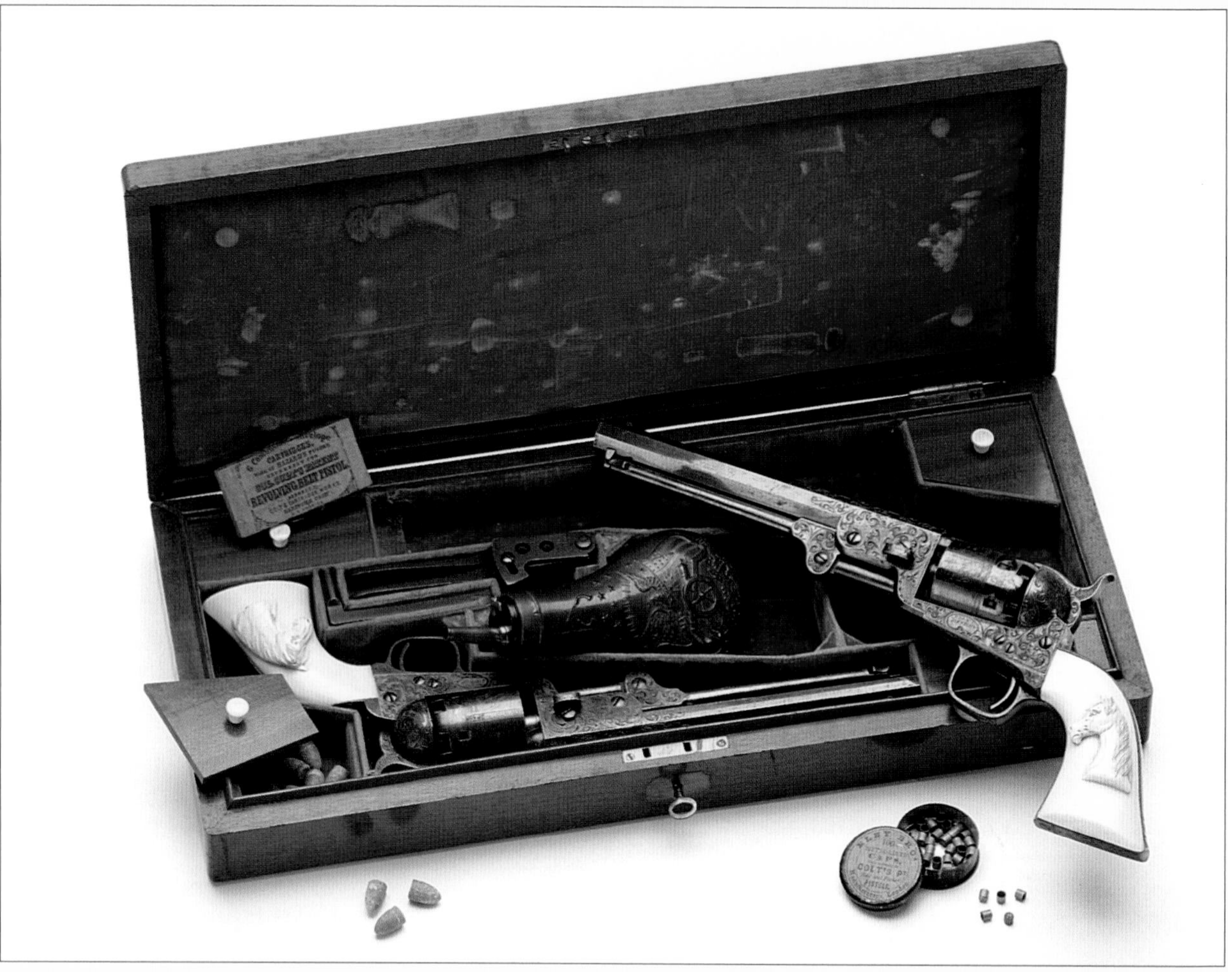

Between the late sixteenth century, when the duel took root in European society, and the late 1700s, dueling was traditionally conducted by the sword. However, as firearms became the principal weapon of war in the nineteenth century, skills of swordsmanship declined and duel by pistol became the preferred method of confrontation. Dueling pistols were not standard military handguns, but custom-designed pieces made specifically for the practice of dueling. They usually came as an expensive matched pair, well made but with minimal decoration. They were finely balanced weapons with heavy barrels about 254 mm (10 in.) long and of 12.7–15.2 mm (0.5–0.6 in.) in bore. Since the penalty for a misfire could be fatal in a duel, special attention was given to producing a very fast and reliable lock system. Some dueling pistols had gold- or platinum-lined touch pans to ensure a more reliable pan ignition.

The design of dueling pistols had to satisfy the needs of probity as well as function. Therefore, while the weapons featured front and rear sights and sensitive trigger pulls, the barrels were left unrifled. A rifled barrel was seen as a dishonorable attempt at accuracy—the purpose of a duel was more to fire a shot and test the bravery of the opponent than meticulously place a killing round. The duelists' seconds would check the opponent's gun for rifling by inserting a finger into the barrel before loading. Some duplicitous pistol manufacturers, however, might half-rifle the back end of the barrel, beyond the reach of the finger.

Duels following circumscribed dueling codes, such as the "Code Duello" of 1777, and were usually performed at a range of twelve paces—roughly 25–30 ft. (8–9 m). The dueling parties might either take turns to fire or fire simultaneously, and shots might be repeated until one party was dead, wounded, or a reconciliation took place. Dueling, although illegal, was tolerated for 200 years as part of a gentlemanly code, until the mid-1850s, when changing social values removed this archaic practice from European society.

Above: *When are dueling pistols not dueling pistols? It would be hard to argue that men such as Jesse James were duelists in the European sense, but dueling was a actually a popular method of resolving disputes in the West. The California lawyer Will Hicks Graham fought several duels using Colt 1851 revolvers like these. He challenged his love rival George Lemon in the 1850s. When Graham missed with all five of his shots, he backed away and fell. Lemon rushed up and shot him in the mouth from point-blank range. Graham survived.*

UNITED KINGDOM

LANCASTER FOUR-BARRELED 0.476 IN. PISTOL 1881

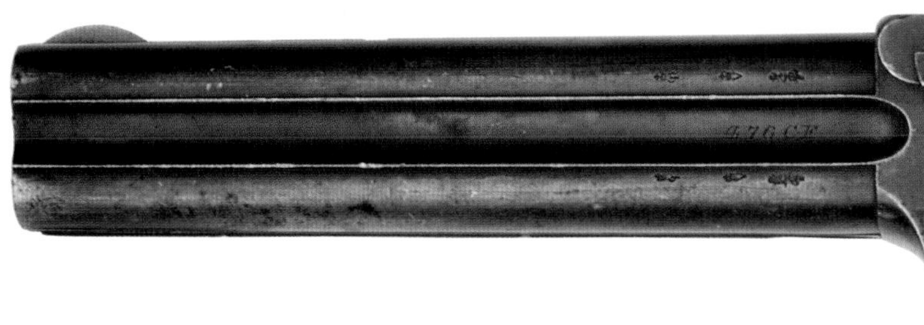

Length (gun): 11.0 in. (279 mm)
Barrel: 6.3 in. (159 mm)
Weight: 40.0 oz. (1.1 kg)
Caliber: 0.476 in. (12.1 mm)
Rifling: oval
Capacity: four
Muz vel: 750 ft./sec. (229 m/sec.)

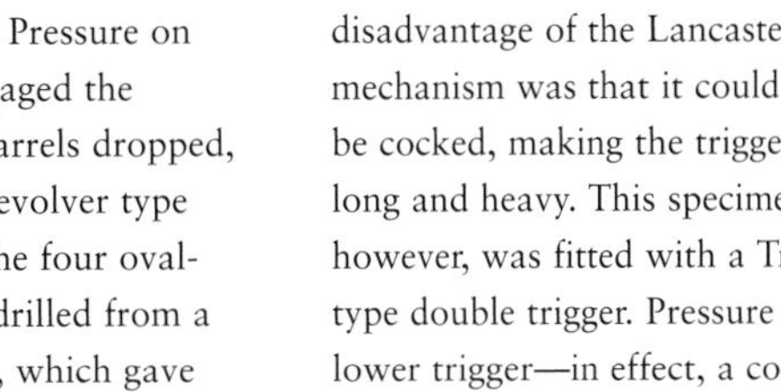

When Charles Lancaster died in 1878, the business was bought by his partner, Henry A. A. Thorn, who continued to run it under Lancaster's name. It was Thorn who developed the Lancaster pistol shown here, which he patented in 1881. The advantage of the Lancaster pistol lay in its stopping power and it was particularly popular with officers of the British Army and big-game hunters. The cluster of barrels was hinged at the bottom and was held in place by two hooks engaging over studs on either side of the barrels; one such hook is visible here. Pressure on the side lever disengaged the hooks, and as the barrels dropped, a star extractor of revolver type came into action. The four oval-bored barrels were drilled from a single block of steel, which gave them great intrinsic strength. One disadvantage of the Lancaster lock mechanism was that it could not be cocked, making the trigger pull long and heavy. This specimen, however, was fitted with a Tranter-type double trigger. Pressure on the lower trigger—in effect, a cocking lever—brought the striker mechanism to the rear, after which a very light touch on the upper trigger sufficed to fire the shot without disturbing the aim.

UNITED KINGDOM

LANCASTER FOUR-BARRELED 0.38 IN. PISTOL 1881

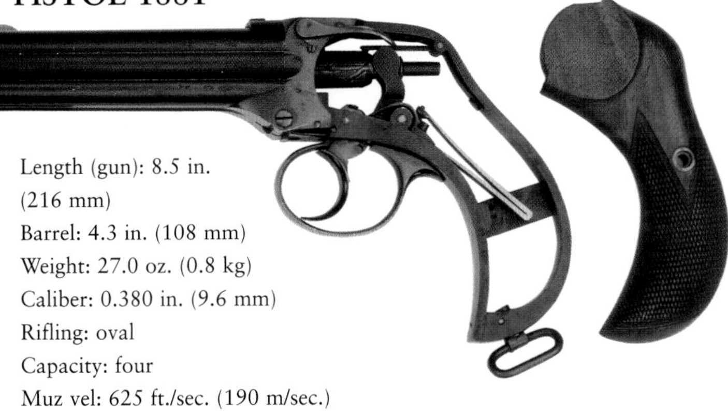

Length (gun): 8.5 in. (216 mm)
Barrel: 4.3 in. (108 mm)
Weight: 27.0 oz. (0.8 kg)
Caliber: 0.380 in. (9.6 mm)
Rifling: oval
Capacity: four
Muz vel: 625 ft./sec. (190 m/sec.)

This Lancaster had a single trigger. The butt plates have been removed in order to show the lock mechanism. Pressure on the trigger caused the vertical hammer-like lever to move to the rear, taking with it the grooved cylinder, which was fitted with a fixed striker on its forward circumference. The cylinder slid along a fixed horizontal rod, the rear end of which can be seen. In the course of its rearward movement, the cylinder was turned through ninety degrees by the guide in one of the transverse grooves. When this cycle was complete, the mechanism tripped, allowing the cylinder to go forward under the impetus of the mainspring. During this forward movement, the guide was engaged in one of the slots parallel to the axis, so that there was no resistance. The striker fired the cartridge and then revolved a further 90 degrees by the next pressure on the trigger, bringing it into line with the next cartridge.

FRANCE

TURBIAUX PALM-SQUEEZER PISTOL 1882

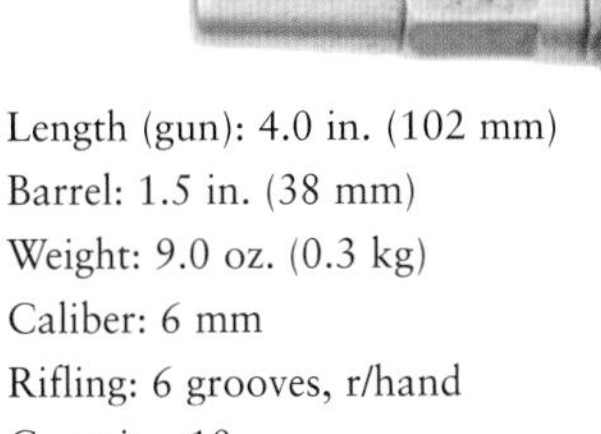

Length (gun): 4.0 in. (102 mm)
Barrel: 1.5 in. (38 mm)
Weight: 9.0 oz. (0.3 kg)
Caliber: 6 mm
Rifling: 6 grooves, r/hand
Capacity: 10
Muz vel: 650 ft./sec. (198 m/sec.)

This was a most unorthodox type of pistol: it was held in the palm of the hand, with the barrel protruding between the fingers, and fired by squeezing in a trigger device. It was invented by Jaques Turbiaux, a Parisian, who patented it in 1882. These pistols were briefly popular in Europe; some were made in the United States, but failed to sell. It is difficult to see anything this weapon offered that a derringer could not. In order to load, it was necessary to remove the top cover and insert the cartridges into the body of the pistol, where they lay radially, bullets outward. The specimen illustrated here was of French origin; American versions had a ring on each side of the barrel for the user's first and second fingers, and a safety.

UNITED KINGDOM

WEBLEY GOVERNMENT (WEBLEY-GREEN) REVOLVER 1882

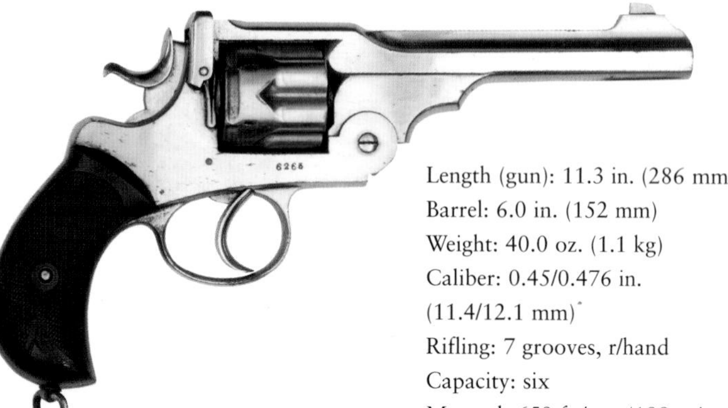

Length (gun): 11.3 in. (286 mm)
Barrel: 6.0 in. (152 mm)
Weight: 40.0 oz. (1.1 kg)
Caliber: 0.45/0.476 in. (11.4/12.1 mm)*
Rifling: 7 grooves, r/hand
Capacity: six
Muz vel: 650 ft./sec. (198 m/sec.)

This revolver, frequently known as the "W.G.," is a development of the Webley-Kaufmann weapon. It is a break-open type, although the barrel is of slightly different section: the lower part is rounded. The six-chambered cylinder is fluted in the manner sometimes referred to as "church steeple," and it is fitted with the usual spring extractor. The locking system is different from that of the Webley-Kaufmann. The top strap of the Webley-Green has a rear extension with a rectangular slot that fits closely over an upper projection from the standing breech. A stirrup-type catch, essentially similar to the one on the Webley-Wilkinson, fits over this whole assembly, and was activated by a lever on the left side. Unless the catch was properly home, the nose of the hammer could not reach the cartridges; this made it strong and also very safe. The lock is usual double-action.

GERMANY

COMMISSION REICHS REVOLVER M1883

Length (gun): 10.0 in. (254 mm)
Barrel: 4.75 in. (121 mm)
Weight: 35.0 oz. (1.0 kg)
Caliber: 0.455 in. (11.5 mm)
Rifling: 3 grooves, l/hand
Capacity: six
Muz vel: 650 ft./sec. (198 m/sec.)

In 1879, several commissions supervised the re-equipment of the German Army. This revolver, sometimes called the "Reichs revolver," was one of the results. There were two models, the 1879 and the 1883. It has a solid frame with a short stem into which the barrel is screwed. The six-chambered cylinder was removed by pressing in the spring stud on the front of the frame, pulling the axis pin forward, and opening the loading gate. There was no integral system for ejection. The breech ends of the chambers are recessed so that the heads of the cartridges were fully supported—a sensible precaution with most of the earlier metallic cartridges. The lock is single-action with a half-cock. Unusually in a revolver, there is a safety catch on the left side of the frame. This specimen was made at Erfurt in 1894; since this was after the passing of the German Proof Act, the revolver bears a number of proof marks.

UNITED KINGDOM

COPY OF WEBLEY R.I.C. REVOLVER 1884

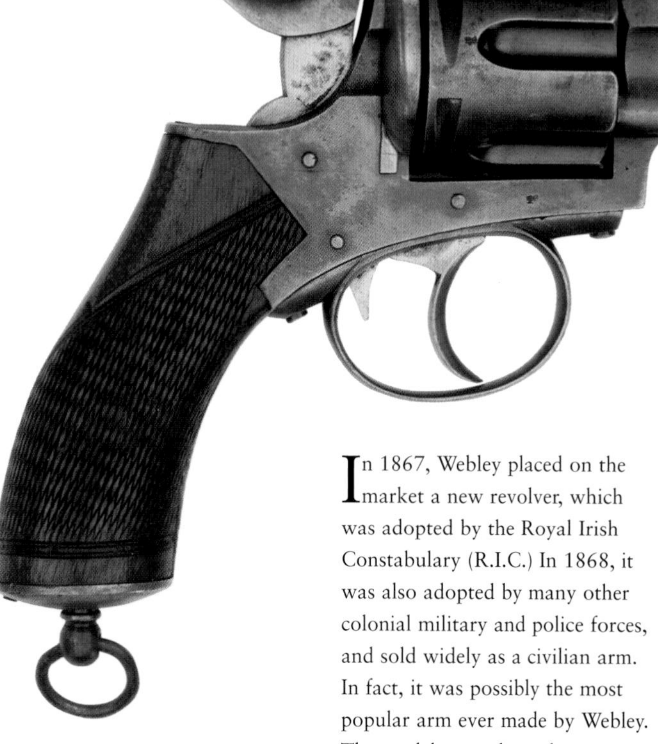

Length (gun): 8.8 in. (222 mm)
Barrel: 4.0 in. (102 mm)
Weight: 30.0 oz. (0.9 kg)
Caliber: 0.45 in. (11.4 mm)
Rifling: 7 grooves, r/hand
Capacity: five
Muz vel: 650 ft./sec. (198 m/sec.)

In 1867, Webley placed on the market a new revolver, which was adopted by the Royal Irish Constabulary (R.I.C.) In 1868, it was also adopted by many other colonial military and police forces, and sold widely as a civilian arm. In fact, it was possibly the most popular arm ever made by Webley. The model went through many variations and was widely copied. The weapon shown is a very close copy of the original: this particular example is based on the Webley No. 1 New Model of 1883. The weapon has a solid frame; the barrel (unlike that of the original Webley) is integral with it and not screwed in. The barrel is practically cylindrical, but its upper part is drawn to a rib, making it basically ovate in section, with a very slight taper toward the breech end. The five-chambered cylinder has the half-fluting associated with later Webley models. There is the usual bottom-hinged loading gate on the right-hand side of the frame, with a deep groove to facilitate loading. The extractor pin was normally housed in the hollow cylinder axis pin, but it could be withdrawn and swiveled out to the right so as to align with the chamber opposite the loading gate.

Early Unitary Cartridges

The first definitive step toward the unitary cartridge came from the Swiss gun designer Samuel Johannes Pauly in 1812. He invented a cartridge to fit a new breech-loading sporting gun he was developing at the time. The cartridge had a cardboard body containing powder and ball and a brass base incorporating a percussion cap. On firing, a firing pin (driven by a falling hammer) drove into the percussion cap to ignite the priming mixture and detonate the main charge. The brass base expanded to provide obturation.

The next step was taken by the Frenchman Lefaucheux, who developed the pinfire cartridge in the mid 1830s. Lefaucheux produced a brass cartridge holding the powder, cap, and bullet, and which featured a metal pin projecting upward from the base of the case. This pin was exposed outside of Lefaucheux's breech-loading rifle through a slot. When the trigger was pulled, the hammer fell on the pin, driving it down onto the cap to fire. The pinfire system achieved popularity in Europe, especially in sporting guns and revolvers, and would endure until the late 1930s.

After pinfire came centerfire and rimfire cartridges in the second half of the nineteenth century. Daniel Wesson of the Smith & Wesson concern built upon the rimfire principle developed by Frenchman Louis Flobert to produce a .22 caliber rimfire with a copper case and the percussion powder concentrated around the rim, which also aided ejection. Rimfire was really only suitable for small calibers because the case had to be soft enough for the hammer to dent.

A far more satisfactory cartridge was the centerfire cartridge, so called because a detachable (and hence reloadable) primer was located in the center of the base. Credit for the centerfire cartridge first goes to Englishman Charles Lancaster in 1854, but development of centerfire primer systems passed to Colonel Edward Mounier Boxer, a British military scientist, and Colonel Hiram Berdan, of the US Union Army. Boxer's ammunition, which had coiled brass walls and a separate anvil on which to strike the primer, was less successful than that of Berdan, who made a solid case with integral anvil. All early centerfire cartridges were rimmed to aid extraction.

The centerfire and rimfire cartridges are still with us today, and transformed small arms. Even with Pauly's cardboard cartridges, the rate of fire went from three rounds per minute to, in one demonstration, twenty-two rounds per minute.

Below: *Colt single-action revolver and 0.45 caliber centerfire ammunition; without the invention of centerfire, the famous Colt 45 would have had to have been the rather less impressive Colt 22. Rimfire required soft cases, too soft for the 0.45 in. caliber.*

BELGIUM

COPY OF SMITH & WESSON RUSSIAN MODEL 1885

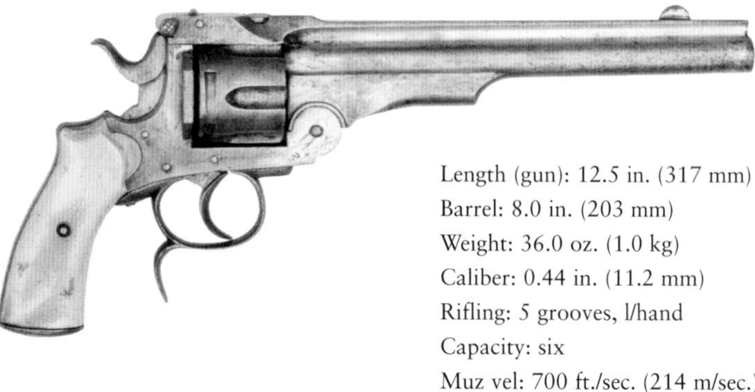

Length (gun): 12.5 in. (317 mm)
Barrel: 8.0 in. (203 mm)
Weight: 36.0 oz. (1.0 kg)
Caliber: 0.44 in. (11.2 mm)
Rifling: 5 grooves, l/hand
Capacity: six
Muz vel: 700 ft./sec. (214 m/sec.)

Smith & Wesson's Russian models were fine weapons of their type, and various European countries, Belgium in particular, were quick to turn out their own versions. These were usually made in small family workshops, where they could be produced much more cheaply than their more reputable prototypes. The copies were of varying quality; some were positively dangerous. This one, based on the various Smith & Wesson Russian models, is of poor quality. The workmanship and general finish are crude. It lacks the groove across the top of the hammer that engaged a flange on the barrel catch—always a feature on the genuine article. The lock is of double-action type; it did not rebound, but was fitted with a manual half-cock. The barrel is spuriously inscribed "SMITH AND WESSON" and there are Belgian proof marks on the cylinder, revealing its true origin.

UNITED KINGDOM

KYNOCH REVOLVER 1885

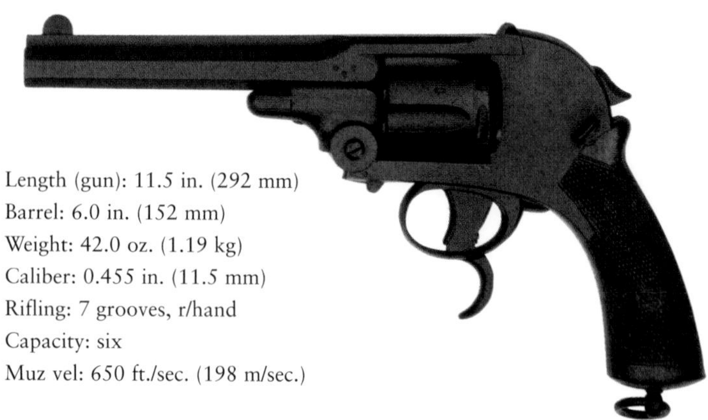

Length (gun): 11.5 in. (292 mm)
Barrel: 6.0 in. (152 mm)
Weight: 42.0 oz. (1.19 kg)
Caliber: 0.455 in. (11.5 mm)
Rifling: 7 grooves, r/hand
Capacity: six
Muz vel: 650 ft./sec. (198 m/sec.)

In 1880, the British government adopted the Enfield revolver but further trials, and combat use, condemned it, and a number of makers developed models they hoped might replace it. One such arm was the Kynoch revolver. It appears to have been patented by a British inventor named H. Schlund in 1885 and 1886, and it was manufactured in a wide variety of calibers by George Kynoch in his Birmingham gun factory. It has an octagonal barrel with a top rib and an integral, half-round foresight. It is of hinged-frame construction, and was opened by pushing forward the catch which can be seen at the rear of the frame. When the weapon was opened thus, the automatic extractor was brought into play. Its lock is based closely on the type originally invented by William Tranter. Pressure on the lower trigger—in effect, a cocking lever—brought the concealed hammer to full-cock.

UNITED KINGDOM

WEBLEY MK I SERVICE REVOLVER 1887

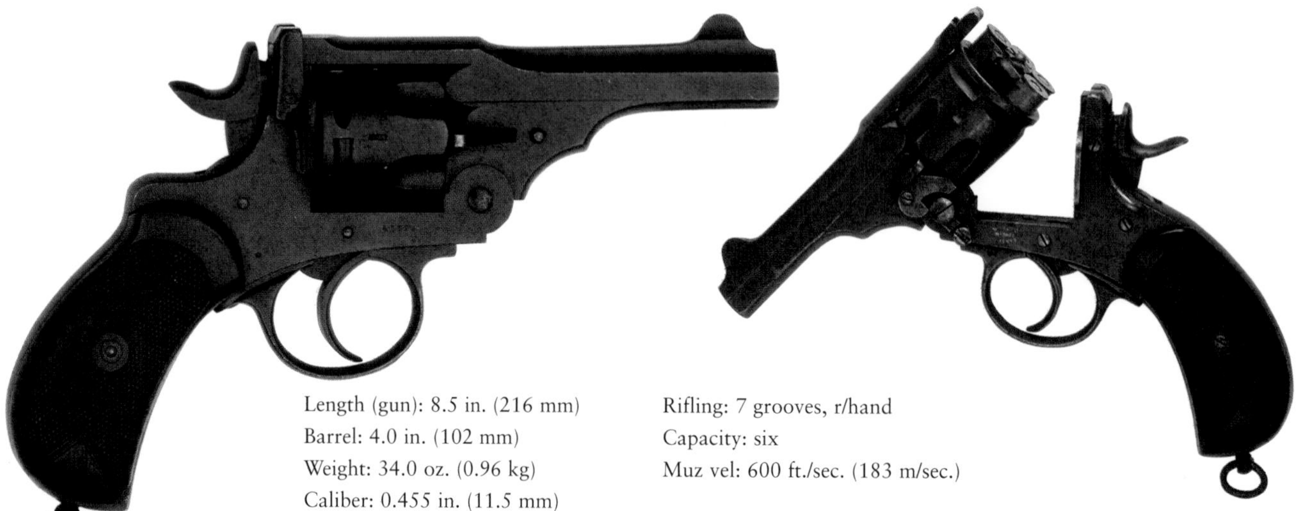

Length (gun): 8.5 in. (216 mm)
Barrel: 4.0 in. (102 mm)
Weight: 34.0 oz. (0.96 kg)
Caliber: 0.455 in. (11.5 mm)
Rifling: 7 grooves, r/hand
Capacity: six
Muz vel: 600 ft./sec. (183 m/sec.)

The Enfield Mark II revolver was felt to be inadequate for service use. Two new weapons were therefore tested: a Smith & Wesson, and a Webley. After exhaustive trials, it was decided in 1887 to adopt the Webley. Since both were of break-open type, the principal factor bearing on the decision was the reliability of the method of holding the weapons closed. Tests found the Webley system to be strong and absolutely safe; if the stirrup catch was not properly fastened, either the projection on the upper part of the hammer knocked the catch safely into position, allowing the revolver to be fired, or it fouled the catch and prevented the hammer nose from reaching the cap. The Webley Mark I is a stubby, compact weapon with a short barrel. Its bird-beak butt, of adequate size to afford a good grip, is fitted with plates of brown vulcanite and is provided with a lanyard ring. The horizontal projection visible in front of the cylinder (there is one on the left side also) is a holster guide, designed to prevent the face of the cylinder from catching on the edge of the leather holster. This arm set the style for almost all later Webley service revolvers.

UNITED STATES

SMITH & WESSON NEW MODEL NO. 3 REVOLVER 1887

Length (gun): 12.0 in. (305 mm)
Barrel: 6.5 in. (165 mm)
Weight: 44.0 oz. (1.3 kg)
Caliber: 0.32 in. (8.1 mm)
Rifling: 5 grooves, r/hand
Capacity: six
Muz vel: 800 ft./sec. (244 m/sec.)

Smith & Wesson's No. 3 First Model American, a bottom-hinged, break-open revolver with a system of simultaneous extraction, attracted the attention of Russia, in the process of re-equipping its Army. By 1871, a contract had been signed for 20,000 revolvers of a type known as Model No. 3, Russian 1st Model. A second model and a third model followed; the order was completed in 1878. The firm then turned to the home market with its New Model No. 3, produced from 1878 to 1912, and later with the New Model 3 Frontier. This was intended as a rival to the Colt, but it never became popular. The single-action arm illustrated first appeared in 1887. It is broadly similar to its predecessors. When the milled catch in front of the hammer was pushed upward, the barrel and cylinder could be pushed downward, causing the star-shaped ejector to be forced outward, allowing very fast reloading.

UNITED STATES

SMITH & WESSON MODEL 0.38 IN. CALIBER SAFETY REVOLVER (FIRST MODEL) 1887

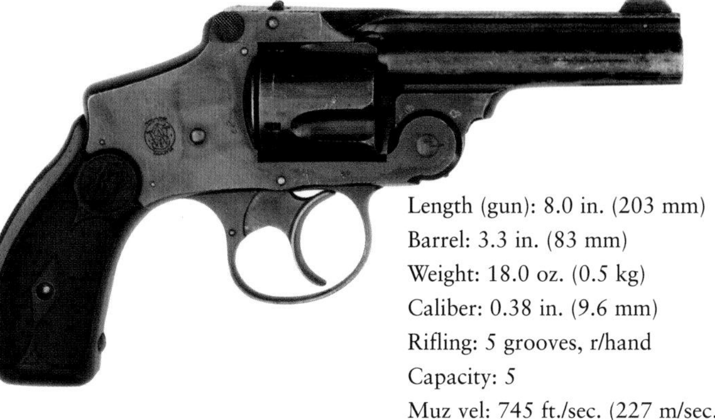

Length (gun): 8.0 in. (203 mm)
Barrel: 3.3 in. (83 mm)
Weight: 18.0 oz. (0.5 kg)
Caliber: 0.38 in. (9.6 mm)
Rifling: 5 grooves, r/hand
Capacity: 5
Muz vel: 745 ft./sec. (227 m/sec.)

Late nineteenth-century American revolvers certainly were carried Western-style, openly in holsters on the belt, but a great many more firearms were carried covertly by townspeople and city dwellers. The demand for a small, compact pocket revolver in which reliability and reasonable stopping power were more important than long-range accuracy, was great. Weapons of this type were turned out by a wide variety of gunmakers, and in 1887 Smith & Wesson introduced the hammerless weapon seen here, which quickly became very popular, since it had no hammer to catch in the lining of the pocket. It was also safe for the wearer, since the grip safety on the back of the butt had to be pressed before the weapon would fire. Indeed, as a last resort it could be fired through a pocket without any risk of jamming. The original weapon was in 0.38 in. caliber, and it was succeeded in 1902 by the second model (qv).

ITALY

BODEO MODEL 1889 SERVICE REVOLVER

Length (gun): 10.5 in. (267 mm)
Barrel: 4.5 in. (114 mm)
Weight: 32.0 oz. (0.9 kg)
Caliber: 0.41 in. (10.4 mm)
Rifling: 4 grooves, r/hand
Capacity: six
Muz vel: 650 ft./sec. (198 m/sec.)

The Bodeo revolver took its name from the head of the Italian commission that recommended its adoption in 1889. By 1891, it had become the standard Italian service revolver, remaining in service for at least fifty years. The Model 1889 was made in two distinct types: a round-barreled version with a trigger guard, and an octagonal-barreled version with a folding trigger. The revolver seen here is of the latter type. Although not an arm of particular distinction, the Bodeo was simple and robust. The barrel is screwed into the frame, and the cylinder was loaded through a bottom-hinged gate that was drawn backward to open it. Ejection was by means of a rod which was normally housed in the hollow axis pin. As in the Rast-Gasser revolver (qv), the loading gate was connected to the hammer in such a way that, when it was opened, the hammer would not function, although the action of the trigger still turned the cylinder. This arrangement, which is known as the Abadie system, was frequently found on European weapons. Revolvers of this type were made in a variety of Italian factories, and during World War I a number were also manufactured in Spain for use by the Italian Army.

HANDGUNS AND THE WILD WEST

The testing ground for the early revolvers of Colt and Smith & Wesson was the nineteenth-century United States, a place of war, frontier violence and, in the far western territories, a fragile rule of law. (By the 1850s, Texas had as many handguns in circulation as there were adult males.) Hollywood has done much to mythologize the gunfighting culture of the Wild West, but as always the films do not fully represent the reality, either of the people involved or the way revolvers were actually used.

The Wild West street duel is one of the subjects most fascinating to movie makers. Between 1850 and 1890 it has been estimated that some twenty thousand men were killed in one-on-one street fights. The quick-draw gunfight was a common method of resolving disputes between parties, especially in areas weakly represented by the law.

Shooting someone through ambush or surprise assassination was looked on as cowardly, though a large number of killings were conducted by this method. The law maker and gunfighter James Butler "Wild Bill" Hickok, who had killed many men in open fight, was himself killed by a shot in the back from Jack McCall in Deadwood, South Dakota. Pat Garrett, John Wesley, and Jesse James shared similar fates. Garrett shot Billy the Kid with a .45 caliber single-action Colt under the cover of darkness.

The Kid had carried a variety of Winchester rifles and Colt revolvers, and it is thought that he exchanged his Peacemaker for a Colt .41 caliber double-action Thunderer in about 1880, the year before his death.

When gunfights occurred, the participants would draw their guns from their holsters, worn on the belt or high up on the hip, rather than low-slung as depicted by Hollywood. Although speed was important, accuracy was more so. The gunfighter Bartholomew "Bat" Masterson ordered a Colt Peacemaker revolver in 1885 and requested that "the front sight [be] a little higher and thicker than the ordinary pistol of this kind," indicating that aim was as important a part of his job as speed.

Many individuals achieved fame in the Wild West through their gun exploits, men such as Wyatt Earp, Pat Garrett, Billy the Kid, and Jesse and Frank James.

Interestingly, many outlaws could become lawmen and vice versa, depending on where they were in the United States. Most would end up dying by the guns they lived by.

Above: *Captain John Jarrett, a former guerilla of the American Civil War and later member of the Jesse James gang. He was present when the James-Younger gang robbed the Russellville, Kentucky, bank on March 21, 1868. The Colt Navy revolver was the weapon of choice of the guerillas on both sides that had fought a vicious war in southwest Missouri, eastern Kansas, and much of Arkansas.*

BELGIUM

COPY OF SMITH & WESSON MODEL NO. 3 REVOLVER 1890

Length (gun): 8.0 in. (203 mm)
Barrel: 4.0 in. (102 mm)
Weight: 22.0 oz. (0.6 kg)
Caliber: 0.38 in. (9.6 mm)
Rifling: 5 grooves, l/hand
Capacity: six
Muz vel: 740 ft./sec. (226 m/sec.)

The Smith & Wesson double-action, break-open pocket revolvers in 0.38 in. (9.6 mm) caliber were widely copied, particularly in Belgium, where the revolver seen here originated. Although there were large factories, a very considerable part of the Belgian output came from small, anonymous back-street workshops. The people employed in such workshops were often skilled as well as hard-working; and although some unreliable arms were produced, most were adequate—and certainly as good as could be expected at the low price. This is a copy of the Smith & Wesson third model, produced from 1884 until 1895, and is a good specimen, considering its origins. It has a round barrel with a top rib and a round brass foresight; the backsight is a notch cut in the front of the barrel catch, which is of the usual T-shape. The lock mechanism is of the orthodox double-action type.

BELGIUM

GALAND VELO-DOG REVOLVER 1890

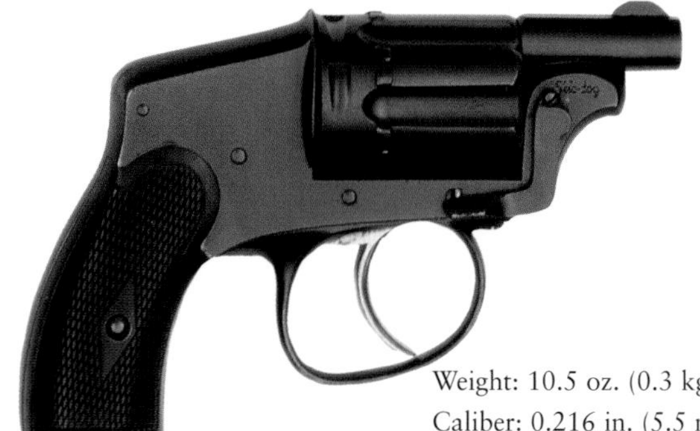

Length (gun): 4.7 in. (119 mm)
Barrel: 1.2 in. (30 mm)
Weight: 10.5 oz. (0.3 kg)
Caliber: 0.216 in. (5.5 mm)
Rifling: 4 grooves, r/hand
Capacity: six
Muz vel: 600 ft./sec. (183 m/sec.)

The term "Velo-Dog" is used to describe a group of cheap pocket revolvers which were made in very considerable numbers at the end of the nineteenth century in Belgium, France, Germany, Italy, and especially Spain. Charles François Galand's first model was of open-frame type, with an orthodox trigger and guard, as seen here; but later models tended to have solid frames, completely enclosed hammers, and folding triggers. The earliest Velo-Dogs fired a long 5.5 mm cartridge with a light bullet; later they were designed to fire 0.22 in. (5.6 mm), 6 mm, and 8 mm Lebel rimmed cartridges, and even 6.35 mm and 7.65 mm rimless rounds. There is little doubt that these revolvers were designed principally for the pioneer cyclists, who appear to have been much troubled by fierce dogs, hence the name. Special deterrent, but less lethal, cartridges loaded with salt, pepper or dust shot, were also supplied.

FRANCE

SINGLE-SHOT PISTOL 1890

Length (gun): 5.5 in. (140 mm)
Barrel: 4.0 in. (102 mm)
Weight: 3.0 oz. (0.08 kg)
Caliber: 0.22 in. (5.6 mm)
Rifling: none
Capacity: one
Muz vel: 450 ft./sec. (137 m/sec.)

This tiny pistol can be only marginally described as a weapon: it should, strictly, be classified as a dangerous toy! Nevertheless, it was a firearm by definition and has been included accordingly. Although it is thought to be of French origin, the marks on it are so faint that it is impossible to be sure. However, it was probably made toward the end of the nineteenth century, when it could have been purchased for a few cents in a gunsmith or hardware store without any kind of formality—together with a supply of bulleted caps for which it was designed. These consisted of a short rimfire case, containing fulminate compound but no powder, with a spherical lead ball as projectile. The round probably equaled the pellet from a modern air rifle in terms of hitting power.

FRANCE

ST. ETIENNE 8 MM MODÈLE 1892 (LEBEL)

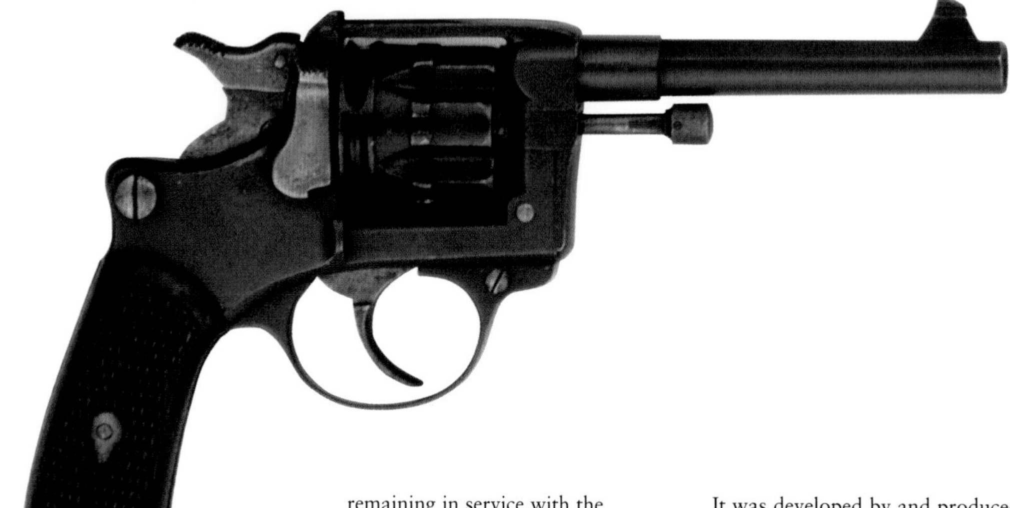

Length (gun): 9.3 in. (237 mm)
Barrel: 4.6 in. (117 mm)
Weight: 30.0 oz. (0.8 kg)
Caliber: 8 mm
Rifling: 6 grooves, r/hand
Capacity: six
Muz vel: 720 ft./sec. (219 m/sec.)

This revolver was a development of the Mle 1873 and was fielded in 1893, remaining in service with the French Army until World War I and with the French police for some years after. Its official designation was the "Revolveur 8mm Modèle d'Ordonnance M1892," although it was usually known simply as the "Lebel" after a colonel of that name who was deeply involved with military weapons at the time of its design. It was developed by and produced at the government arsenal at St. Etienne. It was a solid frame pistol with a cylinder on a separate frame, which, somewhat unusually, swung out to the right for loading and unloading. When closed, the cylinder was held in place by a large, hinged lever on the right-hand side of the frame, while the mechanism could be inspected by removing a plate on the left-hand side. The revolver was reliable, but its cartridge—the 8 x 27mm Lebel—was generally considered to be somewhat underpowered. The Mle 1892 was also produced in Belgium and Spain, and there were some minor variations over the years; for example, some have round barrels, while others have hexagonal.

UNITED STATES

STEVENS BICYCLE RIFLE PISTOL 1890

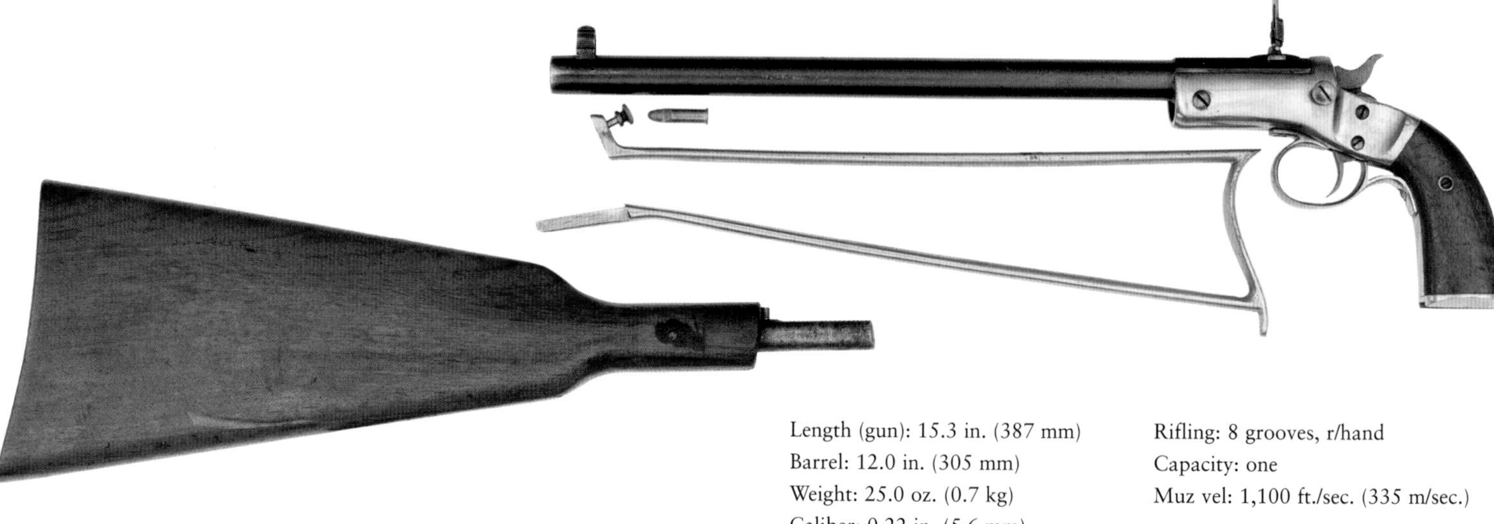

Length (gun): 15.3 in. (387 mm)
Barrel: 12.0 in. (305 mm)
Weight: 25.0 oz. (0.7 kg)
Caliber: 0.22 in. (5.6 mm)
Rifling: 8 grooves, r/hand
Capacity: one
Muz vel: 1,100 ft./sec. (335 m/sec.)

Weapons of this type achieved popularity in the United States toward the end of the nineteenth century, when the bicycle had established itself as a cheap and popular means of transport. The arms presumably got their generic name from the ease with which they could be carried, either assembled or with the wire butt removed, attached to the crossbar of a bicycle. When small game abounded near most country roads, a small, light rifle was a convenient thing to have to hand. The barrel of this specimen was hinged: pressure on the spotted stud below the hammer allowed the barrel to drop, giving access to the breech. It was made by the Stevens Company of Chicopee Falls, Massachusetts.

SPAIN

ARANZABAL EIBAR 11 MM REVOLVER 1890

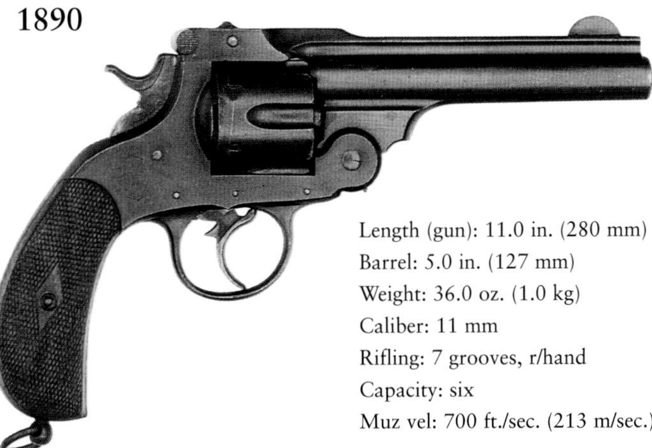

Length (gun): 11.0 in. (280 mm)
Barrel: 5.0 in. (127 mm)
Weight: 36.0 oz. (1.0 kg)
Caliber: 11 mm
Rifling: 7 grooves, r/hand
Capacity: six
Muz vel: 700 ft./sec. (213 m/sec.)

In the nineteenth century, the Spaniards, like the Belgians, were producing large quantities of handguns, most of which were no better than medium quality. They were, however, cheap and therefore popular, particularly in South American countries, which provided obvious markets for Spanish arms of all types. In spite of the extent of their manufacture, it is probable that most Spanish service weapons were imported at that time, and it is equally clear that many of these were later copied. The weapon shown, which was made by Aranzabal, is a break-down self-ejector. It is a heavy and apparently robust weapon, although the lockwork is relatively poor, and bore a general resemblance to the products of Smith & Wesson.

UNITED STATES

SMITH & WESSON SINGLE-SHOT MODEL 91 PISTOL 1891

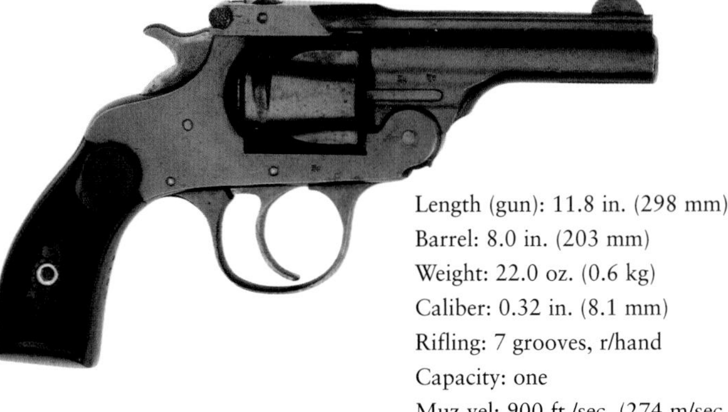

Length (gun): 11.8 in. (298 mm)
Barrel: 8.0 in. (203 mm)
Weight: 22.0 oz. (0.6 kg)
Caliber: 0.32 in. (8.1 mm)
Rifling: 7 grooves, r/hand
Capacity: one
Muz vel: 900 ft./sec. (274 m/sec.)

This handsome weapon was first produced with the object of providing an accurate and well-balanced target pistol with most of the characteristics of a long-barreled revolver. The first model was made in three barrel lengths—6.0 in. (152 mm), 8.0 in. (203 mm), and 10.0 in. (254 mm)—and in three calibers—0.22 in. rimfire and 0.32 in. and 0.38 in. centerfire. It could be obtained with an interchangeable revolver barrel and cylinder assembly, in 0.38 in. caliber only but with several barrel lengths. Its assembly could be mounted onto the existing frame, easily converting the arm into an orthodox revolver. In 1905 there appeared a second model in 0.22 in. caliber, with a 10.0 in. (254 mm) barrel only, but so designed that the earlier revolver assembly could be fitted to it. The pistol shown here is the third model, a single shot. Most of this series were blued, but they could be nickel-plated to order.

UNITED STATES

HOPKINS AND ALLEN FOREHAND MODEL 1891 REVOLVER

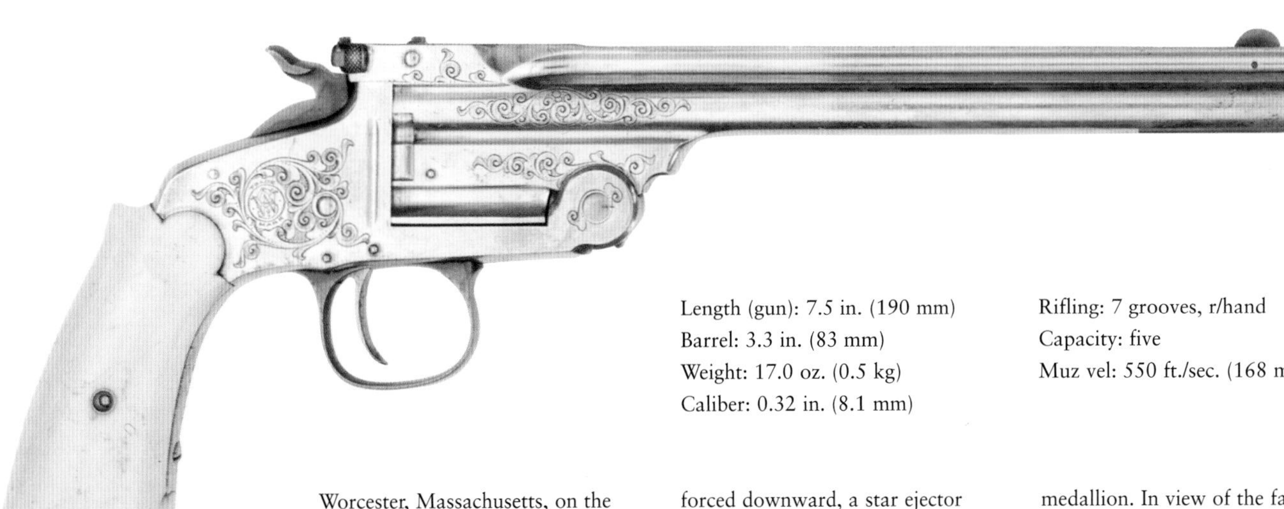

Length (gun): 7.5 in. (190 mm)
Barrel: 3.3 in. (83 mm)
Weight: 17.0 oz. (0.5 kg)
Caliber: 0.32 in. (8.1 mm)
Rifling: 7 grooves, r/hand
Capacity: five
Muz vel: 550 ft./sec. (168 m/sec.)

Hopkins and Allen came into existence in Norwich, Connecticut, in 1868, and manufactured a variety of arms, mainly revolvers. It took over the Forehand Arms Company of Worcester, Massachusetts, on the death of Sullivan Forehand. Soon afterward, Hopkins and Allen began to make the so-called Forehand Model 1891. It is a neat, compact, hinged-frame weapon for pocket use. It was opened by lifting a Smith & Wesson-type T-shaped catch (one of the milled ends of the catch is visible in the photograph). When the barrel was forced downward, a star ejector was brought into play. The five-chambered cylinder could be removed from its axis pin by pressing in the front end of the horizontal lever. The lock is of double-action type and a separate striker is built into the standing breech. The butt plates are of a black vulcanite composition and bear the initials "H & R" in a medallion. In view of the fact that arms made in the United States bore no proof marks acceptable in Britain, all such weapons imported into the United Kingdom had to be legally reproofed: this particular revolver bears the marks of the Birmingham Proof House, which indicates that it was proved for black powder only.

UNITED STATES

IVER JOHNSON REVOLVER 1891

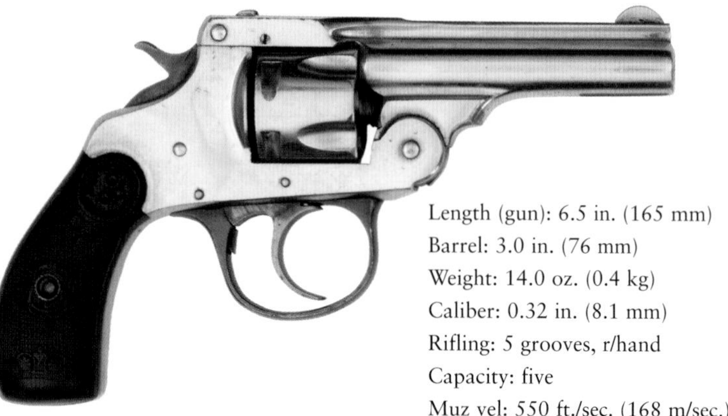

Length (gun): 6.5 in. (165 mm)
Barrel: 3.0 in. (76 mm)
Weight: 14.0 oz. (0.4 kg)
Caliber: 0.32 in. (8.1 mm)
Rifling: 5 grooves, r/hand
Capacity: five
Muz vel: 550 ft./sec. (168 m/sec.)

In 1871, Iver Johnson and Martin Bye set up a company to make cheap revolvers. These were mostly pocket revolvers. In 1883, Johnson bought out his partner and opened his own company in Worcester, Massachusetts, moving to Fitchburg, in the same state, in 1891. There he made revolvers of a somewhat better quality. This revolver is of break-open pattern. It has a round barrel with a rib, the foresight being slotted in. The backsight is a notch on the top extension of the standing breech; the standing breech passes through a rectangular aperture in the top frame, where it was necessary to push up a small, milled catch on the top left side of the frame, which allowed the barrel to drop down. Opening the revolver forced out the extractor. The frame is nickel-plated, the trigger guard is blued, and the hammer and trigger are of hard rubber with an owl's head in a circular escutcheon at the top of each.

UNITED STATES

FOREHAND ARMS COMPANY REVOLVER 1891

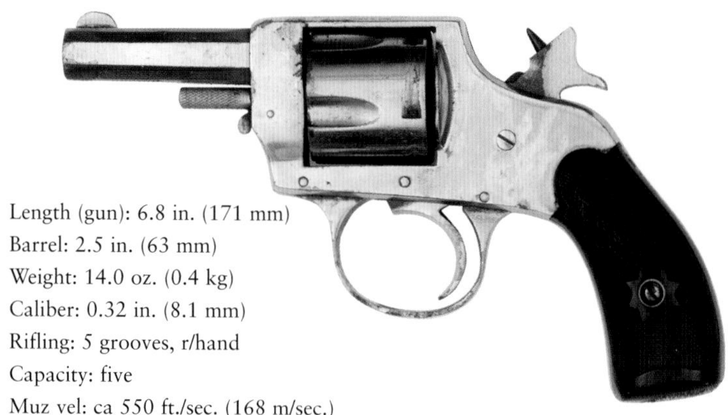

Length (gun): 6.8 in. (171 mm)
Barrel: 2.5 in. (63 mm)
Weight: 14.0 oz. (0.4 kg)
Caliber: 0.32 in. (8.1 mm)
Rifling: 5 grooves, r/hand
Capacity: five
Muz vel: ca 550 ft./sec. (168 m/sec.)

When Ethan Allen died in 1871, his business passed to his daughters, Mrs. Forehand and Mrs. Wadsworth, and was run by their husbands. After Wadsworth left the company in 1890, it was renamed the Forehand Arms Company. The arms it produced in the period 1871–98 were mainly revolvers for the cheaper end of the market. This one is inscribed with the words "FOREHAND ARMS COMPANY" on its top strap, together with the address, "WORCESTER MASS," the words "DOUBLE-ACTION," and a patent date. It is a cheap and poorly finished arm with a solid frame and a five-chambered cylinder without a loading gate: the only provision being a gap left in the shield. It may with justice be classed as a "Saturday night special." In the summer of 1940, Britain lay under threat of invasion by the German Army, and this was sent to help repel the invaders.

GERMANY

MAUSER MODEL 1898 SELF-LOADING PISTOL

Length (gun): 11.8 in. (298 mm)
Barrel: 5.5 in. (140 mm)
Weight: 40.0 oz. (1.1 kg)
Caliber: 7.63 mm
Rifling: 4 grooves, r/hand
Capacity: ten

The Mauser self-loading model appeared in 1896; relatively minor improvements led to the Model 1898. It operated on the short recoil system: the barrel and bolt recoil locked together for a short distance, after which the bolt was unlocked and continued its rearward movement, while the barrel stopped. The return spring, inside the bolt, was compressed during this rearward travel, which also cocked the hammer. The compressed spring then drove the bolt forward, picking up a cartridge from the magazine and chambering it. The closure of the bolt locked it to the barrel—and the pistol was then ready to fire. The hammer struck an inertia firing pin in the bolt, which fired the cartridge. Initial cocking was necessary before the first shot, by pulling back the milled ears at the rear of the frame. The box magazine in front of the trigger guard was loaded from a ten-round clip. When the last round was fired, the magazine platform held the bolt open. The Mauser was the first to feature this system. It took a stock, which acted as a holster. It had an adjustable leaf backsight, graduated to 492 yd. (450 m); the scale on some guns goes up to 766 yd. (700 m).

COLT'S EARLY REVOLVERS

The first revolver was actually of flintlock action and was patented in 1818 by Elisha Collier, a US citizen living in London. It featured a five-chambered cylinder mechanically rotated to align each chamber, and its own vent hole, in turn with the barrel and the pan respectively. Although ingenious, Collier's revolver was already being superseded by the percussion system, and it was left to one Samuel Colt to turn the revolver principle into a viable modern weapon.

During a period at sea, Colt sketched out a number of revolver designs (he is supposed to have gained inspiration from observing the turning of the ship's wheel), which were fleshed out into actual firearms by gunsmiths Anson Chase, then John Pearson. Colt had two main challenges to overcome. First, each chamber had to be held rigidly and accurately in line with the barrel at the moment of firing.

Second, the cylinder had to be structured so that the flash from one of the nipples being fired would not simultaneously detonate its neighbors, thus resulting in a catastrophic firing of all the cylinders simultaneously.

The first problem was overcome simply with a rigid mechanism of quality engineering. The second was negated by putting partitions between each of the nipples. By 1836, Colt had taken out patents and set up a factory in Paterson, New Jersey, to manufacture his first production weapon, the Paterson-Colt revolver (Colt's factory was moved to Hartford, Connecticut, in 1848). Although the weapon was a fine one, demand was low (mainly because of the contemporary American's affection for rifles), and Colt went bankrupt in 1841. However, military interest in his revolvers—especially for use by mounted cavalry—was heightened by the impending Mexican War of 1846–48, and Colt began to produce a series of heavy-caliber models with or without detachable stocks. These caught hold in the US military, and established Colt as one of the largest weapons manufacturers in the United States by the outbreak of the Civil War in 1861.

Below: *Police forces have been a major customer for Colt almost since the beginning, buying revolvers like this one from the 1850s onward; though it was military orders that really established the company.*

THE HANDGUN IN CAVALRY USE

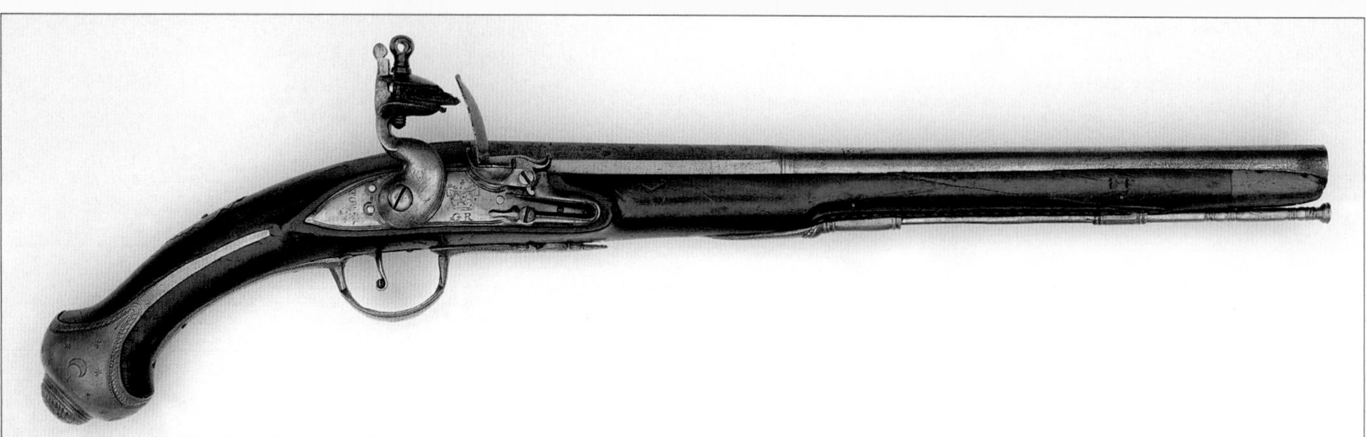

It was the advent of the wheel-lock pistol in the mid-fifteenth century that allowed cavalry to participate in the firearms battle. Early experiments in pistol- or carbine-armed cavalry were conducted in France as early as 1445, when Charles II attempted to create a regiment of "carabineers," but the first effective system of gun-armed cavalry did not emerge until the middle of the next century.

From the mid-sixteenth century, cavalry were faced with a fearsome challenge to their role as shock troops. New infantry formations evolved which placed harqeubusiers and musketeers behind walls of pikeman, all packed tightly in a defensive square known as a *tercio*. The combination of shot and pike in a concentrated mass meant that it was almost impossible for the cavalry to break up the formation. The pistol seemed to offer a solution.

The cavalry could utilize their pistols in an attack formation known as a caracole. Here a rank of cavalry would charge to within about thirty feet of the enemy infantry and musketeers, fire their pistols into the enemy mass, then wheel away to reload further back and resume the attack. New mounted troops were created to effect these tactics, most famously "dragoons," first formed into a corps by Marshall de Brissac in 1554. By the early seventeenth century, guns had almost entirely replaced the lance traditionally employed by mounted troops. The typical weaponry wielded by a cuirassier was a broad-edged sword backed by a pair of pistols.

Above: *The length (21 in./ 550 mm), the back-curled tip of the trigger, and the long ears on the brass butt cap indicate that this British heavy cavalry pistol was made in about 1720. The cypher "GR" indicates that it was certainly made after the death of Queen Anne in 1714. It could fire spherical lead balls of about 0.8 oz. (23 g) each.*

Below: *This cavalry pistol was probably made in Germany in about 1715. It is rifled with seven rounded grooves and the octagonal barrel is sturdy enough to take the consequent pressure. This weapon is a step up from the usual cavalry pistol of the time and would have been supplied to a select few well-trained flankers.*

The pistol–cavalry combination had a questionable effect on the battlefield. The cavalry remained outgunned and outranged by the musketeers, and as the percentage of infantry longarms on the battlefield grew, the caracole became a beleaguered formation. As a countermeasure, cavalry adopted more linear formations. A regiment of cuirassiers would form itself into about ten ranks, which alternated their firing positions to keep up a near-constant fire. When not in such formal structures, the cavalry found their pistols ideal for skirmishing with infantry or other mounted troops.

The sword and pistol combination served the cavalry until the mid 1800s, when the sheer firepower and accuracy of massed infantry weapons meant that close-quarters firing was almost suicidal. Ironically, there was a return to the old sword and lance combination, the infantry taking responsibility for supporting firepower, until the cavalry as a military formation became untenable with the advent of the weaponry of the early twentieth century.

UNITED KINGDOM

WEBLEY WILKINSON SERVICE REVOLVER 1892

Length (gun): 11.0 in. (279mm)
Barrel: 6.0 in. (152 mm)
Weight: 38.0 oz. (1.08 kg)
Caliber: 0.455/0.476 in. (11.5/12.1 mm)
Rifling: 7 grooves, r/hand
Capacity: six
Muz vel: 650 ft./sec. (198 m/sec.)

This service revolver is very similar to the earlier Webley-Pryse model. It is a break-open type. Its octagonal barrel has a very high top rib with a bead foresight inset. The backsight is a simple U on the barrel catch. A rear extension on the top strap fits over a raised part of the standing breech and is held in place by a spring top latch. This was worked by a lever on the left-hand side. The revolver could not be fired when it was open, for unless the latch was fully in position, the upper part of the hammer fouled it, preventing the hammer nose reaching the cartridge. When the revolver was opened, a star extractor threw out the empty cases. The one-piece, wrap-around butt is of fine checkered walnut, with an escutcheon plate. The weapon is particularly well finished, made for retail by the famous Wilkinson Sword Company of Pall Mall, London, which also provided the fine finish.

JAPAN

NAMBU MEIJI 26TH YEAR SERVICE REVOLVER 1893

Length (gun): 9.3 in. (235 mm)
Barrel: 4.7 in. (119mm)
Weight: 32.0 oz. (0.9 kg)
Caliber: 9mm
Rifling: 4 grooves, r/hand
Capacity: six
Muz vel: 600 ft./sec. (183 m/sec.)

There is nothing original about this weapon, which is an amalgam of ideas culled from a careful study of contemporary European and American weapons. The Imperial Japanese Navy had purchased a quantity of Smith & Wesson No. 3 Models, which had been found satisfactory, so it is not surprising that the Colt formed the basis for this Japanese revolver, but there were also ideas gained from Galand (Belgium), Nagant (Russia), and others. It had an octagonal barrel with a foresight bed into which the blade was pinned, while the backsight was incorporated into the top frame. The weapon was opened by lifting the top latch, after which the barrel was swung downward, activating the automatic ejector. The lock was self-cocking, and as the mechanism was slow to respond, accurate shooting was virtually impossible. This was a good effort, in view of the state of Japanese industry.

GERMANY

BORCHARDT SELF-LOADING PISTOL 1894

Length (gun): 13.8 in. (349mm)
Barrel: 6.5 in. (165 mm)
Weight: 46.0 oz. (1.3 kg)
Caliber: 7.65 mm
Rifling: 4 grooves, r/hand
Capacity: eight
Muz vel: 1,100 ft./sec. (335 m/sec.)

This weapon was only moderately successful commercially. It harnessed the backward thrust of a fired cartridge to reload and recock the weapon, firing from a locked breech which worked roughly on the principle of the knee joint. When it was straight and locked it was virtually immovable, but as soon as the joint was pushed upward it opened easily and smoothly. When the cartridge was fired, the recoil drove back the barrel and bolt until lugs on the receiver caused the joint to rise, allowing it to break. The barrel then stopped, but the bolt continued backward against a spring. When the bolt's rearward impetus was exhausted, the compressed spring drove it forward again, stripping a round from the magazine and chambering it. This was the first time such a principle had been applied to a pistol; it worked well, but the weapon was expensive to make, since it called for fine workmanship and the use of steel of very high quality, especially for joint pins. The arm was also very bulky and was practically impossible to fire with one hand. To surmount this difficulty, it was provided with a strong and well-fitting stock: it seems to have been generally regarded more as a light carbine than as a pistol.

UNITED STATES

IVER JOHNSON HAMMERLESS REVOLVER 1894

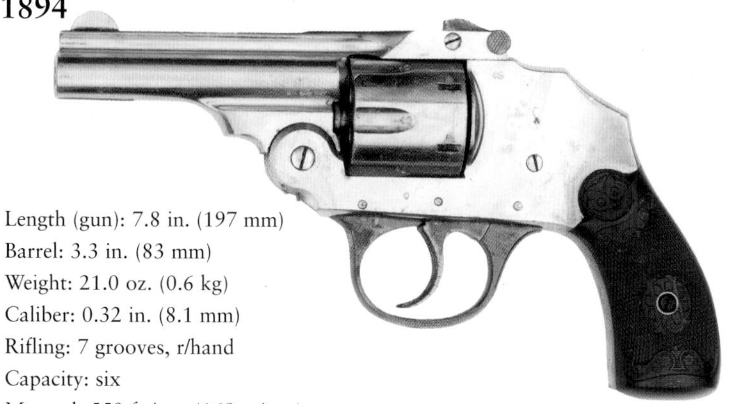

Length (gun): 7.8 in. (197 mm)
Barrel: 3.3 in. (83 mm)
Weight: 21.0 oz. (0.6 kg)
Caliber: 0.32 in. (8.1 mm)
Rifling: 7 grooves, r/hand
Capacity: six
Muz vel: 550 ft./sec. (168 m/sec.)

In 1893, Johnson patented a weapon that he had developed with other gunmakers: the Safety Automatic Double-Action Model. This is the 1894 hammerless version. It was opened by lifting the T-shaped catch, which allowed two projections on the upper part of the standing breech to separate from an aperture in the top strap. Then the barrel could be pushed downward, activating a star extractor—hence "automatic." The most important feature of the weapon was the safety device. The firing pin was mounted separately on the standing breech, so that the rear end of it was struck by the hammer. A transfer bar in the lock mechanism rose to its proper position only when the trigger had been fully and properly pulled; thus, ingeniously, the revolver could not be fired involuntarily.

BELGIUM

MINIATURE PISTOL 1895

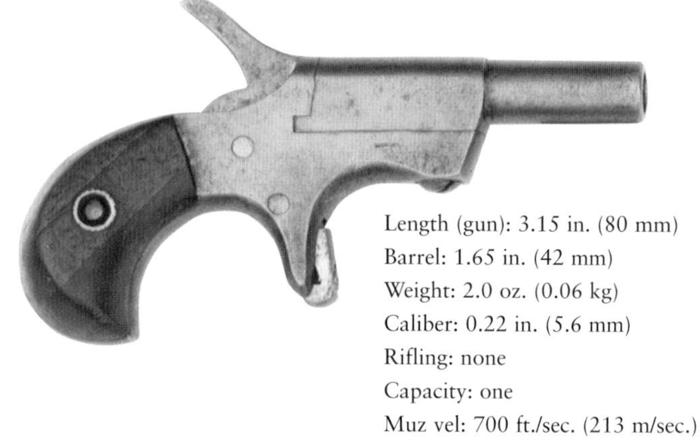

Length (gun): 3.15 in. (80 mm)
Barrel: 1.65 in. (42 mm)
Weight: 2.0 oz. (0.06 kg)
Caliber: 0.22 in. (5.6 mm)
Rifling: none
Capacity: one
Muz vel: 700 ft./sec. (213 m/sec.)

The process of miniaturization has always fascinated designers. Gun products fall into two main categories. There are so-called apprentice pieces, made by young men in the gunmakers' workshops to demonstrate their skills. These are often small works of art in themselves. There are also production-line weapons which have simply been made on a reduced scale, but which will fire commercially available cartridges. This little pistol was the latter, made in Belgium. It was of very simple construction, with a single-action hammer and a sheathed trigger. The barrel was mounted on a horizontal pivot, the head of the screw just visible in the photograph. In order to load, the hammer was cocked and the breech swiveled to the right to allow a cartridge to be inserted.

BELGIUM

SALOON PISTOL 1895

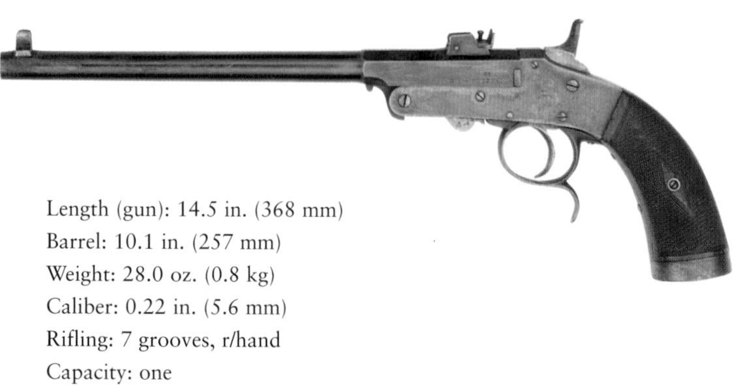

Length (gun): 14.5 in. (368 mm)
Barrel: 10.1 in. (257 mm)
Weight: 28.0 oz. (0.8 kg)
Caliber: 0.22 in. (5.6 mm)
Rifling: 7 grooves, r/hand
Capacity: one
Muz vel: 750 ft./sec. (229 m/sec.)

Pistols of this kind were popular for target practice in Europe in the late nineteenth-century. Duels were by then still quite common in continental Europe, where young men of fashion considered it prudent to keep in practice in case of a challenge. Small-bore weapons firing bulleted caps were adequate for this kind of exercise; their relative lack of noise and smoke made them eminently suitable for practice in an indoor saloon, hence their name. Although this particular specimen, which is of Belgian origin, bears no maker's name, it was well made and finished. The barrel was hinged and was broken by pressing forward the catch protruding from the frame in front of the trigger guard. It was provided with an extractor.

BELGIUM

DOUBLE-BARRELED REVOLVER 1895

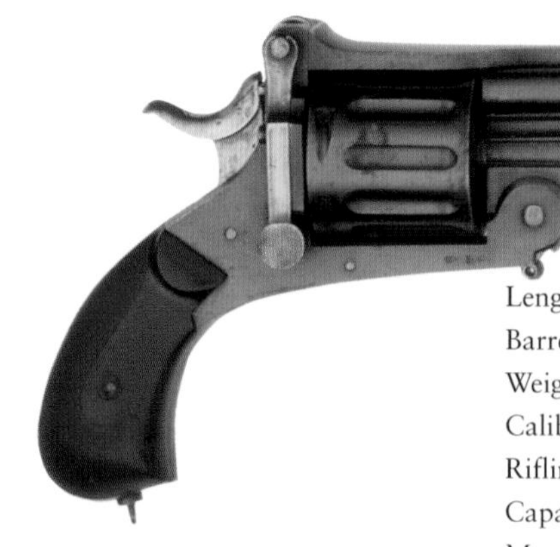

Length (gun): 7.5 in. (190 mm)
Barrels: 3.8 in. (95 mm)
Weight: 18.0 oz. (0.5 kg)
Caliber: 0.22 in. (5.6 mm)
Rifling: 5 grooves, r/hand
Capacity: twelve
Muz vel: 650 ft./sec. (198 m/sec.)

This late nineteenth century side-by-side, double-barreled revolver fired both barrels simultaneously. The barrels, which are round, appear to have been machined out of a single piece of metal and the top rib then attached. The frame is bottom-hinged, the locking device being of the Pryse type, involving the use of two centrally hinged vertical arms. Each arm has a stud at the top of its inner side; the studs were forced inward under the pressure of a spring, so that they passed through holes at the top of the standing breech and engaged a rearward extension of the top rib. The lock is double-action, with a folding trigger. The hammer nose is flat and acted on a pair of firing pins mounted in the rear of the standing breech. The large fluted cylinder is hollow in the center to reduce weight. It is fitted with a star-shaped extractor. The bird-beak butt has wooden side plates. The top rib bears Belgian inspection marks. The weapon is of good quality and well finished.

RUSSIA

NAGANT MODEL 1895 REVOLVER

Length (gun): 9.1 in. (230 mm)
Barrel: 4.4 in. (110 mm)
Weight: 28.0 oz. (0.8 kg)
Caliber: 7.62 mm
Rifling: 4 grooves, r/hand
Capacity: seven
Muz vel: 1,000 ft./sec. (305 m/sec.)

The Belgian brothers, Emil and Leon Nagant, cooperated with the Russian S. I. Mosin to design and produce the Mosin-Nagant Model 1891 rifle, and went on to design this revolver, which was adopted by the Imperial Russian Army in 1895. This weapon was chambered for the 7.62 x 38R Nagant round. Virtually all revolvers had a small gap between the rear end of the barrel and the front face of the chamber, through which a small proportion of the propellant gases escape. The Model 1895 is one of the very few weapons to overcome this problem. It used a specially designed cartridge with a narrowed neck, which fitted snugly into the rear of the barrel and expanded on firing to create a gas-tight seal. The mechanism rotated the cylinder and pressed it home on aligning a new chamber, later withdrawing it slightly before rotating for the next round, thus enhancing the integrity of the seal.

UNITED STATES

COLT NEW NAVY M1895 REVOLVER

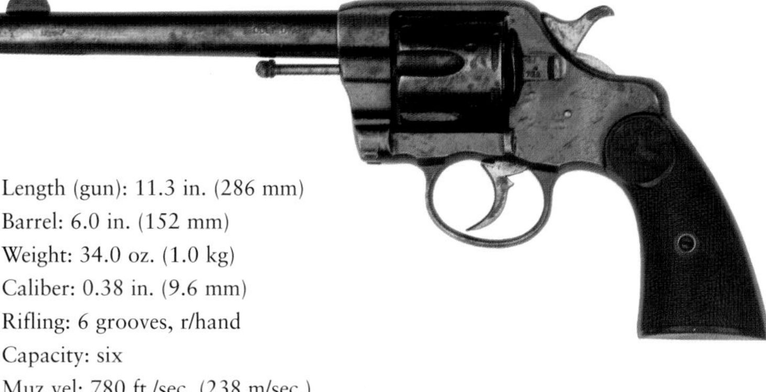

Length (gun): 11.3 in. (286 mm)
Barrel: 6.0 in. (152 mm)
Weight: 34.0 oz. (1.0 kg)
Caliber: 0.38 in. (9.6 mm)
Rifling: 6 grooves, r/hand
Capacity: six
Muz vel: 780 ft./sec. (238 m/sec.)

The New Navy was introduced by Colt, 1889–97, made in 0.38 in. (9.6 mm) and 0.41 in. (10.4 mm) calibers, and in barrel lengths of 3.0 in. (76 mm), 4.5 in. (114 mm) and 6.0 in. (152 mm). The six-chambered cylinder is fluted and has two separate sets of slots for the cylinder stops. When the arm was cocked, the rear stop rose; when the trigger was released, the rear stop dropped and a forward stop came up in its turn to engage the horizontal slots about 0.5 in. (12.7 mm) from the back of the cylinder. The thumb catch was drawn back to allow the cylinder to swing out; the fit between the yoke and the main frame is so good that the joint is difficult to detect. The lock is double-action. The US Navy adopted this revolver in 1892, and the Army soon afterward, calling it the New Army. A variation with a different butt shape and plain walnut grips was produced for the Marine Corps from 1905 to 1910.

UNITED STATES

SMITH & WESSON NEW MODEL DOUBLE-ACTION .38 IN. REVOLVER 1895

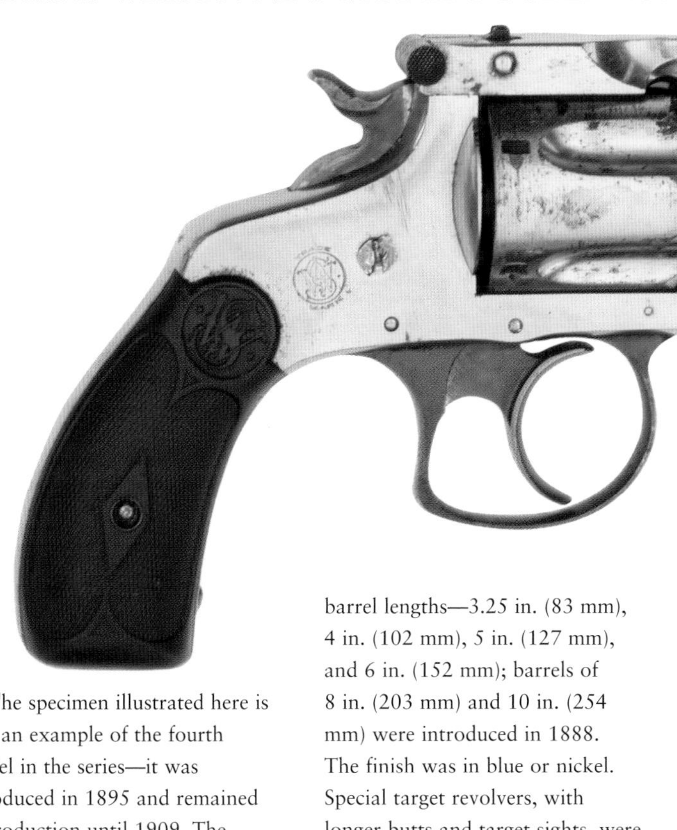

Length (gun): 7.5 in. (190 mm)
Barrel: 3.3 in. (83 mm)
Weight: 18.0 oz. (0.5 kg)
Caliber: 0.38 in. (9.6 mm)
Rifling: 5 grooves, r/hand
Capacity: five
Muz vel: 625 ft./sec. (190 m/sec.)

The specimen illustrated here is an example of the fourth model in the series—it was introduced in 1895 and remained in production until 1909. The model was originally made in four barrel lengths—3.25 in. (83 mm), 4 in. (102 mm), 5 in. (127 mm), and 6 in. (152 mm); barrels of 8 in. (203 mm) and 10 in. (254 mm) were introduced in 1888. The finish was in blue or nickel. Special target revolvers, with longer butts and target sights, were also available. This one has the conventional round sight, pinned into a groove on the top rib; the backsight is a simple V-notch in a raised part of the barrel catch. The earlier models had a rocker-type cylinder stop, which necessitated two sets of notches or grooves on the cylinder; but in the fourth model this was abandoned, so that only one set of notches was required. In revolvers in the series made after 1889, the notches were lined with a special hard-steel shim to prevent undue wear; but this practice, too, was later discontinued, although the lined notches are present on the model shown. The left side of the frame has an access plate to the mechanism. The frame is plated, except for the trigger guard, and the butt is of the usual hard rubber.

SMITH & WESSON: THE EARLY HANDGUNS

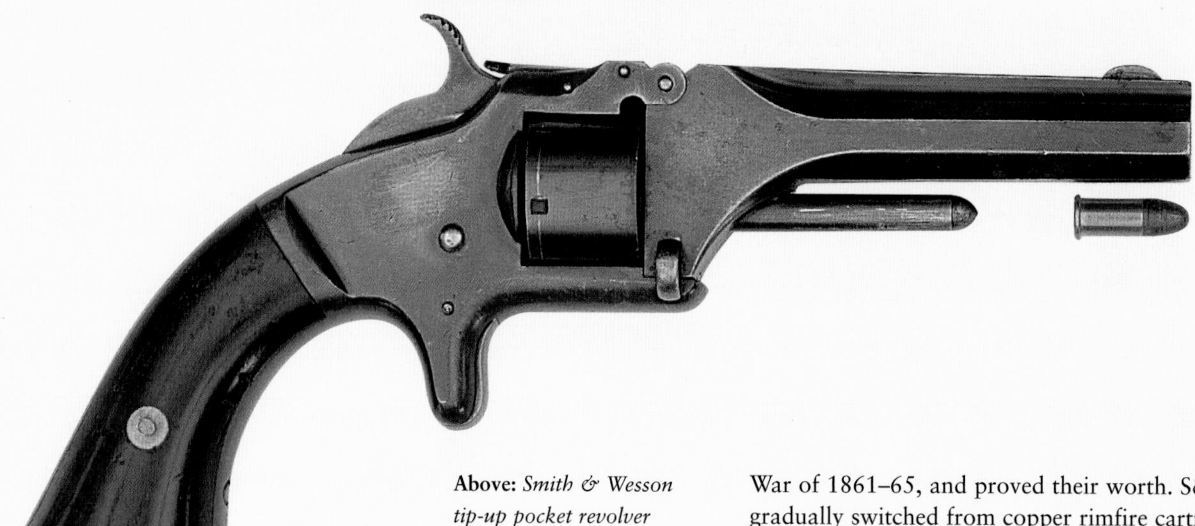

Above: *Smith & Wesson tip-up pocket revolver model No. 1 Second Issue revolver, 1860; this 0.22 in. caliber weapon has three patent dates on its cylinder. The company stole a march on Colt by anticipating the success of self-contained cartridges and the consequent need for bored-through chambers in the cylinder.*

Below: *The more attractive Third Issue was released by Smith & Wesson after the Civil War, when there was something of a revolver recession. The plating and the bird's-beak butt changed the appearance of what was mechanically a very similar gun.*

In 1857 the then little-known US gunmakers Horace Smith and Daniel B. Wesson, who had formed the Smith & Wesson partnership in 1852, took out patents for a revolver (Colt's patent on the revolver expired in 1856) that fired metallic unitary cartridges rather than using the percussion cap system. The cartridges featured a copper case of rimfire design—the percussion powder was located around the rim of the cartridge, the point at which the hammer struck. The new S&W revolvers offered easy-loading, quick-firing reliability. The only drawback was that the soft copper cases might bulge backward after firing and prevent cylinder rotation, but this problem was much reduced by manufacturing pistols only in small calibers, typically 8 mm (0.32 in.).

S&W weapons and the self-contained cartridge were thoroughly tested during the Civil War of 1861–65, and proved their worth. S&W gradually switched from copper rimfire cartridges to centerfire brass cartridges, which were more robust than copper, removing the problem of the backward bulge and so enabling the production of larger caliber weapons. Also, the greater elasticity of brass meant that it provided a perfect gas seal against the wall of the chamber, before contracting to allow easy round ejection.

Smith & Wesson's early revolvers were of tip-up design; the barrel tilted upward to allow the cylinder to be removed and reloaded. In 1870, S&W made another breakthrough by introducing a revolver frame hinged at the bottom to allow the barrel to drop downward (which meant a horseman could do this with one hand while riding) and expose the cylinders for reloading. Easy reloading was enhanced by incorporating a star-shaped extractor that ejected all spent cases simultaneously when the gun was opened.

Throughout the rest of the 1800s, Smith & Wesson innovated and improved on its designs, introducing double-action guns in 1880, and adopting Colt's solid-frame hinged-cylinder design in 1896.

UNITED STATES

IVER JOHNSON SAFETY AUTOMATIC DOUBLE-ACTION REVOLVER 1895

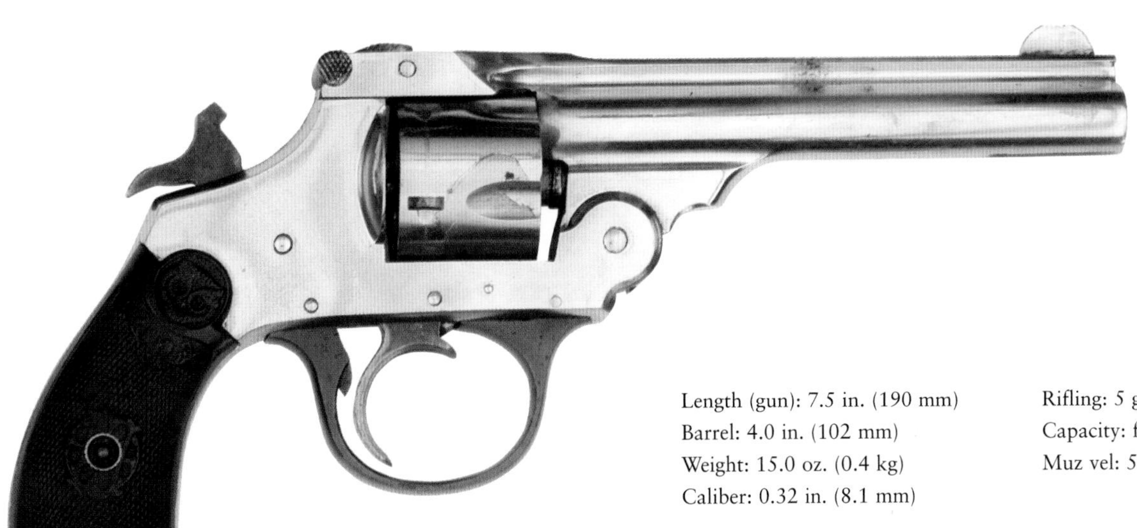

Length (gun): 7.5 in. (190 mm)
Barrel: 4.0 in. (102 mm)
Weight: 15.0 oz. (0.4 kg)
Caliber: 0.32 in. (8.1 mm)

Rifling: 5 grooves, r/hand
Capacity: five
Muz vel: 550 ft./sec. (168 m/sec.)

The Iver Johnson arm illustrated here is a compact and well-made double-action revolver of pocket type. It was opened by lifting the top catch, which caused two parallel projections on the upper part of the standing breech to separate from two corresponding apertures on the top frame. This allowed the barrel to be pushed downward and brought the automatic extractor into play. A very interesting feature of this weapon is that it is of the type known as Safety Automatic Double-Action, a form of lock mechanism developed by Johnson and others in the 1890s and patented to the Johnson company. The firing pin was mounted on the standing breech; its rear end was struck by the flat head of the hammer by means of a flat transfer bar that rose into position only when the trigger was properly pulled. If the bar did not rise, the hammer was held clear of the actual pin by fouling the top of the breech. This was an ingenious and reliable system, which remained in use unchanged for many years. The revolver is well finished, with blued trigger guard and case-hardened lock mechanism, and has the usual hard rubber grips with the familiar owl's-head motif.

GERMANY

MAUSER MODEL 1896 SELF-LOADING PISTOL

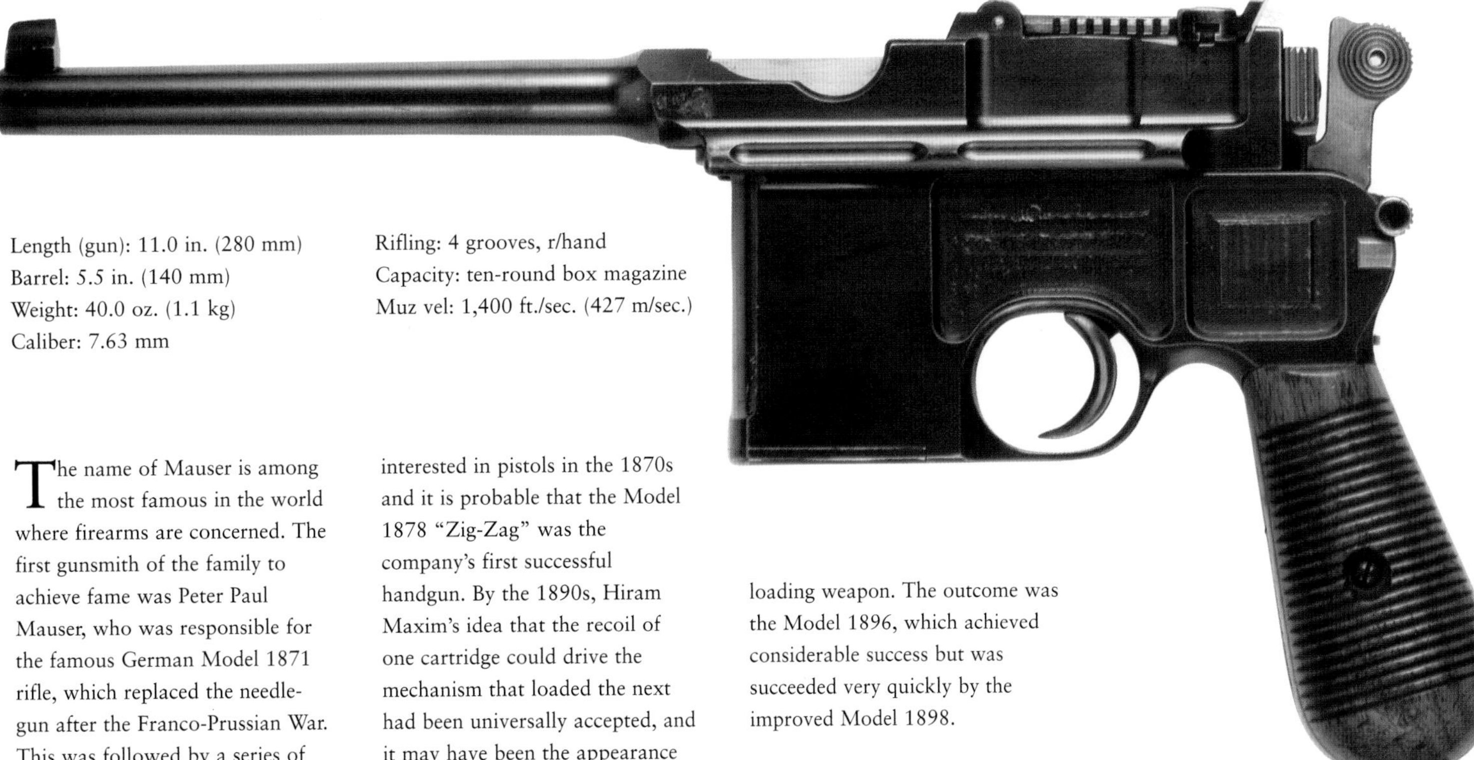

Length (gun): 11.0 in. (280 mm)
Barrel: 5.5 in. (140 mm)
Weight: 40.0 oz. (1.1 kg)
Caliber: 7.63 mm

Rifling: 4 grooves, r/hand
Capacity: ten-round box magazine
Muz vel: 1,400 ft./sec. (427 m/sec.)

The name of Mauser is among the most famous in the world where firearms are concerned. The first gunsmith of the family to achieve fame was Peter Paul Mauser, who was responsible for the famous German Model 1871 rifle, which replaced the needle-gun after the Franco-Prussian War. This was followed by a series of progressively better rifles, culminating in the Model 1898 rifle. The company first became interested in pistols in the 1870s and it is probable that the Model 1878 "Zig-Zag" was the company's first successful handgun. By the 1890s, Hiram Maxim's idea that the recoil of one cartridge could drive the mechanism that loaded the next had been universally accepted, and it may have been the appearance of the Borchardt pistol that inspired the Mauser company to try its hand at a similar, self-loading weapon. The outcome was the Model 1896, which achieved considerable success but was succeeded very quickly by the improved Model 1898.

GERMANY

BERGMANN 1896 (NO. 3) PISTOL

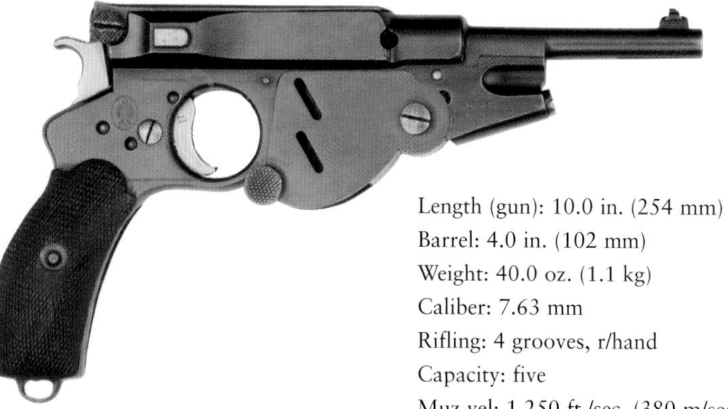

Length (gun): 10.0 in. (254 mm)
Barrel: 4.0 in. (102 mm)
Weight: 40.0 oz. (1.1 kg)
Caliber: 7.63 mm
Rifling: 4 grooves, r/hand
Capacity: five
Muz vel: 1,250 ft./sec. (380 m/sec.)

By 1894, Theodor Bergmann had developed a reasonably successful self-loading pistol; an improved version appeared in 1896. It was a well-made, simple blowback arm; the early versions lacked any mechanical system of extraction or ejection. The action was so designed that the bolt opened while there was still sufficient gas available to blow out the cartridge case. This case struck the next round in the magazine and, in theory, bounced clear; in practice, this process was somewhat unpredictable. A gas escape port in the chamber served as a safety device should the case rupture under pressure. The early cartridges had no rim and were quite sharply tapered to avoid any risk of sticking. However, the system was not considered to be reliable, and later versions were fitted with mechanical extractors, necessitating the use of cartridges with grooved rims. It took a five-round clip.

UNITED STATES

WEBLEY MK III POLICE AND CIVILIAN REVOLVER 1898

Length (gun): 8.3 in. (210 mm)
Barrel: 4.0 in. (102 mm)
Weight: 19.0 oz. (0.54 kg)
Caliber: 0.38 in. (9.6 mm)
Rifling: 7 grooves, r/hand
Capacity: six
Muz vel: 600 ft./sec. (183 m/sec.)

In 1896 Webley introduced a series of 0.38 in. (9.6 mm) caliber pocket revolvers. The Mark III differed from the Mark II (actually the first model) chiefly in the shape of its butt and in its cylinder release system. Like the Mark II, it had two types of hammer. The revolver illustrated has a flat-headed hammer with a separate striker. It has an octagonal barrel with a foresight; the backsight is a V-shaped notch on the barrel catch. The arm has a double cylinder stop: a forward stop, which worked when the hammer was down, and a rear stop, which operated when the trigger was pressed. It is a compact and handy little weapon and proved popular; its only disadvantage lay in its rather small butt. This fault was rectified in a later model, which first appeared in 1932; this had a very much larger butt and was fitted with a safety catch, positioned on the right-hand side of the frame.

GERMANY

BERGMANN 1897 (NO. 5) PISTOL

Length (gun): 10.5 in. (267 mm)
Barrel: 4.4 in. (112 mm)
Weight: 26.5 oz. (0.8 kg)
Caliber: 7.63 mm
Rifling: 4 grooves, r/hand
Capacity: five
Muz vel: 1,100 ft./sec. (335 m/sec.)

Apart from small, pocket arms, it was clear that the main users for self-loading pistols would be the military—and as they were always required to fire a powerful cartridge, it was necessary that their weapons should fire with the breech locked; otherwise, the cartridge case would be pushed out of the chamber when the gas pressure was still high and, unsupported by the walls of the chamber, it was likely to rupture. Therefore, in 1897, Theodore Bergmann patented a pistol of the type seen here. The barrel and bolt were locked together at the instant of firing and remained so during the first 0.24 in. (6 mm) of recoil. A cam in the frame then forced the bolt slightly sideways and unlocked it from the barrel, which then stopped. The bolt continued to the rear, to cock the hammer, and then came forward, stripped a round from the magazine, chambered it, locked onto the barrel, and forced it back to its forward firing position. The magazine was of detachable box type, incorporating its own platform and spring. The pistol could, however, also be loaded through the top of the frame by means of a charger. Much to Bergmann's disappointment, no country adopted this arm, although several experimented with it.

UNITED STATES

HARRINGTON AND RICHARDSON REVOLVER 1897

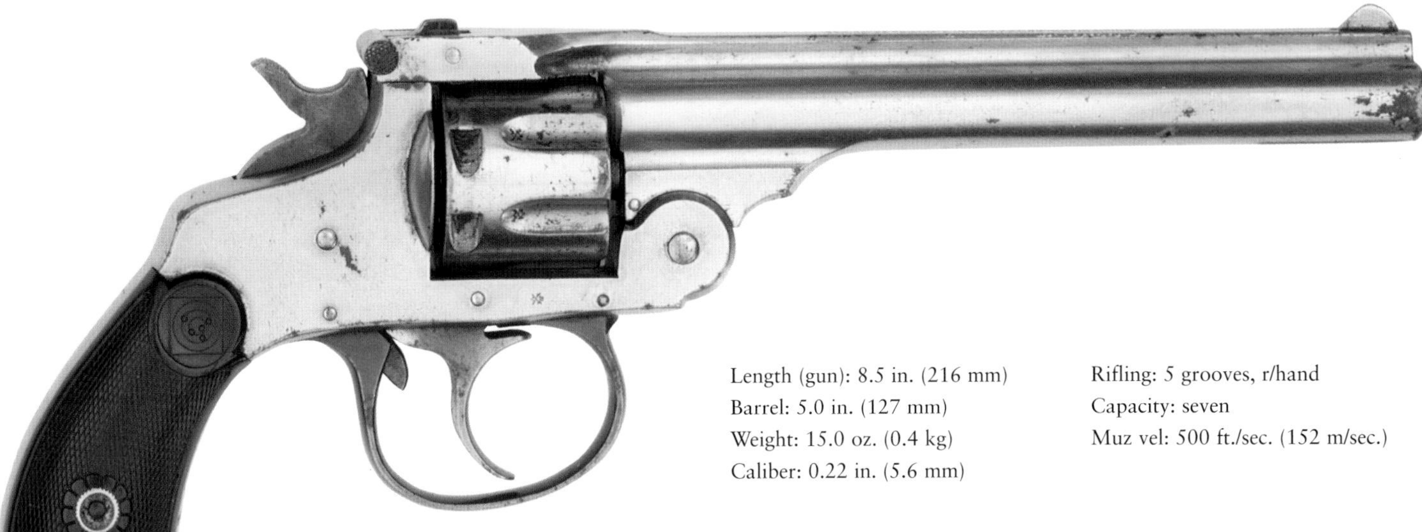

Length (gun): 8.5 in. (216 mm)
Barrel: 5.0 in. (127 mm)
Weight: 15.0 oz. (0.4 kg)
Caliber: 0.22 in. (5.6 mm)
Rifling: 5 grooves, r/hand
Capacity: seven
Muz vel: 500 ft./sec. (152 m/sec.)

The well-known firm of Harrington and Richardson was originally formed in 1874 for the manufacture of revolvers. Its first products were of the orthodox solid-frame type, but by 1897 the company was also producing a range of hinged-frame revolvers in a variety of calibers and barrel lengths. The arm illustrated here is well made and finished, and closely resembles the famous Smith & Wesson No. 3 revolver. This weapon has a round barrel with a top rib, the foresight being slotted in; the backsight is a notch in a raised part of the barrel catch. When the barrel catch was raised, the barrel could be forced downward through about 90 degrees, bringing the automatic ejector into action. It has a seven-chambered cylinder that could be removed by opening the revolver, lifting the barrel catch, and pressing in a small stud on the left side of the top strap; this allowed the cylinder to be lifted off its axis pin. The lock is of double-action type. The butt grips are of black vulcanite; both bear the Harrington and Richardson trademark of a target pierced with five shots. Like all weapons made in the United States (however reputable the company) and sold in the United Kingdom, it was reproofed and bears Birmingham marks.

GERMANY

BERGMANN-BAYARD SELF-LOADING PISTOL 1903

Length: 9.9 in. (251 mm)
Barrel: 4.0 in. (102 mm)
Weight: 35.5 oz. (1.0 kg)
Caliber: 9 mm
Rifling: 6 grooves, l/hand
Capacity: six
Muz vel: 1,000 ft./sec. (305 m/sec.)

This Bergmann-Bayard pistol was designed as a military arm, originally under the trade name Mars, and was the first European pistol of its kind to fire a 9 mm cartridge, a very powerful round. The Spanish Army put in a considerable order, but Bergmann had trouble with contractors and few, if any, pistols were ever actually supplied by him. He eventually sold the rights to Pieper of Liège, who completed the order and also sold some of these arms to the Greek and Danish armies. Once these orders were completed, Pieper put an improved version on the market as the Bergmann-Bayard. The pistol worked on a system of short recoil. The barrel and bolt recoiled together for about 0.25 in. (6 mm); the barrel stopped, and the bolt was unlocked by being forced downward and continued to the rear, extracting the empty case and compressing the return spring which was contained within it, coiled around the long striker. On its forward movement, the bolt stripped a cartridge from the magazine in front of the trigger guard and chambered it. The pistol was considered to be clumsy, and recoil from its powerful cartridge was considerable. Military models were often fitted with a detachable holster stock of hard leather, to improve long-range accuracy.

AUSTRIA-HUNGARY

RAST-GASSER MODEL 1898 REVOLVER

Length (gun): 8.8 in. (222 mm)
Barrel: 4.5 in. (114 mm)
Weight: 34.0 oz. (1.0 kg)
Caliber: 0.31 in. (8 mm)
Rifling: 4 grooves, r/hand
Capacity: eight
Muz vel: 700 ft./sec. (213 m/sec.)

Leopold Gasser's revolvers were widely used by the armed forces of many Balkan states. This service revolver is of solid-frame type, with a round barrel screwed in; its eight-chambered cylinder is plain, except for slots for the stop. The revolver was loaded through a bottom-hinged loading gate, the inside of which is fitted with a small projection which engaged the frame and prevented it from being drawn farther back than the horizontal. When the loading gate was open, the hammer was disconnected, but the cylinder could still be rotated by the action of the trigger, which speeded up loading. The ejector rod is hollow and worked over a rod which was connected to the projection below the barrel; this projection also housed the front end of the axis pin. When it was not in use, the handle of the ejector rod fitted around the axis pin. The lock is of double-action type and there is a separate firing pin on the frame.

UNITED KINGDOM

WEBLEY 0.38 IN. MARK IV REVOLVER (DAMAGED) 1899

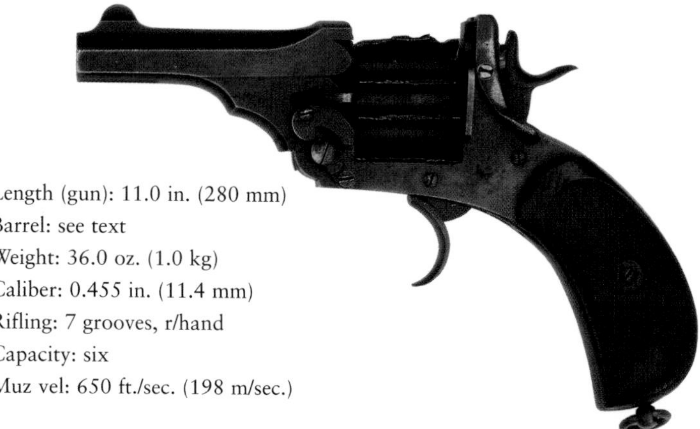

Length (gun): 11.0 in. (280 mm)
Barrel: see text
Weight: 36.0 oz. (1.0 kg)
Caliber: 0.455 in. (11.4 mm)
Rifling: 7 grooves, r/hand
Capacity: six
Muz vel: 650 ft./sec. (198 m/sec.)

The Webley & Scott Mark IV represented a substantial improvement over its forerunners. It was widely used in the South African War, where it was carried by all officers, non-commissioned officers, and trumpeters of cavalry regiments, and by some artillery drivers; indeed, it was so popular that it earned the nickname of the "Boer War Model." It was made in four barrel lengths—3.0 in. (76 mm), 4.0 in. (102 mm), 5.0 in. (127 mm), and 6.0 in. (152 mm). The trigger guard of this one has been removed. Rather more significant, the weapon has suffered catastrophic damage, three of its six chambers having been blown out. The top strap has disappeared completely. The neat way in which the outer walls of the chambers have been removed suggests that the cause was an internal explosion, almost certainly in the central chamber, which was probably under the hammer at the time.

BELGIUM

BROWNING MODEL 1900 ("OLD MODEL") PISTOL 1900

Length (gun): 6.4 in. (163 mm)
Barrel: 4.0 in. (102 mm)
Weight: 22.0 oz. (0.6 kg)
Caliber: 7.65 mm
Rifling: 5 grooves, r/hand
Capacity: seven
Muz vel: 850 ft./sec. (259 m/sec.)

John Moses Browning's first successful venture was a machine gun made by Colt and adopted by the US Navy in 1898. Two years later he produced a self-loading pistol, of the type shown here. However, after a disagreement with Winchester, with whom he had worked for some years, Browning came to the conclusion that more interest might be shown in his pistol in Europe than in the United States—where, of course, the revolver was almost universally predominant. In this he was right: the Belgian firm Fabrique Nationale (FN) of Liège showed immediate interest, and the weapon was soon in production in great quantity. It is robust, reliable and mechanically simple; and although it has not been made since 1912, many are still to be found in collections today. The barrel is fastened to the frame; above it is a moving slide that contains the recoil spring. The slide had to be operated manually to load the first round. When this was fired, gas pressure forced the empty case backward, taking with it the breechblock and slide, compressing the recoil spring, which also operated the striker. The spring then forced the whole assembly forward, stripping a cartridge from the box magazine in the butt and chambering it.

BELGIUM

BROWNING MODEL 1900 PISTOL

Length (gun): 6.8 in. (171 mm)
Barrel: 4.0 in. (102 mm)
Weight: 22.0 oz. (0.6 kg)
Caliber: 7.65 mm
Rifling: 6 grooves, r/hand
Capacity: seven
Muz vel: 940 ft./sec. (287 m/sec.)

This model was the first of a long series of self-loading pistols to be made by Fabrique Nationale. It fired a cartridge originally designed by Browning for use in this particular model; the same round is now widely used in numerous other self-loading pistols. The magazine fitted into the butt. The pistol is numbered (not dated) "1948" and thus must be from one of the very earliest batches produced. The original design on the butt plate incorporated a replica of the weapon and the letters "F.N." On later examples the engraving was omitted. This particular specimen has been fitted at some time with nonregulation aluminum grips. It is known to have been carried as a private weapon by a French infantry officer during the Algerian Insurrection, 1954–62. A pistol of this type was used by the student Gavrilo Princip, who assassinated the Archduke Ferdinand and his wife at Sarajevo in June 1914.

UNITED KINGDOM

WEBLEY SELF-COCKING REVOLVER (WEBLEY-FOSBERY) 1900

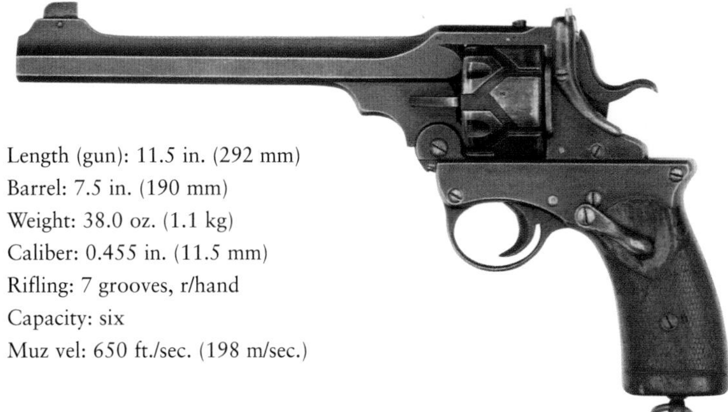

Length (gun): 11.5 in. (292 mm)
Barrel: 7.5 in. (190 mm)
Weight: 38.0 oz. (1.1 kg)
Caliber: 0.455 in. (11.5 mm)
Rifling: 7 grooves, r/hand
Capacity: six
Muz vel: 650 ft./sec. (198 m/sec.)

Colonel George Vincent Fosbery, VC, invented this unique revolver, which used recoil to rotate the cylinder and cock the hammer. It handled and loaded in the same way as the standard issue revolver, but after the first shot the recoil did much of the work: all the firer needed to do was apply light pressure to the trigger. The barrel and cylinder were free to recoil along guide ribs on the butt and trigger component, a stud working in zigzag cylinder grooves rotating the cylinder one-twelfth, cocking the action; going forward, the cylinder turned another one-twelfth, bringing the next chamber into line with the hammer. The revolver was fast and accurate: Walter Winans, one of the finest ever pistol shots, was able to put six shots into a 2.0 in. (51 mm) bull's-eye at twelve paces in seven seconds. The Webley-Fosbery was, however, never popular as a service weapon—mud and dirt tended to clog it.

UNITED STATES

WEBLEY-MARS 0.38 IN. PISTOL 1900

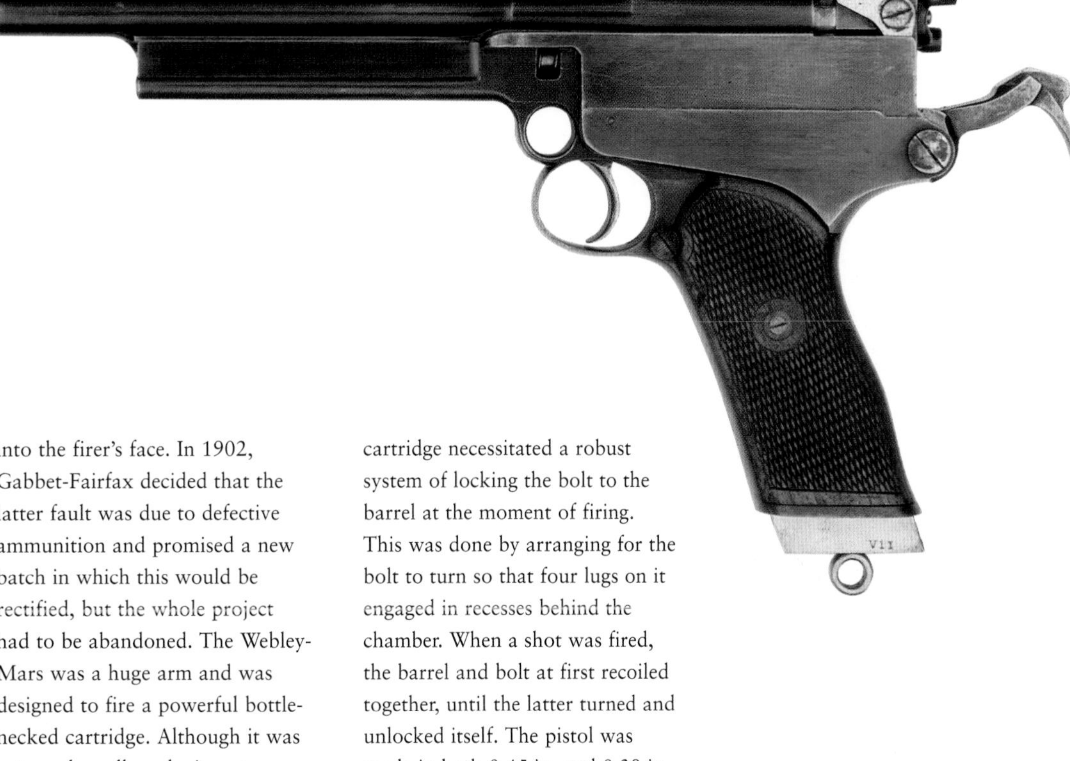

Length (gun): 12.25 in. (311 mm)
Barrel: 9.5 in. (241 mm)
Weight: 48.0 oz. (1.36 kg)
Caliber: 0.38 in. (9.6 mm)
Rifling: 7 grooves, r/hand
Capacity: seven
Muz vel: 1,750 ft./sec. (533 m/sec.)

In 1898, Hugh Gabbet-Fairfax submitted a design to Webley and Scott, which was seeking a suitable design for a self-loading arm. The firm agreed to manufacture it for the inventor, presumably on a commission basis. The British Army tested it in the period 1901–03 but did not adopt it, partly due to its heavy recoil, and partly to its tendency to fail to eject empty cases or to eject them into the firer's face. In 1902, Gabbet-Fairfax decided that the latter fault was due to defective ammunition and promised a new batch in which this would be rectified, but the whole project had to be abandoned. The Webley-Mars was a huge arm and was designed to fire a powerful bottle-necked cartridge. Although it was extremely well made, it was mechanically complex, since the cartridge necessitated a robust system of locking the bolt to the barrel at the moment of firing. This was done by arranging for the bolt to turn so that four lugs on it engaged in recesses behind the chamber. When a shot was fired, the barrel and bolt at first recoiled together, until the latter turned and unlocked itself. The pistol was made in both 0.45 in. and 0.38 in. calibers.

UNITED STATES

COLT NEW SERVICE TARGET REVOLVER 1900

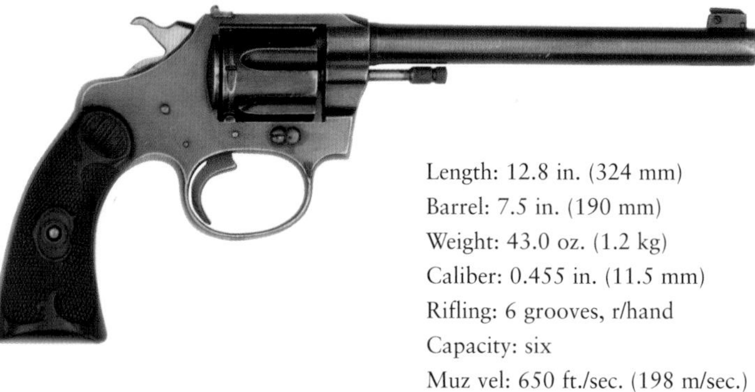

Length: 12.8 in. (324 mm)
Barrel: 7.5 in. (190 mm)
Weight: 43.0 oz. (1.2 kg)
Caliber: 0.455 in. (11.5 mm)
Rifling: 6 grooves, r/hand
Capacity: six
Muz vel: 650 ft./sec. (198 m/sec.)

Colt did not abandon its earlier fixed-cylinder type when it started making swing-out cylinders. Although the new models were made in considerable variety, they were all basically built upon four frame sizes only. The last of the frames to appear was also the largest, and it is on this frame that the New Service revolver was built. It first appeared in 1897 and is still manufactured, with only minor changes to its original specification. It has been made in barrel lengths from 4.0 in. (102 mm) to 7.5 in. (190 mm) and in numerous calibers. In 1900, a new service target revolver was introduced; the revolver shown here is of this type. It has a rectangular blade foresight screwed into its bed, and a laterally adjustable U-backsight at the rear of the frame. The hand-finished lock worked very smoothly and the trigger was checkered to prevent the finger from slipping.

AUSTRIA-HUNGARY

MANNLICHER MODEL 1901 PISTOL

Length (gun): 9.4 in. (239mm)
Barrel: 6.5 in. (165 mm)
Weight: 33.0 oz. (0.9 kg)
Caliber: 7.63 mm
Rifling: 4 grooves, r/hand
Capacity: eight
Muz vel: 1,025 ft./sec. (312 m/sec.)

The Steyr factory first made self-loading pistols in 1894, designed by the German Ferdinand Ritter von Mannlicher. Several models were made. This one was basically of blowback design, but of the type known as retarded blowback. There was no positive locked-breech system: the rearward movement of the slide was mechanically retarded for a very brief period to ensure that the gas pressure in the barrel fell to a safe level. This system permitted the use of a relatively light slide without engendering excessive recoil. Although the magazine was located in the butt—in the modern style—it was not, in fact, a detachable box but an integral part of the arm, and it was loaded from the top by means of a charger. To empty the magazine, the slide was drawn back and pressure was put on the small milled catch above the right butt plate to allow the magazine spring to force out unexpended rounds.

GERMANY

BERGMANN SIMPLEX PISTOL 1901

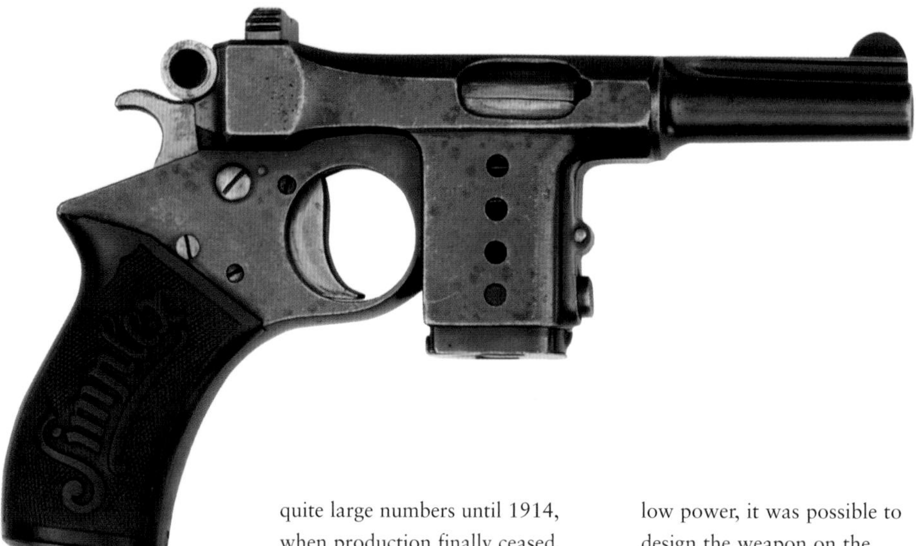

Length (gun): 7.5 in. (190 mm)
Barrel: 2.8 in. (70 mm)
Weight: 21.0 oz. (0.6 kg)
Caliber: 8 mm
Rifling: 6 grooves, r/hand
Capacity: six or eight
Muz vel: 650 ft./sec. (198 m/sec.)

The Bergmann Simplex pistol was patented in 1901. A few were made in Austria, but in 1904 the design was licensed to a company in Belgium, which thereafter turned the arm out in quite large numbers until 1914, when production finally ceased. Although the general shape of this weapon characterizes it as a Bergmann, it is much smaller than the designer's other weapons: the Simplex was originated as a pocket arm. It fired a specially designed cartridge (which is no longer available) and, because it was of low power, it was possible to design the weapon on the blowback principle, with no need for a locked breech. The pistol was cocked by pulling back the bolt by means of the cylindrical cocking piece. When released, the bolt went forward under its recoil spring, stripped a round from the magazine, and chambered it. The weapon had a detachable box magazine in front of the trigger: it was removed by pressing the small stud on the front of the magazine housing. On Belgian-made examples, the barrel was screwed into the frame, whereas the Austrian arms had their barrels forged integrally. The Bergmann was reliable: it sold well.

UNITED STATES

SMITH & WESSON MODEL 0.38 IN. SAFETY REVOLVER (THIRD MODEL) 1902

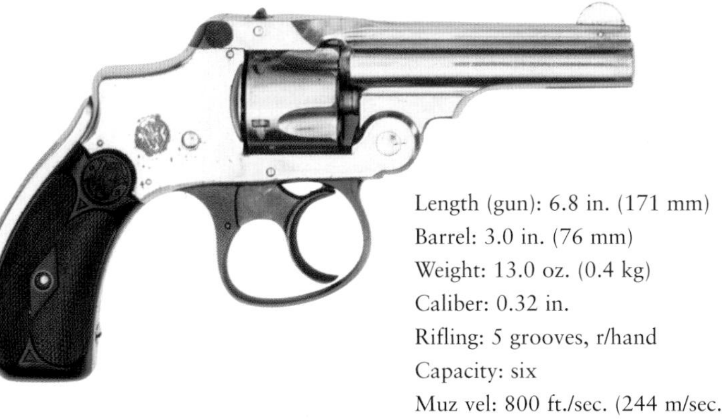

Length (gun): 6.8 in. (171 mm)
Barrel: 3.0 in. (76 mm)
Weight: 13.0 oz. (0.4 kg)
Caliber: 0.32 in.
Rifling: 5 grooves, r/hand
Capacity: six
Muz vel: 800 ft./sec. (244 m/sec.)

This third model was produced in three barrel lengths: 2.0 in. (51 mm); 3.0 in. (76 mm); and 3.5 in. (89mm). The barrel was round with a top rib and a round blade foresight, which in some cases was forged integrally with the barrel and in others was inserted into a slot and pinned. The weapon was opened by pushing up a T-shaped catch with a knurled knob on each side. This allowed the barrel to be forced down and operated the ejector. As on the earlier model, there was a grip safety that, when the butt was properly gripped, was forced in, allowing the lock mechanism to function, making it a very safe weapon. The stocks were of hard, black rubber and were rounded to ensure that there was no risk of snagging on the shooter's pockets. The picture shows an example of the third model whose barrel, frame, and grip safety have been nickel-plated. There is an inspection plate on the left side of the weapon.

AUSTRIA-HUNGARY

MANNLICHER MODEL 1903 PISTOL

Length (gun): 10.5 in. (267 mm)
Barrel: 4.5 in. (114 mm)
Weight: 35.0 oz. (1.0 kg)
Caliber: 7.65 mm
Rifling: 5 grooves, r/hand
Capacity: six
Muz vel: 1,090 ft./sec. (332 m/sec.)

The Mannlicher company realized that the future of self-loading weapons lay in the military sphere, which meant weapons firing powerful cartridges from locked-breech systems, like this one. It was cocked by drawing back the bolt using the milled knob visible on top of the frame. When released, the bolt went forward, stripping a cartridge from the magazine and chambering it. When the bolt was fully forward, a bolt-stop rose from the frame and supported it while the round was fired. Then barrel and bolt recoiled for about 0.2 in. (5 mm), after which the bolt-stop fell. The barrel now stopped, but the bolt continued backward to complete the recocking and reloading cycle. An internal hammer acted on the firing pin; it also had an external cocking device in the form of the curved lever above the trigger. It was not considered safe to fire the 7.65 mm round used in the Mauser self-loading pistol.

UNITED STATES

COLT MODEL 1903 POCKET PISTOL

Length (gun): 6.8 in. (171 mm)
Barrel: 3.8 in. (95 mm)
Weight: 24.0 oz. (0.7 kg)
Caliber: 0.32 in. (8.1 mm)
Rifling: 6 grooves, l/hand
Capacity: eight
Muz vel: 900 ft./sec. (274 m/sec.)

Colt's first pocket self-loading pistol appeared in 1903, but it did not prove entirely popular and was replaced in the same year by a new weapon designed by the famous John M. Browning. This was a success—and with various modifications it remained in production for many years. The example of the Model 1903 illustrated here is of post-1911 manufacture: before that date, the barrel, which was rather thin, was held in place by a barrel bushing, which is absent from this specimen. It worked by blowback, no locking device being required for the 0.32 ACP cartridge, and had a concealed hammer. It was also the first Colt self-loading pistol to be fitted with a grip safety. Most models have vulcanite grips bearing the word "COLT" and the rearing-horse trademark, and it is not clear whether the wooden grips on the arm seen here were optional or are a private replacement. In 1926, a safety disconnecter, which separated the sear from the trigger when the magazine was removed, was incorporated into the design, but this feature is not present in the example shown here. This was an unusually handy and well-balanced pistol and well deserved its popularity.

UNITED KINGDOM

WEBLEY AND SCOTT 0.455 IN. MODEL 1904 PISTOL

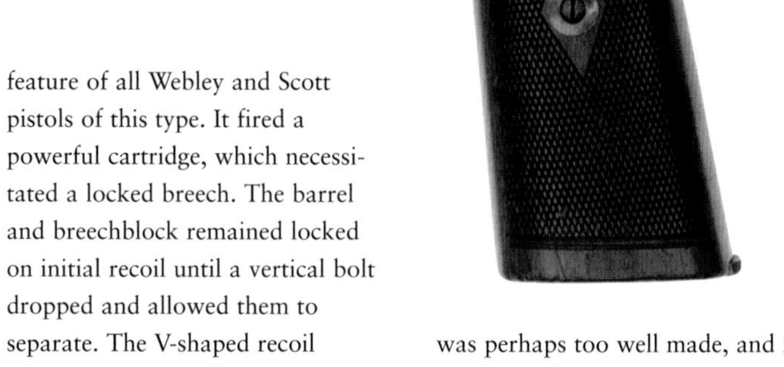

Length (gun): 10.0 in. (254 mm)
Barrel: 6.5 in. (165 mm)
Weight: 48.0 oz. (1.4 kg)
Caliber: 0.455 in. (11.5 mm)
Rifling: 7 grooves, r/hand
Capacity: seven
Muz vel: 750 ft./sec. (229 m/sec.)

By the end of the nineteenth century it had become clear that the self-loading pistol had a future. Much of the work of development was done in Western Europe and, initially, neither the United States nor Britain showed much interest; both countries preferred to stick to their various revolvers, which had proved to be powerful and reliable weapons. However, the new system could not be ignored completely, and as early as 1898 Webley and Scott had sought a suitable design. Apart from the Webley-Mars, they found nothing to its liking until they saw the model shown here, which first went onto the market in 1904. As may be seen, it is of the typical square style that was later to become a noticeable feature of all Webley and Scott pistols of this type. It fired a powerful cartridge, which necessitated a locked breech. The barrel and breechblock remained locked on initial recoil until a vertical bolt dropped and allowed them to separate. The V-shaped recoil spring was situated under the right butt plate. Overall, the weapon was of rather complex design; it was perhaps too well made, and is said to have been susceptible to stoppages caused by dirt; but it set the style for Webley self-loaders.

JAPAN

NAMBU 4TH YEAR 8 MM TYPE A SELF-LOADING PISTOL 1904

Length (gun): 9.0 in. (229mm)
Barrel: 4.7 in. (122 mm)
Weight: 31.0 oz. (0.9 kg)
Caliber: 8 mm
Rifling: 6 grooves, r/hand
Capacity: eight-round box magazine
Muz vel: 1,100 ft./sec. (335 m/sec.)

This was the first Japanese semiautomatic pistol, designed by a retired army officer, Colonel Kirijo Nambu. At the time Japanese officers had to buy their own weapons (a custom learned from the British). The weapon used a locked breech, which was locked by a floating block attached to the barrel extension. As the barrel moved forward, this locking block was lifted as it rode across the frame, forcing a lug upward to engage and lock into a recess in the bolt. The weapon had a grip safety but no holding-open lock, so that when the last round had been fired, the bolt was held open by the magazine lips, but when the magazine was removed, the bolt closed, needing to be recocked after reloading. This model was adopted by the Imperial Japanese Navy in 1909 and by the Thai Army in the early 1920s, but never formally by the Japanese Army.

UNITED KINGDOM

WEBLEY AND SCOTT 0.32 IN. PISTOL 1905

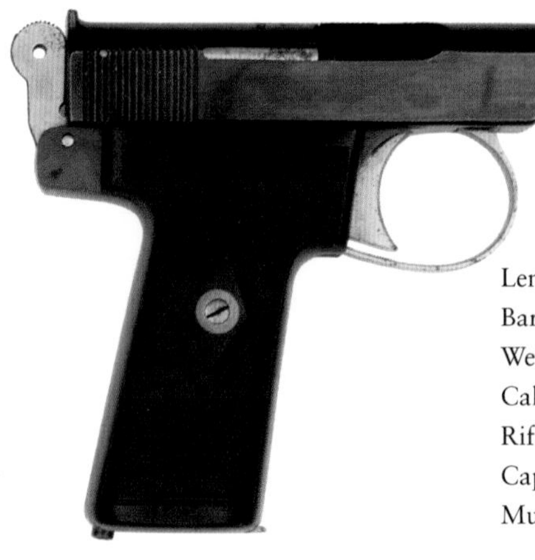

Length (gun): 6.3 in. (159mm)
Barrel: 3.5 in. (89mm)
Weight: 20.0 oz. (0.6 kg)
Caliber: 0.32 in. (8.1 mm)
Rifling: 7 grooves, r/hand
Capacity: eight
Muz vel: 900 ft./sec. (274 m/sec.)

This arm proved so popular that its manufacture continued for almost thirty-five years. It was of simple blowback type with an external hammer; the recoil spring was V-shaped and fitted to the frame inside the right butt plate. Once the magazine was in position, all that was necessary was to pull back the slide by the ribbed finger pieces, push up the safety catch, and fire. The original model had a safety on the left side of the hammer, but most had the safety on the left side of the frame, where it also locked the slide. The trigger guard was hinged at its top end and held into a socket at its lower end by the natural spring of its metal. Although this pistol was small, many officers carried one as a secondary arm in the two world wars. It was adopted in 1911 as the pistol of the Metropolitan Police of London: this particular specimen was a police arm.

UNITED STATES

COLT POLICE POSITIVE REVOLVER 1905

Length (gun): 10.3 in. (260 mm)
Barrel: 6.0 in. (152 mm)
Weight: 24.0 oz. (0.7 kg)
Caliber: 0.22 in. (5.6 mm)
Rifling: 6 grooves, r/hand
Capacity: six
Muz vel: 700 ft./sec. (213 m/sec.)

The original 0.32 in. (8.1 mm) Police Positive revolver was produced in 1905. Two years later a heavier version was produced, chambered for the 0.38 in. (9.6 mm) special cartridge. Their success led to a demand for a lighter version for target shooting. In 1910 the Colt Police Positive Target revolver (above) went into production in both 0.32 in. (8.1 mm) and 0.22 in. (5.6 mm) calibers. The larger caliber was discontinued in 1915, but the smaller version remained in production until 1935. The arm has a round barrel with a blade-type foresight, and an adjustable U-shaped backsight. When a catch on the left side of the frame was drawn back, the cylinder could be swung out to the left. The empty cases were ejected manually with the extractor pin. The rims of the 0.22 in. (5.6 mm) cartridges lacked strength; in 1932, countersinks were added to the chambers, fully enclosing the cartridge rims.

UNITED STATES

MERIDEN POCKET REVOLVER 1905

Length (gun): 6.5 in. (165 mm)
Barrel: 3.0 in. (76 mm)
Weight: 14.0 oz. (0.4 kg)
Caliber: 0.32 in. (8.1 mm)
Rifling: 5 grooves, r/hand
Capacity: five
Muz vel: 550 ft./sec. (168 m/sec.)

The weapons produced by Meriden were mostly pocket models, including some hammerless versions; this revolver is typical. It is of hinged-frame type with a sprung, T-shaped barrel catch, the backsight being a simple V-notch in the raised portion of the catch. It has a round barrel with a top rib of slightly peculiar section, being wider at the top than at its junction with the barrel. Its somewhat unusual foresight has a shape reminiscent of a cocked hat. The lock is double-action, and the butt grips are of black vulcanite. The top flat of the barrel is marked "MERIDEN FIREARMS CO. MERIDEN CONN UNITED STATES," and on the base of the butt is the number "284035" (the figure "8" being stamped upside down on this one). It is cheap and nasty. The workmanship is crude and the components shoddy, but these mail-order revolvers probably only cost a few dollars.

UNITED KINGDOM

WEBLEY NO. 1 MARK I 0.455 IN. PISTOL 1906

Length (gun): 8.5 in. (216 mm)
Barrel: 5.0 in. (127 mm)
Weight: 39.0 oz. (1.1 kg)
Caliber: 0.455 in. (11.5 mm)
Rifling: 7 grooves, r/hand
Capacity: seven
Muz vel: 750 ft./sec. (229 m/sec.)

This Webley was developed from about 1906 onward and was officially adopted as the standard pistol of Britain's Royal Navy in 1913. It was a heavy and robust arm with all the Webley characteristics. It worked, as usual, by recoil. When a loaded magazine was inserted into the butt and the slide pulled back and released, a round was chambered and the hammer cocked. At the moment of firing, the barrel was locked to the slide—a lug on the barrel engaging in a recess in the upper part of the slide—and the two recoiled briefly together. Once the gas pressure had dropped to a safe level (a process measured in thousandths of a second), the barrel was forced downward by a cam-way and disengaged from the slide, which continued to the rear, cocking the hammer as it did so. The slide's forward movement, under the impetus of the V-spring behind the right butt plate, stripped the top round from the magazine and chambered it. A Mark II version, fitted with a stock, was issued to the Royal Flying Corps in 1915. This would be withdrawn upon the introduction of the aerial machine gun.

SMITH & WESSON: FROM REVOLVERS TO AUTOMATICS

Above: *Remarkably, the 1911 is a best seller for Smith & Wesson in 2004, having been brought back after a long absence; the slide and frame are made in-house, and other parts by aftermarket vendors. The single-action .45 has an eight-shot capacity.*

Sensing that the automatic pistol would be an important part of the future of firearms—especially after witnessing the success of Colt's M1911—Smith & Wesson began development of automatic handguns shortly before World War I. Co-president Jo Wesson met with the Belgian gun designer Philibert Clement in 1909 to discuss his automatic designs, and the following year Wesson purchased Clement's patent for a small .35 in. caliber automatic pistol. This was an unusual weapon in that the recoil spring was set above the barrel, this reducing the recoil by setting the barrel closer to the firer's hand. The gun was promising, but S&W stopped production after only six months to concentrate on revolver production for the British Army with the onset of war in 1914.

S&W was not to revisit automatic handgun designs until 1921, when it took the original automatic and reworked it for the .32 in. ACP cartridge. Sales of this gun, arriving as it did during a time of depression, were slow, and S&W boosted its gun sales with a powerful new revolver type, the .357 in. Magnum. The .357 Magnum was a revolution in handguns, giving the user an extremely powerful firearm that became loved by police officers, hunters, and others. S&W introduced other enormously successful revolver weapons, and during World War II manufactured 1.1 million military and police .38 in. revolvers.

It was after the war that S&W revisited the automatic handgun, and during the 1950s a new range of S&W autos was selling well, particularly its .22 Model 41. S&W also introduced its first double-action handgun, the 9 mm Model 39, in 1955, which was taken up as the standard sidearm for the Illinois Police Department in 1967. Since then, S&W has brought out an endless series of superb automatics and pistols, including the high power Series 1000, firing an awesome 10 mm Magnum cartridge, and the modern SW99, a collaborative venture between S&W and Walther.

UNITED KINGDOM

WEBLEY AND SCOTT 0.25 IN. PISTOL 1906

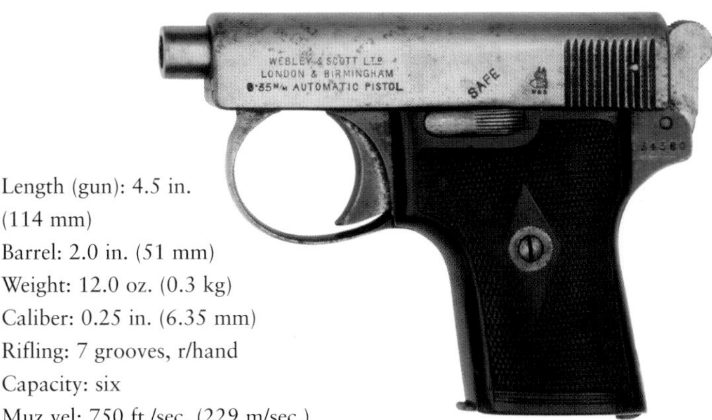

Length (gun): 4.5 in. (114 mm)
Barrel: 2.0 in. (51 mm)
Weight: 12.0 oz. (0.3 kg)
Caliber: 0.25 in. (6.35 mm)
Rifling: 7 grooves, r/hand
Capacity: six
Muz vel: 750 ft./sec. (229 m/sec.)

Since laws for the control of firearms hardly existed in 1906, there appears to have been a very large market for pocket arms of this type. There were, however, numerous makers in Belgium, Germany, and elsewhere who were turning out such weapons at competitive prices; thus, it was necessary for the British company to produce its version as cheaply as possible. This pistol was essentially a scaled-down version of the 0.32 in. model. It was well and simply made. Because it was of small caliber and fired a low-powered cartridge, it was of simple blowback design. The main difference between this and other Webley self-loaders is that the V-spring under the grip was replaced by two coil springs in the slide, one on each side of the firing pin. It was fitted with a safety catch, and this example bears the usual Webley markings. It was strictly a pocket pistol, designed to fit into a waistcoat pocket or handbag.

AUSTRIA-HUNGARY

ROTH-STEYR MODEL 1907 PISTOL

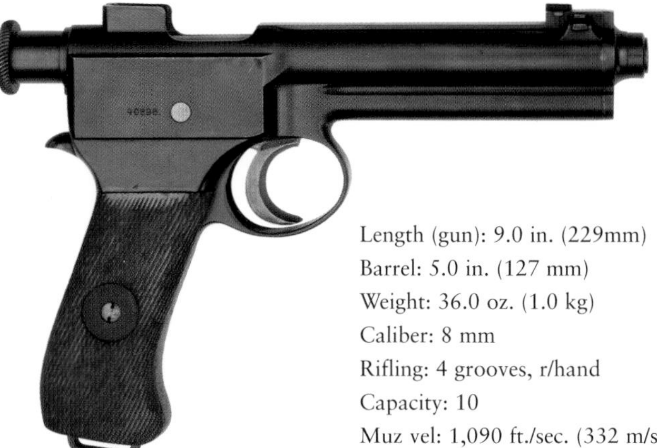

Length (gun): 9.0 in. (229mm)
Barrel: 5.0 in. (127 mm)
Weight: 36.0 oz. (1.0 kg)
Caliber: 8 mm
Rifling: 4 grooves, r/hand
Capacity: 10
Muz vel: 1,090 ft./sec. (332 m/sec.)

This pistol was taken into service by the Austro-Hungarian Army, mainly for use as a cavalry arm, the first time a major power adopted a self-loading pistol. The locked breech was very unusual. The bolt was very long: its rear end was solid, except for the striker sleeve, but its front part was hollow and of sufficient diameter to fit closely over the barrel. The interior of the bolt had cam grooves cut into it, and the barrel had studs of appropriate size to fit the grooves. On firing, the barrel and bolt recoiled together within the hollow receiver for about 0.5 in. (12.7 mm). The grooves in the bolt caused the barrel to turn through 90 degrees, after which it was held while the bolt continued to the rear, cocking the action as it did so. Going forward, the bolt picked up a cartridge through a slot on its lower surface and chambered it, while the studs in the grooves turned the barrel back to locked.

DENMARK

DANSK SCHOUBOE MODEL 1907 PISTOL

Length (gun): 8.8 in. (224 mm)
Barrel: 5.0 in. (127 mm)
Weight: 42.0 oz. (1.2 kg)
Caliber: 11.35 mm
Rifling: 6 grooves, r/hand
Capacity: six
Muz vel: 1,600 ft./sec. (488 m/sec.)

Lieutenant Jens Torring Schouboe was an officer in the Danish Army and a director of the Dansk Rekylriffel Syndikat; he was closely involved with the development of the famous Madsen light machine gun. In 1903, Schouboe patented a self-loading pistol, but although it was well made and reliable, it failed to sell. He then designed a heavier arm of the same general type but of service caliber, the result being the weapon illustrated here. Like his earlier arms, this was of simple blowback design, without any breech-locking mechanism, easy enough to incorporate into small pocket pistols firing low-powered cartridges, but very hard to do in a service-type arm without making it extremely heavy. Schouboe's answer was to produce a cartridge firing an extremely lightweight bullet, which would reduce recoil and leave the barrel faster, thus reducing the period of maximum pressure. The bullet was basically a wooden round with a thin metal jacket. Schouboe's solution worked. The weapon was very satisfactory from the purely mechanical point of view, but it had two serious defects as a military arm: the bullet was too light to have much stopping power, and it lost accuracy very quickly. Although Schouboe produced improved versions, it was never popular, and manufacture ceased in 1917.

GERMANY

RHEINMETALL 7.65 MM DREYSE PISTOL 1907

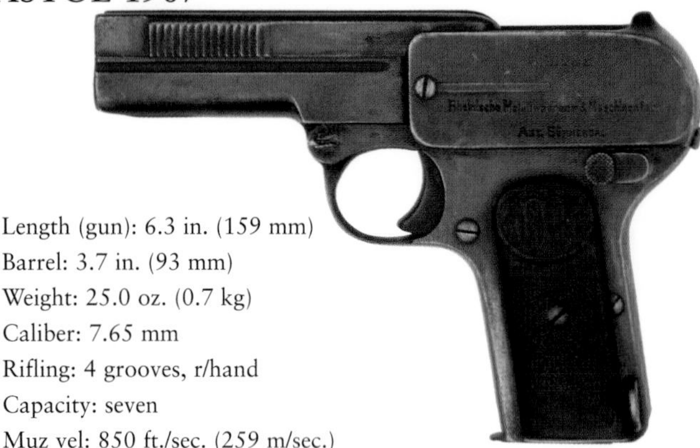

Length (gun): 6.3 in. (159 mm)
Barrel: 3.7 in. (93 mm)
Weight: 25.0 oz. (0.7 kg)
Caliber: 7.65 mm
Rifling: 4 grooves, r/hand
Capacity: seven
Muz vel: 850 ft./sec. (259 m/sec.)

In 1901, Rheinmetall took over Waffenfabrik von Dreyse, which had been founded in 1841 to manufacture the Prussian needle-rifles and needle-revolvers. This pistol is of a type designed by Louis Schmeisser; it was named after Nikolaus von Dreyse. The slide was positioned above the barrel, which lay in a trough in the main frame. At the back of the frame were two parallel rectangular plates, joined at the rear to provide a backsight, but otherwise open to allow the slide to pass between them. The top of the breechblock, integral with the slide (but lower, so as to align with the chamber), could be seen between these plates when the slide was forward. When the slide was drawn back to chamber a round, the breechblock protruded through the rear of the frame; when the slide went forward, the end of the striker protruded slightly as an indication that the arm was cocked.

UNITED STATES

SAVAGE MODEL 1907 PISTOL

Length (gun): 6.5 in. (165 mm)
Barrel: 3.8 in. (95 mm)
Weight: 20.0 oz. (0.6 kg)
Caliber: 0.32 in. (8.1 mm)
Rifling: 6 grooves, r/hand
Capacity: ten
Muz vel: 800 ft./sec. (244 m/sec.)

This is the first self-loading pistol from Savage Arms. It is of unusual design, and was the subject of much controversy. The slide covered the entire top of the weapon, including the barrel proper. The pistol was loaded in the orthodox way, and the slide was pulled back and released to feed the first round into the chamber. A lug on top of the barrel fitted into a curved slot on the top of the slide: when the cartridge was fired, the rearward movement of the barrel and slide was briefly checked by the cam, but the barrel overcame this by twisting slightly until the lug reached a straight stretch of groove, when the slide was again free to move to the rear. The disputed theory was that the counterrotation of the bullet in the rifling was sufficient to prevent the barrel from twisting. It reached the finals of the 1907 competition for the US Army, but lost to the Colt M1911.

UNITED KINGDOM

WEBLEY AND SCOTT TARGET PISTOL 1907

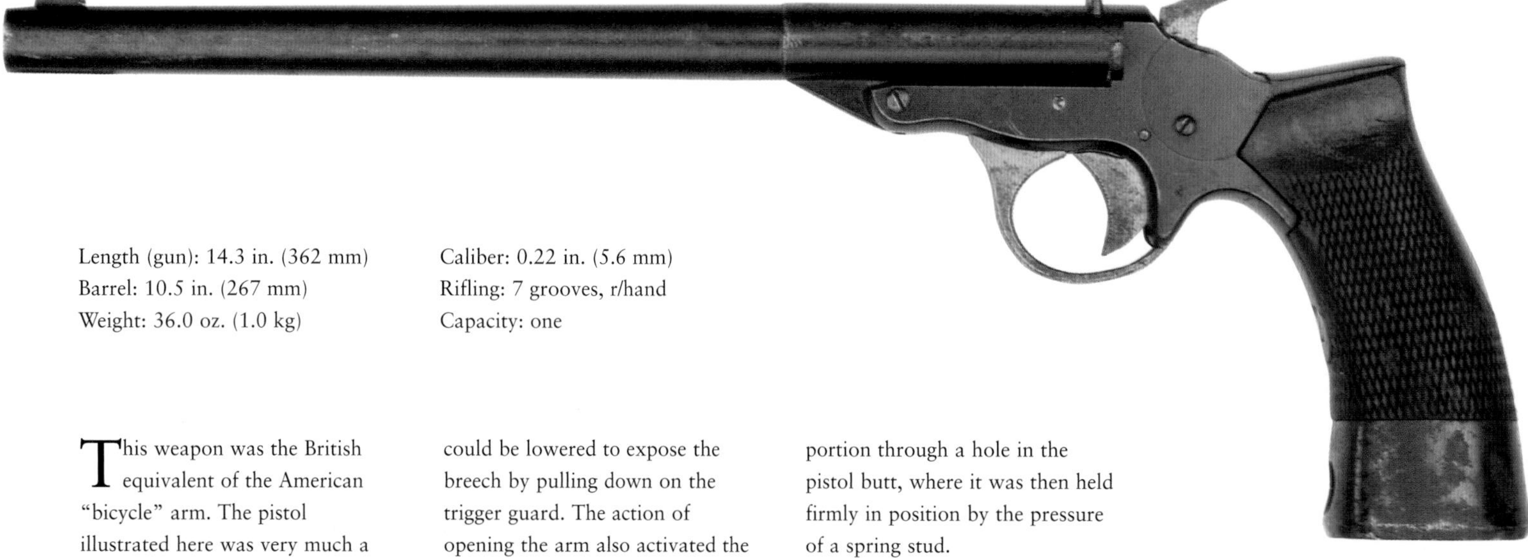

Length (gun): 14.3 in. (362 mm)
Barrel: 10.5 in. (267 mm)
Weight: 36.0 oz. (1.0 kg)
Caliber: 0.22 in. (5.6 mm)
Rifling: 7 grooves, r/hand
Capacity: one

This weapon was the British equivalent of the American "bicycle" arm. The pistol illustrated here was very much a dual-purpose weapon: when used single-handed, without the butt, it was well balanced and suitable for normal practice; the addition of the butt at once converted it to a useful arm for small game or vermin. The barrel was hinged and could be lowered to expose the breech by pulling down on the trigger guard. The action of opening the arm also activated the extractor, which was semicircular and occupied half of the end of the barrel. There was an inspection plate on the left side of the frame, just below the hammer. The rifle butt (not shown here) was attached by pushing its rod portion through a hole in the pistol butt, where it was then held firmly in position by the pressure of a spring stud.

The Beretta Company

Beretta is a name synonymous with the manufacturer of quality firearms, and the Beretta company is the oldest extant manufacturing company in the world. The first record of the Beretta name can be dated to October 3, 1526, when Bartolomeo Beretta of Gardone Val Trompia, near Milan, was commissioned by the Senate of the Republic of Venice to manufacture 185 arquebus barrels. The Beretta business was already thriving when Bartolomeo's son Jacomo joined the company in the mid-1500s. Subsequent generations of Berettas ensured a continuity of the family name, which exists to this day.

The key figure in the story of the modern Beretta company is Pietro Beretta, another Beretta master gunsmith who took over the company in 1903 and ran it until 1957. Pietro oversaw a huge expansion of Beretta production, and pushed Beretta heavily into overseas markets, particularly the United States.

In terms of handguns, this period was extremely fruitful, seeing the production of the Beretta Models 1915, 1915/19, 1923, 1931, and 1934. These weapons equipped the Italian army through the war years and, following Italy's move to the Allied side in 1943, became increasingly popular with US soldiers. Much of the success of these designs can be traced to Pietro's visionary senior gun designer, Tullio Marengoni. The pistols laid the groundwork for future Beretta pistol types.

After Pietro's reign, Beretta increased its penetration of the US markets. In 1975, the US Army announced that it intended to replace the Colt M1911 as its standard infantry sidearm. Committed to chasing the contract, Beretta established a subsidiary in Maryland in 1977, and produced the Beretta Model 92 handgun as its contender. Despite competing against famous US names such as Colt and Smith & Wesson, Beretta won after its gun displayed phenomenal reliability in US Army tests. (As part of the evaluation 12 production standard 92FS pistols fired 168,000 rounds without stoppage or other failure.) The Beretta 92 finally became the US Army's new standard handgun in 1985.

Since 1985, Beretta has consolidated its hold over huge swathes of the international firearms markets. Beretta today, as always, produces the full range of military and civil weaponry, from shotguns to submachine guns. The latest models of handguns, such as the Model 9000S, feature new ergonomic designs with ambidextrous controls and increased use of polymers and fiberglass in the design to reduce weight.

Below: *It was reliability that won the Beretta 92 its place as the US Army's sidearm. Magazine capacity was thirteen, which necessitated a bulkier butt than the earlier Beretta model 1951, with eight-magazine capacity.*

AUSTRIA-HUNGARY

TOMISKA LITTLE TOM PISTOL 1908

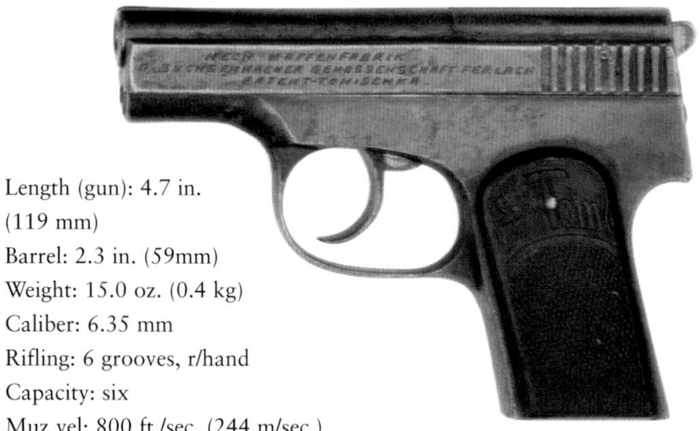

Length (gun): 4.7 in. (119 mm)
Barrel: 2.3 in. (59mm)
Weight: 15.0 oz. (0.4 kg)
Caliber: 6.35 mm
Rifling: 6 grooves, r/hand
Capacity: six
Muz vel: 800 ft./sec. (244 m/sec.)

Alois Tomiska, a Viennese gunsmith, designed a self-loading pistol that he patented in 1908 as the Little Tom. It had a fixed barrel and an open-topped slide; the recoil spring was contained in a sleeve below the barrel. It had a double-action lock; thus, its external hammer could be cocked either by the rearward movement of the slide or by direct pressure on the trigger. The greater part of the hammer lay within a recess at the rear of the frame, but enough of its milled comb protruded to make thumb-cocking possible. When the slide was removed, it was possible to gain access to the lock by pushing up the right butt plate. Pistols of this type appear to have been made by several European factories after the end of World War I, when Tomiska himself worked for Jihoceská Zbrojovka (later Ceská Zbrojovka) in Czechoslovakia. Tomiska's long career did not end until 1946.

GERMANY

LUGER PARABELLUM MODEL 1908 (PO8) PISTOL

Length (gun): 8.8 in. (222 mm)
Barrel: 4.0 in. (102 mm)
Weight: 30.0 oz. (0.9 kg)
Caliber: 9mm
Rifling: 8 grooves, r/hand
Capacity: eight
Muz vel: 1,150 ft./sec. (315 m/sec.)

The Luger pistol was basically similar to the Borchardt, the design having been modified and improved by Georg Luger, and was put onto the market at the very end of the nineteenth century. After several earlier models, there appeared the pistol illustrated here. It was put into production in 1908 and was almost immediately adopted by the German Army, which was then seeking a self-loader. Of course, this assured the arm's success, as many smaller countries followed Germany's lead and purchased large numbers of Lugers for their armed forces. It served the Germans well during World War I and, like the Mauser, became something of a household word, establishing a popular reputation that is, perhaps, greater than its real merit. After World War I, its manufacture was taken over by Mauser, who continued to make both military and civilian models. This is one of those made by Mauser and is dated "1940."

GERMANY

SCHWARZLOSE MODEL 1908 PISTOL

Length (gun): 6.4 in. (163 mm)
Barrel: 3.8 in. (97 mm)
Weight: 25.0 oz. (0.7 kg)
Caliber: 7.65 mm
Rifling: 6 grooves, r/hand
Capacity: eight
Muz vel: 1,000 ft./sec. (305 m/sec.)

The Carl Walther Waffenfabrik (weapons factory) was established in 1886 but did not begin to make self-loading pistols until 1908. Its first nine models were numbered, but in 1929 it produced a tenth model designed specifically for police work, and this was designated the Polizei Pistole or "PP." It was of a new and, to some extent, revolutionary design, and rapidly achieved popularity after its appearance in 1929. It was very soon adopted as a holster arm by several European police forces, and later also became the standard pistol of the German Luftwaffe. Its main feature was its double-action lock, which was basically of revolver type and had an external hammer. A considerable risk was involved in carrying hammerless self-loaders—and even, to a lesser extent, many earlier hammer versions—with a round in the chamber. However, when a round had been loaded into the chamber of a Walther and the safety catch applied, the fall of the trigger could be disconcerting but was completely safe, for the action of the safety placed a steel guard between the hammer and the firing pin. The pistol was easily stripped by pulling down the trigger guard and pushing very slightly to the left, and easing off the slide.

UNITED KINGDOM

WEBLEY 0.45 IN. TARGET MODEL REVOLVER 1908

Length (gun): 13.3 in. (337 mm)
Barrel: 7.5 in. (191 mm)
Weight: 42.0 oz. (1.2 kg)
Caliber: 11.4 mM
Rifling: 7 grooves, r/hand
Capacity: six
Muz vel: 650 ft./sec. (198 m/sec.)

Most specialists regard the Webley WG Model (Webley-Government/Webley-Green) as the finest production revolver ever made. The WG went through several evolutions until it was eventually replaced after World War II by the WS Model, which used the same frame and mechanism as the Mark VI Service revolver. The WG was produced in two versions: "service," for purchase by army officers; and "target." The latter dominated the pistol competition scene for several years, and it is generally agreed that it possessed one of the finest trigger actions ever. The WG introduced the famous Webley stirrup latch, with the thumb lever on the left of the frame. When the Webley horseshoe cylinder retainer was introduced, the WG was fitted with that as well. Unlike the Government revolver, the WG had a sideplate on the left of the receiver, which permitted access to the mechanism.

UNITED STATES

COLT MODEL 1908 PISTOL

Length (gun):
4.5 in. (114 mm)
Barrel: 2.1 in. (53 mm)
Weight: 14.0 oz. (0.4 kg)
Caliber: 0.25 in. (6.35 mm)
Rifling: 6 grooves, l/hand
Capacity: six
Muz vel: 800 ft./sec. (244 m/sec.)

Colt began to make self-loading pistols in 1900, and this weapon was a very small pocket pistol designed by John M. Browning and was originally made in Belgium, until Colt bought the patent and made it in the United States. It was of blowback type and orthodox operation; unusually for a pocket pistol, it was fitted with a grip safety in addition to a second safety catch on the frame. The pistol was so small that only the second finger could be placed around the butt—but its recoil was, of course, negligible. It has sights situated in a groove on the top of the slide.

UNITED STATES

COLT ARMY SPECIAL M1908 REVOLVER

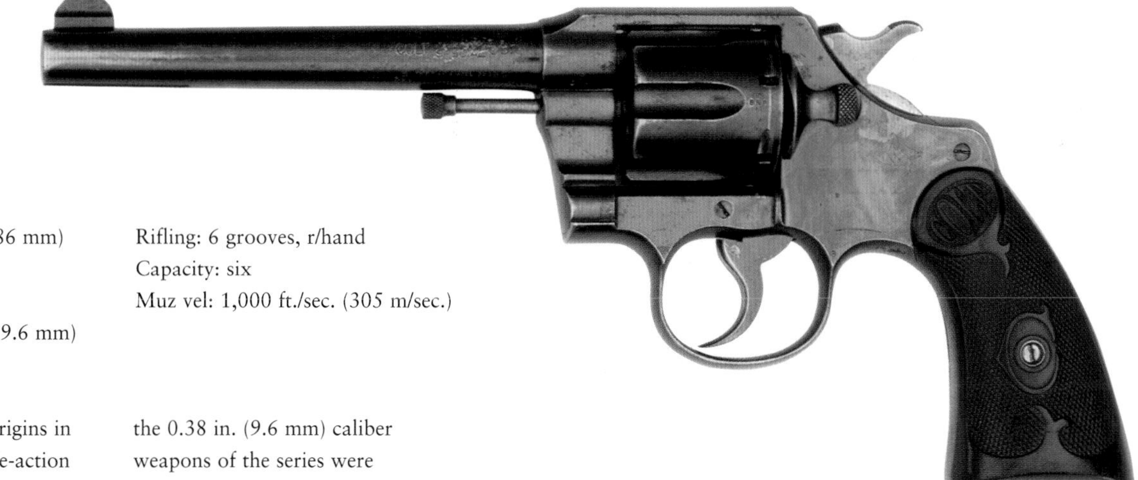

Length (gun): 11.3 in. (286 mm)
Barrel: 6.0 in. (152 mm)
Weight: 35.0 oz. (1.0 kg)
Caliber: 0.38 in. Special (9.6 mm)
Rifling: 6 grooves, r/hand
Capacity: six
Muz vel: 1,000 ft./sec. (305 m/sec.)

This revolver had its origins in the New Navy double-action arm. The Army quickly followed suit and large numbers were made. In 1904, a new version, the Officer's Model Target, was introduced. This was essentially similar to the original model, except for a slight difference in the lower front silhouette of the frame and the addition of adjustable target sights. At the same time, all the 0.38 in. (9.6 mm) caliber weapons of the series were chambered to take the 0.38 in. (9.6 mm) Special cartridge, firing smokeless powder. In 1908, some changes were made both to the lock mechanism and to the cylinder locking system; the latter was reduced to a single stop, instead of the front and rear alternating stops on the original arm. The revolver illustrated here is of post-1908 pattern. After 1908, this revolver was usually known as the "Army Special"; then, in 1926, the type became generally classed as "Official Police" (a version in 0.22 in./5.6 mm caliber was produced in 1930). The 0.41 in. (10.4 mm) caliber was discontinued at the same time. The 0.38 in. (9.6 mm) Special cartridge for which the arm was rechambered differed considerably from the 0.38 in. (9.6 mm) Long Colt for which it was originally intended, principally in power.

UNITED STATES

SMITH & WESSON NEW CENTURY REVOLVER 1908

Length (gun): 11.8 in. (298 mm)
Barrel: 6.5 in. (165 mm)
Weight: 38.0 oz. (1.08 kg)
Caliber: 0.455 in. (11.5 mm)
Rifling: 6 grooves, r/hand
Capacity: six
Muz vel: 650 ft./sec. (198 m/sec.)

The solid-frame revolver seen here first appeared in 1908 and was variously known as the "0.44 Hand Ejector First Model," the "New Century," the "Gold Seal," or the "Triple Lock." The latter name came from the fact that the cylinder locked not only at the rear, but also by means of one bolt into the front end of the rod and a second that emerged from the casing below it. The lock is of rebounding, double-action type and, as with all Smith & Wesson arms, worked very smoothly. The standard production caliber was 0.44 in. (11.2 mm), and it was chambered for the special cartridge, but arms in other calibers were made. A small number of original 0.44 in. (11.2 mm) caliber revolvers were converted to fire the British 0.455 in. (11.5 mm) Eley cartridge, mostly at the outbreak of World War I, but later a special version was made and sold to the British Army. The specimen shown is one of these, bearing the serial number "1068," and also has what is apparently a British number on the bottom of the butt-strap, together with London proof marks. It is in every respect a beautiful weapon.

UNITED STATES

COLT NEW SERVICE REVOLVER M1909

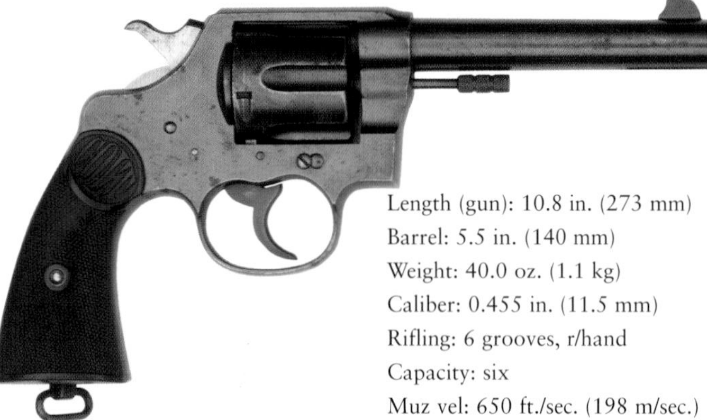

Length (gun): 10.8 in. (273 mm)
Barrel: 5.5 in. (140 mm)
Weight: 40.0 oz. (1.1 kg)
Caliber: 0.455 in. (11.5 mm)
Rifling: 6 grooves, r/hand
Capacity: six
Muz vel: 650 ft./sec. (198 m/sec.)

The Colt New Service revolver was made in six barrel lengths from 4.0 in. (102 mm) to 7.5 in. (190 mm). It was used as a United States service arm from 1907 onward, until it was superseded by a self-loading pistol. Even after that, many continued to be carried privately. This one is of the usual solid-frame type and has as round, 5.5 in. (140 mm) barrel. Access to its six-chambered cylinder was obtained by pulling back a thumb-catch on the left side of the frame. This allowed the cylinder to be swung out sideways, to the left, on its separate yoke. The well-known trademark of the rearing horse is borne on the left side of the frame, below the hammer. The revolver was made in a variety of calibers: the one shown here is chambered for the British 0.455 in. (11.5 mm) Eley cartridge. This arm bears the view marks of the Royal Small Arms Factory, Enfield, showing that it was imported for the British Army in World War I.

UNITED STATES

COLT NEW SERVICE REVOLVER (CUT-DOWN) M1909

Length (gun): 6.8 in. (171 mm)
Barrel: 1.5 in. (38 mm)
Weight: 32.0 oz. (0.9 kg)
Caliber: 0.455 in. (11.5 mm)
Rifling: 6 grooves, r/hand
Capacity: six
Muz vel: not available

The weapon seen here has, obviously, been crudely shortened. It is chambered for the British 0.455 in. (11.5 mm) Eley cartridge, the word "ELEY" being just visible on the stump of the barrel. Its origins are not known, but it bears British government proof marks and also the double-arrow condemnation mark, which suggests that it saw service (as many of this type did) in World War I. It is in a poor state, and as the cylinder is irretrievably jammed in the frame, it is impossible to ascertain its number. The reasons for which it was cut down are not known. It may have had a bulged barrel, or the truncation may have been performed simply to make the arm easier to conceal—although even in its present state it hardly qualifies as a pocket weapon! The drastic reduction of the barrel must have had a very serious effect on the accuracy of the weapon, except at point-blank range.

UNITED KINGDOM

WEBLEY MODEL 1909 0.38 IN. PISTOL

Length (gun): 8.0 in. (203 mm)
Barrel: 5.0 in. (127 mm)
Weight: 34.0 oz. (1.0 kg)
Caliber: 0.38 in. (9.6 mm)
Rifling: 7 grooves, r/hand
Capacity: seven
Muz vel: 750 ft./sec. (229 m/sec.)

In 1908, Webley began work on a pistol of international caliber, to meet the needs of civilian customers who did not require anything quite so powerful as the 0.455 in. cartridge used in the firm's various military models. The new weapon was on the market by 1909, and designed principally to handle the 9 mm Browning long cartridge. The weapon was of a simple blowback design. When the first round was fired it blew back the slide, cocked the hammer, and compressed the recoil spring in the butt. The spring then drove the action forward and stripped and chambered the next cartridge. In this model, the barrel was held in position by a lug on top of the trigger guard, pulled forward to strip the weapon. It was adopted by the South African Police in 1920; production ended in 1930.

JAPAN

NAMBU 7 MM TYPE B (NAMBU "BABY") PISTOL 1909

Length (gun): 6.7 in. (171 mm)
Barrel: 3.3 in. (83 mm)
Weight: 21.0 oz. (0.6 kg)
Caliber: 7 mm
Rifling: 6 grooves, r/hand
Capacity: 7-round box magazine
Muz vel: 950 ft./sec. (290 m/sec.)

As mentioned previously, Japanese officers had to buy their service revolvers, and when the Type 4 failed to sell well, Colonel Nambu was forced to reexamine the product. As a result, he discovered that most officers considered the Type 4 to be too large and cumbersome, so he designed a smaller, neater weapon, chambered for a 7 x 19.5 mm round, which he designed specifically for this weapon. The result was the Nambu "Baby," a short recoil weapon that appeared in 1909 and was, in effect, simply a scaled-down Type 4. The "Baby" had no advantages to offer over European and American pistols and was much more expensive, so it never achieved much success; it remained in low-volume production until the early 1930s.

UNITED KINGDOM

WEBLEY 0.22 IN. MARK III SINGLE-SHOT TARGET PISTOL 1909

Length (gun): 14.25 in. (362 mm)
Barrel: 10.5 in. (267 mm)
Weight: 36.0 oz. (1.0g)
Caliber: 0.22 in. (5.56 mm)
Rifling: 7 grooves, r/hand
Capacity: one
Muz vel: 1,100 ft./sec. (335 m/sec.)

This target pistol remained in production with only the most minor changes from 1909 until 1965. The gun was of all-steel construction and was famed for the simplicity of its mechanism, which consisted of the hammer, trigger, and mainspring guide. The hammer had to be cocked for each shot, and the gun was opened by pressing forward on the trigger guard, which released the barrel to tip forward, pivoting on the hinge at the front of the frame. Shown here is an early production version. In the opinion of shooters Webley showed a curious lack of ambition about this gun, never developing and offering trigger adjustments, decent sights, or choices of barrel length or weights. Indeed, very skilled shooters regarded it as on the light side and rather whippy, and many taped spare wheelweights under the barrel in an attempt to tame these characteristics. The sights were in square format; on the backsight, the windage and elevation were adjustable by opposing screws.

BELGIUM

BROWNING 7.65 MODEL 1910 PISTOL

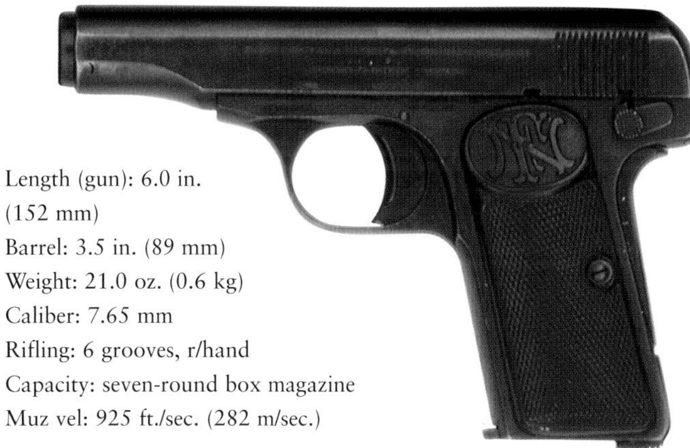

Length (gun): 6.0 in. (152 mm)
Barrel: 3.5 in. (89 mm)
Weight: 21.0 oz. (0.6 kg)
Caliber: 7.65 mm
Rifling: 6 grooves, r/hand
Capacity: seven-round box magazine
Muz vel: 925 ft./sec. (282 m/sec.)

Following their acquisition of John M. Browning's patents, Fabrique Nationale (FN) developed the design, leading to the Model 1910, which was first produced to take the 7.65 x 17 mm Browning round, although it was later also available in 9 x 17 mm Short caliber. The weapon was blowback operated, and the fore-end was tubular in shape because the recoil spring was mounted around the barrel and held in place by a nosecap with a bayonet fastening, resulting in an unusual and easily identifiable profile. It had a grip safety. The Model 1910 had only limited military success, although some were taken into German service during World War I, but it was widely used by police forces and sold well commercially.

ITALY

GLISENTE 9 MM MODEL 1910 PISTOL

Length (gun): 8.3 in. (210 mm)
Barrel: 3.9 in. (99 mm)
Weight: 29.0 oz. (0.8 kg)
Caliber: 9 mm
Rifling: 6 grooves, r/hand
Capacity: seven
Muz vel: 1,000 ft./sec. (305 m/sec.)

Real Fabbricca d'Armi Glisenti (later Siderurgica Glisenti) began operations in about 1889. After some earlier experiments with self-loading pistols, this weapon was put into production in 1910 and was adopted by the Italian Army. The pistol fired from a locked breech. When the first shot was fired, barrel and bolt recoiled briefly together. The barrel then stopped in its rearward position, while the bolt, having unlocked itself, continued to travel. As it came forward, it stripped and chambered the next round and drove the barrel forward. As it did so, a wedge rose from the frame and locked the whole frame into position. The system was complex and not very strong; thus, its cartridges were less powerful than the Parabellum of comparable caliber. The pistol's trigger mechanism was peculiar: the striker was not cocked by the moving parts, but by a projection on the trigger; the striker was forced backward against a spring until it tripped and came forward to fire the round. This made the trigger-pull very long. The milled screw at the front of the frame held in position a plate covering much of the left side; its removal gave access to the working parts. Although this weapon became obsolete in 1934, some were in service in World War II.

UNITED STATES

HARRINGTON AND RICHARDSON 0.25 IN. PISTOL 1910

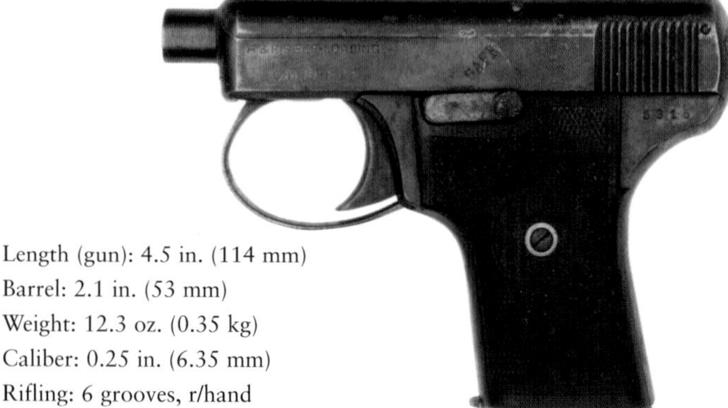

Length (gun): 4.5 in. (114 mm)
Barrel: 2.1 in. (53 mm)
Weight: 12.3 oz. (0.35 kg)
Caliber: 0.25 in. (6.35 mm)
Rifling: 6 grooves, r/hand
Capacity: six
Muz vel: 700 ft./sec. (213 m/sec.)

This particular arm was first produced by Webley and Scott in 1909 and was later made in the United States by Harrington and Richardson under agreement with the British firm. The two weapons were basically similar, but the Webley arm has a full slide with only an aperture for extraction, whereas, in the pistol seen here, the slide is partially open-topped and the rear section of the barrel is built up to conform to the general shape. Unlike its Webley prototype, the US version utilizes two parallel coil springs, one on each side of the firing pin, instead of the more usual Webley V-spring under the grip. It has no sight of any kind, which is understandable for a low-powered pocket arm. It did not prove popular in the United States and was not manufactured after 1914. The left side of the slide is marked "H & R Self-Loading."

GERMANY

WALTHER MODEL 9 POCKET PISTOL 1911

Length (gun): 4.0 in. (102 mm)
Barrel: 2.0 in. (51 mm)
Weight: 9.5 oz. (0.3 kg)
Caliber: 6.35 mm
Rifling: 6 grooves, r/hand
Capacity: six
Muz vel: 800 ft./sec. (244 m/sec.)

Carl Walther Waffenfabrik has produced numerous self-loading pistols since 1908, and this was the ninth in the series, the last before the introduction of the famous PP. It was one of the smallest and neatest self-loading pistols ever made, well-suited for concealment in a waistcoat pocket or in a lady's handbag. It had a fixed barrel with an open-topped slide and was of simple blowback type. The slide was retained on the frame by a dumbbell-shaped catch at the rear, which was held in place by a small spring catch. When this was raised, the entire assembly was forced out to the rear under the pressure of the striker spring. When the weapon was cocked, the rear end of the striker protruded slightly through a hole in the upper circle of the catch to indicate that the arm was ready for action.

SPAIN

UNCETA MODEL 1911 VICTORIA PISTOL

Length (gun): 5.8 in. (146 mm)
Barrel: 3.2 in. (81 mm)
Weight: 20.0 oz. (0.6 kg)
Caliber: 7.65 mm
Rifling: 7 grooves, r/hand
Capacity: seven
Muz vel: 750 ft./sec. (229 m/sec.)

Unceta Y Esperanza was set up in Eibar, Spain, in 1908. This specimen is an example of the first pistol of the type made by the firm under the trade names "Victoria" or "1911 Model"; a virtually identical type was also produced in 6.35 mm caliber. It is a close copy of the 1903 Browning and worked on simple blowback, the recoil spring being housed round a rod below the barrel. When the safety catch, located on the left side of the frame, was set at "safe," it engaged a notch almost in the exact center of the frame. If the slide was drawn to the rear with the catch still at "safe," a second notch about 1.2 in. (30 mm) farther forward engaged the safety and held the slide to the rear; the barrel could then be removed by rotating it and drawing it forward. Between the World Wars, Unceta took advantage of the restrictions imposed on German armaments firms to manufacture a close copy of the Mauser Model 1896.

UNITED STATES

COLT GOVERNMENT 0.45 IN. MODEL M1911 PISTOL

Length (gun): 8.5 in. (216 mm)
Barrel: 5.0 in. (127 mm)
Weight: 39.0 oz. (1.1 kg)
Caliber: 0.45 in. (11.4 mm)
Rifling: 6 grooves, l/hand
Capacity: seven-round box magazine
Muz vel: 860 ft./sec. (262 m/sec.)

The Colt M1911 is one of the classic weapons, having remained in frontline service with the US armed forces for over eighty years. In 1905 Colt made a prototype pistol chambered for the 0.45 in. round. This was entered in a US government competition in 1907, which it won, and went into production as the Model 1911.The weapon is very simple, consisting of three main parts: the receiver, the barrel, and the slide, which runs on ribs machined into the receiver. When the slide is fully forward, the barrel is locked to it by lugs on its upper surface that engage in slots on the slide. When the slide is forced to the rear the barrel moves only a very short distance before its rear end drops, disengaging it from the slide, which continues to the rear, ejecting the empty case. On completion of the permitted travel, it is then driven forward again, driving the top round from the magazine into the chamber.

UNITED KINGDOM

WEBLEY & SCOTT SINGLE-SHOT 0.22 IN. TARGET PISTOL 1911

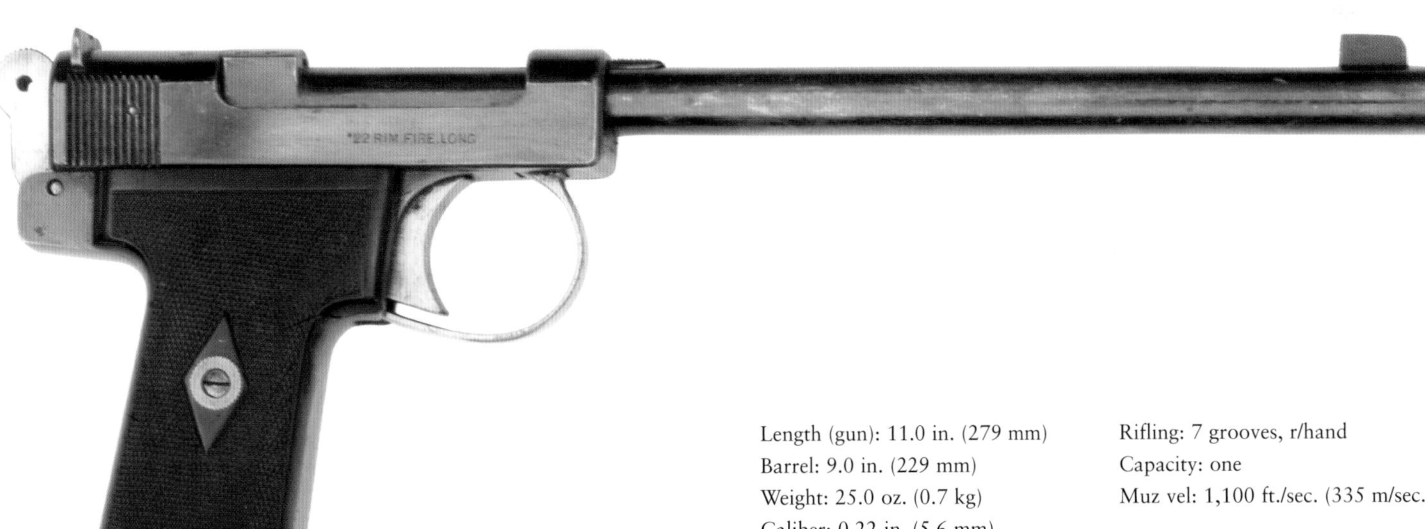

Length (gun): 11.0 in. (279 mm)
Barrel: 9.0 in. (229 mm)
Weight: 25.0 oz. (0.7 kg)
Caliber: 0.22 in. (5.6 mm)
Rifling: 7 grooves, r/hand
Capacity: one
Muz vel: 1,100 ft./sec. (335 m/sec.)

This somewhat unusual weapon was produced by Webley & Scott in 1911 to provide a means of cheap target practice for users of the firm's 0.32 in. self-loading pistol, the two weapons having a strong similarity in all but barrel length. The frame of the single-shot pistol was the same as that of the self-loader, although it was modified to accept a different barrel. The single-shot arm was made in two barrel lengths, 4.5 in. (114 mm) and 9.0 in. (229 mm). To load the pistol, the slide was drawn back a distance of about 1.7 in. (44 mm), exposing the breech and cocking the hammer. A cartridge was pushed into the chamber and the slide was pushed forward manually. Pulling the slide back again ejected the case. At the moment of firing, the slide was held in position by a very light spring latch, situated on the bottom of the slide, which engaged in a groove in the body. There was a machined groove in the bottom of the butt where the magazine opening would normally be; this was intended for the attachment of a rifle-type butt.

UNITED STATES

COLT M1911/1911A1 (NON-COLT VERSIONS) 1911/1940

Length (gun): 8.5 in. (216 mm)
Barrel: 5.0 in. (127 mm)
Weight: 39.0 oz. (1.1 kg)
Caliber: 0.45 in. (mm)
Rifling: 6 grooves, l/hand
Capacity: seven-round box magazine
Muz vel: 860 ft./sec. (262 m/sec)

The Colt M1911 was placed in immediate production for the US Army, but demand was greatly increased during World War I, when manufacture was undertaken in the US by Colt, Remington, and the Springfield Armory. Small-scale manufacture was also undertaken in Canada for the Canadian Army; this was a slightly different weapon, being chambered for the British 0.455 in. Webley round. The weapon was also manufactured under license in Norway as the Pistol m/1914. In 1927, the Hispano-Argentine Fabricas De Automobiles SA (HAFDASA) of Buenos Aires, Argentina, started to produce a version of the M1911 designated the Model 1927; internally this was identical to the M1911, but there were minor external differences. This was widely used by the Argentine armed forces and police, and a number were purchased by the British Government in 1940–41. During World War II, production of the Model 1911A1 was stepped up, with lines at Colt, Ithaca, Remington, Singer, and Union Switch operating throughout the war. The photographs show the HAFDASA Model 1927 (top) and the Colt Remington M1911A1 (bottom).

GERMANY

MAUSER MODEL 1912 SELF-LOADING PISTOL

Length (gun): 11.8 in. (298 mm)
Barrel: 5.5 in. (140 mm)
Weight: 44.0 oz. (1.25 kg)
Caliber: 7.63 mm
Rifling: 6 grooves, r/hand
Capacity: ten
Muz vel: 1,400 ft./sec. (427 m/sec.)

The Model 1912 did not differ significantly from its predecessor of fourteen years before. Weapons of this type were made by the thousands in World War I. In 1916 the German Army required Mauser pistols to fire the straight-sided 9 mm Parabellum cartridge, and it was quickly realized that conversion of the standard Model 1912 would be relatively simple. The arms thus altered were all distinguished by a large figure "9" cut into the butt grips and painted red. The Mauser pistol was widely used in World War I. The emphasis as far as the infantry was concerned was, of course, on the rifle, light machine gun, and medium machine gun. Nevertheless, it was found that a Mauser pistol with its shoulder-stock attached was a handy weapon for raids and clearing trenches. It was used in very similar fashion to the submachine gun, which the Germans finally adopted in 1918. A Mauser-type pistol with a capability for automatic fire was, in fact, made in Spain in the 1930s. The light bolt traveling over a very short distance plus a powerful cartridge was not successful, and the arm's rate of fire made it impossible to shoot with very much accuracy.

THE COLT M1911 REVOLUTION

Above: *In the 1980s, Colt introduced a new series of all their models, with an additional safety device, a firing-pin safety. This stopped the pistol firing if the trigger was not pulled to the end of its free travel. The guns produced thereafter are called Colt Mark IV, Series 80. This system was controversial with shooters who wanted a positive trigger pull. In the 1990s, the "Enhanced Series" of M1911s brought a beveled magazine well, flared ejection port, and a cut beneath the trigger guard that allowed the weapon to sit lower in the hand.*

It is not an overstatement to say that the .45 Colt M1911 transformed the history of handgun design. The M1911 was the brainchild of John Moses Browning, who began work on automatic pistols in 1894 and the following year completed a .38 caliber automatic for Colt. (Browning licensed all his patents for automatic handguns to Colt, and received a royalty contract in 1896.)

The .38 handgun lay the foundations for the M1911, but it had one problem—caliber. From US combat experience in the Philippines against local tribesman, it was felt that the .38 in. round did not have sufficient stopping power for a military handgun. In 1904, General John T. Thompson of the Army Ordnance Board and Major Louise Anatole La Garde of the Medical Corps conducted ammunition trials at the Nelson Morris Company Union Stockyards in Chicago to discover the ideal combat round by firing at inanimate and animal targets. The result was that Browning designed the 230 grain .45 ACP round. Fired from a pistol, this round generates a muzzle velocity of 253 m/sec (830 ft./sec.) carrying 350 ft./lb. of energy at 25 yards (23 m), more than enough to provide a decisive knockdown. Indeed, over penetration has been a problem of the .45 ACP. In modern tests, a .45 ACP cartridge fired at around 49 ft. (15 m) penetrates 26 in. (660 mm) of ballistic gelatin, although this penetration is reduced by using hollow-point rounds.

Colt upgraded the Browning handgun to .45 ACP in 1906, after which it went through a series of modifications until, on March 29, 1911, the final design was approved for United States Army service as the "US Pistol, Automatic, Caliber .45 Model 1911." It would remain the standard United States Army handgun until 1985, when it was replaced by the Beretta 92. The reason for its longevity is a simple design with decisive stopping power. Browning was the first handgun designer to produce a handgun with a slide separate from the barrel, and the lug locking system ensures a very positive lock for the barrel and breech mechanism during firing.

The Colt/Browning short-recoil system is still a dominant operating system in modern handguns, with numerous modifications. Modern Colt handguns such as the Delta Elite, the Double Eagle and the Colt Government are visually and mechanically indebted to the M1911. The M1911 has its faults—particularly a heavy recoil and a low magazine capacity—but debate still rages in the US about whether its replacement by the Beretta in the 1980s was actually a retrograde step in terms of combat performance.

AUSTRIA-HUNGARY

STEYR MODEL 1912 PISTOL

Length (gun): 8.5 in. (216 mm)
Barrel: 5.1 in. (130 mm)
Weight: 35.0 oz. (1.0 kg)
Caliber: 0.357 in.
Rifling: 4 grooves, r/hand
Capacity: eight
Muz vel: 1,100 ft./sec. (335 m/sec)

The Model 1912 is a solid, square-looking arm with some external resemblance to the famous Colt self-loader of the previous year. It has the same heavy slide with the barrel inside it, which covers the whole of the frame. When the action was in the forward position, two lugs on the top of the barrel engaged in two corresponding slots in the slide. When the slide was drawn back for initial loading, the barrel moved with it for a short distance and was rotated sufficiently to disengage it from the slots. The barrel then stopped, but the slide continued to the rear and cocked the hammer. It then moved forward, driven by the recoil spring, stripping a round from the magazine and chambering it. During this forward movement, the barrel rotated back into the locked position in readiness for the next shot. The magazine was loaded by a clip from the top of the frame, the slide to the rear.

HUNGARY

FEGYVERGYAR PISZTOLY 12 M/19 M (FROMMER STOP) PISTOL 1912

Length (gun): 7.5 in. (190 mm)
Barrel: 4.3 in. (120 mm)
Weight: 21.0 oz. (0.6 kg)
Caliber: 7.65 mm
Rifling: 5 grooves, r/hand
Capacity: seven-round box magazine
Muz vel: 1,200 ft./sec. (366 m/sec)

The Pistol 12 m was designed by a team led by Rudolf Frommer and was made at the Royal Hungarian Arsenal at Fegyvergyar. It was a simplified version of a 1903 design and worked on the long recoil principle: the barrel and bolt remained locked together as they traveled rearward for a distance marginally greater than the length of the cartridge. The two were then unlocked and the barrel returned to its forward position, extracting and ejecting the empty case, while the bolt remained locked. On completion of its travel the barrel tripped the bolt stop, releasing the bolt which then traveled forward, stripping a round from the magazine and chambering it. This involved the use of two return springs: one to draw the barrel forward and another to make the breechblock follow it. The Model 12 m was followed by the virtually identical 19 m, in production until 1930.

HUNGARY

FEGYVERGYAR FROMMER BABY 1912

Length (gun): 4.8 in. (121 mm)
Barrel: 2.3 in. (57 mm)
Weight: 14.0 oz. (0.4 kg)
Caliber: 6.35 mm
Rifling: 4 grooves, r/hand
Capacity: six
Muz vel: 800 ft./sec. (244 m/sec)

Rudolf Frommer, one of Fegyvergyar's designers and engineers, was with the firm from 1896 until 1935. This "Baby" of 1912 was basically a smaller type of the Frommer "Stop" service pistol of the same year. It worked on the same system known as long recoil, in which the barrel recoiled almost its full length before returning, leaving the breechblock to come forward after it, stripping a cartridge from the magazine and chambering it. This independent movement of barrel and breechblock made it necessary to have two separate springs, both of which were housed in the separate cylindrical tunnel, visible above the barrel.

UNITED KINGDOM

WEBLEY & SCOTT MARK V 0.455 IN. REVOLVER 1913

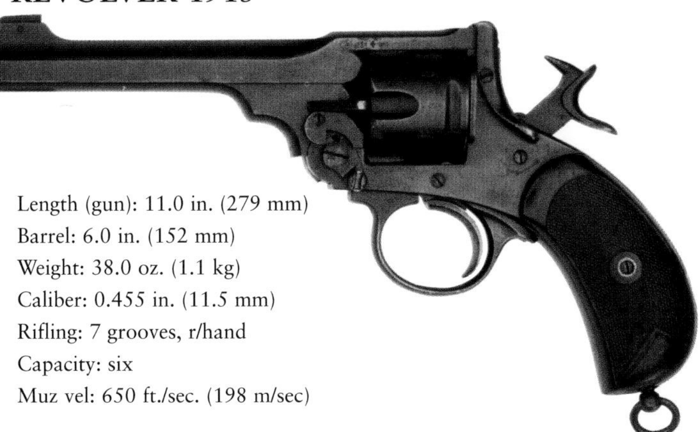

Length (gun): 11.0 in. (279 mm)
Barrel: 6.0 in. (152 mm)
Weight: 38.0 oz. (1.1 kg)
Caliber: 0.455 in. (11.5 mm)
Rifling: 7 grooves, r/hand
Capacity: six
Muz vel: 650 ft./sec. (198 m/sec)

The Webley Mark I was replaced in 1894 by a Mark II, which gave place in 1897 to a Mark III with a different system of releasing the cylinder. The Mark IV followed in 1899. In December 1913, the Mark V was sealed as the standard government pistol, but only 20,000 were made before it was superseded in 1915 by the Mark VI. Thus, the Mark V is the rarest of all the Webley and Scott government series. It resembles its predecessors. It has an octagonal barrel with an integral foresight bed, the blade being inserted separately and held in place by a small screw. The locking system is unchanged from earlier marks, as is the lock mechanism. The Mark III system for removing the cylinder was retained. It consists of a cam (visible below the holster guide), which engaged a slot in the front of the cylinder. Loosening the screw allowed it to be pushed downward: the cylinder could then be lifted clear.

SPAIN

GABILONDO RUBY PISTOL 1914

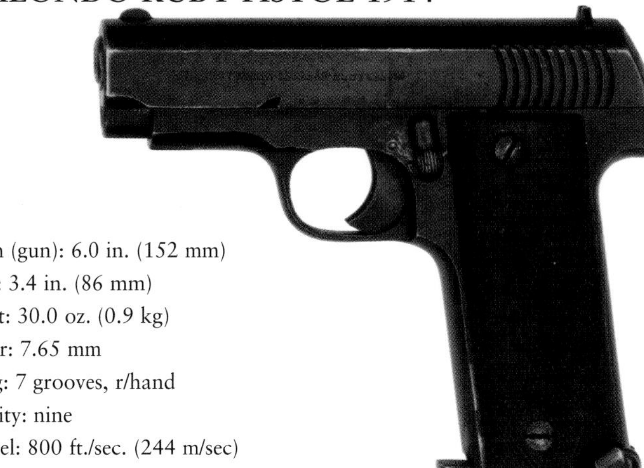

Length (gun): 6.0 in. (152 mm)
Barrel: 3.4 in. (86 mm)
Weight: 30.0 oz. (0.9 kg)
Caliber: 7.65 mm
Rifling: 7 grooves, r/hand
Capacity: nine
Muz vel: 800 ft./sec. (244 m/sec)

The Spanish firm of Gabilondo began to manufacture a pistol of the type shown here in 1914 under the trade name "Ruby." It was not a particularly distinguished weapon in any sense of the word, but it appeared on the market at a time when many countries urgently needed arms; thus, a contract for a large number was soon placed by the French government. The demand was, in fact, so large that Gabilondo was soon forced to put the manufacture of these arms out to subcontractors. The model was discontinued in 1919, although a smaller version in 6.35 mm caliber continued in production under the same name for several years.

UNITED STATES

HARRINGTON AND RICHARDSON 0.32 IN. PISTOL 1913

Length (gun): 6.5 in. (165 mm)
Barrel: 3.5 in. (89 mm)
Weight: 20.0 oz. (0.6 kg)
Caliber: 0.32 in. (8.1 mm)
Rifling: 6 grooves, r/hand
Capacity: six
Muz vel: 980 ft./sec. (299 m/sec)

Harrington and Richardson was set up at Worcester, Massachusetts, in 1874 to make revolvers. In 1910, it began to manufacture a small self-loader based on the Webley and Scott 0.25 in. Model 1909. Two or three years later, Harrington and Richardson put into production this slightly larger self-loading model, which closely resembled the 0.32 in. Webley and Scott Model 1905 pistol, although it was by no means an exact copy. Its principal external difference is that it lacks the characteristic hammer of the Webley pistol. The slide, too, is of a different shape: it has an open top, whereas the Webley's slide has no more than an aperture of sufficient size to allow the empty cases to be ejected. A third difference is the existence on this arm of a grip safety, in addition to an orthodox safety catch. Internally, the weapon is of simple blowback design, but the recoil spring is of the coiled type, while the Webley has a V-spring under the butt plate. The right-hand side of the pistol bears the name and address of the company, together with indications that it was made in accordance with patents of August 20, 1907, and April 18 and November 9, 1909. Manufacture continued into the 1920s.

SPAIN

TROCAOLA BRITISH ARMY REVOLVER 1915

Length (gun): 10.0 in. (254 mm)
Barrel: 5.0 in. (127 mm)
Weight: 40.0 oz. (1.1 kg)
Caliber: 0.455 in. (11.5 mm)
Rifling: 8 grooves, r/hand
Capacity: six
Muz vel: 650 ft./sec. (198 m/sec)

This revolver is marked "TROCAOLA, ARANZABAL y CIA, EIBAR, ESPANA" along the top rib of the barrel. This firm is believed to have started making revolvers soon after 1900, and almost all its arms were close copies of other manufacturers' designs—principally Colt and Smith & Wesson. In 1915 a quantity of Trocaola arms was bought for use by the British Army. These were given the British designation of "Pistol OP, 5 in. Barrel, No. 2 Mark 1." The revolver shown is a copy of a Smith & Wesson. It has a round barrel with a foresight pinned into a slot on the top rib. The backsight is a notch in the barrel catch of standard T-shape and was opened by upward thumb-pressure on the milled studs above the hammer. The revolver is blued, except for the case-hardened lock mechanism, and appears to be of sound construction. It is numbered "1389" and the left side of the barrel is stamped with an Enfield inspector's mark of crossed flags. Trocaola's trademark, visible on the frame below the hammer, was very closely modeled on that of Smith & Wesson—and could easily be mistaken for it at a glance.

SPAIN

BERNEDO 6.35 MM POCKET PISTOL 1915

Length (gun): 4.5 in. (114 mm)
Barrel: 2.0 in. (51 mm)
Weight: 15.0 oz. (0.4 kg)
Caliber: 6.35 mm
Rifling: 6 grooves, r/hand
Capacity: six
Muz vel: 800 ft./sec. (244 m/sec)

Vincenzo Bernedo y Cia of Eibar was one of the many small Spanish firms to produce cheap self-loading pistols. During World War I, the company was involved in the manufacture of Ruby pistols, but after the war had ended Bernedo developed a new design, a specimen of which is illustrated here. The weapon was of pocket type and of the usual blowback design. The barrel was almost fully exposed, with the slide to the rear of it. A small catch was situated just below the barrel; when the cylindrical part of this was lifted, it could be pushed out through a loop on the lower part of the barrel, and the barrel could then be drawn forward. This was facilitated by the fact that the lower part of the loop had flanges which fitted into grooves in the frame of the weapon. This weapon's slide bears many Eibar proof marks, and the butt grips are marked "V BERNEDO."

BRITISH MILITARY HANDGUNS WORLD WAR I–WORLD WAR II

Above: *Cavalry charge in North Africa, presumably with Enfield Mark I and Webley Mark IV small arms, photographed in 1940. Whether this was a publicity exercise or a training exercise, it was not combat.*

The evolution of British handguns over the course of the two world wars is essentially a debate about caliber. During the late 1800s, the British developed a fairly justifiable love of large caliber handguns, as these had proved their decisive stopping power during the Boer War and various other imperial conflicts around the turn of the century. By 1914, the .455 in. round was the favorite, this generating 248 ft./lb. of striking energy—vastly exceeding the theoretical models of 50 ft./lb. as the minimum knockdown force.

The standard models in World War I were the Webley & Scott Mark V and the Mark VI, both hinge-framed .455 in. revolvers. These were manufactured in prolific numbers: 20,000 Mark Vs were made between 1913 and 1915, but from 1915 2,500 Mark VIs were produced each week as war demand rose. Both the Mark V and Mark VI were excellent revolvers, the mechanisms being very resilient against mud and the cartridge providing true killing force during close-quarter combat. For trench raids, the Mark VI could also be fitted with a short bayonet and detachable butt stock, but this feature never caught on.

The large caliber of British handguns, however, was a curse as well as a blessing. It made the guns difficult to shoot well, and it prolonged training times. (Webley & Scott did introduce a .22 in. rimfire version of the Mark VI for training purposes.) After 1918, the British Army reviewed its commitment to the .455 round and decided to shift towards the smaller .38 in. round which generated 187ft./lb. of knockdown force. The wisdom of this is still debated today, modern expert critics such as Ian Hogg arguing that the .38 had markedly reduced killing power in actual combat conditions. Nevertheless, the .38 went into service in Enfield and Webley versions such as the Webley Mark IV and the Enfield Mark I and (after British equipment losses following Dunkirk) the imported US Smith & Wesson .38. All were decent weapons, although the Enfield Mark I's 11 lb. (5 kg) trigger pull combined with double-action made it hard to shoot accurately. British officers, pilots, artillerymen, drivers, and other personnel were issued revolvers until the end of World War II, although by 1945 the Browning HP automatic was also being trialed.

UNITED KINGDOM

WEBLEY & SCOTT MARK VI 0.455 IN. REVOLVER 1915

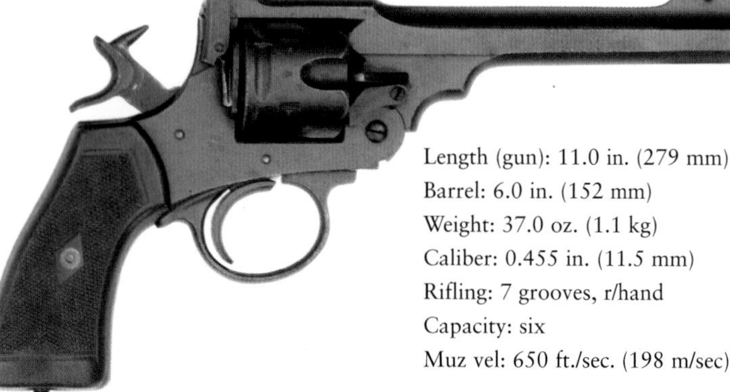

Length (gun): 11.0 in. (279 mm)
Barrel: 6.0 in. (152 mm)
Weight: 37.0 oz. (1.1 kg)
Caliber: 0.455 in. (11.5 mm)
Rifling: 7 grooves, r/hand
Capacity: six
Muz vel: 650 ft./sec. (198 m/sec)

P. Webley and Son (later Webley & Scott) had a virtual monopoly in the supply of British government revolvers for very many years. The company's last, and probably best-known, service arm was the Webley & Scott Mark VI. It did not differ very much from its predecessors, except that the earlier bird-beak butt had been abandoned in favor of the more conventional squared-off style. It is of standard hinged-frame type, with a robust stirrup type, barrel catch: a tough and durable arm. Certainly, it stood up remarkably well to trench warfare. A bayonet was developed for it, many of which were bought privately. A detachable butt, as for the Mauser and Luger, was also provided, but it was not widely used. It was officially abandoned in 1932 in favor of a similar arm in 0.38 in. (9.6 mm) caliber, but many reserve officers still carried Mark VIs in 0.455 in. (11.5 mm) caliber when they were recalled in 1939.

UNITED KINGDOM

WEBLEY AND SCOTT 0.22 IN. MARK VI REVOLVER 1915

Length (gun): 11.0 in. (279 mm)
Barrel: 6.0 in. (152 mm)
Weight: 38.0 oz. (1.08 kg)
Caliber: 0.22 in. (5.6 mm)
Rifling: 7 grooves, r/hand
Capacity: six
Muz vel: 600 ft./sec. (183 m/sec)

The Mark VI revolver was made in large numbers, Webley having a contract to deliver 2,500 weekly. To give individuals some preliminary practice, a small-caliber version (illustrated here) was made. It fired 0.22 in. (5.6 mm) rimfire cartridges, allowing the revolver to be used on indoor ranges, and was economical in ammunition. It bears a strong resemblance to its parent arm. The main differences are its round barrel and its stepped cylinder, but its locking system, trigger pull, and method of ejection resemble the orthodox Mark VI. There was a slightly different version, which was sometimes fitted with a shorter cylinder, the barrel extended to the rear. It was a very accurate and well-balanced weapon and proved to be suitable for beginners; but it was not of much instructional value otherwise, because of the absence of recoil. Recoil is the chief difficulty for the novice.

GERMANY

LUGER ARTILLERY MODEL 1917 SELF-LOADING PISTOL

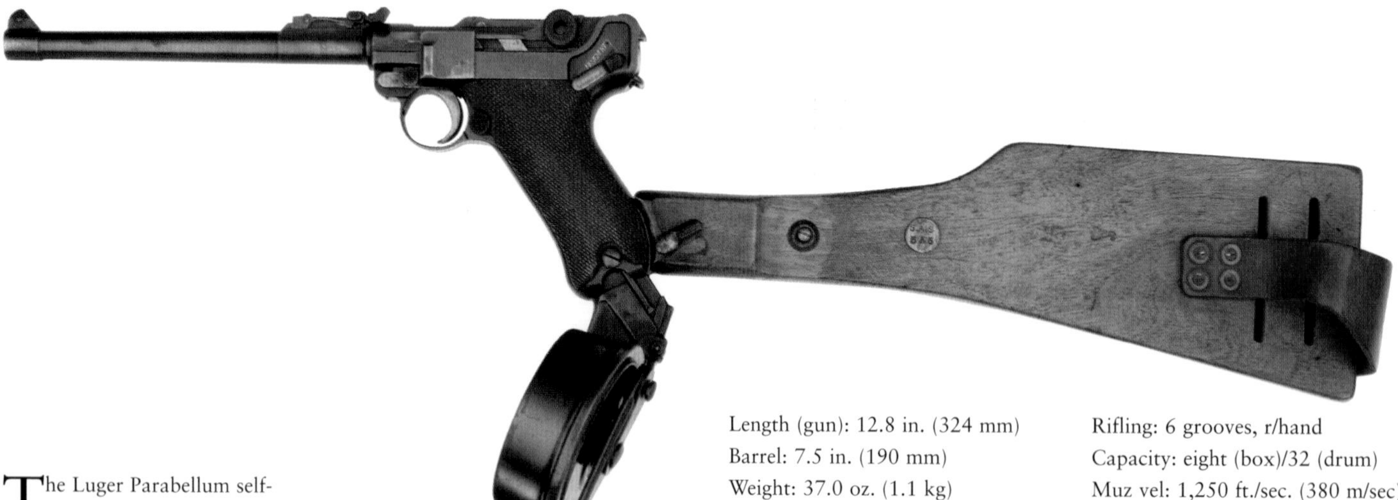

Length (gun): 12.8 in. (324 mm)
Barrel: 7.5 in. (190 mm)
Weight: 37.0 oz. (1.1 kg)
Caliber: 9 mm
Rifling: 6 grooves, r/hand
Capacity: eight (box)/32 (drum)
Muz vel: 1,250 ft./sec. (380 m/sec)

The Luger Parabellum self-loading pistol was adopted by the German Army in 1908, and its subsequent record in World War I made it a household name. In 1917, this was followed by the Artillery Model, illustrated here. The Luger worked on a system of short recoil, during which the barrel and bolt remained locked together. The toggle joint then passed over curved ramps and opened upward, detaching itself from the barrel. When the bolt had reached its rearmost position, it was forced forward again by a return spring, stripping a cartridge from the magazine and forcing it into the chamber en route. It then locked, and could be fired again in the normal way. The standard Luger had a box magazine in the butt, but the example seen here is fitted with an extension type, the so-called "snail drum" magazine with a capacity of 32 rounds. A special tool was needed to load this magazine, which tended to jam: this was cured by replacing the original round-nosed bullet with a pointed one. The Luger also had a detachable stock, which converted it into a carbine and made it a very light and handy weapon for local defense. It was originally issued to machine gun detachments and artillery observers in exposed forward positions.

GERMANY

LIGNOSE EINHAND MODEL 3A PISTOL 1917

Length (gun): 4.6 in. (117 mm)
Barrel: 2.1 in. (53 mm)
Weight: 18.0 oz. (0.5 kg)
Caliber: 6.35 mm
Rifling: 6 grooves, r/hand
Capacity: nine
Muz vel: 800 ft./sec. (244 m/sec)

This pistol was originally manufactured by the Bergmann company in about 1917, but the rights were then sold to the Lignose company, under whose name it is better known. A notable problem of the days before self-loading pistols were provided with double-action locks and other refinements was that it was dangerous to carry such a pistol with a round in the chamber—but, at the same time, it was a relatively slow, two-handed business to prepare it for action. Lignose sought to overcome this problem, and the word *Einhand* (one hand) suggests the method. The front end of the trigger guard of this weapon was very far forward because the brass section was attached to the slide, which thus could be drawn back by the pressure of the first finger. The finger could then be swiftly moved back to the trigger, to fire.

UNITED STATES

SMITH & WESSON REVOLVER M1917

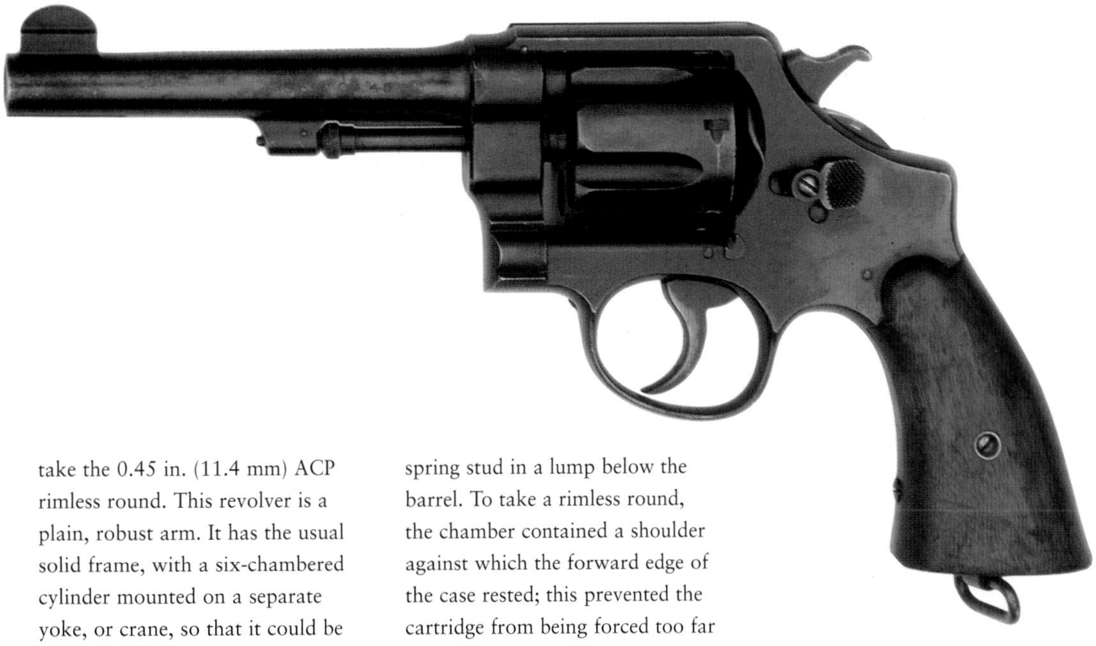

Length (gun): 9.6 in. (244 mm)
Barrel: 5.5 in. (140 mm)
Weight: 34.0 oz. (1.0 kg)
Caliber: 0.45 in. (11.4 mm)
Rifling: 6 grooves, l/hand
Capacity: six
Muz vel: 700 ft./sec. (213 m/sec)

When the United States entered World War I in 1917, she was not well equipped; all available weapons of suitable type had to be pressed into service. It was, however, considered essential to have uniformity of cartridge and, as the standard service pistol was the Model 1911 Colt, a considerable number of revolvers were manufactured to take the 0.45 in. (11.4 mm) ACP rimless round. This revolver is a plain, robust arm. It has the usual solid frame, with a six-chambered cylinder mounted on a separate yoke, or crane, so that it could be swung out to the left after the milled catch below the hammer had been pushed forward. When the cylinder was closed, the end of the extractor pin engaged with a spring stud in a lump below the barrel. To take a rimless round, the chamber contained a shoulder against which the forward edge of the case rested; this prevented the cartridge from being forced too far in. The star extractor would not work with rimless rounds, so the empty cases had to be pushed out with a pencil or some similar instrument. An improvement was to have the cartridges in flat half-moon clips of three, on which the extractor could grip; these were extensively used.

German Military Handguns World War I–World War II

The development of German handguns between 1914 and 1945 is a story of steady rationalization, from a multiplicity of types used in World War I, to the two or three mainstream types in service from 1939. German armaments production and issue of all weaponry during both world wars tended toward excessive numbers of variants, and this was particularly pronounced in handguns between 1914 and 1918. The German Army entered the war with around thirteen different types of handgun produced in many different calibers including 10.6 x 25 mm Deutsche Ordonnance, 7.63 x 25 mm Mauser, 7.65 x 21.5 mm Parabellum, 9 x 19 mm Parabellum, and 7.65 x 17 mm (.32 ACP).

The multiplicity of types complicated logistics and thinned manufacturing focus, but from the mass of weapons, however, emerged two clear frontrunners: the 7.63 mm Mauser C/96 and the 9 mm Parabellum Model 08 (the Luger). Both pistols had their advantages as combat weapons. The C/96 enjoyed a good magazine capacity of ten rounds, which could even be enhanced by a twenty-round extended magazine (although these were not popular). The Model 08 was more compact, with an empty weight of 1.92 lb. (0.87 kg) as opposed to the C/96's 2.75 lb. (1.25 kg) bulk.

Both pistols could be used in long-barrel variants fitted with detachable buttstocks as forms of semiautomatic assault carbine. While some officers found this combination useful in close-quarters combat, most were issued to mortar and machine-gun crews for light defensive purposes.

Although they gave reasonable service, both the 08 and the C/96 were vulnerable to stoppages resulting from dirt intrusion—a perennial problem in the trenches of the conflict—and were expensive to manufacture. Other World War I handguns, such as the 9 mm Dreyse and 7.65 mm Beholla, had proved similarly unreliable and so the interwar years saw the pursuit of cheaper, more rugged weapons types. This was pursued within the limitations of the Versailles Treaty, which restricted handguns to 8 mm caliber and below and barrel lengths to less than 100 mm (3.9 in.). Walther produced two excellent guns, the PP and PPK in 7.65 mm caliber and, once Germany stepped clearly outside the Treaty limits in the late 1930s, there emerged the estimable Walther P38. The P38 became the standard German pistol of World War II, although the 08 remained in theater in huge numbers. It was easy to produce, relying heavily on sheet metal construction, was reliable even under Eastern Front conditions, and rarely suffered from any mechanical failure. The 08 and P38 became cherished souvenirs of the war with many Allied soldiers, and are still fired today by enthusiasts.

Above: *For the SS, pistols were badges of rank and prestige, or weapons of coercion.*

UNITED STATES

REMINGTON MODEL 51 PISTOL 1919

Length (gun): 6.5 in. (165 mm)
Barrel: 3.5 in. (89 mm)
Weight: 21.0 oz. (0.6 kg)
Caliber: 0.38 in. (9.6 mm)
Rifling: 7 grooves, r/hand
Capacity: seven
Muz vel: 900 ft./sec. (274 m/sec)

Remington's first entry into the field of self-loading pistols occurred in 1917, when the company received a contract to manufacture Model 1911 Colts. When this ended, the company had plans for a self-loading pistol of its own, based on the designs of J. D. Pedersen. This was the excellent but expensive Model 51. It was made in two calibers: 0.38 in. auto (illustrated here) and, in much smaller numbers, 0.32 in. The mechanism was of the type known as delayed blowback. When the cartridge was fired, the slide and its internal breechblock recoiled briefly together; the block then stopped, allowing the slide to continue to the rear, but after a brief pause, the block was released and rejoined the slide. Both came forward under the influence of the recoil spring, which was fitted round the fixed barrel. It was fitted with a grip safety and also had a normal safety at the rear left end of the frame.

GERMANY

LUGER 08/20 PISTOL 1920

Length (gun): 8.8 in. (222 mm)
Barrel: 3.8 in. (95 mm)
Weight: 30.0 oz. (0.9 kg)
Caliber: 7.65 mm
Rifling: 8 grooves, r/hand
Capacity: eight
Muz vel: 1,150 ft./sec. (351 m/sec)

Post–World War I, Germany was allowed some degree of manufacture for export, and since vast stocks of components were still hidden away, a good deal of cannibalization went on, while many salvaged weapons were also reconditioned and found their way onto the world markets. The original title of "Parabellum" for DWM's Model 1908 had by then largely given way to that of "Luger," while the suffix "/20" indicated postwar manufacture. The demand for this arm was considerable—partly for use and partly because it was a popular souvenir. The pistol illustrated here appears to be one of the post-1918 arms put together by DWM, whose monogram appears on the toggle joint. One way of circumventing the restrictions imposed by the Treaty of Versailles, which laid down that all weapons made must be of less than 9 mm caliber, was to bore 9 mm barrel blanks for smaller-caliber rounds.

SPAIN

UNCETA ASTRA 400 PISTOL 1921

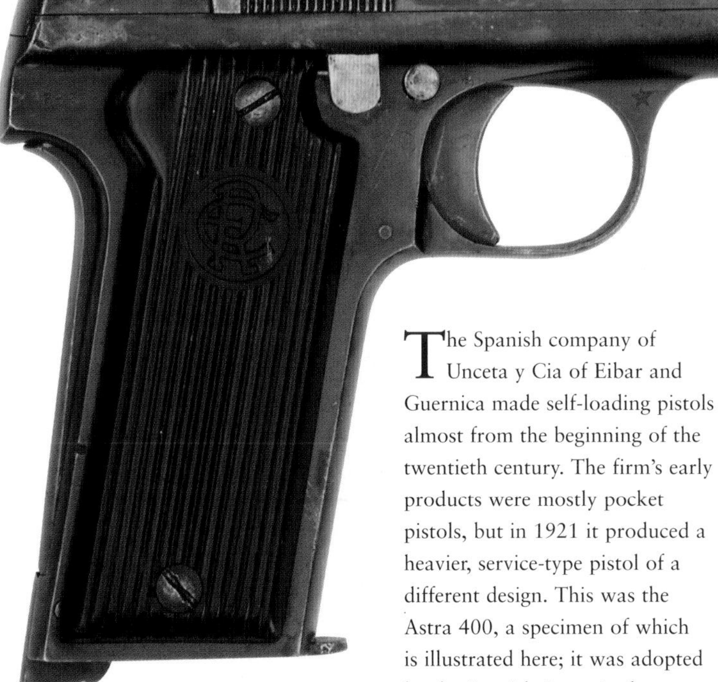

Length (gun): 9.3 in. (235 mm)
Barrel: 5.5 in. (140 mm)
Weight: 38.0 oz. (1.1 kg)
Caliber: 9 mm
Rifling: 6 grooves, r/hand
Capacity: eight
Muz vel: 1,100 ft./sec. (335 m/sec)

The Spanish company of Unceta y Cia of Eibar and Guernica made self-loading pistols almost from the beginning of the twentieth century. The firm's early products were mostly pocket pistols, but in 1921 it produced a heavier, service-type pistol of a different design. This was the Astra 400, a specimen of which is illustrated here; it was adopted by the Spanish Army in the same year it appeared. The pistol had a stepped slide of tubular form: its front end enveloped the barrel, while its rear end acted as breechblock. The recoil spring was positioned around the barrel and inside the slide, and was held in place by the bush visible at the muzzle. The pistol had an internal hammer and a grip safety. Probably the main point of interest is that although it fired a cartridge of considerable power, it worked on straight blowback, without any form of breech-locking device. This was made possible by the use of a heavy slide and an unusually strong recoil spring, which between them reduced the backward action to within safe limits. This made the pistol rather heavy and, in spite of the grooved finger grips on its slide, it was quite hard to cock.

BELGIUM

BROWNING 7.65 MM MODEL 1910/22 PISTOL

Length (gun): 7.0 in. (178 mm)
Barrel: 4.5 in. (114 mm)
Weight: 25.0 oz. (0.7 kg)
Caliber: 9 mm
Rifling: 4 grooves, r/hand
Capacity: nine-round box magazine
Muz vel: 875 ft./sec. (266 m/sec)

In 1922 the FN designers produced a modified version of the M1910, known as the M1910/22. In the modified weapon, the barrel was lengthened to improve accuracy, which, in order to avoid lengthening the existing slide, was achieved by adding an extension to the nosepiece. The butt was also extended to accommodate a larger magazine. The M1910/22 was originally produced in 7.65 mm, but was later also produced in 9 x 17 mm short, this being the maximum caliber considered safe for a blowback weapon. This weapon was adopted by the Belgian, French, Greek, Netherlands, Turkish, and Yugoslavian armies in the 1920s and by the German Luftwaffe in World War II, to which it was known as Pistole 626(b).

UNITED KINGDOM

WEBLEY 0.38 IN. MARK IV REVOLVER 1923

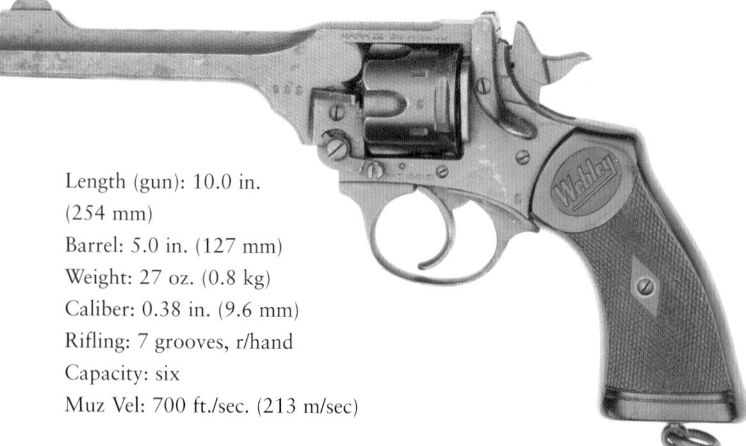

Length (gun): 10.0 in. (254 mm)
Barrel: 5.0 in. (127 mm)
Weight: 27 oz. (0.8 kg)
Caliber: 0.38 in. (9.6 mm)
Rifling: 7 grooves, r/hand
Capacity: six
Muz Vel: 700 ft./sec. (213 m/sec)

The introduction of the Enfield No. 2 Mark I in 1932 marked the end of a long line of British service revolvers made by Webley and Scott. However, the firm still had a great many other customers, and in 1923 it produced a Mark IV revolver in 0.38 in. (9.6 mm) caliber to meet the demands of various military and police forces. It was a robust and reliable arm, and would chamber a variety of 0.38 in. (9.6 mm) cartridges, making it suitable for worldwide use. The lead bullet originally used in the British Enfield had been abandoned in 1938 because of doubts over whether it breached the St. Petersburg convention. By the end of World War II, the supply of Enfield revolvers (many of which were made by outside contractors) was beginning to lag: thus, in 1945 the British government placed a large order with Webley & Scott for the Mark IV. This was not only a reliable arm, but was so like the Enfield in handling that no retraining was needed.

CZECH REPUBLIC

CESKÁ ZBROJOVKA MODEL 1924 PISTOL

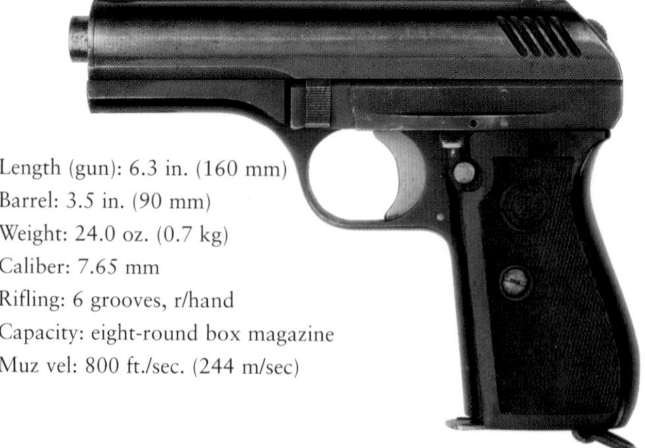

Length (gun): 6.3 in. (160 mm)
Barrel: 3.5 in. (90 mm)
Weight: 24.0 oz. (0.7 kg)
Caliber: 7.65 mm
Rifling: 6 grooves, r/hand
Capacity: eight-round box magazine
Muz vel: 800 ft./sec. (244 m/sec)

The design of this pistol originated in Germany with an engineer named Nickl, who worked for Mauser. In the early 1920s, the company sent Nickl to Czechoslovakia to help establish a Mauser rifle production line, and when he learned that the Czechoslovak Army was looking for a pistol he recast his design to take the 9 mm short round, and the weapon went into production at Brno in 1922, as the Vz-22. This had a slightly complicated method of operation: at the moment of firing, the barrel and slide were locked to each other and as the slide moved to the rear it caused the barrel to rotate slightly and unlock itself, following which the reloading cycle carried on in the usual way. It had an external hammer, and a safety catch was fitted on the left side of the frame, which was released by pressing the circular stud immediately below it. The simplified second model, the Vz-24, remained in production until the mid-1930s.

JAPAN

NAMBU 14TH YEAR 8 MM PISTOL 1925

Length (gun): 8.9 in. (226 mm)
Barrel: 4.8 in. (120 mm)
Weight: 32.0 oz. (0.9g)
Caliber: 8 mm
Rifling: 6 grooves, r/hand
Capacity: 8-round box magazine
Muz vel: 950 ft./sec. (290 m/sec)

The 14th Year pistol, which appeared in 1925, was an improved, cheaper 4th Year. The grip safety was replaced by a safety catch, although this could not be operated by the thumb of the firing hand. When the pistol was fired, the barrel, bolt, and receiver recoiled together for about 0.2 in. (5 mm), the movement of the barrel causing a block in the receiver to rotate, unlocking the bolt, which then continued to the rear. The bolt was then driven forward by two recoil springs until it relocked. There was a large, cylindrical cocking-piece at the rear; early versions had three grooves around, while later versions were knurled. The magazine catch was a circular stud on the left of the frame, but there was also a small retaining spring in the front strap of the butt; one of many shortcomings of this weapon was that the magazine was difficult to remove, especially if dirty or damp. An enlarged trigger guard was introduced in the late 1930s, after it had been found in the Manchurian campaign that the weapon could not be properly controlled if the shooter was wearing gloves. This pistol remained in service until the end of World War II.

JAPAN

NAMBU 14TH YEAR 8 MM PISTOL/SWORD COMBINATION 1925

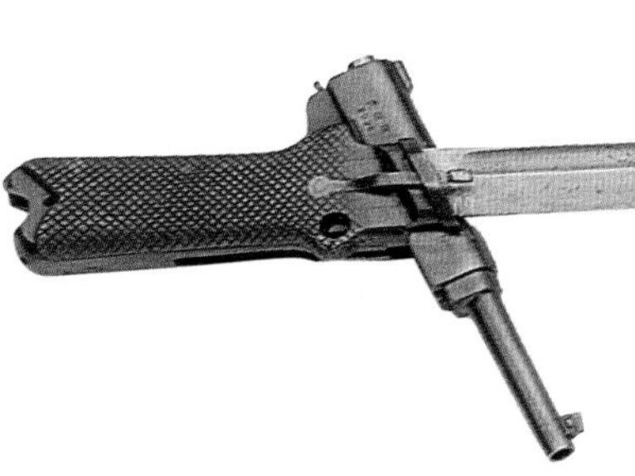

Length (gun): 8.9 in. (226 mm)
Barrel: 4.8 in. (120 mm)
Weight (gun): 32.0 oz. (0.9g)
Caliber: 8 mm
Rifling: 6 grooves, r/hand
Capacity: 8-round box magazine
Muz vel: 950 ft./sec. (290 m/sec)

This amazing combination weapon is included for its curiosity value, since, although there are examples of pistols being fitted with short bayonets or dagger blades, this is the only known example of a combined automatic pistol and sword. The pistol was a Nambu 14th Year and it should be noted that in the picture the trigger group and magazine are both missing. The sword blade was some 29.0 in. (744 mm) long, and the scabbard was modified slightly to accommodate the pistol. In normal sword construction there is an extension, known as a *tang*, around which the handgrip is constructed, but whether or not in this case the tang extended down the side of the pistol into the stock is not apparent. This was probably a "one-off" constructed to satisfy the whim of a traditionally minded officer, but it would seem that the sword blade would have made firing the pistol rather difficult, while the weight and size of the pistol would have made the use of the sword problematical as well. Like just about every combination, it would have been most unsatisfactory, and its tactical value must have been minimal.

UNITED STATES

COLT OFFICIAL POLICE REVOLVER 1926

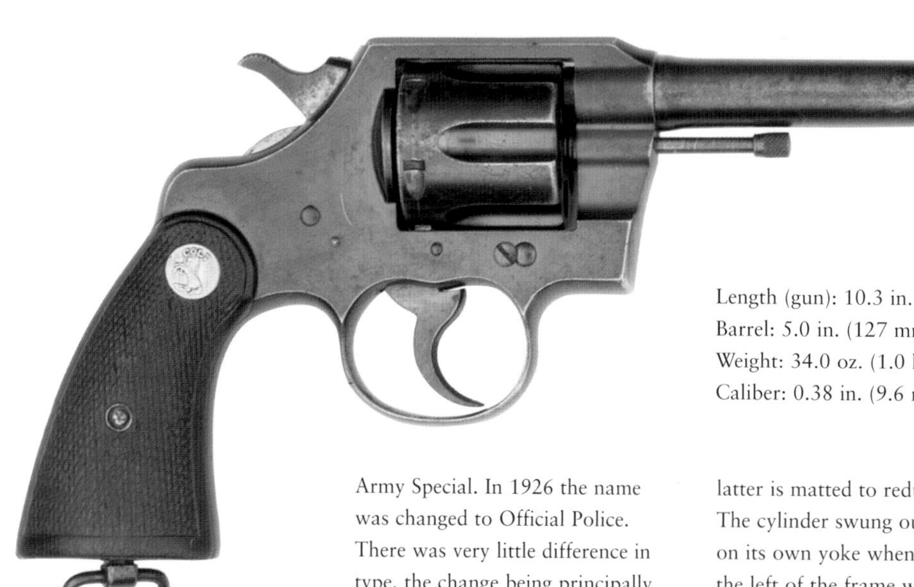

Length (gun): 10.3 in. (260 mm)
Barrel: 5.0 in. (127 mm)
Weight: 34.0 oz. (1.0 kg)
Caliber: 0.38 in. (9.6 mm)
Rifling: 6 grooves, l/hand
Capacity: six
Muz vel: 700 ft./sec. (213 m/sec)

This revolver had its origins in the Colt New Navy model. This was later reclassified as the New Army model; a later, slightly different version was known as the Army Special. In 1926 the name was changed to Official Police. There was very little difference in type, the change being principally made because at that time the US police forces were markedly better customers than the US Army. The round barrel has an integral, semiround foresight and a square backsight notch and groove on the top strap; the upper surface of the latter is matted to reduce the shine. The cylinder swung out sideways on its own yoke when a catch on the left of the frame was pulled back; cartridges or cases could then be ejected simultaneously by pushing the pin. The lock is of rebounding, double-action type, with a separate hammer nose, and access to the mechanism was via an irregularly shaped inspection plate on the left-hand side of the frame. The butt plates are of checkered walnut and bear the famous Colt trademark in white metal medallions. Large numbers of Official Police revolvers were supplied to the British Army during World War II. It was made also in a smaller 0.22 in. caliber version.

UNITED STATES

COLT OFFICIAL POLICE REVOLVER (DAMAGED) 1926

Length (gun): 10.3 in. (260 mm)
Barrel: 5.0 in. (127 mm)
Weight: 34.0 oz. (1.0 kg)
Caliber: 0.38 in. (9.6 mm)
Rifling: 6 grooves, l/hand
Capacity: six
Muz vel: 700 ft./sec. (213 m/sec)

This revolver was purchased by the British government, together with thousands more, during World War II. The damage to it was caused by the firing of a weak cartridge, which drove its bullet only sufficiently far forward to lodge in the barrel. Poor rounds of this kind are very rare in peacetime; but they are sometimes met with in war, when standards of inspection are less stringent. It may also happen that cartridges deteriorate through having been stored for too long or in exceptionally bad conditions. When a second round was fired, its bullet, traveling at normal velocity, struck the one in the barrel and pushed it forward. This probably had no effect on the barrel, partly because of the relatively low velocity of this type of 0.38 in. (9.6 mm) cartridge and partly because of the existence of a means of escape for gas between the face of the cylinder and the barrel. The third round, also traveling normally, hit the first two and pushed them a little farther, as did the fourth—but the resistance was, of course, increasing every time: the fifth round hit the solid blockage and caused the barrel to split.

UNITED STATES

COLT GOVERNMENT MODEL M1911 A1 PISTOL 1926

Length (gun): 8.5 in. (216 mm)
Barrel: 5.0 in. (127 mm)
Weight: 39.0 oz. (1.1 kg)
Caliber: 0.45 in. (11.4 mm)
Rifling: 6 grooves, l/hand
Capacity: seven-round box magazine
Muz vel: 860 ft./sec. (262 m/sec)

The immediate success of the Colt Model 1911 led to its full-scale production throughout World War I, which resulted in a vast body of user experience. As a result, a number of relatively minor improvements were incorporated in a new production model. These changes included: a longer horn on the safety grip, the shape of the handgrip was altered slightly, the trigger was shortened and chamfered, the hammer was shortened, and arc-shaped grooves were chamfered into the frame behind the trigger. There were also minor internal improvements. Apart from this, the weapon remained essentially unchanged and no more modifications were introduced for the remainder of its very long production life. It was popular because it was good at so many things, being compact, easy to handle, reliable, robust, accurate, easy to reload, and with good stopping power. Such was the overall feeling of satisfaction with the M1911 A1 that several attempts to start developing a successor were strongly resisted—not least in Congress—and it was not until the mid-1980s that the US armed forces eventually managed to obtain authorization to procure a successor. Well over three million M1911s and M1911 A1s were manufactured in the United States alone.

CZECH REPUBLIC

CESKÁ ZBROJOVKA CZ27 PISTOL 1927

Length (gun): 6.3 in. (159 mm)
Barrel: 4.0 in. (102 mm)
Weight: 25.5 oz. (0.7 kg)
Caliber: 9 mm
Rifling: 6 grooves, r/hand
Capacity: eight
Muz vel: 900 ft./sec. (274 m/sec)

Following the introduction of the CZ 24, the designer decided that the locking system was unnecessary for such a relatively low-powered round and redesigned the pistol to eliminate this feature and simplify the design. The result was the CZ 27. Externally it appears to be almost identical to the 1924 model, the main apparent difference being that the finger-grooves at the rear of the slide were vertical rather than diagonal. The pistol worked on straight blowback, with its recoil spring mounted around a rod situated below and parallel with the barrel. It had an external hammer, and there was a magazine safety on the left-hand side of the frame, just above the magazine release stud. When the Germans occupied Czechoslovakia, manufacture was continued on a considerable scale. Weapons made during that period, like this one, are marked "BOHMISCH WAFFEN FABRIK AG IN PRAG."

GERMANY

ERMA CONVERSION UNIT 1927

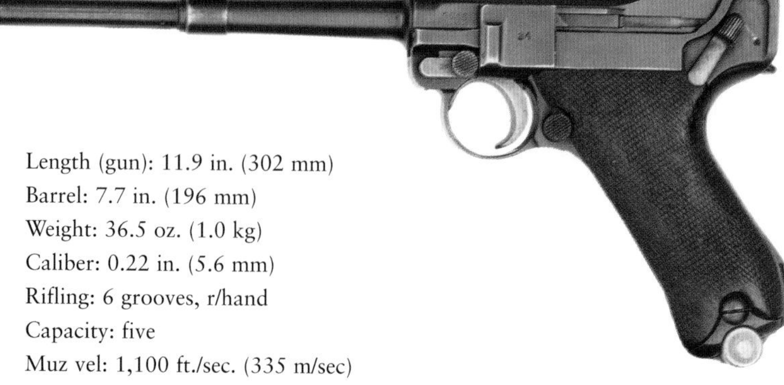

Length (gun): 11.9 in. (302 mm)
Barrel: 7.7 in. (196 mm)
Weight: 36.5 oz. (1.0 kg)
Caliber: 0.22 in. (5.6 mm)
Rifling: 6 grooves, r/hand
Capacity: five
Muz vel: 1,100 ft./sec. (335 m/sec)

When Germany began to rearm, it was decided that there was a requirement for a means of converting the then-standard Luger service pistol to fire 0.22 in. ammunition, for the purpose of small-range practice. Whereas this can be accomplished in a revolver by no more than an easily removed barrel liner and an alternative cylinder, a self-loading pistol requires a more sophisticated arrangement. The solution was provided by the Ermawerke company of Erfurt, which produced a conversion kit. This included an insert barrel, a light breechblock containing its own mainspring, a toggle unit, and a magazine of the appropriate size. The kit had been invented by an Ermawerke employee named Kulisch and patented as early as 1927, so there were few delays in putting it into production. The Erma conversion unit was highly effective in transforming a locked-breech arm into a blowback type.

FRANCE

ST. ETIENNE MODEL 28 PISTOL 1928

Length (gun): 7.9 in. (210 mm)
Barrel: 5.0 in. (127 mm)
Weight: 35.0 oz. (1.0 kg)
Caliber: 9 mm
Rifling: 6 grooves, r/hand
Capacity: eight
Muz vel: 1,100 ft./sec. (335 m/sec)

Française d'Armes et Cycles de St. Etienne began making self-loading pistols just before World War I. These arms were all of similar design and of broadly similar type small-caliber pocket arms. In 1928, it produced its Military Model. Like all the manufacturer's later pistols, the arm was of a very distinctive type. The barrel was hinged at the front end, and when a catch on the frame was pressed, the breech end rose clear of the slide. The magazine carried an extra round in its base. When the magazine had been pushed home, this extra round was withdrawn and placed in the breech, the barrel was closed, and the pistol was ready. When the magazine was withdrawn, the breech rose automatically. It was possible to withdraw it partially, then load and fire single rounds, leaving the magazine's contents as a reserve. No extractor was fitted: the empty cases were blown clear by the residual gas pressure. There was no locking system, the pistol functioning by blowback only—and it was probably this factor which doomed it, for the system meant that it had to fire a cartridge too weak for service use. A misfired cartridge could not be extracted without the use of some improvised tool.

SPAIN

ECHEVERRIA STAR MODEL B 9 MM PISTOL 1928

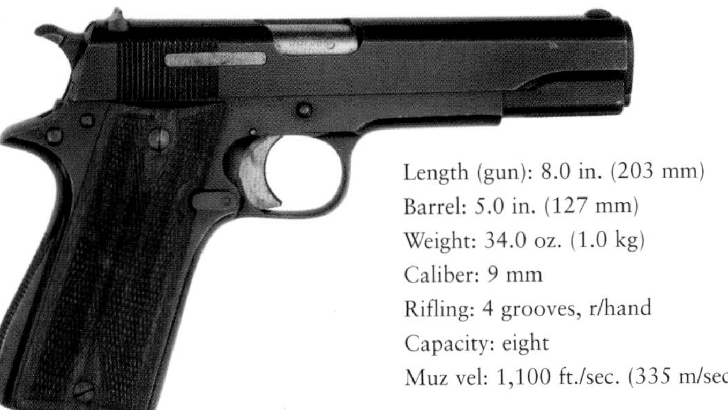

Length (gun): 8.0 in. (203 mm)
Barrel: 5.0 in. (127 mm)
Weight: 34.0 oz. (1.0 kg)
Caliber: 9 mm
Rifling: 4 grooves, r/hand
Capacity: eight
Muz vel: 1,100 ft./sec. (335 m/sec)

This arm is another of the Spanish self-loading pistols based more or less on the Colt Model 1911 and its variants. The firm of Echeverria came into existence in about 1908 in Eibar, and has been making self-loading pistols of one kind or another ever since. The trade name of "Star" was adopted in 1919 and has been in use ever since on a quite bewildering variety of pistols of various types, sizes, calibers, and systems of numbering and classification. The pistol illustrated here is a Star Model B, introduced in about 1928. It was fairly closely based on the Colt, but lacked the grip safety peculiar to that arm. It was a robust and well-made weapon, and since it was chambered for the powerful 9 mm Parabellum cartridge, it necessarily fired from a locked breech. This model pistol was still used by the Spanish armed forces into the 1980s.

JAPAN

NAMBU TYPE 94 8 MM PISTOL 1929

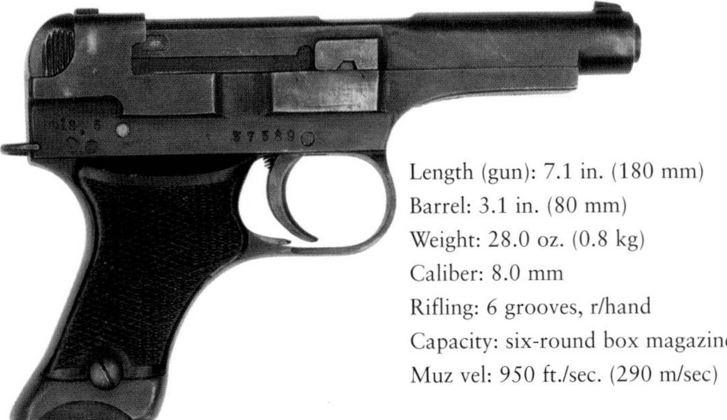

Length (gun): 7.1 in. (180 mm)
Barrel: 3.1 in. (80 mm)
Weight: 28.0 oz. (0.8 kg)
Caliber: 8.0 mm
Rifling: 6 grooves, r/hand
Capacity: six-round box magazine
Muz vel: 950 ft./sec. (290 m/sec)

This weapon is one of the worst pistols ever made. In 1929, Colonel Kirijo Nambu set out to produce a simpler and cheaper self-loading pistol, and the Army Ordnance Department showed considerable interest in the prototypes. Unfortunately, the department then assumed that this gave it the right to interfere in the design and the result was disastrous. The slide covered the entire top of the frame and barrel and the weapon was cocked by pulling this back by means of the milled ears at the rear, but unfortunately, this also exposed the sear bar which was situated on the left-hand side of the frame, so that it protruded slightly, making it possible to discharge the weapon accidentally by a blow. The trigger mechanism was unreliable, and it was possible to fire the pistol prematurely, before the breech was locked. These problems were inherent in the design, but all were exacerbated by poor workmanship.

GERMANY

WALTHER PPK PISTOL 1930

Length (gun): 5.8 in. (147 mm)
Barrel: 3.2 in. (80 mm)
Weight: 20.0 oz. (0.6 kg)
Caliber: 7.65 mm
Rifling: 6 grooves, r/hand
Capacity: seven
Muz vel: 1,000 ft./sec. (305 m/sec)

The Walther PP was immediately popular, and two years later a smaller version was made for concealed use. It was intended for plain-clothes police work and was known as the "PPK," the "K" standing, it is said, for *Kriminappolizei* (criminal police). The Walther PPK pistol was of blowback type, and it had several interesting and important features. The most notable, perhaps, is that it was provided with an external hammer activated by a double-action lock; this allowed the pistol to be carried safely with a round in the chamber and the hammer down. Thus, all that was necessary to bring it into action was to push off the safety catch and press the trigger. It also had an indicator pin that protruded through the top of the slide when there was a cartridge in the chamber—a very useful feature in any self-loading pistol, where the rounds cannot be seen as they can in a revolver. The earliest versions of this pistol had complete butt frames with a pair of grips, but later examples had a front strap only, with a one-piece, molded, wraparound plastic grip. Most also had a plastic extension on the bottom of the magazine, to increase the area of grip.

RUSSIA

TULA-TOKAREV TT-30/TT-33 AUTOMATIC PISTOL 1930

Length (gun): 7.7 in. (196 mm)
Barrel: 4.6 in. (117 mm)
Weight: 29.0 oz. (0.8 kg)
Caliber: 9 mm
Rifling: 4 grooves, l/hand
Capacity: eight-round box magazine
Muz vel: 1,350 ft./sec. (411 m/sec)

These pistols were manufactured at the Tula State Arsenal, designed by Feodor Tokarev. The recoil-operated, single-action TT-30 was mechanically a copy of various Colt-Browning types, chambered for the Russian 7.62 x 25 mm pistol round. Tokarev incorporated one or two minor modifications to simplify manufacture. In 1933, the TT-33 appeared, which incorporated more improvements, and farther simplification to speed up production. In the TT-30, for example, the barrel locking lugs were machined onto the barrel's upper surface, but in the TT-33 these were replaced by bands which went completely around the barrel; this involved no mechanical changes, but cut out a time-consuming milling process during manufacture. Another improvement in the TT-33 was that the entire lock mechanism could be easily removed, greatly facilitating maintenance.

JAPAN

SUGIURA 7.65 MM SEMIAUTOMATIC PISTOL 1931

Length (gun): not available
Barrel: not available
Weight: not available
Caliber: 7.65 mm
Rifling: not available
Capacity: not available
Muz vel: not available

This very rare pistol was manufactured in a Japanese Army arsenal in Manchuria during the Japanese occupation of that country in the 1930s and early 1940s. A 7.65 mm caliber weapon, its design appears to have been based upon that of the Colt Model 1903, which was in service with both Chinese and Japanese armies at that time. The fact that its design and production was undertaken at all exhibits a degree of dissatisfaction and distrust of the Imperial authorities in the home country, and of their procurement policies. Apart from its caliber, no details of this weapon are known with any degree of certainty.

SPAIN

GABILONDO LLAMA 9 MM PISTOL 1931

Length (gun): 9.5 in. (241 mm)
Barrel: 5.0 in. (127 mm)
Weight: 40.0 oz. (1.1 kg)
Caliber: 9 mm
Rifling: 6 grooves, l/hand
Capacity: seven
Muz vel: 850 ft./sec. (259 m/sec)

The great success and wide acceptance of the Colt Model 1911 self-loading pistol and its successive variations made it inevitable that the arm should become the subject of extensive copying. In this field, Spanish manufacturers were particularly active. In 1931 the Spanish firm of Gabilondo y Cia began to manufacture a new range of Colt-type pistols under the general trade name of "Llama," and these arms have continued in production until the present day. They are, in general, very well-made and reliable weapons and sell in considerable quantities. They have been produced in a wide variety of models and calibers—some of blowback type, some with locked breeches, and yet others with grip safeties—so that individual models are not always easy to identify. The pistol illustrated here appears to be a model produced in about 1939. Its general style, which very closely resembles that of the Colt, is clear from the photograph. It was designed to fire the 0.38 in. Colt Super cartridge—a very powerful round, and one which, of course, necessitates a locked breech. This pistol has no grip safety but is fitted with an orthodox safety catch on the left, below the hammer.

UNITED KINGDOM

ENFIELD NO. 2 MARK I REVOLVER 1932

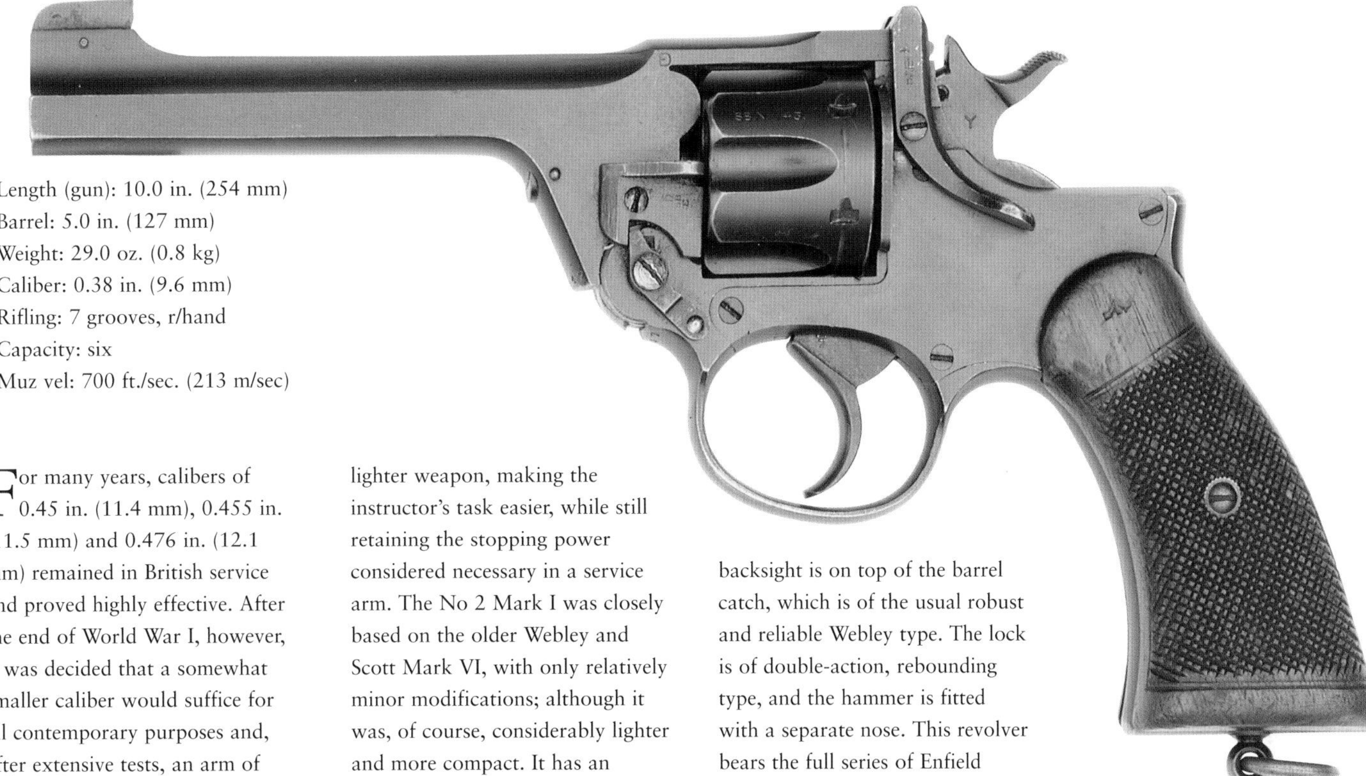

Length (gun): 10.0 in. (254 mm)
Barrel: 5.0 in. (127 mm)
Weight: 29.0 oz. (0.8 kg)
Caliber: 0.38 in. (9.6 mm)
Rifling: 7 grooves, r/hand
Capacity: six
Muz vel: 700 ft./sec. (213 m/sec)

For many years, calibers of 0.45 in. (11.4 mm), 0.455 in. (11.5 mm) and 0.476 in. (12.1 mm) remained in British service and proved highly effective. After the end of World War I, however, it was decided that a somewhat smaller caliber would suffice for all contemporary purposes and, after extensive tests, an arm of 0.38 in. (9.6 mm) caliber was decided upon. This would be a lighter weapon, making the instructor's task easier, while still retaining the stopping power considered necessary in a service arm. The No 2 Mark I was closely based on the older Webley and Scott Mark VI, with only relatively minor modifications; although it was, of course, considerably lighter and more compact. It has an octagonal barrel with a screwed-in blade foresight. The rectangular backsight is on top of the barrel catch, which is of the usual robust and reliable Webley type. The lock is of double-action, rebounding type, and the hammer is fitted with a separate nose. This revolver bears the full series of Enfield proof and view marks, date "1932" and number "B4447."

GERMANY

WALTHER P38 PISTOL 1932

Length (gun): 8.4 in. (213 mm)
Barrel: 5.0 in. (127 mm)
Weight: 34.0 oz. (1.0 kg)
Caliber: 9 mm
Rifling: 6 grooves, r/hand
Capacity: eight
Muz vel: 1,150 ft./sec. (315 m/sec)

In the early 1930s, Carl Walther Waffenfabrik developed two prototype military self-loading pistols, the Model AP Armee Pistole (Army Pistol) and HP Heeres Pistole (also Army Pistol). The AP was hammerless and the HP had an external hammer; since the latter was preferred by the military authorities, the final model was thus equipped. The P38 was easier to manufacture than the Luger P08, and by 1943 it had largely superseded it. The type of cartridge used made it necessary to employ a locked breech. When a cartridge was fired, the barrel and slide recoiled briefly together, until the locking block lugs were carried out of the slide; then the barrel stopped, allowing the slide to continue to the rear to cock the hammer. The slide then traveled forward under the pressure of the recoil spring, chambering another cartridge. So to fire the loaded pistol, one only had to push up the safety catch with the thumb to the "fire" position and press the trigger.

UNITED STATES

COLT 0.22 IN. SERVICE MODEL ACE PISTOL 1931

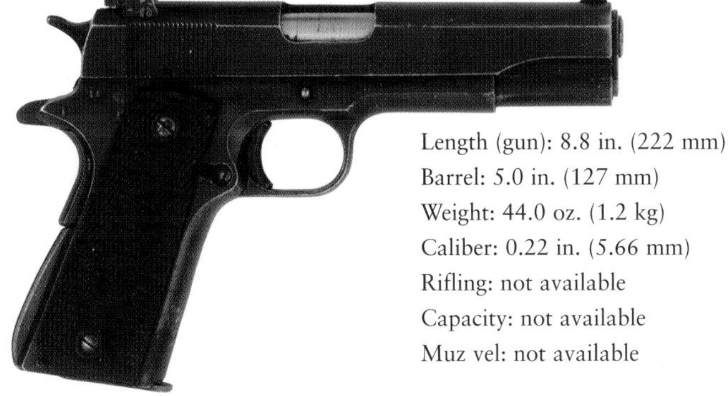

Length (gun): 8.8 in. (222 mm)
Barrel: 5.0 in. (127 mm)
Weight: 44.0 oz. (1.2 kg)
Caliber: 0.22 in. (5.66 mm)
Rifling: not available
Capacity: not available
Muz vel: not available

One of a number of 0.22 in. LR pistols developed for training, the Colt Service Model Ace was designed to provide realistic training for shooters intending to use the Colt Model 1911. The company actually started work on a smaller caliber design in 1910, but the first production model, the 0.22 in. Ace did not appear until 1931—a lengthy gestation period by any standard—and some 11,000 were produced. This was followed by the improved version shown here—the Service Model Ace—in 1937. The Service Model Ace used a Williams patented floating chamber, which, in effect, magnified the breech thrust of the 0.22 in. cartridge to the point where it would cycle the full-weight slide with full-strength springs. Two options were available, the first being a conversion unit, but the changeover proved somewhat complicated and was not popular. The preferred option was the factory-produced 0.22 in. weapon.

UNITED STATES

ENFIELD 0.38 IN. NO. 2 MARK I* REVOLVER 1932 (1938)

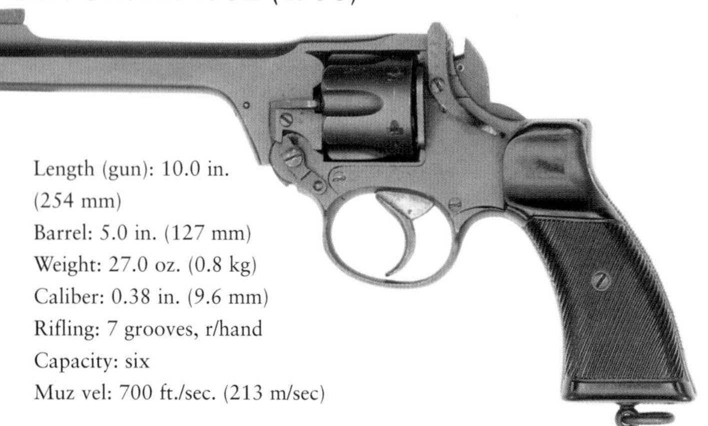

Length (gun): 10.0 in. (254 mm)
Barrel: 5.0 in. (127 mm)
Weight: 27.0 oz. (0.8 kg)
Caliber: 0.38 in. (9.6 mm)
Rifling: 7 grooves, r/hand
Capacity: six
Muz vel: 700 ft./sec. (213 m/sec)

The Enfield No. 2 Mark I revolver issued in 1932 was popular with the British Army. However, complaints were received from the Royal Tank Regiment (whose personnel carried their revolvers in open-topped holsters) that the hammer spur of the Enfield tended to catch on various fittings in the tanks while mounting or dismounting. In 1938 the Mark I* was introduced. The new model had no hammer comb. It could thus only be fired by pressure on the trigger. As a contribution toward accuracy, the weight of the mainspring was lightened to reduce the trigger pull to about 12.0 lb. (5.4 kg), a reduction of 2.0 lb. (0.9 kg) from the earlier model. The butt plates were modified by the addition of thumb grooves to give a better grip, identical on each side, so that the revolver could be used in either hand. The self-cocking concept was not popular—imported American revolvers were preferred.

FRANCE

MAB MODEL D PISTOL 1933

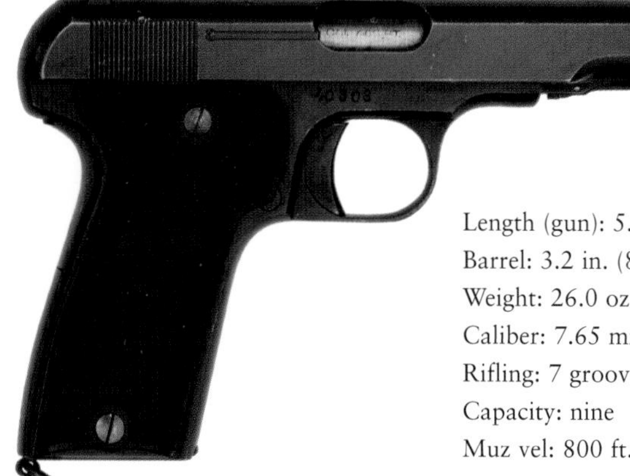

Length (gun): 5.8 in. (147 mm)
Barrel: 3.2 in. (81 mm)
Weight: 26.0 oz. (0.7 kg)
Caliber: 7.65 mm
Rifling: 7 grooves, r/hand
Capacity: nine
Muz vel: 800 ft./sec. (244 m/sec)

MAB is the Manufacture d'Armes de Bayonne, a company which, since 1921, was chiefly concerned with the manufacture of self-loading pocket pistols. The company's products were well made, but most of them were based on the designs of others: this weapon, for example, bears a resemblance to the Browning. It was first put on the market in 1933 as the Model C but, enlarged and with a better-shaped butt, reappeared as the Model D—still in production up to 1988. It is of simple blowback design: when the cartridge is fired, the slide and block are forced to the rear, compressing the coil spring located around the barrel. The forward movement strips a round from the magazine and chambers it. Access to the recoil spring is obtained by pressing up the rear end of the small bar visible under the muzzle: the nose cap can then be turned and removed, taking the spring with it.

ITALY

BERETTA MODEL 1934 PISTOL

Length (gun): 6.0 in. (152 mm)
Barrel: 3.8 in. (95 mm)
Weight: 23.0 oz. (0.7 kg)
Caliber: 9 mm
Rifling: 4 grooves, r/hand
Capacity: nine
Muz vel: 750 ft./sec. (229 m/sec)

The first Beretta self-loading pistol, the Model 1915, was of wartime quality and designed to take a 7.65 mm cartridge; this was soon replaced by a 9 mm version. Development continued after World War I, with a steady improvement in design until 1934, when this weapon appeared. Like its predecessors, the Model 1934 worked by blowback and fired a short cartridge in order to keep the gas pressure within safe limits. As may be seen, it had an external hammer: this could be cocked either by the rearward movement of the slide, or manually, and it had a half-cock position. Most examples were fitted with a curved lower extension to the magazine to ensure a firm grip for a user with a large hand, but some (like this one) were fitted with plain magazines. This arm became the standard Italian service pistol in 1935: this particular example is marked with the letters "RE" surmounted by a crown, indicating that it is a military model. During the course of World War II, many British officers acquired Beretta pistols of this model in the expectation that they would be able to fire standard 9 mm Parabellum Sten-gun ammunition through them, but they found that this ammunition would not fit.

US GUN LAW DEBATE

The "right to bear arms" is one of the most controversial political topics in the United States. The US is a country that evolved with gun in hand as its early citizens relied on firearms for food, protection, and law enforcement. However, in modern times the citizen has fallen under the protection of a large and sophisticated state, while at the same time firearms deaths have reached epidemic proportions—roughly 40,000 each year (including around 9,000 homicides). Such figures have led many bodies to call for greater restrictions on the ownership and usage of firearms.

The gun debate in the US is a long-running and complex one. The debate is constitutional, centering around interpretations of the Second Amendment ratified by Congress on December 15, 1791. The text runs: "A well regulated Militia, being necessary to the security of a free State, the right of the people to keep and bear Arms, shall not be infringed." The pro-gun lobby sees this amendment as enshrining gun ownership, whereas the gun-control lobby interprets the amendment as a historical text relating purely to the need for militia protection for the fledgling nation.

Both sides of the debate have powerful political bodies behind them, and the clash is as much a matter of ideology as practical debate. The pro-gun lobby is dominated by the National Rifle Association, an immensely influential organization formed following the Civil War and today numbering around four million members. Gun-control organizations tend to be less individually strong, but they exist in substantial numbers and include the Brady Campaign to End Gun Violence, the Million Mom March, the Coalition to Stop Gun Violence, and the Violence Policy Center.

The gun debate over the last decade has been more about the types of gun owned rather than the justification for gun ownership per se. Particularly during the Clinton administration, the focus was on banning the sale of semi-automatic assault rifles, of which there are roughly four million in the US. European commentators sometimes depict the US as being almost lawless when it comes to firearms ownership. This is far from the case, however. While long rifles for hunting and target use are easily accessible, handgun owners have to undergo a fairly intensive background screening, and the concealed handgun permit requires the user to undergo in-depth safety training and legal instruction.

The gun control debate will, however, remain a divisive one, and shows no signs of long-term resolution.

Above: *On April 20, 1999, two students, Eric Harris, 18, and Dylan Klebold, 17, killed fifteen people at their high school in Jefferson County, Colorado, before committing suicide. They were armed with a modified TEC-DC9 semiautomatic handgun, a rifle, two sawed-off shotguns, and as many as ninety-seven improvised explosive devices. Was this the terrible result of the antidepressant drugs one or maybe both boys were taking? Or a diet of violent video games? And would stricter gun laws have prevented, or had any effect on, the tragedy?*

BELGIUM

FABRIQUE NATIONALE/BROWNING 9 MM GP35 "HIGH POWER" PISTOL 1935

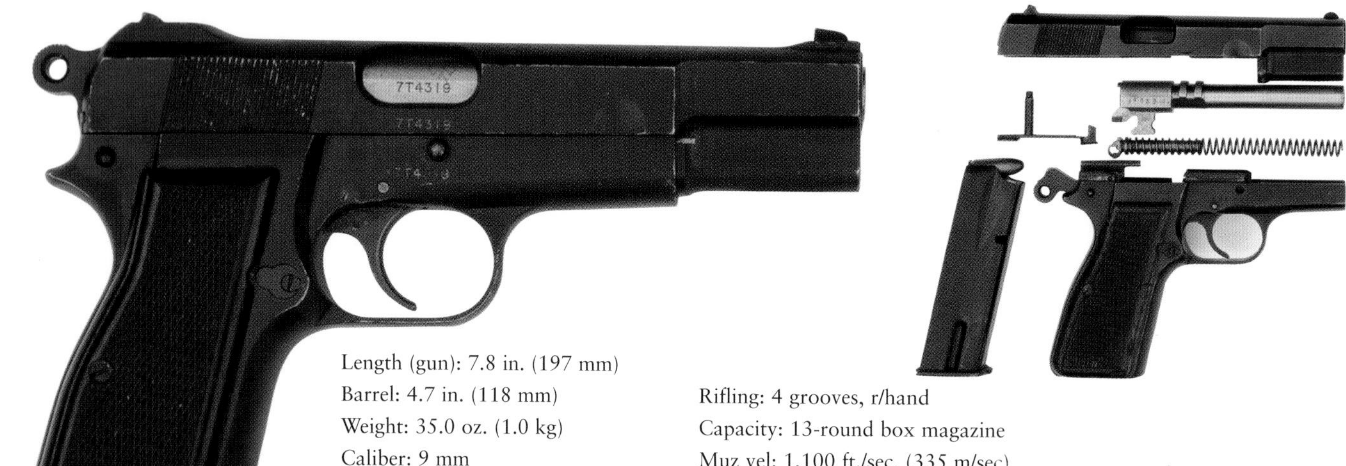

Length (gun): 7.8 in. (197 mm)
Barrel: 4.7 in. (118 mm)
Weight: 35.0 oz. (1.0 kg)
Caliber: 9 mm
Rifling: 4 grooves, r/hand
Capacity: 13-round box magazine
Muz vel: 1,100 ft./sec. (335 m/sec)

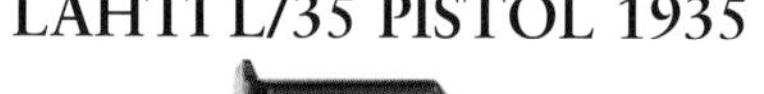

This was the last of John Browning's pistol designs, which he worked on from 1914 until his death in 1926, and is, in essence, a logical development of the M1911. His work was continued within the FN factory and, after several modifications, it introduced the "High Power" in 1935, when it was adopted by numerous armies. It was made in various versions, including one with an adjustable sight and a combined holster/stock of the type found on the original Mausers. When the Germans occupied Belgium in 1940, they continued the production of these weapons for the Wehrmacht as the Pistole 640(b). Meanwhile, a number of FN engineers had escaped to Britain, taking the drawings with them, and in 1942 they were sent to Canada where the John Inglis factory undertook production for the Allies. After the war manufacture reverted to the FN factory at Liège, and the weapon was also put on the civil market as the "High Power." The weapon was adopted by the British Army in 1954 as the "Pistol, 9 mm, Browning, Mark 1*" and has served with over fifty armies since. It is, undoubtedly, one of the greatest pistol designs.

FINLAND

LAHTI L/35 PISTOL 1935

Length (gun): 9.4 in. (239 mm)
Barrel: 4.7 in. (119 mm)
Weight: 44.0 oz. (1.3 kg)
Caliber: 9 mm
Rifling: 6 grooves, r/hand
Capacity: eight
Muz vel: 1,100 ft./sec. (335 m/sec)

This pistol was invented by Aimo Lahti of Finland and was produced by Valtion, the Finnish state factory. The arm was adopted as the official pistol of the Finnish armed forces in 1935; it gave good service in the Finnish campaign against the Russians in the early part of World War II, when it was found to be particularly reliable in very low temperatures. Although, as may be seen, it bore a general resemblance to the Luger, this is misleading: the two were quite different mechanically. The Lahti fired from a closed breech, the bolt being unlocked after a brief rearward travel and going on to complete the usual cycle. The mechanism incorporated a bolt accelerator—a curved arm so designed that it increased the rearward velocity of the bolt. A version of the Lahti was also used by the Swedish forces, who called it the M/40. The Swedes had originally settled for the German Walther P38, but when war intervened, they turned instead to Finland. The Finns supplied some, but later they were made under license by the Swedish firm of Husqvarna Vapenfabrik. Although the Swedes made good weapons, their M/40 was considered inferior to its Finnish prototype.

Japanese Military Handguns World War I–World War II

Japan has the dubious honor of producing some of the world's worst-ever handguns during the wartime years. There were five basic models in use between 1914 and 1945: the Meiji 26 revolver and the Taisho 04, Taisho 14, Small Nambu, and Type 94 automatic pistols.

A major problem prevailing through all Japanese wartime pistols was poorly selected ammunition types. The Meiji 26 used the 9 x 22R cartridge; the Taisho 04, 14, and the Type 94 used the 8 x 21.5 mm Nambu, while the Small Nambu fired the 7 x 19.5 mm Nambu. All these cartridges, when fired from short Japanese pistol barrels, had woefully deficient stopping power, typically generating only around 130–180 ft./lb. of force at the muzzle. This made the guns poor combat weapons in the jungle conditions of the Pacific war between 1941 and 1945, where leaves and twigs would be quite capable of deviating the bullet in flight. In addition, the 9 x 22R and the 8 x 21.5 mm Nambu were unusually shaped cartridges suitable only for Japanese weapons, meaning that captured Allied 9 mm or .45 in. rounds could not be used.

However, inaccurate firing could be the least of a Japanese soldier's problems. Most Japanese sidearms had quite shocking mechanical and design deficiencies. The Meiji 26 was imbalanced and awkward to fire because of a double-action lock, despite being modeled on reliable Smith & Wessons of the late 1800s. The Taisho 04 suffered from a weak striker spring (causing misfires) and could, with catastrophic effect, be assembled and fired without the breech lock in place. The Taisho 14 was fitted with a fearsomely powerful magazine retaining spring, which made changing the magazine a difficult process, especially with sweaty or oily hands. Ian Hogg in his *Infantry Weapons of WWII* (1997) relates a story from Lieutenant Colonel R. K. Wilson, who witnessed a Japanese officer shooting himself while struggling to remove the stubborn magazine of his Taisho 14.

By far the worst offender against quality and common sense among Japanese pistols was the Type 94. Not only could it fire before the barrel and breech were locked into place, its exposed sear along the side of the receiver also meant it could be fired simply by squeezing the gun body.

Explaining the inferiority of Japanese wartime handguns is difficult, especially as some of them began life as copies of perfectly reliable Western weapons. Wartime exigencies doubtless contributed toward inferior metals often used, especially as around 80 percent of Japanese metals were imported.

Handguns, however, tended to have more of a role as status symbols in the Japanese forces, issued to officers throughout the three armed services. It may well be that simply carrying a handgun was enough, and its practical combat usage was secondary.

Above: *The worst pistol of the twentieth century—or even of all time? The dangerously unreliable Nambu Type 94 8 mm did not even fulfill the criterion of cheapness: it was more expensive to build than its shoddy, but better, predecesssors.*

FRANCE

ST. ETIENNE (MAS) 7.65 MM MODÈLE 1935A/1935S PISTOL

Length (gun): 7.5 in. (190 mm)
Barrel: 4.3 in. (110 mm)
Weight: 25.7oz. (0.7 kg)
Caliber: 7.65 mm
Rifling: 4 grooves, r/hand
Capacity: eight-round box magazine
Muz vel: 1,000 ft./sec. (305 m/sec.)

The French state factory, Manufacture d'Armes de St. Etienne (MAS), worked for some years on an automatic pistol following World War I, eventually selecting a design from the Société Alsacienne de Construction Mécanique (SACM). This bore some similarities to the Colt M1911, but there were differences, principally that the weapon was chambered for the French Army's 7.65 x 19.5 mm Longue round, which was not particularly powerful and used only by French forces. The new pistol had a magazine safety, a safety catch on the slide, and a revised firing lock. The original production version was the Modèle 1935A, which was produced only by SACM, and can be recognized by the curved lines of its butt and the fact that the muzzle is flush with the front of the slide (left picture). In 1938, it was decided to simplify the design for manufacture, which resulted in a revised barrel-locking system. It can be recognized by its straight-sided butt, the muzzle sticking out slightly from the front of the slide, and a generally lower standard of finish. This version, Modèle 1935S (right picture), was produced at four factories in France.

ITALY

BERETTA MODEL 1935 PISTOL

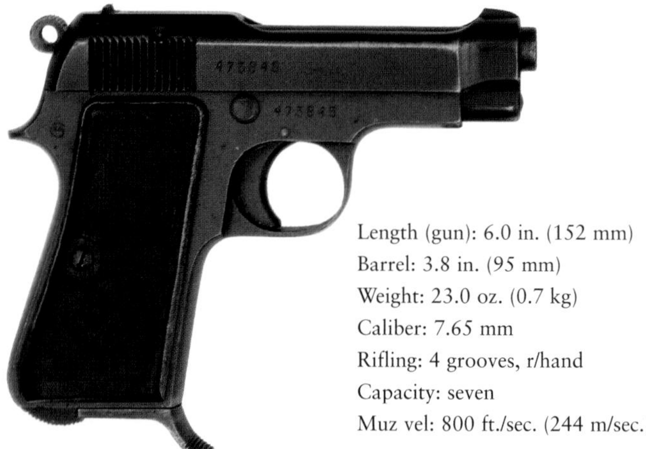

Length (gun): 6.0 in. (152 mm)
Barrel: 3.8 in. (95 mm)
Weight: 23.0 oz. (0.7 kg)
Caliber: 7.65 mm
Rifling: 4 grooves, r/hand
Capacity: seven
Muz vel: 800 ft./sec. (244 m/sec.)

The Model 1935 was very similar in all essentials to the earlier Model 1934 but was of the smaller caliber of 7.65 mm. The specimen illustrated is fitted with a spur-shaped extension below the magazine to offer added support for the little finger of the firer's hand. Like the Model 1934, the Model 1935 had a safety catch on the left side of the frame and was usually fitted with a loop for a lanyard on the lower part of the butt. It was extensively issued to the Italian Navy and Air Force and was also used by the Italian police. The specimen illustrated bears the initials "PS" (*Publica Sicurreza*), indicating that it is a police weapon. Like most Berettas of the period, this arm bears details of the caliber on the left side of the slide, which is also dated "1941." The date is followed by the Roman numerals "XIX," its date in the Fascist Calendar of 1922.

POLAND

RADOM WZ MODEL 1935 9 MM PISTOL

Length (gun): 8.3 in. (211 mm)
Barrel: 4.5 in. (114 mm)
Weight: 37.0 oz. (1.1 kg)
Caliber: 9 mm
Rifling: 6 grooves, r/hand
Capacity: eight
Muz vel: 1,150 ft./sec. (351 m/sec.)

Soon after 1930, the Polish Army required a self-loading pistol. By 1935, the Wz-35 was in extensive production at the Radom factory. Like most later self-loading pistols, it was based on Browning's designs, with some relatively minor changes either for ease of manufacture or actual improvements incorporated in the light of experience. The pistol worked in the orthodox way: lugs on the upper surface of the barrel engaged corresponding slots in the slide when it was locked; the barrel recoiled briefly and then dropped to disengage when the slide was either drawn to the rear manually or blown back by the gases produced by the explosion of the cartridge. The weapon had a grip safety at the rear of the butt. No manual safety as such was fitted, but the arm had a device for retracting the firing pin, and this allowed it to be carried safely with a round in the chamber and the hammer down.

GERMANY

SAUER MODEL 38H PISTOL 1938

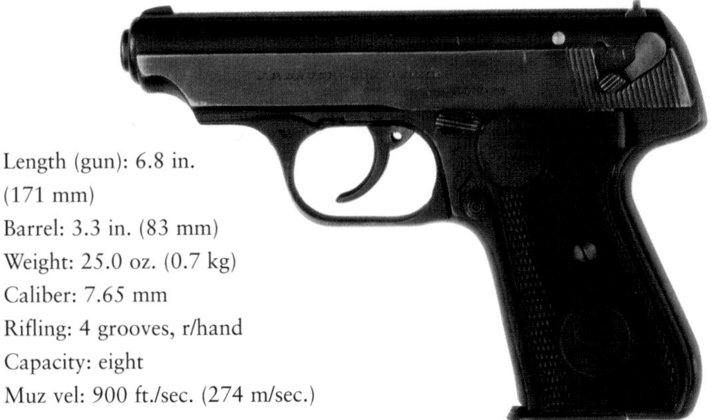

Length (gun): 6.8 in. (171 mm)
Barrel: 3.3 in. (83 mm)
Weight: 25.0 oz. (0.7 kg)
Caliber: 7.65 mm
Rifling: 4 grooves, r/hand
Capacity: eight
Muz vel: 900 ft./sec. (274 m/sec.)

J. P. Sauer & Sohn had a reputation for producing high-quality sporting guns and rifles. The company began to make self-loading pistols in 1913 and continued to do so until after World War II. This is one of Sauer's best products. It was first put on the market in 1938, but the outbreak of war restricted its use to German forces. Manufacture was not resumed afterward. It worked on the blowback principle, having a fixed barrel and an overall slide with the breech-block inside it. It had an internal hammer (hence "H"—for *hahn*, hammer). The first round was chambered in the usual way, but then there were various options. The hammer could be lowered by pressing the trigger, with the thumb on the catch behind it, allowing the catch to rise slowly. To fire then, the pistol could be cocked by depressing the catch with the thumb, or fired double-action by pressing the trigger.

GERMANY

MAUSER 7.65 MM MODEL HSC SELF-LOADING PISTOL 1938

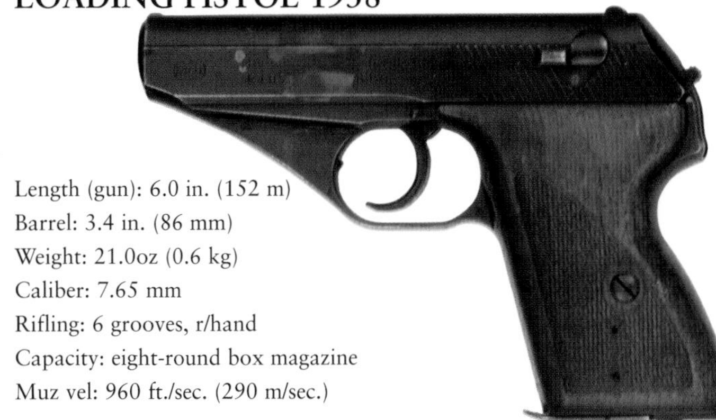

Length (gun): 6.0 in. (152 m)
Barrel: 3.4 in. (86 mm)
Weight: 21.0oz (0.6 kg)
Caliber: 7.65 mm
Rifling: 6 grooves, r/hand
Capacity: eight-round box magazine
Muz vel: 960 ft./sec. (290 m/sec.)

The HSc (*Hahnlos Selbstladung Model c*, Hammerless Self-Loading Model c) was developed by Mauser in the late 1930s for the civilian market, but with the outbreak of war it was quickly taken into military use. It was of modern appearance, but it was not actually hammerless, since the hammer was virtually out of sight in the slide with a small spur protruding which enabled the firer to cock the weapon with his thumb. The Mauser Hsc was mainly produced in 7.65 x 17 mm caliber, but some examples in 9 mm short and 0.22 in. were also manufactured. Following the end of the war production continued in France and was later restarted by Mauser, until they licensed production to an Italian company in the 1970s.

HUNGARY

FEGVERGYAR MODEL 37M/PISTOLE 37 (U) PISTOL 1937

Length (gun): 7.2 in. (183 mm)
Barrel: 4.3 in. (110 mm)
Weight: 27.0oz (0.8 kg)
Caliber: 9 mm
Rifling: 6 grooves, r/hand
Capacity: 7-round box magazine
Muz vel: 900 ft./sec. (274 m/sec.)

The Model 37M was a simple blowback weapon with a fixed barrel and an overall slide, with the recoil spring situated on a rod beneath the barrel. The first round was chambered in the normal way by the manual operation of the slide, which also cocked the external hammer. There was a prominent spur on the magazine to extend the butt length and improve the firer's grip. This version fired a 9 mm short cartridge suitable for a blowback design, and its only safety device was its grip safety. In 1941 the German Wehrmacht placed a contract for a 7.65 mm version, which, apart from the first few, were all fitted with a safety catch of orthodox type on the left-hand side of the frame and did not have the spur. These were used mainly, but not exclusively, by the Luftwaffe, and were designated "Pistole 37 U" by the Germans; the "U" stood for *Ungarisch* (Hungarian). The slide was marked "P MOD 37 Kal 7.65" together with the manufacturer's code "j.h.v." and the last two digits of the year of manufacture. It was used almost exclusively on the Eastern Front and is now rather rare, making the weapon much sought after by weapons collectors.

UNITED KINGDOM

WELROD 0.32 IN. SILENT PISTOL 1940

Length (gun): 12.0 in. (305 mm)
Barrel: 5.0 in. (127 mm)
Weight: 32.0 oz. (0.9 kg)
Caliber: 0.32 in. (8.1 mm)
Rifling: 4 grooves, r/hand
Capacity: one
Muz vel: 700 ft./sec. (213 m/sec.)

Technically, it is not very difficult to silence a weapon; what is difficult is to make an effective silencer that is not so bulky as to make the weapon hopelessly clumsy in use. One requirement is to suppress the noise of the explosion; the other is to conceal what amounts to a sonic boom when the bullet breaks the sound barrier (assuming that it is of such velocity). Many pistol bullets do not exceed the speed of sound, which reduces the problem very considerably, as was the case with the cartridge fired by the Welrod pistol. The pistol's barrel was relatively short, but the outer casing in front of it was fitted with a series of self-sealing, oil-impregnated, leather washers. These closed behind the passage of the bullet and trapped the sound; but, of course, they tended to burn out after comparatively few shots. This would, naturally, have been a great disadvantage in a weapon designed for general use. However, in the case of the Welrod, the situation presumably never arose, because it was a weapon for use by special forces only.

UNITED STATES

SMITH & WESSON BRITISH SERVICE REVOLVER 1940

Length (gun): 10.0 in. (254 mm)
Barrel: 5.0 in. (127 mm)
Weight: 29.0 oz. (0.8 kg)
Caliber: 0.38 in. (9.6 mm)
Rifling: 5 grooves, r/hand
Capacity: six
Muz vel: 650 ft./sec. (198 m/sec.)

In 1940, Smith & Wesson began producing for the British Army a revolver based closely on its Military and Police models. Until 1928, the official British service revolver was the Webley and Scott in 0.455 in. (11.5 mm) caliber, but in that year a change was made to a 0.38 in. (9.6 mm) model made at Enfield. Since the 0.38 in. (9.6 mm) Smith & Wesson would take the new British cartridge, no difficulties were experienced in respect of ammunition. The Smith & Wesson British Service revolver, sometimes known as the "0.38/200" (from its 200-grain, 13-gram bullet), or the Pistol No. 2, was of orthodox solid-frame construction. The arm shown here has a round barrel with an integral half-round foresight; the backsight consists of a notch and groove on the top strap. The milled cylinder catch was pushed forward to allow the six-chambered cylinder to be swung out on its yoke. There is a projection below the barrel, with a spring-loaded stud that engaged with the end of the ejector pin when the revolver was closed. The lock is of double-action, rebounding type, and the hammer has a separate nose held by a pin. The butt plates are of checkered walnut, bearing the company's monogram in a small, silvered medallion.

CZECH REPUBLIC

CESKÁ ZBROJOVKA MODEL 39 PISTOL 1939

Length (gun): 8.1 in. (206 mm)
Barrel: 4.7 in. (118 mm)
Weight: 33.0 oz. (0.9 kg)
Caliber: 9 mm
Rifling: 6 grooves, r/hand
Capacity: eight
Muz vel: 950 ft./sec. (290 m/sec.)

An arms manufactory was established at Pilsen in Czechoslovakia in 1919 and moved to Strakonitz in 1921. It made a wide variety of weapons and accessories for the Czechoslovak Army. Under Communist control, weapons production was greatly reduced in favor of other items. Between the two world wars, however, the company made a whole series of pistols, both small-caliber pocket types and arms in heavier calibers for military use. The earliest of these fired from a locked breech, but as the short cartridge employed hardly warranted the use of this system, subsequent models reverted to simple blowback. The pistol was very well made and finished, but it was not a success as a military arm. In spite of its weight and bulk, it fired only a low-powered round, and its exposed hammer could not be cocked: the arm had to be fired by a quite heavy pull on the trigger.

UNITED STATES

SMITH & WESSON VICTORY MODEL REVOLVER 1942

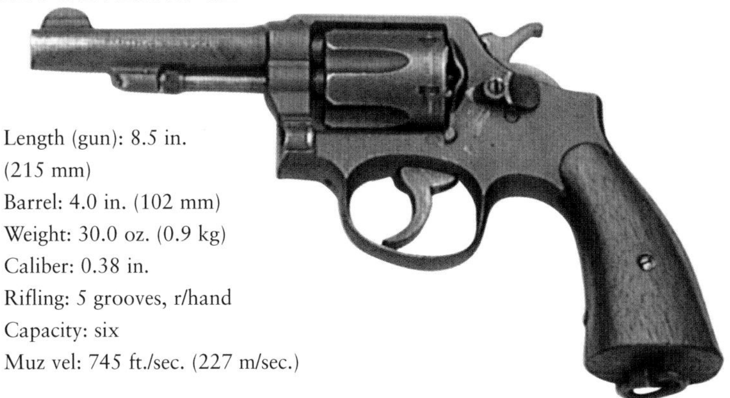

Length (gun): 8.5 in. (215 mm)
Barrel: 4.0 in. (102 mm)
Weight: 30.0 oz. (0.9 kg)
Caliber: 0.38 in.
Rifling: 5 grooves, r/hand
Capacity: six
Muz vel: 745 ft./sec. (227 m/sec.)

This was another World War II version of a well-established handgun, which, like the 0.38/200 for Britain, was based on the well-established Military & Police pistol. Anything fancy was removed, and the result was a utilitarian weapon that was manufactured in large numbers for the U.S. government service, with 4.0 in. (101 mm) versions mainly for the armed forces and 2.0 in. (51 mm) versions mainly for civilian organizations, such as the Justice Department

UNITED STATES

SMITH & WESSON MILITARY AND POLICE FIRST MODEL (CUT-DOWN) REVOLVER 1940

Length (gun): 8.0 in. (203 mm)
Barrel: 3.3 in. (83 mm)
Weight: 28.0 oz. (0.8 kg)
Caliber: 0.38 in. (9.6 mm)
Rifling: 7 grooves, r/hand
Capacity: six
Muz vel: 600 ft./sec. (183 m/sec.)

This revolver is one of those made for the British government during World War II, at a time when the hard-pressed British were desperately short of arms and matériel of all kinds. This arm was known variously as the British Service, the Model No. 2, or the 0.38/200; the latter figure refers to the bullet weight (200 grains, 13 grams) which, by British calculations, provided much the same stopping power as that fired from the earlier 0.455 in. (11.5 mm) caliber Webley service arms. The lead bullet of this type had to be abandoned just before World War II because it contravened the international conventions of warfare; it was replaced by a lighter, 178-grain (11.5 gram) jacketed bullet. The weapon is of orthodox solid-frame type, but it is of interest because at some stage of its career its barrel, originally 5.0 in. (127 mm) long, was cut down to 3.25 in. (83 mm) and a ramp foresight added. The work was quite well done and is difficult to detect at a glance, but it is clear on close examination.

CANADA

INGLIS BROWNING 0.455 IN. NO. 1 MARK 1 (BROWNING GP35) PISTOL 1942

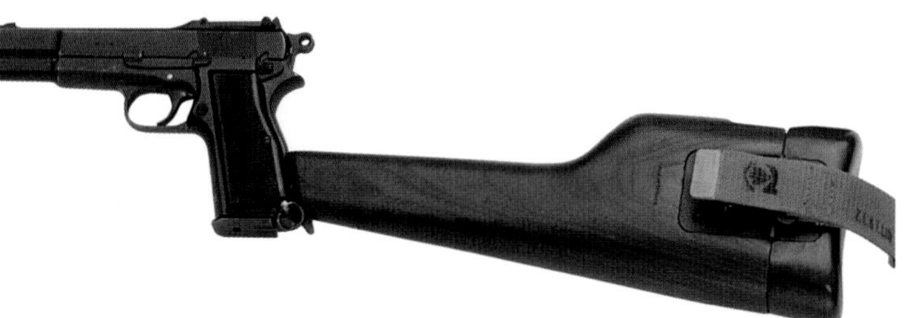

Length (gun): 7.8 in. (197 mm)
Barrel: 4.7 in. (118 mm)
Weight: 35.0 oz. (1.0 kg)
Caliber: 9 mm
Rifling: 4 grooves, r/hand
Capacity: 13-round box magazine
Muz vel: 1,100 ft./sec. (335 m/sec.)

A team of Belgian engineers from the Fabrique Nationale escaped to Britain in 1940, taking with them a number of designs, including those for the Browning GP35. In 1942 they were sent across the Atlantic, where they helped to establish a production line for the Browning GP35, which was designated the Pistol, Canadian, No. 1 Mark 1 and rechambered to take the British 0.455 in. round. Shown here is an Inglis-produced Browning together with, rather unusually, a wooden holster-cum-stock.

UNITED STATES

SMITH & WESSON MODEL 14 K38 MASTERPIECE REVOLVER 1947

Length (gun): 11.1 in. (280 mm)
Barrel: 6.0 in. (152 mm)
Weight: 36.0 oz. (1.1 kg)
Caliber: 0.38 in.
Rifling: not available
Capacity: six
Muz vel: not available

The Smith & Wesson K38 was one of the most successful and popular target revolvers ever made. Part of the reason for its popularity was that it appeared just as revolver shooting was fading from the scene in National Match Course events, only to be replaced, rather by chance, by the growth of nationwide police revolver shooting competitions. Its only serious competitor was the Colt Python. The K38 fired the 0.38 in. Special round and most models used selective double-action, although single-action versions were also available. The crane-mounted cylinder was released by a thumb catch and then swung to the left for loading and unloading. The weapon came with two barrel sizes: 6.0 in. (152 mm) and 8.4 in. (213 mm). It was fitted with a square post foresight and a square notch backsight, click adjustable for elevation and windage. Production of the K38 ceased in 1982.

UNITED STATES

GUIDE LAMP LIBERATOR PISTOL 1942

Length (gun): 5.5 in. (140 mm)
Barrel: 3.5 in. (89 mm)
Weight: 16.0 oz. (0.5 kg)
Caliber: 0.45 in. (11.4 mm)
Rifling: none
Capacity: one
Muz vel: 800 ft./sec. (244 m/sec.)

In 1942 the United States Office of Strategic Services (OSS) asked the Guide Lamp division of General Motors to design a cheap, simple handgun that could be produced in large numbers. The company knew little about guns, but it knew a great deal about the mass production of small metal items, and within about three months it had produced about one million crude pistols. To load the pistol, it was necessary first to pull back the cocking piece and turn it counterclockwise through ninety degrees. The breech was covered by a vertically sliding shutter with a hole for the striker, and was opened by pulling upward on the backsight. A 0.45 in. ACP cartridge was inserted, the shutter was pushed down, and the cocking piece was returned to its original position. There was no safety catch, although a pin on the upper part of the cocking piece passed through a hole in the backsight, presumably to ensure that the shutter did not open and foul the striker. It had no extractor. A few extra cartridges were packed into the butt, access to them being through a sliding trap at the base. After assembly, the arm was packed into a waterproof bag, with a sheet of comic-strip-type instructions with no words, to be air-dropped where required.

RUSSIAN MILITARY HANDGUNS WORLD WAR I–WORLD WAR II

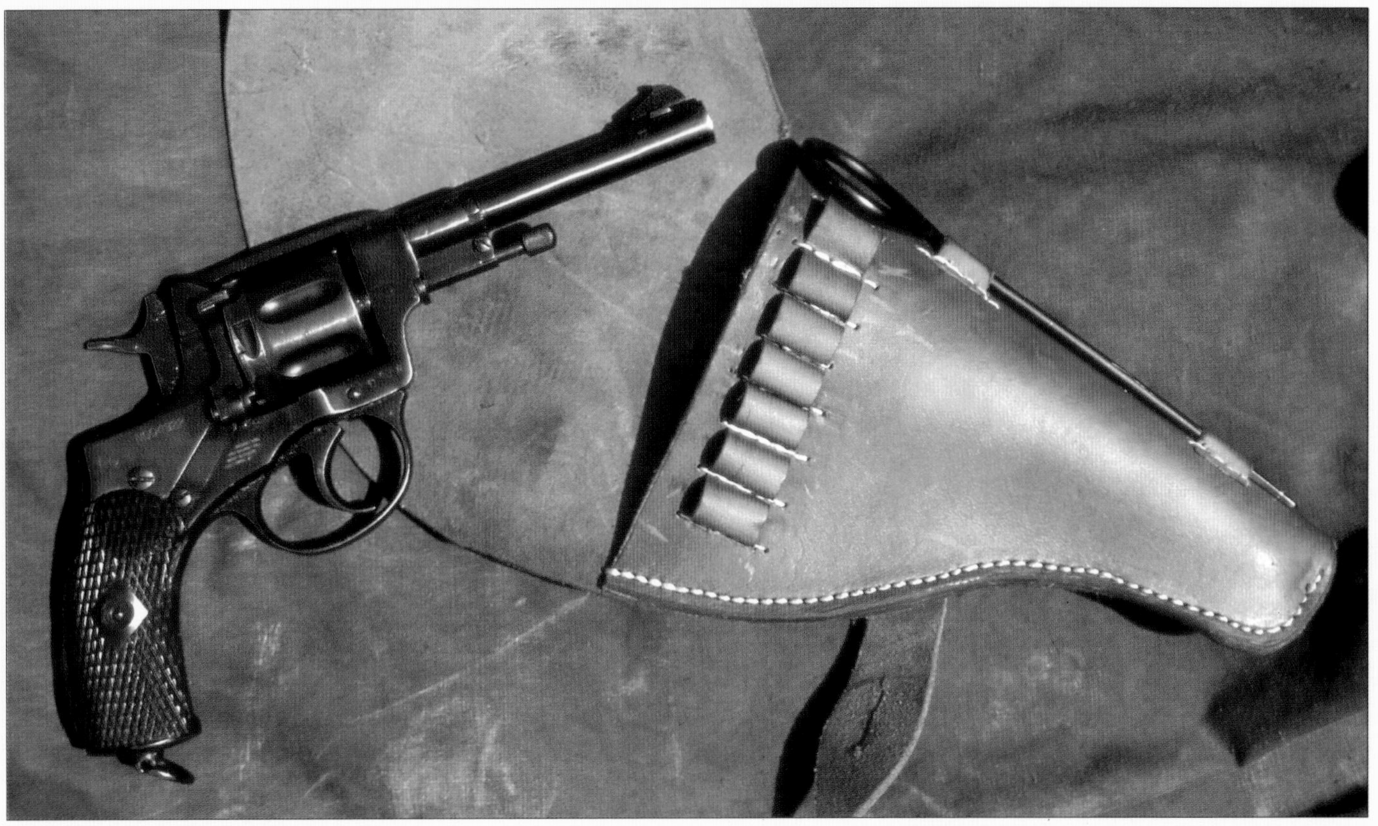

Russian forces of both world wars had only two main types of revolver, though this may not imply limitations in design and production capacity: it may have been merely the logical outcome, because of the excellent quality of the weapons themselves.

The first, and oldest, of these weapons was the Model 1895 Nagant. This excellent revolver, which originated in Belgium, had an advanced gas-seal feature.

Most revolvers lose a portion of the firing gases through the minute gas leak between cylinder and barrel. The Nagant overcame this problem through two methods. First, on cocking, the cylinder was actually pushed forward as well as rotated, allowing the back of the barrel to actually enter the chamber. Second, the cartridge case entirely enclosed the bullet, meaning that the front end of the case would provide obturation against the chamber.

These innovations, and the Nagant's superb reliability, made the revolver a fine combat weapon. It had decisive knockdown force and stood up to the typical severity of weather conditions on the Eastern Front. The numbers manufactured in Russia declined after the Revolution of 1917, but it still served throughout World War II.

Above: *The Model 1895 Nagant was a fine firearm, but would see limited distribution in Russia's huge armies. There was no time for relatively complex handgun training, not when even the most basic understanding of the submachine gun offered greater military advantage.*

However, World War II saw the Nagant challenged by a new weapon type, the Tokarev Model TT33. The automatic TT33 had entered service in 1933, and one glance tells of its Colt M1911 influence. The TT33 used the same swinging-link system as the Colt, with the slide and barrel locking together. With a typical eye for reliability, the Russians also made the feed lips an integral part of the frame, thus making the magazine feed far more dependable (feed lips on magazines are notorious for being damaged).

The Tokarev and the Nagant served the Russians well during the war years, and they reveal some interesting points about Russian combat perspectives and weapons design. Pistols tended to be distributed to officers and some types of NCO (mainly those performing specialist tasks like driving and radio operating), but had almost no distribution among regular soldiers. In World War II, submachine guns dominated among regular troops, as they generated more effective firepower and, crucially for Russia's enormous armies, took far less training time than a handgun. A final interesting point is that the Russians stuck with the 7.62 mm caliber for their handguns. Although small compared to the .45 ACP, the Russian round was still powerful, the Tokarev having a striking energy of 365 ft./lb.

SWITZERLAND

SIG 9 MM P-210 (MODEL 1949) PISTOL

Length (gun): 8.5 in. (215 mm)
Barrel: 4.7 in. (120 mm)
Weight: 32.0 oz. (0.9 kg)
Caliber: 9 mm
Rifling: 6 grooves, r/hand
Capacity: 8-round box magazine
Muz vel: 1,100 ft./sec. (335 m/sec.)

The French Army's Model 1935A 7.65 mm semi-automatic pistol was designed by the French company SACM, based on patents held by a Swiss named Petter. The rights were purchased by Schweizerisches Industrie Gesellschaft (SIG). In 1946, the Swiss Army stated a requirement for a new pistol and SIG had a design ready. This was accepted into service as the Model 1949. The great majority of semi-automatic pistols have a slide which moves along rails machined outside the frame, but in the P-210 these rails are inside the frame, giving much improved support to the slide; this design can be credited with a large contribution to this weapon's famed accuracy and smoothness of operation. The P-210 uses the Browning locking system, with a lug underneath the breech that moves the barrel out of engagement with the slide. Models within the P-201 range included the P-210-1 (polished finish, wooden grips), P-210-2 (matt finish, plastic grips), P-210-4 (a special version for the German border police), P-210-5 (a target pistol with a 6 in./150 mm barrel), and the P-210-6 (a target version with a 4.7 in./120 mm barrel). Models P-210-1, -2, and -6 can be converted between 7.65 mm to 9 mm Parabellum by changing the barrel and return spring.

BELGIUM

FABRIQUE NATIONALE/BROWNING 9 MM "FAST ACTION" PISTOL 1950

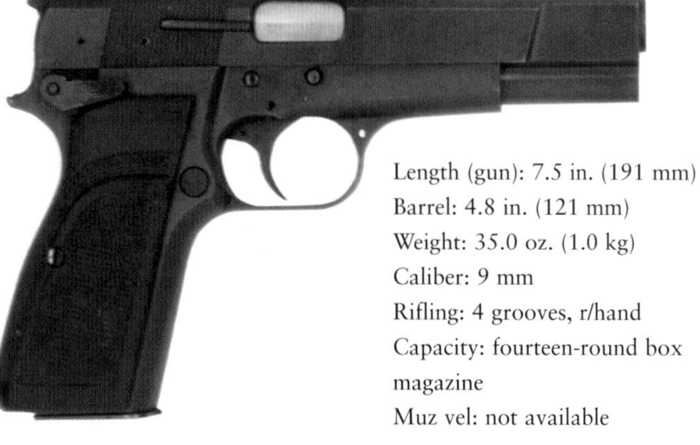

Length (gun): 7.5 in. (191 mm)
Barrel: 4.8 in. (121 mm)
Weight: 35.0 oz. (1.0 kg)
Caliber: 9 mm
Rifling: 4 grooves, r/hand
Capacity: fourteen-round box magazine
Muz vel: not available

This was one of several attempts by Fabrique Nationale to produce a successor to the Browning GP35. The Browning Fast Action, of which some twelve prototypes were built, was intended to afford the safety in carry of a double-action arm, but preserve the speed and accuracy on the first and second shots of a cocked-and-locked single action. In brief, the hammer was mounted round a large hub, which carried the sear engagement. The hammer was pushed forward over a latch for the carry; the first pressure on the trigger released it to spring back around the hub before the sear was released to fire. As a result, trigger pressure was light and easy for each shot, rather than being rough and heavy for the first shot with a drastic change of system for the second shot, which is the case with most double-action pistols.

CZECH REPUBLIC

CESKÁ ZBROJOVKA CZ 1950 PISTOL

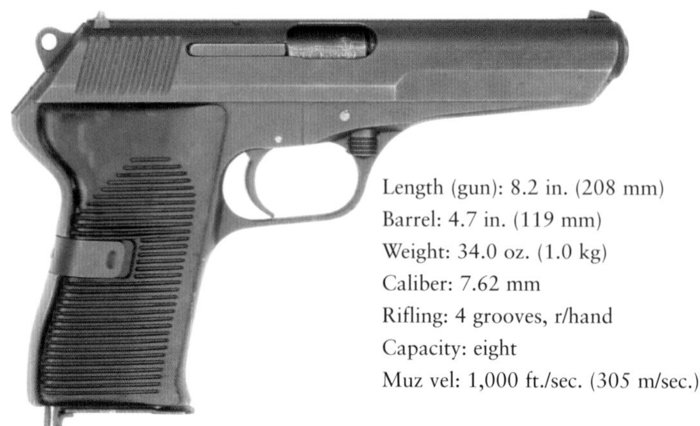

Length (gun): 8.2 in. (208 mm)
Barrel: 4.7 in. (119 mm)
Weight: 34.0 oz. (1.0 kg)
Caliber: 7.62 mm
Rifling: 4 grooves, r/hand
Capacity: eight
Muz vel: 1,000 ft./sec. (305 m/sec.)

This self-loading pistol had its origins after the end of the World War II, when the Czech Army decided that it needed a new pistol. The new weapon was in production by 1950. It was basically similar to the German Walther PP although there were some manufacturing differences. It was a reasonably effective pistol but, like many European service arms, its caliber lacked the essential stopping power for service use; therefore, within a very short period, it had been replaced as a military arm, although it continued in use for police purposes. It was replaced by the Ceská Zbrojovka CZ 1952, which, although of the same caliber, fired a much more powerful round from a locked breech, working by means of a roller device similar to that on the German MG 42 machine gun. This pistol was, in its turn, replaced by the Russian Makarov.

HANDGUNS, THE LAW, AND CRIME IN THE UK

On March 13, 1996, forty-four-year-old Thomas Hamilton walked into the Dunblane Primary School in Stirling, Scotland. He was carrying on his person two Browning automatic handguns and two Smith & Wesson revolvers with 501 rounds of 9 mm and 242 rounds of .357 Magnum ammunition. In under four minutes of carnage, Hamilton killed one teacher and sixteen schoolchildren. All Hamilton's weapons were legally owned, and the government immediately set up a major public inquiry headed by Lord Cullen, which published its results on October 14, 1996. In response to the report, and to the massive public outcry against handgun ownership, in 1997 the government implemented a complete ban on the ownership of handguns, with the exclusion of air pistols and .22 target pistols.

The problem for the government since 1997 has been that handgun crime has risen quite sharply. There were 2,648 handgun crimes committed in the UK in the 1997–98 period, but in the 1999–2000 period the figure rose to 3,685 (data from the Centre for Defence Studies, Kings College, London). Other statistics showed that of the twenty police areas with the lowest number of legally held weapons, ten had above-average levels of gun crimes.

Below: *Police in the UK have consistently voted against being universally armed in referendums. Remarkably, the number of officers authorized to use firearms actually went down, from 7,738 in 1996 to 6,267 in 2000, as did the number of operations in which arms were issued. Of the 10,915 armed responses in 2000, the police discharged their weapons just seven times. These statistics, of course, predate 9/11 and the war on terror.*

The causes of the rise are several. First, there has been a large increase in the number of smuggled weapons illegally entering the UK, especially since the end of the war in the Balkans resulted in huge military surpluses. Second, there has been a rise in the popularity of deactivated and imitation handguns in the UK, and these weapons, although not capable of firing lethal rounds, accounted for a full 12 percent of all gun crime in the UK in 2001–02. The popularity of these weapons has led to the further problem of criminal gunsmiths reactivating deactivated weapons and converting high-quality imitation handguns to fully functioning weapons. The final ingredient is the rise of handgun crime in the UK has been cultural. Most of the eighty or so gun-related deaths each year in the UK are within criminal communities such as drug gangs, although innocent bystanders have been victims. A worrying trend toward gun carrying has risen among males sixteen to nineteen years old, and also markedly among males of African descent. Carrying an illegal firearm now carries a five-year jail sentence, and some recent figures have suggested that handgun crime is starting to fall. The next few years will be the acid test of government firearms policy.

FRANCE

ST. ETIENNE MODEL 1950 PISTOL

Length (gun): 7.6 in. (193 mm)
Barrel: 4.3 in. (109 mm)
Weight: 34.0 oz. (1.0 kg)
Caliber: 9 mm
Rifling: 4 grooves, l/hand
Capacity: nine
Muz vel: 1,100 ft./sec. (335 m/sec.)

The revolvers originally used by the French armed forces all suffered from the defect of firing weak cartridges. After the end of World War I, therefore, France decided to follow the example of virtually every other country on the continent and change to a self-loading pistol. There followed a period of sporadic and leisurely experiment—at a time when another war was unthinkable—and it was not until 1935 that a self-loader was adopted. This, the MAS Model 1935, was a very sound and well-made weapon of basic Browning type—but it suffered from the same defect as the French revolvers: its 7.65 mm round lacked stopping power. After 1945, one of the requirements was for a new pistol. The arm chosen was a redesigned Model 1935, capable of firing the standard 9 mm Parabellum cartridge. This was a success and at last placed a good pistol into the hands of French servicemen.

UNITED KINGDOM

PODSENKOWSKY MCEM 2 PISTOL 1950

Length (gun): 14.0 in. (356 mm)
Barrel: 9.0 in. (229 mm)
Weight: 88.0 oz. (2.5 kg)
Caliber: 0.35 in. (9 mm)
Rifling: 6 grooves, r/hand
Capacity: eighteen
Muz vel: 1,200 ft./sec. (366 m/sec.)

Although the Sten gun had given good service, something better was needed for the postwar British Army. All potential successors were given the title of Machine Carbine Experimental Model (MCEM), with a serial number. The MCEM No. 2 was designed by a Polish officer, Lieutenant Podsenkowsky. Its magazine fitted into the butt, making it more a pistol than a submachine gun. The bolt was made to what was then an advanced design and consisted of a half-cylinder 8.5 in. (216 mm) long; the striker was at the rear, so that at the moment of firing, almost the entire barrel was inside the bolt. There was no cocking handle: the bolt was drawn to the rear by hooking a finger through a slot above the muzzle. Because of its light weight and rate of fire, vibration was considerable, and a rigid-canvas butt was provided, converting it to a true submachine gun. It was never adopted.

RUSSIA

MAKAROV 9 MM PISTOL 1951

Length (gun): 6.4 in. (161 mm)
Barrel: 3.8 in. (97 mm)
Weight: 25.0 oz. (0.7 kg)
Caliber: 9 mm
Rifling: 4 grooves, r/hand
Capacity: eight
Muz vel: 1,075 ft./sec. (328 m/sec.

The Makarov pistol became the standard pistol for both the Soviet forces and the Warsaw Pact. Externally it was a copy of the German Walther PP, but it had no locking system, firing on a simple blowback action. The slide was blown back by the rearward movement of the case. To avoid excessively stiff springs and heavy slides or breechblocks, the cartridge used was intermediate. The pistol had an external hammer with a double-action lock; this meant that it could be carried safely with a round in the chamber and the hammer down. When the pistol had been loaded, the movement of the safety catch—situated on the left rear of the slide, above the butt plate—to the "safe" position allowed the hammer to drop safely and locked the slide. When the last round in the magazine had been fired, the magazine follower pushed up the slide stop and held the slide to the rear. To strip, the magazine was removed. The front of the trigger guard was pulled down and twisted slightly to bear on the frame; the slide could now be removed to the rear.

UNITED STATES

COLT MODEL 1873 SINGLE-ACTION ARMY REVOLVER (MODERN PRODUCTION) 1953

Length: 10.9 in. (274 mm)
Barrel: 5.5 in. (140 mm)
Weight: 37 oz. (1.0 kg)
Caliber: 0.45 in. (11.4 mm)
Rifling: 6 grooves, r/hand
Capacity: six
Muz vel: 650 ft./sec. (198 m/sec.)

This weapon is not, strictly speaking, a replica, since it comes from the same company, Colt, and the same production line that have always produced the genuine Colt Model 1873 Single-Action Army. Series production continued from 1873 to 1942, when it was suspended (note, not terminated) due to the United States joining World War II, by which time some 357,859 had been made. Due to public demand, production restarted in 1953 and ran to 1982, but even after that these revolvers continue to be available as a special order item from the company. The Model 1873 was made in some thirty-six calibers, and the modern example shown here is available in 0.357 Magnum caliber and 0.45 in. caliber (see specifications). This gun has been known under a variety of names: the military version, and the general name, is the "Model 1873 Single-Action Army," while in the Old West the two most widely used models were the "Peacemaker" (0.45 in. caliber) and the "Frontier" (0.44-40 in. caliber). To the company itself, however, it has always been the "Model P."

UNITED STATES

SMITH & WESSON 9 MM MODEL 39 PISTOL 1954

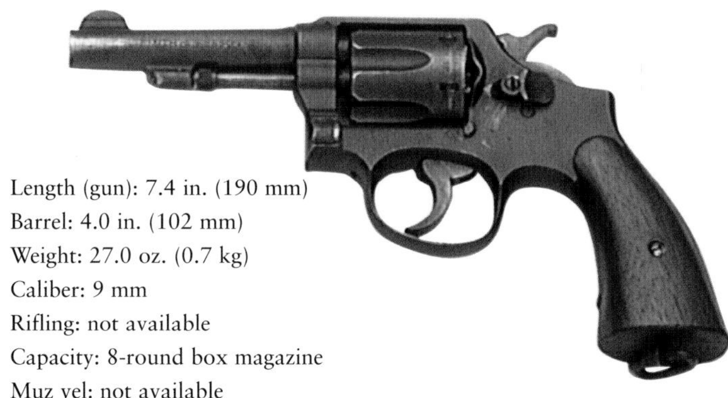

Length (gun): 7.4 in. (190 mm)
Barrel: 4.0 in. (102 mm)
Weight: 27.0 oz. (0.7 kg)
Caliber: 9 mm
Rifling: not available
Capacity: 8-round box magazine
Muz vel: not available

When NATO decided to standardize the 9 mm Parabellum round in 1954, Smith & Wesson quickly produced their Model 39 for possible military adoption but, although it failed in this aim, it was adopted by the Illinois State Police, which enhanced its prospects, and it quickly became popular. The Model 39 has been succeeded by models with improved sights, extractors, and slide bushings, as well as large capacity magazines (Model 59) and stainless steel construction (Models 639 and 659). Later, Smith & Wesson was the only serious American contender for the U.S. Services pistol contract which resulted in the adoption of the Beretta 92SB. The Model 39 worked on double-action for the first shot, followed by single-action for following shots. There was a square ramp foresight and square notch backsight.

UNITED STATES

COLT 0.22 IN. TROOPER REVOLVER 1955

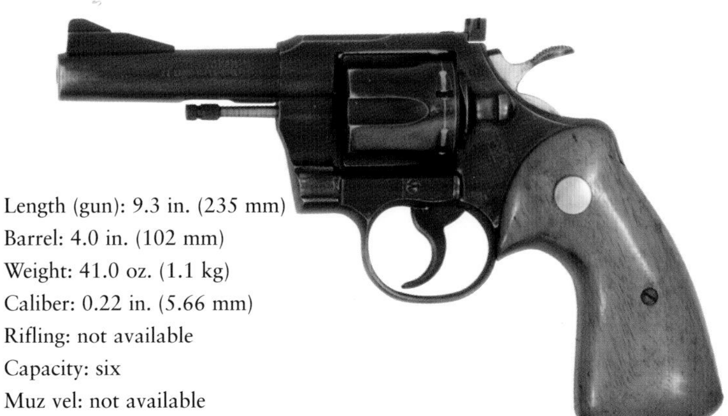

Length (gun): 9.3 in. (235 mm)
Barrel: 4.0 in. (102 mm)
Weight: 41.0 oz. (1.1 kg)
Caliber: 0.22 in. (5.66 mm)
Rifling: not available
Capacity: six
Muz vel: not available

As with pistols, there are two options for a 0.22 in. revolver: to produce a conversion kit that will adapt the barrel and chamber to the smaller round, or to produce a specialist weapon. The latter is general judged to be the most satisfactory solution and the Colt Trooper is an excellent example of the breed. Firing the 0.22 in. Long Rifle round, this is a selective double-action weapon, with a thumb latch on the left of the frame that releases the cylinder to swing out on its yoke. The sights are square format with a large blade foresight and a backsight that is click adjustable for windage and elevation.

UNITED STATES

SMITH & WESSON MODEL 29 REVOLVER 1955

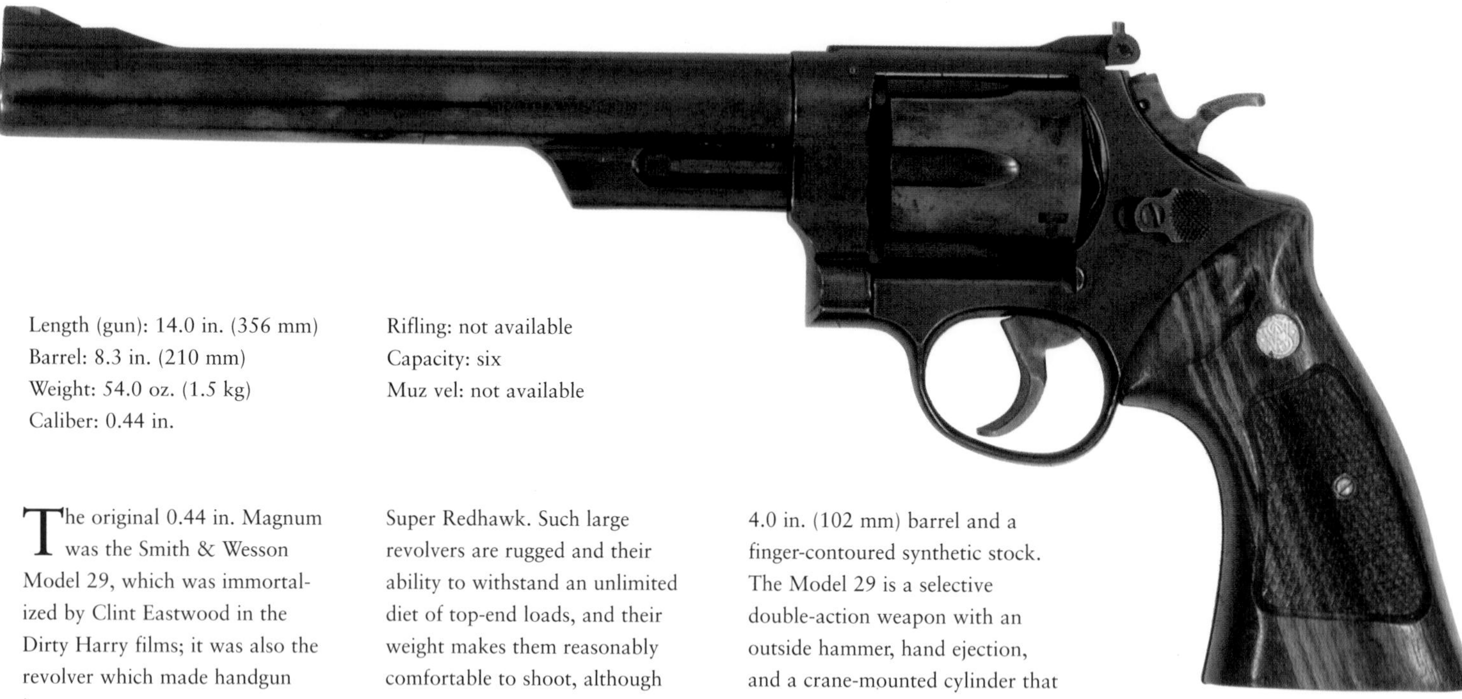

Length (gun): 14.0 in. (356 mm)
Barrel: 8.3 in. (210 mm)
Weight: 54.0 oz. (1.5 kg)
Caliber: 0.44 in.
Rifling: not available
Capacity: six
Muz vel: not available

The original 0.44 in. Magnum was the Smith & Wesson Model 29, which was immortalized by Clint Eastwood in the Dirty Harry films; it was also the revolver which made handgun hunting a recognized sport. The Model 29 was considered to be a large gun when it appeared, although it has been dwarfed by later models such as the Ruger Super Redhawk. Such large revolvers are rugged and their ability to withstand an unlimited diet of top-end loads, and their weight makes them reasonably comfortable to shoot, although there seems little to chose between them and a rifle. The picture shows a Model 29 with an 8.3 in. (210 mm) barrel and wooden stock. Another version has a 4.0 in. (102 mm) barrel and a finger-contoured synthetic stock. The Model 29 is a selective double-action weapon with an outside hammer, hand ejection, and a crane-mounted cylinder that swings leftward out of frame for loading and unloading. There is a square ramp foresight with a square notch backsight that is click-adjustable for elevation and windage. The French Gendarmerie's special operations force, GIGN, showed considerable interest in this weapon.

UNITED STATES

COLT PYTHON TARGET REVOLVER 1955

Length (gun): 11.5 in. (292 mm)
Barrel: 6.0 in. (152 mm)
Weight: 44.0 oz. (1.2 kg)
Caliber: 0.357 in. Magnum
Rifling: not available
Capacity: 6
Muz vel: not available

The Colt Python revolver appeared in 1955, with company advertisements stating confidently that it was "the world's finest revolver." Whether that was true or not is a matter of personal opinion, but it was certainly extremely good and in its heyday—the 1960s and 1970s—its only serious competitor in revolver competitions was the Smith & Wesson Model 14K38. The Python was of all-steel construction (stainless steel was available as an option), and it came in four barrel lengths: 2.5 in. (63.5 mm), 4.0 in. (102 mm), 6.0 in. (152 mm), and 8.0 in. (203 mm). The Python used selective double action and a thumb latch on the left of the frame pulled rearward to release the crane-mounted cylinder, which swung to the left. Spent cartridges were then removed by hand. There was a square ramp foresight pinned to the barrel rib while the backsight was click-adjustable for windage and elevation. The Colt was very popular, and among its advantages over the Smith & Wesson competition were its muzzle heaviness and slightly greater overall weight.

CZECH REPUBLIC

CESKÁ ZBROJOVKA 0.38 IN. ZKR-551 REVOLVER 1957

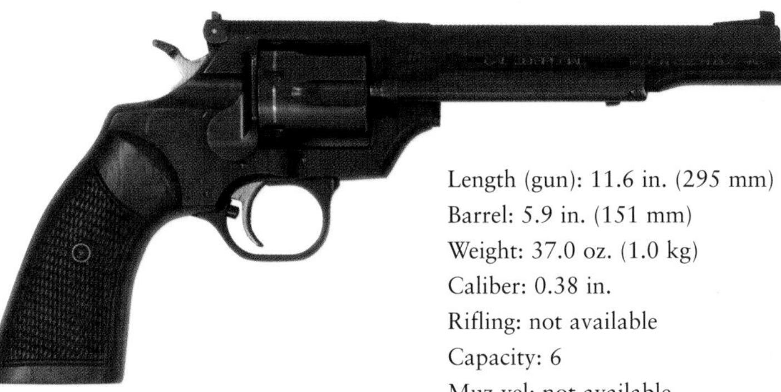

Length (gun): 11.6 in. (295 mm)
Barrel: 5.9 in. (151 mm)
Weight: 37.0 oz. (1.0 kg)
Caliber: 0.38 in.
Rifling: not available
Capacity: 6
Muz vel: not available

The Czechoslovak ZKR-551 was introduced in 1957 and was a six-shot target revolver, chambered for 0.38 in. Special caliber. A competition weapon, it was, in fact, intended for just one event, the UIT Centerfire, which involves one shot per exposure of the target. It was an elegant and impeccably built weapon, distinguished by a low bore line and a fast lock time, with no serious vices. It has a solid frame with gate loading, using a gate to the right of the frame that rocks rearward, locking the action and freeing the cylinder to rotate clockwise. The cases are manually ejected by a sprung-rod ejector mounted offset to the right under the barrel, as in the 1873 Colt.

UNITED STATES

SMITH & WESSON MODEL 41 PISTOL 1957

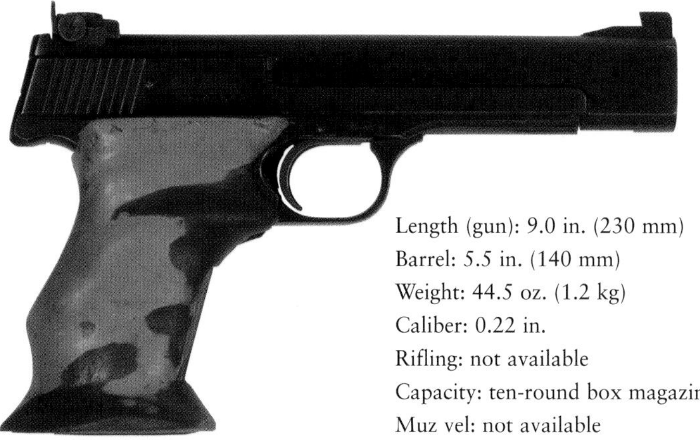

Length (gun): 9.0 in. (230 mm)
Barrel: 5.5 in. (140 mm)
Weight: 44.5 oz. (1.2 kg)
Caliber: 0.22 in.
Rifling: not available
Capacity: ten-round box magazine
Muz vel: not available

The blowback-operated Model 41 was introduced in about 1957 for use in the U.S. National Match Course competition, as well as the UIT Standard Pistol, Standard Handgun, and Ladies matches. The weapon set the fashion for rimfire target pistols with a grip angle duplicating that of the 0.45 in. pistol. The gunmaking company High Standard soon followed suit with upright handles for their very popular and successful Supermatic Trophy and Citation models. The Model 41 has an undercut square post foresight, but its backsight attracted interest since it is mounted on a rib extending rearward from the barrel. Slide-mounted rear sights tended to be viewed with suspicion, and High Standard soon started to mount theirs on a frame-mounted stirrup that encircled the rear of the slide, much the same system that was used by Hämmerli on their Model 208.

SPAIN

ECHEVERRIA MODEL DK (STARFIRE) PISTOL 1958

Length (gun): 5.7 in. (145 mm)
Barrel: 3.1 in. (79 mm)
Weight: 15.0 oz. (0.4 kg)
Caliber: 9 mm
Rifling: 6 grooves, r/hand
Capacity: seven
Muz vel: 1,000 ft./sec. (305 m/sec.)

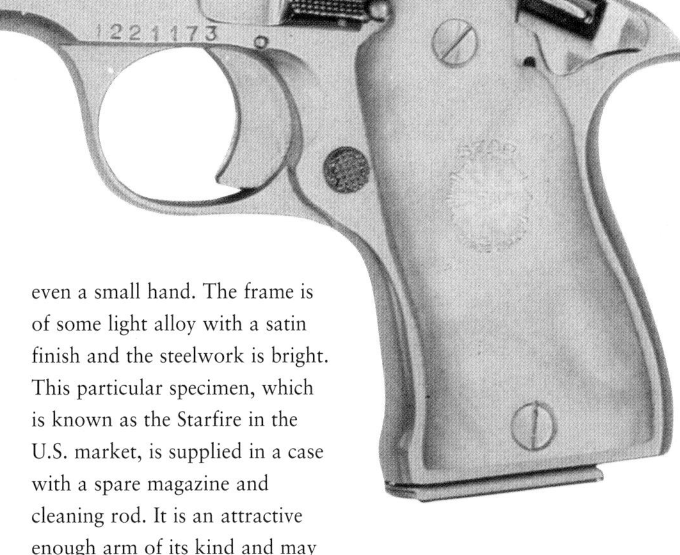

This pistol is based on the company's Model D of about 1930—although the design has been considerably modernized—and appeared in 1958 under the designation of DK. It is of fairly orthodox type, firing from a locked breech of Browning type, the barrel and slide being fixed at the moment of firing. They recoil briefly together until the rear end of the barrel drops, disengages and stops; the slide continues rearward to cock the hammer. It is forced forward again under the influence of the recoil spring (which is located beneath, and parallel to, the barrel), stripping and chambering a cartridge and relocking the breech in readiness for the next shot. The weapon is quite well made; the butt is comfortably shaped, although inevitably on the short side for even a small hand. The frame is of some light alloy with a satin finish and the steelwork is bright. This particular specimen, which is known as the Starfire in the U.S. market, is supplied in a case with a spare magazine and cleaning rod. It is an attractive enough arm of its kind and may be said to justify Echeverria's modern reputation for reliability.

SWITZERLAND

HÄMMERLI MODEL 208 TARGET PISTOL 1958

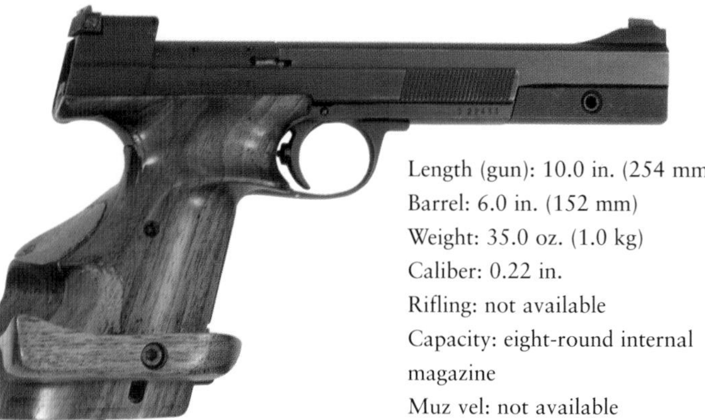

Length (gun): 10.0 in. (254 mm)
Barrel: 6.0 in. (152 mm)
Weight: 35.0 oz. (1.0 kg)
Caliber: 0.22 in.
Rifling: not available
Capacity: eight-round internal magazine
Muz vel: not available

The successor to the Model 207, Hämmerli's Model 208 was introduced in 1958. It was a semi-automatic weapon, blowback operated, using an unlocked breech. It was of all steel construction, being machined from a solid block, and was chambered for the 0.22 in. Long Rifle cartridge. This was the mandatory round for the Standard Pistol event, which involved firing five rounds in ten seconds at a range of 27.3 yd. (25 m) at the international precision target, and required very tight grouping for a good score. Sights consisted of a square post foresight and a square notch backsight, which was click adjustable for elevation and windage. The Model 208 was very successful, although it was constantly being challenged by the FAS Model 601 and Britarms Model 2000.

UNITED STATES

M.B.A. 13 MM GYROJET PISTOL 1960

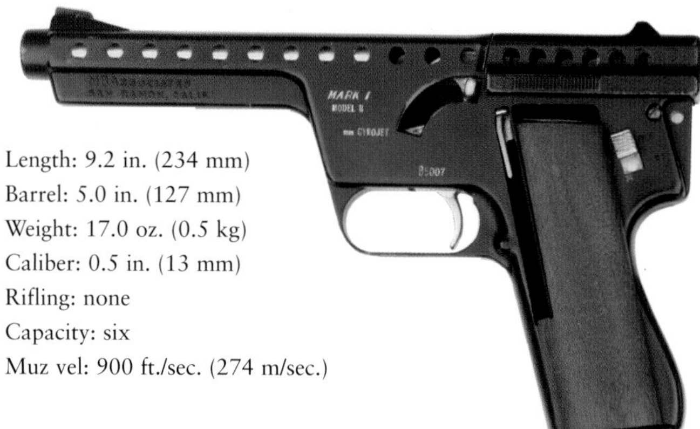

Length: 9.2 in. (234 mm)
Barrel: 5.0 in. (127 mm)
Weight: 17.0 oz. (0.5 kg)
Caliber: 0.5 in. (13 mm)
Rifling: none
Capacity: six
Muz vel: 900 ft./sec. (274 m/sec.)

There had been virtually no significant developments in hand firearms for very many years. Arguably they had reached their full development. In 1960, however, two enterprising Americans, Robert Mainhardt and Art Biehl, found this so hard to accept that they produced this weapon, which although it looks at first glance very like an orthodox self-loading pistol was, in fact, a rocket-launcher! The rocket was of 13 mm caliber: it was about 1.5 in. (38 mm) long, with a solid head as the actual projectile and a tubular body containing a propellant charge. The base was closed, but it had four jets to provide thrust; these were also angled to impart spin to the rocket, in order to ensure stability. Once the rocket had been loaded, pressure on the trigger caused the hammer to drive it to the rear so that the cap in its base struck a fixed pin in the breech. It had neither power nor accuracy.

UNITED KINGDOM

EDGECUMBE ARMS COMBAT TEN REVOLVER 1961

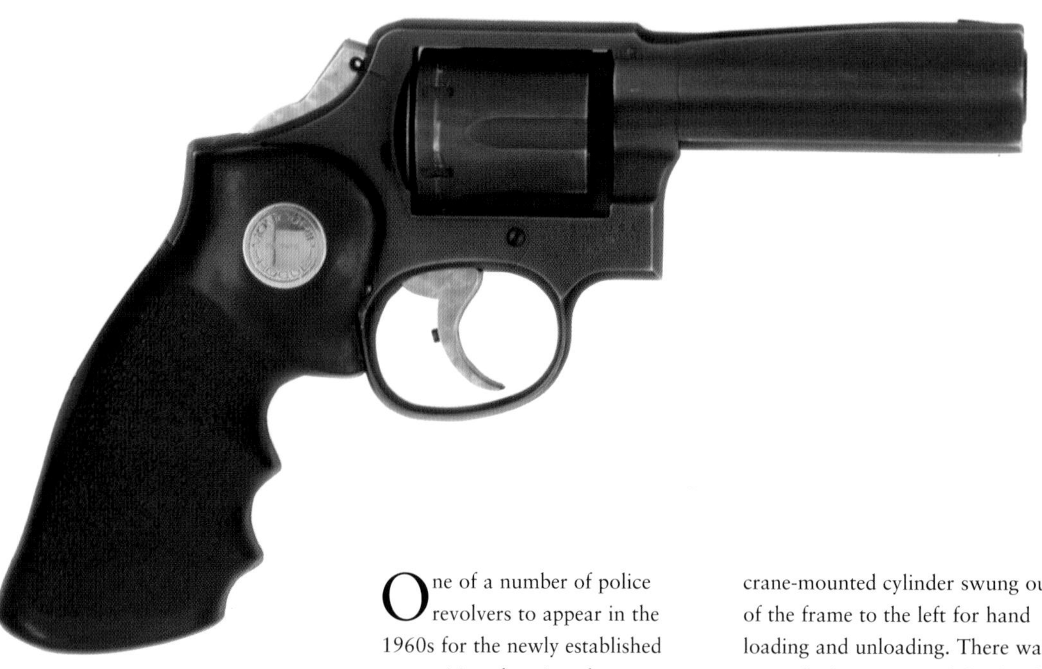

Length (gun): 9.3 in. (263 mm)
Barrel: 4.0 in. (102 mm)
Weight: 40.0 oz. (1.1 kg)
Caliber: 0.38 in.
Rifling: not available
Capacity: six
Muz vel: not available

One of a number of police revolvers to appear in the 1960s for the newly established competition shooting, the Edgecumbe Combat Ten was built on a Smith & Wesson Model 10 frame, with a Douglas barrel. The crane-mounted cylinder swung out of the frame to the left for hand loading and unloading. There was a standard square notch backsight, while the square ramp foresight was integrally milled into the barrel between integral protective ribs. Early products had an Edgecumbe roller-bearing action, but this was subsequently replaced by a reworked standard action. Hogue grips were fitted as standard.

Silenced Weapons

Guns produce a noise upon firing for two main reasons: first, the sudden rapid expansion of hot propellant gases into the air as the bullet emerges from the end of the barrel; second, the sonic boom produced by the bullet as it breaks the sound barrier. A typical silencer concentrates on the first issue only and consists of two sections: a forward expansion chamber situated just in front of the muzzle, then a section fitted with a series of baffles with a hole through the center to allow the passage of the bullet.

When the gun is fired, the muzzle gases first emerge from the muzzle into the expansion chamber where they lose some of their energy. (Criminals have improvised expansion chambers using empty plastic drink bottles to form temporary, though surprisingly effective, silencers.) On some silencers, the expansion chamber contains a cylinder of wire mesh to further fragment the gas movement and also draw off some the gas heat. After passing through the expansion chamber, the bullet then travels through the baffled section, each baffled section slowing, cooling, and deflecting the gases so that when they finally emerge from the silencer, they have a dramatically reduced noise signature. Some extremely modern "wet-type" silencers even contain water or lubricating oil to effect a heat transfer between the gas and the liquid. Other silencer types also slow the velocity of the bullet by porting off gas through vents in the side of the silencer. Silenced pistols are generally used with subsonic ammunition to negate the sound of the bullet passing through the sound barrier. Note that silencers are generally applied to automatic handguns rather than revolvers. Revolvers create some of their noise signature through the escape of gases between the cylinder and the barrel, not just at the muzzle.

Although in use in military special operations units and the criminal fraternity, silencers on pistols have not achieved widespread use because of the bulk they add to a weapon, their limited durability, and the deterioration in bullet performance. Most silencers in use today are applied to hunting rifles.

Above: *Beloved of the movies, the ideal silencer is nevertheless not available because the more effective it is, to some extent, the less effective is the bullet. Weapons such as those pictured were supplied to the OSS and SOE in World War II. Clockwise from top left: the Liberator single-shot 0.45 designed for partisans, with packing case and instructions; Welrod 9 mm single-shot silenced pistol; High Standard Model H-D 0.22 semi-automatic pistol; High Standard Model B 0.22 semi-automatic pistol.*

UNITED KINGDOM

PETER WEST "EXCELSIOR"/"SOUVERAIN" REVOLVER 1961

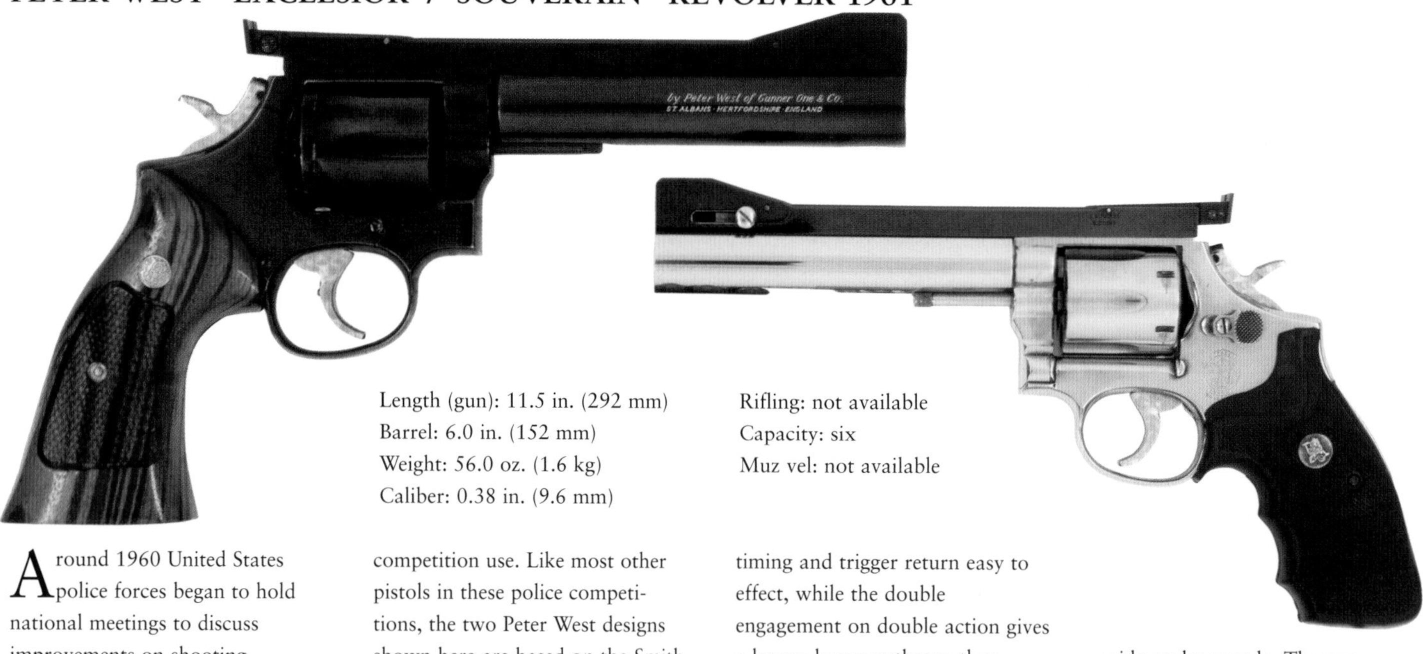

Length (gun): 11.5 in. (292 mm)
Barrel: 6.0 in. (152 mm)
Weight: 56.0 oz. (1.6 kg)
Caliber: 0.38 in. (9.6 mm)
Rifling: not available
Capacity: six
Muz vel: not available

Around 1960 United States police forces began to hold national meetings to discuss improvements on shooting techniques and this led to the idea of competitions with the intention of such improvement. Then the "experts" became involved, rules were written, and designers started to design handguns specifically for competition use. Like most other pistols in these police competitions, the two Peter West designs shown here are based on the Smith & Wesson Model 586/686, which was chosen because of its excellent mechanical design. This mechanism is comparatively straightforward to work on, with the crucial adjustments of cylinder timing and trigger return easy to effect, while the double engagement on double action gives a longer hammer throw, thus allowing a somewhat softer mainspring to be used. Both weapons have the Smith & Wesson frame and mechanism, coupled to a 6.0 in. (152 mm) long Douglas barrel, which is 1.0 in. (25 mm) wide at the muzzle. The two weapons differ slightly in their sighting arrangements, and the Excelsior (see specifications) is blued with wooden grips, while the Souverain is of polished steel finish with Pachmayr grips.

UNITED KINGDOM

STERLING 9 MM MARK VII PISTOL 1961

Length (gun): 14.8 in. (375 mm)
Barrel: 4.0 in. (102 mm)
Weight: 88.0 oz. (2.5 kg)
Caliber: 9 mm
Rifling: 6 grooves, r/hand
Capacity: ten-round box magazine (see below)
Muz vel: 984 ft./sec. (300 m/sec.)

This weapon was developed from the Sterling submachine gun, the essential differences being a much shorter barrel (4.0 in./ 102 mm compared to 7.8 in./ 198 mm) and the lack of a buttstock. The Mark VII fired the 9 mm Parabellum round and, as issued, it had a ten-round magazine, although the housing accepted the usual twenty- and thirty-four-round magazines as well. The Mark VII fired from a closed bolt and was recoil operated. The Mark VII had many shortcomings as a pistol and offered no advantages over the submachine gun version. The sights are the same as on the submachine gun, consisting of a square post foresight and a flip-over aperture backsight.

SWITZERLAND

HÄMMERLI MODEL 207 OLYMPIA TARGET PISTOL 1964

Length (gun): 12.9 in. (328 mm)
Barrel: 7.1 in. (180 mm)
Weight: 39.0 oz. (1.1 kg)
Caliber: 0.22 in.
Rifling: not available
Capacity: 8-round internal magazine
Muz vel: not available

The Hämmerli 200-series owed its origins to the Walther Olympia pistol, used by the German team in the 1936 Berlin Olympics; it was the starting point for the Hämmerli Model 200, introduced in 1952. This led to Model 207. For many years the gun used in the UIT Rapid Fire competition was one or other of the Hämmerli 200-series. The Model 207 is semiautomatic, using the propellant gases to drive the spent cartridge case rearward, and is fitted with a square post foresight and a square notch backsight, which is click adjustable for elevation and windage. The design objective in all Rapid Fire pistols is to minimize the muzzle lift caused by recoil forces on discharge. One way of achieving this is to carry a barrel weight, and the Hämmerli Model 207 carries quite a heavy one. In addition, there is a series of ports drilled through the top of the barrel down into the bore, through which peak pressure gases are vented upward as the bullet travels down the bore.

UNITED STATES

SMITH & WESSON MODEL 57 REVOLVER 1964

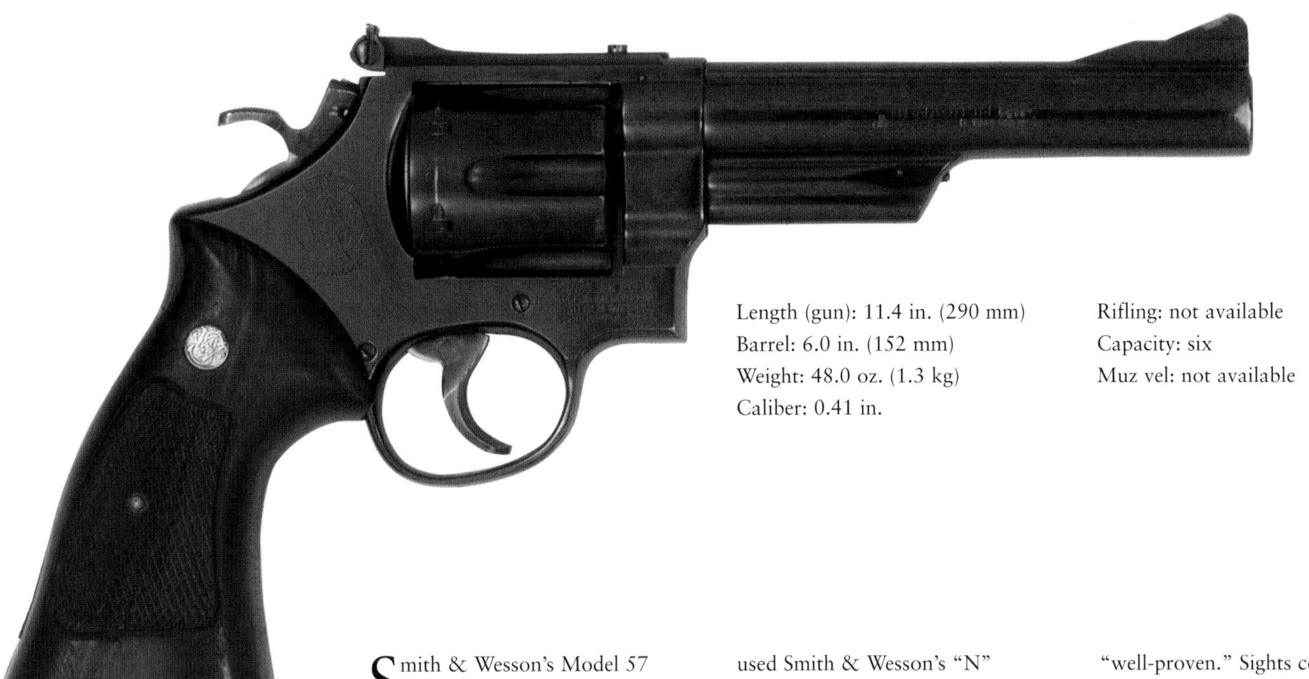

Length (gun): 11.4 in. (290 mm)
Barrel: 6.0 in. (152 mm)
Weight: 48.0 oz. (1.3 kg)
Caliber: 0.41 in.
Rifling: not available
Capacity: six
Muz vel: not available

Smith & Wesson's Model 57 was fielded in 1964 to introduce the 0.41 Magnum round, and apart from the caliber was virtually identical to the Model 29 of 1957. Both weapons used Smith & Wesson's "N" frame, which dated from 1907, when it was used in the New Century revolver and it seems safe to say that by the late 1950s the design could be described as "well-proven." Sights comprised a square ramp foresight with red inset and a square notch backsight, click adjustable for both elevation and windage.

UNITED STATES

HARRINGTON AND RICHARDSON DEFENDER POCKET REVOLVER 1964

Length (gun): 8.8 in. (222 mm)
Barrel: 4.0 in. (102 mm)
Weight: 23.0 oz. (0.7 kg)
Caliber: 0.38 in. (9.6 mm)
Rifling: 7 grooves, r/hand
Capacity: six
Muz vel: 625 ft./sec. (190 m/sec.)

The weapon illustrated here had the trade name of "Defender." There were, in fact, several versions, with a variety of butts, calibers, and barrel lengths: this one is the 0.38 in. (9.6 mm) caliber version with a plain butt. The shape of the barrel is somewhat difficult to characterize: it is basically round, but has flattened sides and a very solid top rib, with a round foresight slotted in. The weapon was opened in the same way as a Smith & Wesson, by pushing up a T-shaped catch: this allowed the barrel to be forced downward and brought the automatic ejector into action. Although basically a pocket arm, it has a very large butt; this, although bulky, provided a very comfortable grip. The butt is of one-piece construction and is held to the weapon by a screw that passes through the back of the butt and into the tang. The revolver is of plain but robust construction.

UNITED STATES

THOMPSON/CENTER CONTENDER TARGET PISTOL 1967

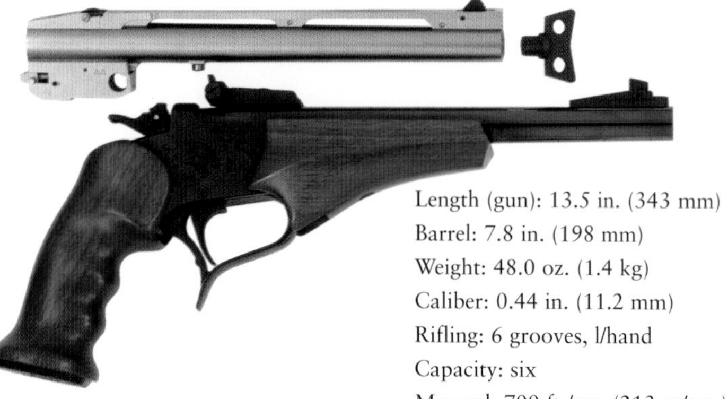

Length (gun): 13.5 in. (343 mm)
Barrel: 7.8 in. (198 mm)
Weight: 48.0 oz. (1.4 kg)
Caliber: 0.44 in. (11.2 mm)
Rifling: 6 grooves, l/hand
Capacity: six
Muz vel: 700 ft./sec. (213 m/sec.)

This remarkable pistol was introduced by Ken Thompson and Warren Center in 1967 as a highly specialized single-shot pistol for competition. Sales were initially poor, being confined mainly to ballistics experts who needed a test bed. By the early 1990s, however, nearly half-a-million had been sold. It owes its popularity to a number of factors, including the great flexibility of the design in which barrels can be changed with ease. It is a single-action, break-open pistol, in which forward pressure on the trigger guard spur releases the barrel to hinge down from the frame. There is a vast range of barrels for different calibers. Thompson/Center itself produces twenty-three different chamberings, but other manufacturers offer many more. Top is 0.45 in. Colt/0.410 in. shotshell chambering and screw-in choke-type key.

GERMANY

WALTHER 0.25 IN. TPH POCKET PISTOL 1969

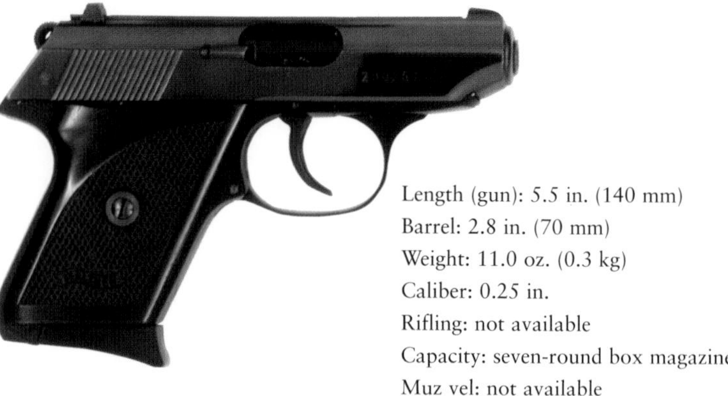

Length (gun): 5.5 in. (140 mm)
Barrel: 2.8 in. (70 mm)
Weight: 11.0 oz. (0.3 kg)
Caliber: 0.25 in.
Rifling: not available
Capacity: seven-round box magazine
Muz vel: not available

The Walther Taschenpistole mit Hahn (pocket pistol with hammer), introduced in 1969, is a short, stubby pistol of the traditional "vest pocket" variety, but built to very modern standards. It is normally chambered for the 0.25 in. ACP round, although 0.22 in. LR is also available. It has a fixed barrel and is blowback operated without any provision for "cocked-and-locked" carry. There is an outside hammer, with a hammer trip safety on the left-hand side. Sights are square post foresight, square notch backsight. Both foresight and backsight have white dots for low-light use and the weapon is remarkably accurate at ranges up to 100 yd. (91 m).

GERMANY

HECKLER & KOCH VP-70 1970

Length (gun): 8.6 in. (218 mm)
Barrel: 4.5 in. (114 mm)
Weight: 34.5 oz. (1.0 kg)
Caliber: 9 mm
Rifling: 6 grooves, r/hand
Capacity: eighteen
Muz vel: 1,100 ft./sec. (335 m/sec.)

Heckler & Koch was established at Oberndorf-Neckar as soon as the manufacture of arms was again permitted in Germany after World War II. It quickly established a reputation for military firearms. This is the VP-70, a blowback weapon that fires a 9 mm Parabellum cartridge of considerable power. The lock is of double-action pattern only, but in order to facilitate deliberate shooting, it is fitted with a type of hesitation lock. This allows a pause between a fairly heavy first-pressure cocking and a much lighter second pressure on the trigger for actual firing. This system makes it safe to carry the pistol with a round in the chamber: a safety catch is not normally fitted. The gun is fitted with a detachable holster-stock; when this is attached, the weapon can be used either for single shots or three-round bursts. The merit of this system is that the bullets are clear of the barrel before the muzzle has a chance to rise, thus removing the basic disadvantage of the so-called machine pistol. The VP-70 magazine accommodates eighteen rounds, and although this can only be achieved by staggering the rounds, it does not make the butt unduly bulky.

GERMANY

HECKLER & KOCH 9 MM P7 SERIES 1970

Length (gun): 6.8 in. (171 mm)
Barrel: 4.2 in. (105 mm)
Weight: 27.0 oz. (0.8 kg)
Caliber: 9 mm
Rifling: 4 grooves, r/hand
Capacity: See below
Muz vel: 1,155 ft./sec. (350 m/sec.)

Heckler & Koch's P7 series uses a gas-retarded blowback system; a proportion of the propellant gas is bled through a port immediately ahead of the chamber into an expansion chamber beneath the barrel, where it acts against a piston attached to the nose of the slide, retarding the slide's rearward movement. As soon as the bullet leaves the muzzle, the pressure inside the barrel drops and the gas seeps back into the barrel, enabling the slide to continue its rearward journey, ejecting the used case and loading the next round. Cocking is achieved by squeezing the lever, which runs the length of the forward face of the butt: recocking is then automatic for as long as the lever remains depressed; releasing it decocks the piece. No separate safety lever is required. There are five weapons in the P7 series: P7 m8 (above) and P7 m13 differ only in their magazine capacities, eight and thirteen, respectively; the P7K3 is the smallest, has a blowback action, and fires 9 mm Parabellum, but can be converted to fire 0.22 in. LR or 0.32 in. (7.65 mm) ACP; the P7 m10 fires 0.40 in. Smith & Wesson; the P7 m7 fires 0.45 in. ACP and employs a unique oil-buffered delay system.

UNITED STATES

COLT 0.45 IN. MODEL 15 GENERAL OFFICERS' PISTOL 1972

Length (gun): 7.9 in. (200 mm)
Barrel: 4.2 in. (106 mm)
Weight: 35.0 oz. (1.0 kg)
Caliber: 0.45 in. (11.4 mm)
Rifling: 6 grooves, l/hand
Capacity: seven-round box magazine
Muz vel: 800 ft./sec. (245 m/sec.)

The United States Army has a tradition of issuing personal weapons to its general officers and from the 1940s to the early 1970s this was the Colt 0.38 in. Pocket Automatic. Production of this weapon ended in 1946 and by the late 1960s there were few remaining in stock; as a result a requirement was issued in 1972 for a replacement, which had to be small and unobtrusive, but effective in emergencies. The winning design came from Rock Island Arsenal and is an M1911 A1 which has been dismantled and rebuilt with all dimensions reduced, operating in the same way as the original. The slide is inscribed in italic script on the left side with "General Officer Model" with the abbreviation "RIA" (Rock Island Arsenal) below. On the grip the left panel has a small inlaid brass plate upon which is inscribed the holder's name, and on the right grip is the badge of Rock Island Arsenal. The pistol was in production from 1972 to 1984. The barrel is somewhat shorter than that of the M1911 A1, but since the same 0.45 in. ACP round is used, this results in greater flash, bang, and muzzle blast, which some observers might consider to be appropriate to the rank of the users.

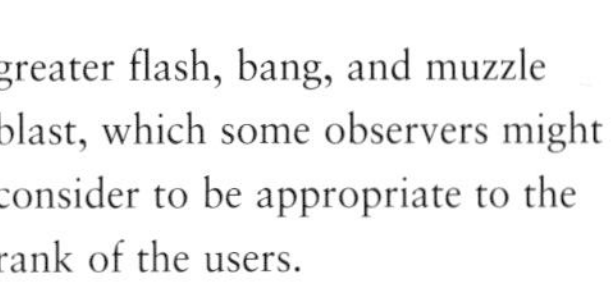

GERMANY

HECKLER & KOCH 9 MM P9/P9S PISTOL 1972

Length (gun): 7.7 in. (192 mm)
Barrel: 4.1 in. (102 mm)
Weight: 31.0 oz. (0.9 kg)
Caliber: 9 mm
Rifling: 4 grooves, r/hand
Capacity: nine-round box magazine
Muz vel: 386 ft./sec. (351 m/sec.)

In the late 1960s, Heckler & Koch undertook a major re-examination of current pistol design, which resulted in the 1972 announcement of the company's P9S, which adapted the roller-locked bolt of its G3 rifle and MP submachine gun to the configuration of a reliable delayed blow-back system of operation. The P9S has a concealed double-action hammer, with an indicator pin that protrudes when the hammer is cocked, and a decocking lever in the right front of the butt group. The P9S pistol has polygonal rifling, which is claimed to reduce deformation of the bullet, thus increasing the muzzle velocity, while the absence of corners at the bottom of the grooves means less fouling accumulation and improvements in accuracy. The P9S was adopted by the *Bundes-grenzschutzpolizei* (German Border Police) and numerous other police and paramilitary forces, and while production has ended in Germany, it continues under license in Greece. The basic model was the double-action lock P9S in 9 mm; another version, the P9 was single-action. A few were chambered for 7.65 mm Parabellum, while the export version, intended primarily for the U.S., was chambered for 0.45 in., in which case the magazine held only seven rounds and muzzle velocity was reduced to 286 ft./sec. (260 m/sec.).

ITALY

FABBRICA ARMI SPORTIVE (FAS) MODEL 601 COMPETITION PISTOL 1972

Length (gun): 11.3 in. (287 mm)
Barrel: 6.0 in. (152 mm)
Weight: 40.0 oz. (1.1 kg)
Caliber: 0.22 in.
Rifling: not available
Capacity: five-round box magazine
Muz vel: not available

This weapon was originally marketed in the early 1970s as the IGI Domino, but was then modified and renamed the Fabbrica Armi Sportive (FAS) Model 601. It is a very sophisticated weapon and was one of the first of the new generation of low bore axis competition pistols. Early examples were plagued by parts breakages and it took several years fully to debug the design; thereafter, however, it became a top-level competition gun. The Model 601 is a semi-automatic, blowback-operated competition pistol chambered for the 0.22 in. Short cartridge. Notable developments include significantly greater hand support, a more steeply raked grip, and a much lower bore line, which significantly reduces muzzle torque on recoil. It also dispenses with the muzzle brake fitted on the earlier model, but introduces large ports running the length of the barrel, with the venting adjustable by plug screws.

POLAND

BRITARMS MODEL 2000 PISTOL 1972

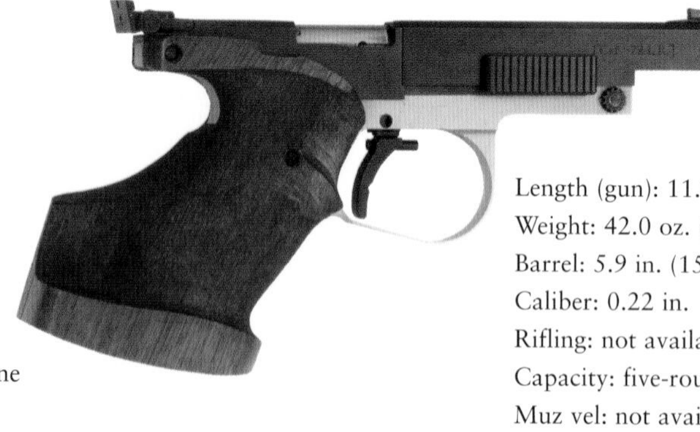

Length (gun): 11.0 in. (280 mm)
Weight: 42.0 oz. (1.2 kg)
Barrel: 5.9 in. (150 mm)
Caliber: 0.22 in.
Rifling: not available
Capacity: five-round box magazine
Muz vel: not available

The Britarms Model 2000 was designed by Chris Valentine in the early 1970s as a state-of-the-art Standard Pistol and may be broadly be described as an upmarket equivalent of the FabBrica Armi Sportive Model 601 (FAS). The Model 2000 is a sophisticated design, rendered in the finest steels, and is highly regarded, although the firm was plagued for over a decade by changes of ownership and low volume production, and as a result it took longer than usual to work the bugs out of this fascinating design. It is a semi-automatic, blow-back weapon, firing from an unlocked breech, using gas pressure in the bore to act on the cartridge case, which then acts as a piston to drive the slide to the rear. It is of all steel construction, machined from the solid. Sights are square post foresight and square notch backsight.

UNITED STATES

RUGER 0.45 IN. "OLD ARMY" PERCUSSION REVOLVER 1972

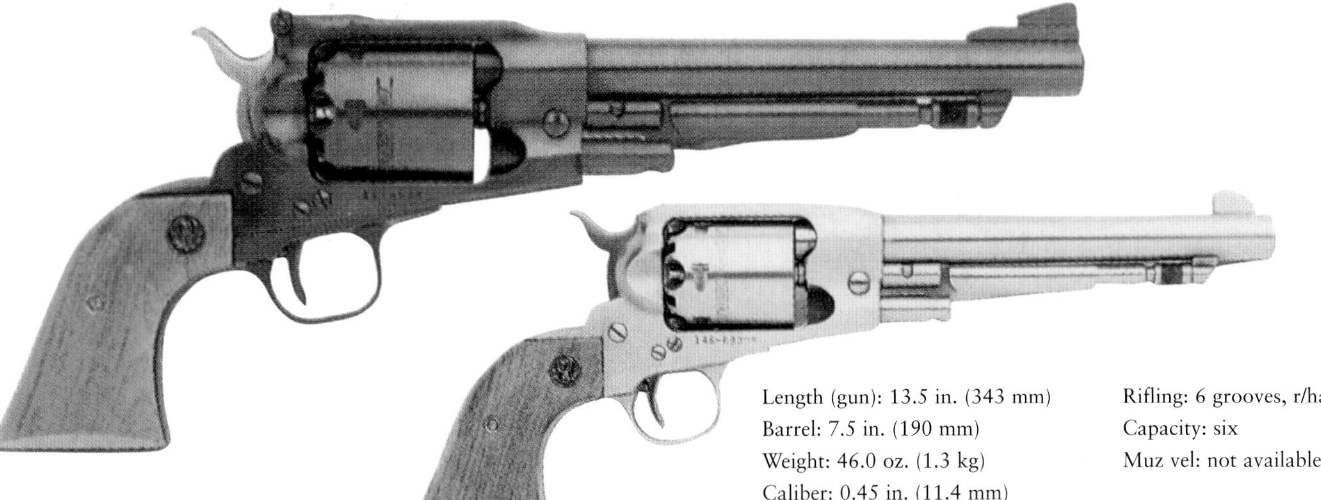

Length (gun): 13.5 in. (343 mm)
Barrel: 7.5 in. (190 mm)
Weight: 46.0 oz. (1.3 kg)
Caliber: 0.45 in. (11.4 mm)
Rifling: 6 grooves, r/hand
Capacity: six
Muz vel: not available

This splendid "cap-and-ball" weapon is a re-creation of the Colt Model 1860 Army Percussion Revolver, but manufactured to modern standards of precision, tolerance, and finish. The unique rammer and base-pin assembly allows easy disassembly without the need for tools, because the base-pin, loading-lever, and rammer are held together by an interlocking arrangement instead of pins or screws. When the cylindrical loading lever catch is engaged with the stud on the barrel lug, the loading lever is locked both laterally and vertically, thus preventing any sideways movement. The nipples are deeply recessed to prevent cap fragments from flying to the side. There are four weapons in the series, all of 0.44 in. caliber: two have adjustable sights and two have fixed sights, with a choice of either blued or stainless steel finish; all have American walnut stock grips. Shown here are the blued finish, adjustable-sight version (above); and the stainless steel finish, fixed-sight version (below).

UNITED STATES

RUGER NEW MODEL BLACKHAWK/SUPER BLACKHAWK REVOLVER 1973

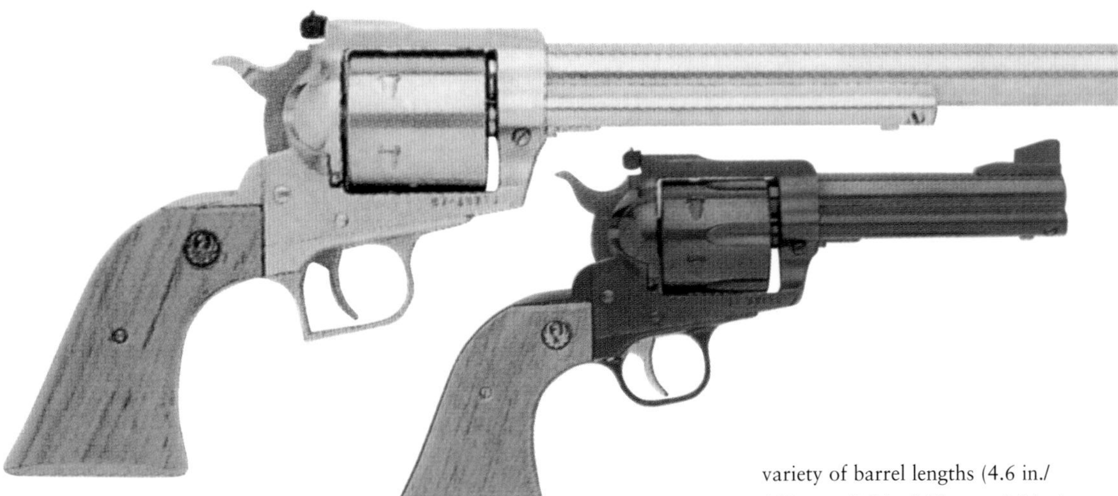

(0.44 in. Magnum version)
Length (gun): 13.4 in. (340 mm)
Barrel: 7.5 in. (191 mm)
Weight: 48.0 oz. (1.4 kg)
Caliber: 0.44 in. (11.2 mm)
Rifling: not available
Capacity: six
Muz vel: not available

The "New Model" range with an interlocking system was known as the "transfer bar mechanism," which ensures an unprecedented degree of safety even though all six chambers are carried loaded. The loading gate freezes the hammer and releases the cylinder for loading and unloading. There is an "1873-pattern" sprung ejector rod in a housing on the lower right side of the barrel. The New Model Blackhawk range covers three calibers: 0.30 in. Carbine (one model), 0.357 in. Magnum (six models), and 0.45 in. Long Colt (seven models). These feature a variety of barrel lengths (4.6 in./117 mm, 5.5 in./140 mm, 6.5 in./165 mm, and 7.5 in./190 mm) and a choice of blued or stainless steel finishes. One model, the New Model Blackhawk Convertible, has two cylinders, one for 0.357 in. Magnum, the other for 9 mm, which can be exchanged without any tools or changes to the weapon. There are eight models in the New Model Super Blackhawk range, all in 0.44 in. Magnum, with a choice of cylinder and styles and round or square-backed trigger guards. Shown are: the New Model Super Blackhawk with 10.5 in. (267 mm) barrel, unfluted cylinder, and square-backed trigger guard (top); and the Blackhawk Convertible (bottom), which can fire either 0.357 in. or 9 mm Parabellum simply by changing the cylinder.

HUNGARY

FEGYVERGYAR FEG P9R 1973

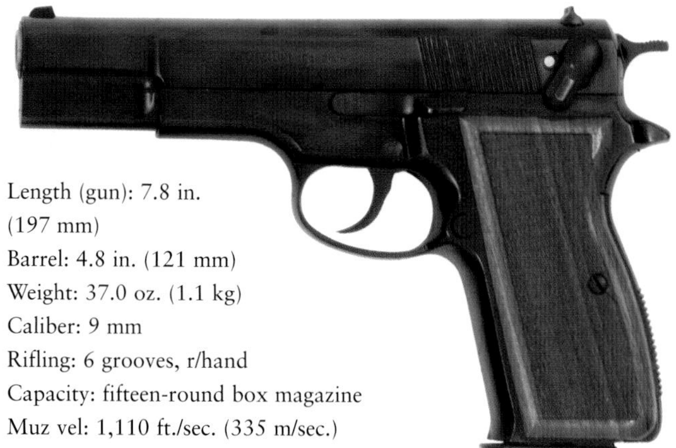

Length (gun): 7.8 in. (197 mm)
Barrel: 4.8 in. (121 mm)
Weight: 37.0 oz. (1.1 kg)
Caliber: 9 mm
Rifling: 6 grooves, r/hand
Capacity: fifteen-round box magazine
Muz vel: 1,110 ft./sec. (335 m/sec.)

The Hungarian State Arsenal carried out an exercise in "reverse engineering" in the 1970s. They started producing copies of Fabrique Nationale's 9 mm GP35 (Browning High Power) under the designation FEG 9; indeed, the copies were so precise that many of the parts were interchangeable. This was offered to, but rejected by, the Hungarian Army, as a result of which the FEG 9 was offered for sale commercially in both Eastern and Western Europe. This was followed by the FEG 9R, which was essentially the same pistol, but with a number of significant modifications. This involved deleting the GP25's transverse cam bar, camming the barrel into lockup with the back of the recoil spring guide rod, which is secured in place by the slide latch crosspin. The P9R has a steel frame, while the otherwise identical P9RA has a light alloy frame, making it some 6.3 oz. (180 g) lighter.

UNITED STATES

COLT 0.22 IN. NEW FRONTIER REVOLVER 1973

Length (gun): 9.9 in. (251 mm)
Barrel: 4.4 in. (111 mm)
Weight: 29.5 oz. (0.8)
Caliber: 0.22 in. (5.6 mm)
Rifling: not available
Capacity: six
Muz vel: not available

Another purpose-built 0.22 in. revolver, this is basically a 7/8th scale model of the Single-Action Army, which was introduced in 1973 and given the name "New Frontier" in tribute to John F. Kennedy's campaign slogan. One difference from the original Single-Action Army was that the New Frontier had an up-dated mechanism, with gate loading and rod ejection and a frame-mounted floating firing pin. Construction was of steel, with blight alloy grip straps and trigger guard. It was fitted with a ramp foresight and a click adjustable square-notch backsight. Apart from 0.22 in. Long Rifle form, the New Frontier was also available in 0.22 in. Magnum, and with 6.0 in. (152 mm) or 7.5 in. (191 mm) barrels.

UNITED STATES

CHARTER ARMS 0.44 IN. BULLDOG REVOLVER 1973

Length (gun): 7.6 in. (193 mm)
Barrel: 3.0 in. (76 mm)
Weight: 24.0 oz. (0.7 kg)
Caliber: 0.44 in. (11.2 mm)
Rifling: not available
Capacity: five
Muz vel: not available

Practice aside, the 0.44 in. Special round's primary modern role is defensive, and the gun most frequently selected by American users in the 1970s and 1980s was the Charter Arms Bulldog. This was introduced in 1973 and proved to be a great success, with well over half-a-million made in the mid-1980s, with production running at some 37,000 per year. It is a selective double-action weapon with an outside hammer and a solid frame (of stainless steel in the picture above), with a thumb latch on the left which releases the crane-mounted cylinder to swing out to the left for loading and unloading. There is a square concave foresight and a square notch backsight milled into the top of the receiver. The Bulldog makes an interesting comparison with the 0.44 in. Smith & Wesson "Horton Special."

HANDGUNS AND FORENSICS

Above: *This is not a forensic scientist at work, but in fact a tester at the Swiss target pistol company of Hämmerli. A similar setup is required by forensics. While the firer here is checking the grouping of the target pistol, the ballistics expert collects information about the rifling on the bullet and characteristic deformations of the cartridge.*

Whenever a firearm is used in a crime in developed countries, a complex forensic operation attempts to identify the characteristics of the firearm used and apply this information to the tracking or the prosecution of the criminal. If the weapon is not available, then the bullets themselves will be the primary route of inquiry. The first stage in analyzing a spent bullet is to pattern the rifling. Although bullets, even those fired from relatively low-velocity handguns, move at incredible speeds down the barrel, the expansion of the bullet under high gas pressure against the rifling means that there will be a negative impression of the grooves in the bullet wall. These impressions are most visible on metal-jacketed ball rounds that have suffered minimal distortion upon impact with the target, but may be entirely obscured when bullets are heavily damaged, as is often the case with hollow-point rounds.

By identifying the rifling type, the forensic scientist will often be able to match the bullet against a database of known rifling configurations, and so move closer to identifying the weapon. Because of minute imperfections in the rifling—which also leave their mark on the bullet—the forensic scientist may be able to match the bullet with a specific gun.

As well as the bullets, empty cartridge cases provide further vital clues to identify the weapon. Cartridge cases from handguns bear distinctive minute markings on the surface caused by the breech, firing pin, magazine lips, and feed, extractor, and ejector.

For example, the incredible pressure under which a cartridge is forced back against the breech when fired results in minute impressions from the breech face being left in the base of the cartridge. Extractors and ejectors, by contrast, make striations and gouging marks on the rim and the head of the case.

All information gleaned from bullet or case is compared against a database and repository of existing ammunition types. The FBI, for example, keeps samples of every US ammunition type fired from hundreds of different weapons into water so that there is no distortion of the round, and clear rifling patterns are preserved. Known and questioned rounds are compared microscopically until a match is secured.

BRAZIL

TAURUS MAGNUM MODEL 86 REVOLVER 1975

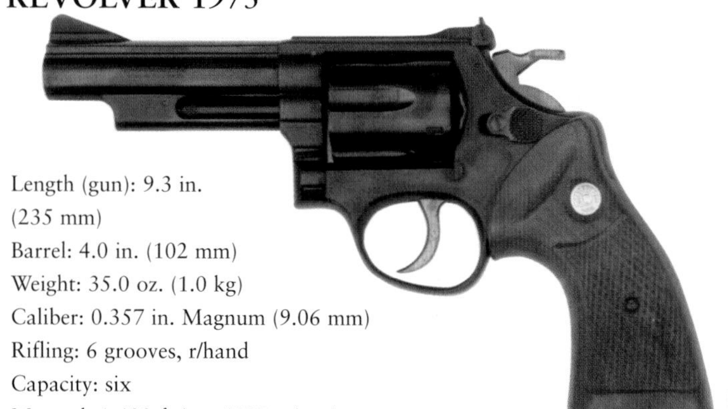

Length (gun): 9.3 in. (235 mm)
Barrel: 4.0 in. (102 mm)
Weight: 35.0 oz. (1.0 kg)
Caliber: 0.357 in. Magnum (9.06 mm)
Rifling: 6 grooves, r/hand
Capacity: six
Muz vel: 1,400 ft./sec. (427 m/sec.)

The weapon illustrated was manufactured by Taurus of Brazil, who began to make revolvers of this caliber in 1975. It is of solid-frame type and has a round barrel with a very wide top rib; the foresight is of ramp type and the arm is fitted with a micrometer backsight, the whole sighting plane being milled to reduce reflection. The cylinder holds six cartridges, the ends of the chambers being recessed to enclose the cartridge heads, and it swings out to the left on its own separate yoke. It has the usual pin-operated extractor; the pin is located in a housing beneath the barrel when the cylinder is in position. There is a separate firing-pin in the standing breech, and the hammer has a wide, flat comb for ease of cocking. Small white-metal medallions in the butt are marked "Taurus Brasil," with a bull's head in the center.

RUSSIA

MARGOLIN "VOSTOK" MTs 0.22 IN. SELF-LOADING TARGET PISTOL 1975

Length (gun): 10.9 in. (276 mm)
Barrel: 7.4 in. (187 mm)
Weight: 37.0 oz. (1.0 kg)
Caliber: 0.22 in.
Rifling: not available
Capacity: six-round box magazine
Muz vel: not available

As competition pistols became more sophisticated and expensive, club-level shooters, particularly in Britain, turned to less expensive weapons. One of the most highly regarded of these was the Russian MTs pistol, not only relatively cheap but also of very high quality. In those Cold War days, even the place of manufacture of a target pistol was highly classified by the Soviet authorities, but British shooters believed that the MTs was built at the State Armaments factory at Tula; what they did not know was that the MTs was designed by a blind man, Mikhail Margolin, a remarkable achievement. The MTs was blowback-operated using an unlocked breech, and had an external hammer. It had a square foresight blade, which was click adjustable for elevation, and a U-notch backsight, click adjustable for windage.

SWITZERLAND

SIG-SAUER 9 MM P-220 (MODEL 1975) PISTOL

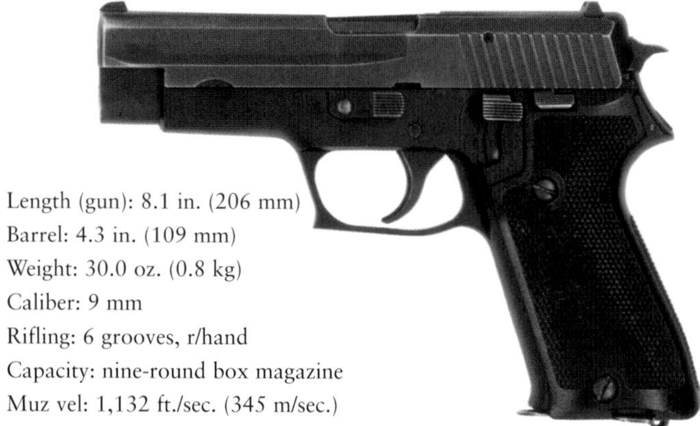

Length (gun): 8.1 in. (206 mm)
Barrel: 4.3 in. (109 mm)
Weight: 30.0 oz. (0.8 kg)
Caliber: 9 mm
Rifling: 6 grooves, r/hand
Capacity: nine-round box magazine
Muz vel: 1,132 ft./sec. (345 m/sec.)

The P-220 is built on a rugged aluminum frame and uses a heavy-gauge stamped slide with a welded nosepiece. The breechblock is a separate machined part keyed into the slide and retained by a rollpin. It is made in a variety of calibers: 9 x 19 mm Parabellum, 7.65 mm Parabellum, 0.45 in. ACP, and 0.38 in. Super. There are three controls on the left of the frame: slide latch, decocking lever, and disassembly lever. The P-200 series conforms to a 1975 requirement of the West German police for a self-loading pistol that could be carried safely, but fired without disengaging a manual safety. Pulling the slide to the rear and releasing it chambers a round and cocks the action. Pressing the decocking lever raises the sear from the hammer, which rotates under pressure from a spring until the sear engages the safety notch, holding the hammer clear of the firing pin. The firing pin is held down by a locking pin.

SWITZERLAND

SIG-SAUER 9 MM P-225 PISTOL 1975

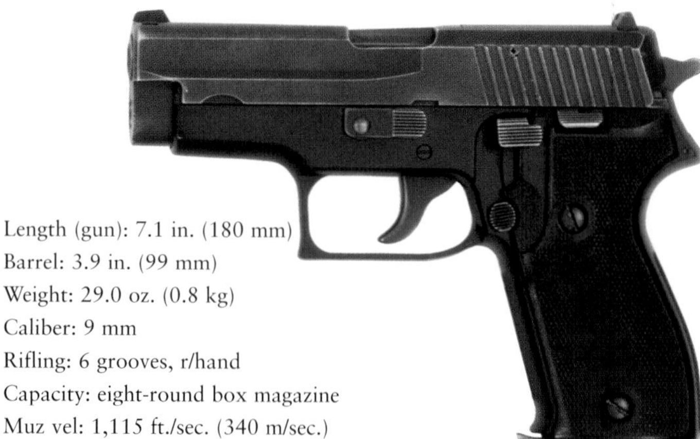

Length (gun): 7.1 in. (180 mm)
Barrel: 3.9 in. (99 mm)
Weight: 29.0 oz. (0.8 kg)
Caliber: 9 mm
Rifling: 6 grooves, r/hand
Capacity: eight-round box magazine
Muz vel: 1,115 ft./sec. (340 m/sec.)

The P-225 is a foreshortened and redesigned version of the P-220 (left). In the competition to meet that requirement the SIG P-225 competed against weapons from Mauser, Walther, and Heckler & Koch and was the only one to pass the 10,000-round test. It was then ordered by the West German police (to whom it is known as the P6) and set the pattern for the new generation of pistols. It is almost totally safe to carry with a round in the chamber, but can be used instantly, without having to disengage latches, and requires only pressure on the trigger to shoot. The controls on the left of the receiver are the slide hold-open (rearmost), then the decocking lever that lets the hammer down safely, and beneath that the push-button magazine release, while in the center of the weapon is the stripping (takedown) lever. The single-stack eight-round magazine offers a comfortable, compact grip.

ITALY

BERETTA MODEL 81 7.65 MM PISTOL 1976

Length (gun): 6.8 in. (171 mm)
Barrel: 3.8 in. (95 mm)
Weight: 24.0 oz. (0.7 kg)
Caliber: 7.65 mm
Rifling: 6 grooves, r/hand
Capacity: twelve-round box magazine
Muz vel: 985 ft./sec. (300 m/sec.)

In 1976 Beretta put no fewer than three new pistols into production: Model 81, Model 84, and Model 92. The Model 81 fires the 7.65 mm cartridge and operates on the straight-forward blowback principle. The slide is pulled to the rear manually, which cocks the hammer, and on release the slide is driven forward by the recoil spring, chambering a round as it moves. The recoil from the fired case thrusts the slide to the rear, compressing the recoil spring as it does so, and allows the firing cycle to continue. When the slide is forward and the pistol ready to fire, the extractor protrudes slightly from the side in order to give the firer a visual indication of the weapon's readiness to fire. There is also a manual safety, which can be operated by either left or right hand. The pistol has a double-column magazine, which holds twelve rounds and is virtually identical with that of the Model 84, except that it has long deep grooves along each side to hold the smaller rounds.

ITALY

BERETTA MODEL 84 9 MM PISTOL 1976

Length (gun): 6.8 in. (171 mm)
Barrel: 3.8 in. (95 mm)
Weight: 22.0 oz. (0.6 kg)
Caliber: 9 mm
Rifling: 6 grooves, r/hand
Capacity: 13-round box magazine
Muz vel: 920 ft./sec. (280 m/sec.)

The second in this series of Beretta pistols, the Model 84 is chambered to fire the 9 mm short cartridge and, since this is a relatively low-powered round, the weapon works on the simple blowback principle, without any requirement for breech locking. Manual retraction of the slide cocks the hammer and chambers a round on its forward motion. The recoil from the fired case thrusts the slide to the rear, compressing the recoil spring as it does so, and allows the firing cycle to continue. When the slide is forward and the pistol is ready to fire, the extractor protrudes slightly from the side in order to give the firer a visual indication of the weapon's readiness to fire. There is also a manual safety, which can be operated by either left or right hand. The pistol has a double-column magazine, but without the long grooves which characterize the magazine of the Model 81.

Both Models 81 and 84 have anodized aluminum frames, and are very reliable mechanically.

Competition Handgun Shooting

Above: *Sydney Olympics, 2000: twelve years after winning his first gold medal, Tanyu Kiriakov of Bulgaria added a second, this time around in the men's 50-meter pistol competition. Kiriakov, a gold medalist in the 10-meter air pistol at the Seoul Games in 1988, won the 50-meter event with 666 points.*

The world of competitive pistol shooting is one of diverse disciplines, ranging from the controlled practice of Free Pistol through to the combat shooting of Practical. Counting the full range of international disciplines lifts the number to well over 100. Despite the antiquity of handguns, many of the disciplines are of fairly recent date. Flintlock and Percussion Pistol, for example, dates only from the 1960s, Practical handgunning started in the late 1950s, while Handgun Metallic Silhouette competition was launched in the U.S. in 1971. However, the first regular handgun competitions began in the U.S. and UK during the mid to late 1800s.

In 1896 the first modern Olympics featured five different shooting events: Free Rifle (200 m), Free Rifle (300 m), Rapid-Fire Pistol (25 m), Military Revolver (25 m) and Free Pistol (50 m). The Rapid-Fire event was particularly exciting. The shooter faced a bank of six silhouettes at 25 m (82 ft.), and simply had to hit each target. Each competitor began by firing eighteen rounds (one shot per target on each of three ten-second exposures). Those with no misses then attempted a single pass of the targets at eight second exposures, then another at six seconds, and a final pass at four seconds. The times would be reduced, even down to two seconds, until a winner was left.

Today there are five main international standard pistol disciplines: Standard Pistol (25 m), Free Pistol (50 m), Rapid-Fire Pistol (25 m), Air Pistol (10 m) and Sport Pistol. Apart from the men's element of Sport Pistol, most of these events are shot with .22 caliber guns, either magazine-fed or single-shot. The shooters of Free Pistol use sophisticated .22 single-shot handguns with a wraparound grip that fits like a glove, and an electrical or multilever mechanical set trigger that can be adjusted to fractions of an ounce. During firing, the shooter is not allowed to use the free hand as a support; instead, it must be tucked into the belt or placed in a pocket.

Sporting handgun shooting has been hampered or curtailed in many European countries, particularly the UK, by stringent gun laws that prohibit the ownership of handguns over .22 caliber. However, shooting's status as an Olympic sport should ensure the continuity of pistol sports for the foreseeable future.

UNITED KINGDOM

ZIP GUNS 1970s

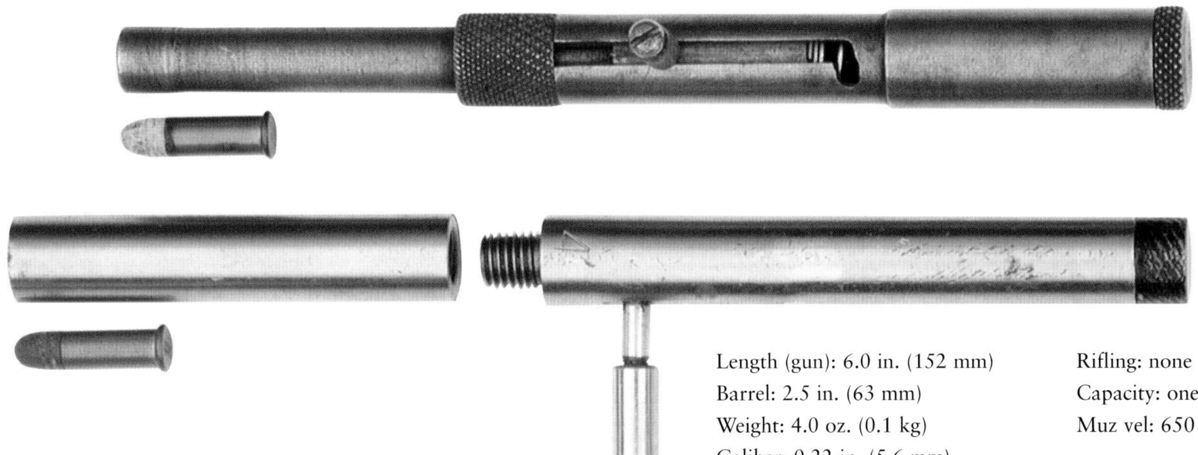

Length (gun): 6.0 in. (152 mm)
Barrel: 2.5 in. (63 mm)
Weight: 4.0 oz. (0.1 kg)
Caliber: 0.22 in. (5.6 mm)
Rifling: none
Capacity: one
Muz vel: 650 ft./sec. (198 m/sec.)

Homemade firearms are relatively common, and it is difficult to generalize about their genesis. The really difficult thing for an amateur gunsmith is to obtain a supply of modern cartridges, but if these can be obtained, it is relatively simple for anyone with some basic skills in the use of metal-working tools to produce a device from which they may be fired. Such improvised weapons are usually of a two-piece construction, with a smooth-bored screw-off barrel and a simple striker mechanism in the handle. Some, however, are more sophisticated: they may be disguised as pens, torches, screwdrivers, or some other apparently harmless piece of equipment. The two specimens illustrated here originated in Northern Ireland, where they were found in about 1976. The data given, of course, apply only to the arms shown; naturally, individual weapons vary considerably.

ITALY

BERETTA MODEL 92/92S 9 MM PISTOL 1976

Length (gun): 8.5 in. (217 mm)
Barrel: 4.9 in. (125 mm)
Weight: 35.0 oz. (1.0 kg)
Caliber: 9 mm
Rifling: 6 grooves, r/hand
Capacity: fifteen-round box magazine
Muz vel: 1,280 ft./sec. (390 m/sec.)

In the 1970s Beretta updated their Model 1951 to produce the Model 92; first fielded in 1976, this was taken into service by various armies and was also sold commercially under the trade name of "Brigadier." The Model 92 differed from the Model 1951 in having a double-action trigger and magazine capacity was increased from eight to thirteen, necessitating a somewhat bulkier butt. The powerful 9 mm Parabellum meant that the Model 92 needed a locked-breech mechanism, in which the rearward pressure of the fired case drove back the barrel and slide, which were locked together by a block. Having traveled about 0.3 in. (8 mm) the locking block pivoted downward to disengage from the slide, whereupon the barrel stopped but the slide continued to the rear to complete the reloading cycle. Next to appear was the Model 92S, identical to the Model 92 apart from the safety catch, which was situated on the slide instead of the frame and which could also be used as a decocking lever. Both the Model 92 and 92S were sold to numerous military and police users and remained in production until the mid-1980s.

UNITED STATES

DETONICS 0.45 IN. COMBAT MASTER MARK I PISTOL 1977

Length (gun): 7.0 in. (178 mm)
Barrel: 3.4 in. (87 mm)
Weight: 30.0 oz. (0.8 kg)
Caliber: 0.45 in.
Rifling: not available
Capacity: six-round box magazine
Muz vel: not available

In the mid-1960s Major George C. Nonte carried out a design exercise to investigate how far the Model 1911 A1 could be reduced in size and weight, while still remaining capable of firing a 0.45 in. ACP round. The Detonics Combat Master Mark I, which was introduced in 1977, draws on Nonte's experiences and is one of the smallest automatic 0.45 in. pistols ever built. It is of all-steel construction and is a single-action weapon with an outside hammer. It is recoil operated and the Colt/Browning-type link-unlocking barrel locks the ribs on the barrel top into corresponding recesses in the roof of the slide. It has a square post foresight and a square notch backsight that is drift-adjustable for windage. This was the first of the ultracompact production automatics and quickly established an excellent reputation.

UNITED STATES

RUGER REDHAWK/SUPER REDHAWK REVOLVER 1979

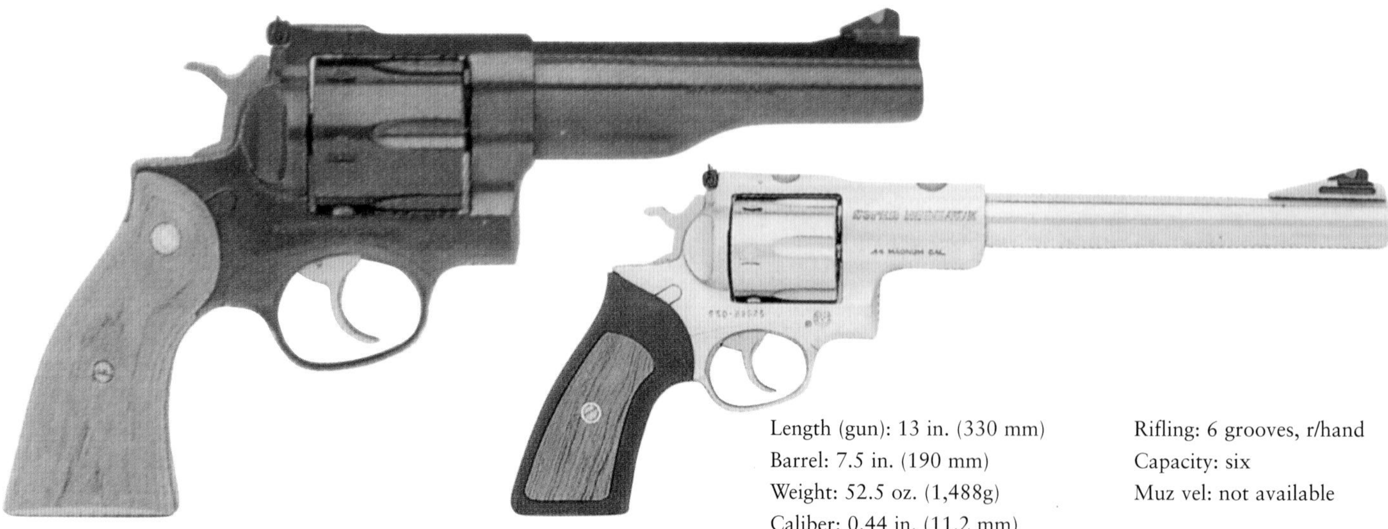

Length (gun): 13 in. (330 mm)
Barrel: 7.5 in. (190 mm)
Weight: 52.5 oz. (1,488g)
Caliber: 0.44 in. (11.2 mm)
Rifling: 6 grooves, r/hand
Capacity: six
Muz vel: not available

The Ruger Redhawk, which was introduced in 1979, was the first revolver designed to use the 0.44 in. Magnum round, and is a large and heavy handgun designed for hunting, particularly of dangerous game. It has the Ruger double-action mechanism, the single-spring mechanism for both hammer and trigger, and a crane-locking system for positive cylinder alignment. There is a wide and substantial extra top strap, and the critical areas under and surrounding the barrel threads are particularly strong. It is available with 5.5 in. (140 mm) and 7.5 in. (190 mm) barrels, chambered for 0.44 in. Magnum or 0.45 in. Long Colt. The Super Blackhawk is available with 7.5 in. (190 mm) or 9.5 in. (241 mm) barrels chambered for 0.44 in. Magnum, but the latest version, with a 7.5 in. (190 mm) barrel only, is chambered for the new and very powerful 0.454 in. Cassul round (although it also accepts the 0.45 in. Long Colt). The Super Redhawk has stainless steel finishes only and features a new cushioned grip made of rubber with wooden inserts. The 0.45 in. Magnum Super Redhawk with 9.5 in. (241 mm) barrel weighs 3.6 lb. (1,644 g) unloaded.

Automatic Pistol Operating Systems

There are two basic systems of cycling an automatic handgun in widespread use today: blowback and recoil. Blowback is a simple system relying on the rearward pressure of the propellant gases impinging upon the breechblock. The breech itself is not locked into place upon firing—the weight of the bolt and the pressure of the return spring alone secure the cartridge. Upon firing, the gas pressure builds up against the slide until the inertia is overcome and the slide is pushed backward to permit ejection and the loading of a new cartridge from the magazine as the slide returns forward.

Note that the bullet has always left the barrel before cycling takes place, allowing the gases to dip to a safe level of pressure.

Blowback tends to be restricted to fairly small caliber weapons, typically 9 mm and below. A more advanced system suitable for larger caliber weapons is the recoil system. Recoil operation for the automatic relies on the recoil of the barrel upon firing. The barrel and slide together move backward until the pressure in the chamber reaches safe levels. At this point, the barrel stops its movement, but the slide continues its rearward movement to open the chamber, eject the cartridge, and then return to its locked position with a new cartridge ready to fire.

Recoil weapons, and some types of blowback gun require locking systems to hold the cartridge securely in the breech until the gas pressure has dropped to allow safe operation. Locking mechanisms are numerous and quite varied, and different companies have developed different signature methods.

The Browning-Colt locking system, for example, utilizes cams or lugs which lock into recesses on the inside of the slide. When the gun is fired, the barrel moves back a few millimeters and is dropped by a hinge, which results in the cams disengaging from the slide to allow the slide to complete its movement. Other locking systems include toggle locking, roller locking, rotation locking, and gas-retarded locking.

Above: *The Israeli Jericho 941 stripped down; the sturdy and comfortable Jericho is a locked-breech, recoil-operated firearm, In the United States, the different members of the quite extensive Jericho family are marketed under the names of "Baby Eagle," "Uzi Eagle," or "Baby Desert Eagle." They are also used by the Israeli Defense Forces and by the Israeli Police.*

UNITED KINGDOM

HOMEMADE SINGLE-SHOT PISTOL 1970s

Length (gun): 13.0 in. (330 mm)
Barrel: 8.0 in. (203 mm)
Weight: 23.0 oz. (0.7 kg)
Caliber: 0.22 in. (5.6 mm)
Rifling: none
Capacity: one
Muz vel: 650 ft./sec. (198 m/sec.)

Firearms have a certain fascination for many people, but because of the need for strict controls over their ownership and use, relatively few people are able to possess conventional weapons of their own. This leads on occasion to attempts to make them, but although this is to some extent understandable, it is a highly dangerous occupation, which has in the past resulted in many cases of death or serious injury. Very few people realize the enormous power concealed in even a small cartridge. A bullet from a 0.22 in. cartridge, propelled by the gases resulting from no more than a pinch of explosive, can kill at ranges in excess of 880 yd. (805 m); this gives at least some indication of the pressures developed in the breech of a firearm. It will, therefore, be obvious that materials intended to stand such internal stresses must be specially made—and such materials are rarely available to the amateur gunmaker. The fact that a cartridge fits a tube of some kind is no guarantee of that tube's strength: in these circumstances, a homemade weapon becomes as dangerous to the firer as a grenade. The crude weapon shown here is, in all essentials, a zip-gun with a butt; its trigger is a dummy.

UNITED KINGDOM

HOMEMADE REVOLVER 1970s

Length (gun): 7.5 in. (190 mm)
Barrel: 3.3 in. (83 mm)
Weight: 25.0 oz. (0.71 kg)
Caliber: 0.22 in. (5.6 mm)
Rifling: none
Capacity: six
Muz vel: not available

The homemade arm illustrated originated in Northern Ireland, although it is not known whether it was meant for serious use, or if it is simply the essay of an amateur gunsmith. It has a solid frame of heavy but crude construction. The round barrel has been bored very wide of center and it is not rifled. The cylinder has a capacity of six and its chambers are countersunk to cover the rims of the cartridges. The lump of metal below the cylinder contains a spring plunger; this engages in the circular depressions in the cylinder and thus ensures that the chamber under the hammer is aligned with the barrel. The cylinder itself must be rotated manually. As may be seen, the revolver has no trigger: the hammer is so designed that it must be drawn back by the thumb and then released, when a spring drives it forward with enough force to fire a 0.22 in. (5.6 mm) rimfire round. This caliber was presumably chosen because such cartridges are easily obtained.

UNITED STATES

SMITH & WESSON 9 MM MODEL 469 AUTOMATIC PISTOL 1980

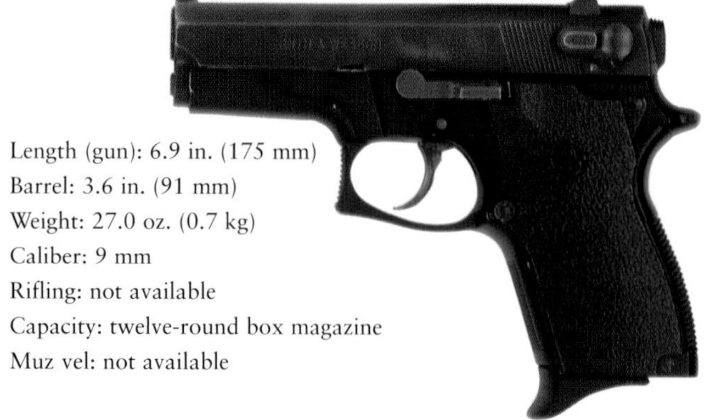

Length (gun): 6.9 in. (175 mm)
Barrel: 3.6 in. (91 mm)
Weight: 27.0 oz. (0.7 kg)
Caliber: 9 mm
Rifling: not available
Capacity: twelve-round box magazine
Muz vel: not available

The Model 469 appeared in the 1980s to meet requests for a smaller ("chopped") automatic pistol and was based on the fourteen-shot Model 459. The 469's barrel was 0.5 in. (12.7 mm) shorter than that on the 459, while bobbing the tang and using a spurless hammer helped to achieve a reduction in overall length of about 0.8 in. (21 mm), which was about all that could be done while still retaining a conventional recoil spring. The Model 469 used a selective double action, with no provision for "cocked-and-locked" carry and was recoil-operated with a locked breech and cam unlocking. A rib on top of the barrel locked into a mortise in the roof of the slide and the rear of the barrel, then cammed downward to unlock. There was a hammer trip safety on the left side, and the receiver was made of light alloy, all other parts of steel. The 469 accepted the 459's fourteen-round magazine, although its own standard magazine was a shorter one of twelve-round capacity.

SWITZERLAND

SIG-SAUER 9 MM P-226 PISTOL 1981

Length (gun): 7.7 in. (196 mm)
Barrel: 4.4 in. (112 mm)
Weight: 26.4oz (0.7 kg)
Caliber: 9 mm
Rifling: 6 grooves, r/hand
Capacity: fifteen-round box magazine
Muz vel: 1,148 ft./sec. (350 m/sec.)

When the U.S. Army, acting as agent for all U.S. armed forces, issued its requirement for a new pistol to replace the Colt M1911 A1, SIG-Sauer entered the competition with their P-226, with many of the parts taken from the existing P-220 and P-225 designs. It is chambered for the standard NATO 9 x 19 mm Parabellum round and is fitted with a detachable box magazine housing fifteen rounds. Mechanically, the P-226 is virtually identical to the P-220, from which it differs in having a wider butt to house a fifteen-round magazine and in the magazine catch, which can be operated by either left- or right-handed shooters. The weapon lost out in the finals of the competition to the Beretta 92SB (M9) but, despite this, large numbers have been sold to, among others, the U.S. Coast Guard, British Ministry of Defence, and the New Zealand armed forces. A sporting model has been developed.

UNITED STATES

SMITH & WESSON MODELS 586/686 REVOLVERS 1981

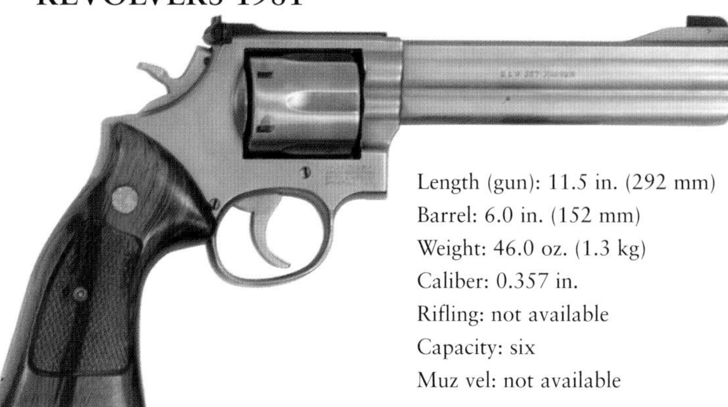

Length (gun): 11.5 in. (292 mm)
Barrel: 6.0 in. (152 mm)
Weight: 46.0 oz. (1.3 kg)
Caliber: 0.357 in.
Rifling: not available
Capacity: six
Muz vel: not available

This revolver was produced in two guises, the blued steel Model 586 and the stainless steel Model 686, both of which were introduced in 1981 and were in direct competition with the Colt Python and Ruger GP-100. Smith & Wesson designed a new frame for these two weapons, designated the "L" frame, which was developed from the earlier "K" frame and slightly enlarged. The weapons use selective double action, with a crane-mounted cylinder that swings to the left for loading and unloading. There is a square ramp foresight with a red plastic insert, and a square notch backsight that is click adjustable for windage and elevation.

UNITED STATES

SMITH & WESSON MODEL 64 MILITARY & POLICE REVOLVER 1981

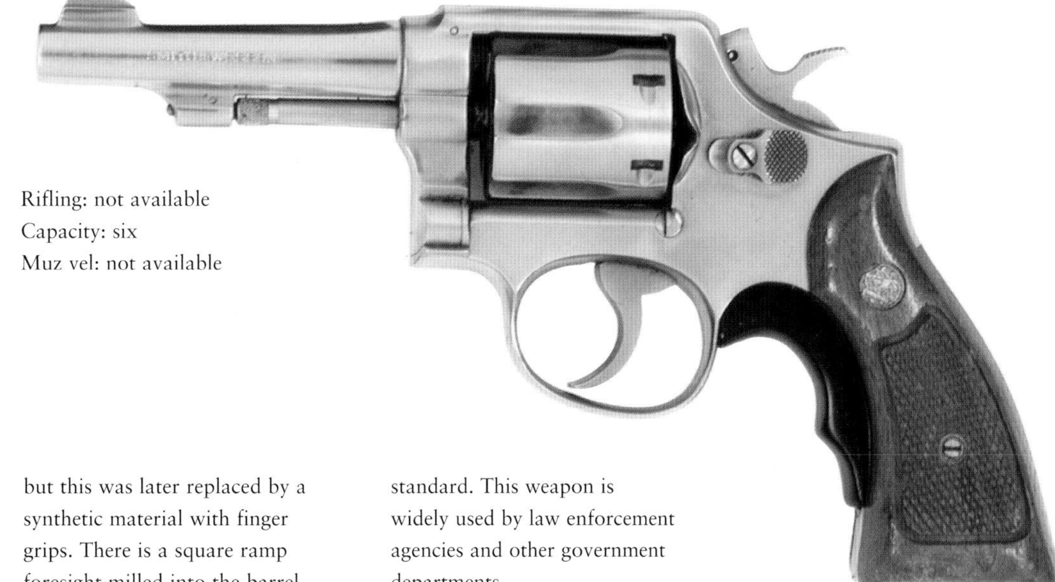

Length (gun): 8.8 in. (222 mm)
Barrel: 4.0 in. (102 mm)
Weight: 32.0 oz. (0.9 kg)
Caliber: 0.38 in.
Rifling: not available
Capacity: six
Muz vel: not available

The Model 64 was introduced in 1981, and is the stainless steel version of the company's Model 10 Military & Police that dated from 1902 (see also Model 1). The weapon is made entirely of stainless steel, except for the hammer and trigger, which are chrome-plated. The stock grips were originally of polished walnut, but this was later replaced by a synthetic material with finger grips. There is a square ramp foresight milled into the barrel and a square notch backsight milled into the frame; neither is adjustable. The picture shows a Model 64 with a Tyler T-Grip adapter added between the stock and trigger guard, but is otherwise standard. This weapon is widely used by law enforcement agencies and other government departments.

ISRAEL

IMI DESERT EAGLE PISTOL 1983

Length (gun): 10.6 in. (270 mm)
Barrel: 6.0 in. (153 mm)
Weight (loaded): 67.4 oz. (1.9 kg)
Caliber: 0.357 in. Magnum
Rifling: 6 grooves, r/hand
Capacity: nine-round box magazine (see below)
Muz vel: not available

The Israeli Military Industries (IMI) Desert Eagle was developed as a sporting weapon. It has a fixed barrel. Some of the propellant gases are diverted through a gas port in front of the chamber into a duct that channels the gas to a point just beneath the muzzle where it enters a gas cylinder containing a short-stroke piston. This is driven to the rear, where it drives the slide, whose first action is to rotate and unlock the bolt, which then withdraws, extracting and ejecting the empty case. The slide is then pushed forward by the return-spring rod, strips off and chambers a round, and rotates the bolt into the locked position ready for firing. The standard version of the Desert Eagle is chambered for 0.357 in. Magnum, but three calibers are available, each having different capacity magazines: 0.357 in. Magnum (nine rounds); 0.44 in. Magnum (eight rounds); and 0.50 in. Action Express (seven rounds).

ITALY

BERNARDELLI P018-9 9 MM PISTOL 1984

Length (gun): 8.4 in. (213 mm)
Barrel: 4.8 in. (122 mm)
Weight: 36.0 oz. (1.0 kg)
Caliber: 9 mm
Rifling: 6 grooves, r/hand
Capacity: fourteen-round box magazine
Muz vel: 1,150 ft./sec. (350 m/sec.)

Introduced in 1984, the Bernardelli is an all-steel automatic pistol, with major components machined from forgings. It is recoil-operated, using a locked breech with cam unlocking. Ribs on top of the barrel at the breech end seat in the roof slide. It has a post foresight and a square-notch backsight, laterally dovetailed, which can be adjusted for windage using an Allen key. It has selective double action. In its standard form, it is chambered for the 9 mm Parabellum round, but is also available for 7.65 mm Luger. There is a compact version of the P018/9, which is also available in both 9 mm and 7.65 mm calibers.

SWITZERLAND

SPHINX 9 MM AT-2000S PISTOL 1984

Length (gun): 8.0 in. (204 mm)
Barrel: 4.5 in. (115 mm)
Weight: 36.3 oz. (1.0 kg)
Caliber: 9 mm
Rifling: 6 grooves, r/hand
Capacity: fifteen-round box magazine
Muz vel: 1,155 ft./sec. (352 m/sec.)

Sphinx Engineering SA of Porrentruy in Switzerland originally manufactured the Czech CZ Model 75 pistol under license, but then developed so many improvements to that design that the outcome was an entirely new design, designated the AT-88S. This pistol was successful and attracted orders from numerous police forces. Further minor improvements then led to the AT-2000, of which there are many minor variants. The AT 2000S is a recoil-operated, semiautomatic, double-action pistol, using Browning cam locking, and is available in either 9 x 19 mm Parabellum (see specifications) or 0.40 in. S&W calibers. The various versions include: AT 2000P (shorter and lighter), AT2000H (compact version), AT2000SDA/PDA/HDA (identical to -S, -P and -H versions above, but double- rather than single-action, together with a new Sphinx-developed safety system), and the AT 2000PS (police special, with sixteen-round magazine).

MODERN PISTOL AMMUNITION

Modern pistol ammunition tends to be of centerfire rimless or rimmed rimfire configuration, with a straight-walled cartridge case. The power of a round in terms of its muzzle velocity and terminal power depends not only on the cartridge and bullet weight, but also on the weapon firing it—longer barrels tend to increase range and sustain a higher muzzle velocity. The range and terminal effect are also affected by the type of bullet. There are around fifteen different types of handgun bullets, the following five being among the most popular:

- Lead round nose (LRN)—a simple and economical lead round with a rounded nose.
- Lead wadcutter (LW)—a lead round with a flattened nose to arrest the bullet more quickly upon impact with the target.
- Full metal jacket (FMJ)—the lead core of the bullet is completely encased in a copper/steel jacket, resulting in excellent flight properties, a reduction of fouling in the barrel and little deformation upon impact with the target. This type is known by the military as "ball."
- Jacketed hollow point (JHP)—here the bullet is jacketed, but unlike the FMJ, the tip of the jacket is open to expose the inner lead core. On impact, the open tip mushrooms outward, deforming the bullet severely and (against a living target) causing extensive tissue damage. The JHP has the advantage that it usually stops inside the target, delivering all of its kinetic energy into terminal force.
- Semijacketed hollow point (SJHP)—part jacketed, but with a section of the lead core exposed at the tip of the round to create some deformation upon impact. This round is often found in magnum type handguns.

As well as such basic bullet types, there are numerous advanced types, particularly for use in combat/law enforcement roles. The Winchester SXT frangible round, for example, produces six uniform radial jacket pellets with perpendicular tips to arrest the round hard when it hits a target and maximize takedown force A similar round, "Black Talon," was voluntarily withdrawn from sale in the U.S. in the 1990s because of bad publicity.

Below: *A range of modern handgun ammunication for comparison: the 9 mm Parabellum round has a flat "wadcutter" bullet, whereas the two Magnum rounds feature hollow-point bullets.*

9mm PARABELLUM

.38 SPECIAL

.357 MAGNUM

.44 MAGNUM

PISTOL SIGHTS

Left: *Not a sight of course, but the "Crimson Trace" laser on the Smith & Wesson Model 642 .38 is presumably an effective aid to accuracy: though at what distance in broad daylight it is difficult to guess.*

Pistol sights have traditionally been extremely basic in type, usually consisting of little more than a notch-and-post configuration. This reflects the fact that expectations of long-range handgun shooting are low, and sights are designed more for quick target acquisition than for laborious alignment (except in the case of match pistols). Open sights, however, can present a problem for handgun use. The eye has to flit between rear sight, front sight, and target to achieve target alignment and this compromises accuracy. Notch-and-post sights become even more difficult to use in low-light conditions. This being said, modern open sights have achieved high standards, including features such as microadjustable rear sights for windage and elevation, and luminous tritium spots on the front and occasionally rear sights to aid rapid target acquisition and low-light shooting.

Simple open steel sights are only one of the options available to handgunners today. A large range of optical sights is now available for handguns, designed for either hunting or target shooting. Electronic red-dot sights for handguns emerged in the late 1970s, and achieved prominence in the United States after U.S. Army Reserve Sgt. Joe Pascarelli won the National Pistol Championship at Camp Perry in 1979 with an Aimpoint sight on his 1911 Government Model .45 ACP pistol.

Since then, electronic sights have reached a high degree of sophistication, using optical tube configurations with holographic or laser reticles. For example, the Bushnell HOLOsight II presents a "floating" reticle (the dot appears to be in front of the weapon) created by a Class II laser, and the sight is powered by two 1.5-volt batteries that give around forty hours of use.

Simple telescopic sights are also available for handguns. These differ from rifle scopes in the "eye relief" settings—the distance from the eye to the scope. Handgun optical sights will have an eye relief of around 508 mm (20 in.) at arm's length, and this means that the field of view is very restricted. The bulk and weight of an optical sight also means that the gun has an additional handling burden, so these sights are rarely suitable for beginners. Having said this, with a good scope of any type a handgunner can extend the accurate range of the weapon out to and beyond 80 ft. (25 m).

FRANCE

MANURHIN MR-32 "MATCH" REVOLVER 1985

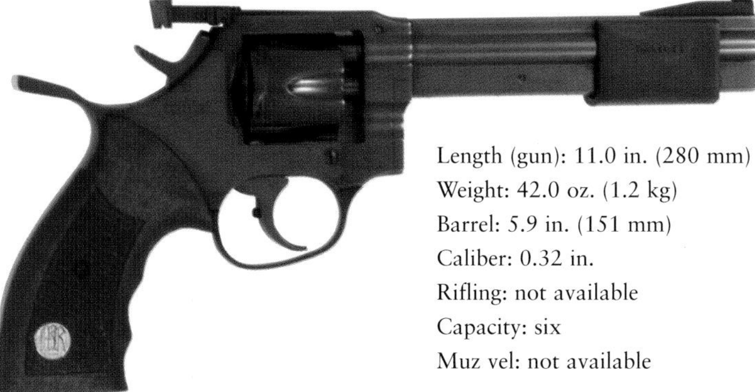

Length (gun): 11.0 in. (280 mm)
Weight: 42.0 oz. (1.2 kg)
Barrel: 5.9 in. (151 mm)
Caliber: 0.32 in.
Rifling: not available
Capacity: six
Muz vel: not available

Manurhin (Manufacture des Machines du Haut-Rhin) was a French company that produced a range of very high quality pistols for both service and target use. The MR-32 "Match" was designed specifically for UIT Centerfire match competitions and was based on the Manurhin MR-73, which was produced in both 0.357 in. Magnum and 0.38 in. Special versions. The MR-32 fires 0.32 Smith & Wesson Long cartridges and is single action only, with a distinctive tang, which is designed to enable the firer to place his or her hand very precisely on the backstrap, a major problem with target revolvers. The crane-mounted cylinder swings to the left and the Smith & Wesson–type thumb latch clears locks at the rear of the cylinder and at the ejector rod tip. The pistol-making facility at Manurhin was purchased by the Belgian Fabrique Nationale in the early 1990s.

ITALY

BERETTA U.S. ARMY M9 (MODEL 92SB/92F) 9 MM 1985

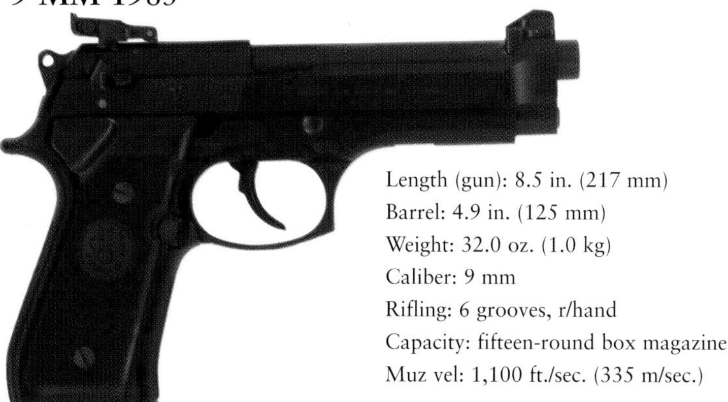

Length (gun): 8.5 in. (217 mm)
Barrel: 4.9 in. (125 mm)
Weight: 32.0 oz. (1.0 kg)
Caliber: 9 mm
Rifling: 6 grooves, r/hand
Capacity: fifteen-round box magazine
Muz vel: 1,100 ft./sec. (335 m/sec.)

The Beretta 92SB entered service with the U.S. Army as the Pistol M9 in 1985, with initial orders for some 500,000. The pistol is entirely coated in a Teflon-derived material and the barrel is chrome-plated. Its action uses the locked-wedge design. The weapon is loaded in the orthodox manner by inserting a magazine into the butt, following which the slide grip is used to pull the action to the rear, cocking the hammer, and released to chamber a round. Gas pressure drives the barrel and slide to the rear, locked together by a wedge; having traveled some 0.3 in. (8 mm), the locking wedge pivots downward, disengaging from the slide; the barrel immediately stops but the slide continues rearward to complete the reloading cycle. The changes required by the U.S. Army included an enlarged trigger guard to enable a two-handed grip, and an extension to the base of the magazine.

ITALY

BERETTA MODEL 93R 9 MM PISTOL 1985

Length (gun): 9.5 in. (240 mm)
Barrel: 6.1 in. (156 mm)
Weight: 39.5 oz. (1,120g)
Caliber: 9 mm
Rifling: 6 grooves, r/hand
Capacity: fifteen- or twenty-round box magazine
Muz vel: 1,230 ft./sec. (375 m/sec.)

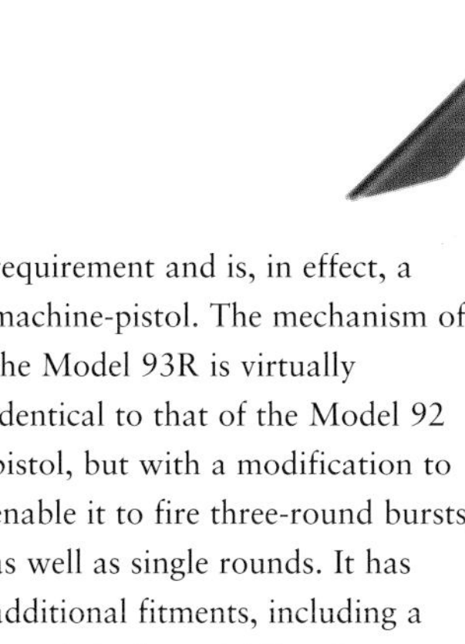

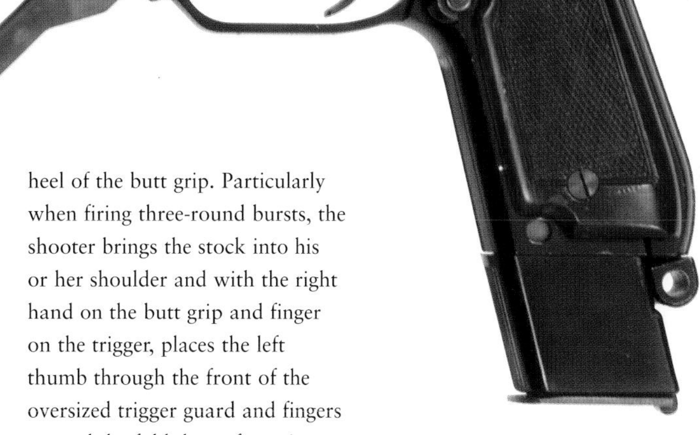

The Beretta Model 1951R was developed in the 1970s for the Carabinieri, special forces, and government close-protection squads. It was a modified version of the Model 1951. Firing 9 mm Parabellum rounds, it had a large, wooden foregrip at the front of the slide and could fire single rounds or fully automatic; it did not have a buttstock. The Model 93R is designed to meet a similar requirement and is, in effect, a machine-pistol. The mechanism of the Model 93R is virtually identical to that of the Model 92 pistol, but with a modification to enable it to fire three-round bursts, as well as single rounds. It has additional fitments, including a muzzle brake, a folding-down metal forestock, enlarged trigger guard, and a folding steel-skeleton buttstock, which clips onto the heel of the butt grip. Particularly when firing three-round bursts, the shooter brings the stock into his or her shoulder and with the right hand on the butt grip and finger on the trigger, places the left thumb through the front of the oversized trigger guard and fingers around the fold-down foregrip. The 93R has been taken into service by Italian and other national special forces.

United States

SMITH & WESSON MODEL 624 "HORTON SPECIAL" REVOLVER 1985

Length (gun): 7.8 in. (197 mm)
Barrel: 3 in. (76 mm)
Weight: 40.0 oz. (1.1 kg)
Caliber: 0.44 in.
Rifling: not available
Capacity: six
Muz vel: not available

Smith & Wesson's Model 24, firing the 0.44 in. Special round, ended its first production run in 1958, but was reintroduced in 1983 and an initial run of 7,500 was sold out within months. A special chrome-plated version was put into production in 1985 to meet an order from a Massachusetts gun distributor, Lew Horton, following which the weapon was known as the "Horton Special." This had a very short, 3.0 in. (76 mm) barrel and a very smooth, chrome-plated finish, with a "bird's-head" grip and deep finger grooves. The weapon has a solid frame, with hand ejection from a crane-mounted cylinder, which swings out to the left following release by a thumb catch. Sights consisted of a square ramp foresight and a square notch backsight, click adjustable for elevation and windage. The "Horton Special" makes an interesting comparison with its contemporary, the Charter Arms Bulldog, designed to fill the same niche in the market.

United States

RUGER BISLEY REVOLVER 1985

Length (gun): 13.0 in. (330 mm)
Barrel: 7.5 in. (191 mm)
Weight: 48 oz. (1.4 kg)
Caliber: 0.357 in. Magnum
Rifling: not available
Capacity: six
Muz vel: not available

The outline of Ruger's Bisley Model, introduced in 1985, closely resembles that of Colt's 1890s Bisley model, a single-action-only weapon, designed for Edwardian-era competition shooting. The modern weapon, however, has a slightly more upright handle and a lower hammer spur, which enable the shooter to recock it using the right thumb without shifting the grip, a considerable advantage in timed competitions. It is produced in four models, chambered for 0.22 in. LR, 0.357 in. Magnum (see specifications), 0.44 in. Magnum, and 0.45 in. Long Colt. The 0.22 in. version has a 6.5 in. (165 mm) barrel; the remainder have 7.5 in. (191 mm) barrels. The Bisley has a ramp foresight and click adjustable Partridge backsight. Pictures show the 0.45 in. Long Colt version (above), and 0.22 in. Long Rifle version (below).

UNITED STATES

RUGER 0.22 IN. NEW MODEL SINGLE-SIX REVOLVER 1985

Length (gun): 14.9 in. (378 mm)
Barrel: 9.5 in. (241 mm)
Weight: 38.0 oz. (1.1 kg)
Caliber: 0.22 in. (5.56 mm)
Rifling: not available
Capacity: six
Muz vel: not available

The Ruger New Model Single-Six is a modern 0.22 in. caliber single-action revolver, intended for use either for targets or on the trail. There are two types: the New Model Single-Six with fixed sights and the New Model Super Single-Six (see specifications) with ramp foresight and click adjustable rearsight. As sold, the gun has a cylinder for 0.22 in. Long Rifle, but an extra cylinder is also provided in Winchester Magnum Rimfire (WMR), which can be instantly interchanged without the need for tools. Shown are the New Model Super Six with 9.5 in. (241 mm) barrel in blued finish (top); and the New Model Single-Six with 6.5 in. (165 mm) barrel in stainless steel finish (bottom).

GERMANY

PETERS-STAHL PISTOLE 07 MULTICALIBER TARGET PISTOL 1986

Length (gun): 9.5 in. (241 mm)
Barrel: 6.0 in. (152 mm)
Weight: 43.0 oz. (1.2 kg)
Caliber: 0.45 in. (see text)
Rifling: not available
Capacity: eight-round box magazine
Muz vel: not available

This competition handgun was introduced in 1986. It uses a Caspian Arms 1911 receiver, but the upper structure is a new design manufactured by Peters-Stahl. The weapon is of all-steel construction, with a hammer-forged barrel with polygonal rifling. The trigger has been finely tuned, and the long slide shifts the center of balance forward, helping the gun hold more solidly on target and dampening the recoil of light loads. The extension of the tang should also be noted. As is to be expected on a competition weapon, the backsight is click adjustable in small increments for windage and elevation. The undercut, interchangeable post foresight gives a dead black Partridge picture. The Pistole 07 can be converted quickly from one caliber to another by replacing the barrel and magazine, while the same breechblock, recoil spring, and all other elements are retained unchanged. The calibers covered are: 0.45 in. ACP, 9 mm Parabellum, 0.38 in. Super, and 0.38 in. Special Wadcutter. In 0.45 in. and 9 mm caliber, the weapon operates with a locked breech; in 0.38 in. caliber, it operates as a blowback weapon and the magazine capacity is reduced to five rounds. Shown here are the 0.45 in. version (left) and the 0.38 in. Special Wadcutter with wooden butt plates (right).

UNITED STATES

RUGER 0.357 IN. GP-100 REVOLVER 1986

Length (gun): 9.3 in. (236 mm)
Barrel: 4.0 in. (102 mm)
Weight: 41.0 oz. (1.1 kg)
Caliber: 0.357 in. Magnum
Rifling: 5 grooves, r/hand
Capacity: six
Muz vel: not available

Ruger introduced the Security-Six, Police Service-Six, and Speed-Six revolvers in 1971, but these were replaced in 1986 by the GP-100 series, which has the same layout as the Service-Six, but with improvements in the mechanism and distribution of the metal. A double-action gun, the cylinder locking notches are offset and cut into the thick part of the cylinder walls between the chambers rather than over them. In the firing position, the cylinder is securely locked into the frame in two places: at the rear by the traditional cylinder pin and at the front of the crane by a large spring-loaded latch. All models are fitted with the Ruger cushioned grip. The cylinder crane locks directly to the frame with an offset, shrouded ejection rod that allows a thicker, stronger frame under the barrel threads. Models are available with 3.0 in. (76 mm), 4.0 in. (102 mm), and 6.0 in. (152 mm) barrels and with fixed or adjustable sights. All are chambered for the 0.357 in. Magnum except one that takes the 0.38 in. Special. Shown here are: 0.357 in. caliber, 3.0 in. barrel, blued finish (top left); 0.357 in. caliber, 6.0 in. barrel, stainless steel finish (above); and 0.38 in. Special, 4.0 in. barrel (below left).

UNITED STATES

RUGER 0.22 IN. MARK II GOVERNMENT TARGET PISTOL 1986

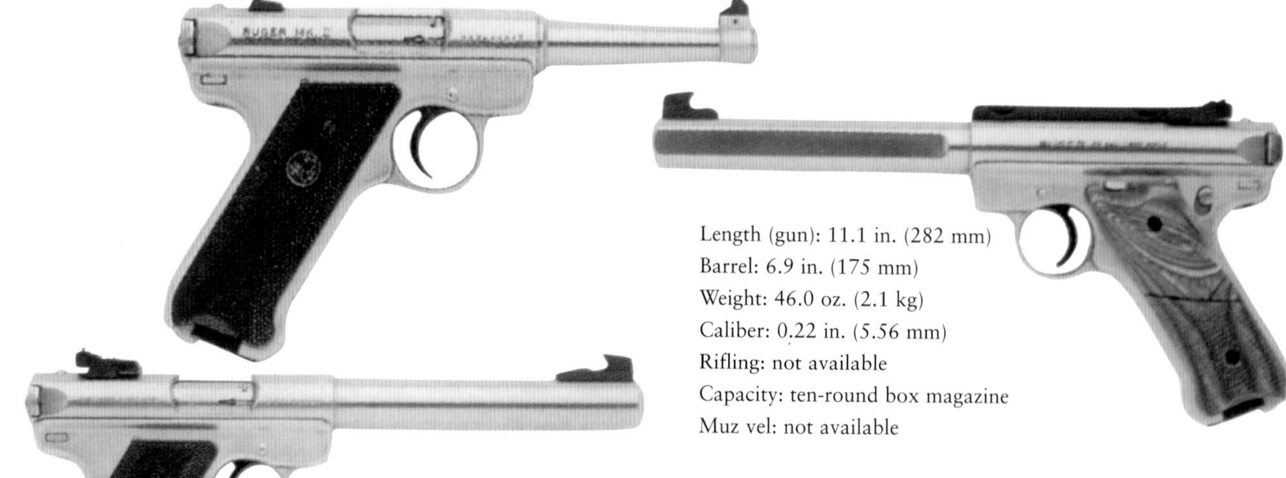

Length (gun): 11.1 in. (282 mm)
Barrel: 6.9 in. (175 mm)
Weight: 46.0 oz. (2.1 kg)
Caliber: 0.22 in. (5.56 mm)
Rifling: not available
Capacity: ten-round box magazine
Muz vel: not available

The Ruger 0.22 in. Long Rifle target pistol was introduced in 1949. The Mark II comprises eighteen pistols in five ranges: Standard, Target, Bull, Government, and Competition, in blued or stainless steel finishes, and a variety of barrel lengths. The safety positively locks to the rear, but the bolt can be manually operated with the safety in the "on" position for added security while loading and unloading. A bolt stop locks the pistol automatically when the last cartridge has been fired (provided that the magazine is in the weapon); the bolt stop can be manually activated by a thumb piece on the left of the weapon to aid loading, cleaning, and inspection. The Target series has a heavier, less-tapered barrel and competition sights, with a rear sight that is click adjustable for windage and elevation, while the front sight is a Partridge type blade (0.125 in. wide), undercut to prevent glare. The Government Target model is standard issue to U.S. armed forces, and all weapons are individually targeted before leaving the factory using a patented laser sighting device, and this factory-test target is enclosed with each pistol before delivery. Shown are the Standard Model with 4.75 in. (121 mm) barrel (top left); Government Target Model with 6.9 in. (175 mm) barrel (below left); and the Competition Model (right).

SWITZERLAND

SIG-SAUER 9 MM P-228/P-229 PISTOL 1988

Length (gun): 7.1 in. (180 mm)
Barrel: 3.9 in. (96 mm)
Weight: 29.0 oz. (0.8 kg)
Caliber: 9 mm
Rifling: 6 grooves, r/hand
Capacity: thirteen-round box magazine
Muz vel: 1,115 ft./sec. (340 m/sec.)

These two pistols are virtually identical, except that the SIG-Sauer P-228 (see specifications) fires the 9 mm Parabellum round, while the P-229 fires the 0.40 S&W or 0.357 in. SIG round. They are, in essence, a P-225 with larger magazines, and there is a substantial commonality of parts between the three weapons. The P-228 has been purchased by the U.S. Army (9 mm Compact Pistol M11), FBI, and DEA, and the British MoD. The P-229 is chambered for 0.40 in. S&W or 0.357 in. SIG; only a change of barrel is needed. It uses a machined, stainless steel slide, manufactured in the United States, with an aluminum alloy frame manufactured in Germany. There are three control levers, all on the left side of the weapon. Nearest the muzzle is the release lever for stripping; the middle lever, just below the slide, is the decocking lever; the rearmost lever is the slide latch. Like all SIG pistols, the P-229 has an automatic firing-pin safety, operating without a traditional safety-control lever, with the first shot when the hammer is at half-cock requiring a longer trigger pull. The P-228 and P-229 (pictured) are fitted with high contrast Stavenhagen sights; a tritium-enhanced foresight and luminous rearsights can also be fitted.

UNITED KINGDOM

SHIELD MODIFIED 0.357 IN. RUGER BLACKHAWK TARGET REVOLVER 1988

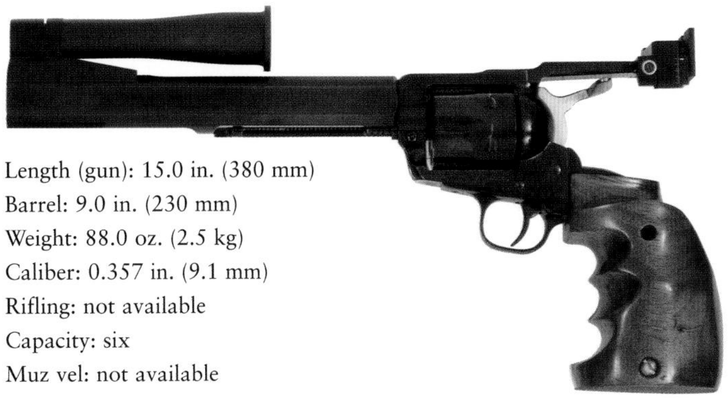

Length (gun): 15.0 in. (380 mm)
Barrel: 9.0 in. (230 mm)
Weight: 88.0 oz. (2.5 kg)
Caliber: 0.357 in. (9.1 mm)
Rifling: not available
Capacity: six
Muz vel: not available

This weapon is designed for the All Comers category competition, which is shot in three stages, starting at 100 meters, where two sets of five shots are shot in thirty seconds, followed by two identical stages at 200 meters and 300 meters, each consisting of twelve shots in twelve minutes, with two sighters permitted prior to each stage. The gun is a Ruger Blackhawk, rechambered from 0.30 in. M1 carbine and rebarreled with a Douglas premium 1.25 in. (3.2 cm) outside diameter blank, machined square, of 0.357 in. (9.1 mm) bore diameter with a one-in-ten twist. There are different rounds for each of the three ranges. The foresight is a 0.14 in. (3.6 mm) blade in a Parker-Hale tunnel, with custom adapter block and extended sunshade. The Beeman backsight is mounted on a 3.5 in. (88.9 mm) extension, with a custom backplate and 3.32 x 0.085 in. (84.3 x 2.2 mm) notch.

UNITED KINGDOM

SHIELD 0.357 IN. MAGNUM LONG-RANGE FREE PISTOL 1988

Length (gun): 15.3 in. (387 mm)
Barrel: 10.0 in. (254 mm)
Weight: 135.0 oz. (3.8 kg)
Caliber: 0.357 in. Magnum
Rifling: not available
Capacity: one
Muz vel: not available

This unusual-looking pistol was designed specifically for the International Long-Range Pistol Shooter's Association (ILRPSA) Free Pistol "B" competition, and was designed and built by Andy Wooldridge of the British company Shield Gunmakers. The pistol is chambered for 0.357 in. Magnum, loaded to maximum allowable length overall with 180-grain Speer 0.358 rifle bullets ahead of 16.5 grains of H4227 with CCI Bench rest primers. It will hold a 4.5 in. (114 mm) group at 200 meters. It is side-lever operated and is fired by an internal hammer operating over a forty-seven-degree arc. The trigger engages a free-floating sear, and is adjustable between 16.0–32.0 oz. (0.45–0.9 kg) let-off weight, but the rules admit any safe trigger weight, and most shooters seem to prefer releases in the region of 16.0 oz. (0.45 kg). Sights are Leopold M8 4x scope.

Basic Handgun Technique

Above: *The standard double-handed grip, with the nonshooting hand cupping the hand on the grip; here the supporting hand index finger is in front of the trigger guard, suggesting that the firer is pulling back with that hand, pushing forward with the firing hand, to increase stability.*

Handgun technique varies according to the weapon and the user's requirements, but during the second half of the twentieth century the fundamentals of handgun shooting were laid down in military units and police forces. Grip tension on the gun is important—too tight, and you introduce tremble into the firing hand (which disturbs accuracy), too loose, and the gun's recoil is inadequately controlled. To achieve the correct tension, squeeze the gun with increased pressure until tremble is felt, then relax the hand just enough for the tremble to subside. You now have the correct grip tension.

The non-firing hand should support the firing hand by cupping the fingers around those on the pistol grip, with the option of curling the lower fingers beneath the grip to form a cup-and-saucer support. Some shooters extend the index finger of the shooting hand along the side of the trigger to enhance accurate aiming through utilizing a natural pointing action. This is a valid technique, but on an automatic pistol, make sure both hands are clear of the gun's slide when it recoils. Applying isometric tension between the two hands (the firing hand pushing forward, the supporting hand pulling backward) will further stabilize the gun.

In terms of general stance, extend the firing arm straight out with the elbow of the supporting arm bent and pointing downward. The head should remain upright, looking straight down the arm of the firing hand. Feet should be shoulder width apart, with the supporting-arm foot extended forward to bring the body into a forty-five-degree angle to the shooting plane. This posture not only generates stability, but also makes you less of a target to a responding shooter.

When firing, keep both eyes open and concentrate hard on the target rather than make a deliberate sight/target alignment. Utilize the natural pointing computer of the brain—if your stance and grip are correct, you will shoot where you look. Squeeze the trigger—which should be pulled with the padded tip of the index finger—firmly but without jerking or the firer is flinching. A common cause of flinching is anticipating the recoil, but instead let your hand ride back naturally with the recoil before returning to the firing position.

UNITED KINGDOM

SHIELD 0.45 IN. NEW SERVICE LONG-RANGE FREE PISTOL 1988

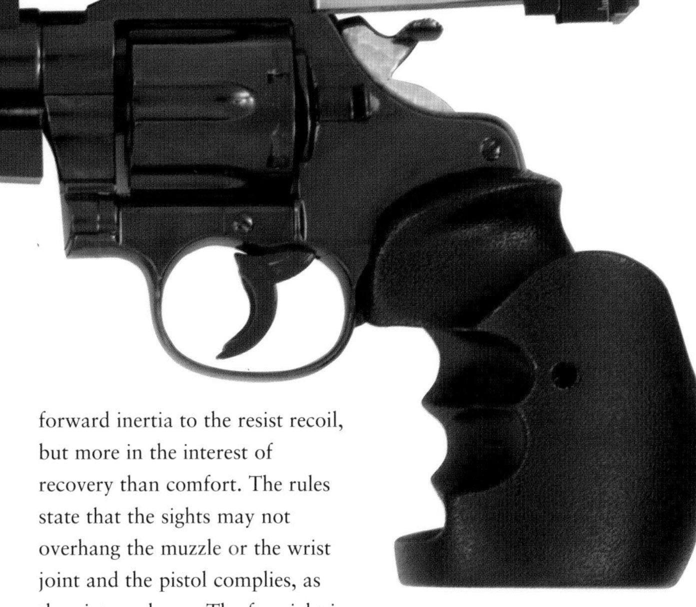

Length (gun): 9.5 in. (241 mm)
Barrel: 3.6 in. (90 mm)
Weight: 71.0 oz. (2.0 kg)
Caliber: 0.45 in. (11.43 mm)
Rifling: not available
Capacity: six-round box magazine
Muz vel: not available

This curious weapon started life as a Colt New Service revolver, which the builder found discarded in a gunsmith's workshop. The builder used this as the basis of a weapon designed to produce a weapon for the ILRPSA Pocket Pistol competition, which calls for two sighters followed by two sets of five shots in thirty seconds at 100 meters. It has a 3.6 in. (90 mm) barrel with a grip of maximum 10.0 in. (254 mm) circumference, with no wrist support. The gun operates on selective double-action. The retracting thumb latch on the left of the frame frees the crane-mounted cylinder to swing out for loading or unloading. The 0.45 in. (11.4 mm) barrel is machined from a Douglas blank and has 1-in-16 in. (406 mm) rifling, with its massive underlug giving some forward inertia to the resist recoil, but more in the interest of recovery than comfort. The rules state that the sights may not overhang the muzzle or the wrist joint and the pistol complies, as the picture shows. The foresight is a 0.14 in. (3.6 mm) post in a short Parker-Hale tunnel, with a custom adapter block, while the Beeman backsight is mounted on a short extension, with a custom backplate and 1.2 in. (30.5 mm) notch.

UNITED STATES

RUGER SP-101 REVOLVER 1989

Length (gun): not available
Barrel: 3.1 in. (79 mm)
Weight: 27.0 oz. (0.8 kg)
Caliber: 9 mm
Rifling: not available
Capacity: five
Muz vel: not available

The SP-101 series are small revolvers in calibers ranging from 0.22–32 in. Magnum, 9 mm and 0.357 Magnum, to 0.38+P with a six- or five-round cylinder, depending on caliber. The SP-101 series are all double-action, with offset cylinder-locking notches cut into the thick part of the cylinder walls between the chambers. The cylinder is securely locked into the frame at the rear with a traditional cylinder pin, and at the front by a large, spring-loaded latch. All models are fitted with a hardened rubber grip without wooden inserts. The cylinder crane locks directly to the frame with an offset, shrouded ejection rod that enables a thicker, stronger frame to be mounted under the barrel threads. The hammer, trigger, and most small internal components are stainless steel. Some models are double-action only and have a spurless hammer. Barrels, in stainless steel, available in 2.25 in. (57 mm), 3.1 in. (79 mm), and 4.0 in. (102 mm) lengths. The 0.22 in. Long Rifle and 0.32 in. Magnum versions have six-round cylinders; 9 mm, 0.38+P, and 0.357 in. Magnum have five. Shown are the KSP-240 0.22 in. caliber, 4.0 in. barrel (above left); KSP-93 9 mm, 3.1 in. barrel (right); KSP-321XL 0.357 in. Magnum, 2.25 in. barrel (below left).

UNITED KINGDOM

HOMEMADE SINGLE-SHOT 0.41 IN. PISTOL 1980S

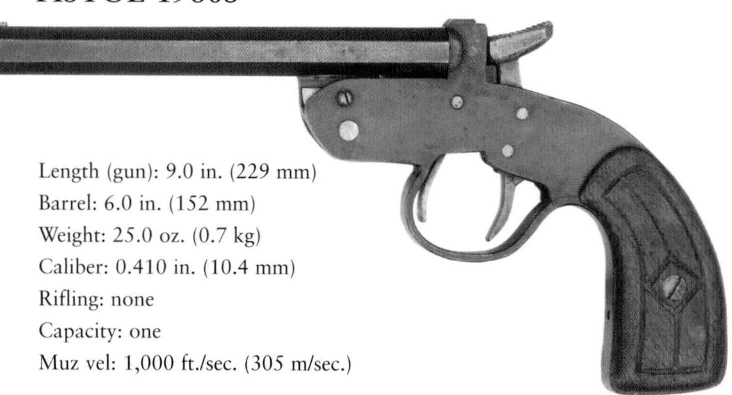

Length (gun): 9.0 in. (229 mm)
Barrel: 6.0 in. (152 mm)
Weight: 25.0 oz. (0.7 kg)
Caliber: 0.410 in. (10.4 mm)
Rifling: none
Capacity: one
Muz vel: 1,000 ft./sec. (305 m/sec.)

It will, perhaps, surprise many to learn that a diminutive 0.410 in. cartridge of the type fired by this weapon develops appreciably higher pressures than those normally produced by the much larger twelve-bore cartridge. The reason for this is that, in order to produce an effective shot pattern, the column of shot in the smaller cartridge has to be very long in relation to its diameter. Sufficient force must then be applied to the very small area at the base of this column of shot to force it from the barrel at a lethal velocity of something in the region of 1,200 ft./sec. (366 m/sec.); thus, the charge must be a comparatively large one. The weapon shown here was made with the cut-down barrel of a 0.410 in. shotgun, but the locking system was fundamentally weak and the metal used in it was inadequate both in weight and quality. It was probable that a few shots would have been enough to destroy it.

SWITZERLAND

SIG-SAUER 9 MM P239 PISTOL 1990

Length (gun): 6.8 in. (172 mm)
Barrel: 3.6 in. (92 mm)
Weight: 23.0 oz. (0.8 kg)
Caliber: 9 mm, 0.40 in. Smith & Wesson, or SIG's own 0.357 in.
Rifling: 6 grooves, r/hand
Capacity: seven-round box magazine
Muz vel: 1,115 ft./sec. (340 m/sec.)

The SIG-Sauer P-239 was specifically designed to meet the increasing requirement created by female shooters in armed forces, law enforcement agencies, etc. Research established that because most women's hands are smaller than men's, they needed a pistol with the same performance, but in a physically smaller package. The smaller size also makes the pistol easier to conceal. This size reduction has been achieved by restricting the number of rounds in the magazine to eight in the 9 mm version (seven in the 0.40 S&W and 0.357SIG versions) in order to eliminate the double-stacking of rounds and thus produce a smaller butt. The P-239 is a mechanically locked, recoil-operated, auto-loading weapon. The sights are adjustable, the rear sight having six notches, while five different foresight posts are available. It has a machined, stainless steel slide with a light alloy frame and is black anodized.

GERMANY

WALTHER 0.32 IN. GSP-C TARGET PISTOL 1990

Length (gun): 11.5 in. (292 mm)
Barrel: 4.3 in. (108 mm)
Weight: 45.5 oz. (1.3 kg)
Caliber: 0.32 in.
Rifling: not available
Capacity: five-round box magazine
Muz vel: not available

The Walther GSP is a highly specialized target competition weapon, and is generally considered to be a brilliant design in every respect; it has certainly proved very successful in competition shooting. The weapon has a die-cast aluminum frame, and the forward mounting of the magazine gives it a distinctive profile and solved a lot of design problems, but nothing is ever gained without penalty and this made overall length a critical dimension. Thus, in order for the Walther GSP to comply with the rules by fitting inside the referee's box magazine and still have a barrel of sufficient length to reassure shooters (who expect to see a long barrel on a target pistol), the heel support has been cut short, thus sacrificing some stability of hold. Sights are interchangeable post foresight, square notch backsight. The GSP is available as a three-caliber kit, with conversions to 0.22 in. LR or 0.22 in. short for Standard Pistol, Standard Handgun, Ladies Match, and Rapid Fire Pistol events.

UNITED STATES

SMITH & WESSON 0.45 IN. MODEL 4500 SERIES PISTOL 1990

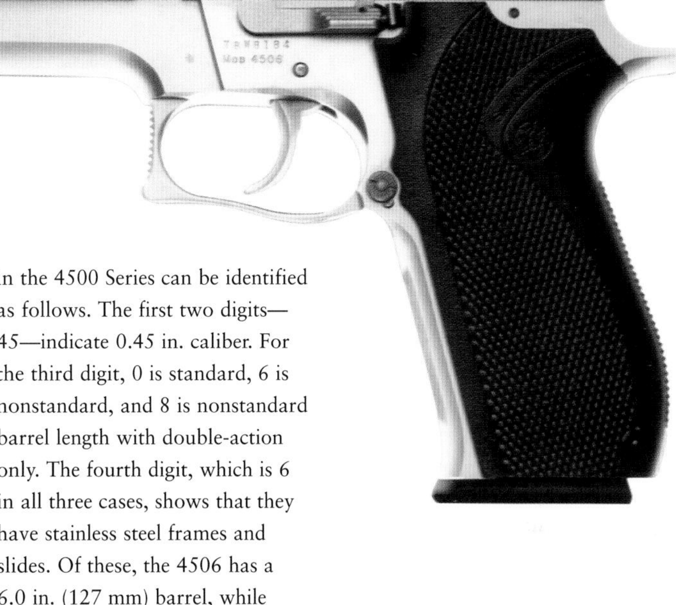

Length (gun): 8.6 in. (219 mm)
Barrel: 5.0 in. (127 mm)
Weight: 40.9 oz. (1.1 kg)
Caliber: 0.45 in.
Rifling: not available
Capacity: eight-round box magazine
Muz vel: not available

Smith & Wesson involved U.S. government and law enforcement agencies in a major redesign exercise, which resulted in a new range of automatic pistols, known as the "Third Generation." Most of the resulting pistols fire 9 x 19 mm Parabellum, but the heaviest, the Model 4500 series, fires 0.45 in. ACP. There are currently three weapons in the series: Models 4506 (see specifications), 4566, and 4586; the numbers, under the Smith & Wesson system for their Third Generation pistols, provide information about the weapons. The first two digits indicate the caliber, except in 9 mm where the first digit indicates the model number and the second digit (always "9") the caliber. The third digit indicates the type—e.g., standard, compact, or nonstandard barrel length. The fourth digit indicates the finish. The weapons in the 4500 Series can be identified as follows. The first two digits—45—indicate 0.45 in. caliber. For the third digit, 0 is standard, 6 is nonstandard, and 8 is nonstandard barrel length with double-action only. The fourth digit, which is 6 in all three cases, shows that they have stainless steel frames and slides. Of these, the 4506 has a 6.0 in. (127 mm) barrel, while the 4566 and 4586 both have a 4.25 in. (108 mm) barrel.

GERMANY

HECKLER & KOCH 0.45 IN. MARK 23 (SOCOM) PISTOL 1991

Length (gun): 9.7 in. (245 mm)
Barrel: 5.9 in. (150 mm)
Weight: 42.0 oz. (1.2 kg)
Caliber: 0.45 in.
Rifling: Polygonal; r/hand
Capacity: twelve-round box magazine
Muz vel: 850 ft./sec. (260 m/sec.)

In 1990 U.S. Special Forces Command (SOCOM) issued a new operational requirement for an Offensive Handgun Weapon System consisting of three elements: handgun, laser-aiming module (LAM), and sound/flash suppressor. Some very demanding criteria were announced, and any arms manufacturer was allowed to enter the competition; the Heckler & Koch pistol, with the Knight suppressor, was the winner. The pistol was a development of H&K's 0.45 in. version of the USP, but with a longer slide, a slight extension of the barrel for the screw attachment for the suppressor, and mountings for the LAM. It was accepted for service as the "Pistol, Caliber .45, Mark 23 Mod 0" (known simply as the "SOCOM Pistol") and deliveries started in May 1996. The LAM is attached to the underside of the pistol ahead of the trigger guard and projects a red spot onto the target, enabling the weapon to be sighted with great accuracy. The suppressor screws onto the muzzle and provides a substantial reduction in both flash and noise, the latter being aided by the fact that the bullet is just subsonic, thus avoiding the characteristic "crack" of a supersonic bullet. Specifications relate to the weapon without suppressor.

SWAT
HANDGUNS

Above: *These SWAT team officers in Massachusetts are guarding a courthouse, a duty for which the handgun has little relevance—though some retain a sidearm as a back-up weapon.*

The U.S. Special Weapons and Tactics (SWAT) units are among the best equipped law enforcement organizations in the world, especially in terms of their weaponry. The handguns carried are selected on the basis of reliability, accuracy, ease of handling, and takedown power. The officers of the Los Angeles Police Department SWAT, for example, tend to carry the Colt Government Model .45 ACP. This weapon, although having a limited magazine capacity (eight rounds) when compared to, say, the 9 mm Beretta 92 (fifteen rounds), it has a decisive terminal effect on a human target. It features accurate high-visibility sights, a polished feed ramp, and throated chamber and, on some models, an ambidextrous safety catch for good combat handling. It should be noted that the Para-Ordnance version of the Colt Government features a high-capacity fourteen-round magazine.

SWAT team members, however, are generally allowed to select the weaponry with which they are most comfortable. The Las Vegas SWAT, for example, has an arsenal that includes the Heckler & Koch P9 (in 9 mm and .45 in. calibers); the Glock 17, 19, and 21; the SIG Sauer P220 and P226; and the Smith & Wesson 4003. Many weapons receive some level of modification for SWAT use, particularly in terms of sighting. Luminous night-sights for low-light operations are often fitted as standard, and some pistols even have a small high-power torch attached in front of the trigger. This torch not only aids illumination in dark conditions—its beam can also act as an accuracy aid.

All members of a SWAT team, regardless of their primary weapon, will have a handgun as either a principal or backup weapon. During an entry operation conducted by a typical seven-man team, two members usually are exclusively armed with handguns, one being the point man who needs his other hand to carry a ballistic shield. The entire team may opt for handgun armament if it has to infiltrate a building through narrow windows or doorways.

UNITED STATES

RUGER 9 MM P89/0.45 IN. P90 PISTOLS 1991

Length (gun): 7.75 in. (200 mm)
Barrel: 4.5 in. (114 mm)
Weight: 32.0 oz. (0.9 kg)
Caliber: 9 mm
Rifling: 6 grooves, r/hand
Capacity: see below
Muz vel: 1,099 ft./sec. (335 m/sec.)

The P89 and P90 are upgrades of the P85, the P89 (see specifications) chambered for the NATO standard 9 x 19 mm Parabellum round, the P90 for the 0.45 in. ACP round. Most models in the series are available in three different configurations: manual safety, decock only, and double action only. The manual safety models incorporate ambidextrous safety levers, which push the firing pin forward into the slide, out of reach of the hammer, locking the firing pin firmly in position and decocking the hammer. The gun cannot be fired until the safety lever is moved to the "fire" position and the trigger is pulled fully to the rear. In the decock-only models, the hammer is decocked by depressing either of the ambidextrous decocking levers. When released, the lever springs back to the "fire" position; the gun can only be fired by a double-action pull on the trigger without further contact with the decocking lever. In the double-action-only models, all of which have a spurless hammer, the firing pin is blocked from forward movement by an internal safety unless the trigger is completely pulled; operation is "double action only" for all shots. Shown here are the P89D 9 mm Parabellum, blued finish, decock-only (right); and the P90 0.45 in. ACP, blued finish, manual safety (left).

AUSTRIA

STEYR 9 MM SPECIAL PURPOSE PISTOL 1993

Length (gun): 12.7 in. (322 mm)
Barrel: 5.1 in. (130 mm)
Weight: 45.0 oz. (1.3 kg)
Caliber: 9 mm
Rifling: 6 grooves, r/hand
Capacity: fifteen- or thirty-round box magazine
Muz vel: 1,214 ft./sec. (370 m/sec.)

The Steyr 9 mm Special Purpose Pistol (SPP) is generally similar to the Steyr Tactical Machine Pistol (TMP), but whereas the latter, despite its name, is properly categorized as a submachine gun, the SPP is most definitely a pistol. The SPP's frame and top cover are made of a synthetic fiber material, and the weapon does not have the forward grip of the TMP, although there is a small extension of the fore-end of the body, which is intended to keep the firer's fingers away from the muzzle. The SPP fires the 9 x 19 mm Parabellum round in the semiautomatic mode only. The cocking handle is at the rear of the weapon, and the weapon is recoil-operated, the breech being locked by a rotating barrel. The box magazine is housed in the pistol grip, and there are two sizes, fifteen and thirty rounds. They lacked stopping power.

UNITED STATES

HECKLER & KOCH UNIVERSAL SELF-LOADING PISTOL 1993

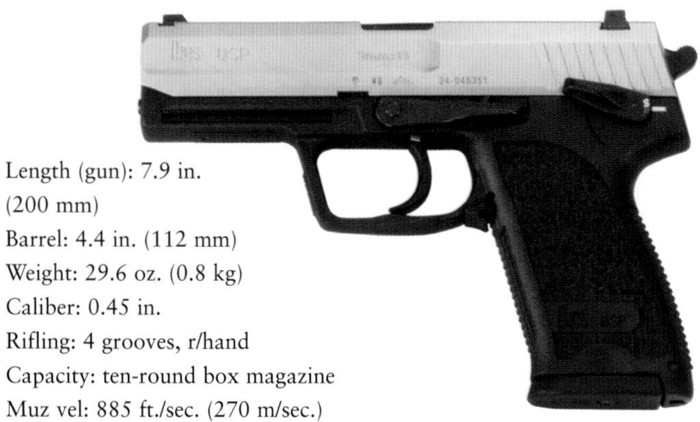

Length (gun): 7.9 in. (200 mm)
Barrel: 4.4 in. (112 mm)
Weight: 29.6 oz. (0.8 kg)
Caliber: 0.45 in.
Rifling: 4 grooves, r/hand
Capacity: ten-round box magazine
Muz vel: 885 ft./sec. (270 m/sec.)

This was initially designed around the 0.40 in. S&W round, but was then adapted to the 9 mm Parabellum round, and then to the 0.45 in. ACP (see specifications), in which case the weapon is marginally larger and heavier. It uses a locked-breech double-action, with a Browning cam lock and a recoil buffering device, but a modular approach to the design has resulted in great flexibility, with customers being able to choose between as many as nine alternative action and safety combinations. Mounting grooves are already fitted for scopes, night sights, and laser spot projectors. Another version, the USP Compact, is identical in all respects to the USP but is dimensionally smaller; the 0.45 in. version, for example, is 7.1 in. (180 mm) long, weighs 28 oz. (0.79 kg) and takes only eight rounds. Like the larger USP, the Compact is also available in 0.40 in. S&W and 9 mm Parabellum.

UNITED STATES

RUGER P93 PISTOL 1994

Length (gun): 7.25 in. (184 mm)
Barrel: 3.9 in. (99 mm)
Weight: 31.0 oz. (0.9 kg)
Caliber: 9 mm
Rifling: 6 grooves, r/hand
Capacity: ten-round box magazine
Muz vel: 1,165 ft./sec. (355 m/sec.)

This is the compact model in the Ruger P-series and is produced in 9 mm caliber only. It is smaller and lighter than the P89 and is available in Decock-only (D) and Double-Action-Only (DAO) versions, but not in Manual Safety. There is no equivalent model chambered for 0.45 in. ACP, but the P93 fires all types of 9 x 19 mm ammunition including those with +P loads. The magazine holds ten rounds and is interoperable with the magazine of the P89. The picture shows the P93D, the Decock-only version.

UNITED STATES

RUGER VAQUERO REVOLVER 1993

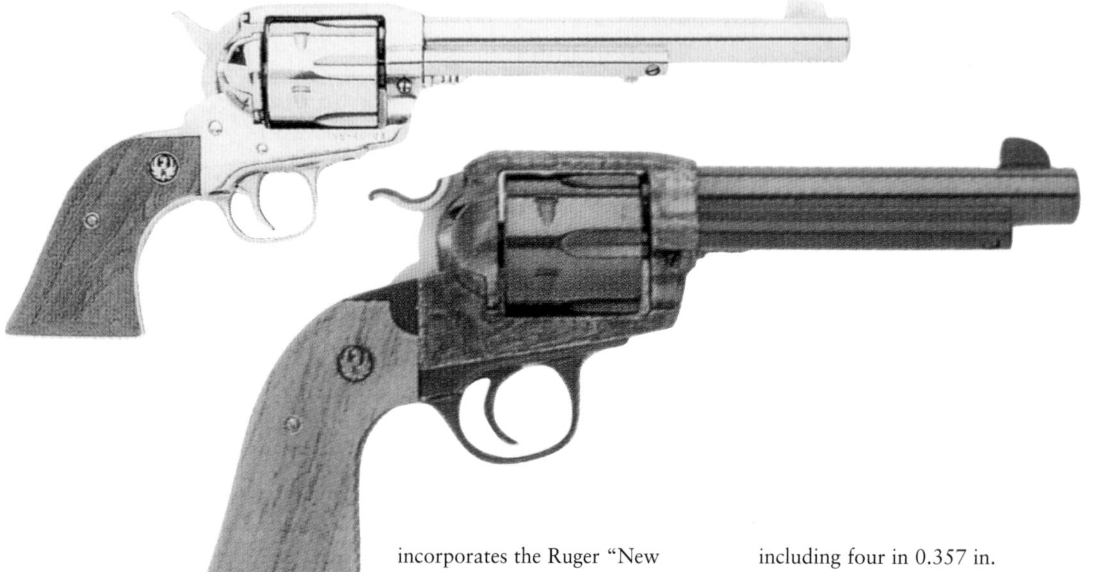

Length (gun): 13.2 in. (335 mm)
Barrel: 7.5 in. (191 mm)
Weight: 41.0 oz. (1.1 kg)
Caliber: 0.44-40 in.
Rifling: not available
Capacity: six
Muz vel: not available

Ruger's Vaquero is a fixed-sight version of the New Model Blackhawk and is outwardly patterned after the traditional pistols of the American West of the mid-1800s. Internally, however, it incorporates the Ruger "New Model" single-action mechanism and is made of modern materials and produced to modern degrees of accuracy and tolerance, resulting in a weapon that is much more reliable and accurate than its predecessors. No fewer than twenty variations are marketed, including four in 0.357 in. Magnum, six in 0.44-40 in. (see specifications), four in 0.44 in. Magnum, and six in 0.45 in. Long Colt. These include the usual selections of barrel length and finishes. The Bisley-Vaquero combines the looks of the Vaquero with the Bisley-style hammer, grip frame, and trigger. Shown here are the 0.44-40 in. Vaquero with 7.5 in. (191 mm) barrel in high-gloss stainless steel finish (top); and 0.44 Magnum Bisley-Vaquero with 5.5 in. (140 mm) barrel in blued finish (bottom).

UNITED STATES

RUGER P94/0.40 AUTO P944 PISTOL 1994

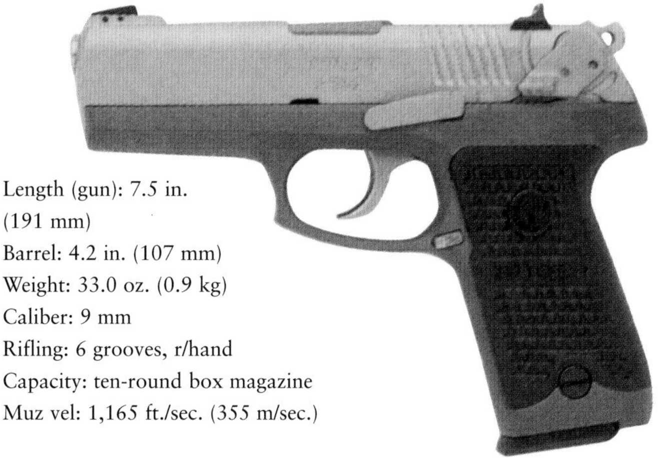

Length (gun): 7.5 in. (191 mm)
Barrel: 4.2 in. (107 mm)
Weight: 33.0 oz. (0.9 kg)
Caliber: 9 mm
Rifling: 6 grooves, r/hand
Capacity: ten-round box magazine
Muz vel: 1,165 ft./sec. (355 m/sec.)

The P94 models are sized between the P89/P90 and the compact P93. Like all other models in the P-series, the blued models in the range P94 are made from chrome-molybdenum steel, while the stainless steel versions are made of aircraft-quality hard-coated A356T6 aluminum alloy and Ruger's proprietary "Terhune-Anticorro" stainless steel. The grips are made of 6123 Xenoy resin, which is claimed to be virtually indestructible. The Model 94 is made in manual safety, decocking-only and double-action-only versions; the manual model is made in both blued steel and stainless steel finishes, the others in stainless steel only. A second version is available, the P944, which is chambered for the 0.40 Auto round and is available in the same models as the P94. The picture shows the P94, the 9 mm weapon with manual safety and stainless steel finish.

UNITED STATES

RUGER 9 MM P95/0.45 IN. P97 PISTOLS 1996

Length: 13.5 in. (343 mm)
Weight: 68 oz. (1.93 kg)
Barrel: 7.5 in. (190 mm)
Caliber: 0.44 in. (11.2 mm)
Rifling: 7 groove, l/hand
Capacity: Six
Muz Vel: 850 ft./sec. (259 m/sec.)

The P95 is chambered for 9 x 19 mm Parabellum (including those with +P loads), and the P97 for 0.45 in. ACP. They are dimensionally identical, but the P95 holds ten rounds, the P97 seven. They are smaller than previous models in the P-range, and weigh 27.0 oz. (0.77 kg) compared to 32.0 oz. (0.91 kg) for the P89 and 31.0 oz. (0.88 kg) for the P93. One of the main reasons is the use of a new compounded polymer for the frames, which incorporates a long-strand fiberglass filler. The mechanism uses the same tilting barrel system, but with a new type of lock which decelerates the fast-moving barrel and brings it to a halt without damage to the frame. Both are available with either decock only (D) or double-action only (DAO) safety features. Shown here are the KP95DAO 9 mm version with stainless steel finish (left); and the KP97D 0.45 in. ACP version, decock-only, with stainless steel finish (right).

BELGIUM

FABRIQUE NATIONALE 5.7 MM FIVE-SEVEN PISTOL 1998

Length (gun): 8.2 in. (208 mm)
Barrel: 4.8 in. (123 mm)
Weight: 22.0 oz. (0.6 kg)
Caliber: 5.7 mm
Rifling: 6 grooves, r/hand
Capacity: twenty-round box magazine
Muz vel: 2,133 ft./sec. (650 m/sec.)

The Five-Seven pistol has been developed by FN as the hand-held element of the company's P90 personal defense weapon system. Much of the Five-Seven is made from synthetic materials, including the outer casing of the slide, and it uses a new type of delayed blowback developed by FN specifically for this application, in which the slide is briefly held by cams until the barrel has withdrawn some 0.12 in. (3 mm), whereupon they unlock. There is provision for mounting a laser target designator (LTD) or a small light in front of the trigger.

Rifles & Shotguns

"With the possible exception of the foreign observers, no one present had previously seen breechloaders in action, and to men accustomed to volleys the fire was frightening in its intensity."

General Napier on the use of the Snider rifle at the Battle of Arogi in Abyssinia, 1868.

Above: *The 7.62 mm Accuracy International L96A1 sniper rifle has all the sophisticated attributes of modern sniper weapons. The heavy barrel is made from durable stainless steel, the stock and cheek piece are fully adjustable, and it has guaranteed first-round accuracy.*

The history of rifles goes back as far as the fourteenth century, when soldiers of northern Europe tucked pike hafts beneath their armpits to which were attached basic, crude "hand gonnes." These weapons were little more than miniaturized cannons, fired by touching a hot iron or match against a vent hole. The next 200 years were essentially spent refining the system of firing. Around the mid 1400s, the matchlock brought controllable ignition by a single individual, and the sixteenth century brought the innovations of wheel-lock and snaphance lock. The snaphance itself evolved into the flintlock around 1612.

The steady progress in firing mechanism and barrel manufacture meant that the early smoothbore weapons had a decent accuracy up to 164 ft. (50 m), but the major leap forward for the rifle in terms of accuracy came with rifling. Rifled firearms had emerged as early as the sixteenth century. Rifling the barrel, which involved cutting spiral parallel grooves into the bore of the weapon, dramatically improved rifle accuracy. In flight, a bullet fired from a smoothbore weapon will flip to present its heaviest side foremost, and this rotation destabilizes the bullet's flight path, as well as shortening its effective range. Rifling, however, imparts spin to the bullet, maintaining its stability in flight through gyroscopic motion around the central axis of the round.

Rifled weapons, initially called "screw guns," were, however, expensive to make and slow to load because of the tight constriction of the barrel around the shot (loading was later speeded up by wrapping the ball in a small patch of oiled leather or linen). They were taken up by wealthy sportsmen but also entered military use during the English Civil War (1642–51) in a sniping role. It was, however, in the early decades of European colonization of the New World that rifled firearms established themselves as important weapons. The rifled gun's extended range was not only practical for the hunters in the vast expanses of North America, but also found ready application in the wars against the Indians. The Indian wars did not involve the formal meeting of column and line of infantry. Instead, US frontiersman valued the rifle for its ability to engage a fast and elusive enemy before he could close to hand-to-hand combat distance. The typical US rifle had a barrel length of up to 4 ft. (1.3 m), giving it a head-shot accuracy at 164 ft. (50 m), and had a caliber of 0.5 in. (12.75 mm) to provide decisive stopping power. The US used the rifle in a much more modern, irregular, manner than many European forces, and US rifleman proved their worth against the French in the Seven Years' War (1756–63) and the British in the Revolutionary War (1775–83).

The move to breech-loading

The British in particular learned many hard lessons from fighting the revolutionary Americans, and in 1800 a Rifle Regiment armed with the new rifled Baker flintlock was created. The Baker was a durable weapon with an accuracy of up to and even beyond 650 ft. (198 m), but it was surpassed in 1853 with the introduction of the Enfield rifle, which had a ladder-type backsight that could be configured to ranges

between 300 ft. (91 m) and 2,650 ft. (807 m). The Enfield took advantage of new elongated projectiles, which had a hollow base. Although the round was loose enough to push quickly down the barrel, on firing the percussion gases expanded the hollow base to grip the rifling. This simple innovation speeded up loading time, although the time was still relatively slow, at about three to four shots each minute.

As the range, reloading time, accuracy, and stopping power of rifles increased, nineteenth-century warfare was transformed. The American Civil War (1861–65) proved the point—frontal attacks were slaughtered, the construction of defensive works became essential, infantry engagements began at greater ranges, and cavalry became increasingly ineffectual.

However, despite the technological advances, muzzle-loading weapons were still restricted by their laborious loading process. In 1838 the Prussian gunsmith Johann von Dreyse designed the infamous "needle gun," a breech-loading single-shot rifle firing a nonmetallic unitary cartridge. By 1880, by which time the needle gun had proved its worth in combat against the Danes, Austrians, and French, bolt-action rifles firing self-contained cartridges were in use throughout Europe and the United States. Such rifles could achieve rates of fire of around ten shots per minute, but these rates were exceeded by repeating rifles such as the Henry/Winchester, which were fed from tubular magazines and operated by lever action.

Above: *A French infantryman shoulders a Lebel M1886/93, This 0.3 in (8 mm) rifle, which was fed from an 8-round under-barrel tube magazine, continued to serve with French forces until the end of World War II.*

From bolt-action to automatic

Bolt-action, magazine-fed rifles gave unprecedented killing power to the common soldier. In tandem with advances in cartridge technology, a rifle such as the Mauser Gewehr 98 or the Lee-Enfield Mk III had a killing range of up to 1 mile (1.6 km) and could be fired every two or three seconds. Less well-armed enemies—such as the Sudanese forces which confronted the colonial British in 1898—were decimated. In 1914, at the onset of World War I, German soldiers cut down the massed ranks of French soldiers attempting bayonet charges with their reliable but old-fashioned Lebel rifles. The Germans themselves suffered at the hands of the British equipped with the superb Short-Magazine Lee-Enfield (SMLE) rifle. The SMLE could fire fifteen aimed rounds a minute, and the British rifle fire in battles such as that at Mons in 1914 was so intense that the Germans interpreted it as machine-gun fire.

Yet although the full-caliber rifle was the most common weapon of World War I, the conflict also revealed the rifle's limitations. Machine-gun fire and artillery took responsibility for most long-range killing, and unless engaged in sniping, an infantryman would be more likely to fight at close quarters in and around trench systems. Rifles measuring in the region of 49 in. (1.25 m) were unwieldy in close-quarter combat. A partial solution to this was the use of more carbine rifles of reduced length, such as the Italian Mannlicher-Carcano M1891 with a length of 36.2 in. (920 mm). Another solution was the use of different weapon types, such as the early submachine guns and the hand grenade.

By the beginning of the next World War in 1939, many of the world's infantrymen were still armed with long-range bolt-action rifles, although submachine guns and light machine guns were now a formal part of the unit arsenal. However, a new weapon had also entered service—the semiautomatic rifle. Semiautomatic rifles had appeared as far back as the late nineteenth century, but none entered widespread service until after World War I. In 1936, the United States Army took the revolutionary step of becoming the first world army to adopt a semi-automatic rifle as its standard infantry weapon. This weapon was the .30 in. M1 Garand, a tough, accurate, gas-operated rifle fed from a charger-loaded eight-round magazine. The Garand was a superb illustration of the advantage conferred on an infantryman through the semi-automatic system. Having the ability to unleash eight rounds in as many seconds enabled US soldiers to generate enormous volumes of small-unit firepower, something that became especially useful in the Pacific War, which often favored firepower over tactical maneuvers because of the difficult terrain.

The assault rifle

Although the Garand was undoubtedly a major step forward in rifle evolution, it was still wedded to the full-power rifle cartridge with a range of 3,200 ft. (1,000 m). In World War II, a typical infantry section would include three different types of weapon: rifles, submachine guns, and light machine guns. The light machine guns provided long-range support fire, the submachine guns close-quarter firepower, while the rationale for the rifle seemed, awkwardly, somewhere in between.

Combat studies by the Germans during the late 1930s revised practical infantry combat ranges to a maximum range of 1,300 ft. (400 m), but usually rifle fire was exchanged at a range of around 320 ft. (100 m). Furthermore, the profusion of different weapon types within an infantry unit increased the logistical burden of ammunition supply.

One option was to enable rifles to fire in full-auto but, apart from superb exceptions like the Russian Tokarev M1938 and the German Fallschirmgewehr 42 (FG42), such weapons were almost uncontrollable because of the high-power rifle round.

What emerged from Germany was a new type of cartridge and the weapons to fire it. The 7.92 x 33 mm "Kurz" (short) round contained 50 percent less powder than the standard Mauser 7.92 x 57 mm rifle round, but still offered plenty of killing power within the 1,300 ft. (400 m) combat range, while also facilitating controllable full-automatic fire.

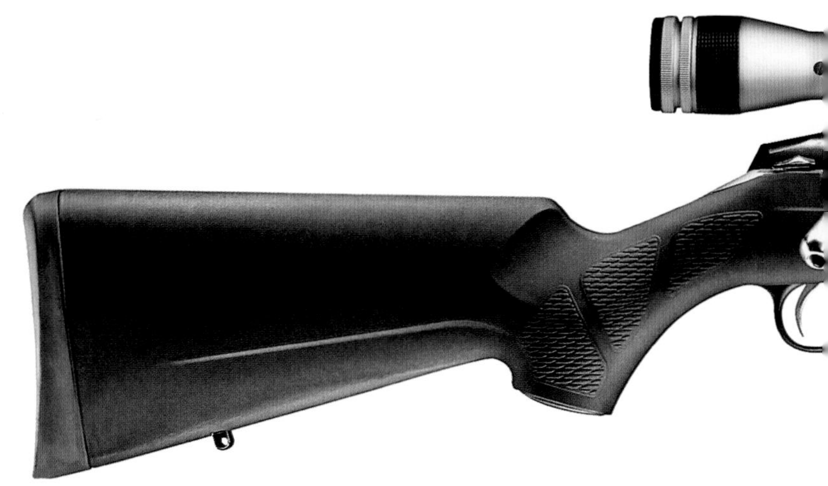

Above: *The Tikka T3 hunting rifle. The classic bolt-action is an ideal system for accuracy weapons, providing a consistent loading of each cartridge, a safe firing of powerful rounds, and a gentle handling of high-quality ammunition.*

The "Kurz" round gave birth to the assault rifle. A series of new gas-operated weapons emerged from Germany industry to take the "Kurz," including the cutting-edge StGG44. Although most of Germany's infantryman still fought World War II with bolt-action rifles—the short round innovation came too late in the war to make a decisive impact—the groundwork was laid for the global switch to the assault rifle type in the postwar world.

In 1947, a 7.62 mm version of the "Kurz" round was applied by one Mikhail Kalashnikov to the most influential assault rifle, indeed arguably the most influential firearm, in history—the AK47. The AK47 was not a sophisticated weapon, but it was extremely reliable, generated heavy firepower, and was easy to mass produce by relying heavily on metal stamping processes. It was adopted as the standard infantry weapon of the Soviet army, and to date some 80 to 100 million AK47s and variants have been distributed around the world into the hands of armies, terrorists, criminals, and militias.

Small-caliber rifles

Western Europe and the United States also opted for the assault rifle, but took a different course and timeline. The full-power 7.62 mm rifle round persisted in many western armies, and indeed equips many armies today. In the US, the M1 Garand was replaced by the M14 in the mid-1950s. The British Army adopted the L1A1 rifle (based on the FN FAL) in 1954 and used it until the late 1980s. Both were excellent semiautomatic weapons, but attempts to apply full-auto settings to these powerful guns were not successful.

In the 1950s, however, the US weapons designer Eugene Stoner designed the Armalite

AR-15. The AR-15 was distinctive not only because of its increased use of plastics in the construction, but also because of its round—the 5.56 x 45 mm M193. While substantially smaller than the 7.62 mm round, the M193 achieved extremely high velocities of around 3,280 fps (1,000 mps), which in terms of terminal ballistics compensated for the reduced size.

The smaller round also enabled the infantryman to carry more ammunition, and the US Army eventually adopted the AR-15, renamed the M16, as the standard US Army rifle from 1967. It is still with the US Army in the form of the M16A2.

Increased requirements for NATO standardization in the 1960s and '70s led the rest of NATO nations down the 5.56 mm route. France replaced its MAS 49 and 49/56 rifles with the 5.56 mm Fusil Automatique MAS (FAMAS) in the early 1980s.

In the late 1980s the British Army was re-equipped with the controversial SA80 bullpup weapon, firing the now standard 5.56 x 45 mm NATO round. In the 1970s, even the Russians produced the AK74 variant firing a 5.45 x 39 mm high-velocity round.

The future

The future of rifle development is difficult to predict. The basic metallic cartridge, gas-operated design shows little sign of succumbing to a technological revolution. Heckler & Koch did attempt an advance with the 4.7 mm G11 rifle, firing caseless ammunition: the round is embedded in a block of propellant rather than fitted into a cartridge. The G11 is a remarkable weapon, with unsurpassed control of recoil in full-auto mode (owing to the fact it has no extraction and ejection phase), yet politics rather than pragmatism has delayed its intended issue to the German forces.

The significant future changes for the rifle seems to lie in the word "modularity." The capabilities of rifles are being enhanced not so much by changes to their intrinsic mechanisms, but through fitting modular components which enhance the weapon's performance or change its role. The US Army's Land Warrior program, for example, has the M16/M-4 rifle fitted with a video-camera sight attached to a monocular head-up display unit, allowing the soldier to fire his weapon accurately around corners. The weapon is also fitted with a laser rangefinder /digital compass (LRF/DC) to provide range and direction information. Other modular weapons such as the OICW and the XM8 are already threatening the future of the M16A2 as the standard US rifle. Whatever the outcome, the common assault rifle is becoming much more than just a standard infantry weapon, but a complete weapons system in its own right.

Above: *A US soldier opens fire with his .30 in. Garand rifle during fighting on Bougainville in March 1944. The Garand was the first semi-auto rifle to be adopted for standard military use, and gave reliable service in all theaters, from the Arctic conditions of the Aleutians to the tropical jungles of the South Pacific.*

RUGER RED LABEL SHOTGUN

The Ruger is an over-and-under 12-gauge shotgun fitted with a hammer interrupter which is only lifted clear of the hammers by a deliberate pull of the trigger, a valuable safety device similar in its effect to the intercepting safety sears found on most quality sidelock guns and some high-quality boxlocks. The automatic safety catch incorporates the barrel selector, which pivots from one side to the other and, unlike other over-and-unders, indicates the barrel to be fired first by the unmistakeable letters "B" and "T," for bottom and top, rather than the letters "U" and "O" or other symbols that may be more ambiguous.

The Red Label is manufactured using stainless steel in the receiver, trigger, and forend iron. The stock and semi-beavertail forearm are produced from American walnut. The weapon is taken down by opening the latch and pivoting the barrels off the frame, then removing the forend. The barrels pivot on trunnions, one piece with the frame.

This weapon lends itself well to sporting clay shooting; the over-and-under design provides a sighting plane, and the rugged construction allows the shotgun to stand up to the continual shooting of thousands of shells.

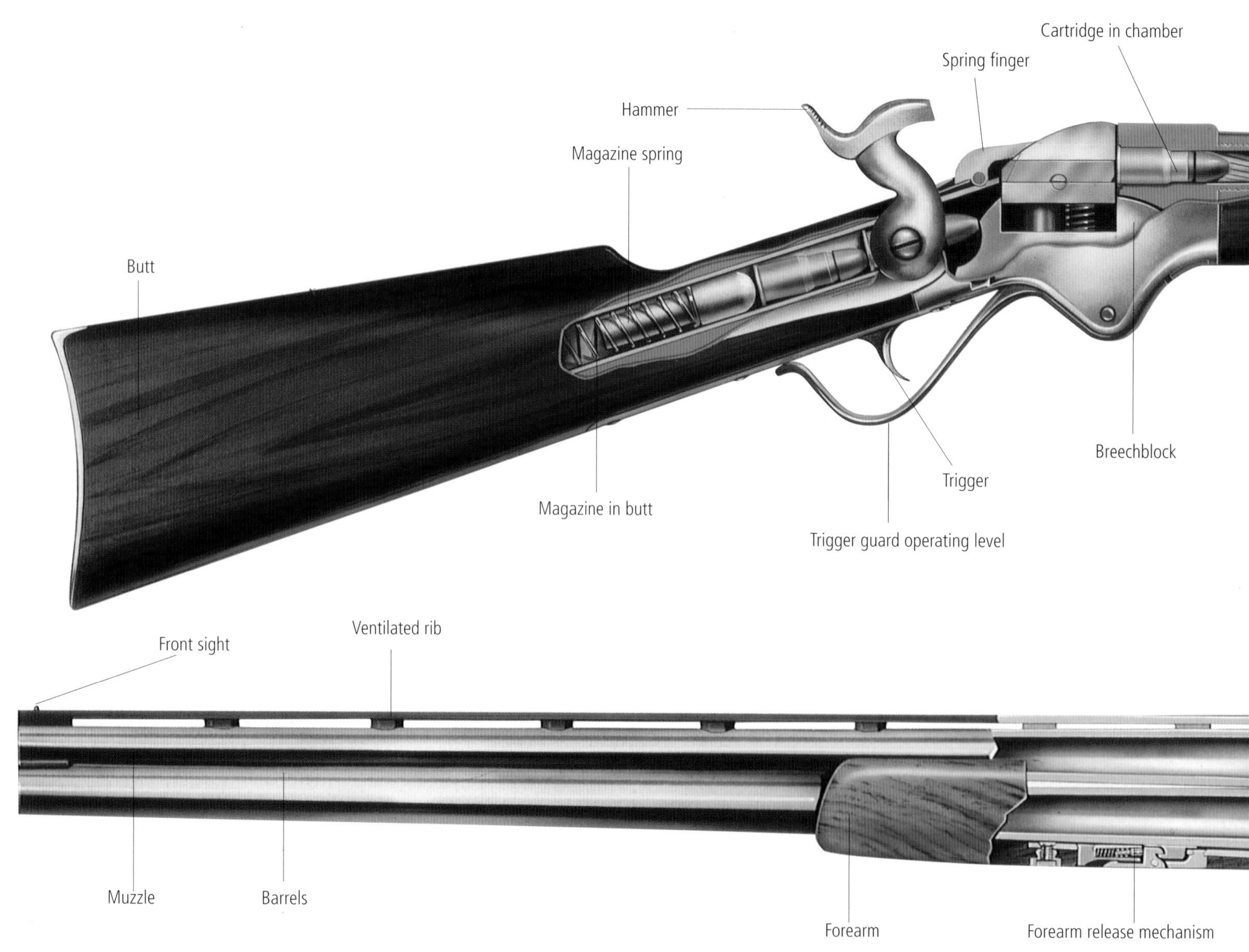

RUGER RED LABEL SHOTGUN

SPENCER RIFLE 1860

In March 1860, Christopher Spencer, a remarkable American who had little formal education but was endowed with great inventive genius and energy, produced the repeating arm named after him. It had a removable tubular magazine in the butt which took seven copper rimfire cartridges and was worked by a lever which also acted as a trigger guard. Downward pressure ejected the empty case (if any) in the chamber and upward pressure loaded the next round, after which the external hammer had to be cocked in readiness for firing.

It was a simple, reliable arm, cheap to make and sufficiently robust for service use. Its appearance coincided closely with the outbreak of the American Civil War. At that time the breechloader firing modern cartridges was a rarity; the armies on both sides were armed with percussion rifles of Enfield type. Although it was quickly officially adopted there were considerable delays in issuing it to the Union Army. Some states purchased Spencer's arms privately and their value in battle soon became apparent. In 1863, Spencer approached President Lincoln personally, and the president tried out the Spencer by taking the rifle into a neighboring park and firing it at a plank leant against a tree. Lincoln was duly impressed; by the end of the war the United States government had bought upwards of 100,000 of the arms.

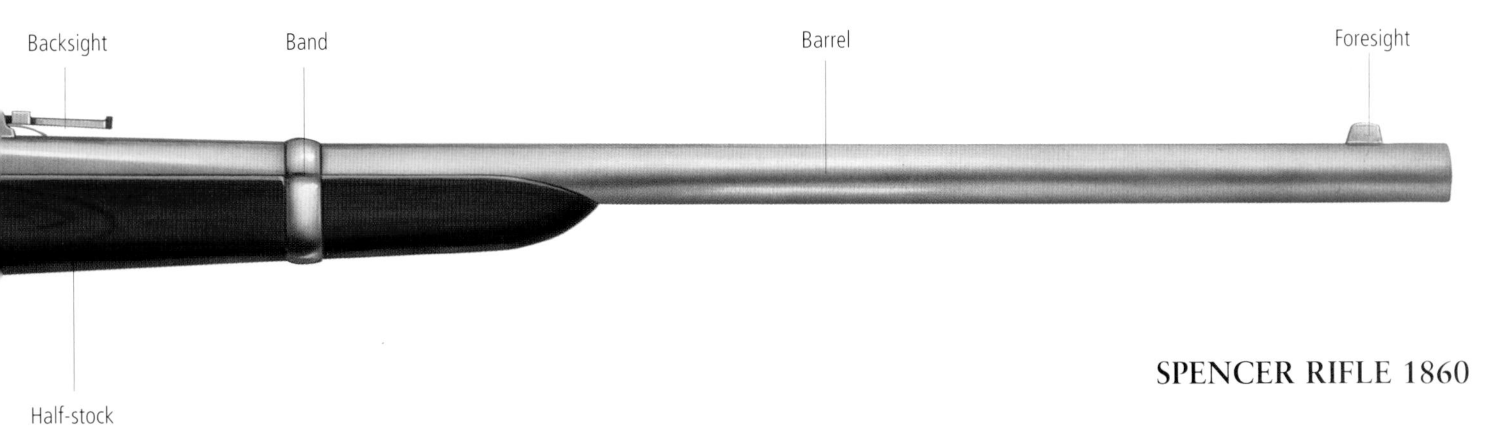

SPENCER RIFLE 1860

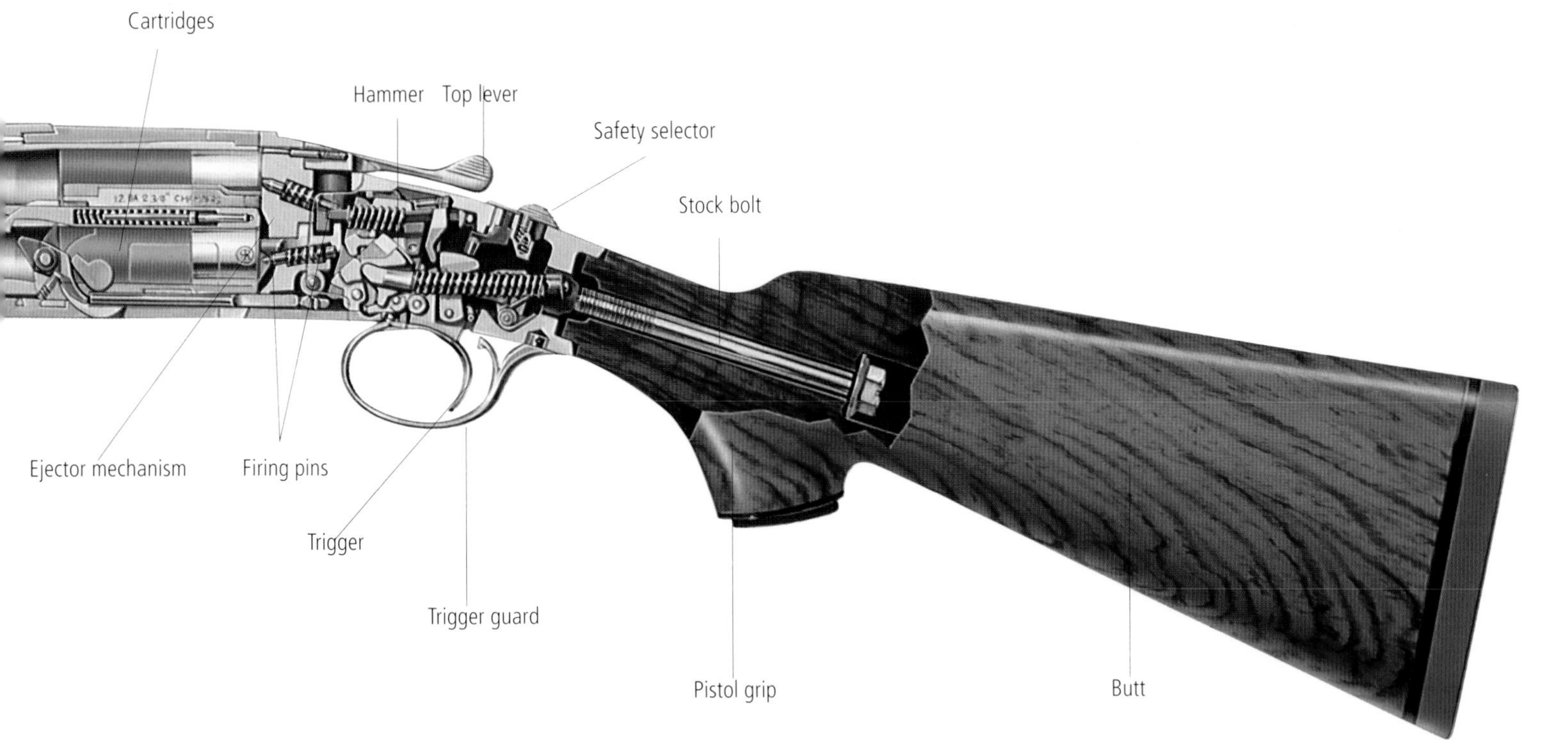

ITALY

BROWN BESS FLINTLOCK MUSKET (REPRODUCTION) 1768

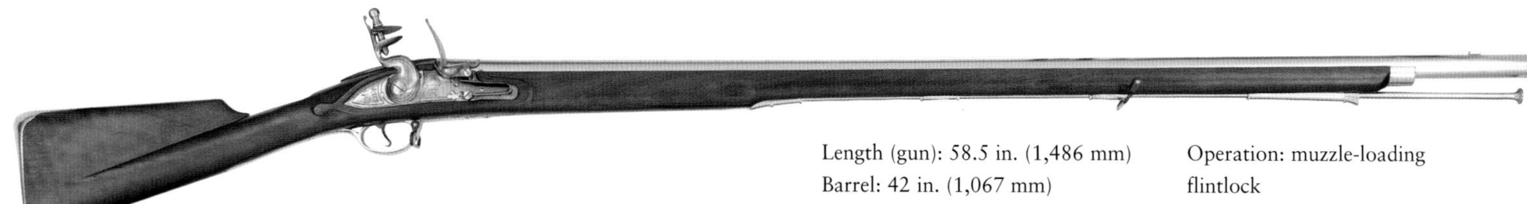

Length (gun): 58.5 in. (1,486 mm)
Barrel: 42 in. (1,067 mm)
Weight (gun): 9.4 lb. (4.3 kg)
Caliber: 0.75 in. (19.1 mm)
Rifling: none
Operation: muzzle-loading flintlock
Feed: single-round, muzzle-loader
Muz vel: n.k.

This Perdosoli reproduction is of the famous British "Brown Bess" (qv), the standard British infantry long-arm for some 130 years. The reproduction is closely based on a model made for use by the militia by a firm named Grice in 1762, although the iron ramrod and forward ferrule have been taken from the Short Land Pattern Musket of 1768. Modern smoothbore musket competitive shooting began in 1958 with the introduction of the Brown Bess Cup, which called for the firing of ten shots in ten minutes at a distance of 75 yd. (69 m). The demand for weapons for such competitions remained limited for some years, but wider interest was generated by the growth of historical battle re-enactments, which led to the formation of various display societies. This Brown Bess replica is, admittedly, somewhat out-of-period for that conflict.

ITALY

KENTUCKY FLINTLOCK RIFLE (REPRODUCTION) 1785

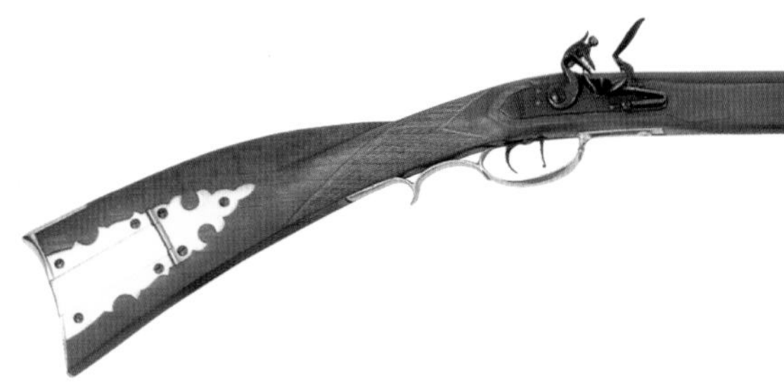

Length (gun): 57.5 in. (1,460 mm)
Barrel: 40.5 in. (1,030 mm)
Weight (gun): 7.6 lb. (3.5 kg)
Caliber: 0.45 in. (11.4 mm)
Rifling: n.k.
Operation: flintlock
Feed: single-round, manual
Muz vel: n.k.

Many copies of early American firearms are made in Europe for collectors who cannot afford a rare and expensive original, although, according to experts, the quality of such reproductions varies widely. This particular example, made in Italy by the Palmetto Armory, is a replica of the generic "Kentucky rifle" which, despite its name, actually originated in the New England states. Rifles of this type featured an unusually long barrel of very small bore, typically between 0.400 in. (10.2 mm) and 0.450 in. (11.4 mm), and were reputed to be extremely accurate as well as economical in their use of powder and lead. Their range was, however, somewhat limited, probably of the order of 80 yards (73 m), although this would have been perfectly adequate for the purpose for which they were intended—shooting game for the pot at close range in the New England forests.

UNITED KINGDOM

INDIA PATTERN BROWN BESS MUSKET 1793

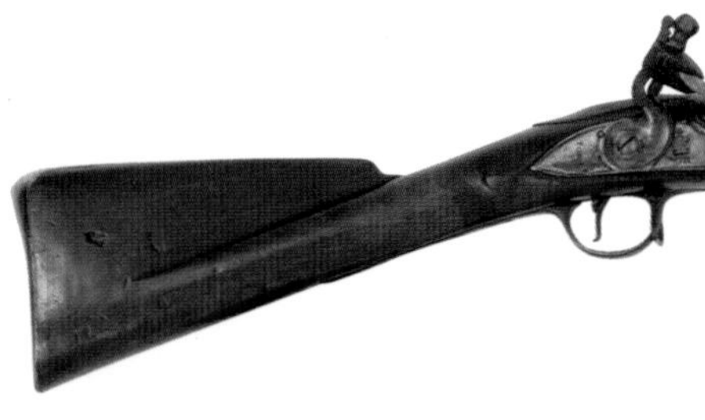

Length (gun): 54.3 in. (1,378 mm)
Barrel: 38.6 in. (921 mm)
Weight (gun): 9.9 lb. (4.5 kg)
Caliber: 0.753 in. (19.1 mm)
Rifling: none
Operation: flintlock
Feed: manual, muzzle-loading
Muz vel: n.k.

The "Brown Bess" was the standard British Army infantry weapon throughout the Napoleonic Wars, with a maximum rate of fire of about 4 rpm. Its accuracy was estimated as being capable of hitting a man-size target at 75 yards (69 m). The reason for the title "India Pattern" is that when the French Revolutionary Wars started in 1793, the British Army was short of weapons and turned to the Honorable East India Company, which handed over what muskets it had in stock in Britain, and armories throughout the country were encouraged to produce the "India Pattern Brown Bess." This remained the standard British infantry musket well into the nineteenth century and was in production at the start Queen Victoria's reign. The weapon illustrated carries the Tower Ordnance Store Keeper's Stamp dated 1800, indicating that it was accepted for service in that year.

THE MATCHLOCK AND ARQUEBUS

The earliest handguns of the fifteenth century utilized the application of a hand-held slow match or hot iron to the touchhole to achieve ignition. However, this process was far from satisfactory, as it required a two-man effort—one man would steady and aim the weapon, and another would fire it. This compromised accuracy, producing an inevitable delay between achieving the sight picture and firing the weapon. What was required was a mechanism by which the gun could be handled and fired by one person.

The matchlock provided the solution and was utterly simple. A curved metal arm was fitted to the side of the weapon, the lower portion acting as the trigger, while the upper end held a smoldering slow match. All it required the soldier to do to fire the weapon was to pull on the trigger in order to drop the slow match forward onto the touchhole.

The matchlock facilitated the birth of true small arms, as it enabled single-operator firearms, in particular the arquebus rifle. The term "arquebus" comes from the German "hakbusche" meaning hook gun, possibly a reference to the early weapons that featured hooks beneath the barrels to lock onto solid objects, such as walls or trees, to aid aiming.

The arquebus was undoubtedly a revelation in firearms design but had severe limitations. The weapons were time-consuming to load and prone to misfires (both gunpowder and slow match were very vulnerable to damp) and so tended to be used on the battlefields of late-fifteenth-century Europe for isolated salvoes only.

More innovative military leaders, such as Charles the Bold of Burgundy, combined gunners and English archers into what were in effect prototype combined-arms units.

Moreover, compared to the bow the arquebus was inaccurate, although the best weapons in trained hands could hit a cavalry horse or even a man at around 130 feet (40 m). Accuracy was assisted by a special forked support on which the arquebus was set prior to firing.

Although limited, the matchlock sowed the seeds of future firearms and effectively transformed the face of warfare and personal defense.

Above: *Loading the arquebus was a time-consuming process, a competent rifleman achieving little more than two shots per minute. Note the monopod stand used to assist accurate firing, essential in a weapon often weighing more than 12 lb. (5.5 kg).*

Left: *By the middle of the sixteenth century, the matchlock had evolved into "snapping matchlock" varieties. Here, the slow match was held by a hammer cocked under spring tension and released into the pan by pulling the trigger. The snapping matchblock gave much faster ignition times than the earlier matchlocks, which operated simply via a pivoted arm.*

European Rifle Combat in the 18th Century

The key restriction upon the tactical employment of muskets in the eighteenth century was accuracy, or rather, the lack of it. The limits of an individual musket's firepower were commented on by British colonel Georg Hanger in 1814:

> A soldier's musket, if not exceedingly ill-bored (as many are), will strike the figure of a man at 80 yards; it may even at a hundred; but a soldier must be very unfortunate indeed who shall be wounded by a common musket at 150 yards ... and as to firing at a man at 200 yards, you may as well fire at the moon.

This statement of the inaccuracy of musket fire is borne out by an accuracy test conducted by the Prussian army toward the end of the eighteenth century. A whole battalion, firing at a target 100 ft. (30 m) long by 6 ft. (2 m) high, managed 60 percent hits at 75 yd. (66 m) and only 40 percent hits at 150 yd. (137 m).

The inaccuracy of the musket at range meant that volley fire was the only practical engagement method for the armies of Europe in the eighteenth century. War was conducted by drill, typically the musketeers moving into battle in column, then positioning themselves in a ranked line or square for firing. The ideal was that all fire would be synchronized, one rank firing while another reloaded, discharging hails of shot at an enemy often about 160 ft. (50 m) away.

Above: *A contemporary illustration of fighting around the Tuileries in Paris during the Revolution in 1792 depicts something of the reality of musket warfare. The soldiers are deployed in ranked squares to present sequential volley fire against the enemy. Note the vast billows of smoke. The visibility on eighteenth-century battlefields could be reduced to a matter of yards by black powder smoke, and prolonged exposure to such smoke resulted in headaches, nausea, and vomiting.*

Theoretically, a two-rank line should have been able to deliver six volleys a minute (based on a trained musketeer firing three rounds per minute), but the reality of combat was, not surprisingly, very different.

Inequalities in loading speed, misfires (often running at a rate of one in five, more if the weather was damp), and casualties among the riflemen meant that after the initial volleys, rifle fire became far more sporadic, each rifleman firing at targets as the opportunity arose.

Apart from his fire, the most important contribution a soldier could make would be with his bayonet, which had replaced the need for separate riflemen and pikemen in the seventeenth century. Enemy cavalry found it extremely hard to penetrate a martial square of riflemen, the mounted troops being either shot at distance or their horses stuck by the enemy bayonets. Also, many eighteenth-century tacticians generally mistrusted the musket to win battles and felt that cold steel was the way to actually dominate the enemy. Only by the end of the next century did firepower alone appear unassailable.

UNITED KINGDOM

BAKER RIFLE 1800

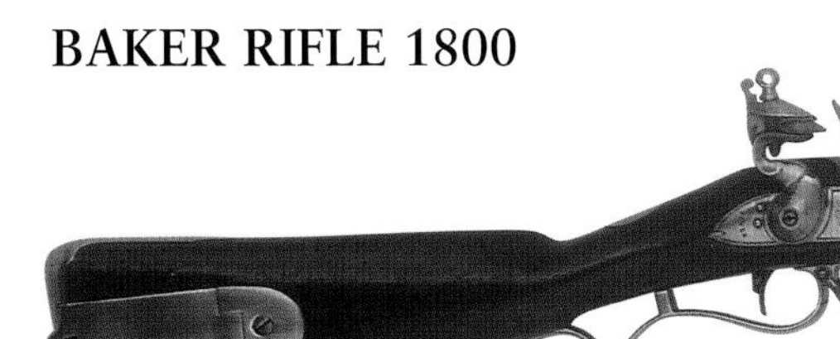

Length (gun): 46.0 in. (1,168 mm)
Barrel: 30.0 in. (762 mm)
Weight (gun): 9.1 lb. (4.1 kg)
Caliber: 0.614 in. (15.6 mm)
Rifling: 7 grooves, r/hand
Operation: flint
Feed: muzzle-loading
Muz vel: ca 1,000 ft./sec. (305 m/sec.)

The Baker rifle was designed by Ezekiel Baker and submitted to the tests that were held at the Royal Arsenal, Woolwich, England, in February 1800. It duly won and was ordered into production, entering service with the British Army in 1801. It was the weapon with which the specialty "rifle" regiments fought in the Peninsular War and at the Battle of Waterloo in 1815. For its day it was a light, robust, handy, and well-made weapon, in which its users had great confidence. It was usually fitted with fixed sights with which targets could be engaged with reasonable accuracy up to ranges of some 200 yd. (183 m), although marksmen might be able to achieve 300 yd. (274 m) on a windless day. A few examples have been found with a folding rear sight. It remained in service until 1838, when it was replaced by the Brunswick rifle (qv).

UNITED KINGDOM

SAMUEL STAUDENMAYER TARGET RIFLE 1805

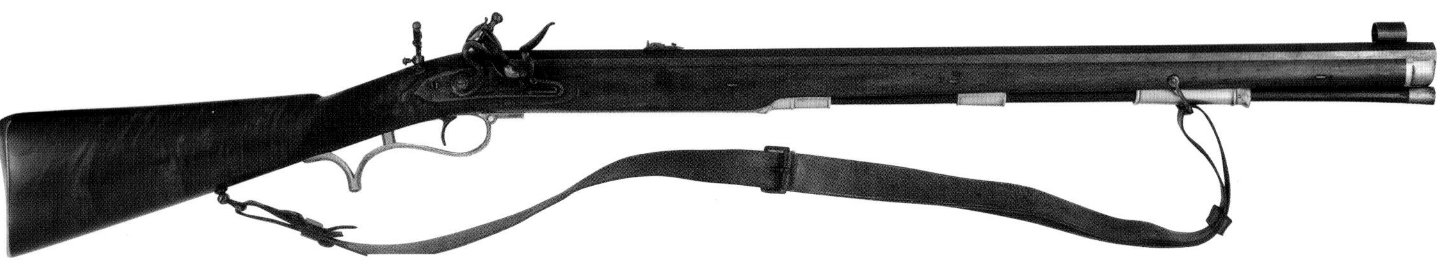

Length (gun): 45.5 in. (1,158 mm)
Barrel: 30.0 in. (762 mm)
Weight (gun): 8.9 lb. (4.0 kg)
Caliber: 0.615 in. (15.6 mm)
Rifling: n.k.
Operation: muzzle-loading, flintlock
Feed: single-round, manual
Muz vel: n.k.

This Regency-period target rifle was made by celebrated London gunsmith Samuel Staudenmayer in about 1805. It has a walnut stock, brass mounts, and a wooden ramrod. The fore sight is a plain blade protected by a sunshade. It has two back sights, the forward of which is a notched sight mounted atop the barrel, with blades for 100 yd. (91 m), 200 yd. (183 m), and 300 yd. (274 m), which can be moved along two mounting grooves. The second rear sight is a tang-mounted aperture sight adjustable for both windage and elevation. Such an accurate weapon would have been used by Regency-period marksmen corps, among which were the splendidly named Duke of Cumberland's Sharpshooters and the Acrotomentarian Society of Riflemen.

UNITED KINGDOM

THEOPHILUS RICHARDS MUZZLE-LOADING SPORTING SHOTGUN 1815

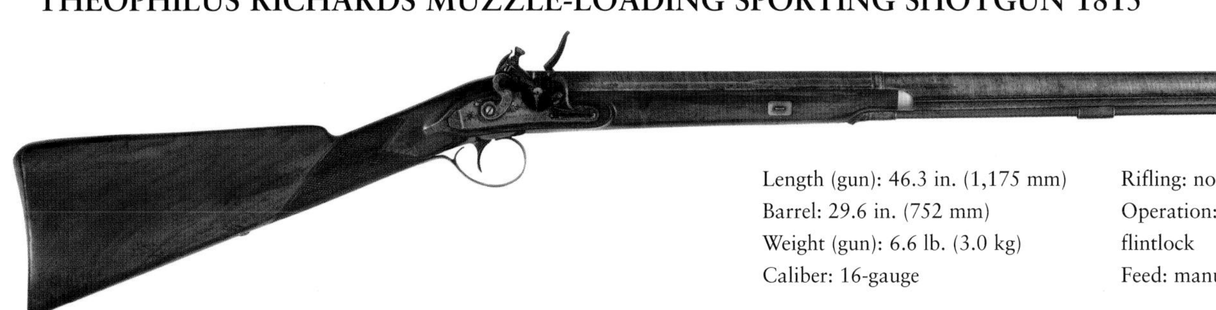

Length (gun): 46.3 in. (1,175 mm)
Barrel: 29.6 in. (752 mm)
Weight (gun): 6.6 lb. (3.0 kg)
Caliber: 16-gauge
Rifling: none
Operation: muzzle-loading, flintlock
Feed: manual

This single-barrel, sporting, muzzle-loading shotgun was made by the British gunsmith Theophilus Richards and has a post-1813 Birmingham proof mark, suggesting that it was probably made in 1815, the year of the Battle of Waterloo. It has a twist barrel manufactured from horseshoe nails and stamped "Stubs twisted," being octagonal at the breech, changing to 16-sided, and then, after a baluster turn, is round. The stock is made from walnut and the mounts are iron. The shooter of such a weapon would have needed to carry a number of accessories with him, including powder, flask, shot flask, wads, spare flints, and a third flask for fine-grain powder.

SPAIN

HAWKEN PERCUSSION RIFLE (REPRODUCTION) 1832

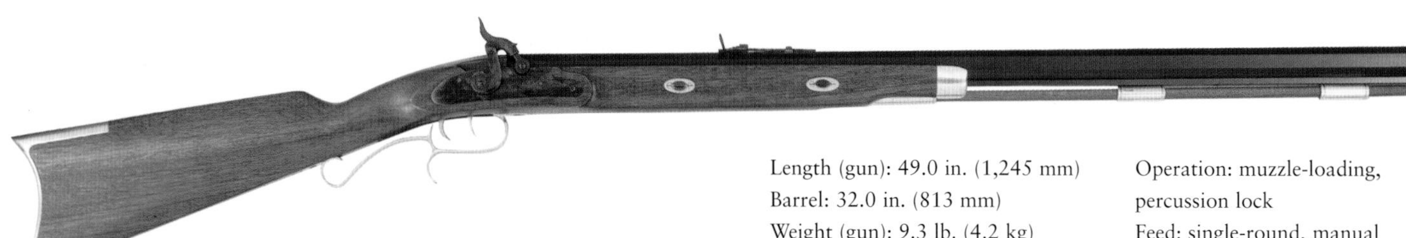

Length (gun): 49.0 in. (1,245 mm)
Barrel: 32.0 in. (813 mm)
Weight (gun): 9.3 lb. (4.2 kg)
Caliber: 0.54 in. (13.7 mm)
Rifling n.k.

Operation: muzzle-loading, percussion lock
Feed: single-round, manual
Muz vel: n.k.

During the early nineteenth century, as exploration opened up the "plains" areas of Midwestern America and explorers started to encounter larger game, it became necessary to enhance the power of rifles by increasing both their bore and their powder charges. Among the most prolific gunsmiths of the time were the Hawken brothers of St Louis, and a new type of rifle came to have the generic name "Hawken" regardless of whether or not it was made by the brothers. Such weapons had larger caliber than their predecessors, which meant that the barrel was much heavier; to compensate, the overall length of the barrel had to be reduced to enable the frontiersman to handle it. The weapon shown here is a replica of a typical "Hawken Rifle" made by Ardesa of Spain.

ITALY

INTERMARCO MUZZLE-LOADING SHOTGUN (REPRODUCTION) 1836

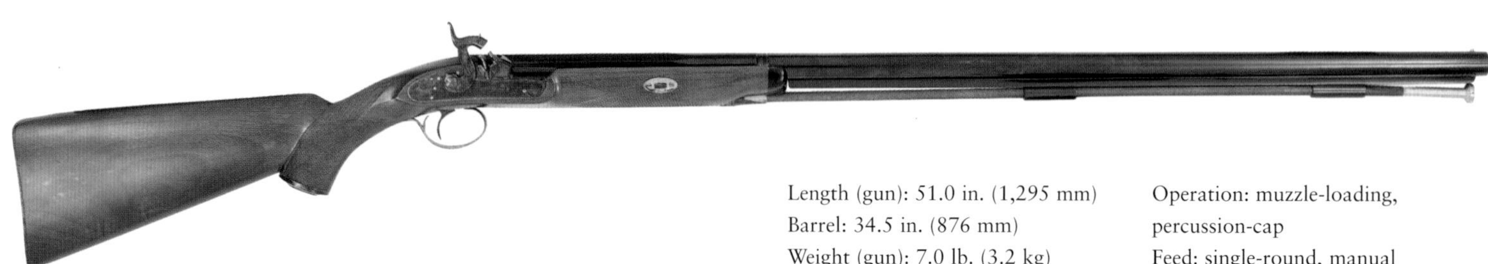

Length (gun): 51.0 in. (1,295 mm)
Barrel: 34.5 in. (876 mm)
Weight (gun): 7.0 lb. (3.2 kg)
Caliber: 12-gauge
Rifling: n.k.

Operation: muzzle-loading, percussion-cap
Feed: single-round, manual
Muz vel: n.k.

An original flintlock sporting gun would be too valuable to actually shoot, so there are now reproductions available for enthusiasts to discover what such weapons felt like to use. This reproduction by the Italian company Interarmco is modeled on an original by the great Scottish gun-maker Alexander Henry. It is a beautifully made, single-barrel, muzzle-loading weapon, using a percussion firing system. Percussion shooting was a vast improvement on the flintlock but had only a relatively brief lifespan, from about 1836 until the first breech-loaders with pinfire, rim-fire, and centerfire came onto the market in the late 1860s.

UNITED KINGDOM

SHORT SEA SERVICE MUSKET 1839

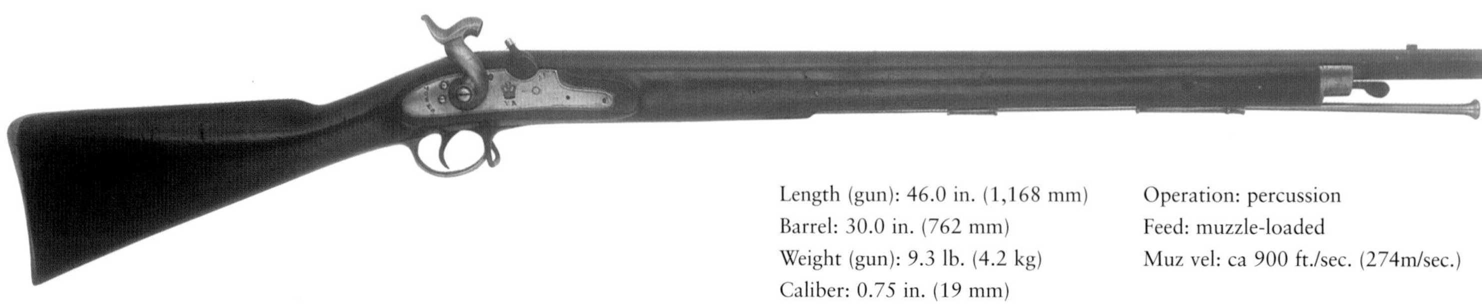

Length (gun): 46.0 in. (1,168 mm)
Barrel: 30.0 in. (762 mm)
Weight (gun): 9.3 lb. (4.2 kg)
Caliber: 0.75 in. (19 mm)
Rifling: none

Operation: percussion
Feed: muzzle-loaded
Muz vel: ca 900 ft./sec. (274m/sec.)

The Short Sea Service Musket of the type used by the British Royal Navy was originally issued as a flintlock but was altered to percussion by means of a conversion lock, designed by George Lovell of the Royal Small Arms Factory at Enfield in 1839. The lock plate has on its upper surface the depression that once housed the pan, but it is now filled by the nipple lump and the holes for the frizzen spring. Note also the Royal Crown and initials "VR" (Victoria Regina).

UNITED KINGDOM

BRUNSWICK RIFLE 1845

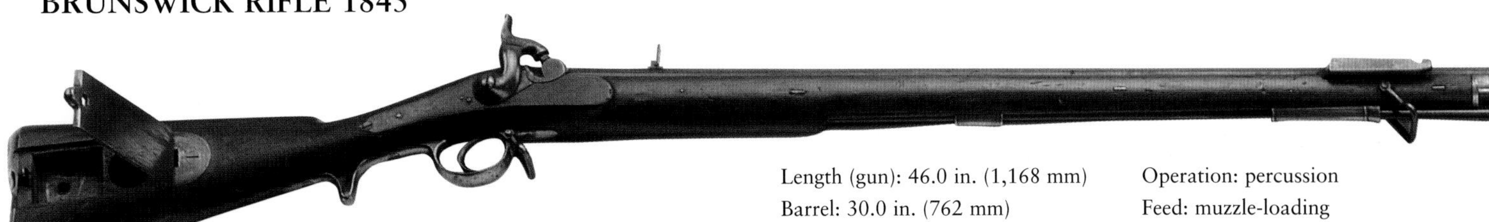

Length (gun): 46.0 in. (1,168 mm)
Barrel: 30.0 in. (762 mm)
Weight (gun): 9.1 lb. (4.1 kg)
Caliber: 0.704 in. (17.88 mm)
Rifling: n.k.

Operation: percussion
Feed: muzzle-loading
Muz vel: ca 1,000 ft./sec. (305 m/sec.)

The Brunswick replaced the Baker rifle. Its barrel had two deep grooves 180 degrees apart and fired a spherical ball with a belt cast around its circumference, the intention was, when the ball was held between forefinger and thumb with the belt horizontal, the edges of the belt would fit the grooves, which were cut away into semicircular notches at the muzzle to facilitate loading. Before the rifle was put into production, the caliber was increased to 0.704 in. (17.88 mm) so that it could also take the standard musket ball. Details of tests survive to show that the Brunswick would place the majority of its shots into a 2 ft. (610 mm) target at 200 yd. (183 m) and just over 50 percent into a 3 ft. (914 mm) target at 300 yd. (274 m). To facilitate shooting at longer ranges, the rifle had a fixed back sight for 200 yards and a folding-leaf back sight for 300 yards.

FRANCE

THOUVENIN PILLAR-BREECH RIFLE 1846

Length (gun): 49.3 in. (1,251 mm)
Barrel: 34.0 in. (864 mm)
Weight (gun): 9.0 lb. (4.1 kg)
Caliber: 0.7 in. (17.5 mm)
Rifling: 4 grooves, r/hand

Operation: percussion
Feed: muzzle-loading
Muz vel: ca 1,000 ft./sec. (305 m/sec.)

Colonel Thouvenin, a senior officer in the French Army, designed a rifle that was fitted with a "pillar-breech." In this, a small metal rod—the pillar—was inserted inside the breech so that it left precisely the necessary space for the powder charge. When the spherical ball was inserted in the muzzle and pushed down the barrel, it was eventually stopped by the pillar, at which point the rifleman gave a number of firm taps on the ramrod with a mallet, forcing the ball to spread slightly, thus fitting into the rifling grooves. This rifle came into service with the French Army in 1846, and the idea was later improved by using elongated, rather than spherical, bullets. In service, however, it was found that repeated explosions tended to weaken and distort the pillar, while fouling quickly built up in the confined spaces.

UNITED STATES

PRUSSIAN MODEL 1849 NEEDLE GUN

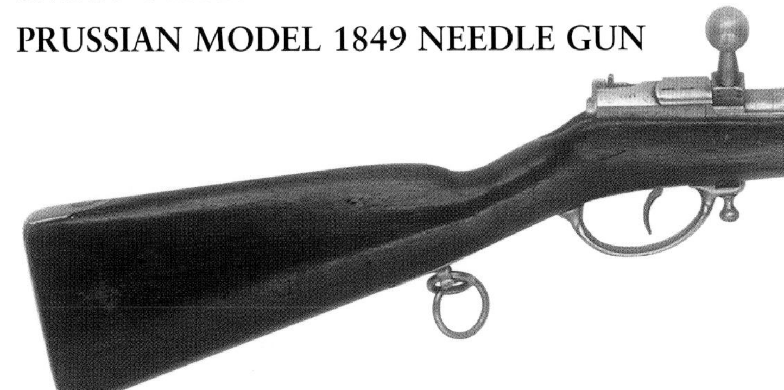

Length (gun): 56.0 in. (1,422 mm)
Barrel: 38.0 in. (964 mm)
Weight (gun): 9.0 lb. (4.1 kg)
Caliber: 0.607 in. (15.43 mm)
Rifling: 4 grooves, r/hand

Operation: breech-loading
Feed: single-round, manual
Muz vel: ca 950 ft./sec. (290 m/sec.)

The famous Prussian needle gun stemmed from a design produced by Johann von Dreyse in 1838, which was approved for production as the Model 1841, although it was not formally issued to the army until 1848. It was a solid weapon and its breech mechanism consisted of an enormous bolt, the lever of which stuck up at an angle of about 10 degrees vertically when closed. The bolt contained an inner sleeve with the firing pin and spring, which had to be drawn back by means of a thumb piece before the breech could be opened; this was done by turning the bolt lever to the vertical and then pulling it back. After the cartridge was inserted, the breech was closed and the inner sleeve pushed forward until it was caught by a spring, leaving the striker protruding from the back end.

UNITED KINGDOM

1853 PATTERN ENFIELD RIFLE

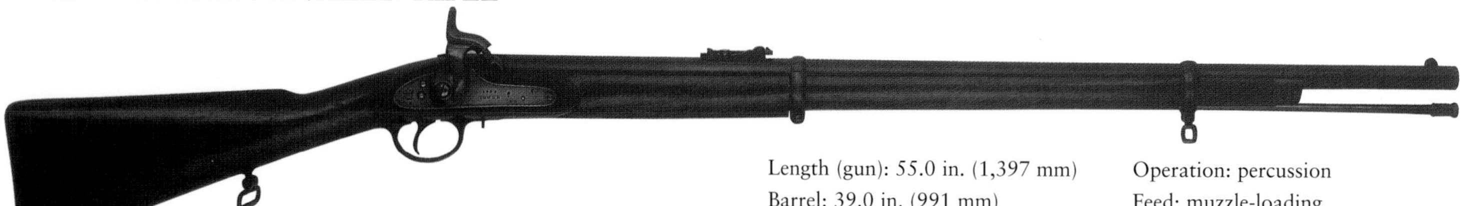

Length (gun): 55.0 in. (1,397 mm)
Barrel: 39.0 in. (991 mm)
Weight (gun): 8.6 lb. (3.9 kg)
Caliber: 0.577 in. (14.6 mm)
Rifling: 3 grooves, l/hand

Operation: percussion
Feed: muzzle-loading
Muz vel: n.k.

The Enfield had a 39.0 in. (991 mm) barrel and was rifled with three grooves, which made one complete turn in 78.0 inches (1,982 mm). It was light in comparison to other service rifles, weighing 8.6 lb. (3.9 kg), and for the first time, the barrel was secured to the stock by bands rather than the traditional pins. (The shorter, two-band version of 1856 is shown.) The back sight was a ladder, hinged at the rear and with a notch on the bridge; at rest it was set for 100 yd. (91.4 m) and the slider could be pushed forward and set for 200 yd. (183 m), 300 yd. (274 m), and, finally, 400 yd. (366 m). At ranges greater than 400 yards, the ladder was raised to the vertical and the slider set according to the range, with the firer using a second notch, which was in the slider itself. There were different bullets, but a typical round was just over 1.0 in. (25.4 mm) in length and weighed about 530 grains.

ITALY

ENFIELD PATTERN 1853 PERCUSSION RIFLE (REPRODUCTION)

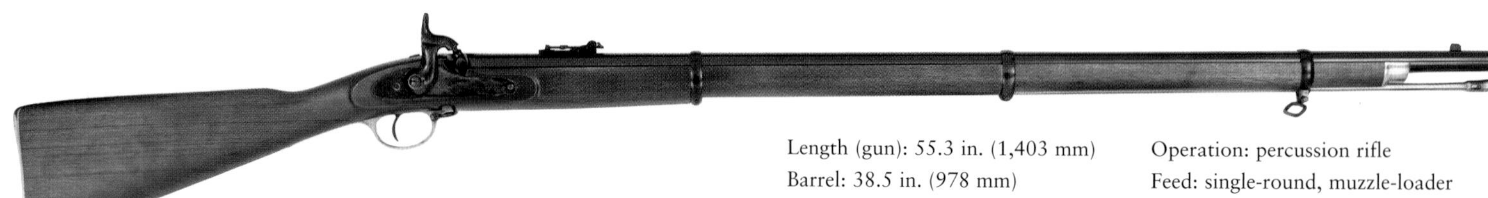

Length (gun): 55.3 in. (1,403 mm)
Barrel: 38.5 in. (978 mm)
Weight (gun): 9.94 lb. (4.5 kg)
Caliber: 0.577 in. (14.7 mm)
Rifling: n.k.

Operation: percussion rifle
Feed: single-round, muzzle-loader
Muz vel: n.k.

The demand for replicas of nineteenth-century rifles was slow to materialize in the UK because of the comparatively easy availability of good shooting originals, and also because of a lack of interest in American-style shooting. In the 1970s, however, there was perceived to be a substantial market for the Enfield series of rifles in the United States, created by the increasingly popular American Civil War re-enactment societies, who needed the rifles for parades and re-enactments, and also shot them competitively. The greatest original production was of the Pattern 1853 Infantry Rifle-Musket (also known as the Long Enfield and the Three-Band Enfield). The Italian replica shown here was made for a company named Euroarms in the United States, but perhaps the most famous Enfield replicas were made by Parker-Hale of Birmingham, England.

UNITED KINGDOM

WEBLEY REVOLVING RIFLE 1853

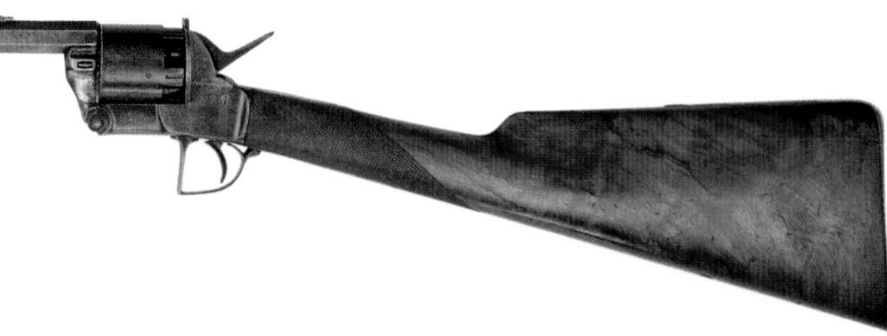

Length (gun): 45.5 in. (1,156 mm)
Barrel: 27.8 in. (705 mm)
Weight (gun): 4.5 lb. (2.0 kg)
Caliber: 0.500 in. (12.7 mm)

Rifling: 18 grooves, r/hand
Capacity: five
Muz vel: ca 800 ft./sec. (244 m/sec.)

The weapon illustrated was made by James Webley in 1853. It is an extension arm with very strong family resemblance to the Webley Longspur revolver (qv). It has a 27 in. (686 mm), octagonal, rifled barrel with a fore sight and two back sights—one fixed and one hinged. The barrel lump is hinged to the lower part of the frame, held rigid by a wedge through the cylinder axis pin. The plain cylinder has five chambers, each serially numbered. Because no rammer was provided, the flash of firing could occasionally leach to the neighboring chambers and cause a multiple discharge—a fault by no means unknown, even with Colt's rammer. In order to minimize the risk of damage, the barrel lump is grooved so that the mouths of the two chambers are not obstructed; and it was usual for the firer to hold his left hand back, around the trigger guard.

UNITED STATES

JENNINGS RIFLE 1853

Length (gun): 43.0 in. (1,092 mm)
Barrel: 24.5 in. (622 mm)
Weight (gun): 7.8 lb. (3.5 kg)
Caliber: 0.55 in. (14 mm)
Rifling: 7 grooves, l/hand
Operation: breech-loading
Feed: tube magazine
Muz vel: ca 600 ft./sec. (183 m/sec.)

By 1848, Walter Hunt invented a bullet with its own charge of powder, the base sealed by a thin piece of cork and pierced at the center to allow the flash of a cap to reach the contents. Lewis Jennings, a highly skilled mechanic, produced a fully operational weapon for this round, the "Jennings' Magazine Rifle." Ignition was via percussion pills held in a flat, cylindrical container just above the breech. When the ring trigger was pushed forward, the rearmost round in the magazine was forced into a scoop-shaped carrier by the magazine spring. The hammer was then cocked and the ring trigger drawn to the rear, which lifted the carrier into line with the breech, chambered the round, and dropped a percussion pill into position. A final, harder pull then fired the round and the process was repeated; with no separate case, no extraction was required.

UNITED KINGDOM

CONVERTED SHORT SEA SERVICE MUSKET 1855

Length (gun): 46.0 in. (1,168 mm)
Barrel: 30.0 in. (762 mm)
Weight (gun): 9.3 lb. (4.2 kg)
Caliber: 0.76 in. (19.3 mm)
Rifling: 3 or 4 grooves, r/hand
Operation: percussion
Feed: muzzle-loaded
Muz vel: ca 1,000 ft./sec. (305 m/sec.)

News of the success of the French Minié system, with a rifled barrel and percussion firing, came to the notice of British authorities in 1850 and led to the conversion of a number of existing weapons, among them those then used by the Royal Marines, which became the "Altered Pattern 1842 Rifle-Muskets." Once this conversion proved successful, the Admiralty authorized the conversion of most of the Sea Service muskets (qv) then in use. These converted weapons were fitted with an adjustable-leaf back sight and issued to sailors when required for arming landing parties or in ship-to-ship duels.

UNITED STATES

SHARPS CARBINE 1855

Length (gun): 35.0 in. (889 mm)
Barrel: 21.3 in. (540 mm)
Weight (gun): 7.6 lb. (3.4 kg)
Caliber: 0.577 in. (14.7 mm)
Rifling: 3 grooves, l/hand
Operation: capping breech-loading
Feed: single-round, manual
Muz vel: ca 1,100 ft./sec. (335 m/sec.)

The Sharps carbine was one of a number of weapons that saw service in the mid-nineteenth century, known as "capping breech-loaders." In these weapons, a made-up cartridge of powder and bullet was wrapped in some combustible material, loaded into the breech, and then fired by a separate percussion cap, as in a muzzle-loader. In the American Sharps, the breech mechanism was a vertical sliding block working in grooves in the receiver by means of a lever, which also acted as a trigger guard. This system leaked some gas but had the advantage of a dual system of ignition; it took the ordinary percussion cap and was also fitted with a tape primer. This took rolls of caps, rather like those used today in children's pistols. A fresh one was pushed over the nipple when the hammer was cocked, which meant that a mounted soldier did not have to fumble with relatively small caps when he had to prime.

UNITED KINGDOM

SAMUEL AND CHARLES SMITH SPORTING MUZZLE-LOADING SHOTGUN 1858

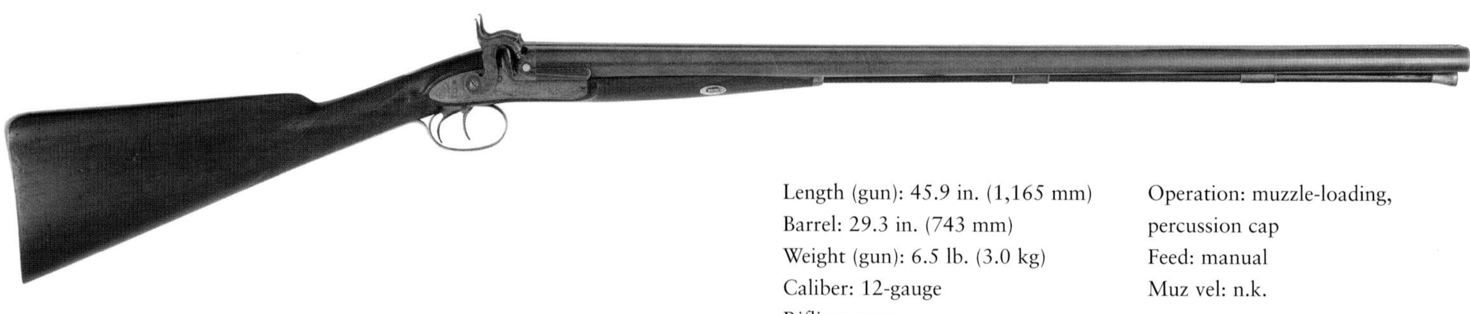

Length (gun): 45.9 in. (1,165 mm)
Barrel: 29.3 in. (743 mm)
Weight (gun): 6.5 lb. (3.0 kg)
Caliber: 12-gauge
Rifling: none
Operation: muzzle-loading, percussion cap
Feed: manual
Muz vel: n.k.

This 12-bore, double-barrel, percussion-cap game gun was made by leading London gunmakers of their time (about 1858), the brothers Samuel and Charles Smith. It consists of a pair of Damascus barrels with a walnut stock and iron mounts. The history of this particular gun is recorded: it was one of a pair made in 1858 for the Chaworth Musters family, who lived in Nottinghamshire, England.

UNITED STATES

GREEN'S CARBINE 1858

Length (gun): 34.0 in. (837 mm)
Barrel: 18.0 in. (457 mm)
Weight (gun): 7.5 lb. (3.4 kg)
Caliber: 0.55 in. (14 mm)
Rifling: 3 grooves, l/hand
Operation: capping breech-loading
Feed: single-round, manual
Muz vel: ca 1,000 ft./sec. (305 m/sec.)

Like the Sharps carbine (qv), the Green's carbine was an American-designed capping breech-loader, and in many ways one of the best. In this case the barrel was undocked from the breech by pressure on the forward trigger; it was then given a counterclockwise twist, pushed forward, and then swung out sideways for reloading. The reverse procedure then locked the barrel back into position, and the then pushed the cartridge onto a spike in the standing breech, which tore the cartridge cover so that the flash could reach the powder. It was gas-tight and had a tape primer on a wheel, like the Sharps. Unfortunately, because of ignition difficulties, the cartridge had to be made in very thin material, which made it too flimsy for military use.

UNITED KINGDOM

JACOB'S RIFLE 1860

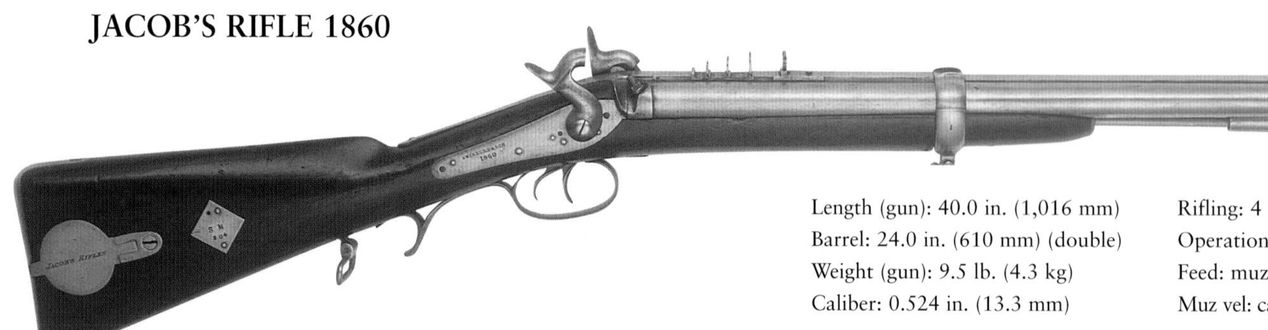

Length (gun): 40.0 in. (1,016 mm)
Barrel: 24.0 in. (610 mm) (double)
Weight (gun): 9.5 lb. (4.3 kg)
Caliber: 0.524 in. (13.3 mm)
Rifling: 4 grooves, l/hand
Operation: percussion
Feed: muzzle-loading
Muz vel: ca 1,000 ft./sec. (305 m/sec.)

The Jacob's Rifle was designed by Brigadier General John Jacob, a British officer who originally served in the Bombay Artillery but later commanded a cavalry regiment, the Scinde Horse. His early work was devoted to improving the existing Brunswick rifle, but he then went on to design his own, one of which was this double-barrel weapon that was adopted for use by some regiments of the British Indian Army. The problem in the early nineteenth century was the long time it took for an infantryman to reload his weapon. By giving him a second barrel, the Jacob's rifle did at least double the number of rounds immediately available—although it also took double the usual time to reload! The two barrels were both rifled, with four grooves to take flanged bullets. And it had a variety of back sights, including one 4.5 inches (114.3 mm) high and graduated up to 2,000 yd. (1,828 m).

UNITED STATES

SPENCER REPEATING RIFLE 1860

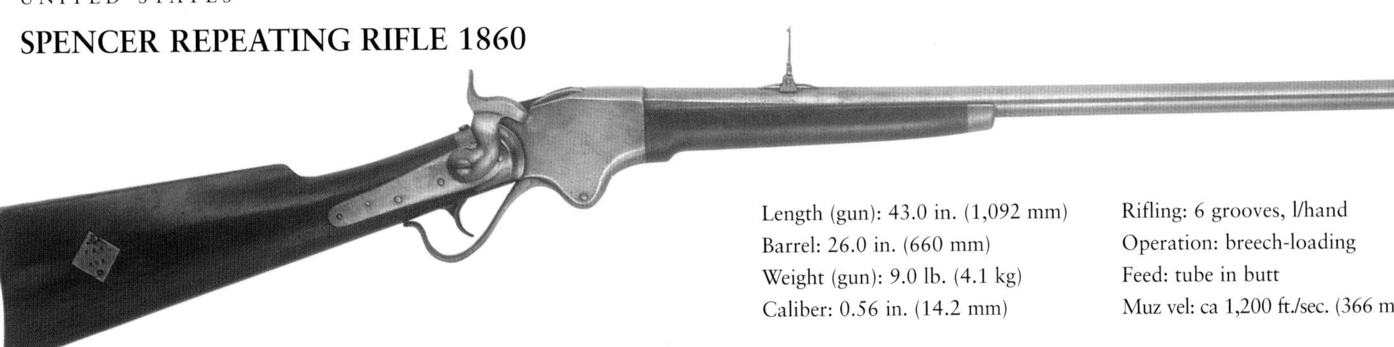

Length (gun): 43.0 in. (1,092 mm)
Barrel: 26.0 in. (660 mm)
Weight (gun): 9.0 lb. (4.1 kg)
Caliber: 0.56 in. (14.2 mm)
Rifling: 6 grooves, l/hand
Operation: breech-loading
Feed: tube in butt
Muz vel: ca 1,200 ft./sec. (366 m/sec.)

In March 1860, Christopher Spencer (1833–1922) produced the repeating rifle that bears his name. It used a removable tubular magazine in the butt, which housed seven copper rimfire cartridges. It was worked by a lever-cum-trigger-guard. Downward pressure ejected the empty case, and upward pressure loaded the next round, after which the external hammer had to be cocked. It was a simple, reliable weapon, cheap to manufacture and robust. The Spencer Repeater was adopted by the Union Army soon after the outbreak of the Civil War in 1861, but nothing much seemed to have happened until Spencer demonstrated it to President Lincoln in 1863; by the following year one division of 12,000 men had been equipped with the rifle. The Spencer Repeater was also made in carbine form and a number were converted by Springfield. A few were produced in the immediate post-war years for sporting use. The illustration shows the carbine with a shortened forestock; the tubular device underneath is the magazine, usually housed in the butt. Considerable numbers were purchased during the war, but the factory went out of business in 1869 and most of its stock and machinery were purchased by Oliver Winchester.

UNITED KINGDOM

PATTERN 1861 ENFIELD SHORT RIFLE

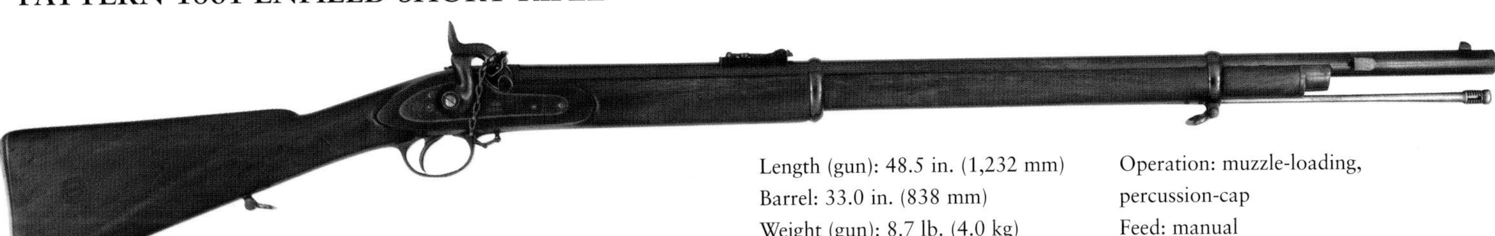

Length (gun): 48.5 in. (1,232 mm)
Barrel: 33.0 in. (838 mm)
Weight (gun): 8.7 lb. (4.0 kg)
Caliber: 0.577 in.
Rifling: n.k.
Operation: muzzle-loading, percussion-cap
Feed: manual
Muz vel: ca 1,000 ft./sec. (305 m/sec.)

In 1859, the British government and people became obsessed by an apparent threat of invasion by the French, since the improved railways systems and steamships made it possible to concentrate and move a large body of troops with unprecedented speed. The majority of the regular army was overseas in India and the colonies, and as a result many hundreds of volunteer rifle corps were formed. These volunteers were largely middle-class and used their own money to obtain weapons. A vast number of rifles were manufactured over a short period. Typical of these is this "Pattern 1861 Short Enfield" (also known as the "Two-Band Enfield"), which was made to government design by a private contractor, the London Armory Company. A muzzle-loader, it had an iron barrel with five-groove rifling in a 48 in. (1,129 mm) spiral. It was fitted with a barleycorn fore sight and a rear sight that was adjustable for elevation only from 100 yd. (91 m) to 1,250 yd. (1,143 mm). This particular rifle is known to have been used in the Ashburton Shield, one of Britain's premier shooting competitions, in 1866. (Note that this "Short Enfield" should not be confused with the "Short Magazine Lee-Enfield," which was a totally different weapon.)

1803–74
WEAPONS OF THE AMERICAN WEST—1

The men who penetrated, settled, and eventually "won" the West needed firearms for protection from competitors, enemies, and wild animals, and for game hunting in order to obtain food for survival. Weapons were thus an essential, and not an optional, part of their lives. Among the earliest of these men were the members of the Lewis and Clark expedition, which was a direct outcome of the Louisiana Purchase in 1803 and involved trekking from St Louis, Missouri, then a frontier town, to the Pacific Coast and back, through country never previously explored by white men. Their weapons were rifles and muskets, some from reputable gun-makers in the United States or Great Britain, but others from anonymous gunsmiths who, either by accident or design, failed to put their names on their products. After the explorers came the hunters and trappers, who, quite literally, lived by their guns, and for whom Samuel Hawken of St Louis produced some excellent weapons. These were followed by men armed with carbines like the Spencer and the Sharps, and, above all, by the "gun that won the West"—the Winchester '73.

1. Harper's Ferry Model 1803. A 0.54-in.-caliber (13.7 mm) flintlock rifle manufactured at the government arsenal at Harper's Ferry in West Virginia. It is shown with a powder horn with turned wood plug and carved neck. Such weapons are known to have been included among those carried by members of the Lewis and Clark expedition.
2. Flintlock (ca 1820). A flintlock from an unidentified manufacturer. Brass- mounted, with plain brass patch box.
3. Kuntz air rifle. The air reservoir was contained in the hollow metal butt and the false flint cocking action actuated the release of air, firing the weapon. This type of weapon was taken on the Lewis and Clark expedition.
4. Sam Hawken rifle. Brass-mounted, half-stocked plains rifle made by Samuel Hawken, a gunsmith of St Louis, Missouri.
5. Sam Hawken rifle. An iron-mounted plains rifle, also made by Sam Hawken.
6. Winchester Model 1873 rifle. A lever-action Model 1873. caliber, 0.45–60 in.
7. Winchester Model 1873 rifle. This lever-action Model 1873 differs from the above model in being 0.44–40 in. in caliber. It is believed to have been used to enforce the rules in a Western gambling saloon.
8. Modified Spencer rifle. This Spencer rifle has been modified to take a 0.50-in.-caliber (12.7 mm) cartridge. Octagonal barrel and a set trigger.
9. Sharps Model 1874 carbine. A 0.45-in.-caliber (11.4 mm) carbine with heavy octagonal barrel. The branded "S" on the butt is an owner's rather than maker's mark.
10. English shotgun. A double-barrel 12-gauge shotgun, manufactured by W. and O. Scott, a firm of English gun-makers.
11. Ballard sporting rifle. A high-quality, light, lever-action rifle made by the Brown Manufacturing Co. and intended for hunting game.

1841–66
WEAPONS OF THE AMERICAN WEST—2

Prior to the Civil War, the US Army's presence on the frontier was limited, and the units were small in size and widely scattered. Their mission was to protect civilians in their area of responsibility and to look after immigrants passing through on their way westward. Compared with those of the people they had to fight, their weapons were sophisticated and up-to-date. Their resupply of ammunition was guaranteed and maintenance facilities were of a high standard. A selection of the arms they used up to 1871 is shown here, together with a selection of firearms used by Native Americans, most of them readily identifiable by their characteristic use of brass studs as decorations, their generally well-used condition, and their use of rawhide to effect all types of repair. The Native Americans did not have any manufacturing facilities and acquired all their weapons from trading posts or by purchase from individuals, although usually only antiquated flint and percussion muzzle-loading weapons could be obtained in this way. The most modern weapons were usually acquired by capture, although these became useless once the ammunition was expended.

1. Spencer Model 1865 carbine. As used by the US Army, this has the standard barrel, rather than the modified barrel shown on the preceding pages. Note the half stock, neat action, and back sight, which has been raised for long-range shooting.
2. Springfield Model 1884 carbine. Note that the "trapdoor" breech cover is raised.
3. US Army Model 1861 rifle musket. Of 0.58 in. caliber, made by an unidentified contractor.
4. Colt Third Model Dragoon revolver. The shoulder stock is mounted to convert it to a carbine, although the absence of any sights would have precluded any great accuracy.
5. Percussion rifle. An unmarked percussion rifle of 0.45 in. caliber. One of the owners has used rawhide to make repairs around the lock area and at the rear of the barrel.
6. Percussion rifle. Another of the many types of percussion rifles used by Plains Indian warriors.
7. US Army Model 1841 percussion rifle. Probably captured in a frontier engagement, it is identifiable as an "Indian" weapon by its brass stud decorations.
8. Winchester Model 1866 rifle. Probably also captured from the Army, this Winchester has added brass stud decorations.

1855–95
WEAPONS OF THE AMERICAN WEST—3

The name "Winchester" is synonymous with the "Wild West," the American frontier, and all the romance that has been attached to the subject by Hollywood filmmakers and generations of writers. The company that eventually bore the Winchester name was originally called "Volcanic" but was later taken over by Oliver Winchester, who had earlier been involved in manufacturing shirts. The company was renamed the Winchester Repeating Arms Company in 1866 and concentrated its efforts on the design, development, and production of long-arms, the most popular caliber being 0.44–0.40, which was also the same as that used by the Colt single-action handgun. On the right-hand page below are rifles produced by lesser-known companies and several of the less popular products of the larger companies, all of which played their part in the "taming of the West."

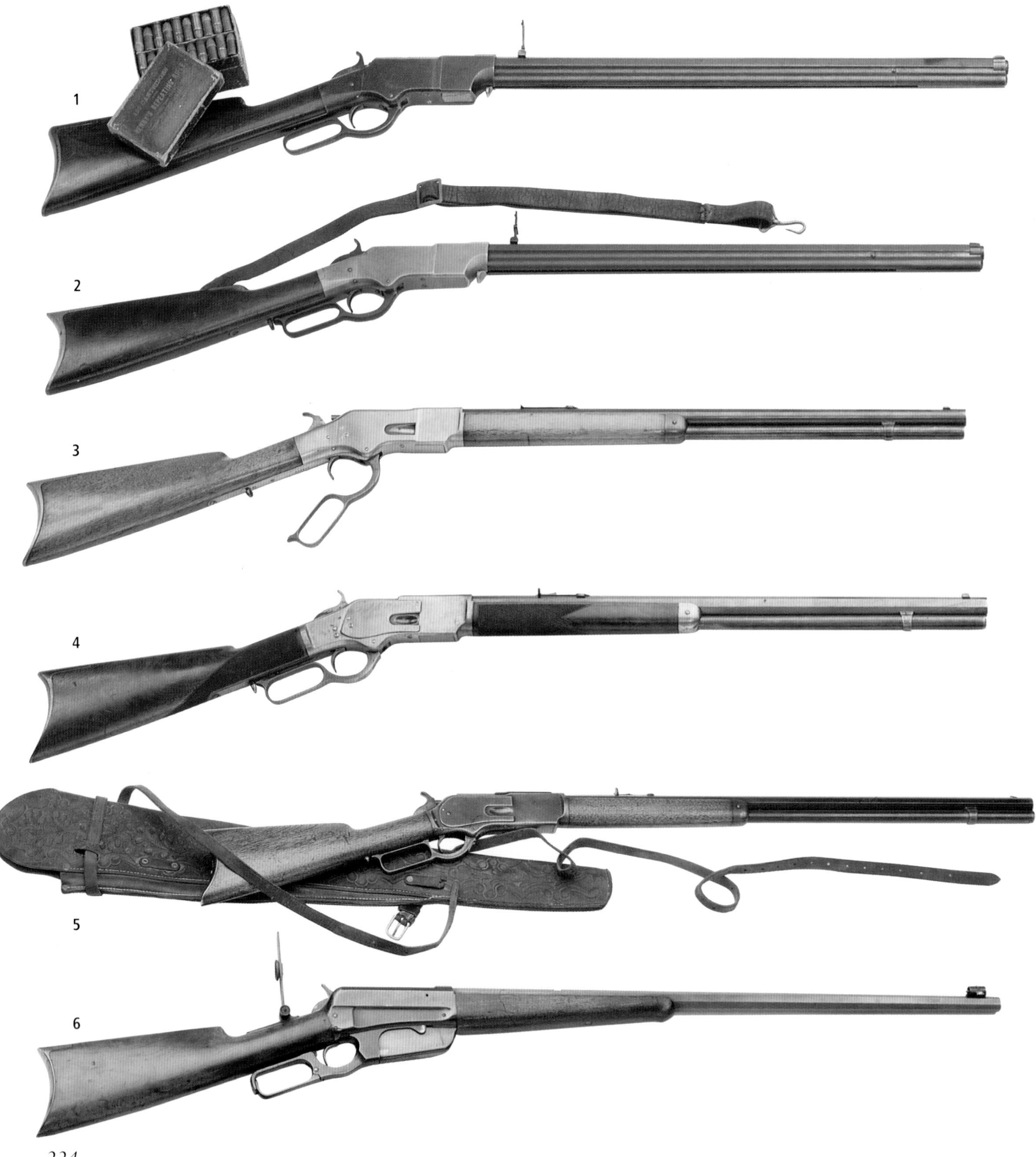

1. Henry rifle. An early iron-framed Henry lever-action repeating rifle, with its rear sight raised for long-range firing, shown with 100-round box of cartridges.
2. Henry rifle, generally similar to the one above, but with a brass frame.
3. Winchester Model 1866 rifle. This Winchester 1866 clearly shows its development from the Henry rifles above, but with the addition of the loading gate and lever action, which transformed a good weapon into an outstanding one.
4. Winchester Model 1873 rifle with the round barrel replaced by an octagonal one. In general, this was the most popular weapon in the West, combining reliability and accuracy with a high rate of fire. A military version was sold to several overseas armies, including those of Spain and Turkey. It was similar to the civilian model except for a longer forestock, which extended forward almost to the muzzle.
5. Winchester Model 1876 rifle shown with leather saddle scabbard. This weapon is a development of the Model 1873, with a longer barrel.
6. Winchester Model 1895 rifle. This rifle incorporated significant changes, with the tubular magazine replaced by a box containing five rounds. Note also the tang back sight, here in the raised position. In its military version, this rifle was purchased in large quantities by Imperial Russia.
7. Colt Lightning Repeater rifle. Unlike most of the others shown on these pages, this weapon worked by slide (pump) action. Though reasonably effective, this system was never as popular as the lever action, marketed by firms such as Winchester and Marlin.
8. Remington-Creedmore rifle. This particular weapon is significant because it was once owned by General George Armstrong Custer. With a 0.44-100 caliber, it is generally acknowledged to have been one of the finest weapons ever made by Remington.
9. Marlin Model 1881 rifle. This lever-action rifle had a half-length magazine and an octagonal barrel. It was a serious competitor for the contemporary Winchesters, but never triumphed over its rival.
10. Colt Model 1855 rifle. This half-stock percussion sporting rifle was made between 1857 and 1864 and operated on the revolver principle, with four rounds in the revolving chamber. Such "revolver rifles" were never entirely successful, as they were prone to mechanical failure, often at the worst possible moment.
11. Remington-Keane rifle. This bolt-action, magazine-fed rifle is shown with its bolt open. Note the short, vertical bolt handle and the cocking lever on the rear of the bolt. This weapon was popular with frontiersmen and was purchased by the Department of the Interior to arm "Indian police."
12. Roper revolving shotgun. This was one of many attempts to find an efficient repeating action. A 12-gauge weapon, the cylinder housed four cartridges, but overall the weapon proved to be fragile.

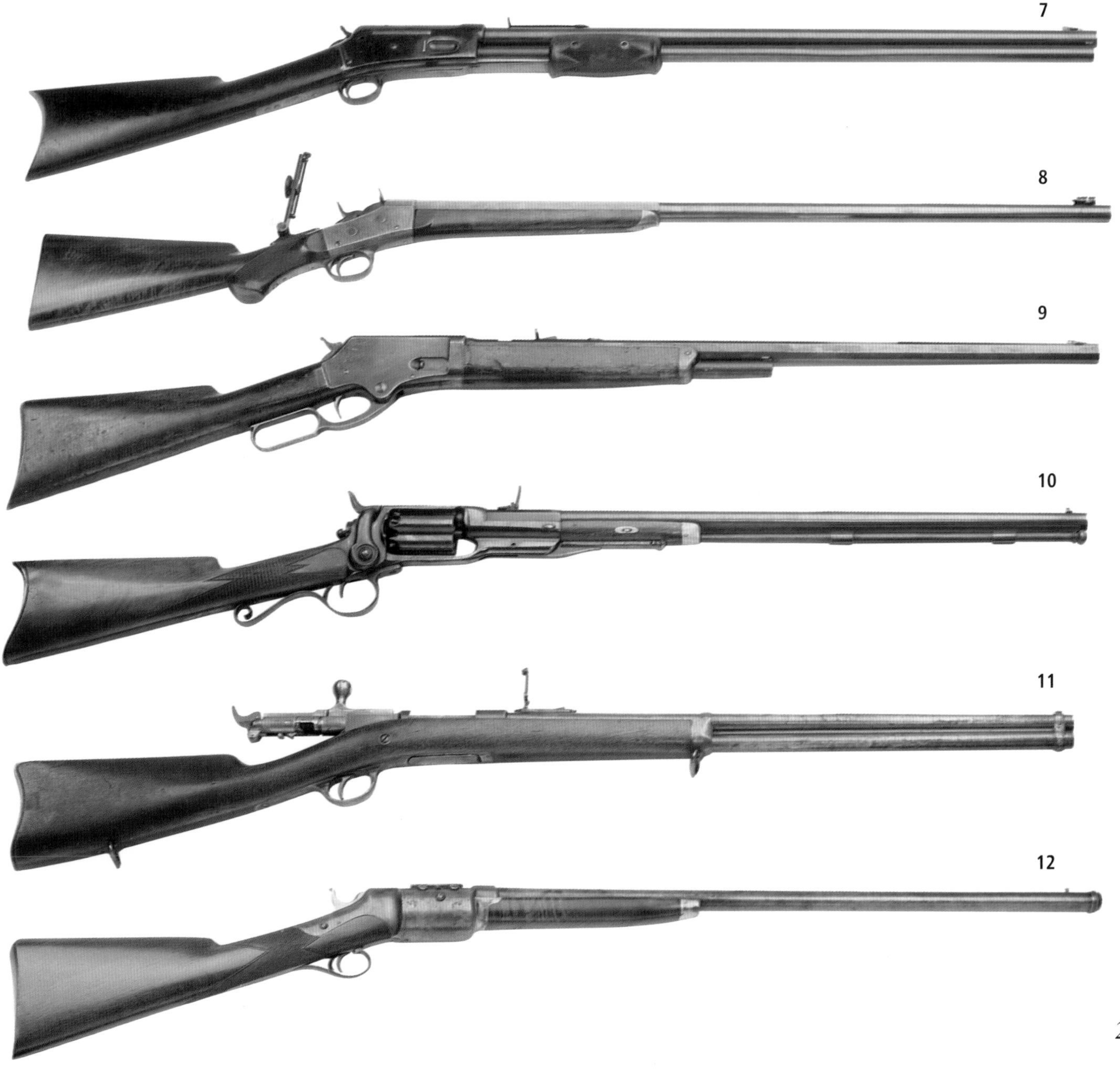

1849–74
SHARPS RIFLES

Christian Sharps (1811–1874) produced his first breech-loading single-shot rifle in the late 1840s, and by the mid-1850s had established himself as one of America's premier gun-makers and even sold several thousand to the British Army for cavalry use in India. By the late 1850s, the weapon was a firm favorite on the American frontier and the Model 1853 carbine was shipped in Kansas territory by the Reverend Beecher and other abolitionists in crates marked "Bibles," leading to Sharps rifles being nicknamed "Beecher Bibles." By the time of the Civil War, Sharps rifles and carbines were in great demand, and Colonel Hiram Berman, chief of the celebrated "Sharpshooters," used a number of Model 1859 rifles in 0.52 in. (13.2 mm) caliber, some with set triggers that enhanced accuracy. Sharps dissolved his own company in the early 1860s and entered into partnership with William Hankins, with whom he manufactured small four-barrel pistols, breech-loading rifles, and carbines. The partnership was dissolved in 1866 and Sharps set out on his own again to produce small pistols and long-arms. After his death, the company began producing powerful rifles that bore his name, among them the celebrated 0.50-in.-caliber buffalo rifle known as the "Big Fifty." The accuracy and stopping power of the large-caliber Sharps rifles are legendary, and at ranges of 1,000 yd. (915 m) they were reckoned to be deadly.

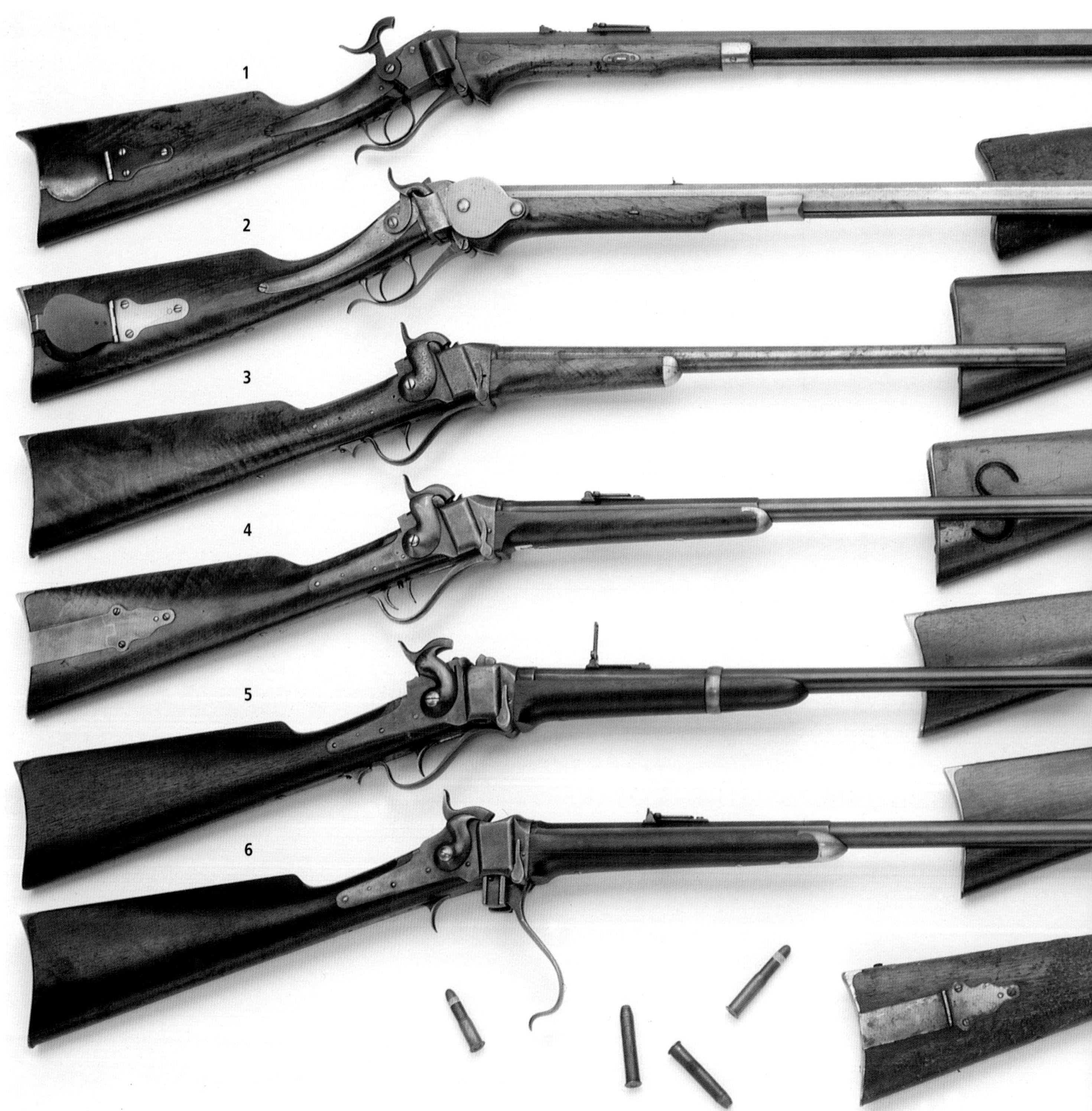

1. Sharps Model 1850 rifle complete with Maynard's tape primer.
2. Model 1849 with circular disk automatic capping device.
3. Model 1852 carbine in 0.52 in. caliber and slanting breech.
4. The rifle version complete with set triggers for targets and hunting.
5. 1869 carbine, produced in calibers as large as 0.60 inches.
6. Rifle version of the Model 1869.
7. This 1874 Sharps rifle has a repaired stock. Many rifles were prone to breakage at this point due to recoil.
8. Version of 1874 model with blade fore sight.
9. A fine Sharps in "as new" condition.
10. This rifle has normal rear sights on the barrel and peep or adjustable sights on the stock
11. Round-barrel Sharps rifle, which is uncommon.
12. New Model 1863 rifle with, above it, a box of 0.40-caliber shells 1.875 inches long; below it, a plains cartridge belt.

1855–90
COLT LONG-ARMS

Throughout the nineteenth century, a wide variety of long-arms found favor in the American West, including the trappers' Hawken rifle, the buffalo hunters' Sharps, the soldiers' Springfield, and, of course, the Winchester. Prior to the Civil War, Samuel Colt had included in the company's lineup various rifles, carbines, and shotguns with revolving cylinders, but many of these were not practical until the advent of metallic cartridges after the war, after which Colt began to develop and produce more successful shoulder arms. Single-shot military rifles sold worldwide helped to keep the firm in business through hard economic times. From 1883 until just after 1900, Samuel Colt tried to compete with Winchester in the rifle market. Thus, the Burgess lever-action 0.44–40 in. (11.2 mm) rifle was introduced in 1883 in an effort to compete with Winchester's Models 1873 and 1876, and the first slide-action Colt Lightning rifles followed in 1884. Winchester countered with several prototype revolvers, sending a very clear message to Colt, which forced the latter to abandon the rifle market. Numbers of Westerners did, however, use Colt long-arms and these became important additions to the armory of many law officers, outlaws, and (see example 2) even performers.

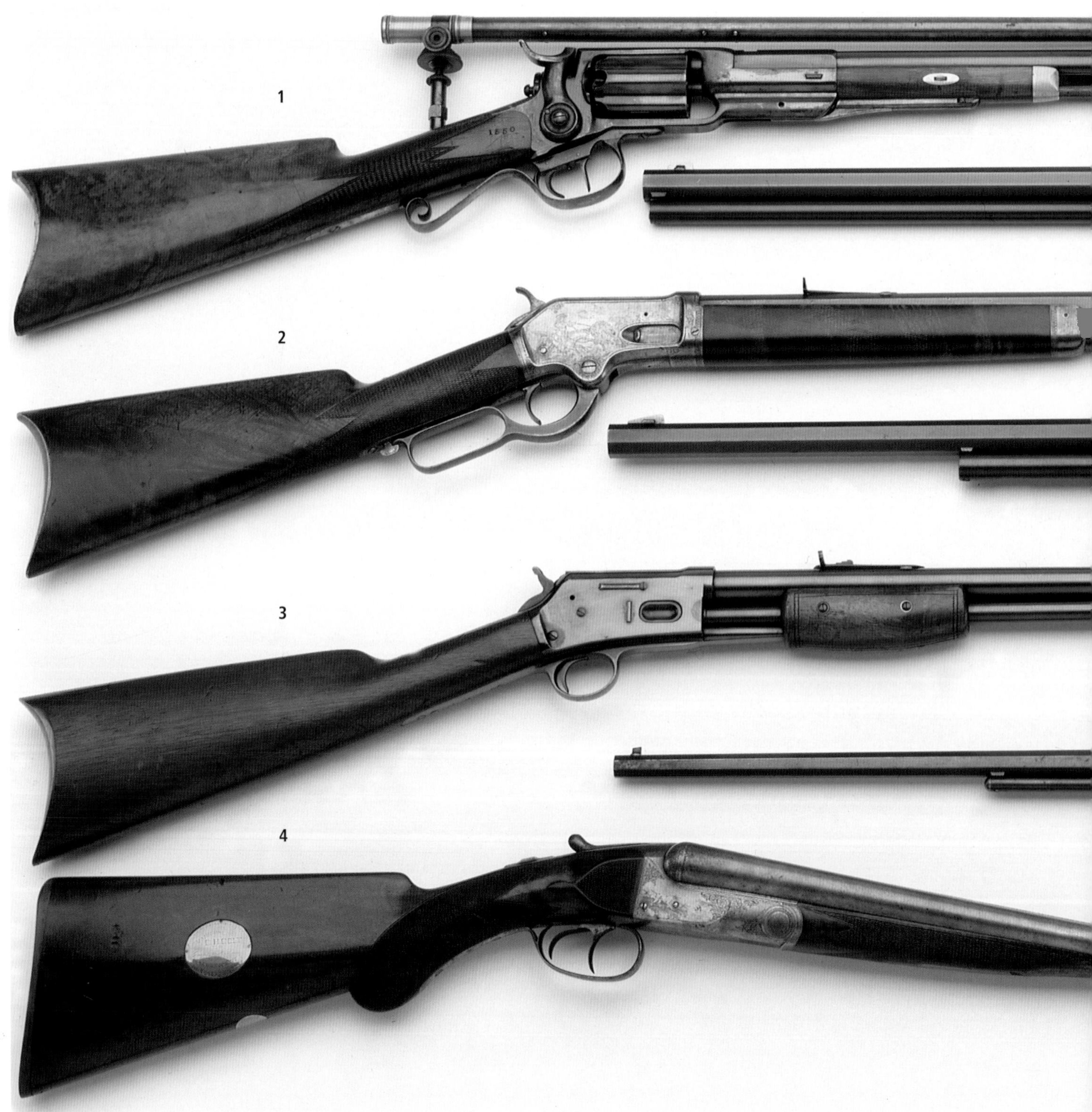

1. This half-stock Colt revolving sporting rifle version of the Model 1855 is equipped with a sighting scope and has a special finish and set triggers. It was the top of the Colt company's rifle line at the time.
2. Colt Burgess, deluxe engraved, inlaid with gold, presentation inscribed from the Colt factory to William F. "Buffalo Bill" Cody in 1883, the first year his famed Wild West show traveled to the East.
3. Lightning slide-action rifle, medium frame, 0.44–40 caliber, purchased around 1898 for the San Francisco Police Department.
4. This hammerless model 1883 Colt shotgun was a presentation from Samuel Colt's son Caldwell in about 1891.
5. Lever-action 0.44-caliber Colt Burgess rifle, manufactured between 1883 and 1885. Fewer than 7,000 were made.
6. Lightning slide-action rifle, large frame, 0.40–60–260 caliber, half magazine, peep sight.
7. Lightning slide-action rifle, small frame, 0.22 caliber, made in 1890.

1861–1865
WEAPONS OF THE AMERICAN CIVIL WAR: CONFEDERATE STATES ARMY WEAPONS

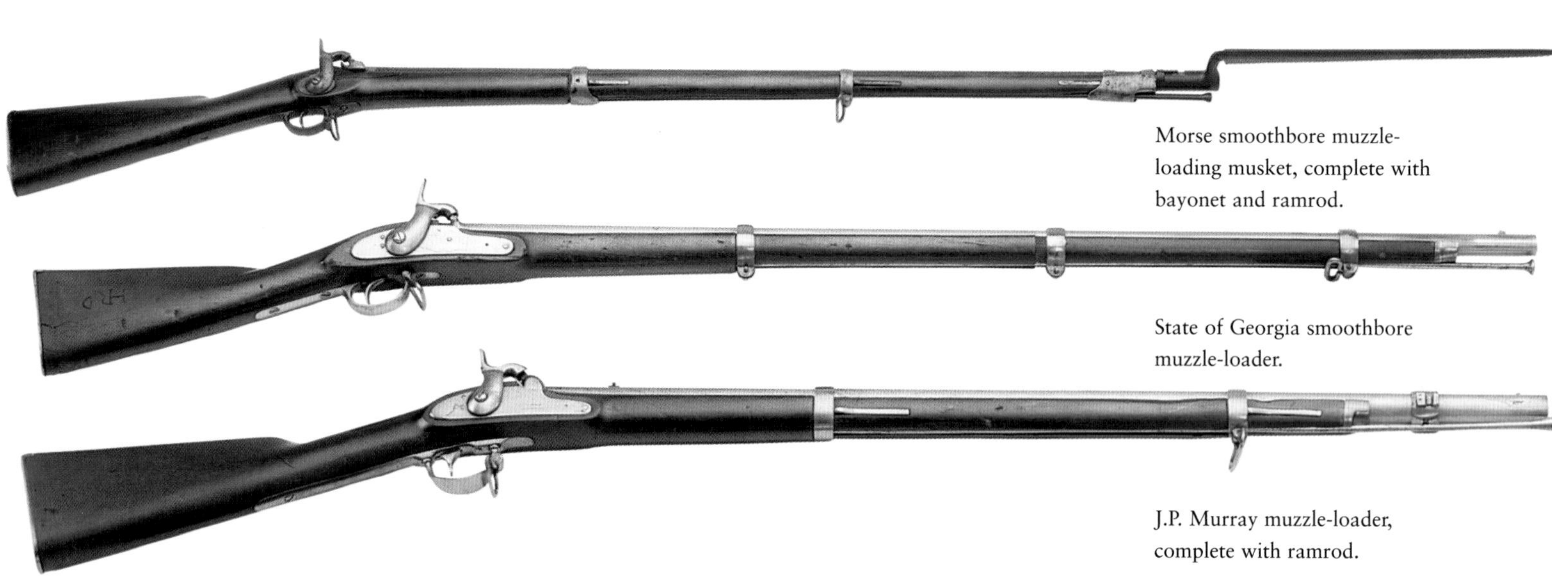

Morse smoothbore muzzle-loading musket, complete with bayonet and ramrod.

State of Georgia smoothbore muzzle-loader.

J.P. Murray muzzle-loader, complete with ramrod.

1861–1865
WEAPONS OF THE AMERICAN CIVIL WAR: AFTER THE BATTLE

Many tens of thousands of artifacts of the Civil War have been found and continue to be found, even today. These six rifles were dropped on various battlefields, almost certainly as the owners were wounded or killed. The metal parts have shown remarkable endurance but the woodwork has gone forever.

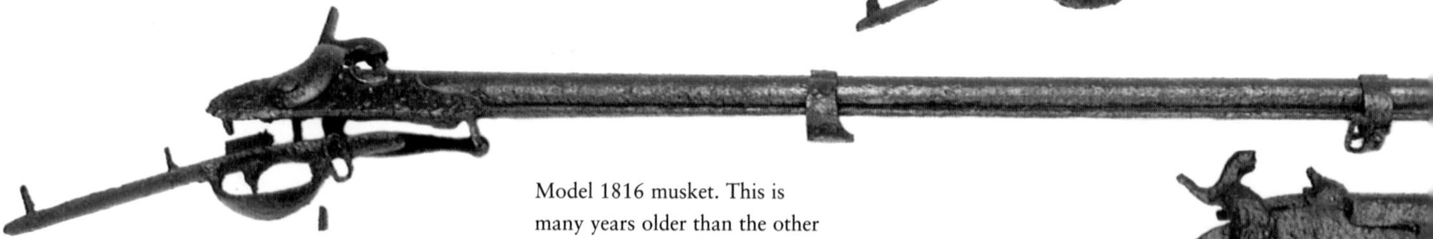

Model 1816 musket. This is many years older than the other weapons shown on this page.

Model 1842 rifle. This was found on the battlefield of Shiloh in Tennessee.

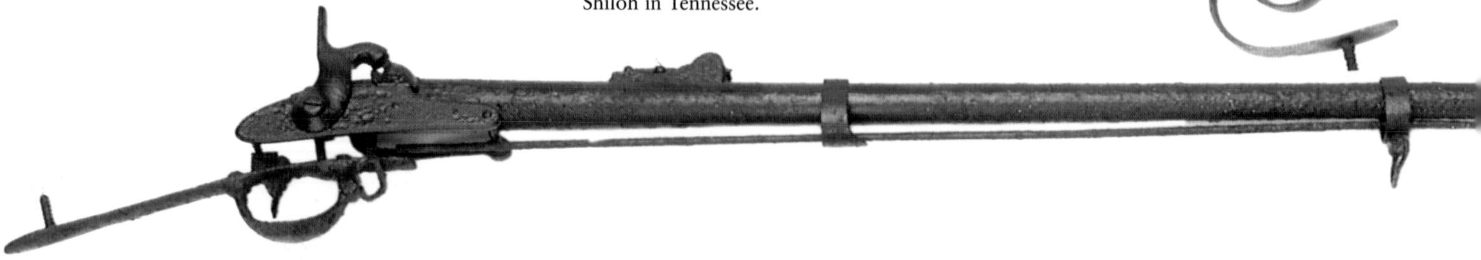

Model 1855 rifle, found in Kennesaw, Georgia.

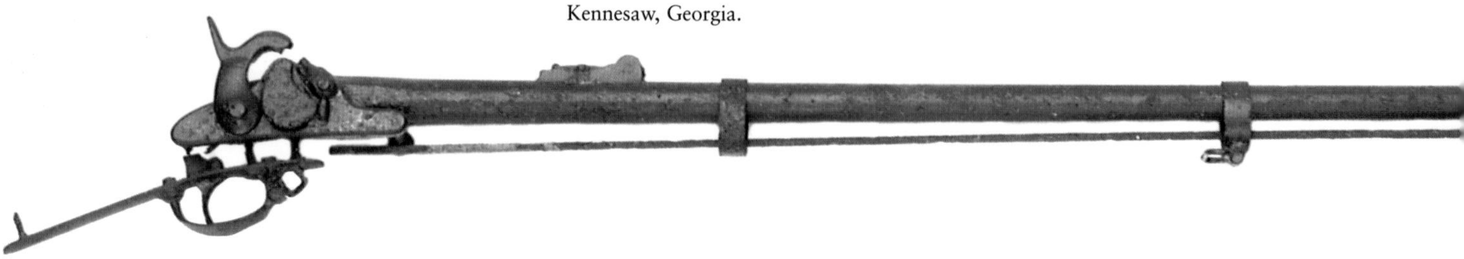

Pulaski muzzle-loading rifle.

Read and Watson late design muzzle-loading rifle.

H.C. Lamb muzzle-loader.

Model 1861 rifle musket, found near Bethesda Church, Virginia.

Model 1841 rifle, found in Wilderness, Virginia. Note that the muzzle is split, suggesting that the weapon may have been deliberately thrown away.

Sharps Model 1859 rifle. Note that even the back sight leaf is still preserved.

1861–65
WEAPONS OF THE AMERICAN CIVIL WAR: CONFEDERACY CAVALRY WEAPONS

Both sides in the Civil War had large forces of cavalry who required weapons that were lighter and shorter than the infantry rifles. Their rifles needed to be fired from horseback and carried without snagging. Some such weapons were simple adaptations of infantry rifles, but a few were specifically designed for cavalry use. As in other spheres, the Confederacy was poorly provided for compared to the Union, and much use was made of weapons imported from Europe.

1. Dickson, Nelson, and Company carbine. The ramrod is in the stowed position, but note the retaining swivel below the muzzle, which prevented it from being lost.
2. British Enfield Pattern 1853 musketoon. This is an adaptation of the standard British rifle, cut back for cavalry use.
3. J.P. Murray musketoon.
4. Tallahassee carbine. Note the ramrod and retaining swivel, and the raised leaf back sight.
5. Tarpley carbine.
6. J.P. Murray carbine.
7. Terry Pattern 1860 carbine. A British design, the Terry carbine had an early form of bolt action, with the device seen here in the open position.
8. C. Chapman musketoon.
9. Bilharz, Hall, and Company carbine. This rising breech carbine shows the lever depressed and the breech in its raised position for reloading.
10. Bilharz, Hall, and Company carbine. This is a muzzle-loading carbine.
11. Richmond carbine. Made in the capital of the Confederacy, this carbine includes the original ramrod and carrying sling.
12. Morse carbine. Another very early breech-loader, this example has its breech open for reloading.

1861–65
WEAPONS OF THE AMERICAN CIVIL WAR: CONFEDERACY INFANTRY WEAPONS

The Confederate States' Army had to take its weapons from wherever it could find them, whether from abroad, from existing prewar stocks found in Confederate territory on the outbreak of the Civil War, or from local manufacture once the war had started. Here are a miscellany of weapons from all three such sources. Numerically, the most important source was none of these: it was the Union Army.

1. Belgian Pattern 1842 short rifle. A number of Belgian rifles were imported for use by the CSA, where they gained a reputation for a heavy recoil (earning the nickname "mules") and shoddy workmanship.
2. Kerr's Patent rifle. This was a product of one of Britain's many small gunsmiths of the middle nineteenth century, but certainly appears to be of good-quality workmanship.
3. Palmetto Armory Model 1842 musket. A prewar musket manufactured in the United States but used by the Confederate Army. Note the very dangerous-looking bayonet, ramrod in place beneath the muzzle, and raised leaf back sight.
4. Dickson, Nelson, and Company muzzle-loader, an undistinguished and very conventional muzzle-loading design.
5. Davis, Bozeman, and Company muzzle-loader.
6. Mendenhall, Jones, and Gardner muzzle-loading rifle, complete with ramrod and carrying sling.
7. Richmond rifle-musket. Early type of rifled musket, with sling.
8. Fayetteville rifle, shown with CS-embossed cartridge box complete with strap; an early-model muzzle-loading rifle that could also have been fitted with a bayonet.
9. Fayetteville rifle. Later-model muzzle-loading rifle from Fayetteville. This does not have a bayonet fitting and has a modified rear sight.
10. Richmond rifle-musket. Later type of rifled musket from the Confederate capital's arsenal, with minor improvements as a result of combat experience.
11. Cook and Brother rifle, produced in a small gunsmith's shop.

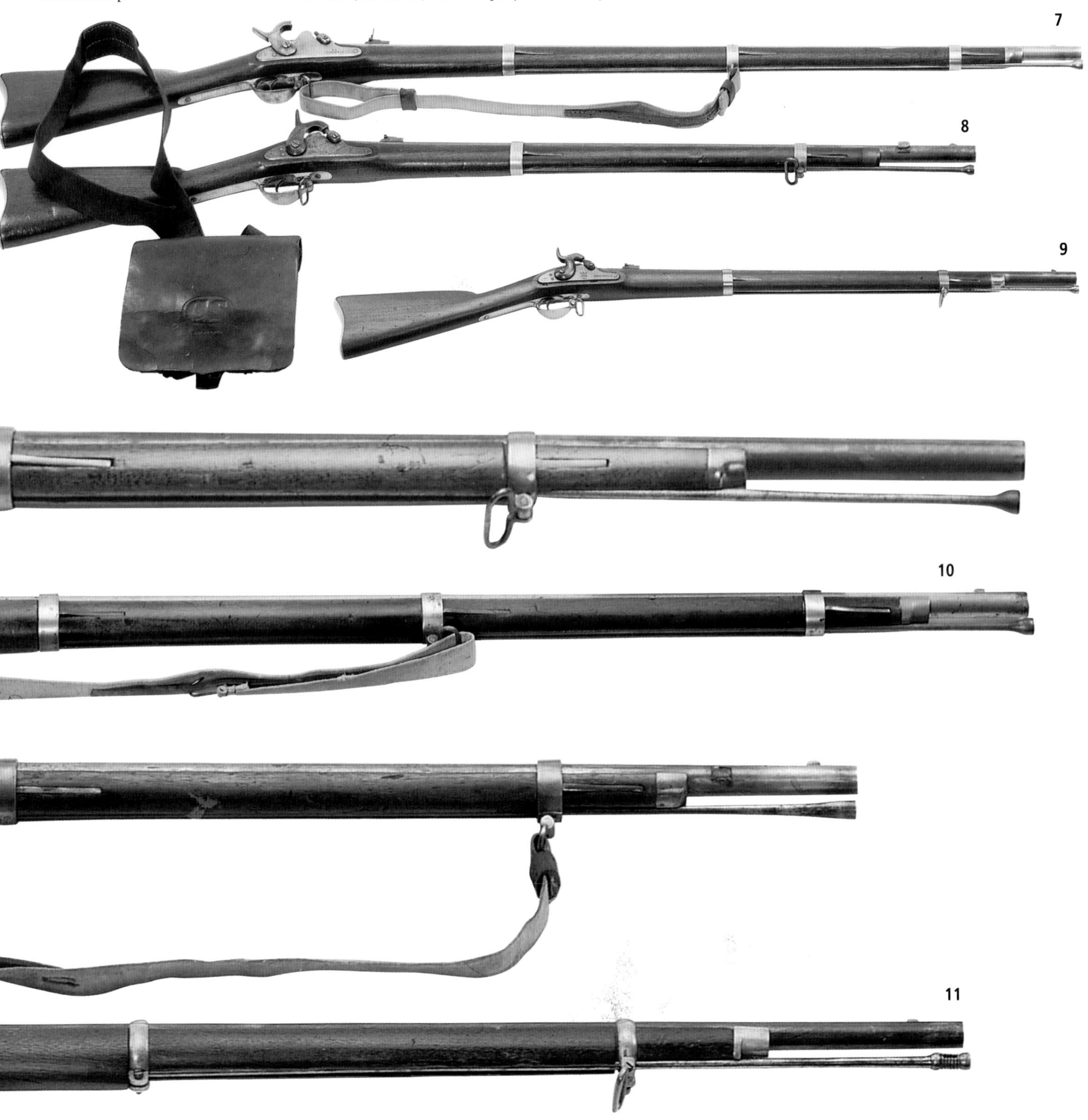

1861–65
WEAPONS OF THE AMERICAN CIVIL WAR: US ARMY WEAPONS

The US Army had the advantage over the CSA in that it had and retained control over the great majority of the prewar arsenals, and thus not only was able to maintain production, but was also able to make do with far fewer makes of weapon. Here some representative types of cavalry carbine are shown on the left, and infantry rifles on the right.

1. Starr cavalry carbine. A conventional, lever-action, breech-loading carbine.
2. Maynard 1st Model carbine. An unusual type of carbine in which the lever action released a lock so that the gun could be "broken" (as shown here) to enable it to be reloaded.
3. Merril carbine. A late-model Merril carbine, with the unusual breech mechanism open for reloading.
4. Joslin Model 1864 carbine.
5. Burnside 4th Model carbine. Note that the breech mechanism has been opened to show its operation.
6. Spencer carbine. On this weapon the back sight has been raised and the breech opened to show its action. Note also the spring-fed tubular magazine, which is partially withdrawn from its housing in the butt.
7. US Army Model 1816 musket. A smoothbore weapon, shown here with its bayonet in place.
8. US Army Model 1855 rifle-musket, shown with rifle-musket cartridge box with shoulder belt. The successor to the Model 1842, the Model 1855 had a rifled barrel, which necessitated proper sights (note the raised back sight).
9. US Army Model 1842 musket. The successor to the weapon shown immediately below, the Model 1842 offered little improvement in any department.
10. US Army Model 1861 rifle-musket. Again, this seems to have offered only marginal improvements over its three predecessors.
11. British Pattern 1853 rifle-musket. Although this has been shown elsewhere in this book, the British Enfield muzzle-loading rifle-musket is shown here for comparison with its two United States contemporaries, the Model 1855 and the Model 1861 shown above.
12. Justice rifle-musket. US Army rifle-musket from a private contractor.

1862–1866
HENRY RIFLES

The Henry rifle was a derivative of the Smith and Wesson/Volcanic arms, with Henry's modified action and improved cartridge revolutionizing the concept. The latter consisted of a brass casing with the propellant in its base and a 216-grain bullet and 25 grains of powder. The Henry was fitted with a tubular magazine holding sixteen rounds. The "rimfire" round proved successful, and tests by the US Army's Ordnance Department were encouraging, showing that at a range of 400 yd. (365 m) the bullet could embed itself 5.0 in. (127 mm) in a wooden post. Despite this success, the US government was somewhat slow in accepting the Henry rifle, but by 1863 a large number had been purchased and issued to volunteer and state troops; the state of Kansas, in particular, took to the Henry. The only real problem lay in the price: in October 1862, the rifle was listed at $42, while ammunition cost $10 per thousand. Even though the dealers failed to get a good discount, demand was sufficient to keep the company busy. One particular weakness was the magazine spring, which was exposed by a slot underneath through which dust and dirt could enter. This was cured in 1866 when a "gate" was placed in the receiver, which enabled the firer to charge the magazine from the receiver rather than from the muzzle end. This invention came too late for Henry, however, and the device was incorporated in its successor, the Winchester Model 1866.

1. An early brass-frame Henry rifle (serial no. 14).
2. Iron-frame Henry rifle, levered for loading.
3. Iron-frame Henry rifle (serial no. 155).
4. Early-production (rounded-butt) brass-framed, engraved Henry rifle (serial no. 172).
5. Early-production brass-framed, silver-plated Henry (serial no. 2115) with, above, a box of early cartridges, and, below, a box of post-Civil War cartridges, both 0.44 -caliber Henry rimfire.
6. Early-production brass-frame, silver-plated, engraved Henry rifle.
7. Early-production brass-frame Henry military rifle (serial no. 2928), with, below it, a four-piece wooden cleaning rod normally stored in the butt trap.
8. Later-production (crescent-butt) brass-frame Henry military rifle (serial no. 6734).
9. Later-production silver-plated Henry military rifle (serial no.7001) with leather sling.
10. Later-production brass-frame Henry military rifle (serial no. 9120).
11. Later-production brass-frame Henry military rifle (serial no. 12832) with, below it, a quartet of 0.44-caliber Henry flat nosed cartridges.

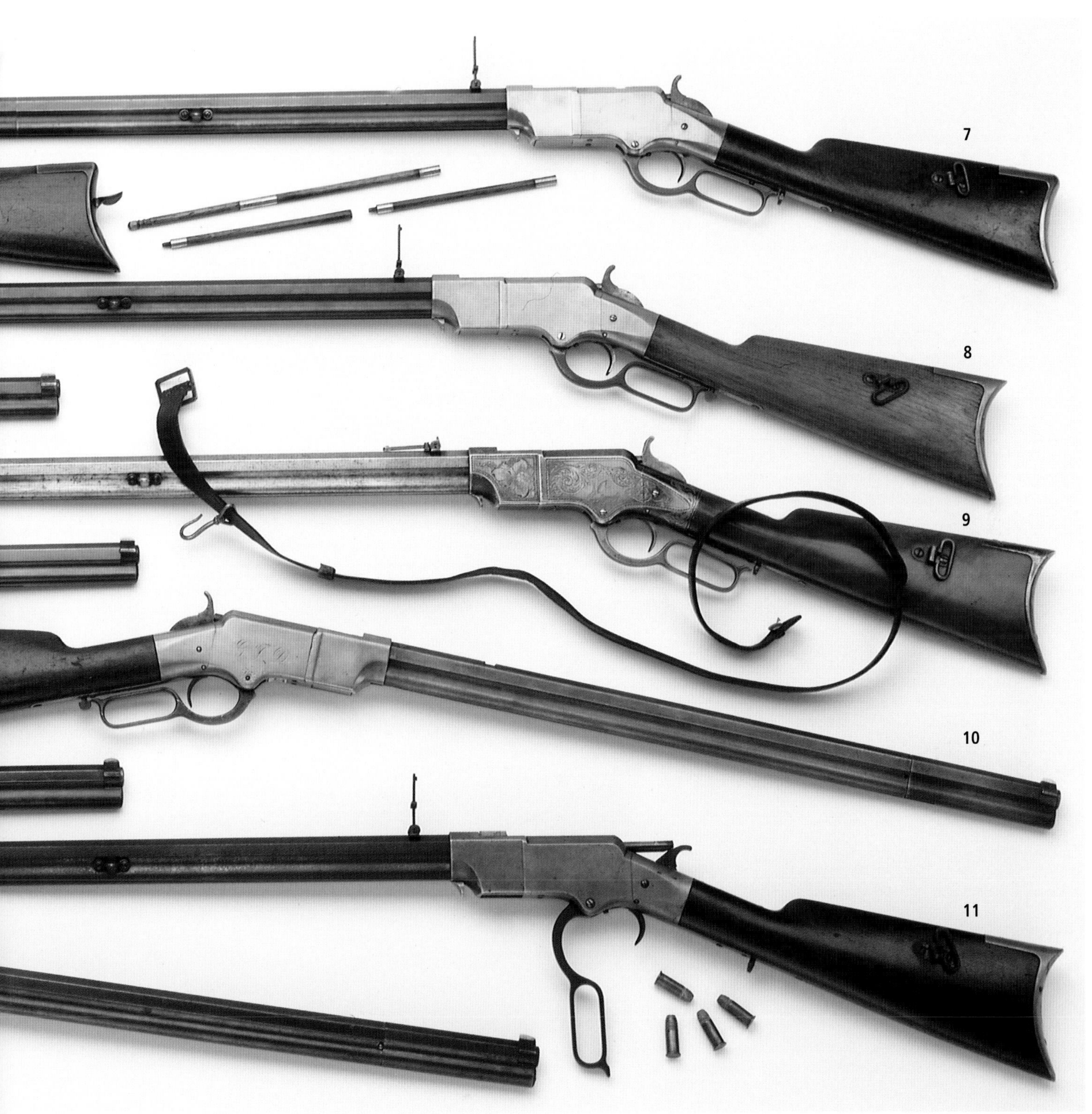

1870–1885
HUNTING AND BUFFALO RIFLES

While Sharps' weapons dominated the American hunting scene in the 1860s, by the early 1870s a number of serious competitors had appeared, seeking to break into this specialized but lucrative market, especially among those hunters who seemed determined to exterminate the West's vast herds of buffalo. Ballard, in particular, produced a number of "hunting" rifles in calibers ranging from 0.32 in. (8.1 mm) to 0.44 in. (11.2 mm), which met with some success. But Sharps' main competition came from Remington, whose sporting and hunting rifles, with their calibers ranging from 0.40 in. (10.2 mm) to 0.50 in. (12.7 mm), and their powerful cartridges, proved ideal for hunting buffalo and other big game.

No matter who the makers were, however, rifles for hunting large animals were expensive, usually between $100 and $300, depending upon the maker and the quality of the weapon. Further, the addition of special iron sights or even of the early telescopic sights added yet more to the hunter's outlay. Ammunition also aroused controversy, although hunters generally loaded their own most of the time and paid particular attention to the black powder they used: American powders tended to burn "hot and dry" and to cake up the bore, whereas British powders, particularly that made by Curtis and Harvey, burned "moist."

1. Maynard 0.50-caliber rifle in fitted case with reloading tools, powder flask, and cartridges. Note the second barrel, normally supplied in different calibers from 0.32 to 0.44 rim- or centerfire.
2. Maynard rifle cartridge box.
3. Remington-Hepburn rifle with pistol grip.
4. Fine example of Frank Wesson's two-trigger rifle.
5. The outside-hammer Peabody hunting rifle appeared in 0.44- to 0.45-caliber models.
6. Remington Rolling Block short-range rifle in the "Light Baby Carbine" model.
7. Winchester single-shot rifle Model 1885 with a 20 in. round barrel.
8. Similar Winchester to that above, with 30 in. octagonal barrel. Both weapons have adjustable rear sights.
9. Fine Marlin-Ballard No. 2 sporting rifle in 0.38 in. centerfire, with "shells" for it below.
10. Sturdy breech-loader by the Brown Mfg. Company.
11. Remington No. 1 Rolling Block sporting rifle. It was chambered for various calibers from 0.40 to 0.50, and was popular with hunters and plainsmen alike.

1866–1873 WINCHESTER RIFLES

The legendary Winchester rifle owed its origin to the early Smith and Wesson, and later Volcanic, arms. But by the mid-1860s it was a much-improved weapon and the Model 1866 (called the "Yellow Boy" on account of its brass receiver) could be loaded with fifteen cartridges. By far the most popular model was the standard rifle with a 24.0 in. (610 mm) octagonal barrel, followed by the carbine, which had a somewhat shorter, 2.0 in. (508 mm), round barrel. Early advertisements for the Model 1866 made much of the fact that an expert shot could empty the magazine in fifteen seconds, giving a remarkable, if theoretical, rate of fire of sixty shots a minute.

By the late 1860s, however, rimfire ammunition for rifles and other large arms was in decline. With the centerfire cartridge came the the legendary Model 1873, usually known as the Winchester '73. In this model, Winchester improved the mechanism and replaced the brass lever with an iron one, while the new 0.44 in.-40 (10.2 mm) cartridge was a great improvement, even if it failed to impress the Army's Ordnance Department because it was a pistol round and the Army wanted something much more powerful. The civilian market, however, welcomed the new cartridge, and in 1878 Colt chambered some of their Peacemakers and double-action Army pistols in 0.44-I, which were marked "Frontier Six-Shooter."

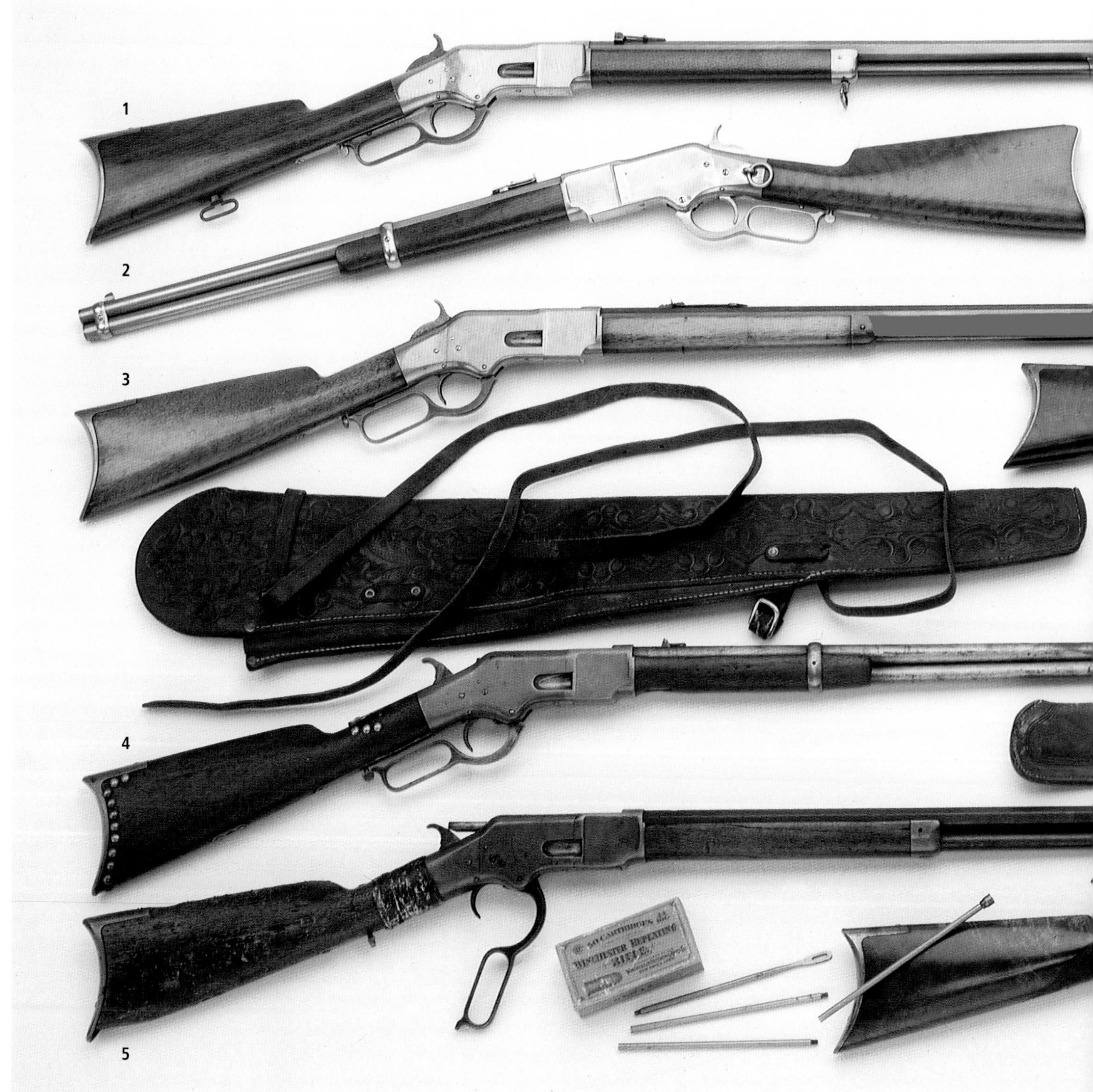

1. A fine Winchester Model 1866, 0.44-caliber, with 24 in. octagonal barrel and sling swivels.
2. Carbine version with a saddle ring and a round 20 in. barrel.
3. Some Model '66 rifles were made with round barrels on request. Below it is a fine hand-carved leather scabbard.
4. This Model 1866 was once Indian-owned—note the typical brass-tack design.
5. Model 1866 with broken stock, repaired with wet rawhide strips.
6. Cocking action of the Winchester—note how the breech-pin cocks the hammer as the lever drops.
7. Typical 1873 carbine with the round barrel and saddle ring. Above it are a box of original "shells" for the '73, and two-part cleaning rod.
8. A '73 with round barrel and shortened magazine.
9. A fine '73 carbine with, below it, a typical saddle scabbard for a Winchester rifle.
10. Fine example of the Winchester '73 target rifle with additional sights set behind the hammer and, at its butt, its cleaning rod and an original box of 50 0.44-100 rifle cartridges.

1876–1886
WINCHESTER RIFLES

Faced with the rejection of the Model 1873 by the US Army because of its ammunition, Winchester produced a modified version, known as the Model 1876. This had a receiver that was able to accept the pressures generated by the Army's 0.45-in.-70 (11.4 mm) cartridge which was 2.0 inches (50.8 mm) long—almost twice the length of the standard 0.44-in.-40 (10.2 mm) round. In fact, the Model 1876 could accept a 0.45-in.-75 (11.4 mm) cartridge with a bullet weight of 350 grains, which was more powerful than the government version. This rifle never achieved the fame of the '73, but it was accepted by the Northwest Mounted Police and, like its predecessor, enjoyed a good reputation among frontiersmen.

John M. Browning, whose brilliant designs would later enhance Colt's reputation, completely redesigned the Winchester rifle to produce the most powerful of them all, the Model 1886. Chambered for 0.45 inch-90 (11.4 mm), it also appeared in 0.50 inch-110-300 (12.7 mm) Express, which proved to be a very popular caliber. The Browning-inspired Models 1877, 1892, and 1894 also met with great success. Many old-time gunfighters and plainsmen carried Winchesters. The Model 1873 and the 1886, or even the Henry rifle, were used by buffalo hunters, but most hunters preferred larger-caliber rifles.

1. Superficially similar to the Model '73, the '76 had an enlarged receiver and bigger loading-slot plate.
2. Like the '73, some Model '76s were sold with short magazines. Above the rifle is a box of cartridges for the '76.
3. Fine example of the Model 1876 carbine (serial no. 45569).
4. Fully blued '76 rifle (serial no. 40330), with a pair of ladies' buckskin gauntlets.
5. A '76 (serial no. 10018) equipped with a checkered pistol stock and target sights; below it are two 0.45-70 cartridges for the '76.
6. The Browning-designed Model 1886 rifle, a big improvement on earlier models.
7. A similar 1886 rifle, with choice wood pistol stock and target sights. Note the long "shell" case below it.
8. An "as new" carbine version of the Model 1886 (serial no. 8484).
9. The short-magazine 1886 rifle (serial no. 57909) and, below it, high-powered cartridges.
10. Model 1886 carbine with a ring that allowed it to be slung over a saddle or shoulder and, above it, a silver-embossed, hand-tooled rifle scabbard for the 1886.

1861–1873
SPENCER RIFLES AND CARBINES

In 1864, Brigadier General James W. Ripley, Chief of the US Army's Ordnance Department, submitted a report to the Secretary of War in which he stated that the Spencer rifles and carbines were the "cheapest" and the "most efficient" of the many weapons in use by the Union forces, and that they enjoyed an excellent reputation among cavalry regiments. This seven-shot weapon, fitted with a Blakeslee quick-loader, was designed so that the ammunition was contained in a tube set into the stock. It took a matter of seconds to remove an empty tube and replace it with a fully charged one.

More than 90,000 carbines were purchased during the Civil War, and following the conflict, the Spencer enjoyed a great reputation on the frontier. In 1865 the company introduced a 0.50 in. caliber (12.7 mm) version, complete with magazine cut-off that enabled it to be used as a single-shot weapon, if required. Issued to various regiments, including the legendary Seventh Cavalry, the Spencer was considered to be the finest weapon of its type available at the time, and what it lacked in magazine capacity compared with the Winchester it made up for by being easier and faster to load. In 1874 the Spencer was superseded by the Springfield Model 1873, a single-shot carbine in 0.45-70 caliber capable of firing twelve or thirteen rounds a minute.

1. Spencer 0.36-caliber light sporting rifle (serial no. 15).
2. Spencer 0.44-caliber light carbine (serial no. 5) and, below it, a seven-round tubular magazine for Spencer rifles and carbines.
3. Spencer US Navy contract 0.36-56-caliber military rifle and, below it, four rounds of Spencer 0.56-52-caliber rimfire ammunition.
4. Spencer US Army 0.56-56 military carbine (serial no. 30670) carried at the Battle of the Little Bighorn by a Cheyenne warrior.
5. Spencer US Army Model 1865 0.56-50-caliber military carbine (serial no. 5909) and, below it, 0.56-56 Spencer rimfire cartridges.
6. Spencer 0.56-46 caliber sporting rifle (serial no. 17444).
7. Spencer 0.38-caliber prototype sporting rifle (no serial no.).
8. Spencer 0.56-50-caliber carbine (serial no. obliterated) rebarreled to a sporting rifle. Above it are a pair of typical Western saddle boxes that might have carried loose ammunition.
9. Spencer 0.56-46-caliber sporting rifle (no serial no.).
10. Spencer 0.56-56-caliber carbine (serial no. 35862) rebarreled to 0.56-50 by John Gemmer of St Louis under S. Hawken's stamp.

1873–1888
BURGESS-WHITNEY RIFLES

Andrew Burgess, a prolific inventor, took out patents in 1873 and 1875 on a lever action for rifles, parts of which included features patented by G.W. Morse in 1856. Burgess then contracted with Eli Whitney Jr. (whose company had made Sam Colt's Walker pistols back in 1847) to produce a magazine lever-action rifle based on these patents, which would compete with the Winchester. The venture was not a success and in the mid-1880s Burgess turned to Samuel Colt, who then manufactured an improved version of the lever-action rifle; but apparently, Winchester threatened to start producing revolvers unless Colt ceased production of the Burgess. Whatever the reason, production suddenly stopped! Whitney, however, went on to produce other lever-action weapons, notably the Whitney-Kennedy series, one of which was owned by "Billy the Kid."

The Whitney range of lever-action rifles was designed for frontier or sporting rather than military use, and an estimated 20,000 were made, Like the Winchester arms, the carbine version had a 20.0 in. (508 mm) barrel, and the rifle had a 24.0 in. (610 mm) barrel. The company also produced several bolt-action military models, but none was ever ordered into production by the Ordnance Department. There were reports that a number of these military rifles later found favor among Central and South American armies. In 1888 Whitney sold out to Winchester.

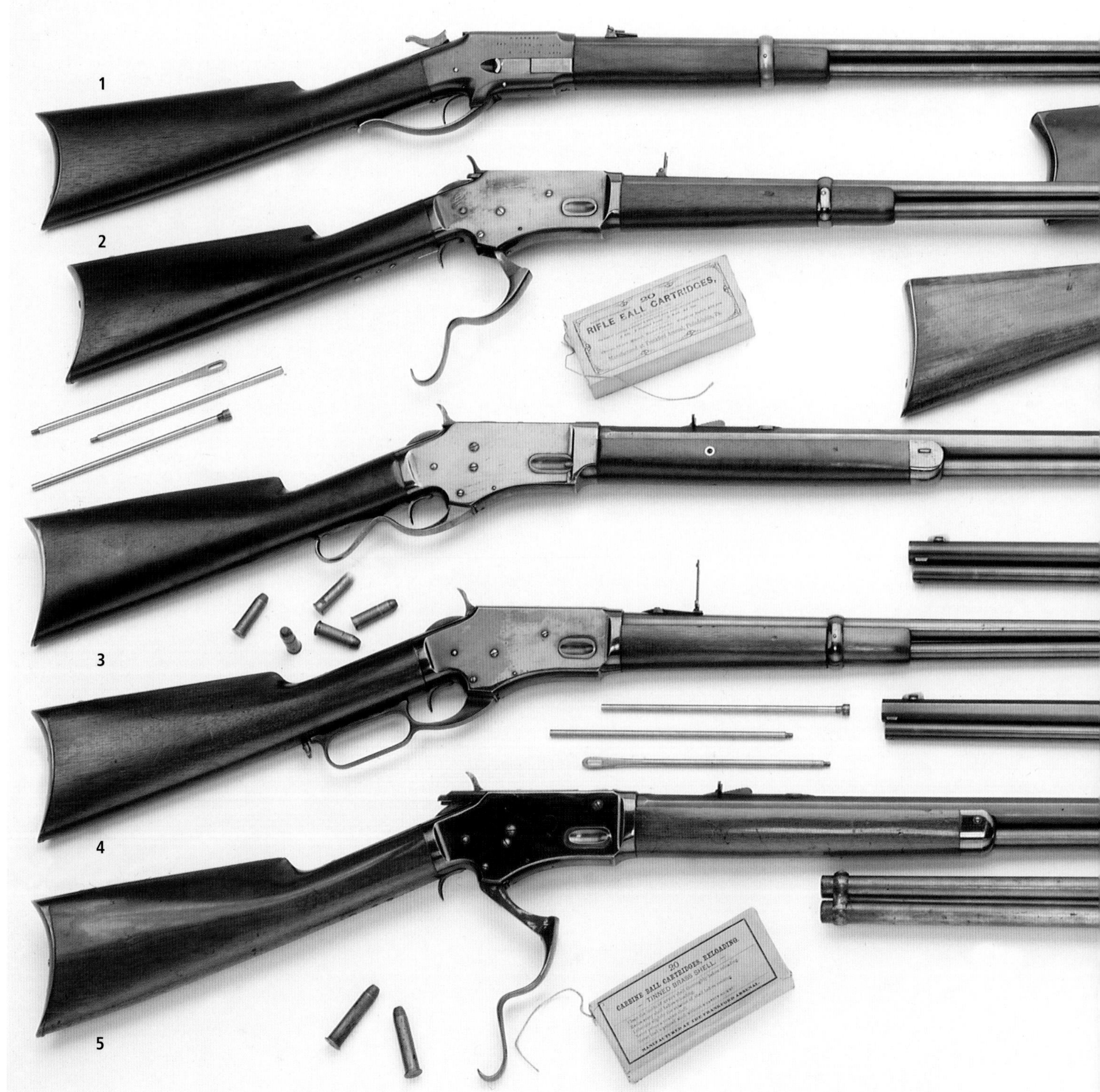

1. Whitney-Burgess carbine in 0.40 caliber.
2. Whitney-Kennedy lever-action carbine showing the "S" lever on early models and, below it, its three-part cleaning rod and a box of 0.45-caliber rifle cartridges.
3. A Whitney-Burgess-Morse lever-action rifle in 0.44 caliber. Whitney-Kennedy carbine fitted with a full loop lever and, below it, a cleaning rod for it .
5. Whitney-Kennedy rifle in 0.40-60 caliber and, below it, cartridges for it.
6. Whitney-Scharf lever-action hunting rifle. It was sold in 0.32-20, 0.38-40, and 0.44-40 calibers. Below it are hunting cartridges.
7. Another version of the sporting rifle and, below it, a box of government cartridges and a fine example of a typical Stetson-type broad-rimmed hat.
8. Colt-Burgess lever-action rifle, with cleaning rods below it.
9. Colt Lightning slide-operated rifle. Colt produced a number of variants of this rifle.
10. Remington-Keene magazine bolt-action rifle in 0.45-79 caliber.

UNITED STATES

REMINGTON RIFLE 1863

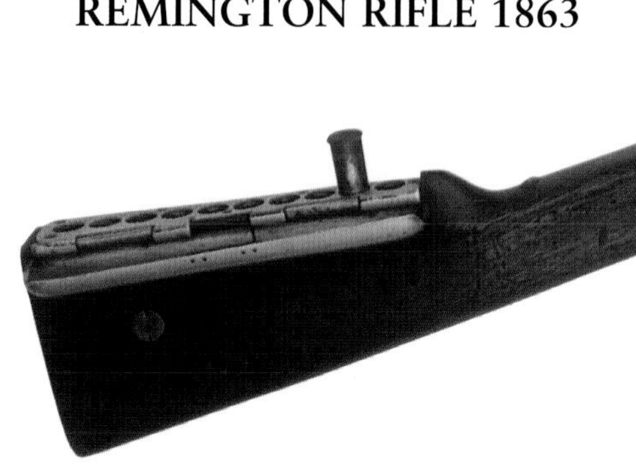

Length (gun): 50.5 in. (1,283 mm)
Barrel: 35.0 in. (889 mm)
Weight (gun): 9.3 lb. (4.2 kg)
Caliber: 0.45 in. (11.4 mm)
Rifling: 5 grooves, l/hand
Operation: breech-loading
Feed: single-round, manual
Muz vel: ca 350 ft./sec. (411 m/sec.)

Leonard Geiger patented a rifle mechanism in 1863, but when he was subsequently employed by Remington, that company's name was applied to the resulting weapon. An order was placed by the US Army during the Civil War, but the war ended before any deliveries had been made, and despite its success elsewhere, the Remington rifle was never adopted by the US Army. After some improvements, it was exhibited at the 1867 Paris Imperial Exposition, where it won a silver medal, attracting a number of overseas orders. In the Remington action, the breast of the hammer and the rear of the block were so designed that the former wedged so closely behind the latter that together they made an absolutely rigid support for the cartridge, a support strengthened by the nose of the hammer engaging a recess at the rear of the striker. The Remington Rifle was normally sighted to 1,000 yd. (914 m).

UNITED KINGDOM

WHITWORTH RIFLE 1864

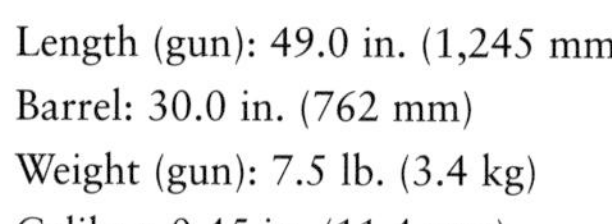

Length (gun): 49.0 in. (1,245 mm)
Barrel: 30.0 in. (762 mm)
Weight (gun): 7.5 lb. (3.4 kg)
Caliber: 0.45 in. (11.4 mm)
Rifling: n.k.
Operation: percussion
Feed: muzzle loading
Muz vel: ca 1,000 ft./sec. (305 m/sec.)

In 1854 the British government asked Sir Joseph Whitworth to design machinery for the mass production of service rifles, which he agreed to do. He then went one step further and undertook the design of his own rifle as well. With the help of an experienced small-arms designer and two Army officers, he produced a rifle with a caliber of 0.451 in. (11.45 mm), somewhat smaller than other contemporary weapons, a change that was not greeted with any marked enthusiasm by British Army "experts." Whitworth's rifles proved to be exceptionally accurate but were considered to be too well made and also suffered from such excessive fouling that they had to be cleaned regularly with a special scraper. Despite this, an order was placed in 1864 and some 8,000 were delivered to the British Army. This particular example was used by the Confederate Army in the American Civil War.

FRANCE

MODEL 66 "CHASSEPOT" RIFLE 1866

Length (gun): 51.8 in. (1,314 mm)
Barrel: 36.0 in. (914 mm)
Weight (gun): 9.8 lb. (4.5 kg)
Caliber: 0.461 in. (11.7 mm)
Rifling: n.k.
Operation: muzzle-loading, percussion-cap
Feed: manual
Muz vel: n.k.

The Model 1866 Rifle, designed by Antoine Alphonse Chassepot, was the French answer to the Prussian "needle gun." This was a single-shot, bolt-action weapon, although it was not cocked by the bolt; it was necessary to pull the cocking piece to the rear with thumb and forefinger before the breech could be opened. The bolt lever normally projected horizontally to the right and had to be turned upward through 90 degrees to open it. The barrel was of 0.433 in. (11 mm) caliber, but the bullet, unlike that of the Prussian needle gun, did not have a sabot but fitted the barrel. The rifle was sighted to a maximum of 1,312 yd. (1,200 m). One of the Chassepot's surprising features was its consumable cartridge, although it was somewhat fragile and caused heavy fouling, resulting in an escape of gases rearward, despite the fitting of a rubber obturating ring on the bolt.

Rifle Warfare in The American Civil War

The American Civil War (1861–65) straddled an interesting period in rifle history, as the shift from muzzle-loader to breech-loader was taking place. The Civil War armies were equipped with a multiplicity of different weapons, each with its own combat properties. There were several reasons for this variety, including the sudden need for equipping mass conscription armies, the sheer number of sources available for armaments purchase (both indigenous and across Europe), and the use of civilian stocks.

The most common type of rifles used were percussion-cap muzzle-loading rifle-muskets, such as the British Enfield Model 1853 and the US Springfield Model 1861. About 1.5 million of these weapons were distributed throughout the armies of the North and South, and with a .58 in. caliber and a range of up to 1,640 ft. (500 m), they were deadly weapons, although restrained by their slow rate of fire of about three rounds per minute. Breech-loaders were also making their presence felt, though the newness of the cartridges for these and their consequent scarcity meant that such guns were not as widespread as percussion-cap weapons. However, Union forces used more than 90,000 Sharps single-shot breech-loaders, and the Confederates manufactured their own copy. The Civil War also saw the emergence of the repeater as a new tool of infantry warfare. Combat usage of the Spencer and Henry repeaters showed it capable of generating heavy volumes of firepower against massed troops. The numbers distributed were comparatively small—only 10,000 Henry repeaters were used in the war—but when they were used in action they had a shattering effect.

Above: *Union troops unleash a barrage of rifle fire. Although most Civil War rifles were still muzzle-loaders, the rate of fire and the accuracy of such weapons were improved by general adoption of the cylindro-conoidal Minié round in 1855. The round had a hollow base that expanded on firing to fit the bore. Therefore, before firing, the round was relatively loose in the bore and could be loaded quickly without excessive force.*

At Hoover's Gap, Tennessee, on June 24, 1863, for example, the Union 17th Indiana Brigade used Henry repeaters to engage a heavily superior Confederate force, inflicting 500 enemy casualties for only forty-seven dead.

The power of contemporary rifles, regardless of type, along with improved artillery, led to important tactical changes for both North and South. Frontal assaults were far too costly, so fire and maneuver tactics became dominant, with units spread more widely over a battlefield and utilizing cover more effectively. Cavalry actions were also curtailed; instead of being applied in shock assaults, they were used more in reconnaissance, probing, pursuit, and screening actions. Finally, as exposure on open land became suicidal, defensive earthworks and fortifications were necessary, often constructed while under fire.

UNITED KINGDOM

GEORGE GIBBS LONG-RANGE TARGET RIFLE 1866

Length (gun): 51.8 in. (1,314 mm)
Barrel: 36.0 in. (914 mm)
Weight (gun): 9.8 lb. (4.5 kg)
Caliber: 0.461 in. (11.7 mm)
Rifling: n.k.
Operation: muzzle-loading, percussion-cap
Feed: manual
Muz vel: n.k.

This Metford Rifle by George Gibbs of Bristol, England, was made in about 1866 and was intended for accurate shooting at ranges up to 1,000 yd. (914 m). The rifling was Metford's pattern with shallow grooves and a gaining twist, and the barrel was fitted with a muzzle extension, designed to protect the end of the rifling when the weapon was being loaded and cleaned. The long-range back sight was mounted on a tang behind the action and had a vernier adjustment for elevation only. The variable aperture fore sight was adjustable for windage and had a cross-leveling spirit level; there was also provision for different fore sight blades. The caliber of this example was 0.461 in. (11.7 mm) and it fired a hardened cylindrical, paper-patched slug of 550 grains (6 g), which was driven by 90 grains (6 g) of the finest-quality black powder available.

UNITED KINGDOM

HILL DOUBLE 10-BORE SHOTGUN 1866

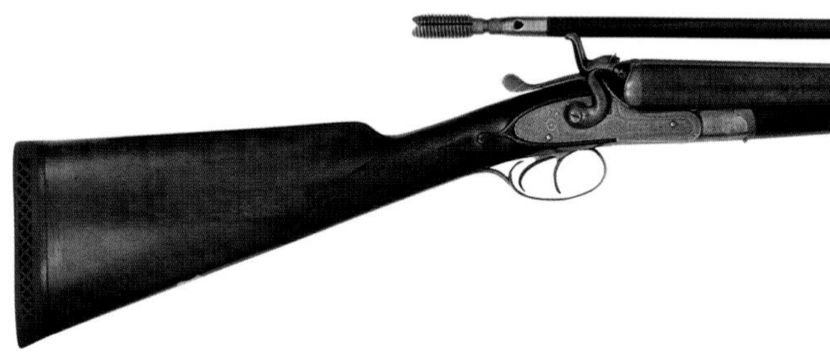

Length (gun): 47.3 in. (1,200 mm)
Barrel: 31.3 in. (794 mm)
Weight (gun): 9.7 lb. (4.4 kg)
Caliber: 10-gauge
Rifling: none
Operation: external-hammer, breech-loading
Feed: manual
Muz vel: n.k.

The double-trigger side-by-side Hill shotgun is a good example of an early breech-loading wild-fowling gun of the "black powder" era, before the appearance of inside-hammer mechanisms. It is capable of projecting 2 oz. (57 g) of shot, somewhat more than that fired by the average modern 10-bore shotgun, which uses a nitro powder cartridge, although in the Hill's case the firer has to load his own cartridge. The shotgun shown in the picture is in original condition, except for the butt pad, which had to be replaced as the older one had crumbled away.

UNITED KINGDOM

SNIDER RIFLE 1866

Length (gun): 48.0 in. (1,219 mm)
Barrel: 33.0 in. (838 mm)
Weight (gun): 8.3 lb. (3.7 kg)
Caliber: 0.577 in. (14.7 mm)
Rifling: 3 grooves, l/hand
Operation: breech-loading
Feed: single-round, manual
Muz vel: ca 1,100 ft./sec. (335 m/sec.)

By 1864, the British Army had concluded that breech-loading rifles were essential, and that the quickest way to re-equip the troops was to convert the existing stock. In August 1864, leading British gun-makers were invited to submit mechanisms for converting the existing Enfield muzzle-loading rifles; the clear winner was the Snider, but it was only accepted for service in May 1866 after lengthy tests. The breechblock was hinged on the right and opened sideways to enable the firer to load a single cartridge, which he placed in the trough and pushed home, then closed the breech. He then cocked the action. Pulling the trigger released the striker, which struck the firing pin, which, in turn, hit the cap in the base of the cartridge. The main problem lay with the ammunition; finally, the Mk IX was deemed fully acceptable. Large numbers of rifles were converted in a remarkably short amount of time.

UNITED STATES

US ARMY MODEL 1866 RIFLE (SPRINGFIELD-ALLIN CONVERSION) 1866

Length (gun): 51.0 in. (1.295 mm)
Barrel: 32.5 in. (825 mm)
Weight (gun): 8.3 lb. (3.7 kg)
Caliber: 0.45 in. (11.4 mm)

Rifling: 6 grooves, l/hand
Operation: breech-loading
Feed: single-round, manual
Muz vel: ca 1,350 ft./sec. (411 m/sec.)

The Springfield-Allin conversion was of fairly standard type. There was a trough leading into the breech, which was closed by a front-hinged block containing a striker, the end of which was so positioned that it could be struck by the original percussion hammer. To load, it was necessary to place the hammer at half-cock, release a spring catch on the right-hand side, and raise the block until it was inclined forward at an angle of about 45 degrees; this action also worked the extractor. When the cartridge was in the breech, the block was pulled back into position and the trigger pressed in the usual way. The nose of the hammer fit exactly into a recess around the end of the striker, which effectively locked the block at the moment of firing. This rifle, with only minor modifications, remained in service until replaced by the Krag-Jörgensen magazine rifle.

UNITED STATES

WINCHESTER MODEL 1866 RIFLE

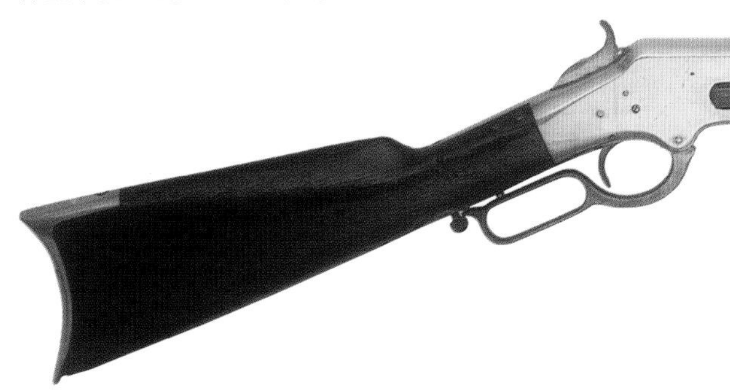

Length (gun): 39.0 in. (991 mm)
Barrel: 20.0 in. (508 mm)
Weight (gun): 7.8 lb. (3.5 kg)
Caliber: 0.44 in. (11.2 mm)

Rifling: 5 grooves, l/hand
Operation: breech-loading
Feed: 16-round tubular magazine
Muz vel: ca 1,125 ft./sec. (343 m/sec.)

Following the collapse of his unsuccessful "Volcanic Rifle" venture in 1857, Oliver Winchester brought in a skilled and experienced weapons engineer, Benjamin Tyler, who quickly analyzed the problems and designed and developed a new, self-contained, much more powerful and very reliable 0.44 in. (11 mm) cartridge. Henry also refined the design of the Volcanic rifle, which held sixteen of the new rounds in a tubular magazine beneath the barrel. The new weapon, dubbed the "Henry repeater," was introduced in 1862. By 1866 Winchester had created the Winchester Repeating Arms Company. A loading gate on the right-hand side of the rifle was introduced, and the famous Winchester Rifle, with its distinctive brass receiver (hence its nickname "Yellow-boy") was complete. The Model 1866 remained in production until 1898.

AUSTRIA

M1867 INFANTRY RIFLE (WERNDL)

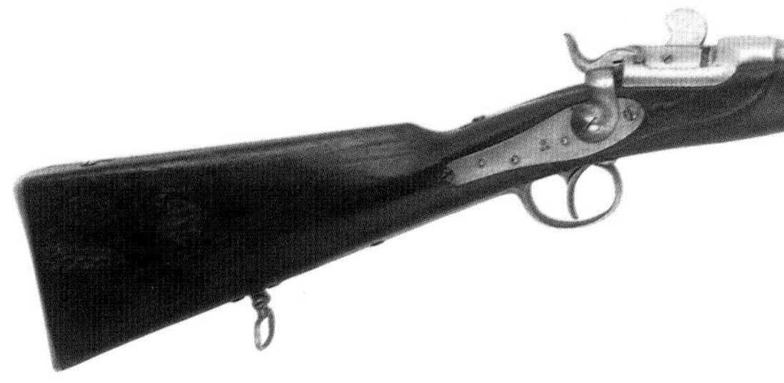

Length (gun): 50.5 in. (1,283 mm)
Barrel: 33.0 in. (838 mm)
Weight (gun): 9.0 lb. (4.1 kg)
Caliber: 0.42 in. (10.7 mm)

Rifling: 6 grooves, l/hand
Operation: breech-loading
Feed: single-round, manual
Muz vel: ca 1,350 ft./sec. (411m/sec.)

The M1867 Infantry Rifle, the brainchild of Joseph Werndl, was more commonly known as the Werndl Rifle. It had a cylindrical breechblock mounted on a pin parallel to and just below the line of the barrel, designed to move 90 degrees. A deep semicircular groove was cut out of one side of the block; when it was turned level with the chamber, it acted as a guide for the cartridge, this action only being possible when the action was at half-cock. The block was then turned back to the closed position by a protruding thumb-piece, the hammer drawn back to full cock, and the trigger pulled. Developments included the M1873 (improved action with a central hammer) and M1877 (new cartridge, sights). A cavalry carbine was produced by shortening the barrel. This is the M1867 version. The Werndl was optimistically sighted to 1,750 yd. (1,600 m).

SWITZERLAND

M1869 VETTERLI INFANTRY RIFLE

Length (gun): 52.0 in. (1,320 mm)
Barrel: 33.1 in. (841 mm)
Weight (gun): 10.3 lb. (4.7 kg)
Caliber: 0.41 in. (10.4 mm)
Rifling: 4 grooves, l/hand
Operation: breech-loading
Feed: 12-round, tube
Muz vel: ca 1,427 ft./sec. (435 m/sec.)

Vetterli's breech-loading rifle was adopted by Italy as the M1870. It was manufactured by Beretta under license in four versions: M1870 Infantry Rifle with a 53.0 in. (1,345 mm) barrel; M1870 Short Rifle with a 43.1 in. (1,095 mm) barrel; M1870 Cavalry Carbine with an even shorter 36.8 in. (929 mm) barrel; and the M1882 Naval Rifle, which was the M1870 with an eight-round tube magazine. It was later converted to take a four-round Vitali box magazine, when it was designated the M1870/87 Infantry Rifle (Vetterli-Vitali). Another model was produced in1915, when the 1870/87 conversions were reconverted, being fitted with a 6.5-mm-caliber barrel and a new type of clip-loaded magazine. The Vetterli was a bolt-action rifle with four locking lugs at the rear of the bolt, which locked into the recesses in the body. Its unusual safety device consisted of a small catch below the bolt lever.

SPAIN

CREEDMORE MATCH, RIGBY-TYPE PERCUSSION RIFLE (REPRODUCTION) 1877

Length (gun): 49.0 in. (1,245 mm)
Barrel: 32.5 in. (825 mm)
Weight (gun): 8.2 lb. (3.7 kg)
Caliber: 0.45 in. (11.4 mm)
Rifling: n.k.
Operation: muzzle-loading, percussion-cap
Feed: single-round, manual
Muz vel: n.k.

The name "Creedmore" derives from a place on Long Island, New York, where a British and a US team competed in 1877 for what was called, perhaps immodestly, the "Championship of the World." This is a replica of the British Rigby muzzle-loader used in that event. The barrel of this example is some 4 inches (102 mm) shorter than would normally be expected in a long-range rifle of this kind, although it is perfectly adequate for shooting at 109 yd. (100 m), the range at which the vast majority of rifles of this type might be expected to be used. The advent on the "black powder" scene of English-style replicas, such as this, including the Enfield as well as the German Schützen rifles, marked a clear break with the American concept of the replica arm.

UNITED KINGDOM

WILLIAM EVANS FARQUARSON ACTION RIFLE 1878

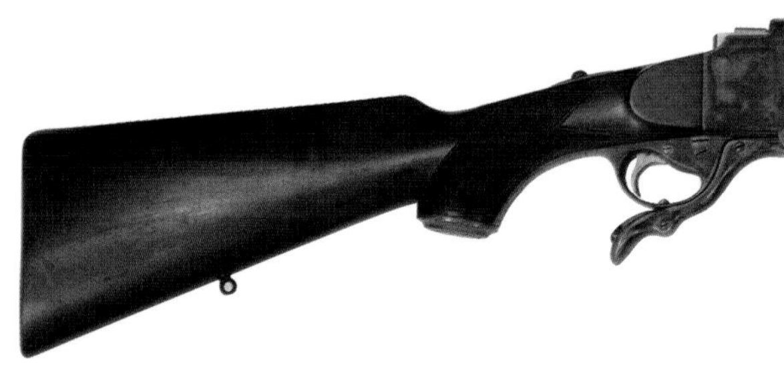

Length (gun): 43.5 in. (1,105 mm)
Barrel: 26.8 in. (680 mm)
Weight (gun): 9.8 lb. (4.5 kg)
Caliber: 0.577-3 in.
Rifling: 7 grooves, r/hand
Operation: lever-operated
Feed: manual
Muz vel: n.k.

Farquarson, a Scotsman, was the most famous poacher of his age; a record of his exploits in this sphere eventually was published in a book. He was a superb marksman, winning the Scottish rifle championship in 1863 and the "King of the Belgians" prize in 1869. He invented the "Farquarson action," which he patented. The Farquarson action involved a lever under the trigger guard, which is pushed down and forward, recocking the striker and activating the ejector. The Farquarson was made under license until the patent expired, when it was marketed by Webley using actions bought in from Francotte of Italy. The weapon shown here was made by William Evans of 63 Pall Mall, London. Using a 3.0 in. (76 mm) case and 100 grains of cordite, it fired a 750-grain bullet, either full-jacketed or soft-point, against heavy or dangerous game.

UNITED KINGDOM

MARTINI-HENRY RIFLE 1882

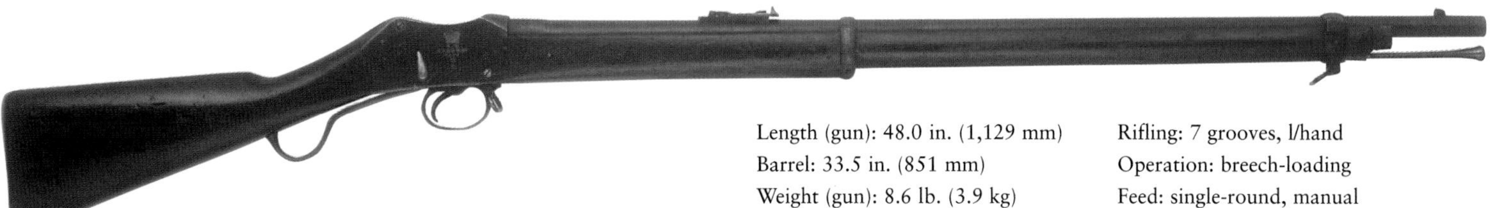

Length (gun): 48.0 in. (1,129 mm)
Barrel: 33.5 in. (851 mm)
Weight (gun): 8.6 lb. (3.9 kg)
Caliber: 0.45 in. (11.4 mm)
Rifling: 7 grooves, l/hand
Operation: breech-loading
Feed: single-round, manual
Muz vel: 1,350 ft./sec. (411 m/sec.)

In the Martini system, the block, which had a scoop-like top, was hinged at the rear, and a sharp pull on the lever caused the front of the block to drop, exposing the breech, partially extracting the empty cartridge case, and cocking the striker. The firer then removed the empty cartridge case, inserted a new one, and pulled the lever back against the stock. The barrel was designed by Alexander Henry (see Farquarson rifle). His steel barrel was 0.45 in. (11.43 mm) in caliber and fired 0.5 in. (12.7 mm) bullets, with seven grooves making a left-hand turn in every 22.0 in. (559 mm). The bullet weighed 480 grains (31.1 g) and was hardened by the addition of small amounts of tin; it had a slightly hollow base. Trials found shortcomings in the cartridge and a new design was developed: it was bottle-shaped and fit into an enlarged and slightly tapered chamber. The new weapon was accepted into service in 1871 as the "Rifle, Martini-Henry Mk1."

FRANCE

MODÈLE 1886 (LEBEL) RIFLE

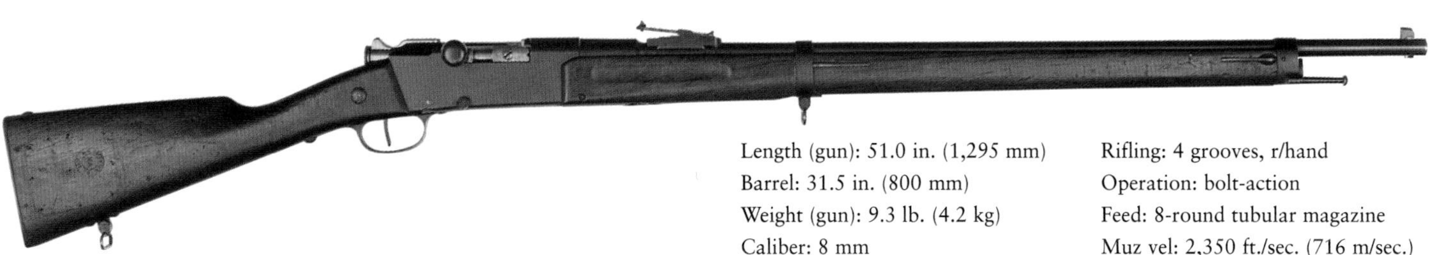

Length (gun): 51.0 in. (1,295 mm)
Barrel: 31.5 in. (800 mm)
Weight (gun): 9.3 lb. (4.2 kg)
Caliber: 8 mm
Rifling: 4 grooves, r/hand
Operation: bolt-action
Feed: 8-round tubular magazine
Muz vel: 2,350 ft./sec. (716 m/sec.)

The Modèle 1886 (Lebel) was based on the Austrian Kropatschek rifle, with which the French Marine Infantry was equipped in 1878. The Lebel was a bolt-action rifle with a tubular magazine concealed in the woodwork below the barrel. The magazine incorporated a powerful coil spring at its front; the rear end of the spring was fitted with a close fitting plug. The rifle was loaded by pushing the rounds nose-first into the magazine opening below the chamber; it had a capacity of eight. The contents of the magazine could be kept in reserve by a cut-off device, allowing the rifle to be used as a single-loader. The most important feature of the Lebel was undoubtedly the fact that its cartridges were loaded with a recently developed smokeless propellant instead of black powder; the French were the first to make this important change.

GERMANY

MODEL 1888 COMMISSION RIFLE

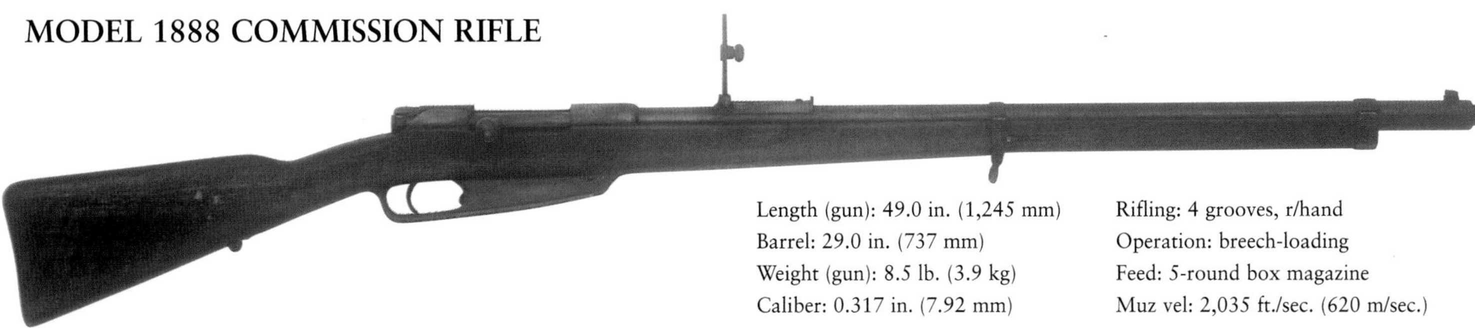

Length (gun): 49.0 in. (1,245 mm)
Barrel: 29.0 in. (737 mm)
Weight (gun): 8.5 lb. (3.9 kg)
Caliber: 0.317 in. (7.92 mm)
Rifling: 4 grooves, r/hand
Operation: breech-loading
Feed: 5-round box magazine
Muz vel: 2,035 ft./sec. (620 m/sec.)

The Lebel rifle caused the Germans to look at their own rifles, and in 1888 they set up a Small Arms Commission to chart the way ahead. The group designed an effective and modern weapon that, although designated the Model 1888, became known as the "Commission Rifle." It was part Mauser, firing the 7.92 x 57 mm Mauser smokeless round, and part Mannlicher (for example, the box magazine holding five 0.317 in./7.92 mm rounds). The magazine protruded a short distance below the receiver but was nonremovable. There were two shortened versions: the M1888 Cavalry Carbine and the M1891 Artillery Carbine. The rifle was used by various armies and was also manufactured in Austria by Steyr. An export model for China, however, the M1907, failed to win an order, although a number were later impressed into German service in 1914.

UNITED STATES

WINCHESTER .22 IN. SINGLE-SHOT MUSKET 1888

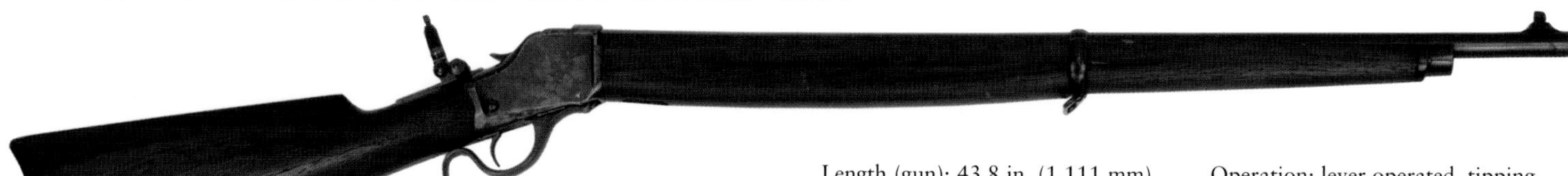

Length (gun): 43.8 in. (1,111 mm)
Barrel: 28.0 in. (711 mm)
Weight (gun): 8.4 lb. (3.8 kg)
Caliber: 0.22 LR
Rifling: n.k.
Operation: lever-operated, tipping-block
Feed: single-round, manual
Muz vel: n.k.

Naming this weapon a "musket" is slightly misleading, since it is not a muzzle-loading, nonrifled weapon as the name would normally imply. Instead, the name, which was given in the late 1880s, derived from what was considered to be the military-style woodwork and general appearance of the weapon. This was one of a number of "miniature" (i.e., 0.22 in.) weapons that appeared in the United States toward the end of the nineteenth century in response to a popular movement for the widespread training of civilians in the shooting arts. Indeed, the National Rifle Association of America had been lobbying to have shooting with such weapons included in all school curriculums. This weapon, of which some 109,327 were manufactured in twenty-eight years of production, was made of either steel or iron, with wooden furniture, and in a wide variety of calibers.

NORWAY

KRAG-JÖRGENSEN RIFLE 1889

This rifle was of turn-bolt design, locked by a single lug on the bolt head, which engaged a recess behind the chamber. Further support was provided by a rib on the bolt, the rear end of which rested on a shoulder on the body. The sheet-steel box magazine was L-shaped, curving under the action with a loading gate on the right-hand side of the body. The gate was hinged at the front and was held in position by a spring catch at the rear; inside the gate was a

FRANCE

M1890 CAVALRY CARBINE

Length (gun): 37.2 in. (945 mm)
Barrel: 17.9 in. (453 mm)
Weight (gun): 6.6 lb. (3.0 kg)
Caliber: 0.32 in. (8 mm)
Rifling: 4 grooves, l/hand
Operation: bolt-action
Feed: 3-round box magazine
Muz vel: ca 2,000 ft./sec. (609 m/sec.)

In 1890, the French adopted a Berthier carbine intended for mounted troops. It had a three-round box magazine, and it loaded from a single charger, which was pushed out through a hole in the bottom of the magazine when the last round had been fired; the entire charger could also be ejected by pressing a catch inside the trigger guard. The bolt was similar to that of the Lebel except that it was turned down close to the body, which was considered more convenient for cavalry use. The cartridge was the same as that used in the Lebel. There were special versions, including the M1890 Cuirassier Carbine and the M1892 Artillery Musketoon (the French name for a carbine fitted with a bayonet). The carbine was later converted to a rifle, initially for use by colonial troops, but the M1907/15 was a World War I version rushed into production to replace the aged Lebel as the standard infantry rifle.

ITALY

MANNLICHER-CARCANO CARBINE M1891

Length (gun): 36.2 in. (920 mm)
Barrel: 17.1 in. (444 mm)
Weight (gun): 6.6 lb. (3 kg)
Caliber: 6.5 mm
Rifling: 4 grooves, r/hand
Operation: bolt-action
Feed: 6-round magazine
Muz vel: 2,300 ft./sec. (701 m/sec.)

The Model 91 weapons were the first of a series developed for the Italian Army toward the end of the nineteenth century. It was primarily of Mauser design; the only feature of Mannlicher origin was the six-round clip. They were developed at Turin by S. Carcano, a designer at the Italian Government Arsenal. The first of the series was a full-length infantry rifle, closely followed by the weapon illustrated, the Model 91 cavalry carbine, which went into service in 1893. Most cavalry of that time deluded themselves as to the superiority of the sword and professed to regard firearms as of little importance, but the pretense was wearing thin. One feature of the Model 91 carbine is its folding bayonet, which indicates that even then the Italian Cavalry understood that it might have to act as mounted infantry and fight on foot. One interesting feature of these early models was the progressive twist rifling.

Length (gun): 49.0 in. (1,245 mm)
Barrel: 30.0 in. (762 mm)
Weight (gun): 9.35 lb. (4.2 kg)
Caliber: 0.30 in. (7.62 mm)
Rifling: 6 grooves, l/hand
Operation: breech-loading
Feed: 5-round integral magazine
Muz vel: 2,480 ft./sec. (756 m/sec.)

spring and a follower (platform). To load the rifle, the gate was pushed fully open, causing the follower and spring to be held back. The rifle was then tilted slightly to the left, five rounds introduced singly into the magazine opening, and the gate closed; this also released the spring, thus pushing the rounds up, the topmost into the shorter arm of the magazine, where it was ready to be pushed into the chamber by the bolt. The Krag-Jörgensen was adopted by Denmark in 1889 and the US Army in 1892, although the required modifications delayed its introduction until 1896. Norway adopted the weapon in 1894. The picture and specifications relate to the US Army's "Model 1896 Krag Rifle."

UNITED STATES

MARLIN MODEL 39A RIFLE 1891

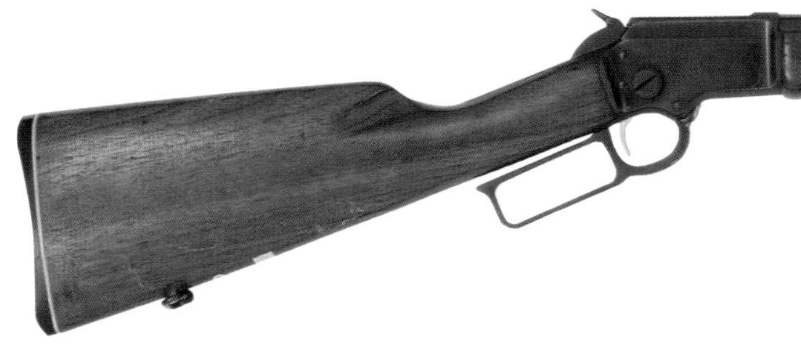

Length (gun): 36.5 in. (927 mm)
Barrel: 20.5 in. (521 mm)
Weight (gun): 6.0 lb. (2.7 kg)
Caliber: 0.22 in. (see text)
Rifling: n.k.
Operation: lever-action, tilting-bolt
Feed: see text
Muz vel: n.k.

The 0.22 in. Marlin Model 39A was introduced in 1891 and has been in continuous production ever since. In fact, like its near contemporary, the Savage (qv), it is a well-loved classic. The Model 39A was innovative in the 1890s as the first rifle with a front-loading, tubular magazine, which can take twenty-six 0.22 short or nineteen long/long rifle rounds. The nose of the lever locks the bolt, and pulling the lever down and forward drives the bolt to the rear, overriding and cocking the hammer, extracting and ejecting the spent case, and raising the cartridge lever, which elevates a new round from the magazine. Then, as the lever is closed, the new round is chambered ready for firing. There is a bead fore sight with an open-notch back sight, which has a notched elevation ladder, drift-adjustable for windage. There is a large screw on the right of the receiver, which allows disassembly into two parts.

Breech-loaders in Action

Above: *Soldiers of the Royal Munster Fusiliers stand guard at Honey Kloof, South Africa, during the Boer War (1899–1902). By the time of the Boer War, breech-loaders were the standard infantry weapons on the battlefield. The British Army relied especially on the .45 in. Martini-Henry rifle. This powerful weapon was a single-shot breech-loader with a hinged breechblock operated by an underaction lever. The Martini-Henry was a decisive man-stopper but was replaced by the magazine-fed Short Magazine Lee-Enfield in 1907.*

Breech-loading signaled the true advent of modern weapons, particularly when employed with the unitary cartridge. Breech-loaders emerged in the 1840s–50s; one of the first practical examples was the Sharps rifle of 1848, named after its inventor, Christian Sharps. The Sharps rifle utilized a linen cartridge, the base of which was shorn off when the lever-operated breechblock was closed, exposing the powder for percussion ignition. The Sharps rifle was a solid performer, and during the Civil War (1861–65) Colonel Hiram Berdan's 1st Union Sharpshooters demonstrated superb sniper skills with the weapons, killing at ranges of up to 1,640 feet (500 m).

Breech-loaders offered several advantages over muzzle-loaders other than speed of loading, one of which was that when using metallic cartridges, the breech-loader could accept magazine feed. The most famous of the magazine-fed breech-loaders was the Henry rifle. The Henry was a lever-action rifle, and operating the lever ejected spent cartridges and fed new ones in from a spring-loaded tubular magazine underneath the barrel. The Henry rifle was patented in 1860, and was later known as the Winchester rifle (the Winchester company would handle production and sales).

The Henry/Winchester rifles served in limited numbers in the American Civil War and in larger numbers in the frontier wars against the Native Americans. A true testament to the performance of this weapon comes from its use in Turkish hands at the siege of Plevna in the Russo-Turkish war of 1877. There, exported Winchesters shared the front line with another early breech-loading weapon, the Peabody-Martini rifle. Unlike the magazine-fed Winchester, the Peabody-Martini was a single-shot weapon loaded via a hinged breechblock. It was a rugged weapon, and the drop-breech action was strong enough to take heavy long-range loads. At the Bulgarian town of Plevna, 14,000 Turkish troops occupied the town against besieging Russian troops, who were armed with Colt Berdan rifles and Krenka conversion muskets. The Russians sent in a mass assault, but at range the Turks opened up with the Martini rifles. When the surviving Russians had closed to less than 200 yd. (190 m), the Turks switched to the Winchester rifles to deliver heavy close-range firepower. Two Russian mass assaults resulted in 26,000 casualties.

Plevna proved the efficiency of the breech-loader, and the world's armies began the scramble to either re-equip with breech-loaders or convert existing weapons.

ITALY

CEI-RIGOTTI AUTOMATIC RIFLE 1895

Length (gun): 39.4 in. (1,000 mm)
Barrel: 19.0 in. (483 mm)
Weight (gun): 9.6 lb. (4.3 kg)
Caliber: 6.5 mm
Rifling: 4 grooves, r/hand
Operation: gas
Feed: 25-round box
Cyclic rate: up to 900 rpm
Muz vel: 2,400 ft./sec. (730 m/sec.)

Captain Cei-Rigotti, an officer in the Italian Army, carried out experiments with gas-operated automatic rifles. In 1895 he demonstrated one to his Divisional Commander, the Prince of Naples. It was not until 1900 that his efforts were made public in a Roman newspaper, which included a reference to the use of mounted infantry in the war in South Africa. This most likely drew British attention to the new weapon, and specimens were obtained and a series of tests carried out by both Army and Navy experts. The rifle worked by a short-stroke piston from the barrel to a rod connected to the bolt, this rod and the cocking handle at its rear clearly visible in the photograph; it was designed to fire both single shots and bursts. The tests were generally unfavorable, both authorities commenting on the difficulties of ejection and the high rate of misfires.

UNITED KINGDOM

PURDEY DOUBLE RIFLE 1895

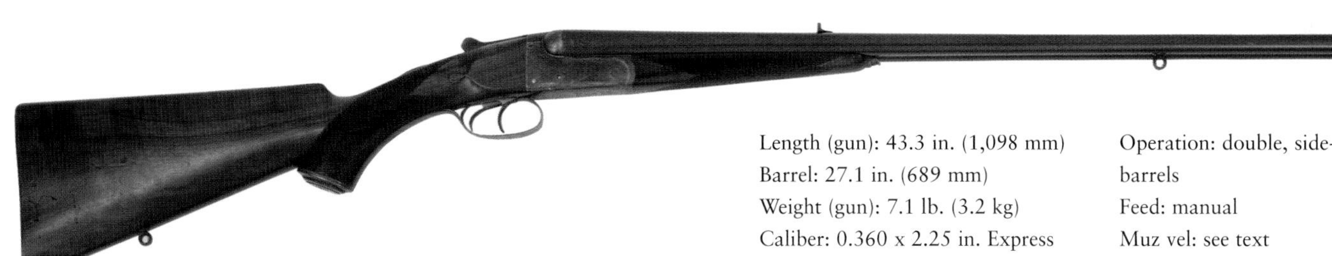

Length (gun): 43.3 in. (1,098 mm)
Barrel: 27.1 in. (689 mm)
Weight (gun): 7.1 lb. (3.2 kg)
Caliber: 0.360 x 2.25 in. Express
Rifling: 17 grooves, r/hand
Operation: double, side-by-side barrels
Feed: manual
Muz vel: see text

This is a double-barrel, side-by-side, rifled, hammerless, boxlock made by J. Purdey and Sons of South Audley Street, London, in the 1890s. It was chambered for the 0.360 x 2.25 in. Express, a cartridge that threw a 190-grain bullet, often paper-patched, at about 1,700 ft./sec. (518 m/sec.), and was probably used for culling fallow deer in the parkland of some great house. In general, side-by-sides such as this are preferred to over-and-unders, such as the Gebrüder Merkel (qv), when dealing with dangerous game because of their greater reliability and speed of fire. The Purdey operates by pushing the top lever to the right, which allows the barrels to open on a hinge, recocking the internal hammers and activating the extractors. The barrels are made of steel and are rifled, with a seven-grooved right-hand twist. Trigger guard and butt straps are of brass, and the butt has walnut side plates.

UNITED STATES

LEE MODEL 1895 (US NAVY) RIFLE

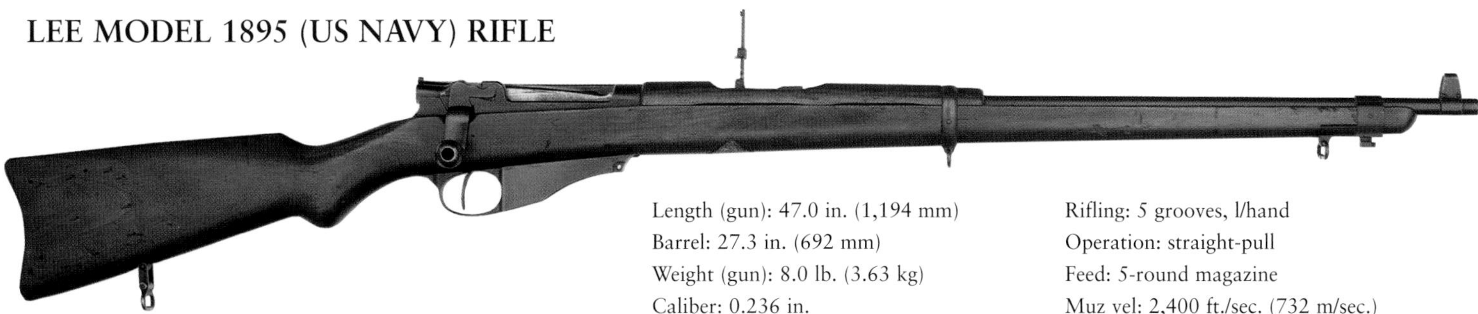

Length (gun): 47.0 in. (1,194 mm)
Barrel: 27.3 in. (692 mm)
Weight (gun): 8.0 lb. (3.63 kg)
Caliber: 0.236 in.
Rifling: 5 grooves, l/hand
Operation: straight-pull
Feed: 5-round magazine
Muz vel: 2,400 ft./sec. (732 m/sec.)

James Lee is probably best known for his box magazine for bolt-action rifles. Toward the end of the nineteenth century he invented a rifle that in 1895 was adopted by the US Navy, which ordered 10,000. The rifle incorporated a "straight-pull" breech in which direct backward pressure on the lever caused the breech to rise slightly, opening as it did so. Locking worked by an arrangement of cams on the bolt. It was of unusually small caliber and had a magazine capacity of five rounds. It was the first US service rifle to be loaded by a charger. Unfortunately, straight-pull rifles have no advantage over the turn-bolt types, but they do have several disadvantages, such as their complex structure and tiring operation. The US Navy disliked it and it soon disappeared from the service. A sporting version was made, but this also proved unpopular and the model was soon withdrawn.

GERMANY

GEWEHR 98 RIFLE 1898

Length (gun): 49.3 in. (1,250 mm)
Barrel: 29.0 in. (740 mm)
Weight (gun): 9.0 lb. (4.1 kg)
Caliber: 7.92 mm
Rifling: 4 grooves, r/hand
Operation: bolt-action
Feed: 5-round box
Muz vel: 2,850 ft./sec. (870 m/sec.)

The Mauser Gewehr 98 was strong and reliable with the forward-locking lugs made famous by the makers, and a five-round magazine, the bottom of which was flush with the stock. Although its straight bolt lever was clumsy and not well adapted to fast fire, it remained popular. In one form or another it was sold to a great number of different countries; there have been few rifles produced in such large quantities. A considerable number of the earliest ones were bought by the Boers, who used them with tremendous effect in their war with the British, which broke out a year later; and it served the German Army well in World War I. In 1918 the Germans experimented with a twenty-round magazine to prevent the constant entry of mud from the continuous reloading of the five-round magazine, but this was not a success. The lower photo shows the K98k version.

INDIA

MANTON MAUSER 98 1898

Length (gun): 44.8 in. (1,137 mm)
Barrel: 23.8 in. (603 mm)
Weight (gun): 7.7 lb. (3.5 kg)
Caliber: 0.30-06
Rifling: n.k.
Operation: bolt-action
Feed: 4-round internal magazine
Muz vel: n.k.

Joseph Manton set up his own company in 1792 and became the most celebrated gun-maker of his time. A designer of genius, he defined the form of the classic English shotgun, which remains essentially unchanged to this day. In his time, a Manton gun cost £73.10, the equivalent of £2,750 (ca $4,400) at today's prices, a sum that was willingly paid by rich sportsmen of the time. Manton's gun-making genius was not, however, matched by his business acumen; he went to debtor's prison twice and died poor. In 1825, however, he sent his son, Frederick, to Calcutta, where he founded the Indian branch of the business, which flourished under the patronage of successive British viceroys. The gun shown was made by Manton in India from parts supplied by Mauser, whose crest appears on the receiver ring. It has the standard Mauser Model 98 bolt-action.

UNITED STATES

SAVAGE MODEL 99A RIFLE 1899

Length (gun): 39.5 in. (1,003 mm)
Barrel: 20.0 in. (508 mm)
Weight (gun): 6.3 lb. (2.9 kg)
Caliber: 0.30-30 in. Winchester
Rifling: n.k.
Operation: lever-action, tipping-bolt
Feed: 5-round rotary magazine
Muz vel: see text

The Savage was introduced in 1895 and improved in 1899; over 1.5 million have been subsequently produced. For the first fifteen years or so, the '99 was chambered for the usual run of low-pressure, lever-action cartridges: 0.30-30, 0.25-35 and 0.32-40. But the breakthrough came in 1915 with the introduction of the 0.250-300, which put this rifle in a class of its own. Charles Newton designed the 0.250 on a cut-down 0.30-40 Krag case as a useful deer-hunting cartridge. Then Harvey Donaldson, another leading ballistic experimenter, suggested basing it on the 0.30-06 instead, and Arthur Savage cut the bullet weight from 100 to 87 grains, enabling him to launch the first commercially loaded American cartridge with a muzzle velocity in excess of 3,000 feet/second (914 m/sec.), hence the cartridge's designation.

BELGIUM

BROWNING A5 SELF-LOADING SHOTGUNS 1900

Length (gun): 44.5 in. (1,130 mm)
Barrel: 24.8 in. (629 mm)
Weight (gun): 8.6 lb. (3.9 kg)
Caliber: 12-gauge (see text)
Rifling: none
Operation: long-recoil, locked-breech
Feed: tubular magazine
Muz vel: n.k.

John Browning patented his self-loading shotgun design in 1900 and production started at FN in Belgium in 1903. The A5 became one of the classic guns; millions were made over the following eighty years by FN, and from 1905 to 1948 by Remington in the United States (Model 11). Its long-recoil action was copied by almost every rival gun-making factory. On firing, the barrel and bolt both recoiled, locked together, over the full length of the receiver. The barrel then returned forward alone, ejecting the spent shell; the bolt followed, loading a fresh shell. At 8.6 lb. (3.9 kg), the A5 was heavy but it was solid and reliable, and it easily adjusted to suit different loads. It was made in almost every format: Magnum; police guns; riot guns; and barrels with or without ribs. It was also produced in 12-, 16- and 20-gauge. The example illustrated is fitted with the optional Cutts Compensator.

SWITZERLAND

M1889 SCHMIDT-RUBIN INFANTRY RIFLE 1900

Length (gun): 43.0 in. (1,092 mm)
Barrel: 23.3 in. (592 mm)
Weight (gun): 8.0 lb. (3.6 kg)
Caliber: 0.295 in. (7.5 mm)
Rifling: 3 grooves, r/hand
Operation: breech-loading
Feed: 12-round box magazine
Muz vel: 1,920 ft./sec. (585 m/sec.)

The Model 1889 employed a straight-pull breech mechanism. The bolt consisted of a long-bolt cylinder, over the rear half of which was fitted a sleeve with two locking lugs; the operating rod was parallel to it and in its own housing. The receiver was unusually long; the rear end consisted of a complete cylinder, on the inside of which were two recesses for the locking lugs. A straight pull on the handle brought it to the rear, with its unlocking stud traveling in a slot on the locking sleeve, which was curved in such a way that the pressure of the stud caused the sleeve to rotate and unlock the locking lugs. The forward movement of the operating rod reversed the process and cocked the striker, which was fitted with a ring-type cocking piece, allowing it to be cocked without opening the breech. The magazine held two chargers of six cartridges each.

UNITED KINGDOM

GREENER GP SHOTGUN 1900

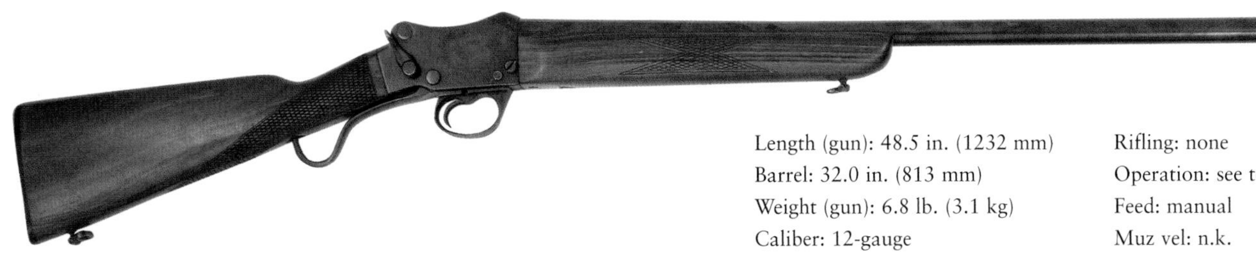

Length (gun): 48.5 in. (1232 mm)
Barrel: 32.0 in. (813 mm)
Weight (gun): 6.8 lb. (3.1 kg)
Caliber: 12-gauge
Rifling: none
Operation: see text
Feed: manual
Muz vel: n.k.

This Greener used the rugged and reliable Martini tipping-block mechanism to produce an extremely robust sporting gun, and the "GP" in the designation is believed to have stood for "General Purpose." The manufacturer, W.W. Greener and Company, has long since gone out of business. It was bought out by the British Webley Company, which was still manufacturing this gun on a small scale in the early 1990s. It is also said to be manufactured in the Philippines. The picture shows an original Greener model, with a tubular steel operating lever under the small of the butt and a large safety lever on the side of the receiver, above and to the rear of the trigger. Lowering the operating lever ejected the spent case and cocked the striker.

FABRIQUE NATIONALE

Fabrique Nationale d'Armes de Guerre is one of the truly great names of modern firearms design. The company was formed on July 3, 1889, to fulfill an order from the Belgian government for 150,000 Mauser magazine rifles. The company consisted of influential gun-makers from the Liégeois, and a factory was built at Herstal, Belgium, where the headquarters of the FN industry remain to this day.

FN fulfilled the order for the Mauser rifles between its foundation and 1894, after which there was a period of political readjustment that saw FN become part of a cartel; the other members were Deutsche Waffen and Munitionsfabriken, Waffenfabrik Mauser, and Österreichische Waffenfabriks-Gesellschaft.

The period around the turn of the century saw FN involved in the production of more military rifles, plus .22 rimfire sporting rifles. More significantly, by 1898 FN was working with John Moses Browning, producing one million Browning handguns by 1912.

The First World War saw an abrupt change in FN's fortunes, as in 1917, when Germany took over the factory for the production of its arms. With the end of the war in 1918, however, FN was returned to Belgian. The list of guns produced by FN before 1940 includes the Browning Hi-Power 9 mm handgun; the Browning M1917, M1919, and M2 machine guns; the Browning BAR; and the Mauser Mle 1924 rifle. Even 40 mm Bofors anti-aircraft guns were manufactured from 1936 on. Export clients stretched across Europe and throughout the Americas.

During World War II, some FN staff who had escaped to the UK invested their time designing a new semi-automatic rifle, which, after the war became the 7.62 mm FN FAL rifle, one of the most successful weapons in history.

More than one million FN FALs were produced, and it came to be the standard infantry weapon of fifty countries worldwide. FN reinforced this success by producing, starting in 1957, the superb FN MAG machine gun, which ultimately supplied a client list of seventy different countries.

In the 1980s FN further extended into US markets by purchasing the US Repeating Arms Company, the makers of Winchester rifles and ammunition. There followed a dip in fortunes during the 1990s, when FN was sold to the French Giat concern, but FN moved back to Belgian ownership in 1997. Since then it has focused on producing a new line of personal defense weapons, and also makes many firearms from across the world under license.

Above: *Following the failure of their previous 5.56 mm caliber assault rifle, the CAL, Fabrique Nationale began to develop a new assault rifle to take the 5.56 mm NATO cartridge in the early 1970s. The final design, called the FNC (Fabrique Nationale Carbine), was produced in 1978 and was adopted by the Belgian Armed forces. It was also adopted by Sweden and Indonesia, and both countries purchased licenses to build modified FNCs. The gas drive and rotating bolt resemble the AK-47 system, and have the same durability.*

UNITED STATES

HARRINGTON AND RICHARDSON TOPPER SINGLE-BARREL SHOTGUN 1900

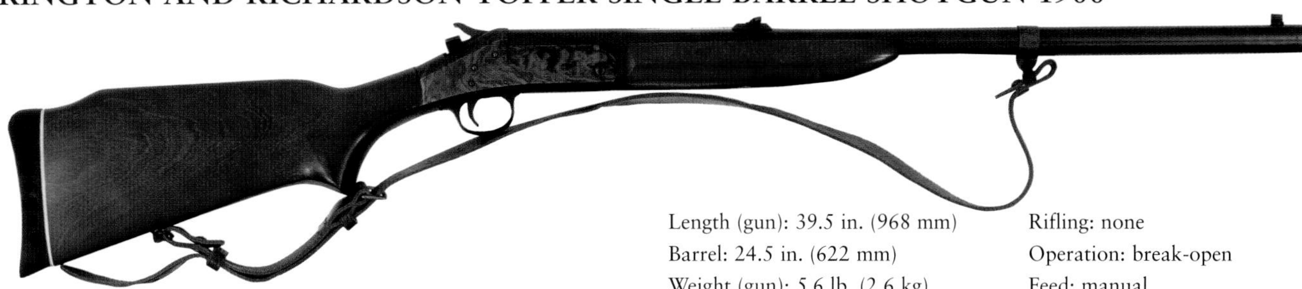

Length (gun): 39.5 in. (968 mm)
Barrel: 24.5 in. (622 mm)
Weight (gun): 5.6 lb. (2.6 kg)
Caliber: 12-gauge
Rifling: none
Operation: break-open
Feed: manual
Muz vel: n.k.

The most basic form of working gun is the break-open, single-shot weapon with simple accessories such as sling, recoil pad and iron sights. Pump actions and other types of repeater give much greater firepower, but at a considerable increase in price. As a result, the single-shot was an integral element of every American small farm, regarded as almost as much of a tool as an axe or a spade. One reason for the cheapness of these weapons was that they could be made almost entirely by machine, and the Harrington and Richardson gun shown here is typical of the breed. Such guns were widely used in Britain by small farmers and small-holders for pest control, and for a long time, particularly in the wars before World War I, between the two wars, and from 1945 to the early 1980s, American guns such as this were popular in Britain because of their simplicity, efficiency, and cheapness.

UNITED KINGDOM

VICKERS-ARMSTRONG JUBILEE MODEL RIFLE 1901

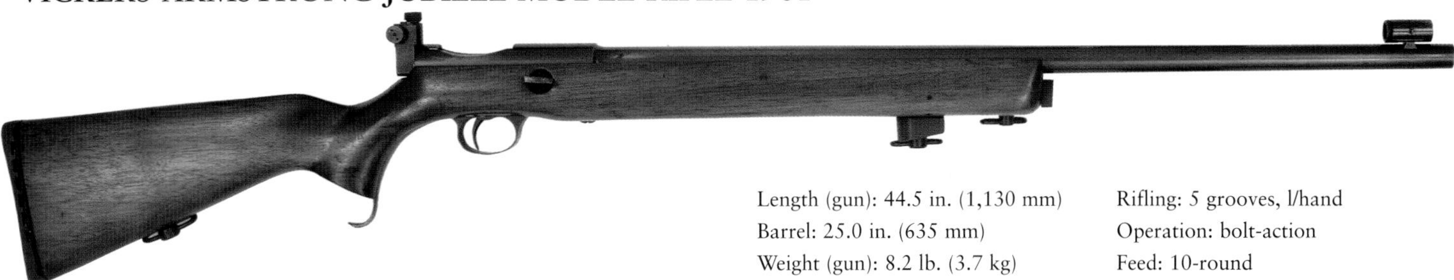

Length (gun): 44.5 in. (1,130 mm)
Barrel: 25.0 in. (635 mm)
Weight (gun): 8.2 lb. (3.7 kg)
Caliber: 0.303 in.
Rifling: 5 grooves, l/hand
Operation: bolt-action
Feed: 10-round
Muz vel: 2,440 ft./sec. (738 m/sec.)

The British heavy engineering firm of Vickers-Armstrong has involved itself only sporadically in the small arms business. It produced the Vickers-Maxim machine gun, for example, and some Luger pistols under license, but why they should have produced this 0.22 in. marksman's rifle at the beginning of the twentieth century is not clear. The "Jubilee" is a lever-operated, tipping-block, single-shot rifle whose operation bears a passing resemblance to the Martini action, and it was one of the leading target rifles of its day. The stock is one piece, which made it easier to bed, and the receiver and barrel are one piece as well. A wing screw on the right side frees the action to drop out for cleaning or adjustment. A brass cap screw on the fore-end top houses nine interchangeable fore sight elements. Ring fore sights of various diameters were used at different ranges and in differing light conditions.

UNITED STATES

SPRINGFIELD RIFLE MODEL 1903

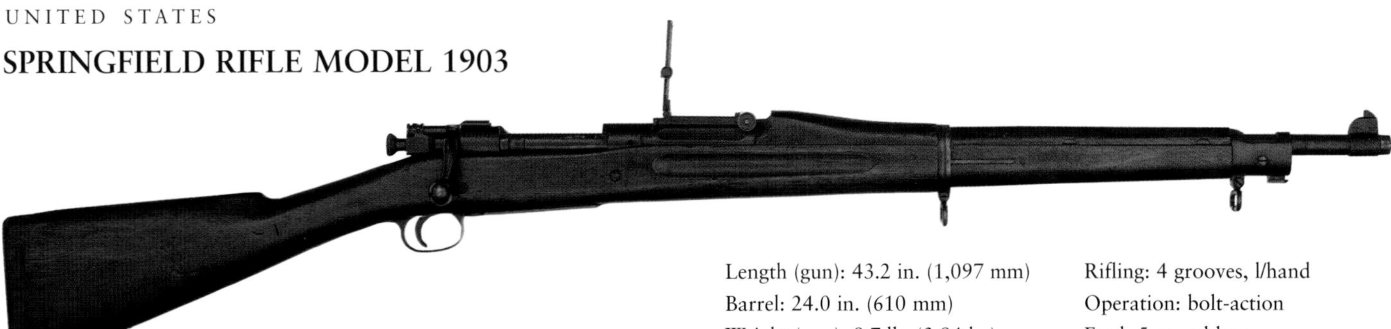

Length (gun): 43.2 in. (1,097 mm)
Barrel: 24.0 in. (610 mm)
Weight (gun): 8.7 lb. (3.94 kg)
Caliber: 0.30 in.
Rifling: 4 grooves, l/hand
Operation: bolt-action
Feed: 5-round box
Muz vel: 2,800 ft./sec. (813 m/sec.)

The Springfield had a Mauser-type bolt and a five-round magazine with a cut-off, and after some basic modifications, notably the introduction of a lighter, pointed bullet in place of the earlier round-nosed variety, it was brought into general issue by 1906. It proved to be a very popular rifle, its chief disadvantage, a minor one: its small magazine capacity; it remained in use for many years. In this time it underwent various modifications, notably one to allow it to be converted to an automatic weapon by the addition of the Pedersen device of 1918, and another that added a pistol grip to the stock in 1929. There was also a target variety, equipped with a Weaver telescopic sight, which was used successfully as the sniping rifle in World War II, together with a variety of other sporting variations, many of which are still in use. The picture shows the original production M1903.

CANADA

ROSS RIFLE MARK III 1905

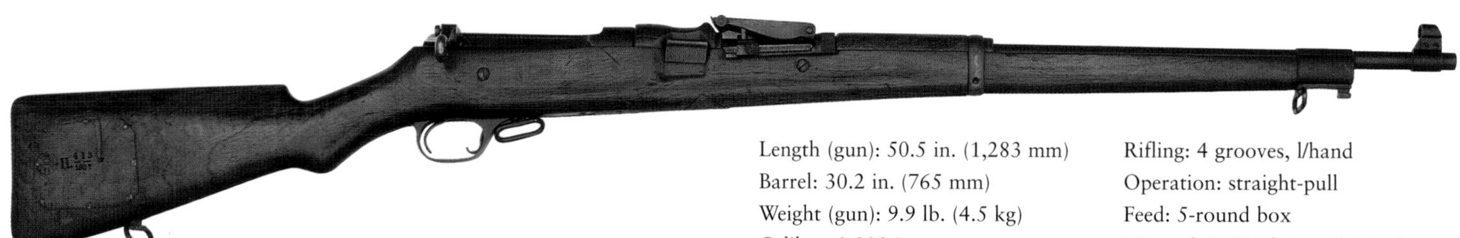

Length (gun): 50.5 in. (1,283 mm)
Barrel: 30.2 in. (765 mm)
Weight (gun): 9.9 lb. (4.5 kg)
Caliber: 0.303 in.
Rifling: 4 grooves, l/hand
Operation: straight-pull
Feed: 5-round box
Muz vel: 2,600 ft./sec. (794 m/sec.)

This rifle was designed by Sir Charles Ross, with first issues made in 1905 to the Royal Canadian Mounted Police. The rifle was unusual in being of the "straight-pull" type, in which the bolt handle was drawn straight back, the breech unlocked by the rotation of the locking lugs by means of cams. It proved to be an excellent target rifle. There were, however, fundamental defects in its design that rendered it unsuitable as a service rifle. The British School of Musketry reported unfavorably on it, but in spite of this the Canadian Army went to war with Mark III in 1914, which could be loaded by charger. Its main fault, that the bolt stop bore on one of the locking lugs, causing it to burr, led to disastrous consequences, particularly in the trenches when Canadian soldiers were seen kicking their rifle bolts to open them during German attacks.

GERMANY

GLASER HEEREN SYSTEM RIFLE 1905

Length (gun): 42 in. (1.067 mm)
Barrel: 27.5 in. (698 mm)
Weight (gun): 8.3 lb. (3.8 kg)
Caliber: 8 x 68 mm
Rifling: n.k.
Operation: see text
Feed: single-shot, manual-feed
Muz vel: n.k.

The Heeren action was patented in Paris and is still built by Glaser of Zurich, Switzerland, as well as by various small makers in Ferlach and Kufstein in Austria. The Heeren has an integral set trigger, and the trigger guard, hinged at the rear, forms the operating lever. The lever draws the breechblock downward, recocks the striker, and activates the extractor. The release latch is in the bow of the guard. The Heeren is a strong, efficient, and extremely compact action. It lacks the Farquarson's (qv) elegance and powerful extractor.

JAPAN

MEIJI 38TH YEAR CAVALRY CARBINE 1905

Length (gun): 34.2 in. (868 mm)
Barrel: 19.2 in. (487 mm)
Weight (gun): 7.3 lb. (3.3 kg)
Caliber: 6.5 mm
Rifling: 4 grooves, r/hand
Operation: bolt-action
Feed: 5-round magazine
Muz vel: 2,400 ft./sec. (732 m/sec.)

Japan's war with China in 1894 showed some defects in her infantry's rifle armament, and a commission headed by Colonel Arisaka made recommendations for improvement. The result was a series of Mauser-type rifles, first adopted in 1897 and often known as Arisaka rifles. But their title was the Meiji 30th Year type, having been made in the thirtieth year of the rule of Emperor Meiji. Rifles of this type were used in the war against Russia in 1904–05, and a number were purchased by the British in 1914 to train their new armies. The 38th Year type came into use in 1905 and was an improved version of the earlier model. It was used in World War II. The 38th Year carbine was a shortened version of the rifle. It had a metal dustcover over its bolt that proved very noisy in close-quarter jungle fighting. Like most carbines, it suffered from fairly heavy recoil. A 1944 version had a folding bayonet.

GRENADE-LAUNCHING SYSTEMS

Grenade-launching attachments on rifles were used extensively in World War II. Whereas an infantryman throwing a standard hand grenade could achieve a maximum distance of only about 160 ft. (50 m) with questionable accuracy, a rifle grenade could be fired to around 320 ft. (100 m), though accuracy was also limited. Rifles require temporary modification to fire grenades, and the firing process can be clumsy, violent, and of limited value.

Since World War II, the tendency has been for armies to employ separate grenade launchers either as stand-alone weapons (such as the US M79 grenade launcher) or as underbarrel attachments upon rifles (such as the M203 grenade launcher, which replaced the M79).

Rifle-fired grenades work in one of several ways. Early rifle grenades were fired from cup-dischargers, the rifle firing the cup using a ballistite cartridge (a blank cartridge designed to provide a form of blast propulsion). However, these systems could either damage the user's shoulder or break his weapon, such were the forces of recoil, and the cup-discharger was generally replaced in the postwar world by the bullet-trap grenade. Here a bullet is actually fired into the grenade, which has a trap system at its base to contain the round. The impact of the bullet gives about 65 ft. (20 m) of projection, but the gases from the cartridge can throw the grenade up to 1,000 ft. (320 m). (Data: Allsop and Toomey, 1999.)

Another type of rifle-grenade operation is the bullet-through grenade. As with the bullet-trap type, this grenade uses the gases of firing to achieve projection, but has a tube running through its center through which the bullet passes and exits, rather than getting trapped.

Rifle grenades have yet to become mainstream combat weapons, yet future developments could change that. The Objective Individual Combat Weapon, a prototype modular firearm system for the US Army, combined a 0.219 in. (5.56 mm) assault rifle with a .787 in. (20 mm) advanced grenade launcher capable of firing magazine-fed programmable (a laser range-finder feeds distance information to the ammunition-fuzing system), air-bursting munitions at 10 rpm out to 1,640 feet (500m).

Above: *An armored vehicle crewman operates a Heckler and Koch HK 69A1 40 mm grenade launcher. It is a single-shot break-open weapon with a maximum range of around 1,150 ft. (350 m) and is fitted with a retractable stock.*

Left: *The M203 grenade launcher is fitted beneath the barrel of the M16A2 rifle, adding 3 lb. (1.36 kg) to the weight of the rifle.*

RIFLE COMBAT IN WORLD WAR I

Left: *Soldiers of the Russian Army man a trench on the Eastern Front during World War I. The rifles on the parapet are 7.92 mm Mosin-Nagant M1891 rifles, a simple bolt-action rifle that was fed from a five-round internal box magazine. The M1891 went through numerous modifications and served with Russian forces during the next World War.*

The First World War was a conflict in which the infantryman's classic weapon, the rifle, found itself up against the new forms of small arms and heavy-caliber weaponry that would ultimately dominate the battlefields. The rifle was still the primary infantryman's weapon during the conflict, and it had been refined to a high degree of lethality. Britain's .303 in. (7.69 mm) Short Magazine Lee-Enfield (SMLE), Germany's 0.319 in. (7.92 mm) Mauser 1898, and the French .315 in. (8 mm) Lebel all had a lethal range of around 1 mile (1.6 km) and fed from three- or five-round box magazines to produce respectable volumes of fire.

The killing range of these rifles meant that during the long years of trench deadlock along the Western Front, the infantryman could still deliver accurate fire between opposing trench systems, even when they were many hundreds of yards apart. Their range indirectly caused a problem in training. A high-power rifle delivers substantial recoil and is usually heavy; the Mauser 1898 weighed 9 lb. (4.8 kg). Training times were frequently too short to teach effective control.

Of all the combatants, the British were most successful at bringing its excellent SMLE to full potential, mainly to compensate for the lack of machine guns available in the early years of the war. Before the war, in 1909, the chief instructor of the School of Musketry in Hythe reinvigorated army rifle shooting with a drill that emphasized rapid, accurate shooting.

Aided by the swift bolt action of the SMLE, a trained British infantryman could produce 15–20 aimed rounds per minute; and during the British retreat through France in 1914, the Germans suffered dreadfully from the British fire. In one incident, on August 24, one battalion of the Duke of Wellington's Regiment defeated six German battalions around Mons.

Yet the rifle's use in World War I on both sides showed key deficiencies. It was unwieldy in close-quarter trench combat, where handguns and submachine guns were preferable. It was also overpowerful in these situations, likely to go through a close-range enemy and kill one of your own. Furthermore, new weapons were now commanding the long-range combat distances. Tripod-mounted heavy machine guns such as the Maxim and Vickers could put out a battalion's worth of rifle fire, while artillery meant that engagement distance was now well beyond even the rifle's range. Around 80 percent of all World War I casualties were caused by artillery and machine guns.

JAPAN

ARISAKA MEIJI 44 CAVALRY CARBINE (MODEL 1911)

Length (gun): 38.5 in. (978 mm)
Barrel: 18.5 in. (470 mm)
Weight (gun): 8.9 lb. (4.0 kg)
Caliber: 6.5 mm
Rifling: 6 grooves, r/hand
Operation: bolt-action
Feed: 5-round integral magazine
Muz vel: 2,250 ft./sec. (685 m/sec.)

The Meiji 44th Year Cavalry Carbine (Model 1911) was accepted for service in 1911 and actually reached the Imperial Japanese Army in 1912, replacing the Meiji 38th year Carbine (Model 1905) (qv), and it remained in production until 1942. It was essentially similar to the Meiji 38, with the same bolt action. Most unusually for a weapon intended for horsed cavalry, though, it was fitted with a permanently attached bayonet, which, when not in use, folded downward and to the rear, where it was secured below the barrel. Even more surprising is that in successive modifications, even longer bayonets were fitted. The picture shows the bayonet in the folded position.

UNITED KINGDOM

HOLLAND AND HOLLAND 0.375 IN. MAGAZINE RIFLE 1912

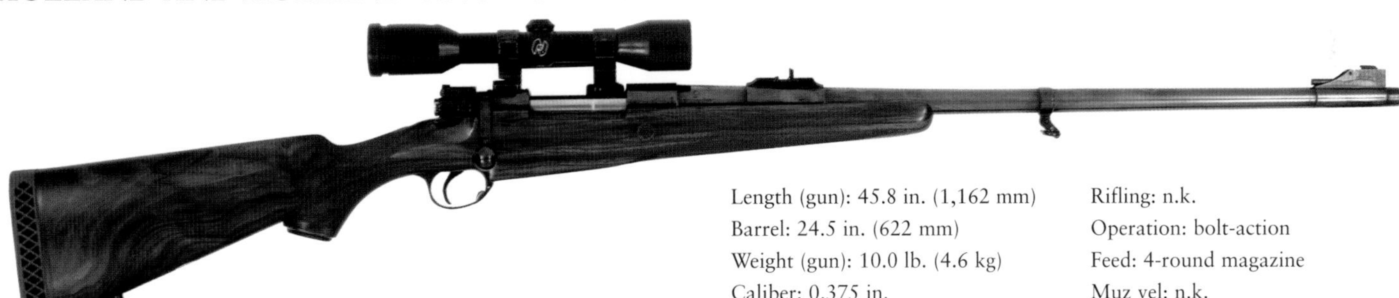

Length (gun): 45.8 in. (1,162 mm)
Barrel: 24.5 in. (622 mm)
Weight (gun): 10.0 lb. (4.6 kg)
Caliber: 0.375 in.
Rifling: n.k.
Operation: bolt-action
Feed: 4-round magazine
Muz vel: n.k.

Holland and Holland was founded in 1835 by Harris J. Holland and took its present name in 1877. The rifle illustrated here was intended primarily for use in big-game hunting, an activity that does not meet with approval today except under carefully monitored conditions. Holland and Holland also designed and produced its own cartridges, and this rifle was designed around the company's 0.375 in. round, which was introduced in 1912 and is generally considered to have been the finest big-game round of its time. This weapon had a Mauser 98 turn-bolt action, with two forward lugs locking into the receiver ring. The normal sights were two leaf rear sights, which were marked "50/200 yards" and "300 yards," respectively (46/183 m and 274 m), and a gold post and folding "big bead" fore sight. The weapon illustrated, however, is fitted with a Zeiss Diatal-C 4 x 32 telescopic sight.

UNITED KINGDOM

PATTERN 1913 RIFLE 1912

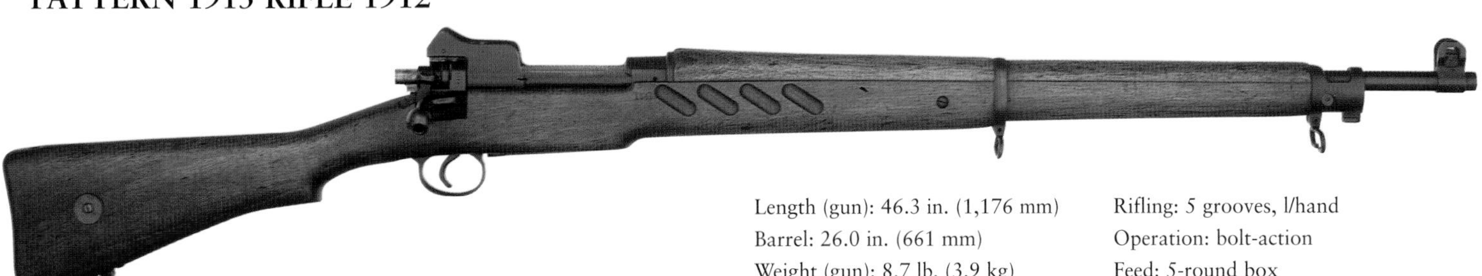

Length (gun): 46.3 in. (1,176 mm)
Barrel: 26.0 in. (661 mm)
Weight (gun): 8.7 lb. (3.9 kg)
Caliber: 0.276 in.
Rifling: 5 grooves, l/hand
Operation: bolt-action
Feed: 5-round box
Muz vel: 2,785 ft./sec. (843 m/sec.)

The Pattern 1913 differed from earlier Enfields in that it had a Mauser-type bolt and fired a new rimless Enfield 0.276 in. cartridge from an integral five-round magazine. It had an aperture back sight protected by a somewhat bulky extension on the body above the boltway. Although it was very accurate, the Pattern 1913 was clumsy to manipulate and subject to excessive metallic fouling in the bore; it had a tremendous flash and loud report; and the breech heated so fast that after about fifteen rounds there was a risk of the round firing as it went into the chamber. The project was shelved by the outbreak of World War I. The rifle was then converted to the standard British 0.303 in. service round and manufactured in the United States by Winchester, Eddystone, and Remington. This rifle was designated the Pattern 1914; because of its accuracy it was used as a sniping rifle.

UNITED KINGDOM

SHORT MAGAZINE LEE-ENFIELD MARKS III AND III* RIFLES 1916

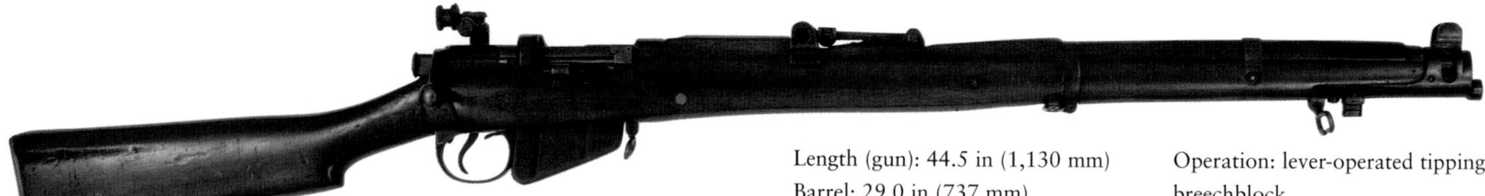

Length (gun): 44.5 in (1,130 mm)
Barrel: 29.0 in (737 mm)
Weight (gun): 9.6 lb (4.3 kg)
Caliber: 0.22 in. LR
Rifling: n.k.
Operation: lever-operated tipping-breechblock
Feed: single-round, manual
Muz vel: n.k.

In 1903, 1,000 Short Magazine Lee-Enfield Mark I's were made for trials. The model was also tested operationally in the Somaliland, and after modification it emerged as the Short Magazine Lee-Enfield (SMLE) Mark III, in 1907. It was an excellent weapon, and although slightly less accurate than its predecessor, it had certain compensating advantages, notably its fast rate of manipulation. The Mark III was a complex weapon to make, and in 1916 various simplifications were introduced, notably the abolition of the magazine cut-off and the disappearance of the special long-range collective fire sight, clearly unnecessary in the machine-gun age. These changed its designation to the Mark III*, perhaps the most famous rifle in British history. It remained an excellent weapon with an 18 in. (457 mm) sword bayonet for close-quarter work and the ability to project grenades, either rodded or from a screw-on cup.

GERMANY

MAUSER TANK-GEWEHR MODEL 1918 ANTITANK RIFLE

Length (gun): 66.0 in. (1,676 mm)
Barrel: 38.7 in. (983 mm)
Weight (gun): 39.0 lb. (17.7 kg)
Caliber: 0.51 in. (13 mm)
Rifling: 4 grooves, r/hand
Operation: bolt-action
Feed: single-shot
Muz vel: 3,000 ft./sec. (913 m/sec.)

The Germans soon found that high-velocity rifle bullets would often penetrate a tank. The Model 1918 antitank rifle was basically a large-scale version of the standard service rifle, designed to fire a special 0.51 in.-caliber (13 mm) round, which itself had to be invented since nothing of that size existed in the German armory. Although of normal bolt action, it was a single-shot weapon, half-stocked and with a simple bipod and an unusually long barrel, and as it was impossible to grasp it with the right hand in the normal way a pistol grip was added. As was to be expected, this rifle had a fearsome recoil and was not universally popular with the Germans. It came far too late to have any seriously adverse effect on the bigger and better tanks then in production.

BELGIUM

BROWNING 125 SHOTGUN 1922

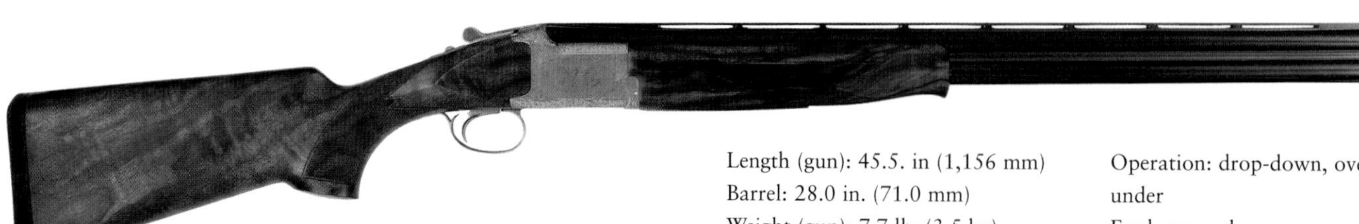

Length (gun): 45.5. in (1,156 mm)
Barrel: 28.0 in. (71.0 mm)
Weight (gun): 7.7 lb. (3.5 kg)
Caliber: 12-gauge
Rifling: none
Operation: drop-down, over-and-under
Feed: manual
Muz vel: n.k.

John Browning died in 1926, but his last design, which appeared in the early 1920s, was his first over-and-under shotgun, which, as so often happened with his designs, turned out to be a most influential design that had a major effect on the shooting world. Prior to Browning's design, a few famous London gun-makers had produced over-and-unders, but they had been very expensive, and it was FN and Browning that made it possible for such a weapon to be manufactured at an affordable price. By the 1930s these over-and-unders were selling in substantial numbers in both Europe and the United States, and they were still in production in the 1980s, being made in Liège, Belgium, by Fabrique National (FN), and by B.C. Miroku in Japan. These guns were made both with standard barrels and with internally threaded variable chokes, a device that Browning called the "Invector" system.

UNITED KINGDOM

BSA 0.260 IN. MODEL 1922 SPORTING RIFLE

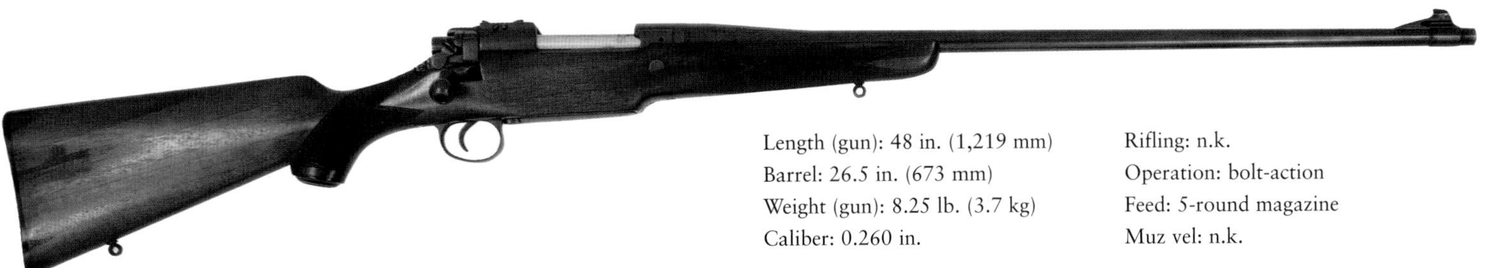

Length (gun): 48 in. (1,219 mm)
Barrel: 26.5 in. (673 mm)
Weight (gun): 8.25 lb. (3.7 kg)
Caliber: 0.260 in.
Rifling: n.k.
Operation: bolt-action
Feed: 5-round magazine
Muz vel: n.k.

The British developed a 0.280 in. rifle prior to World War I. This became the 0.303 in. Pattern 1914 and was eventually adapted by US manufacturers to take the 0.30-06 round and adopted by the US Army as the Enfield M1917. By late 1918, when Remington ran production down to peacetime levels, it had a vast stock of parts left over. For some reason, the British firm BSA (Birmingham, Small Arms) decided to produce a sporting rifle based on M1917 components, which, presumably, the company acquired as surplus from the United States. It also designed a new round for the rifle—the 0.260 in. Rimless Nitro Express—which was a Holland and Holland 0.375 in. round necked down to 0.256 in. (6.5 mm) and shortened, driving a 110-grain (7.1 g) bullet at 3,100 ft./second (945 m/sec.), giving a level of performance largely wasted in a rifle, as seen here, without telescopic sights.

UNITED KINGDOM

SHORT MAGAZINE LEE-ENFIELD MARK V RIFLE 1923

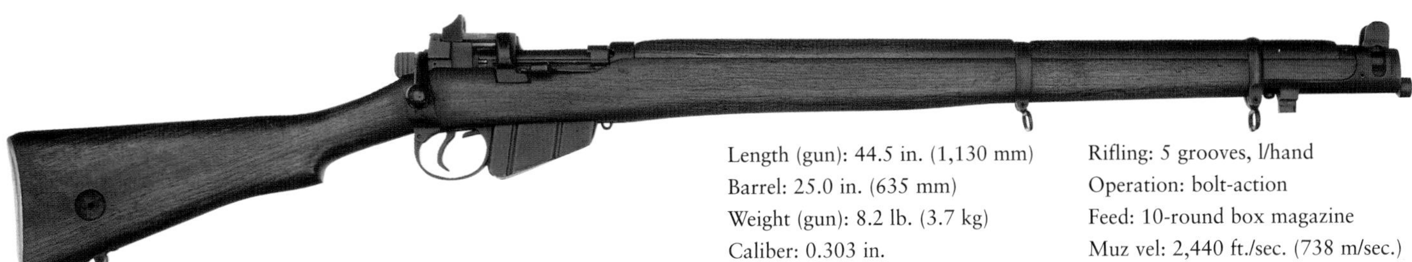

Length (gun): 44.5 in. (1,130 mm)
Barrel: 25.0 in. (635 mm)
Weight (gun): 8.2 lb. (3.7 kg)
Caliber: 0.303 in.
Rifling: 5 grooves, l/hand
Operation: bolt-action
Feed: 10-round box magazine
Muz vel: 2,440 ft./sec. (738 m/sec.)

Soon after the end of World War I, the British Army began to consider a new rifle, similar to its predecessor, but easier to make by modern mass-production methods. The resulting Short Magazine Lee-Enfield Mk V appeared as early as 1923. Apart from an extra barrel band just in front of the forward sling swivel, the main difference was that it had an aperture back sight that was moved much farther back, on the bridge above the bolt. The sight was graduated only as far as 1,400 yd. (1,280 m), and coupled with the increased distance between the fore and rear sights, this made for more accurate shooting. After trials with the Mk V, it was decided that conversion of the large existing stocks of rifles would be too expensive, and although the development of a new rifle was continued (which led eventually to the Number 4 Rifle), large numbers of SMLEs remained in service well into World War II.

UNITED STATES

FARQUHAR-HILL RIFLE 1924

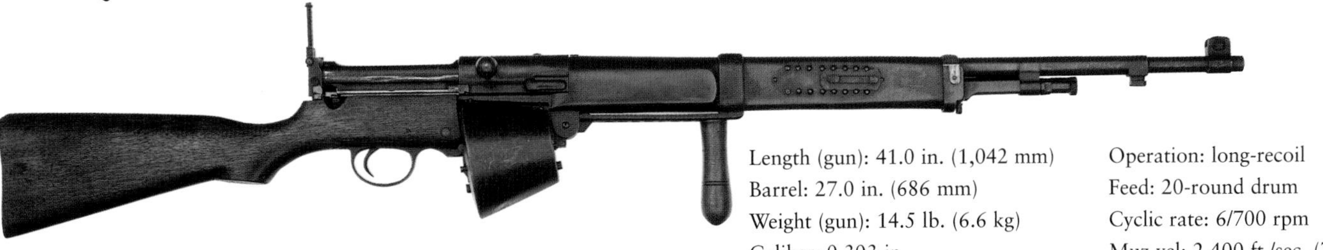

Length (gun): 41.0 in. (1,042 mm)
Barrel: 27.0 in. (686 mm)
Weight (gun): 14.5 lb. (6.6 kg)
Caliber: 0.303 in.
Rifling: 5 grooves, l/hand
Operation: long-recoil
Feed: 20-round drum
Cyclic rate: 6/700 rpm
Muz vel: 2,400 ft./sec. (732 m/sec.)

In 1908, Major Farquhar and Mr. Hill produced an automatic rifle that was tested by the Automatic Rifle Committee of the British Army. The Farquhar-Hill was an extremely complex weapon. It utilized long recoil, but faulty design kept the barrel and breech locked together long after the bullet had left the muzzle. The gun was rejected and nothing more was heard of it until 1917, when a second version appeared. The main difference was its unusual magazine, which was in the shape of a truncated cone, powered by a clockwork spring. This version was also tested and rejected, as it was prone to fouling and to a variety of complex stoppages. The inventors were persistent, and as late as 1924 they submitted the weapon above. This had a similar but much smaller magazine with a capacity of ten rounds (there were up to sixty-five in the earlier versions), but again it was unsatisfactory.

Mauser Bolt-action Rifles

The name Mauser is practically synonymous with the bolt-action rifle, and the legacy of Paul and Wilhelm Mauser lives on to this day in many military and hunting weapons. The two brothers were born into the world of firearms, joining their father working in the Royal Württemburg Rifle Factory on Oberndorf am Neckar in the 1850s when each turned 12 years old. Having undertaken apprenticeships, the two young men set about designing weapons, and their first accepted rifle began the process of revolutionizing rifle design. The M/71 rifle was a breech-loading rotating-bolt rifle that made improvements over the then-popular Dreyse needle gun and the Chassepot. On opening the bolt, the firing pin was drawn backward, being cocked when the bolt was pushed forward.

The weapon was not perfect, but the Prussian government recognized its qualities and ordered substantial numbers. Unfortunately for the Mauser brothers, the state appropriated production of the weapon (in the late 1800s governments quite often claimed the rights of production over weaponry), although production orders with the brothers increased in 1873.

Soon the M/71, and a carbine version that emerged in 1875, were selling well at home and worldwide. Over the next twenty years, Mauser produced more refined bolt-action rifles, introducing box magazines from 1887 (earlier experiments with tube magazines were not wholly effective) and, in 1888, a charger-loaded Mauser, the .302 in. (7.65 mm) M/88.

The M/88 had an excellent feed system, as it allowed the user to top up the loaded rifle with single rounds, and it was copied in many other weapons. It also used a three-lug bolt-locking action, a particularly safe form of locking, and still the most important method of locking bolt-action rifles. Yet the perfection of the Mauser bolt-action rifle came with the Mauser M/98 (Gewehr 98), which had an improved spring extractor and a staggered column magazine that held all rounds within the body of the weapon. The M/98 also featured a short-travel firing pin, giving it a very fast lock time appreciated by combat soldiers. The Kar98k variant became the standard infantry firearm for the German army over the next forty years.

The M/98 represents the height of Mauser's achievement. Modern bolt-action rifles are indebted to the Mauser action, and it is widely recognized as one of the truly enduring features of weapons design.

Above: *The Mauser bolt-action, shown here with a cartridge about to be chambered. The Mauser action on the M/71 rifle achieved locking through a rear lug turned down in front of the receiver bridge. Locking and weapon safety were considerably improved in the M/88 version with the introduction of the three-lug bolt.*

UNITED KINGDOM

NUMBER 4 RIFLE 1928

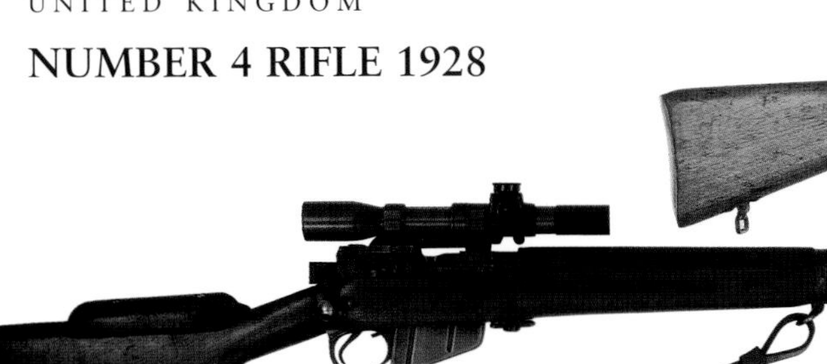

Length (gun): 44.5 in. (1,130 mm)
Barrel: 25.2 in. (640 mm)
Weight (gun): 9.1 lb. (4.1 kg)
Caliber: 0.303 in.
Rifling: 5 grooves, l/hand
Operation: bolt-action
Feed: 10-round
Muz vel: 2,440 ft./sec. (743 m/sec.)

By 1928, the British government had developed a new service rifle, similar in general appearance and capacity to the Lee-Enfield but a good deal easier to mass-produce. This new rifle, the Number 4, was a most serviceable arm, its main difference from its predecessor being its aperture sight. It was produced from 1941 onward mainly in Canada and the United States, although some were made in England. It underwent some modifications, mainly in the substitution of a simple two-range flip back sight for the earlier and more complex one, and some were made with two-groove rifling. Otherwise the remained substantially unchanged, the main feature perhaps the variety of bayonets made to fit it. Selected specimens were fitted with No. 32 telescopic sights and detachable cheek rests and were successfully used as sniper rifles. It remained in British service until 1957.

UNITED STATES

SPRINGFIELD M1903A3 RIFLE 1929

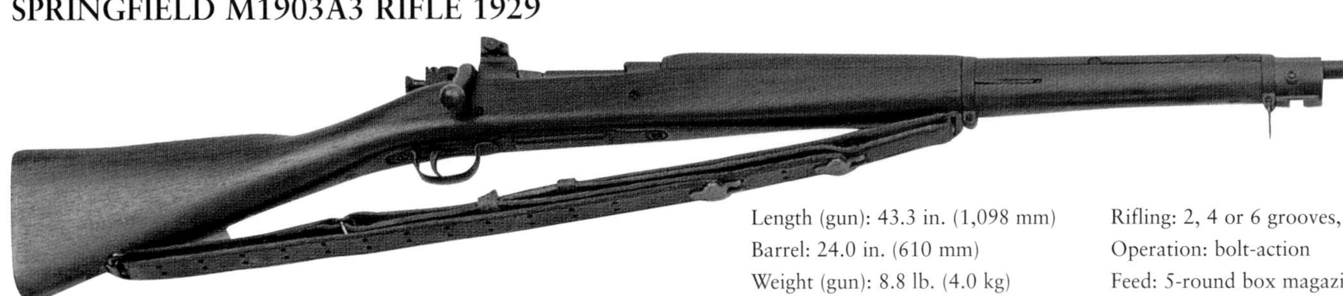

Length (gun): 43.3 in. (1,098 mm)
Barrel: 24.0 in. (610 mm)
Weight (gun): 8.8 lb. (4.0 kg)
Caliber: 0.30 in. (7.6 mm)
Rifling: 2, 4 or 6 grooves, r/hand
Operation: bolt-action
Feed: 5-round box magazine
Muz vel: 2,805 ft./sec. (855 m/sec.)

The Springfield M1903 remained in service throughout World War I and was given a minor facelift in 1929 when it was fitted with a different type of butt stock and became the M1903A1. With the outbreak of World War II, however, there was a requirement for infantry rifles in vast numbers and the M1903 was re-engineered for mass production. Among the changes were the substitution of sheet metal stampings wherever feasible, but the most obvious external changes were the removal of the leaf back sight on top of the barrel and its replacement by an aperture sight atop the receiver bridge, as well as the deletion of the grasping groove for the fingers on the forestock. The new sight, which was adjustable for windage, was graduated up to 800 yd. (732 m). About 950,000 of these weapons were produced between 1942 and 1944, when production switched to the Garand rifle.

RUSSIA

MOSIN-NAGANT 7.62 MM MODEL 1891/30 RIFLE 1930

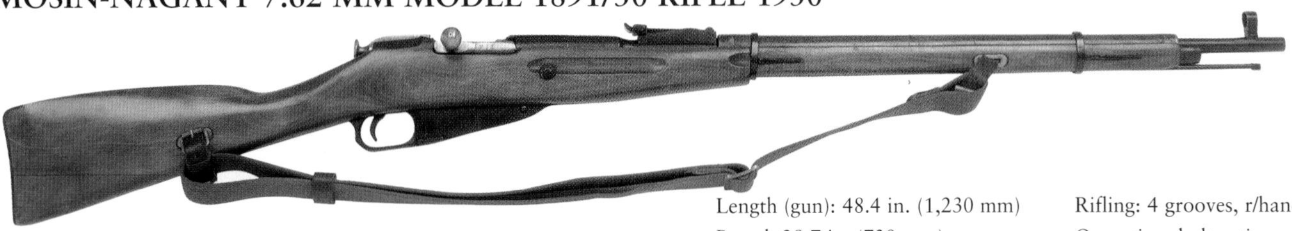

Length (gun): 48.4 in. (1,230 mm)
Barrel: 28.7 in. (730 mm)
Weight (gun): 8.6 lb. (4.0 kg)
Caliber: 7.62 mm
Rifling: 4 grooves, r/hand
Operation: bolt action
Feed: 5-round internal box
Muz vel: 2,575 ft./sec. (785 m/sec.)

The Mosin-Nagant Model 1891 first entered service with the Tsarist Army in 1891, and the final model, the Carbine M1944, was phased out of production in the Soviet Union in the late 1940s. The original M1891 was a straightforward bolt-action rifle with an internal five-round magazine. The basic infantry version had a 31.6 in. (802 mm) barrel, and the Dragoon and Cossack versions had a shorter (28.8 in./730 mm) barrel. The latter two differed only in that the Dragoon came with a bayonet, and the Cossack did not. Next came the Carbine M1910, which had a much shorter barrel—20.0 in. (510 mm)—but was otherwise the Dragoon. Following the Revolution in 1917, the rifle remained unchanged until the M1891/1930, in which the barrel was shortened to 28.8 in. (730 mm), the receiver changed from hexagonal to circular profile, and new sights were fitted.

GERMANY

HALGER NO. 7 RIFLE 1933

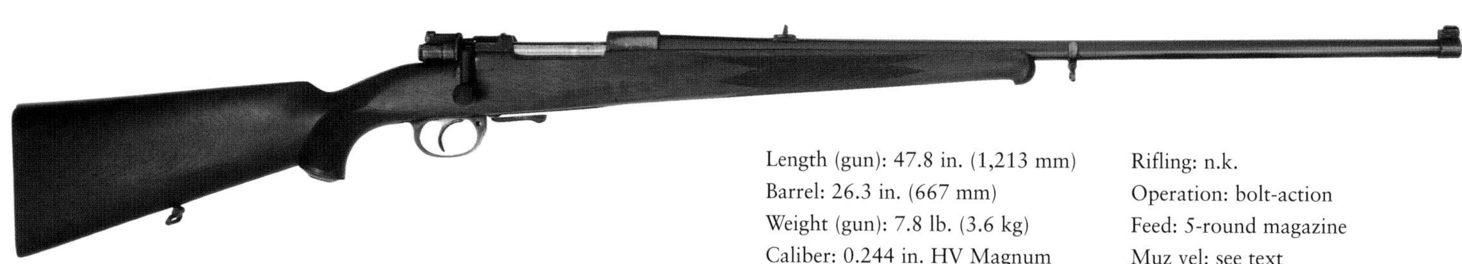

Length (gun): 47.8 in. (1,213 mm)
Barrel: 26.3 in. (667 mm)
Weight (gun): 7.8 lb. (3.6 kg)
Caliber: 0.244 in. HV Magnum

Rifling: n.k.
Operation: bolt-action
Feed: 5-round magazine
Muz vel: see text

Halger was run by the famous designer Harold Gerlich, who was born of German parents in the United States. He was working in London, England, when World War I broke out, so he went to Germany to enlist in the Imperial Army but was turned down as a "foreigner." He returned to England and in the early 1930s was working at Woolwich Arsenal. He had a fascination with ever-higher muzzle velocities and designed the 0.224 in. HV Magnum round, with which he claimed to achieve 3,700 feet/second (1,128 m/sec.), and the 0.280 Magnum, for which he claimed 3,900 feet/second (1,189 m/sec.). As Halger made only about 150 rifles, however, and not a single loaded cartridge survives, these claims are impossible to substantiate. The rifle shown is somewhat crude, having a rough trigger, nonadjustable iron sights, and no provision for mounting a scope.

FRANCE

FUSIL MAS 36 RIFLE 1935

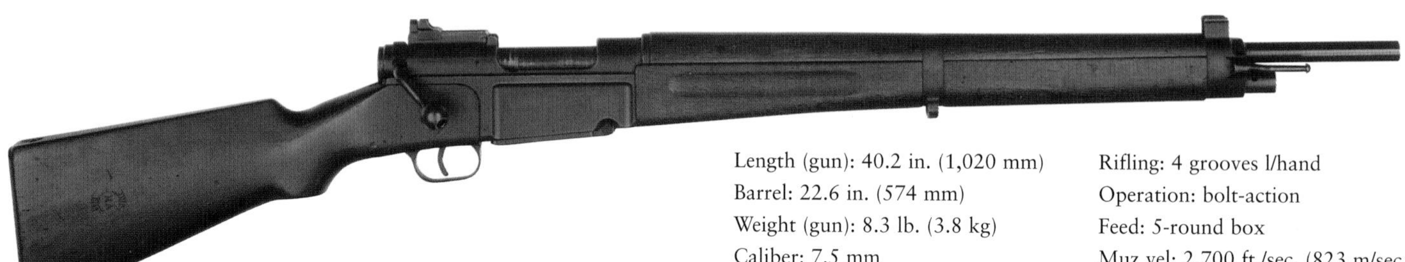

Length (gun): 40.2 in. (1,020 mm)
Barrel: 22.6 in. (574 mm)
Weight (gun): 8.3 lb. (3.8 kg)
Caliber: 7.5 mm

Rifling: 4 grooves l/hand
Operation: bolt-action
Feed: 5-round box
Muz vel: 2,700 ft./sec. (823 m/sec.)

The MAS 36 was produced to use the new 7.5 mm round developed in France in 1924. It was a bolt-action rifle of modified Mauser type, but with the bolt designed to lock into the top of the body behind the magazine. This made it necessary to angle the bolt lever forward so as to be in reach of the firer's hand, the general effect being rather ugly. The magazine was of standard integral box type with a capacity of five rounds, and there was no manual safety catch. The rifle had a cruciform bayonet carried in a tube beneath the barrel. It was fixed by withdrawing it and plugging its cylindrical handle into the mouth of the tube, where it was held in place by a spring. Small numbers of a modified MAS 36 were later made for airborne troops; they had shorter barrels and folding butts and were designated the MAS 36 CR39.

GERMANY

GEBRÜDER MERKEL DOUBLE RIFLE 1935

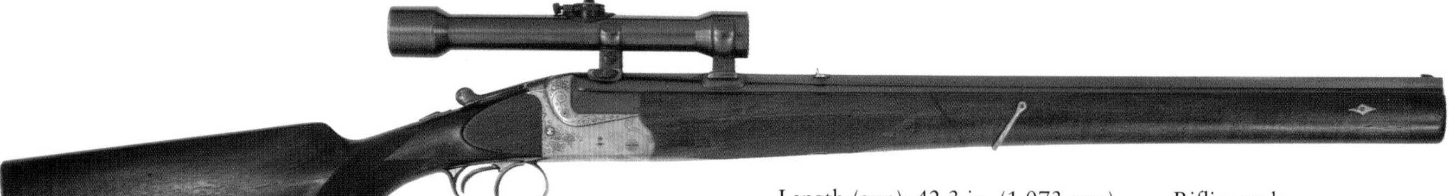

Length (gun): 42.3 in. (1,073 mm)
Barrel: 25.5 in. (648 mm)
Weight (gun): 9.3 lb. (4.2 kg)
Caliber: 7 x 57R

Rifling: n.k.
Operation: double, over-and-under
Feed: manual
Muz vel: n.k.

The Merkel is chambered for the 7 x 57R Normaliziert, a round specially loaded by Dynamit Nobel and guaranteed for ballistic uniformity. With loads of comparable uniformity, this rifle will pattern shots from alternate barrels into 1.5 inches (38 mm) at 109 yd. (100 m), and will hold excellent groups even farther. The rifle is fitted with a telescopic sight made by Carl Zeiss, of Jena, Germany, and a 4x scope featuring a three-post reticle, and it is fitted to the rifle by means of the integral claw mounts. The full-length fore end is an unusual feature. It should be noted that over-and-under weapons have to hinge over a much greater arc for the lower barrel to clear the standing breech. Also, the top chamber is high enough over the hinge to put a great strain on the lower lock-up, which, in effect, requires an extended rib to lock into the end of the standing breech.

THE SNIPER

Above: *A New Zealand sniper takes aim in the rubble of Monte Cassino, March 1944. His rifle, the .303 in. Lee-Enfield Number 4, was not designed as a sniper weapon but fitted with a No. 32 telescopic sight and an adjustable cheek rest (both seen here). It was an accurate sniper tool out to 3,280 ft. (1,000 m).*

Although tiny numbers of skilled individuals with specialized equipment have featured in warfare almost since the invention of the firearm, sniping as a specific military tactic emerged in North America during the 1700s. Whereas European armies concentrated on volley fire from smoothbore weapons, the combination of the hunting capabilities of the frontiersmen with the invention of the rifled Kentucky weapon produced skirmishing militias during the American War of Independence (1775–83). These militias employed irregular tactics, shooting British officers from hidden positions within woodland at ranges of up to 1,000 ft. (320 m). On October 7, 1777, Timothy Murphy of Morgan's Kentucky Riflemen shot and killed British General Simon Fraser. Murphy was reported to have taken the shot at roughly 1,500 ft. (457 m). At the time, General Fraser was leading a reconnaissance in force against the rebels at Bemis Heights in New York. The British withdrew, having suffered heavy losses, to their fortified positions; ten days later, 6,000 British troops would surrender at Saratoga, and the colonists' victory is seen as a crucial turning point in the War of Independence. A single shot may start a war, but it cannot win one; this incident is about as close as possible to such an outcome.

The British formed similar units of sharpshooters in response, including the 95th Rifles—known as the "Greenjackets"—and used them to telling effect in the Peninsular War against Napoleon. Snipers also started to take their place among navies. When opposing warships closed to boarding distance, snipers hiding in the rigging would attempt to shoot down enemy officers. The most famous victim of a maritime sniper was Admiral Horatio Nelson, killed on the quarterdeck of HMS Victory by a sniper on the French ship, the Redoubtable.

Yet throughout even the nineteenth century, the sniper did not have an official role in the army, and sharpshooters would effect group actions, not work as isolated individuals tracking individual targets. Nevertheless, sharpshooters had a powerful impact in battle.

In the American Civil War, the Confederate side produced hundreds of first-rate snipers (often to compensate for inadequacies in conventional forces) and claimed some very high-ranking victims. During the Boer War, Dutch units of "Kommandos" decimated ranks of British troops from hidden positions using .315 in. (8 mm) Mauser rifles and smokeless powders to hide the shot signature. However, it was World War I that saw the development of the true modern sniper. To maintain harassment of the enemy during trench deadlock, the German Army formed groups of dedicated marksmen armed with telescoped hunting rifles (thousands were requisitioned from civilian sources at the start of the war) or accurized .319 in. (7.92 mm) Mauser Gewehr 1898 rifles firing nonstandard SmK long-range ammunition.

British war reports soon noted thousands of headshot deaths among British troops along the Western Front. Sniper and counter-sniper units were soon part of the British response, often drawing personnel from former deer-stalkers who had previously worked on Highland estates in Scotland.

Sniping now became a true military art, the sniper working alone with specialized weapons, training in dedicated sniper schools, moving to whatever position the shot required, and marked out by separate uniform insignia. Since World War II, sniping has simply seen a refinement of tactics and sniping technologies, not a fundamental change of role.

UNITED STATES

GARAND RIFLE 0.30 IN. CAL M1 1936

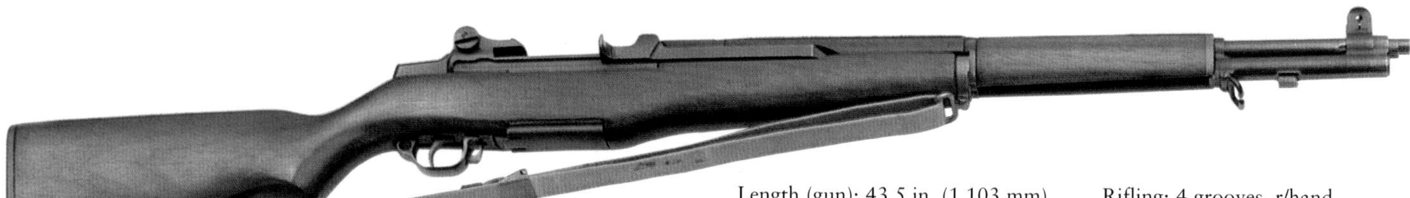

Length (gun): 43.5 in. (1,103 mm)
Barrel: 24.0 in. (610 mm)
Weight (gun): 9.5 lb. (4.4 kg)
Caliber: 0.30 in.

Rifling: 4 grooves, r/hand
Operation: gas
Feed: 8-round internal box
Muz vel: 2,800 ft./sec. (853 m/sec.)

The Garand was the first self-loader to be adopted (in 1936) by any army as a standard weapon. It was a good weapon, robust, simple and reliable; it operated by gas and piston. The eight-round magazine had to be loaded by a special charger holding the cartridges in two staggered rows of four each. When the last round had been fired, the empty clip was automatically ejected and the bolt remained open. The Garand was the standard rifle of the US Army in World War II, and was the only self-loader generally used. They were made mainly by the Springfield Armory and the Winchester Repeating Arms Company, with smaller numbers by other American arms companies; after the war a quantity were made by Beretta. When manufacture finally ceased in the middle of the 1950s, an astonishing total of some 5.5 million had been produced.

JAPAN

TYPE 97 20 MM ANTI-TANK RIFLE 1937

Length (gun): 80.1 in. (2,035 mm)
Barrel: 47.0 in. (1,200 mm)
Weight (gun): 152 lb. (69.0 kg)
Caliber: 20 mm

Rifling: n.k.
Operation: gas
Feed: 7-round box magazine
Muz vel: 2,510 ft./sec. (990 m/sec.)

The Type 97 entered service in 1937 and was a gas-operated, fully automatic weapon, firing a specially developed 20 x 124 mm round that was available in armor-piercing (solid shot) and high-explosive natures. The weapon fired from a closed bolt, which was unlocked by a gas piston and then driven to the rear by blowback forces, with the entire barrel and receiver moving some 6 inches (150 mm) along a track in the stock. It was very heavy—no less than four times the weight of the Boys Rifle (which the British Army considered excessively heavy) and required a four-man crew to carry it, using two crossbar-type carrying handles. In action, the gun rested on a forward bipod and rear monopod and was fired by one man. Despite the muzzle brake, the recoil must have been very heavy and the full-auto mode would have been ferocious.

UNITED KINGDOM

BOYS ANTITANK RIFLE 1937

Length (gun): 63.5 in. (1,613 mm)
Barrel: 36.0 in. (914 mm)
Weight (gun): 36.0 lb. (16.3 kg)
Caliber: 0.55 in. (13.97 mm)

Rifling: 7 grooves, r/hand
Operation: bolt-action
Feed: 5-round box
Muz vel: 3,250 ft./sec. (990 m/sec.)

The Boys Rifle was essentially a large-scale, large-caliber version of a service rifle with a spring absorber, a muzzle brake, and a front support. In the original weapon, the muzzle brake was circular, and the front support was a monopod, like an inverted T. In the second version, the one illustrated, the muzzle brake was flat with holes on each side, and the monopod had been replaced by a bipod. Both models were bolt-action weapons with detachable top-mounted box magazines holding five rounds, but whereas the first model had a double sight for 300 and 500 yd. (274 and 457 m), the second had a fixed sight. The first few were in the hands of the infantry by 1937, but tank design had advanced; soon after the outbreak of war it was clear that the weapon was of limited use. It was uncomfortable to fire due to its enormous recoil, and by 1943 it had largely been replaced.

UNITED STATES

ITHACA 37 SHOTGUN 1937

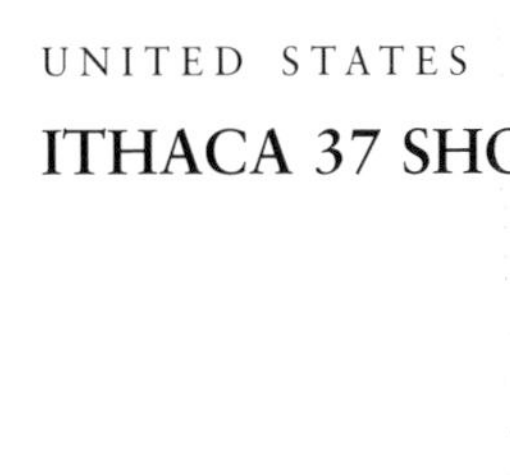

Length (gun): 44.0 in. (1,118 mm)
Barrel: 24.3 in. (616 mm)
Weight (gun): 6.8 lb. (3.1 kg)
Caliber: 12-gauge
Rifling: none
Operation: slide-action, repeater shotgun
Feed: 8-round tubular magazine
Muz vel: n.k.

The Ithaca Gun Company of Ithaca, New York, was founded in 1880 and is best known for its trap guns and slide (pump-action) shotguns. In 1937 Ithaca introduced this slide-action gun, the Model 37 Featherlight, which has become a classic. Unlike other weapons in its field, it used bottom ejection for spent cartridges, which had four benefits: it gave protection in rain and snow; in the event of a burst cartridge the debris was ejected downward; the gun could be used with equal ease by either right- or left-handed shooters; and the shorter receiver resulted in a lighter weapon. It was, in fact, more than 1.0 lb. (0.45 kg) lighter than any competitor. The Model 37 was made in 12-, 16-, and 20-gauge, and in many formats. The "Stakeout" police shotgun, for example, had a pistol grip, no stock, and a shorter barrel with a magazine holding just four rounds.

BELGIUM

SELF-LOADING EXPERIMENTAL RIFLE 1938

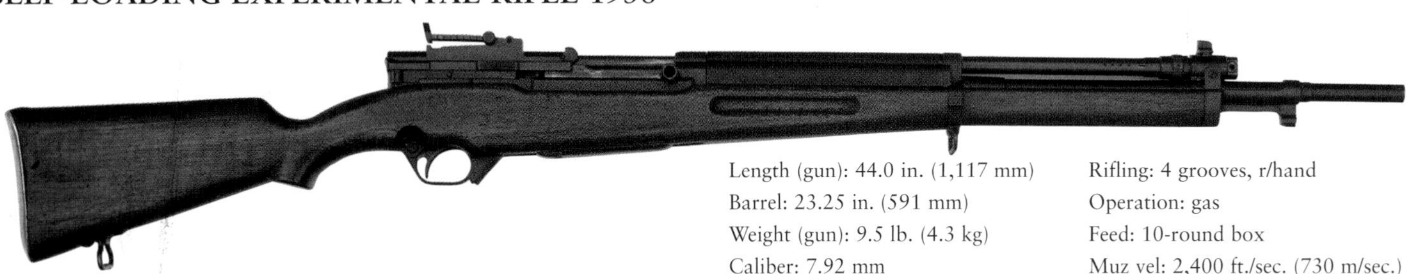

Length (gun): 44.0 in. (1,117 mm)
Barrel: 23.25 in. (591 mm)
Weight (gun): 9.5 lb. (4.3 kg)
Caliber: 7.92 mm
Rifling: 4 grooves, r/hand
Operation: gas
Feed: 10-round box
Muz vel: 2,400 ft./sec. (730 m/sec.)

Designed by a M. Saive in the 1930s, the Self-Loading Experimental Model (SLEM) was gas-operated and had a bolt very similar to that of the Russian Tokarev rifle. They were well made and full-stocked in walnut, and all made to fire the 7.92 mm Mauser round. Although they were successfully tested, nothing came of the project. When Saive returned to Belgium after the war, however, he perfected an improved model known as the Model 49. This was a time when many countries were looking for cheap and reliable self-loaders, and the Model 49 was an immediate success. It was sold to a considerable number of countries including Columbia, Venezuela, Egypt and Luxemburg. The Model 49 was manufactured in a variety of calibers. The Belgian Army adopted it and it saw service in Korea. It was subsequently developed into the FAL.

ITALY

MANNLICHER-CARCANO CARBINE MODEL M1938

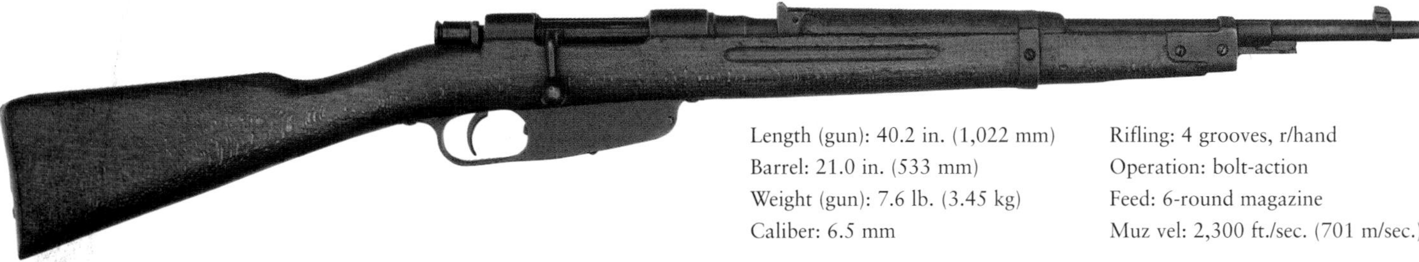

Length (gun): 40.2 in. (1,022 mm)
Barrel: 21.0 in. (533 mm)
Weight (gun): 7.6 lb. (3.45 kg)
Caliber: 6.5 mm
Rifling: 4 grooves, r/hand
Operation: bolt-action
Feed: 6-round magazine
Muz vel: 2,300 ft./sec. (701 m/sec.)

There are two versions of the Model 1938 carbine, which, except for caliber (6.5 mm and 7.35 mm), are virtually indistinguishable. The one illustrated is an example of the later reversion to the small caliber. One of its unusual features was the abandonment of the tangent back sight in favor of a fixed one, set at 328 yd. (300 m). This Model 1938 carbine is of considerable interest, as it is the type used to assassinate President Kennedy in November 1963. The particular weapon was an item of Italian war surplus fitted with a cheap Japanese telescope and purchased by mail order for a few dollars. It seems to have been an odd choice for that dreadful deed, since the Carcano has no great reputation for accuracy, and although its bolt works smoothly enough, the rate of fire would have been slowed down by the telescope. It is notoriously difficult to shoot rapidly using such a sight.

Antitank Rifles

Antitank rifles have been one of the least successful lines of firearms development since 1914. They first appeared during World War I, when the Germans attempted to counter British tanks with the fearsome 13 mm Tank-Gewehr Modell 1918, developed by Mauser and Polte-Werke. Nicknamed "Elefantenbüsche" (Elephant Gun), it was introduced into service in May 1918, two issued to each infantry regiment. The Model 1918 was little more than an enlarged Mauser rifle firing a .319 in. (13 mm) round with a steel core, lead/antimony liner, and a copper jacket. It could penetrate 1.18 in. (30 mm) of steel at 164 ft. (50 m) and had some success in the early days of armored warfare, although it came too late to influence the battlefields of World War I.

By the next World War, most of the world's armies had equipped themselves with antitank rifles. The British developed the Boys Mark I, a 0.55-in.-caliber (13.97 mm) weapon with 0.78 in. (20 mm) of penetration at 1,640 ft. (500 m). The Russians opted for the 0.57 in. (14.5 mm) PTRD (bolt-action) and PTRS (semi-automatic). Germany scaled back the caliber of its antitank weapons in the 0.319 in. (7.92 mm) Panzerbüsche 38 and 39, generating a muzzle velocity of around 3,975 feet/second (1,211 m/sec.) and about 1 in. (25 mm) of penetration at 984 ft. (300 m). Conversely, the Japanese produced the 0.78 in. (20 mm) Type 97 weapon, a semi-/full-automatic weapon operating off a gas/blowback hybrid system. Despite its fearsome credentials, the Type 97 was an impotent weapon, producing only 0.47 in. (12 mm) of penetration at 656 ft. (200 m).

Above: *The top photograph is of a Mauser K98k 7.92 mm rifle with grenade launcher and sight. The ubiquitous German rifle of World War II, the K98 in K98k form could fire both explosive and armor-piercing grenades with the addition of a shot cup. The first antitank rifle of 1918 had also been a Mauser, a conventional bolt-action rifle scaled up to take a new 13 x 92SR cartridge. The picture below is of the 0.319 in. (7.92 mm) Panzerbüsche 39 antitank rifle.*

World War II saw the peak and the demise of the antitank rifle. Although many such weapons had respectable penetration in relation to existing armor types at the beginning of the war, by 1942–43 the depth of tank armor had increased tremendously to counter antitank artillery. Moreover, antitank rifles were extremely cumbersome battlefield weapons—the lightest Russian models weighed around 38 lb. (17 kg) and the Japanese Type 97 weighed in at 115 lb. (52 kg). Antitank rifles quickly lost their rationale, although the principle of a vehicle-disabling rifle has not died out altogether. The modern US 0.50 in. (12.7 mm) caliber Barrett M82A1 sniper weapon was originally designed to destroy the engines of soft-skinned vehicles at long ranges, and it found application in this role in the 1990–91 and 2003 wars in Iraq.

RUSSIA

MOSIN-NAGANT CARBINE MODEL 1938

Length (gun): 40.2 in. (1,020 mm)
Barrel: 20.1 in. (510 mm)
Weight (gun): 7.7 lb. (3.5 kg)
Caliber: 7.62 mm
Rifling: 4 grooves, r/hand
Operation: bolt-action
Feed: 5-round integral magazine
Muz vel: 2,575 ft./sec. (785 m/sec.)

Following the Mosin-Nagant M1891/1930 (qv), the next in the series was the weapon illustrated here, the Mosin-Nagant 7.62 mm Carbine M1938, which was, in essence, the Carbine M1910 incorporating the same modifications that had been made to produce the M1891/1930. This weapon was specifically intended for use by front line troops other than infantry, such as artillery, engineers, cavalry, and communications, and certain logistics troops such as supply-vehicle drivers, all of whom needed a lighter, handy weapon, basically for self-defense. As the illustration shows, this was simply a shorter, handier version of the M1819/1930. The final version was the Carbine M1934, which was simply the Carbine M1938 with a permanently attached, folding bayonet, which, it should be noted, was anchored to a block on the right-hand side of the barrel and did not fit over the muzzle.

JAPAN

TYPE 99 RIFLE 1939

Length (gun): 44.0 in. (1,117 mm)
Barrel: 25.8 in. (655 mm)
Weight (gun): 8.6 lb. (3.9 kg)
Caliber: 7.7 mm
Rifling: 4 grooves, r/hand
Operation: bolt-action
Feed: 5-round box
Muz vel: 2,350 ft./sec. (715 m/sec.)

Japanese experience in China in the 1930s showed the need for a more powerful cartridge than the 0.256 in. (6.5 mm) they then used, and after a good deal of experiment they settled in 1939 for a rifle built to fire a rimless version of their 0.303 in. (7.7 mm) round. The original intention of the Japanese had been to use a carbine, but when firing powerful rounds, carbines inevitably have increased recoil. As a compromise, the new rifle, designated the Type 99, was made in two lengths: a "short" rifle in line with modern European custom, and a "normal" version some 6 in. (152 mm) longer; the one illustrated is the shorter type. This new rifle had a rather odd attachment in the shape of a folding wire monopod (seen in top photograph), designed to support the rifle when fired from the prone position, but it was of little practical value due to its lack of rigidity. The back sight was also fitted with two graduated horizontal extensions to the right and the left, intended to be used to give a degree of lead when firing at crossing aircraft; nothing is known regarding their effectiveness. The Type 99 was not widely used in World War II.

RUSSIA

TOKAREV 7.62 MM SVT-40 RIFLE 1940

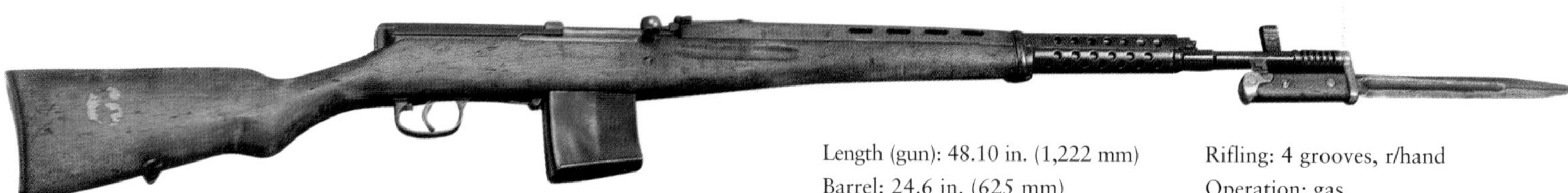

Length (gun): 48.10 in. (1,222 mm)
Barrel: 24.6 in. (625 mm)
Weight (gun): 8.6 lb. (3.9 kg)
Caliber: 7.62 x 54R

Rifling: 4 grooves, r/hand
Operation: gas
Feed: 10-round box magazine
Muz vel: 2,725 ft./sec. (830 m/sec.)

Designed by Fedor Tokarev, the self-loading SVT-40 was the outcome of a development process that started in the early 1920s. Tokarev submitted several prototypes for state trials in the 1920s and 1930s. He achieved some success with his Model 1938. When early production weapons were used in the 1940 "Winter War" against Finland, yet more shortcomings were identified. When solutions had been found, the SVT Model 1940 was ordered into full production, and some two million were produced. The Samozaryadnaya i avtomatich-eskaya Vintovky sistemy Tokareva (semiautomatic and automatic rifle, Tokarev pattern) utilized a gas-operation, with locking achieved by the tail of the breechblock dropping into a recess in the receiver. The SVT-40 was not a success; the weapon was complicated, making manufacture and field-stripping difficult. Production ended in 1944.

GERMANY

GEWEHR 41 (W) RIFLE 1941

Length (gun): 44.5 in. (1,130 mm)
Barrel: 21.5 in. (546 mm)
Weight (gun): 11.0 lb. (5.0 kg)
Caliber: 7.92 mm

Rifling: 4 grooves, r/hand
Operation: gas
Feed: 10-round box
Muz vel: 2,550 ft./sec. (776 m/sec.)

The Germans were among the pioneers of self-loading rifles. By 1941, two separate models were undergoing tests. The first was the Gewehr 41 (Mauser), which incorporated a bolt similar to that of the manually operated rifle; it was never a success and was soon abandoned. The second was the Gewehr 41 (Walther), an example of which is shown here; this was a good deal more successful. It incorporated a muzzle cap that deflected part of the gases back on to an annular piston that worked a rod placed above the barrel; its return spring however was below it. This piston rod worked the bolt and the concept was reasonably satisfactory, although the arm had certain defects, notably its weight and balance, together with a serious tendency to foul very badly around the muzzle cap. It was manufactured in some quantity and issued chiefly to units on the Russian Front.

UNITED STATES

US CARBINE 0.30 IN. CALIBER M1 1941

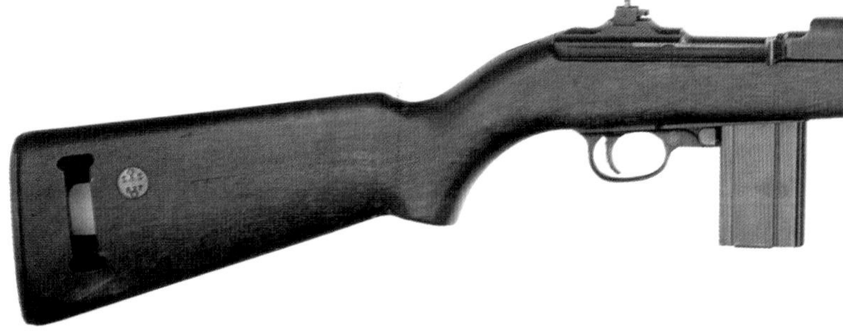

Length (gun): 35.7 in. (905 mm)
Barrel: 18.0 in. (458 mm)
Weight (gun): 5.5 lb. (25 kg)
Caliber: 0.30 in.

Rifling: 4 grooves, r/hand
Operation: gas
Feed: 15-/30-round box
Muz vel: 1,950 ft./sec. (585 m/sec.)

Just before World War II, the US Army decided that it needed a new light weapon, an intermediate between the pistol and the rifle, as a convenient arm for officers and noncommissioned officers, and as a secondary weapon for mortar men, drivers, and similar categories for whom the service rifle would have been awkward. By the end of 1941 the Army had settled for the M1 carbine, and the weapon had gone into large-scale production. The M1 was a short, light, self-loading rifle, and although its caliber was the same as that of the service rifle, it fired a different, pistol-type cartridge so that there was no question of interchangeability between the two. The M1 carbine was an odd weapon, since in a very real sense it looked back toward the arms of the stocked Luger or Mauser pistol-type, rather than forward to the submachine gun.

GERMANY

FALLSCHIRMJÄGERGEWEHR 42 RIFLE 1942

Length (gun): 37.0 in. (940 mm)
Barrel: 20.0 in. (508 mm)
Weight (gun): 9.9 lb. (4.5 kg)
Caliber: 7.92 mm
Rifling: 4 grooves, r/hand
Operation: gas
Feed: 20-round box
Cyclic rate: 750 rpm
Muz vel: 2,500 ft./sec. (762 m/sec.)

The Fallschirmjägergewehr 42 (Paratroop Rifle, Model 1942) was one of the earliest assault rifles, introduced in 1942. Its main disadvantage was that, although the Germans had gained some success with intermediate cartridges, this particular arm fired the full-sized 7.92 x 57 mm rifle round, which was too powerful for it; but it proved to be a very good weapon to the limited number of troops armed with it, most parachutists. It was capable of single rounds or bursts. Bursts were fired from an open bolt—that is, there was no round in the chamber until the bolt drove one in and fired it in the same movement; the reason was that the chamber tended to get hot enough to fire a cartridge left in it even for a very short time.

JAPAN

TYPE 0/12 PARACHUTIST RIFLE 1942

Length (gun): 45.3 in. (1,150 mm)
Barrel: 25.4 in. (645 mm)
Weight (gun): 8.9 lb. (4.1 kg)
Caliber: 7.7 mm
Rifling: 4 grooves, r/hand
Operation: bolt-action
Feed: 5-round integral magazine
Muz vel: 2,368 ft./sec. (722 m/sec.)

The Type 99 rifle (qv) was far too long to be carried in an aircraft, so the first attempt was the Parachutist Rifle Type 0, which consisted of a Type 99 rifle divided into two parts. The inner end of each was fitted with an interrupted screw thread; this allowed the weapon to be carried in two parts during the flight and the subsequent jump, and then reassembled immediately after landing. This was not a success, and the next attempt was the Type 2, again a two-piece rifle. This time there was a wedge above the front of the receiver that had to be inserted into a receptacle above the barrel. Although trials were reasonably successful, only a few were produced, probably because by the time this weapon was available for production, in late 1942, the need for parachute troops in the Japanese Army had passed. The Type 1 Parachutist Rifle was developed as a fall-back in case the Types 0 and 2 failed, and was a Meiji 38th Year carbine with a folding butt; it never served with paratroop units, but the few that were manufactured were pressed into service in the desperate final months of the war.

UNITED STATES

US CARBINE 0.30-IN.-CALIBER M1A1 1943

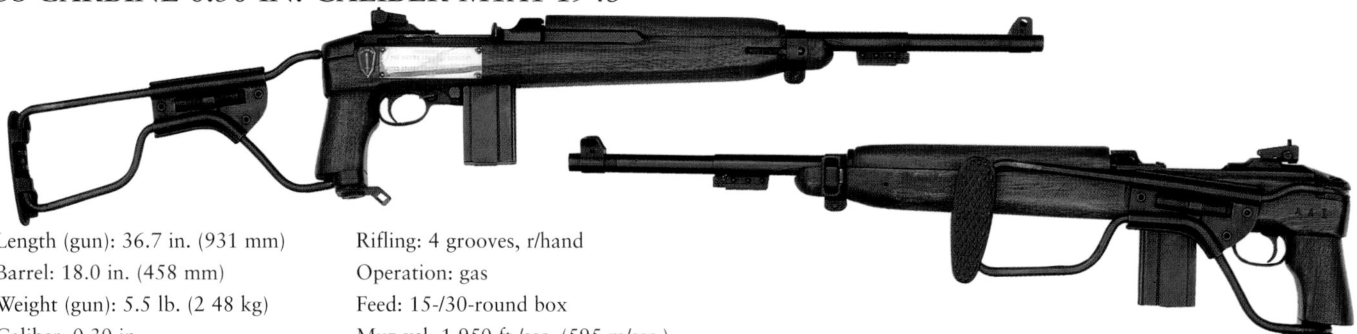

Length (gun): 36.7 in. (931 mm)
Barrel: 18.0 in. (458 mm)
Weight (gun): 5.5 lb. (2 48 kg)
Caliber: 0.30 in.
Rifling: 4 grooves, r/hand
Operation: gas
Feed: 15-/30-round box
Muz vel: 1,950 ft./sec. (595 m/sec.)

The M1A1, although the same basic weapon as the M1, was equipped with a folding stock, the central bracing plate of which carried an oil bottle. This skeleton stock was pivoted on a pistol grip so that the carbine could be fired with the stock folded, making it a convenient weapon for parachute and airborne forces. The M1 carbine in its various forms was the most common weapon produced by the United States, the total production reaching the astonishing figure of just over seven million. At one stage a selective-fire version was produced, which in effect converted the carbine into a submachine gun. There was also a version designed to take various types of night sight, with no conventional sights fitted.

GERMANY

MASCHINENPISTOLE MP 44 RIFLE 1944

Length (gun): 37.0 in. (940 mm)
Barrel: 16.5 in. (420 mm)
Weight (gun): 11.3 lb. (5.1 kg)
Caliber: 7.92 mm
Rifling: 4 grooves, r/hand
Operation: gas
Feed: 30-round box
Cyclic rate: 500 rpm
Muz vel: 2,125 ft./sec. (647 m/sec.)

The MP 43(H) was developed in 1943. This new "machine carbine," which was gas-operated, was an immediate success, and by the end of 1943 the German Army had received 14,000. The long-term idea seems to have been to make the MP 43 a universal weapon at squad or section level, doing away with rifles, submachine guns, and light machine guns. Production declined rapidly after the first few months of 1944, and the new concept was never realized. There were some variations to the standard type, notably an MP 43(1), which had a fixture allowing it to fire grenades. In 1944 the designation was changed to MP 44, and by the end of the same year the weapon had been given the additional title "Sturmgewehr," (assault rifle).

RUSSIA

MOSIN-NAGANT CARBINE MODEL 1944

Length (gun): 40.0 in. (1,016 mm)
Barrel: 20.4 in. (518 mm)
Weight (gun): 8.9 lb. (4 kg)
Caliber: 7.62 mm
Rifling: 4 grooves, r/hand
Operation: bolt-action
Feed: 5-round magazine
Muz vel: 2,700 ft./sec. (823 m/sec.)

The first Mosin-Nagant arms were developed by Colonel Sergei Mosin of the Russian Artillery and a Belgian designer named Nagant. The 1891 model was the first of the modern smallbore bolt-action magazine rifles to be used by Russia, and virtually all her later rifles of the type are based on it. The caliber was originally measured in an old Russian unit known as a line and equivalent to 1/10 in. As a result they were often known as "three-line" rifles. Their sights were also calibrated in arshins, another ancient measurement based on the human pace. Many of these earlier rifles were made in other European countries, and during World War I the United States manufactured 1.5 million of them for Russia. The next major change came in 1930, although even this was little more than a general modernization of the early type. It led to the production of a sniper version with a telescopic sight.

Snipers of Stalingrad

The battle of Stalingrad in the winter of 1942–43 was a war of small arms. The deliberate Soviet tactic of maintaining close proximity with German troops to obviate the advantage of air, artillery, and armor support meant that rifles, submachine guns, and grenades became the most influential combat weapons.

The sniper also came into his own. The shattered urban landscape provided ideal cover for both sniper positions and covert movement between those positions. Thousands of snipers were employed on both sides, their missions being to kill enemy officers, restrict enemy unit movement, and to kill runners or supply carriers to interfere with enemy communications and logistics.

Stalingrad was also the setting for the most infamous, and apocryphal, sniper duel in history, involving the Soviets' premier sniper, Vasili Zaitsev. Zaitsev was a national hero, the Soviet Army's most successful sniper with more than 100 kills. In Stalingrad he added another 242 kills to his credit, and his military and propaganda value to the Soviets led the Germans to dispatch a counter-sniper to kill him. This German sniper is usually identified as a Major Konings of the Berlin Sniper School, but detailed research does not confirm this. Suffice to say, that the German was a man of some talent. A captured German prisoner gave Zaitsev forewarning, and so the two men began tracking each other.

Zaitsev and a group of fellow snipers began an almost academic study of all German snipers operating in the Stalingrad theater, noting their modus operandi and attempting to identify those with exceptional talent. The shooting of Zaitsev's comrades Morozov and Sheykin, both veteran snipers, led Zaitsev to conclude that they were in the presence of the German "super-sniper," and Zaitsev, Nikolay Kulikov, and a Soviet political officer staked out the area over the next few days. The political officer was seriously wounded after being shot by a sniper, having raised his head for only a brief second above the parapet. To Zaitsev, this phenomenal shooting confirmed that his man was out there.

Zaitsev deduced the only hiding place for the German was under a sheet of metal between a destroyed tank and a ruined pillbox. He tested his theory by holding up a mitten on the end of a stick, provoking a shot. Zaitsev shifted his position during the night. In the morning, a glint of reflected sunlight suggested a rifle sight, and Kulikov raised his helmet fractionally above a trench parapet to test the response. The German immediately shot the helmet and, believing he had got Zaitsev, raised his head fractionally. It was all Zaitsev needed. He killed the German with a head shot and secured another propaganda victory for the Soviets.

Below: *Russian infantry move across the blasted landscape of Stalingrad, clutching Mosin-Nagant rifles. Soviet snipers would often use the standard army rifle fitted with telescopic sights, whereas others preferred civilian hunting rifles. The Soviets often fielded dedicated units of snipers, working independently, rather than in support of conventional forces.*

WORLD WAR II AND THE BIRTH OF THE ASSAULT RIFLE

The emergence of the assault rifle was in many ways the result of ammunition development rather than firearms design. In Germany during the interwar years, the German military establishment conducted a review of combat ranges and rifle ammunition. The conclusion was that the standard 0.319 in. (7.92 mm) rifle round was too powerful. Most actual combat, the officers concluded, was conducted at ranges of less than half the 7.92 mm's 3,280-plus ft. (1,000-plus m) range, and the heavy recoil of the round increased training times, marred accurate shooting, and even made soldiers less willing to shoot their weapons because of shoulder bruising.

The review led German ammunition designers to produce so-called "intermediate" rounds, ammunition of rifle caliber but with a reduced case length and propellant charge. The first of these, the 0.30 x 1.55 in. (7.75 x 39.5 mm) M35 from Gustave Genschow and Company, had a muzzle velocity of 2,296 ft./second (700 m/sec.) as opposed to the 2,788 ft./second (850 m/sec.) of the Mauser 0.319 x 2.24 in. (7.92 x 57 mm) round. The M35 was not a success mainly because the gun designed for it, the MKb35, was expensive and a poor performer, but a subsequent cartridge produced by Polte Werke of Magdeburg went on to greater achievements. This round was the 0.319 x 1.3 in. (7.92 x 33 mm) "Kurz" (short) round. With a 33-grain propellant load and a muzzle velocity the same as that of the M35, the short round gave good performance over a practical 1,640-ft. (500m) range, with a recoil that could be controlled even when using full-auto fire. The Kurz was lucky to receive an excellent weapon to fire it: the MP43/44 (or StG44). This gas-operated weapon, developed from the earlier MKb42H, was the first weapon to receive the title "assault rifle" (Sturmgewehr), a name given by Hitler himself.

The principle of the short cartridge soon caught on with the Russians. In 1943, the M43 0.30 x 1.54 in. (7.62 x 39 mm) cartridge was produced by N.M. Elizarov and B.V. Semin, and this went into the Simonov SKS and, shortly after the war, into the AK-47, the archetypal assault rifle. Shortened cartridges gave the user a controllable fire, and the postwar world would, eventually, accept almost universally either shortened rounds or small-caliber rounds as the standard infantry rifle ammunition.

Above: *The MP43/44 was arguably the world's first true assault rifle. It utilized gas-operation to cycle the weapon and was fed from a 30-round detachable box magazine with cyclical full-auto rates of fire of 500 rpm. Although it looks like, and in some senses is, an ancestor of the AK-47, it used a tipping bolt rather than the rotating bolt of the AK weapons.*

UNITED KINGDOM

NUMBER 5 0.303 IN. RIFLE 1944

Length (gun): 39.5 in. (1,003 mm)
Barrel: 18.8 in. (475 mm)
Weight (gun): 7.2 lb. (3.3 kg)
Caliber: 0.303 in.

Rifling: 5 grooves, l/hand
Operation: bolt-action
Feed: 10-round box magazine
Muz vel: 2,400 ft./sec. (731 m/sec.)

The British Empire forces took readily to jungle warfare. It was, however, quickly found that the standard infantry rifles—the Rifle Number 4 and Short Magazine Lee-Enfield—were too long and heavy for jungle fighting. This led to the development of the Rifle, Number 5, Mk 1, in essence a cut-down Number 4, some 5.0 inches (127 mm) shorter and 1.9 lb. (0.85 kg) lighter. The shorter barrel necessitated a flash suppressor and a new type of bayonet; in addition, the fore-end stock was cut back. The working parts were identical to those of the Number 4, but a rubber butt pad was fitted to protect the firer's shoulder from the increased recoil, and the rear sling swivel was replaced by a different type of hook. The result was an excellent weapon, which was very popular with all those who used it in the Burma campaign during World War II and in the postwar Malayan Emergency.

UNITED KINGDOM

EM 2 RIFLE 1948

Length (gun): 35.0 in. (889 mm)
Barrel: 24.5 in. (623 mm)
Weight (gun): 7.6 lb. (3.42 kg)
Caliber: 0.280 in.

Rifling: 4 grooves, r/hand
Operation: gas
Feed: 20-round box
Cyclic rate: 450 rpm
Muz vel: 2,530 ft./sec. (772 m/sec.)

Soon after 1945, work began at the Royal Small Arms Factory in Enfield on a new assault rifle to replace the Number 4. The new arm had the working parts and magazine housed behind the trigger in a rearward extension of the body, which also had the butt plate attached to it. As the butt plate was in line with the axis of the barrel, it was necessary to elevate the line of sight by incorporating an optical sight as part of the carrying handle. It did very well on trials, its only minor disadvantage that the ejection opening on the right side above the magazine meant the rifle could not be fired from the left shoulder. In spite of its effectiveness, NATO rejected it mainly because of American reluctance to change caliber. A few EM 2s were rebarreled to take the 7.62 mm round, but the rifle needed a major redesign, and the UK reluctantly abandoned it in favor of the L1A1.

RUSSIA

7.62 SKS CARBINE (SIMONOV) 1949

Length (gun): 40.2 in. (1,022 mm)
Barrel: 20.5 in. (521 mm)
Weight (gun): 8.5 lb. (3.9 kg)
Caliber: 7.62 mm

Rifling: 4 grooves, r/hand
Operation: gas
Feed: 10-round box
Muz vel: 2,410 ft./sec. (735 m/sec.)

This was an early type of self-loader, developed and produced by Russia in the course of World War II. It was a gas-operated weapon of orthodox appearance and was designed to fire an "intermediate" round of the type originally developed by the German Army for its MP 43/44. It had a magazine capacity of 10 rounds, which could be loaded either separately or by clips, and it was equipped with a folding bayonet of bladed type, which turned back under the barrel when not required. The woodwork was of laminated beech and heavily varnished. The SKS was an efficient weapon, if somewhat heavy, and the cartridge gave adequate power at the sort of ranges envisaged in modern war, which by Russian techniques were of the order of 330–440 yd. (300–400 m). The SKS was used and manufactured by many countries but was superseded by the AK-47.

BELGIUM

FN FAL (MODEL 50) 7.62 MM RIFLE 1950

Length (gun): 41.5 in. (1,054 mm)
Barrel: 21.0 in. (533 mm)
Weight (gun): 9.5 lb. (4.3 kg)
Caliber: 7.62 mm

Rifling: 4 grooves, r/hand
Operation: gas
Feed: 20-round box
Muz vel: 2,800 ft./sec. (853 m/sec.)

The 7.62 mm FAL was a great success: it was gas-operated, could fire automatic or single shots as required, and was generally a robust and effective arm. It was sold to a great many countries. Although it had the capability to fire bursts, this led to problems of accuracy due to the inevitable rise of the muzzle, and most countries therefore had their rifles permanently set at semi-automatic, which still allowed 20 to 30 well-aimed shots to be fired in one minute. There was also a heavy-barreled version with a bipod, which was adopted by some countries as a section automatic weapon. When the UK abandoned development of the EM2 (qv), it adopted a version of the FAL and purchased 1,000 for trials, one of which is shown here. These were tested in the UK, Germany, Kenya, and Malaya, which led to the modified version that was produced in the UK as the L1A2.

UNITED STATES

REMINGTON 870 WINGMASTER SLIDE-ACTION SHOTGUN 1950

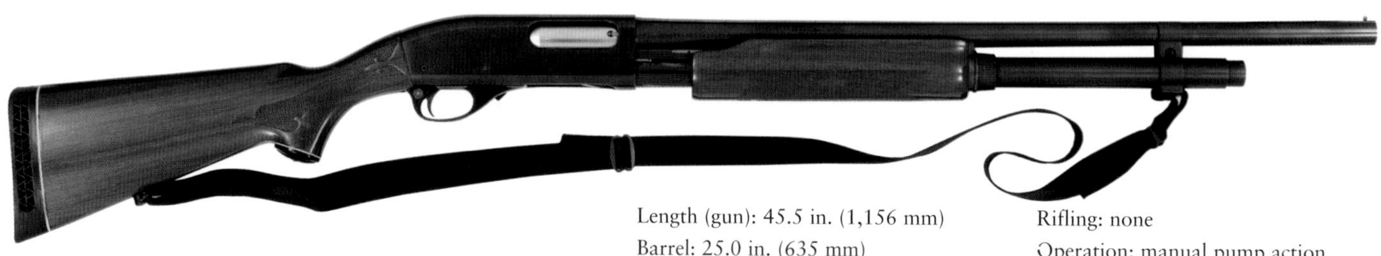

Length (gun): 45.5 in. (1,156 mm)
Barrel: 25.0 in. (635 mm)
Weight (gun): 7.5 lb. (3.4 kg)
Caliber: 12-, 20-, 28- or 40-gauge

Rifling: none
Operation: manual pump action
Feed: 5- or 8-round tubular magazine
Muz vel: n.k.

The Remington 870 was introduced in 1950, and more than four million have been made since then. It is produced in a wide variety of models and in four gauges: 12-, 20-, 28-, and 40-gauge. Normal magazine capacity is five rounds, but an extension giving eight-round capacity is also available. It has a strong and positive action, with double-action bars, and all except the Police and Special-Purpose models are fitted with walnut stocks and fore ends. One shortcoming in earlier models occurred when cartridges that were not pushed fully into the magazine might slip and cause a stoppage, but this was rectified in later versions. Other later modifications included fitting the "Rem" internally threaded choke system, and recoil pads on the 12- and 20-gauge models.

BELGIUM

FN FAL (MODEL 50) 0.280 IN. RIFLE 1951

Length (gun): ca 40.0 in. (1,016 mm)
Barrel: 19.0 in. (483 mm)
Weight (gun): ca 10.0 lb. (4.5 kg)
Caliber: 0.280 in. (7 mm)

Rifling: 4 grooves, r/hand
Operation: gas
Feed: 20-round box
Muz vel: n.k.

After World War II, the British expended a great deal of development effort on the Enfield 0.280 (7 mm Mk1Z) round and two new rifles to fire it: the EM1 and EM2. NATO standardized on the Belgian 7.62 x 51 mm round, but during this period the Belgian FN factory developed a version of its new Model 50 (FAL) chambered to fire the British 0.280 in. round, presumably intended as a safeguard against the possibility that the British round was selected instead, in which case the Belgians would have offered this weapon to third parties in competition with the British "bullpup" EM2. Note that, unlike the Model 50 (FAL), this weapon has a shorter barrel fitted with a flash suppressor and a different fore handgrip, which has grooves for the fingers and does not fully enclose the gas cylinder. It also lacks a carrying handle and has a plainer and less angled pistol grip.

THE GARAND RIFLE IN WORLD WAR II

The M1 Garand was adopted by the US Army in 1936, thus becoming the world's first semi-automatic rifle to enter service as a standard army weapon. The Garand's proving ground would be the battlefields of World War II, and military analysts watched closely to see how the semi-auto would perform in actual combat conditions. At the outset, the Garand had its critics. Some felt the Garand was too heavy; it was nearly the same weight as a Springfield 03 but more than 3 in. (76 mm) shorter. Others thought that the semi-auto action would encourage ammunition wastage among infantry troops already liable to expel all their ammunition too quickly even with bolt-action weapons, and that the fire would be undisciplined and inaccurate.

The Garand, however, proved its critics wrong on numerous counts. The Garand was heavy, but its engineering wasn't wasted. With legendary reliability, the Garand performed without problems in all terrains: the arid conditions of West Africa, the temperate/winter climates of northern Europe, and the tropical extremes of the Pacific War. It was accurate out to 1,960 ft. (600 m) and was as precise in practical terms as a Mauser 98k. Admittedly, Garand users could quickly run through their stock of eight-round clips in action, although in many theaters the high volumes of fire produced by the Garand were a blessing. In the Pacific theater, jungle terrain often precluded flanking attacks against Japanese positions. Instead, frontal attacks had to be used, relying upon dense volumes of lead to perform leapfrogging fire-and-maneuver actions. The Garand was ideal for this role, as a squad of eight men could unleash more than 400 rounds a minute.

If there were problems with the Garand, they were to be found in the feed system. A half-spent clip could not be topped up with individual rounds; the gun had to be emptied and then reloaded with a fresh full clip. This did indeed encourage ammunition wastage, as troops were more likely to empty their weapons against nothing so they could reload. Also, when a soldier fired the last round in the clip, the metal clip would be expelled with a load "ping" sound. This noise signaled to the enemy that his opponent's gun was empty, and so it was temporarily safe to charge. Some canny US troops took to throwing an empty clip on the ground after firing only a few rounds, fooling the enemy into thinking he was empty, then shooting the enemy as he moved from cover.

Right and below: *The Garand rifle demonstrated the superiority of the self-loading rifle over bolt-action weapons as standard-issue rifles. General George S. Patton, not an easy man to impress with military technology, even went so far as to describe the rifle as "the greatest battlefield implement ever devised." Garands were capable of use as straightforward infantry weapons or as precision sniper, and even competition guns.*

RUSSIA

KALASHNIKOV AK-47 ASSAULT RIFLE 1947

Length: 13.5 in. (343 mm)
Barrel: 7.5 in. (190 mm)
Weight (gun): 4.25 lb. (1.93 kg)
Caliber: .44 in. (11.2 mm)
Rifling: 7 groove, l/hand
Capacity: 6
Muz Vel: ca 850 ft./sec. (259 m/sec.)
Sights: fixed

Mikhail Kalashnikov's AK-47 was officially adopted for the Russian Army in 1951. It was in every way an exceptionally fine assault rifle. It worked by gas, tapped off from the barrel and impinging on a piston working in a cylinder above the barrel. This piston took with it the rotating bolt, the whole being thrust forward again by the coiled return spring at the proper time. The AK-47 is sufficiently heavy to shoot well at automatic up to the sort of ranges likely in modern war, that is, about 330 yd. (300 m). The bore is chromed and the weapon is easy to strip and handle. It is designed to take a knife-type bayonet and in later models the wooden butt has been replaced by a folding metal one. The AK-47 was manufactured extensively by various countries of the former Soviet Bloc. It was replaced by an improved version, the AKM, but is still an almost universal arm for subversive and terrorist groups.

RUSSIA

AK-47 (FOLDING-BUTT) (AUTOMATIC-KALASHNIKOV) RIFLE 1952

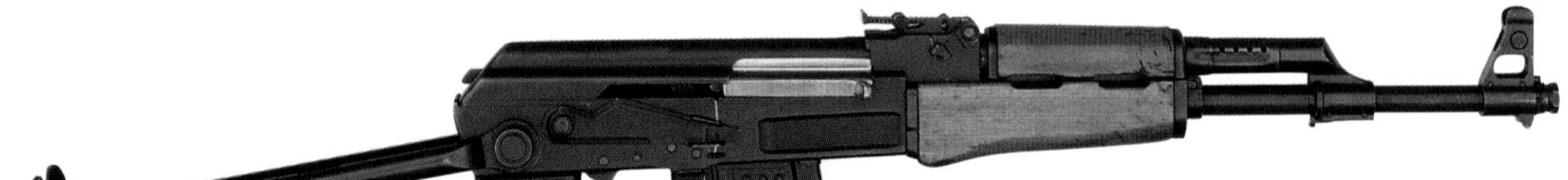

Length (gun): 34.7 in. (880 mm)
Barrel: 16.3 in. (415 mm)
Weight (gun): 9.5 lb. (4.3 kg)
Caliber: 7.62 mm
Rifling: 4 grooves, r/hand
Operation: gas
Feed: 30-round box
Cyclic rate: 600 rpm
Muz vel: 2,350 ft./sec. (717 m/sec)

The earliest versions of the AK-47, which came into use in the Russian Army in 1951, had wooden butts. These, like many other Soviet arms of their era, were of poor-quality timber, which detracted greatly from the otherwise excellent quality and finish. Soon afterward there appeared an alternative version with a folding metal butt that could, if required, be turned forward under the weapon without affecting its use. This type was probably originally intended for use by airborne troops, but its compactness made it easily concealed and therefore an obvious weapon for guerrillas, terrorists, and similar irregular organizations, and it now appears to be used all over the world. Apart from its compactness, the AK-47 has certain other obvious advantages: it is strongly made and it shoots as well as an orthodox rifle to 437 yd. (400 m).

CZECH REPUBLIC

MODEL VZ-52 ASSAULT RIFLE 1952

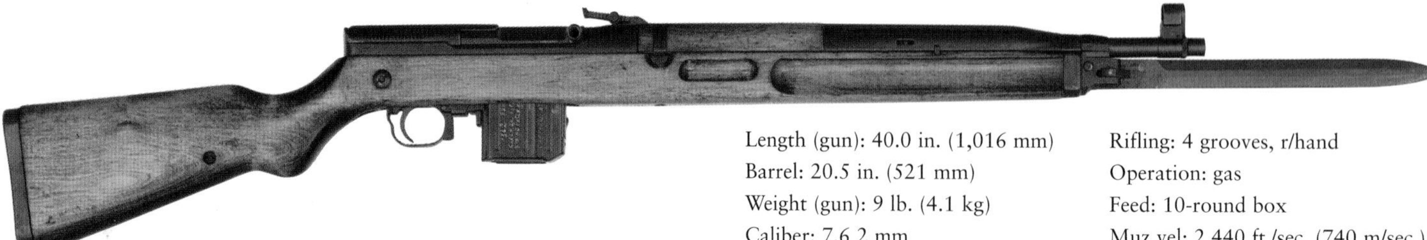

Length (gun): 40.0 in. (1,016 mm)
Barrel: 20.5 in. (521 mm)
Weight (gun): 9 lb. (4.1 kg)
Caliber: 7.6 2 mm
Rifling: 4 grooves, r/hand
Operation: gas
Feed: 10-round box
Muz vel: 2,440 ft./sec. (740 m/sec.)

This self-loading rifle was originally designed to fire the Czech 7.62 x 45 mm cartridge. It was gas-operated, with power transmitted by a sleeve around the barrel, which was forced to the rear by the pressure of the gas tapped off from the bore, taking the bolt with it. The bolt worked on the tilting principle under which its front end dropped into a recess in the bottom of the body; this had the effect of locking it at the instant of firing. The rifle performed well with the cartridge for which it was designed, but the Russians later compelled the Czechs to adopt their own less powerful 7.62 x 39 mm round, which adversely affected its performance. The modified rifle was the Model 52/57. The original VZ-52 was relatively heavy, which reduced recoil. It lacked any simple system of gas regulation, so that any change involved the removal of the foregrip before the gas stop could be adjusted.

UNITED KINGDOM

L1A1 RIFLE 1953

Length (gun): 44.5 in. (1,130 mm)
Barrel: 31.0 in. (787 mm)
Weight (gun): 9.5 lb. (4.3 kg)
Caliber: 7.62 mm
Rifling: 4 grooves, r/hand
Operation: gas
Feed: 20-round box
Muz vel: 2,800 ft./sec. (854 m/sec.)

Once the EM 2 rifle (qv) had been rejected, the British Army decided to adopt the Belgian FN FAL rifle, and this, with a number of modifications, became the L1A1. The British version was a self-loader only and would not fire bursts. The early rifle was modified in some respects, particularly with regard to the use of glass fiber instead of wood, but it remained unchanged in principle. It was gas-operated and generally a sound and reliable weapon. The specimen illustrated is fitted with a night sight. A variety were available, varying from the simple fore sight with a self-powered light source to the Trilux sight shown, which could be quickly and easily mounted. It was self-energizing and easily adjusted for intensity and was useful not only for night work, but also against indistinct targets by day. It entered service in 1974; its official designation was the Sight Unit Infantry Trilux.

AUSTRALIA

LITHGOW L1A1 1954

Length (gun): 45.0 in. (1,143 mm)
Barrel: 24.4 in. (618 mm)
Weight (gun): 9.8 lb. (4.5 kg)
Caliber: 7.62 mm
Rifling: 4 grooves, r/hand
Operation: gas-operated
Feed: 20-round box magazine
Cyclic rate: 700 rpm
Muz vel: 2,756 ft./sec. (840 m/sec.)

The 7.62 mm FN FAL was, with some modifications, adopted by the British as the L1A1. This was a gas-operated weapon with a tipping bolt and a short-stroke piston that acted on the bolt carrier. Lock-up was against a shelf in the lower receiver. The gas regulator had six positions so that the rifle and ammunition could be exactly matched. The recoil spring was in the butt, the folding cocking handle on the left of the gun. The axis of the bore was as low as possible without turning to a straight stock with raised sights. In the 1950s most commonwealth countries still continued to follow the lead set by the UK in military matters, so when the British adopted the FN FAL as the L1A1, the Australians and Canadians followed suit. The weapon illustrated here is the Australian Army's Lithgow L1A1, which was very similar to the British original, but with furniture made of ICI Maranyl nylon.

DENMARK

SCHULTZ AND LARSEN MODEL 68DL RIFLE 1954

Length (gun): 46.0 in. (1,168 mm)
Barrel: 26.0 in. (660 mm)
Weight (gun): 9.7 lb. (4.4 kg)
Caliber: 0.264 in. Winchester
Rifling: n.k.
Operation: bolt-action
Feed: 3-round magazine
Muz vel: n.k.

The Schultz and Larsen Model 68DL was an exceptionally fine weapon, but a commercial disaster. It was designed in the late 1940s and introduced in 1954 in match-target and hunting versions as the Model 54. A number of subsequent modifications were intended to make it more appealing to the North American market, including changing from cock-on-closing to cock-on-opening and a faster lock time. It was one of the most accurate, safe, and smooth-operating rifles ever made, combining fine metallurgy with exquisite workmanship. Four equidistantly spaced locking lugs mounted just ahead of the bolt handle permitted an extremely stiff enveloping receiver to guide the ground-and-lapped bolt throughout the operating stroke. Some 3,000 were made, of which only a pitiful 200-odd of the perfected Model 68DL were delivered to the United States.

BELGIUM

BROWNING SPECIAL SKEET GUN 1955

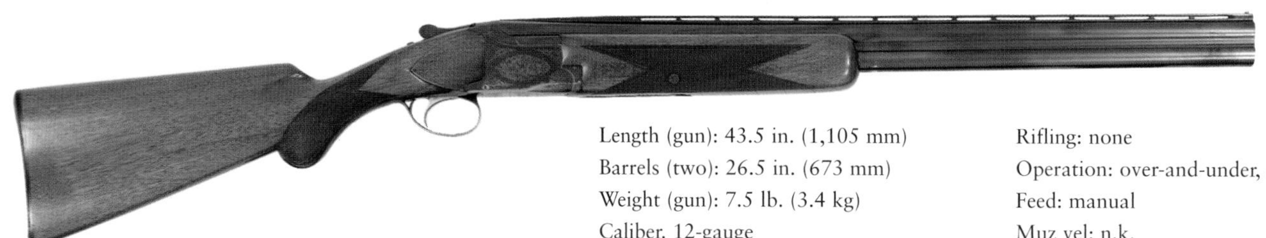

Length (gun): 43.5 in. (1,105 mm)
Barrels (two): 26.5 in. (673 mm)
Weight (gun): 7.5 lb. (3.4 kg)
Caliber. 12-gauge

Rifling: none
Operation: over-and-under, drop-down
Feed: manual
Muz vel: n.k.

Despite the simplicity and elegance of the side-by-side double-barrel gun, the over-and-under (also known as the "stacked-barrel") continues to be popular. This is the Special Skeet Model, which was manufactured in the 1950s and 1960s by Fabrique Nationale (FN) of Belgium, chiefly for North American customers, where it was marketed under the Browning label. The stock has a half pistol grip rather than the full pistol grip now almost universal on over-and-unders. Like all Browning skeet guns of this period, this gun has four points of choke in each barrel, so that the selection of which barrel to fire first is of little consequence. Over the thirty years or so since this gun was made, skeet guns have tended to be made with no choke at all in the barrels; in fact, even "trumpet" choking has been seen, whereby the barrels actually open out at the muzzles to give the widest possible spread.

SPAIN

AYA NUMBER ONE SHOTGUN 1955

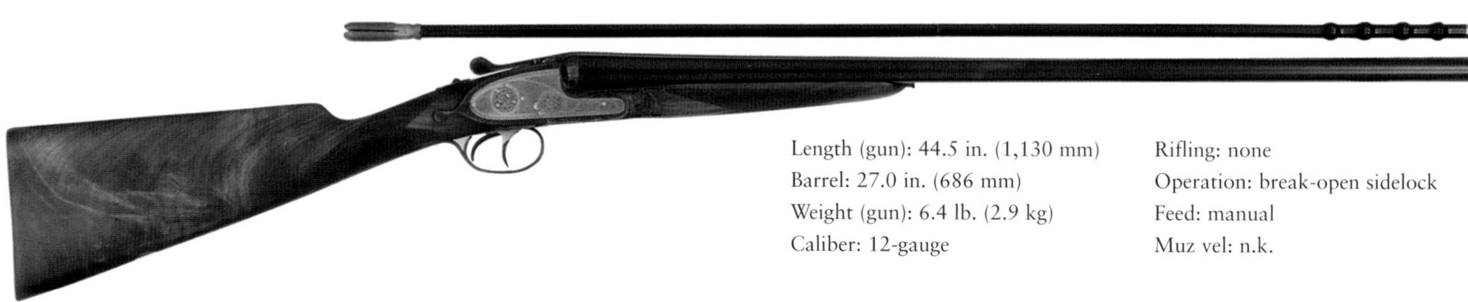

Length (gun): 44.5 in. (1,130 mm)
Barrel: 27.0 in. (686 mm)
Weight (gun): 6.4 lb. (2.9 kg)
Caliber: 12-gauge

Rifling: none
Operation: break-open sidelock
Feed: manual
Muz vel: n.k.

In the 1950s, a company known as Anglo-Spanish Imports of Ipswich, England, placed a contract with AYA, a Spanish gun-making company, to produce guns for the British market. The guns were to be virtual copies of British guns but at a fraction of the contemporary prices. Prior to this, Spanish guns exported to the UK had been rather heavy, often fitted with sling swivels roughly finished. The 1950s contract saw a complete change, and AYA was soon exporting a variety of quality guns, ranging from a box-lock nonejector through several box-lock ejectors to the gun shown here, the Number One model, double-barrel, break-open, side-lock ejector. With an assisted opening system fitted, it can be made in more than one caliber if required, at a quarter of the price of the equivalent British gun. The illustration shows the excellent finish of this weapon.

UNITED KINGDOM

HOLLAND AND HOLLAND 0.458 IN. MAGAZINE RIFLE 1955

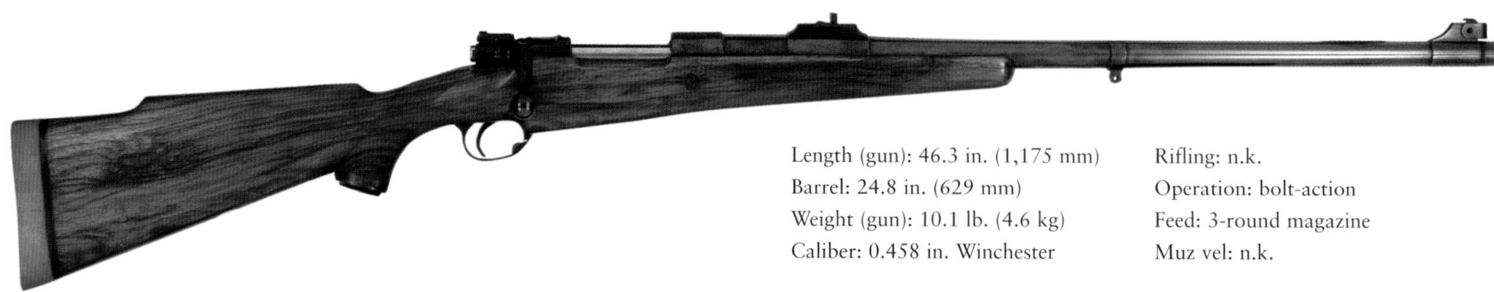

Length (gun): 46.3 in. (1,175 mm)
Barrel: 24.8 in. (629 mm)
Weight (gun): 10.1 lb. (4.6 kg)
Caliber: 0.458 in. Winchester

Rifling: n.k.
Operation: bolt-action
Feed: 3-round magazine
Muz vel: n.k.

When the American company Winchester decided around 1955 to seek a slice of the then very profitable African market, the cartridge case firm looked to the venerable rimless 0.375 in. round. The company blew this out, straight-walled it, and trimmed its length to 2.5 in. (63.5 mm) overall, and arrived at the 0.458 inch. The round quickly became the world standard in its category and is used by this Holland and Holland rifle. Part of the reason for the popularity of this round lay in its dimensional compatibility with standard-length, bolt-action receivers, another with the excellent performance of its 510 grain (33 g) bullets. This rifle's action is Mauser 98 turn-bolt, with two forward lugs locking in the receiver ring. The weapon has a single-stage trigger, with rocking safety on the right of the receiver. It has a gold bead fore sight with folding guard and a two-leaf back sight.

UNITED KINGDOM

THOMAS WILD SIDELOCK EJECTOR SHOTGUN 1955

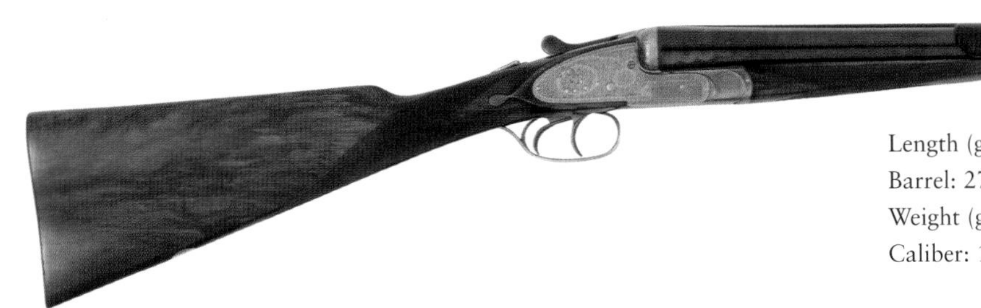

Length (gun): 44.5 in. (130 mm)
Barrel: 27.0 in. (886 mm)
Weight (gun): 6.4 lb. (2.9 kg)
Caliber: 12-gauge
Rifling: none
Operation: break-open, sidelock
Feed: manual
Muz vel: n.k.

This is a good-quality sporting gun by a well-known British gunsmith, and it was made as one of a pair in 1955. The firm Thomas Wild and Company operated from Whitehall Street in Birmingham in what was once a very busy gun-making area, but has long since succumbed to "inner city development." The double-barrel gun is light, with 2.75 in. (70 mm) chambers and a sidelock, but is so well balanced that shooting even 1.125 oz. (32 g) loads from it does not produce any unacceptable recoil.

CHINA (PRC)

TYPE 56 RIFLE 1956

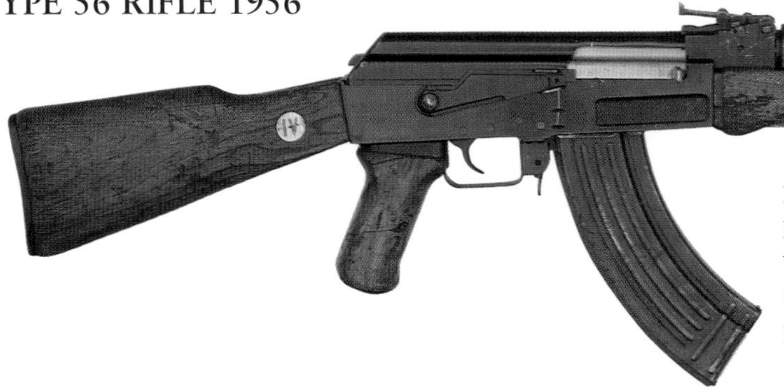

Length (gun): 34.7 in. (880 mm)
Barrel: 16.3 in. (415 mm)
Weight (gun): 9.5 lb. (4.3 kg)
Caliber: 7.62 mm intermediate
Rifling: 4 grooves, r/hand
Operation: gas
Feed: 30-round box
Cyclic rate: 600 rpm
Muz vel: 2,350 ft./sec (717 m/sec.)

The Type 56 assault rifle is a mechanically close copy of the original AK-47, the principal difference being a permanently attached folding bayonet of cruciform section. Although it was a very old idea, the Chinese were the only country still using it in the 1960s; all others had opted for a detachable knife-type bayonet that the soldier could use as a general-purpose implement. Chinese-made Type 56 rifles were extensively used in Vietnam by the Viet Cong, who found them to be ideal weapons for soldiers who were mostly small and slight by Western standards; the specimen illustrated is one of the many captured there by the US Army. They are also found in large numbers in Middle East and African countries.

SWITZERLAND

SIG 7.5 MM SG-57 RIFLE 1957

Length (gun): 43.4 in (1.102 mm)
Barrel: 20.5 in (520 mm)
Weight (gun): 12.3 lb (5.6 kg)
Caliber: 7.5 mm
Rifling: 4 grooves, r/hand
Operation: delayed blowback
Feed: 24-round box
Cyclic rate: 475 rpm
Muz vel: 2,493 ft./sec. (760 m/sec.)

The SG-57 was designed specifically for the Swiss militia, whose troops kept their rifles at home. It had an integral bipod, semi-/full-automatic selector lever, and straight-line stock, and fired the 7.5 x 55 mm Swiss M1911 round. The weapon used the roller-delayed system pioneered in the Mauser StG-45, which had been further developed in the late 1940s by German designers in Spain (see G3 rifle). The SG-57 had a pressed-steel receiver, a vented foregrip, a bipod, a wooden butt with a rubber butt pad, and a carrying handle, and it was capable of launching grenades. Some 600,000 were manufactured for the Swiss defense forces and another 100,000 for export. The weapon illustrated is the SG-510-4 AMT (American Match Target), and the white tab above the pistol grip denotes that the full-automatic facility has been deactivated.

UNITED STATES

7.62 MM M14 RIFLE 1957

Length (gun): 44.0 in. (1,117 mm)
Barrel: 22.0 in. (558 mm)
Weight (gun): 8.6 lb. (3.9 kg)
Caliber: 7.62 mm
Rifling: 4 grooves, r/hand
Operation: gas
Feed: 20-round box
Cyclic rate: 750 rpm
Muz vel: 2,800 ft./sec. (853 m/sec.)

By 1953, NATO had settled on a common cartridge, and the US Army developed the M14 as a selective fire weapon of assault-rifle type. It was a logical development of the Garand. A number of important improvements were made, notably the abolition of the awkward eight-round clip and the substitution of a prefilled detachable box magazine holding twenty rounds. The new rifle was capable of firing single shots or bursts, and although most were issued permanently set for semi-automatic fire only, a number were fitted with light bipods with a view to being used as squad or section light automatics. They were, however, only marginally suitable for this role because sustained fire caused them to overheat and there was no provision for changing barrels. There was also an excellent sniper version. Some 1.5 million M14s were made in all.

CZECH REPUBLIC

VZ-58 7.62 MM ASSAULT RIFLE 1958

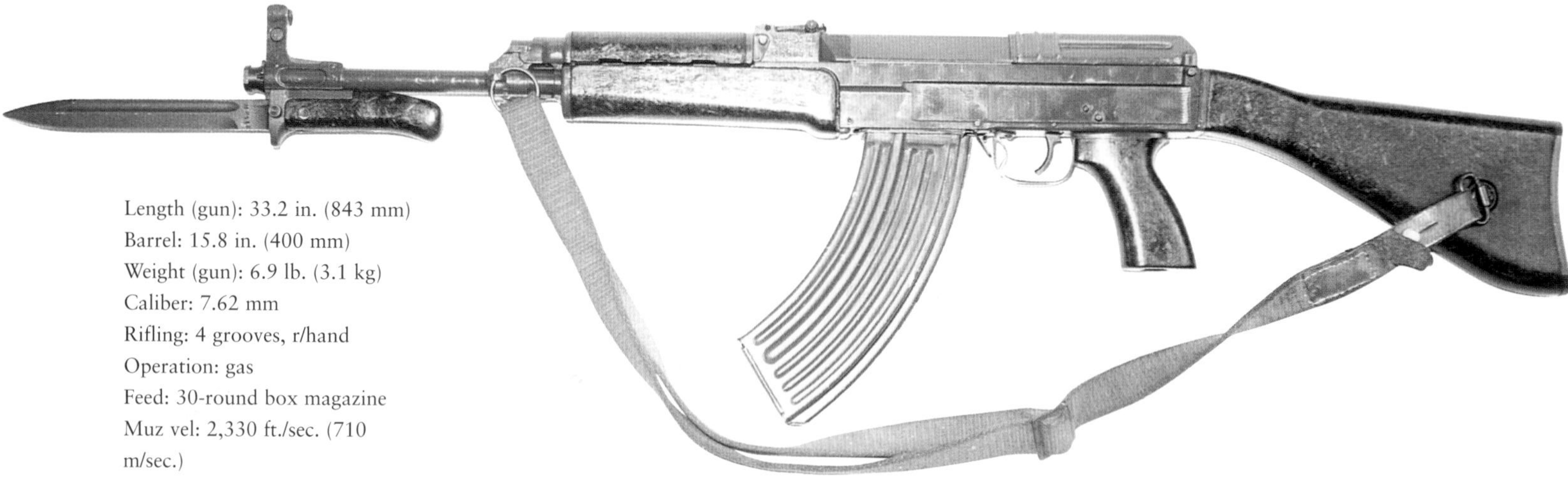

Length (gun): 33.2 in. (843 mm)
Barrel: 15.8 in. (400 mm)
Weight (gun): 6.9 lb. (3.1 kg)
Caliber: 7.62 mm
Rifling: 4 grooves, r/hand
Operation: gas
Feed: 30-round box magazine
Muz vel: 2,330 ft./sec. (710 m/sec.)

Another product of the Czech Republic's imaginative arms industry, the VZ-58 assault rifle appears at first glance to be based on the Kalashnikov series of rifles, but it is, in fact, a completely different weapon. Internally, it has a gas-operated tilting bolt, similar to that used in the earlier VZ-52 (qv), and no gas regulator; all the gas force is brought to bear on the piston head, and the entire piston system is chrome-plated to prevent fouling. Externally, early production models were fitted with wooden furniture, but this was later replaced with plastic-impregnated wood fiber, and later still by plastic. Three versions were produced: one with a fixed butt (VZ-58P, shown in the photographs); one with a fixed butt, bipod, and special attachment for a night sight (VZ-58Pi); and one with a single-strut, side-folding butt (VZ-58V). All versions were chambered for the 7.62 x 39 mm M1943 Soviet round. The VZ-58 was used to equip the then-Czechoslovak armed forces, and a few were sold on the commercial market.

KALASHNIKOV AND THE AK-47

Mikhail Timofeyevich Kalashnikov designed the AK-47 from his hospital bed after being wounded in a tank action near Bryansk in October 1941. Although the weapon came too late for World War II service, in 1949 it was accepted as the standard infantry rifle for the entire Soviet Army. It has since become the most numerous weapon of any type in history—some 100 million (including foreign copies and variants) have been produced since 1947—and it is also has possibly the most tragic legacy. Distribution of Kalashnikov's gun has been particularly unrestrained, and it has equipped armies, terrorists, and criminals alike.

There are many reasons for its prolific spread. Poor Soviet/post-Soviet stock control has certainly been to blame, especially since the 1990s, as poorly paid Russian soldiers supplement their wages by illegally selling AKs. (In 1993 alone more than 3,000 Soviet officers were found to have been involved in illegally trading small arms.) Also, the AK has been extensively copied either through licensed production or by unlicensed imitation in countries ranging from Armenia to Korea. Because of the sheer number of countries producing AK-type weapons, the network of trade links has meant that almost anyone who wants to obtain AKs can do so. Furthermore, the fall of the Soviet Union means that there are now many former Soviet republics trying to relieve poverty by selling their arms stocks to the highest bidder.

Possibly the biggest factor in AK distribution, however, was the active distribution of AKs across the globe during the many conflicts of the Cold War. AKs are durable weapons that last for decades, so arms shipped into, say, Africa in the 1970s are still in full working order today. In Mozambique, for example, AKs are now so common that they exchange hands for around $6, or are swapped for a bag of maize. They are so abundant in Africa that China has even built an AK ammunition factory in Uganda. Neither is the West blameless. During the Soviet occupation of Afghanistan (1979–89), the CIA sponsored the passage of around three million AK weapons across the Pakistan/Afghan border for distribution to the Mujahedeen resistance. When the occupation ended, these weapons simply disappeared into the Central Asian hinterland.

It is impossible to know how many people have been killed with AKs, possibly millions. With AKs still being produced, and older weapons still having many more years of working life, the death toll will only rise.

Above: *AK rifles have become preferred weapons with revolutionary, guerrilla, and terrorist groups. Their popularity is down to several key factors. First, the huge numbers of AKs worldwide means they are cheap. Second, the AK's extreme strength and durability reduce maintenance times. Third, the simplicity of operation combined with powerful automatic fire mode appeals to nonprofessional users.*

CLAY TARGET SHOOTING

The sport of clay target shooting developed during the late nineteenth century. There had been a massive growth in the popularity of game shooting, and shooters looked for ways to improve their skills in more predictable ways than on an actual shoot. Initially, this involved little more than releasing game under controlled conditions. The shooter might cover a bird (usually a starling, sparrow, or pigeon) with his top hat on the ground, then pick up the hat, releasing the bird, at which point he would mount the gun and fire. A more sophisticated practice was to have five birds in five separate boxes, or traps, set in a row in front of the shooter, one bird at a time being released in no predictable order by a "trapper."

These methods, however, had pretty obvious drawbacks. The shooting ground had to find a constant supply of animal life to fulfill the shooters' requirements. Also, the unpredictable flight paths of the birds meant that there was no consistent way of training specific types of shots. (Oh, and you need a big hat to cover a pheasant). The solution came from a US inventor named George Ligowsky in the late 1880s. Ligowsky sought to design an inanimate object that could be thrown a sufficient distance and that had aerodynamic flight properties to simulate the flight path of a bird. He produced a disk of baked clay that could be thrown from the spring-loaded arm of one of his new "traps." The angle and power of the throw could be varied to replicate varieties of bird flight. Hence, by the early 1900s different types of clay-target throws were described by equivalent bird types, such as "springing teal" and "driven partridge."

Clay-target shooting quickly caught on, especially among the big shooting schools, such as the Holland and Holland school in the UK. Initially, live birds and clay targets were commonly mixed on the layouts, but gradually clay target layouts reached such levels of sophistication and challenge that they were shot for their own pleasure alone. Since the early 1900s, clay target shooting has established itself as the world's most popular form of sport shooting, with numerous disciplines and Olympic-level competitive events.

Right: *Receiving tuition in clay shooting. The most important element of clay shooting is the gun mount. The shotgun should be mounted consistently time after time, the dominant eye looking straight along the rib, the cheek pressed solidly against the stock, and the upper body leaning forward slightly into the shot.*

DENMARK

SCHULTZ AND LARSEN UIT FREE RIFLE 1958

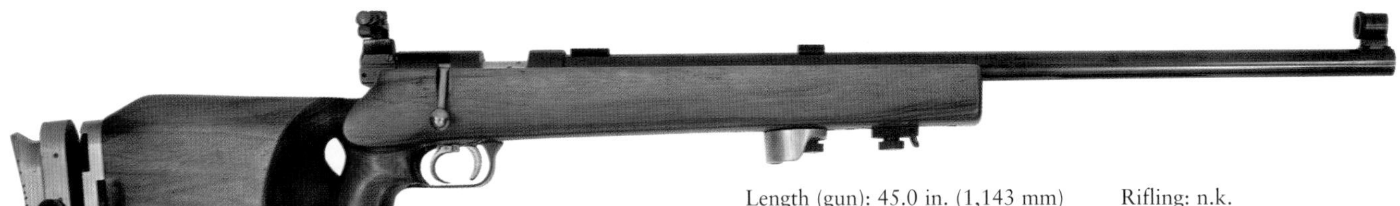

Length (gun): 45.0 in. (1,143 mm)
Barrel: 28.3 in. (718 mm)
Weight (gun): 13.9 lb. (6.3 kg)
Caliber: 0.22 in. LR
Rifling: n.k.
Operation: bolt
Feed: single-round, manual
Muz vel: n.k.

The Danish weapons firm Schultz and Larsen was established around the beginning of the twentieth century and produced some fine competition rifles. The rifle shown here was introduced in the late 1940s to meet the requirements of the UIT "Free" competitions and remained in production, with improvements, into the 1970s. It was the outcome of the pressure of competition and the search for improvements that reached a degree of sophistication that was eventually difficult to exceed. This particular weapon, which was made in the 1960s, had working parts of all-steel construction, with wooden furniture and an aluminum butt plate assembly. Operation was by lifting the bolt handle, which unlocked the breech and cocked the striker. There was no magazine, and reloading was by hand. There was a micrometer rear sight and a tunnel fore sight with interchangeable elements.

SPAIN

CETME 7.62 MM MODEL 58 SELF-LOADING RIFLE 1958

Length (gun): 39.4 in. (1,000 mm)
Barrel: 17.0 in. (432 mm)
Weight (gun): 11.4 lb. (5.1 kg)
Caliber: 7.62 mm
Rifling: 4 grooves, r/hand
Operation: see text
Feed: 20-round box magazine
Cyclic rate: 600 rpm
Muz vel: 2,493 ft./sec. (760 m/sec.)

The Spanish Army's Model 58 was developed at CETME from the German World War II Mauser StG45. This rifle had reached the prototype stage in 1945, but when the war ended the design team took it to Spain to continue working on the unique roller-locked, delayed-action breech mechanism. This resulted in a self-loading rifle firing the specially developed 7.92 x 40 mm CETME round. CETME produced a 7.62 mm version, the Model 58, but although it appeared externally similar to the G3 9 (qv), the Spanish rifle fired the 7.62 x 51 mm CETME round, which contained a reduced charge. The Model 58 used the Mauser system, with fluted chamber walls, and fired single rounds with a closed bolt and full automatic with an open bolt; it also had a flash suppressor and a bipod. Subsequent versions were the Model C, which fired the standard 7.62 mm NATO round, and the 5.56 mm Model L.

UNITED STATES

ARMALITE AR15 (M16) RIFLE 1959

Length (gun): 39.0 in. (991 mm)
Barrel: 20.0 in. (508 mm)
Weight (gun): 6.4 lb. (2.9 kg)
Caliber: 0.233 in. (5.56 mm)
Rifling: 4 grooves, r/hand
Operation: gas
Feed: 30-round magazine
Cyclic rate: 800 rpm
Muz vel: 3,250 ft./sec. (991 m/sec.)

The prototype for this weapon was the AR-10, which first went into production in 1955. It was an advanced arm employing plastic and aluminum wherever possible, but it proved too light to fire the powerful NATO 7.62 mm cartridge for which it was designed, and manufacture ceased in 1962. It was soon followed by the small-caliber high-velocity AR-15, designed by Eugene Stoner and made under license by the Colt company from July 1959 on. This new weapon soon became popular. It was a good jungle rifle and, as it was light and easy to handle by small men, it soon found favor in various countries in the Far East. It was quickly adopted by the United States after the country's intervention in Vietnam and, as the M16, is now its standard rifle. It has no piston; the gases simply pass through a tube and strike directly onto the bolt.

GERMANY

HECKLER AND KOCH G3 7.62 MM RIFLE 1960

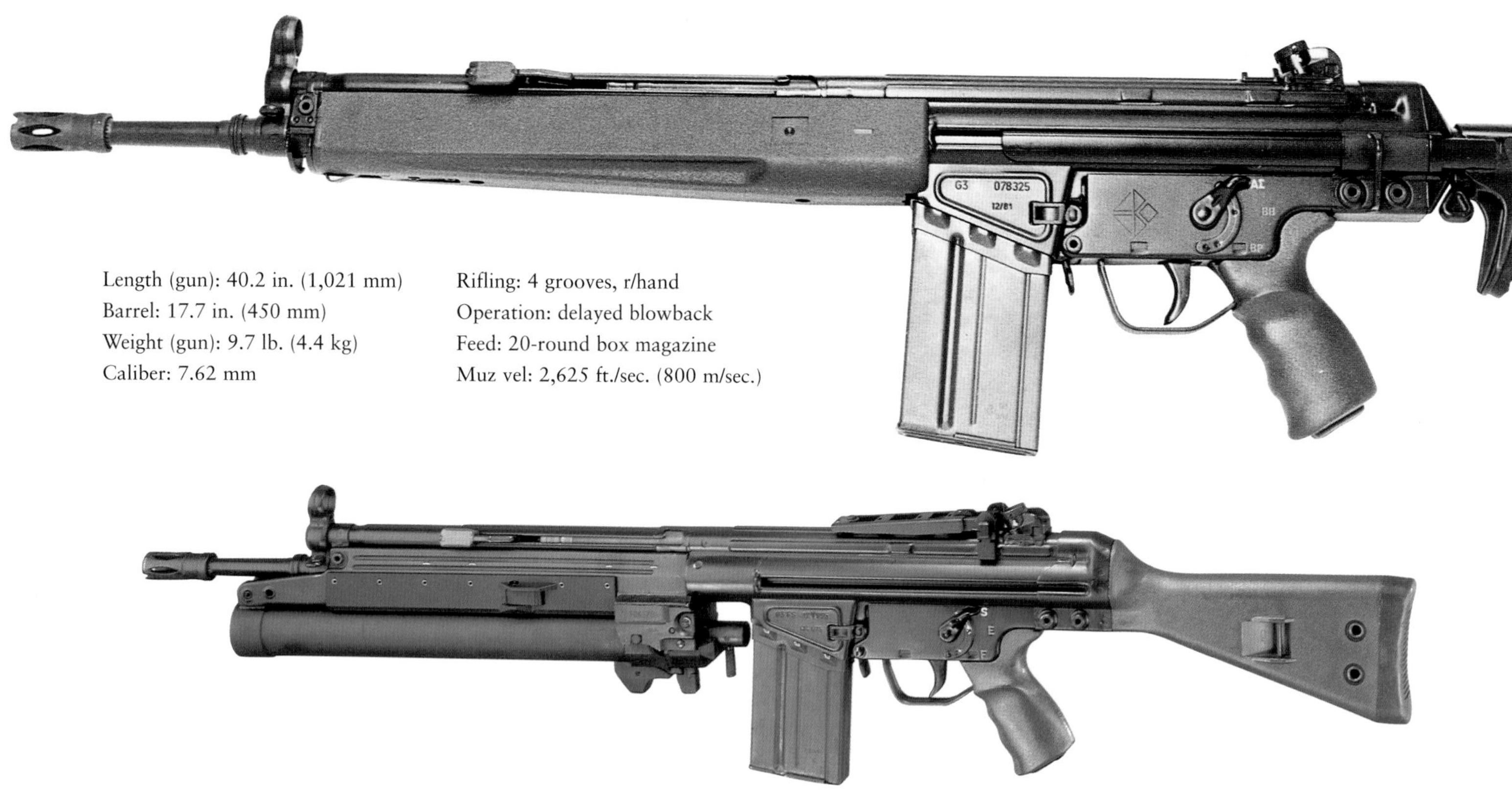

Length (gun): 40.2 in. (1,021 mm)
Barrel: 17.7 in. (450 mm)
Weight (gun): 9.7 lb. (4.4 kg)
Caliber: 7.62 mm

Rifling: 4 grooves, r/hand
Operation: delayed blowback
Feed: 20-round box magazine
Muz vel: 2,625 ft./sec. (800 m/sec.)

After World War II, a group of German weapons designers set themselves up in Spain, where they worked for CETME developing a new rifle for the Spanish Army. This rifle worked on the roller-delayed blowback system and was subsequently used as the basis for a new German rifle for the recently re-established West German Army. This weapon, the G3, was then the basis for every German rifle design until the G36, which appeared in the mid-1990s. The G3 design (shown in bottom photo with 1.57 mm/40 mm grenade launcher) subsequently went through a number of developments. The G3A1 was identical to the original except that it had a folding butt; the G3A2 introduced a free-floating barrel; the great majority of G3s were modified to this standard. The G3A3, fielded in 1964, had a new flash suppressor and drum rear sight, and the butt and forward handgrip were made of plastic instead of wood. The G3A4 was a G3A3 with a retracting butt. Several countries undertook licensed production of the G3A3, including Turkey (G3A7) and Iran (G3A6). Other Heckler and Koch projects included the HK32A2, which was a G3A2 rechambered to take the Russian 7.62 x 39 mm round, and the HK32A3, which was an HK32A2 with a retracting butt.

FINLAND

VALMET M1962 ASSAULT RIFLE 1962

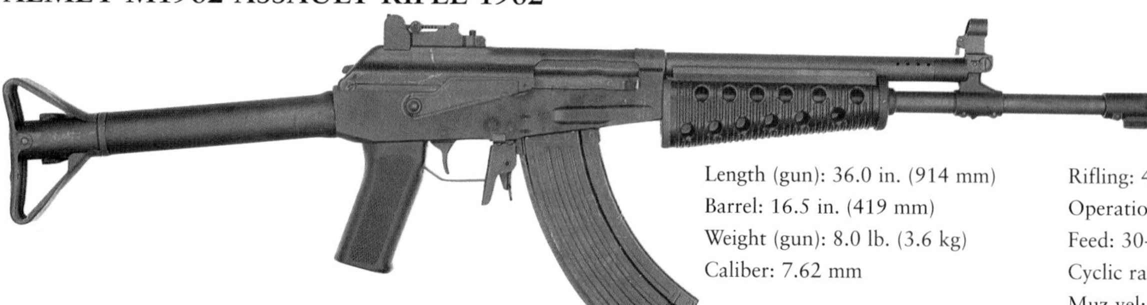

Length (gun): 36.0 in. (914 mm)
Barrel: 16.5 in. (419 mm)
Weight (gun): 8.0 lb. (3.6 kg)
Caliber: 7.62 mm

Rifling: 4 grooves r/hand
Operation: gas
Feed: 30-round box
Cyclic rate: 650 rpm
Muz vel: 2,350 ft./sec. (718 m/sec.)

The first Soviet-type assault rifle made by the Finns was developed in the late 1950s and appeared as the Model 1960. Mechanically it was virtually identical to the Russian AK-47, but there were many external differences. The M1960, which was made at Valmet, hence its name, had no woodwork on it; everything was made of metal, much of it plastic-covered. It had a plastic forehand grip ventilated with a series of holes and a rather ugly tubular butt with a shoulder piece welded on to the end of it. This early model was unusual in that it had no trigger guard in the accepted sense of the term, only a vertical bar in front of the trigger to allow the weapon to be fired by a soldier wearing heavy winter gloves. The Model 1962 illustrated was essentially similar but made increased use of pressings and riveting.

ILLEGAL GUN TRADING

Above: *A consignment of illegal weapons seized by British customs officials in 1993. The haul—which includes handguns and fragmentation grenades—was destined for the hands of Loyalist terrorist groups in Northern Ireland before the seizure.*

Systematic illegal gun trading has actually been a fairly recent phenomenon, a legacy of the Cold War. From the 1950s on, the Soviet Union and the West were locked in military competition, constantly attempting to develop superior weapons technologies. This race led to both a surplus of small arms as the competitors maintained production at war levels, and stockpiles of obsolete weaponry. The solution to handling these unwanted arms was twofold: sell the weapons to approved purchasers and/or distribute them to forces engaged in proxy wars.

What began as legal arms sales fueled the illegal arms trade for several reasons. First, many of these arms were exported to countries with either weak or corrupt state control of weapons distribution, or to countries in that were states of conflict and could not guarantee who would control future weapons stocks. These problems were particularly acute in Africa, the Middle East, and Southeast Asia, all of which received massive military support from abroad from the 1960s on. For example, during the Soviet occupation of Afghanistan between 1979 and 1989, the Mujahedeen guerrillas received $2 billion in weapons aid from the CIA, much of which was channeled into unaccountable stocks of AK-47s moved from over the Pakistan border. In a terrible irony, many of these weapons would be turned against the United States during the 2002 war in Afghanistan. An estimated 80 percent of illegal gun sales originate in state-sanctioned deals.

The 1990s saw a massive acceleration in illegal worldwide gun trading following the dissolution of the Soviet Union. Subsequent poverty among serving soldiers and former Soviet republics meant that selling off Soviet weaponry became a popular method of raising income. Furthermore, the 1990s saw a huge growth in worldwide firearms manufacturers, as countries began to make license-built firearms or simple copies of existing weapons. In the 1960s, Africa had one weapons-producing company; by the 1990s it had twenty-two. South and Central America went from two producers to seventeen over the same period. This growth in the arms-producing network has meant that it is possible for almost any regime, criminal group, or terrorist faction to access arms if they want to.

The scale of the problem regarding the proliferation of small arms is immense. Approximately 500,000 people are killed with conventional arms each year, and every year eight million new weapons are produced. Of all these weapons, 60 percent will end up in civilian hands, fueling civil wars and criminality.

UNITED KINGDOM

ENFIELD 7.62 MM L39A1 TARGET RIFLE 1962

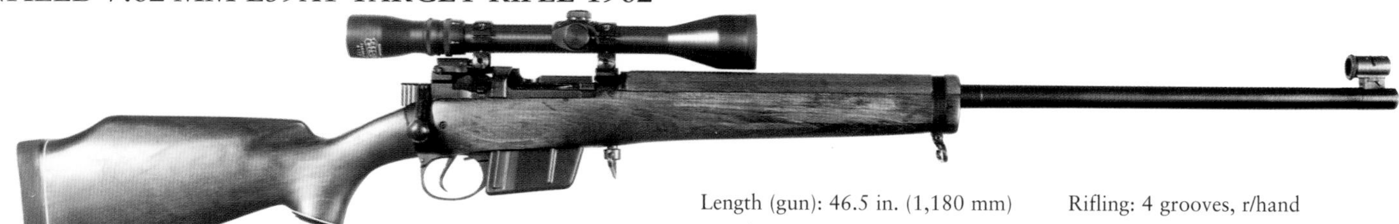

Length (gun): 46.5 in. (1,180 mm)
Barrel: 27.6 in. (700 mm)
Weight (gun): 9.7 lb. (4.4 kg)
Caliber: 7.62 x 51 mm
Rifling: 4 grooves, r/hand
Operation: bolt-action
Feed: 10-round box magazine
Muz vel: ca 2,758 ft./sec. (841 m/sec.)

When the British Army adopted the 7.62 mm L1A1 rifle, it was discovered that, while it was sufficiently accurate for use in combat, it was not up to the standard required for competition firing. As there were many service teams that wanted to take part in such competitions, it was decided to produce such a weapon by taking carefully selected 0.303 in. Number 4 rifles (qv) and modifying them to competition standards, firing the new 7.62 x 51 mm NATO rimless round. This involved fitting a new, heavy, cold-forged, 27.6 in. (700 mm) barrel. The forward stock was cut back, leaving some 15 in. (380 mm) of the barrel exposed. The receiver and bolt were modified to take the 7.62 mm rimless round. The Number 4 butt was retained unchanged, apart from a new recess, which was intended to accommodate spare fore sight blades (although these were never provided).

GERMANY

HECKLER AND KOCH HK 33 RIFLE 1963

Length (gun): 37.0 in. (940 mm)
Barrel: 15.0 in. (382 mm)
Weight (gun): 7.7 lb. (3.5 kg)
Caliber: 5.56 mm
Rifling: 6 grooves, r/hand
Operation: blowback
Feed: 20-, 30-, 40-round box
Cyclic rate: 600 rpm
Muz vel: 3,145 ft./sec. (960 m/sec.)

The HK 33 was a logical development of the G3, to which it bears a strong resemblance both externally and mechanically. This worked on delayed blowback. The breech was never fully locked in the strictest sense of the word; it was equipped with rollers that the forward movement of the firing pin forced outward into the recesses in the receiver. The breech was held closed until the pressure dropped to a safe level when the rollers were forced out of the recesses. The residual gas pressure in the chamber blew the empty case backward, taking the bolt with it and compressing the return spring, which caused the cycle to be repeated. The chief difference between the HK 33 and the G3 was that the HK 33 was designed to fire the 5.56 mm round, giving good performance at reasonable ranges and more accurate automatic fire than was possible with the more powerful 7.62 mm cartridge.

RUSSIA

BAIKAL MODEL 628 (MC-8-0) SHOTGUN 1964

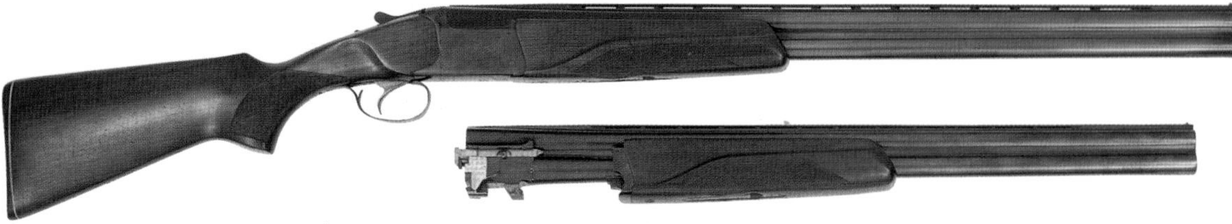

Length (gun): 43.0 in. (1,092 mm) (with longer barrels)
Barrel: long, 28.0 in. (711 mm); short, 26.0 in. (660 mm)
Weight (gun): 7.0 lb. (3.2 kg)
Caliber: 12-gauge
Rifling: none
Operation: boxlock, over-and-under
Feed: manual
Muz vel: n.k.

This gun was manufactured in the Soviet Union during the Cold War and was sold in Western countries at a low price, undercutting weapons made in Europe or North America. The Model 628 was a 12-bore with two sets of boxlock, over-and-under barrels, both of which are shown here. The longer (28 in./711 mm) set (shown here mounted) was more tightly bored and was used for trap and wild-fowling, while the shorter (26 in./660 mm), more open set (shown dismounted, below) served for skeets and upland game. The quality varied from one gun to another, but in general they were well made and had chrome-lined barrels. They were well regarded and popular with users.

GERMANY

WALTHER UIT BV UNIVERSAL 1965

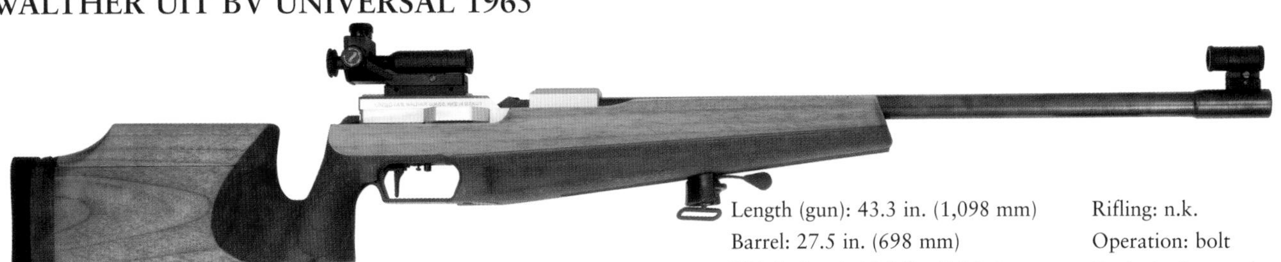

Length (gun): 43.3 in. (1,098 mm)
Barrel: 27.5 in. (698 mm)
Weight (gun): 10.5 lb. (4.8 kg)
Caliber: 0.22 LR
Rifling: n.k.
Operation: bolt
Feed: single-round, manual
Muz vel: n.k.

This rifle is made by the famous German firm Walther, of Ulm an der Donau. The Standard Rifle was introduced in the 1960s in an effort to simplify the Free Rifle designs that had become somewhat outlandish. Thus, the Standard Rifle rules banned butt plate extensions, external adjustable weights, thumbhole stocks, adjustable palm rests and cheek pieces, and forward hand rests. In addition, the maximum weight was lowered to 11 lb. (5 kg). The weapon shown here was built to Standard Rifle configuration, although the cheek piece and butt plate are capable of considerable adjustment; once set, however, they must be locked in place for the remainder of that particular competition. In the designation, "BV" stands for Blockverschluss ("block lock"). "BVE" indicated an electric trigger system, which did not prove very popular.

UNITED STATES

ARMALITE AR18 1965

Length (gun): 37.0 in. (940 mm)
Barrel: 10.1 in. (257 mm)
Weight (gun): 6.9 lb. (3 kg)
Caliber: 5.56 mm
Rifling: 6 grooves, r/hand
Operation: gas operated
Feed: 20-, 30-, 40-round box magazine
Cyclic rate: 800 rpm
Muz vel: 3,280 ft/sec. (1,000 m/sec.)

The AR18 was intended to be a cheaper alternative to the AR15, and in particular it was meant to be suitable for production in Third World countries that might lack the sophisticated tooling necessary to deal with the forged-aluminum receiver of the AR15. It used a seven-lugged rotating bolt locking into the breech end of the barrel, with a short-stroke piston driving the bolt-carrier rearward. Twin recoil springs, running on guides through the upper part of the carrier on each side, gave a well-supported, straight-line return from recoil, permitting a rigid, folding buttstock to be fitted. Construction was all steel, with extensive use made of sheet steel pressings for the upper and power receiver bodies, and for a number of external and internal parts; all furniture was plastic.

UNITED STATES

REMINGTON MODEL 1100 SHOTGUN 1965

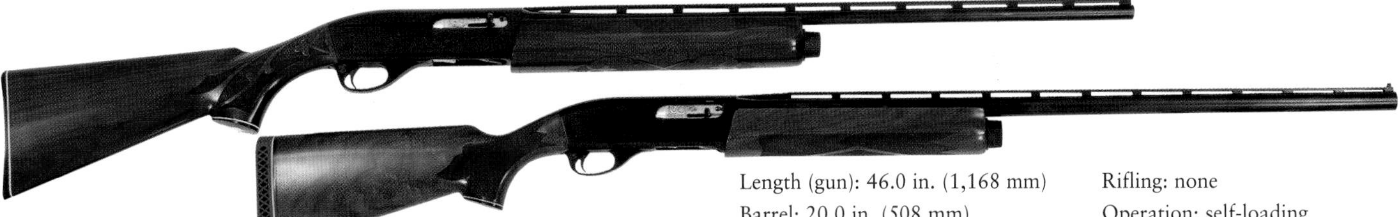

Length (gun): 46.0 in. (1,168 mm)
Barrel: 20.0 in. (508 mm)
Weight (gun): 6.0 lb. (2.72 kg)
Caliber: 0.410-gauge
Rifling: none
Operation: self-loading
Feed: 3-round tubular magazine
Muz vel: n.k.

The Model 1100 was distinguished by its piston, which surrounded the magazine tube and was impaled on two rather long and narrow gas ports. This had a "metering" effect, delivering a uniform impulse over a wide range of cartridge pressures. Remington offered the Model 1100 in four gauges—12, 20, 0.28, and 0.410—and in a host of configurations, including goose guns, quail guns, skeet guns, trap guns, deer guns, riot guns, and youth guns. There were straight-grip stocks, folding stocks, Monte Carlo stocks, and mirror-image actions for left-handers. The guns shown here are 0.410-gauge skeet gun (top, see specifications), and wild-fowler (bottom), which has a longer 30 in. (762 mm) full-choked barrel chambered for 3 in. (76.2 mm) shells.

THE M16 IN VIETNAM

Above: *A US infantryman opens up with a burst of fire from his M16 during a Vietnam firefight. Though the M16's image was undoubtedly shaken by initial reliability issues and questions over the efficacy of the 5.56 mm round, in full-auto modes it was undoubtedly a more controllable weapon than the M14 rifle.*

The war in Vietnam between 1963 and 1975 saw the clash of two contrasting types of assault rifles. On the US side was the newly introduced 5.56 mm M16A1, and the Viet Cong and the NVA generally used the Soviet AK-47. The contrasting performance of these weapons sparked a passionate argument that continues even today among Vietnam War veterans.

Although the M16 is today one of the most successful rifle types ever, its entrance into the conflict in Vietnam was not auspicious. Previously, the US infantryman had been armed with the powerful 0.30 in. (7.62 mm) M14 rifle, a heavy but robust weapon based on the redoubtable M1 Garand mechanism. For US soldiers, the switch from the M14 to the light, plastic-furniture small-caliber M16 was culture shock enough. Soon, however, the M16 began to show major deficiencies in combat.

In early actions there were reports of up to 50 percent of weapons jamming in combat, either through excessive carbon fouling in the chamber or through a spent cartridge case remaining stuck in the mouth of the chamber. Gradual analysis of the problem revealed a host of issues. First, although the powder used in the cartridges in the test and development phases of the M16 worked perfectly, the powder type was switched in the issue weapons without further testing. Not only did this powder cause excessive carbon buildup, it also worked under higher pressure, and so extraction might begin when the cartridge case was still obturated to the chamber wall. The US Army eventually introduced a cleaner-burning powder and chrome-lined the M16's chamber to reduce friction between case and the chamber. These measures solved many of the problems but others emerged, including alarming incidents of rounds being fired by bolt slam before they were properly chambered, resulting in the weapons being blown apart.

Such failings, in addition to the fact that many soldiers felt the M16 had too little killing force, initially made it an unpopular weapon. The M16A1 variant (introduced in 1967) finally seemed to make the M16 a dependable weapon with regular cleaning, but not before many US soldiers had either reclaimed their old M14s or even acquired AK-47s as combat weapons. However, the M16A2 was especially popular among South Vietnamese troops; the weapon's lightness and controllability was enjoyed by soldiers of shorter height and more slender frame than most US servicemen.

UNITED STATES

SPRINGFIELD ARMORY 7.62 MM M1A RIFLE 1965

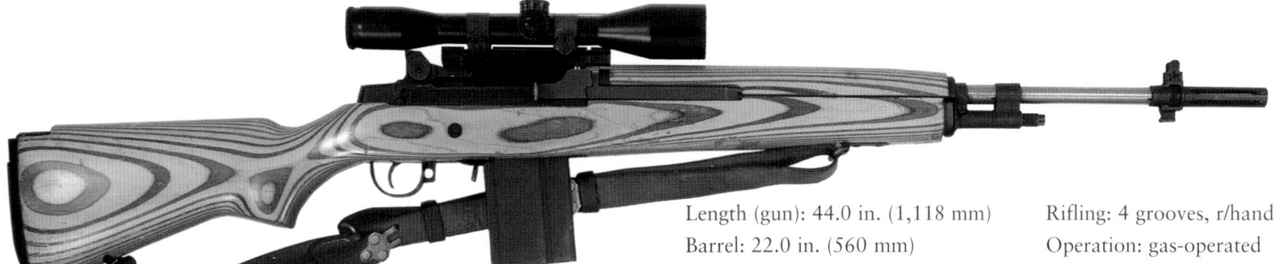

Length (gun): 44.0 in. (1,118 mm)
Barrel: 22.0 in. (560 mm)
Weight (gun): 13.5 lb. (6.1 kg)
Caliber: 7.62 mm
Rifling: 4 grooves, r/hand
Operation: gas-operated
Feed: 20-round box magazine
Muz vel: 2,800 ft./sec. (853 m/sec.)

When the Springfield Armory was closed, the name itself was sold to an Illinois-based light engineering firm that saw a golden opportunity on the civil market for the M14 rifle (qv). This weapon, developed from the Garand series, had been produced in only small numbers for the US Army when production was halted and switched to the 5.56 mm M16 (AR15 Armalite). The new company, however, placed the M14 rifle back in production for the civilian market under the company designation M1A, and this has proved to be a superb and very popular target performer.

RUSSIAN FEDERATION

DRAGUNOV 7.62 MM SNIPER RIFLE (SVD) 1967

Length (gun): 48.2 in. (1,225 mm)
Barrel: 24.5 in. (622 mm)
Weight (gun): 9.5 lb. (4.3 kg)
Caliber: 7.62 mm
Rifling: 4 grooves, r/hand
Operation: gas
Feed: 10-round box magazine
Muz vel: 2,723 ft./sec. (830 m/sec.)

Development of the SVD began in 1965, and the weapon entered service with the Soviet Army in 1967. It became the standard sniper rifle of most Warsaw Pact armies and was built under license in China, Iraq, and Romania. The SVD is gas-operated and uses a system similar to that of the AKM assault rifle, but modified to take a short-stroke piston in order to avoid the shift of balance inherent in long-stroke systems; this would upset a sniper's point of aim. The SVD has a combined flash suppressor/compensator and can mount the standard AKM bayonet. There is a cheek pad atop the open buttstock and it is fitted with a detachable, nonvariable, 4x telescopic sight, with an extension tube for eye relief. The SVD, shown in Afghan (left) and Russian (right) hands, was generally considered one of the best sniper rifles of its era.

UNITED STATES

REMINGTON 40XB BR RIFLE 1969

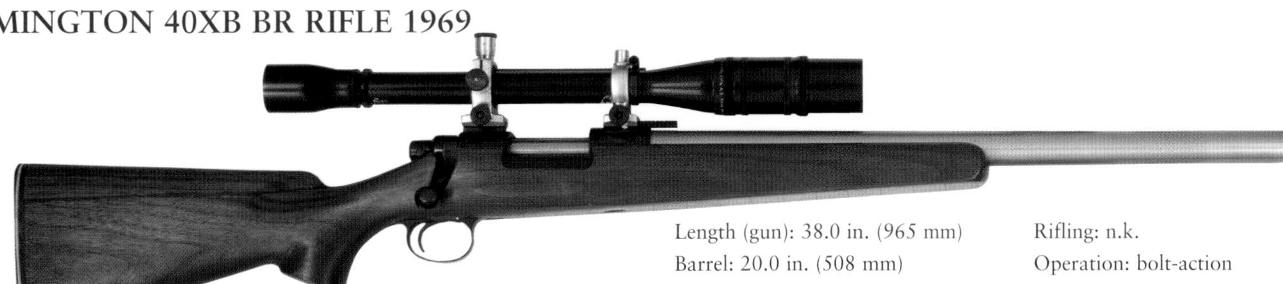

Length (gun): 38.0 in. (965 mm)
Barrel: 20.0 in. (508 mm)
Weight (gun): 10.5 lb. (4.8 kg)
Caliber: 0.222 Remington
Rifling: n.k.
Operation: bolt-action
Feed: single-round, manual
Muz vel: n.k.

Bench Rest shooting is devoted to the elimination of skill and as many variables as possible, and the promotion of accuracy and consistency. The Remington Model 40XB BR in 0.222 in. Remington caliber dominated the sport for a decade starting in 1969. It offered "out-of-the-box" accuracy of 0.4MOA and used the 0.222 cartridge with a 0.378 in. (9.6 mm) head diameter and 1.7 in. (43 mm) length, which is generally regarded as the most accurate factory cartridge ever produced. A slightly lengthened version, with the shoulder moved forward, was adopted by the US armed forces, and subsequently by NATO. The 40XB BR as shown typifies the "light varminter" of the 1970s with a short, massive, free-floating stainless-steel barrel, glass-bedded action, and walnut stock with a broad flat fore end to lie steadier on the sandbags. The telescope is a x20 Remington-Unertl with adjustments in the back mount.

ITALY

BERETTA 5.56 MM AR-70 ASSAULT RIFLE 1970

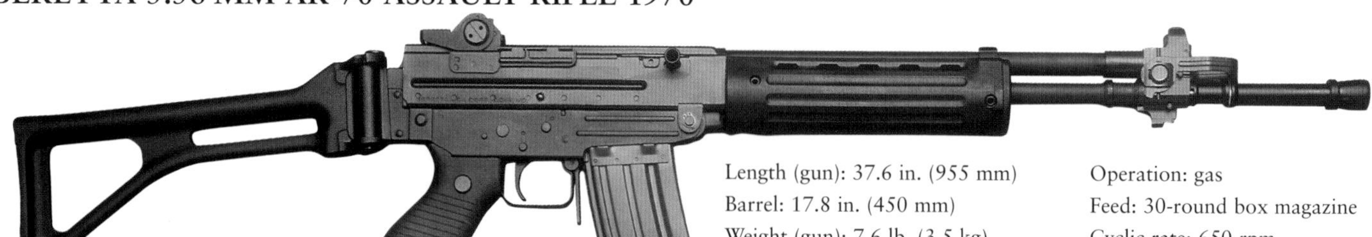

Length (gun): 37.6 in. (955 mm)
Barrel: 17.8 in. (450 mm)
Weight (gun): 7.6 lb. (3.5 kg)
Caliber: 5.56 mm
Rifling: 4 grooves, r/hand
Operation: gas
Feed: 30-round box magazine
Cyclic rate: 650 rpm
Muz vel: 3,116 ft./sec. (950 m/sec.)

The AR-70 weapon fires the 5.56 x 45 mm M193 round from a closed bolt and is gas-operated. Since the gas port has been placed close to the muzzle end of the barrel, the system needs a relatively long (14 in./355 mm) piston. Semi-automatic fire is obtained by the usual disconnector between the trigger and sear. Upper and lower receiver bodies are sheet-metal stampings, and guide rails and ejector are welded and riveted to the upper receiver shell. The hold-open system that retains the bolt group in the rearward position after the magazine has been emptied is almost identical to that used on the M16. There are two easily interchangeable buttstock configurations, with a high-impact rigid plastic stock with a steel butt plate being used in the AR-70 assault rifle version (see specifications) and a folding, tubular strutted stock in the SC-70 (special carbine).

UNITED KINGDOM

SNIPER RIFLE L42A1 1970

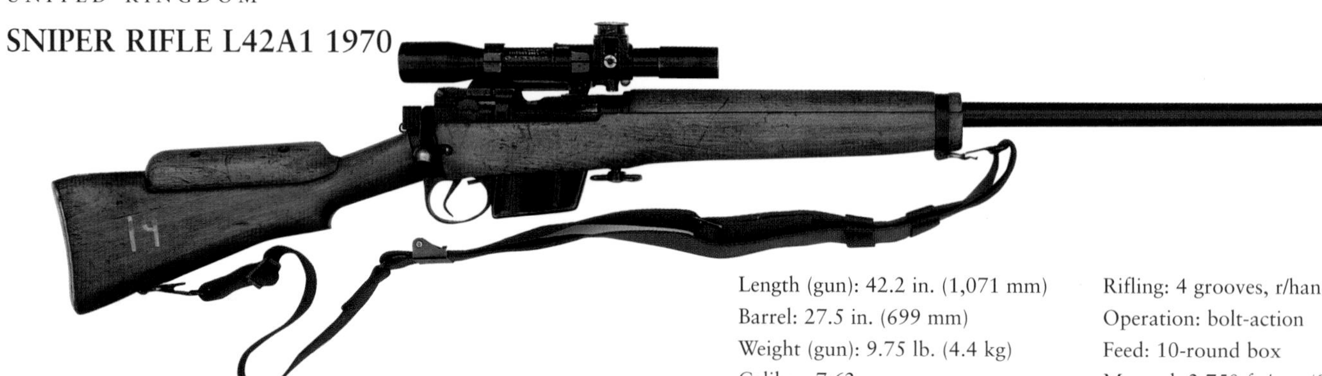

Length (gun): 42.2 in. (1,071 mm)
Barrel: 27.5 in. (699 mm)
Weight (gun): 9.75 lb. (4.4 kg)
Caliber: 7.62 mm
Rifling: 4 grooves, r/hand
Operation: bolt-action
Feed: 10-round box
Muz vel: 2,750 ft./sec. (838 m/sec.)

After 1945, the British Army neglected sniping until its long experience in internal security duties around the world made it think differently. Self-loading rifles of the time were not well suited to a telescopic sight, so it therefore became necessary to look back rather than forward for a suitable weapon. It so happened that a commercial conversion of the Number 4 rifle, the Enfield Envoy, was available; it had been developed for target use, principally by being rebarreled to fire the standard NATO rifle cartridge and by cutting it down to half stock. The Royal Small Arms Factory at Enfield then converted a number of specially selected Number 4s in similar fashion and fitted them with sights that are a modified version of the original No 32 telescopic sight.

UNITED KINGDOM

HOLLAND AND HOLLAND 0.264 IN. MAGAZINE RIFLE 1972

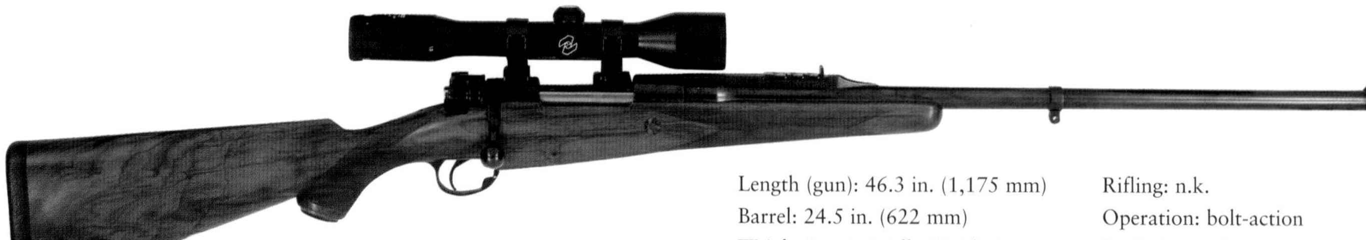

Length (gun): 46.3 in. (1,175 mm)
Barrel: 24.5 in. (622 mm)
Weight (gun): 9.6 lb. (4.4 kg)
Caliber: 0.264 in.
Rifling: n.k.
Operation: bolt-action
Feed: 4-round magazine
Muz vel: n.k.

The 0.264 in. Winchester round used in this rifle is ultimately of Holland and Holland parentage, being nothing more than the 0.458 in. necked to 0.256 in. (6.5 mm). The capacious case is doubtless somewhat over bore capacity, but the ballistics are nevertheless impressive. The standard load throws a 100-grain (6.5g) bullet at 3,700 ft./second (1,128 m/sec.), or a 140-grain (9.1g) bullet at 3,200 ft./second (975 m/sec.). Excellent sectional density helps the projectile hold its velocity and deliver a very fast trajectory. With the heavier bullet, it should be suitable for most plains game. The rifle shown has a Zeiss scope, although careful inspection will reveal an array of four V-notch back sights mounted on a quarter-rib, which are graduated to 450 yd. (411 m).

RIFLE SIGHTS

Most rifles, except those sniper/accuracy weapons intended for use with scopes only, come prefitted with one of several types of "iron" sight. By far the simplest type of open sight on modern weapons is the tangent sight at the rear, which features a V-shaped notch combined with a simple post over the muzzle. More advanced rear sights include adjustment for windage, elevation, and range, usually up to around 1,640 feet (500 m) for a standard military weapon. Guns like the AK-47 go, with wild optimism, up to 2,624 feet (800 m) in range. Improved target acquisition is gained by using an aperture ring sight at the rear, with the front post held in the center of the rear ring, which then "ghosts" out to present a clear sight picture. Aperture sights are useful for rapid target acquisition, as they allow better use of peripheral vision and provide for easier rapid target alignment; hence, they are common on military weapons such as the M16, as well as on riot weapons.

The front sight on a rifle is often a simple post, sometimes with a bead at its top, mounted flat to the barrel or set on a raised platform; on military rifles it is usually set in a steel ring to protect it from damage. Luminous Tritium dots are now frequently used to delineate the front post for low-light work.

Above: *A US infantryman holds an M16 rifle fitted with an AN/PVS-2 image-intensifying scope. This first-generation Vietnam-era Starlight scope was shock- and water-resistant, had a x4 magnification- and was powered by four AA batteries.*

Beyond open sights there are a massive range of scope options. Straightforward optical scopes are improved with various features. The reticles may feature range-finding indicators, be luminous, or have LED center dots for shooting in low-light conditions. Some sights are of the "red dot" type, with no reticle but simply a luminous red dot, which is superimposed on the target when the sight is used with both eyes open. True night-sights tend to be of either passive light-amplification (using infrared imaging) or thermal-imaging type; the former is more common. A good modern light-intensifying sight like the Zeiss Orion 80II will magnify existing light levels 20,000 times when viewed through the scope. In conditions of absolute darkness, however, more advanced IR scopes are required, which use an IR flashlight to provide a light source. Thermal-imaging devices read heat contrast signatures in the environment, and are both bulky and expensive, so they tend to be used only by police or special forces. Another useful night-aiming device is the laser sight, which projects a laser dot onto the target at the aiming point.

FEED SYSTEMS

Feed systems in rifles are often the most basic elements of the design but are among the most crucial components. The simplest of all feed systems is the manual feed used on single-shot weapons, usually on bolt-action hunting rifles. This system involves the user simply opening the bolt, inserting a round into the chamber, and closing the bolt. Opening the bolt after firing ejects the cartridge. Such a feed is obviously unsuitable for military weapons, which require a higher magazine capacity.

A far more advantageous system is magazine feed, as this permits the continuous feed of multiple rounds. Magazines can be either integral or detachable. An integral magazine is, as the name suggests, a fixed part of the weapon and is generally replenished by the user pushing either a clip or charger of rounds down through the open bolt. Note that a charger simply controls the flow of rounds down into the magazine before being discarded. A clip holds the rounds and is actually pushed into the magazine itself, and it is ejected after the last round is fired. Integral magazines have the advantage of protecting the rounds within the body of the weapon, but have they also have a limited ammunition capacity. Some integral magazines may be hinged to the weapon, allowing them to swing open for reloading or maintenance.

The detachable magazine is by far the most popular type of feed system on modern assault weapons, as it permits large ammunition capacities, typically of twenty to thirty rounds. A magazine usually consists of a rectangular metal box featuring a spring-loaded platform inside, onto which the rounds are loaded in single column or staggered double column. The wall of the magazine is usually fullered; that is, indented ribs are pressed into the wall to reduce friction against the sides of the rounds and provide a clearance space for any dirt inside the magazine. The magazine lips must place each round precisely in front of the bolt ready to be stripped off and fed into the chamber. Shooters must take good care of magazines if the gun is to function correctly, emptying them when not in use to preserve the strength of the spring, and taking care to avoid damage to the feed lips.

Top and above: *The Steyr AUG (Armee Universal Gewehr) rifle was first taken up by the Austrian Army in 1977. By changing barrels and using a bipod, this bullpup rifle can be transformed into an assault rifle, a carbine, or a light machine gun. The stock and magazine are of high-grade plastic. The 30- or 42-shot box is transparent.*

GERMANY

HECKLER AND KOCH G3SG/1 7.62 MM SNIPER RIFLE 1973

Length (gun): 40.2 in. (1,021 mm)
Barrel: 17.7 in. (450 mm)
Weight (gun): 12.2 lb. (5.5 kg)
Caliber: 7.62 mm
Rifling: 4 grooves, r/hand
Operation: delayed blowback
Feed: 20-round box magazine
Muz vel: 2,625 ft./sec. (800 m/sec.)

The Heckler and Koch G3 rifle (qv) replaced the FN FAL in the West German Army from 1959 on. The first sniper version was the G3A3ZF, introduced in 1964, which was simply a G3 with a telescopic sight. A more substantial modification came with the G3SG/1 in 1973, when specially selected specimens of the G3A3 version were converted for use as sniper rifles. This version retains the great majority of the features of the G3 but has a new trigger, buttstock, and bipod. The G3SG/1 retains the G3's iron sights but also has a mounting rail for a Zeiss 1.5-6x scope. There is a modified trigger that features a "set" lever behind the trigger itself, the use of which reduces the pull to 2.8 lb. (1.3 kg). The buttstock is fitted with a detachable comb that allows for up to 1 in. (25.4 mm) of variation for proper eye-to-scope orientation. There is also a detachable cheek rest.

ISRAEL

GALIL 7.62/5.56 MM ARM ASSAULT RIFLE 1973

Length (gun): 38.6 in. (979 mm)
Barrel: 18.1 in. (460 mm)
Weight (gun): 9.6 lb. (4.4 kg)
Caliber: 5.56 mm
Rifling: 6 grooves, r/hand
Operation: gas
Feed: 35- or 50-round box magazine
Cyclic rate: 700 rpm
Muz vel: 3,116 ft./sec. (950 m/sec.)

Israel's Galil 7.62 mm assault rifle operates using a rotating-bolt gas system, and with the exception of the stamped-steel breech cover, the Galil is fully machined. The foregrip is wood, lined with Dural, and has ample clearance around the barrel for heat dissipation. When extended, the buttstock has a positive latching system that prevents wobble by wedging the hinge end's tapered latching lugs into corresponding slots. The ambidextrous safety switch on the left side is a small lever, but its reciprocal right-side member also acts as an ejection port cover. The Galil ARM originally appeared in 1973 as a 7.62 mm (lower photo) weapon, firing the NATO standard round, in three versions: assault rifle/light machine gun (as described above); assault rifle (basically the ARM, but minus the bipod); and the SAR (short assault rifle), which had a shorter barrel (15.8 inches/400 mm). This series was followed by the 5.56 mm weapon (see top photo and specifications), which was a scaled-down version of the 7.62 mm weapon.

UNITED KINGDOM

WEBLEY AND SCOTT MODEL 700 SHOTGUN c. 1970

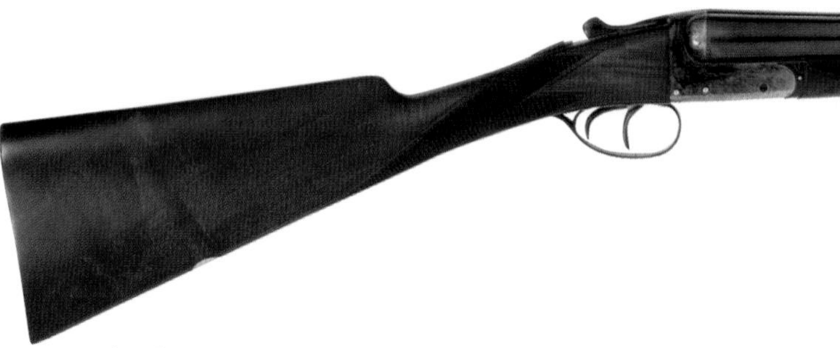

Length (gun): 43.0 in. (1,092 mm)
Barrel: 26.0 in. (660 mm)
Weight (gun): 6.3 lb. (2.9 kg)
Caliber: 12-gauge
Rifling: none
Operation: break-open, boxlock
Feed: manual
Muz vel: n.k.

The internationally respected British firm Webley and Scott was founded in about 1900. The company was well known for its action, in which the forward lump of the barrels showed through the action body—a method not commonly used by other makers of boxlock guns. When production of sporting guns resumed after World War II, demand quickly outstripped supply and production delays led to an increasing number of imports, particularly from Spain. The gun-making business was sold off to a group of former employees, who created a new company with the much earlier name of W. and C. Scott Ltd., although this has since been taken over by Holland and Holland (qv). By the late 1980s the Model 700 seen here (which is also known as the "Kinmount") was one of the cheapest British-made double guns still on the market. The rare (just 40 made) Model 710 was an upgraded version of the 700.

RUSSIAN FEDERATION

5.45 MM AK-74 ASSAULT RIFLE 1973

Length (gun): 37.6 in. (950 mm)
Barrel: 16.3 in. (415 mm)
Weight (gun): 10.7 lb. (4.85 kg)
Caliber: 5.45 mm
Rifling: 4 grooves, r/hand
Operation: gas
Magazine: 30-round box
Cyclic rate: 650 rpm
Muz vel: 2.953 ft./sec. (900 m/sec.)

The AK-74 was introduced in 1973, chambered for 5.54 mm, following examination of captured US M16s from Vietnam. Compared to the earlier AK-47 and AKM rifles, it had a larger muzzle brake, and a groove in each side of the butt allowed the AK-74 to be identified by feel; otherwise it looks identical to the earlier, larger-caliber rifles. The early AK-74s had laminated wood or composite furniture; later models used plastic. As many as thirteen variants have been made, including the AK-74M, with a folding butt, which replaced the 74 in the late 1980s; it had a rail for light intensifier, optical, or passive infrared sights. The AKS-74 was a shortened version with a folding skeleton butt for crews of armored vehicles and paratroops. The AKS-74U was an even shorter version, introduced in 1979; it is only 26.55 in. (67.5cm) long.

GERMANY

MAUSER SP-66 1976

Length (gun): 44.29 in. (1,120 mm)
Barrel: 25.59 in. (650 mm)
Weight (gun): 13.5 lb. (6.12 kg)
Caliber: 7.62 x 51 mm NATO
Rifling: 4 grooves, r/hand
Operation: bolt-action
Feed: 3-round integral box magazine
Muz vel: 2848 ft./sec. (868 m/sec.)

The Mauser SP-66 emerged in 1976 as a military/police sniper variant of the Mauser Model 66 Super Match competition rifle. It utilizes a short-throw bolt-action system to achieve cartridge ejection with minimal operator movement (the cocking handling is set toward the front of the bolt), and bolt locking is accomplished by two lugs that engage with the barrel extension. Ammunition is fed from a three-round integral box magazine. The heavy match-grade barrel is made from rustproof steel and is fitted with a flash-hider/muzzle-brake combination. The gun's furniture is of laminated wood and features a fully adjustable stock and cheek pad with a thumbhole-type configuration. Standard sighting fitment on the rifle is the Zeiss Diavari ZA telescopic sight with a x1.5–6 variable power (there are no iron sight fittings). The SP-66 is used by the German military and security forces in Israel and Italy.

UNITED KINGDOM

4.85 MM INDIVIDUAL WEAPON 1976

Length (gun): 30.3 in. (770 mm)
Barrel: 20.4 in. (518 mm)
Weight (gun): 8.5 lb. (3.9 kg)
Caliber: 4.85 mm
Rifling: 4 grooves, r/hand
Operation: gas
Feed: 20-round box
Cyclic rate: n.k.
Muz vel: 2,952 ft./sec. (900 m/sec.)

By the early 1970s it was clear that an assault rifle was necessary because the existing rifle was too long and bulky for modern armored warfare. The weapon developed bears a strong outward resemblance to the EM 2 but is smaller, lighter, and more advanced. It is gas-operated with a rotating bolt, has an optical sight, and fires single rounds or bursts. There is a heavy-barreled version with a light tripod, and about 80 percent of the components are common to both weapons. A thirty-round magazine is available for a grenade-firing type, although each version will take both kinds of magazine. The gun fires from a closed bolt, i.e., the round is prepositioned in the chamber ready to fire. When NATO decided to standardize on the 5.56 x 45 mm SS109 cartridge, the British ceased development of their 4.85 mm cartridge and produced a new weapon, based on the 4.85 IW.

AUSTRIA

STEYR AUG 5.56 MM 1977

Length (gun): 31.1 in. (790 mm)
Barrel: 20.0 in. (508 mm)
Weight (gun): 7.9 lb. (3.6 kg)
Caliber: 5.56 mm
Rifling: 6 grooves, r/hand
Operation: gas
Feed: 30-round box magazine
Cyclic rate: 650 rpm
Muz vel: 3,182 ft./sec. (970 m/sec.)

The excellent Armee Universal Gewehr (universal army rifle) was designed to meet an Austrian Army requirement and entered service in 1977 (designated the StuG-77). It is fitted with a Swarovski x1.5 scope mounted in the carrying handle. Barrels can be changed rapidly, locking into a machined steel ring contained within the cast-aluminum breech housing; the bolt-head locks into the same steel ring. The gun uses a rotating bolt that recoils along two substantial guide rods, the right one housing the operating rod. Both rods impinge on recoil springs contained with the buttstock. The use of polymers extends to the firing unit, most components of which were originally plastic, although some were later replaced by metal parts. The magazine is translucent to enable the firer to see how many rounds remain unfired.

ITALY

FRANCHI SPAS 12 SHOTGUN 1979

Length (gun): 41.0 in. (1,041 mm)
Barrel: 21.5 in. (546 mm)
Weight (gun): 9.6 lb. (4.4 kg)
Caliber: 12-gauge
Rifling: none

Operation: see text
Feed: 8-round tubular magazine
Cyclic rate 24–30 rpm (practical)
Muz vel: n.k.

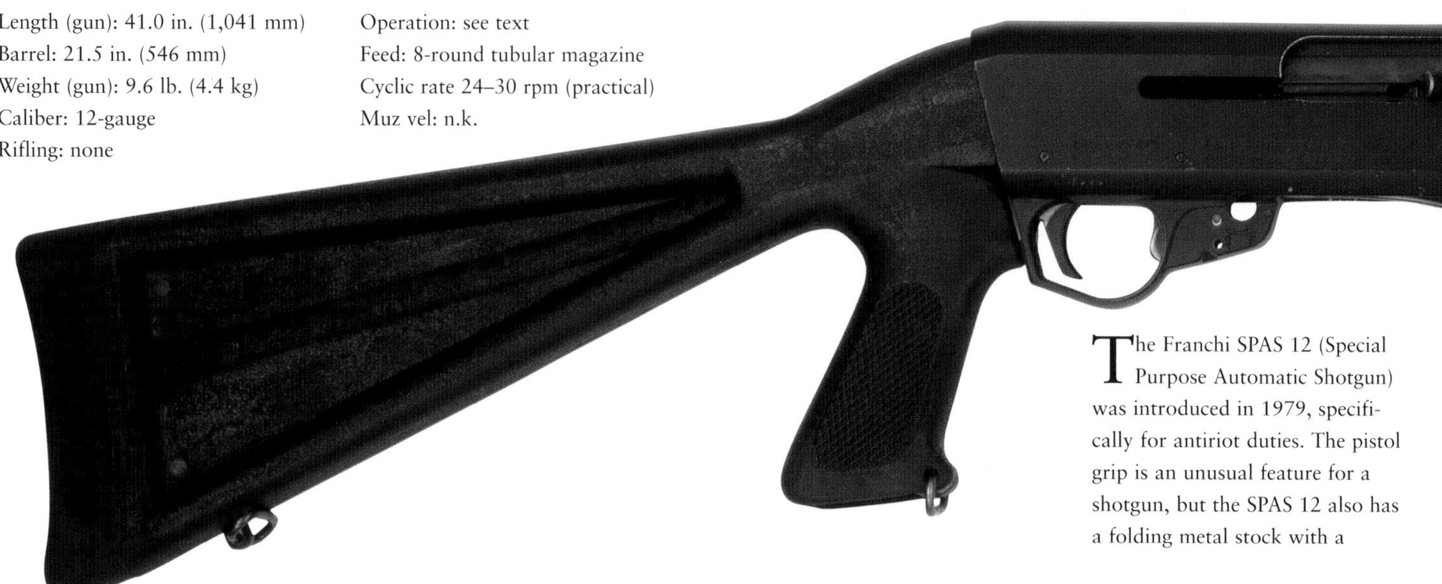

The Franchi SPAS 12 (Special Purpose Automatic Shotgun) was introduced in 1979, specifically for antiriot duties. The pistol grip is an unusual feature for a shotgun, but the SPAS 12 also has a folding metal stock with a

FRANCE

FA MAS 5.56 MM ASSAULT RIFLE 1980

Length (gun): 29.8 in. (757 mm)
Barrel: 19.2 in. (488 mm)
Weight (gun): 8.1 lb. (3.7 kg)
Caliber: 5.56 mm
Rifling: 4 grooves, r/hand

Operation: delayed blowback
Feed: 25-round box magazine
Cyclic rate 950 rpm
Muz vel: 3,150 ft./sec. (960 m/sec.)

The FA MAS (Fusil Automatique, Manufacture d'Armes de St Etienne) was introduced into service in 1980 and has proven to be an effective and generally well-conceived weapon. It fires the 5.56 x 45 mm French round from the closed-bolt position, using a delayed blowback mechanism that was derived from the French AA-52 general-purpose machine gun. Because it has a "bullpup" configuration, the trigger mechanism and pistol grip have been mounted to the lower hand guard, forward of the magazine housing. Among the features of the FA MAS are the prominent carrying handle (which also houses the sight), left- or right-side ejection, a three-round burst option, and a built-in biped, whose legs fold individually against the receiver when not in use. A slightly modified export version has a revised trigger guard and fires the standard 5.56 x 45 mm NATO round.

pivoting "shepherd's crook," which hooks under the forearm; holding the pistol grip, the shooter can fire the gun single-handed. The massive front end derives from the fact that the SPAS 12 is a dual-function gun, capable of operating with pump action or as a gas-operated self-loader. An inset pushbutton in the fore end can be clicked rearward, closing the gas system for manual operation. The purpose of this is to allow the gun to be used as a manual repeater with special low-pressure ammunition, which would not be sufficiently powerful to cycle it as a self-loader. Examples are gas munitions, plastic baton rounds, high explosives, and flares. A launcher can be fitted to the muzzle, enabling grenades to be fired to a range of 165 yd. (150 m). The gun shown here has a molded Choate replacement stock, minus the hook.

GERMANY

WALTHER KK MATCH GX1 1980

Length (gun): 43.2 in. (1,098 mm)
Barrel: 25.8 in.(654 mm)
Weight (gun): 12.4 lb. (5.6 kg)
Caliber: 0.22 in. LR
Rifling: n.k.
Operation: bolt
Feed: single-round, manual
Muz vel: n.k.

The UIT Free Rifle is a sophisticated piece of engineering; because it is fired from the standing position, its engineering must compensate for the lack of a solid rest. A Free Rifle is so called because it is relatively free of restriction. It must have no optical sight, the pistol grip may not contact the sling, weight must not exceed 17.6 lb. (8 kg), butt hooks must not exceed 6 inches (153 mm), and the forward palm rest must not extend more than 7.9 inches (200 mm) below the centerline of the barrel. The picture shows the Walther KK Match GX1, a top-quality UIT Free Rifle made of steel, with a one-piece walnut stock. This is the bare rifle; for competition it would have a number of accessories, including a long armpit prong extending from the butt plate and a black elastic tape some 2 inches (51 mm) wide along the complete length of the barrel to break heatwaves.

UNITED KINGDOM

PARKER-HALE MODEL 81 CLASSIC 1981

Length (gun): 44.5 in. (1,130 mm)
Barrel: 24.0 in. (610 mm)
Weight (gun): 7.8 lb. (3.5 kg)
Caliber: 0.30-06
Rifling: n.k.
Operation: bolt-action
Feed: 4-round magazine
Muz vel: n.k.

The Model 81 Classic was made by Parker-Hale in Birmingham, England, using that company's hammer-forged barrels and a new commercial receiver made by the La Coruna arsenal in Spain. The Model 81 was manufactured by Parker-Hale and then bought by the London firm Rigby, which then did some additional work on it before marketing it under their combined names. The Model 81 was rated as a fine rifle, the only noteworthy modification a side-mounted safety, which became necessary if a scope was fitted. This picture shows such a rifle, fitted with a Pecar 1 x 4 variable, although it also carries the standard ("as supplied") gold-bead fore sight and Williams semi-buckhorn U-notch back sight; the latter is adjustable for windage and elevation.

SOUTH AFRICA

VEKTOR 5.56 MM R4/R5/R6 RIFLES 1982

Length (gun): 39. in. (1,005 mm)
Barrel: 18.1 in. (460 mm)
Weight (gun): 9.4 lb. (4.3 kg)
Caliber: 7.62 mm
Rifling: 6 grooves, r/hand

Operation: gas
Feed: 35-round box magazine
Cyclic rate: 700 rpm
Muz vel: 3,215 ft./sec. (980 m/sec.)

In the 1970s and 1980s, there was close cooperation in defense matters between Israel and South Africa, one fruit of which was the 5.56 mm R4 rifle (see specifications), which was, in essence, a modified version of the Israeli Galil rifle (qv). The R4 was first fielded in 1982 and replaced the Belgian FN FAL and Heckler and Koch G3 in South African service. The modifications were intended to make the weapon easier to use by the South African troops, who were taller and more heavily built than the Israelis, and also to meet the more stringent demands of bush warfare. The R5 (top photo) was a shorter version of the R4 (bottom photo) used by the South African Marine Corps and Air Force. The R6 was an even shorter version, 31.7 in. (805 mm) overall, intended for use by airborne troops and tank/vehicle crewmen.

GERMANY

HECKLER AND KOCH PSG-1 7.62 MM SNIPER RIFLE 1982

Length (gun): 47.6 in. (1,208 mm)
Barrel: 25.6 in. (650 mm)
Weight (gun): 17.0 lb. (8.1kg)
Caliber: 7.62 mm
Rifling: 4 grooves, r/hand, polygonal

Operation: delayed blowback
Feed: 5- or 20-round box magazine
Muz vel: 2,723 ft./sec. (830 m/sec.)

The PSG-1 was developed in the early 1980s to meet the renewed military and police requirement for a long-range and very accurate weapon. The PSG-1 uses Heckler and Koch's roller-locked bolt system and fires semi-automatic single shots only. Its design was based on that of the G3 military assault rifle (qv), but it is fitted with a polygonally bored, heavy, free-floating barrel; the trigger, fitted with an adjustable trigger shoe, is normally set to break at 3.3 lb. (1.5 kg). A special low-noise, bolt-closing device is fitted, and the stock has an adjustable comb and a butt pad that allow fitting to individual shooters. A bipod attaches directly to the stock. The PSG-1 is normally fitted with the Hensoldt 6 x 42 scope with LED-enhanced manual reticle. The scope-mounted activator produces a helpful red dot for approximately thirty seconds, plenty of time to get off that critical shot.

BULLPUP DESIGNS

A bullpup weapon is a firearm that locates the rifle operating mechanism between the grip and the butt plate, thereby utilizing space that on an ordinary rifle is simply taken up by a wooden or plastic stock. Bullpup systems offer several key advantages. First, the weapon can be dramatically shortened while retaining a long barrel length. The British SA80, for example, has a barrel of 20.4 inches (518 mm) in a weapon that has a total length of 30.9 inches (785 mm). Compare this to the XM16A2—with a barrel length of 20 inches (510 mm) in a gun 44.2 inches (1,122 mm) long. Furthermore, because the weight of the mechanism is set to the rear, the weapon's center of gravity is closer to the user, making it easy to hold in a stable, aimed position.

It was not until after World War II that bullpup weapons emerged as a full-fledged concept. The first was Enfield's 7 mm EM2, a gas-operated weapon with the magazine set well behind the pistol grip. Trials showed the EM2 to be reliable and accurate, but because of political resistance to the short-range cartridge concept used in the weapon, the EM2 never got beyond the prototype stage.

The bullpup concept remained in the background of weapons design until the 1970s, when France, Austria, and the UK all produced new designs. France developed the 5.56 mm FAMAS rifle, a delayed-blowback weapon of such quality that it became the standard French army rifle from the early 1980s. Austria also produced an excellent weapon, the 5.56 mm Steyr AUG, a futuristic-looking, tough weapon featuring a x1.4 optical sight built into the carrying handle. The AUG has been adopted by several armies, including those of Australia, New Zealand, Ireland, and Austria itself.

The most controversial bullpup weapon has been the British SA80, adopted as a replacement for the 7.62 mm SLR in 1985. The development phase of the SA80 saw some unwanted political influence, and as a consequence the weapon was pushed into production with many reliability problems outstanding. Deficiencies included poor-quality magazines, bolt bounce, and weak ejection and extraction systems. Over recent years the SA80 has been revamped, resulting in the SA80A2. Very thorough testing of this weapon in arctic, desert, and jungle conditions showed a Mean Round Between Failure (MRBF) of a phenomenal 6,745 rounds. If it continues to prove itself in action, the SA80A2 may well confirm the bullpup system as the future direction for many assault rifle systems.

Above: *The French FAMAS (Fusil Automatique Manufacture d'Armes de St Etienne) assault rifle has been one of the most successful bullpup weapons since World War II. It was adopted as the standard French Army rifle in the late 1970s and is a delayed-blowback weapon firing from a closed-bolt position. Despite its relatively short length of only 29.8 inches (757 mm), it can also be fired from a bipod.*

CHINA (PRC)

NORINCO 7.62 MM TYPE 81 ASSAULT RIFLE 144

Length (gun): 37.6 in. (955 mm)
Barrel: 15.8 in. (400 mm)
Weight (gun): 7.5 lb. (3.4 kg)
Caliber: 7.62 mm
Rifling: 4 grooves, r/hand
Operation: gas
Feed: 30-round box magazine (see text)
Cyclic rate: 750 rpm
Muz vel: 2,395 ft./sec. (730 m/sec.)

The People's Liberation Army (PLA) commenced indigenous rifle production with the Type 56 assault rifle, a Kalashnikov clone, and the Type 56 Carbine, which was a direct copy of the Russian Simonov SKS. The first Chinese weapon was the Type 68 Rifle, which combined features of the Simonov and Kalashnikov systems; but with the Type 81 Chinese designers began to innovate. The Type 81 is based on the Type 68 and used the Kalashnikov receiver and stock. It has a gas-operated action and is normally fed from a thirty-round box magazine, although a seventy-five-round drum magazine can also be fitted. The Type 81 has a solid butt, whereas the Type 81-1 has a frame butt that folds sideways to the right, although in other respects it appears no different from the Type 81. There is also a Type 81 light machine gun, with most components being interchangeable.

UNITED STATES

BARRETT 0.50 IN. MODEL 82A1 "LIGHT FIFTY" 1983

Length (gun): 61.0 in. (1,550 mm)
Barrel: 29.0 in. (737 mm)
Weight (gun): 44 lb. (13.4 kg)
Caliber: 0.50 in. (12.7 mm)
Rifling: 8 grooves, r/hand
Operation: recoil-operated
Feed: 11-round box magazine
Muz vel: 2,798 ft./sec. (853 m/sec.)

Introduced in 1983, the Barrett "Light Fifty" fires the 0.50 in. Browning (12.7 x 9 mm) round and was intended for use as a high-power, long-range sniper weapon. It operates on the short-recoil principle, with a substantial amount of energy imparted by the cartridge to the bolt face when barrel and bolt carrier start to travel to the rear. Once the bolt carrier disengages from the barrel, the latter is moved forward again by a spring, while the bolt carrier extracts and ejects the spent case, then loads a new round. Maximum effective range is 1,970 yd. (1,800 m). The next version, the M82A2, was introduced in 1992. This has a bullpup configuration. The shoulder rest is beneath the butt, immediately behind the magazine housing; this allows the rear end of the receiver to pass over the firer's shoulder. The pistol grip/trigger group is forward of the magazine housing, and a reversed pistol grip serves as the forward hand grip. There is no built-in bipod, as the weapon can be fired without one. The overall result is slightly smaller, lighter, and simpler than the M82A1: length, 55.5 in. (1,410 mm); weight 29.0 lb. (12.2 kg).

GERMANY

BLASER "ULTIMATE" SR830 RIFLE 1984

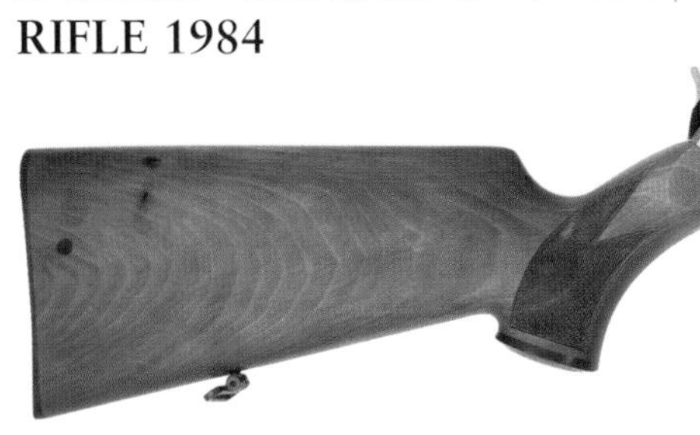

Length (gun): 40.3 in. (1,022 mm)
Barrel: 22.0 in. (559 mm)
Weight (gun): 7.7 lb. (3.5 kg)
Caliber: 0.270 Winchester (see text)
Rifling: n.k.
Operation: bolt
Feed: 2-round magazine
Muz vel: n.k.

The Blaser "Ultimate" entered the market in 1984. It incorporated some novel ideas in the search for a "take-down" rifle that worked. Mauser re-entered this field some thirty years ago with its Model 66, which had no receiver in the traditional sense but rather a set of rails that carried a bolt head mounted on a pistol-like slide. The bolt head locked into the barrel extension, and all the stress of the discharge was taken there. Recoil transfer to the stock was a problem, which took several redesigns to solve. Blaser built on Mauser's experience, using a two-piece stock and a bolt-bearing slide mounted on an aluminum receiver, with the barrel mounted on a forward extension of the receiver. The gun comes apart in a moment; the barrels interchange with a hexagonal (Allen) screw and are said to return to zero and shoot subminute of angle groups. Ten different-caliber barrels are offered for the SR830.

ITALY

BERETTA SPECIAL TRAP MODEL 682 1984

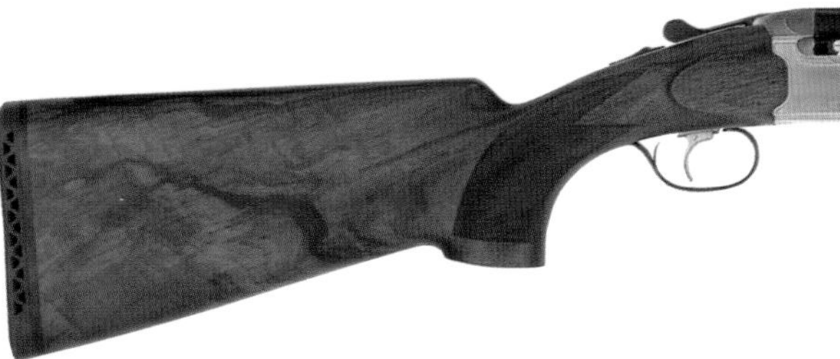

Length (gun): 47.0 in. (1,194 mm)
Barrel: 30.0 in. (762 mm)
Weight (gun): 8.0 lb. (3.6 kg)
Caliber: 12-gauge
Rifling: none
Operation: dropdown
Feed: manual
Muz vel: n.k.

Trap shooting, or, as it was called in Britain, "down-the-line" shooting, evolved directly from the nineteenth-century sport of putting a live, specially bred pigeon under an old top hat, which was then pulled away by a cord, thus releasing the bird. The gun (there was only one shooter at a time) then fired at the bird. By the 1890s the sport had spread over most of Europe, and special guns were being designed and made for it. Often known as "pigeon guns," these were generally heavier than game guns because the shot loads allowed for trap shooting were usually 1.25 ounces (35.5 g), and the extra weight of the gun counteracted the extra recoil. When the shooting of live pigeons from traps was banned, it gave a great boost to the sport of clay-pigeon shooting, which had, in fact, begun in the 1880s. This very modern Beretta trap-shooting gun is an over-and-under weapon, specifically designed for this sport.

UNITED KINGDOM

5.56 MM L85A1 INDIVIDUAL WEAPON 1984

Length (gun): 30.9 in. (785 mm)
Barrel: 20.4 in. (518 mm)
Weight (gun): 8.4 lb. (3.8 kg)
Caliber: 5.56 mm
Rifling: 6 grooves, r/hand
Operation: gas
Feed: 30-round box magazine
Cyclic rate: 800 rpm
Muz vel: 3,084 ft./sec. (940 m/sec.)

The 5.56 mm L85A1 Individual Weapon, also known as the SA80, entered British Army service in 1985. It is a bullpup design using conventional gas operation, with a rotating bolt that engages in lugs in the rear of the breech. The design makes maximum use of stampings, pressings, and spot-welding for the metal components, and of high-impact plastic elsewhere. It was designed to use an optical sight—the Sight Unit, Small Arms, Trilux (SUSAT)—which enables trainee infantrymen to attain a high standard of accuracy very quickly; soldiers of other arms are issued weapons with iron sights. Over the first decade of service it received a good deal of criticism, especially concerning its reliability and the fact that it cannot be fired satisfactorily by left-handers. With time, experience, and numerous minor modifications, it is now, in the form of the SA80A2, a satisfactory weapon.

ITALY

BERETTA SPECIAL SKEET MODEL 682 1985

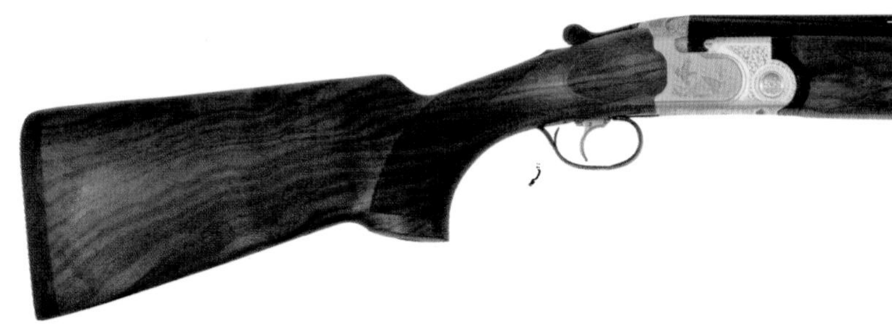

Length (gun): 45.3 in. (1,149 mm)
Barrel: 28.0 in. (711 mm)
Weight (gun): 7.8 lb. (3.5 kg)
Caliber: 12-gauge
Rifling: none
Operation: over-and-under dropdown
Feed: single round, manual
Muz vel: n.k.

Beretta is one of the largest firearms-manufacturing companies in the world and for many years claimed to be the oldest in continuous existence, dating back to 1680. Further records have, however, been discovered relating to a Bartolomeo Beretta (1490–1567), a master barrel-maker in Brescia, Italy, showing that the company is even older than the Beretta family itself, which still runs the company, had known. The Skeet Model 682 is one of several skeet models offered by the company and is an over-and-under weapon with a dropdown operation. The weapon has fully interchangeable multichokes to adjust the shot spread, the skeet discipline usually requiring fairly wide choking to maximize the spread of shot.

UNITED KINGDOM

ACCURACY INTERNATIONAL L96A1 7.62 MM SNIPER RIFLE 1985

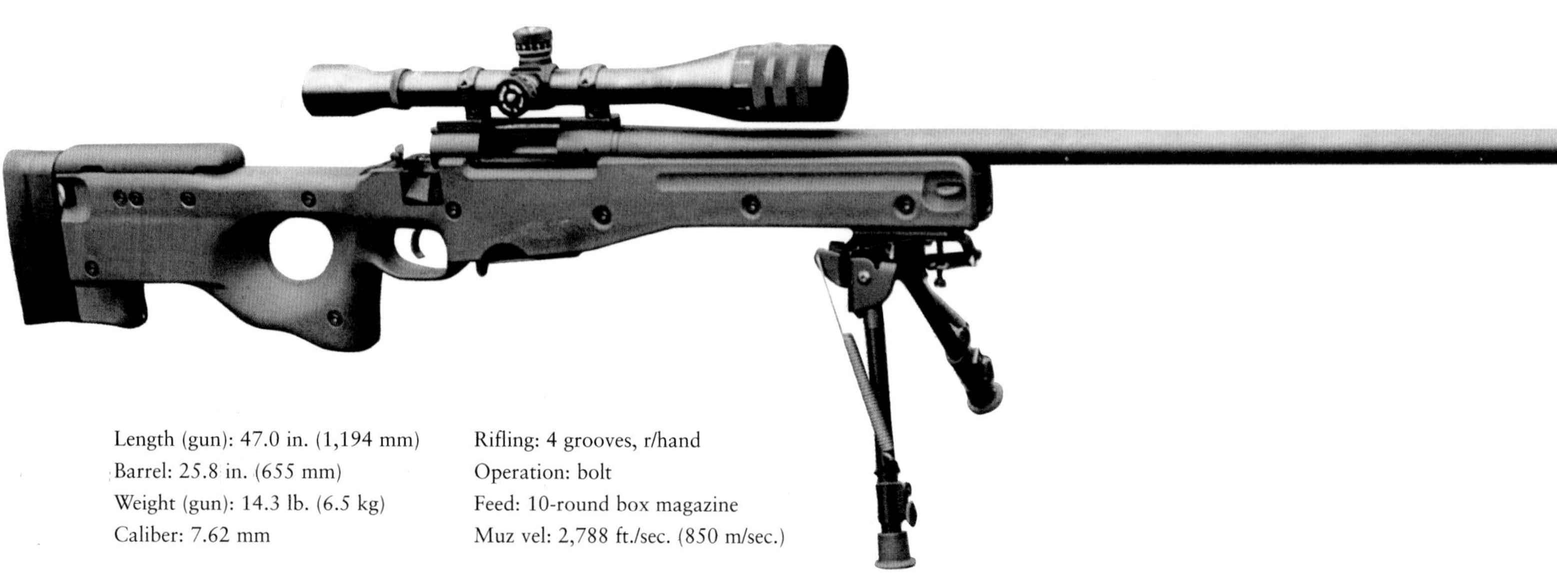

Length (gun): 47.0 in. (1,194 mm)
Barrel: 25.8 in. (655 mm)
Weight (gun): 14.3 lb. (6.5 kg)
Caliber: 7.62 mm
Rifling: 4 grooves, r/hand
Operation: bolt
Feed: 10-round box magazine
Muz vel: 2,788 ft./sec. (850 m/sec.)

Sniper rifles went out of fashion in the 1960s and 1970s, but in the 1980s and early 1990s there was a strong resurgence, with many models becoming available. One weapon designed from the start for sniping is the Accuracy International Model PM. This was designed to meet challenging criteria: guaranteed first-round accuracy; unchanging zero; a stock unaffected by environmental changes; bipod; stock and trigger adjustable to meet an individual firer's requirements; telescopic sight; reliability; interoperability; and economy. The solution fixed upon by A.I. was to use a massive and very stiff integral chassis, which is impervious to environmental changes and is precisely reproducible. The barrel is made of stainless steel and has a normal accuracy life in excess of 5,000 rounds. It attaches to the action by a screw thread bedding against a locking ring and can be changed in about five minutes without stripping the rifle. The sniper can carry out all but the most major repairs on his weapon himself with three Allen keys and a screwdriver. All accessories mate directly to the chassis, including the stock, butt, spacers, sling swivels, trigger unit, magazine and catch, hand stop, and bipod. The weapon entered service with the British armed forces in 1985 as the L96A1.

THE SWITCH TO SMALL CALIBER

During the 1960s, designers of small arms were faced with several problems concerning rifle ammunition. The 0.30 x 2.0 in. (7.62 x 51 mm) NATO round was dominant, with a killing range in excess of one mile (1.6 km) and a muzzle velocity of about 2,723 feet/second (830 m/sec.). While the knockdown power of the 7.62 mm round was not to be doubted, it did present problems. It generated heavy recoil forces, making it unsuited to three-round burst and full-auto fire in an assault rifle, extending the training times required to reach competency and making accurate shooting more difficult.

The solution was a smaller caliber round. NATO ammunition trials were conducted between 1977 and 1980 with three main competitors: the 0.22 x 1.77 in. (5.56 x 45 mm) M193, the 0.22 x 1.77 in. (5.56 x 45 mm) SS109, and the 0.19 in. (4.75 mm) caseless (fired from the Heckler and Koch G11). The SS109, which was already serving the US Army in its M16 rifles, won and became the standard NATO round.

Controversy has dogged the shift away from the 7.62 mm round to this day, the dispute concerning "terminal ballistics" (the effect a bullet has on its target). At combat ranges of around 984 feet (300 m), the 55g SS109/M855 (the M855 is the current M16A2 round) is undoubtedly a powerful killing round. Its 3,280-feet/second (1,000 m/sec.) muzzle velocity translates into a large temporary cavitation in the target, owing to supersonic shockwaves pushing the tissue apart, and because the round usually fragments within 656 feet (200 m), stripping off metal and tumbling when it moves through a heavier-than-air medium. The takedown power is ensured if a vital area is struck. At long ranges the picture changes slightly to favor the 7.62 mm round, which causes cavitation more through tumbling rather than fragmentation. In British Army tests, the 7.62 mm round penetrated a CRISAT (NATO-sponsored Collaborative Research into Small Arms Technology) armored vest at up to 1,968 feet (600 m), the SS109 up to 1,870 feet (570 m). The crucial point is that the SS109 loses velocity far quicker than the 7.62 mm round, although its bullet-drop rates are roughly the same as those of the larger round. The 5.56 mm round appears perfectly adequate for standard infantry range engagements. The most important factor in the debate, however, is that any bullet must hit a vital physical structure to guarantee a kill on a human target; cavitation or physical shock are not sufficient in themselves.

Below: *The M16 rifle led the way in the adoption of the 5.56 x 45 mm round as the standard NATO cartridge. Today almost all major Western armies use the 5.56 mm round in their standard rifles. There is little sign of dissatisfaction with 5.56 mm, and the XM8, the US Army's prototype replacement for the M16A2, is also chambered for the standard 5.5 mm cartridge.*

FINLAND

TIKKA T3 TACTICAL 1985

Length (gun): 40 in. (1,020 mm)
Barrel: 20 in. (510 mm)
Weight (gun): 8 lb. (3 kg)
Caliber: .223 Remington

Rifling: 5 grooves
Operation: bolt
Feed: 6-round clip
Muz vel: n.k.

The Tikka T3 Tactical is one of the highly successful T3 range. It is a bolt-action rifle with a two-lug locking action and is fed from a five- or six-cartridge single-column detachable clip, the ammunition capacity depending on the caliber (five-clip magazine for the .308 Winchester and .300 Winchester Magnum versions, and six-clip magazine for the .223 Remington version). For enhanced accuracy, the barrel is of a heavy free-floating design and is cold-hammer forged. If required, the muzzle can be fitted with a suppressor or muzzle brake. The trigger pull is fully adjustable between 2 and 4 lb. (1–2 kg). No open sights are supplied with the standard T3 Tactical, although these can be fitted as an option. As with most modern accuracy rifles, the furniture is highly adjustable. The stock has an adjustable butt plate and cheek piece to achieve a perfect fit with the user (even left-handed shooters), and also has an ambidextrous palm swell. Close attention has been paid in the T3 Tactical to quality of materials. The bolt is Teflon-coated stainless steel, and the stock is made from durable glass-fiber reinforced copolymer polypropylene.

GERMANY

HECKLER AND KOCH G11 1985

Length (gun): 29.63 in. (752.5 mm)
Barrel: 21.16 in. (538 mm)
Weight (gun): 8.38 lb. (3.80 kg)
Caliber: 4.7 x 33 DM11 caseless

Rifling: 6 grooves, r/hand
Operation: recoil-operated, rotating-breech
Feed: 50-round detachable box
Muz vel: 3,050 ft./sec. (930 m/sec.)

The G11 represents possibly the next stage in the evolution of the assault rifle, and even firearms in general. It fires 4.7 x 33 DM11 caseless ammunition, each bullet embedded straight into a block of propellant with a percussion cap in the rear of the block. The caseless round removes the extraction and ejection phases of firearm operation, giving the weapon exceptional full-auto control. Cook-off is controlled by using a special heat-resistant propellant that has, according to some sources, reduced the incidence of cook-off to one round every 150 when firing at sixty rpm. The G11's internal mechanism is as revolutionary as its cartridge. Fifty rounds are held in a rectangular magazine that sits parallel to the top of the barrel. Cartridges are fed into the chamber by a rotating breech piece, with recoil flipping the breech piece through a 90-degree cycle to maintain ammunition feed. However, in three-round burst mode, the second round is chambered before recoil is complete, thus compressing the whole sequence into a 2,200-rpm burst that imparts only one recoil sensation to the user. The G11 was meant for service with the German army in the mid-1990s, but so far only special-forces soldiers have been issued the weapons.

UNITED STATES

RUGER RED LABEL SHOTGUN 1985

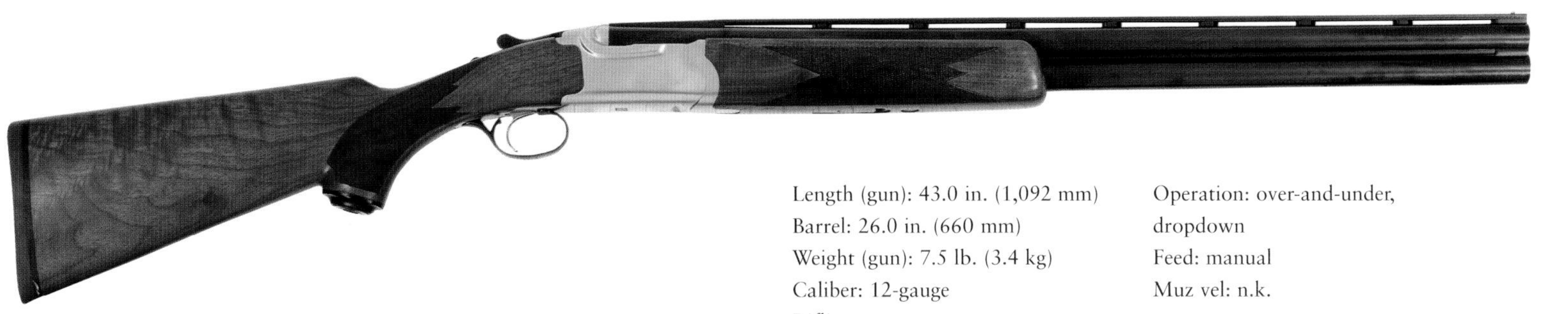

Length (gun): 43.0 in. (1,092 mm)
Barrel: 26.0 in. (660 mm)
Weight (gun): 7.5 lb. (3.4 kg)
Caliber: 12-gauge
Rifling: none
Operation: over-and-under, dropdown
Feed: manual
Muz vel: n.k.

Rivaling the traditional Browning for popularity in the United States is Ruger's elegant Red Label, the firm's first shotgun, an over-and-under 20-bore that was followed some years later by a 12-bore. Both guns come in several barrel lengths and degrees of choke boring, with the actions offered in both blued and stainless-steel finishes. There are no visible screws or pins on the actions, which, although devoid of any engraving, still manage to look very handsome. Both the 20-bore and 12-bore are available in two barrel lengths: 26.0 inches (660 mm) and 28.0 inches (711 mm), and two Field choke borings, plus a skeet gun, and are chambered for 3.0 inch (76 mm) cartridges. The guns are fitted with a hammer interrupter that is only lifted clear of the hammers by a deliberate pull of the trigger, a valuable safety device similar in its effect to the intercepting safety sears found on most quality sidelock guns and some high-quality boxlocks. The automatic safety catch incorporates the barrel selector, which indicates the barrel to be fired first by the unmistakable letters "B" and "T" for bottom and top, rather than the letters "U" and "O" or other symbols.

SWITZERLAND

SIG SSG 550 1986

Length (gun): 39.29 in. (998 mm)
Barrel: 20.79 in. (528 mm)
Weight (gun): 9.04 lb. (4.1kg)
Caliber: 5.56 x 45 mm NATO
Rifling: 6 grooves, r/hand
Operation: gas-operated, rotating-bolt
Feed: 20- or 30-round detachable box magazine
Muz vel: 3000 ft./sec. (915 m/sec.)

Like many assault rifles developed during the 1980s, the SG 550 was designed as a replacement for a large-caliber rifle, in this case the Swiss Army's 7.5 mm Stgw57. It built upon earlier designs—the SG 540 and the SG 541—and was successful in becoming the replacement army weapon from 1986 on (in military service it has the designation Stgw90). Much about the SG 550 is familiar territory in terms of modern assault weapons, though with some sophisticated refinements. The weapon is gas-operated with a rotating bolt along the lines of the AK, and the bolt is locked by two large lugs. A gas regulator allows three different settings, including a closed setting for use when firing rifle grenades. The SSG 550 is a sniper variant of this basic assault rifle. The basic mechanism of the rifle is the same; the main differences is that the SSG 550 has a hammer-forged heavy barrel and the full-auto mode is removed to leave a semi-auto weapon. As with most modern sniper weapons, the furniture is fully adjustable, as is the telescopic sight on its mount. In the photograph here, an antireflective screen is fitted over the barrel. This prevents thermal heat waves rising off a hot barrel from interfering with the sniper's sighting of the weapon. Feed is from the standard 20- or 30-round box magazines, which are made from transparent plastic so the ammunition usage can be checked.

SHOTGUN DEVELOPMENT

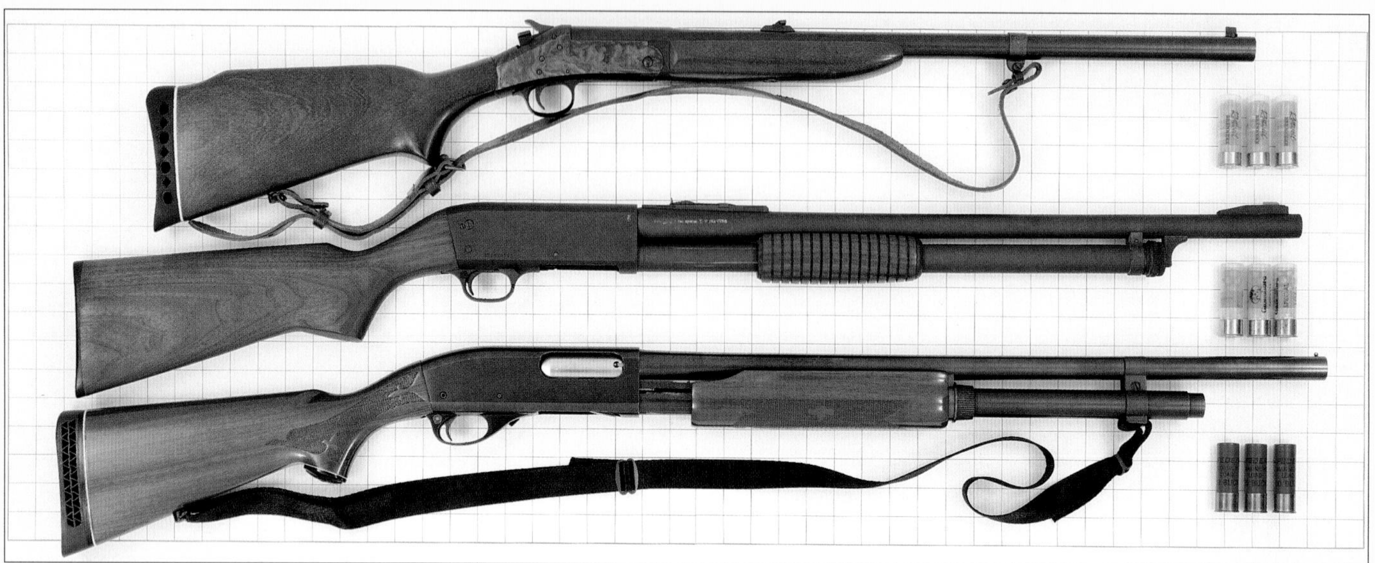

By definition, shotguns enter into firearms history as far back as the sixteenth century, when standard arquebus matchlock weapons were loaded with lead shot or scrap metal as a combat load or as a gaming load. The first depiction of a shotgun load being used in hunting is in a German engraving of 1545. By the 1600s the landed gentry of Europe had established game shooting with smoothbore shotguns as an important social activity; the guns were exquisitely decorated and extremely expensive. However, the system of flintlock ignition was still far from ideal for hunting—the time lag between the falling flint and the bullet leaving the muzzle could allow an alert animal to escape. With the development of the percussion cap, then the unitary cartridge during the 1800s, shotguns could fulfill a practical hunting function far more efficiently. In 1858 Englishman Westley Richards patented the top lever form of breech-loading, and the 1850s also saw the establishment of the T-form locking system. Efficient locking was the biggest challenge for shotgun-makers. Westley Richards led the way when, in 1862, he patented the Doll's Head locking system. The next year the famous James Purdey introduced underbolt locking. Variations on locking systems continue to this day and include sidelocking, pinlocking, breechblock locking. The 1870s saw the introduction of hammerless guns, which became the dominant type by the twentieth century. By the early years of the century, shotguns were also being produced in over-and-under, pump, and repeating configurations.

Modern shotguns have reached a high level of sophistication, although it is arguable whether there have been any major advances in shotgun design since the early twentieth century. One of the key advances has been multichoke guns. Here the shotgun has a set of removable chokes, which can be screwed into the end of the barrel, or barrels, to alter the spread of shot to adapt to the sport or target type.

Above: *Hunting shotguns from the United States. Top, the Harrington and Richardson Topper single-barrel gun, the basic break-open single-shot working man's (or woman's) 12-bore. Middle, the Ithaca Model 37 Deerslayer, with rifle-type sights and a cylinder barrel designed to shoot slug loads for deer. Bottom, the most popular pump gun, the Remington 870 Wingmaster.*

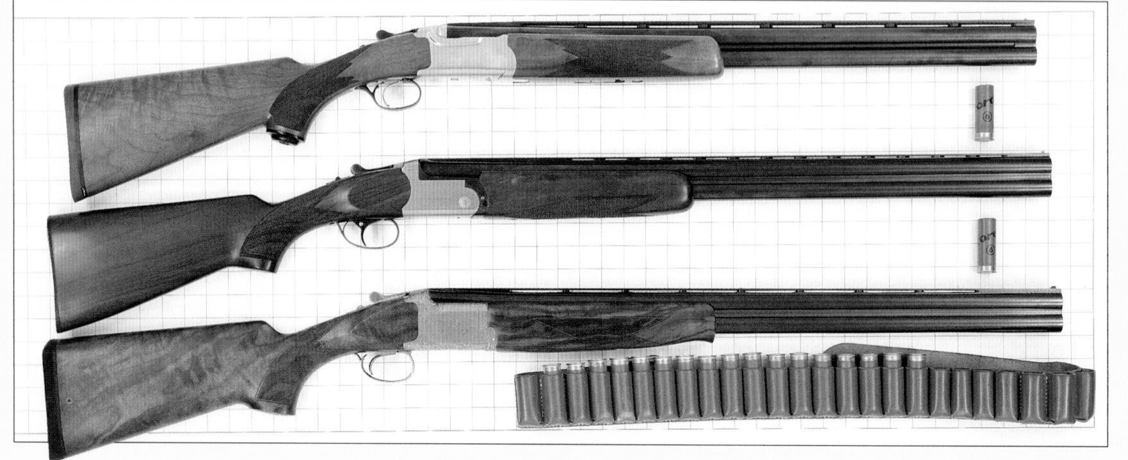

Left: *Target shotguns. Top, the Ruger Red Label, a handsome, unadorned over-and-under. Middle, the value-for-money Aya Yeoman from Spain, aimed at the clay-shooting market rather than the game shot. Bottom, the last gun from arguably the most influential designer of all, the Browning 125.*

SPAIN

AYA YEOMAN SHOTGUN 1986

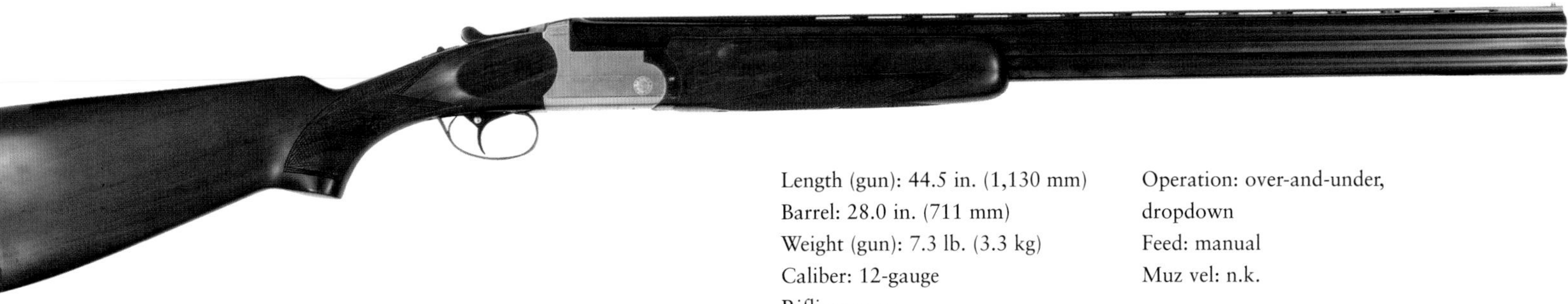

Length (gun): 44.5 in. (1,130 mm)
Barrel: 28.0 in. (711 mm)
Weight (gun): 7.3 lb. (3.3 kg)
Caliber: 12-gauge
Rifling: none

Operation: over-and-under, dropdown
Feed: manual
Muz vel: n.k.

Spanish gun-making company AYA moved to a new factory in 1986 and shortly thereafter introduced this new over-and-under 12-gauge shotgun, the Yeoman, which was intended for the clay-pigeon shooting market rather than the game shot. There were two models, one with standard barrels bored 1/2 and full chokes, and the other a multichoke version, with three internally threaded choke tubes supplied with the gun; others were available at extra cost. The selector for the selective single trigger was a button on the actual trigger rather than the more conventional device fitted to the strap. A free or nonauto safety catch was fitted as standard, but an automatic one was available at slightly extra cost.

ROK SOUTH KOREA

DAEWOO 5.56 MM K2 ASSAULT RIFLE 1987

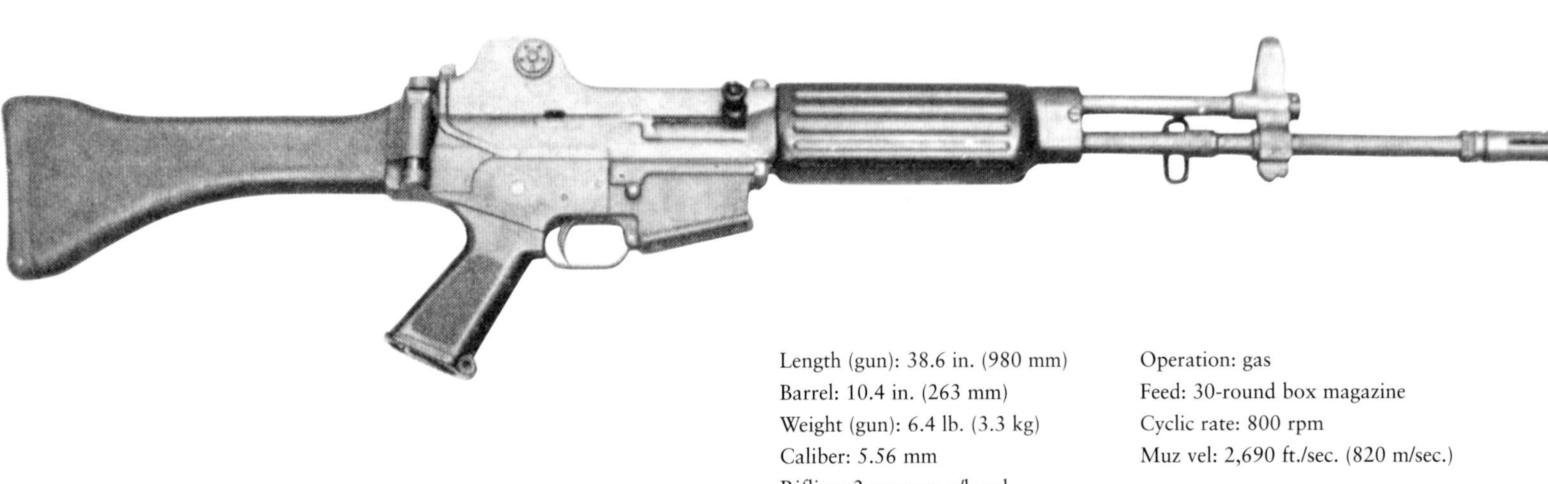

Length (gun): 38.6 in. (980 mm)
Barrel: 10.4 in. (263 mm)
Weight (gun): 6.4 lb. (3.3 kg)
Caliber: 5.56 mm
Rifling: 2 grooves, r/hand

Operation: gas
Feed: 30-round box magazine
Cyclic rate: 800 rpm
Muz vel: 2,690 ft./sec. (820 m/sec.)

The K2 Rifle, which appears to have been an original Korean design, also incorporates ideas from foreign designs. The K1 entered service with the RoK Army in 1987; it is 5.56 mm in caliber and can fire either M193 or SS109 rounds. The K1 action has a long-stroke piston, similar in many respects to that used in Russian Kalashnikov rifles, and it operates a rotating bolt. The weapon is capable of full-automatic, semi-automatic, and three-round burst fire, although a curious feature of the latter is that instead of resetting when the trigger is released, as in most other actions with a burst facility, when the trigger is pressed again the cycle simply carries on from where it left off in the previous burst. The receiver, which is made from two separate aluminum forgings, appears at first to be similar to that of the M16, but there are many differences. The back sight is housed between two prominent protectors and can be set to a maximum of 655 yd. (600 m). The K2 has a solid butt, which folds sideways to the right. The Daewoo K1A1 Short Carbine is based on the K2 but has a shorter barrel and uses direct gas action rather than a piston.

SPAIN

LANBER 12-GAUGE OVER-AND-UNDER SPORTING SHOTGUN 1987

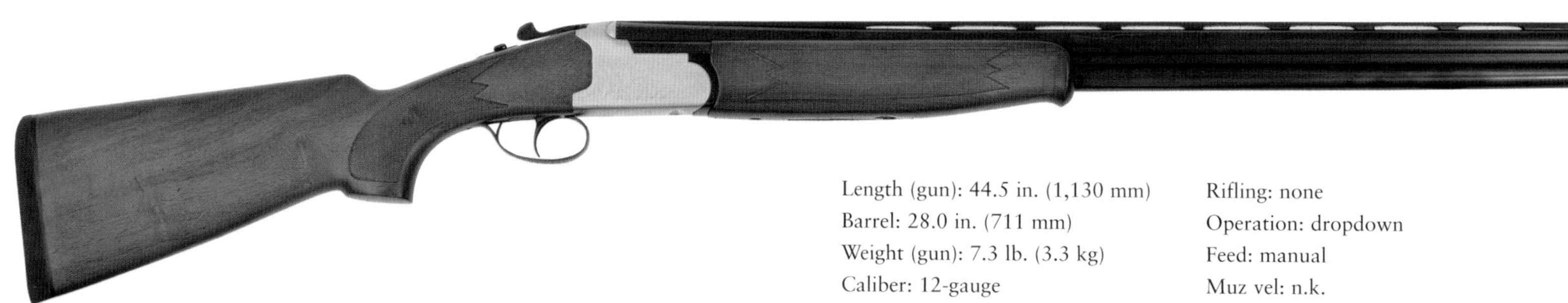

Length (gun): 44.5 in. (1,130 mm)
Barrel: 28.0 in. (711 mm)
Weight (gun): 7.3 lb. (3.3 kg)
Caliber: 12-gauge
Rifling: none
Operation: dropdown
Feed: manual
Muz vel: n.k.

The ubiquitous over-and-under sporting weapon comes at all levels of sophistication from rustic to exquisite, passing through the category of "sound but unexciting." This label fits this Lanber clay-pigeon target gun quite well. Built by one of Spain's largest makers of "over-and-unders," it has the reputation of being a "good gun for the money." There are six guns in the range; one of their features is that, except for the 3 in. (76 mm) Magnum model, the field models have more open boring than some others at the inexpensive end of the market, where the half- and full-chokes seem to be the norm. The multichoke models come with five different chokes and a hefty spanner to assist in screwing or unscrewing them. The engraving, although done by machine, is at least respectable.

SINGAPORE

CIS 5.56 MM SR-88 1988

Length (gun): 38.1 in. (970 m)
Barrel: 18.1 in. (459 mm)
Weight (gun): 8.1 lb. (3.7 kg)
Caliber: 5.56 mm
Rifling: 6 grooves, r/hand
Operation: gas
Feed: 20- or 30-round box magazine
Cyclic rate 750 rpm
Muz vel: 3,182 ft./sec. (970 m/sec.)

Like many other countries, Singapore entered the arms business by undertaking license production in the 1960s of the US 5.56 mm M16. A factory being set up for this purpose by Chartered Industries of Singapore (CIS). In the early 1970s the Singapore Armed Forces (SAF) asked CIS to develop a more cost-effective rifle, which had to be simple, rugged, reliable, economical to manufacture, and, at the very least, as good as the M16. This led to the SAR-80, which was produced in some numbers. Next came the SR-88, which was conventional in design but thoroughly sensible in approach. The SR-88 is built on the straight-line principle, with barrel, bolt, recoil mechanism, and stock all inline, dispersing the recoil straight into the firer's shoulder, minimizing barrel climb, and increasing controllability and accuracy. There are four main assemblies: upper receiver, gas piston, bolt group, and stock/lower receiver. (The removable-butt version is shown in lower photo.) There are two versions of the rifle: one has a fixed glass-fiber stock, the other a folding twin-strut stock. There is also a carbine (top photo), which has a shorter barrel and a folding stock. A model with further improvements, designated SR-88-A, was fielded in 1990 in both rifle and carbine versions.

Rifle Target Shooting

Target shooting with rifles is a precision sport that requires an exacting control over the body, as well as a high-quality weapon. For the rifle itself, adjustability is the principal quality required. The buttstock will usually be adjustable for stock length and comb drop and cast, and the gun may feature a fore-end palm rest. The barrel will be of a heavy type, sometimes of "free-floating: design—the barrel is not attached to the fore end to prevent the wood from distorting the barrel—and depending on the event, sights will be either micrometer-adjustable aperture back sights with tunnel fore sight, or powerful optical scopes (usually x20–x36 in power). Any sort of muzzle brake or compensator is usually prohibited.

For international target events, the regulations on everything from stance to clothing are extensive. In Olympic-style smallbore Free Rifle, for example, optical sights are permitted as long as they do not magnify. Clothing is heavily regulated, as the judges want to see that no item of clothing will provide artificial support for either the gun or the body. The shooter will make a total of 120 shots at 50m targets. Forty rounds will be fired in one hour from a prone position, the shooter resting on a regulation shooting mat. The prone position allows for the strap of the rifle to act as a support around the upper arm, but forearms are not allowed to touch the ground; they must be held at an angle of at least 30 degrees to the floor. The second shooting position for another forty shots is kneeling, with only three points of ground contact permitted: left foot, right knee, and toes of right foot (for right-handed shooter). The left elbow can be in contact with the left knee but must not extend more that 4 inches (10 cm) in front of the knee. The final forty shots are taken from a standing position, a straight-legged posture with only the arms supporting the weight of the gun; however, the elbow of the front arm may be tucked back onto the hip.

Events such as Free Rifle are incredibly demanding. Physical control is the key, and many shooters will even train themselves to shoot between heartbeats to achieve optimal accuracy.

Right: *The top picture shows a diverse range of Beretta accuracy/hunting weapons. From top to bottom: Super Sport .22LR; Express S689; Rifle Series 500; and AR70 Sport. Target shooting has become a huge international sport with many different disciplines. In the bottom photograph, the shooter is using a standard 7.62 mm M14 rifle, firing over open sights in what some argue is a purer test of marksmanship skills than using advanced optical sights.*

UNITED KINGDOM

SWING SIN 71 M5 RIFLE 1988

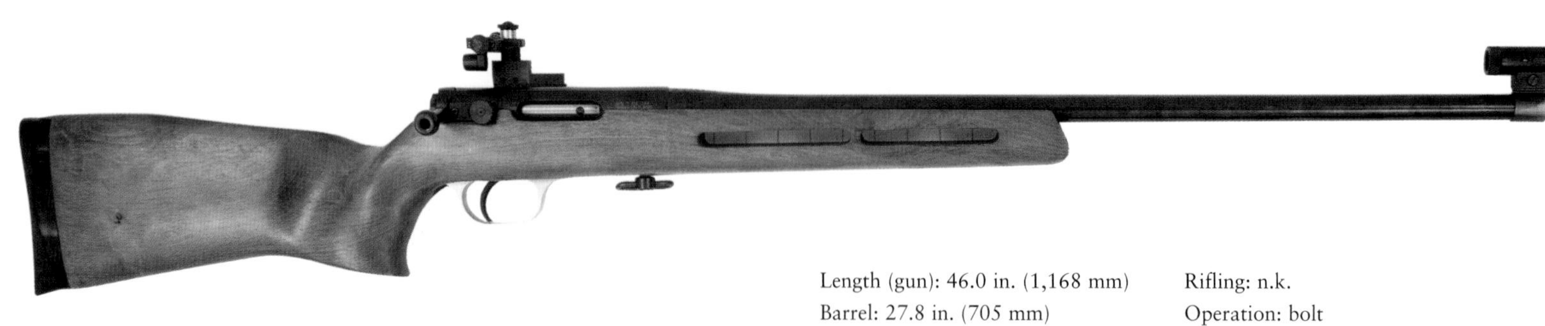

Length (gun): 46.0 in. (1,168 mm)
Barrel: 27.8 in. (705 mm)
Weight (gun): 11.2 lb. (5.1 kg)
Caliber: 7.62 mm
Rifling: n.k.
Operation: bolt
Feed: single-round, manual
Muz vel: n.k.

In the late 1980s most top British marksmen were using the Swing SIN 71 M5 rifle, designed by George Swenson. It has an ultrastiff action delivering dense and round (as opposed to elliptical) groups, with a very fast lock time to minimize shooter-related departure error. The M5 has a massively rigid, round-bottomed action, with the smallest possible loading/ejection port, and two massive recoil lugs (one at the back, underneath the bolt handle, the other just to the rear of the locking engagements). Vertical bedding bolts engage each lug. The rifle is Devcon-bedded up to the bore line, and the positioning of the recoil lugs is intended to minimize torquing of the receiver within the bedding. The bolt head carries four large, equally spaced locking lugs, with a plunger-ejector. The extractor is set into the right lug, and by using titanium components and a massive main spring, the lock time has been reduced to 1.24 milliseconds. The trigger unit, which is an adaptation of a Montari design of the 1930s, is adjustable down to 1.0 lb. (0.45 kg) and is a much sought-after item in its own right, as are the Swing's micrometer sights (back sight, adjustable aperture; fore sight, tunnel with interchangeable elements). The rifle is normally fitted with 28.0 in. (711 mm) or 30.0 in. (762 mm) Schultz and Larsen barrels.

ITALY

BERETTA SO4 SPORTING MULTICHOKE SPORTING GUN 1970s/80s

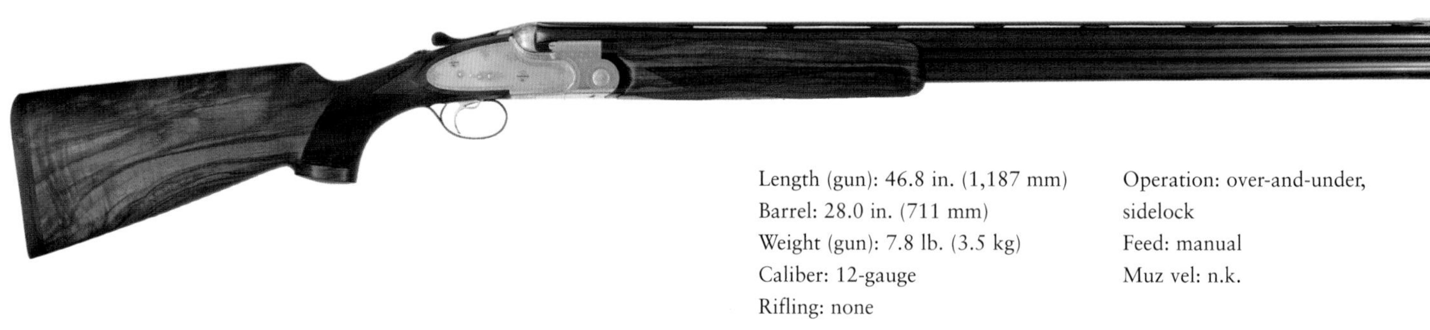

Length (gun): 46.8 in. (1,187 mm)
Barrel: 28.0 in. (711 mm)
Weight (gun): 7.8 lb. (3.5 kg)
Caliber: 12-gauge
Rifling: none
Operation: over-and-under, sidelock
Feed: manual
Muz vel: n.k.

Much of Beretta's success in the modern era can be put down to Tullio Marengoni (often referred to by firearms historians as Europe's John Browning), whose run of new products began with a hammerless shotgun in the first decade of the twentieth century and covered nearly every important Beretta firearm until 1960. The company's ability to innovate and lead the market is symbolized by this elegant sidelock, one of the most popular models in a comparatively new breed of competition gun. The game of sporting clays had always been shot with a variety of guns, most of them skeet guns, field guns, or even trap guns from which some of the choke had been bored out. After World War II sporting shooting began to increase, and by the early 1970s such events as the British Open Sporting Championship were attracting many hundreds of entries. Gun-makers realized that shooters wanted a gun not bored as open as a skeet gun and not as tightly choked as a trap gun. And so sporting guns such as this were born, with fixed borings of $^1/_4$ and $^1/_2$ choke, or $^1/_4$ and $^3/_4$, but at some time thereafter multichoke models were also introduced. In this particular case, the Beretta SO4 has an internally threaded multichoke system.

SWITZERLAND

SIG SSG 3000 1990

Length (gun): 45.45 in. (1,180 mm)
Barrel: 24 in. (610 mm)
Weight (gun): 11.90 lb. (5.40 kg)
Calibre: 7.62 x 51 mm NATO
Rifling: 4 grooves, r/hand
Operation: bolt-action
Feed: 5-round box
Muz vel: 2460 ft./sec. (750 m/sec.)

The SIG SSG 3000 is a pure sniper weapon used by military, police, and security forces. It shoots the standard 7.62 x 51 mm NATO round from a heavy cold-hammer-forged barrel with integral muzzle brake (the muzzle brake has no vents on its underside to prevent raising a dust signature on firing) and set into a stock that is ventilated to prevent heat buildup warping the wood and thereby distorting the barrel. The gun also comes with fittings to attach an antimirage ribbon along the top of the barrel. Bolt action is of standard Mauser type with six locking lugs and a plunger-type ejector system. The SSG 3000 is a modular weapon, with parts such as the barrel, receiver, and trigger/magazine system easily removed or replaced. The McMillan Fibreglass Tactical Stock is fully adjustable, and the weapon, depending on the configuration, comes supplied with a variety of scopes, including the Leupold Vari-X III 3.5–10x 40 mm Duplex Reticle Scope and the Leupold Mark 4 M1 10x 40 mm Mil-Dot Scope.

JAPAN

HOWA TYPE 89 5.56 MM ASSAULT RIFLE 1989

Length (gun): 36.1 in. (916 mm)
Barrel: 16.5 in. (420 mm)
Weight (gun): 7.7 lb. (3.5 kg)
Caliber: 5.56 mm
Rifling: 6 grooves, r/hand
Operation: gas
Feed: 20- or 30-round box magazine
Cyclic rate: 750 rpm
Muz vel: 3020 ft./sec. (920 m/sec.)

The Japanese Ground Self-Defense Force (JGSDF) realized in the late 1950s that the rifle of the future had to be self-loading, and in the early 1960s it authorized the development of a self-loading rifle by a project team that included the civilian arms firm, Howa. This resulted in the 7.62 mm Type 64, which in turn evolved into the 5.56 mm Type 89. The Type 89 fires the standard NATO 5.56 x 45 mm round and comes in two versions: one with a fixed butt, the other with a twin-strut, folding butt. The absence of an M16 (AR-15) type buffer assembly and tube extending into the butt stock permitted the design team at Howa to create a side-folding stock model. Both versions have a folding bipod. The Type 89 uses an unusual method of operation, in which the piston head is slightly narrower than the diameter of the gas cylinder, with a full-bore collar behind it. The result is that when the gas hits the piston head it imparts an initial low momentum to the bolt carrier (a form of "kick-start") so that when, microseconds later, the full gas pressure moves past the piston head to the collar and the full momentum is passed to the bolt carrier, the latter is already in motion. This, it is claimed, results in a smoother motion and also reduces wear and tear on the working parts, thus enhancing reliability. The Type 89 has a slotted flash suppressor and is capable of accepting a bayonet. It is in service only with the JGSDF.

Shotgun Ammunition

Shotgun cartridges are far more complex in composition than bullet ammunition types. The outer shell of the cartridge is usually made of plastic, although cardboard is sometimes still used. At the base of the cartridge is a steel or brass head, which contains the percussion cap. The base swells upon firing to provide a gas-tight seal against the chamber walls. Inside the case, directly in front of the cap, is the main powder charge. The weight of powder charge varies according to the gun and its role, but loads of 28–32 grams are the most typical for clay shooting and general hunting applications.

Between the powder charge and the shot is probably the most important component of a shotgun shell, the wad. Wads come in two varieties: felt or plastic. Felt is the traditional wad and simply sits as a disk between powder and shot, which disintegrates upon firing. The plastic wads form a cup around the shot, often featuring a shock-absorbing section to reduce felt recoil and shot deformation; the wad will carry the shot up and out of the barrel without disintegrating.

Above: *The Ferret Liquid Agent Barricade Penetrating Cartridge is one of the many specialist shotgun cartridges in use for military/security tasks. Rather than holding shot, the cartridge contains a liquid-irritant CS agent within a plastic projectile; the agent is released in an aerosol form after penetrating a structure.*

Plastic wads undoubtedly have advantages over felt wads. They cause less deformation of the shot on firing (deformed shot will slow more quickly in flight and keep a less consistent pattern) and also make a more effective obturation along the barrel. Felt wads, however, are fully biodegradable, so they are becomingly used more often to reduce plastic pollution over shooting grounds.

The shot is usually made of either lead/antimony or steel depending on use and regulations (lead has been banned in many hunting grounds because of its polluting effect), but hunting shot may be found in bismuth, Molyshot, tin, or zinc.

The shotgun pellets are produced in a range of graded sizes, formed by dropping molten lead through mesh then into water to cool and harden it. Typically, No.8 shot has around about 400 pellets in a 12-gauge cartridge with a 28 g load and is suitable only for clay-pigeon shooting or small vermin or birds. No.3 shot contains about 140 balls in the cartridge and is used to hunt goose or fox.

CANADA

DIEMACO C7A1 5.56 MM ASSAULT RIFLE 1990

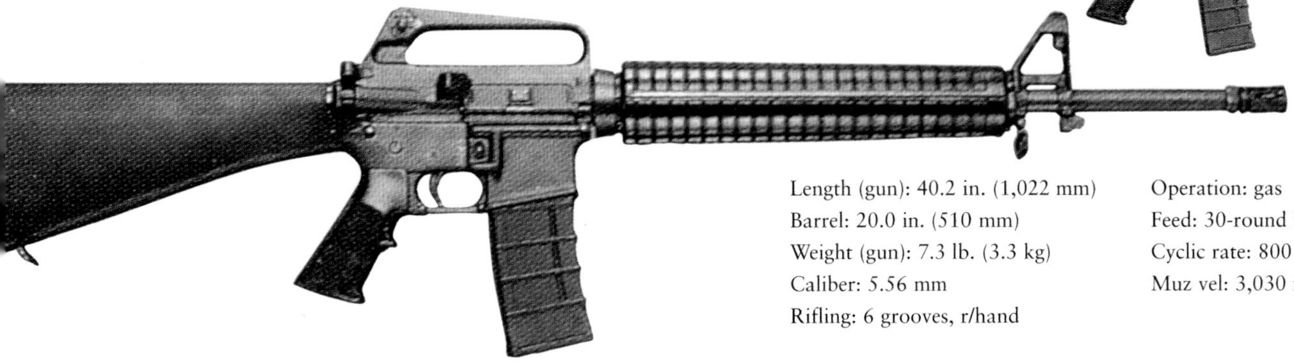

Length (gun): 40.2 in. (1,022 mm)
Barrel: 20.0 in. (510 mm)
Weight (gun): 7.3 lb. (3.3 kg)
Caliber: 5.56 mm
Rifling: 6 grooves, r/hand

Operation: gas
Feed: 30-round box magazine
Cyclic rate: 800 rpm
Muz vel: 3,030 ft./sec. (920 m/sec.)

When the Canadian armed forces adopted the NATO 5.56 mm round, Diemaco commenced production of the US 5.56 mm Colt M16A2. The latest series of weapons are a development of this, designated C7 Combat Rifle (lower photo) and C8 Carbine (top). The C7 has three modes: safe, single rounds, and fully automatic. It does not have a three-round burst mode. It uses a simple, two-position rear sight on top of the rear of the receiver, between two prominent protectors. The barrel is cold-forged and chrome-lined, and the weapon fires NATO SS109 or US M193 5.56 mm rounds. The C7 is used by the Canadian armed forces and the Royal Netherlands Army, and a small quantity were purchased by Denmark for its forces deployed in Bosnia. The C7A1 is an improved version with a low-mounted optical sight mounted atop the receiver rail; it is used by the Dutch special forces. The C8 is a compact version of the C7, with a telescopic butt, a butt pad, and a shorter barrel (14.6 inches/370 mm long), for armored crews, engineers, and signalers. Both take the Diemaco-made version of the M203 40mm underbarrel grenade launcher.

FINLAND

VALMET M90 7.62 MM ASSAULT RIFLE 1990

Length (gun): 36.6 in. (930 mm)
Barrel: 16.4 in. (416 mm)
Weight (gun): 8.5 lb. (3.9 kg)
Caliber: 7.62 mm
Rifling: 4 grooves, r/hand

Operation: gas
Feed: 30-round box
Cyclic rate: 700 rpm
Muz vel: 2,625 ft./sec. (800 m/sec.)

The Valmet M90, firing the 7.62 x 39 mm Soviet M1943 round, followed the earlier Valmet M60, M62, and M70 series into service with the Finnish Army. It was designed around the basic and well proven Kalashnikov gas-operated, rotating-bolt system, but with a much improved and lighter receiver. At the muzzle is a prominent cylindrical device that serves as a combined flash suppressor and grenade launcher. It had a new pattern, side-folding, tubular steel butt. The M90 was developed in both 7.62 x 3 mm and 5.56 x 45 mm versions, but as far as is known, only the former was ever put into production. The manufacturer, Sako, also developed a special hard-core bullet for this rifle. Designated K413, it was made of special alloy steel and was intended to penetrate targets not vulnerable to the normal 7.62 mm round.

FRANCE

BRETTON DOUBLE-BARREL ("BABY BRETTON") SHOTGUN 1990

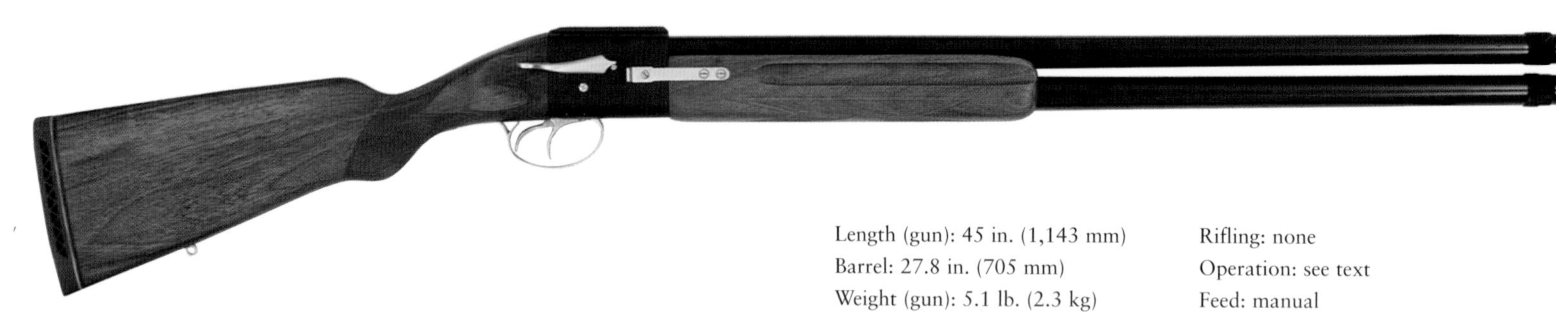

Length (gun): 45 in. (1,143 mm)
Barrel: 27.8 in. (705 mm)
Weight (gun): 5.1 lb. (2.3 kg)
Caliber: 12-gauge
Rifling: none
Operation: see text
Feed: manual
Muz vel: n.k.

This bizarre French 12-gauge weapon is more of a "garden gun" but is of interest because of its very unusual action and lightness. The two over-and-under barrels are unlocked by means of the large lever seen on the right of the weapon and are then slid forward, which ejects the spent cartridge cases, although not forcibly. The barrels are secured to each other at the breech with a detachable twin collar at the muzzle, which is not fitted in this photograph. There are two triggers, one for each barrel, but there are no sights, not even a bead on the muzzle. The main claim to fame for the "Baby Bretton" is its extraordinary lightness—just 5.1 lb. (2.3 kg)—although this results in a more powerful recoil than would be found in a heavier weapon. The Bretton trademark was first seen in 1934. The company specialized in lightweight shotguns from the outset. In 2000 the company merged with the far older French gunmaker Gaucher.

HUNGARY

M1/M2 GEPARD 12.7 MM ANTIMATERIEL RIFLE 1990

Length (gun): 60.2 in. (1,53 0 mm)
Barrel: 43.4 in. (1,100 mm)
Weight (gun): 26.5 lb. (12.0 kg)
Caliber: 12.7 mm
Rifling: 8 grooves, r/hand
Operation: long-recoil, semi-automatic
Feed: 5- or 10-round box magazine
Muz vel: 2,756 ft./sec. (840 m/sec.)

The Technika-produced Gepard M1 is a bolt-action, single-shot weapon firing the Russian 12.7 x 108 mm DshK round. The pistol grip doubles as the bolt handle, which, reload the weapon, is rotated counterclockwise and pulled to the rear, ejecting the spent cartridge; a new cartridge is then inserted, the bolt closed, and the hammer cocked (this requires a separate action). The Gepard M1A1 is essentially the same but includes a frame that can be used to carry the weapon or as a firing rest. The Gepard M2 (see specifications) was developed from the M1 but has an entirely different, semi-automatic, action, using a positive-locking, long-recoil system, fed from a five- or ten-round box magazine. The M2 has a cylindrical receiver and a cylindrical cradle that extends almost to the muzzle, together with a built-in bipod and a short butt. The M2A1 is a shortened version intended for use by airborne troops. The makers have said that both the M1/M1A1 and the M2/M2A1 (shown in lower photo) could easily be converted to take the 12.7 x 99 mm (0.50 in. Browning) round. A Gepard M3 (upper photo) is chambered for the 14.5 x 114 mm Russian round.

RIFLES IN URBAN COMBAT

Urban combat places unusual demands on both rifleman and rifle. For the rifleman, targets are presented at close ranges, 90 percent at less than 164 feet (50 m), but the time window in which to fire is usually only a few seconds as the target passes between positions of cover. The US Army Field Manual FM90-10 recommends that for combat within building interiors, the gun be held up ready either to the shoulder or in an underarm position (not from the hip) and, when a target appears, fired instinctively with both eyes open rather than meticulously sighted. Short full-auto or three-round bursts are used for room-clearance operations.

Rifle shooters have to shoot from numerous angles and elevations, often through limiting apertures, which degrade both visual target acquisition and free barrel movement. Target acquisition is also hampered by the airborne detritus of urban combat, such as smoke and dust. For this reason, modern armies train their soldiers to use rifles while wearing respirators or using thermal imaging sights.

One other factor that distinguishes urban combat from open-space combat is the effect of urban structures on terminal ballistics. Rifle rounds fired in urban combat strike solid surfaces, usually at angles of less than 90 degrees, and this decreases the penetrative effect of the round while increasing the percentage of ricochets (hence fratricide can be common among units engaged in urban fighting). A 5.56 mm M16A2 rifle will have almost no penetrative ability against solid masonry and/or steel structures, although the round is quite capable of punching through interior partitions, wood paneling and plasterwork.

Interestingly, the penetration improves with distance. At close ranges of, say, 32 feet (10 m), the high-velocity round is unable to cope with the massive impact and fragments into pieces (the maximum penetration range of an M16A2 is around 656 feet/200 m). Penetration can be improved by using armor-piercing rounds, but these tend to have a higher percentage of ricochets than standard ball rounds, and may even rebound straight back at the firer if they do not penetrate.

Below: *A US serviceman engages in MOUT (Mounting Operations in Urban Terrain) training. The M16A2 rifle he carries has little penetrative potential against urban structures, more destructive fire being the role of larger-caliber weapons such as the 7.62 mm M60 or .50-caliber Browning M2HB machine guns.*

ITALY

BERETTA 5.56 MM AR-70/90 ASSAULT RIFLE 1990

Length (gun): 39.3 in. (998 mm)
Barrel: 17.7 in. (450 mm)
Weight (gun): 8.8 lb. (4.0 kg)
Caliber: 5.56 mm
Rifling: 6 grooves, r/hand

Operation: gas
Feed: 30-round box magazine
Cyclic rate: 625 rpm
Muz vel: 3,050 ft./sec. (930 m/sec.)

The Beretta AR-70/90 is an updated version of the AR-70 (qv), which incorporates a number of significant improvements, the most important of which is that the cranked butt-stock is replaced by a new butt, giving a straight-line configuration. The weapon retains the same system of gas operation with a rotating bolt, but now includes a three-round burst capability. It can accommodate any standard M16 magazine. In addition to the AR-70/90 assault rifle, there are three other versions. The SC-70/90 is identical to the AR-70 apart from a twin-strut folding butt, which makes it slightly shorter in overall length, but some 0.4 lb. (0.2 kg) heavier. The SCS-70/90 and SCP-70/90 are for use by special forces and both have a shorter (13.9 in./352 mm) barrel and a folding butt; they differ in that the SCS-70/90 does not have a gas regulator and is not capable of launching grenades; the SCP-70/90 does have a gas-regulator and can launch grenades.

ITALY

FABRICCA NAZIONALE COMBINATION GUN 1990

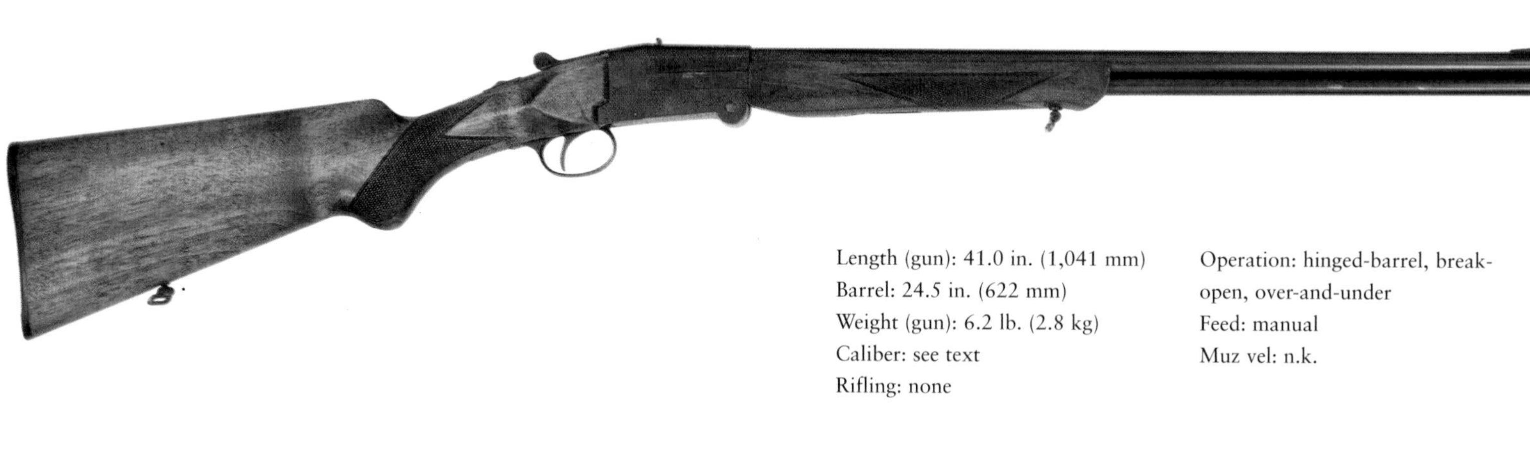

Length (gun): 41.0 in. (1,041 mm)
Barrel: 24.5 in. (622 mm)
Weight (gun): 6.2 lb. (2.8 kg)
Caliber: see text
Rifling: none

Operation: hinged-barrel, break-open, over-and-under
Feed: manual
Muz vel: n.k.

The Fabricca Nazionale Combination Gun has two up-and-over barrels of different calibers, the upper a 0.410 in. gauge and the lower a 0.22 in. LR. It is commonly used by trappers, farmers, ornithologists, and those who might need an easily packed survival gun. The thumb lever releases the barrels to pivot downward, and the oversized hinge allows the gun to be folded up on itself, making for easy stowage. The chambering makes the gun ideal for shooting rats and most garden pests, although it may be a little light for larger species such as crows or foxes.

UNITED STATES

WINCHESTER 8500 SPECIAL TRAP SHOTGUN 1990

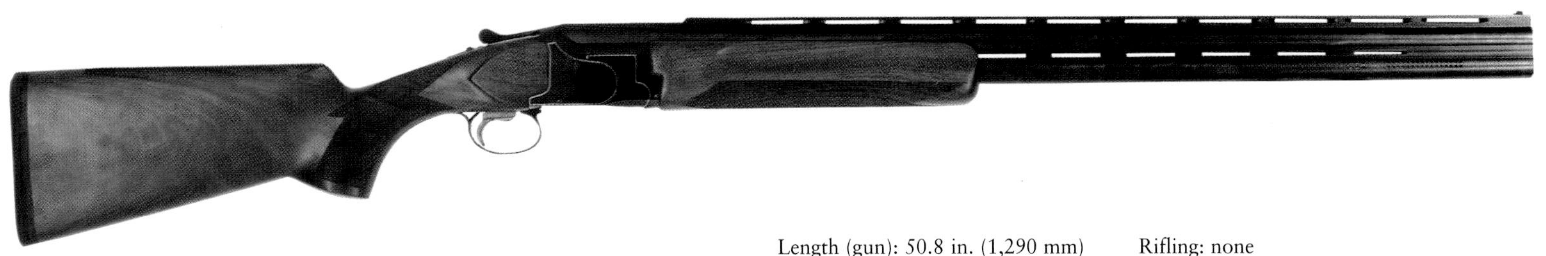

Length (gun): 50.8 in. (1,290 mm)
Barrel: 30.0 in. (762 mm)
Weight (gun): 8.3 lb. (3.8 kg)
Caliber: 12-gauge

Rifling: none
Operation: standard
Feed: manual
Muz vel: n.k.

At the other end of the target-shooting spectrum from the French "Baby Bretton" (qv) is this Winchester 8500 Special Trap, which is quite distinctive in appearance with a plain black action, high trap rib, and ventilated mid-rib. An unusual feature is that the bottom barrel is "ported"—in other words, it has a series of small round holes running along the barrel for some 4.0 inches (102 mm) to the rear from a point around 3.0 inches (76 mm) from the muzzle. The theory behind this is that the gases, or some portion of them, are vented through these ports before they leave the muzzle, thus helping to reduce muzzle "flip" and assisting in keeping the gun on target for the second shot. The method has been used before, mainly by means of venting right at the end of the barrels, but "porting" is supposed to be more effective and less noisy.

UNITED STATES

MOSSBERG 500ATP SHOTGUN 1992

Length (gun): 40.3 in. (1,009 mm)
Barrel: 20.3 in. (308 mm)
Weight (gun): 6.7 lb. (3.1 kg)
Caliber: 12-gauge

Rifling: none
Operation: pump-action shotgun
Feed: 8-round tubular magazine
Muz vel: n.k.

The basic series of Mossberg 500 sporting shotguns was specially modified for police and military use, and the guns are described in some circles as "reloadable Claymores." There are two main types: the six- and eight-shot models. The latter is generally used by military forces. Its design ensures maximum reliability in use and has an aluminum receiver for good balance and light weight. The cylinder-bored barrel is proof-tested to full Magnum loads, provides optimum dispersion patterns, and permits firing of a variety of ammunition. The shotgun has two extractors, and the slide mechanism has twin guide bars, which help prevent twisting or jamming during rapid operation. A later modification was the creation of a muzzle brake by cutting slots in the upper surface, thus allowing gas to escape upward and exerting a downward force that prevented the muzzle from lifting during firing. The ATP-8 version has no buttstock; a pistol grip is added, resulting in an extremely compact weapon that can be stowed more easily inside a vehicle.

CZECH REPUBLIC

CZ 2000 5.56 MM WEAPONS FAMILY 1993

Length (gun): 33.5 in. (850 mm)
Barrel: 15.0 in. (382 mm)
Weight (gun): 6.6 lb. (3.0 kg)
Caliber: 5.56 x 45 mm
Rifling: 6 grooves, r/hand
Operation: gas
Feed: 30-round box
Cyclic rate: 800 rpm
Muz vel: 2,985 ft./sec. (910 m/sec.)

The Czech Republic's new range of infantry weapons was revealed in 1993, in NATO 5.56 x 45 mm, clearly in anticipation of Czech membership of NATO. The family was known as the "Lada" system, but that name has since been dropped in favor of "CZ 2000." The system is gas-operated and uses a rotating bolt, derived from that used in the Kalashnikov, which locks into the barrel at the moment of firing. The weapon fires full-automatic single rounds or three-round bursts, and it has a pressed-steel receiver with plastic furniture and a twin-tubed, side-folding butt (there is no solid-butt version). The 30-round magazine is made of clear plastic so that the firer can see how many rounds it contains, but the US M16 magazine can also be used. The sights are of open type, with hooded front post and open notch adjustable rear. The CZ 2000 Short Assault Rifle appeared in 1995 and is a lighter and shorter version; indeed, it is virtually a submachine gun. The receiver, butt, trigger group, and pistol grip are the same, but the barrel is considerably shorter (7.3 in./185 mm compared to 15.0 in./382 mm), which has resulted in a shorter gas cylinder. The slotted flash suppressor has been replaced by a more conventional coned type. The CZ 2000 series includes a light machine gun version.

UNITED KINGDOM

PSG-90 7.62 SNIPER RIFLE 1993

Length (gun): 47.25 in. (1,200 mm)
Barrel: 25.6 in. (650 mm)
Weight (gun): 14.3 lb. (6.5 kg)
Caliber: 7.62 mm
Rifling: 4 grooves, r/hand
Operation: bolt
Feed: 9-round box magazine
Muz vel: 2,788 ft./sec. (850 m/sec.)

The PSG-90 7.62 mm sniper rifle is the Swedish designation for the British L96A1, which has been described elsewhere in this book. In 1993 the Swedish Army ran a competition for a new sniper rifle. The competition was won by the British company Accuracy International with a development of the L96A1, which was updated and modified to meet the Swedish requirement. As with the L96A1, the PSG-90 is a precision bolt-action weapon fed from a nine-round magazine. Standard sighting fitment is the x10 Hensoldt (Zeiss) telescopic scope, but many other different scope types can be fitted according to the preference of the sniper. The Hensoldt sight has excellent light intensification properties, making it ideal for use in the extreme winter conditions that can prevail in Sweden. It also has variable illumination adjustment for the crosshairs. The PSG-90 fires a range of different ammunition types to suit the objective, including full metal jacket, armor piercing, tracer and subcaliber discarding sabot.

RUSSIA

AN-94 ABAKAN 1994

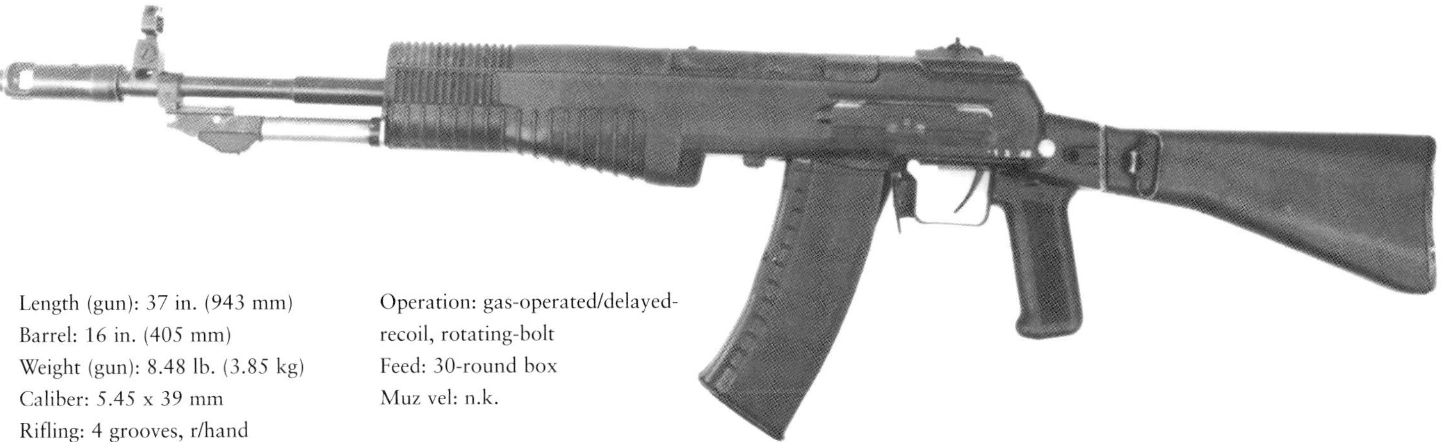

Length (gun): 37 in. (943 mm)
Barrel: 16 in. (405 mm)
Weight (gun): 8.48 lb. (3.85 kg)
Caliber: 5.45 x 39 mm
Rifling: 4 grooves, r/hand

Operation: gas-operated/delayed-recoil, rotating-bolt
Feed: 30-round box
Muz vel: n.k.

The Avtomat Nikonova-94 (AN-94) Abakan is the potential replacement for the Kalashnikov AK-74 in Russian forces and heralds a controversial step away from the simplicity of the AK design. The most unusual feature of the AN-94 is its operation, which is described in technical manuals as "blowback shifted pulse," although it is actually more of a modified standard gas-operated rotating-bolt action. When the gun is fired on two-round burst or full-auto mode, the bolt group and barrel receiver assembly begin to move backward, ejecting the spent case. As it does this, a cartridge rammer actually feeds another round into the chamber, which is fired by the returning bolt before the receiver assembly has finished its return journey. Only after the second shot—both shots are fired at rate of 1800 rpm—does the user feel the recoil impulse. Consequently, the automatic modes of fire are extremely accurate, increasing killing power and body armor penetration. However, this does not make the AN-94 a worthy successor to the AK. Reports indicate that this complex weapon is difficult to clean and maintain, has awkward ergonomics, and is very expensive to make. Currently it serves only with elite military units and police squads. The AN-94 can accept standard AK-74-compatible magazines with 30 or 45 rounds as well as the more recent 60-rounds four-stack box magazines.

GERMANY

HECKLER AND KOCH G36 1994

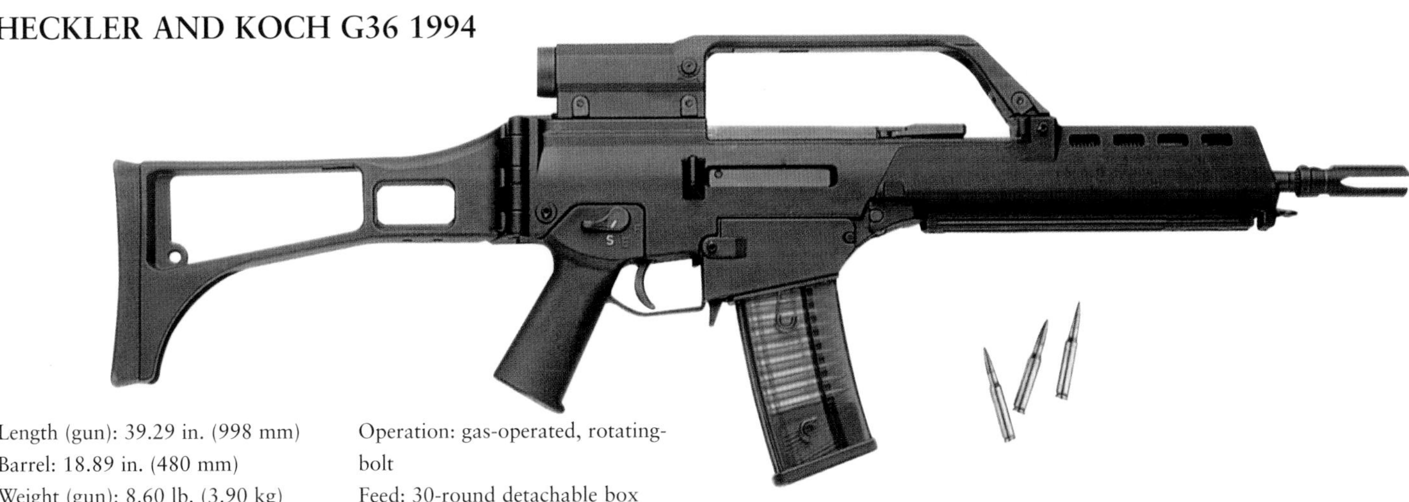

Length (gun): 39.29 in. (998 mm)
Barrel: 18.89 in. (480 mm)
Weight (gun): 8.60 lb. (3.90 kg)
Caliber: 5.56 x 45 mm NATO
Rifling: 6 grooves, r/hand

Operation: gas-operated, rotating-bolt
Feed: 30-round detachable box magazine
Muz vel: 3050 ft./sec. (930 m/sec.)

The H. and K. G36 began its development life in the 1990s when the Bundeswehr looked for a replacement for the G3 rifle. The weapon is of conventional gas-operated, rotating-bolt design, moving away from the roller-delayed system of the G3. The bolt has a total of seven locking lugs, and the square-section bolt carrier moves on a single guide rod. An interesting feature is the charging handle at the top of the bolt carrier, which can be rotated to the left or the right. Trigger units are interchangeable on the G36, allowing different fire-mode configurations made up of single-shot, two- or three-round burst, and full auto; the fire selector is of ambidextrous fitting. The gun is fed from transparent thirty-round box magazines, and these feature clip fittings that allow two or three magazines to be connected side by side for fast reloading. The standard G36 is sighted through a two-scope combination: a 3.5x telescopic sight with a red dot sight set above it. Such is the advanced nature of the G36, it is the basis of the US Army's XM8 project.

ITALY

BENELLI MODEL 121-M1 SHOTGUN 1994

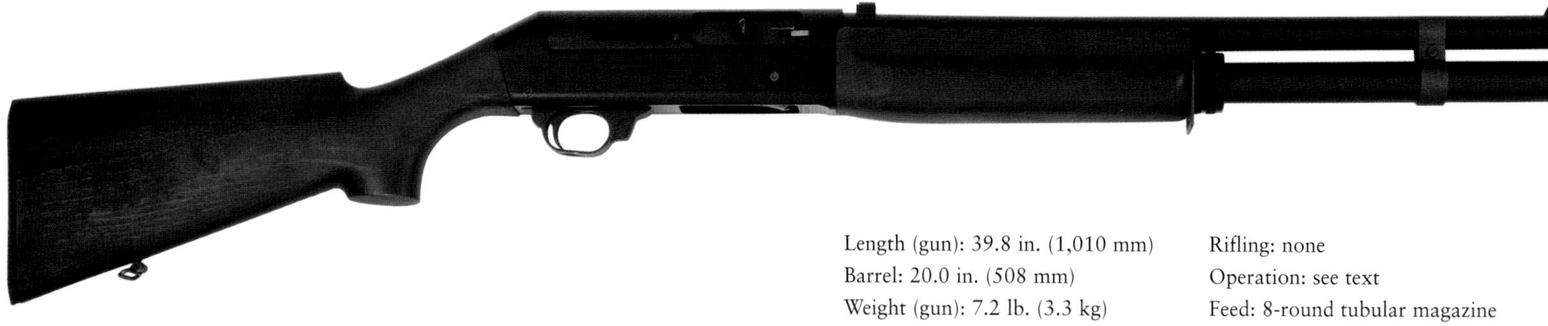

Length (gun): 39.8 in. (1,010 mm)
Barrel: 20.0 in. (508 mm)
Weight (gun): 7.2 lb. (3.3 kg)
Caliber: 12-gauge
Rifling: none
Operation: see text
Feed: 8-round tubular magazine
Muz vel: n.k.

The Benelli Model 121 is an elegant weapon, beautifully styled and technically radical. The use of upper and lower receiver assemblies, which slide apart on disassembly, makes maintenance easy, and the locking system confuses even engineers. The lower receiver is made of aluminum; all other parts are of steel. Basically, the Model 121 is recoil-operated but with a static barrel, and the bolt is cammed out of engagement by an inertial piece. That this works is undeniable, but the cyclic speed suggests semi-blowback operation; one professional shooter is reputed to fire so rapidly that all eight spent cartridge cases are in the air at the same time. This rapid-fire capability made the Benelli the first choice in the United States for shotgun skittles matches. The modifications consist of porting, muzzle brakes, and weights, all calculated to diminish muzzle lift, allowing the gun's potential rate of fire to be deployed in a lateral sweep along the tabletop. Most Benelli aficionados claim that they can deliver five shots per second if everything goes right.

CZECH REPUBLIC

MODEL 96 FALCON 12.7 MM ANTIMATERIEL RIFLE 1996

Length (gun): 54.3 in. (1,380 mm)
Barrel: 36.5 in. (927 mm)
Weight (gun, loaded): 32.9 lb. (14.9 kg)
Caliber: 12.7 mm
Rifling: 8 grooves, r/hand
Operation: bolt
Feed: 5-round box or manual
Muz vel: 2,790 ft/.sec. (850 m/sec.)

The Model 96 was originally designated the OPV 12.7 mm and was fitted with a 140.4 in. (1,027 mm) barrel, capable of firing either the 12.7 x 99 mm (0.50 in. Browning) or the 12.7 x 108 mm Russian DshK rounds. The production weapons have two barrels: one is 36.5 inches (927 mm) long for the 12.7 x 108 mm round, the other 33.0 in. (838 mm) long for the 12.7 x 99 mm round. The weapon is bolt action, and the considerable recoil from the 12.7 mm round is attenuated by a large four-baffle muzzle brake and a buffer spring in the tubular, detachable butt. The barrel screws on to the receiver and is locked by a spring-actuated lever. There is a detachable five-round box magazine, but if the firer wishes to use manual feeding, he can insert a cover over the magazine well. Maximum effective range is claimed to be 2,187 yd. (2,000 m) with the optical sight, 1,094 yd. (1,000 m) at night. A 10 x 40 scope is supplied with the weapon, with a sight reticle that can be illuminated by internal batteries. Iron sights are also fitted. Specifications above relate to the 12.7 x 108 mm DshK version.

UNITED STATES

XM8 1996

Length (gun): 29.8 in. (757 mm)
Barrel: 12.5 in. (317 mm)
Weight (gun): 6.2 lb. (2.8 kg)
Caliber: 5.56 x 45 mm
Rifling: n.k.
Operation: gas-operated rotating-bolt
Feed: 10- or 30-round box magazine or 100-round drum magazine
Muz vel: n.k.

The XM8 Lightweight Modular Carbine Weapon is a prototype weapon that is earmarked to be a future replacement for the M16A2 beginning in 2005. Designed by Heckler and Koch, this ultramodern assault rifle is actually the 5.56 mm kinetic energy element of the Objective Individual Combat Weapon. Internally the XM8 is simply a rotating-bolt gas-operated rifle. Unlike the M16A2, however, the XM8 does not channel gases back into the receiver, therefore reducing carbon fouling and consequently increasing the weapon's reliability. H. and K. also states that "this system also allows the weapon to fire more than 15,000 rounds without lubrication or cleaning in even the worst operational environments." The XM8 is a modular weapon, and the XM320 40 mm grenade launcher and LSS lightweight 12-gauge shotgun can be attached to the XM8 without tools. Most of the rifle's components are interchangeable, including the barrel (the XM8 is intended to be caliber-convertible), receiver and buttstock. Ammunition feed is from 10- or 30-round box magazines or 100-round drum magazines. The standard sight is an optical red-dot sight that uses an IR laser aimer and laser illuminator. The sight rails allow the sight to be removed and refitted without losing zero.

ITALY

FALCO ALBERTI GARDEN GUN 1997

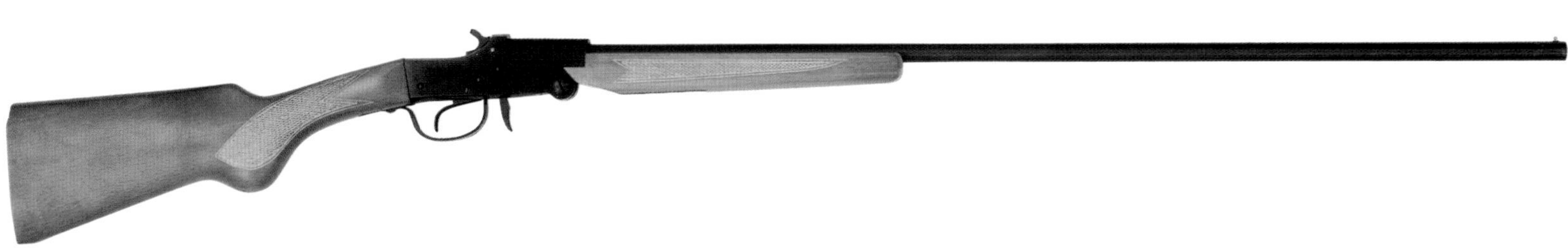

Length (gun): 40.5 in. (1,030 mm)
Barrel: 27.6 in. (702 mm)
Weight (gun): 2.9 lb. (1.3 kg)
Caliber: 9 mm, rimfire
Rifling: none
Operation: single-action, exposed-hammer
Feed: single-round, manual
Muz vel: n.k.

The little 9 mm Falco Alberti garden gun is basic, with little to go wrong. The 9 mm rimfire shells put little strain on the mechanism and pose little in the way of public hazard, although they are sufficient for small vermin at close range. The spur ahead of the trigger guard presses rearward to release the barrel, which can then fold back over the gun for easy transport. The ludicrously long barrel is fitted solely for qualifying as a shotgun under British firearms laws; otherwise it would be about 12 inches (305 mm) shorter. The hammer must be thumb-cocked. Under British law, a shotgun is defined as a smoothbore gun with a barrel length of not less than 24 inches. Semi-automatic shotguns must not have a magazine capacity in excess of two cartridges. Shotguns with a shorter barrel or a greater magazine capacity are classified as firearms and are subject to stricter licensing regulations.

HUNTING WITH RIFLES AND SHOTGUNS

Hunting is an activity requiring skill, training, and a knowledge of wildlife. It also requires a firearm that suits the prey type. The following are some of the classic prey types for hunters, with recommendations about the type of firearm and ammunition required to produce a clean and efficient kill.

Small game (rabbits, squirrels, etc.)
Three types of weapons are commonly used against small game: air rifles, shotguns, and .22 rifles. Air rifles have the advantage of limited noise, so they don't scare off other animals after the first shot. Generally, .22-caliber air rifles are preferred, and a gun with around 12 foot/lb. of pressure is recommended to produce a clean kill. Shotguns are excellent small-game weapons, as (in the case of modern double-barrel weapons) they can be choked according to range (modified and improved cylinder is a good combination). Shot size should be #6–#8, as larger shot will probably destroy too much meat. For rifles, a .22 Long Rifle caliber is ideal, giving a decisive shot at ranges of 100 m (328 feet).

Ducks
Duck shooting requires a shotgun, usually a 12-, 16- or 20-gauge weapon (.410 is not generally recommended). Double-barrel guns can offer the advantage of multichoking, whereas single-barrel pump-action or repeating weapons provide more shots through the magazine feed. Shot size depends on the range of shot, the size of the bird, and the season (in winter many ducks have thicker feather coverings). Many veteran duck hunters recommend #4 or #5 shot for long-range ducks, the larger shot size for winter use, although for smaller varieties of duck at close ranges a smaller shot load (such as #6 or #7.5) might be used.

Deer
Deer rifles are typically bolt-action, lever-action, pump-action, or semi-auto weapons fitted with optical scopes. The caliber of an ideal deer rifle is hotly debated, but the most popular calibers in US sales are the .30-06 Springfield, .270 Winchester, .30-30 Winchester, .308 Winchester, .243 Winchester, and 7 mm Remington Magnum. The .30-06 is one of the most useful all-purpose rounds, capable of tackling everything from small deer to bear.

Above: *A hunter displays a deer kill. The deer was shot at a range of 440 yd. with a .25-caliber Winchester M70 carbine. The M70 series is popular with hunters, featuring a a strong claw ejector and high-quality furniture.*

INDIA

INSAS 1997

Length (gun): 38.97 in. (990 mm)
Barrel: 18.26 in. (464 mm)
Weight (gun): 7.05 lb. (3.20 kg)
Caliber: 5.56 x 45 mm NATO
Rifling: 6 grooves, r/hand
Operation: gas-operated
Feed: 20- or 30-round detachable box magazine
Muz vel: 2,903 ft./sec. (885 m/sec.)

The INSAS (Indian Small Arms System) assault rifle entered service with the Indian Army in 1997 and was intended as a replacement for the 7.62 mm Ishapore FN FAL. Development actually began in the mid 1980s, when the Ordnance Factory Board (OFB) and Armaments Research and Development Establishment (ARDE), Pune, was commissioned to design a replacement for the older weapon that was more in line with modern small-caliber, high-velocity weapons such as the M16 and utilize the 5.56 x 45 mm SS109 NATO round (the INSAS can take the standard M16 magazine, although the indigenous standard magazine is of transparent plastic design). The INSAS is a fairly standard rotating-bolt gas-operated assault rifle that combines different elements from other successful weapons. The receiver and pistol grip are indebted to the AKM, the stock, flash hider (which also acts as a rifle grenade launcher), and regulator to the FN FAL, the fore end to the M16, and the cocking handle to those of H. and K. (For interest, the picture at left shows a 30 mm AG-17 automatic grenade launcher.) Construction materials include plastics for the furniture and sheet-metal pressings for the receiver. The barrel is chrome-lined. Fire selection is single or three-round burst. Optical and passive night sights can be fitted. Built at the Rifle Factory, Ishapore, at least 300,000 are in service with the Indian Army.

SOUTH AFRICA

VEKTOR 5.56 MM CR-21 ASSAULT RIFLE 1997

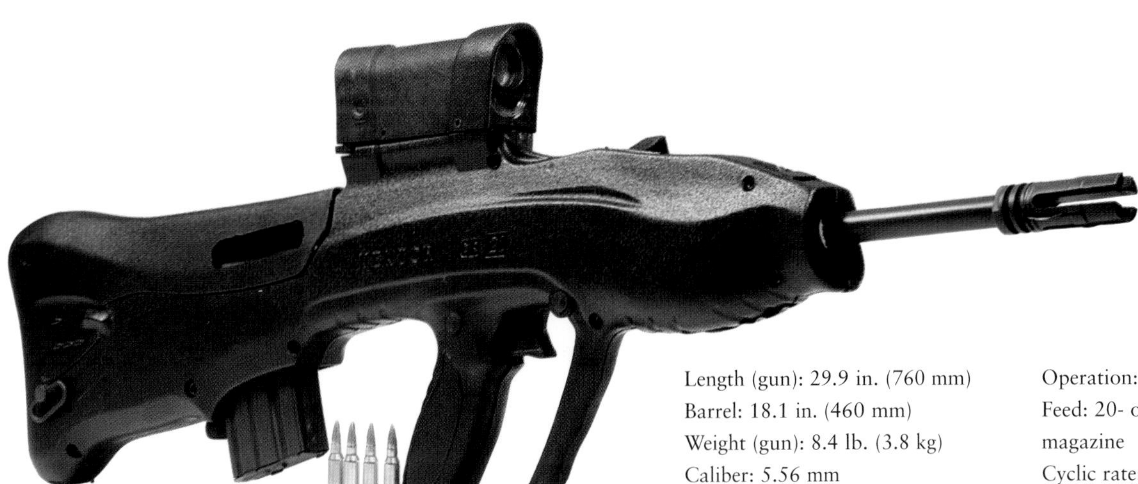

Length (gun): 29.9 in. (760 mm)
Barrel: 18.1 in. (460 mm)
Weight (gun): 8.4 lb. (3.8 kg)
Caliber: 5.56 mm
Rifling: 6 grooves, r/hand
Operation: gas, bullpup
Feed: 20- or 35-round box magazine
Cyclic rate: 700 rpm
Muz vel: 3,215 ft./sec. (980 m/sec.)

One of the "new look" assault rifles, The South African CR-21 (Combat Rifle for the 21st Century) was revealed in 1997. It is designed on the "bullpup" principle, with a short butt and the magazine housing behind the trigger group. Handling and strength considerations have been optimized in the design, making extensive use of modern synthetic polymer-based materials; it is very light, just 8.4 lb. (3.8 kg) fully loaded. It is gas-operated, with a rotating bolt and has its center of gravity above the pistol grip, making it easy for the firer to control. The carrying grip contains the x1 reflex optical sight, made by Vektor, which is intended to be used with both eyes open and is claimed to make training easy and to improve the probability of a first-round hit in combat. The sight also includes a unique, Vektor-developed adjustment mechanism for zeroing. The CR-21 can fire both SS109 and M193 series 5.56 x 45 mm ammunition, and the muzzle has a pronged flash suppressor that claims to virtually eliminate flash, even at night, and can also be used as a grenade launcher. Maximum effective range is about 500 yd. (457 m).

UNITED STATES

REMINGTON 40XB RANGEMASTER TARGET RIFLE 1998

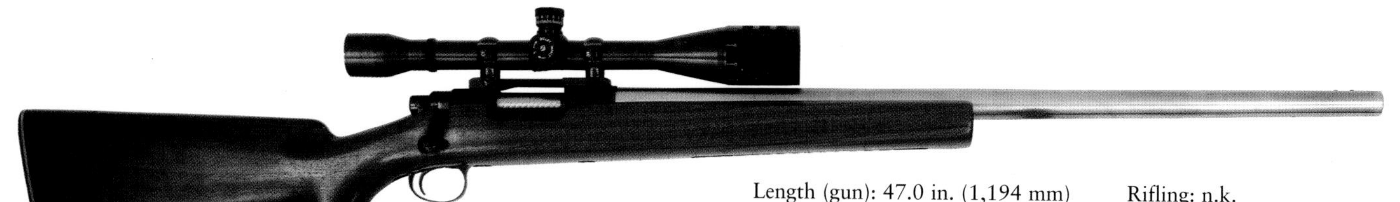

Length (gun): 47.0 in. (1,194 mm)
Barrel: 27.3 in. (692 mm)
Weight (gun): 13.0 lb. (5.6 kg)
Caliber: 0.30-338 Magnum
Rifling: n.k.
Operation: bolt-action
Feed: single-round, manual
Muz vel: n.k.

The Model 40XB is built in Remington's "Custom Shop" on Model 700 receivers taken from the production line before the magazine opening is cut. They are then lathe-turned to very tight standards of concentricity and fitted with special barrels, with barrel and receiver trued square and adjusted for minimum head space. The bolt lugs are lapped for full bearing contact, and most of these guns carry Remington's 2-ounce (57g) trigger. They come with guaranteed accuracy of a minute of angle (1MOA) or less. In 0.222 or 0.223, Remington guarantees 0.45 in. (11 mm) groups; in 7.62 mm, 0.75 in. (19 mm) groups at 100 yd. (91 m). The illustration shows a Remington Model 40X in 0.30-338—a 0.38 Winchester Magnum necked to 0.30 cal.

SINGAPORE

CIS 5.56 MM SAR-21 ASSAULT RIFLE 1999

Length (gun): 31.7 in. (805 mm)
Barrel: 20.0 in. (508 mm)
Weight (gun): 8.4 lb. (3.8 kg)
Caliber: 5.56 mm
Rifling: n.k.
Operation: gas-operated, bullpup
Feed: 30-round box magazine
Cyclic rate: 650 rpm
Muz vel: n.k.

The SAR-21 is a 5.56 mm gas-operated "bullpup" weapon, with a maximum use of high-strength engineering plastics and composites. It consists of four main elements: barrel group, which includes the main part of the body and the carrying handle; bolt group; upper receiver group, including the trigger and magazine housing; and the lower receiver group, which includes the butt plate. The weapon has a rotating bolt and can fire either full- or semi-automatic. One unusual feature is the patented high-pressure vent hole in the chamber wall, which is designed to release high-pressure gas harmlessly into the atmosphere in the event of a chamber explosion. There is a x1.5 optical scope (x3 optional) integrated into the carrying handle with backup iron sights on the top. A laser-aiming device is mounted in the front plate of the body and powered by one AA-size battery.

UNITED STATES

HART MODEL 2 1998

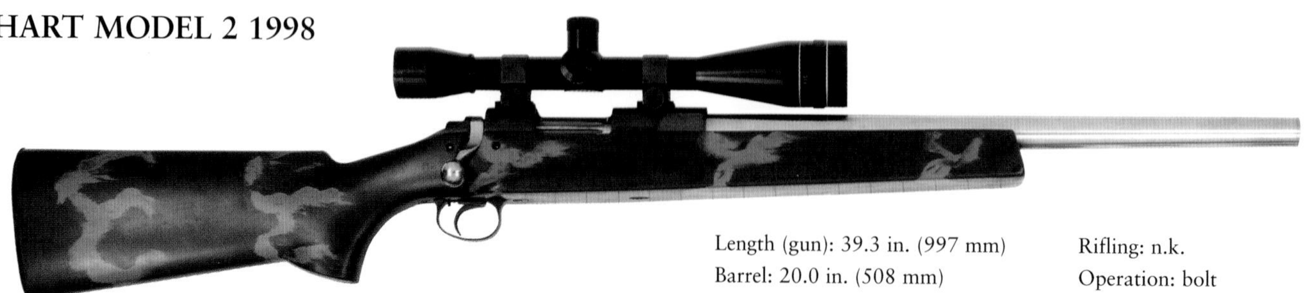

Length (gun): 39.3 in. (997 mm)
Barrel: 20.0 in. (508 mm)
Weight (gun): 10.4 lb. (4.7 kg)
Caliber: 0.22 PPC
Rifling: n.k.
Operation: bolt
Feed: single-round, manual
Muz vel: n.k.

The successor to the Remington 40XB BR as top rifle was the Model 2, built by Robert Hart of Pennsylvania. This used a fluted bolt (to save weight) and a massive action, with thick receiver walls and a receiver ring nearly twice the length of that on the Remington. The barrel unscrewed by hand, but all the engagements of barrel, bolt, and receiver were machined to be absolutely true. Operation is by bolt-action, with the bolt handle lifted to unlock the breech and cock the striker. Each round must be placed in the breech by hand, as there is no magazine. The Hart is chambered for the 0.22 PPC, the initials taken from the surnames of the designers, Pindell and Palmisano, together with "C" for cartridge. This was derived from a necked-down 7.62 x 39 mm Soviet case and was based on computer calculations concerning the most efficient combustion chamber configuration for a given projectile.

THE FUTURE OF MILITARY RIFLES

The future of military weapons is, of course extremely hard to predict. The gas- or recoil-operated weapon firing unitary metal cartridges is certainly going to be with us for a lot longer, such is its success and the political/industrial force stacked behind it. The real changes will probably lie within one word: modularity.

Modularity is the buzz word among US military weapons designers, referring to a weapon's ability to alter its function or range of capabilities through interchangeable components or via the influence of ancillary devices. The assault rifle may no longer be a separate piece of kit, but part of an integrated combat system. Such is typified by the US Army's Land Warrior program. Land Warrior was a program that began in 1991 and looked to transform the infantryman into a total combat system through technology. At the heart of this system is a "ruggedized" portable computer that uses a secure wireless link to transmit combat data direct to and from the infantryman—data such as real-time maps of forces deployments, GPS information, artillery coordinates, etc. The M16A2 rifle is upgraded to receive a Thermal Weapon Sight (TWS) and video camera sight. Both relay pictures to a monocular visual display unit worn as part of the soldier's Integrated Helmet Assembly Subsystem. The infantryman can use the video camera and TWS as gun sights, enabling him to shoot around corners and at night. Also, a laser range-finder fitted to the weapon provides the soldier with accurate distance information either for personal engagement or to provide artillery support with range data.

Land Warrior boosts the capabilities of the assault rifle through ancillary technologies, but the United States is also introducing new weapon types that may replace the M16A2. These are the Objective Individual Combat Weapon (OICW) and the XM8, both of which are covered in separate entries in this book. These weapons emphasize modularity: the OICW has a 5.56 mm kinetic energy weapon and a magazine-fed 20 mm grenade launcher in one unit; the XM8 (purely a 5.56 mm assault rifle) uses interchangeable parts and additional sighting/weapon subsystems. The question remains whether the advances in technology will be a help or a hindrance on the actual battlefield. All is speculation; perhaps Einstein was right: "I know not with what weapons World War III will be fought, but World War IV will be fought with sticks and stones."

Above: *A vision of the future infantryman? This US Army Infantryman 2000 concept features a soldier with modular rifle/grenade launcher linked to an eyes-up display in the helmet. The rifle sight can feed back images to the eyepiece, enabling the soldier to look or fire around corners while remaining behind cover. Other weapons systems include antitank missiles (seen carried on this soldier's back).*

SUBMACHINE GUNS

> *"With its small size, its light weight, its tremendous rate of fire, and its ease of control, the Thompson Gun is probably the most efficient man killer of any firearms yet produced."*
>
> FROM AN ARTICLE IN THE JOURNAL *SCIENTIFIC AMERICAN*, 1921.

Above: *The ultimate portable firepower. The VZ 61 Skorpion measures only 10 in. (271 mm) with the stock folded, but can empty its 20-round magazine in around three seconds, operating at a cyclical rate of 700rpm.*

Close-quarter combat places unusual burdens on firearms. Achieving accurate shooting at close-quarters can, despite the short range, be difficult because targets are usually presented for fleeting durations. Close-quarters combat also requires a weapon that is easily handled, something that excludes many rifles, because of their extended length. Power is also a problem. Firing rounds which are too powerful—particularly long-range rifle rounds such as the 7.62 x 51 mm NATO—within the confines of, say, a building or a trench system means that bullets will likely travel straight through their targets and increase the numbers of ricochets and friendly fatalities.

It was these issues, among others, which saw the rise of the submachine gun as a weapons system in the twentieth century. Submachine guns are single-operator automatic weapons firing pistol cartridges, fed from box or drum magazines. They are lighter and shorter than rifles but provide heavier and more accurate volumes of fire than a pistol. This "intermediate" role has, as we shall see, made the submachine gun a practical yet simultaneously problematic weapon to issue to units. Modern assault rifles can take the roles of rifles, SMGs, and in some cases light machine guns, which complicates production and supply. Although the popularity of the form reached a low point shortly after World War II, it has today experienced a resurgence in certain contexts.

The tool for the job

Unlike most other small-arms types, the SMG evolved in a very specific time frame to meet unique combat conditions. In World War I (1914–1918), it soon became apparent to the principal combatants that a new system of firepower was required to fulfil the requirements of trench combat. Rifles such as the Mauser 98 and the SMLE were fine combat weapons at range, but in the confines of a trench they were unwieldy, excessively powerful (a typical Mauser 98 had a killing range of 1 mile), their reloading actions were too slow, and magazine capacity too limited. Also, better support weapons were required for the advance across no-man's land, when the support fire from machine guns had often stopped.

The submachine gun was the answer. Italy led the way, producing the double-barrelled Villar-Perosa weapon in 1915, a delayed blowback weapon firing 9mm Glisenti pistol cartridges and which, with the help of a support strap, could be fired from the hip. With its 1200rpm rate of fire, the Villar-Perosa was a powerful weapon, and other nations took notice of the SMG form—especially Germany.

Germany had attempted to make a light assault weapon out of its C/96 Mauser pistol and its Luger 08 Parabellum simply by elongating the barrels of both and fitting extended magazines and detachable buttstocks. This arrangement, however, was not satisfactory, and most models of the pistol were not fully automatic (an automatic version of the C/96 was produced, known as the M712). However, German gun designers soon realized that it would be more productive to design a specific full-auto weapon rather than modify pistols, and this resulted in the first true SMG, designed by Hugo

Schmeisser, the Bergman MP18. The blowback-operated MP18 featured a 32-round "snail-drum" magazine that fed 9 mm Parabellum rounds at a rate of 400 rpm (there was no single-shot setting).

In a clear indication that the long-range psychology had yet to be overcome, the sights were set to 3,280 ft. (1,000 m), although its effective combat range was actually around 656 ft. (200 m). The MP18 was descriptively known as the "trench broom," and it certainly must have been a potent weapon within those confines. However, the weapon came too late, some 35,000 being produced in the last year of the war, so its battlefield effect was limited.

The inter-war years

The Bergman had no real equivalent among the Allies in World War I. The only similar effort was the unsuccessful US Pedersen Device, a curious blowback mechanism which could be fitted in about 15 seconds into the breech of a Springfield 03 rifle to covert it into a semi- or full-automatic weapon. The Pedersen was not a success, but in the interwar years the US more than caught up with the SMG principle. In 1921 Colonel J.T. Thompson unveiled the M1921 .45 caliber SMG, the cartridge combined with an 800rpm rate of fire making it a fearsome weapon.

Europe was also pushing ahead with SMG technology in the interwar years. Italy maintained its lead in SMGs by producing a series of fine Beretta weapons (the Model 18, Model 1918/30, and Model 38A), although, typical of many Italian firearms, they required demanding engineering, unsuited for wartime production. Switzerland, used by Germany as a weapons producer to circumvent the prohibitions of the Versailles Treaty, produced the 9 mm Steyr-Solothurn SI-100, a blowback weapon of superior quality. In 1938 France issued the 7.65 mm MAS 38, a controllable and light weapon with a simple, reliable mechanism. Spain developed the 9 mm Labora and the 9 mm SI35 in the late 1930s, the former being used heavily in the

Below: *A British patrol mixes Sten SMGs and various handguns to create a powerful close-range fighting capability during action in Oosterbeck in September 1944.*

Spanish Civil War while the latter never made it to large-scale production. The Russians also entered the SMG age with the 7.65 mm PPD-34/38 series of weapons, which fired from either a 25-round box magazine or a 71-round drum magazine, and proved to be a solid and reliable performer.

It was Germany, however, which would enter World War II with probably the most widely recognized SMG. The Germans modified the MP18 in 1928 to take more convenient box magazines and fire on either single-shot or full-auto, and this model, the MP28, would later become the the inspiration for the British Lanchester SMG of 1940. However, in 1938 German's infamous MP38 went in to production, and this would become a defining weapon of World War II.

World War II submachine guns

What made the MP38 and its successor, the MP40, notable was not so much their performance, which was rivaled by many other weapons, but their construction process. The MP38 was machined from steel, but the MP40 was produced using pressings and sub-assemblies, making it ideal for mass production. Thus the German army fought its way through the war equipped with around one million MP38/40s, and although crude, they were potent short-range killing weapons, working off 32-round box magazines and firing at a cyclical rate of 500 rpm.

Below: *A soldier armed with a 9mm Sten Mk III forms part of a patrol in France in 1944. In terms of use, the submachine gun reached its high point during World War II, as in the postwar years SMGs were steadily replaced by assault rifles as the standard infantry weapon.*

The rest of the world looked at the German SMGs and realized that an effective submachine gun was not only one that worked well, it also had to be in the hands of as many soldiers as possible. So World War II saw the SMG enter its mass-production era, as the combatants churned out crude weapons in their millions, most of which, like the German weapons, replaced wooden furniture with wire stocks.

The British introduced the 9 mm Sten in 1941, a crude blowback weapon with unfiled weldings and a single strut stock with a buttplate welded to it. More than two million Mk II Stens were produced in three years. The US put the .45 ACP M3 "Grease Gun" SMG into service in 1942, improving this with the M3A1 in 1944, and 700,000 of both types were made, with each unit costing only around twenty five dollars.

The Soviets also pushed ahead with SMG design during the war, and in many ways their weapons were superior to those in the west, as they combined simplicity of manufacture with a tremendous reliability and solidity. The PPSh-41 was arguably the finest SMG of the war, cheap and quick to make, dependable in action, and effective when firing at a 900 rpm cyclical rate from a 35-round box magazine or the 71-round drum. A total of five million were made, and the numbers alone gave the Soviets a distinct advantage in urban battles such as occurred in Stalingrad and Kharkov.

The war ended with the SMG having served with distinction, but changes in the post-war world would see a major decline in the use of the SMG as a military firearm.

Postwar fall and rise

The postwar climate saw the rise of a new weapon type—the assault rifle and the consequent decline of SMG usage as a military weapon. The assault rifle fused the capabilities of the rifle and the SMG into one, and outperformed the SMG at every level. Assault rifles had selective-fire modes often including full-auto options, were accurate up to and over 1640 ft. (500 m), and had more powerful terminal ballistics.

Throughout the 1950s and 1960s the SMGs were steadily replaced by assault rifles in most world armies. The Red Army withdrew all SMGs from service by 1950, despite the fact that they had previously made more use of SMGs than any other nation. Other armies kept SMGs in service, but in a reduced role. The British and French armies, for example, issued the Sterling and the MAT-49 weapons respectively to one member among each squad, when the L1A1 SLR (the British version of the FN FAL) and the MAS-49/56 were the standard issue rifles. Also, US Army M3s were to be found in service in various roles until the 1970s, and were especially popular with US troops in Vietnam, having already proved their tropical credentials during the World War II Pacific campaign.

Despite some SMGs hanging on in certain armies, it was standardization of the 5.56 mm round in NATO in 1980 that finally took the SMG out of mainstream military use. The new round was perfectly controllable even in full-auto fire, and could be fired from carbine models of rifles, which had the dimensions of SMGs but with significantly improved performance. However, although the modern assault rifle definitely did reduce the number of SMGs in circulation, it did not spell the end.

Submachine guns have experienced a major revival over the last twenty years in police and security work. SMGs offer some important advantages in internal security operations, they give the officers heavy firepower but the pistol-calibre rounds are not over-powered for close-quarters urban actions. This means that an officer can, say, shoot a terrorist in reasonable confidence that his rounds will not pass straight through and hit hostages.

The advantages of the 9 mm round are such that both the M16 and the Steyr AUG are available chambered for 9 mm (the 9mm M16 was used by US Marines in Panama in 1989, an operation in which tens of thousands of potential US hostages were at stake).

The supreme modern submachine gun is the 9mm Heckler & Koch MP5, a state-of-the-art weapon used by counter-terrorist and police forces the world over, including the SAS, Delta Force, SWAT teams, and many others. The MP5 fires from a closed bolt, which makes it highly accurate, and is reliable and easy to control on full auto, a key consideration. Other first-class SMGs include the Italian Beretta PM12 and the Polish RAK PM-63.

Very small machine pistols such as the Ingram MAC 10, the Uzi, and the Czech Skorpion, are also easily concealed under a jacket, so are ideal for undercover deployments.

Submachine guns are once again a respected weapons system and have had their role in law enforcement and military operations defined and rationalized. We will surely never see the time again where entire armies have SMGs as a high percentage of their small arms, but as the weapons of some of the world's most professional and expert combatants, the SMG will always be a respected weapon of undoubted close-range power.

Above: *An Italian Folgore paratrooper takes aim with a Beretta PM 12. Submachine guns have traditionally been popular with paratroopers and Special Forces soldiers, as they offer heavy firepower but with convenient portability.*

STERLING L34A1 SUBMACHINE GUN (SILENCED)

The L34A1 is the silenced version of the British Sterling SMG adopted in 1954, which is itself the successor to the Sten gun, which was used widely during World War II and since. The Sterling has a normal blowback mechanism but is unusual in having a ribbed bolt which cuts away dirt and fouling as it accumulates and forces it out of the receiver. In the L34A1 the barrel jacket is covered by a silencer casing, with front and rear supports. The barrel has 72 radial holes drilled through it, which permits propellant gas to escape, thus reducing the muzzle velocity of the bullet. The barrel has a metal wrap and diffuser tube; the extension tube goes beyond the silencer casing and barrel. A spiral diffuser beyond the barrel is a series of disks, which has a hole through the center that allows passage of the round. Gas follows the round closely and is deflected back by the end cap; it mingles with the gases that are coming forward—with the result that the gas velocity leaving the weapon is correspondingly low.

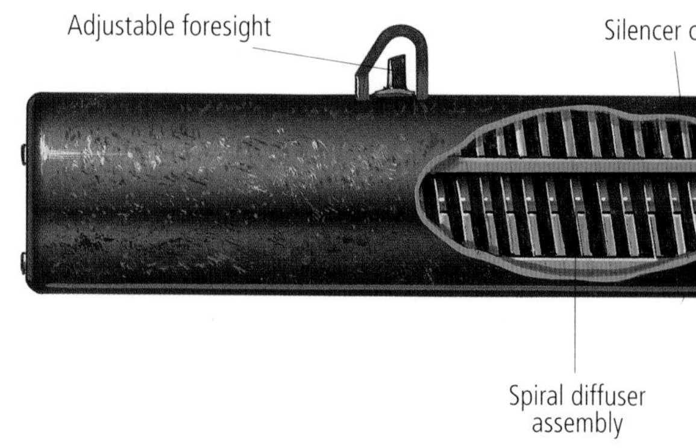

STERLING L34A1 SUBMACHINE GUN (SILENCED)

UZI SUBMACHINE GUN

Designed by Uziel Gal (who died in 2002 at the age of 78) and based on post-World War II Czechoslovakian 9mm Models 23 and 25, the Uzi was developed to fill the Israeli requirement to arm her defense forces with reliable, home-produced guns following the establishment of the state of Israel in 1948. It is now probably the most widely used submachine gun in the Western world, in service with, in addition to Israeli forces, Belgium, Germany, Iran, the Netherlands, Thailand, Venezuela, and other countries, and many paramilitary forces and terrorist groups. A Mini-Uzi has been developed, smaller, lighter, and with different firing characteristics.

It is of simple blowback design. The bolt is cocked by drawing it to the rear. The sear rotates up to engage and hold it open. A coil spring is used to tension the sear; pulling the trigger to the rear allows the sear to move down and rotate out of engagement with the bolt. The bolt's own coil spring drives it forward, stripping a cartridge from the magazine, chambering it and firing it as the striker in the bolt face impacts the primer. The momentum generated by the exploding cartridge then drives the bolt to the rear, extracting and ejecting the fired case—until it comes up against the bolt stop. Its spring then drives it forward again in a repeat cycle. Current Uzis are fitted with a grip safety, which blocks the trigger unless depressed.

Foresight protectors
Barrel nut
Barrel
Forehand grip

UZI SUBMACHINE GUN

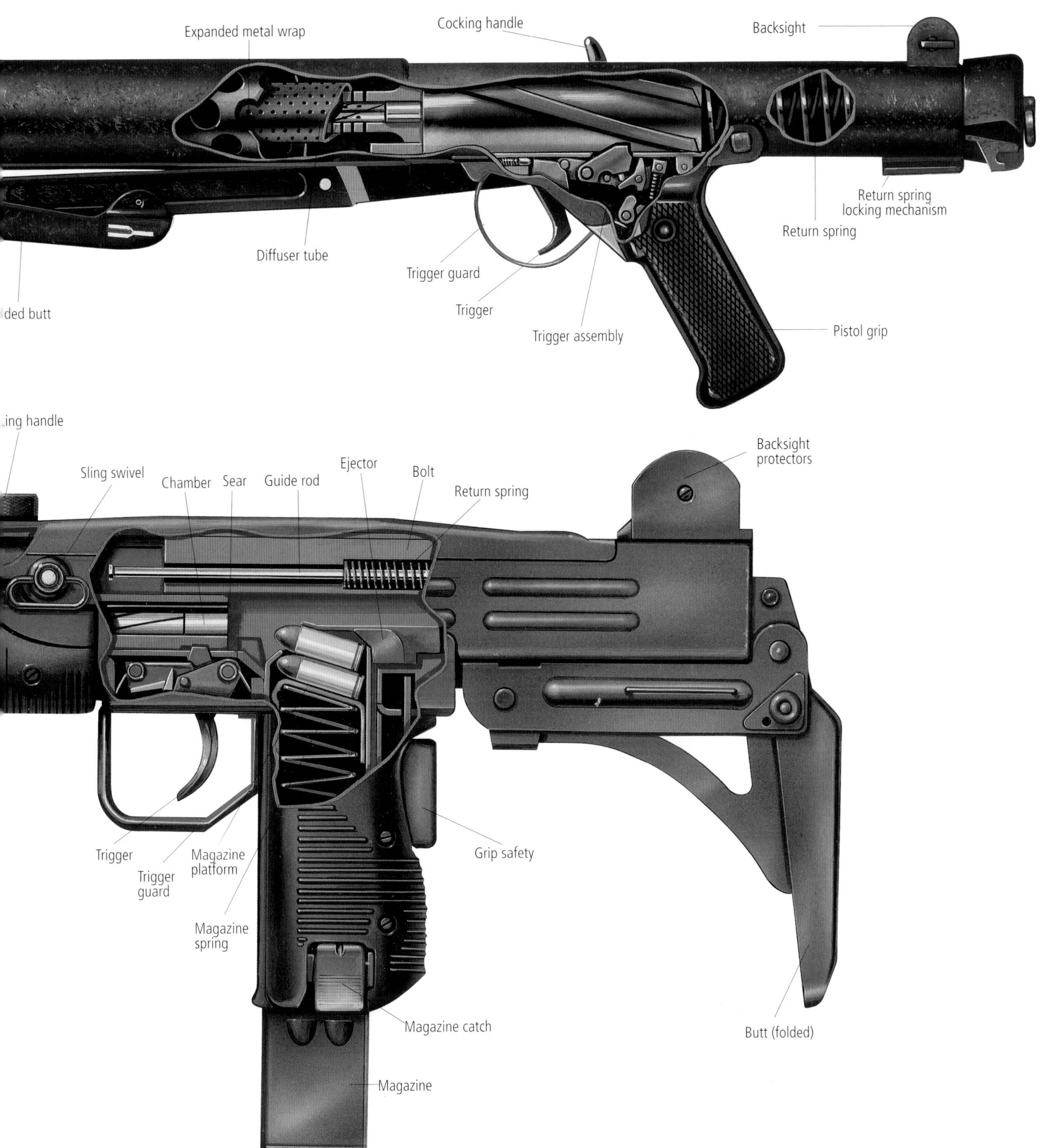
Expanded metal wrap
Cocking handle
Backsight
Return spring
locking mechanism
Return spring
Diffuser tube
Trigger guard
Trigger
ded butt
Trigger assembly
Pistol grip
ing handle
Sling swivel
Chamber
Sear
Guide rod
Ejector
Bolt
Return spring
Backsight
protectors
Trigger
Trigger
guard
Magazine
platform
Magazine
spring
Grip safety
Magazine catch
Butt (folded)
Magazine

GERMANY

BERGMANN MP 18.I 1918

Length (gun): 32.0 in. (813 mm)
Barrel: 7.9 in. (200 mm)
Weight: 9.2 lb. (4.9 kg)
Caliber: 9 mm
Rifling: 6 grooves, r/hand

Operation: blowback
Feed: 32-round snail drum
Cyclic rate: 400 rpm
Muz vel: 1,250 ft./sec. (365 m/sec.)

One of the genuinely new weapons to appear in World War I was the submachine gun. Work on a prototype weapon started in 1916 at the Bergmann factory, designed by Hugo Schmeisser. By the early months of 1918, it was in limited production. The Germans appreciated that, at that late stage of the war, when their manufacturing capacity was fully extended, any new weapon would have to be simple to make and the MP 18.I fulfilled that requirement. The techniques of mass production by the use of pressings, spot-welding, and pinning were, however, hardly developed, so "simple" is a relative term compared with, say, the Sten gun of a quarter century later. The Bergmann was machined, and although elaborate milling had been abandoned by necessity, its general finish was relatively good. Its weakest component was its magazine, which originally developed for the Luger pistol, and too complex and prone to stoppage to be fully reliable. The Germans proposed to have six guns per company. Each was to have a number two to carry ammunition, and there were to be three hand carts in addition, which presupposed a type of barrage fire, but the weapon came too late.

GERMANY

BERGMANN MP 28.II 1928

Length (gun): 32.0 in. (812 mm)
Barrel: 7.8 in. (199 mm)
Weight: 8.8 lb (4 kg)
Caliber: 9 mm
Rifling: 6 grooves, r/hand

Operation: blowback
Feed: 20/30/50-round box
Cyclic rate: 500 rpm
Muz vel: 1,250 ft./sec. (365 m/sec.)

A modified MP 18.I appeared in 1928 as the MP 28.II, the II denoting two minor modifications to the prototype. The new gun could fire bursts or single shots; a circular stud above the trigger had to be pushed in from the right for automatic, and from the left for single shots. The gun incorporated an elaborate tangent back sight optimistically graduated by hundreds up to 1,094 yd. (1,000 m). It was equipped with straight box magazines, but the magazine housing would also accept the old snail-drum type. The Bergmann MP 28.II was produced in Germany by Haenel at Suhl, but as there were still some restrictions on domestic production of military firearms, a great many more were produced under license by a Belgian company in Herstal. The gun was adopted by the Belgian Army in small numbers in 1934. The Bergmann soon established a reputation for reliability and was purchased in South America and by the Portuguese, who used it as a police weapon. Although it was mainly manufactured in 9 mm Parabellum, it also appeared in 9 mm Bergmann, 7.65 mm Parabellum, 7.63 mm, and even for the American 0.45 in. cartridge. It seems probable that its main use was in the Spanish Civil War of 1936–39, where its robustness made it an ideal weapon for the militias.

SUBMACHINE GUNS AND THE BLOWBACK ACTION

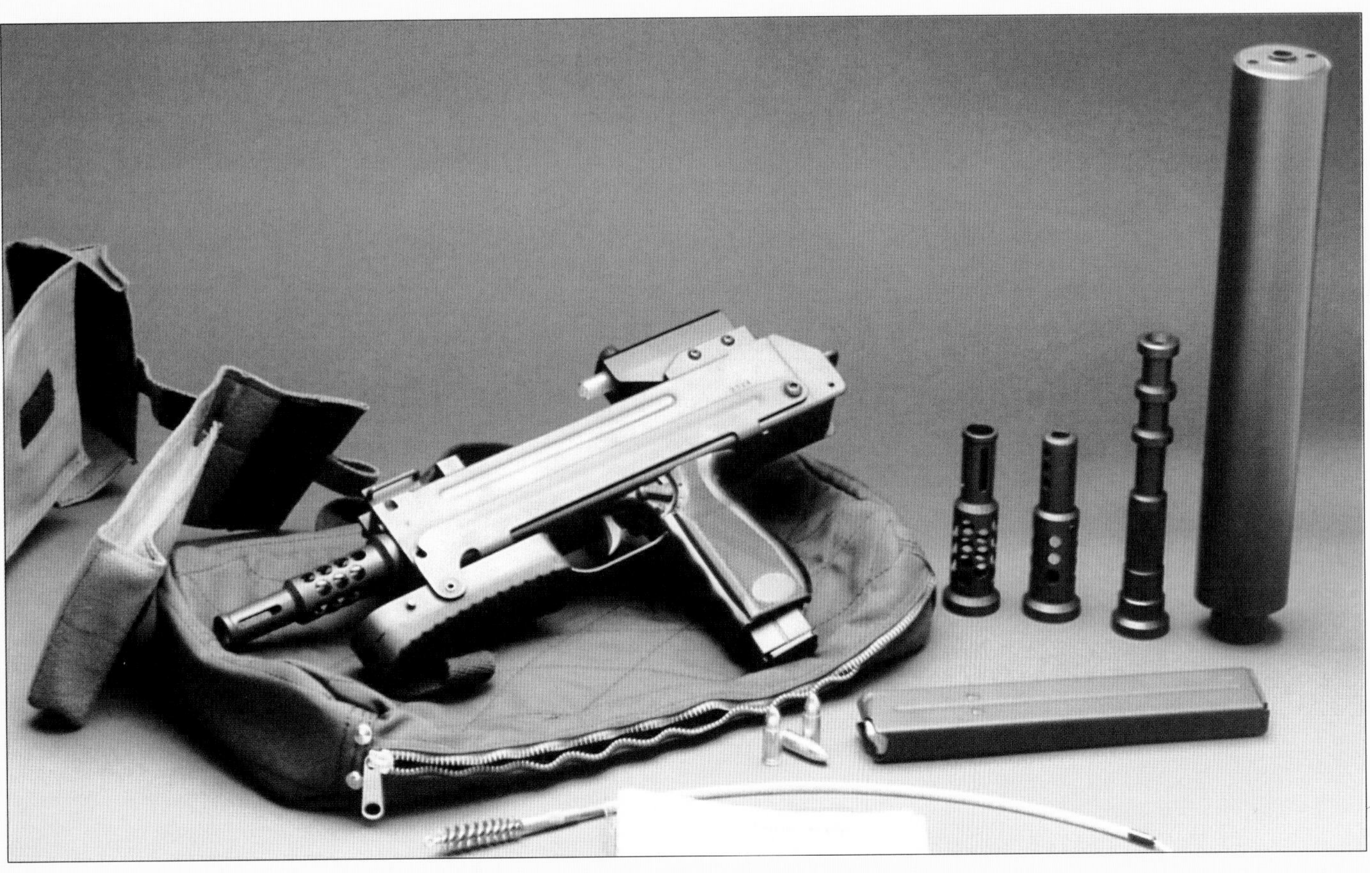

Above: *The South African BXP submachine gun is a classic blowback weapon. It uses a telescoping bolt, the front part of the bolt hollowed out to wrap around the rear portion of the barrel, thus reducing overall dimensions. Using the standard 9 mm Parabellum, the BXP can achieve rates of fire of between 1,000 and 1,200 rpm.*

The blowback action is ideal for submachine guns. It is well suited to pistol-caliber rounds as it is a relatively cheap system to manufacture (so it was ideal for the mass-production SMGs of World War II) and can allow high rates of fire. The basic blowback operating system is explained in the handguns chapter, but to achieve a fast full-auto fire, many submachine guns apply an advanced primer ignition (API) variant on pure blowback. In pure blowback, such as that used in handguns, the bolt is stationary when the gun is fired, serving to hold the cartridge in place in the chamber. However, pure blowback in weapons of larger caliber requires a very heavy bolt that, when oscillating, creates intense vibration and unsettles the stability and, therefore, accuracy of the weapon. API differs in that the bolt is still moving forward when the firing pin is released and fires the cartridge. Note that the bolt is far enough forward to ensure that the cartridge is adequately chambered; the firing pin is released when friction between the round and the chamber is sufficient.

On a 9 mm Sterling L2A3 submachine gun, for example, firing takes place when the bolt is approximately 0.03 in. (0.76 mm) from the breech face. The result is that the rearward force applied to the cartridge base on firing serves two functions: first, it must arrest the forward movement of the bolt; second, it must then drive the bolt backward to cycle the weapon.

API has fundamental advantages for submachine guns. The bolt can be lighter and its movement faster than the bolt in a pure blowback weapon, thereby allowing for higher rates of fire and more stability in the weapon. It is also a simple and reliable design, though not without occasional fault. If there is an accretion of carbon deposits in the chamber, or if ammunition is dirty, friction levels between round and the chamber may build up too early and the cartridge may be fired before it is fully chambered, producing a burst case. Conversely, the bolt can hit the breech face and bounce back slightly before firing, resulting in the bolt being driven backward at nine times its normal kinetic energy (data: Allsop and Toomey, 1999).

Note that API weapons must fire from an open-bolt position, which reduces the accuracy of first shots as the bolt mass has to shift forward before firing. Submachine guns of greater accuracy fire from the closed-bolt position, imposing a mechanical delay on the bolt return to allow gases to drop to safe levels.

UNITED STATES

THOMPSON M1928AI 1928

Length (gun): 33.8 in. (857 mm)
Barrel: 10.5 in. (267 mm)
Weight: 10.8 lb. (4.9 kg)
Caliber: 0.45 in.
Rifling: 6 grooves, r/hand
Operation: blowback
Feed: 50-round drum/20-round box
Cyclic rate: 800 rpm
Muz vel: 920 ft./sec. (281 m/sec.)

The Thompson ("Tommy") gun was developed in the course of World War I but came too late to be used in action. After the war ended, good advertising and publicity ensured a small but steady sale to law enforcement agencies as well as criminals. The weapon illustrated is the M1928A1. The gun worked by the blowback system, but it had a delay device to prevent the bolt from opening until the barrel pressure had dropped. Two squared grooves were cut into the sides of the bolt at an angle of 45 degrees, the lower ends nearer the face of the bolt, and an H-shaped fitted into these. When the bolt was fully home, the bottom ends of the H-piece engaged in recesses in the receiver. When the cartridge fired, the pressure was enough to cause it to rise, thus allowing the bolt to go back after a brief delay. It slowed the cyclic rate, which assisted accurate firing.

AUSTRIA/GERMANY/SWITZERLAND

STEYR SOLOTHURN S100 1929

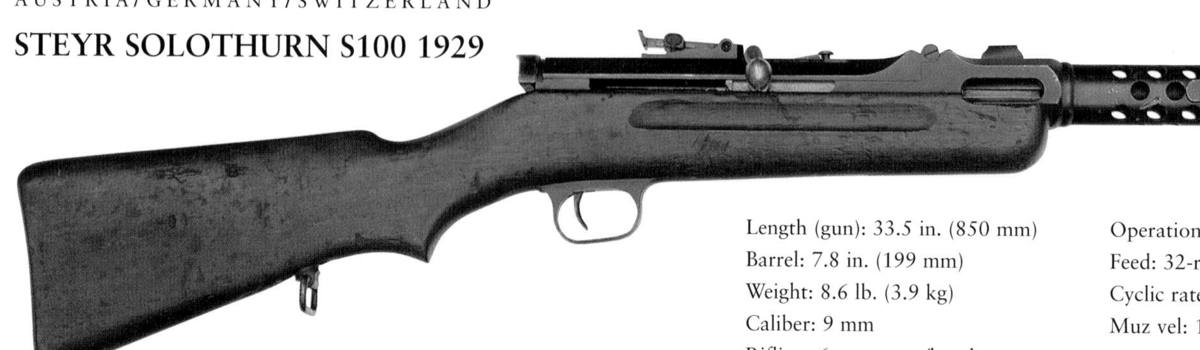

Length (gun): 33.5 in. (850 mm)
Barrel: 7.8 in. (199 mm)
Weight: 8.6 lb. (3.9 kg)
Caliber: 9 mm
Rifling: 6 grooves, r/hand
Operation: blowback
Feed: 32-round box
Cyclic rate: 500 rpm
Muz vel: 1,375 ft./sec. (417 m/sec.)

German arms production was seriously restricted in the years following World War I by the Treaty of Versailles, so in 1929 Rheinmetall acquired the Swiss firm Solothurn to allow it to make and sell arms legally. One of the first projects was the S100, which had been destroyed by Rheinmetall. Through Solothurn, the company subcontracted actual production to the Austrian firm Steyr, which started work in 1929. The S100 was of orthodox mechanism but extremely well made; the machining, milling, and general finish were of an unusually high standard, which must have made it expensive to produce. Most of the production models were fitted with an unusual device in the shape of a built-in magazine filler. The magazine housing had a slot on top with recesses to take the Mauser pistol-type clip, and a magazine locking device underneath.

FINLAND

SUOMI MODEL 1931

Length (gun): 34.3 in. (870 mm)
Barrel: 12.5 in. (317 mm)
Weight: 10.3 lb. (4.7 kg)
Caliber: 9 mm
Rifling: 6 grooves, r/hand
Operation: blowback
Feed: (see text)
Cyclic rate: 900 rpm
Muz vel: 1,312 ft./sec. (400 m/sec.)

The model illustrated was designed by Johannes Lahti. Although patents were not finally granted until 1932, the gun was in use by the Finnish Army the previous year, hence its final designation "Model 31." It worked by normal blowback system and had no fewer than four different magazines, a single 20-round box, a double 50-round box, and two drums—one of 40-round capacity and one of 71. It was well made of good steel, heavily machined and milled, and unusually well finished. The end product was an exceptionally reliable and robust weapon, although it was very heavy by modern standards; with the bigger drum magazine it weighed more than 15 lb. (6.8 kg). This at least had the merit of reducing recoil and vibration, thus increasing accuracy. It was made under license in Sweden, Denmark, and Switzerland, and in addition to Finland was also used by Sweden, Switzerland, Norway, and Poland. The Suomi was still used in many units of the Finnish Army as late as the 1980s.

CZECH REPUBLIC

ZK 383 1933

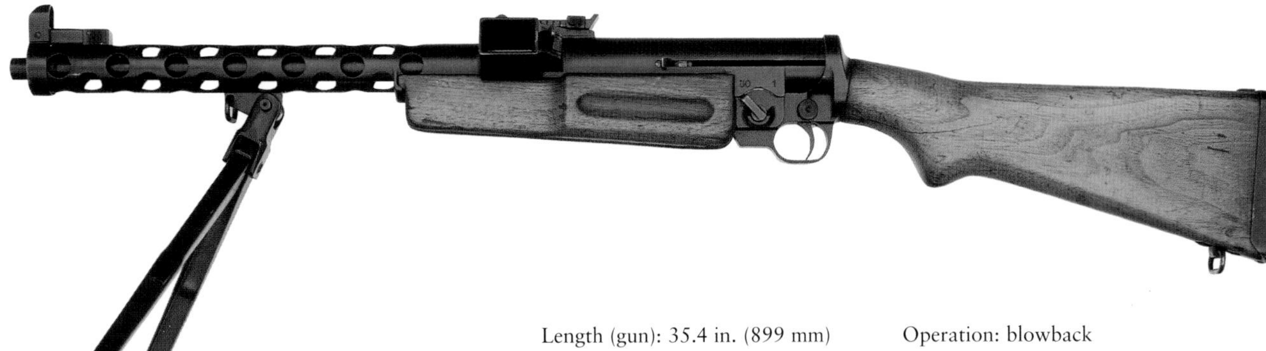

Length (gun): 35.4 in. (899 mm)
Barrel: 12.8 in. (325 mm)
Weight: 9.4 lb. (4.3 kg)
Caliber: 9 mm
Rifling: 6 grooves, r/hand

Operation: blowback
Feed: 30-round box
Cyclic rate: 500 and 700 rpm
Muz vel: 1,250 ft./sec. (365 m/sec.)

This weapon, designed by the Koucky brothers at Brno, was still in production three years after the end of World War II. It was a most sophisticated and well made weapon, manufactured of precision castings of excellent finish. It is of particular interest in that it has a dual rate of fire, achieved by removing a weight on the bolt, which increased its rate of functioning. There was also a quick-release barrel. The ZK 383 fired single rounds or automatic, the change lever above the trigger pushed back or forward as necessary. The stud behind it was the push-in safety. The pierced barrel casing carried the fore sight and a well-made tangent back sight. Another unusual feature was the folding bipod, which made a considerable improvement in the accuracy of the gun. Even so, it is likely that the maximum setting of 2,620 ft. (800 m) was optimistic. This was the standard submachine gun used by the Bulgarian Army during and after World War II. The Germans continued to manufacture it after they had overrun Czechoslovakia and it was used by their SS troops. A modified version was also produced for police use, which had no bipod and no tangent sight. Some models took a bayonet.

RUSSIA

PPD 34/38 1934

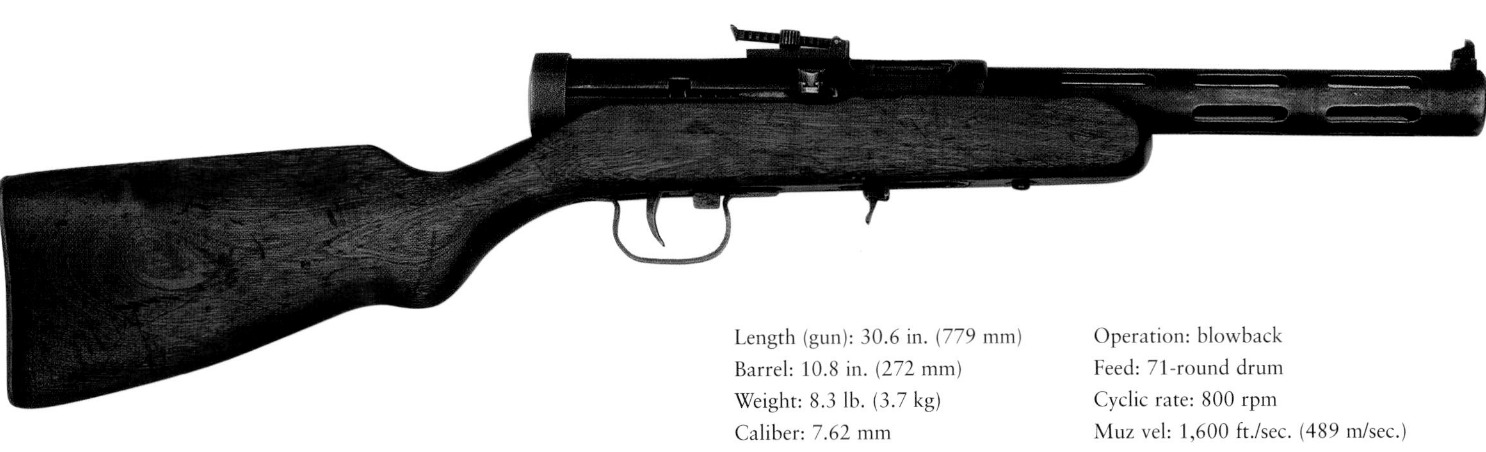

Length (gun): 30.6 in. (779 mm)
Barrel: 10.8 in. (272 mm)
Weight: 8.3 lb. (3.7 kg)
Caliber: 7.62 mm
Rifling: 4 grooves, r/hand

Operation: blowback
Feed: 71-round drum
Cyclic rate: 800 rpm
Muz vel: 1,600 ft./sec. (489 m/sec.)

This weapon, designed by Vasily Degtyaryev, appeared in 1934 and was the first successful weapon of its type to be used in the Soviet Army. It was based closely on the German MP 28.II and was reasonably well made and finished. The PPD worked by normal blowback on the open-bolt principle, single rounds or bursts being obtained with a selector in front of the trigger. Both bore and chamber were chromed to prevent undue wear. The cartridges were fed from a near-vertical drum with an unusual extension piece that fitted into the bottom of the receiver; this drum was worked by clockwork, was similar mechanically to that of the Finnish Suomi (qv), and held 71 rounds. As drum magazines are susceptible to dirt, there were likely problems over stoppages; there was also a curved box magazine, but this was very rarely used. One or two minor variations to the original model were made, the most obvious being the reduction in the number of jacket slots from rows of eight small ones to three larger ones. Although the gun was technically replaced by the PPD 40 in 1940, it was used in the Finnish campaign of World War II and probably also saw later service elsewhere.

THE 9 MM PARABELLUM

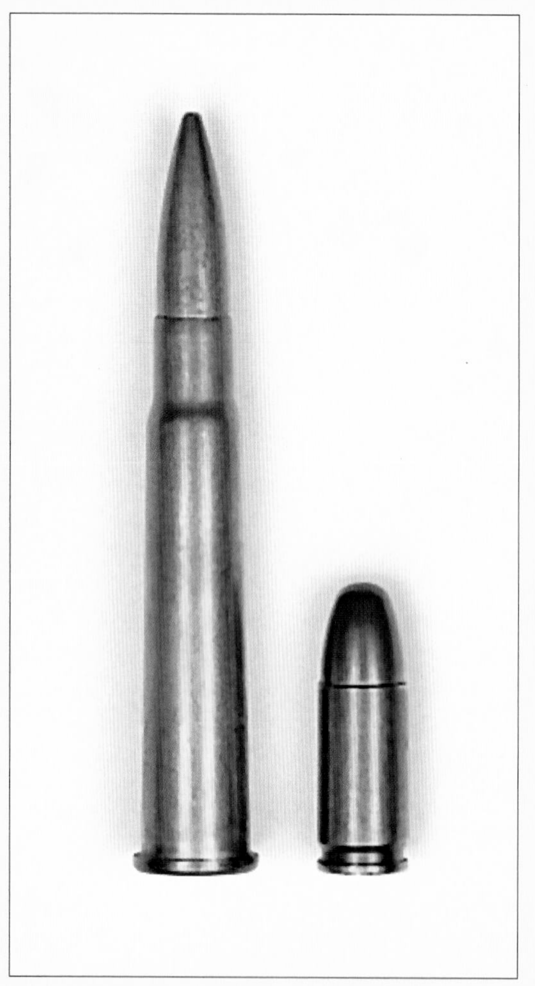

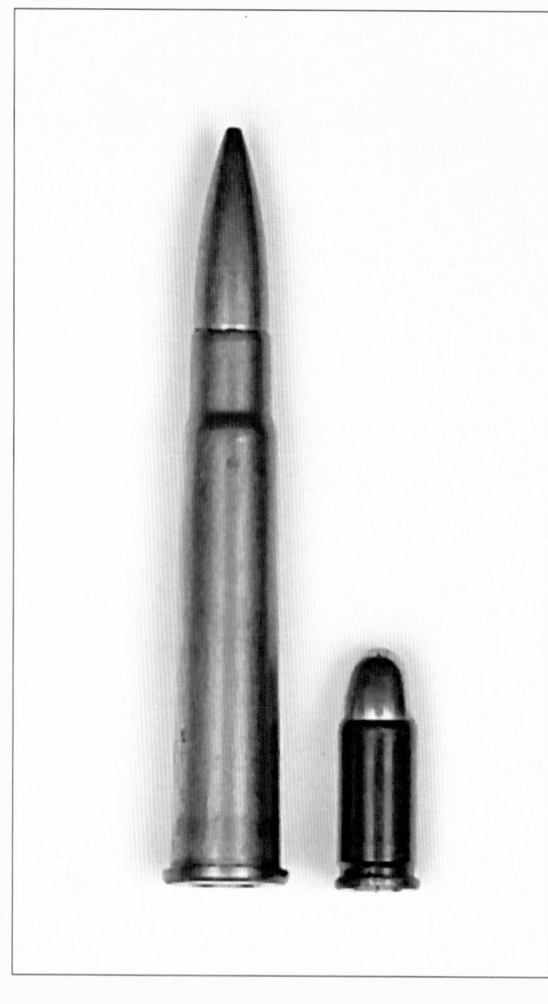

Left: *The 9 mm pistol round has been produced in numerous subtle variations. The 9 mm Parabellum is by far the most widely used, and is pictured on the left set in comparison with a 7.62 mm rifle round. The small cartridge on the right in the 9 mm Short cartridge generates around 25 percent less muzzle velocity than the Parabellum.*

The 9 mm Parabellum pistol round is an ideal cartridge for submachine guns, creating a manageable recoil suited to full-auto fire in blowback- and recoil-operated weapons, and providing sufficient penetration and killing force at close quarters. Although World War II saw the US submachine guns chambered for the .45 ACP, and Russian submachine guns using the 7.62 x 25 mm Soviet, the post-war world almost universally came round to the 9 mm Parabellum for its submachine guns.

The invention of the Parabellum round came from none other than Georg Luger, who in the 1890s was an employee of Ludwig Loewe and Company in Berlin, which produced \ the Borchardt self-loading pistol. Luger worked on developing a replacement for the Borchardt, which went out of production in 1898. The result was the Pistole 1900 in 7.65 mm Parabellum ("Parabellum" is Latin, meaning "for war"). However, many felt that the 7.65 mm round was too small for combat use, so by 1902 he had developed a new 9 mm Parabellum round. Luger's route to the 9 mm round was simply to remove the bottleneck from the 7.65 mm cartridge to create a larger-caliber round that did not require extensive recalibration of the production equipment at Ludwig Loewe and Company.

Although there are many other types of 9 mm round available, the 9 mm Parabellum has been particularly enduring. A basic 9 mm Parabellum NATO standard round has the following statistics: The round length is 1.15 in. (29.28 mm), with the case taking up 0.76 in. (19.35 mm) of a total length. Rim diameter is 0.39 in. (9.94 mm) and bullet weight is 0.27 oz. (7.78 g). In terms of muzzle velocity, the 9 mm Parabellum is one of the faster of the pistol-caliber cartridges at 1299 feet/second (396 m/sec.). By way of comparison, the .45 ACP has a muzzle velocity of 820 feet/second (250 m/sec.). Although muzzle velocity does not equate with take-down force, in a submachine gun the full-auto mode makes a hail of 9 mm rounds a lethal prospect. In terms of terminal ballistics, tests with a 9 mm NATO Ball M882 FMJ round show a generally straight passage through a gelatin block; the larger areas of cavitation are caused by the round tumbling as it passes through the medium.

ITALY

BERETTA MODELLO 38A 1938

Length (gun): 37.3 in. (946 mm)
Barrel: 12.4 in. (315 mm)
Weight: 9.3 lb. (5.0 kg)
Caliber: 9 mm
Rifling: 6 grooves, r/hand

Operation: blowback
Feed: 10/20/40-round box
Cyclic rate: 600 rpm
Muz vel: 1,378 ft./sec. (420 m/sec.)

The Modello 38A had its origins in a self-loading carbine first produced in small numbers for police use in 1935. By 1938 it had been discharged into a true submachine gun. It was well machined and finished, which made it expensive to produce but resulted in a most reliable and accurate arm. It functioned by normal blowback and had a separate firing pin, again a somewhat unusual refinement. Its forward trigger was for single shots, the other for bursts. The first model can be distinguished by the elongated slots in its jacket, by its compensator, which consisted of a single large hole in the top of the muzzle with a bar across it, and a folding, knife-type bayonet. Not many of these were produced before the elongated cooling slots were replaced by round holes, which thereafter remained standard. The third version, seen here, had a new compensator consisting of four separate cuts across the muzzle but no bayonet. This version remained in production for the remainder of the war, used by both the Italian and the German armies; captured specimens were popular with Allied soldiers. The Beretta Modello 38A was also used by a number of other countries, notably Romania and Argentina.

UNITED STATES

UNITED DEFENSE MODEL 42 1938

Length (gun): 32.3 in. (820 mm)
Barrel: 11.0 in. (279 mm)
Weight: 9.1 lb. (4.1 kg)
Caliber: 9 mm/0.45 in.
Rifling: 6 grooves, r/hand

Operation: blowback
Feed: 20-round box
Cyclic rate: 700 rpm
Muz vel: 1,312 ft./sec. (400 m/sec.)

The United States Defense Supply Corporation, a US government corporation, was formed in 1941 to supply weapons to the various Allied nations involved in World War II. The UDM42 (illustrated) was designed in about 1938 by Carl Swebilius and was manufactured by the Marlin Firearms Company. The Model 42 was of normal blowback operation with a separate firing pin inside the bolt, and after one or two modifications it performed particularly well. It was accurate, easy to handle, and almost impervious to dirt. The original models were of 0.45 in. caliber and took a 20-round box magazine, but the production models were all 9 mm and were fitted with double back-to-back magazines, with a total capacity of 40 rounds. The gun was one of the best produced in the United States at that period. It was of the pre-war style of manufacture, made of machined steel and well finished. Its main problem was that it came at a time when the United States was already well equipped with submachine guns. Simplified wartime versions of the Thompson were available, and the mass-produced M3 gun was in an advanced stated of preparation

GERMANY

MASCHINENPISTOLE MP 40 1940

Length (gun): 32.8 in. (833 mm)
Barrel: 9.9 in. (251 mm)
Weight: 8.9 lb. (4.0 kg)
Caliber: 9 mm
Rifling: 6 grooves, r/hand
Operation: blowback
Feed: 32-round box
Cyclic rate: 500 rpm
Muz vel: 1,250 ft./sec. (365 m/sec.)

The MP 38 was the first weapon of its type to be adopted by the German Army since 1918, and was the first arm of its type ever to be made entirely from metal and plastic, with no woodwork of any kind. Gone were the heavy butt and carefully machined body, and in their place had come a folding tubular metal stock and a receiver of steel tube, slotted to reduce weight. The MP 38, although an excellent weapon, was relatively slow and expensive to produce. This led to the gun illustrated, the MP 40, which made more extensive use of pressing, spot-welding, and brazing. Perhaps its most important change was the introduction of a safety device; it had been found (like the Sten) that a moderately severe jolt was sometimes enough to bounce the bolt back and fire a round. A number of the earlier 1938 models were also modified in this way as a result of active service experience. Most of the later MP 40s were made with horizontal ribs on the magazine housing. Only a few, like the one illustrated, were made without them. A later model was fitted with a double side-by-side magazine in a sliding housing. More than a one million had been produced by 1945.

JAPAN

8 MM TYPE 100/40 AND TYPE 100/44 1940

Length (gun): 35.0 in. (890 mm)
Barrel: 9.0 in. (228 mm)
Weight (gun): 8.4 lb. (3.8 kg)
Caliber: 8 mm
Rifling: 6 grooves, r/hand
Operation: blowback
Magazine: 30-round box
Cyclic rate: 450 rpm
Muz vel: 1,100 ft./sec. (335 m/sec.)

The Imperial Japanese Army was very slow to adopt the submachine gun. The Type 100 was introduced in 1940. It had a tubular receiver and a perforated jacket around the barrel, which was fitted with a muzzle compensator. It was an Army requirement, based on Japanese tradition, that as many weapons as possible be fitted with bayonets, so the Type 100/40 (see specifications) had a long bayonet bar under the barrel. The Type 100/40 fired the 8 x 21 mm Nambu round, with 30 rounds carried in a forward-curving box magazine. There were two versions: one with a fixed stock made at Kokura State Arsenals, the other (in top photo) with a folding stock, which was manufactured at Nagoya. The Type 100/40 proved unsatisfactory for a variety of reasons, including frequent stoppages and being too complicated to manufacture; and combat experience showed that the bayonet was of very limited value. As a result, a modified version entered service in 1944, known as the Type 100/44 (bottom photo), which was simpler to produce due to the substitution, wherever possible, of machining by welding, and the removal of the bayonet bar. The cyclic firing rate was also increased to 800 rpm.

AXIS SUBMACHINE GUNS IN WORLD WAR II

Above: *The MP38 and the MP40 submachine guns were excellent additions to the German arsenal. The MP38's appearance in combat in 1939 jolted all of the world's arms manufacturers, who realized that metal stampings and pressings, rather than expensive machining processes, offered better methods of putting SMGs into mass production and into the hands of as many soldiers as possible.*

In 1939, only Germany had convincingly built up its stocks and distribution of submachine guns throughout its military forces. In the context of Blitzkrieg doctrine, they were ideal weapon systems for equipping troops who would be deployed by vehicle, where space would be at a premium and guns might have to be fired through gun ports. (The underbarrel lug on the MP38/40 was meant to sit against the lip of a gun port to stop the weapon moving around under fire and when being fired.)

At the beginning of WW II, the Wehrmacht had equipped itself substantially with the MP38, whereas the Waffen-SS armed its ranks mainly with the Bergmann MP34 (the improved variant MP35 became the Waffen-SS's standard submachine gun in 1940). The MP40 upgrade switched away from the MP38's time-consuming machining production processes to more use of pressings and stampings, dramatically improving cost and production time.

Yet despite the shift to mass-production technologies, only about one million MP38/40s were manufactured between 1938 and 1945 (compared with four million British Sten guns made between 1940 and 1945). German war industry tended toward scattering its energies between too many sophisticated weapons systems, diluting the scale of its projects.

In combat, the MP38/40 was a generally solid performer, although the magazines were vulnerable to dirt ingress, which, in the filthy conditions of the Eastern Front, led to many stoppages. German soldiers also complained that their firepower was inferior to the Russians' PPSh-41s fed with 71-round drum magazines. In response, the MP40/II with a double magazine was introduced, but this was an unpopular configuration as it unbalanced the weapon.

The two other major Axis forces of World War II, Italy and Japan, had entirely contrasting approaches to SMG development. The Italians tended to make high-quality machined weapons such as the Beretta Model 38 and variants. Although wartime exigencies did introduce stampings and pressing into the production process, numbers made were still quite small,and the Italian infantryman would typically be armed with a Mannlicher-Carcano Modello 91 rifle.

Even fewer Japanese infantry would have seen use of their homegrown SMGs, the Type 100/40 and Type 100/44 variant. Only around 10,000 of these weapons were made, despite there being reasonably sound firearms. Possibly many thousands of Allied lives were saved by the Japanese reticence to invest in submachine guns, as they proved to be one of the best weapons for close-quarters jungle warfare.

ITALY

LANCHESTER MARK I 1940

Length (gun): 33.5 in. (851 mm)
Barrel: 7.9 in. (200 mm)
Weight: 9.7 lb. (4.38 kg)
Caliber: 9 mm
Rifling: 6 grooves, r/hand

Operation: blowback
Feed: 50-round box
Cyclic rate: 600 rpm
Muz vel: 1,200 ft./sec. (365 m/sec.)

In 1940, arrangements were hastily made to copy the German MP 28, which was known to be reliable; a British version was designed by George Lanchester of the Sterling Armament Company. The new weapon was intended for the Royal Air Force and the Royal Navy, but most went to the latter. The Lanchester was a robust and reliable gun; British industry had not then been converted totally to a war footing so the machining and finish of the weapon were very high quality, with a walnut stock (complete with brass butt plate) and a brass magazine housing. It was fitted with a standard boss to allow the ordinary Lee Enfield bayonet to be fixed. It had a simple blowback mechanism and could fire single rounds or automatic. It functioned well with most of the standard makes of 9 mm rimless cartridge. There was also a later version that fired automatic only. The Lanchester saw little service except with the occasional boat or landing party, but it remained in service with the Royal Navy for a long time. Many years after the war, most HM ships carried racks of them chained for security.

UNITED STATES

SMITH AND WESSON LIGHT RIFLE MODEL 1940

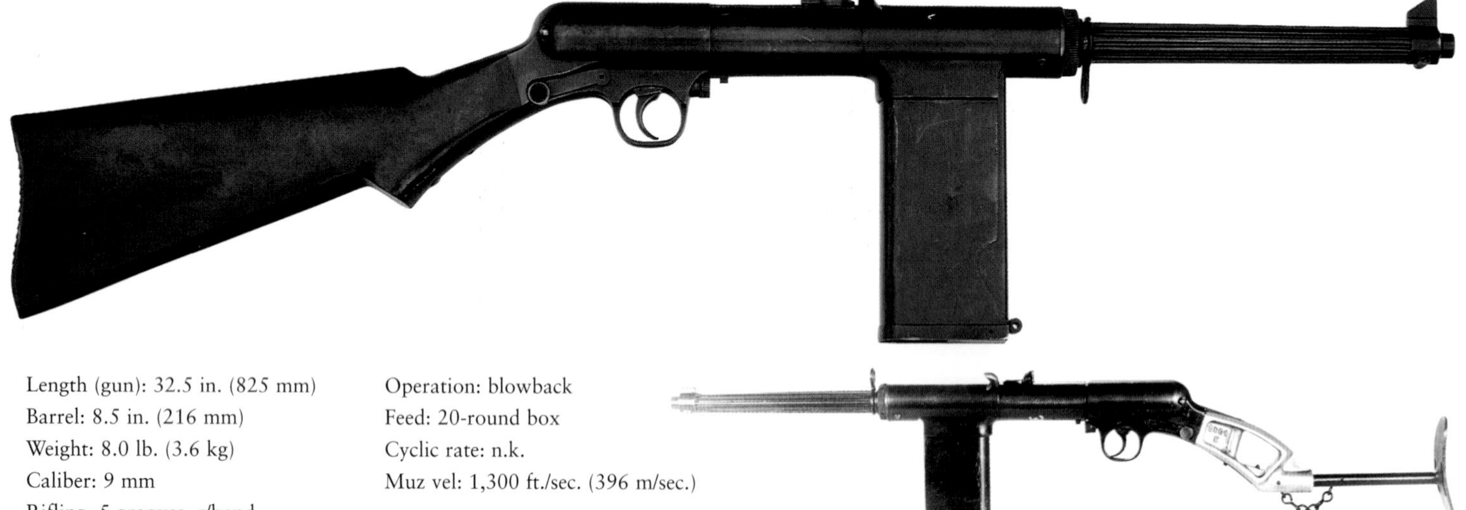

Length (gun): 32.5 in. (825 mm)
Barrel: 8.5 in. (216 mm)
Weight: 8.0 lb. (3.6 kg)
Caliber: 9 mm
Rifling: 5 grooves, r/hand

Operation: blowback
Feed: 20-round box
Cyclic rate: n.k.
Muz vel: 1,300 ft./sec. (396 m/sec.)

This weapon, believed to have been invented by a designer named Edward Pomeroy, was made in small numbers just before the outbreak of World War II. One was tested at the US Army Proving Grounds at the end of the same year but was rejected, partly because it fired a 9 mm round whereas the American Army favored 0.45 in., and partly because it was only semi-automatic. Smith and Wesson were advised to convert it to a full-automatic weapon in the larger caliber and resubmit it. It is said that a few of the original prototypes were made to fire automatic, which marginally justifies its inclusion here as a submachine gun. A slightly modified version of the type illustrated was reissued in 1940, when Great Britain, desperate for arms, bought the whole batch of 2,000 for the Royal Navy. The bolt and barrel were made of chrome nickel steel, the remainder of the metalwork was of manganese steel, and the machining, bluing, and general finishing are fully up to the peacetime standards. It worked on the blowback system and fired from an open bolt. The back of the very wide magazine housing contained an ejector tube, down which the empty cases passed after firing.

AUSTRALIA

OWEN MACHINE CARBINE 1941

Length (gun): 32.0 in. (813 mm)
Barrel: 9.8 in. (250 mm)
Weight: 9.4 lb. (4.2 kg)
Caliber: 9 mm
Rifling: 7 grooves, r/hand
Operation: blowback
Feed: 32-round box
Cyclic rate: 700 rpm
Muz vel: 1,375 ft./sec. (420 m/sec.)

Although there was a well established arms factory at Lithgow, Australia was not a very industrialized country; it began to produce arms as a matter of hard necessity. One of the country's first efforts was an Australian Sten known, perhaps inevitably, as the Austen (qv), but it was never popular with the Australian Army. The first locally designed submachine gun was the work of Lieutenant E. Owen, of the Australian Army, which was adopted in November 1941 and put into production immediately. It was a well made weapon, if a little on the heavy side, and was an immediate success with the soldiers. It was of fairly orthodox design and its point of balance was immediately above the pistol grip, which allowed it to be fired one-handed if necessary. The magazine was vertically above the gun, and although this involved offset sights, the idea was popular because it helped when moving through thick cover. Some early weapons had cooling fins on the barrel, but this was found to be unnecessary and discontinued. All were camouflaged after 1943. A prototype version (Mark 2) was fitted with a different method of attaching the butt and a bayonet lug above the muzzle compensator to receive a special tubular-haft bayonet. Overall weight was also reduced to 7.6 lb. (3.5 kg).

RUSSIA

PPSH 41 1941

Length (gun): 33.1 in. (841 mm)
Barrel: 10.6 in. (269 mm)
Weight: 8.0 lb. (3.6 kg)
Caliber: 7.62 mm
Rifling: 4 grooves, r/hand
Operation: blowback
Feed: 71-round drum/35-round box
Cyclic rate: 900 rpm
Muz vel: 1,600 ft./sec. (489 m/sec.)

The PPSh 41, designed by Georgii Shpagin, was put into limited production in 1941. After stringent testing by the Soviet Army it was finally approved early in 1942, after which production was on a vast scale. The PPSh was an early and successful example of the application of mass-production techniques to the manufacture of firearms. As much as possible it was made from sheet-metal stampings, welding, and riveting, although it retained the wooden butt. It worked on the blowback system with a buffer at the rear of the receiver to reduce vibrations and had a selector lever in front of the trigger to give single rounds or burst. As its cyclic rate of fire was high and would have tended to make the muzzle rise when firing bursts, the front of the barrel jacket was sloped backward to act as a compensator. Feed was either by a 71-round drum, similar to that of the earlier PPD series but not interchangeable, or by a 35-round box. The bore and chamber were chromed. There were two models: the first (illustrated) had a complicated tangent back sight, and the second had a two-aperture flip sight.

UNITED KINGDOM

STEN MARK 1 1941

Length (gun): 35.3 in. (896 mm)
Barrel: 7.8 in. (198 mm)
Weight: 7.2 lb. (3.8 kg)
Caliber: 9 mm
Rifling: 6 grooves, r/hand

Operation: blowback
Feed: 32-round box
Cyclic rate: 550 rpm
Muz vel: 1,200 ft./sec. (365 m/sec.)

There was an urgent requirement for a simple, home-produced submachine gun, and by the middle of 1941 a weapon had been designed, was in limited production, and undergoing trials. The Sten took its name from the initial letters of the surnames of the two people mostly closely concerned with its development (Major Shepherd and Mr. Turpin), plus the first two letters of Enfield, the location of the Royal Small Arms factory where it was first produced. As soon as the few weaknesses revealed by the trials had been rectified, the Sten gun went into large-scale production. The Sten worked on a simple blowback system using a heavy bolt with a coiled return spring, but in spite of its simple concept the first models made were still relatively elaborate. They had a cone-shaped flash hider and a rather crude forward pistol grip, which could be folded up underneath the barrel when not in use.

UNITED STATES

REISING MODEL 50 1941

Length (gun): 35.8 in. (908 mm)
Barrel: 11.0 in. (279 mm)
Weight: 6.8 in. (3.1 kg)
Caliber: 0.45 in.
Rifling: 6 grooves, r/hand

Operation: delayed blowback
Feed: 12- or 20-round box
Cyclic rate: 550 rpm
Muz vel: 920 ft./sec. (280 m/sec.)

Eugene Reising produced the weapon named after him in 1938, with Harrington and Richardson beginning manufacture at the end of 1941. Tests led to minor improvements, and it was accepted for service by the US Marine Corps and first used in action on Guadalcanal, where it proved to be a complete failure, jamming so frequently that the exasperated Marines, who were fighting desperately, threw it away in disgust. The problems were due mostly to the complexity of the mechanism and its susceptibility to dirt. The gun fired with the breech locked; this was achieved by the action of a ramp that raised the rear of the bolt into a recess in the top of the receiver after the moment of firing. This would have been acceptable if there had been some self-clearing device, but the bolt recess soon filled with dirt, particularly in hot, dry climates, rendering the weapon useless.

ITALY

BERETTA MODELLO 38/42 1942

Length (gun): 31.5 in. (800 mm)
Barrel: 8.4 in. (216 mm)
Weight: 7.2 lb. (3.3 kg)
Caliber: 9 mm
Rifling: 6 grooves, r/hand

Operation: blowback
Feed: 20/40-round box
Cyclic rate: 550 rpm
Muz vel: 1,250 ft./sec. (381 m/sec.)

The Beretta Modello 38/42 was a utility version of the Modello 38, the whole weapon simplified for mass-production. The rifle-type stock was cut short at the magazine housing, and the adjustable rear sight disappeared, as did the perforated jacket that had been such a notable feature of many Beretta guns. The barrel had deep parallel fluting along its whole length to assist the dissipation of heat in the absence of the jacket, and the compensator was reduced to two cuts. Later productions had plain barrels and were sometimes referred to as the Modello 38/44. There was a later variation still, in which the weight and dimensions of the bolt were reduced; this led to a somewhat shorter return spring and rod, which did not protrude beyond the rear of the receiver. The Beretta 38/42 was widely used by the Italians and Germans, and after the war a number of 38/44 Models were sold to various countries, including Syria and Pakistan.

ALLIED SUBMACHINE GUNS IN WORLD WAR II

Above left: *The Sten gun embodied a new philosophy of weaponry suited to the age of total war. The most important considerations behind its creation was that it should work and that it should be suited to mass production. Any sophisticated features were omitted, and a Sten Mk I could be produced for around £2.50 ($10). The soldier here is using a Sten Mk II, of which two million were produced during the World War II.*

As with the Axis powers of World War II, the influence of submachine guns among the Allies was as much about industrial warfare as frontline combat. In 1939, when war broke out across Europe, the UK did not have a submachine gun type to distribute to its soldiers. During government defense budget distributions in 1938, new small arms technologies took a low priority, and many in the British military establishment saw submachine guns as nothing more than a way of increasing ammunition expenditure. However, German use of the MP38 in the offensive of 1939–40 proved this perspective backward, and in 1940 the British government ordered the development and production of an indigenous submachine gun.

The first of these was the Lanchester, a copy of the German MP28, which, although undoubtedly a fine weapon, was far too slow to produce under wartime urgency. The solution was the Sten gun, the brainchild of Major R.V. Shepherd and Mr. H.J. Turpin, which emerged for trial in January 1941 and entered production in June. The Sten, with its simple blowback action, absence of wooden furniture, and crude metal stampings and pressings, could be manufactured rapidly in enormous numbers, and that was what was needed. Nearly four million were produced during the war, and one British factory was producing 20,000 per week.

The US took a similar route to the UK's during the war, entering it with the expensive Thompson M1928 but simplifying it into the M1 in 1941, then the M1A1 in 1942. However, the Thompson weapons, although superb combat tools, remained expensive productions. US industrial might compensated for this and produced more than one million Thompson guns. A weapon more in line with the British Sten and German MP38/40 was the M3 "Grease Gun," adopted for service in December 1942. The M3 was another all-metal stamping and pressing design, crude but reliable, and in only two years more than 600,000 were made.

Of all the Allies, it was the Soviet Union that bought into the submachine gun philosophy most readily. Submachine guns such as the PPSh-41 were produced in countless millions in large factories and small workshops alike across the Soviet Union. In contrast to the UK and US, the Soviet military equipped entire divisions with submachine guns alone. This reflects an important tactical mindset, which preferred soldiers to engage at close range with maximum firepower rather than conduct precision warfare at a distance. Furthermore, the massive manpower of the Soviet Army meant that weapons training was brief, so the submachine gun was seen as a way of making an untrained soldier's firepower as effective as possible, the spray of full-auto fire compensating for inaccuracy. In many ways that remains the essence of the SMG.

UNITED KINGDOM

STEN MARK 2 1942

Length (gun): 30.0 in. (762 mm)
Barrel: 7.8 in. (197 mm)
Weight: 6.7 lb. (3.0 kg)
Caliber: 9 mm
Rifling: 6/2 grooves, r/hand

Operation: blowback
Feed: 32-round box
Cyclic rate: 550 rpm
Muz vel: 1,200 ft./sec. (365 m/sec.)

The Mark 2 was a somewhat stripped-down version of the Mark 1 to simplify manufacture. It looked cheap because it was cheap. Nevertheless, it not only worked but managed to incorporate one or two improvements over the Mark 1, notably by attaching the magazine housing to a rotatable sleeve, held by a spring, so that in bad conditions it could be turned upward through 90 degrees, thus acting as a dustcover for the ejection opening. One of the most persistent weaknesses of the Sten was the poor quality of its magazine. In particular, the lips were very susceptible to damage, which had a serious effect on the feed and led to endless stoppages. It was also found that dirt tended to clog the magazine, and although careful attention to cleanliness helped in this respect, the problem was never really solved. Despite these drawbacks, the Mark 2 was an important weapon.

UNITED KINGDOM

STEN MARK 2 (CANADIAN PATTERN) 1942

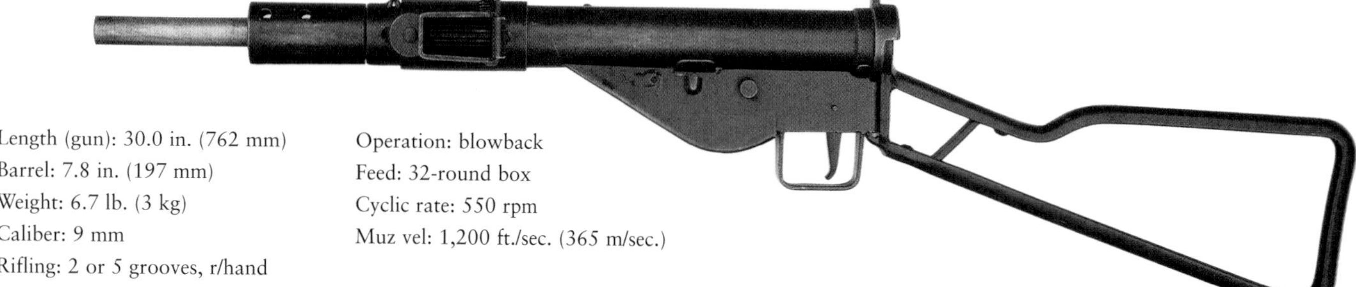

Length (gun): 30.0 in. (762 mm)
Barrel: 7.8 in. (197 mm)
Weight: 6.7 lb. (3 kg)
Caliber: 9 mm
Rifling: 2 or 5 grooves, r/hand

Operation: blowback
Feed: 32-round box
Cyclic rate: 550 rpm
Muz vel: 1,200 ft./sec. (365 m/sec.)

British and Colonial forces had an insatiable appetite for Sten guns. More than 100,000 of the earlier Marks had been produced by early 1942, and there was still no slackening of the demand. Apart from the inevitable loss and damage in action, more troops were being raised and trained; and as the prospect of an Allied invasion of North West Europe drew closer, the need for submachine guns continued to increase. There was also an increasing demand for light, easily concealed automatic weapons for the various Resistance movements in German-occupied Europe. Much help was given by Canada, and the weapon illustrated is an example of the type made at the famous Long Branch factory. Although made to specifications similar to those of the British Mark 2, it was of somewhat better finish, with a more robust butt. It also had a bayonet, and examples of this are now very rare.

UNITED STATES

M3A1 1942

Length (gun): 29.8 in. (757 mm)
Barrel: 8.0 in. (203 mm)
Weight: 8.7 lb. (3.7 kg)
Caliber: 0.45 in.
Rifling: 4 grooves, r/hand

Operation: blowback
Feed: 30-round
Cyclic rate: 400 rpm
Muz vel: 920 ft./sec. (280 m/sec.)

The M3 was made as much as possible from stampings, with practically no machining except for the barrel and bolt. It worked by blowback and had no provision for firing single rounds. Its stock was of retractable wire and the caliber was 0.45 in. It bore a strong resemblance to a garage mechanic's grease gun, from which it derived its famous nickname. Large-scale use revealed some defects in the gun, and further successful attempts to simply it were initiated, resulting in the M3A1 (illustrated). It had no cocking handle; the firer inserted a finger into a slot in the receiver to withdraw the bolt, which had an integral firing pin. It worked on guide rods, which saved complicated finishing of the inside of the receiver and gave smooth functioning with little interruption from dirt. By the end of 1944, the new gun officially replaced the Thompson as the standard US Army submachine gun.

UNITED KINGDOM

DE LISLE SILENT CARBINE 1942

Length (gun): 35.0 in. (889 mm)
Barrel: 9.0 in. (228 mm)
Weight: 7.0 lb. (3.18 kg)
Caliber: 0.45 in.
Rifling: 7 grooves, l/hand
Operation: bolt-feed
Feed: 10-round magazine
Muz vel: ca 1,200 ft./sec. (366 m/sec.)

The de Lisle was an SMLE rifle (qv) converted to fire a rimless pistol cartridge. The bolt and the chamber were shortened. The new short barrel of .45 in. caliber was screwed into this, and a new magazine opening fitted. The sheet-metal tube housed the silencer, which included ten metal disks, each with a central hole just over 0.5 in. (12.7 mm) in diameter with a smaller hole on each side, and cut along one radius. The pieces on each side of the cut were then pulled apart so that when the disks were strung along two parallel rods, one on each side of the barrel 0.75 in. (19 mm) apart and with stops between, they formed a continuous Archimedes screw. The front end of the casing was closed by a circular plug with a hole for the bullet to leave by, and two small screw sockets to hold the front ends of the silencer rods. The bullet never exceeded the speed of sound, so there was no "sonic boom." This system worked remarkably well—the sound of the discharge was quite inaudible a short distance away. The carbine shot accurately to about 300 yd. (274 m). Although not an automatic, this seems a suitable place for a weapon that is in a category of its own.

UNITED STATES

THOMPSON M1A1 1942

Length (gun): 32.0 in. (813 mm)
Barrel: 10.5 in. (267 mm)
Weight: 10.5 lb. (4.7 kg)
Caliber: 0.45 in.
Rifling: 6 grooves, r/hand
Operation: blowback
Feed: 20/30-round box
Cyclic rate: 700 rpm
Muz vel: 920 ft./sec. (281 m/sec.)

As with most other prewar weapons, the M1928A1 had been luxuriously made, and to speed up production some simplification became essential. The first result was the M1, the main mechanical difference being the abolition of the H-piece and the substitution of a heavier bolt to compensate for it. The main external differences were the absence of the compensator on the muzzle, the substitution of a straight forehand for the forward pistol grip (although this had been optional on the Model 28), the removal of the rather complex back sight, and its replacement by a simple flip. The new gun would not take the 50-round drum, but this had never been very reliable in dirty conditions so it was no loss. A new 30-round box magazine was introduced, and the earlier 20-round magazine would also fit the new model. There was yet another simplification, the incorporation of a fixed firing pin on the face of the bolt; this resulted in the M1A1, the weapon illustrated. Although the basic design was almost a quarter century old by then, the Thompson gave excellent service in 1939–45. Even if it was heavy to carry it was reliable, and its bullets had considerable stopping power.

AUSTRALIA

AUSTEN 1943

Length (gun): 33.3 in. (845 mm)
Barrel: 7.8 in. (198 mm)
Weight (gun): 8.66 lb. (3.97 kg)
Caliber: 9 mm
Rifling: 6 grooves, r/hand
Operation: blowback
Magazine: 20-round box
Cyclic rate: 500 rpm
Muz vel: 1,200 ft./sec. (366 m/sec.)

This effective weapon owed its design to a combination of the best features of the British Sten gun (qv) and the German Erma MP40 (qv), which had been encountered and admired by Australian troops in the Middle East. Some 25,000–30,000 were produced in Australia from 1943 to 1946; the name Austen combed "Australia" and "Sten." Mechanically, the Austen took the telescopic mainspring housing and bolt from the MP40 and married them to the Sten, but with some additional refinements, including a forward grip and a folding butt. The Mark II differed in that it had a two-piece cast-aluminum receiver and overall weight was reduced to 8.5 lb. (3.86 kg). The Austen was never as popular with Australian troops as the Owen (qv).

UNITED KINGDOM

STEN MARK 6(S) 1944

Length (silenced): 35.8 in. (908 mm)
Barrel: 7.8 in. (198 mm)
Weight: 9.8 lb. (4.45 kg)
Caliber: 9 mm
Rifling: 6 grooves, r/hand
Operation: blowback
Feed: 32-round box
Cyclic rate: 550 rpm
Muz vel: ca 1,000 ft./sec. (305 m/sec.)

Probably the best Sten was the Mark 5, which would see service from 1944 until well into the 1950s. Although very similar to its predecessors, it was of more robust construction with a wooden butt and pistol grip, and there was provision for a bayonet. Experiments had been conducted earlier with a silenced Sten, and in 1944 it was decided that a weapon of this type was again required. The standard Mark 2 silencer was thus fitted to the Mark 5, which was then redesignated Mark 6(S). The muzzle velocity of the Mark 5 bullet was in excess of the speed of sound, but by drilling gas-escape holes in the barrel, the velocity was brought down to subsonic. The silencer tended to heat rapidly so a canvas hand guard was laced over it, and it was not advisable to fire bursts except in emergencies. The Mark 6 Sten was used mainly by airborne forces and Resistance fighters in World War II, and as late as 1953.

ITALY

TZ 45 1945

Length (gun): 33.5 in. (851 mm)
Barrel: 9.0 in. (229 mm)
Weight: 7.2 lb. (3.3 kg)
Caliber: 9 mm
Rifling: 6 grooves, r/hand
Operation: blowback
Feed: 20/40-round box
Cyclic rate: 550 rpm
Muz vel: 1,250 ft./sec. (365 m/sec.)

The TZ 45 first went into limited production in 1945. It was crudely made and finished, partly of roughly machined parts and partly of stampings. It incorporated a grip safety, an L-shaped lever just behind the magazine housing (which also acted as a forward handgrip). Firm pressure on the vertical part of the lever caused the horizontal arm to be depressed sufficiently to withdraw an upper stud from the boltway, thus allowing the working parts to function. The TZ 45 had a retractable stock made of light tubing. There were parallel slots cut into the top of the barrel at the muzzle end, which acted as a crude compensator. The TZ 45 came too late in the war to be of much use, and only about 6,000 were made. These were chiefly used by Italian troops on internal security duties. After the war the gun was offered commercially, but only the Burmese showed interest. A number were made there in the early 1950s under the title BA 52.

JAPAN

8 MM TYPE 11 1945

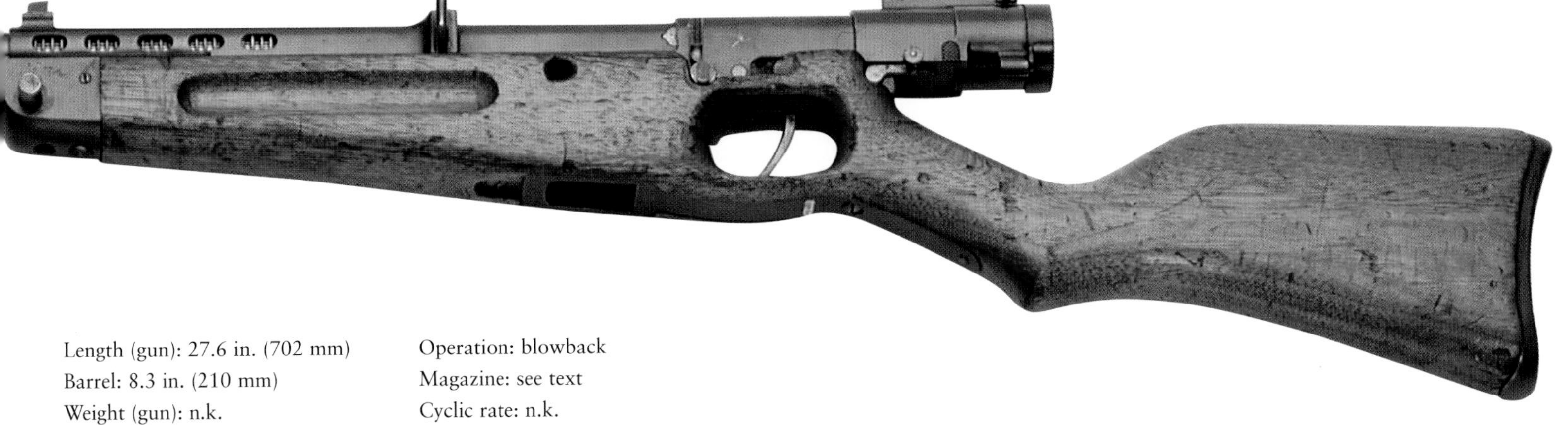

Length (gun): 27.6 in. (702 mm)
Barrel: 8.3 in. (210 mm)
Weight (gun): n.k.
Caliber: 8 mm
Rifling: 6 grooves, r/hand

Operation: blowback
Magazine: see text
Cyclic rate: n.k.
Muz vel: n.k.

At the end of World War II, a new Japanese submachine gun design was just entering service, the Type 11. It was one of the most unusual-looking submachine guns ever made. The wooden furniture of the Type 10 was retained, albeit somewhat shorter, but with the working parts sitting along the top, as shown in the picture. The weapon was of bullpup configuration, with the box magazine (missing in the example shown) inserted from beneath the weapon. The return spring fitted around the barrel and the trigger was inset so that the stock provided the guard. There was a fixed fore sight but the back sight was mounted on a ramp, suggesting a somewhat optimistic assessment of the weapon's accuracy at longer ranges.

SWEDEN

CARL GUSTAV MODEL 45 1945

Length (gun): 31.8 in. (808 mm)
Barrel: 8.0 in. (203 mm)
Weight: 7.6 lb. (3.5 kg)
Caliber: 9mm
Rifling: 6 grooves, r/hand

Operation: blowback
Feed: 36/50-round box
Cyclic rate: 600 rpm
Muz vel: 1,210 ft./sec. (369 m/sec.)

In the course of World War II, Sweden, although neutral, increased its army considerably to defend itself if necessary. This led to the realization that the country had no simple submachine gun for mass production. Sweden set out to rectify this but the result, the Model 1945, was not put into production until after the war. The Model 1945 was made of stampings from heavy-gauge steel, riveted or welded as necessary, and within the limits imposed by these methods was a sound and reliable weapon. Mechanically it bore a strong resemblance to the British Sten gun, but it had a rectangular stock of tubular metal that could be folded forward on the right of the gun without interfering with its working. Although it was designed for firing on automatic only, single rounds could be fired by anyone with a reasonably sensitive trigger finger. It fired a special high-velocity cartridge, and the original model used the old Suomi 5-round magazine. Later versions fired a new 36-round type, but as large stocks of the older magazines, which were not interchangeable, remained, the new gun had an easily detached magazine housing, which could be replaced by one of the older type if required.

UNITED KINGDOM

MCEM 2 1945

Length (gun): 23.5 in. (598 mm)
Barrel: 8.5 in. (216 mm)
Weight: 6.0 lb. (2.7 kg)
Caliber: 9 mm
Rifling: 6 grooves, r/hand

Operation: blowback
Feed: 18-round box
Cyclic rate: 1,000 rpm
Muz vel: 1,200 ft./sec. (365 m/sec.)

Among the postwar designs to replace the Sten gun was the Military Carbine Experimental Model (MCEM) series produced at Enfield. The first in the series (MCEM 1) was the work of H. J. Turpin, who had been instrumental in designing the original Sten gun. The weapon illustrated, the MCEM 2, was the work of another designer, a Polish officer named Lieutenant Podsenkowsky, and it was a very unusual weapon. It was less than 15 in. (380 mm) long and its magazine fit into the pistol grip; it was also well balanced, which meant that it could be fired one-handed like an automatic pistol. The bolt was of advanced design and consisted of a half cylinder 8.5 in. (216 mm) long with the striker at the rear, so that at the instant of firing almost the whole of the barrel was inside it. The gun had a wire-framed canvas holster that could also be used as a butt. It fired at a cyclic rate of 1,000 rounds per minute, which made it very hard to control and may have led to its rejection.

CZECHOSLOVAKIA

CZ-23, CZ-24, CZ-25, CZ-26 9 MM/7.62 MM 1948

Length (gun): 27.0 in. (685 mm)
Barrel: 11.2 in. (284 mm)
Weight (gun): 6.8 lb. (3.1 kg)
Caliber: 9 mm
Rifling: 4 grooves, r/hand

Operation: blowback
Magazine: 24- or 4-round box
Cyclic rate: 600 rpm
Muz vel: 1,250 ft./sec. (380 m/sec.)

This series of four weapons began with the CZ-23 (see top photo and specifications), which appeared in 1948 and continued until the CZ-26 was produced. The CZ-23 entered service in 1951 and the CZ-25 (bottom left) in 1952, both firing the 9 mm Parabellum round, which was available in vast quantities in the early post-World War II years. The two weapons differed only in that the CZ-23 had a wooden stock, whereas the CZ-25 had no stock. Following the formation of the Warsaw Pact in 1955, however, came standardization, which meant in essence that all the other members adopted Soviet standards and weapons. One result was the replacement of the 9 mm round by the Soviet Tokarev 7.62 x 25 mm pistol round, which led to two new Czech submachine guns chambered for the new round: the CZ-24, which replaced the CZ-23, and the CZ-26, which replaced the CZ-25. The adoption of the new round meant that the CZ-24 and CZ-26 were slightly heavier (7.25 lb. or 3.3 kg) and had a higher muzzle velocity (1,800 feet/second or 550 m/sec.); they were also provided with a 32-round box magazine. These weapons were all used by the Czech Army until the mid-1960s, and were also exported, especially those firing the Soviet round.

FRANCE

MAT49 1949

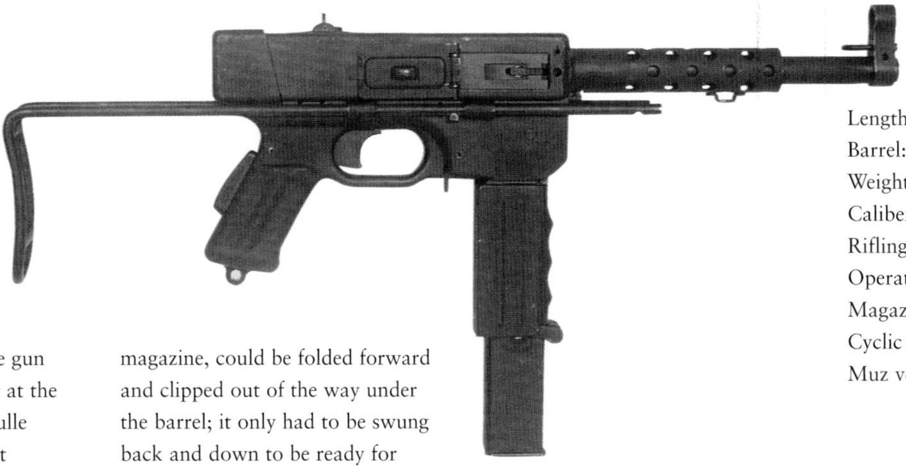

Length (gun): 28.8 in. (720 mm)
Barrel: 9.0 in. (228 mm)
Weight (gun): 7.9 lb. (3.6 kg)
Caliber: 9 mm
Rifling: 4 grooves, r/hand
Operation: blowback
Magazine: 20- or 32-round box
Cyclic rate: 600 rpm
Muz vel: 1,279 ft./sec. (390 m/sec.)

The MAT49 submachine gun was designed and built at the Manufacture d'Armes de Tulle (MAT) and had an excellent reputation among French troops. It was adopted by the French Army in 1949 and subsequently saw considerable service in Indochina and Algeria. The MAT49 had a conventional blowback design. The magazine housing, complete with magazine, could be folded forward and clipped out of the way under the barrel; it only had to be swung back and down to be ready for instant use. This, combined with the telescopic steel stock, made the weapon particularly suitable for use by paratroops and special forces. The safety in the rear of the pistol grip had to be squeezed to enable the weapon to fire. An ejection port cover helped keep dirt out of the gun. The 9 mm MAT49 may still be in use by the armies of many former French colonies. A large number of MAT49s were captured by the Viet Minh and Viet Cong during the Indochina wars and later converted to take the Soviet 7.76 mm Type P round. These weapons could be recognized by the longer barrel and 35-round magazine, and were also capable of around 900-rpm auto fire.

UNITED KINGDOM

BSA EXPERIMENTAL 1949

Length (gun): 27.9 in. (697 mm)
Barrel: 8.0 in. (203 mm)
Weight: 6.5 lb. (2.9 kg)
Caliber: 9 mm
Rifling: 6 grooves, r/hand
Operation: blowback
Feed: 32-round box
Cyclic rate: 600 rpm
Muz vel: 1,200 ft./sec. (365 m/sec.)

Between 1947 and 1952, various new submachine guns were tested, among them the BSA's weapon of the type illustrated here. All were designed to a specification that included maximum weight of 6 lb. (2.7 kg) without magazine, a rate of fire not more than 600 rpm, a magazine capacity of 30–60 rounds, and to take the No. 5 rifle bayonet. The BSA was of conventional blowback but had no cocking handle; that function was performed by a flat rod attached to the plastic-covered fore-end grip. When the grip was twisted and pushed forward, the end of the rod engaged the bolt, which was then in the forward position. As the grip was pulled back, the rod forced the bolt back until it was caught by the sear and disengaged from the rod. The magazine housing could be released and swung forward on a hinge without removing the magazine, which was thought to facilitate the clearing of stoppages.

CHINA (PRC)

TYPE 50 1950

Length (gun): 33.8 in. (858 mm)
Barrel: 10.8 in. (273 mm)
Weight: 8.0 lb. (3.6 kg)
Caliber: 7.62 mm
Rifling: 4 grooves, r/hand
Operation: blowback
Feed: 35-round box
Cyclic rate: 900 rpm
Muz vel: 1,400 ft./sec. (472 m/sec.)

The Type 50 had its origins in the Soviet Union's PPSh 41. The new gun was largely made of heavy-gauge stampings, welded, pinned, and brazed as necessary. The gun was of normal blowback mechanism and had the interior of the barrel chromed. The front end of the perforated barrel casing sloped steeply backward from top to bottom, acting as a compensator to keep the muzzle down. In spite of its high cyclic rate of fire, the gun was reasonably accurate and could be fired in single rounds if required. The Type 50 had a somewhat lighter stock than the PPSh 41. It was also designed to take a curved box magazine, though it could also fire the 71-round drum, the standard magazine on the original Russian model. All Chinese versions had a two-range flip sight. The Type 50 was used extensively by the Chinese in the Korean War, and by the Viet Minh against the French in Indochina.

THE MACHINE PISTOL

The terms "machine pistol" and "submachine gun" are often treated as interchangeable, particularly within the context of World War II weaponry when the Germans used "machine pistol" as a prefix for all its submachine gun types. However, in the postwar world we can pull the two terms apart to distinguish between traditional submachine guns and full-auto weapons of reduced dimensions that can be held and fired with one hand.

The concept of the machine pistol actually stretches back to the 1930s, when full-auto variations/imitations of the Mauser C/96 were produced. Mauser issued its own full-auto weapon, the Schnellfeuerpistole M712 ("Rapid-Fire Pistol" M712), which had a selective-fire mechanism that allowed full-auto bursts of 850 rpm. The typical ten-round C/96 box magazine could be used, but a twenty-round magazine was also made. It was during the 1950s and 60s, however, that the machine pistol concept took popular hold, led by the need to equip armored vehicle crews with personal firepower in cramped conditions, and also to provide security police and special forces with portable weapons for urban/covert operations.

The Czechs led the way with the CZ-23 of 1948, which featured two key innovations. First, the magazine was inserted into the pistol grip. Second, the CZ-23 used a wraparound bolt, where a semitubular bolt encloses the rear end of the barrel at firing, with slots for feed and ejection. This system allowed for significant reduction in overall gun length: the CZ-23 was only 25 in. (686 mm) long. Yet these dimensions were surpassed by the remarkable vz/62 Skorpion, which emerged in the early 1960s. Although a conventional front-magazine-loading blowback 7.65 mm weapon, the Skorpion had a stock-folded length of only 10.6 in. (270 mm) and could be fired full-auto with one hand.

Other nations soon joined the Czechs with machine-pistol designs. Israel produced the Uzi in the 1950s using the Czech wraparound-bolt principle, a principle also applied in the United States to the Ingram MAC 10. New designs continued into the 1980s with weapons such as the Italian Socimi Type 821, the Peruvian MGP-84, and the South African BXP. These weapons all offered compact dimensions with heavy firepower—the Micro-Uzi, for example, is only 9.8 in. (250 mm) long with the stock folded and fires at 1,250 rpm—but they have fallen out of fashion with professional forces (not criminals, however) because of their difficult fire control.

Above: *The CZ-25, seen here in the hands of a Cuban militia, entered service in 1952 and was distributed in large numbers among the member states of the Warsaw Pact. The Czech Army also used the CZ range of weapons as standard SMGs, as they were ideally suited for use aboard armored vehicles because of the compact dimensions. The later CZ-26, for instance, had a length of only 17.75 in. (445 mm) with the stock folded.*

DENMARK

MADSEN MODEL 46/50 1950

Length (gun): 31.3 in. (794 mm)
Barrel: 7.8 in. (199 mm)
Weight: 7.0 lb. (3.15 kg)
Caliber: 9 mm
Rifling: 4 grooves, r/hand
Operation: blowback
Feed: 32-round box
Cyclic rate: 550 rpm
Muz vel: 1,250 ft./sec. (365 m/sec.)

The main body of the Madsen Model 46, including the pistol grip, is made from two side pieces hinged together at the rear, so that the weapon can be easily opened for repair, cleaning, or inspection. The disadvantage is that springs are likely to fall out unless care is taken. One of the Madsen's unusual features is a grip safety behind the magazine housing that (with the magazine itself) acts as a forward handgrip. The Model 50, the gun illustrated, is similar to the Model 46; the main difference is the milled knob cocking handle that replaced the flat plate of the earlier model. The curved magazine belongs to the later model. When the new model was demonstrated in 1950, many countries showed great interest but few orders were placed.

ISRAEL

UZI, MINI-UZI, AND MICRO-UZI 1950

Length (gun): 25.2 in. (640 mm)
Barrel: 10.2 in. (260 mm)
Weight: 7.7 lb. (3.5 kg)
Caliber: 9 mm
Rifling: 4 grooves, r/hand
Operation: blowback
Feed: 25/32/40-round box
Cyclic rate: 600 rpm
Muz vel: 1,280 ft./sec. (390 m/sec.)

By 1950, Major Uziel Gal of the Israeli Army had designed the weapon illustrated here, and production continues to date. The Uzi is a blowback weapon made from heavy pressings in conjunction with certain heat-resistant plastics. The rear end of the barrel extends backward into the body, and the front of the bolt is hollowed out so as to wrap round this rear projection. The magazine fits into the pistol grip, affording firm support and also keeping the point of balance above it, so that the gun can be fired one-handed if necessary. It fires single rounds or bursts. Most of the early Uzis had a short wooden butt 8 in. (203 mm) long, but a very few were made longer. Later models have a folding metal stock, and other versions include the Mini-Uzi (1981, illustrated) and Micro-Uzi (1982). The Uzi is also manufactured in Croatia as the ER09, and the Mini-Uzi as the Mini ERO9.

CHINA (PRC)

TYPE 43 1953

Length (gun): 32.3 in. (819 mm)
Barrel: 10.0 in. (254 mm)
Weight: 7.5 lb. (3.4 kg)
Caliber: 7.62 mm
Rifling: 4 grooves, r/hand
Operation: blowback
Feed: 35-round box
Cyclic rate: 700 rpm
Muz vel: 1,600 ft./sec. (488 m/sec.)

This weapon was designed by A. Sudarev during the 1942 siege of Leningrad. The gun, originally known as the PPS 42, was designed and made in the city. It was made of stampings, using any suitable grade of metal, held together by rivetings, welding, and pinning. It was a cheap but effective blowback weapon and would fire automatic only; its oddest feature was its semicircular compensator, which helped to keep the muzzle down but increased blast considerably. The PPS 42 was followed by the PPS 43. This had no separate ejector. The bolt moved backward and forward along a guide rod that was of such a length that, as the bolt came back with the empty case, the end of the rod caught a sharp blow and knocked it clear. From 1949 the Soviet Union supplied China with large numbers of the PPS 43; by 1943 the Chinese had begun large-scale manufacture of these weapons.

SWITZERLAND

REXIM-FAVOR 1953

Length (gun): 32.0 in. (813 mm)
Barrel: 10.8 in. (273 mm)
Weight: 7.0 lb. (3.2 kg)
Caliber: 9 mm
Rifling: 5 grooves, r/hand

Operation: see text
Feed: 20-round box
Cyclic rate: 600 rpm
Muz vel: 1,300 ft./sec. (396 m/sec.)

The Rexim submachine gun appeared in 1953 and fired from a closed bolt; the round was fed into the chamber by the action of the cocking handle and remained there until pressure on the trigger allowed the firing pin to go forward. Motive power was provided by two coiled springs, one working inside the other with an intermediate hollow hammer. When the trigger was pressed, the depression of the sear released the hammer, which went forward under the force of the large outer spring and struck the firing pin. Normal blowback then followed and the cycle continued. The gun was well made, chiefly of pressings, but with a superior finish. It had a quick-release barrel in which the withdrawal of the small catch under the milled nut allowed the nut to be unscrewed and the barrel pulled out forward. In the model illustrated the butt had a separate pistol grip.

UNITED KINGDOM

STERLING L2A1/L2A3 1953

Length (gun): 28.0 in. (800 mm)
Barrel: 7.8 in. (198 mm)
Weight: 6.0 lb. (2.8 kg)
Caliber: 9 mm
Rifling: 6 grooves, r/hand

Operation: blowback
Feed: 32-round box
Cyclic rate: 550 rpm
Muz vel: 1,200 ft./sec. (365 m/sec.)

This gun was designed by George Patchett and was at first known as the Patchett submachine gun. It was originally patented in 1942, and by the end of the war a small number had been made by the Sterling Engineering Company. After tests between 1947 and 1953, the gun was finally accepted for service in the British Army. Its official title was the SMG L2A1, but it was commonly known as the Sterling. The gun was of normal blowback mechanism but had a ribbed bolt that cut away dirt and fouling as it accumulated and forced it out of the receiver. This allowed the gun to function well under adverse conditions. The gun underwent many modifications after its initial introduction, notably in the addition of fore-sight protectors, varying shapes of muzzle and butt, and, on one light version, a spring-loaded bayonet. Some of the earlier models also took a straight magazine.

AUSTRALIA

F1 SUBMACHINE GUN 1959

Length (gun): 28.1 in. (925 mm)
Barrel: 8.0 in. (203 mm)
Weight: 7.2 lb. (3.3 kg)
Caliber: 9 mm
Rifling: 6 grooves, r/hand

Operation: blowback
Feed: 34-round box
Cyclic rate: 600 rpm
Muz vel: 1,200 ft./sec. (365 m/sec.)

The Australian Army canvassed the views of battle-experienced soldiers to what an ideal submachine gun should be. The first gun based on these ideas was similar to the Owen. This model was not a success and was not developed. However, in 1959 and 1960, two additional models were produced. Known provisionally as the X1 and X2, after minor modifications the gun became the weapon illustrated, the F1. It was based on the originally specification and was light in weight and with a much lower cyclic rate than its predecessor. It retained the top magazine of the Owen, which was universally popular. The back sight was a shaped metal flap that folded forward over the receiver when not required. The cocking handle, on the left of the body, had a cover attached to it to keep dirt out of the cocking slot. Although the cocking handle was normally nonreciprocating, the F1 incorporated a device by which it could be made to engage the bolt. This meant that if the mechanism became jammed with dirt, the bolt could be worked backward and forward using the handle in order to loosen it.

ISRAELI SMALL ARMS DEVELOPMENT

Above: *Two Israeli infantrymen disembark from an armored personnel carrier with Uzi submachine guns at the ready. During the Six-Day War of 1967, the Uzi was particularly useful in the mountain combat around the Golan Heights and in urban fighting, at close quarters more than holding its own against the opposing Arab forces' Soviet-made AK-47 and AKM rifles.*

The defense forces of the modern State of Israel, when it emerged in 1947, had a woeful inadequacy of personal weapons. The Hagana (a Jewish self-defense force formed in 1920) had managed to build up a stockpile of 3,600 submachine guns, 8,000 rifles, and 200 machine guns (data: Ian Hogg, 1983). These weapons were a diverse mix of World War II surplus, a typical infantry unit being armed with Mauser and Lee-Enfield rifles, Sten guns, and Browning M1919 machine guns.

Despite the deficiency in firearms, Israel managed to survive the attacks from the professional armies of six Arab states in its War of Independence. Israel endured its baptism of fire by grit and ingenuity. During the 1950s, the Israeli Defence Force (IDF) sought to standardize and rationalize all its weapons, including small arms. Two excellent firearms went to equip the Israeli infantry. For a rifle, the Israelis chose the FN FAL rifle chambered to fire the 7.62 x 51 mm NATO standard round.

The FN FAL was a good initial choice, as it easily had the range to command the distances involved with desert warfare and had excellent resistance to the dust and dirt of the environment.

From the 1960s, Israel also purchased large numbers of the US M16A1, taking advantage of favorable trade agreements with the United States. For a submachine gun, the Israelis turned to an indigenous design: the 9 mm Uzi designed in 1949 by Lieutenant Uziel Gal. The Uzi was also an excellent desert weapon, the grooved bodywork providing escape channels for dust and dirt, and it gave sterling service in the Six-Day War of 1967 and an ongoing internal security operations.

Following the Six-Day War, Israel was impressed by both the performance of the Arabs' Soviet-made AKM assault rifles and the M16's small-caliber round. In the late 1960s and early 1970s, several 5.56 mm rifles were tested to find a new standard infantry weapon; the winner was the Galil rifle designed by Yaakov Lior and Israel Galili. The Galil replaced both the Uzi and the FN FAL, and in the trials it outperformed both the Kalashnikov and the M16A1.

The Galil remains the standard Israeli weapon and is issued in various formats including a heavy-barrel bipod-mounted support weapon version, as well as carbine and submachine gun versions.

The most recent development among Israeli small arms is the 5.56 mm Tavor rifle, a bullpup weapon that will be of advanced modular design to receive the latest sighting, fire-control, and tactical technologies. The Tavor is earmarked to replace the M16, which has not demonstrated the same reliability as the Galil in desert combat. At the time of writing 15,000 Tavors have been issued among Israeli special forces.

ITALY

BERETTA 9 MM MODEL 12 1959

Length (gun): 26.0 in. (660 mm)
Barrel: 7.9 in. (3.4 kg)
Weight (gun): 6.6 lb. (3.0 kg)
Caliber: 9 mm
Rifling: 6 grooves, r/hand
Operation: blowback
Magazine: 20-, 32- or 40-round box
Cyclic rate: 550 rpm
Muz vel: 1,250 ft./sec. (380 m/sec.)

The Model 12 entered service with the Italian Army in 1959. It was widely exported, and although production in Italy ended in 1980, the Model 12 remained in license production in Brazil and Indonesia for many years afterward. The Model 12 is of all-metal construction except for the optional wooden butt. The gun is fabricated from sheet-metal stampings, which are spot-welded to form the tubular receiver, the combined trigger housing and pistol grip, and the rectangular magazine housing. The breechblock is the wraparound type, with a fixed firing pin, and there is a separate forward handgrip. There are two safety systems: a grip safety on the front of the pistol grip, which must be depressed before the action can be cocked, and a button safety that controls safe, semi-automatic or automatic fire. The normal stock is a metal tube and a metal butt plate, which can be folded to the right. Alternatively, a detachable wooden stock can be used. The Model 12S (the S2 is shown in the bottom photo), introduced in 1983, is very similar to the earlier weapon but has an altered safety system, different sights, and an improved overall finish.

CZECH REPUBLIC

VZ61 (THE SKORPION) 1960

Length (gun, folded): 10.0 in. (271 mm)
Barrel: 4.5 in. (114 mm)
Weight: 2.9 lb. (1.31 kg)
Caliber: 7.65 mm
Rifling: 6 grooves, r/hand
Operation: blowback
Feed: 10/20-round box
Cyclic rate: 700 rpm
Muz vel: 970 ft./sec. (294 m/sec.)

This was a good example of the small number of true machine pistols, its general dimensions comparable to those of the Mauser pistol Model 1896. It was of relatively limited use as a military weapon. Its small caliber also reduced its stopping power, although automatic fire helped in this respect. There was also a bigger version, made only in limited quantities, which fired a 9 mm round and was a good deal heavier. The Skorpion worked on the blowback system. Very light automatic weapons often have the disadvantage that their cyclic rate of fire is unacceptably high, but in this weapon the problem was largely overcome by a buffer device in the butt. It had a light wire butt for use from the shoulder that could be folded forward when not required without affecting the working of the weapon. Although the size and capacity of the Skorpion reduced its military efficiency, it was an excellent weapon for police or other forms of internal security work since it was inconspicuous and easily concealed. Its low muzzle velocity also made it relatively easy to silence. The VZ61 was sold to many African countries. Other versions fired the 9 mm short round (VZ63), the 9 mm Mokarov (VZ65), or the 9 mm Parabellum (VZ68).

CHINA (PRC)

NORINCO TYPE 64/TYPE 85 (SILENCED) 1966

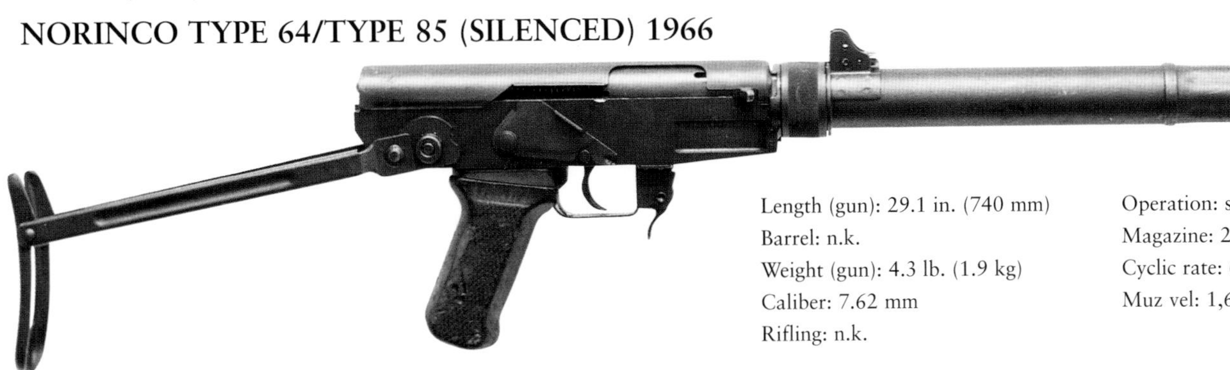

Length (gun): 29.1 in. (740 mm)
Barrel: n.k.
Weight (gun): 4.3 lb. (1.9 kg)
Caliber: 7.62 mm
Rifling: n.k.

Operation: see text
Magazine: 20-round box
Cyclic rate: 650 rpm
Muz vel: 1,640 ft./sec. (500 m/sec.)

The Chinese NORINCO Type 64 uses the Chinese Type 51 7.62 x 25 mm pistol round in a weapon that incorporated a number of features taken from weapons already produced in China. Thus, the bolt mechanism comes from the Type 43 (qv), and the trigger group comes from Czechoslovakian ZB VZ/26 7.92 mm machine gun, which was produced under license in China in the 1930s as the Type 26. The weapon operates by blowback and takes a curved 30-round box magazine. The Maxim-type noise suppressor is 14.4 in. (365 mm) long and screws on to the weapon. The outer third of the barrel is perforated with thirty-six holes, allowing a proportion of the gas to escape. On leaving the barrel, the round passes through a stack of disk-shaped baffles, which have a 9 mm-diameter hole in their centers and are held in place by two long rods. The suppressor was fairly efficient for its time.

GERMANY

HECKLER AND KOCH MP5 1965

Length (gun): 26.0 in. (660 mm)
Barrel: 8.9 in. (225 mm)
Weight (gun): 5.6 lb. (2.6 kg)
Caliber: 9 mm
Rifling: 6 grooves, r/hand

Operation: delayed blowback
Magazine: 15- or 30-round box
Cyclic rate: 800 rpm
Muz vel: 1,312 ft./sec. (400 m/sec.)

The MP5 uses the same roller-delayed blowback system as the G3 rifle; most parts are interchangeable with other weapons in the H. and K. range. The MP5 can fire semi-automatic, fully automatic, or three-, four- or five-round bursts. Burst control is by a small ratchet interacting with the sear; each time the bolt cycles to the rear, the ratchet advances one notch until the third, fourth or fifth cycle allows re-engagement of the sear. Firing ceases the instant the trigger is released, regardless of how many rounds have been discharged. The specifications above refer to the MP5A3, which has a shorter barrel with a vertical foregrip underneath, and its butt is replaced by a simple cap. MP5SD is a series of silenced weapons: MP5SD1 has no stock; MP5SD2 has a fixed stock; MP5SD3 has a retractable stock. The photo at left shows the MP5SD, with silencer and special laser sight.

UNITED KINGDOM

L34A1 STERLING SILENCED SMG 1966

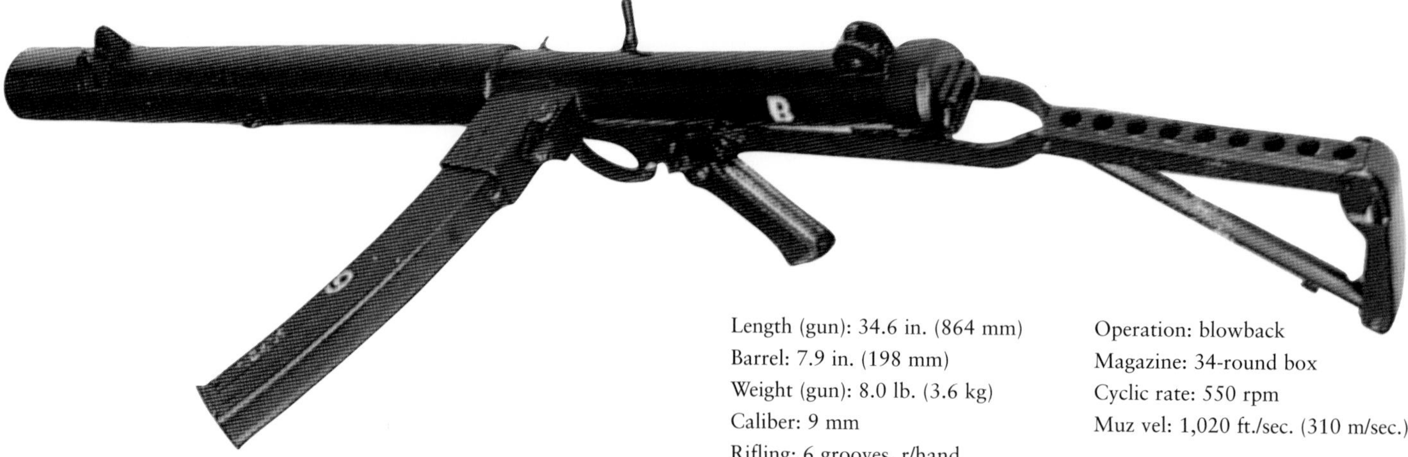

Length (gun): 34.6 in. (864 mm)
Barrel: 7.9 in. (198 mm)
Weight (gun): 8.0 lb. (3.6 kg)
Caliber: 9 mm
Rifling: 6 grooves, r/hand
Operation: blowback
Magazine: 34-round box
Cyclic rate: 550 rpm
Muz vel: 1,020 ft./sec. (310 m/sec.)

The L34A1, which entered service in 1966, was the silenced version of the British L2A3 Sterling, with which it shared many components. The silenced weapon was, however, almost 2 lb. (1 kg) heavier and considerably longer due to the large silencing device fitted around and beyond the barrel. The barrel itself was the same length as that on the unsilenced version, but had seventy-two radial holes drilled in its walls to allow the propellant gases to escape, thus reducing the muzzle velocity of the bullet. Beyond the end of the barrel there was a spiral diffuser, which consisted of a series of disks, each with a hole in the center through which the bullet passed. Propellant gas followed the round but was deflected back by the end cap to mingle with the advancing gases, ensuring that the gases leaving the barrel did so at a low velocity. The silenced Sterling was very effective and was used by the British and other armies, principally by special forces, although some also got into the hands of various terrorist groups. Most silenced weapons require special rounds, but the L34A1 was unusual in firing standard 9 mm Parabellum ammunition.

UNITED STATES

5.56 MM COLT COMMANDO 1965

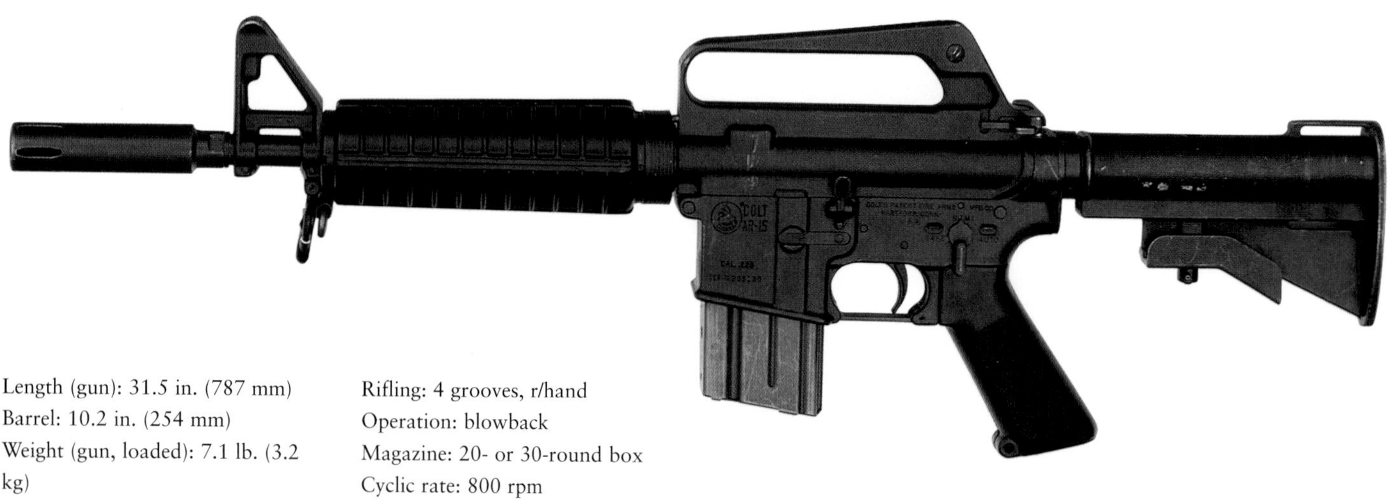

Length (gun): 31.5 in. (787 mm)
Barrel: 10.2 in. (254 mm)
Weight (gun, loaded): 7.1 lb. (3.2 kg)
Caliber: 5.56 mm
Rifling: 4 grooves, r/hand
Operation: blowback
Magazine: 20- or 30-round box
Cyclic rate: 800 rpm
Muz vel: 3,050 ft./sec. (924 m/sec.)

The Colt Commando is a weapon that does not fit neatly into any one category and is variously described as an assault rifle, carbine, and submachine gun; here it is treated as a submachine gun. The weapon was a shorter, handier version of the M16 rifle (qv), intended for use in the Vietnam War as a close-quarter survival weapon. Mechanically it was identical to the M16, but with a much shorter barrel, which reduced the muzzle velocity slightly and also reduced its accuracy at longer ranges. The short barrel also caused considerable muzzle flash, which had to be overcome by a 4 in. (100 mm) flash suppressor that could be unscrewed, if necessary. The Colt Commando had a telescopic butt that could be extended when it was necessary to fire the weapon from the shoulder. It featured selective fire and a holding-open device, and it was actuated by the same direct gas action as the M16. In spite of the limitations on range, the weapon proved useful in Indochina. And although it had been designed as a survival weapon, it fit the submachine gun role so well that it was later issued to the US Special Operations Forces and also used in small numbers by the British SAS.

AUSTRIA

STEYR 9 MM MPI-69 AND –81 1969

Length (gun): 26.4 in. (670 mm)
Barrel: 10.2 in. (260 mm)
Weight (gun): 6.9 lb. (3.1 kg)
Caliber: 9 mm
Rifling: 6 grooves, r/hand
Operation: blowback
Magazine: 25- or 32-round box
Cyclic rate: 550 rpm
Muz vel: 1,250 ft./sec. (381 m/sec.)

Steyr-Mannlicher started production of the MPi-69 in 1969, superseded in 1981 by a slightly modified version, the MPi-81; production ended in 1993. It was of straightforward but rugged design and consisted of a square-sectioned body with a trigger group and a pistol grip containing the housing for either a 25-round or 32-round box magazine. The barrel was easily changed and there were two lengths: the standard barrel at 10.2 in. (260 mm) and a second and considerably longer barrel, used in conjunction with an optical sight. The longer barrel had a flash suppressor and required a heavier bolt. The MPi-69 had a unique cocking system in which the forward end of the sling was attached to the cocking lever; the weapon was cocked by the firer gripping the sling, holding it at 90 degrees to the weapon, and pulling it to the rear. The MPi-81 had a conventional cocking handle, with the forward end of the sling attached to a swivel anchored to the front of the weapon. The MPi-81 also had an increased rate of fire: 700 rounds per minute compared to 550. Both MPi-69 and MPi-81 had a sliding, steel wire butt.

UNITED STATES

INGRAM MODELS 10 AND 11 1970

Length (gun): 10.5 in. (267 mm)
Barrel: 5.75 in. (146 mm)
Weight: 6.4 lb. (2.8 kg)
Caliber: 0.45 in.
Rifling: 5 grooves, r/hand
Operation: blowback
Feed: 30-round box
Cyclic rate: 1,100 rpm
Muz vel: 900 ft./sec. (275 m/sec.)

Gordon Ingram's first submachine gun design, the M5, never got beyond a single model. He then worked on a new model for two years, producing his Model 6 in 1949. By 1959, he had produced Models 7, 8 and 9, all of which were sufficiently successful to encourage him to continue. In 1970, he began to design weapons entirely different from his earlier ones, and two Models, Numbers 10 and 11, soon appeared. These were virtually identical except the Number 10 was 0.45 in. and the smaller Number 11 was 0.38 in. They worked on blowback but had wraparound bolts, which made it possible to keep the weapon short, and improved control at full-automatic fire. The cocking handle, which was on the top, was equally convenient for right- or left-handed firers; it had a slot cut in the center of it so as not to interfere with the line of sight. The magazine fitted into the pistol grip and the gun had a simple retractable butt. The whole thing was made of stampings with the exception of the barrel—even the bolt was made of sheet metal and filled with lead. The Models 10 and 11 were both fitted with suppressors, which reduced the sound considerably.

SUBMACHINE GUNS AND CRIME

Submachine guns have long been portrayed by Hollywood as the weapon of choice for criminals, although the reality is somewhat different. The earliest documented criminal use of submachine guns occurred in the United States during the 1920s, when Thompson M1921 submachine guns fell into the hands of gangland criminals. Actual distribution of Thompsons among this community was limited—a production of parts for 15,000 Thompsons in 1921 was not fully used up for another twenty years. However, high-profile criminals and crimes turned General Thompson's invention, intended in his own words to be a "trench broom" to hasten the end of World War I, into a legend.

The St. Valentine's Day Massacre in 1929, during which seven members of the "Bugs" Moran gang were gunned down by Thompsons in a Chicago garage courtesy of Al Capone's henchmen, put the power of the Thompson on the map. Other big-name criminals, such as John Dillinger (who made a "concealed" Thompson by removing the buttstock and replacing the drum magazine with a twenty-round clip) and "Baby Face" Nelson, reinforced the notoriety. Yet submachine guns were still relatively rare in armed crime, as they were difficult to conceal and apt to provoke a vigorous response from the police.

The same is true today. In the United States, laws introduced in 1934 have made it an offense to own a submachine gun without federal authorization, although in 1995 there were 240,000 full-auto weapons registered with the Bureau of Alcohol, Tobacco, and Firearms. In the same year, 7,700 machine guns and submachine guns were reported as stolen. However, a study of US prison inmates found that although 8 percent of firearm offenders owned an assault-type weapon, less than 1 percent used it in a crime because of its impracticality.

Despite the relatively low rate of usage of submachine guns in crime in the Western world, there is still some room for concern. The conversion of deactivated and replica submachine guns, particularly simple blowback weapons like the Uzi and the Ingram MAC 10, into fully functioning weapons has increased, with criminals taking advantage of the legal purchase of such weapons.

Furthermore, stocks of submachine guns from the Balkans are currently flooding across Europe. In November 2002, for example, British customs officers found thirty Uzis aboard a truck from Croatia bound for London. Such hauls are extremely worrying and could herald a rise in submachine gun crime.

Above: *General John T. Thompson and his invention. Despite the image of the Thompson submachine gun as the archetypal gangster weapon, actual criminal use of the Thompson was relatively rare. Thompsons were heavy, were difficult to conceal, and had unnecessarily heavy firepower for most criminal purposes. Handguns were, and remain, far more popular firearms for criminals.*

SPAIN

STAR 9 MM MODEL Z-70 1971

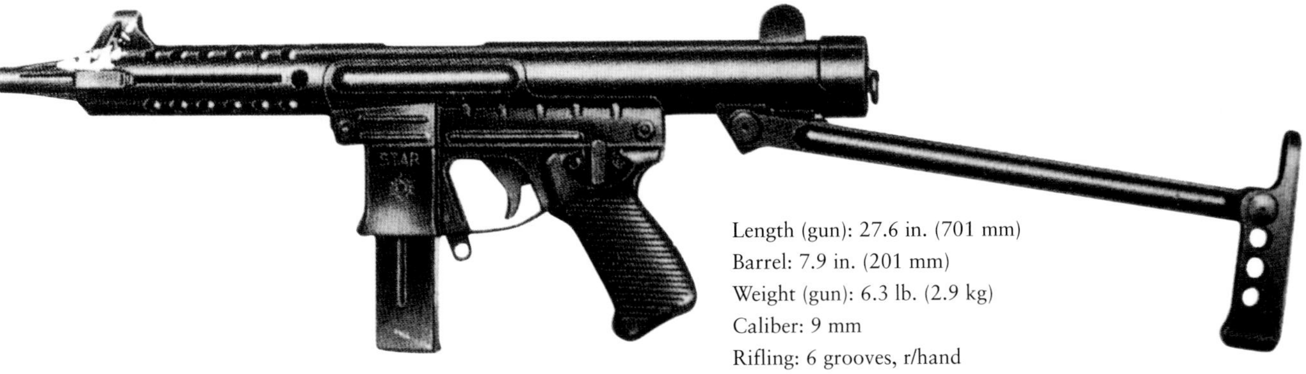

Length (gun): 27.6 in. (701 mm)
Barrel: 7.9 in. (201 mm)
Weight (gun): 6.3 lb. (2.9 kg)
Caliber: 9 mm
Rifling: 6 grooves, r/hand
Operation: blowback
Magazine: 20-, 30- or 40-round box
Cyclic rate: 550 rpm
Muz vel: 1,250 ft./sec. (380 m/sec.)

Star Bonifacio Echeverria, of Eibar, has produced a series of submachine guns dating back to the SI-35, introduced in 1935. Most have been the company's own design except for the Z-45 of 1944, which was loosely based on the German MP-40. The Z-62 of 1960 was a company design, with two models produced: one fired 9 x 19 mm Parabellum, the other 9 x 23 mm Largo. The Z-62 appears to have had some problems with the trigger group, and the Star Model Z-70/B was brought into service in 1971 to overcome them. The Z-70/B has a cylindrical receiver with a perforated barrel jacket, with the muzzle protruding several inches. The butt has two parallel steel struts with a centrally pivoted plate at the end; it folds down and forward. In the Z-62 the trigger was solid and two pressures were used for single shot or automatic, but in the Z-70/B there is a more conventional change lever and a stand-alone trigger. The Z-70/B was used by the Spanish armed forces and police but has been superseded by the Z-84. Most Z-70/Bs take the 9 x 19 mm Parabellum round, but some take the 9 x 23 mm Largo round.

BRAZIL

URU 9 MM MODEL 2 1974

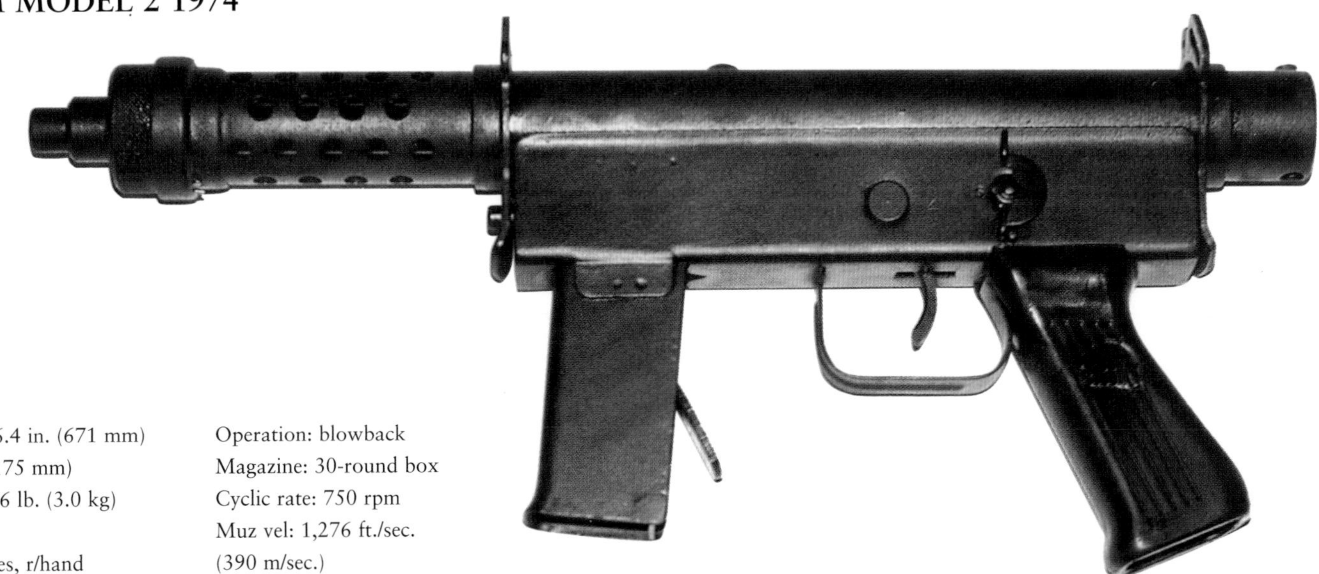

Length (gun): 26.4 in. (671 mm)
Barrel: 6.9 in. (175 mm)
Weight (gun): 6.6 lb. (3.0 kg)
Caliber: 9 mm
Rifling: 6 grooves, r/hand
Operation: blowback
Magazine: 30-round box
Cyclic rate: 750 rpm
Muz vel: 1,276 ft./sec. (390 m/sec.)

The Uru Model 2 was developed from the Model 1, which was designed in 1974 and placed in production by a company called Mekanika in 1977 to meet orders placed by Brazil's Army and police forces. All design and production rights to the weapon were acquired by the FAU Guns division of Bilbao SA in 1988, which developed the weapon into the Model 2. The Model 2 has a cylindrical body; the forward end is drilled with vents for cooling the barrel and the rear end is closed with a cap, which can be replaced by a butt stock, either solid or a single-strut tubular-steel assembly, if required. Beneath the tubular assembly is a box-like feature that includes the magazine housing (which also serves as the forward handgrip), the trigger and pistol grip (which incorporates a grip safety), and the change lever (which can be set to safe, semi-automatic, or full automatic). A silencer can be screwed onto the muzzle. Other versions include one firing the 0.38 ACP round, as well as a carbine with a wooden stock that is also available in either 9 mm Parabellum or 0.38 ACP versions.

CHINA (PRC)

NORINCO 7.62 MM TYPE 79/TYPE 85 1979

Length (gun): 29.1 in. (740 mm)
Barrel: n.k.
Weight (gun): 4.3 lb. (1.9 kg)
Caliber: 7.62 mm
Rifling: n.k.

Operation: see text
Magazine: 20-round box
Cyclic rate: 650 rpm
Muz vel: 1,640 ft./sec. (500 m/sec.)

The Chinese designers employed an unusual mechanism in the Type 79 (see specifications) in which a tappet above the barrel was activated by the projectile gases to drive rearward a short-stroke piston attached to the bolt carrier. Because of the short distances traveled, the components are smaller and lighter than usual, resulting in a very light weapon that weighs (with an empty magazine) just 4.33 lb. (1.9kg). The Type 79 uses the Chinese Type 51 7.62 x 25 mm pistol round. The weapon has a folding butt, although the strut is box-shaped rather than the more common tube. Despite the apparent advantages of the Type 79, a modified version appeared as the Type 85, using a straightforward blowback operation with a cylindrical receiver. The Type 85 has the same folding butt as the Type 79 and uses the same 30-round box magazine.

RUSSIA

5.45 MM AK-74-SU 1979

Length (gun): 26.6 in. (675 mm)
Barrel: 8.1 in. (206 mm)
Weight (gun): 5.9 lb. (2.7 kg)
Caliber: 5.45 mm
Rifling: 4 grooves, r/hand

Operation: blowback
Magazine: 30-round box
Cyclic rate: 700 rpm
Muz vel: 2,411 ft./sec. (735 m/sec.)

In the 1970s, a new Soviet SMG based on the Kalashnikov AKS-74 assault rifle made its appearance. The barrel was only 8.1 in. (206 mm) long and was fitted with a screw-on, cylindrical attachment at the front of which was a cone-shaped flash suppressor. Unlike the majority of SMGs, the AK-74-SU fired standard, full-charge rifle ammunition, in this case the Russian 5.45 x 39.5 mm. In addition, due to the shortness of the barrel, the gas was tapped off very close to the chamber, resulting in a very high pressure for such a small weapon. The muzzle attachment was an expansion chamber, designed to reduce the pressure acting on the gas piston; it also served as a flame damper. The weapon was fitted with basic iron sights, the rear sight a basic flip-over device that was somewhat optimistically marked for 220 yd. (200 m) and 440 yd. (400 m).

POLAND

GLAUBERYT PM-84 1984

Length (gun): 22.6 in. (575 mm)
Barrel: 7.3 in. (185 mm)
Weight (gun): 4.6 lb. (2.1 kg)
Caliber: 9 mm
Rifling: 6 grooves, r/hand

Operation: blowback
Magazine: 15- or 25-round box
Cyclic rate: 600 rpm
Muz vel: 1,083 ft./sec. (330 m/sec.)

The PM-63 (also designated the Wz-63), fielded in 1963, was notable for its unusual reciprocating receiver. The PM-84 is an updated version of the PM-63, in which the major change is that the bolt and other moving elements are housed inside the receiver. The butt strut is hinged just behind the pistol grip and folds down and forward until it clips below the receiver, with the butt plate acting as the forward handgrip. With the butt folded, the pistol grip is at the point of balance, enabling single rounds to be fired with one hand. The PM-84 is chambered for the 9 x 18 mm Makarov round, and this version is widely used in the Polish forces. A new version, the PM-84P, appeared in 1985 for the export market. It is chambered for the 9 mm Parabellum round, and the weapon is slightly heavier at 4.75 lb. (2.2 kg). The latest version, the PM-98, is an updated version of the PM-84P and is slightly larger still, weighing 5.1 lb. (2.3 kg).

Submachine Gun Use in the Iranian Embassy Siege

Above: *Hostages make their escape during the SAS storming of the Iranian embassy. The rescue mission was problematic because of the number of hostages, but the accuracy of the H. and K. MP5s used by the SAS soldiers ensured that their was no collateral damage from SAS fire, despite the SAS using full-auto firing modes.*

The SAS hostage-rescue action at the Iranian Embassy in London in 1980 not only gave the SAS public notoriety, but also brought attention to a specific weapon: the 9 mm Heckler and Koch MP5. The MP5 had been selected for the SAS counter-terrorist unit during the 1970s on the basis of its reliability, ease of handling, and accuracy that came from its closed-bolt firing position. In May 1980, the SAS gave the weapon its first combat testing in public.

On the morning of April 30, 1980, six terrorists took over the Iranian Embassy at No.16 Princes Gate, London, taking twenty-six hostages. Within twenty-five minutes the SAS antiterrorist unit in Hereford had been informed, and on May 1, following increased threats of violence against the hostages, an SAS team was deployed in the vicinity of the building. The team immediately set up observation posts overlooking the embassy, and the next day a covert entry point into the building through a roof skylight, plus rappel ropes for a rapid assault, were secured ready for action.

The siege dragged on for three more days, but on May 5 the embassy press officer was summarily executed and thrown from the embassy door. The SAS was given the green light. Armed with the MP5 and with Browning Hi-Power handguns as backup weapons, they began their assault at 7.23 P.M.

SAS teams, their MP5s slung over the shoulders, rappelled down from the roof to all balcony levels, making multipoint entries around the building by blowing out the windows with frame charges. Another squad entered through the roof skylight, and still another went in at basement level. Once the teams were inside, each room and floor was systematically cleared with stun grenades and with MP5 fire.

The MP5 demonstrated the benefits of the closed-bolt accuracy and its sustained 9 mm firepower. The terrorists were mown down in extremely close proximity to the hostages. Oan, the terrorist leader, was killed while grappling with a British policeman who had been one of the hostages. Another two were shot dead while pretending to be hostages themselves by mingling in with the terrified prisoners. One other terrorist was killed with concentrated auto bursts as he attempted to deploy a hand grenade.

The whole action, which took seventeen minutes, resulted in five out of six terrorists killed, two dead hostages, and no SAS combat casualties. The MP5 had proved itself, and it remains a standard SAS counter-terrorist firearm.

ITALY

SITES SPECTRE 9 MM M-4 1983

Length (gun): 22.8 in. (580 mm)
Barrel: 5.1 in. (130 mm)
Weight (gun): 6.3 lb. (2.9 kg)
Caliber: 9 mm
Rifling: 4 grooves, r/hand
Operation: blowback
Magazine: 30- or 50-round
Cyclic rate: 850 rpm
Muz vel: 1,312 ft./sec. (400 m/sec.)

The Spectre M-4, announced in 1983, is made by SITES of Turin. It uses a blowback system but fires from a closed bolt. The gun is cocked as normal, allowing the bolt to move forward, driving a round into the chamber but leaving the hammer to the rear. The decocking lever is now pressed and the hammer moves forward until it is a short distance behind the bolt. Pulling the trigger allows the hammer to go forward to strike the firing pin. This arrangement overcomes the problem inherent in the closed-bolt system of having to cock the weapon before firing, and it allows the weapon to be carried safely with "one round up the spout." The bolt and the interior of the receiver are so designed that as the bolt travels forward, it forces air ahead of it and around the barrel, thus cooling it. The magazine is thicker than normal since it accommodates fifty rounds in four vertical rows. The Model C is a carbine firing single rounds only; the Model P is a pistol (qv); and the Model PCC is for police use and can be chambered for 9 mm Parabellum or 0.45 in. ACP.

SOUTH AFRICA

MECHEM BXP 9 MM 1984

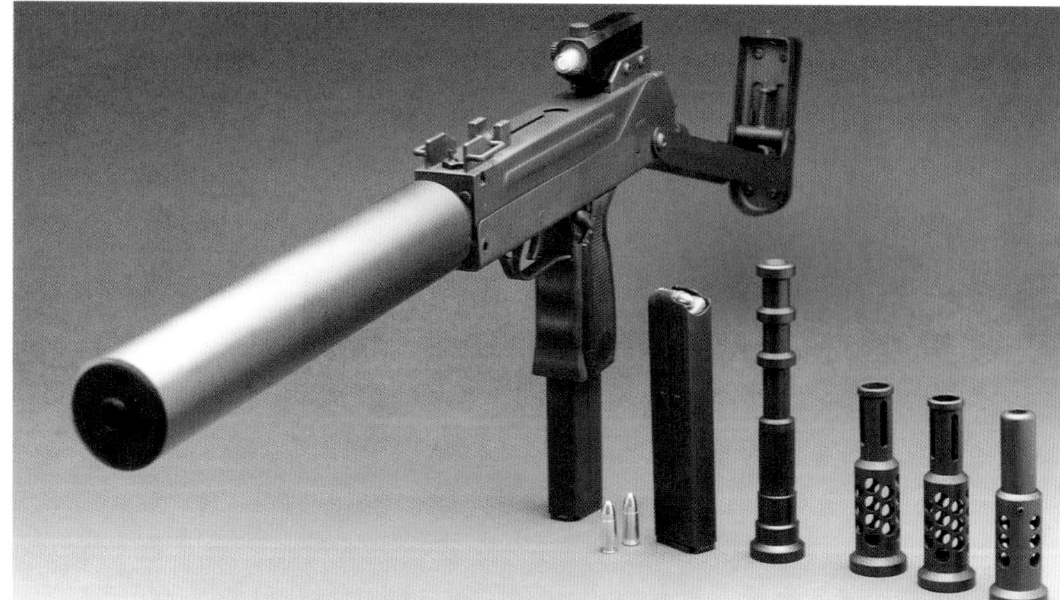

Length (gun): 23.9 in. (607 mm)
Barrel: 8.2 in. (208 mm)
Weight (gun): 5.8 lb. (2.7 kg)
Caliber: 9 mm
Rifling: 6 grooves, r/hand
Operation: blowback
Magazine: 22- or 32-round box
Cyclic rate: 800 rpm
Muz vel: 1,250 ft./sec. (380 m/sec.)

The BXP 9 mm submachine gun, which entered service in 1984, is one of a number of weapons developed in South Africa during the period when that country was subjected to an international arms embargo while concurrently involved in a series of conflicts in the southern part of the continent. The BXP has a short, box-shaped receiver and a very short barrel with a screw-on flash suppressor, which can be removed and replaced by a large, cylindrical noise suppressor. In its normal mode the barrel is fitted with a short, vented jacket. One very unusual feature for a submachine gun is that the BXP can be fitted with a grenade-launcher attachment for use in antiriot situations to project CS and other types of grenade. The twin-strut butt folds down and forward, with the butt plate swiveling to lie under the receiver and act as a foregrip. The BXP is used by the South African armed forces and police, and has also been exported to a number of other countries

SPAIN

STAR 9 MM MODEL Z-84 1984

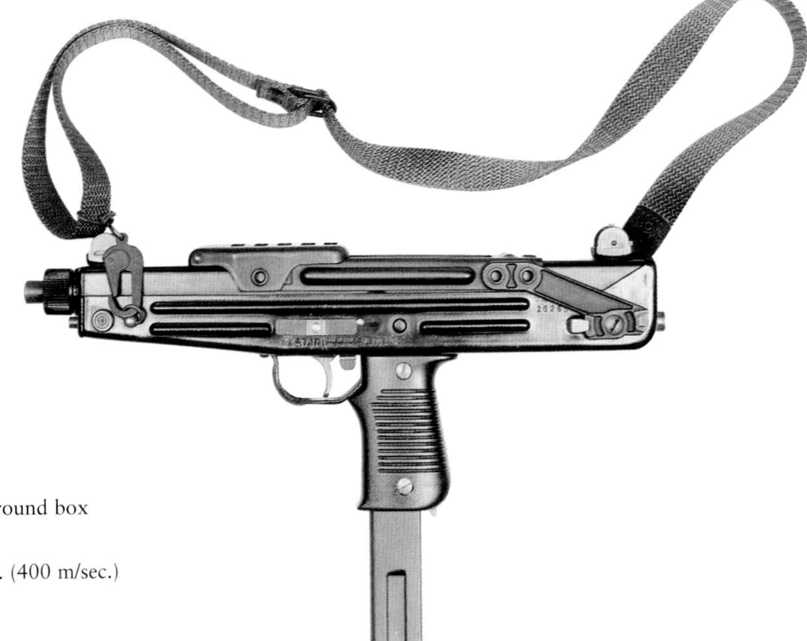

Length (gun): 24.2 in. (615 mm)
Barrel: 8.5 in. (215 mm)
Weight (gun): 6.6 lb. (3.0 kg)
Caliber: 9 mm
Rifling: n.k.

Operation: blowback
Magazine: 25- or 30-round box
Cyclic rate: 600 rpm
Muz vel: 1,312 ft./sec. (400 m/sec.)

The Star Z-84 is a totally new design first seen in public in 1984. It has a box-shaped receiver with the muzzle protruding a short distance from the barrel nut at the front. At the rear is a twin-strut butt, similar to that on the Z-70B, which folds down and forward when not required. Beneath the receiver is the pistol grip, which contains the magazine housing and is at the point of balance to ensure good control when firing, even when single-handed. One unusual feature is that the ejection slot is on the top of the receiver. Particular care has been taken to ensure that no dust or dirt can be admitted to the working parts and that, even if it is, the weapon will continue to operate efficiently

AUSTRIA

STEYR AUG 9 MM PARA 1986

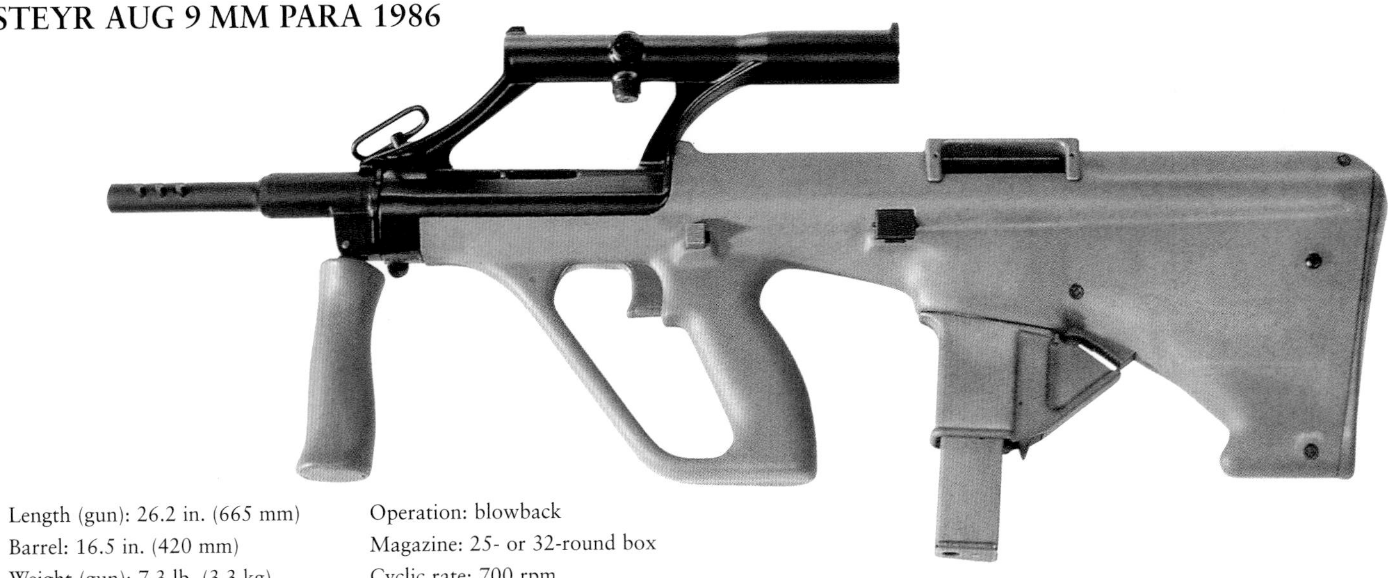

Length (gun): 26.2 in. (665 mm)
Barrel: 16.5 in. (420 mm)
Weight (gun): 7.3 lb. (3.3 kg)
Caliber: 9 mm
Rifling: 6 grooves, r/hand

Operation: blowback
Magazine: 25- or 32-round box
Cyclic rate: 700 rpm
Muz vel: 1,312 ft./sec. (400 m/sec.)

Steyr-Mannlicher produces the AUG assault rifle (qv), and this weapon, introduced in 1986, is the submachine gun model in that range. Externally they appear very similar and many elements are common to both weapons, including the bullpup layout, plastic casing, canted carrying handle with built-in x1.5 optical sight, forward handgrip, and pistol grip with hand guard. Although it bears an outward resemblance to the assault rifle, the submachine gun has substantial differences internally. It fires the 9 x 19 mm Parabellum round rather than the rifle's 5.56 mm, and the barrel is shorter: 16.5 in. (420 mm) compared to 20.0 in. (508 mm). The method of operation is also different in that the submachine gun version has a new bolt and operates by blowback from a closed bolt. The magazine housing is fitted with an adapter that allows it to accommodate the new magazine holding 9 mm rounds. The submachine gun's barrel can be fitted with a screw-on silencer.

BELGIUM

FN 5.7 MM P-90 1988

Length (gun): 19.7 in. (500 mm)
Barrel: 10.4 in. (263 mm)
Weight (gun): 5.5 lb. (2.5 kg)
Caliber: 5.7 mm
Rifling: 8 grooves, r/hand

Operation: blowback, closed-bolt
Magazine: 50-round box
Cyclic rate: 900 rpm
Muz vel: 2,345 ft./sec. (715 m/sec.)

The futuristic-looking FN P-90 was designed as a self-defense weapon for support and technical troops. It has been designed from basic principles and incorporates a host of new and imaginative ideas. The shape is based on extensive ergonomic research, and care has been taken to ensure that it can be used by left- or right-handed firers; its smooth contours ensure that it will not snag on clothing or equipment. The clear plastic magazine is positioned along the top of the receiver and contains fifty rounds that lie in two rows. These are pushed forward by a spring and fed into a single row, then rotated 90 degrees, aligning them with the chamber, into which they are then fed. The carrying handle incorporates a tritium-illuminated sight, but there are also conventional iron sights on the top of the receiver. A totally new round was designed by FN for use in this weapon: the 5.7 x 28 mm. This is lead-free and causes extensive wounds to humans, since it is designed not only to transfer the maximum energy to the target, but also to "tumble" inside the target. Two versions also available for special forces include a number of optional accessories, including a silencer.

AUSTRIA

STEYR 9 MM TACTICAL MACHINE PISTOL (TMP) 1989

Length (gun): 11.1 in. (282 mm)
Barrel: 5.1 in. (130 mm)
Weight (gun): 2.9 lb. (1.3 kg)
Caliber: 9 mm
Rifling: 6 grooves, r/hand

Operation: locked-breach
Magazine: 15- or 30-round box
Cyclic rate: 900 rpm
Muz vel: 1,180 ft./sec. (360 m/sec.)

The TMP is another weapon that does not fit neatly into any one category, its small size and lack of a buttstock suggesting a pistol, while its full-automatic firing and forward handgrip are more akin to a submachine gun; it is treated as such here. The receiver is made from a synthetic material and incorporates a rail along the top for an optical sight, if required. Internally, there is a guiderail for the bolt, and the operating system consists of a locking breech and a rotating barrel. There is no buttstock, which allows the cocking handle to be mounted at the foot of the back plate; the weapon is cocked by pulling it straight to the rear. The barrel is threaded to accommodate a cylindrical sound suppressor (left), which is longer than the weapon itself.

CHILE

SAF 9 1990

Length (gun): 25.3 in. (640 mm)
Barrel: 7.9 in. (200 mm)
Weight (gun): 5.9 lb. (2.7 kg)
Caliber: 9 mm
Rifling: 6 grooves, r/hand
Operation: blowback
Magazine: 30- or 20-round
Cyclic rate: 1,200 rpm
Muz vel: 1,280 ft./sec. (390 m/sec.)

The Swiss SIG 540 is manufactured under license by Fabricas y Maestranzas del Ejercito (FAMAE) at Santiago, Chile. FAMAE has developed a new submachine gun, the SAF 9 mm, which uses a large number of features from the SIG 540. The weapon works by blowback, both barrel and chamber are chrome-plated, and, unlike the SIG 540, it has a three-round burst capability. There are three basic models: standard, with fixed or folding stock; silenced, with fixed (lower left) or folding (top left) stocks; and Mini-SAF (top right), which is intended for concealed carriage.

The Mini-SAF has the same basic mechanism as the larger weapon, but with a very short barrel (4.5 in./115 mm), a forward handgrip, and no buttstock. It takes the standard 30-round translucent magazine, but there is also a 20-round version for maximum compactness. Both magazines have slots and studs so they can be connected back-to-back, effectively doubling the capacity. The Mini-SAF is in service with the Chilean armed forces and police, but as far as is known, it has not been exported

UNITED STATES

CALICO M960A 1990

Length (gun): 32.9 in. (835 mm)
Barrel: 13 in. (330 mm)
Weight (gun): 4.78 lb. (2.17 kg)
Caliber: 9 mm Parabellum
Rifling: 6 grooves, r/hand
Operation: roller-delayed blowback
Feed: 25- or 100-round helical box magazine
Muz vel: n.a.

The Calico M960A began life as the Calico M950 single-shot semi-automatic produced in 1988. Both of these 9 mm Parabellum weapons are immediately distinguished by unusual magazine feed—a 50- or 100-round plastic helical magazine sits horizontally atop the weapon above the receiver (the 100-round magazine actually extends out over the back of the receiver). The rounds within the magazine are fed along a helical track, pushed by a spiral spring that can be externally unwound to save spring tension when the magazine is not in use. Because of the positioning of the magazine, the Calico's rounds are ejected downward from a port just in front of the trigger guard. Internally the mechanism is roller-delayed blowback, indebted to the Heckler and Koch design. The M960A is distinguished from the M950 as a full-auto weapon, with a cyclical rate of fire of 750 rpm, and it features a pistol-grip fore end to allow users to control it in this mode. Although the Caliço weapons are both ingenious and functional, lack of interest on the part of the US military and a US ban on certain types of assault weapon meant that the guns had no market, and the Calico Light Weapons Systems Company was sold in the mid-1990s

RUSSIAN FEDERATION

OTS-02 (KIPARIS) 9 MM 1992

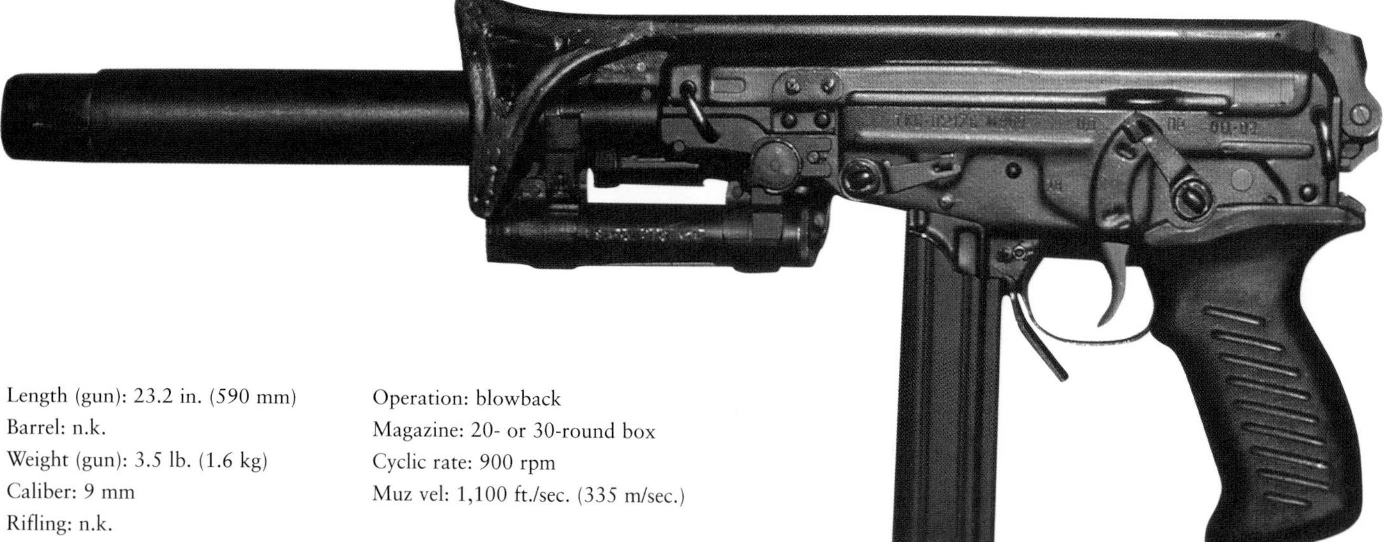

Length (gun): 23.2 in. (590 mm)
Barrel: n.k.
Weight (gun): 3.5 lb. (1.6 kg)
Caliber: 9 mm
Rifling: n.k.

Operation: blowback
Magazine: 20- or 30-round box
Cyclic rate: 900 rpm
Muz vel: 1,100 ft./sec. (335 m/sec.)

The OTS-02 9 mm submachine gun, also known as Kiparis (cypress tree), was developed in Kazakhstan, one of the republics of the Russian Federation. The weapon works on the standard blowback principle and fires the standard Russian 9 x 18 mm Makarov round. The change lever is to the left of the trigger group and has three positions: safe, single rounds, and fully automatic. The receiver is made from pressed steel and the twin-strut butt folds upward and over the top of the receiver, with the butt plate straddling the barrel. A laser-aiming device can be fitted, which sits below the barrel and also serves as a forward handgrip. The weapon is intended primarily for use by police and other internal security troops.

RUSSIAN FEDERATION

BISON 9 MM 1993

Length (gun): 26.0 in. (660 mm)
Barrel: n.k.
Weight (gun): 4.6 lb. (2.1 kg)
Caliber: 9 mm
Rifling: n.k.

Operation: blowback
Magazine: 64-round helical
Cyclic rate: 700 rpm
Muz vel: 1,115 ft./sec. (340 m/sec.)

The Bison submachine gun was designed by a team led by Viktor Kalashnikov, the son of Mikhail Kalashnikov, who was responsible for weapons such as the AK-47 and AK-74. It operates on the blowback principle; the left-folding twin-strut butt stock, trigger mechanism, receiver cover, and magazine catch all come straight from other Kalashnikov designs. The barrel protrudes a considerable distance from the front of the receiver and is completely surrounded by a forestock, which has three horizontal cooling slots in each side. The most unusual feature is the magazine, helical in shape and secured under the forestock with its rear end engaged in the magazine feed and held in place by a Kalashnikov magazine catch. The magazine holds sixty-four rounds, and while the prototype was made from pressed steel, production versions will be made of translucent plastic. The first prototype (Bison 1) fires either 9 x 18 mm Makarov pistol rounds or the newer and more powerful 9 x 18 mm "Special." Bison 2 fires the newer "Special" round only, as does the Bison 3, but the latter also has a different-style folding butt. The weapon is ready for production, but as of late 1999 no orders had been announced.

PORTUGAL

INDEP 9 MM LUSA A2 1994

Length (gun): 23.0 in. (585 mm)
Barrel: 6.3 in. (160 mm)
Weight (gun): 6.2 lb. (2.9 kg)
Caliber: 9 mm
Rifling: 6 grooves, r/hand
Operation: blowback
Magazine: 30-round box
Cyclic rate: 900 rpm
Muz vel: 1,280 ft./sec. (390 m/sec.)

The first submachine gun to be manufactured in Portugal was the M-948, and the design included features of the US M3A1, the German MP 40, and some local parts. It fired the 9 mm Parabellum round. This was followed by an improved M-976, but in 1986 a totally new weapon was introduced, the Lusa A1. This blowback weapon had a receiver with a figure-of-eight cross-section, with the overhung bolt in the top cylinder; the lower cylinder contained the trigger group and the feed mechanism, with the barrel at the fore end. The telescopic stock retracted along the waist between the upper and lower cylinders, and the magazine housing acted as the forward handgrip. Firing modes were fully automatic, single-rounds, and three-round bursts. There were two versions: one with a plain, detachable barrel, the other with a fixed barrel surrounded by a vented cooling jacket. The Lusa A2 (see specifications) appeared in 1994 and is an improved version of the A1. It has a stronger butt and a detachable barrel, which comes in two versions: one a normal barrel, the other a long cylindrical silencer, which incorporates a special barrel. The A2 also has a mounting for a laser-aiming device.

ROMANIA

RATMIL 9 MM 1995

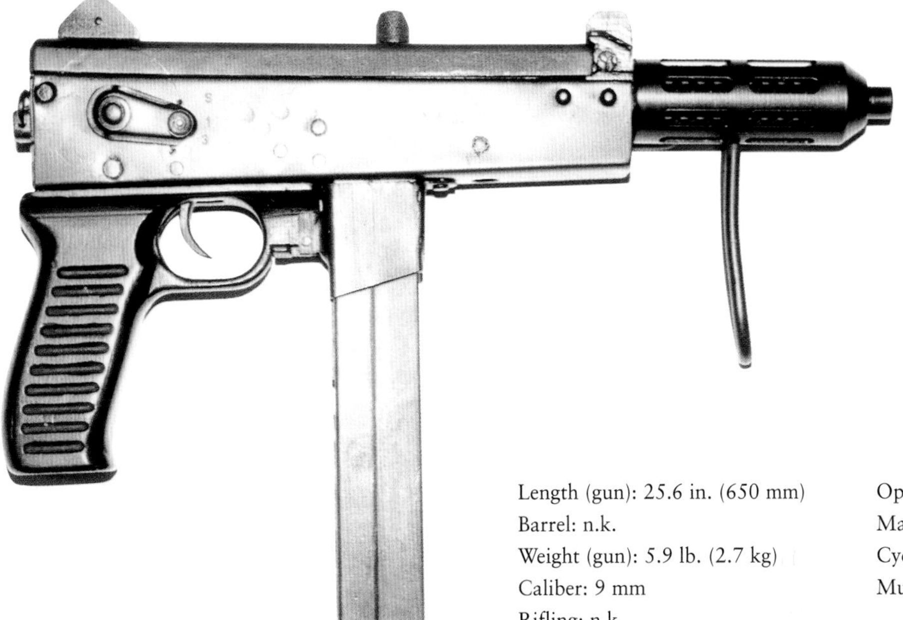

Length (gun): 25.6 in. (650 mm)
Barrel: n.k.
Weight (gun): 5.9 lb. (2.7 kg)
Caliber: 9 mm
Rifling: n.k.
Operation: blowback
Magazine: 30-round box
Cyclic rate: 650 rpm
Muz vel: 1,214 ft./sec. (370 m/sec.)

The Romanian Ratmil, which appeared in 1995, is another of weapon that slips into the gray area between pistols and submachine guns. It has a box-shaped receiver with a wraparound bolt and a barrel that protrudes from the front end; the barrel is ribbed and surrounded by a vented cooling jacket, which also serves as a handgrip. The weapon has a cyclic rate of fire of 650 rounds per minute, but the change lever, which is situated on the right of the receiver above the pistol grip, has three positions: safe, single rounds, and three-round bursts. The wire stock swings to the left to be secured against the receiver. The cocking handle is on the top of the receiver and includes a longitudinal slot, which allows it to be used as a rudimentary sight.

TACTICS AND SUBMACHINE GUNS

Submachine guns have their own distinct set of tactical considerations. Shooting full-auto certainly produces a lethal spray of bullets but reduces accuracy considerably. The general rule taught among military units is that up to 160 feet (50 m), full-auto fire is practical against close-spaced multiple targets, but above that range semi-auto fire has a better chance of securing kills. At individual human targets, submachine guns are best used at ranges of less than 80 feet (25 m). Submachine guns should not be used if the target is too far away to observe the impact of the rounds; much of the aiming process of the submachine gun comes from "walking" the observed round impacts onto the target. The limit of the visual range can, of course, be improved with the use of tracers.

Full-auto fire should not be employed when ammunition is in short supply, or if resupply is uncertain. In such situations the single-shot setting (if the weapon has one) should be applied, or the user should pull the trigger sensitively to fire only one shot at a time.

In these modes, however, the weapon should not be treated like a rifle. Submachine gun sights are generally not set with the accuracy of rifle sights; in addition, the pistol-caliber round does not carry the range, penetration, or killing power of a rifle round.

Submachine guns are best used in situations where ammunition supply is not a problem, and where concentrated devastating firepower is required in close-quarters combat. These qualifications demonstrate why submachine guns are a weapon of choice for counter-terrorist forces working in urban assault scenarios, where terrorists and hijackers must be emphatically downed before they can either deploy weapons or kill hostages. The key talent to wielding a submachine gun is control. If a submachine is not rigorously controlled during full-auto fire, the percentage of bullets that miss the target will be increased, causing potential danger to bystanders or hostages. When firing from a standing position, two thirds of body weight should be on the bent front leg, with (in the case of a right-handed shooter) the right shoulder pushed forward into the stock. This position pushes the body weight into the weapon, helping to control recoil and muzzle lift. When fired from the hip, the submachine gun should be clamped firmly under the armpit or against the waist from the same reasons. Submachine guns do take training time to handle properly, hence they are usually seen today in the hands of specialists.

Below: *A unit of British Army soldiers makes a cautious advance through a battle-scarred village. Two of the soldiers are armed with 9 mm Sten Mk III submachine guns, which appeared in British and Canadian service from 1943 on. Weapons such as the Sten were ideal for urban warfare because they can generate heavy volumes of firepower in rapid-response close-range combat situations, whereas rifles such as the .303 Lee-Enfield No.4 (in the hands of the third soldier) covered long-range tactical distances.*

UNITED STATES

RUGER MP-9 9 MM 1994

Length (gun): 21.9 in. (556 mm)
Barrel: 6.8 in. (173 mm)
Weight (gun): 6.6 lb. (3.0 kg)
Caliber: 9 mm
Rifling: 6 grooves, r/hand
Operation: blowback
Magazine: 32-round box
Cyclic rate: 600 rpm
Muz vel: 1,148 ft./sec. (350 m/sec.)

The Ruger MP-9 is, in effect, an updated and improved Uzi (qv). The design work was carried out by Uzi Gal in the mid-1980s and was then passed to the Ruger Company for final touches and production, which started in 1994. Unlike the Uzi, the MP-9 fires from a closed bolt. The upper part of the receiver is made of polished and treated steel alloy, and the lower part is fabricated from glass-fiber-reinforced synthetic material. The chrome/molybdenum steel barrel is detachable and can be fitted with a noise suppressor. The folding butt telescopes and then folds downward to combine with the frame behind the pistol grip/magazine housing. The MP-9 is in production, but the identity of the customers has not been revealed.

UNITED KINGDOM

PARKER-HALE PERSONAL DEFENSE WEAPON (PDW) 1999

Length (gun) (stock extended): 22.0 in. (560 mm)
Barrel: 4.0 in. (108 mm) (see text)
Weight (gun) (pistol configuration): 4.75 lb. (2.1 kg)
Caliber: 9 mm
Rifling: see text
Operation: blowback
Magazine: 12-/20-/32-round boxes
Cyclic rate: 400 rpm
Muz vel: 1,155 ft./sec. (352 m/sec.)

The Personal Defense Weapon (PDW) is clearly targeted at the market currently dominated by the Heckler and Koch MP5. The PDW can be fitted with a variety of barrels, which simply screw on to the front of the receiver. The standard barrel is 4.0 in. (108 mm) with barrel twist of one turn in ten, but there are also 6.0 in. (152 mm), 10.0 in. (254 mm), 12 in. (305 mm), and 14 in. (356 mm) versions. All except the 4.0 in. and 6.0 in. barrels are fitted with a cylindrical heat shroud and can accept a bipod, enabling the weapon to be used as a light machine gun. A noise-suppressed barrel is also available. Iron ring sights are fitted as standard, but a Picatinny Arsenal rail on top of the receiver accepts a wide variety of sights, and a flashlight, red dot, or laser designator can be fitted beneath the barrel. Effective range is claimed to be 164 yd. (150 m). In the PDW, the rate of fire has been restricted to 400 rounds per minute. The weapon can be fired in single rounds, or two- or three-round bursts, using finger control. Full automatic is not available. The PDW fires standard 9 x 19 mm Parabellum, and magazines housing 12, 20, or 32 rounds are available.

Light Machine Guns

"The .303 Lewis should be fired in bursts of four or five rounds at the most and never until the target is sufficiently large and vulnerable."

Official British Army instruction on the use of the Lewis Gun, World War II.

Light machine guns (LMGs) are by definition air-cooled man-portable weapons with a caliber not more than 7.62 mm (0.3 in.). The term "light," however, can be misleading, as it carries with it connotations of inferior levels of firepower when compared to medium/heavy machine guns. Although in many cases this is true, especially when applied to the new generation of 5.56 mm squad weapons, some light machine guns are neither light in weight nor moderate in force. The FN MAG general-purpose machine gun, for example, weighs 22.25 lb. (10.15 kg) and can fire 7.62 mm NATO rounds at a rate of 850 rpm for a range of 10,000 ft. (3000 m)+. This performance actually equals that of many heavy machine guns, including weapons such as the Vickers .303 in. machine gun, the Browning Model 1917 and the German MG34. Indeed, when mounted on a tripod the FN MAG is more than capable of performing the sustained-fire role often adopted by the heavier weapons.

Above: *The M249 Squad Automatic Weapon is one of the new generation of light machine guns. Firing the standard 5.56 mm NATO round, it can accept either belt feed or magazine feed and weighs only 22 lb. (10 kg) fully loaded with a 200-round belt.*

Development

The first light machine guns appeared in the opening decade of the twentieth century, as gun designers sought to make heavy firepower more portable for infantry soldiers. One of the earliest models was the Danish Madsen 1902, a prototype long-recoil weapon which weighed 22 lb. (10 kg) and was fed from a top-mounted box magazine containing thirty 8 mm rounds. The Madsen was not a commercial success, but the principle of the LMG was established and this approach was pushed with vigor during World War I (1914–18).

Although heavy and medium machine guns proved extremely valuable in World War I, they were large and weighty items of equipment, and required a tripod which made them difficult to conceal in the forward areas. As a result, inventors started to design lighter automatic weapons which could be carried by one man and fired from cover, mounted on a bipod, and used the same ammunition as the infantry they supported. Air-cooling was also used rather than the cumbersome water-cooling of heavy machine guns.

The result was light machine guns. These consisted of either entirely new models, such as the British Lewis Gun, or modified versions of existing heavy machine guns, such as the German Light Maxim MG08/15 which dispensed with the heavier weapon's water-cooling pump in preference for a self-contained water jacket, and added a buttstock and pistol grip . The performance of these early weapons was intensely variable. The Allied Hotchkiss weapon was a solid performer alongside the Lewis, whereas the French Chauchat M1915 is justifiably regarded as one of the worst guns ever to enter production. The US entered the war in 1917 with their own LMG, the Browning Automatic Rifle (BAR). In terms of capabilities, the BAR was probably more akin to the squad automatic weapon of modern times, essentially being little more than a heavy-barrelled automatic rifle firing standard .30 caliber ammunition from a magazine of just 20 rounds capacity.

During the inter-war years, the US Army took the BAR on as a standard weapon, while

Above: *A team of German paratroopers take up positions with an MG42. The MG42 is known as a general-purpose machine gun, being suitable for light-, medium- or heavy-machine gun roles according to its mount and tactical usage.*

other nations refined the technology and capabilities of this new weapon form. Germany, although its army was prohibited under the Versailles Treaty from owning more than 1,134 light machine guns and 792 medium machine guns, covertly pushed ahead with LMG design, often relocating their expertise to Switzerland to develop weapons there. Rheinmetall design staff working through the Swiss Solothurn concern produced the MG15 aviation machine gun, a weapon which in turn evolved into the MG34 in 1934, one of the finest machine guns ever produced. In the UK, the estimable Bren gun emerged, based on the Czech ZB30, and the Bren would set a gold standard for LMG performance which lasted for decades to come.

Into the modern era

World War II saw the light machine gun become a fully integrated part of infantry warfare. The conflict also saw a new category of weapon—the general-purpose machine gun (GPMG)—take the stage in superlative guns like the German MG42. A GPMG could take light, medium, and heavy machine-gun roles depending upon its mount (bipod, pintle, or tripod). As a concept, the GPMG was one of the dominant themes in postwar machine gun development in weapons such as the US M60 and the German MG3.

Post-1945, the Cold War military environment was one of increasing standardization in weapons, as the Western and Eastern blocs sought to produce weapons conformity among their member states. GPMGs still occupied a great deal of gun design output, but new generations of light machine guns emerged based around existing assault rifle models. Heckler & Koch, for example brought out a succession of magazine-fed bipod-mounted versions of the G3 rifle with heavy, interchangeable barrels, the HK11 (7.62mm NATO), the HK12 (7.62 x 39 mm Soviet) and the HK13 (5.56 x 45 mm NATO). The later HK21, HK22, and HK23 are essentially the same weapons, but are belt fed instead of magazine fed to provide more sustained fire.

The Soviets produced an enlarged rifle/light machine gun, in the 7.62 mm RPK (*Ruchnoi Pulemyot Kalashnikova*—Kalashnikov's Light Machine Gun) of the 1960s, basically an elongated Kalashnikov AK rifle with a fixed barrel and attached bipod. The RPK demonstrates one useful principle of many modern light machine guns in that it can accept magazines from the standard infantry rifle, (and some parts) although to increase fire support 40-round box or 75-round drum magazines are also available. Weapons such as the RPK belong more to the classification "squad automatic weapon" rather than machine gun.

In the West, the adoption of the 5.56 mm round as the standard NATO cartridge in the early 1980s had a marked effect on light machine guns. A 5.56 mm machine gun, even one with a very high rate of fire, does not have the destructive force of a 7.62 mm weapon. The squad automatic weapon (SAW) concept, however, is perfectly suited to the smaller cartridge, as the SAW's role is more to boost levels of squad firepower rather than ensure material destruction. To adapt to the new round, the UK developed the L86A1 Light Support Weapon (LSW), which is a heavy-barreled version of the standard L86A1 (SA80) rifle. The extended barrel gives the LSW a longer range than the standard rifle, although it is fed from the same size of magazine. It is as much used as a long-range sniper weapon as a machine gun. The US Army also has a heavy-barrelled version of the M16A2 rifle.

A more sophisticated range of SAWs can be found in modular firearms such as the Belgian FN Minimi (and its US variant, the M249 SAW) and the Israeli Negev. The Minimi is a 5.56 mm weapon that can be fired either from the standard M16 rifle magazine or a 200-round belt without having to make any engineering adjustment. The weapon, which has a rate of fire of up to 1,000 rpm, is also light enough 15 lb. (6.8 kg) to be fired from the hip, making it an ideal assault weapon to bolster squad fire during engagements.

The SAW concept is keeping the light machine gun alive in modern times, but what actually are the specific roles of the LMG in modern warfare?

LMGs and tactics

Light machine guns have tactical roles distinct from heavy machine guns. Heavy machine guns are designed for sustained attritional fire against enemy personnel, vehicles, and equipment. Usually they are set up in fixed defensive emplacements or as weapons on board armored vehicles. Light machine guns, by contrast, should be as mobile as the infantryman. The general application of LMGs is to give infantry units man-portable support fire in localized sectors, and increase the enemy casualty count rather than destroy his physical defenses.

Within the light machine gun category, however, the type and configuration of the weapon alter the tactical remit. More powerful 7.62 mm machine guns such as the FN MAG and the US M60, which are often classified as medium machine guns, combine high-powered long-range rounds fired from a changeable barrel. This means that such weapons can be used to establish ad hoc sustained-fire positions in offensive or defensive situations, and hit an enemy with suppressive fire at ranges in excess of 3,300 ft. (1,000 m). Also, such weapons have more potency against structural targets, a typical 7.62 mm round capable of penetrating 2 in. (50 mm) of concrete or a single layer of sandbags at 660 ft. (200 m) range. The downside of medium machine guns is that even though they are perfectly transportable by one man, they are often heavy enough to slow him down on foot, and generally require a two-man team to operate.

A different category of light machine gun is those with fixed barrels, usually firing 5.56 mm rounds or shortened 7.62 mm rounds such as the Soviet 7.62 x 39 mm (in the case of weapons such as the RPK). The fixed barrel markedly limits the amount of firepower these weapons can produce, as prolonged bouts of sustained fire will result in the barrel overheating and weapon malfunction.

Tactically, therefore, this category of light machine gun is more practical for mobile assault, the infantryman supporting fire-and-maneuver deployments with intermittent bursts of heavy fire. Alternatively, accurate weapons such as the British LSW will provide roughly the same intensity of fire as a standard rifle, but simply extend the range of fire up to around 2,600–3,300 ft. (800–1,000 m). The 5.56 mm light machine guns also have different structural

Below: *A British infantryman deploys a Bren LMG in the Far Eastern theater. The Bren was an extremely accurate weapon, more suited to hitting specific targets at range rather than producing general sprays of attritional firepower.*

penetration properties when compared to the 7.62 mm weapons. At ranges of less than 164 ft. (50 m), most urban structures will stop a 5.56 mm round—at this distance a 5.56 mm bullet will not penetrate a single layer of sandbags, a 2 in. (50 mm) concrete wall, or even a strong plate glass window, if the round strikes at a forty-five-degree angle or less.

However, concentrated fire can produce structural penetration, and belt-fed weapons like the M249 SAW can be used in this role. US Army tests have showed that it takes about 250 rounds of 5.56 mm to make a 7 in. (177 mm) loophole in 8 in. (203 mm) reinforced concrete and 220 rounds to make a penetration of a 24 in. (609 mm) double sandbag wall. In most cases, such heavy expenditure of ammunition is not recommended, and the light machine gun will instead be used for targeting personnel or soft-skinned vehicles.

As with many small-arms systems, light machine guns have reached such a level of

perfection that it is difficult to see where the future lies. As with other small arms, modularity is probably the future, a light machine gun being created by taking a rifle and simply switching the barrel and possibly the feed mechanism. Such was the principle behind the Stoner M63, which combined SMG, assault rifle, LMG, and even sustained-fire machine gun through changing system components. Although the M63 was not a commercial success, the principle of modularity is apparent in the US XM8 assault rifle, which may be the future replacement for the M16A2. As with most small arms we do not know what will happen with the light machine gun, although the versatility of the weapon type ensures its future.

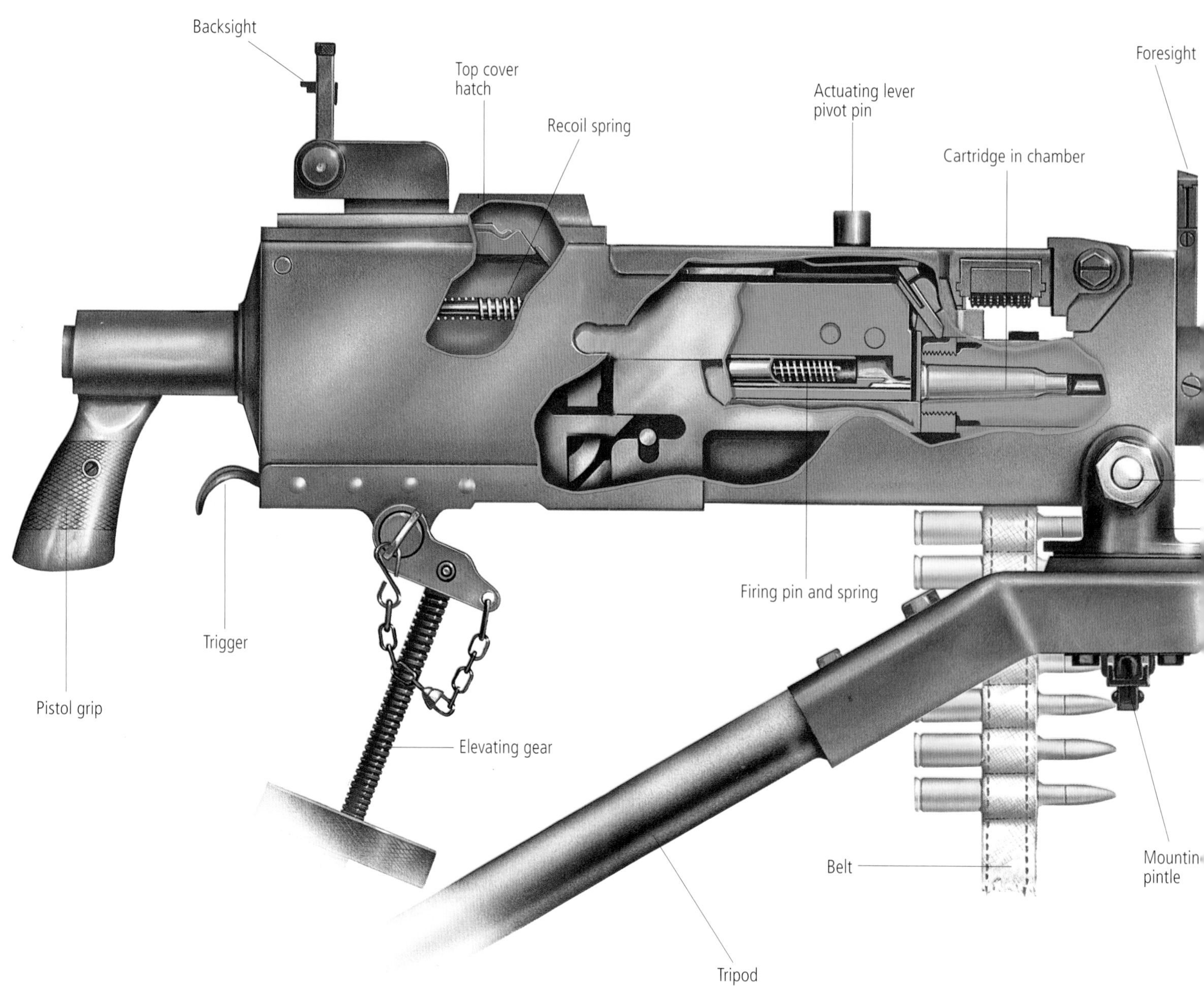

BROWNING 0.30 IN M1919A4 LIGHT MACHINE GUN

One of the most successful machine guns ever produced, the Browning 0.30 in. M1919A4 is recoil-operated and usually employed as a light machine gun, although it could also be employed in the heavy/medium role (as seen here). The method of operation enabled the mechanical elements to be housed in a neat, box-like structure and there was no requirement for a gas-tube along the barrel. The M1919A4 entered service with the US Army in 1934 and remains in large-scale use with many armies at the start of the twenty-first century. It was developed from the air-cooled 0.30 in. M1919 tank machine gun, although many elements of its design dated back to the water-cooled weapon first produced in 1910. The 24 in. (610 mm) barrel is surrounded by a slotted jacket, which provides all the necessary cooling. The gun is not light, weighing 31 lb. (14 kg), while the tripod, which is required for the sustained fire role, weighs 14 lb. (6.4 kg). The M1919A4 has a pistol grip with the horizontal trigger mounted on the back-plate, but another version, the M1919A6, which appeared during World War II, was fitted with a butt, a bipod, and a carrying handle, thus enabling it to be used as a light machine gun by an infantry squad. The M1919A4 fires the Springfield 0.30-06 round, which is normally supplied in a 250-round cloth belt; firing rate is 500 rounds per minute.

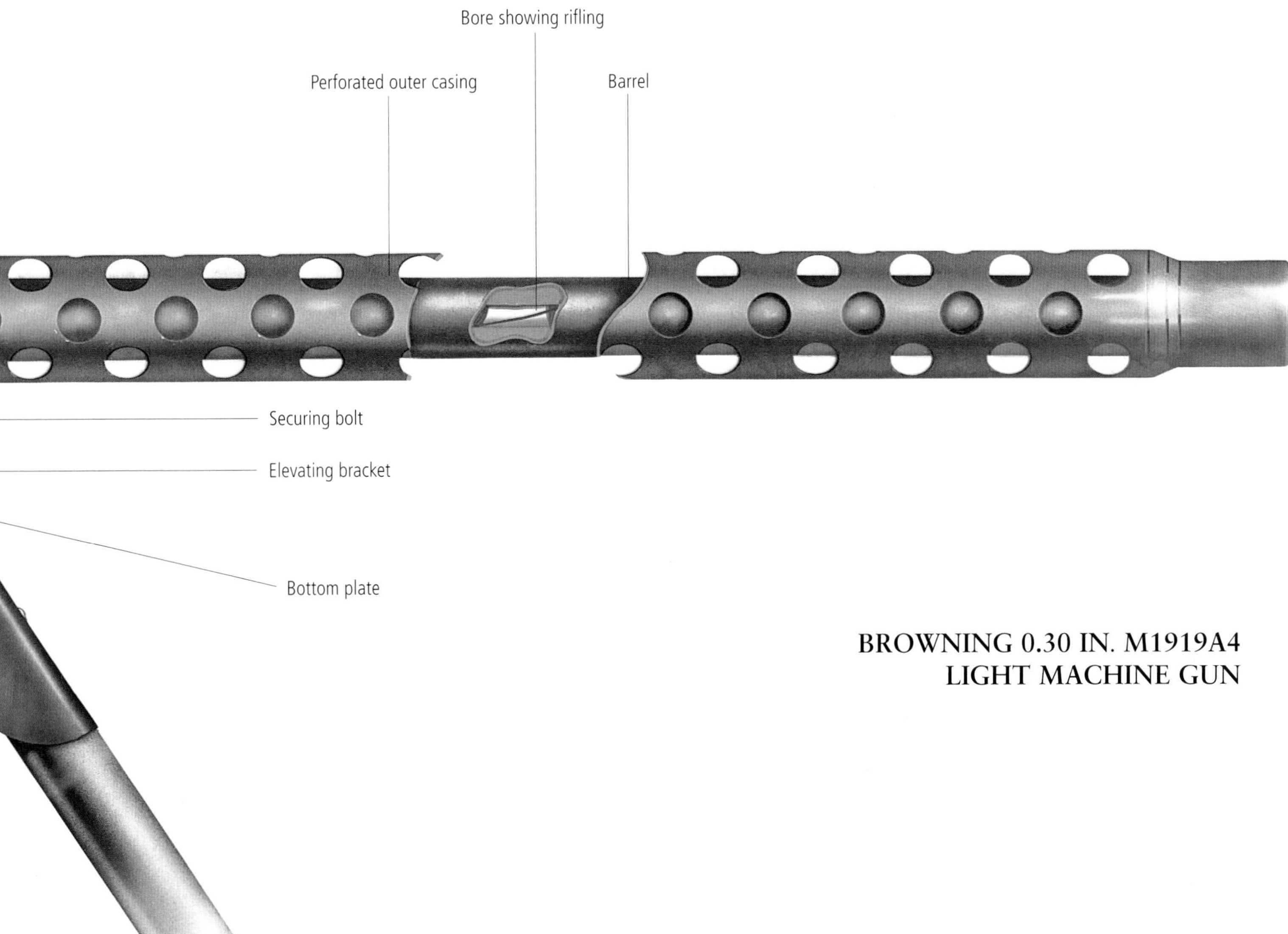

BROWNING 0.30 IN. M1919A4
LIGHT MACHINE GUN

DENMARK

MADSEN 1902

Length (gun): 46.0 in. (1,169 mm)
Barrel: 19.0 in. (483 mm)
Weight: 22.0 lb. (10.0 kg)
Caliber: 8 mm
Rifling: 4 grooves, r/hand
Operation: long recoil
Feed: 30-round box
Cyclic rate: 400 rpm
Muz vel: 2,700 ft./sec. (824 m/sec.)

This gun was known as the Madsen after a Danish Minister of War, but the British called it the Rexer. The breech mechanism consisted of a rectangular steel frame sliding on ribs in the main body of the gun. Inside this steel frame, a breechblock pivoted in the vertical plane, locked, dropped, or raised. This movement was controlled by a curved feed arm attached to the left-hand side of the box. The gun was of the long-recoil type. The first round had to be located manually by a lever, and when it was fired, the barrel and breech mechanism recoiled together, causing the front of the breechblock to rise, extracting and ejecting the case underneath it. When the rearward action was complete, a return spring forced the mechanism forward, stripping the next round from the magazine. The round was carried forward on top of the breechblock, which acted as a feed tray. At the proper time the feed arm depressed the front of the block so that the chamber was exposed and forced the cartridge in, after which the block rose to the locked position and the round was fired. The Madsen was tested by many armies between 1903 and 1917 but was not adopted in any numbers.

UNITED KINGDOM

VICKERS-BERTHIER 1908

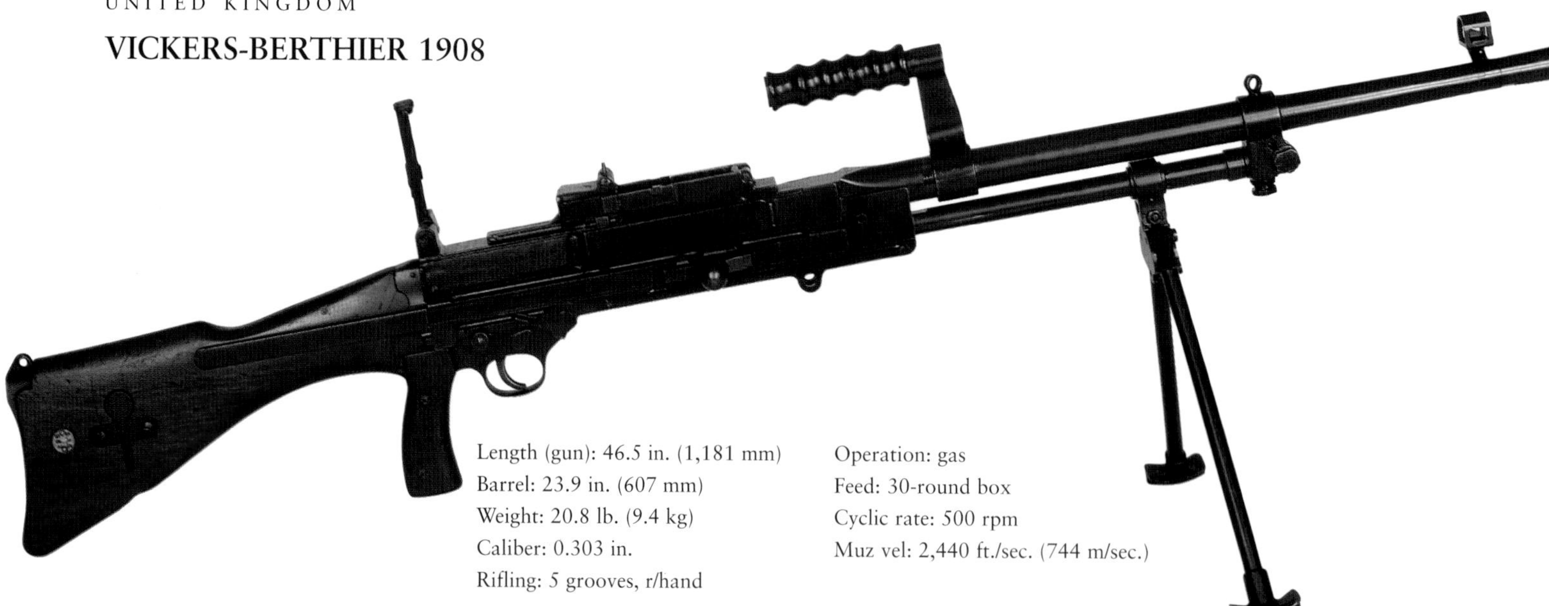

Length (gun): 46.5 in. (1,181 mm)
Barrel: 23.9 in. (607 mm)
Weight: 20.8 lb. (9.4 kg)
Caliber: 0.303 in.
Rifling: 5 grooves, r/hand
Operation: gas
Feed: 30-round box
Cyclic rate: 500 rpm
Muz vel: 2,440 ft./sec. (744 m/sec.)

This gun was designed by a French officer, Lieutenant André Berthier, in 1908 but failed to win any orders. In the early 1920s, Vickers bought the manufacturing rights and began to make a modified version of the 1908 model. In 1925 Vickers demonstrated the gun to the Small Arms Committee. Apart from some minor points, it was reported as efficient and referred to as a serious rival to the Browning Automatic Rifle, which was also being considered. Two more guns, complete with spare barrels and accessories, were bought, and at the end of this series of tests the Vickers-Berthier came out best. The next year there were further tests, the stated need being for a gun that could fire 1,500 rounds in fifteen minutes and 5,000 in thirty. The general opinion was that the Vickers-Berthier could be improved to this standard. In 1933, the Indian Army settled unilaterally on the Vickers-Berthier Mark 3 as a replacement for the Lewis gun, but the British Army was more cautious and decided to proceed with the testing. In 1934 the final endurance trials were held, and the Czech ZB gun began to demonstrate its unmistakable superiority.

UNITED KINGDOM

LEWIS MACHINE GUN 1912

Length (gun): 50.5 in. (1,282 mm)
Barrel: 26.0 in. (660 mm)
Weight: 27.0 lb. (12.3 kg)
Caliber: 0.303 in.
Rifling: 4 grooves, r/hand
Operation: gas
Feed: 47-round drum
Cyclic rate: 550 rpm
Muz vel: 2,440 ft./sec. (744 m/sec.)

The principle on which the Lewis gun worked was simple: Gases were tapped off from the barrel to drive back a piston, which took the bolt with it, extracting and ejecting the empty case. A stud on top of the bolt activated a feed arm that took the next round from the double-layer, circular magazine on top of the gun; the mechanism was equipped with two stop pawls that ensured the magazine rotated the correct amount only. During this backward movement, a rack on the underside of the piston engaged a pinion, which wound a clock-type spring that drove the working parts forward, chambering and firing the round. The bolt was of the turning variety with lugs that locked into recesses in the barrel extension. The barrel was kept cool by radial fins that surrounded it; the fins, in turn, were surrounded by a light outer casing to keep the whole thing clean.

FRANCE

CHAUCHAT MODÈLE 1914 (CSRG)

Length (gun): 45.0 in. (1,143 mm)
Barrel: 18.5 in. (470 mm)
Weight: 19.0 lb. (8.6 kg)
Caliber: 8 mm
Rifling: 4 grooves, r/hand
Operation: long- recoil
Feed: 20-round box
Cyclic rate: 250 rpm
Muz vel: 2,300 ft./sec. (700 m/sec.)

The Chauchat was rushed into production in 1914. Much of it was constructed of ordinary commercial tubing never intended for the strains in an automatic weapon firing a full-sized rifle cartridge; even locking lugs and similar essentials were stamped, pressed, and screwed together. The pistol grip was rough wood, the forehand grip no more than a crudely shaped tool handle. When the gun was fired (assuming that it did fire, which was not always the case) the barrel and bolt recoiled together, the bolt locked to the barrel by locking lugs. This action continued for the entire backward phase, when the bolt was turned and unlocked allowing the barrel to go forward. The bolt then followed, taking a round, chambering it, and firing it. The long recoil caused a great deal of vibration, making it virtually impossible to hold the weapon on a target when firing automatic.

GERMANY

LIGHT MAXIM MG08/15 1915

Length (gun): 55.0 in. (1,398 mm)
Barrel: 24.0 in. (610 mm)
Weight: 39.0 lb. (17.7 kg)
Caliber: 7.92 mm
Rifling: 4 grooves, r/hand
Operation: recoil
Feed: 250-round box
Cyclic rate: 400 rpm
Muz vel: 2,900 ft./sec. (885 m/sec.)

The Maschinengewehr 08/15, or "Light Maxim," was water-cooled like its larger counterpart. But whereas the 08 Maxim had a pump that kept the water moving, the light model had a plain but effective water jacket. It fired a fifty-round belt, which avoided any major redesign of the original mechanism, and was equipped with a belt box that was fitted to the right-hand side of the gun and allowed it to be moved rapidly. It was an effective weapon and soon became popular with the German Infantry. Light Maxims were used in Zeppelins, the bulky and heavy water jacket replaced by a simple ventilated casing, as the movement of airships through the air was sufficient for cooling. A version of this air-cooled Maxim was issued to the German Army under the designation 08/18. It was not a success. When used on the ground, this air-cooled version overheated rapidly.

LIGHT MACHINE GUNS IN WORLD WAR I

During World War I, it became apparent to armies on both sides that heavy machine guns had severe tactical limitations. Though they were eminently suited to long-range attrition fire from static positions, their weight meant that they were unable to provide effective support to a mobile assault. The British Vickers 0.303 in. machine gun, for example, weighed 40 lb. (18 kg), and the German 7.92 mm Maxim 08 weighed 58.3 lb. (26.4 kg), precluding easy portability.

Although World War I is commonly represented as a conflict of trench deadlock, fire-and-maneuver assaults and fighting patrols were common in localized sectors, and light machine guns provided the support fire within these contexts. For the British, the most successful light machine gun was the Lewis gun, a gas-operated .303 in. weapon fed from a forty-seven-round drum magazine and weighing a still heavy but perfectly transportable 26 lb. (1.8 kg). The Lewis found a vital application within the context of fighting patrols: patrols sent to neutralize a specific enemy objective, often a machine gun post or artillery position. A typical British fighting patrol would consist of sixteen personnel: one patrol leader, one runner, seven scouts, four grenade-armed bombers, and three Lewis gunners. The basic purpose of the Lewis gunners was to provide a base of fire for the attacking infantry when contact with the enemy was made, with three Lewis guns providing a combined 1,800 rpm cyclical rate of fire.

The British fighting patrol illustrates how effective light machine guns must be part of a combined-arms unit, the heavy firepower of the machine gun supporting the lighter firepower carried by the assault troops. This principle steadily took root in the German Army also, particularly during the last year of the war. Germany did not have a particularly successful light machine gun design during World War I; the chief land-warfare weapon was the Maxim 08/15, which is basically the standard MG08 but fitted with a pistol grip, a shoulder stock, and a bipod. It was still extremely heavy, about 39 lb. (18 kg), and later removal of the water jacket to produce the 08/18 version saved only 2.2 lb. (1 kg) in weight.

However, the Germans did apply these "light" machine guns with effect in the Stormtrooper assaults of 1918. Stormtrooper assault divisions mixed grenades, submachine guns, flamethrowers, mortars, and light machine guns among their ranks, and used the mixed firepower to blast open enemy trench systems. Light machine guns were particularly concentrated on the flanks to protect the main spearhead from side attacks. Although the German light machine guns had a long way to evolve, along with the LMGs of other nations they proved that this versatile weapon type had a firm future in infantry warfare.

Above: *An early French armored car, dating from around 1915, is armed with the dreadful Saint-Etienne Modele 1907 in an antiaircraft mount. The M1907 and the more successful Hotchkiss weapons were fed from 24- or 30-round metallic strips of ammunition, but in the interwar years this system was dropped in favor of belt-feed and magazine-feed in machine gun systems.*

UNITED KINGDOM

HOTCHKISS MARK 1 1915

Length (gun): 46.7 in. (1,187 mm)
Barrel: 23.5 in. (597 mm)
Weight: 27.6 lb. (12.2 kg)
Caliber: 0.303 in.
Rifling: 4 grooves, r/hand
Operation: gas
Feed: 30-round strip
Cyclic rate: 500 rpm
Muz vel: 2,440 ft./sec. (744 m/sec.)

In 1915, the British cavalry needed a light machine gun and selected the French Benet-Mercie, which was put into production as the Hotchkiss Machine Gun Mark 1, chambered for the British 0.303 in. cartridge. The Mark 1 operated by the action of gas tapped off from the bore and striking a piston to which the breechblock was attached. The forward action of the mechanism under the impulse of the return spring caused the bolt to turn and lock into a fitting, forming part of the barrel extension (known by its French term, fermeture nut). The cocking handle was a long rod, and its rear end, similar in appearance to a rifle bolt, is just above the pistol grip in the photograph. It was pulled back to its full extent (almost 6 in./152 mm) to cock and then forced forward again. When it was fully home it could be turned to the right until a line on it coincided with either A, R, or S on the receiver, which gave automatic fire, rounds only, or safe, as required. It was considered best to use both hands to cock the gun. The Hotchkiss gun was also a tank gun. It remained in service with cavalry units until World War II.

UNITED STATES

BROWNING AUTOMATIC RIFLE 1918A2

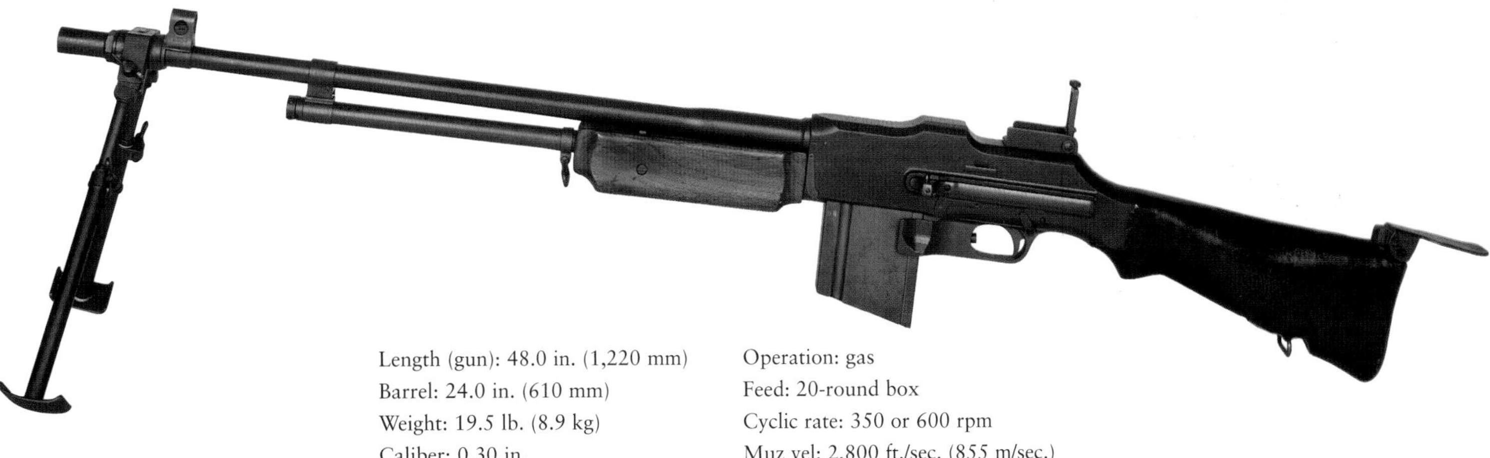

Length (gun): 48.0 in. (1,220 mm)
Barrel: 24.0 in. (610 mm)
Weight: 19.5 lb. (8.9 kg)
Caliber: 0.30 in.
Rifling: 4 grooves, r/hand
Operation: gas
Feed: 20-round box
Cyclic rate: 350 or 600 rpm
Muz vel: 2,800 ft./sec. (855 m/sec.)

Much of Browning's original work on the automatic rifle, which was of normal gas and piston operation, had been done at the Colt factory, but Winchester also gave a good deal of assistance later. Manufacture started early in 1918, with total production in excess of 50,000. The BAR was received enthusiastically by the Allies, none of whom had a weapon of quite the same type, and they were ordered in large numbers. Model 1918A, like the original, was able to fire bursts or single rounds and had a bipod. The next change came in 1940 with the introduction of the Model 1918A2, which had a light bipod attached to the tubular flash hider. Although it would fire bursts only, it incorporated a selector that allowed two cyclic rates: the higher was some 600, the lower 350 rpm. The BAR was used by many countries and was made in Belgium as the Herstal. A number were sold to Great Britain in 1940 and were used to arm the Home Guard, where they gave good service but caused some problems over caliber. The BAR Model 1922 was used by the US Cavalry and had a heavier, finned barrel, a bipod, and a butt rest; it fired automatic only.

UNITED KINGDOM

BEARDMORE-FARQUHAR EXPERIMENTAL 1919

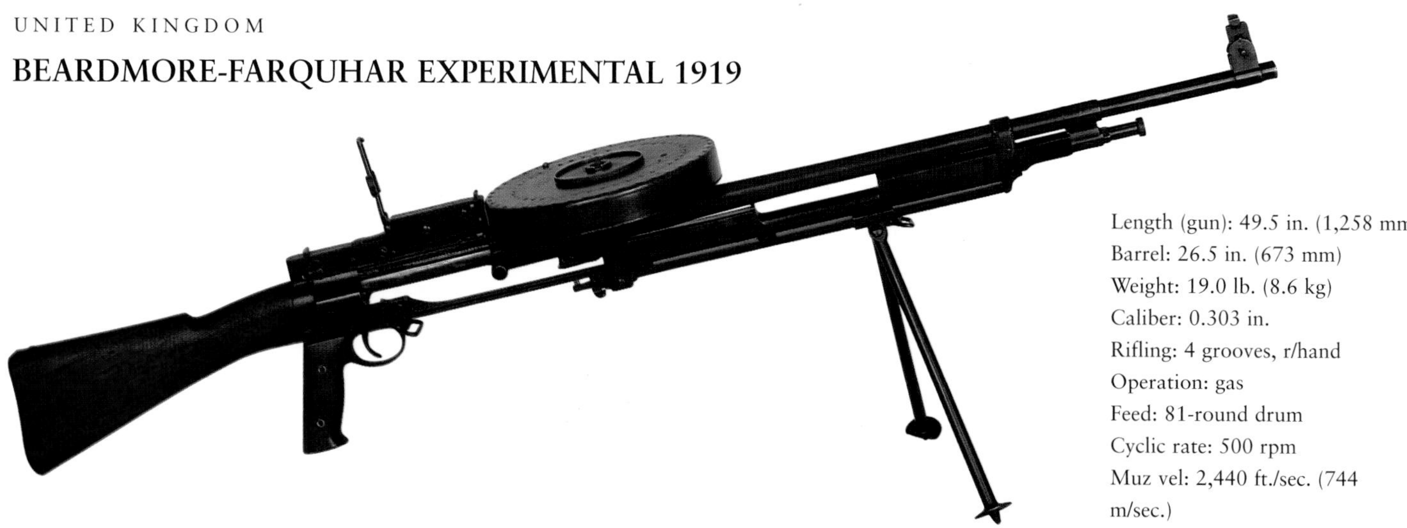

Length (gun): 49.5 in. (1,258 mm)
Barrel: 26.5 in. (673 mm)
Weight: 19.0 lb. (8.6 kg)
Caliber: 0.303 in.
Rifling: 4 grooves, r/hand
Operation: gas
Feed: 81-round drum
Cyclic rate: 500 rpm
Muz vel: 2,440 ft./sec. (744 m/sec.)

The Beardmore-Farquhar Experimental light machine gun was based on a mixture of gas and spring operation. In the Beardmore the piston was not directly connected to the bolt. Instead of an operating rod there was a coil spring, and when the piston moved back it compressed this spring. The other end bore against the bolt, and this bolt was so designed that the pressure of the gas helped to keep it locked. When the pressure had dropped to a safe level, the piston spring overcame the bolt locking and the usual reciprocating motion began. When the bolt reached the buffer, it tripped the piston sear and the return spring could then force bolt and piston forward again. The usual feed action took place on the forward stroke, but another peculiarity was that the return spring was stretched, not compressed as on all other guns. One consequence of this was a smooth action with much less likelihood of stoppages and extraction problems. But it also had a much slower rate of fire than its rivals. This weapon was officially tested in late 1922, and although it had some good features, its overall performance was poor and it was not developed further.

UNITED STATES

BROWNING MODEL 1919A4

Length (gun): 41.0 i.n (1,041 mm)
Barrel: 24.0 in. (610 mm)
Weight (gun): 31.0 lb. (14.0 kg)
Weight (tripod): 14.0 lb. (6.4 kg)
Caliber: 0.30 in.
Rifling: 4 grooves, r/hand
Operation: recoil
Feed: belt
Muz vel: 2,800 ft./sec. (854 m/sec.)

The Browning Model 1919A4 was a sort of general-purpose light machine gun that, with minor changes in mounts, could be used in tanks and armored cars, as a multiple antiaircraft gun, and in a ground role. The mechanism of this gun was similar to that of the Model 1917 water-cooled Browning, working by the recoil power of the barrel, which, in a brief rearward thrust, unlocked the breechblock and sent it to the rear, extracting the case. The force of the compressed return spring provided the motive power for the forward action in which a new round was stripped from the belt, chambered, and fired. It had a heavy barrel enclosed in a light perforated outer casing. Feed was by a woven-fabric belt holding 150 rounds, with brass tags at each end to facilitate loading. The weapon had a single pistol-type grip, very similar to that of the Colt revolver, and its trigger, which had no guard, protruded almost horizontally from the rear of the receiver. When used in the ground role, the gun was mounted on the standard M2 tripod. The lower photo shows the improved model, that M1919A6, with rifle-type butt and pistol grip and a flash hider.

GAS OPERATION IN LIGHT MACHINE GUNS

Most modern light machine guns are gas-operated weapons, and gas operation is also the dominant system in modern assault rifles. At their most basic, gas-operated systems work by tapping off some of the propellant gas via a port in the barrel. The gas enters a cylinder where is impinges on a piston head (although in some weapons the gas is channeled directly back against the bolt carrier); the piston is connected to the bolt, so when the piston is forced back, the bolt is driven rearward to eject the spent cartridge. The bolt then moves forward under the pressure of the return spring, a new round is chambered, and the cycle can begin again.

A crucial element of gas operation is the positioning of the gas port along the barrel. If the gas port is located near the muzzle, there is less effect on the gas pressure behind the bullet, although the volume of gas required to cycle the weapon is greater because of the lower gas pressure at the muzzle end. Also, the gases at the muzzle will produce heavier carbon deposits, which are taken back into the gun through the gas cylinder. Situating the gas port near the breech produces higher gas pressures, which are more punishing on mechanisms, and also extreme high temperatures, which can wear the gas-port aperture. However, such a configuration can produce a very high rate of fire owing to the short delay between cartridge ignition and piston activation. Usually a light machine gun has its gas port about 6.9–12 in. (177–305 mm) from the muzzle, the gases reaching the gas port about a millisecond after cartridge ignition.

The forces at work in a gas-operated system are extremely violent, the piston and connected parts driven back at high speed under enormous forces of pressure. Therefore, much effort is expended by gun designers attempting to moderate and control the forces at work. For a start, a period of free travel is built into the piston movement to allow time for the bullet to exit the muzzle, and the gases to drop to a safe level before the bolt is engaged and moved backward. Also, various gas-control devices are often fitted. Gas regulators can be fitted which either alter the size of the track from the port through to the pistol, hence altering the gas pressure, or regulate the amount of gas vented into the atmosphere.

Generally, the weapon operator adjusts the regulator to supply more gas to the piston as the weapon becomes hotter and dirtier, and the additional power is used to overcome the increased friction within a dirty gun.

Below: *The Lewis gun was one of the earliest gas-operated weapons to enter widespread service. Gas-operated weapons usually have less felt recoil than recoil-operated weapons, as part of the gas-pressure buildup is diverted to operate the gas mechanism. The controllability of gas-operated machine guns makes them ideal for multirole uses. Here this Lewis gun is used in an anti-aircraft role.*

JAPAN

TYPE 11 (NAMBU) 1922

Length (gun): 43.5 in. (1,104 mm)
Barrel: 19.0 in. (482 mm)
Weight (gun): 22.7 lb. (10.2 kg)
Caliber: 6.5 mm
Rifling: 4 grooves, r/hand
Operation: gas-piston
Feed: see text
Cyclic rate: 500 rpm
Muz vel: 2,300 ft./sec. (701 m/sec.)

The Type 11 was an air-cooled, gas-operated gun with a finned barrel. Its feed system was a large hopper on the left-hand side of the gun, which contained six five-round rifle chargers. The six chargers were held down by a strong spring-loaded arm, and on the backward action of the gun a sliding ratchet drew the rounds into the gun, discarding the clip as it did so. The theory was that any infantryman could contribute loaded chargers to the hopper, thus overcoming the need for belts or magazines. But experience showed that the hopper accumulated mud and dust, which it then pushed through the mechanism, causing very heavy wear. This was overcome by introducing a less powerful round, but this meant that the infantryman now had to carry two different types of round: one for his rifle and one for the machine gun, thus getting away from the original intention of the system.

FRANCE

CHÂTELLERAULT MODÈLE 1924-9

Length (gun): 42.5 in. (1,080 mm)
Barrel: 19.7 in. (500 mm)
Weight: 20.3 lb. (9.1 kg)
Caliber: 7.5 mm
Rifling: 4 grooves, r/hand
Operation: gas
Feed: 25-round box
Cyclic rate: 550 rpm
Muz vel: 2,590 ft./sec. (790 m/sec.)

The 1924 Model Châtellerault light machine gun was gas- and piston-operated with a mechanism very similar to that of the Browning Automatic Rifle. It had two triggers, the forward one for automatic fire, and with a selector that had to be previously set for the type of fire required. It had a gas regulator that could be used in conjunction with an adjustable buffer to allow the firer to vary his cyclic rate. It was designed to fire the new 7.5 mm rimless round, similar in type and general performance to the German 7.92 mm cartridge. There was a further modification in 1928, when the round was shortened slightly, after which the gun functioned with great efficiency. To increase the firepower of the infantry garrisons in the Maginot Line, the French produced that Modèle 31. This was fundamentally the same weapon but had a huge side-mounted 150-round drum.

RUSSIA

DEGTYAREV PAKHONTNYI (DP) 1926

Length (gun): 50.3 in. (1,290 mm)
Barrel: 23.8 in. (605 mm)
Weight: 20.5 lb. (9.3 kg)
Caliber: 7.62 m
Rifling: 4 grooves, r/hand
Operation: gas
Feed: 47-round box
Cyclic rate: 500 rpm
Muz vel: 2,730 ft./sec. (849 m/sec.)

The original DP contained only sixty-five parts, as it was designed for assembly by semi-skilled labor. The gun had some defects: in its very large bearing surfaces, which caused undue friction; its susceptibility to dirt; and overheating. The earliest guns had finned barrels to help dissipate the heat, but this problem was never fully overcome except by restricting the rate of fire. The gun was used extensively in the Spanish Civil War (1936–39) as a result of certain improvements that eliminated its worst faults. The gun worked by tapped-off gas driving back a piston, taking the bolt with it, which was forced forward again by a compressed return spring. The magazine was a large, flat, single-deck drum; its size and thinness made it susceptible to damage. It had an integral clockwork mechanism and a capacity of forty-nine, but this was later reduced by two. The modified guns (the one illustrated is an example) had removable barrels, and the mainspring was placed in its own sleeve below the receiver and suffered from the effects of heat. The gun worked on the open-bolt system and fired automatic only. The weapon gave good service in World War II and was used in Korea and Vietnam.

CZECH REPUBLIC

ZB 26 AND ZGB VZ30 SERIES 1930

Length (gun): 45.3 in. (1,150 mm)
Barrel: 25.0 in. (635 mm)
Weight: 22.5 lb. (10.2 kg)
Caliber: 0.303 in.
Rifling: 6 grooves, r/hand
Operation: gas
Feed: 30-round box
Cyclic rate: 500 rpm
Muz vel: 2,440 ft./sec. (744 m/sec.)

Having started in the ZB works at Brno as an ordinary workman, Vaclac Holek rose rapidly, and the Czechoslovakian Army's request for a new light automatic gave him his chance. His team included his brother Emmanuel and two expatriate Poles, Marek and Podrabsky. The result, the ZB 26, was gas-operated, with a piston working to a tilting breechblock. It had an easily removed barrel and a vertical box magazine, and it was chambered for the rimless 7.92 mm German round. After exhaustive tests by the British in 1932, it was clear that they had found a potential winner. After some modifications to allow the gun to fire the British 0.303 in. rimmed round, it became the ZGB vz30 series. The barrel finning was dispensed with, but otherwise there were no fundamental changes. The weapon illustrated is one of the final modified models made in Czechoslovakia. Once the gun was accepted, the British Government decided that it should be made at Enfield. The body of the new gun, which was cut from solid metal, required 270 operations, involving 550 gauges accurate to 1/2000 inch, which gives some idea of the complexity of the undertaking. The new gun entered British service in 1938 and was one of the finest infantry weapons used in World War II.

ITALY

BREDA MODELLO 30 1930

Length (gun): 48.5 in. (1,232 mm)
Barrel: 20.5 in. (520 mm)
Weight: 22.7 lb. (10.3 kg)
Caliber: 6.5 mm
Rifling: 4 grooves, r/hand
Operation: blowback
Feed: 20-round box
Cyclic rate: 500 rpm
Muz vel: 2,063 ft./sec. (618 m/sec.)

The Modello 30 was a light machine gun weighing less than 23 lb. (10.4 kg), and fired from a bipod. Mechanically it was similar to the earlier Revelli gun, since it worked on a combination of gas and recoil. When the round was fired, the barrel recoiled for about 0.5 in. (12.7 mm), then stopped; this allowed the breech to unlock, the working parts moving farther backward, partly due to the recoil and partly due to the residual gas pressure in the barrel. On striking the buffer, the compressed recoil spring thrust them forward again, allowing the bolt to strip a round from the magazine, chamber it, lock itself to the barrel, and allow the firing pin to function. The gun would fire automatic only. The use of direct blowback led to the continued use of an oiler to lubricate the rounds as they went into the chamber. The feed system consisted of a box magazine on the right side but hinged to the gun at its front corner so that by releasing a catch, the whole magazine could be pivoted forward until it was parallel with the barrel. It was the standard light machine gun of the Italian Army in Abyssinia, as well as in its campaigns in North and East Africa during World War II.

JAPAN

TYPE 91 6.5 MM 1931

Length (gun): 42.0 in. (1,066 mm)
Barrel: 19.2 in. (488 mm)
Weight (gun): 24.4 lb. (11.0 kg)
Caliber: 6.50 mm
Rifling: 4 grooves, r/hand
Operation: gas-piston
Capacity: 50-round hopper
Muz vel: 2,300 ft./sec. (701 m/sec.)

The Type 91 light machine gun was fielded in 1931 and was a tank version of the Type 11 infantry LMG. It used the same type of hopper-feeding system, but in a larger size, taking fifty rounds in clips. This seems to have been a somewhat pointless exercise since the ability to accept infantrymen's clipped ammunition simply did not exist in a tank, and the restricted space in a turret made refilling the hopper a complicated task. Then, in a curious reversal, most of these Type 91s were removed from tanks and returned to the infantry, who mounted a rather inelegant cranked butt stock, bipod, and x1.5 telescopic sight (shown in the top photo of weapon without its wooden stock). The Type 91 fired the 6.5 x 51SR Arisaka round, and was rather heavy for an LMG, weighing 24.4 lb. (11.0 kg) compared to 22 lb. (9.9 kg) for the British Bren.

JAPAN

TYPE 96 1936

Length (gun): 41.5 in. (1,054 mm)
Barrel: 21.7 in. (553 mm)
Weight: 20.0 lb. (9.1 kg)
Caliber: 6.5 mm
Rifling: 4 grooves, r/hand
Operation: gas
Feed: 30-round box
Cyclic rate: 550 rpm
Muz vel: 2,400 ft./sec. (732 m/sec.)

The Type 96 replaced the Type 11 when the Japanese were fighting the Chinese. It was of basic Hotchkiss design, to which the Japanese usually remained faithful. One of the principal differences from its predecessor was the abolition of the inefficient system of loading and the substitution of a more orthodox top-mounted box magazine. It still fired the rather unsatisfactory 6.5 mm cartridge, but the oil pump was situated in the magazine loader, thus completely divorced from the gun itself—a considerable improvement. The gun had a quick system for changing barrels, which helped its capacity for sustained fire. It had a carrying handle and a distinctive one-piece butt and pistol grip combined, and it would take the infantry bayonet; although a 20 lb. (9.1 kg) gun makes a poor thrusting weapon. Perhaps its oddest feature was the frequent incorporation of a low-powered telescopic sight, which is not usually considered to be of great value on an automatic weapon. The cartridge used was still the reduced-charge pattern used in the previous gun, which must have continued to cause complications over resupply of ammunition.

JAPAN

TYPE 99 1937

Length (gun): 46.5 in. (1,181 mm)
Barrel: 23.6 in. (600 mm)
Weight (gun): 23.0 lb. (10.4 kg)
Caliber: 7.7 mm rimless
Rifling: 4 grooves, r/hand
Operation: gas
Feed: magazine (30 rounds)
Cyclic rate: 850 rpm
Muz vel: 2,350 ft./sec. (715 m/sec.)

Japanese experience fighting the Chinese in Manchuria in 1936 highlighted a number of problems with the Type 96, and work began in 1937 to produce a new weapon. This resulted in the Type 99, which fired a new and better round, the 7.7 mm Arisaka rimless round, fed from an overhead magazine containing thirty rounds. There was also a new method of adjusting the headspace, and together with the new round, this did away with the need for lubrication. The Type 99 had a finned barrel and a bipod, but also had a monopod under the butt so the weapon could be fired on fixed lines, although in practice vibration soon shook it off target. The Type 99 could be fitted with a bayonet, in line with the Japanese Army's very aggressive tactics, which required light machine gunners to accompany the riflemen in a charge. Large numbers of Type 99s were abandoned by the Japanese following their defeat in 1945 and were left all over Southeast Asia. The Chinese Army collected many of these and modified them to take the standard Russian-pattern 7.62 mm round. The bottom photo shows the breakdown of parts for paratroop use.

UNITED KINGDOM

BREN 1938

Length (gun): 45.5 in. (1,156 mm)
Barrel: 25.0 in. (635 mm)
Weight (gun): 22.5 lb. (10.2 kg)
Weight (tripod): 26.5 lb. (12.0 kg)
Caliber: 0.303 in.
Rifling: 6 grooves, r/hand
Operation: gas
Feed: 30-round box
Cyclic rate: 500 rpm
Muz vel: 2,440 ft./sec. (744 m/sec.)

The Bren gun was developed from the Czechoslovakian ZB 26 in the mid-1930s. It was designed for single rounds or bursts controlled by a change lever; the trigger pull was noticeably longer for single rounds than for automatic fire. There was an elaborate back sight with a drum and a pivoted lever carrying the aperture, and because the magazine was top-mounted, the sights were offset to the left. The barrel could be replaced in two or three seconds. Although the magazine capacity was nominally thirty, it was reduced to twenty-eight; but magazines with rimmed cartridges had to be loaded carefully and the most common stoppage on the gun, fortunately easy to clear, was caused by careless loading. The Bren could be mounted on a tripod for firing on a fixed line. It proved to be a most reliable and efficient gun, and all who used it had great confidence in it. When the UK adopted the 7.62 mm NATO round a number of the later, many Brens were converted to fire it. Designated L4A1 to L4A6, these have a cone-shaped flash hider and a straight magazine, the latter necessary because of the rimless NATO round.

Light Machine Guns in World War II

Above: *The Bren light machine gun was one of the superior weapons of its type in World War II. Here it is deployed in the rubble of Monte Cassino, the Bren operator hanging back ready to provide immediate support fire for his Thompson M1A1-armed companion, advancing forward.*

In World War II, the nation least wedded to the LMG idea was the United States. The standard infantry firearm, the M1 Garand, was semi-automatic, and it was felt by many that the infantry could generate sufficient heavy firepower without LMG assistance. This view was reflected in the US LMG designs. One was the Browning Automatic Rifle (BAR), which had a limited fire-support capacity because of its twenty-round magazine. The other was the Browning M1919, more of a medium machine gun at 30.7 lb. (14 kg). An attempt was made to turn the M1919 into a true LMG by fitting a shoulder stock, pistol grip, carrying handle, and bipod, but it was still too heavy for the task.

By contrast, the British Army had an excellent LMG, the Bren gun. The Bren weighed just over 22 lb. (10 kg), had an effective bipod-mounted range of 3,280 ft. (1,000 m), was very reliable, and was highly accurate. Barrel change could be achieved in seconds and was normally performed after ten thirty-round magazines had been fired. Like the Browning M1919, and also German weapons such as the MG42, the Bren found itself in all sorts of vehicular mounts. The increased mechanization of armies in World War II led to LMGs being fitted as either secondary weapons to tanks or primary defense weapons on gun carriers, trucks, etc. The Bren even had its own dedicated vehicle, the Bren Gun Carrier.

Like the British, the Soviets bought into the idea of a single mass-produced LMG, in their case the DP1928, a typically robust gas-operated Russian weapon with only six moving parts. Its only real deficiency was the cylindrical top magazine, which was easily damaged. The French also produced a serviceable type, the Châtellerault M1929, which used a BAR action and had a double trigger for switching between single-shot and full-auto fire. Probably the most inconsistently served of all the combatants in terms of LMGs was Japan, which had three basic types: the Taisho 11, the Type 96, and the Type 99. Both the Taisho 11 and Type 96 had, among other problems, oil-lubricated feeds. In battle conditions this resulted in grit-filled chambers and stoppages. The Type 99, by contrast, was a truly reliable weapon, which had better extraction (a common cause of trouble in Japanese LMGs) and no oiler, but was produced in too few numbers at the end of the war to make a real impact.

UNITED KINGDOM

BESAL MK 2 1939

Length (gun): 46.6 in. (1,185 mm)
Barrel: 22.0 in. (559 mm)
Weight: 21.5 lb. (9.8 kg)
Caliber: 0.303 in.
Rifling: 4 grooves, r/hand
Operation: gas
Feed: 30-round box
Cyclic rate: 600 rpm
Muz vel: 2,440 ft./sec. (744 m/sec.)

The Bren gun, adopted by the British in the 1930s, required a complicated production process. Thought was therefore given to a gun based on the Bren but requiring much simpler production processes. H. Faulkoner, chief designer at the Birmingham Small Arms Company, created the Besal as a result. The body was made entirely of pressings, riveted and spot-welded with a nonadjustable bipod fitted over a sleeve at the forward end. The barrel was roughly finished externally, with a handle, a simple tubular flash hider, and a fore sight on a bracket. The gas passed to the piston through a simple flanged gas regulator that could be turned by the point of a bullet and was held in place by a pin suspended by a link chain from the fore-sight block. The piston held the return spring; as the piston blew back, the end of the return spring frame was held firmly by a vertical pin, allowing the spring to be compressed. The back sight consisted of an L-shaped flip. There were two Marks that differed in their method of cocking. The Mark 1 had a skeleton butt, and the Mark 2 (seen here) had a solid butt.

UNITED STATES

CRANSTON AND JOHNSON MODEL 1941

Length (gun): 42.3 in. (1,074 mm)
Barrel: 22.0 in. (558 mm)
Weight (gun): 14.3 lb. (6.5 kg)
Caliber: 0.30 in.
Rifling: 4-grooves, r/hand
Operation: recoil
Feed: box magazine
Cyclic rate: 600 rpm
Muz vel: 2,800 ft./sec. (853 m/sec.)

The M1941 was noted for its simplicity, ease of handling, accuracy and reliability, and it was light for a machine gun: 14.3 lb. (6.5 kg) empty and 15.9 lb. (7.2 kg) with sling and loaded magazine. One unusual feature was that in single-round mode it used a closed bolt, which locked before firing; but in automatic it used an open bolt. It had a quick detachable barrel. It was also designed for ease of manufacture, as it was produced using conventional lathes and milling machines. The Mannlicher-type box magazine was on the left side of the weapon, and a unique feature was that reloading could be achieved using rifle chargers from the right-hand side without removing the magazine. The automatic firing rate could be adjusted by altering the tension in the buffer spring, with a theoretical maximum of 900 rpm. The Johnson appeared in two versions, which differed only in minor details: the M1941 had a bipod and a wooden butt (as shown in the photographs, the upper one with bipod folded under); the M1944 had a monopod made of light tubing, while the butt was fabricated from two parallel pieces of tubing closed by a butt plate.

FRANCE

MAS AA-52 7.5/7.62 MM 1952

Length (gun): 49.0 in. (1,245 mm)
Barrel: 23.6 in. (600 mm)
Weight (gun): 25.1 lb. (11.37 kg)
Weight (tripod): 23.4 lb. (10.6 kg)
Caliber: 7.5 x 54 mm M1929
Rifling: 4 grooves, r/hand
Operation: gas
Feed: belt
Cyclic rate: 700 rpm
Muz vel: 2,756 ft./sec. (840 m/sec.)

The Arme Automatique Transformable Modèle 52 was first fielded in the French Army in 1952. The original AAT-52 was designed to fire the elderly French 7.5 x 54 mm M1929 round, but when NATO standardized on the 7.62 x 51 mm NATO cartridge, the majority of in-service guns were converted and designated AA-7.62 F1. The general-support version had a light barrel and a bipod that could be supplemented by a rear-mounted monopod for firing on fixed lines. The second version had a heavier barrel and the US M2 tripod for the sustained fire role. The gun was air-cooled and -operated using delayed blowback with a two-piece bolt; the chamber was fluted so gas could aid extraction. The 7.62 mm version can use either a French or the NATO M13 belts; when the gun is carried with a belt in place, it must be cocked. Specifications here are for the AA-52 Heavy Barrel version.

RUSSIA

RUCHNOI PULEMYOT DEGTYARYEV (RPD) 1953

Length (gun): 40.8 in. (1,036 mm)
Barrel: 20.5 in. (520 mm)
Weight: 15.6 lb. (7.0 kg)
Caliber: 7.62 mm
Rifling: 4 grooves, r/hand
Operation: gas
Feed: belt
Cyclic rate: 700 rpm
Muz vel: 2,400 ft./sec. (732 m/sec.)

The RPD's chief merits were its lightness and simplicity. The gun was belt fed, and each belt held fifty rounds. Belts could easily be connected to each other or coiled and fitted into a sheet-metal drum (see picture). The gun was fitted with a rotatable gas regulator, had a fixed barrel, and would fire only automatic; overheating was avoided by the gunner ensuring that he did not exceed 100 rpm. The first model had a reciprocating cocking handle. The piston had a hollow head that fit over the gas spigot. The second model revised the piston-head arrangements and added protectors for the back sights. The third model incorporated a folding, nonreciprocating handle and a much-needed dustcover over the ejector opening.

UNITED STATES

M60 1960

Length (gun): 43.8 in. (1,111 mm)
Barrel: 25.5 in. (647 mm)
Weight: 23.0 lb. (10.4 kg)
Caliber: 7.62 mm
Rifling: 4 grooves, r/hand
Operation: gas
Feed: belt
Cyclic rate: 600 rpm
Muz vel: 2,800 ft./sec. (853 m/sec.)

The M60 was based on the best features of the German MG 42 and FG 42. IT used stampings, rubber, and plastics, but it had a somewhat fussy, cluttered look about it. There was no gas regulator. Under certain conditions the gun stopped, or in some instances, kept firing uncontrollably. With the M60's slow rate it was possible for a good gunner to fire single rounds by quick trigger release. No barrel handle was fitted, and as the barrel might well have reached a temperature of 932°F (500°C), great care had to be taken in changing it. An asbestos mitten was issued with each gun but was lost easily in action. Barrels were chromium-plated and had Stellite liners for the first 6 in. (152 mm) from the chamber. The M60 was used extensively in Vietnam and improved considerably; the resulting weapon was the M60E1.

RUSSIA

RUCHNOI PULEMYOT KALASHNIKOVA (RPK) 1961

Length (gun): 40.5 in. (1,029 mm)
Barrel: 23.3 in. (592 mm)
Weight: 11.0 lb. (5.0 kg)
Caliber: 7.62 mm
Rifling: 4 grooves, r/hand
Operation: gas
Feed: 30-round box or 75-round drum
Cyclic rate: 600 rpm
Muz vel: 2,410 ft./sec. (735 m/sec.)

This weapon is similar in general appearance to the AK-47, from which it was developed. Its principal external differences are its characteristic club butt and its longer and heavier barrel. It is equipped with a bipod, fitted well forward and designed to be folded back and held by a clip when not required. The weapon is gas-operated; when the first manually loaded round is fired, part of the gases pass through a vent in the barrel and into the cylinder above it, where they force back the piston. The initial rearward action of the piston causes the bolt-locking lugs to rotate counter-clockwise, allowing the breech to open, after which the bolt continues to the rear with the piston compressing the return spring. The return spring drives the mechanism forward, the bolt stripping a round from the magazine and chambering it. The mechanism then stops, but the piston continues sufficiently to cause the locking lugs to engage with the locking shoulders, after which the striker is free to fire the round and the cycle continues. There is a change lever on the right-hand side of the receiver above the trigger. The RPK takes the same thirty-round magazine as the rifle or a seventy-five-round drum.

UNITED KINGDOM/BELGIUM

GPMG L7A1 AND L7A2 1963

Length (gun): 49.8 in. (1,264 mm)
Barrel: 24.8 in. (629 mm)
Weight (gun): 24.0 lb. (10.9 kg)
Weight (tripod): 29.0 lb. (13.2 kg)
Caliber: 7.62 mm
Rifling: 4 grooves, r/hand
Operation: gas
Feed: belt
Cyclic rate: 800/900 rpm
Muz vel: 2,800 ft./sec. (855 m/sec.)

The British carried out a series of trials in the late 1950s to find a new machine gun firing the newly adopted NATO standard 7.62 mm round. The winner was the Belgian FN MAG. The British-made gun is designated the L7A1,but is generally referred to as the GPMG. The new gun, like many original FN products, owes a great deal to the patents of American John M. Browning, one of the most prolific and most successful designers in the field of firearms that the world has ever seen. It is gas-operated with a bolt-locking system similar to that of the original Browning Automatic Rifle of 1917. its feed mechanism is virtually identical to that the German MG42, as is its trigger. The original idea was to have two different barrels for the gun, a plain steel one for the light role and a heavy barrel with a special liner for the sustained fire role, but the latter was abandoned. Other versions include L8A1 (coaxial gun in tanks); L37A1 (for use in vehicles or on the ground); and L2OA1 (for use in helicopters). The L7A2 model (in photographs) has modified trigger and feed mechanisms, fitting of a belt box to the left side, and other minor changes.

UNITED STATES

STONER 5.56 MM 1963

Length (gun): see text
Barrel: 21.7 in. (550 mm)
Weight (gun): 10.4 lb. (4.7 kg)
Caliber: 5.45 mm
Rifling: 6 grooves, r/hand
Operation: gas
Feed: belt
Cyclic rate: 700 rpm
Muz vel: 3,270 ft./sec. (990 m/sec.)

Eugene Stoner was responsible for a number of revolutionary weapons in the latter half of the twentieth century, the most famous being the Armalite rifle, which saw worldwide service as the M16. He also designed numerous other weapons, including light machine guns. The Stoner 63 was manufactured by Cadillac-Gage, and a later design was prepared for production by ARES. This latter weapon has subsequently been updated to produce the weapon now known as the Stoner 5.56 mm LMG. The Stoner LMG is remarkably light, the bare weapon weighing just 10.4 lb. (4.7 kg), and only 16.1 lb. (7.3 kg) loaded with a 200-round belt, which is fed from a 200-round box attached to the left side of the weapon. There are two barrels: one is 21.7 in. (551 mm) long, but the other (shown in lower photograph) is much shorter, 15.6 in. (397 mm); with this barrel and the detachable buttstock removed, overall length is 26 in. (660 mm). The forward grip can be positioned either vertically downward or at 90 degrees to the left to suit the firer's requirements. There is a mounting on top of the receiver for optical or night sights.

CHINA (PRC)

NORINCO 7.62 MM TYPE 67-2C 1970

Length (gun): 49 in. (1,254 mm)
Barrel: 23.9 in. (606 mm)
Weight (gun): 36.4 lb. (16.5 kg)
Weight (tripod): 12.3 lb. (5.6 kg)
Caliber: 7.62 mm
Rifling: 4 grooves, r/hand
Operation: gas
Feed: belt
Cyclic rate: 650 rpm
Muz vel: 2,755 ft./sec. (840 m/sec.)

The weapons used by the People's Republic of China in the 1940s and 1950s were mostly Russian, although there were many others, particularly of US origin, which had been captured from the Nationalists. The Type 67 was the first Chinese-designed LMG and incorporates a number of features from other weapons that were in PRC service at the time. This would include the feed mechanism from the Maxim (Chinese Type 24), the gas regulator from the RPD (Type 56), and the piston and flash suppressor from the Czech ZB-26 (Type 26). The result was a thoroughly practical and very reliable weapon that has subsequently seen a lot of service with the People's Liberation Army (PLA); some were also supplied to North Vietnam during the 1970s. The original Type 67 was fired from a bipod, but a new version appeared in the late 1980s—Type 67-2C—which can be fired from a specially designed tripod and used in the sustained-fire role. The new weapon also includes a number of other improvements including a barrel made from a new type of steel alloy. As with all Chinese infantry weapons, the Type 67 and Type 67-2C are also intended for use in the anti-aircraft role.

THE M60 IN VIETNAM

The M60 machine gun became infamous among the US soldiers serving in Vietnam between 1963 and 1973, earning the affectionate title "the Pig." It was introduced into the US Army in 1957 as an attempt to replicate the general-purpose machine gun concept demonstrated by the German MG42 in World War II. By the advent of US involvement in Vietnam, the M60 had become the standard squad support weapon.

The M60's Vietnam service brought it a mix of dislike and respect. As a squad automatic the weapon was, and remains, excessively heavy. To compare it with a contemporary squad weapon, the US M249 SAW, the M60E1's empty weight was 23.15 lb. (10.5 kg) whereas the SAW weighs 15 lb. (6.8 kg). For a US infantryman or Marine on patrol in the Vietnamese jungle, already carrying about 60 lb. (27 kg) of pack, the weight was not popular, so relatively few wanted to take on the M60.

Furthermore, the M60E1 had a chronic defect in its barrel change. The barrel and bipod on the first-generation weapons were united, so performing a barrel change required the gunner to life the weapon out of the jungle mud by the carrying handle while the ammunition handler changed the barrel/bipod assembly for a new one. This was an awkward process and could not be performed easily by one person, or under firefight conditions. The barrel-change problem was eventually solved by attaching the bipod to the gas mechanism and fitting a change handle to the barrel.

For all its awkwardness, the M60 was a formidable weapon. It was ideal for jungle reconnaissance by fire, ambush/ambush-defense, and fixed-position defense roles. Its 550-rpm rate of fire meant it was controllable and accurate, and its 7.62 mm round had the extended penetration through jungle foliage and through urban structures that the M16 lacked. M60 users had to be careful of their fire control, however, as prolonged bursts would inform VC/NVA opponents of the machine gun's location, which would then attract heavy rifle, machine gun, and RPG return fire. Short sustained bursts were more advisable and reduced the frequency of barrel changes.

The M60C and D version were used on helicopter gunships, while the M60E2 was the coaxial MG on the M60 tank.

Below: *The M60 machine gun was a powerful infantry weapon in Vietnam. Dragging it through the hot and humid Vietnamese jungles, however, required an operator with great stamina and endurance, and he would generally be the slowest-moving member of a fire team.*

LMG
LOCKING MECHANISMS

Above: *The Bren gun uses tilting-block locking, the rear of the breech block being driven upwards into a recess in the top of the receiver while a ramp is pushed beneath the block to hold it firm into the recess. Tilting-block locking is a reliable and durable mechanical process, and helped make the Bren one of the world's finest LMGs.*

Locking is one of the most critical phases in the firing cycle of almost all firearms. Locking refers to the act of mechanically securing the cartridge in place in the chamber before the firing pin is released. The only weapons that do not use locking systems are the simplest blowback weapons, which hold the cartridge in place purely by the inertia of the bolt and spring, but these are generally chambered only for small-caliber pistol rounds. With high-powered rifle-caliber ammunition, locking must take place; otherwise the violent forces of ignition would result in damaged bolts, split cartridge cases. and serious weapon malfunction.

In LMGs the primary methods of locking are rotating-bolt, lug, and tilting-block locking. Rotating-bolt locking, which is generally applied to gas-operated weapons such as the GPMG and M60, functions by rotating the bolt as it travels forward using a piston post that fits into a curved cam path in the surface of the bolt. At the front of the bolt are two or more locking lugs that twist around to lock into recesses on the barrel extension or receiver. Once the lugs are securely in place, firing can take place. Unlocking takes place by a reverse process, although the return cam path will often feature a short straight section to allow the bullet to exit the gun and pressure to drop to safe levels before the curved cam section rotates the lugs out of the recesses.

Lug locking has a similar principle to rotating-bolt locking in the sense that locking lugs are forced from the breechblock into recesses in the barrel extension or receiver. There are many lug-locking methods. The German MG3, for example, uses roller locking, with two rollers attached to the bolt-head being forced outward into recesses in the barrel extension. Heckler and Koch has used roller locking very successfully on many of its rifle and LMG types; the rollers delayed the recoil of the bolt after firing to allow pressure against the bolt to drop to safe levels for recoil and ejection. By contrast, the .30 in. caliber Browning M1919 has a single locking lug attached to the barrel extension. The lug is moved via ramps to either drop into a recess to provide locking or be lifted free of the recess for unlocking. Although the Browning system is reliable, many LMGs using lug locking have two locking lugs to provide stable support to the bolt.

Tilting-block locking has been applied to many military rifles, but also to the Bren LMG. In this case, a ramp at the rear of the piston extension (the Bren is a gas-operated weapon) pushes the rear of the breechblock upward to drop into a recess in the top of the receiver body. Further forward movement of the piston-extension pushes the extension under the block to lock the block into place. Tilting-block locking is a very safe method of locking, as the firing pin and cartridge are not aligned until locking has taken place.

GERMANY

HECKLER AND KOCH 7.62 MM HK11 1971

Length (gun): 40.2 in. (1,020.mm)
Barrel: 17.7 in. (450 mm)
Weight (gun): 15.0 lb. (6.8 kg)
Caliber: 7.62 mm
Rifling: 4 grooves, r/hand
Operation: delayed-blowback
Feed: box or drum
Cyclic rate: 850 rpm
Muz vel: 2,560 ft./sec. (780 m/sec.)

The HK11 series has consisted of two parallel developments, one belt-fed and the other magazine-fed. The first in the 7.62 mm magazine-fed series was the HK11 (see specifications), which could accept either the G3 twenty-round box or a fifty-round drum magazine. Internally, it used the normal H. and K. delayed blowback system. The next model in the series was the HK11A1, which did away with the fifty-round drum magazine option, depending solely upon the depending-round box magazine. Next to appear was the HK11E, which had the same internal improvements as the HK21E (qv), including a three-round burst capability, a drum rear sight, and a forward handgrip midway under the barrel. The HK11E also had a new trigger and trigger guard for operation while wearing heavy Arctic gloves.

GERMANY

HECKLER AND KOCH 7.62 MM HK21 AND HK23 1971

Length (gun): 40.2 in. (1,020 mm)
Barrel: 17.7 in. (450 mm)
Weight (gun): 16.2 lb. (7.3 kg)
Caliber: 7.62 mm
Rifling: 4 grooves, r/rand
Operation: delayed-blowback
Feed: belt (metal links)
Cyclic rate: 900 rpm
Muz vel: 2,625 ft./sec. (800 m/sec.)

The HK21 (specifications are for basic model) was the second version of the H. and K. machine guns using the 7.62 mm NATO cartridge. The gun was designed to be belt-fed, but an adapter could be fitted for box or drum magazines. Other rounds, such as the 7.62 x 39 mm or 5.56 x 45 mm, could be fired by changing the barrel, feed plate, and bolt. The HK21A1 lacked the magazine and 7.62 x 39 mm options, and had an improved belt-feed mechanism. The final gun in the series was the HK21E (left photo), which had a longer receiver, a longer barrel (26.4 in./560 mm compared to 17.7 in./450 mm), a new forward handgrip, a three-round burst capability, and a new trigger enabling the firer to use Arctic gloves. The HK21 series were used by many armies and were produced in Germany (all models), Greece (HK21A) and Portugal (HK21). The HK23E (right photo fired the 5.56 x 45 mm cartridge.

BELGIUM

FN 5.56 MM MINIMI 1974

Length (gun): 40.9 in. (1,040 mm)
Barrel: 18.4 in. (466 mm)
Weight (gun): 15.2 lb. (6.8 kg)
Caliber: 5.56 mm
Rifling: 6 grooves, r/hand
Operation: gas-piston
Feed: magazine or belt
Cyclic rate: 850 rpm
Muz vel: 3,000 ft./sec. (915 m/sec.)

The Minimi uses gas operation and a rotating bolt that's locked by a patented FN system. The weapon is belt-fed, with the belt normally housed in a large, lightweight, 200-round plastic box. The Minimi Para features a shorter barrel (13.7 in./347 mm) and a telescopic butt. A Minimi Mark 2 incorporates a number of minor improvements (such as a folding cocking handle) intended to make it easier to handle without changing its major features or any loss in interchangeability of components. The weapon has been adopted by many armed forces, including those of Australia, Belgium, Canada, France, Indonesia, Italy, New Zealand, Sri Lanka, Sweden, and the United Arab Emirates. Production takes place in Australia (as Type 89 Minimi) and the United States (as M249 SAW). The Minimi is normally fired from its bipod, but a tripod is also available for the sustained-fire role.

CHINA (PRC)

NORINCO 7.62 MM TYPE 74 1973

Length (gun): 43.6 in. (1,107 mm)
Barrel: 20.8 in. (528 mm)
Weight (gun): 14.1 lb. (6. 4kg)
Caliber: 7.62 mm

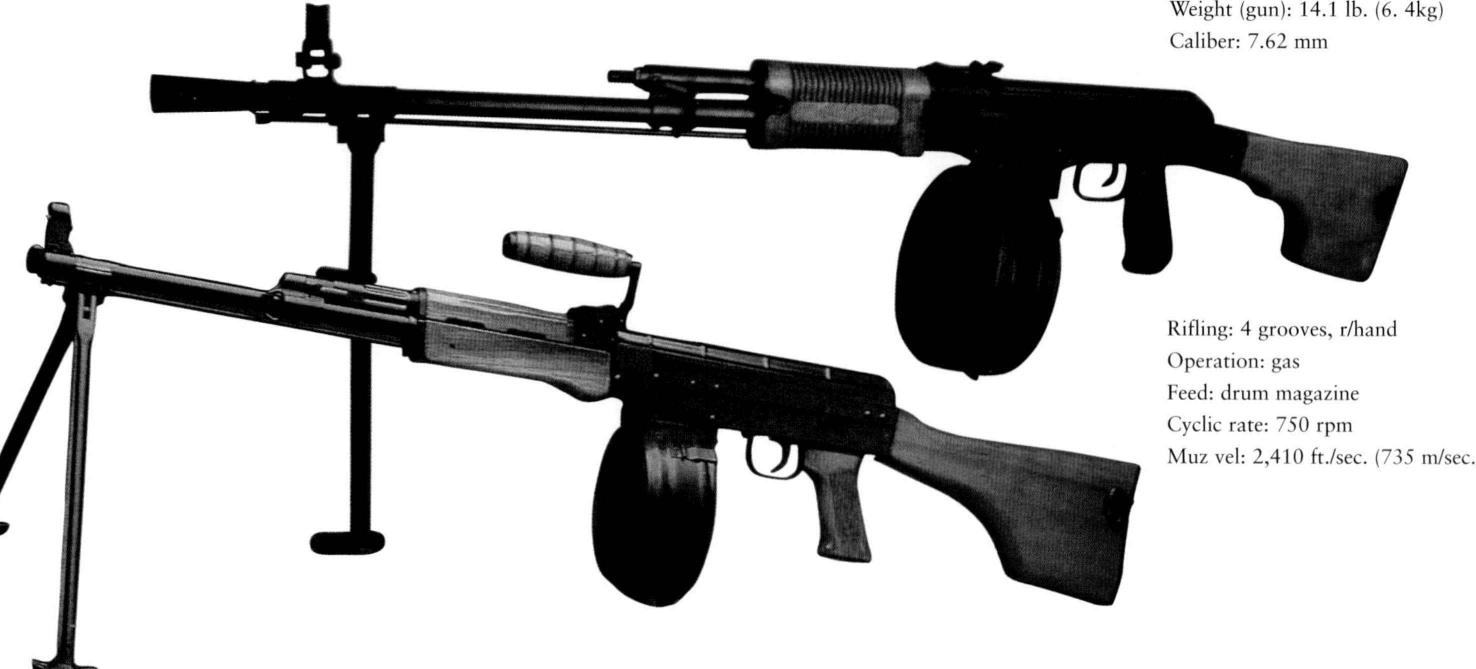

Rifling: 4 grooves, r/hand
Operation: gas
Feed: drum magazine
Cyclic rate: 750 rpm
Muz vel: 2,410 ft./sec. (735 m/sec.)

The Type 74 is intended as a section/squad LMG and entered service in the mid-1970s. The weapon is gas-operated, using a piston mounted above the barrel, with a four-position gas regulator. The barrel is 20.8 in. (528 mm) long and is fitted with a ZB-type flash suppressor; the barrel is chrome-plated, as is the chamber. The Type 74 (upper photo) is fed from a vertically mounted 101-round drum magazine, which is attached below the weapon, and the magazine from the Type 56 rifle (qv) can also be used. Newer types of Chinese LMGs are the Type 80, a copy of the Russian PK (qv), and the Type 81 (lower photo), a 7.62 mm weapon apparently intended primarily for export.

SPAIN

SANTA BARBARA 5.56 MM AMELI 1982

Length (gun): 38.2 in. (970 mm)
Barrel: 15.8 in. (400 mm)
Weight (gun): 11.4 lb. (5.2 kg)
Caliber: 5.56 mm
Rifling: 6 grooves, r/hand
Operation: gas
Feed: magazine or belt
Cyclic rate: 900 rpm
Muz vel: 2,870 ft./sec. (875 m/sec.)

The Spanish Ameli light machine gun is produced by the Santa Barbara Company, which is named after the patron saint of artillerymen. The Ameli, which appeared in 1981, was designed around the NATO 5.56 x 45 mm round and uses a delayed-blowback system with a two-part bolt, similar to that used in all Spanish automatic weapons for many years. Feed is by magazines holding either 100 or 200 rounds, or by a disintegrating metal link belt. Unusual among modern light machine guns, the Ameli has a slotted barrel jacket, which incorporates the fore sight, carrying handle and flash suppressor.

SINGAPORE

CIS 5.56 MM ULTIMAX 100 1982

Length (gun): 40.3 in. (1,024 mm)
Barrel: 20.0 in. (508 mm)
Weight (gun): 10.8 lb. (4.9 kg)
Caliber: 5.56 mm
Rifling: 6 grooves, r/hand
Operation: gas-piston
Feed: 20/30-round boxes; 100-round drum
Cyclic rate: 500 rpm
Muz vel: 3,182 ft./sec. (970 m/sec.)

The Ultimax 100 was fielded in 1982 and is in service with the Singapore Armed Forces and several other armies, including at least one in Europe. Entirely of Singaporean design, the Ultimax 100 has a rotating bolt, uses the open bolt position, and fires automatic only, at a rate that can be varied between 400 and 600 rounds per minute by use of the three-position gas regulator. Feed is from either twenty- or thirty-round box magazines or a clockwork-powered 100-round drum. The bipod is positively locked in either up or down position and allows 30-degree movement without adjusting the feet. The barrel is designed for quick changes, and two models are available: the normal barrel is 20.0 in. (508 mm) long, but this can be replaced by a short "Para" barrel that's 12.9 in. (330 mm) long for use by special forces or in tight spaces. The weapon can also be fired without the butt, if necessary, and is fitted (unusual for an LMG) with a forward pistol grip. The Mark III version is shown in the photo at left.

UNITED STATES

M249 SQUAD AUTOMATIC WEAPON (SAW) 1982

Length (gun): 40.9 in. (1,040 mm)
Barrel: 20.6 in. (523 mm)
Weight (gun): 15.1 lb. (6.9 kg)
Caliber: 5.56 mm
Rifling: 6 grooves, r/hand
Operation: gas
Feed: metal-link or magazine
Cyclic rate: 750 rpm
Muz vel: 3,000 ft./sec. (915 m/sec.)

The M249 SAW is a development of the "Minimi" for the US Army and Marine Corps. Original orders were met from the FN factory, but a production line was subsequently established in the United States. The US Army's concept for a Squad Automatic Weapon (SAW) was formulated in the 1960s, when a requirement was established for a weapon that would have greater range than the M16 but would be lighter and easier to handle than the 7.62 mm M60. The weapon selected, the Minimi, needed certain minor changes to meet US military requirements and suit US manufacturing processes. The main external differences were in the shape of the butt and the hand guard. The M249 is very smooth in operation and displays an exceptional degree of reliability. Fully combat ready with a magazine of 200 rounds, bipod, sling, and cleaning kit, the M249 weighs 22 lb. (9.97 kg), which is still 1 lb. (0.4 kg) less than an empty M60! The Minimi can accept magazine- or belt-fed ammunition without modification. It is normally fired using the built-in bipod, but a tripod is available. FN also markets a "Para" model with a sliding stock and shorter barrel; it is a little lighter than the standard weapon but is shorter and easier to handle in confined spaces.

SOUTH AFRICA

VEKTOR 7.62 MM SS-77 GPMG/5.56 MM MINI-SS 1986

Length (gun): 45.5 in. (1,155 mm)
Barrel: 21.7 in. (550 mm)
Weight (gun): 21.2 lb. (9.6 kg)
Caliber: 7.62 mm
Rifling: 4 grooves, r/hand
Operation: gas-piston
Feed: belt (metal-link)
Cyclic rate: 750 rpm
Muz vel: 2,756 ft./sec. (840 m/sec.)

The South African company Vektor has produced a series of weapons designs, all of them based on some thirty years of combat experience by the South African Army. Most of them were also produced to overcome the effects of the international arms embargo that was imposed prior to the end of Apartheid. The Vektor SS-77 general-purpose machine gun was one of these weapons and was designed around the NATO 7.62 mm round; it entered service in 1985. The SS-77 was not fitted with a gas regulator, which meant that the cyclic rate could not be varied, but eased the maintenance requirements. The 7.62 mm SS-77 could be converted into the Mini-SS (pictured) to take the new NATO standard 5.56 mm round by means of a relatively simple kit. This consisted of a gas piston, a feed cover, and a 5.56 mm barrel, which was chrome-plated; it also included a new-style flash suppressor and a new integral bipod.

SOUTH KOREA (ROK)

DAEWOO 5.56 MM K3 LMG 1982

Length (gun): 40.6 in. (1,030 mm)
Barrel: 21.0 in. (533 mm)
Weight (gun): 15.1 lb. (6.9 kg)
Caliber: 5.56 mm
Rifling: 6 grooves, r/hand
Operation: gas-piston
Feed: belt or magazine
Cyclic rate: 850 rpm
Muz vel: 3,000 ft./sec. (915 m/sec.)

The weapons industry in South Korea expanded with great speed from the 1970s on, and the K3 was the first indigenously designed light machine gun, designed to fire the NATO 5.56 x 45 mm M193 and SS109 rounds. Outwardly it bears a resemblance to the Belgian FN Minimi. The weapon fires on full automatic only and can be fired either from the integral bipod or from an M122 tripod. The gas regulator can be adjusted among three positions, giving rates of fire between 700 and 1,000 rounds per minute. Feed is from either a 200-round metal-link belt or a 30-round box magazine mounted on the left of the gun.

ISRAEL

IMI 5.56 MM NEGEV 1990

Length (gun): 40.2 in. (1,020 mm)
Barrel: 18.1 in. (460 mm)
Weight (gun): 16.5 lb. (750 kg)
Caliber: 5.56 mm
Rifling: 6 grooves, r/hand
Operation: gas-piston
Feed: magazine or belt
Cyclic rate: 1,000 rpm
Muz vel: 3,280 ft./sec. (1,000 m/sec.)

The Israeli Army used the Galil (qv) family of small arms from the 1960s on. The light machine gun version (ARM) differed only minimally from the assault rifle. The Negev, announced in 1990, was designed as a multipurpose light machine gun and is not an adaptation of an assault rifle. The Negev is gas-operated, fires from an open bolt, and employs a rotating bolt that locks into a barrel extension. It is normally fed by magazines, but an adapter enables it to fire 200-round belts. A bipod with finned legs is fitted as standard. The Assault Negev is an assault rifle version, which has the same internal mechanisms but a shorter barrel, forward handgrip, and folding butt; the bipod is not fitted. This brings overall length with butt folded down to 25.6 in. (650 mm), and the total weight is reduced to 15.4 lb. (7.0 kg), which allows the weapon to be used as an assault rifle.

SMALL ARMS WITHIN INFANTRY UNITS

The type and distribution of small arms among an infantry unit is meant to produce well balanced firepower capability. This capability must allow for maximum operational flexibility, combining individual rifle fire with support-fire elements such as light machine guns and, usually in platoon- or company-size units, also heavy machine guns.

The small-arms distribution among military units varies according to country, time, and tactics. In the modern US Army, a typical infantry squad consists of nine personnel. A squad leader, armed with an M16A2 rifle, is in charge of the entire unit, with the remaining eight soldiers split into two fire teams.

Each team consists of a leader, a rifleman, an automatic rifleman, and a grenadier. The team leader and the rifleman are both armed with M16A2 rifles, as is the grenadier, although his weapon also has an M203 grenade launcher. Team support fire is provided by the automatic rifleman, whose typical weapon is the M249 Squad Automatic Weapon (SAW).

The fire composition of a US Army squad contains all the basic small-arms types to effect any small-unit mission. Whereas the M16A2s provide personal offensive and defensive capability, and the M203s give additional firepower against enemy personnel, positions and vehicles, the M249 "in the hands of a rifleman can provide mobility and a high volume of fire up front in the assault or across the squad's position in the defense" (US Army FM 3-21-9). In a defensive position the M249 "adds the firepower of 10 or 20 riflemen without the addition of manpower" (US Army FM 3-21-9).

As the unit size increases, so different small-arms types are introduced. In a US Army platoon (made up of three or four squads) heavier firepower is required to support its broader operational remit. The key addition to platoon firepower is typically two machine-gun teams (each comprising two soldiers) to provide sustained fire roles; the machine gun usually is a 7.62 mm M240B.

Anti-armor teams may also be present in a platoon, armed with infantry guided-missile technologies such as the TOW or Dragon.

The distribution of firepower in US Army platoons and squads is paralleled in most other modern armies, although the role of the grenadier is less common. The British Army infantry section, for example, has two four-man fire teams, each team having one soldier armed with the LSW version of the SA80 to provide light support fire.

Below: *A British Army infantry squad conducts an exercise armed with SA80 assault rifles. Usually one soldier on a four-man team will be armed with the extended-barrel version of the SA80, the Light Support Weapon (LSW), to provide general support fire. Heavier firepower will come from company-level machine gun teams armed with the 7.62 mm General Purpose Machine Gun (GPMG).*

ITALY

BERETTA AR70/90 1990

Length (gun): 39.4 in. (1,000 mm)
Barrel: 18.3 in. (465 mm)
Weight (gun): 11.8 lb. (5.3 kg)
Caliber: 5.56 mm
Rifling: 6 grooves, r/hand
Operation: gas-piston
Feed: box magazine
Cyclic rate: 800 rpm
Muz vel: 3,215 ft./sec. (980 m/sec.)

Following the adoption of the NATO standard 5.56 x 45 mm round, the Italian Army adopted the Belgian Minimi (qv). Despite this Beretta has designed a series of light machine guns for the new caliber, although, as far as is known, none of these has yet been put into full production. First was the AR70/78, which was designed around the US M193 5.56 x 45 mm round, and was, in essence, a heavy-barrel version of the AR70 assault rifle. This design was then adapted to produce the AR70/84, which took the 5.56 x 45 mm NATO round and also incorporated some other modifications such as the deletion of the rapid-change barrel facility. Next in the series was this weapon, the AS70/90, which is the light-machine-gun version of the AR70/90 assault rifle (qv), with a heavy barrel and various other modifications. Feed is from a thirty-round box magazine and the AS70/90 can also fire grenades, but from a different launcher from that used on the AR70/90. There is a large, fixed carrying handle that can accommodate optical sights, if required, although metal sights are commonly used.

CZECH REPUBLIC

CZ 2000 5.45 MM/5.56 MM 1993

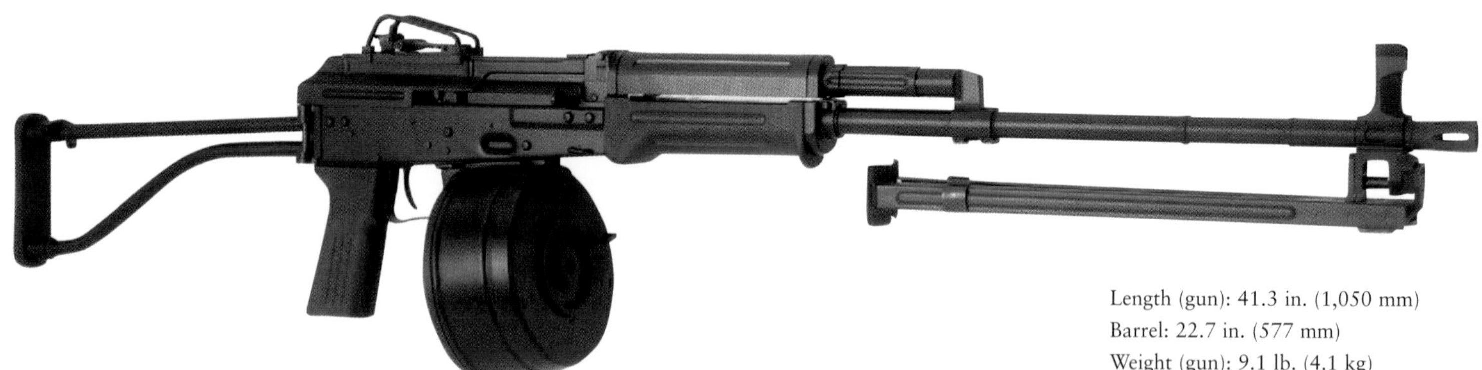

Length (gun): 41.3 in. (1,050 mm)
Barrel: 22.7 in. (577 mm)
Weight (gun): 9.1 lb. (4.1 kg)
Caliber: 5.45 mm
Rifling: 6 grooves, r/hand
Operation: gas
Feed: magazine
Cyclic rate: 800 rpm
Muz vel: 3,150 ft./sec. (960 m/sec.)

This LMG is one of three elements of the CZ 2000 weapons system, which includes an assault rifle and a carbine (qv). The LMG is similar to the rifle, but with a heavy barrel and bipod for the support role. The CZ 2000 LMG has three modes of fire, controlled by a lever moved by the firer's right thumb: fully automatic, three-round bursts, and single-round semi-automatic. There is a skeleton stock formed by two tubular steel struts and a base plate, which folds sideways to the right. It can be fed from a thirty-round curved box, as used in the CZ 2000 assault rifle, or a seventy-five-round drum magazine. The fore and rear sights are fitted with luminous blades; optical and night sights can be mounted. The weapons in the CZ 2000 system can be chambered for the Russian 5.45 mm round or the NATO 5.56 mm round, and although the latter must be the long-term choice, it seems that simple economics will force the Czech armed forces to retain the 5.45 mm caliber for several years to come. A limited number of 5.45 mm CZ 2000 weapons have been produced for the Czech armed forces and the design has been offered to countries still using the Russian round, such as North Korea.

INDIA

INSAS 5.56 MM 1993

Length (gun): 41.3 in. (1,050 mm)
Barrel: 21.1 in. (535 mm)
Weight (gun): 13.5 lb. (6.1 kg)
Caliber: 5.56 mm
Rifling: 4 grooves, r/hand
Operation: gas-piston
Feed: magazine
Cyclic rate: 650 rpm
Muz vel: 3,130 ft./sec.
(954 m/sec.)

The INSAS (Indian Small Arms System) is a family of weapons with two basic models: an assault rifle and an LMG. All these weapons fire a 5.56 x 45 mm cartridge, but it is not to the NATO standard. The INSAS family appears to share a number of features with other weapons that have been manufactured in India. Mechanically the operation appears to resemble that of the Kalashnikov family, while the solid butt resembles that used on the Bren gun. As with other families of weapons, the INSAS LMG has a different barrel from the assault rifle, heavier, longer (21.1 in./535 mm compared to 18.3 in. /464 mm) and chrome-plated. The LMG has a bipod (based on that used by the Indian-produced Bren gun) and has a special thirty-round magazine, although the twenty-two-round rifle magazine can also be used; both types of magazines are made of clear plastic. As with the assault rifle, the LMG is available in fixed- and folding-butt versions, and the INSAS Para LMG also has a shorter barrel (20.1 in. /510 mm), although this is still longer than the rifle barrel. The LMG fire selector can be used for either single rounds or full automatic.

GERMANY

HECKLER AND KOCH G36 1995

Length (gun): 39.0 in. (990 mm)
Barrel: 18.9 in. (480 mm)
Weight (gun): 7.7 lb. (3.5 kg)
Caliber: 5.56 mm
Rifling: 6 grooves, r/hand
Operation: gas
Feed: magazine
Cyclic rate: 750 rpm
Muz vel: 3,020 ft./sec. (920 m/sec.)

Following the modern trend, the G36 is the light support weapon (LSW) version of the Heckler and Koch G36 rifle and is identical in most respects to that weapon. The differences lie in optimizing it for the support role (i.e., in giving sustained automatic fire) with a different barrel, which has the same dimensions but is of thicker construction, particularly at the chamber end. It is also permanently fitted with a bipod, which is optional in the rifle. Like the assault rifle version, the LSW has a large carrying handle with a built-in x3 optical sight; a folding, skeleton butt; and a muzzle compensator/flash suppressor. It is magazine-fed, using a thirty-round box. There is also a G36E export version, which differs mainly in that is has a less powerful x1.5 optical sight.

Heavy Machine Guns

"To see the bullets making a clean cut across the trunk and to soon witness the fall of the tree was a spectacle that invariably seemed to fully drive home a sense of my gun's ability."

Hiram Maxim, writing on his sales promotion technique for the Maxim gun, c.1888.

Above: *The 12.7 mm NORINCO Type 85 is a Chinese heavy machine gun. Its skeletal appearance makes it very light; the gun itself weighs only 41 lb. (18.5 kg). Compare this with the Browning M2HB, which weighs 84 lb. (38.1 kg).*

It is not an overstatement to say that machine guns have shaped the face of modern infantry warfare. Prior to the 1850s, the volume of fire generated by a unit of infantry was constrained by the number of infantryman who were actually on the field. Even the most highly trained rifleman operating a flintlock musket could fire only about three to four rounds each minute. A select group of gun designers soon realized that what was required was a mechanical system for rapid fire that would give individual infantryman a fire capability beyond what was "naturally" achievable.

The first machine guns

Although the search for an automatic weapon that would enable one gunner to emulate the fire of twenty or more riflemen started at the early as the seventeenth century, it was the invention of the percussion cap in the early 1800s that galvanized machine gun design. Some of the earliest machine guns were surprisingly effective. The Agar "Coffee Mill" gun, designed around the time of the US Civil War, was a hopper-fed weapon that was operated by a rotating handle; turning the handle dropped preloaded tubes (containing ball and powder) and a nipple for the percussion cap into the gun's chamber one at a time for firing, achieving a 100-rpm rate of fire.

Other hand-cranked machine guns soon emerged, many of them working on the "battery gun" principle of fixed multiple barrels, each barrel with its own firing-pin mechanism. Metal unitary cartridges, which were becoming the dominant firearms ammunition, were also put to good use. The Montigny Mitrailleuse, for example, had twenty-five rifle barrels that were discharged one at a time using a crank handle (the feed mechanism was a metal plate holding twenty-five cartridges), and with efficient reloading up to 250 rounds could be fired each minute.

A major leap toward the modern design of the machine gun came with Dr. Richard Gatling's infamous Gatling Gun of 1861. Gatling applied a hopper-feed mechanism to a weapon featuring six barrels in a rotary arrangement; the weapon was fired by hand cranking as well. The Gatling Gun also automatically ejected spent cartridges, thus allowing prolonged sustained fire. Gatling's weapon was powerful, and combat testing in the Civil War proved its worth: the US Army adopted the Gatling in 1866, and the British Royal Navy followed suit in the 1870s.

The Royal Navy also acquired the multibarrel Nordenfelt machine gun designed by Heldge Palmcrantz, which simultaneously loaded a horizontal arrangement of barrels with cartridges that were fired by a ripple of firing pins when the operator turned the crank handle. With a reliable 4,000-rpm rate of fire, some have claimed that Nordenfelt surpasses the Gatling in the race for an effective machine gun.

Whatever the case, guns like the Gatling and Nordenfelt awoke the world for the possibilities of mechanized firepower. It would, however, take one Hiram Maxim to introduce the first true machine gun.

From Maxim to Browning

The Gatling and other early mechanical firearms were not machine guns in the truest sense. A machine gun must function using self-generated power, and that was exactly what US inventor Hiram Maxim demonstrated in 1884. Maxim utilized the force of recoil in a single-barrel .45-caliber machine gun that was fed from a belt of ammunition. The gun worked on the short-recoil system, the barrel and bolt separating on recoil after a short distance to eject the spent cartridge and load a new one, and the barrel cooled by the water jacket.

By 1908 Maxim's weapon had been refined among German forces into the MG08, a 7.92 mm weapon with a 400-rpm rate of fire that could be sustained hour after hour. By this time, however, Maxim had competition. From 1889 American John Moses Browning had developed a machine gun that used ported gas to operate a hinged lever, which in turn cycled the weapon. This gun becoming the Colt "Potato Digger" of 1895. From Austria–Hungary came a blowback-operated machine gun that developed into a series of fairly unreliable Skoda machine guns. Most significant, however, was the gas-operated Hotchkiss machine gun, which emerged around 1893. The Hotchkiss used the gas-piston arrangement, which is still the groundwork for many small arms today, although the weapon used metallic-strip feed rather than belt feed.

Both the Hotchkiss and the Maxim were used in battle during the Russo-Japanese war of 1904, and the conflict decisively demonstrated that a handful of machine guns could dominate or defeat hundreds of enemy troops, such were the volumes of fire. By 1914, and the outbreak of the First World War, machine guns were standard components of infantry firepower, although at

Below: *A group of Berliners man a Maxim MG08 during Germany's inter-war period. Hiram Maxim was the forefather of the modern machine gun, using the force of recoil as an operating energy for his automatic weapons.*

Above: *British soldiers of the 11th Leicestershire Regiment occupy positions in a captured German trench at Cambrai, 1917. The trench is guarded by two .303 in. Vickers machine guns. Together these two weapons could produce a practical volume of fire of around 800 rpm.*

first they were spread rather thinly at around two guns per battalion. Demand soon increased the numbers, and weapons such as the British .303 in. Vickers, the French Hotchkiss, and the German Maxim 08 would soon be accounting for thousands of lives, putting paid to the wisdom of frontal assaults forever. Machine guns such as the Lewis gun and the MG14 also took to the skies in the new fighter aircraft, fitted on flexible or fixed mounts, but eventually attached above the engine cowling, and synchronized to fire through the propeller.

Consolidating the foundations

During the later years of WW I, and in its aftermath, the United States produced a new range of machine guns that would become seminal weapons of the twentieth century. Browning's M1917 appeared in 1917, a water-cooled belt-fed recoil-operated weapon that used a bolt accelerator to throw the bolt to the rear after it had separated from the barrel during recoil. The system was efficient, and it evolved into the air-cooled Browning M1919, a superb .30-caliber general-purpose weapon that would see service for the next five decades and beyond in various world armies. In the 1930s, the awesome .50-caliber Browning M2, then the M2HB (Heavy Barrel), entered the world stage, with their slow rates of fire (around 500 rpm) offset by the huge power of the .50-caliber round up to 6,561 feet (2,000 m). The M2HB, with relatively minor changes, is still a standard heavy machine gun of the US Army and other world forces, a testimony to the success of the Browning design.

Although the foundations of the machine gun were entirely laid by the end of World War I, the interwar and World War II years brought diversifications in the types and roles of machine guns. Magazine-fed light machine guns such as the British Bren were developed for more mobile heavy firepower. Water-cooling, although retained in heavy weapons like the Vickers, was superseded by the more practical air-cooling system, and this in turn entailed more efficient and rapid barrel-change facilities.

One of the general movements in machine gun technology in the 1930s and 1940s was the lightening of the weapon, combined with a dramatic increase in rates of fire.

The defining symbol of this movement is the German MG42, one of the finest machine guns ever made and one that is still basically in use today as the MG3. The MG42 began life as the MG34, an air-cooled 7.92 mm machine gun with an overall weight of 26.7 lb. (12.1 kg) and a rate of fire of 900 rpm. Although a fine weapon, the MG34 was expensive to produce—too expensive for the mass production needs of wartime Germany—and its mechanical complexity was intolerant of dirt.

A revision of the MG34 resulted in the cheaper MG42, which relied more on metal stampings, pressings, and welding in its production process, reduced the weight by nearly a kilogram (2.2 lb.), and utilized roller-locking. Its reliability was also markedly improved, and the rate of fire rose to a potent 1,200 rpm.

What is significant about the MG42 is that it truly occupied the category of "general-purpose machine gun." It was light enough to be carried by the two-man team and established on its bipod in temporary positions to support troop maneuvers with localized bursts of heavy fire. In defensive positions, the weapon could be set on a tripod in a sustained-fire role, complete with periscope optics and separate trigger group for use by a concealed soldier.

The power and range of the weapon also meant it could be mounted in anti-aircraft configurations. Little wonder the MG42 became one of the most feared weapons among Allied soldiers during World War II.

Low-level anti-aircraft fire became one of the major applications of machine guns during the war, usually involving multiple machine guns in a single mobile mount. The US Army assembled four Browning M2HB weapons into what was known as the Maxson Mount. This was effectively an electrically powered turret; the gunner sat between two pairs of Brownings. The firepower from the Maxson Mount was lethal to low-flying aircraft, and the Mount was fitted to the back of everything from half-tracks to Jeeps. If necessary, the weapons of the Maxson Mount could also be depressed to engage ground targets. The United States was not the only country to make such an application of its machine guns. Soviet forces, for example, in the later war years were equipped with the KPV machine gun mount, featuring four 14.5 mm machine guns that not only fired ball rounds, but also could project armor-piercing, incendiary, and high-explosive rounds to range of 26,000 ft. (8,000 m).

Postwar machine guns

From the immediate postwar period to the present day, most of the major advances in machine-gun technology and configurations have been in the realms of the light machine guns (see preceding chapter).

Many machine guns have now little to distinguish them from assault rifles except for heavier, longer barrels and, sometimes, belt feed. Heavy machine guns, like the Browning M2HB, and general-purpose machine guns, like the FN MAG, are either direct descendants of far older weapons or are simply refinements of existing principles of machine-gun technology. Furthermore, revisiting of the concept of multibarrel rotary machine guns over the last four decades (see feature in this chapter) harks back to Gatling's earliest forays into machine-gun type itself. The principal difference today is the rotary-barrel weapons are driven by electric motors to achieve phenomenal rates of fire, rather than laboriously hand-cranked.

The familiar configurations of the heavy machine gun look set to continue for the foreseeable future, although there is one potentially revolutionary new weapon type. From Australia has come "Metal Storm," a multibarrel electro gun that can fire at unimaginable rates of

Below: *The function of a machine gun can change considerably depending on type of mount. Here, an MG42 (bottom) is mounted on a tripod for the sustained fire role, while the same weapon in the top picture is fitted with a periscope aiming device, allowing the gunner to shoot from a concealed position.*

one million rpm and has no separate ammunition feed, magazine or ejection system; it does not fire standard ammunition at all. The bullets are stacked in long barrels with the propellant separating them.

The propellant is ignited by electrical impulse; the round is the propellant, expanding to act as a chamber lock for the fired round. The one million rpm was achieved by the 36-barrel Metal Storm, which is likely to find applications in air defense roles, but other weapons can be designed. The absence of mechanical parts potentially makes Metal Storm extremely reliable, and the weapon keeps pushing the limits of the heavy firepower dream envisioned by the likes of Maxim and Gatling all those decades ago.

MAUSER MG 42 MACHINE GUN

One of the most feared weapons of World War II, the Mauser Maschinengewehr Model 1942 (MG 42) became the German Army's standard machine gun in the latter part of the war, and in various guises it is still in service with many armies today. It was developed from the MG 34 but was designed to be lighter and easier to manufacture, and to have enhanced performance. The MG 42 had slightly lower muzzle velocity (2,480 feet/second [755 m/sec.] compared to 2,780 feet/second [820 m/sec.]), but it had virtually double the rate of fire (1,200 compared to 650 rounds per minute), giving rise to the characteristic sound that was likened by Allied soldiers to the noise of tearing cloth. The MG 42 was recoil-operated, used a roller-locked bolt, and weighed 25.3 lb. (11.5 kg), more than the contemporary British Bren Mk 3, which weighed 19.3 lb. (8.8 kg). The MG 42 could also be employed by an infantry squad as a light machine gun, using a bipod (below) or as a medium/heavy machine gun, using a large and complicated tripod that weighed 42.3 lb. (19.2 kg).

MAUSER MG 42 MACHINE GUN

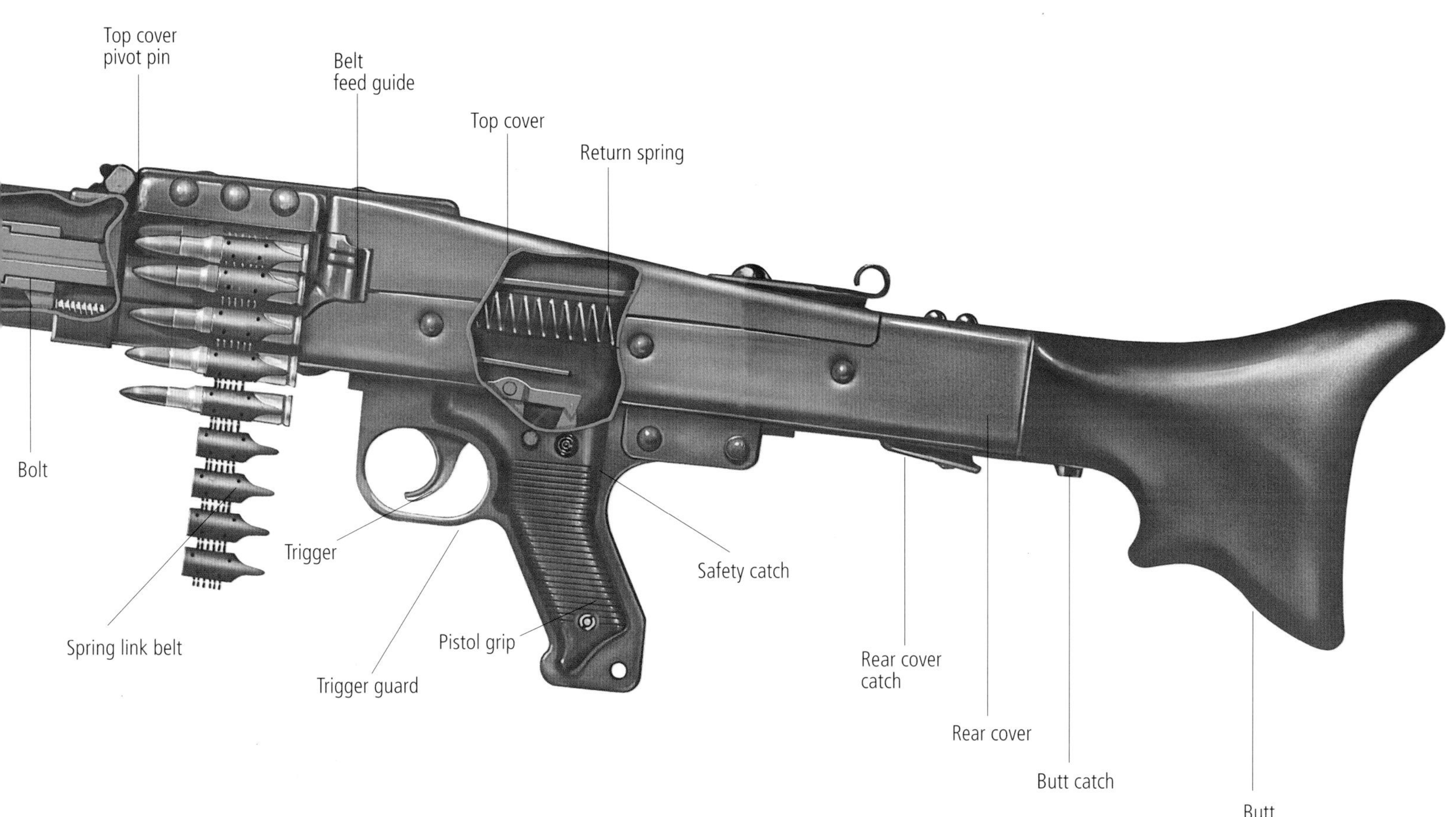

UNITED KINGDOM

PUCKLE REPEATING GUN 1718

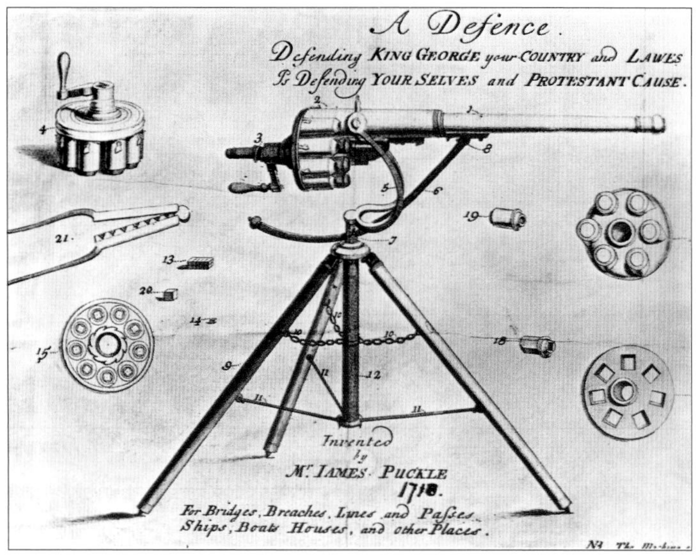

Length (gun): 39 in. (991 mm)
Barrel: 36 in. (914 mm)
Weight (gun): n.k.
Weight (tripod): n.k.
Caliber: 1.0 in. (25.4 mm)
Rifling: none

Operation: see text
Feed: 9-round magazine
Cooling: air
Cyclic rate: ca 628 rpm
Muz vel: n.k.
Range: n.k.

This unusual weapon was invented by Englishman James Puckle in 1718. The Puckle gun was intended for repelling naval borders by producing a larger volume of fire than was possible with a blunderbuss. The gun consisted of a single, long, brass barrel fed by a nine-round, circular magazine rotated by a handle. On loading the magazine, the first round was aligned with the barrel, then fired by the flintlock; the magazine was rotated until the next round was aligned, the flintlock was recocked, and the second round was fired. The rate of fire could not have been high. A note on the drawing indicates that the machine could be made to discharge grenades as well as bullets. The gun was mounted on a well designed tripod with metal stays, giving a firm base, while the cradle allowed the gun to be elevated and traversed. Puckle decided that round bullets were only for use against Christians, and that for engagements against Muslims (for example, in the Mediterranean) square bullets should be used! Why a man who had the intelligence and imagination to design such an innovative weapon should then come to such an extraordinary conclusion is not recorded. The Puckle gun certainly worked but was never adopted by either the British Navy or Army.

UNITED STATES

GATLING, 0.45 IN., MODEL 1875

Length (gun): 59.4 in. (1,360 mm)
Barrel: 31.9 in. (812 mm)
Weight (with carriage): 444.0 lb. (201.4 kg)
Number of barrels: 6
Caliber: 0.45 in. (11.43 mm)
Rifling: 7 grooves, r/hand

Operation: mechanical
Feed: various (see text)
Cooling: air
Cyclic rate: 800 rpm
Muz vel: n.k.
Range: n.k.

This famous weapon was designed and patented by Richard Jordan Gatling of Maney's Neck, North Carolina. The example shown here is the Model 1875, manufactured by the Colt Patent Firearms Manufacturing Company. The weapon had ten barrels that were mechanically rotated and fired using a lever on the right-hand side of the weapon. The weapon used the US Army standard 0.45 in. cartridge, and rounds were gravity-fed from a box magazine mounted on top of the bronze breech housing. The Gatling was, in effect, six rifles, each with its own bolt, striker, and extractor, and each of them firing in rapid succession. The weapon was mounted on either a two-wheel, a horse-drawn trailer, or a simple tripod (as shown here). Early Gatlings were widely distributed within the US Army, and most garrisons in the West had at least one; most field expeditions included one or more. Three were available to Major-General George Custer in June 1876, but he decided to leave them behind as he felt that they would slow down his rate of march; had he taken them the outcome of the battle of the Little Bighorn might have been different. (See page 418 for early battlefield deployments.)

UNITED STATES

VANDENBURGH VOLLEY GUN 1860

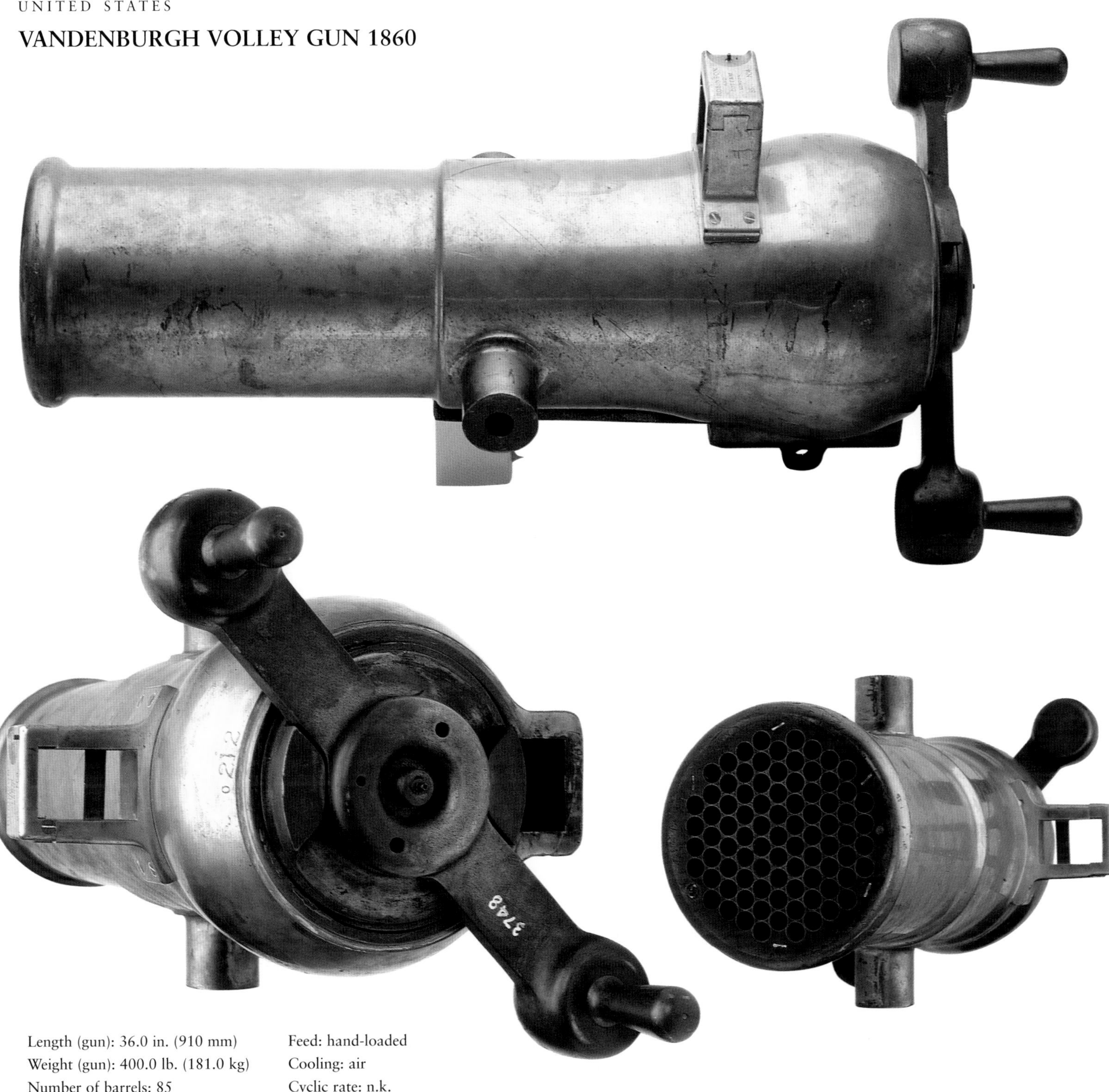

Length (gun): 36.0 in. (910 mm)
Weight (gun): 400.0 lb. (181.0 kg)
Number of barrels: 85
Caliber: 0.50 in. (12.7 mm)
Rifling: n.k.
Operation: n.k.
Feed: hand-loaded
Cooling: air
Cyclic rate: n.k.
Muz vel: n.k.
Range: n.k.

The Volley Gun was a step on the way to automatic weapons. It was designed and developed in 1860 by General Origen Vandenburgh of the New York State Militia. Having failed to find a manufacturer in America, the gun was produced in small numbers by British gunsmith Robinson and Cottam of London. When it failed to find a market in Europe, Vandenburgh sold it to the Confederate Army! The weapon consisted of a cast-brass barrel containing eighty-five individual 0.50 in. (12.7 mm) rifled barrels, each of which had to be individually loaded by hand. The screw breech was then closed and secured using the large handles, which made an airtight seal with the firing chamber. A single percussion cap in the center of the breech fired all rounds simultaneously. The weapon would have had a devastating effect on densely packed infantry at close quarters. The square device above the breech is a sight, and the trunnions show that the weapon must have rested on a simple artillery mount, in the same manner as the contemporary Gatling (qv). This particular example was captured by Union Cavalry near Salisbury, North Carolina, in April 1865 and is now exhibited in the museum at the United States Military Academy, West Point.

THE GATLING GUN IN BATTLEFIELD USAGE

Many myths have been built around the Gatling gun, courtesy of wartime press, and then Hollywood. The question remains: how effective was the Gatling in combat, and how much did it change the face of warfare?

Gatling's invention arrived just in time for it to see limited use during the Civil War. When applied properly, the Gatling could be devastating, but the use of fragile paper cartridges resulted in frequent stoppages, bolstering the Gatling's many detractors. A poem by Henry Newbolt (1862–1938) even makes reference: "The sand of the desert is sodden red/Red with the blood of a square that broke/The Gatling's jammed and the Colonel dead/And the regiment blind with dust and smoke." However, from 1865 Gatling switched to more dependable rimfire copper-cased cartridges, and the gun started to show its true worth. In the many trials undertaken by the Gatling, its volume-fire supremacy quickly emerged. In Prussia in 1869, for example, 100 Prussian infantry armed with rifles fired 721 rounds in one minute at a target 6 ft. (1.8 m) by 72 ft. (22 m) from a range of 875 yd. (800 m). They hit the target 196 times. A single Gatling, operated by only two men, performed the same test, firing 246 rounds and hitting the target 216 times.

Tactically, the Gatlings were at first used in the same manner as cannons. Yet in the Spanish-American War of 1898, Gatling Gun Detachment commander Lieutenant John H. Parker actually took his guns forward with the infantry during an assault on San Juan Hill in Cuba, utilizing the weapon successfully in a mobile support role. With four Gatling guns used in this way, San Juan Hill was captured. The action was an important lesson in the new tactical considerations for machine guns.

Above and below left: *The Gatling's chief virtue was its rugged simplicity; inconsistency in ammunition was one of the main reasons for any stoppages. Here the weapon is pictured with its breech cover open. The picture at bottom left shows a cartridge entering the breech during loading. A well trained team of men could achieve a rate of fire of about 1,000 rpm.*

UNITED KINGDOM

GARDNER MACHINE GUN, 2-BARREL, 0.45 IN. 1880

Length (gun): 47.0 in. (1,193 mm)
Barrels: 30.0 in. (762 mm)
Weight (gun): 218.0 lb. (98.9 kg)
Caliber: 0.45 in.
Operation: mechanical
Feed: see text
Cooling: air
Cyclic rate: up to 250 rpm
Muz vel: n.k.
Max range: 2,000 yd. (1,830 m)

American William Gardner designed a series of mechanically cranked guns between 1874 and 1900. Although his designs were tested by the US Army and Navy, they failed to attract significant orders, so Gardner moved to England. The main Gardner design consisted of two parallel barrels, 1.25 in. (32 mm) apart; in earlier versions the barrels were supported at both ends, but in later versions they were secured at the barrel end only. They were housed inside a bronze casing through which cooling water could be passed. Each barrel was loaded, fired, and extracted in turn, with a cam system so ordered that one bolt was withdrawn as the other was pushed in. There was a two-man crew, one aiming and cranking the gun, the second responsible for ensuring that the rounds fed correctly and topping up the hopper. The Gardner was adopted by the Royal Navy in 1880 and later by the British Army; it was manufactured at the Royal Small Arms Factory at Enfield and used in various colonial campaigns. The Gardner was also produced by Pratt and Whitney, for whom Gardner had worked when he designed the gun. That company sold small numbers of the twin-barrel version to the US Army and a single-barreled version to the US Navy.

UNITED STATES

GATLING, 0.45 IN., MODEL 1883

Length (gun): 42.5 in. (1,080 mm)
Barrel: 24 in. (610 mm)
Weight (gun): 260.0 lb. (118.0 kg)
Number of barrels: 10
Caliber: 0.45 in (11.4 mm)
Rifling: n.k.
Operation: mechanical
Feed: circular magazine
Cooling: air
Cyclic rate: ca 200 rpm
Muz vel: n.k.
Range: n.k.

Gatling and Colt produced several improved versions of the Gatling machine gun. The model 1883 had ten barrels enclosed in a brass casing. These barrels were fed by a circular Accles patent magazine placed centrally above the gun, which meant that the sights were displaced to the right. The doughnut-shaped Accles mechanical drum feeder was a complex mechanism subject to jamming. In 1898, the US Army refitted its model 1883 Gatlings with a Bruce feeder adapter. The model 1883 had a new flexible yoke that permitted a wider angle of traverse and elevations. The vertical feed did not work as well it did with wider range in elevation. The weapon rested in an artillery-type trunnion mounting and was lockable in elevation. Gatlings were regularly used by late-Victorian armies against unsophisticated enemies, by the US Army in the American West, and by European armies in their colonial wars in Africa and Asia. They also found naval use mounted in the fighting tops and intended for use in sweeping the decks of enemy ships or repelling boarders, although the rapidly increasing range of ships' main guns meant that this role diminished. Gatlings could be used in close-range naval engagements against torpedo boats, for which 0.65 in. (16.5 mm) and even 1 in. (25 mm) Gatlings were developed. Ship-mounted Gatlings were used against land-artillery crews serving open batteries.

UNITED KINGDOM

MAXIM GUN 1884

Length (gun): 46.0 in. (1,169 mm)
Barrel: 24.0 in. (610 mm)
Weight (gun): 26.0 lb. (11.8 kg)
Weight (tripod): 15.0 lb. (6.8 kg)
Caliber: 0.45 in.
Rifling: 4 grooves, r/hand
Operation: recoil
Feed: belt
Cooling: water
Cyclic rate: 500/600 rpm
Muz vel: 1,600 ft./sec. (488 m/sec.)
Range: 1,500 yd. (1,372 m)

Hiram Maxim (above, showing the lightness of his gun), born in Maine, moved to England in the 1880s where he designed, built, and patented a true automatic gun, in which the recoil of the first manually loaded round was used to fire the next. The principle was that the barrel recoiled a short distance before unlocking the breechblock from it and allowing the breechblock to continue backward under its momentum, extending a strong fusee spring as it did so and drawing a cartridge from the belt. When the bolt reached its most rearward position, the extended fusee spring drew it forward again so that it chambered and fired the cartridge, after which the process was repeated. The cyclic rate of fire was about 600 rpm; the cartridges were 0.45 in. Boxer type loaded with black powder. The barrel got so hot that it was necessary to surround it with a water jacket. The gun was mounted on a long tubular metal tripod with a canvas seat for the firer. It was fitted with elevating and traversing gear and was sighted to 1,000 yd. (914 m). The British Army used the rifle-caliber gun of the type illustrated (mounted on a light two-wheel artillery type carriage instead of the tripod) in its various colonial wars, where it proved effective in breaking up mass attacks.

UNITED KINGDOM

0.303 IN. VICKERS-MAXIM 1895

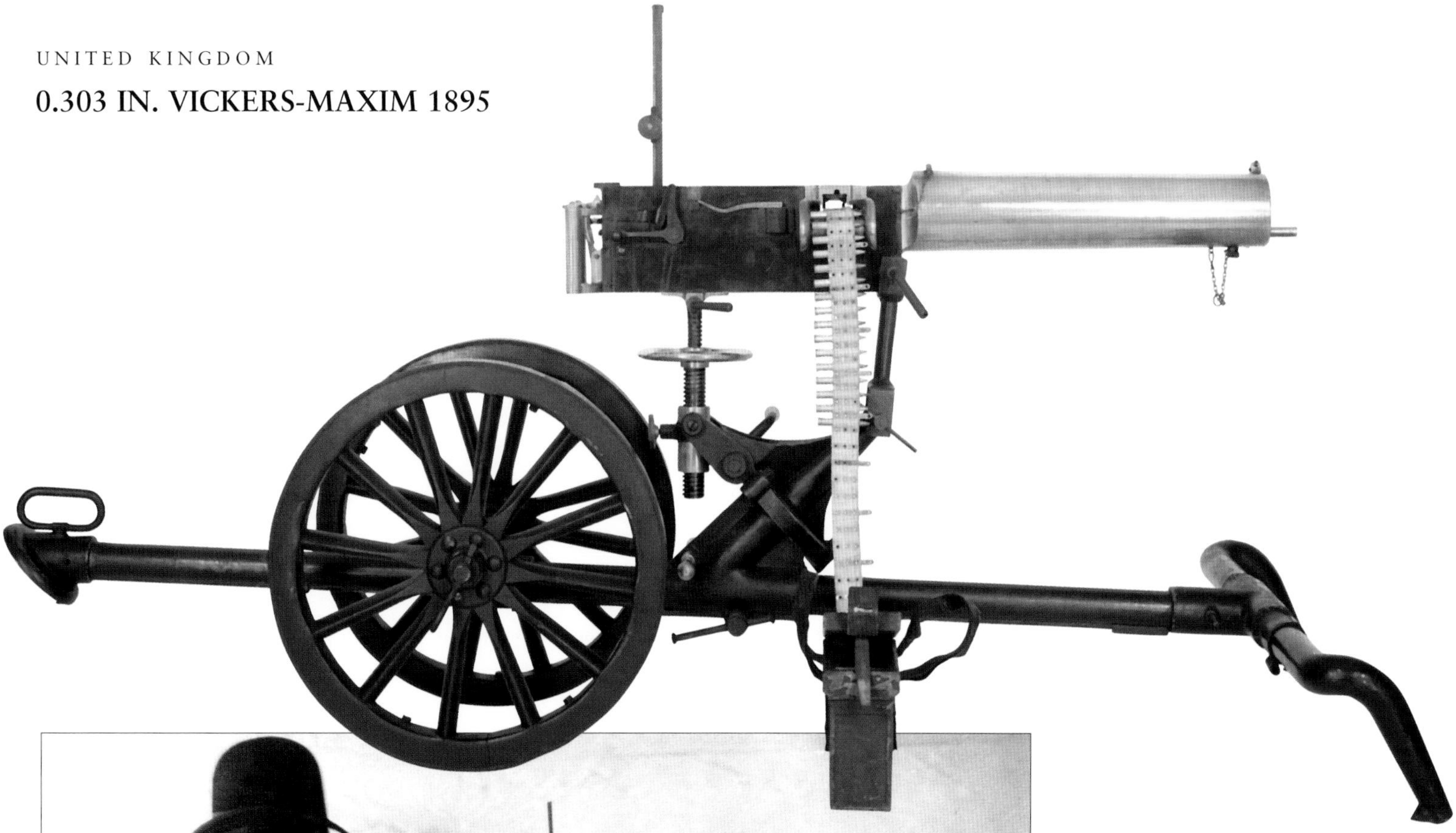

Length (gun): 42.5 in. (1,079 mm)
Barrel: 26.5 in. (673 mm)
Weight (gun): 60.0 lb. (27.2 kg)
Length (mounting): 75.0 in. (1,905 mm)
Weight (mounting): 178.0 lb. (80.7 kg)
Caliber: 0.303 in.
Rifling: 4 grooves, r/hand
Operation: recoil
Feed: belt
Cooling: water
Cyclic rate: ca 550 rpm
Muz vel: 2,440 ft./sec. (744 m/sec)
Range: 2,900 yd. (2,652 m)

The British Army changed to smokeless propellant in 1891 and found that the greater heat and pressures necessitated a new type of rifling. This change was particularly beneficial to the Vickers-Maxim because, apart from better range and flatter trajectory, the more powerful propellant increased the recoil and, thus, the amount of power for smooth operation. The new rifle-caliber cordite cartridge gun soon showed its fearful capacity. At Omdurman, the huge Dervish armies, charging across flat, open desert, sustained hideous casualties in their fruitless attempts to reach the British firing line. The weapon proved somewhat less useful in South Africa, but it was in the trench warfare of 1914–18 that its power was fully recognized. The weapon illustrated has been selected because of its "parapet" carriage, in which the two horn-shaped projections at the front could be raised and hooked into the top of a wall or earth parapet. This allowed the gun, mounted on a sleeve that could be slipped up and down the central pole, to be raised to fire over defenses with a reasonably wide arc of traverse. The plate at the rear of the central pole was a foot to give the third point of support. It had two holes in it, about 1 in. (25.4 mm) in diameter, so that it could be held rigidly in place by pegs.

UNITED STATES

COLT-BROWNING MODEL 1895/1904/1917

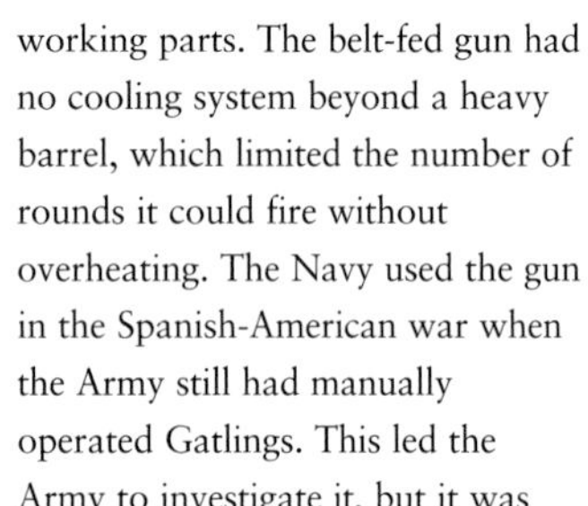

Length (gun): 40.8 in. (1,035 mm)
Barrel: 28.0 in. (712 mm)
Weight (gun): 35.0 lb. (15.9 kg)
Weight (tripod): 61.3 lb. (27.8 kg)
Caliber: 0.30 in.
Rifling: 4 grooves, r/hand
Operation: gas
Feed: belt
Cooling: air
Cyclic rate: 480 rpm
Muz vel: 2,800 ft./sec. (855 m/sec.)
Range: 2,000 yd. (1,829 m)

Invented by John Browning and produced by Colt, this gun equipped the US Navy by 1898. It worked by gas and the piston was hinged at the rear. A gas port in the bottom of the bore allowed gas to strike the front of the piston and blow it downward through ninety degrees; a lever then activated the working parts. The belt-fed gun had no cooling system beyond a heavy barrel, which limited the number of rounds it could fire without overheating. The Navy used the gun in the Spanish-American war when the Army still had manually operated Gatlings. This led the Army to investigate it, but it was finally decided that it was too complex for land service. Modifications led to the Model 1904, which was bought by some countries. When the United States entered World War I in 1917, its Army had no modern machine guns. A new model, the 1917 (Army), was ordered, and about 1,500 were supplied before the end of the war. One serious defect was that it could not be used in the prone position because the 10 in. (254 mm) piston hit the ground if the gun was too low. This tendency inevitably led the United States infantrymen to nickname it the "potato digger."

SWEDEN

NORDENFELT MULTIBARREL VOLLEY GUN 1898

Length (gun): 41.5 in. (1,054 mm)
Barrels: 28.5 in. (724 mm)
Weight (gun): 93.0 lb. (42.2 kg)
Caliber: 0.577 in.
Rifling: 5 grooves, r/hand
Operation: mechanical
Feed: 27-round, gravity
Cooling: air
Cyclic rate: 300 rpm
Muz vel: ca 1,350 ft./sec. (411 m/sec.)
Range: n.k.

These guns were designed by Swedish engineer Palmcrantz and were produced in England in 1898 by the Maxim-Nordenfelt Company. The gunner operated a lever, which carried the required number of cartridges from an overhead hopper to the breechblock, which then chambered them. A block containing the firing pins then moved in and lined up with the cartridge caps. As the handle reached the end of the forward stroke, it tripped the firing pins in rapid succession. The operator then pulled the handle to the rear, extracting the empty cases and restarting the sequence. The Nordenfelts had the first-ever armor-piercing round with a hard steel core. A facility in models with five or more barrels was an "automatic scattering gear." This allowed each barrel to be adjusted manually so that at a range of 300 yd. (275 m) there would be a spread of some 3 ft. (0.9 m) between rounds, which was calculated to cover up to ten men advancing in line. At 500 yd. (457 m) or more, it was believed that natural dispersion achieved the same effect. Five- and three-barreled Nordenfelts were adopted in 1878 by the British Army and the Navy, in both 0.45-in and 0.303-in calibers. These guns were somewhat clumsy in design, but effective; the twelve-barreled gun could fire at about 4,000 rpm.

AUSTRIA-HUNGARY

SCHWARZLOSE MASCHINEGEWEHR MODEL 05 1905

Length (gun): 42.0 in. (1,067 mm)
Barrel: 20.7 in. (527 mm)
Weight (gun): 44.0 lb. (20.0 kg)
Weight (tripod): 44.0 lb. (20.0 kg)
Caliber: 8 mm
Rifling: 4 grooves, r/hand
Operation: blowback
Feed: belt
Cooling: water
Cyclic rate: 400 rpm
Muz vel: 2,000 ft./sec. (610 m/sec.)
Range: 3,062 yd. (2,800 m)

The Schwarzlose machine gun had a characteristically slow cyclic rate of fire, about 400 rpm. The system of lubricating the cartridge case to assist its extraction, although widely used in those days, was undesirable one as it was likely to lead to difficulties in very dry or dusty countries. After some further work, Schwarzlose finally succeeded in eliminating this feature by increasing the weight of the breechblock and the strength of the spring, as well as by increasing the various mechanical disadvantages working against the bolt during the initial stages of its rearward action. These improvements resulted in a second model of his gun, which first appeared in 1912. The new Schwarzlose proved to be a reliable weapon from the beginning, when two of the early models fired 35,000 rounds each with minimal stoppages under test, and with no apparent loss of accuracy. It was also simple to fire and maintain and was soon in service with the Austro-Hungarian Army, where it was used with considerable success. The Austrians calculated the fire of a single well-handled gun as being equivalent to that of eighty riflemen. The weapon is now officially obsolete, but there may be a few still in use in remote areas of the world.

FRANCE

SAINT-ETIENNE MODÈLE 1907

Length (gun): 46.5 in. (1,181 mm)
Barrel: 28.0 in. (711 mm)
Weight (gun): 56.8 lb. (25.7 kg)
Weight (tripod): 60.0 lb. (27.2 kg)
Caliber: 8 mm
Rifling: 4 grooves, r/hand
Operation: gas
Feed: strip
Cooling: air
Cyclic rate: 4/500 rpm
Muz vel: 2,300 ft./sec. (700 m/sec.)
Range: 2,625 yd. (2,400 m)

In 1893, a captain in the Austrian Army, Baron von Odkolek, invented a new type of automatic weapon that utilized part of the gases from one round to load and fire the next. With no manufacturing facilities of his own, he turned to French gun-making firm Hotchkiss, which showed great interest not only in the completed weapon, which they decided was of quite impracticable design, but in one of its components, the system of tapping gases from the barrel to activate the piston. After many years of work, the company produced this weapon. Although basically of Hotchkiss type, the piston was blown forward instead of backward to activate a mechanism of astonishing complexity. For example, the reversed piston operation necessitated the introduction of a rack-and-pinion mechanism to reverse the motion again. The mainspring, which was coiled on a steel rod, was largely exposed below the massive brass receiver so as to keep it cool, and the gun was fed by thirty-round strips of standard Lebel rifle cartridges. The gun shown is mounted on a 1914 pattern tripod; this was interchangeable with the 1907 pattern, the main difference being the very large brass wheel, which was essentially used for clamping the elevating gear in the earlier model.

GERMANY

MAXIM MG08 1908

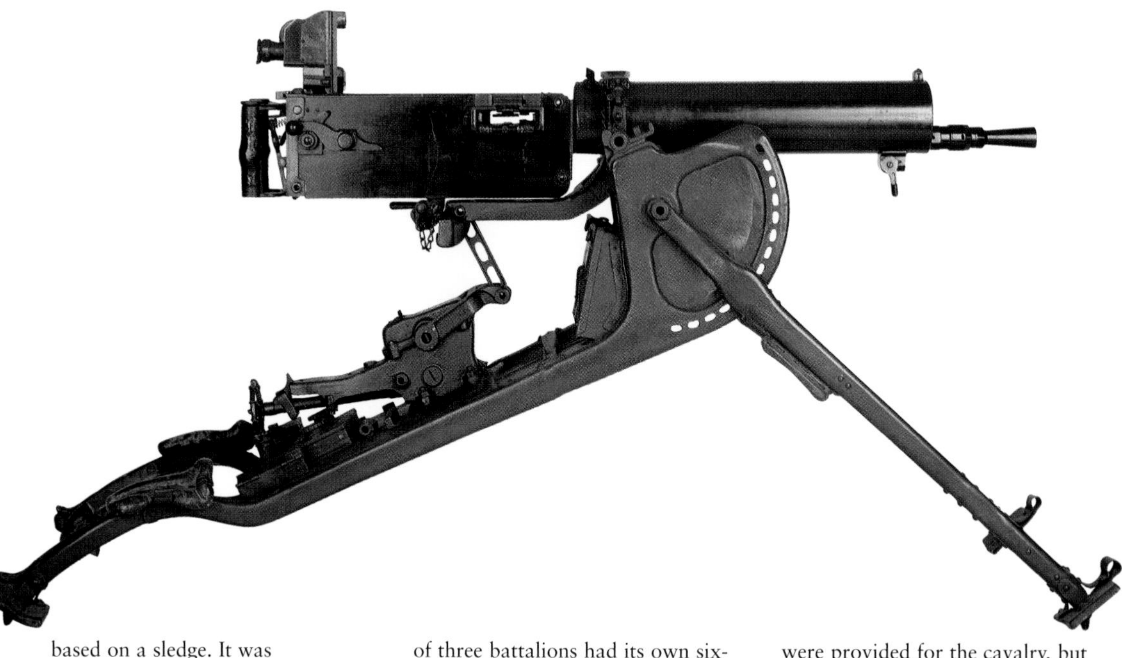

Length (gun): 46.3 in. (1,175 mm)
Barrel: 28.3 in. (719 mm)
Weight (gun): 58.5 lb. (26.5 kg)
Weight (tripod): 70.5 lb. (32.0 kg)
Caliber: 7.92 mm
Rifling: 4 grooves, r/hand
Operation: recoil
Feed: belt
Cooling: water
Cyclic rate: 3/400 rpm
Muz vel: 2,925 ft./sec. (892 m/sec.)
Range: 2,188 yd. (2,000 m)

In 1899, a number of Maxim batteries, each of four guns, were tried out at the Imperial maneuvers. A Maxim gun was subsequently developed at the factory at Spandau and came into service in 1908. Instead of a wheeled artillery-type carriage or a tripod, it had a solid heavy mount based on a sledge. It was necessary only to elevate the gun and swing the forward legs over it to have it ready to drag along. When the legs were down they could easily be adjusted so that the firers could sit, kneel, or lie down as appropriate. By the end of 1908, every German regiment of three battalions had its own six-gun battery. The guns were carried on light horse-drawn carts and the detachments, usually of four men each, marched; extra vehicles were provided for ammunition. The German battery was under the direct hand of the Regimental Commander and similar batteries were provided for the cavalry, but these were more mobile, as the wagons had four horses instead of two and the detachments were mounted on horses. A modified sledge mount was also introduced at this time, which reduced the total weight and allowed the individual guns to be manhandled.

UNITED KINGDOM

VICKERS 0.303 IN. 1912

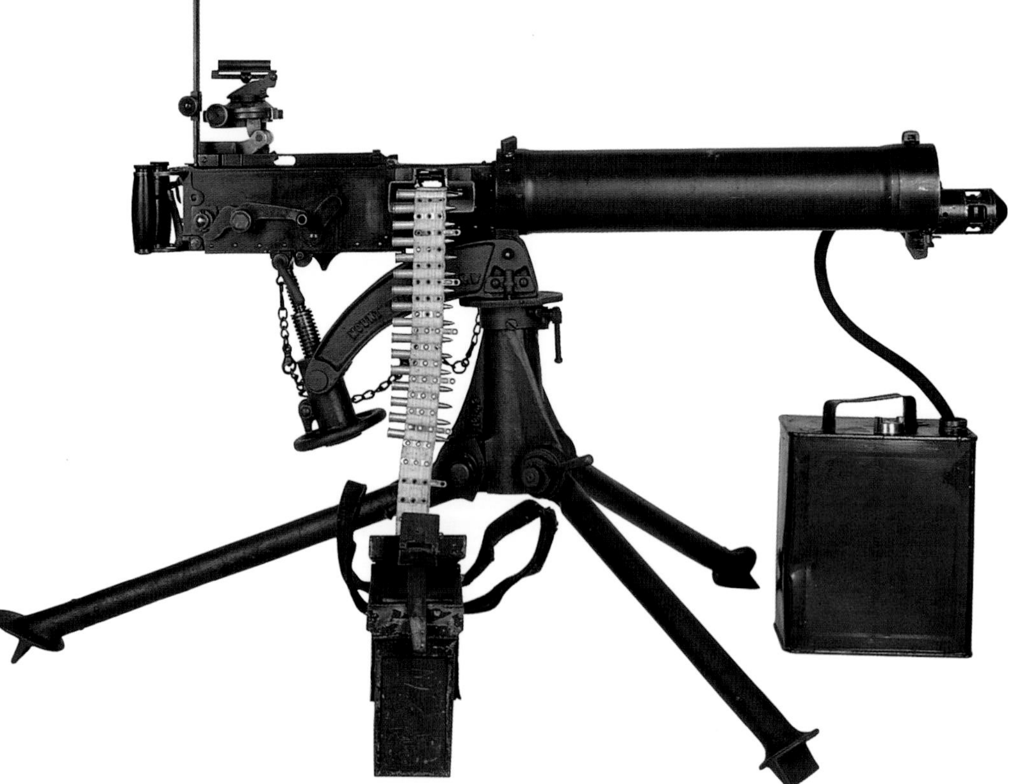

Length (gun): 43.0 in. (1,092 mm)
Barrel: 28.4 in. (722 mm)
Weight (gun): 33.0 lb. (15.0 kg)
Weight (tripod): 50.0 lb. (22.7 kg)
Caliber: 0.303 in.
Rifling: 4 grooves, r/hand
Operation: recoil
Feed: belt
Cooling: water
Cyclic rate: 500 rpm
Muz vel: 2,440 ft./sec. (744 m/sec.)
Range: 3,800 yd. (3,475 m)

Mechanically, the Vickers was similar to the Maxim. The rear impulse was produced by recoil supplemented by the action of a muzzle attachment, which deflected some of the gas. This thrust the lock backward, taking with it a round from the belt and extending the fusee spring situated in an elongated box on the left-hand side. The spring then forced the bolt forward and the cycle was repeated. The gun had a superb capacity for sustained fire but this led to problems of wear. A barrel would last for about 10,000 rounds at 200 rpm, after which the rifling was so worn that the bullet ceased to be spun effectively and lost accuracy. The barrel could be changed very quickly. The gun was water-cooled with a jacket capacity of about 7 pints (4 l). This began to boil after 3,000 rounds of steady fire, evaporating at the rate of 1 or 2 pints per 1,000 rounds depending on the rate of fire and the climatic conditions. The gun had a condenser tube leading into an old-fashioned 1-gallon petrol can, and if some water was put into the can first and the steam passed through it, a considerable amount of the water lost could be used again.

The Heavy Machine Gun in World War I

Above: *A British Vickers machine gun team lays down sustained fire while wearing elementary gas masks. Heavy machine guns were, when used in trench warfare, usually set in locked angles on their tripods to establish a lethal beaten zone extending several hundred yards out from the enemy trenches. The MG team simply had to maintain the flow of ammunition and prevent or deal with malfunctions.*

The battlefield tactics of World War I were among the most costly in military history. Although it is fashionable to berate its military leaders for murderous frontal-assault tactics, many of these leaders were struggling to adjust to new realities in weapons systems that had developed with lightning pace. The machine gun was one such weapon system.

During the initial months of the war, when infantry mobility was high, the distribution of heavy machine guns was limited; most battalions usually had two machine gun teams at their disposal. However, by 1915 the war had bogged down into static trench warfare, and the heavy machine gun found its seminal role: sustained defensive firepower from static positions.

The weapons of the time had several characteristics that made them ideal for this role. First, machine guns such as the Vickers and Maxim, being water-cooled, could maintain high rates of fire for prolonged periods with relatively low (compared to air-cooled weapons) numbers of barrel changes, and exhibited exemplary reliability. On the Somme in 1916, ten Vickers guns famously fired over one million rounds in twelve hours, some weapons averaging 10,000 rounds an hour. The second criteria for sustained fire was long range. Flat trajectory killing range from a .303 in. round was in excess of 3,280 ft. (1,000 m), and when fitted on an elevated mount, most World War I machine guns could kill at ranges of up to 8,200 ft. (2,500 m).

Despite the evident lethality of machine guns, it took a long time for military leaders to perceive their overriding significance. British Army commander General Douglas Haig, for example, described the machine gun as a "much overrated weapon," despite the fact that MGs created a significant portion of the 60,000 casualties on the first day of the Somme offensive in 1916. Indeed, the machine gun was second only to artillery in the rankings of most lethal weaponry in WW I. Its lethality was enhanced by intelligent defensive positioning. Along a static trench line, machine guns were set centrally and along the flanks to create interlocking cones of fire that were murderous to exposed infantry. Also, although heavy MGs were weighty weapons, they were still portable enough to be taken into underground bunkers during artillery bombardments, only to re-emerge to face attacking enemy troops when the bombardment lifted.

The counter-tactic of troops advancing just behind a rolling bombardment was intended to help reduce casualties, as the soldiers could attack before the enemy had a chance to emerge from their bunkers and establish their weapons. Yet the machine gun in World War I confirmed that the age of mechanical warfare had truly nullified the significance of individual warriors.

FRANCE

HOTCHKISS MODÈLE 1914

Length (gun): 51.6 in. (1,311 mm)
Barrel: 31.0 in. (787 mm)
Weight (gun): 55.7 lb. (25.3 kg)
Weight (tripod): 60.0 lb. (27.2 kg)
Caliber: 8 mm
Rifling: 4 grooves, r/hand
Operation: gas
Feed: strip
Cooling: air
Cyclic rate: 500 rpm
Muz vel: 2,325 ft./sec. (709 m/sec.)
Range: 2,625 yd. (2,400 m)

The breech end of the barrel of the Hotchkiss was encircled with five solid metal disks to increase the heat-radiating surface by more than ten times its original area. About 3.15 inches (80 mm) in diameter, these disks helped make the gun an extremely serviceable weapon. In the Russo-Japanese War (1904–05), the Russians used a water-cooled belt-fed Maxim and the Japanese used a Hotchkiss; both were capable of standing up to the demands of modern warfare. In 1914 the French Army found itself in serious difficulties over its relative lack of automatic weapons. Fortunately, the reliable Hotchkiss was readily available and manufacture soon started in huge quantities. The earliest models went to reserve units. The regular Army was then largely equipped with the Saint-Etienne 07, but once the Hotchkiss guns began to appear in large numbers, they quickly demonstrated their superiority and the French Army clamored for more of them. In 1916 two Hotchkiss guns remained in almost continuous action for ten days, during which time they fired the astonishing total of more than 150,000 rounds without anything worse than brief and easily cleared stoppages. When the US Army arrived in France in 1918, twelve of its divisions were therefore equipped with the Modèle 1914 Hotchkiss.

UNITED STATES

BROWNING MODEL 1917

Length (gun): 38.5 in. (978 mm)
Barrel: 24.0 in. (610 mm)
Weight (gun): 32.6 lb. (15.0 kg)
Weight (tripod): 53.0 lb. (24.0 kg)
Caliber: 0.30 in.
Rifling: 4 grooves, r/hand
Operation: recoil
Feed: belt
Cooling: water
Cyclic rate: 5/600 rpm
Muz vel: 2,800 ft./sec. (855 m/sec.)
Range: 2,800 yd. (2,560 m)

When the trigger was pressed (the first round was loaded manually with a cocking handle duplicating the action of the recoil) and the round fired, the barrel and breechblock recoiled together, for just over half an inch, until pressure had dropped to a safe level. The barrel and breechblock then unlocked, the barrel stopped, and the block continued backward under its initial power. The empty case was extracted from the breech and ejected, and a fresh cartridge was drawn from the belt. When this backward phase was complete, the return spring drove the working parts forward again, chambering the cartridge, locking the block to the barrel, and firing the round. This cycle continued as long as the trigger was pressed and there were rounds in the belt. The Browning was made in considerable variety, including air-cooled models for use in tanks and aircraft. The final modification before the outbreak of World War II resulted in the Model 1917A1 (lower photos: ground-mounted left, and anti-aircraft mount right), introduced in 1936. World War II was the first real combat test of the Browning since its introduction. It also saw much service in Korea.

MACHINE GUN AMMUNITION

Left: *A two-man machine gun team prepares to fire a Browning .50-caliber M2HB machine gun. The M2HB is usually fed from a 110-round metal-link belt; ammunition types include standard ball rounds, tracer, incendiary, armor-piercing (AP), armor-piercing incendiary (API), armor-piercing incendiary tracer (API-T), saboted light armor-piercing (SLAP), and saboted light armor-piercing tracer (SLAP-T).*

A belt of machine gun ammunition rarely contains one single type of round. Typically the belt will contain standard ball ammunition interspersed every four or five cartridges with a tracer round. Typical ball ammunition is usually a composite structure, such as a lead antimony center and a copper alloy or copper-coated steel jacket. The jacket protects the round from corrosion and reduces deposits in the rifling. There are numerous variations, however, and modern machine gun rounds often contain a steel core to increase penetration.

Much of the targeting of machine guns comes not from sighting but from observing the impact of the rounds and "walking" the bullets onto the target. As a typical 7.62 mm machine gun will fire out to ranges beyond observed impact; tracers provide directional guidance.

Tracers work through a tracer compound that occupies roughly half the length of the round and burns in flight. The operator must use caution when basing his aim point on tracer fall. Tracers have their weight concentrated at the tip (the metal tip is heavier than the compound), which increases their instability, especially as the round loses mass as the tracer compound is burned during flight.

The instability of tracer rounds, particularly over long ranges, means that they will not necessarily follow the same flight as the ball rounds, and the operator may have to aim higher than the fall of the tracers to achieve his target. Modern armies tend to mix dark trace with bright rounds in the belt (some dark trace rounds are only visible through IR scopes), as using only bright trace rounds will of course make it easier for the enemy to target the firer.

As well as ball and tracer rounds, there are a variety of specialist ammunition types fired from machine guns. Armor-piercing rounds usually feature a hardened steel or, more rarely, tungsten core. The metal jacket around the core strips off on impact to leave the core to penetrate the target further. Armor-piercing rounds may also contain an incendiary filler material to define the point of impact and cause fires, and pure incendiary ammunition is available for larger machine guns such as the Browning M2HB. A more expensive armor-piercing type is the discarding sabot variety. This provides excellent penetration through using a subcaliber projectile encased in a sabot, which is jettisoned after the bullet leaves the muzzle. Ammunition types can also be blended, such as the armor-piercing incendiary tracer type.

JAPAN

TAISHO 14 (TYPE 3), TYPE 92 (LEWIS COPY), AND AIR-COOLED TYPE (1941)

This weapon, also known as the Type 3 (right), was based closely on the French Hotchkiss but used the Japanese 6.5 mm round, a poor round of only moderate power and not well adapted to machine guns because the relative lack of taper of its case caused problems of extraction. The Japanese also had difficulties in adjusting their head space, that is, the distance between the base of the round and the face of the bolt. This is very important because if it is too small, the breech will not always close; if it is too great, the cartridge blows back unsupported and is likely to rupture. The Japanese solved the problem by oiling each round as it was fed into the chamber. This allowed the round to slip back easily and be supported by the face of the bolt before the pressure reached its maximum. In view of the propensity of the earlier Hotchkiss to overheat, the Japanese increased the number of cooling rings so that they extended along the full length of the barrel. Mobility was an important feature in Japanese tactics, so the tripod legs had sockets on them into which carrying handles could be inserted.

In 1932 the gun was modified to take the more powerful 7.7 mm cartridge, but apart from the barrel and the breech, it is almost identical to the earlier version; the chief difference is the removal of the old spade grips in favor of a double-pistol type. The new version still incorporated a cartridge oiler. Known as the Type 92 (center right), it was Japan's standard medium machine gun of World War II. It fired a rather heavy thirty-round strip, and due presumably to the inertia of this dead weight, the gun fired its first few rounds hesitantly before picking up speed. It was a characteristic sound that made the presence of the gun easily identified in action. The photo at left shows the Type 92 (Aircraft), a 1932 copy of the Lewis gun (qv) in 7.7 mm caliber, shown in anti-aircraft configuration with its 47-round drum magazine in position and a spare drum beneath the weapon. At the bottom right is an air-cooled Type (1941), also of 7.7 mm caliber, with spade grips and flash suppressor. Above the barrel are stripper ammunition clips of 7.7 mm in their original cardboard packing boxes.

Length (gun): 45.5 in. (1,155 mm)
Barrel: 29.0 in. (737 mm)
Weight (gun): 62.0 lb. (28.1 kg)
Weight (tripod): 60.0 lb. (27.3 kg)
Caliber: 6.5 mm
Rifling: 4 grooves, r/hand
Operation: gas
Feed: 30-round strip
Cooling: air
Cyclic rate: 450 rpm
Muz vel: 2,400 ft./sec. (732 m/sec.)
Range: 2,406 yd. (2,200 m)

UNITED STATES

BROWNING 0.50 IN. CALIBER M2HB 1933

Length (gun): 65.0 in. (1,651 mm)
Barrel: 45.0 in. (1,143 mm)
Weight (gun): 84.0 lb. (38.1 kg)
Weight (tripod): 44.0 lb. (19.09 kg)
Caliber: 0.50 in.
Rifling: 8 grooves, r/hand
Operation: recoil
Feed: belt
Cooling: air
Cyclic rate: 500 rpm
Muz vel: 2,930 ft./sec. (894 m/sec.)
Range: 2,600 yd. (2,378 m)

John Browning's M2 was intended principally for use on multiple anti-aircraft mounts, but there was a version for a tank turret and one on a ground mount. It worked on the usual Browning system of short recoil. When the cartridge was fired, the barrel and breechblock, which were locked together, recoiled for just under an inch when the barrel was stopped by an oil buffer. At this stage the pressure dropped sufficiently for the breechblock to unlock and continue to the rear under the power given to it by the barrel, extracting and ejecting the empty case and extracting the next live round from the belt. The compressed return spring drove the working parts forward, chambering the round, locking the breechblock, and firing the cartridge. The gun would fire automatic only, although some were equipped with bolt latches to allow single rounds to be fired. After seventy or eighty rounds had been fired continuously, it was necessary to pause to allow the barrel to cool. A heavy-barreled version (M2HB) was then adopted. The extra metal in the barrel made a considerable difference, and this new gun was most effective; it was extensively used in World War II and all subsequent campaigns up to the present day. This is a Belgian FN version with quick-change barrel.

GERMANY

MACHINENGEWEHR MG34 1934

Length (gun): 48.0 in. (1,220 mm)
Barrel: 24.8 in. (628 mm)
Weight (gun): 26.7 lb. (12.1 kg)
Weight (tripod): 42.3 lb. (19.2 kg)
Caliber: 7.92 mm
Rifling: 4 grooves, r/hand
Operation: short-recoil
Feed: belt or saddle-drum
Cooling: air
Cyclic rate: 8/900 rpm
Muz vel: 2,480 ft./sec. (75 6m/sec.)
Range: 2,188 yd. (2,000 m)

The MG34 was designed by Louis Stange, who worked for Rheinmetall. It was the first truly modern machine gun the German Army received. The weapon worked by the unusual combination of recoil and gas; when the round was fired, the barrel recoiled and additional thrust was given to this by some of the gases, which were trapped in a muzzle cone and deflected backward. The recoil of the barrel was short, just enough for the bolt-head to be rotated through 90 degrees and unlocked when the pressure was low enough for this to happen safely. This rearward movement of the bolt continued after the barrel had stopped moving, until the return spring was fully compressed, when the forward action started. The bolt then fed the next cartridge from the belt into the chamber, locked itself, and fired the round. This gun had many excellent features including a quick means of changing the barrel, easy stripping, and the use of high-impact plastics. It had no change lever, which was unusual. There was simply a two-part trigger that fired single rounds or automatic according to whether the upper or lower part was pressed. The MG34 would fire either a belt, sometimes coiled inside a drum for transport, or a double-saddle drum. The upper photo shows the bipod folded.

MACHINE GUN COOLING SYSTEMS

Left: *The Vickers machine gun relied on water-cooling; the barrel was surrounded by a water jacket into which water was pumped and circulated as a barrel coolant. Water-cooling is highly efficient for sustained-fire weapons, although the resulting bulkiness inevitably meant it fell out of favor with post-World War II military forces.*

Firing a machine gun results in tremendous heat buildup in the barrel and chamber that, if not controlled, can result in serious malfunction. Running an entire 200-round belt through a 7.62 mm weapon will result in extreme barrel heat, the interior of the barrel momentarily reaching temperatures of around 1,832°F (1,000°C), heat that is conducted through the barrel metal and into the breech. The outer surface of the barrel will be between 212°F and 752°F (100°–400°C) cooler than the inner surface of the barrel. The problem is that the heat rise far outstrips the heat loss through radiation into the atmosphere. A GPMG breech can reach a temperature of 1,112°F (600°C), and rounds cooking off (fired by heat alone) become a dangerous reality.

There are several methods of controlling heat buildup in machine guns, some down to the design of the weapon, others down to operator technique. The earliest true machine guns, such as the Maxim and Vickers, surrounded the barrel in a water jacket, the water conducting heat quickly out of the barrel. Although the Vickers was to serve through the 1940s, the water-jacket arrangement was not satisfactory owing to the excessive weight. (Some modern gun designers are, however, reconsidering water-cooling for chain guns aboard armored vehicles, where the weight is not so disadvantageous.)

For the majority of machine guns, which do not have water jackets, air-cooling and increasing the barrel dimensions are the primary methods of heat control. Some World War II machine guns such as the Hotchkiss had metal fins along the length of the barrel to maximize the surface area exposed to heat exchange with the air, yet this system had little to recommend it in terms of heat-loss efficiency.

Most machine guns follow the simple expedient of having thick barrels, with the barrel acting as a heat sink. For example, a 5.56 mm machine gun with a 4.2-lb. (1.9 kg) barrel will reach 752°F (400°C) in eight minutes, whereas a gun with a 7.3-lb. (3.3 kg) barrel will reach only 572°F (300°C) in the same time.

Most modern field machine guns also have changeable barrels. As a general rule, the operator should change the barrel every 400 rounds. The operator should try to control heat buildup anyway by firing the weapon in short five- to 10-round bursts, periodically opening the top cover and cocking the bolt back to allow the gun mechanism to cool down; easy to recommend, hard to follow in battle.

AVIATION MACHINE GUNS

At the beginning of World War I, in 1914, military aircraft were unarmed; their main roles were reconnaissance and artillery spotting. Yet it steadily became more critical to interdict enemy aircraft, and this led the British to mount Lewis guns on the nose of its "pusher" (the propeller was rear-mounted) Vickers FB5 biplanes. For aircraft with front propellers, machine guns were usually fitted atop the wing, while two-seater aircraft often had a machine gun set on a revolving mount around the secondary cockpit. The Germans also followed suit, fitting their aircraft with either 0.311 in. Parabellum weapons or Gast guns.

As front-mounted propellers became almost standard for performance reasons, a more satisfactory arrangement had to be found for allowing the pilot to take a direct aim. In 1915 Fokker designed an interrupter gear for a Spandau machine gun; a rod linkage between the propeller and the machine gun ensured that the weapon only fired when a propeller blade was not in its way. The interrupter gear gave birth to the true aerial fighter, turning planes into flying guns. Soon every combatant nation had versions of the interrupter gear fitted to their aircraft, the British developing the Constantinesco hydraulic synchronizer to fire two belt-fed Vickers through the propeller.

Since World War I, aircraft-mounted machine guns have followed an interesting evolution. In World War II, both bombers and fighters were laden with heavy weaponry, the former mounting machine guns through fuselage gun ports or mounted in dedicated cupolas (often electrically powered); the latter relocating more firepower in the wings, the weapons arranged to direct their fire at a fixed point usually around 820 ft. (250 m) in front of the aircraft. Putting guns in the wings allowed rates of fire unmoderated by an interrupter gear. The British Spitfire was armed with eight Browning .303 in. machine guns putting out a total rate of fire of 9,600 rpm. World War II fighters also upgraded firepower to mix cannon with machine guns, cannon providing a much more efficient killing force than a stream of ball rounds and making the aircraft ideal for ground-attack roles against vehicles.

In the decades after World War II, however, the aerial gun steadily lost out to air-to-air missiles. An F4 Phantom in the early days of the Vietnam War was armed with nothing more than Sparrow or Sidewinder air-to-air missiles. Yet combat aviators soon complained of this lack, finding themselves in deep trouble in a dogfight when missiles were depleted. Subsequent F4s received a 20 mm cannon in an external pod, and since then almost all combat aircraft have been fitted with a cannon as an auxiliary weapon and a sure dogfight tool. Modern rotary-barreled aircraft cannon such as the Soviet GSh-6-23 and the US M61 Vulcan have phenomenally high rates of fire, the Soviet weapon boasting 12,000 rpm.

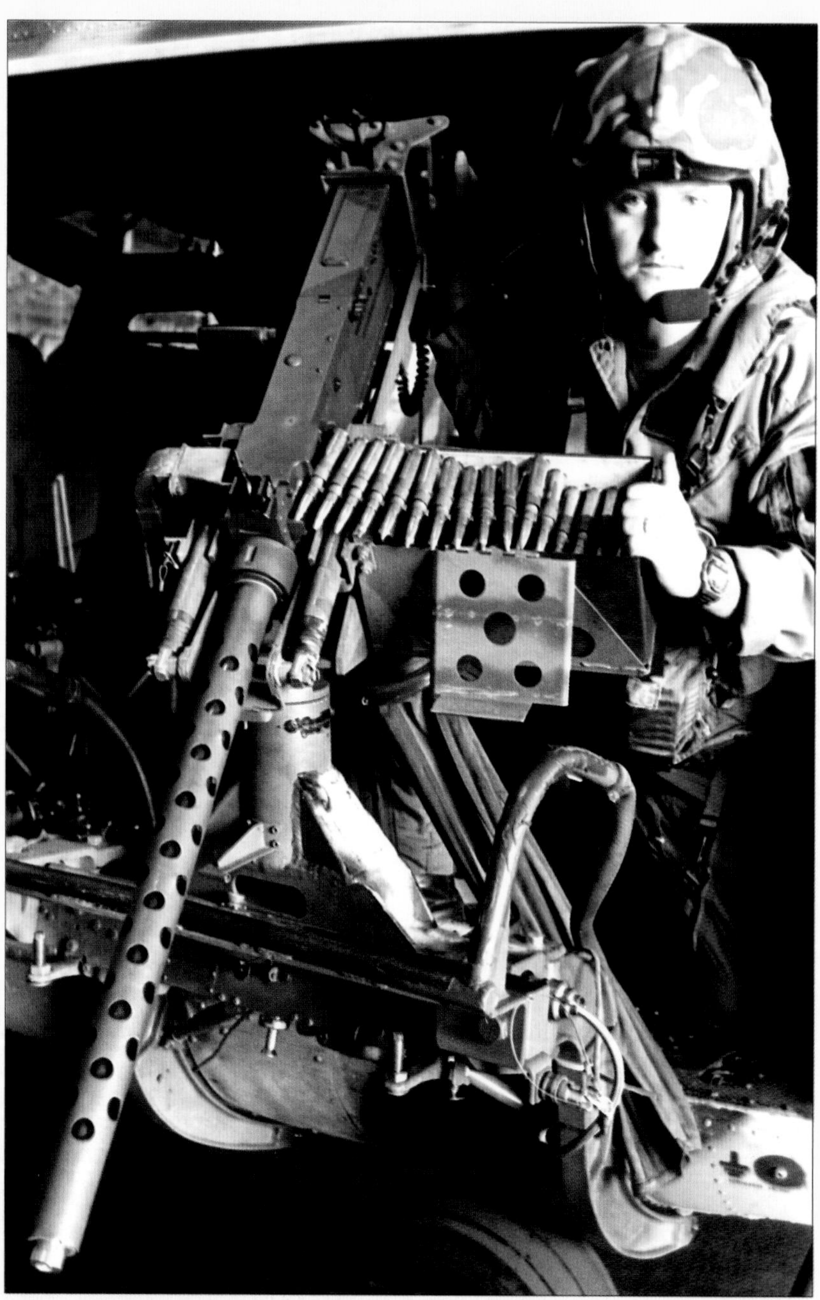

Above: *A US helicopter door gunner with a .50-caliber machine gun. The .50-caliber round has been used in many aircraft-mounted weapons systems, as it has a substantial destructive force against human and material targets and a range in excess of 4,900 ft. (1,500 m). It was, of course, in Vietnam that the concept of air mobility warfare was first put to the test.*

UNITED KINGDOM

BESA 1936

Length (gun): 43.5 in. (1,105 mm)
Barrel: 26.7 in. (679 mm)
Weight (gun): 41.8 lb. (19.0 kg)
Weight (tripod): 38.5 lb. (16.1 kg)
Caliber: 7.92 mm
Rifling: 4 grooves, r/hand
Operation: gas
Feed: belt
Cooling: air
Cyclic rate: 500 or 700 rpm
Muz vel: 2,600 ft./sec. (793 m/sec.)
Range: 2,500 yd. (2,287 m)

The Czech-designed ZB 53 was gas-operated, but the barrel also moved back under the force of the recoil, timed so that the cartridge was fed into the chamber and fired as the barrel went forward. The backward force had to arrest, then reverse, the forward movement, which had the effect of diminishing the next recoil considerably, reducing the general stresses on the weapon. The guns had very heavy barrels, some finned, which allowed sustained fire; the earlier models could vary their cyclic rate from 450 to 850 rpm. The gun was so reliable that in 1937 there was a possibility that it would replace the Vickers in the ground role. Unfortunately, it fired the 7.92 mm rimless round and could not be modified to handle the rimmed 0.303 in. cartridge. This is probably one of the prototypes sent to England for testing. In 1936, BSA arranged with ZB to manufacture the No. 53 gun under the name "Besa," from the initial letters of Brno and Enfield and the last two of BSA. There was a larger 0.59-in.-caliber (15 mm) version.

ITALY

BREDA MODELLO 37 1937

Length (gun): 50.0 in. (1,270 mm)
Barrel: 25.0 in. (635 mm)
Weight (gun): 42.9 lb. (19.9 kg)
Weight (tripod): 41.5 lb. (18.8 kg)
Caliber: 8 mm
Rifling: 4 grooves, r/hand
Operation: gas
Feed: strip
Cooling: air
Cyclic rate: 450 rpm
Muz vel: 2,600 ft./sec. (793 m/sec.)
Range: 3,280 yd. (3,000 m)

In 1931 Breda produced a 13.2 mm caliber gun that it then scaled down to fire the 8 mm Modello 35 cartridge. The simple mechanism used a piston worked by gases tapped off the bore. The piston activated the breechblock, which was locked in the firing position by a ramp acting on the piston that lifted the end of the block into a recess on the top of the body. The gun fired automatic only; the cyclic rate was controlled with a gas regulator through which the gases passed on their way to the interchangeable piston head. The need to keep the gas port correctly aligned with the gas regulator made it impossible to alter the headspace, which was therefore larger than necessary. This gave rise to the risk of ruptured cases, due to the lack of support by the breechblock. Breda overcame this by oiling each case as it entered the chamber, allowing the case to "float" and set back firmly against the block before the pressure got too high. Breda may have gotten the idea from the Schwarzlose, which it had received after World War I. The gun was air-cooled, its heavy barrel of 9.7 lb. (4.4 kg) allowing sustained fire.

RUSSIA

DEGTYAREV DSHK-38 12.7 MM 1939

Length (gun): 62.3 in. (1,582 mm)
Barrel: 39.4 in. (1,000 m)
Weight (gun): 73.3 lb. (33.33 kg)
Weight (tripod): n.k.
Caliber: 12.7 mm
Rifling: 8 grooves, r/hand
Operation: gas
Feed: belt
Cooling: air
Cyclic rate: 575 rpm
Muz vel: 2,805 ft./sec. (855 m/sec.)
Max range: n.k.

The Degtyarev-Shpagin DShK-38 was used in vast numbers during World War II and has remained in widespread use ever since. The trail legs could be opened out to form a tall tripod for the anti-aircraft role. A modified version, the DShK-38/46 (left, also known as DShK-M), appeared after the war and incorporated several minor improvements. The original rotary-ammunition feed system was replaced with a much simpler and more reliable lever system. The DShK-38/46 was widely used for air defense in armored fighting vehicles, particularly tanks from the T-54 to the T-72. In the earlier turreted installations, the commander had to expose his head and upper torso to fire, but later tanks featured a full remote-control facility. The DShK-M was supplied to most pro-Soviet armies during the Cold War. The DShK-M was widely used by North Vietnamese and Viet Cong forces.

RECOIL OPERATION

Recoil operation is one of the most commonly used operating systems for machine guns, utilizing but moderating the great forces of recoil generated by the powerful MG rounds. In its essence, recoil operation is simple. In a recoil-operated weapon, the barrel and bolt are securely locked together for firing, and unlike in other weapons, the barrel has a freedom of movement within the gun body. The recoil force generated on firing pushes the breech rearward, taking the barrel with it. At a designated point, the barrel and bolt are unlocked and separate to allow ejection and reloading to take place.

Recoil operation separates into two basic types: long recoil and short recoil. In long-recoil weapons, the locked barrel and breechblock recoil for a distance greater than the length of an unfired round. At the end of the travel—the point at which loss of energy and the compression of the return spring bring the block to a standstill—the barrel detaches and rides forward. The breechblock follows shortly afterward, but the gap between the two allows the ejection of the empty cartridge and the reloading of a new round.

Long-recoil is seldom used today except in the case of large cannon fitted to armored vehicles, such as the 30 mm Rarden. Because of the extended distance, the barrel and breech must recoil before any operations such as extraction, ejection, and feed can be performed, as long-recoil produces slow rates of fire. Also, long-recoil weapons are expensive to produce, requiring bearings for the barrel movement and buffer systems to control the movement of both breechblock and barrel.

Short-recoil is the preferred recoil system for machine guns. In short-recoil the barrel and breechblock separate after only a short distance, much less than the length of the unfired round, when the pressure has dropped to safe levels. The breechblock continues rearward, often aided by an accelerator lever, with blowback from the cartridge also providing impetus. The breechblock goes back far enough to create space from the barrel for extraction and ejection to occur. The compressed return spring halts the breechblock, then drives it forward to enable reloading. Short-recoil is a very fast process, and therefore ideal for machine guns requiring rapid rates of fire.

Above: *During the interwar years the German Army decided against following the usual light/heavy machine gun division and introduced the radical concept of the general purpose machine gun (GPMG). The result was the MG34 and its easier-to-manufacture sibling, the superb MG42 (above). Its roller-delayed recoil-operation system of firing permitted an awesome 1,550 rpm. Its distinctive firing sound of ripping canvas was horribly recognizable to Allied troops in World War II.*

RUSSIA

GORYUNOV SGM 1943

Length (gun): 44.1 in. (1,120 mm)
Barrel: 28.3 in. (719 mm)
Weight (gun): 29.8 lb. (13.5 kg)
Weight (mount): 50.9 lb. (23.1 kg)
Caliber: 7.72 mm
Rifling: 4 grooves, r/hand
Operation: gas
Feed: belt
Cooling: air
Cyclic rate: 650rpm
Muz vel: 2,700 ft./sec. (823 m/sec.)
Range: 2,187 yd. (2,000 m)

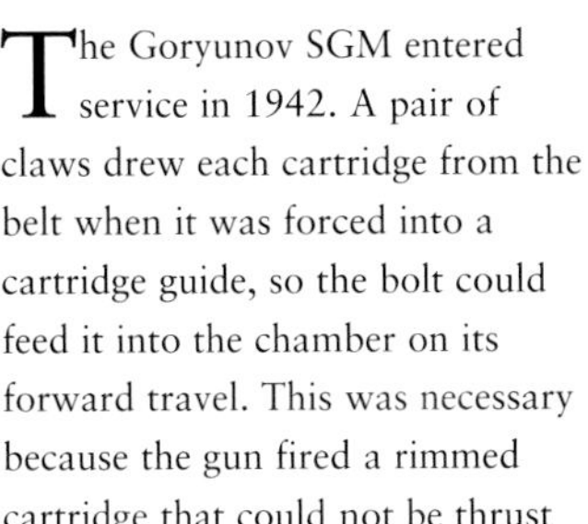

The Goryunov SGM entered service in 1942. A pair of claws drew each cartridge from the belt when it was forced into a cartridge guide, so the bolt could feed it into the chamber on its forward travel. This was necessary because the gun fired a rimmed cartridge that could not be thrust straight forward from the belt. As the bolt approached its forward position, a cam forced it slightly to the right, where it engaged a recess in the body and was locked before the round was fired. This meant that the face of the bolt had to be recessed at an angle so that it gave proper support to the base of the cartridge. Cooling was achieved with a very heavy barrel with a chromed bore. It could be changed very quickly and therefore allowed the gun to fire almost continuously for long periods without undue overheating. Although a number had been made by 1945, the old Maxim remained in service until the end of the war. The gun illustrated is the modernized version of the Goryunov and has some mechanical improvements; its chief distinguishing feature is the distinctive longitudinal flanging of the barrel to assist with cooling.

GERMANY

KPV 14.5 MM 1944

Length (gun): 79.0 in. (2,006 mm)
Barrel: 53.0 in. (1,346 mm)
Weight (gun): 108.2 lb. (49.1 kg)
Caliber: 14.5 mm
Rifling: 4 grooves, r/hand
Operation: recoil
Feed: metal-link belt
Cooling: air
Cyclic rate: 600 rpm
Muz vel: 3,280 ft./sec. (1,000 m/sec.)
Max range: 8,750 yd. (8,000 m)

One of the largest-caliber true machine guns ever to enter service, the 14.5 mm KPV, was designed by Vladimirov. The KPV was the only weapon to use the 14.5 x 114 mm Soviet round. The weapon was recoil-operated, with a rotating bolt and an air-cooled, quick-change barrel mounted in a perforated jacket. The mechanism was very simple, with no adjustments for the headspace or timing. The KPV was used in two principle modes: as a trailer-mounted anti-aircraft weapon, and as a tank-, armored-personnel-carrier-, or armored-car-mounted, dual-purpose (i.e., antiground/anti-air) weapon. The ground version was mounted on a two-wheeled chassis with either one (ZPU-1) or two (ZPU-2) guns, or on a four-wheeled chassis with a quadruple gun installation (ZPU-4). The latter was widely considered to be an effective weapon system, since the 14.5 mm round had a much heavier "punch" than smaller caliber weapons; it was much easier to hide than heavier systems, such as the tracked ZSU-23-4, and the quad installation had a very high rate of fire. The ZU-series was widely used by the North Vietnamese and Viet Cong. A new version of this weapon was later developed in Poland. Designated the Pirat, this comprises KPVT, normally used as a coaxial machine gun in tanks, and is mounted on a newly developed tripod.

UNITED STATES

M134 MINIGUN 1965

Length (gun): 31.5 in. (800 mm)
Barrels: 22 in. (559 mm)
Weight: (gun): 35 lb. (15.9 kg)
Caliber: 7.62 x 51 mm NATO
Rifling: 4 grooves, r/hand
Operation: rotary, electric
Feed: 4,000-round belt
Cooling: air
Cyclic rate: 6,000 rpm
Muz vel: 2,850 ft./sec. (869 m/sec.)
Range: 2,186 yd. (2,000 m)

During the Vietnam War, the US Army sought a weapon to mount on helicopters to give them a powerful ground-attack capability. The solution was the General Electric M134 Minigun, a 7.62 mm rotary-barrel Gatling-type weapon based on the 20 mm Vulcan cannon. With the weapon powered by an electric motor, the Minigun could achieve rates of fire of up to 6,000 rpm, although in many cases the firepower was moderated to more in the region of 2,000–4,000 rpm. The M134 featured six barrels, with a six-bolt rotating unit positioned behind them. As the weapon was rotated, ammunition from a 4,000-round link belt was fed into the action, and each round was fed into a chamber and locked into place by a bolt. When the round reached the top of the weapon's revolution, the firing pin was released to fire the weapon. The barrels themselves could be angled inward from their outmost parallel position to provide converging fire. In Vietnam, the M134s were usually mounted either in the side door of helicopters such as the Bell UH-1, or alternatively in fixed M18 gun pods on gunships such as the AH-1 Cobra.

RUSSIA

NSV 12.7 MM 1971

Length (gun): 61.4 in. (1,560 mm)
Barrel: 44.5 in. (1,130 mm)
Weight (gun): 55.1 lb. (25.0 kg)
Weight (tripod): 35.3 lb. (16.0 kg)
Caliber: 12.7mm
Rifling: 8 grooves, r/hand
Operation: gas
Feed: belt
Cooling: air
Cyclic rate: 750 rpm
Muz vel: 2,772 ft./sec. (845 m/sec.)
Max range: 7,655 yd. (7,000 m)

The NSV used the standard 12.7 x 108 mm Russian round and entered service around 1971. It was basically a scaled-up version of the PKM light machine gun, using the Kalashnikov action, which resulted in a smaller and much lighter weapon than previous 12.7 mm weapons that was also more reliable. As with other Russian heavy machine guns, it was employed either as a ground weapon, mounted on a tripod, or as a pintle-mounted air defense weapon on tank turrets. It was a gas-operated weapon, using a three-piece bolt with locking lugs, plus a quick-change, air-cooled barrel fitted with a carrying handle and a flash hider. The weapon was fitted with either a twin spade grip or a hollow butt. It was manufactured in Russia, and also under license in Bulgaria, Poland, and Yugoslavia.

BELGIUM

FN BRG-15 1983

Length (gun): 83.85 in. (2,150 mm)
Barrel: n.k.
Weight: (gun): 88 lb. (40 kg)
Weight (tripod): 44 lb. (20 kg)
Caliber: 15.5 mm
Rifling: n.k.
Operation: gas
Feed: dual-belt
Cooling: air
Cyclic rate: 600 rpm
Muz vel: 3,460 ft./sec. (1,055 m/sec.)
Range: 2,623 yd. (2,400 m)

The FN BRG 15 is a particularly heavy-caliber machine gun, firing the 15.5 x 106 mm BRG round. When it was introduced in 1983, the BRG-15 was intended as a replacement for the Browning M2HB, although this has not occurred and testing is still underway. Unlike the Browning weapon, the BRG 15 is a gas-operated weapon using a rotating-bolt configuration and has a quick-change barrel (improved barrel change over the M2HB was a major reason behind the development of the BRG 15). However, early tests discovered that the barrel wore out too quickly under sustained fire, so the ammunition was changed to include a plastic driving band that took the caliber from 15 mm to 15.5 mm. An interesting feature of the BRG 15 is the ammunition feed: a dual-feed system allows double-belt feed, one belt entering from each side of the weapon. The operator uses a selector switch to select which belt is fired, allowing mixtures of ammunition types, e.g., standard ball/tracer and ball/armor-piercing.

CHINA (PRC)

NORINCO 12.7 MM TYPE 85 1985

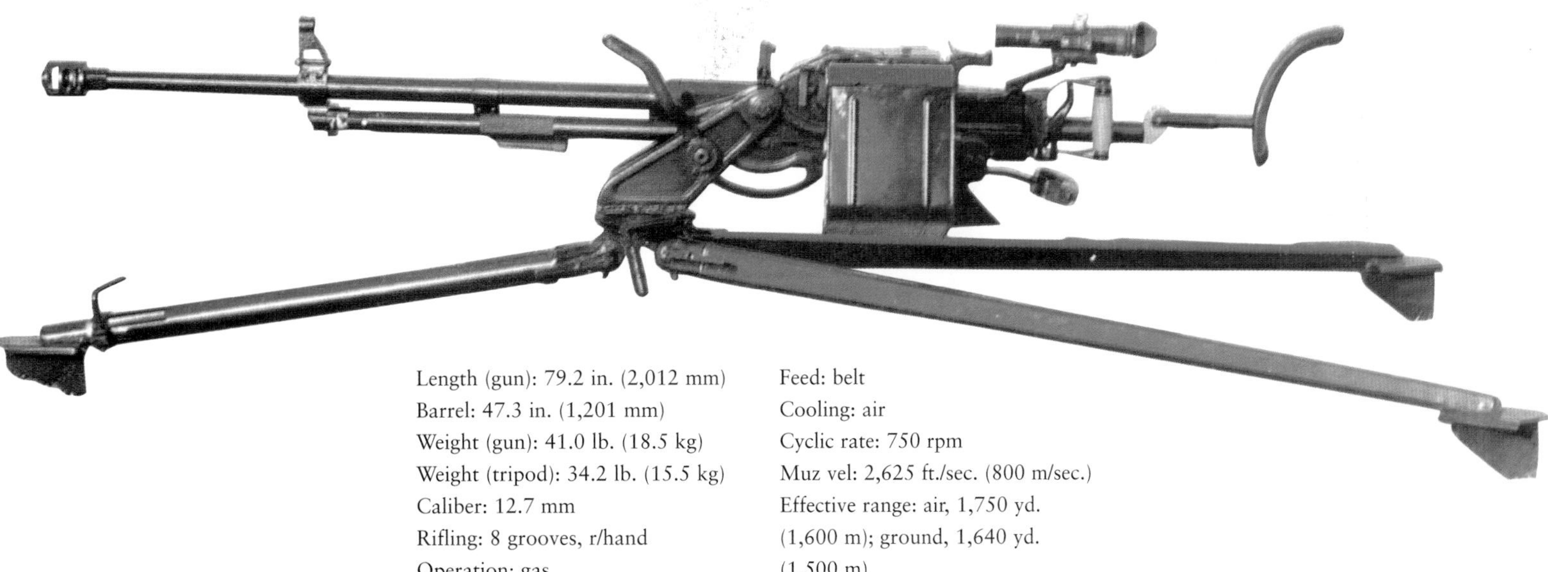

Length (gun): 79.2 in. (2,012 mm)
Barrel: 47.3 in. (1,201 mm)
Weight (gun): 41.0 lb. (18.5 kg)
Weight (tripod): 34.2 lb. (15.5 kg)
Caliber: 12.7 mm
Rifling: 8 grooves, r/hand
Operation: gas
Feed: belt
Cooling: air
Cyclic rate: 750 rpm
Muz vel: 2,625 ft./sec. (800 m/sec.)
Effective range: air, 1,750 yd. (1,600 m); ground, 1,640 yd. (1,500 m)

The Type 54 was a direct copy of the Russian DShk (qv) produced under license. Two more recent heavy machine guns are, however, Chinese designs. The first was the 12.7 mm Type 77, which used an unusual direct-action gas tube, similar in concept to that used in the M16 rifle; this weapon delivered the gas through a tube under the barrel to the forward face of the bolt carrier, thus driving it to the rear. The more recent weapon is the 12.7 mm Type 85, seen here, which is very light; the bare gun weighs only 41 lb. (18.5 kg). The Type 85 uses a new design of tripod that enables the weapon to be used either as an anti-aircraft weapon or in the ground role, and in the latter case it has an especially low profile. All Chinese 12.7 mm machine guns fire the NORINCO Type 54 ammunition, which is available in a variety of types, including armor-piercing discarding sabot (APDS) with tungsten-carbide core for use against lightly armored vehicles such as armored personnel carriers. The Type 85 is belt-fed with the ammunition carried in a metal box on the left side of the weapon. An optical sight is mounted above the spade grips.

UNITED STATES

HUGHES CHAIN GUN 1985

Length (gun): 35 in. (889 mm)
Barrel: 22 in. (558 mm)
Weight: (gun): 29 lb. (13.16 kg)
Caliber: 7.62 x 51 mm NATO
Rifling: 4 grooves, r/hand
Operation: chain, electric
Feed: belt
Cooling: air
Cyclic rate: 100–600 rpm
Muz vel: 2,850 ft./sec. (870 m/sec.)
Range: 2,186 yd. (2,000 m)

The Hughes Chain Gun was designed specifically for use from armored vehicles, and uses an externally powered chain drive to perform all stages of the weapon's operation. The gun is driven by an endless-loop chain, the chain featuring a link which drives the bolt forward, holds it in place for firing (the bolt head is rotated by cams for locking), then retracts the bolt to perform extraction. The Chain Gun has several important advantages for use in armored vehicles. First, the dwell time from firing to unlock is comparatively long at 13 milliseconds, this giving more time for the propellant gases to exit into the atmosphere rather than return to the interior of the vehicle. Also, the Chain Gun uses an ingenious forward ejection system. Here the spent cases are ejected forward up a tube and are thrown around 20 m, this preventing the troublesome build-up of cases on the floor of the armored vehicle. The Chain Gun rate of fire can be easily varied by altering the voltage of the electrical current running to the chain drive, the rpm varying from literally one round to 600 rpm.

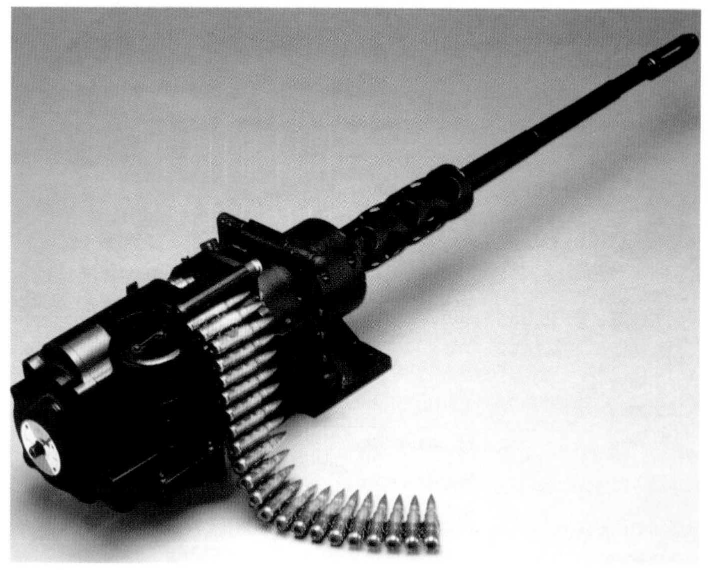

SINGAPORE

CIS 0.50 IN. 1988

Length (gun): 66.0 in. (1,676 mm)
Barrel: 45.0 in. (1,143 mm)
Weight (gun): 66.2 lb. (30.0 kg)
Weight (tripod): 51.0 lb. (23.0 kg)
Caliber: 0.50 in. (12.7 mm)
Rifling: 8 grooves, r/hand
Operation: gas
Feed: belt
Cooling: air
Cyclic rate: 600 rpm
Muz vel: 2,920 ft./sec. (890 m/sec.)
Maximum range: 7,440 yd. (6,800 m)

The State of Singapore developed an efficient and internationally respected weapons industry from scratch in a little more than a couple of decades. In the early 1980s, Singaporean market research identified a continuing requirement for a heavy machine gun and established that, despite its many merits, the US Browning M2 (HB) suffers from some longstanding limitations, including complexity and heavy production costs. The Singaporeans set out to do better—and succeeded. The Chartered Industries of Singapore (CIS) 0.50 in. MG is simple in design and consists of just 210 separate components in five assemblies: receiver body, feed mechanism, trigger module, barrel group, and bolt-carrier group. The weapon has a rotating bolt and the ammunition-feed system uses disintegrating belts that can be fed in from either side. The 0.50 in. MG fires normal Browning 12.7 x 99 mm ammunition, but can also fire the Saboted Light Armor Penetrating (SLAP) round, which was specially developed by CIS.

ROTARY-BARREL WEAPONS

Above: *The GAU-8 Avenger Gatling gun is a 30 mm seven-barrel rotary cannon, chiefly known as the principal weapon of the tank-busting A-10 Thunderbolt ground-attack aircraft. In total the cannon weighs 618 lb. (281 kg), and with the ammunition feed and motor in place (not shown here) the weapon is the size of an average family car.*

Rotary-barrel machine guns were among the earliest examples of machine-gun technology, most famously represented by the Gatling weapons. The Gatling system was a revolutionary way of overcoming the excessive barrel heating that would result from firing multiple rounds from one standard barrel; by having six barrels the heat buildup was distributed among the barrels while maintaining a high rate of fire. Gatling guns were hand-cranked, although in 1893 Gatling produced a shortened "Bulldog" version that, looking far into the future, was powered by an electric motor.

The Gatling gun, while undeniably effective, was extremely heavy and in 1884 was more or less rendered obsolete by Hiram Maxim's recoil-powered single-barrel machine gun. Yet ironically, the principle of rotary-barrel machine guns has been revisited in modern times. This has mainly occurred within the context of aircraft-mounted weaponry, as the jet age requires weapons that, because of the fast air speeds of modern jets, have extremely high rates of fire to make the most of brief target windows.

The Vietnam War also saw the development of helicopter gunships, such as the Bell UH-1 and the AH-1 Cobra, and because many of the gunships' targets lay beyond visual acquisition in dense jungle, massive firepower became the primary tool of successful engagement. Electrically powered rotary-barrel weapons were the best way of achieving the heaviest densities of firepower. The 7.62 mm M134 Minigun, for example, could achieve rates of fire of 6,000 rpm. And like the Gatling a century earlier, it consisted of six barrels, each with its own bolt unit. These Gatling-type weapons often had a separate electrical supply for the ammunition to maintain the highest rates of fire.

Although more in the category of cannon rather than machine gun, one of the greatest rotary-barrel weapons is the 30 mm GAU-8 gun fitted inside the A-10 ground-attack jet. Measuring roughly the same dimensions as a family car, the GAU-8 fires at 3,900 rpm and is fed a mix of depleted uranium armor-piercing rounds mixed with high-explosive shells. A one-second burst from this weapon is enough to destroy a main battle tank fitted with even advanced reactive armor.

Glossary

Action: The mechanism of a firearm involved in presenting the cartridge for firing and in ejecting the spent case and introducing a fresh cartridge.
Aperture sight: A type of iron sight in which the backsight takes the form of a small hole or aperture; also called a "peep sight."
Assault rifle: A rifle capable of controllable full-automatic fire, usually achieved by firing small-caliber rounds or rifle-caliber rounds with reduced case length.
Automatic: A firearm that continues firing for as long as the trigger remains depressed or until the magazine or belt containing extra ammunition runs empty. A machine gun.
Automatic ejection: A system predominantly used on break-open revolvers on which, as the barrel is tipped down, the ejector is automatically activated to clear the chambers. See "Hand ejection" and "Rod ejection."
Automatic revolver: A rare type of revolver, of which the Webley Fosbery and the Union are the best known examples, that uses the recoil energy of cartridge discharge to rotate the cylinder and cock the hammer for each succeeding shot.
Backstrap: The rear of the two gripstraps on a handgun, which lies under the heel of the hand when a firing grip is taken.
Ball: A military term for standard, full-jacketed ammunition.
Ballistics: The science of cartridge discharge and the bullet's flight.
Barrel: A cylindrical part of a firearm through the bore of which the shot is fired. The barrel serves the purposes of imparting direction and velocity to the projectile or projectiles.
Battery: The disposition of parts of a firearm when the breech is locked up, ready for firing.
Bedding: The manner in which the barreled action of a rifle is fitted to the stock.
Birdshot: Shotgun pellets of comparatively small diameter, meant to be used on birds in flight and on small game such as rabbit and squirrel. See "Buckshot."
Black powder: See "Gunpowder."
Blowback: Also called "unlocked breech." Said of a self-loading or automatic firearm whose breechblock and barrel are not mechanically locked together when in battery or at the moment of firing. Used in comparatively low-powered weapons, in which the inertia of the breechblock, and casewall adhesion against the chamber, are sufficient to retard opening until breech pressures have fallen to a safe level.
Bolt: A form of breechblock, usually cylindrical in cross-section, that operates on a prolongation of the bore axis, and is withdrawn over a distance greater than the length of the cartridge, to expose the chamber. Lends itself well to magazine feeding. On a revolver, the cylinder stop.
Bolt action: A firearm that uses a mobile breechblock acting along a linear extension of the bore axis, and hand-operated either on a pull-push basis or on a turnbolt basis.
Bore: The caliber of a shotgun. See "Gauge." The interior of a gun barrel.
Bore diameter: The diameter of the inside of the barrel after boring but before rifling. The land diameter.
Bottle-necked: Said of a cartridge whose projectile diameter is substantially less than the body diameter of the case. Such a case affords adequate power capacity and is necked down as required to grip the projectile.
Boxlock: A firearm—normally a double-barreled shotgun or rifle—on which the firing mechanisms are housed in recesses in the rear of the receiver. See "Sidelock."
Breechblock: The part that seals the rear of the chamber and supports the casehead when the cartridge is fired. Breech-loading firearms are classified according to the type of breech employed, and the mechanical means of locking it into place for firing and displacing it for reloading.
Breech-loader: A firearm that is loaded from the rear. The firing chamber will normally be machined into the rear end of the barrel, but may be a separate piece aligned with the barrel for firing, as is the case with revolvers.
Breech plug: A threaded plug, often incorporating the tang, that closes the breech end of the barrel of most muzzle-loading firearms.
Buckshot: A term for the larger sizes of shotgun pellets, useful against fox and feral dogs, and in an antipersonnel role, but not usually humane on deer.
Bullpup: A shoulder gun in which the receiver is located well back in the stock, so much so that the cheek is alongside the breech on firing.
Burst fire: Said of a firearm the mechanism of which is fitted with a ratchet escapement device that permits a predetermined number of shots (usually three) to be fired each time the trigger is pressed. See "Selective fire."
Buttstock or Butt: That portion of the stock that enables the firearm to be braced against the shoulder and cheek for firing.
Caliber: The diameter, nominal diameter, or designation of a bore, projectile, or cartridge, normally expressed in hundredths of an inch or thousandths of an inch, or in millimeters, although shotgun caliber is usually expressed in a system based on fractions of a pound (e.g., twelve-bore).
Cannelure: A circumferential groove or indentation around a bullet or cartridge case.
Capping breech-loader: A type of early breech-loader circa 1860 that was fired by a standard percussion cap that was placed on an external nipple or chimney after the breech had been closed.
Carbine: A small rifle, shorter, lighter, and handier than a full-size rifle.
Cartridge: A round of ammunition consisting, in modern times, of case, primer, powder, and projectile (either single or multiple). In early gun models, the cartridge (from the French *cartouche*) consisted of the powder and ball in a paper packet, with the percussion cap or priming powder separate.
Case: The metallic body of a cartridge, usually made of brass but sometimes of steel, aluminum, or plastic.
Centerfire: A cartridge in which the primer or primer assembly is seated in a pocket or recess in the center of the base of the case. A firearm that uses centerfire cartridges.

Chamber: The part of a firearm that contains the cartridge when it is fired.
Charger: A device, normally of pressed metal, that holds a group of cartridges for easy and virtually simultaneous loading into the magazine of a firearm.
Choke: A barely discernible construction near the muzzle of a shotgun that has the function and effect of regulating pattern density, as measured by the percentage of pellets that would normally be contained in a 30 in. (762 mm) circle at 400 yd. (366 m). Choke classifications are: cylinder bore (40 percent), improved cylinder (50 percent), quarter choke (55 percent), half choke (60 percent), three-quarter choke (65 percent), full choke (70 percent).
Clip: A device, normally of pressed steel that holds a group of cartridges and which is inserted into the magazine, along with the cartridges it contains, in order to reload the gun.
Cock: A pivoted piece, normally spring-activated, that loads the match, pyrites, or flint on a matchlock, wheellock, or flintlock mechanism; often called the "dog" in Mediterranean countries.
Cook-off: When a chambered round is fired purely by the residual heat that has built up in the breechblock and barrel.
Corned powder: Gunpowder formed into granules to create a consistent mix of elements that do not separate in transit and have more efficient burning characteristics.
CP round: Automatic Colt Pistol, a type of ammunition.
Crane: The pivoting member on which the cylinder is mounted on a revolver, the cylinder of which swings out for loading. Also called the "yoke."
Crown: The form of the muzzle where the bore emerges, normally chamfered or recessed.
Cylinder stop: On a revolver, the part, normally spring activated and housed in the floor of the frame, which engages in the cylinder stop notch (also called "bolt cut"), arresting the cylinder's rotation and locking it so that the chamber to be fired is locked in alignment with the barrel.
Delayed blowback: Also called "retarded blowback" and "hesitation locked." Said of a self-loading or automatic firearm whose breechblock and barrel are not positively locked together, but which incorporates a mechanism that causes the breechblock to operate against an initial mechanical disadvantage, thus delaying its opening.
Double-action: A revolver or pistol on which a long pull-through on the trigger will rock the hammer back against the mainspring and release it at the top of its travel to fire the shot. On a revolver, subsequent shots may be fired the same way; on a pistol, the slide will normally cock the hammer after the first shot so that subsequent shots are taken with just a light pressure on the trigger.
Ejector: A part whose function is to throw a spent case clear of the gun.
Ejector star: On a revolver, the collective ejector, operating through the cylinder axis that, when activated, clears all chambers at once. The ratchet is normally machined as part of the ejector star.
Elevation: Vertical disparity in a bullet's flight, due to errors in range estimation or other factors. See "Windage."
Extractor: A part, normally hook- or crescent-shaped that withdraws a spent case from the chamber.
Face: The front surface of the standing breech on a break-open shotgun—the surface that supports the base of the cartridge. A worn gun with looseness or space at the breech is said to be "off the face."
Falling block: An action type in which the breechblock, usually lever operated, moves vertically (or nearly so) in internal receiver mortises. A very strong, compact, and usually elegant action.
Firearm: A lethal, barreled weapon that uses the pressure of combustion-generated gases to propel a projectile or group of projectiles.
Firing pin: In a hammer-fired gun, that part that physically impacts the primer to detonate it. A striker-fired gun does not have a firing pin. See "Striker."
Flash hider: A device, usually consisting of linear slots or prongs, fitted to the muzzles of some firearms, designed to break up and minimize flash.
Flintlock: A system widely used in the seventeenth to nineteenth centuries, in which ignition is achieved by striking a flint against an upright steel face called the frizzen. The resultant sparks ignite the priming powder in the pan, which burn through the touch hole to ignite the main charge in the barrel.
Fore-end: The portion of a gun or rifle stock located ahead of the receiver, which is normally gripped by the left hand.
Frame: The receiver of a revolver or pistol.
Freebore: The distance between the front of the bearing surface of the chambered bullet and the beginning of the rifling. Zero freebore gives best accuracy.
Frizzen: The vertical iron face of a flintlock gun against which the flint strikes to produce sparks. Usually formed as a vertical extension of the pan cover.
Front-locking: Said of a bolt-action gun that has locking lugs on the front of the bolt that engage in corresponding mortises either in front of the receiver or in the rear of the barrel, or in an intermediate sleeve or collar between the two, and immediately behind the chamber.
Frontstrap: The forward of the two gripstraps on a handgun, that falls underneath the fingers.
Gas-operated: Said of a self-loading or automatic firearm that uses combustion gases, tapped via a port along the barrel, to impulse a piston that cycles the action. Gas-operated systems are classified as long stroke, short stroke, or direct delivery.
Gas-retarded: Said of a firearm if gas bled from the bore is used not to cycle the action but to delay its opening by acting to hold the breech closed. See "Delayed blowback."
Gauge: The caliber of a shotgun, usually expressed in fractions of a pound. British: "bore" as in "twelve bore," "twelve bore," etc. The bore diameter of a twelve-gauge gun would correspond to the diameter of a spherical lead ball weighing 0.5 lb. (0.23 kg).
Grain: An avoirdupois unit of measurement used for expressing the weight of cartridge components. There are 7,000 grains to the pound; one grain = 0.002285 ounce or 64.79891 milligrams.
Groove: Spiral cut produced by a rifling cutter.
Gunpowder: Also called black powder, the standard propellant for firearms from their introduction in the early fourteenth century until the late nineteenth century, when black powder was quickly superseded by smokeless powder.
Hammer: The part, powered by the mainspring, that is driven around its axis of rotation, and drives the firing pin into the base of the chambered cartridge. The firing pin may or may not be part of the hammer. See "Firing pin" and "Striker."
Hammer spur: The thumbpiece on the top rear of the hammer that enables it to be drawn to full cock.
Hammerless: Said of a firearm, particularly a shotgun, without visible, external hammers. Most such guns are in fact hammer fired, but use internal hammers.
Hand ejection: A system most often used on swingout cylinder revolvers, in which the ejector rod is pushed rearward by hand in order to clear the chambers. See "Automatic ejection" and "Rod ejection."
Handgun: A firearm intended to be aimed and fired in the hand or hands, without being braced against the shoulder and cheek. A catch-all term for any pistol or revolver.
Hangfire: A cartridge that discharges after a delay. Dangerous.
Headspace: The distance between the face of the breechblock in battery and the point at which the cartridge case abuts against the chamber, normally the front surface of the rim, belt, shoulder, or mouth.
Heeled bullet: An early type of revolver bullet that had a reduced diameter heel that seated in the mouth of the cartridge case.
Hinged frame: A break-open gun that hinges open for loading or disassembly.
Hollow point: A bullet with a hollow in the

nose, designed to mushroom on impact.
Iron sights: A sighting system consisting normally of a foresight and backsight not containing glass or reflective elements, magnifying or not.
Jacket: The skin or covering of a composite bullet, usually made of copper, gilding metal, cupro-nickel or mild steel. The core, inside the jacket, is normally of a lead alloy. The jacket is hard enough to hold rifling at velocities that would strip a lead bullet.
Lands: The upstanding ridges of metal left between the grooves when a barrel is rifled. The lands bite into the bullet, causing it to spin in flight, thus imparting gyrostatic stability and preventing it from tumbling end over end.
Land Warrior Program: From 1991, a US army program to transform the infantryman into a total combat system through technology, with computer and wireless links to transmit combat data direct, such as real-time maps, GPS, artillery coordinates, etc.
LC: Long Colt, a type of ammunition.
Lever-action: A firearm that uses a breechblock that is operated by a downward rotational action on a sidelever or underlever.
Lock: The ignition mechanism of a firearm, e.g., matchlock, wheellock, flintlock, miquelet lock, percussion lock, sidelock, boxlock, back action lock, etc.
Locked breech: Self-loading or automatic firearm whose breechblock and barrel are mechanically locked together when in battery and at the moment of firing.
Lockplate: The flat metal plate on which the mechanism or lock of the firearm is mounted.
Long recoil: A recoil-operated firearm in which the barrel and breechblock are locked together for the full distance of travel, after which the barrel returns forward while the breechblock is retained rearward. When the barrel has fully returned, the breechblock is released to fly forward, chambering a fresh cartridge in the process.
Long stroke: Said of a gas-operated firearm if the piston is attached to the bolt and accompanies it during the full length of the operating cycle.
LR: Long Rifle, a designation of the most popular variety of 0.22-in. rimfire cartridge, universally used in pistols as well as rifles.
Machine carbine: A submachine gun.
Machine pistol: European continental parlance, a submachine gun, sometimes applied to a pistol, with or without buttstock attachment, capable of fully automatic fire.
Magazine: The part of a firearm containing the reserve ammunition supply, and out of which cartridges are mechanically fed to the chamber for firing.
Magnum: A term borrowed from the vintner's trade to designate a cartridge that is notably powerful.
Mainspring: The spring, in a firearm that powers the hammer or striker.
Matchlock: An early ignition system in which a smoldering "match"—usually a nitrate-soaked cord—was applied directly to the priming powder in the flashpan to ignite it to burn through the touch hole and ignite the main charge.
Mauser type: Said of a bolt-action rifle containing many of the design elements of the Model 1898 Mauser, notably twin forward-locking lugs, an integral double-column magazine, and often a collar-mounted external extractor and fixed ejector.
Misfire: A cartridge that fails to discharge.
Musket: A smoothbore military shoulder gun intended to fire a single projectile, normally a round ball of nearly bore diameter.
Muzzle brake: A device fitted to or machined into the muzzle of a firearm and intended to reduce recoil and muzzle flip by redirecting the combustion gases.
Muzzle-loader: A firearm that loads from the front end: the end of the barrel (muzzle) or, in the case of revolvers, the front of the cylinder.
Muzzle velocity: The speed of the bullet, measured in feet per second or meters per second, a short distance from the muzzle.
Neck (n): The constricted forward section of a bottle-necked cartridge case—the portion that grips the bullet.
Neck (v): To alter the diameter of the neck of a cartridge case so as to change its caliber. Thus, the 0.25-06 is the 0.30-06 necked down to 0.25-in. caliber, while the 0.35 in. Whelen is the 0.30-06 necked out to 0.35 in. caliber.
Needle-fire: A transitional ignition type in which the firing pin took the form of a "needle" that was driven forward through the base of the cartridge, through the powder charge, until it impacted the primer, which was affixed to the base of the bullet.
Ogive: The curved portion of a bullet between the bearing surface and the tip.
Open frame: Said of a revolver frame that has no topstrap.
Open sights: A sighting system consisting of a post or bead foresight and a notch, V, or groove backsight.
Over-and-under: A double-barreled gun on which the two barrels are mounted one above the other.
Pepperbox: A type of early percussion revolver with a barrel cluster rather like a long cylinder (but with no single, separate barrel) and with a bar-type hammer striking from above. Normally double-action only. Popular during the early and mid-nineteenth century.
Pinfire: A metallic cartridge in which the primer is normally contained, cup upward, in a base wad and which is discharged by the blow of the hammer, falling at ninety degrees to the axis of the cartridge, which drives a protruding pin into the primer. A gun which takes cartridges of this type.
Pistol: A handgun. In normal usage, the term "pistol" refers to any handgun except revolvers, and includes self-loaders, manual repeaters, single-shots, double- or multibarreled pistols, and freak types such as belt buckle pistols, cutlass pistols, and so forth.
Pitch: Also called "twist." The rate at which rifling turns, measured in calibers, inches, or centimeters. A typical pitch would be one turn in 14 inches (35.56 cm).
Port pressure: In a gas-operated firearm, the peak pressure over the gas port; determines port diameter.
Primer: The part of the cartridge that ignites the propellant powder. In a metallic cartridge, the primer is part of the assembly, but earlier ignition systems used various types of separate and external primers. A modern primer consists essentially of the cup, anvil, and pellet, the latter usually a lead styphnate–based compound, although mercury fulminate was previously used.
Primer pocket: The counterbore in the center of the base of a centerfire cartridge in which the primer assembly is seated.
Proof: The testing of forearms for their ability to withstand safely the pressure of cartridge discharge.
Proof mark: A mark or symbol stamped or engraved on a firearm to indicate that it has successfully been proof tested.
Pump-action: A firearm that employs a breechblock that is operated by linear manual pressure, normally on a mobile fore-end, although variants with mobile pistol grips or handgrips exist.
Ramrod: A rod, normally of wood or iron, used for loading a muzzle-loading firearm, and normally stored in a groove underneath the barrel.
Rear-locking: Said of a bolt-action gun on which the locking lugs are toward the rear of the bolt and which lock into the receiver behind the magazine well.
Receiver: The principal structural component of a firearm. The buttstock is attached to the back of the receiver, the barrel and fore-end to the front, and the action operates within it. Called the "frame" on a revolver or pistol.
Recoil lug: A lug or face, normally on the underside or rear of a receiver that transfers the forces of recoil from the barrel/receiver group to the stock.
Recoil-operated: Said of a self-loading or automatic firearm operated by mobile components—the barrel and breechblock—which recoil rearward in reaction to the projectile, which is being propelled forward. See "Short recoil" and "Long recoil."
Repeater: A firearm containing reserve ammunition that may be discharged, shot after

shot, until the reserve is exhausted, as opposed to a single-shot firearm, for which the reserve ammunition is normally carried in a belt, pocket, or pouch worn by the shooter.
Revolver: A repeating handgun that carries its cartridges in a cylinder that is drilled linearly with chambers that are disposed around a common central axis. Each chamber contains a cartridge, and is rotated into alignment with the barrel for firing. See "Pistol," "Cylinder," and "Chamber."
Rifle: A shoulder gun intended to fire a solid or composite projectile of bore diameter, and having a rifled barrel designed to impart a spin to the projectile. See "Musket," "Shotgun," and "Carbine."
Rifling: A series of spiral grooves cut or formed into the interior of a barrel. The ridges of metal between the grooves are called "lands."
Rimfire: A metallic cartridge in which the priming compound is deposited centrifugally in the hollow rim of the case around its entire circumference. The firing pin crushes the rim against the rear face of the barrel, which serves as an anvil for the purpose.
Rimless: Said of a cartridge of which the base diameter and body diameter are the same. Such a case will normally have an extraction groove machined around it, yielding a rim of body diameter.
Rod ejection: A system primarily used on solid-frame revolvers, in which ejection is accomplished by rotating the cylinder so that each chamber in turn aligns with the ejector rod mounted under the barrel, and with the loading gate, out through which the spent case may be pushed.
Round: A unit of ammunition consisting of the primer, case, propellant, and bullet. A cartridge.
Safety: A mechanical device intended to prevent accidental discharge; may be either manually operated at will, such as a thumb lever or crossbolt, or an automatic safety such as a firing pin block or magazine disconnector, or something between the two, such as a grip safety.
Sear: The piece—either part of the trigger or an intermediate piece—that holds the hammer or striker at full cock. Pressure on the trigger causes the sear to release the hammer or striker to fly forward and fire the shot.
Selective fire: Said of a firearm capable of either semi- or full automatic fire, or semiautomatic or burst fire, or all three. Most selective-fire weapons have a selector switch or lever; some have separate triggers for each mode while others fire semiauto on short pulls and automatic on a long pull of the same trigger.
Self-loader: A firearm that harnesses the energy of cartridge discharge to extract and eject the spent case and to load a fresh cartridge into the chamber. Also called "semiautomatic" or, sometimes, "automatic."
Semiautomatic: See "Self-loader."
Short recoil: A recoil-operated firearm in which the barrel and breechblock are locked together through a short distance of travel, whereupon the two are uncoupled, the barrel is arrested, and the breechblock continues rearward, extracting the spent case from the chamber. Most self-loading pistols are of short recoil operation. See "Recoil-operated" and "Long recoil."
Short stroke: Said of a gas-operated firearm if the piston operates over only a short distance and impulses the bolt and bolt carrier rearward. Also called "tappet-operated."
Shot: A pellet of a shotgun cartridge; alternatively, all of the pellets or the pattern of the pellets from a shotgun cartridge. The effect of the noise or the incident of a cartridge being fired. Also refers to the person who shoots.
Shotgun: A smoothbore shoulder gun intended for the most part to fire shells containing a number of small, round pellets, the size of which varies according to the application.
Shoulder gun: A firearm meant to be fired supported by the shoulder and cheek, as opposed to a handgun. A catch-all term for any rifle, shotgun, or combination gun.
Side-by-side: A double-barreled gun on which the two barrels are mounted one beside the other, i.e., in a horizontal plane.
Sidelock: A firearm—normally a double-barreled shotgun or rifle—on which the lockwork is mounted on detachable lockplates that are mortised into the stock on either side, just to the rear of the receiver.
Silencer: A sound moderator.
Single-action: A revolver or pistol on which the hammer must be cocked before the first shot can be fired. On single-action revolvers, the hammer must be drawn to full cock for each shot; on pistols, the slide will automatically recock the hammer for the second and subsequent shots. See "Double-action."
Small arm: A firearm capable of being carried and used by one person, as opposed to crew-served weapons.
Smokeless powder: A form of nitrocellulose-based propellant which replaced gunpowder in small-arms cartridges at the end of the nineteenth century. Smokeless powder is classified as single-based or double-based depending on whether the nitrocellulose is used with a nitroglycerine additive.
Smoothbore: A firearm, such as a musket or shotgun that is not rifled. A shotgun.
Snaphaunce: An early type of flintlock in which the frizzen and the pan were separate parts.
Solid frame: Said of a revolver on which the frame window is broached through a solid piece; i.e., the construction is neither break-open nor open-framed. Most swing-out cylinder revolvers have solid frames.
Sound moderator: A device attached to the muzzle of a firearm, and sometimes sleeving the barrel and parts of the breech as well, intended to attenuate the noise of cartridge discharge by containing the expanding gases until they have slowed to subsonic levels. A silencer.
Speedloader: A device that carries revolver cartridges in a circular pattern, enabling a revolver to be reloaded in a single motion.
Standing breech: The receiver face that supports the casehead when the chambered cartridge is fired in certain types of firearms, notably revolvers and break-open shotguns and rifles.
Stock: The part of a firearm that facilitates its being held for firing, notably the butt, fore-end, pistol grip, handguard, etc.
Striker: In a gun that does not have a hammer, the part that impacts the primer to detonate it. A striker is itself powered by the mainspring, and operates linearly; a hammer operates rotationally. See "Firing pin" and "Hammer."
Submachine gun: A fully automatic or selective-fire weapon of pistol caliber.
Tipping block: An action type in which the breechblock, usually lever-operated, is hinged at the back and tips down at the front to expose the chamber.
Tipping bolt: Said of a bolt-type breechblock that tips to lock. Normally a square face on the rear underside of the bolt will lock against a corresponding face on the receiver.
Topstrap: Part of a revolver frame extending over the top of the cylinder and connecting the top of the standing breech with the forward portion of the frame into which the barrel is screwed.
Trajectory: The arc described by a projectile from the muzzle to its point of impact.
Transitional revolver: An early type of percussion revolver with a pepperbox action but with a single, rifled barrel.
Trigger: A part that, when pressed, releases the hammer or striker to fire the gun.
Trigger bar: On a self-loading pistol, or any other firearm in which the trigger is at some distance from the sear, an intermediate piece connecting the two parts.
Twist: The rate at which rifling causes the bullet to rotate. See "Pitch."
Unitary cartridge: A form of ammunition in which a single case holds the bullet, propellant, and primer in one single unit.
WCF: Winchester Center Fire; a type of ammunition.
Web: The wall of brass between the casehead and the combustion chamber or case body.
Wheellock: An early ignition system in which a serrated steel wheel was spun against iron pyrites contained in a clamp in order to generate sparks to ignite the priming charge.
Windage: The lateral deflection in a bullet's flight due to wind drift, the earth's rotation, sighting error, etc. See "Elevation."
Yoke: See "Crane."

INDEX

Entries in **bold** refer to features independent of the individual gun descriptions.

Picture Acknowledgments

All images courtesy of Chrysalis Image Library apart from the following.

T = Top B = Bottom C = Center

© **Art Archive/Gunshots** 23.
© **Bharat Rakshak (www.bharat-rakshat.com)** 333TL, 333TR.
© **Bundesarchiv** 411, 434.
© **Canadian Forces Photo** 427.
© **Colt's Manufacturing Company LLC** 137.
© **Corbis** 258. / Christel Gerstenberg 24. / Ali Meyer 37. / Bettmann 56, 93, 368.
Peter Johnson 59. / Hulton-Deutsch Collection 96,141, 266. / Jacques Langevin/Sygma 182. /
Reuters 200. / Gianni Dagli Orti 212. / Dave G. Houser 292.
© **H&K Defense Inc. (US)** 331T
© **US Department of Defense** 301, 325, 335, 432.
© **www.guns.ru** 392T.
© **Imperial War Museum** 144, 273, 337, 378, 381, 383, 388, 391, 396, 412, 425.
© **Musée de L'Armée** 205.
© **Novosti Picture Library** 281.
© **Rex Features** / Stewart Cook 155. / RYB 165. / The Stewart Bonney Agency 295. / F Zabci 371.
© **Royal Ordnance Factories** 407.
© **2004 Sako Ltd** 314T, 206T.
© **Swiss Target Pistol Company** 179.
© **Smith & Wesson** 126, 190.
© **TRH Pictures** 163, 196, 251, 298, 304B, 314B, 315B, 321T, 329T, 375B, 402, 436T, 437T, 438T.
© **US Army Photograph** / (Ref: SC189099) 207C. / (Ref: CC121254) 313. / (Ref: CC111988) 401.

Books cited in text: **Small Arms and Machine Guns.** Dr. D. F. Allsop and Lt. Col. M. A. Toomey, Brasseys, UK, 1999.
The Israeli War Machine. Ian Hogg, Chartwell Books, UK, 1983.